Genealogies of Kentucky Families

From The Register of the
Kentucky Historical Society

Genealogies of KENTUCKY *F*AMILIES

From The Register of the
Kentucky Historical Society

O – Y
(Owens – Young)

Baltimore
GENEALOGICAL PUBLISHING CO., INC.
1981

Excerpted and reprinted from *The Register of the Kentucky Historical Society* (with added Publisher's Note, Table of Contents, Index, and textual notes) by Genealogical Publishing Co., Inc., Baltimore, 1981. Copyright © 1981, Genealogical Publishing Co., Inc., Baltimore, Maryland. All rights reserved. Library of Congress Catalogue Card Number 80-85395. International Standard Book Number: Vol. O-Y: 0-8063-0932-6. Set Number: 0-8063-0930-X.
Made in the United States of America.

Note to the Reader

THIS VOLUME, covering families ranging in alphabetical sequence from O to Y, and a preceding volume, covering families from A to M (there are no N's except for allied families), consists of articles excerpted from *The Register of the Kentucky Historical Society*. The two volumes together contain all the family history articles published in the *Register* between 1903 and 1965 (when genealogical contributions were discontinued) except for those articles on Woodford County families by William E. Railey which, after their appearance in the *Register,* were collected and published, with additional material, as the *History of Woodford County, Kentucky* (1938, repr. Baltimore: Genealogical Publishing Co., 1975). Also omitted are a few articles which are rather more historical or biographical in nature than genealogical. At the same time, to broaden the genealogical basis of the work, every Bible record and genealogical fragment known to have been published in the *Register* has been included (see Appendices).

A third volume in the series, also published under the title *Genealogies of Kentucky Families,* is composed of articles excerpted from *The Filson Club History Quarterly*. Each volume in the series is published with an index and is complete in itself, so the reader need only consult the particular volume required for his research.

This space affords us an opportunity to thank the various persons who cooperated or assisted in the production of this book, and therefore to all who were involved we offer our thanks. We wish, in particular, to express our gratitude to Gen. William R. Buster, Director of the Kentucky Historical Society, for granting us permission to reproduce articles from the *Register;* to Gary Parks for preparing the Index; and to Joseph Garonzik for collecting and arranging the articles.

Genealogical Publishing Company

Contents

Sketches of the Owens and Tate Families, by R. M. Mayfield, from Vol. 27 (May 1929), 440-442 1

The Pattons: A Pioneer Family in Kentucky and Their Descendants, by Sara G. Clark, from Vol. 35 (April 1937) 131-178, (Oct. 1937) 383-384 4

Captain James Patton of Augusta County, Virginia, and Louisville, Kentucky: Ancestors and Descendants, by William S. Muir, from Vol. 42 (July 1944), 227-255 54

    Gracey 64
    Sawtell 69
    Lindenberger ... 71
    Nelson 73
    Harriman 75
    Low 76
    Muir 78
    Patton 79
    Tracy 80
    Van Buskirk 81
    Wurts 81

The Payne Genealogy, by Judith L. Marshall, from Vol. 2 (May 1904), 53-55 83

Colonel Asa Payne, by J. Stoddard Johnston, from Vol. 26 (Sept. 1928), 319-323 86

The Pogues, by H. M. Williamson, from Vol. 6 (May 1908), 75-76 91

History of William Poage and His Wife, Ann Kennedy Wilson Poage Lindsay McGinty, by Mrs. S. V. Nuckols, from Vol. 11 (Jan. 1913), 101-102 93

The Pryor Ancestry, by Henry Strother, from Vol. 13 (Jan. 1915), 89-91 95

Railey-Randolph History and Genealogy, by William E. Railey, from Vol. 9 (Sept. 1911), 53-83; Vol. 10 (Jan. 1912), 91-135; Corrections: Vol. 11 (Jan. 1913), 103 98

    Brief Sketches of the Randolphs and Their Connections; Also the Owsleys and Whitleys, by William Edward Railey, from Vol. 16 (May 1918), 61-76; Corrections: Vol. 16 (Sept. 1918), 47-49, 50-52; Vol. 32 (Oct. 1934), 368, 370; Vol. 34 (July 1936), 300-305 173

The Flemings of Virginia, by William E. Railey, from Vol. 37 (July 1939), 266 ... 200

The Keiths, by Annie H. Miles, from Vol. 1 (Sept. 1903), 71-73 ... 201

Tuckahoe and the Tuckahoe Randolphs, by Jefferson Randolph Anderson, from Vol. 35 (Jan. 1937), 29-59 ... 204

The Family and Fortune of General James Ray, Pioneer of Fort Harrod, by Kathryn Harrod Mason, from Vol. 43 (Jan. 1945), 59-68 ... 235

The Rennicks, from Vol. 2 (Jan. 1904), 70-74 ... 245

Richardsons in Kentucky, by Jennie C. Morton, from Vol. 7 (Jan. 1909) 75-77, (May 1909) 99-103 ... 250

The Rogers Family, excerpted from "The Rogers Family and Old Cane Ridge," by Julia S. Ardery, from Vol. 53 (July 1955), 234-246 ... 258

Skelton, by Lewis H. Jones, from Vol. 27 (Jan. 1929), 437-439 ... 265

The Slaughter Genealogy, excerpted from "Colonel B. G. Slaughter," by Jennie C. Morton, from Vol. 2 (Jan. 1904), 89-97 ... 270

The Slaughter Family, by W. A. Slaughter, from Vol. 2 (May 1904), 47-50 ... 272

Sir Richard Steele and Descendants in America and Kentucky, by Mrs. Mary Willis Woodson, from Vol. 2 (Jan. 1904), 67-69 ... 276

Captain Andrew Steele, A Revolutionary Soldier and Descendant of Sir Richard Steele of Ireland, by Jennie C. Morton, from Vol. 2 (Jan. 1904), 75-77 ... 279

Thomas Steele, Pioneer, by Jno. A. Steele, from Vol. 2 (Jan. 1904), 81-83 ... 282

Supplement to the "Steele Genealogy," by Idelie Keyes, from Vol. 2 (May 1904), 51-52 ... 286

Mrs. Martha McKamie Steele, by Wm. Edwards Baxter, from Vol. 3 (Jan. 1905) 69-74, (May 1905) 82 ... 288

Stephenson-Lee-Logan-Gilmore Family Records, by L. O. Stephenson, from Vol. 29 (July 1931), 315-329 ... 295

Stephenson Family Records, by L. O. Stephenson, from Vol. 29 (Jan. 1931), 90-94 ... 310

Stephenson Family Bible, from Vol. 30 (April 1932), 201-202 ... 315

A Study of Some Stewart and Allied Families, by William C. Stewart, from Vol. 61 (Jan. 1963) 78-103, (April 1963) 169-190 ... 317

The Strother Family, by Annie Hawkins Miles, from Vol. 1 (Sept. 1903), 67-70 ... 365

The Strothers, by William E. Railey, from Vol. 15 (Sept. 1917), 89-100; Vol. 16 (Jan. 1918), 93-106; Corrections: Vol. 16 (Sept. 1918), 49-50; Vol. 32 (Oct. 1934), 369 ... 369

The Strother Family, by John Chaplin Strother, Henry Strother, and Susan T. Green, from Vol. 25 (Sept. 1927), 293-309 ... 397

Tandy, by Gen. Henry T. Allen, from Vol. 28 (April 1930), 155-174 ... 414

    Bledsoe-Tandy, by Mrs. Arthur Ferguson, from Vol. 29 (April 1931), 228, 329 ... 434

Reminiscences of James Bledsoe Tandy, from Vol. 53 (April 1955), 101-114 ... 435

Ancestors and Descendants of the Rev. John Taylor (1752-1835), by Dorothy Brown Thompson, from Vol. 47 (Jan. 1949), 21-51 ... 451

    Additional Notes on the John Taylor Family, by Dorothy Brown Thompson, from Vol. 53 (Oct. 1955), 348-354 ... 483

Taylor and Morris Families, by Mrs. Henry D. McHenry, from Vol. 3 (May 1905), 81-82 ... 490

Throckmorton and Warner and Descendants, by Sir John Throckmorton, from Vol. 13 (Jan. 1915), 79-80 ... 492

Memorabilia of the Trabue Family, by Mrs. Z. F. Smith, from Vol. 7 (Sept. 1909), 77-87 ... 494

The Genealogy and History of the Trabue Family, by Alice Trabue, from Vol. 17 (May 1919), 47-60 ... 505

Rev. Andrew Tribble, Pioneer, by Bess L. Hawthorne, from Vol. 24 (May 1926), 187-190 ... 521

The Turner Family, by Jozie Mae Turner Matthews, from Vol. 19 (Jan. 1921), 13-19 ... 525

Turner Family, by Samuel Stephen Sargent, from Vol. 45 (April 1947), 166-170 ... 532

History of the Upshaws, Lafons, Jacksons, and Youngs, by Sally Jackson, from Vol. 4 (Jan. 1906) 55-59, (May 1906) 53-55 ... 537

    The Young and Jackson Ancestry of Mrs. Virginia Crittenden and Miss Sally Jackson, Sisters, by Sally Jackson, from Vol. 4 (Sept. 1906), 67-68 ... 544

The Van Meterens of Holland and America, by Amelia Clay Lewis Van Meter Rogers, from Vol. 34 (Jan. 1936), 22-41 ... 546

The Venables, by Miss Morton, from Vol. 9 (Jan. 1911), 67-69   567

The Viley Family, by Martinette Viley Witherspoon, from Vol. 7 (May 1909), 107-118   570

The Thurston-Waddy Family of Shelby County, Kentucky, by George C. Downing, from Vol. 8 (May 1910), 65-70   580

    Notes Concerning the Waddy-Thomson Family, by George C. Downing, from Vol. 8 (Sept. 1910), 105-112   586

    The Robert Thurston Family, excerpted from "Captain Robert Thurston," by George C. Downing, from Vol. 8 (Oct. 1910), 97-101   594

Captain John Wall and Major John Taylor—Sketch of the Revolutionary Ancestry of Mrs. W. W. Longmoor, Sr., of Frankfort, Kentucky, by Jennie C. Morton, from Vol. 3 (Sept. 1905), 79-80   595

The Ward Family, by Mrs. E. W. Doremus, from Vol. 6 (Jan. 1908), 37-47   597

Watlington: History and Genealogy from an Old Family Letter, by Mrs. H. V. McChesney, Sr., from Vol. 47 (Oct. 1949), 309-313   608

The Ancestry of Edward West of Lexington, Kentucky, 1757-1827, by Mabel Van Dyke Baer, from Vol. 58 (Oct. 1960), 354-363   613

The Whittington Family, excerpted from "William Whittington's Book," by Mrs. M. C. Darnell, from Vol. 47 (Oct. 1949), 314-324   623

Biographical Sketch of the Wood Family of Mason County, Kentucky, by Lucy Coleman Lee, from Vol. 4 (Sept. 1906), 61-66   631

The Wood Family of Woodlawn, Kentucky, by Evelyn Crady Adams, from Vol. 47 (July 1949), 171-185   637

Woodson and Watkins, by Miss Morton, from Vol. 9 (May 1911), 69-71   653

Wright-Hamilton Families, by Mrs. W. B. Ardery, from Vol. 33 (Jan. 1935), 78-81   656

    Some Descendants of the Washington Family in Jefferson County, Kentucky, by Stratton O. Hammon, from Vol. 51 (July 1953), 248-259   660

Young Family, by Asa D. Young, from Vol. 52 (Jan. 1954), 248-259   672

Appendix A: Bible Records ... 679

Kentucky Bible Records, from Vol. 26 (May 1928), 155-189

Adams-Hampton	679	Littlepage	696
Alexander	680	Neale	696
Bacon	681	Park	697
Bibb, Richard	682	Pedego	698
Bibb, T. P. Atticus	684	Peyton	698
Boone-Grant-Lemond	686	Redford	698
Cannon	686	Richardson	699
Cox	687	Robertson	700
Crutchfield	687	Scott	702
Dillingham	688	Searcy	702
Elley	688	Smith, Basil G.	704
Everett	689	Smith, Benedict	704
Garrard	689	Snoddy	705
Goodwin-Dobson-Meux	690	Stinson (Stevenson)	706
Griffith	690	Trumbo	707
Haggard	691	Twyman	708
Harlin	691	Waddy	708
Harlow	692	Ware	710
Higdon	693	Wilson-Brinegar-Boone	710
Howard	693	Woodruff	711
Jacobs	694	Young-Proctor	712
Lancaster-Fletcher-West	695		

Kentucky Bible Records—Mercer County, by Lockette Smith, from Vol. 31 (Oct. 1933), 341-349 ... 714

Armstrong and McAfee	714	Dunn	718
Bayse	714	Robb-Coleman	720
Bohon	715	Sharp	720
Bottom-Carpenter	716	Scomp-Van Nuyce	720
Carlisle	716	Van Arsdale	721
Comingo	717	Vanarsdell	722
Davis	717		

Bacon and Ford Families' Bible Records, from Vol. 29 (April 1931), 215-216 ... 723

Cottrell Bible Records and the Smith Family Record, from Vol. 28 (July 1930), 288-289 ... 725

Old Bible Records, by Ruth Beall, from Vol. 29 (Oct. 1931), 417-422 ... 727

Griswold-Parsons	727	Stuart	731
Twyman-Haggard	730	Barkley Grave Yard	732

Bible Record of Robert and Frances Harris, by Mrs. Paul Davis, from Vol. 46 (Jan. 1948), 454-455 ... 733

Bible Records, from Vol. 59 (Jan. 1961), 79-87 ... 735
    Johnson ... 735   Crockett ... 741
    Viley ... 737   Morris ... 743
    Blackburn ... 738

Bible Records, by Mrs. L. N. Taylor, from Vol. 27 (Sept. 1929), 648-650 ... 744
    William Tarlton Taylor and Elizabeth Hampton Taylor ... 744
    Robert Buchanan and Mary Jamison Buchanan ... 745
    Robert Adams and Rebakah Willey Adams ... 745
    Old Newelle Bible Records ... 746

Appendix B: A Few Old Franklin Families Between the Kentucky River and South Elkhorn Creek, and South of the Georgetown Turnpike, by George C. Downing, from Vol. 6 (May 1908), 61-71 ... 747
    Major ... 748   Sanders ... 751
    Trabue ... 749   Crutcher ... 752

Appendix C: The Families Kinkead, Stephenson, Garrett, Martin, and Dunlap, excerpted from "Historic Meeting at Pisgah Church," by Laura Kinkead Walton, from Vol. 37 (Oct. 1939), 283-321 ... 757

Index ... 779

Editors of The Register of the Kentucky Historical Society

Jennie Chinn Morton: Vol. 1 (1903) - Vol. 17 (1919)

Harry V. McChesney: Vol. 18 (1920) - Vol. 44 (1946)

Bayless E. Hardin: Vol. 45 (1947) - Vol. 54 (1956)

Charles F. Hinds: Vol. 55 (1957) - Vol. 56 (1958)

George M. Chinn: Vol. 57 (1959)

G. Glenn Clift: Vol. 58 (1960) - Vol. 68 (1970)

Hambleton Tapp: Vol. 69 (1971) - Vol. 78 (1980)

James C. Klotter: Vol. 79 (1981) -

Genealogies of Kentucky Families

From The Register of the
Kentucky Historical Society

SKETCHES OF OWENS AND TATE FAMILIES.

By R. M. Mayfield, M. D., Seattle, Washington.

OWENS

The Owens family were of Welsh descent. William, born Nov. 10, 1750, and Nancy, born March 15, 1754, were cousins, both born in Shenandoah Valley, Va., where they were married September 30, 1773, and at once moved to Russell Co., Va., and later to Pulaski Co., Ky. William Owens served in Revolutionary War; enlisted June, 1776, for 6 mo. under Capt. John Cook, Col. Brown; 1778, for 9 mo. as sergeant, Capt. James Newell, Col. Preston; 1779, for 9 mo.; 1780, for 12 mo. under Capt. James Maxwell, Col. Preston, from Augusta Co., Va. Pensioned June 20, 1834, from Pulaski Co., Ky. Born Nov. 10, 1750; died, Pulaski Co., Ky., Aug. 9, 1836. His widow, Nancy, whom he married Sept. 20, 1770, (?) was also pensioned (see records in Bureau of Pensions, Washington, D. C., Old Cemetery, Somerset, Ky.). He owned fifteen slaves, who were sold after his death. Their daughter, Rebecca Owens, born Sept. 15, 1782, married Wesley Short, Dec. 20, 17—. Her sister, Jane married Capt. Samuel Tate, born Nov. 11, 1775, who was Robert's brother.

W. Allen Owens now lives on the old homestead, on Pitman Creek, three miles south of Court House, Somerset. Other descendants are: Col. John Owens, 82 yrs.; David D. Owens, 73 yrs.; Perry Owens, 48 yrs.; Dr. J. M. Owens, 42 yrs.; Jack Owens, 45 yrs.; Clarence Owens, 35 yrs.; Wm. K. Owens, 40 yrs.; Martin Owens, 30 yrs.; all of Somerset; James and Samuel Owens, 52 and 50 yrs., Stanford, Lincoln Co., sheriffs. Reuben Owens died, Clinton Co., Ky., near Albany.

William Owens and Nancy Owens' children:

Reuben Owens, b. Nov. 13, 1775; d. Feb. 15, 1843.

Jane Owens, b. Aug. 10, 1778; d. Nov. 24, 1861; m. Samuel Tate b. Nov. 11, 1775, d. May 21, 1845.

Sarah Owens, b. Feb. 15, 1780; d. Feb. 18, 1855. m. Sept. 11, 1800, Wm. H. Price, b. Jan. 10, 1777, d. Jan. 20, 1835.

Rebecca Owens, b. Sept. 15, 1782; d. Sept. 28, 1858; m. Feb. 4, 1802, Wesley Short, b. Dec. 20, 1780, d. Sept. 16, 1852.

Samuel Owens, b. June 19, 1785; d. June 4, 1834; m. Jane Mercer, b. April 4, 1789, d. Nov. 16, 1877.

Nancy Owens, b. Nov. 10, 1787; m. Samuel Newell, April 2, 1809.

Avy Owens, b. Nov. 11, 1789; d. Dec. 31, 1848; m. Feb. 3, 1808, John Short, b. Nov. 11, 1786, d. Mch. 1851.

William Owens, b. Mch. 25, 1792; d. Jan. 3, 1873; m. Margaret Newell, Mch. 9, 1814.

John Owens, b. Mch. 25, 1792; m. Ann Chesney.

Martin Owens, b. April 12, 1796; m. Polly Chesney.

Levina Owens, b. July 15, 1799; d. Mch. 21, 1858; m. Feb. 2, 1817, Reuben Short, b. Oct. 15, 1794.

TATE

The Tates were of Scotch-Irish descent, and came to this country before the Revolutionary War, as many served in that war from Virginia.

     Richmond, Va., Dec. 3, 1901.
"Dr. R. N. Mayfield,
New York City.

Dear Sir:—

I find the following names of Tate in the Revolutionary Records: Jesse and James Tate, Continental line; Capt. M. Tate of militia.
     Yours truly,
     W. G. STANARD,
     Virginia Historical Society."

John and Robert Tate from Washington records War Department. Samuel (Irish) enlisted Sept. 4, 1755. Henry and Robert took oath of allegiance in Henry Co., Va.

John Tate married Mary Bracken, who was of German descent; was three times sheriff of Russell Co., Va., and a Colonel and Whig in time of Washington. On H. John Tate's farm at Zumbeg, near Lebanon, Russell Co., Va., we find a moss-covered slab that reads: "Col. John Tate, died Dec. 15, 1828, aged 85 yrs., and Mary Tate, his wife, died March 13, 1817, aged 75 years." Robert Tate, their son, was born in Russell Co., Va., July 31, 1768, where his parents remained until their death. He married Winnie Atkinson, who was born in South Carolina, Aug., 1766, and was a descendant of the French Huguenots. Soon after their marriage, with brother Samuel they removed to Pulaski Co., Ky. (1806), and lived and died on a farm one-half mile west of Tateville, on Cincinnati Southern Ry., ten miles south of Somerset. The old house, with wooden latches and string, still stands on the old farm, where live John and Reuben Shaddown grandsons of Mattie Buster, built by Robert and Samuel, who lived next farm south. Two miles south of this place is the "Milt Short" bend of the Cumberland River, where the grandfather of the writer lived when in Kentucky. Robert and Samuel are buried at Tateville Cemetery.

Robert Tate was a slave-owner, but would never punish any of his negroes himself; he always sent for his brother Samuel to do all the punishment. He was a great Methodist before the time of Alexander Campbell, when they became Disciples of Christ. He was a very religious man, aways wearing fancy deerskin clothing and hunting shirt at the religious meetings. His brother Samuel after the war of 1812 was made a major, and served for twenty years in the County Courts of Pulaski Co. Samuel's children were: William O.; John; Samuel Bracken; Robt. M. and Bank G. Tate, and three daughters Cecil Geneva.

Isaac Tate, brother of Robert, about the year 1883 left Virginia for Kentucky, then located in Missouri. His sister married, 1758, John Callaway in Virginia. John son of Major Samuel, was a Baptist minister until converted by Alexander Compbell. His two distinguished sons: Samuel, b. Dec. 19, 1825, and Judge S. H. Tate, b. Dec. 5, 1828, still living at Somerset. Samuel married Minerva Martin, 1846; ten children all living. John S , 53 yrs.; Geo. W., 51 yrs.; Robert M., 49; W. S., 36 yrs.; grandson Asar Tate, Somerset. Judge Tate's son Samuel O., member of Kentucky Legislature.

The Tates were a healthy family; none was ever known to have died of consumption; and usually held some office in their county especially sheriff.

Robert's daughter, Mary Tate, b. Dec. 5, 1811; d. Dec. 13, 1864, cem. 1 mile south of Springville; m. Milton Short, Jan. 8, 1829, in Pulaski Co., Ky., where they resided until 1836, when they moved to Indiana. It was here that they freed their slaves they had inherited from the Robert Tate estate.

John Tate and Mary Bracken's children:—

Robt. Tate, b. July 31, 1768; d. Aug. 3, 1844; m. Winnie Atkinson, b. Aug., 1766, d. April 13, 1856.

Samuel Tate, b. Nov. 11, 1775; d. May 21, 1845; m. Jane Owens, b. Aug. 10, 1778, d. Nov. 24 1861.

Homer Tate, m. Cole Fugate.

John Tate.

Lydia Tate, m. William Fugate.

Isaac Tate.

Mattie Tate, d. 1847, m. John Buster.

Hannah, m. Fugate. She lived and died five miles S. W. Tateville. Ch.: Jane, m. Lewis; Polly, m. Geo. Ellis; Winnie, m. Lewis Shaddown; Martha, m. F. Claunch.

Robert Tate and Winnie Atkinson Tate's children:

Lydia Tate, b. Aug. 15, 1808; d. Dec. 9, 1845; m. Joseph Smith, Jan. 1, 1824. Ch. Jane Shaddown, d. Ky.; Rebecca Penky d. Ind.

Mara Bracken Baker, d. Ind. Sam. Killed late war; Penton Smith lives veteran in Lebanon, Ind., 65 yrs. old.

Samuel Tate, b. May 13, 1810; d. Oct. 8, 1828. Mary Tate, b. Dec. 5, 1811; d. Dec. 13, 1864; m. Milton Short, Jan. 8, 1829.

John Tate, b. May 31, 1813; d. Oct. 27, 1823, Somerset, Ky.

Remarks: I have spared no pains or expense to make this report accurate.

R. N. MAYFIELD.

THE PATTONS

A PIONEER FAMILY IN KENTUCKY AND THEIR DESCENDANTS

By SARA G. CLARK

Captain John McKinley Chapter, D. A. R.

It has been said that "He who cares nothing about his ancestors, will rarely achieve anything worthy of being remembered by his descendants". If this be true, those who come after me, will have much to recall, as there are but few things which interest me more than the records of those who have gone before, hence it is a real pleasure to comply with a request to arrange my Patton data for publication. In doing this I think it will be interesting to begin with the family in Virginia.

First I will take up Roger Dyer whose daughter Esther (or Hester) married Matthew Patton. Roger Dyer was one of the early settlers in Pendleton County, West Virginia (then Augusta County, Virginia, and later Rockingham County). He bought over 800 acres of land for twenty pounds current money and his son, William Dyer, bought 350 acres for fourteen pounds. From the same tract of 1850 acres which had been patented to Robert Green on January 12, 1746, four other men, viz. Matthew Patton, John Patton, Jr., John Smith and William Stevenson bought land. On August 28, 1750, Roger Dyer, William Dyer, William Stevenson, Matthew Patton and John Patton "were added to the list of tithables" in Augusta County, Virginia, so it is certain that they had made their settlement by 1750. It was the earliest settlement in that section of the country on the south branch of the Potomac and was known as the "Dyer Settlement".

We know nothing of the early life of Roger Dyer or of his wife. They had the following children:

1. Esther b. 1731, d. between 1816 and 1821. She married Matthew Patton.
2. William Dyer had two sons, Roger b. 1755 and John b. 1757.
3. Hannah Dyer d. between 1815 and 1820, m. Frederick Keister b. 1730, d. 1815. They had three sons and several daughters.
4. Sarah m. Henry Hawes who was dead by 1755. About 1764 Sarah Dyer Hawes m. Robert Davis. Sarah had a daughter Hannah by her first husband, and eight children by her second. Robert Davis was a captain in the Revolutionary Army.
5. James Dyer b. 1744, d. 1807, was married three times, 1st. Ann Harrison, 2nd. Jane Ralston or Rolstone October 13, 1780 and 3rd. Nancy Hall. (This was sent to me by Mrs. Mary Lee Keister Talbot, 2000

Lincoln Park, West Chicago.) James Dyer had 13 children, 9 sons and 4 daughters. He was prominent in Augusta, Rockingham and Pendleton counties; a constable in Augusta, in 1768, one of the first justices of Rockingham County, in 1777, one of the commissioners of Pendleton, when it was organized in 1788.

VIRGINIA FARM IN WEST VIRGINIA
(Third Prize Old Homes Contest)

"In 1763 Robert Davis purchased by deed from his brother-in-law Matthew Patton, a tract of land on the South Fork of the South Branch of the Potomac in what is now Pendleton County, West Virginia, and took up his abode there. To this pioneer home he brought his wife, Sarah, who had seen her father, Roger Dyer, tomahawked at the Fort Seybert massacre, 1758, and who herself had been carried away captive by the Indian chieftain, Kilbuck. Later she escaped and returned to her old home bringing back with her a sole memento of her two years with the Shawnees, a curiously carved Indian spoon, which today is a cherished possession of a descendant. To the original purchase, Robert Davis added to his home by purchasing adjacent desirable lands from 1791 to 1800, three of said patents being signed by James Monroe, one by Henry Lee and one by Beverley Randolph, all governors of Virginia.

Robert Davis was a member of the commission to organize Pendleton County in 1788, and was immediately appointed the first "high sheriff" and later served in the Legislature at Richmond. Today, he and his wife, Sarah, rest in a little family cemetery, just above and in sight of the present Davis residence and in the same plot are the graves of Robert's son, a grandson and their wives, through whom the home passed without break. Today Robert's great-grandson, Laban Davis, 92 years of age who marched with Lee and Jackson, owns and lives on the farm that his great grandfather began to carve out of the wilderness of western Virginia 172 years ago. And I, the present owner's granddaughter, listen to the same pleasing murmur of the river and look up at the same beautiful Shenandoah Mountain crests, that have continuously charmed through six generations.

Margaret Temple,
Pendleton County, West Virginia."

(This is copied from a newspaper clipping sent to me by Mrs. Clay Shropshire, Lemon's Mill Pike, Lexington, Kentucky.)

Fort Seybert and The Death of Roger Dyer. Taken from a newspaper "Moorefield" Hardy County, West Virginia. This was loaned to me by cousin, Mrs. Alla Gay Jones of Winchester, Kentucky.

"Correspondent writes interestingly of Indian Massacre at Fort Seybert."
Much of this information was gathered from the citizens of South Fork

Valley, who had heard from their ancestors the incidents of that early period. The late William C. Miller, whose dwelling stands on the site of the old fort, having possessed more traditional information than any other person.

Settlers came into the South Fork Valley from the region of The Highland, and into the South Branch Valley from the region of Petersburg and Moorefield. By the year 1758 about 200 settlers lived in the two valleys nearby, equally divided between the two, and located chiefly in the vicinity of Upper Tract and Fort Seybert.

Early in the year 1754 hostilities began between the English and French colonies and traders along the Ohio—the beginning of the French and Indian War. Braddock's well known defeat the following year, was fraught with bitter consequences for the English settlers along the northwestern frontier, leaving them exposed to merciless atacks from the French supporting Indians. To provide quickly for their protection the General Assembly in Virginia, in 1756 appropriated $33,333.00 for the construction of twenty-three forts extending from Hampshire to Halifax Counties. These forts were erected as speedily as possible and their defense entrusted to Colonel George Washington, already noted for his military leadership. Among the forts, both probably erected in 1756 were Fort Seybert and Fort Upper Tract. Fort Seybert was located on the left hand side of South Fork River, and situated on an elevation which sloped rapidly to a ravine on the north and descended rapidly over a ledge of rocks to the river bottom southeast. The defense consisted of a circular stockade some twenty yards in diameter, consisting of logs or puncheons, end in the ground side by side, and rising to a height sometimes twelve feet. A puncheon door closed the entrance. Within the stockade stood the two story blockhouse, twenty-one feet square. From the upper loopholes the open space about the fort could be swept by the rifles of the defenders. One weakness of the fort was the absence of water within the stockade. This had to be procured from a spring about seventy-five yards distant, the path to which was unprotected. In times of danger it was expected that the settlers would gather at the fort for protection and that the men would constitute the garrison. The command was entrusted to Jacob Seybert. Even before the line of forts was completed, the expected raids began.

Washington, stationed at Winchester in 1757, writes "Not an hour, yes scarcely a minute passes that does not produce fresh alarms and melancholy accounts". In August, 1756, he wrote "We have built some forts, and altered others, as far south as the Potomac, as settlers have been molested, and there only remains one body of settlers at a place called Upper Tract who need a guard." The next year there were raids in the Upper Tract. One of the leading characters in the Indian raids in Hampshire, Hardy, Grand and Pendleton Counties was Kilbuck. He was of the same trible as Tecumseh. Kilbuck had lived among the settlers and knew most of them. Against one of them at least he had a grudge. Peter Casey engaged him for fourteen shillings to bring back a runaway servant. Kilbuck promptly delivered the servant, but Casey refused to pay the stipulated sum. In the altercation which followed, Casey knocked Kilbuck down with his cane. When war broke out he sought opportunity to kill Casey, but never found it. Many Indians were wronged by unscrupulous settlers, and for this there was a terrible harvest of "blood and tears". Kilbuck had a well known reputation for treachery.

THE MASSACRE

The morning of April 28, 1758 dawned upon Fort Seybert with a fog hanging over the valley of South Fork as if presaging the calamity that hung over the heads of the settlers. By an unfortunate conjunction of events, part of the men were absent from the settlement, having crossed the Shenandoah Mountains the day before. Probably because of their absence, the men, women and children were gathered within the fort. They knew that danger was imminent, but were unaware of the immediate presence of an enemy stealing steathily among them. Concealed by the fog and protected by the forest was a party of forty Shawnee warriors. At their head was the revengeful and treacherous Kilbuck. It is probable that they separated into several groups for the purpose of surprising and capturing the scattered settlers. One of these captured Mrs. Peter Hawes (Sarah Dyer) at her home at what is now the Laban Davis place near Brandywine, opposite the mouth of Hawes Run. She was taken on down the river toward the fort, and as her captors conducted her along the high bank of the river, she suddenly pushed one of the savages next to the river into the water. He returned in a rage threatening to kill her, but his companions restrained him, and laughed at him, calling him a "squaw man".

The first violent act of the savages near the fort was the killing of William Dyer. Mr. Dyer was out hunting when waylaid by the savages. He attempted to fire upon them, but his flint lock missed fire and he was shot dead. Now that the presence of the savages was known, the settlers fastened the gate and put themselves on the defensive. An Indian peering up over the ledge of rocks, under the brow of the hill was espied by Nicholas Seybert, fifteen year old son of Captain Seybert, from his position at a loophole, and fired upon. Kilbuck now changed his attack to strategy, and called out to Captain Seybert in English that they would all be spared. Seybert entered into a parley with Kilbuck as a result of which he agreed to surrender without resistance, and turn over to the Indians the money and valuables in the fort. Kilbuck agreed that the inmates of the fort would not be harmed. Some of the inmates favored this conditional surrender while others opposed it. Nicholas Seybert was bitter in his opposition, and attempted by violence to prevent a surrender. Before the gate was opened he took aim at Kilbuck and would have killed him dead but his gun was knocked aside by his father. The bullet struck at Kilbuck's feet. There has been much conjecture as to why Captain Seybert confided in the promise of an Indian, on the war path, and did the most unparalled thing of surrendering to a savage foe. Whatever his reason or reasons, appears now to have been a mistake. Results might have been better had they resisted and if young Seybert had been permitted to kill the leader, the Indians would have withdrawn, but these things were not known until too late. Events in the past are clearer than in the future. The gate was now thrown open and the Indians begun to enter. Kilbuck greeted Seybert by striking him in the mouth with the pipe end of his tomahawk, knocking loose his front teeth. This deed and the action of the savages showed the settlers, too late, what they might expect, and confusion followed. Young Seybert refused to surrender, and was overpowered. A man named Robertson managed to secrete himself, and was the only one who managed to escape. The inmates were made prisoners, the money and valuables secured, and the block-house set on fire. The Indians took their prisoners up the slope toward the South Fork Mountains about a quarter of a mile. Here they divided the prisoners into two groups, placing in one group those whom they selected as desirables as captives. At some time while the prisoners were being separated, James Dyer, a swift footed youth of fourteen, broke from them and attempted to escape by flight, so swift was he that his pursuers did not overtake him, until he had reached the river three-quarters of a mile distant. Here in a cane-brake, opposite the dwelling of J. W. Conrad, he was taken. Because of his swiftness he was preserved.

Having selected and bound their prisoners, the remaining prisoners doomed to perish were placed in a row, probably seated upon a log.

About this time, Roger Dyer who was among the doomed ones, was struck in the mouth with a tomahawk. His daughter, Mrs. Hawes, also among the victims, saw him spit the broken teeth from his mouth, and fainted. When she had recovered, she had been placed among the captives, and one of them placed in her stead. This change which saved her life, was made because the Indians had among their many superstitions one which prevented their killing a person in a fainting condition. The fatal moment had now come. The unfortunate victims were quickly tomahawked, then scalped, and their bodies left lying where they fell, seventeen in all. The names of three have come down: Captain Sybert, Roger Dyer and the Wallace boy.

The Indians had now done what they came to do, and started quickly on their return. They put their eleven captives in line, bore their wounded warriors, and started Indian file northward up the mountain side.

When they had traveled several days, young Seybert called attention to a flock of young turkeys flying some distance from them. Kilbuck remarked that he had sharp eyes and asked if he was not the one who shot the warrior who died on the way. Seybert replied that he was, and said that he would have killed Kilbuck also, if his father had not knocked his gun aside. Kilbuck complimented the young man's bravery and told him if he had killed him (Kilbuck) the warriors would have given up the attack and fled.

The captives whose names are known as Nicholas Seybert, James Dyer, Mrs. Hawes, Mrs. Peterson and a Miss Hevener. The latter was possibly the first captive to return, but no details of her escape are known. After the lapse of two years, James Dyer had gained the confidence of his captors and was taken by them on trading expeditions. While in Fort Pitt on one of these expeditions, he was sent with an Indian boy to buy bread. Eluding the watchfulness of his companion, he entered a cabin and sought protection. The trader's wife hid him behind a chest and threw a pile of furs over him. The Indians spent the afternoon searching for him. In the course of their search they entered the cabin, and begun throwing the furs off, one by one. When he was almost uncovered they ceased their examination and he was safe. An English trooper conveyed him six or seven miles on horseback from which place he reached his friends in Pennsylvania.

The Rescue of Mrs. Hawes by Her Brother-in-Law, Matthew Patton

When Matthew Patton took his cattle to market at Pittsburgh, the dealer to whom he sold them told him that an Indian tribe there had a red-headed woman among them. Mr. Patton suspected this was his wife's sister and had the dealer to arrange for her to come into his store where he concealed her behind his counter and covered her with furs. The Indians begun to search for her, and entered the store, and as in searching for her brother, threw off part of the covering hides. Thoroughness not being a characteristic of Indian habits, they ceased in both searches before uncovering the fugitives. That night Mr. Patton, accompanied by Mrs. Hawes, left Pittsburgh secretly and traveled until daylight, when he hid her in the thick top of a fallen tree. Night came on and Mr. Patton rejoined her and they traveled again. After that he provided her with other clothes instead of her Indian apparel and they traveled by day until their return. Mrs. Hawes had been with the Indians seven years and had traveled to the Great Lakes, and over much of the prairie of the middle west. She often spoke of the country she had traversed.

Mrs. Hawes had a daughter, just a child at the time of her capture. This child, Hannah, was with relatives near Dayton when her mother was carried away and when she returned from captivity after many years the child had forgotten her, and at first feared her. When Mrs. Hawes returned she brought with her a large spoon which the Indians had carved for her from a buffalo's horn, and this spoon was handed down, and is still possessed by one of her descendants. Another keepsake in the family is the wearing apparel of her little son, Sammy Davis, who was drowned.

While even the names and family ties of most of them are lost yet, "one touch of nature makes the whole world kin" and the story of their unhappy fate will still touch a responsive chord of pity whenever told and implore the passing tribute of a sigh.

> "Tis the wink of an eye, the draft of a breath,
> From the blossom of health, to the paleness of death;
> From the gilded saloon, to the bier and the shroud,
> Oh! Why should the spirit of mortal be proud?"

A fairly authentic story records that Hannah Dyer who had married Frederick Keister, who owned a plantation adjoining Fort Seybert, was in the fort with her two year old son, James, and her baby daughter, Hannah, and escaped in some remarkable manner by seeking cover of a rock near a spring.

Roger Dyer was a Quaker, and first lived in Lancaster County, Pennsylvania. It is said that the Dyers left Pennsylvania because there were too many Germans settling in that vicinity. Two of his daughters later married Germans.

The father of Matthew Patton was Captain John Patton, High Sheriff of Augusta County, Virginia. It seems that he was twice married, 1st. to Miss Rogers. Their children were John, Jr., Matthew and Samuel. Next he married Agnes. Their children were William, James, Margaret, Isabell and Agnes.

The following was sent to me by Mrs. Mary Lee Keister Talbot of Chicago:

Notes from Augusta County Records.
Augusta County Court House, (Augusta 21, 1936. Copied this date).

WILL OF JOHN PATTON

In the Name of God Amen. January the second day in the year of our Lord, One Thousand Seven Hundred and Fifty-six, I, John Patton of the County of Agusta and collony of Virginia ———

Im primus I give and bequeath to Agnese my Dearly beloved wife the use of the Plantation whereon I now Dwell with all the appurtenances thereto belonging during her widowhood Provided that no waste be made thereon, I do also bequeath to her One Large Bay Mare with a White Face and I do put into her Hands my moveable Estate except what is hereafter named. In order to have my five children (to wit) William, James, Margaret, Isabel and Agness Educated and Supported until they come to Age, and when any of my said children come to Age such child is to have an equal Share of the remainder of my sd Estate. Deducting one-third of the whole for the use of my wife, and if she Intermarry before that time I order that my other Executors Lay her off her sd third of my Estate and the remainder to divide Equally amongst my sd five children. * * *

Item: William and James, my beloved sons, Two Hundred Acres of Land on which I now Dwell in Fee Simple.

I do Bequeath to my son, William, a white faced Stallion Colt and I give to my son, James, the Fole which the Bald Mare is now with.

Item: I give and bequeath to each of my above sd. three Daughters a mare now running at the South Branch of the Potowmack.

As my elder children are already Portioned off they are not by this Will Intitled to any Part of what I now Possess. Therefore order that none but such as above named are to have any share of my Estate.

Wife Executrix & Alexander Miller and John Wardlow, Executors.

his
JOHN J   P PATTON
mark

WILL MCCLUNG
JOHN STIEVENSON
MATTHEW LYLE

March 16, 1757

Agnes Patton, Matthew Lyle and Alexr Miller gave bond of Three hundred pounds as Executrix of John Patton.

her
AGNES   PATTON
mark

In this will John Patton names only his second wife, Agness and her children, but near the close he says, "As my elder children are already portioned off, they are not by this will entitled to any part of what I now possess."

WILL OF ROGER DYER

In the name of God, Amen. This twenty-fourth day of February, in the year of our Lord 1757, I, Roger Dyer of Augusta County, being weak in body, but of perfect mind and memory thanks be given to God, thereto calling to mind the mortality of my body, and knowing that is appointed for all men once to dye, do make and ordain this to be my last will and Testament, that is to say principally and first of all, I give and recommend my soul in the hands of God, the hands of God that gave it and my body I recommend to the earth to be buried in a Christian manner Executors nothing doubting but at the Resurrection I shall receive the same again by the mighty power of God. And as touching such worldly estate where with it pleased God to bless me in this life, I give, Devise and dispose of them in the following.

Item. I give and bequeath to my well beloved wife, Hannah Dyer, after debts and charges be paid, the full third part of all my movables estaid of good and Grants whether in this Colloney or any other, and one good bed and one good horse or mare, which she shall use out of my stock, over and above the third part of the plantation I now live on until my son, James, comes of the age of twenty-one years unless my wife marry again then the plantation be rented out for the use of my sd son, James Dyer, I likewise constitute, make and ordain my well beloved wife my only and sole executor of my last will and testament. Item. I give and bequeath to my well beloved son, William Dyer, two shears to be equally divided between him and my three daughters after the rest is paid what is nominated in this will. Item. I give and bequeath to my well beloved son, James Dyer, the plantation that I now live on with all the improvements thereunto belonging and fifty acres serveyed by itself joining the same plantation I live on and not pattoned as yet. Messuages and all profits thereunto belonging in any wise and fifty pounds current money with the sd lands to his Heirs and assigns forever. Item. I give and bequeath unto my well beloved daughter, Hannah Gester, a certain tract of land lying in Hampshire County containing 427 acres of land, more or less, to her, Her heirs and Assigns forever. Item. I give and bequeath unto my grandson, Roger Dyer, son of William Dyer, twenty pounds current money of Virginia. Now after all the above legacies are paid the remainder of my movables is to be divided into five parts, and my beloved son, William Dyer is to have two parts, and my beloved daughters, Hester Patton, Sarah Hase and Hanna Gester, each of them one part. And I do hereby utterly disallow, revoke and disannul all and every other testament ratifying and confirming this and no other to be my last will and Testament in witness thereof I have hereunto set my hand and seal the Day and Year first above written.

ROGER DYER   Seal

Signed sealed in the presence
of us
WILLIAM MILLER
ADAM HIDER
WILLIAM GIBSON

At a Court held for Augusta County March the 21st, 1759. This last will and testament of Roger Dyer dec'd. was proved by the oath of William Gibson one of the witnesses thereto and ordered to lie in the office for further proof.

TESTE—

At a Court held for Augusta County May the 16, 1759. This last will and testament of Roger Dyer dec'd. being this day further proved by the oath of Adam Hider another of the witnesses thereto was admitted to record and on the motion of Hannah Dyer, the executrix, therein named who made oath according to law certificate is granted her for obtaining a probate in due form, she having with Abraham Smith & Ephraim Love, her securities, entered into and acknowledged their bond.

Teste—

Matthew Patton

Matthew Patton was of Scotch descent, but was born in the North of Ireland in 1730 and died in Clark County, Kentucky, May 3rd, 1803. He was a son of John Patton and a Miss Rogers, who came to Virginia in 1740 and settled in Augusta County on land granted to Preston, Breckinridge and Patton (James, a brother of John).

John Patton, Sr., and his sons John, Jr., and Matthew, removed to Orange County, North Carolina. John Patton, Jr., settled in Tyson County and one of his descendants was Lieutenant Governor of that state. Matthew Patton went to Virginia and settled on the south branch of the Potomac. He was a land owner as early as 1747, being then a lad of seventeen years. About 1749 he married Esther Dyer, a daughter of Roger Dyer. She was born 1731 and died in Clark County, Kentucky, September 1820. (A portion of this Matthew Patton data was given me by Cousin Alla Gay Jones.)

From Chalkley's record of Augusta County Order Book, Vol. 1, Page 75: "Matthew Patton qualified Lieutenant of Foot, November 23, 1753."

Page 175: "May 21st, 1768, Matthew Patton qualified Captain of Militia."

From a History of Rockingham County, Virginia, by John W. Wayland, Page 101:

"May 29, 1782, amount for service rendered and supplies furnished during the Revolutionary War allowed to Matthew Patton."

The Virginia Census for 1782 states that there were ten persons comprising the household of Matthew Patton.

When Pendleton County was formed in 1788, Matthew Patton was made one of the first Justices. Serving with him were his two brothers-in-law, James Dyer and Robert Davis, who had married Sarah Dyer Hawes.

This is what Morton says about him in his "History of Pendleton County", Page 91:

"Matthew Patton was one of the very first members of the Dyer Settlement, and after the murder of Roger Dyer he became a leading citizen of the Pendleton territory. He was commissioned justice of the peace, August 19, 1761, and for a number of years he took the list of tithables for this portion of Augusta County."

It seems that Matthew Patton was among the men who had gone over the mountain on business at the time of the Fort Seybert Massacre, and within a month after the massacre he was appointed administrator of the estates of several men, and the guardian of a child whose mother was captured by the Indians; his niece, the daughter of Sarah Dyer Hawes. He was probably one of the few men left after the massacre who could take care of the business of those who had been massacred.

Matthew Patton moved to Clark County, Kentucky, in 1790. He was a very prominent man, and took a leading part in all activities whether in Virginia, North Carolina or Kentucky, but is possibly best remembered for the improvement in the breeding of the Short Horn cattle.

This is quoted from Mr. William Warfield in his article in Fayette County History:

"The first introduction of improved cattle into Kentucky was due to the enterprise of the sons of Matthew Patton, Sr., a resident of the rich valley of the South Fork of the Potomac. In 1783 Mr. Patton had secured for his own use on his plantation in Virginia, a bull imported from England by Mr. Gaugh of Baltimore, Maryland, which was described by Mr. Patton himself as very large and of the Long Horn breed. In 1785 three of Mr. Patton's sons and his son-in-law, Mr. Gay, bought several half breed, the get of this bull, with them to Kentucky. In 1790 Matthew Patton himself emigrated to Clark County, Kentucky, bringing with him several more half breeds, calves of the same Long Horn bull. These cattle were very large and rangy, fattening slowly and late, but at maturity making excellent beef. Some of them were also first rate milkers. Having seen the benefit wrought by one cross of improved stock, Mr. Patton could not fail to try more. Accordingly we find him as soon as 1795, procuring through his son, William, two new animals of the Gaugh and Miller stock.

In all old records a sharp distinction is drawn between these new animals and the bull being used earlier being always identified respectively as Long and Short horns. The bull subsequently entered in the American Short Horn Herd Book as Mars (No. 1850) was a deep red with white face of good size and of round full form, with more bone than the popular stock of the present day. The heifer Venus was a pure white, except her ears which were red, of fine size, high form, short crumply horns, turning downward. Venus produced but two calves, both bulls, one was taken by William Patton to Chillicothe, Ohio, and the other by Roger Patton to Jessamine County. Mars remained in Clark County until the death of Matthew Patton, Sr., in 1803, when he was carried by Mr. Peeples to Montgomery County. In 1803 Daniel Harrison, James Patton and James Gay, sons-in-law and son of Matthew Patton, sent back to Mr. Miller's herd in Virginia for another bull of the "milk" Short Horn breed and got a two year old bull, "Pluto" (No. 850), certified to be by an imported bull, and out of an imported cow. He was dark red or brindle (roan) says Mr. Harrison, and when full grown, was the largest bull I ever saw. In 1810 Pluto went to Ohio, where he soon died.

The importation in 1810 by Captain William Smith of Fayette County of the bull "Buzzard", who was himself of mixed blood; of Inskip's Brindle in 1813; of the Case stock imported by Mr. Daniel Harrison from Maryland in 1814, and of the bull "Shaker" which had come from Mr. Miller's stock through the Ohio Shakers, completed the list of cattle brought to Kentucky previous to the year 1817, and those bulls crossed on native stock of the country, produced the "Patton stock", a great improvement on the old breeds. The superior excellence of the "Patton stock" over native cattle, naturally stimulated the minds of breeders, to attempt the possibility of further improvement.

Matthew Patton died May 3rd, 1803, at his home, "Sycamore", in Clark County, Kentucky. His grave is encased in a wall of rock, laid in cement, and upon this foundation rests a horizontal slab with this inscription:

"To The Memory
Of Matthew Patton
Who departed this life
3rd. day of May 1803
In the 73rd. year of his life."

Surrounding his tomb are many unknown graves, marked with head and foot-stones of native rock. The graves extend over a space of more than an acre.

The Sycamore estate is now owned by Benjamin Douglas Goff. He is a lineal descendant through both his paternal and maternal lines. His wife, Bessie Spahr Goff, is also a scion on her paternal side. "Sycamore" was destroyed by fire years ago.

From records I find Matthew Patton in 1774 furnished supplies for Lord Dunmore; was Captain of Militia in Virginia in 1768. He moved from the South Fork of the South Branch of the Potomac, known as Bull Pasture, about 1785.

Will of Matthew Patton

Clark County, Kentucky, Record Will Book 1, page 315.

In the name of God, Amen. Being old and infirm and weak of body, but of sound mind, I do hereby make and ordain and constitute this my last will and testament, to be executed by sons, hereafter named, to wit Matthew Patton, Jr., Roger Patton and William Patton. It is my will and desire, that after all my just debts are paid, and ample provision made for my beloved wife by my said executors, that all of my estate both real and personal, to be sold to the best advantage for my children, and be equally divided amongst them and that all sums of money, lands and negroes or other property already given them shall be taken into consideration and charged to each legatee, as they may have received, that as equal distribution be made, and that my above named executors shall dispose of my said estate, at the time and the place, and by the way they shall appoint, by way of public sale duly published, previous thereto. It is my will and my desire that my mulatto man, Cript, shall be free in six months after my death. It is also my will and desire that my mulatto woman's oldest children named Ruth and David be free at the age of twenty-four years, and be learned to read the Bible distinctly, also that my negro man, Henry, shall be free in ten years, and that my negro man, David, shall be free in twelve years after my decease, also I give and bequeath my mulatto woman and her youngest children to my beloved wife to dispose of as she may think proper. It is also my will and desire that my son, Matthew, do reside on my home place where he now lives and have the free use of as much as he wishes to occupy, until the land is sold, as may be agreed upon by my executors. Done this second day of May in the year of our Lord, 1803.

MATTHEW PATTON

In the presence of
 RICHARD A.
 THOMAS GOFF
 WILIAM BLACK

N. B. I had forgotten my daughter Sarah's children in the foregoing will, and in order that equal justice be done, it is my will and desire that her four children get a child's part, or one-eighth part of my estate after debts being paid and my wife being provided for as specified in my above will.

Done this third day of May, 1803.

his
MATTHEW   PATTON
mark

(He was now too weak to write his name.)

JAMES CROCKETT
THOMAS GOFF
WILLIAM BLACK

ESTHER PATTON'S WILL, CLARK COUNTY RECORDS, BOOK 5, PAGE 21.

In the name of God, Amen. I, Esther Patton, of the County of Clark, and State of Kentucky, being weak of body, but of sound and perfect mind and memory do make my last will in the manner following, that is to say, first I give and bequeath to Eliza Patton, daughter of Roger Patton, deceased, my saddle and bridle. To Mary Ann Patton, daughter of the said deceased, my bed and bedding. I likewise bequeath to the above Eliza and Mary Ann my negro girl, Nancy, which is not to be sold out of the family. I also bequeath unto Matthew Patton, son of Roger Patton, a note in my possession amounting to forty-nine dollars and ninety-five cents dated the nineteenth day of September, 1811, payable the twentieth day of September, 1812, on the estate of the said Roger Patton. I allow the balance of my estate to be divided as follows: I bequeath to my son, James Patton, one sixth part, and the remainder to be equally divided between my grandchildren William, Sally, John, Matthew, Eliza, and Mary Ann, children of Roger Patton, John, James, Benjamin and Ester Gay, children of James Gay, Ester, Margaret, Sally, Matthew, Ann and Polly Patton, children of John Patton, Sarah, Betsy and Julia Hume, children of John Hume, and Margaret Maxwell, daughter of Daniel Harrison. In witness whereof I have hereunto set my hand and seal the twenty-third day of October, in the year of our Lord, 1816.

ESTHER PATTON

Signed in the presence of us,
    PETER LILE
    CATY SCOBEE
    ROBERT SCOBEE

From a document sent me by S. Holloway of Winchester, and copied from Clark County records, dated January 15, 1817, the following heirs of Matthew Patton are mentioned:

    Heirs of Roger Patton, dec'd. (Matthew's son): Benjamin, James, Margaret, Sarah, William, John, Matthew, Eliza and Mary Ann Patton.
    Heirs of John Patton, dec'd.: Hetty, Margaret, Sarah, Ann, Mary and Matthew.
    Heirs of William Patton, dec'd.: James and Rebecca.
    Heirs of Sally Patton Gay, dec'd.: Benjamin Patton, John and James Gay and Hetty Gay Coffer.
    Heirs of Ann Patton Harrison, dec'd.: Margery, Benjamin, Hannah, Ann and Patton D. Harrison.

Children of Matthew and Esther Dyer Patton:

1. Matthew, Jr., b. 1750. (So stated by his war record.) m. Rebecca.
2. William, Captain of Militia in Pendleton County, West Virginia, married Catherine. Moved from Clark County to Chillicothe, Ohio.
3. Roger Dyer, m. 1st Mary McAfee in Virginia, 2nd. a Miss Fravir, d. in Jessamine County, Kentucky, in 1812.
4. James, m. Elizabeth.
5. John, m. Mary Hopkins August 29, 1786 (Rockingham County Records).
6. Ann, b. April 10, 1763, d. February 7, 1813, m. January 29, 1784, Daniel Harrison.

7. Sarah, b. May 10, 1762, d. November 14, 1795, m. about 1786 to Captain James Gay of Clark County, Kentucky.
8. Esther, b. 1769, d. 1856, m. John Hume, b. 1752, d. May 24, 1824, m. 17—.

Clark County Records, Winchester, Kentucky, Page 142, Benjamin P. Gay m. Polly Anderson October 23, 1816. (He was son of James and Sarah Patton Gay.)

From the same, Page 60, William Patton m. Ann Harrison December 23, 1808. (Ann was daughter of Daniel and Anna Patton Harrison.)

This was sent to me from Mrs. A. S. Frye of Somerset, Kentucky. Now I take up descendants of Matthew Patton, Jr. Children of Matthew and Rebecca Patton:

1. John Dyer, m. Hetty.
2. Benjamin W., b. 1788, m. February 8, 1815, Margaret St. Clair Patton. He d. February 11, 1825, age 37.
3. James, m. Polly Huston.
4. Robert, m. Elizabeth Johnson.
5. William, m. Ann.
6. Matthew, m. Sarah Patton November, 1818, d. October, 1833.
7. David S., m. Hannah Kelley November 14, 1815, d. in Paducah in 1837.
8. Rebecca, m. Edward Palmer.
9. John, m. Ester Patton.

(I believe that Margaret St. Clair Patton, Sarah and Esther were sisters, all daughters of Roger Patton, who died in Jessamine County in 1812. If this be true, then they were first cousins of their husbands.)

RECORDS OF CHRISTIAN COUNTY, KENTUCKY.

Deed Book I, Page 59. Matthew Patton, Sr., and Rebecca, his wife sold to Dennis Payne lot No. 3 in Hopkinsville, March 9, 1818.

Deed Book L, Page 123, February 11, 1820. John D. Patton and Hetty, his wife, sold to Robert P. Henry lot No. 11 in Hopkinsville.

Deed Book L, Page 126, October 9, 1820. Benjamin W. Patton and Peggy, his wife, James Patton and Polly, his wife, sold to Zack Glass a tract of land.

Deed Book N, Page 37, April 28, 1834. John D. Patton appointed his son, St. Clair Patton, his attorney to sell all his land in Kentucky and Illinois.

Deed Book N, Page 323, November 8, 1822. Matthew Patton, Sr., for the love and affection he bears to his son, William Patton, deeds a lot to said William Patton in Hopkinsville.

From the pension papers of Matthew Patton, Sr. (Hopkinsville, Kentucky), Certificate 26880—"Matthew Patton was born May, 1750 (O. S.) in Augusta County, Virginia, that part which was later called Pendleton County, and moved when a young man to Baltimore, Maryland. While a resident of Baltimore, he volunteered, 1775, as one of about sixty gentlemen of handsome property who organized themselves into a company of Infantry under Captain Mordecai Gist . . . served four weeks as a private in said company . . . He then served from 1776 at various times until the surrender of Cornwallis, was in the battles of Brandywine and Germantown."

"He had lived in Christian County, Kentucky," about twenty years when he made application for pension January 8, 1834.

(This Matthew was son of Matthew Patton who died in Clark County, Kentucky, in 1803.)

"Benjamin W. Patton, b. December, 1788, came from Clark County, Kentucky, to Hopkinsville and was a son of Matthew Patton, an early settler from Maryland. He died in 1825, age 37. David S. Patton was his younger brother, who died in Paducah in 1837."

> Copied from the marriage bonds of Christian County:
> "Edward Palmer to Rebecca Patton, November 1, 1812
> Philip Allen to Sally L. Allen, February 16, 1807
> Daniel S. Patton to Hannah Kelley, November 24, 1815
> James Patton to Polly Huston, March 28, 1815
> Matthew D. Patton to Susan Davidge, February 14, 1825
> Susan, a daughter of Judge Benjamin Davidge by his first wife, Elizabeth Bell
> Robert Patton to Elizabeth Johnson, April 11, 1819
> Ira Allen to Polly Patton, March 4, 1811."

Records of Christian County Order Book G, Page 190. Benjamin W. Patton, guardian of Matthew D. Patton, infant and heir of Roger Patton, dec'd.

Order Book J, Page 145. Benjamin W. Patton, guardian of Eliza Patton and Mary Ann Patton, infant heirs of Roger Patton, dec'd. Roger Patton d. in Jessamine County in 1812 and was the father of Mrs. Benjamin W. Patton. Benjamin and Margaret Patton had only one child, Margaret.

Will Book E, Page 193, October 31, 1827. Appraisement of the estate of Robert Patton, dec'd., widow Elizabeth infant heirs, Hester and Mariah, Adms. Matthew Patton, Sr. (husband of Rebecca). Robert was their son.

Order Book G, Page 190, March 6, 1822. Banjamin W. Patton, guardian of Matthew D. Patton, infant and heir of Roger Patton, dec'd.

Matthew D. Patton was then over 14.

Order Book G, Page 145. Benjamin W. Patton, guardian of Eliza and Mary Ann Patton, infant heirs of Roger Patton, dec'd.

Will Book D, Page 291. Will of Benjamin W. Patton, written February 8, 1825, proven May 4, 1825. Daughter Margaret, if she should die during her minority, then everything is left to John D. Patton and John T. Patton. Benjamin W. Patton died February 11, 1825. John D. was his brother (children of Matthew and Rebecca). John T. Patton died before June 1, 1831.

Margaret Patton was an only child of Benjamin W. and Margaret St. Clair Patton, his cousin.

Will Book E, Page 193 and 234, March 14, 1826, and October 31, 1827. Appraisement and settlement of estate of Robert Patton estate, widow Elizabeth, infant heirs Hester and Mariah.

Admr. Matthew Patton (husband of Rebecca). Robert was their son.

Will Book H, Page 51, September 22, 1832, proven October 28, 1833. Will of Matthew Patton, Jr., daughter George Ann, brothers, D. S. Patton, James Patton, sister Rebecca Palmer, other bequests to Matthew Stacy, Rebecca Kenny, Matthew P. Kenny, and Margaret Filson (heirs of James Kenny), Mary, wife of James Lander, and daughter of James Kenny. The wife of this Matthew Patton was Sarah, daughter of Roger Patton.

Deed Book E, Page 1, September 5, 1814. Eleanor Dyer, late wife of Robert Patton, and John Gray, executor of Robert Patton, dec'd, sold to the said John Gray land in Monroe County, Virginia, being part of the dower of said Eleanor.

Deed Book K, Page 420, September 3, 1838. Jesse Patton, James T. Patton, Louisa N. Patton and Mary Ann Patton, heirs and infant children of William Patton, dec'd. Patton D. Harrison, their next friend and guardian, David S. Patton, Administrator of William Patton, dec'd, David S. Patton, Executor of Matthew Patton, Jr., dec'd, and David S. Patton in his own individual rights, and Elizabeth Patton, Administratrix of Robert G. Patton, and A. Hites, Commissioner, sold all interest in a storeroom on Main Street in Hopkinsville to David Glass.

From tombstones in the Old Baptist Graveyard in Hopkinsville:

Ann Patton
Wife of
William Patton
Died March 17, 1822
Age 28 years, 11 months and —— days

Benjamin W. Patton
Born ——, Died February 11, 1825

Mrs. Margaret St. Patton
Wife of
Benjamin W. Patton
Born ——, Dec'd. ——, 1833

From Kentucky D. A. R. Year Book, 1933-34. Matthew Patton, son of Matthew Patton, Jr., a Revolutionary soldier, m. Sally Patton November, 1818, and died October, 1833. Buried in old Baptist graveyard in Hopkinsville.

Benjamin W. Patton, b. ——, m. Margaret St. Clair Patton (cousin) February 8, 1815, d. February 11, 1825. Buried in old Baptist cemetery, Hopkinsville, a son of Matthew Patton, Revolutionary soldier.

From Marriage Records of Jessamine County, Kentucky. (County seat, Nicholasville.)
Benjamin W. Patton and Margaret Patton, February 18, 1815.
James Patton and Sally Bourne, December 8, 1815.

Culpepper County, Virginia, by R. G. Green, Page 74. John Patton married Sally, daughter of Alexander and Mildred C. Taylor.
Page 108. John M. Patton married P. French, daughter of Isaac Hite Williams and Lucy Slaughter.
Page 68. Thomas Patton m. Betsy Moss, 1804.
Page 57. John Bailey m. Alice Patton, 1802.
Page 62. William Embry m. Hannah Patton, 1818.

Copied from graves on the old Harrison farm near Winchester, Kentucky:

In memory of
Ann Harrison
Who departed this life
April 18, 1820
In the 62nd. year of her age
By her nephew, Patton D. Harrison

In memory of
Margaret Maxwell
Late Margaret Harrison
Born May 16, 1785
And departed this life
August 1838
By her brother, Patton D. Harrison

In memory of
Ann Harrison
Consort of
Daniel Harrison
Who departed this life
February 7th, 1813
In the fiftieth year of her age
By her son, Patton D. Harrison

In memory of
Daniel Harrison
Born Sept. 2, 1760
Who departed this life
March ——, 1823
By his son, Patton D. Harrison

Patton Daniel
Son of Daniel and Ann (Patton) Harrison
Born Nov. 2nd., 1795
Died March 26, 1841
Married Mary Elgin, Sept. 28, 1820

(This was all sent to me by Mrs. A. S. Frye, Somerset, Kentucky. Different ones had given it to her.)

James Patton, son of Matthew and Esther Dyer Patton. (This is Mrs. A. S. Frye's line, also sent by her.) James m. Elizabeth.

Children:
1. Matthew
2. John m. Sibbee Holley 20th of December, 1805
3. Polly m. Henry Holley, 2 of May, 1806

Children of John and Sibbee Holley Patton:
1. James
2. Elizabeth m. Fisher November 6, 1827
3. Sarah Ann m. James Dunn
4. Richard
5. John William
6. Polly m. Rice
7. Mackey died young
8. Matthew Thompson died young

Children of James and Sarah Ann Patton Dunn:
1. Elizabeth b. October, 1828, d. very young, m. Baughman
2. Eleanor b. November 18, 1832, d. 19—, m. John Moss
3. Martha b. 1835, d. 1835
4. Sybil b. November 5, 1863, d. 18—, m. Doctor Armstrong
5. Augustine b. November 21, 1838, d. December, 1928, unmarried
6. John b. November 28, 1839, d. 19—, m. 1st Hannah Dunn, 2nd. Edna Sutton

7. Richard b. December 12, 1840, d. 19—, m. Katie Paxton.
8. Joshua b. January 15, 1843, d. young
9. Mary b. December 1, 1845, d. 18—
10. Sarah b. March 26, 1849, m. Thomas Moore
11. James b. September 30, 1851, d. July 29, 1919, m. August 23, 1882 Mamie McRoberts
12. Mackay b. February, 1855, m. Richard Allen McGarth

Children of James and Mamie McRoberts Dunn:
1. Eva b. March 6, 1884, m. J. R. Ridings
2. Margaret McRoberts, b. December 31, 1890, m. January 22, 1912 Archie Spears Frye
3. Mary Harvey b. August 30, 1892, m. E. P. Lane

This is copied from a paper which Miss Julia Spurr loaned me:

Sally Ann Patton married James Dunn of Jessamine County November 26, 1827, at the home of her parents in Clark County, near Winchester, Kentucky, and rode horseback to his home near Bryantsville, the home built by Augustine and Eleanor Dunn, who lived with James until their death.

A wagon loaded with furniture, bedding and two negroes, gifts from her parents, preceded Sally Ann to her new home.

In her trousseau was one checked silk and one woolen dress and a white leghorn hat which her father had brought to her from Philadelphia, on his return from his trip shortly before she was married.

Next I give something of Sarah, daughter of Matthew and Esther Dyer Patton.

Sarah was born May 10, 1762, d. November 14, 1795. About 1786 she m. Captain James Gay of Clark County, Kentucky. Their children were Benjamin P., John, James and Hetty. After the death of his first wife Captain James Gay m. in 1797 Elizabeth Dunlap. The father of James Gay was also James Gay (1719-1776) of Calf Pasture and Gay's Run who came from Ireland to Pennsylvania, thence to Augusta County, Virginia, with his brothers William, John, Robert, Henry and Samuel Gay.

Ann Patton b. April 16, 1763, d. February 7, 1813, m. January 29, 1784.

Daniel Harrison b. September 2, 1760, d. March 16, 1823. Moved to Clark County 1818. The parents of Daniel were Daniel and Sarah Moore Harrison; he was b. 1729, d. 1817. His grandfather was Jesse Harrison, who m. Margaret Cravens. He was b. 1701, d. July 10, 1770. His great-grandfather was Captain Daniel Harrison, son of Isaiah Harrison. Captain Daniel Harrison was b. 1660, d. 1738. Name of wife, Abigail Smith. (D. A. R. records.)

Children of Daniel and Ann Patton Harrison:

Margaret b. May 16, 1785, d. August 5, 1835, m. Maxwell

Benjamin

Hannah

Anna m. William Patton December 22, 1808

Patton D. b. November 2, 1795, d. 1841, m. September 28, 1820

Ann Elgin, who was b. August 9, 1804, d. August 9, 1870

Their daughter, Ann Harrison b. April 14th, 1823, d. February 2, 1844, m. April 19, 1842, John Stuart Williams, b. 1818, d. 1898. General Williams served in the war against Mexico, and for his gallantry at Cerro Gordo he was promoted to the rank of Colonel and ever afterwards he was called "Cerro Gordo Williams". His parents were General Williams and Rebecca Leithell. John Augustus Williams was a nephew of Samuel Williams.

(From Genealogies and Sketches of Old Families.)

The daughter of John Stuart Williams and Ann Harrison was Mollie Elliott Williams, b. September 21st, 1843, d. October 6, 1934.

Their children are:

Mamie m. T. W. L. Van Meter September 24, 1889

James, dec'd.

John m. Anne Fulton October 3, 1906

Patton D. b. 1867, d. December 12, 1935.

Letter written by William Patton of Richmond, Virginia, to his sister, Ester Patton Hume, and her husband, John Hume:

Dear Brother and Sister:

As I have nothing of importance to communicate, I suppose it will give you some satisfaction to hear of your friends on the Western waters. From the last accounts I received, Father's family were all well, though Mother had been very unwell for some time in the fall. The rest of the friends on the branch are well. Brother Matthew arrived in Stanton about the first of November, and he and family have been well, except one of his children who has been unwell, but was recovering when he wrote me last. I believe they are tolerably well pleased with the place and I hope may do pretty well. I was informed by Dervall of your health and safety on the river, in the passage down. The defeat of St. Clair's army will, I suppose, be attained with serious consequences to Kentucky, and I fear will be very injurious to your settlement on strodes, but hope you will not hazard your lives, for the consideration of improving your plantation. I expect to start in a few days for home. The session has been much longer than we expected, when we came and very little done of a general nature.

Give my love to any of my friends who may enquire for me. I remain with esteem and affection

                                Yours,

                                WILLIAM PATTON

This letter was written to John Hume and his wife Esther Patton, from her brother, Hon. William Patton, who was in Richmond, Virginia, as a member of the Legislature. The original of this letter was in the possession of their granddaughter, Jane Rachel Graves, at the time a copy was made by Mrs. Alla Gay Jones.

Some Hume History from Virginia Magazine, Vol. 38:

Sir David Hume of Welderburn and eldest son were slain at the Battle of Flodden Field in 1513. His seven sons were present at this battle and were known as "The Seven Spears of Welderburn" (Lay of the Last Minstrel).

> "The Humes of old were warriors bold
> As are auld Scotland kin'd man.
> Their motto was "Their Country's Cause"
> And "True unto the end man."
> Those nobel men their names be praised
> They died ere they would yield man."

George Hume of Welderburn was married to Margaret, daughter of Sir Patrick Hume in 1695. Patrick Hume d. in 1671. He was fourth in descent from Alexander Hume of Manderston as the sons were called from their service at Flodden.

Ninian Hume (1670–1744), son of Abraham Hume, graduated from Edinburgh in 1695. George Hume and his brother, Frances, m. respectively Margaret and Isabel Hume, daughters of Sir Patrick Hume.

Mention of a marriage contract between Ninian Hume and Margaret Hume (daughter of George) April, 1726. Thompson says that Ninian Hume was the most influential man in Berwickshire in the middle of the eighteenth century. Margaret Hume was b. September 30, 1700. Her husband, Ninian Hume, d. December 17, 1744, age 74 years.

Scottish Notes and Queries for December, 1926, page 246. Ninian Hume was born December 25, 1670.

"Early American History, Hume and Allied Families" by William Evart Brockman.

"Of the family of Dunbar from which the Humes sprang, Douglas in his "Peerage of Scotland" remarks "No surname in Scotland can boast of more noble origin than that of Dunbar, being descended from the Saxon kings of England and the princes and earls of Northumberland. The family has furnished Earls of Northumberland, March and Dunbar, Marchmount, Hume and

Netland, Barons of Melrose, Hume and Polworth, Greenlaw, Douglas and Dundas, Baronets, Knights of the Garter and Thistle, Prime Councilors, Ambassadors, Envoys, Lord Joint Regents of Scotland, Duchess of Landersdale, Countess Joint Regents of Scotland, Countess of Dunbar and Douglass, two of Crawford, Murry and Sutherland Fitswilliam, Suffolk, Ely, Arran, Marshall, Hume and Bute, Viscountess Duncan Seton, Crickton, Erskine, Polworth and Lovat.''

The Humes are the eldest cadets of the family of Dunbar. Hume Castle is one of the most conspicuous forts in the Muse. Here for a long time was the residence of the main line of the family which early rose to eminence in the political life of Scotland being enrolled first as Lords and afterwards as Earls of Hume. It is still represented in the main line by the present Earl of Hume. In America the family has furnished officers in every war fought by the Colonies or the United States.

SCOTTISH KINGS FROM WHICH THE HUME FAMILY SPRANG.*

Kenneth 1st reigned from 850 to 860, Donald from 860 to 864, Constantine, 1st son of Kenneth from 864 to 867, was succeeded by his brother, Donald, who reigned from 889 to 900, he was succeeded by Constantine II, who reigned 42 years. Malcolm, 1st son of Donald, from 954 to 962, a son of Malcolm, 1st reigned from 962 to 971. Kenneth II, son of Malcolm 1st, from 971 to 997, Kenneth III from 997 to 1004, Malcolm II, son of Kenneth II, from 1005 to 1034. Malcolm II had one child, Bethoe, who m. Crinan; to this union were born two children, Duncan, King of Scotland, 1034–1040, and Maldred. Duncan was slain by Macbeth. Maldred m. Aldgatha, daughter Uchtred and granddaughter of King Etheldred of England.

Egbert was the first King of United England, 827-828. His second son, Alfred, known in history as Alfred the Great, who was later King of England. Egbert was a direct ancestor of Etheldred, King of England from 968 to 1013. In the year 1002 he married Enrma, the sister of Richard, Duke of Normandy, a lady who was known as the ''Flower of Normandy''. He was the last of the six early Saxon kings. Elgira, the fifth child of Etheldred m. Uchtred, Prince of Northumberland. Their daughter, Aldgatha, m. Maldred, grandson of Malcolm, second King of Scotland. From these two royal houses sprang the Hume family. Malredus, a son of Malcolm II and Edith, and his wife Aldgatha had one son, Cospatrick, Earl of Northumberland, who fought at the Battle of Hastings, and who was the first Baron of Dunbar, and ancestor of the Barons of Hume. He died in 1081. His son, Cospatrick, was the first Earl of Dunbar and Baron of Hume. He died in 1139 and was succeeded by his son, Cospatrick III, second Earl of Dunbar and Baron of Hume, who m. Ada, daughter of King William.

*For additional information on the Hume family see *Genealogies of Kentucky Families* (Vol. A-M), 524-564.

He d. in 1149 and his son, Colpatrick IV, Earl of Dunbar, d. in 1166 and was succeeded by his son, Sir Patrick, ancestor of Earls of Hume and Hume family. Sir William, son of Sir Patrick, was the first Lord of Hume. He m. his cousin, Ada, daughter of Sir Patrick, fifth Earl of Dunbar.

Sir Patrick de Hume, son of Sir William, was succeeded by his son, Galfridus de Hume, the third Lord of Hume, in 1300. His son, Sir Roger de Hume, was fourth Lord of Hume in 1331, and was succeeded by his son, Sir John de Hume, fifth Lord of Hume. Sir Thomas, son of Sir John, m. Nichola Pepdie. They had five children of whom the second son, Sir David Hume was the first Earl of Welderburn. He was knighted by King James II in 1443 and d. in 1467. Sir David Hume, son of the first Baron of Welderburn, m. Elizabeth Carmichael. He forced Robert Graham, the murderer of King James I, from his hiding place, and brought him to justice. He d. in 1450, before his father, of wounds he received in a fight with robbers. Sir George, the son of Sir David, in 1469 became heir to his father's estate in the lands of Welderburn. Sir George m. Mariotta Sinclair, daughter and coheir of John Sinclair of Hardmanstone, from whom he inherited half the lands of Polworth and Hardmanstone. He built an addition to the house at Welderburn and fortified it with several towers and ditches, and placed over the outer gates his name and arms. Sir George was slain and his body shamefully mangled by some Englishmen who wanted to plunder his house in 1497. The Scots erected a cross upon the spot where Sir George fell, which still remains. Sir David succeeded Sir George as the third Baron of Welderburn in 1499. He was knighted by King James IV of Scotland and was killed with his eldest son, Sir George, in the Battle of Flodden, 1513. Sir David, the second son, succeeded his father in 1513. He rendered such valuable assistance to the King (James V) he was granted an augmentation to his Arms with the motto "Remember". His death was caused by falling from his horse, 1523, in battle. A cross was erected where he fell. His wife was Aleson, sister of Archibald, Earl of Angus. She was brought up in the Catholic Church, but later changed to the Protestant faith. On her death bed a crucifix was brought to her, but she turned her head away and said that her faith was in no such trifle, but in the Lord Jesus Christ, the Saviour of the world.

Sir David was succeeded by his eldest son, George, who was killed at the Battle of Pinkie September 10, 1547, and he, being unmarried, was succeeded by his brother, Sir David Hume of Welderburn.

Sir David was the fifth Baron of Welderburn. He m. Mariota, daughter of Andrew Johnstone. On account of her extended charity work and good influence in the community, she was known as "good Lady Welderburn". Sir David was captured after the Battle of Pinkie and was carried to England, where he remained a prisoner for two years until his ransom was paid. He d. soon afterwards, and was said to have been the first male of his family to die a natural death.

Sir George Hume, son of Sir David, was born in 1550, he d. in 1616 and was succeeded by his son, Sir David.

Sir David, seventh Baron Welderburn, succeeded his father. Sir David was an old man when killed at the Battle of Dunbar, 1650, fighting against Cromwell. His wife was Margaret, daughter of Sir John Hume. Their son, David, did not live to inherit his father's estate, but was killed at the Battle of Dunbar at the same time that his father was. His wife was Catherine Morison. Their son, Sir George, was the eighth Baron of Welderburn, was b. in 1651. He sold half of his land in Polworth to Sir Patrick Hume, who was a distant relative, b. in 1641. He was a son of Sir Patrick Hume of Polworth. In 1690 he was made Lord High Chancellor of Scotland and was created Earl of Marchmount in 1697.

Sir George, son of Sir George, m. Isabel, daughter of Sir Francis Liddell of Ravensworth. He d. in 1715 leaving two sons, George and Francis. Sir George, ninth Baron of Welderburn, m. Margaret, daughter of Sir Patrick Hume and died in 1720.

The Line of Andrew Hume in America by Mrs. Linda Kennedy Wine, Culpeper, Virginia, copied from "Hume History" by Dr. John R. Hume, St. Louis. Alexander II, Earl of Marchmont b. in 1675 m. Margaret, daughter and heiress of Sir George Campbell, was a member of Parliament from Berwickshire in 1704 and resigned in favor of his younger brother, Sir Andrew Hume.

Andrew Hume first appears in the Minute Books of Fauquier County in 1759. Tradition says he came from Scotland to Stafford County but as twenty-seven books of that county were destroyed by Union soldiers who were camping in the clerk's office during the Civil War, many of them being cut to pieces with knives, it is not strange that no records of him can be found there. His home, "Loenst Grove', in Fauquier County, was destroyed by fire and all records burned. In the manuscripts of Colonel Milme Hume of Welderburn of Scotland beginning 1413. There seems to have been an Andrew Hume as witness for George Hume in Welderburn in 1478.

Page 2 says, "The Humes of Welderburn were the olders cadets of the family of Hume" and that there were numerous descendants who shared the honors, etc. . . .

Andrew Hume of Fauquier County is believed to have been the son of Ninian Hume who m. a sister of Emigrant George Hume in 1726. He was about the age of Charles Hume, youngest son of the Emigrant George, who m. Hannah Jones who lived in Fauquier County in 1764. Then Charles, son of Francis Hume, who was second son of George of Welderburn, also m. in Fauquier County, Celia Shumate, showing that Andrew Hume lived among them. It is said that Ninian Hume had sixteen children, but the names of only nine are given: Ninian, **Patrick, David, Abraham, Andrew, Thomas, Isabel, Jean and Margaret.** Each child is accounted for except Andrew. Andrew d. in Fauquier County in 1809. His life corresponds exactly with the Andrew of Ninian's family. It is on record that Ninian Hume came to America to hunt for his Cousin Francis Hume, who d. at the home of his cousin, Governor Spottswood. It is an established fact that many of the Humes besides Emigrant George and his Uncle Francis are closely allied by intermarriage for many generations. We find Patrick Hume in King George County in 1746, where he m. prior to 1753, Frances, daughter of William Pattershall. Alexander and James Hume lived in Fairfax, Fauquier and Spottsylvania Counties. William Hume left a son, James, and a widow, Sarah Hume, in Culpeper in 1753. The author writes "I have been told by my cousin, the late Miss Carrie L. Hume of Orange County, that Jacob Hume, a grandson of Andrew Hume, was a kinsman of the family"—. The relationship to Jacob Hume was always recognized and claimed between the descendants of Emigrant George of Spottsylvania and Culpeper and Andrew of Fauquier County.

In Book 3, Page 382, is the will of Andrew Hume dated March 20, 1802. His wife being dead, he mentions only his children, Robert, Andrew, John, George and Hannah Hume. His sons, George and Andrew were executors of the estate. Children of Andrew Hume were:

1. Robert b. 1744, m. Sarah McKay, d. 1809
2. Andrew
3. John went to Kentucky
4. Hannah
5. George

(End of quotations from William E. Brockman's Early American History of Hume and Allied Families).

The murder of Margaret Hume, sister of Sir George Hume. (From all records I have compared, she was also the wife of Ninian Hume and if so, she was John Hume's grandmother).

This is taken from The Virginia Historical Magazine, Volume 38, Pages 219-220:

From a letter of Alexander Hume:

This murder is one of the celebrated crimes of Scotland, and finds a place in all the works on the subject. Billie Castle was the scene of the crime. Margaret Hume resided here, and had a considerable household of servants, chief of whom was a butler, who had been in her service for a number of years, and in whose integrity she had the utmost confidence. The old lady was in the habit of personally collecting rents from her tenants, and as there were no county banks in which to deposit the money, it was her custom to count it in the presence of her butler, prior to locking the guineas away in a strong cupboard in her room. The door to this bedroom was secured by a very ingenious arrangement whereby a heavy brass bolt was allowed to fall by its own weight into an opening made to fit exactly. To an eye in the head of the bolt was attached a cord which worked through a pulley fastened to the ceiling, and thence by a series of running block passed to the bedside. For years the butler had witnessed the counting of the money, but there came a night when the guineas clinked too seductively, and the devil whispered in the butler's ear. It came to his mind if he would quietly fill up the hole into which in his mistress room door the bolt dropped, he might help himself to as much money as he wished. The time of the year was the cherry season. What was so easy as to fill the hole with cherry stones? At midnight he stole into his mistress chamber, cut her throat from ear to ear, broke into the cabinet, and possessed himself of her money, and although he might have walked down the stairs and out of the door without exciting either alarm or suspicion, he opened the window and let himself down nearly two stories, broke his leg and lay there among the shrubbery until morning without even attempting to crawl away. He was seized, tried, condemned and executed.

This was grisly enough say Andrew and John Long in "Highways and Byways of the Border" (P. 18), but not hardly so grisly as the real story. The old lady's room was entered as described, but the butler, Norman Ross, did not immediately cut her throat. She was awakened by the sound of the rifling of the cupboard, and with that pluck which is characteristic of the Scotch, she jumped up to grapple with the robber, then he cut her throat, and leaving her for dead, in her bed, proceeded with his rifling. A slight noise, however, disturbed him, and looking around a terrifying sight confronted him. The woman whom he believed to be dead was on her feet, blindly groping her way along the wall to the bell. Before he could seize her and finish his work, she had grabbed the cord and pulled with all the strength which she had left, and thus had alarmed the other servants. Thus the murderer had no way of leaving by means of the stairs. He jumped from the window, missed his footing and broke his leg. With painful effort, he dragged himself to a field nearby, where among sweet scented flowers he lay concealed for several days. On the fourth day, he lay groaning, beside a tiny stream of water where he was seen by some children who gave information. The wretched man was taken, tried, condemned and executed. The last instance in Scotland of a criminal being executed in chains.

The blood of a murdered person they say refuses to wash clean from any woodwork into which it may have been soaked. In this instance there is no doubt of the fact, that these marks remain. The prints of the old lady's bloody hands still cling to the oak wainscoating of the gloomy old room where the deed was committed.

Kentucky Historical Register, Vol. 21, Page 274. "John Hume certificate issued for 100 acres of land at the State price in the District of Kentucky which was marked and improved by Chambers in the year 1776 lying on the waters of Salt River, the head of the first big creek that empties into the said river, above Floyd's Fork, to include said Chambers improvements, satisfactory proof being made to the Court, they are of the opinion that the said Hume, Assee. of Chambers has the right to preemption of 1000 acres of land, to include the above location and that a certificate be issued accordingly'' 1779-1780.

Kentucky Historical Register, Page 294. September 1, 1796, The Governor appointed John Hume Justice of the Peace in Bourbon County.

The descendants of John Hume and Esther Patton. John Hume b. 1752, d. May 24, 1824, m. Esther Patton b. 1769, d. 185–

Children:
1. Sally b. May 14, 1790, d. November 1, 1865, m. June 11, 1811, James Ritchie b. November 24, 1778, d. January 25, 1825.

Children:
1. Louise b. March 2, 1, 1812
2. Benjamin Patton Ritchie b. August 12, 1813, d. June 1, 1889. May 6, 1838 he m. Sarah A. Foster b. December 1, 1810, d. February 10, 1878.
3. Mary Esther b. October 8, 1815, d. August 16, 1878
4. Elizabeth Julia b. September 2, 1817
5. Susanna b. July 15, 1819, d. May 21, 1824

Children of Benjamin P. Ritchie and Sarah A. Deadman Foster:
1. James Henry Ritchie b. September 13, 1840, d. September 3, 1871
2. William Hume Ritchie b. April 21, 1842, d. February, 1920.
3. John Silus b. December 28, 1843, d. February 27, 1932
4. Philip Ritchie, b. November 18, 1845
5. Mary Louise Ritchie, b. March 4, 1848, d. November 9, 1909
6. Sarah Lizzie b. October 10, 1850. Still living. February, 1936 m. W. G. Batterton.

Children of Mary Louise Ritchie and Harrison M. Long:
1. Benjamin Ritchie Long b. November 23, 1873
2. Mary Sue b. February 1, 1875, d. August 12, 1913
3. William John Long b. April 21, 1875
4. Harrison Hume Long b. May 28, 1879, m. November 20, 1911, Grace Bassett b. February 11, 1890
5. Lucille Long Martin b. June 5, 1881
6. James Henry Long b. September 8, 1882
7. Esther Long b. November 12, 1885

(This Ritchie data was furnished me by Mrs. Lucille Long Martin, great-granddaughter of Sallie Hume Ritchie of Missouri).

THE SEARCH FOR AN OLD FAMILY BIBLE AND HOW IT ENDED.

My grandmother, Jane Hughes Graves, several years before she died, while talking about her people one day, remarked that her cousin, Ben Ritchie had the old family Bible, but she did not know where he was living at that time.

When I became interested in my ancestors, I asked a number of my relatives if they knew anything about him. Finally, Miss Julia Spurr in looking over some of her mother's papers and letters came across the name Lou Ritchie Long, Sturgeon, Missouri. I at once wrote to this address, saying on the envelope "If she is not living please deliver to her nearest relative". Promptly I received the following reply:

Sturgeon, Missouri
October 4, 1934

Mrs. R. M. Clark
Chilesburg, Ky.

My dear Mrs. Clark:

I have been intending to write to you for some time in regard to the Bible. B. P. Ritchie, my grandfather, had the Bible and gave it to his daughter, Lizzie, now Mrs. W. G. Batterton. She had a fire four years ago, and the Bible was burned, so that is bound to be the end of that. I am very sorry that I cannot give you any of the information that you asked for.

My mother, Lou Ritchie Long, has been dead for 25 years.

It would be one of our greatest pleasures to have you visit us some time. I also assure you it would be a great pleasure to meet some of my mother's people that live there in Kentucky.

Sincerely,
HUME H. LONG

2. William Patton Hume, 2nd. child of John and Esther Patton Hume, b. April 7, 1792, d. March 18, 1875, m. Eliza Hutchcraft, daughter of Thomas Hutchcraft. They had two children, David J. and Mary F. David J. Hume b. October 11, 1824, m. December, 1848 Martha A. Talbot b. May, 1828, daughter of Benjamin and Mary Grimes Talbot, Mary being a daughter of Charles Grimes. They had five sons, William P., Benjamin T., Orlando V., Samuel C. and John S. John S. was drowned at the age of 14. "Inwood" was the name of D. J. Hume's home.

Benjamin Talbot Hume was b. June 30, 1851, m. 1876, Susie McCann b. April 10, 1855, d. May 28, 1931. Her husband d. February 27, 1935.

Thomas Hutchcraft, father of Eliza Hutchcraft Hume m. a Miss Apperson. He served seven years in the Revolution.

Will P. Hume (son of David J.) b. January 4, 1850, m. Sallie Bacon b.

November 2, 1853, daughter of W. A. and Belle Talbot Bacon. Sallie B. Hume d. 1878 leaving two children, David P. and Sallie L.

William P. Hume, Sr.'s, second wife was Matilda Renick, m. July 13, 1829. Their daughter, Martha A. Hume b. May 7, 1830, m. August 5, 1856, James W. Ferguson, son of Abraham L. Ferguson, and Mary Matson. Abraham L. was b. September 27, 1803, d. August 1, 1854. Mary Matson was b. February 9, 1810. James W. Ferguson was b. August 25, 1830. Children of James W. Ferguson and Martha A. Hume: William P., Abraham L., Maggie B., Robert H., Lucy E., Volney W. and Matilda R.

Matilda, second wife of William P. Hume, Sr., d. January, 1870.

Elizabeth Patton Hume, third child of John and Esther Patton Hume b. April 22, 1896, d. December 8, 1827, m. Jacob Hughes February 14, 1815. He was b. March 22, 1791, d. May 15, 1874

Winchester, Kentucky, Clark County Records:

"Jacob Hughes and Elizabeth Hume married February 14, 1815."

Jacob Hughes m. Sarah A. Berryman b. February 1, 1805, d. July 4, 1869. She must have been a wonderful woman, all the grandchildren were devoted to her.

Jacob Hughes was a son of Cornelius Hughes who came from Wales and Rachel Campbell, a Scotch lassie. Mrs. Claude William has Jacob Hughes' Bible and from it the following is copied.

Cornelius Hughes b. 1739, d. 1814, m. Rachel Campbell in 1776. Rachel was b. in Scotland in 1743, d. in Boone County, Kentucky, 1821. (I have been told by many members of the family that she was of the Argyle stock).

Children of Cornelius and Rachel Hughes:
  Mary Hughes b. December 7, 1776
  John Hughes b. February 16, 1778
  George Hughes b. October 17, 1779
  Catherine Hughes, Sr., b. August 12, 1781
  Cornelius Hughes b. 1783. Settled in Gallatin County, Kentucky.
  Robert Hughes b. November 11, 1785
  Ann Hughes b. November 2, 1787, m. Joseph Brown
  Thomas Hughes b. July 20, 1789, d. March 20, 1862
  Jacob Hughes b. March 22, 1791
  Michael Hughes b. January 6, 1793
  Mary Hughes, b. September 15, 1794
  Jane Hughes, b. September 1, 1795
  Catherine Hughes b. April 11, 1798
    Joseph Brown, son-in-law, b. April 3, 1786
    (End of quote from Bible.)

Cornelius Hughes came to Virginia 1757.

From Scotch Irish Records I copied the following Augusta County Administrator Records:

February 20, 1776

"Neil Hughes Administrator of Henry Laughlin".

I had always been told that Cornelius Hughes was with Washington. I know he was given 2000 acres of land in Boone County, Kentucky, for his services. I wrote to Washington, D. C., trying to get some record of his services, also to several other places, without success. Finally I wrote to the State Library, Harrisburg, Pennsylvania, and received the following:

Mrs. Sara G. Clark,
Chilesburg, Kentucky

My dear Mrs. Clark:

The name of Cornelius Hughes appears in the company of Captain Henry Shade 1st Battalion Continental line, known as Colonel Miles Rifles. Reference, Pennsylvania Archives, 5th series, Volume 2, Pages 260–262. On the second list, June 1st, he is marked "sick". Captain Shade was from Northampton County. It is probable Cornelius Hughes was from the same township, as a man by that name is taxed as a carpenter in Macungie Township.

Hoping this information will be of service, I am

Very sincerely yours,
GERTRUDE McKINNEY,
Director of State Library

By JAMES C. FERGUSON, Genealogist.

From this I judge Cornelius must have been in Pennsylvania at one time. His son, Jacob, was born in Spottsylvania County, Virginia. Cornelius Hughes came to Boone County, Kentucky, in 1797.

I have the following Hughes data:

This of John Hughes was given to me by Mrs. Claude Johnston, 33 Oak Ridge, Ft. Thomas, Kentucky.

John Hughes b. February 11, 1778, m. Mary Patterson.

His son, James Henry Hughes, b. April 9, 1824, d. December 3, 1899, m. first Lemira Ann Campbell June 5, 1848. Had one son, John Hughes, who d. in 1934. John Henry Hughes' second wife was Ann Elizabeth Owen, d. March 22, 1920.

Their daughter, Mary Hughes, m. 1st. Marshall Hill, she being his second wife. Marshall Hill's first wife was her younger sister, Annie Hughes.

Annie had two children: (1) Mary Hughes Hill, m. Ellott Clarkson, (2) Annie Marshall Hill, m. W. A. R. Bruehl. They have one son, Robert Bruehl.

Third child of James Henry Hughes was Robert Owen Hughes, whose first wife was Emma Perry, had one son, Roderick Perry Hughes, who m. Marie Menifee and second, Alice Waterhouse.

Robert Perry Hughes and Mary Menifee had two sons, Roderick Perry and Jack Hughes.

James Henry Hughes was youngest son of John and Mary Patterson Hughes. They had two daughters: (1) Mary Christian Hughes, b. August 29, 1810, d. July 28, 1832, (2) Rachel Campbell Hughes, b. June 30, 1816, d. May 20, 1839, m. Waller Herndon.

Third child of John and Mary Patterson Hughes was Caroline Donaldson, d. August 5, 1816.

Fourth, John Christian Hughes, b. September 1, 1817, d. November 10, 1879, m. Amanda Jane Dragoo.

Fifth, Alexander Franklin Hughes, b. March 25, 1830, d. 1872, m. Sarah—. Their daughter, Martha, m. John Woolsiscroft.

Their daughter, Sarah, m. Claude Johnson. They have three children, Louise, Charles and Sarah. Mrs. Johnson has a sister, Sarah, another sister, Helen, died.

Sixth child of John and Mary Patterson Hughes was Rebecca Patterson, b. February 14, 1822, m. W. B. Stevens, b. October 17, 1779.

George Hughes, third child of Cornelius and Rachel Campbell Hughes, m. Mary Case. (This data was furnished by Mrs. Amelia Hughes Britt, granddaughter of George Hughes).

Mary Case, who m. George Hughes, was a daughter of Leonard Case, Jr. Their other children were Bopher, Reuben and Sarah.

Leonard, Jr., was a son of Leonard, Sr., who had another son, William Case. Leonard, Sr., was a son of Meshack Case.

Children of George and Mary Case Hughes:
1. Joseph Case Hughes m. Amanda Tucker
2. Delilah Case Hughes m.— Hume
3. Sallie Case Hughes m.— Ballard

Joseph Hughes b. 1810, d. 1877. His wife Amanda Tucker, b. 1824, d. 1909. They were m. in 1846. Their children were:
1. George Hughes m. Louise Winston. He d. May 12, 1922. They had two children, Mary Hughes Page, who d. as a result of burns when their home was destroyed by fire, June, 1931, and her husband perished in the flames. Mary was so badly burned that she died in a few days. Her husband's name was Frank Page. They left a son, George Hughes Page.

Sarah Hughes, the other daughter, m. 1st Ralph Ackerman. After his death she m. W. F. Price. Sarah has no children of her own, but has taken care of Mary's son.

2. Joseph Coleman Hughes d. November 25, 1925, m. Emma Dickey. Left one daughter, Emily who m. J. F. Cleck.
3. Mary E. Hughes, d. December 23, 1927, m. Dr. W. E. Shaw who d. September 5, 1913. They had four children: (1) Juliet m. S. W. Baker, They have two children, Mary Elizabeth and Sheridan, Jr. (2) Joseph W. Shaw was killed in an automobile accident May 20, 1927. He m. Mrs. Frances Tyler who is also dead. (3) W. E. Shaw, Jr., m. Pauline Schilling. They have two sons, William and Robert. (4) Ruth Shaw d. January 13, 1935, m. Max Cown. Left five children, Max, Sallie Hughes, William E., Donald Joseph and Mary Shaw Cown.
4. Sarah A. Hughes d. January 5, 1935, never married.
5. Amelia Hughes m. William H. Britt. They have one son, G. W. Hughes Britt, m. Hortense Saunders. William H. Britt, d. summer of 1935.
6. Annie Hughes m. R. M. Samuel Hind. They have three children, S. Wayne, Lucile and Lee H.
7. E. Lee Hughes m. C. C. Sleet. They have one daughter, Rebecca.
8. Jacob Hughes d. 1906, m. Sallie Green, have two children, Jacob and Anna Pearl.
9. Pearl Hughes m. John C. Bedinger. They have one daughter, Mary Amanda, m. Russell Yealy. They have one daughter, Mary Russella.

The next is copied from tombstone in the Hughes' lot in the Lexington Cemetery.

Hughes
Michael C. Hughes
Born 1793
Died March 21, 1844

Mary Adams
Wife of Michael C. Hughes
Born Dec. 8, 1812
Died Dec. 16, 1872

Near the graves are Merrett W. Hughes and Mary Frances Hughes.

Then on the front of the large monument:

John T. Hughes, d. August 4, 1924

On the opposite side of the monument from Michael C. Hughes is:

Thomas Hughes
July 20, 1789
March 18, 1862

Julia Ann, wife of
Thomas Hughes
April 9, 1805
March 18, 1846

Near these are two graves marked as follows:

Robert Henry Hughes
Jan. 19, 1837
April 17, 1852

Anna Hughes Ferguson
Dec. 19, 1841
Jan. 24, 1863

Anna Hughes m. Robert Ferguson.

Thomas and Julia Ann Smith Hughes had another daughter, Kate, (or Katherine) who m. James B. McCreary June 12, 1867. He d. 1919. James B. McCreary was twice governor of Kentucky from 1875 to 1879 and from 1911 to 1915.

The Register of Kentucky Historical Society of July, 1935, Page 211, has the following:

"James Bennett McCreary born in Richmond, Kentucky, July 8, 1838, died October 8, 1919. Enlisted as a private in the Civil War, 1862, promoted to Lieutenant Colonel July 4, 1863, captured shortly afterwards and was prisoned for fifteen months. He was exchanged and returned to the Army where he remained until the close of the war. Was a member of Congress 1885 to 1897 and again from 1903 to 1909."

William Hughes, brother of Kate Hughes McCreary, m. Sallie Cooper. They had four children.

Susan who m. Charles J. Bronston May 28, 1874. Charles J. Bronston was b. July 29, 1848, was the only child of Thomas S. and Sallie A. Bronston. He had red hair while his friend, Rev. C. P. Williamson, was quite bald. It is related of Mr. Bronston that one day when he met Mr. Williamson he teasingly said, "My friend, where were you when they were giving out hair?" Quick as a flash Mr. Williamson replied, "Charley, I was right there but they didn't have any left except some red stuff and I didn't want that." Susie Hughes Bronston had three brothers, Cooper, Thomas and Lacy Hughes.

Now we return to Jacob Hughes and his family.

First child of Jacob and Elizabeth Patton Hume Hughes was Augustus, b. April 1, 1816, d. December 12, 1843.

"Leafland," home of Jacob Hughes, built after 1850. Now the home of Miss Julia Spurr (great-granddaughter of Jacob Hughes), and the family of her brother, R. J. Hughes Spurr.

Second child, Julia Mary Hughes, b. January 27, 1819, m. January 9, 1838 to J. Howard Sheffer. She d. Oct. 24, 1872.

Their children were:

1. Ruth Wierman Sheffer b. October 1, 1843, d. July 2, 1928, m. Richard A. Spurr September 4, 1866. He was b. March 18, 1835. His father, Richard Spurr, b. 1809, d. February 8, 1851. December 3, 1830, he m. Martha Prewitt, a daughter of William C. Prewitt and Margaret Montgomery Edmonson. He was b. March 9, 1788 and his wife March 2, 1788. William C. Prewitt d. September 1854, his wife d. October 13, 1830. Martha Prewitt Spurr b. November 11, 1813.

Children of Richard A. and Ruth Sheffer Spurr:

1. Julia Hughes Spurr
2. Laura Sheffer Spurr m. Carl Welch in Mexico November 3, 1925
3. R. J. Hughes Spurr b. January 1881, d. December 30, 1936, m. September 1, 1919, Louise Jennings who was born in Westmoreland County, Virginia. Their children are:
   (1) Carola Jennings Spurr b. July 20, 1920
   (2) Richard Hughes Spurr b. January 7, 1922
   (3) Burgess Hill Spurr b. February 11, 1923
3. Child of J. Howard and Julia M. Sheffer, Elizabeth Hume Shaffer b. December 12, 1845, d. October 14, 1922. October 5, 1864, she m. Richard Hickman Prewitt, a son of William C. Prewitt and his second wife, Catherine Hickman.

Children of Richard H. and Elizabeth Hume Prewitt:

1. Jacob S. Prewitt b. August 7, 1865, d. February 28, 1891.
2. Julia Hughes Prewitt b. December 16, 1866. January 9, 1895 she m Dr. Charles Taylor. Their children are Elizabeth Prewitt Taylor, b. July 2, 1899 and Charles M. Taylor, Jr., b. June 1, 1903. Doctor Taylor is dead.
3. Catherine Hickman Prewitt b. February 22, 1869. November 22, 1890 she m. John G. Winn, a lawyer of Mt. Sterling.

Their children are:

Richard P. Winn b. December 31, 1891, m. Lucy Clay Woodford, February 20, 1919.

Sarah Elizabeth Winn b. February 16, 1895, d. December 11, 1901.

John G. Winn, Jr., b. February 7, 1898, m. Anna Walcott July 22, 1931.

David Prewitt, fourth child of Richard H. and Elizabeth Prewitt b. March 28, 1871, m. Martha Rodes Estill, daughter of Colonel William Rodes Estill and Martha Prewitt Van Meter. (Both of her parents were twice married.) David Prewitt and Martha Estill m. December 26, 1896. She died August, 1903. Several years after the death of his first wife, David m. Mary Graham, granddaughter of Rev. Robert Graham, a celebrated minister of the Christian church.

Children of David and Martha Estill Prewitt:
1. Elizabeth S. Prewitt b. January 28, 1898. July 17, 1926 she m. Dr. A. R. Shands. Have one child, A. R. Shands, Jr., b. December 19, 1928.
2. Martha Rodes Estill Prewitt b. June 11, 1899, m. Clifton Rodes Breckinridge. Have one child Catherine Carson Breckinridge b. February 7, 1930. Martha Prewitt and C. R. Breckinridge were m. March 3, 1928.
3. Richard Hickman Prewitt b. January 22, 1901. August 1, 1930, m. Jean Mary Simpkins.
4. Julia Katherine Prewitt b. December 26, 1902, m. E. S. Dabney November 19, 1929. Have one child, Elizabeth Prewitt Dabney b. August 22, 1931. Kitty Prewitt Dabney d. Autumn of 1935.

4th Child of J. Howard and Julia M. Sheffer was Laura Jane b. June 5, 1848, d. February 14, 1866.

2nd. Jacob Hughes Sheffer b. August 8, 1841, d. January 16, 1863.

5th Harriet Hughes Sheffer b. June 11, 1848, d. January 28, 1927. September 6, 1870 she m. William W. Estill b. April 12, 1848, d. January, 1926.

Children:
1. Jacob S. Estill b. July 24, 1871, d. February 4, 1917.
2. William Rodes Estill b. October 26, 1873, m. Katherine Christian March 17, 1927. They have two children, Anna Price Estill b. April 7, 1928 and Katherine Rodes Estill b. December 20, 1929.
3. Howard S. Estill b. October 16, 1877, m. Annie Adams December 22, 1910.
4. George Castleman Estill b. May 27, 1881, m. Alice D. Garth October 25, 1911. They have one child, Alice Garth Estill b. December 2, 1912.

6th Child of J. Howard and Julia M. Sheffer was Omie Wiermann Sheffer b. October 23, 1855, d. July 8, 1913, m. Robert C. Estill December 3, 1876. He was b. April 22, 1855, d. 1932. W. W. Estill and R. C. Estill were brothers, both being sons of Colonel William R. and Amanda Fry Estill. (These names and dates of descendants of Julia Hughes and J. Howard Sheffer are copied from Jacob Hughes' Bible, now the property of his great granddaughter, Mrs. Claude S. Williams.)

Children of Robert C. and Omie Wierman Sheffer Estill:
1. R. Julian Estill b. October 23, 1877, m. Mrs. Elizabeth W. Hinton June 6, 1925. They have one son, Robert Whitridge Estill b. September 7, 1927.

2. Laura Sheffer Estill b. June 8, 1879, m. Claude S. Williams June 17, 1909. He d. April 6, 1934.
3. Elizabeth Prewitt Estill b. September 14, 1882, m. Fayette Johnson, June 3, 1908, Fayette being a son of Major P. and Sally Chiles Johnson. Sally Chiles was the only child of John Henry Chiles and Mary Rogers who were m. May 14, 1846. John Henry Chiles was a son of Richard and Sarah Johnston Chiles who came to Kentucky in 1810.
4. Daniel Sheffer Estill b. February 23, 1887.
5. Robert Rodes Estill b. November 9, 1890, m. Katherine Headley October 1, 1914. Have one daughter, Naomi Sheffer, b. July 25, 1919.

This next is copied "From Blue Grass Homes and Their Traditions", by Elizabeth Simpson.

Chance Meeting of Two Travelers Results in Life Long Association.

"Life—careless, haphazard wench that she is—has a way now and then of making her little jokes. Ever once in awhile with her tongue in her cheek, and a sly look in her eye, she gathers together the scattered pieces of her jig-saw puzzle and fits them into a pattern with sure deliberate aim. She lines up an incident here, with an episode there, and then sits down to see what happens. Just as she did that morning a hundred or more years ago, when John Howard Sheffer, still in his teens, rode out from Lexington and overtook another young fellow on horseback about three miles out Strode's Station Road which is now the Winchester Pike.

Sheffer had come out from Philadelphia to collect some old accounts for a wholesale dry-goods house. William Estill had come up from Mississippi to buy stock for a great southern plantation and was on his way to Richmond. So the two young companions of the highway drifted into talk of trade and the beauty of Kentucky girls.

"We'll meet back here to get married", one laughingly said at the forks of the road as they parted.

A few years later William Estill returned and married Miss Amanda F. Fry, in front of whose house he and his erstwhile comrade had met, and John Howard Sheffer returned to wed Miss Julia Hughes. Two of the Sheffer daughters, Harriet and Omie married the Estill sons, William W. and Robert C. The two friends through youth and manhood, grew side by side, and both of them died at the house, in front of which they had met that summer morning years and years before."

Jane Hughes, third child of Jacob and Elizabeth Hume Hughes, was b. August 27, 1821, d. January 1, 1903. December 19, 1844, she m. Robert Benjamin Graves b. April 13, 1813, d. September 7, 1887. (More of this family later.)

4th Child, Harriet Amanda Hughes b. December 23, 1824, d. August 13, 1852. January 21, 1851, she m. Joseph B. Stewart. a prominent lawyer of Washington City who collected the largest fee that had ever been collected by a lawyer up to that time. He was a friend of Abraham Lincoln, and was with him in the box the night he was shot.

Copied from a paper loaned me by Miss Julia Spurr, written by her mother, Mrs. Richard A. Spurr.

Harriet Hughes' Wedding

My aunt's wedding I well remember. She wore a white satin dress with a veil. The first soldiers I ever saw were her husband's attendants with their regular dress uniforms. The cake table was set diagonally across the dining room. In the center was a stack of cakes six feet high and a large white cake iced with flowers. Then candy dolphins holding another cake, with pillars holding still another with a little bride in center with a veil on. Then more columns supporting a large basket of colored flowers in candy of every description. At one end of the table was a large black cake iced with cone shaped pyramid of Malaga grapes pulled off and stuck on to a hollow piece of cone shaped tin, when horn heated from inside, when it came off and was then set on cake with two little doves in candy sitting on a twin cake with a little red headed cupid on top swinging. Lemonade in pitchers was on the table, candy kisses, raisins, small cakes and ice cream were handed around. The meat table was the entire length of the porch with turkey, pigs, hams, fowls of all kinds, chicken salad, celery, beaten biscuit and pickle, also oyster soup. Butter about a fourth of a yard high, about as big at the bottom as an ordinary coffee pot, cone shaped with butter run through a colander making designs ornamenting the sides and these were all up and down the table."

As Cornelius Hughes had a large family to support, when Jacob was about fifteen he left home and began life alone. He worked hard, was industrious and economical, as well as a good business man. I have often heard the story told that he was driving hogs to market from Kentucky to Philadelphia, fattening them along the way on acorns, berries and nuts. Arriving at the Potomac, he found the waters out of bounds and a quantity of hogs were collected there. These he bought, and taking a chance of losing a part of his drove, he swam his hogs across. He lost comparatively few and arrived at Philadelphia for a boom market.

He won the second Fair premium on five acres of wheat which averaged thirty-seven bushels and two pounds per acre.

He believed in giving his children the best education possible, and sent them to the finest schools of his day. In his library he had principally histories and such novels as "Days of Bruce", "Scottish Chiefs" and "Children of the

Abbey''. All three of his daughters were married at his first home, ''Hibernia'', and while only the description of Harriet's has been preserved we are sure they were all equally brilliant.

We do not know when ''Hibernia'' was built, but know it was before 1827 as his first wife died that year, was buried there. When he built ''Leafland'' and moved to it early in 1853, he had her body as well as those of Augustus and Harriet, taken up and buried in the garden of his new home.

Hibernia

The first home of Jacob Hughes, ''Hibernia'', was one of the old anti-bellum southern colonial homes. Looking from the hill, in front of it, it seemed like a little villa. A small stream ran just in front several hundred yards from the house which was bridged, with fencing on both sides. The house was a double brick with two stories and porticoes running the entire length of the house in front and the rear, and railing on top of the house enclosing six yards square. To the left was an entry some twenty yards long or perhaps thirty enclosed in front with door opening in front. In the rear it was arched with brick with second story storeroom above. Just out was the old covered well with windlass and bucket attached to a rope. To this day the sound of ''the old oaken bucket'' as it fell to the water is music to my ear. Next, adjoining the entry, was the kitchen with stone and large fireplace with kettles on the crane, a reflector for the Christmas turkey, square waffle irons with handles two yards long to be run in the hot coals. Next in line was the negroes' dining room with good warm fireplace, long table with dishes, knives and forks. They had hot rolls, coffee and indeed all the substantials of the house. My grandfather killed eighty hogs, had numberless orchards with cellar full for all. Killed two and often three beeves in a winter and Cotswold sheep and fowls with a splendid garden. His slaves idolized him. The next room still to the left was the loom room where carpets and woolen clothes for the servants were woven. The next was the house woman's room; these all one story high. To the left still running half the length of the yard down from this room to the front was a ten pin alley built for my aunt who had been at school in New York at Madam Shegarie's school and was not strong. She spent a great deal of money on clothes at A. T. Stewart's, then the leading merchant in New York. Mrs. Colonel Tucker of Winchester said to my daughter, Julia Spurr, that Miss Harriet Hughes was to this part of the country what Sallie Wood Downes was to Louisville. She was beautifully educated and Uncle Robert Prewitt said the smartest woman he ever knew. There my grandfather spent many days with friends. Just in front of this ten pin alley down to the front fence just inside the lawn was a beautiful flower garden where cape jasmine, pinks, daffodils, sweet brier, honeysuckle and all those dear old fashioned flowers bloomed to welcome all those beaux and friends of this family. To the right of this lawn just in front was a small pasture for carriage, buggy and driving horses with carriage house. The carriage was a thousand dollar one; seat in front, very high with seat on the back for trunks, high arms above the seat. It was a very large carriage with steps to fold up and let down. Then just back of the carriage house the vegetable garden with grapevine trellis running both ways from the middle of the garden, very ornamental. In the back of the garden was the family graveyard with monuments. Through this garden running at right angles with the house was a path which led over the style block to the stables, made of hewn logs, separated the two stables by a covered shed which contained a corn mill with beams to hitch the horses to. I have often with the little negroes tumbled down from the loft above when a child and Uncle Jim would say "Dar now, you'll git killed in a minnit." We would jump on the beams for a ride. Just on the hill above was the overseer's house, and between was a pond, the first made in the state. My grandfather tole me if lakes of size could exist why not small ones in this clay soil. His ice house was the first built of hewn logs. Back of the house, to the right was the poultry yard and just back to the left was the negro quarters with brick cabins all in row with porches in front. The parlor was a salon parlor with velvet carpets beautifully papered with large portraits and pictures hanging on the walls, damask and lace curtains. Two large davenports, two large and twelve small chairs, all mahogany; a piano, the first brought to this country, crystal chandeliers, divided mantle mirror, two pier glasses reaching from floor to ceiling on opposite sides of the room. Just back a bedroom in mahogany, the room just across in mahogany and also in dining room. The solid silver, large five hundred dollar silver service. Well do I remember eating and seeing my face long and short in the highly polished urn. The upstairs was all mahogany."

> (This description of "Hibernia" and of Aunt Harriet Hughes' wedding tables was given me by Miss Julia Spurr. It is copied from notes written by her mother, Mrs. Richard A. Spurr.)

4. Julia Hume who m. Colonel Arthur McGaughey was daughter of John and Esther Patton Hume.

Charles McGaughey—1727–1760 died in Ireland. Married Lavinia Wilson (who in 1761 married George Milligan and with her three sons went to America).

This history of Charles McGaughey is from the family record of Arthur McGaughey II written 1835–11–15.

---

2 Generation

1—Lieutenant Arthur McGaughey 1755–8–11—1830–6–23 Married Eleanor Kenton. Died 1830–5–15. (Eleanor was a daughter of a well known trader of Bedford, Pennsylvania, Thos. Kenton who died 1777 and Rachel, his wife, died 1798.)

Arthur McGaughey was a Lieutenant in the Bedford County Rangers and also in the Second Regular Infantry in 1792. David Espy's report of 1796 shows his place filled. After the death of Thomas McGaughey in 1794 the two older brothers left Bedford, Pennsylvania, for Shelby County, Kentucky. Arthur sold his numerous pieces of property and was a wealthy man apparently, as judged by the standards of those days. He served two terms 1787–1788 as High Sheriff of Bedford County. This was the highest position of trust in early county history of Pennsylvania. He was one of the administrators of Thos. McGaughey's estate. Left for Kentucky in 1794. He left Shelby County in 1808. Going to Hardin County (now Hart County) buying land on Bacon Creek, where he died and is buried. He had eleven children. Five only growing to maturity.

3 Generation

1—Ann McGaughey

Married Bradshaw; lived in Illinois.

2—Rachel McGaughey, died before 1735–11–15.

Married—Milliken. (In Rachel Kenton's will dated 1798, a legacy of ten pounds each is left to Ann and Rachel McGaughey.)

3—Lavinia McGaughey.

Married—Blackwell. Lived in Missouri.

4—Jane McGaughey.

Married—Milam. Lived in Kentucky.

5—Eleanor McGaughey.

The youngest child who died at 15 years of age.

6—Colonel Arthur McGaughey, 1790–4–1—1852–8–1.

Married 1818–3–12 to Julia Patten Hume 1799--1–7—1852–7–30. Arthur was born in Bedford County, Pennsylvania, married in Clark County, Kentucky, died in Christian County. In 1825 he bought 1350 acres on Little River, Christian County. His will is recorded at Hopkinsville, Kentucky. He was a Colonel of the War of 1812. He and his wife died of cholera.

4 Generation

1—Lavinia McGaughey, 1819–1–27, Hart County, Kentucky.

2—Ellen Kenton McGaughey, 1821–8–29—1894–6–20.

Married 1846–10–21 to Albert H. Wallace, 1800–1879. Albert Wallace was born in Culpeper County, Virginia. He came to Kentucky years before coming to Hopkinsville and went to Hopkinsville, Kentucky, in 1856 where he died.

5 Generation

1—Julia Hume Wallace, 1848-8-23—1904-9-19.

2—Alfred Horner Wallace, 1855-12-10.
Married Kate Edgar Whitlock on 1879-12-10. Her birth 1859-2-10.

3—Arthur McG. Wallace, 1847-8-26—1847-9-17.

4—Albert Wallace, 1850-5-8—1850-7-23.

5—Robert McG. Wallace, 1851-8-5—1852-7-30.

6—John W. Wallace, 1854-6-6—1855-4-15.

7—Henry Dade Wallace, 1857-12-13—1919-4-18.
Married Mary Campbell who was born ——.

8—Howson Hoe Wallace, M. D., 1860-4-19—1931-12-11.

3—Harriet McGaughey, 1823-1-16.
Married Gano Henry.

5 Generation

1—Thomas Henry.

2—Arthur McG. Henry married Mary Stowe. They had three children.

3—Hallie Henry married Bird Chambers. They had six or seven children.

4—Robert McGaughey, 1826-1-2—1903-11-1.
Married Mrs. Jennie Crumpler Green on 1868-9-27. No children.

5—Arthur Kenton McGaughey, 1828-7-19—1844-12-2.

6—John McGaughey, 1832-7-2—1905-4-9.
Married Hattie Kinkead on 1868-4-7.

5 Generation

1—Hume McGaughey.

2—Norman McGaughey died 1876-9-5.

3—Arthur McGaughey died 1887-4-3.

4—Robert McGaughey, 1883 and died 1919-7-30.
Married Miss Rosalie Adams. They had six children.

6 Generation

Children of Alfred Honer Wallace and Kate E. Whitlock.

1—Nell Kenton Wallace, 1881-7-31.

2—Lucy Whitlock Wallace, 1883-4-27.
Married Thos. H. Wallace who was born 1857-9-20. They have no children.

3—Julia McGaughey Wallace, 1885-2-21.

4—Maria Withrow Wallace, 1887-4-7; died 1903-8-31.

5—Kate Macrae Wallace, 1889–5–1.
   Married Guy Starling on April 10, 1913. He was born 1872–4–4. They have two children, Guy Starling, Jr., 1914–6–19, and Alfred Wallace Starling, 1916–9–13.
6—Alfred Henry Wallace, 1891–10–12.
   Married Mary Louise Cooper on December 15, 1915. She was born on 1889–7–10. They have two children; Mary Wharton Wallace, born 1917–4–19, and Alfred Henry Wallace, Jr., born 1923–10–21.
7—John Whitlock Wallace, 1894–4–10.
   Married Dorothy Jean Marquis on August 5, 1931.
8—Sara Clarke Wallace, 1897–7–18.

6 Generation

Children of Henry Dade Wallace and Mary Campbell.

1—Henry Dade Wallace, Jr., 1888–7–19. Died October, 1918.
2—Mary Amos Wallace, 1889–8–23.
   Married Horace Wilkins of Houston, Texas, on May, 1914.
3—Bessie Beazley Wallace, 1891–12–3.
4—Howeson Hooe Wallace, 1893–10–......
5—Margaret Campbell Wallace, 1897–10–......

This was sent to me by Miss Nell Wallace, great-granddaughter of Julia Hume, fourth child of John and Esther Patton Hume.

5th Child of John and Esther Patton Hume was Matthew D. Hume.

The following dates are copied from tombstones in the graveyard near his old home. This farm now belongs to his grandson, Harry B. Clay. The graveyard is beautifully kept, tombstones all standing, and it is surrounded by a substantial iron fence.

"Matthew Dyer Hume
Born June, 1803
Died May, 1892"

"Maria D. Cunningham
Born Oct., 1810
Died Aug., 1849"

"Elizabeth Hume
Wife of James D. Gay
Born April 11, 1831
Died July 25, 1854"

"Lizzie
Daughter of J. D. and E. Gay
Born July 14, 1854
Died Aug. 3, 1854"

Letter of Matthew D. Hume now in the possession of Mrs. Claude Williams (Laura Estill).

"September 28, 1875

Mr. W. W. Estill,
Dear Sir:

I am sorry it does not suit me to leave home at this time. I do not know that I can this fall. I think that I would enjoy the visit with the folks very much, but circumstances prevent, and the girls will have to excuse me.

Yours respectfully,
MATTHEW D. HUME"

Matthew Dyer Hume, born June 22, 1803, died June, 1892; married Maria Cunningham, November 6, 1827.

Maria Cunningham, born October 10, 1810, died August 7, 1849.

Their children:
Mary C. Hume
Elizabeth Hume
Anne Maria Hume
Laura Frances Hume

Mary C. Hume, born August 4, 1829, died June 30, ... Married Franklin Bedford, March 29, 1849, to which union were born,
Matt H. Bedford
H. Clay Bedford
Franklin Bedford
Henrietta Bedford
Samuel Bedford

Elizabeth Hume, born April 11, 1831, died July 25, 1854. Married Jas. D. Gay, September 5, 1850, to which union were born, Maria Gay, who married George Payne of Scott County, to which union was born,
Elizabeth
J. Walter
June J.
M. Hume.

Maria Gay Payne was later married to Gano Hildreth, no issue.

Anne Maria, born August 11, 1833, died December 8, 1857. Married William Hooker from New York State in 1856, to which union were born twins that did not live.

Laura Frances Hume, born November 12, 1838, died January 28, 1923. Married John Carter Clay, March 27, 1862, to which union were born:

M. Hume Clay, born October 4, 1863, died December 26, 1910; John Frank Clay, born October 4, 1865, died December 27, 1920; m. Miss Turney;

Harry B. Clay, born May 11, 1867, m. Miss Turney.

(This was sent to me by Mrs. Fred Batterton at the request of Mr. Harry B. Clay, Paris, Kentucky, and is copied from a scrapbook compiled by Mrs. Laura Hume Clay, daughter of Matthew D. Hume, mother of Harry B. Clay and grandmother of Mrs. Batterton.)

Robert Hume, 6th child of John and Esther Patton Hume, b. September 7, 1807, d. February 20, 1863, m. Laetitia Flournoy.

The John Hume home is still standing, a wonderful old brick house. Not far from it, and a little to the back was the ice house. The roof is gone, but the stone part remains, so well built it may be there for another hundred years.

Back of the house is the graveyard surrounded by a substantial stone wall. We could decipher but one of the inscriptions on the tombstones:

"Elizabeth Stevens Hume,
Born April 15, 1852
Died June 11, 1852"

After the death of John Hume, his son, Robert, lived in the old home. Some time after this, Esther Patton Hume, built for herself a small house, nearby, calling it "Buckeye Cabin" where she lived, taking her meals with Robert.

Now, I return to Jacob Hughes. As has been stated before he died May 15, 1874. In those days, when there were no telephones, or rapid means of communication, when a death occurred, as soon as the funeral arrangements were completed, the family had "Funeral Notices" printed, which a man on horseback carried to the homes of friends and acquaintances. These notices had a black border about a fourth of an inch wide.

Here is one copied from the scrap-book of Mrs. Lizzie H. Gay:

"Funeral Notice
The funeral services of
JACOB HUGHES
Will take place at his residence
On tomorrow (Sunday) afternoon at 3 o'clock
The friends and acquaintances of the family
Are respectfully invited to attend
Saturday, May 16, 1874"

From a newspaper clipping:

"JACOB HUGHES

The death of this venerable citizen was not unexpected, as he had been in delicate health for several years, and had reached a period in life when slight attacks often prove fatal

He was a native of Spottsylvania County, Virginia, but came with his parents in early childhood to the comparative wilderness of Kentucky. He was the exemplification of what an industrious and energetic young man of good habits and limited opportunities may accomplish in this country. Commencing life with no patrimony and small education he not only gave his children every opportunity, but accumulated the largest landed estate, we believe in the Blue Grass region, and saw his children located upon good farms which he had purchased for them, and all respected, and of fair fame and good habits.

He was a man of kindly disposition, and did not make his large estate by grinding the face of the poor, but by the simple process that agriculture opens to every man who pursues it with diligence and energy.

He has often occupied positions of public trust, and always discharged his duty with fidelity and satisfaction. It was his pride and boast that when he was a candidate for office, he always got every vote in his precinct, and he seemed to value this mark of confidence and attachment from his immediate neighbors more than the largest majorities in the whole county.

It is seldom that a man lives nearly three-quarters of a century, and grows rich in a county, who does not provoke the enmity and jealousy of some, but we have yet to hear the first word of bitterness uttered against this venerable man. Some men acquire greatness, some acquire great wealth, but few have ever lived more blameless to their eighty-fifth year, or retained more entirely the veneration and respect of their descendants and neighbors than did this venerable Jacob Hughes."

(Taken from the scrap-book of his granddaughter, Mrs. Lizzie H. Gay.)

Jacob Hughes organized the First National Bank of Lexington in 1865, and was its first president. All of his children but Jane Rachel have been sketched. She was b. at Hibernia, August 27, 1821, and d. at her home "Edgewood", January 1, 1903. December 19, 1844, she m. Robert Benjamin Graves, a son of Joseph and Mary Goodwin Graves, through the latter the family trace back to Harold Godwyn, which is the Saxon spelling of Goodwin, who was the last Saxon King in England. He was killed at the Battle of Hastings, October 14, 1066. His sister was the wife of King Edward the Confessor, who preceeded Harold on the throne of England.

Robert Benjamin and Jane Rachel Hughes Graves had the following children:

1. Jacob Hughes b. October 25, 1846, d. February 14, 1921.
    September 25, 1866 he m. Jennie McKenney, b. February 26, 1850,

d. December 29, 1928. She was a daughter of William and Sallie Ferguson McKenney.

Children:
1. Sallie Elizabeth b. July 25, 1869, m. Reuben M. Clark, October 12, 1898. He was b. September 18, 1864. Two children, Julius Graves and Virginia Rosalie Clark and one grandson, Julius Graves Clark, Jr.
2. Jane Rachel Graves b. August 2, 1872, d. March 26, 1926.
3. Jacob Hughes, Jr. b. April 22, 1876. April 25, 1917 he m. Julia Thompson b. September 7, 1889, d. January 29, 1919. October 1, 1925, he m. Eran Blackwell b. September, 1903. They have three children, Jacob, Jr., James and Jane.

2. Elizabeth H. Graves b. August 13, 1848, d. February 14, 1917. September 1, 1870 she m. Dr. W. D. Gay. Children:
1. Benjamin Patton b. June 10, 1871, d. February 1, 1905. October 12, 1892, m. Elva Gatewood.

Children: Gatewood b. October 28, 1893, m. Harriet McCreary, granddaughter of James B. McCreary.

> Children: Elva Gatewood d. when about three years old
> Thresa McCreary and Betty Gay.
> Robert McCreary.

2nd Child of Benjamin and Elva Gatewood Gay, Augustus, b. October 28, 1895, m. Elizabeth Sims. They have a son and a daughter, Lucy.

3. Elizabeth Gay b. September, 1900, m. summer of 1936.

2nd. Child of W. D. and Elizabeth H. Gay, Jacob Douglas b. March 24, 1874. June 10, 1906 m. Lucy Graddy. They have one son, J. D. Gay, Jr., b. April 4, 1910, m. November 28, 1936, Elizabeth Caldwell.

3rd. Child of Robert Benjamin and Jane Hughes Graves, Augustus, b. October 23, 1849, d. September 14, 1856.

4th. Eleanora Burnley, b. July 17, 1853, m. John W. Coleman, June 19, 1879. She d. September 14, 1892. They had one child, Louise, b. May 6, 1880, d. July 2, 1880.

5th. Ben b. January 28, 1859, d. February 27, 1859.

6th. Julia Mary b. March 7, 1860, d. May 11, 1884, m. November 9, 1880 Strauder D. Goff, only child of Benjamin and Ann Prewitt Goff. Have one son, Ben Douglas Goff b. December 18, 1882. December 12, 1906 he m. Bessie Spahr b. March 10, 1882, daughter of Asa and Emma French Spahr. Have one son, Ben Douglas, Jr. b. November 5, 1912.

7th. Harriet Amanda Patton Hughes Graves b. July 1863. January 1, 1893, m. James D. Wilson, b. July 15, 1865, d. August 20, 1917. Children: Oscar b. April, 1900, and Edgar b. June, 1902.

Much more might be written of this wonderful pioneer family and their descendants, but as all things in this world, whether good or otherwise, must have have an ending, so I bring my article to a close.

Before doing this, I wish to thank every one who helped me in any way to make this record possible.

"THE PATTONS"

Query and Corrections.*

Kentucky Register, April, 1937.

P. 145. Children of Matthew and Rebecca Patton:
1. John D. m. Hetty.
9. John m. Esther Patton.

Query:

Are not these two the same John?

Miss Nannie Starling, Hopkinsville, Kentucky, compiler of Patton records in Christian County lists only *one* John, though she adds after her list of eight, "Matthew and Rebecca Patton are said to have had *ten* children. These are all I can locate."

Jessamine County Will Book A, p. 387. Will of Roger Patton pro 1812—"daughter, Esther, now wife of John Patton of Christian County."

Christian County Records, Kentucky Register, April, 1937, p. 145, show John D. Patton and wife, Hetty, still living in 1820 and John D. Patton and son at St. Clair in 1834.

Also the names Esther, Hester and Hetty are used interchangeable.

---
*For pp. 145, 146, 149 & 150 see pp. 18, 19, 22 & 23, this volume.

P. 145 and 6. James Patton m. Polly Huston. Should be Polly Husban or Husband.

Kentucky Register, Volume 25, p. 83—Also "Early Settlers of Sangamon County, Illinois" by John C. Powers, states "James Patton —— m. in Christian County, Kentucky 1815, Polly Husband.

P. 146. Philip Allen m. Sally L. Allen. Should be Philip Patton.
Kentucky Register, Volume 25, p. 83. Also Miss Starling's copy of Christian County Marriages.

P. 146. John T. Patton, legatee of Benjamin W. Patton. Should be *executor*. Christian County, Kentucky Will Book D, p. 291. Will of Benjamin W. Patton, 1825. Executors, John D. Patton and John T. Patton.

P. 149. Holley. Should be Halley.

P. 149. November 6, 1827, marriage date of Elizabeth Patton. Should be marriage date of Sarah Ann Patton and James Dunn.

P. 149. Mackey, 7th child of John and Sibbea H. Patton. Should be Nackey. Same correction p. 150.

P. 149. John Dunn, 2nd wife, Edna Sutton. Should be Edna *Salter*.

These corrections pp. 149-150 are substantiated by family records in possession of Margaret Mc. R. D. Frye also by her personal knowledge.

CAPTAIN JAMES PATTON OF AUGUSTA COUNTY, VIRGINIA, AND LOUISVILLE, KENTUCKY ANCESTORS AND DESCENDANTS

Compiled by William S. Muir, of South Orange, New Jersey, in response to a request for information on Capt. Patton. Research made by Miss Ophelia Muir, of Woodstock, Vermont, and Nelson Van Buskirk, of Louisville, Kentucky, great-great-great grandchildren of Capt. Patton.

Copied and prepared for publication by Bayless Hardin, of the Kentucky State Historical Society.

The grandparents of Captain James Patton were Henry Patton and his wife Sarah Lynn, the daughter of the Laird of the Loch Lynn, Scotland—Sarah Lynn's brother was the William Lynn of Fredericksburg, Virginia. The Pattons (Paten or Patis) are supposed to have reached England from Normandy, then to Scotland, and later with many other families induced to leave Northern Scotland to colonize Northern Ireland, with Scotch Presbyterians, for political reasons by James 1st. The parents of Capt. James Patton were Capt. John Patton and his first wife, a Miss Rogers, living, we are informed, in Newtown Timivady, in the County of Donegal, Ireland, near Londonderry.

The children of Henry Patton and wife, Sarah Lynn, who came to Augusta County, Virginia, were all married abroad, and came over, 1736-1740, with their families. A number of the children of Capt. John Patton having, probably, been born abroad, viz: John, Jr., Matthew, born 1730, and possibly others of his eight known children.

The three children of Henry Patton, who came over to Augusta County, were:

Capt. John Patton, with wife, Miss Rogers and several children.

Col. James Patton, with grant of 120,000 acres of land. And Elizabeth Patton, the wife of John Preston. All three settled in Augusta County, Virginia.

Of the eight children of Capt. John Patton, six are believed to be by the 1st wife, Miss Rogers, viz:

(1) John, Jr.
(2) Matthew, born 1730, Ireland; died May 3, 1803, in Kentucky.
(3) Samuel
(4) William
(5) Our Capt. James Patton, born Oct. 12, 1735, or 1748, died Louisville, Kentucky, Dec. 29, 1815, of whom more later.
(6) Margaret.

His 1st wife, Miss Rogers, evidently died before 1754, as we find record of marriage of John Patton on March 23, 1754 to Agnese ———, and it is believed that the following children are daughters of this Agnese, viz:

(7) Isabell

(8) Agnese

Although No. 8 being named Agnese after her mother may well have been the 1st born, and therefore the only child by Agnese.

This Capt. John Patton achieved prominence in Augusta County Virginia. We find him a large land owner, and in 1745 the first High Sheriff of the newly created Augusta County. On Nov. 18, 1752, he qualified as Captain of the "County Foote." He died 1757, having made his will the 2nd of January, 1756. A copy of his will is shown on page 137, Vol. 35, No. 111, April, 1937 issue of the Register of the Kentucky State Historical Society, Frankfort, Kentucky.

By his will, he bequeaths "to Agnese, my dearly beloved wife, the use of the plantation whereon I now dwell, and my moveable estate, in order to have my five children (to wit) William, James, Margaret, Isabel and Agnese educated and supported until they come to age" "Item: William and James (our Capt. James), my beloved sons, two hundred acres of land on which I now dwell, in Fee Simple". Note: in 1777 we find our Capt. James selling this land and on 27th of May, 1778 reaching the Falls of the Ohio, where he lived until his death, acquiring large holdings of land probably from the proceeds of the sale of the Augusta County inheritance. The will states that "my elder children are already portioned off". On March 16, 1757, Agnes Patton, Matthew Lyle and Alexander Miller gave bond for three hundred pounds as Executrix of John Patton. Note: In Jan. 1756, when the will was signed by John Patton, our (Capt.) James Patton, (his son) was under 21 years of age, Whether he was born about 1735-1739, as his newspaper obituary suggests, or in 1748 as was carved on his tombstone. The obituary states he "was nearly 80 years old", which might mean anywhere between 70 and 80, so that his birth was probably between 1735 and 1739.

With the foregoing, which sketches the ancestry of Capt. James Patton, of Louisville, Ky., the following pages will give a short outline of the life of Capt. James Patton, after which the descendants of Capt. James Patton will be enumerated, as fully as known.

Very little is known of the life of Capt. James Patton before the 27th of May, 1778, on which day, as shown by a deposition made by Capt. Patton in Case 531, Old Chancery Court of Louisville, the Expedition led by General George Rogers Clark, with twenty families, and with troops, reached the Falls of the Ohio, opposite the site of the present City of Louisville, therefore the day "which laid the foundation of that City".

Capt. Patton was accompanied by his wife Mary Doherty, and three young daughters, the oldest eight years of age. It has been stated before that deeds in 1777 show the sale by Capt. Patton of his lands in Augusta County, Virginia, inherited under the will dated Jan. 2, 1756, of his father Capt. John Patton, who died 1757, so that these inherited acres in Augusta County had been retained by Capt. Patton for twenty years, but whether he had farmed them and lived there for that period of years, or whether his step-mother had continued to live there until 1777, is not at this time known. Capt. James Patton, born Oct. 12, 1735 or 1748 (see notes and references) died Dec. 29, 1815, in Louisville and is buried in the old Jefferson Street Cemetery, with a stone marker on his grave.

He is represented in the Society of the Cincinnati in the State of Virginia by his great, great, great, grandson, Nelson Van Buskirk McMullin, Pendennis Club, Louisville, Ky. Capt. Patton was spoken of "as a man of fine personal appearance, tall, well formed, with great energy and a man of affairs in the early life of Louisville."

His first wife was Mary Doherty (it is believed) and she may have been the daughter, or sister, of that John Doherty, who is shown by the records of the County Court House Minute Books to have been with Capt. Patton, commissioned in 1779 to get lumber from the forests for the building of Fort Nelson (this building being completed by Capt. Patton in 1782) for the protection of the settlers against the Indians.

Mary Doherty died in 1787—she had been married probably about 1768-69, and probably born in 1750, or thereabouts. She was buried in old Fort Nelson, Louisville, Ky.

Capt. Patton's three daughters, by his first wife, Mary Doherty, were: Martha (Patsy), Margaret (Peggy), and Mary (Polly), and all of them married as follows:

Martha Patton (Patsy), daughter of Capt. James Patton, and his first wife, Mary Doherty, was born in Virginia in 1770. She died in Louisville Dec. 29, 1815. She married first on April 2, 1791, John Laloo, but he died shortly thereafter, leaving no issue; and she married second on March 14, 1793, Capt. John Nelson, and had five children, as follows:

(1) James Nelson, born 1795, married Eliza Cartmill, of Bardstown, Ky., by whom he had Sarah Nelson, who married in 1846, Hon. H. M. Woodward, of Tully, Laura Co., Missouri.

(2) Sarah Nelson, born Nov. 29, 1797 (died Oct. 6, 1869) married Jan. 16, 1813, Cornelius Van Buskirk (born Aug. 22, 1776; died Feb. 20, 1863); they had four children as follows: 1, Ophelia; 2, Emmeline; 3, Charlotte; 4, Mary. (See Van Buskirk descendants, following)

(3) David Patton Nelson, born 1799, died 1845, was living in Warren County, near Cincinnati, Ohio. He married Nancy ————, family name not known, of Bardstown, Kentucky, and had at least six children, as follows:

Augustine O. Nelson, born 1826; Cornelius Van Buskirk Nelson; Benjamin F. Nelson; Marcus L. Nelson; Julia Nelson; Nancy Nelson.

(4) Mary Ann Nelson, born 1800; married Edward Tracy, of St. Louis, Missouri. A grandson of this union, Edward Nelson Tracy, was in 1917 said to be living in New York City with three children, as follows: Charles F. Tracy, John Nelson Tracy and Edward F. Tracy.

(5) Margaret Nelson, Married John Olliver (See Nelson Family genealogy following)

Margaret Patton (Peggy), the daughter of Capt. James Patton, and his first wife, Mary Doherty, married Nathaniel Pryor.

Mary Patton (Polly), daughter of Capt. Patton, and his first wife, Mary Doherty, was born in Virginia in 1773, and died in 1840 at Eddyville, Kentucky. She married first, May 15, 1792, John Vaughn, who died in 1795, leaving one daughter, Nancy Vaughn, born 1793, died 1857, who married Chittenden P. Lyon, of Eddyville, Ky. They had: 1, James Nelson Lyon, who married Catherine E. ———; 2, Chittenden P. Lyon, Jr.; 3, Matthew P. Lyon, who married Sarah R. ————; 4, Martha A. Lyon, who married Willis B. Machen, U. S. Senator; 5, Mary Ann Lyon, who married Reuben R. O'Hara, uncle of the poet. Mary Patton married second in 1796, John McDaugh, who died in 1798, not leaving children.

Mary Patton married third, in 1800, George Gracey, who was born in 1774. He left home in Pennsylvania when about 16 years old, about 1780 (because of the second marriage of his father) with a brother, John or James, who is believed to have settled further West. They left a sister Rebecca at home, who stayed with her father. George Gracey was probably a descendant of the John Gracey who came over with William Penn in 1682-83, and had large land holdings in Haverford Township, Pennsylvania. Mary Patton and George Gracey had four children: 1, James Nelson Gracey, Sr.; 2, Martha Nelson Gracey; 3, Matthew Lyon Gracey; 4, William Gracey.

(See Gracey Genealogy following)

Capt. James Patton (following the death of his first wife, Mary Doherty Patton, which occurred on or about 1787) married a second time, on June 14, 1792, Elizabeth Reager, a widow, and had by her, a son, who died childless; and on the death of this second wife, Capt. James Patton married a third time on July 21, 1804, Phoebe McCausland (born April 27, 1782; died May 22, 1848), the widow of William Basye, and had by her a son, born 1811, who died 1819.

Phoebe McCausland had one daughter by her first husband (Wm. Basye), viz: Sarah Payne Basye, who was born in 1802, and who married in 1819 Dr. John Moil Talbot, and had by him a daughter, Cordelia Lafayette Talbot, who married Dr. Madison Pyles. After the death of Capt. James Patton, his widow, Phoebe McCausland Basye Patton, married for the third time William Marshall, who long survived her.

(Captain James Patton, from the Manuscripts and Writings of Col. R. T. Durrett, Louisville, Kentucky.)

Captain James Patton was born in Virginia in 1735 and died in Louisville, Ky., Dec. 29, 1815.

He came to Louisville in the Spring of 1778 with Gen. George Rogers Clark, while on his way to the conquest of the Illinois Country.

The Expedition reached the Falls of the Ohio and landed on Corn Island on the 27th of May, 1778.

Captain Patton did not accompany the Soldiers to the Illinois Country, but remained on the Island to take care of the stores landed there by Gen. Clark and some families who had accompanied him to Redstone.

The task of Capt. Patton to take care of these families and especially to provide them food from the surrounding country forest, in which Indians lurked, was quite as difficult as that of the Soldiers who went to the conquest of the Illinois Country.

He succeeded however in keeping them in food by having reliable hunters in the woods at the proper time.

There was no attack by the Indians upon the settlement while Gen. Clark was in the Illinois Country.

The Indians seem to have had an impression that Corn Island was a very strongly fortified place and they never assailed it. In 1779 when Gen. Clark had conquered the Illinois Country, the families on Corn Island determined to move to the mainland.

They called a public meeting of the inhabitants then at the Falls, who appointed a committee to plan and establish a town. This committee consisted of seven men, among them Captain James Patton. They established a town and gave it the name of Louisville. The next year 1780 they petitioned the Legislature of Virginia to incorporate the town they had established. Among those who signed the petition, the name of Captain James Patton appears. The Legislature of Virginia incorporated the town in accordance with the petition. After Louisville had thus become an established town, regular Trustees were from 1780 until 1792 appointed by the Legislature, and Captain Patton was so appointed a number of times, and later when Louisville became part of the Commonwealth of Kentucky, Captain Patton was several times elected Trustee of the City of Louisville.

Although Captain James Patton was not in the Illinois Expedition, he performed gallant acts of soldiering in other expeditions against the Indians. In 1779 he was in Bowman's Expedition to the Ohio towns. In 1780 he was in Capt. Wm. Harrod's Company, then stationed at the Falls of the Ohio.

He was in the Expedition of Gen. George Rogers Clark in 1780 against the Ohio Indians, to avenge the taking of Martin's and Ruddell's Stations, which was a brilliant victory. In 1782 he was again in the Expedition of Gen. George Rogers Clark against the Ohio Indians to avenge the disaster at the Blue Licks.

He thus appears to have been in all the expeditions in early times except that of Gen. Clark against Kaskaskia and Vincennes in 1778-79.

At an early date Capt. Patton acquired a half acre lot on Eight Street, between Main Street and the river. The land was heavily timbered and among the trees which grew upon it, was a giant sycamore, which was hollow at the root. This hollow was as large as an ordinary room of a house, and Capt. Patton, taking advantage of this fact, erected a log cabin close to the tree, so as to use the hollow of the sycamore as one room to his cabin. He occupied this cabin and hollow tree until danger from the Indians was gone from the Falls and then he erected upon this piece of ground a large double stone house, in which he lived until he died. On the top of this house was a kind of cupola or balcony, which he added for the purpose of giving himself a view of the Falls of the Ohio. In this little apartment he would sit and watch the rapids of the Ohio. Nothing seemed to delight him more than to occupy the top of his house and look at the Falls of the River. Captain Patton's love for the Falls of the Ohio had made him so familiar with the rapids, that he was considered the most skillful and safest man to conduct a boat over the rapids. The taking of a boat over the rapids was considered a dangerous undertaking and the Legislature in 1798 passed an Act establishing the Office of Falls Pilot. Captain Patton was the first man who ever filled this Office and he remained in it from his first appointment until his death.

Captain Patton was the owner of a great deal of valuable real estate in Louisville and in the surrounding country. He was also the owner of Square No. 9, which he purchased of James Morrison but for which he failed to secure a deed during his life. This was the property on part of which his original log cabin beside the hollow sycamore was built and on which he afterwards reared his stone mansion.

It required a suit in chancery, after his death, to secure the property for his heirs.

A rare relic of the Patton's is the hymn book, which the first Mrs. James Patton (Mary Doherty) brought with her to Corn Island in the Spring of 1778. It is an edition of Watt's Hymns, bound in plain leather and much worn by use. Mrs. Patton used to gather the Colonists together on Corn Island on Sunday during the Summer of 1778 and have hymns sung from this book. "As it was the only hymn book present, the hymns had to be lined from it while they were being sung."

The following obituary notice appeared in the Western Courier Jan. 4, 1816, a weekly paper published at that time in the City of Louisville:

"Died in this town on Friday last, Dec. 29, 1815, Captain James Patton, aged nearly eighty years. He was one of the earliest settlers of Louisville, and came to this City with General Clark as Captain in the Illinois Regiment. He was the first authorized Pilot over the Falls and ever sustained the character of an upright, worthy citizen."

His gravestone in the old Jefferson St. graveyard contains the inscription that he was born in 1748, which would make him 67 years old at death, and the statement quoted above from the Western Courier that he was nearly eighty years old can perhaps only be proven false or otherwise by the discovery of Capt. Patton's birth date record. If born in 1735, he was probably born in Ireland or Scotland, while, if born in 1748, it was probably in Augusta County, Virginia.

NOTES AND REFERENCES

Augusta County, Virginia, Records of the Scotch Irish. Nov. 20, 1752, Capt. John Patton, Surety on Wm. Preston's bonds as Assistant Surveyor. (Capt.) John Patton's will dated Jan. 2, 1756, and proved Nov. 26, 1757, p. 44 (183). Proved by Witnesses March 16, 1757.

Homes "History of Virginia". In 1736-40 Benjamin Burden brought over upwards of 100 families and among them was (Capt.) John Patton and his brother (Col.) James Patton, of Augusta County, the latter received a grant of 120,000 acres of land. page 453.

Campbell's "History of Virginia"—Capt. John and (Col.) James Patton, brothers of Elizabeth Patton, wife of John Preston.

Chalkley refers to him as (Col.) James Patton, Gent. in his chronicles of the Scotch Irish. Vol. 3, 457. "Chronicles of the Scotch Irish" in Virginia. Vol. 1, pages 56-378—John Patton qualified, Captain, Co. Foote, Nov. 18, 1752 to 1754. "Annals of Augusta County, Virginia" gives lengthy detail of Patton family, from Ireland early in 1700's. Vol. 3, p. 106, Agnese of the will of (Capt.) John Patton (dated Jan. 2, 1756) was probably a second wife, as we find marriage license to John Patton March 23, 1754 (John Patton died 1757).

Peyton's "History of Augusta County Virginia", page 32—meanwhile the legal business of the people west of the Blue Ridge continued to be transacted at the Orange Court House and led to the organization of the County (Augusta, at Staunton) in 1745. (Capt.) John Patton was appointed High Sheriff, and John Madison, Clerk.

Cartmell's "History Shenandoah Valley and Descendants", Vol. 1, page 446—(Capt.) John Patton was the first Sheriff, 1745, Augusta County, Virginia.

"Corners of Ancestry"—(Capt.) John Patton, his brother (Col.) James Patton, and their sister Elizabeth, wife of John Preston, all married, came from Ireland.

1914, from Courier Journal of Louisville, Ky., gives Londonderry, North Ireland, for James, John and Elizabeth Patton. Another letter names Donegal, Ireland.

Richmond, Virginia, Standard, 1880—letters state James Patton (Col.) brought over many in his own ships and sister Elizabeth Patton, wife of John Preston.

"Life of General George Rogers Clark", by Wm. Hayden English, President of the Indiana Historical Society—"Capt. James Patton remained in the vicinity of the Falls (of the Ohio, Louisville) the rest of his life and was a useful and respected citizen."

Henning's Virginia Statutes—"(Capt.) James Patton, appointed Trustee of Louisville (by the Virginia Assembly) in 1786. Vol. 7—(Capt.) James Patton appointed by the Assembly of Virginia at Williamsburg, as a Trustee of Kentucky County, at Louisville, Falls of the Ohio, 1786, and he served until 1792, when Kentucky State was admitted into the Union."

Deeds showing sale by (Capt.) James Patton of the home place (left to James by his father (Capt.) John) in the year 1777. Note: Shortly thereafter in 1778 Capt. James Patton appeared at the Falls of the Ohio with General George Rogers Clark, and later bought extensive tracts of land, probably from the proceeds of the sale of his inherited property.

Deeds. Other deeds, between Col. James and brother Capt. John, and between Capt. James and Col. James.

William Hayden English's "Conquest of the Northwest", Vol. 1, page 147 —(Capt.) James Patton's birth Oct. 12, 1748; died Dec. 29, 1815. Vol. 2, page 848—Capt. James Patton served under General George Rogers Clark.

Society of the Cincinnati in the State of Virginia Capt. James Patton is represented in this Society by his great great great grandson, Nelson Van Buskirk McMullin, Pendennis Club, Louisville, Ky.

Note: Capt. James Patton was a man of fine personal appearance, tall, well formed and of great energy. He performed other military services after the close of the Illinois campaign and is said to have been the first authorized Pilot of the Falls of the Ohio. He was granted 100 acres of land in Gen. George Rogers Clark's grant in tract No. 309 and 8 acres in tract No. 101 on account of his services in the Illinois Campaign. He was a man of affairs and one of the early lot owners in Louisville.

Virginia State Library has under a glass case a letter from General George Rogers Clark addressed to the Governor of Virginia, telling of the good work done in building Fort Nelson. This Fort Nelson was built by Capt. James Patton.

The Kentucky Historical Society is reported to have received, as a gift, from Cordelia La Fayette Talbot (Mrs. (Dr.) Madison Pyles), the grand daughter of Capt. James Patton's third wife, Phoebe McCausland, by her first husband, William Basye, the sword of Capt. James Patton, with blade thirty inches long and one and a quarter inches wide, with ivory handle and silver guard.

Richmond Virginia Standard, June 1880, letters refer to Vol. 3, page 63, "Sketch of Col. James Patton", giving birthplace of Col. James, his brother, Capt. John and their sister, Elizabeth, wife of John Preston, as Newtown Timivady, in County Donegal, Ireland, and article under the date of Sept. 1880 says the Pattons emigrated from near Londonderry 1736-40, and gives the parents of Col. James, Capt. John and Elizabeth as Henry Patton and Sarah Lynn, the daughter of the Laird of Loch Lynn, Scotland.

The Sun, Baltimore, Nov. 6, 1904—a letter from "Descendant" quoting letters from her great grandmother, Letitia Preston (who married Governor John Floyd, son of Col. Floyd, the first "Colonial Governor" of Kentucky) the daughter of the only son of John Preston, the Emigrant, viz: William Preston and wife Susannah Smith, says John Preston (the husband of Elizabeth Patton and brother-in-law of Col. James Patton, and Capt. John Patton) was born in Newtown Timivady, in County Donegal, Ireland. The letters of Letitia Preston also confirm the parentage of Col. James, Capt. John and Elizabeth Patton as given in the Richmond Virginia Standard June 1880 and Sept. 1880. She states further that Col. James Patton was a former officer in the Royal Navy.

Encyclopedia Brittanica—An Act of the Virginia Legislature in 1780 (following the receipt from the inhabitants of a signed petition, among the signers being (Capt.) James Patton, gave the little settlement of Louisville the rank of town.

Encyclopedia Brittanica—The rank of City was conferred upon Louisville by the Kentucky State Legislature in 1828, following the receipt of the Resolutions prepared by a committee appointed at a town meeting, as follows:

1st Resolved: That Public Convenience renders it important that we ask for a passage of an Act incorporating Louisville with its enlargements and giving a City Court for the speedy punishment of crimes and the speedy trial of Civil Suits. 2nd Resolved: That a Committee of five citizens be appointed to draft an Act of incorporation and to submit the same at an adjournment of this meeting. The Committee, under 2nd Resolution, was composed of Daniel Wurts, Thomas Anderson, S. S. Goodwin, S. S. Nichols and Garrett Duncan.

Pattons of Virginia, see Waddells "Annals of Augusta County"; Foote's "Sketches"; Richmond Standard, Vol. 1 to 4; Slaughter's "St. Marks Parish."

Note: Col. James Patton, who brought many families to Virginia, was killed by the Indians July 8, 1755. His only children were two daughters, viz: Mary, the wife of William Thompson, and Margaret, the wife of Col. John Buchanan.

Note: Henry Patton (the father of Col. James, Capt. John and Elizabeth Preston) with three brothers, are said to have served under King William in the defense of Londonderry in 1698, when it was besieged by the Roman Catholic Party.

"Centenary of Louisville," May 1, 1880—p. 29—In May 1778 General George Rogers Clark, under orders of Patrick Henry, Governor of Virginia, sailed (down the Ohio river) for what is now the City of Louisville, with some 20 families and troops.

Page 3—Case 531 Old Chancery Court of Louisville, a deposition of Capt. James Patton, that he reached the Falls of the Ohio on May 27, 1778, "which day laid the foundation of Louisville."

Page 33—The inhabitants held a public meeting April 17, 1779, and appointed seven trustees for the town, among whom was Capt. James Patton.

Page 24—The Louisville Trustees on April 24, 1779, James Patton among them, made some rules for the sale of lots.

Page 37—Mentions H. Marshall's "History of Kentucky", written in 1812; McMurtries "History of Louisville, published in 1819; Butler's "History of Louisville", published in 1832; Cassady's Histories.

Page 93—Lewis Collin's history, published in 1847; Richard Collin's Jefferson County History.

Page 38—Mentions that only five (5) names have been preserved by Dr. McMurtrie in his book on the "First Settlers" "James Patton being the first named of the five mentioned."

Page 39—Mentions James Patton, his wife Mary, and their three daughters, Martha (Patsy), Margaret (Peggy) and Mary, (Polly).

Page 42—Fort Nelson was erected in 1792.

Page 48—"All these early settlers have undistinguished graves with the exception of Gen. George Rogers Clark and Capt. James Patton, the latter resting in the old Jefferson Street Graveyard, between 16th and 18th Streets, surmounted by a stone monument."

Virginia Magazine of History and Biography, April issue, 1939: Col. James Patton (the uncle of Capt. James Patton) was the son of Henry Patton and his wife, Sarah Lynn (daughter of the Laird of Loch Lynn, and sister of William Lynn, who came to Fredericksburg, Virginia) and was born in Ireland in 1690, in the town of Newtown Timivady, near Londonderry, County Donegal. The Pattons were a prominent family in the North of Ireland and (Col.) James Patton was bred to the sea and served as an Officer in the Royal Navy in Queen Anne's War with the French, which ended with the treaty of Utrecht in 1713. After that Col. James Patton owned a line of ships, which plied between Ireland and Scotland and later to Virginia. He came to Hobb's Hole on the Rappahannock River (now Tappahannock) bringing settlers to the new World, making as many as twenty-five trips across the Atlantic and long voyages they were in those days. Col. James Patton was granted for himself and his associates, by King George 2nd of England, "120,000 acres of the best land lying above the Blue Ridge". He lived at "Springhill", near Staunton, Augusta County, Virginia.

"We have read of his vast enterprise to open up and settle the Western lands in Virginia. He directed the affairs of the James River and Roanoke Company, and he was the connecting link between Eastern Virginia and the great Southwest Virginia". In July 1755 he was killed by the Indians.

GRACEY GENEALOGY

Furnished by Mrs. William McClure Drane, Madison St., Clarksville, Tennessee.

George Gracey married Mary Patton (Polly)

born 1774, probably in Pennsylvania; died Feb. 5, 1828, Eddyville, Kentucky. Settled in Louisville about 1790. Probably descended from John Gracey, who came to America with William Penn, sailing from Deal on the ship "Welcome", on Sept. 1, 1682, with 100 associates landing at Newcastle on the Delaware River Oct. 27, 1682 or later. This John Gracey was granted 960 acres of land in Haverford County, adjoining, or part of, the City of Philadelphia. George Gracey left his home in Pennsylvania with his brother John or James, leaving a sister, Rebecca, at home with his father, and the latters 2nd wife. William Adolph Gracey, owner of "Geneva Times", of Geneva, New York, is a direct descendant from the first John (above) through four generations of John Graceys.

born 1773 in Virginia; died Nov. 26, 1838, in Eddyville, Kentucky. She was the daughter of Capt. James Patton (Patten) and Mary Dougherty (Doherty) This was her third marriage in 1803 to George Gracey. (See Patton (or Patten) Genealogy)

George Gracey and Mary Patton had five children, viz.:
1 James Nelson Gracey married Zarilda O'Hara
born about 1804 born about 1810

They had among probably other children:

Mildred Gracey married W. M. Kelly the inventor of the
born 1830 "Bessemer Steel" process and a partner of Carnegie and Frick. Mrs. W. M. Kelley (Mildred Gracey) was living in 1917 at 954 S. 4th St. Louisville, Ky.

They had two daughters and two sons, viz;

(1) Zarilda (Lily) Kelly, married Robert Coleman Thompson,
born 1851 born 1839, died 1927

They had daughter

Blanche Kelly Thompson, born 1888, who married Clarence Dudley Maffitt, living in 1939 at 219 S. 5th Ave., Wilmington, North Carolina.

(2) William C. Kelly, married May ———
President Kelly
Axe Company.

They had one son, William, Jr.

(3) Blanche Kelly, married William Ballard Lockett. Mrs. William Ballard Lockett was living in 1939 on Rittenhouse Square, 19th and Walnut Sts. Philadelphia, Pennsylvania.

(4) James Kelly, married ———————————————. He died in 1916 in New York, leaving widow, one son and one daughter.

2 Martha Nelson Gracey married J. M. Marshall prominent lawyer
born Sept. 13, 1806, in Tennessee, and cousin of Chief
died Feb. 17, 1893 Justice Marshall.
married about 1820

They are said to have had 13 children.

3 Matthew Lyon Gracey married Maria Tilford
born Dec. 13, 1809 born June 15, 1813
died Jan. 2, 1850 died Nov. 16, 1847
married about 1829-30. She was the daughter of John Tilford and Elizabeth Crumbaugh, of Russellville, Ky.

They had:

(1) George Tilford Gracey, married Mary Barnes in
born 1832 1864-65.

They lived at Summit, Mississippi. Had Charles, Matthew, Kate and William.

(2) Frank Patton Gracey, married Irene Cobb in 1857
born 1834; died
April 27, 1895 in
Clarksville, Tenn.

They had son Julius, who married Minnie Thomas, and they had Louise, Hope, Julien, Minnie, Frank and Irene.
(3) William Robert Gracey, married 1st, Miss White
    born 1836   2nd, Laura Scott
        Children by 2nd marriage, Iola, Laura and Frank.
(4) Mary Gracey   married   John Stacker
    born May 3, 1838
    married Jan. 17, 1854
    died Nov. 14, 1899
        They had two children, George, and Mary. Mary died in infancy.
(5) Lucy Gracey,   married   James Francis Wm. Childers
    born March 12, 1840
    married Oct. 1, 1857
    died Eddyville, Ky.
        They had William, Elizabeth, Gracey, Mary Stacker, Lula and Irene.
(6) Ellen Gracey,   married   Russell Wake
    born March 19, 1842
    died April, 1865
        They had son, Frank Wake, who had no children.
(7) Maria Tilford Gracey   married   Thomas Dade Luckett
    born Dec. 16, 1843   born Nov. 4, 1843
    married Dec. 2, 1869   died May 24, 1913
    died Jan. 18, 1910   The 7th generation of Lucketts in America. From Normandy at time of the Conquest, when the name was Lockett. The emigrant ancestor was Samuel Luckett 1, who settled at Post-Au-Tobac, Maryland; was a large land owner and planter. Had sons Samuel II, and William. William moved to Frederick County; was wealthy; was Lieutenant-Colonel in Revolutionary Army, and Captain in the French and Indian Wars. William married Charity Middleton, daughter of John Middleton. Their son, Leven Luckett married Letitia Peyton, descendant of Col. Valentine Peyton and also of Capt. Francis Peyton, the

latter marrying Frances Dade, and this latters son marrying Susan E. Hobbs, connecting the prominent families of Hobbs, Dorsey and Lawrence in Maryland and Virginia; and these latter three families came to Kentucky about 1799, settling on connecting large plantations near Louisville, Ky. Thomas Dade Luckett (above) was son of Alfred Luckett, and was born at Middletown, near Louisville, Ky. Thos. Dade Luckett moved to Clarksville, Tennessee, in 1876.

They had 4 children

1 Mary Stacker Luckett married Wm. McClure Drane
born Jan. 4, 1872   born May 23, 1866
married Dec. 14, 1899   died June 2, 1931.
Living 1939, Madison St.
Clarksville, Tennessee.

They had

(1) Roberta Luckett Drane, married Hilliard O. Wood,
born Mar. 11, 1911   born 1911, son of Dr. Hilliard
m. Nov. 16, 1935   Wood, and his wife,
                           Martha O. —————,
                           of Nashville, Tenn.

They had
Hilliard O. Wood, Jr., born Aug 15, 1938.

(2) William McClure Drane
born Oct. 4, 1912
died Oct. 23, 1938
not married.

(3) Walter Harding Drane
born Feb. 18, 1915;
lives Cleveland, Ohio.

2 Lou Lue Luckett
born Jan. 4, 1872,
the twin sister of Mary Stacker Luckett, (No. 1, above). Lou Lue died in 1872.

3 Gracey Hobbs Luckett   married   Edmonia Rankin
born Apr. 28, 1877,   of Henderson, Ky.
lives Louisville, Ky.

                          They had
        (1) Thomas Dade Luckett
            born Nov. 4, 1908
        (2) Edward Rankin Luckett
            born Nov. 15, 1910.

(3) Frances Luckett   married   Carlyle Bethel
    born Dec. 20, 1912
    married in 1935
                          had
      Gracey Hobbs Luckett Bethel, born Sept., 1938.
        (4) Gracey Hobbs Luckett
            born May 2, 1918

4 Roberta Lucket   William Edwin Baldwin
born Dec. 6, 1878   President of Banks-Baldwin
married Nov. 8, 1913   Law Publishing Co., Cleveland,
                                      Ohio.

    Children of Matthew Lyon Gracey and Maria Tilford, Continued—
8 Elizabeth Gracey   married   1st Urey Henry, in 1863; had
born Jan. 13, 1845   son Robert Henry.
died Aug. 15, 1914   2nd John Boyd, March 12, 1872;
                                        had Marie and Bessie, who married Mr. Travis.

9 Matthew Gracey   married   Marion Castner, Nov. 3, 1876.
born Mar. 4, 1847
died Aug. 21, 1907.

                         They had
(1) Lucy Castner Gracey, married Chas. Haddox Drane. They had Charles, Mary Louise, William and Lucy.
(2) Frank Patton Gracey, married Judith Bright. They had Sarah Bright Gracey who married Frank Haskell; also Frank, Judith, Matthew and Robert.
(3) Mary Beaumont Gracey, never married
(4) Matthew Gracey, never married.

      Children of George Gracey and Mary Patton, continued—
4 William Gracey   married   Caroline Tubbs
   born 1811
                             No Children

5 George Gracey, not married
born March 29, 1813
died July 19, 1834

SAWTELL GENEALOGY

A. Richard Sawtell   married   Elizabeth Post, daughter of Thomas Post; she died Oct. 18, 1694
Town Clerk Groton, Mass. 1662-64
Watertown, Mass. 1636-1651
died Aug. 21, 1694

had

B. Obadiah Sawtell, born 1648, oldest son; died March 20, 1740   married Hannah Lawrence, dau. of George Lawrence, born March 21, 1661

had

C. Lieut. Hezekiah Sawtell born March 2, 1703; of Groton, Mass; died March 18, 1779; in King George War.   married Joanna Wilson, born Jan. 6, 1701; died Sept. 11, 1786; dau. of John Wilson and Elizabeth Foster.

had

D. Lieut. Ephraim Sawtell born Jan. 18, 1734 living in 1785 married Dec. 22, 1757   married Abigail Stone, born Dec. 2, 1736; daughter of Deacon James Stone and Mary Farwell

had

E. John Sawtell, born Oct. 15, 1773; of Milford; died 1828 married April 19, 1797   married Martha Wallingford, born March 26, 1774; died Feb. 18, 1834; daughter of Lieut. David Wallingford and Elizabeth Leeman

(see Muir Genealogy)

F. Rev. Dr. Eli Newton Sawtell born Sept. 8, 1799 married Sept. 8, 1829 died Apr. 6, 1885   married Ophelia Van Buskirk (see Van Buskirk Genealogy)

they had ten children:

1. Cornelius Sawtell, died in infancy
2. Sarah Ann Huntingdon Sawtell M. Aug. 2, 1859   married Joseph Tate Tompkins of Louisville, who died 1877.

they had nine children:
   (1) Sarah Tompkins, died in infancy
   (2) Lucy Tompkins, died in infancy
   (3) Samuel Tompkins, died unmarried
   (4) Ophelia Tompkins, married William Jones, and had one daughter, Ethel Jones.

- (5) Joseph Tompkins, died unmarried
- (6) Julia Tompkins, married Elisha Kelly and had Warfield, Julia and Annie Kelly
- (7) Emma Tompkins, married Denison Hurlbut and had Emma, Jr.
- (8) George Stuart Tompkins, who died young
- (9) Annie Elizabeth Tompkins, married Emmett Foy and had Winthrop and Virginia Foy

3. Albert Barnes Sawtell,   died unmarried in Civil War, Feb. 18, 1864.

4. Edward Newton Sawtell,   died unmarried Nov. 16, 1879, Bartlett Falls, California

5. Augusta Elizabeth Sawtell, born Havre, France, Oct. 21, 1838; died Mass. Sept. 3, 1929

    Married William Muir, Sept. 27 1859; he born Louisville, Ky. July 2, 1834; died Philadelphia June 7, 1908.
    (see Muir Genealogy)

6. Ophelia Sawtell, died in infancy

7. Frederic Henri Sawtell named for Rev. Frederic Monod of Paris and Henri Monod of Havre, a French family of note and beloved friends of his parents. Note: the above named Rev. (or french style "Pasteur") Frederic M o n o d is named more than a dozen times in Rachel Field's popular story of the life of her great Aunt Henriette Desportes under the title of "All This and Heaven Too"

    married Martha Blair in 1873 daughter of Thomas Johnston Blair of Illinois
    born Illinois June 12, 1830
    died Aug. 1, 1900
    and his wife Lucinda Montgomery of Iowa
    born Iowa, June 30, 1829
    died July 4, 1881
    the daughter of John Gilbert Montgomery and wife Martha Neely who were married Oct. 30, 1826 granddaughter of Colbert Powell Blair of Raleigh, N. C.
    born N. C., Decr. 29, 1805
    died June 18, 1906
    aged 101 years.
    and his wife Elizabeth Hill of Virginia
    born Ky. Feby. 13, 1805
    died Oct. 12, 1869
    Family tradition is that the above Colbert Powell Blair was the son of

———————Blair, who married Molly Morgan, the daughter of the Revolutionary hero.

they had six children

(1) Edward Newton Sawtell
(2) Walter Sawtell, living 1939 California unmarried
(3) Ophelia Sawtell, died in infancy
(4) Royal Montgomery Sawtell, born Oct. 20, 1880 in Oregon; died Nov. 13, 1937 in California; married Oct. 14, 1914 to Fay Lenora Hewett, daughter of Alfred W. Hewett and Emily Cook Hewett. They had Richard Blair Sawtell, born May 29, 1917; and Emily Martha Sawtell, born June 21, 1918.
(5) Esma Sawtell married Ralph B. Wade in 1907 and had Norman Sawtell Wade, born April 16, 1911; and Martha Sawtell Wade, born Dec. 31, 1916
(6) Augusta Elizabeth Sawtell, unmarried 1939 living at Portland, Oregon.

Children of Rev. Dr. Eli Newton Sawtell and Ophelia Van Buskirk, continued

8. Emma Sawtell, died unmarried
9. Julia Coster Sawtell, married Rev. John Boyd, May 11, 1875 they had two children Alice Webster Boyd, living 1939, unmarried; and Sallie Anna Shipton Boyd, who married William C. Montignani; she was born Nov. 1882. No children.
10. James Low Sawtell, married, and left one daughter, Ophelia Sawtell.

LINDENBERGER GENEALOGY

A. Jacob Hopewell Lindenberger living Baltimore Maryland in 1750. Very large property owner married Anna Emory of Baltimore, Maryland

they had

1. J. Hopewell Lindenberger, Jr. (descendants not known)
2. Eliza Lindenberger. (descendants, if any, not known)
3. Wm. Jas. Lindenberger of Louisville, Ky. married Mary Van Buskirk, May 14, 1839, daughter of Cornelius Van Buskirk (see Van Buskirk Genealogy)

Children of William James Lindenberger and Mary Van Buskirk:
1. Dr. William H. Lindenberger, unmarried
2. Edward Lindenberger, married; descendants not known
3. George Lindenberger, who married ——————— Bailey

they had

    Lily Lindenberger, died, unmarried
    Laura Lindenberger, died, unmarried
    George Lindenberger, died, unmarried
    Harry Lindenberger, believed living in 1939
4. Mary Lindenberger   married John H. McMullin
            | April 5, 1870
           they had
  Nelson Van Buskirk McMullin (Norval) unmarried living in 1939
  Florence McMullin, died young, unmarried
  Clarence McMullin, died in infancy
  Alvinx McMullin, died in infancy
  Beverly McMullin, died unmarried

5. Sarah Lindenberger, unmarried

6. Anna Emory Lindenberger,   married John English Green son of
  born June 20, 1850 Louis-   Norvin Green and Martha Ann
  ville, Ky; died Jan. 3, 1933   English; the son of Joseph Strother
  Nyack, N. Y.   Green and his wife Susan Martha
               Ball; and he was the son of Francis
               Wyatt Green and wife Lucy
               Strother; and he was the son of
               William Green and his wife Ann
               Coleman; and he was the son of
               Robert Green and his wife Eleanor
               Dunn

          they had
1. Ethel Green,   married Baron Ernest von Schilling
           | living 1939 Copenhagen, Denmark

          they have
Cecilia von Schilling,   married Marcus Wilson Acheson,
           | living in Yonkers, N. Y.

     and they have one daughter, Benedicta von Schilling
    Acheson, born 1939
Nicholas von Schilling,   married Margaretta Calendar, of Sweden

Ernst John von Schilling, unmarried
Children of Anna Emory Lindenberger and John English Green: Continued
2. Mable Green, unmarried, living 1939, Southampton, Long Island.
3. Mildred Green,   married Abram Owen Brand, of Louisville,
  Living London, England, | deceased.
  1939
          they have one son

Abram Owen Brand, Jr., unmarried in 1939 a missionary to Africa

4. Martha Nelson Green, who married 1st, George Floyd Crego, who died New York 193—. She married 2nd, Ledyard Heckscher, of Radnor, Pa. 1939 no issue

NELSON GENEALOGY

A. John Nelson married Hendrica Jansen Vander Vliet, daughter of Dirck Jansen Vander Vliet. She died 1694
In Mamaroneck, N. Y., 1683 married about 1670(?); died after March 28, 1713

had son

B. Polycarpus Nelson married Ruth Gedney daughter of Eleazer Gedney, and his wife Mary Ann Mott
born July 17, 1680
died Dec. 17, 1738

had son

C. Thomas Nelson married Mary ————
made a Deed in 1766

had son

D. Capt. John Nelson, of Louisville; Born N. Y. 1761; Married March 14, 1793; died Louisville, Ky., 1845. married Martha Patton, daughter of Capt. James Patton. She was born Va., 1770; died Louisville, Nov. 9, 1815

Children of Capt. John Nelson and Martha Patton:

1. James Nelson married Eliza Cartmill, of Bardstown, Ky., Aug. 24, 1815; she was daughter of Jacob Cartmill
born 1795
Student Princeton College

They had Sarah Nelson, who married Hon. H. M. Woodward, of Tully, Lewis County, Mo., in 1846.

2. Sarah Nelson married Cornelius Van Buskirk, of Louisville (see Van Buskirk Genealogy)
born 1797
married Jan. 16, 1813
died Oct. 6, 1869

3. David Patton Nelson married Nancy ————
born 1799

He died in 1845, leaving wife Nancy and six children:
  1. Augustine O. Nelson, born 1826
  2. Cornelius Van Buskirk Nelson

3. Benjamin F. Nelson
4. Marcus L. Nelson
5. Julia Nelson
6. Nancy Nelson

4. Mary Ann Nelson   married   Edward Tracy, of St. Louis, Mo.; a
   born, 1800   grandson of Edward Tracy and
                                   Mary Ann Nelson in 1917 was said
                                   to be living in New York City, and
                                   had
                                   1. Charles F. Tracy
                                   2. John Nelson Tracy
                                   3. Edward F. Tracy
                                   (See Tracy Genealogy following)

5. Margaret Nelson   married   John Oliver

WAR SERVICE OF CAPTAIN JOHN NELSON OF LOUISVILLE, KENTUCKY

In view of the letter from a Department of the U. S. Government, which is quoted below, it is believed that the Revolutionary war service of Captain John Nelson of Louisville, Ky., is confirmed. He enlisted when very young (he was born in 1761) as a drummer boy in Colonel Lamb's Regiment of Artillery, for which service he was issued pension Certificate No. 932 on Sept. 19, 1829 for $104.00 per annum and Land Warrants Nos. 7554 and 7555, each for 100 acres of land.

His title of Captain is believed to have been acquired solely from one of his business activities, as owner and builder of several steamboats, one of them, the "Independent," plying between Louisville and St. Louis. There were a number of men by the name of John Nelson in the war and therefore some confusion in records, but the letter following appears to make the record clear, as to Capt. John Nelson of Louisville, Ky., Pensioner No. 932. It is believed that he came to Louisville, Ky., in 1786 or 1790; was elected Trustee of Louisville in 1807, and was prominent in the affairs of that City.

"General Accounting Office, Washington, D. C.
Aug. 25, 1939 (Records Division—In reply please quote R-120310h11)
Sir: In reply to your letter dated Aug. 25, 1939 requesting information concerning John Nelson, a pensioner of the Revolutionary War, Certificate No. 932 Kentucky Agency, you are advised the records on file in this office show that pensioner died on Sept. 25, 1845 in Louisville, Jefferson County, Kentucky, and left no widow (note: wife had died in 1815)

On April 9, 1846, the Clerk of the Court for Jefferson County, State of Kentucky, certified that execution of the will of John Nelson was granted to Elon

W. Rupert and W. J. Lindenberger. The arrears of Pension covering the period from Sept. 3, 1845 to Sept. 25, 1845 were made at Louisville, Ky., on April 10, 1846 to W. J. Lindenberger, one of the Executors of the Estate of John Nelson. No further information has been found of record in this office.— Signed P. D. Fallon, Asst. Chief, Records Division."

Note: The above named W. J. Lindenberger was the husband of a granddaughter of Capt. John Nelson and the latter died on the date named in the above letter, so that Capt. John Nelson of Louisville, Ky., is accurately identified as Pensioner No. 932.

HARRIMAN GENEALOGY

A. Oliver Harriman 1st;   married   Laura Low
   born Sept. 18, 1826   the daughter of James Low and
   died March 12, 1904   Emmeline Van Buskirk of Louisville, Ky., and New York City. (See Low Genealogy and Van Buskirk Genealogy)

   Children of Oliver Harriman and Laura Low believed to be as follows:

1. James Harriman
2. Oliver Harriman 2nd   married   Grace Carley
                                     of Louisville, Ky., have children
3. J. Borden Harriman, married Florence Jaffray
   died Dec. 1, 1914
   have daughter Ethel Borden Harriman
4. Joseph Harriman
5. Emmeline Harriman, married, in sequence not known—
                                     Howard Spencer
                                     Mr. Dodge
                                     Mr. Olin

6. Anne Harriman married 1st Samuel Stevens Sands I; he was killed in a hunting accident in 1888 at Meadow Brook, Long Island, N. Y.
   Children of Anne Harriman and Samuel Stevens Sands I:
   1 Samuel Stevens Sands II, who married Oct. 18, 1910 Gertrude Sheldon, daughter of George R. Sheldon. They had Samuel Stevens Sands III. Samuel Stevens Sands II died in 1913 in an automobile accident near Westhampton, Long Island, N. Y.
   2 George Winthrop Sands, who married ——————. He was killed in an automobile accident in 1908, leaving a widow, a daughter and a son.

Anne Harriman married 2nd Lewis Maurice Rutherford in 1890 in London, England

    Their children were:
1. Margaret Rutherford, who married 1st Ogden Mills, Jr. On his death, she married 2nd Frederick L. Sprague.
2. Barbara Rutherford, who married 1st Cyril Hatch, and 2nd Winfield J. Nicholls. She died in 1939.

Anne Harriman married 3rd William Kissam Vanderbilt, Sr., April 23, 1903; he died in 1920. There were no children by this marriage. Anne Harriman died April 20, 1940 (see newspaper pictures and sketch of her life in New York Herald Tribune, Sunday April 21, 1940) From the statements contained in this newspaper sketch it will be seen that six grandchildren of Anne Harriman-Sands-Rutherford-Vanderbilt attended her funeral services in April, 1940, viz: Rutherford Hatch, Miss Mary Margaret Nicholls, Guy Winthrop Nicholls, Mrs. Geo. Raymond Burgess, Geo. Winthrop Sands, Jr., and Samuel Stevens Sands III.

7. Lillie Harriman, married 1st William Travers; no children
    married 2nd—Havermyer; no children.
8. Herbert Harriman

LOW GENEALOGY

A. Thomas Low — married Susanna, who died Aug. 6, 1684
   born in England 1605
   died Sept. 8, 1677

had son

B. John Low — married Sarah Thorndike
   born about 1635
   married Dec. 10, 1661
   in Beverly, Mass.
   died about 1695

had son

C. John Low — married Anne ———
   born April 24, 1665

had son

D. Nathaniel Low — married Abigail Riggs, born in Newbury, Mass., and died Aug., 1774 in Salisbury, Mass.
   born Nov. 15, 1695

had son

E. Edward Low   married   Rachel Baker; born Oct. 31 —
   born Feb. 1, 1743 in Ipswich,   died April 13, 1792
   Mass. Died Feb. 14, 1823 in
   Leominster, Mass. Married
   Jan. 9, 1772
                        had son
F. Jabez Baker Low   married   Sophia Sawyer
   born May 24, 1778
   died Oct. 3, 1867
G. James Low   married   Emmeline Van Buskirk
   born Nov. 27, 1809   daughter of Cornelius Van Buskirk
   married May 10, 1832   of Louisville, Ky. Born Oct. 10,
   died May 21, 1898   1815; died New York City, May 4,
   in New York City   1870

              Children of James Low
              and Emmeline Van Buskirk

1. Laura Low   married   Oliver Harriman, 1st, of New York,
   born Oct. 2, 1834   born Sept. 18, 1820; died March
   died May 31, 1901   12, 1904
                                 (see Harriman Genealogy)

2. James Low, Jr.
              Lived abroad
3. Nelson Low
4. Joseph Tompkins Low, 1st; married Mary Varum Mott
   born Aug. 2, 1846   born July 31, 1848
   died Nov. 13, 1932   died Sept. 8, 1922
   married Feb. 17, 1870

     Children of Joseph Tompkins Low and Mary Varum Mott:
1. Dr. Joseph Tompkins Low, 2nd; married Edith Joyce of Winchester, Mass.
        They have three children:
        1. Edith Low Hovey
        2. Joseph Tompkins Low, 3rd
        3. Frederick Joyce Low
2. Laura Low married Richard G. Babbage
        Living in New York City—no children
3. Mary Mott Low, married Henry Gansevoort Sanford, Sr.
                 have children:
        1. Henry Gansevoort Sanford, Jr., died 1920
        2. Louise Mott Sanford, who married Theodore
           Pearson, and have two children:
           1. Victoria Evans Pearson
           2. Laura Louise Pearson

MUIR GENEALOGY

A. William Muir   married   Mary Ritchie,
born about 1754, Anwoth, Scotland; came to America 1774 and entered Washington's Army. Died New York City, Feb. 9, 1809. Married Dec. 24, 1786. | who was born Sept. 19, 1764; daughter of George Ritchie and Katherine Vigneau Tillou who were married April 26, 1760 in New York.

had son

B. Lieutenant John Muir,   married   Maria Wade Wurts,
who served in the War of 1812; born New York City Jan. 17, 1793; married 1829, Louisville, Ky., where he lived all of his business life. Died in Philadelphia, Aug. 21, 1870. | born May 7, 1807; died Atlantic City, Sept. 15, 1900; daughter of Daniel Wurts and his wife, Phoebe Wade, of Louisville, Ky. (See Wurts Genealogy following)

(NOTE: William Muir and Mary Ritchie had also one daughter, who married and had a daughter, who married the Rev. Fergerson)

Children of Lt. John Muir and Maria Wade Wurts:
1. Clara Muir died unmarried
2. Mary Muir died unmarried
3. William Muir, of Louisville, Ky., and Philadelphia (see C following)

C. William Muir (No. 3 above)   married   Augusta Elizabeth Sawtell,
born Louisville, Ky., July 2, 1834; married Louisville, Sept. 27, 1859; died Philadelphia, June 7, 1908. | born Havre, France, Oct. 21, 1838. Died Mass., Sept. 3, 1929; daughter of Rev. Dr. E. N. Sawtell (See Sawtell Genealogy)

They had five children, viz:

1. Maria Wurts Muir   married   Rev. Frank S. Ballantine,
born Louisville, Ky. | June 1, 1908; died 1930 childless.

2. William Sawtell Muir   married   1st Lydia W. Chichester,
born Chicago May 6, 1864; living South Orange, N. J. in 1939 | June 6, 1894, daughter of Washington Bowie Chichester, of Olńey, Maryland; niece of Capt. Arthur Mason Chichester of Leesburg, Va.

William Sawtell Muir married 2nd Caroline Bruce Morton, Oct. 17, 1914, the daughter of Judge James Williams Morton, of Orange, Virginia. They have one son, William Morton Muir, born Nov. 27, 1915.

3. Ophelia Muir, born Louisville, Ky.; unmarried; living in 1939 at Woodstock, Vermont.
4. John Wallingford Muir; married Mary Frothingham Brinley, born Saratoga Springs March Nov. 15, 1905
   3, 1871; living in Philadelphia, 1939

   They have two children:
   1. John Brinley Muir, born 1907
   2. Alice King Muir, married Rev. Russell Clapp, June, 1938
5. Augusta Elizabeth Muir, married John Haines Lippincott, born Harrisburg, Pa. Nov. 18, 1902. Died

   They have three daughters:
   1. Augusta Elizabeth Lippincott, born May 15, 1904 unmarried in 1939
   2. Deborah Scull Lippincott, born July 23, 1906; married Guy Currier, of Boston; no children 1939.
   3. Dorothy Muir Lippincott, born Dec. 13, 1909; married Francis Barton Gummere; they have one son, Francis Barton Gummere, Jr., born April 5, 1939.

SOCIETY OF THE CINCINNATI

NOTE: Lieutenant David Wallingford (see Sawtell Genealogy preceding), the father of Martha, who married John Sawtell, is represented in the "Society of the Cincinnati for the State of New Hampshire," by William Sawtell Muir, above, the hereditary successor being William Morton Muir, above.

It will be seen from the foregoing record, that there are three soldiers of the Revolutionary War, who are represented in the Societies of the Cincinnati by descendants, viz;
1. Captain James Patton (see Patton Genealogy)
2. Captain John Nelson (see Nelson Genealogy)
3. Lieutenant David Wallingford (see Sawtell Genealogy)

PATTON GENEALOGY

A. Henry Patton married Sarah Lynn, daughter of the Laird of Newtown, Timivady of Loch Lynn, Scotland and sister County Donegal, Ireland of Wm. Lynn, of Fredericksburg, Virginia.

had son

B. John Patton married 1st. Miss Rogers in Ireland; she
of Augusta County, Va. died before 1754; married 2nd,
Emigrant 1736-40 Agnese ———— on March 23,
died 1757. 1754.
Had brother, Col. James and
sister, Elizabeth, wife of John
Preston

had son

C. Captain James Patton, married 1st Mary Doherty
born Oct. 12, 1735 or 1748, 2nd, Elizabeth Reager, widow
Augusta County, Virginia, 3rd, Phoebe McCausland Basye,
and Louisville, Ky., died Dec. widow
29, 1815.

Children of Capt. James Patton and 1st wife,
Mary Doherty, as given previously:

1. Martha (Patsy) married Capt. John Nelson
    (See Nelson Genealogy)
2. Margaret (Peggy married Nathaniel Pryor
3. Mary (Polly) married 1st John Vaughn
    married 2nd John McDough
    married 3rd George Gracey
    (see Gracey Genealogy)

TRACY GENEALOGY

Edward Tracy, married Mary Ann Nelson,
born March 2, 1782, at Nor- born 1800, daughter of Capt. John
wich, Conn. The 3rd son of Nelson and Martha Patton
Capt. Frederick and Deborah
Thomas Tracy. He died Nov.
6, 1852 in Louisville, Ky.

Children of Edward Tracy and Mary Ann Nelson

1. Charles Frederick Tracy
2. Edward Nelson Tracy
3. John Nelson Tracy
4. Henry Nelson Tracy
5. Augustus Early Tracy
6. William Thomas Tracy
7. Alfred Ripley Tracy
8. William Thomas Tracy
9. Eliza Ripley Tracy

A grandson of Edward Tracy and Mary Ann Nelson, named Edward Nelson Tracy, and therefore probably the son of No. 2 Edward Nelson Tracy, above, was in 1917 said to be living in New York City with three children, as follows:

Charles F. Tracy
John Nelson Tracy
Edward F. Tracy

VAN BUSKIRK GENEALOGY

A. John Van Buskirk, married ——————————
born 1736; died Dec. 16, 1814. Buried St. Paul's Church Yard; see Trinity Church Records, New York City.

had son

B. Cornelius Van Buskirk married Sarah Nelson
born Aug. 22, 1776 (see Nelson Genealogy)
Died Feb. 20, 1863
Married Jan. 16, 1813

Children of Cornelius Van Buskirk and Sarah Nelson:

1. Ophelia Van Buskirk married Rev. Dr. Eli Newton Sawtell
born Sept. 20, 1813 born Sept. 8, 1799
died Oct. 5, 1899 died April 6, 1885
married Sept. 8, 1829 (see Sawtell Genealogy)

2. Emmeline Van Buskirk married James Low
born Oct. 10, 1816 born Nov. 27, 1809
died May 4, 1870 died May 21, 1898
married March 9, 1832 (see Low Genealogy)

3. Charlotte Van Buskirk married Edward Rupert
born 1818 (descendants live in Western
died 1844 State)
married May 7, 1834

4. Mary Van Buskirk married Wm. James Lindenberger
born 1823 son of Jacob Hopewell Lindenberger of Baltimore, Md.
died 1882
married May 13, 1839 (see Lindenberger Generalogy)

WURTS GENEALOGY

This Wurts line descends authentically from 1020 A. D. (see Wurts printed Genealogy) in Switzerland. The immigrant Wurts sire came to Pennsylvania in 1735, viz;

A. Rev. John Conrad Wurts   married   Anna Goetschie,
born Switzerland, Nov. 30, 1706; died Pennsylvania Sept. 30, 1763.   1724, daughter of Rev. Maurice Goetschie

had son

B. John Wurts,   married   Sarah Grandin,
born June 30, 1744; married June 8, 1773; died Sept. 14, 1793.   daughter of Samuel Grandin, of New Jersey.

had son

C. Daniel Wurts,   married   Phebe Wade,
Lieutenant in Navy; born Sept. 8, 1779; married July 5, 1806; died Merion, Pa., May 1841; he lived for many years in Louisville, Ky. We find him appointed by a Louisville town meeting on a committee of five citizens to draw up a petition to the Kentucky State Legislature to pass an Act to incorporate Louisville with the rank of a City, which was duly legislated in 1828   who was born Oct. 3, 1782 in New Jersey, daughter of Jonas Wade; she died Aug. 21, 1867. This Phebe Wade has illustrious ancestry, through her grandmother, Rebecca Bruen, and the latter's 4th great grandmother, Lady Dorothy Holford, who married John Bruen of Bruen Stapleford (b. 1510, d. 1580). This ancestry runs back to Charlemagne, William the Conqueror, Alfred the Great, Anne of Russia, who married Henry 1st of France, and many other well authenticated and well known historic lines.

had daughter

D. Maria Wade Wurts   married   John Muir
born May 7, 1807 married in Louisville in 1829; died Sept. 15, 1900   born New York, Jan. 17, 1793; died Philadelphia, Aug. 21, 1870; Lieutenant in War of 1812; spent all his business life in Louisville

had son

E. William Muir   married   Augusta Elizabeth Sawtell
born Louisville, July 2, 1834; married Louisville Sept. 27, 1859; died Philadelphia June 7, 1908.
(see Muir Genealogy)   born Havre, France, Oct. 21, 1838; died Mass., Sept. 3, 1929, the daughter of Rev. Dr. Eli Newton Sawtell, and his wife Ophelia Van Buskirk, of Louisville.
(see Van Buskirk and Sawtell Genealogies)

The Payne Genealogy.

Descendants in Kentucky of John and William Payne, sons of Sir Robert Payne, of England. They came to America in 1694, and both were from England. James I. to conciliate them did especially mention them in a land charter granted to a company, May 23, 16—.

Genealogy published by permission of Mrs. Judith L. Marshall, a descendant.

CHAPTER I.

The Paynes were a powerful tribe in Wales, and one part of the tribe was never willing to submit to the king of England. James I to conciliate them gave them a special grant of land twelve miles square, near Alexandria, Va., known as Payne's Manor.

Their coat of arms. Gn (red) fesse; two lions passant. Ar (blue).

Crest. A lion's gamb erased and erect. Ar. (blue) grasping a broken tilting spear." Motto—"Malo mori quam foedari" (Death before dishonor).

Sir John Payne settled in Fairfax county, on the manorial estate, at least in what was then known as Fairfax county, Va.

Sir William Payne settled in Maryland, near a town, now called Leonardstown. He never married.

Sir John Payne had one son, William Payne, born August 10, 1671, died August 24, 1776.

Alicia Payne, first wife of Wm. Payne, died October 31, 1760.

Children of William Payne and Alicia, his first wife, were:

Edward Payne;
William Payne, Jr.;
Sanford Payne.

William Payne, Sr., married for his second wife, Ann Jennings. Had one son by this marriage, John Payne. He settled near Georgetown, Scott county, Kentucky.

Edward Payne, eldest son of William, Sr., and Alicia, his wife, was the last owner of Payne's Manor in Virginia. He sold it in 1785, and moved to Kentucky the same year and settled on Town Fork, one and a half miles from Lexington, Kentucky. He died in 1806.

Edward Payne married Lady Ann Holland Conyers, who was related to Lord Holland, Henry Fox, the Duke of Richmond, and Earl of Leinster. Their children were:

1. Henry Payne, who married Ann Lane.
2. William Payne married (1) Miss Grimes; (2) Miss Harrison, sister of Governor Benjamin Harrison, a signer of the Declaration of Independence.
3. Daniel McCarty Payne, who married Miss Given.
4. Edward Payne.
5. Jilson Payne married Miss Harrison.
6. James Payne.
7. Theodosia Payne married Mr. Turner.
8. Elizabeth Payne married Mr. Lewis.

William Payne, Jr., second son of William and Alicia Payne, was born July 31, 1724, was married 3d of February, 1748, to Susan Clarke, by Rev. Charles Green. She died July 19, 1782. Susan Clarke, wife of William Payne, Jr., born December 17, 1721; died February 22, 1771. Their children were:

1. Alicia, born Dec. 17, 1749; married to Giles Cooke Nov. 30, 1775, by Rev. Townsend Drake; died Feb. 27, 1837.
2. William Payne, born Feb. 14, 1751; married Polly Robinson, of Princess Ann Co., Va., on July 20, 1777. He died Sept. 23, 1813.
3. Mary Payne, born Feb. 23, 1753; married Pearce Bayley Feb. 23, 1772. Pearce Bayley died Oct. 7, 1860.
4. Benj. Clark Payne, born Dec. 28, 1755; married to Miss Jane Campbell by Rev. Lee Massey Dec. 24, 1778; died April 29, 1789.
5. Penelope Payne, born Dec. 7, 1757; married Col. George West Jan. 8, ——; died Aug. 2, 1785.
6. Anna Payne, born July 4, 1757; married Captain Thomas West Jan. 31, 1779; died May 5, 1788.
7. Devall Payne, born Jan. 1, 1764; married to Hannah Brent Dec. 15, 1785.

Sanford Payne (third son of William Payne, Sr., and Alicia, his wife), settled near Richmond, Virginia. Their daughter, Dolly Payne, married James Madison, president of the United States; another daughter married John G. Jackson, from whom descended Stonewall Jackson, the famous Confederate general.

John Payne (son of William Payne, Sr., by his second wife, Ann Jennings), married Miss Johnson, a sister of Colonel Richard M. Johnson, of Georgetown, Kentucky. They had fifteen children, four of them surviving.

John Payne's descendants:

1. Asa Payne lives at Payne's Depot, Scott Co., Ky. His first wife Theodosia Turner, was a grand-daughter of Edward Payne, Sr. His second wife, Mrs. Offutt, was Miss Sallie Vance.
2. John or Jack Payne, Warsaw, Ky.
3. Jeff. Payne, Howard Co., Missouri.
4. A daughter, Mrs. Offutt.

The children of Devall Payne and Hannah Brent, his wife:

1. Penelope Payne, born Sept. 19, 1786; married Daniel Vertner.
2. John Payne; married (1) Eliza Sprigg; (2) Letitia Whiteman; born Feb. 18, 1788.
3. Mary Payne, born June 20, 1789; married William Morris.
4. Margaret Payne, born Oct. 10, 1791; never married.
5. James Payne, born Oct. 21, 1793; married (1) Miss Logan; (2) Eliza Somers.
6. Hugh Payne, born July 16, 1795; married Amanda Davis.
7. William P. Payne; married (1) Lucinda Payne; (2) Mary Bayley.
8. Elizabeth Baxter Payne, born Nov. 20, 1798; married John T. Langhorn.
9. Susan C. Payne, born Nov. 5, 1800; married Samuel Boude.
10. Thomas T. Payne, born Nov. 11, 1802; married Elizabeth Turner.
11. Devall Payne, Jr., born Feb. 6, 1808; married (1) Miss Taylor, by whom he had an only child, Bell, who married Mr. Parker; (2) Mary Wilson, daughter of Hamilton Wilson, of Bourbon Co., Ky.
12. Benj. Payne; died young.
13. Alicia Ann Payne, born June 22, 1809; married James Boude.
Penelope Payne and Daniel Vertner had only one child, John D. Vertner.

The children of John Payne and Letitia Whiteman:

1. Penelope Payne married Matthew Hopple.
2. Eliza Payne married John C. Bull.
3. Clara Payne married Mr. — Willis.
4. Twins, Matilda and Letitia Payne; Letitia Payne married Mr. Schofield; one son, Benj. Payne, died.

The children of Mary Payne and Wm. Morris:

1. Penelope; married Mr. ——'.
2. Hannah Ann Morris; married Hiram Wallingsford.
3. Susan Morris.
4. Alicia Morris.
5. Mary Morris.
6. William Morris.
7. Hugh Morris.
8. Asa Morris.

Children of Innis Payne and his wife, Eliza:

1. William Payne.
2. Cornelia Payne.
3. Benj. Payne.

The children of Thomas Payne and his wife, Elizabeth:

1. John Payne.
2. Mary Payne; married Mr. Lemon.
3. William Payne.
4. Thomas Payne.
5. Letitia Payne; married James Wood.

The children of Susan Payne and Samuel Boude:

John Boude.
Devall Boude.
Eliza Boude; married Mr. McKibben.

Children of Alice Payne and James Boude:

1. Henry Boude.
2. Annie Boude.
3. Hannah Boude.
4. Benjamin Boude.
5. Susan Boude.
6. Letitia Boude.
7. Eliza Boude.
8. Jack Boude.

Devall Payne, Jr., had by his first wife, Miss Taylor, a daughter, Bell, who married Mr. Parker, of Howard Co., Mo.

By his second wife, Mary Wilson, his children were:

2. Thomas Payne.
3. Edwin Payne.
4. Henry Payne.
5. James Payne.
6. Mary Payne.
7. George Payne.

Children of Hugh Payne and his wife, Amanda:

1. Sallie Payne.
2. Eloise Payne; never married.

3. Margaret Payne; married Mr. James Polk; Julia Payne married Dr. Driggs.

Children of William Payne and first wife, Lucinda:

1. Edwin Payne.
2. William Payne.
3. Benjamin Payne.

By second wife, Mary Bayley:

1. Mollie Payne; married Mr. Reno.
2. George Payne.

Elizabeth Baxter Payne married John Trotter Langhorne, November 23, 1815. He was the son of John Langhorne and Sarah Bell. The children of Elizabeth Baxter Payne and John Trotter Langhorne were:

1. Elizabeth Brent; married (1) Allen Stockwell; (2) William N. Green, Nov. 11, 1840.
2. Maurice Langhorne; married Eve Anna Greaff.
3. Sarah Bell Langhorne; married Henry Waller.
4. John Devall Langhorne; married (1) Mary Potter; (2) Nannie Taylor.
5. Judith Fry Langhorne, born June 15, 1826; married Charles Edward Marshall, son of Judge John James Marshall.
6. Penelope Vertner Langhorne.
7. William David Langhorne.
8. Thomas Young Langhorne.

NOTE: The American Langhornes were descended from Sir William Langhorne, first Earl of Gainsborough, who resided at Hamstead Heath, near London, England.

Mrs. Judith L. Marshall, of Louisville, Ky., born in Mason county, Ky., daughter of Elizabeth Baxter Payne and John Trotter Langhorne, is a member of the Kentucky State Historical Society, a member of the Jemima Johnson Chapter of the Daughters of American Revolution at Paris, Ky., and a member of the Albert Sydney Johnston Chapter of the Confederate Daughters.

COLONEL ASA PAYNE

By J. Stoddard Johnston

(Copied from Georgetown Times of Sept. 20, 1898. Contributed by Mrs. W. H. Coffman, Georgetown, Ky.)

In pursuance of my promise, I venture to give you a brief sketch of my old friend, Asa Payne, Sr., a native and long a resident of Scott county, who died near Burgin, Kentucky, in 1887, in the 99th year of his age. It was my fortune to have known him for more than thirty years before he died and to have found him one of the best men and most interesting companions I ever met. He was no blood kin, but being related to my wife it was my habit to call him Uncle Asa, in deference to his age and the respect and affection I bore him. It was my habit to visit him at intervals of a year or two for a long time before he died upon which occasions I got much information concerning the early history of the state, his own and other families of the same connection. Much of this I made note of, as it was unwritten history.

Asa Payne was born in Scott county on the 19th day of March, 1788 and was the son of John Payne and Betsy Johnson. His paternal grandfather was that William Johnson of whom it is said that upon being given the lie by Washington, he knocked the father of his country down, whereupon Washington apologized and they made friends. His father was General John Payne who commanded the Kentucky troops in the first expedition against the Indians in the war of 1812, dying in 1837 in the 76th year of his age. His mother was the eldest child of Robert Johnson, familiarly known as Robin, and Jemima Suggett, and was the sister of Richard M. Johnson, Vice-President of the United States. He was the eldest of thirteen children, nine sons and four daughters. The names of his brothers and sisters, in order were: Asa, Robert, Nancy, Sally, John, Betsey, Newton, William J., Thomas Jefferson, Franklin, Richard, Cyrus and Emmeline.

Robert married Maria Williams, daughter of Minor and Merritt Williams and moved to Howard county, Missouri, where he left a large number of descendants. Judge George V. Payne of Georgetown is a grandson and the only resident in Kentucky.

Nancy married Robert Offutt, of Scott county and died in 1882, aged 91. She was a fine type of womanhood and had nine children, all of whom but one survive her.

Sallie married Charles Thomson of Scott county and was the mother of Pres. and Sid Thompson and Mrs. Betsey Worthington.

John, known as General John Payne of Warsaw, Ky., married Mary Stevenson, and died in 1887, aged 92. He left two sons, William and Robert, of Warsaw. W. F. DeLong, of Scott county, who owns the Frank Payne place is his great-grand-son.

Betsey married Maj. Uriel Sebree of Howard county, Mo., and left a number of descendants, some of them of prominence in public life. Among them is Hon. Uriel Sebree Hall, member of Congress in the present (44th) Congress from the Second Missouri District. His father William A. Hall, was also a member from the same District from 1860 to 1865, and was thirty years Circuit Judge.

Newton Payne married first Louisa Nuckles, second Susan Spencer, and lived in Warsaw, Ky. His descendants live in Missouri.

William J. Payne died in 1813 when eleven years old.

Thomas Jefferson married first Leticia Thompson, second Mary Wright. He died in Howard county, Mo., in 1880, aged 76 years. He formerly lived on the John Parrish place on the Payne's Depot pike.

Franklin married Polly Rogers, resided in Scott county on the Frankfort pike, one mile from Georgetown and died without issue in 1874. He adopted his grand niece, Bettie Payne DeLong, whom he made his heir.

Richard died in 1823, at 15 years of age.

Cyrus died in 1848 a soldier in the Mexican War, aged 36, unmarried.

Emeline married James Peak of Scott county, and died in 1851, aged 38. She had eight children, five of whom are dead. Her descendants live in Chicot county, Ark.

I have given this list at the risk of being tedious, on account of the prominence of this family in Scott county and because from the large number of descendants, without it, none but the oldest citizens can keep the run of them.

Asa Payne, the subject of this sketch, was educated at West Point, and was among the first pupils at that institution. In fact, it was not formally organized into graded classes until a period subsequent to the date at which he left there. In 1810 he was appointed an Indian sub-agent by President Madison, and was stationed at Fort Madison and Fort Snelling on the Upper Mississippi, remaining there until the summer of 1811, when on the 13th of August he married Theodocia Turner, daughter of Louis E. Turner of Fayette county, Ky. He then began life as a farmer, but in 1812 when the war began, he became aide-de-Camp to his father, Gen. John Payne and was at Fort Meigs during its siege by the British and Indians. On one occasion he gave me an interesting account of the rendezvous of the Kentucky troops at Georgetown prior to their departure for the seat of war August 12, 1812. They were camped on what was then called Craig's Hill, just above the Big Spring. He described to me John Allen of Shelby who commanded a regiment, Capt. Paschal Hickman and others of prominence who afterwards fell in battle. There are few living now who witnessed this gathering. I know of but one, your venerable and well preserved townsman, my old friend, Dr. Stephen F. Gano, who at eighty-seven is in possession of all his faculties and as active as most men of sixty. He visited the camp with his father at a most impressionable age of childhood, and remembers the stirring scene vividly heightened by a speech made by Henry Clay who was then speaker of the House of Congress.

After the war Mr. Payne devoted himself to farming in Scott county, living the greater part of his life on a farm near Payne's Depot. Though a man of education and one who took interest in public affairs, he never held any office except that of Justice of the Peace, in which capacity he served fifteen years. For a number of years, as he informed me, he used to ship his bacon and other farm products down to New Orleans, hauling them to Leestown, just below Frankfort, and transporting them by flatboat and returning afoot from Natchez through what was termed the Wilderness. It is not my purpose to go into the details of his life since it was uneventful and comprised only the incidents of an active, industrious farmer, a Christian gentleman who discharged conscientiously his duties to his neighbor, his family and his friends. His industry never flagged. Long after he had given up the active management of the farm, he took it upon himself to keep the drives and fence corners free from weeds, a pursuit which he followed until within a short time of his death.

His family was one of remarkable longevity. I asked him once in what year his father died. He said 1837. "Then," I said, "he must have been an old man." "Oh, no," said he, "he was only seventy-six. He bid fair to live to an advanced age, but was thrown from a horse and died several months after from the effects of the fall." When asked what year his grandfather William Payne died, he said in 1776. I ventured to ask if he had not died young, as more than a hundred years had elapsed. "Oh, no," said he, "he was 105 years old. He was born in 1671." This nearly took my breath away, as the three lives—his own, his father's and his grandfather's —occupied more than two hundred years. The average, taken from 1671, the time of his grandfather's birth to 1887, the time of his own death, would be 72 years. It would take only 26 such lives to have reached back to the time of Christ—more than one-ninth of which was covered by the lives of these three. He then informed me that his grandfather, who lived in Orange county, Virginia, was married twice, the first time to an English lady, named Conyers, being called Lady Conyers. From this marriage, as he expressed it, came the light-haired, florid-complexioned Paynes of Lexington, the grandfather of Col. Thomas H. Payne of Scott, Edward Payne of Shelby and others, being sons of William Payne. And thence came the middle names of Madison Conyers Johnson and Henry Conyers Payne. The grandmother of my wife and the mother of Gen. William Johnson and Col. L. L. Johnson were grand-daughters of William Payne of this marriage. The second wife of William Payne, he said, was a Miss Jennings, "an English spinster, supposed to be the heiress of the Jennings estate." At the time of this marriage he was 92, yet two children were born to him— Gen. John Payne whom he lived to see twelve years old, and a daughter, who married a man by the name of Riley, from whom were descended the Rileys in the northern part of Scott. The descendants of Gen. John Payne, he said, were generally dark-haired.

The last time but one before his death that I saw him he said to me, "I see, Stoddard, you have been to Washington." I told him I had, when he remarked that he expected Washington had improved a good deal since he had been there. Thinking he had been there within twenty or thirty years, I assented, saying it had progressed wonderfully since the war, and was now one of the handsomest cities in the Union. "Is Gadsby's tavern there yet?" he then asked, remarking that when he was there on his last visit he had put up there. I told him it had long ago been merged into one of the older hotels and asked him when was the last time he had been there. "It was in the winter of 1809," he said, "when I went from West Point to see my Uncle Richard (R. M. Johnson) who was then a member of Congress. The tavern was kept by a Mrs. Williams, a clever lady who had two nice daughters, one of whom, Mary, I was very fond of." And then in all simplicity and earnestness he asked me if I had ever heard who Mary married. More than three-quarters of a century had elapsed, and yet the young West Point cadet's interest in the pretty girl had not died out. I told him if I had the opportunity when I went to Washington again I would inquire, but it did not occur. A year or two afterwards when I was with him again he suddenly turned from the subject we were discussing, and resuming our former conversation as if there had been no interval of time, he said: "Mr. McDaniel told me he thought Mary had married a man named Graham, and I have been anxious to find out if it could have been our Dr. Graham." The latter to whom he referred was Dr. C. C. Graham, who had but recently died, a centenarian. The McDaniel I knew without inquiry was Uncle William McDaniel, long postmaster at Georgetown, who had come from the vicinity of Washington, and who had been dead forty years. I told him I was quite sure it was not our Dr. Graham. Within the year he died with the mystery unsolved.

Mr. Payne had three sons—his only children. The youngest, Henry, died unmarried in 1845, in his 26th year. The eldest, Mr. Louis T. Payne, who for a long time was a prominent farmer in Woodford and Scott, is now living in Mercer county in his 79th year. His second son, John F. Payne, died in 1876, aged 61. He was a prosperous and energetic farmer, a director in the Farmers' Bank and a worthy son of such a father. His death made a great void in the community in which he lived, and I know few men whose memory is kept so green. He was my neighbor, and I never knew a better one.

In 1852 Mr. Payne married a second time, Mrs. Nuckols, a lady of much worth, whom he survived many years.

In thus discharging my labor of love to the memory of a noble man for whom

I had so much respect and admiration, I feel conscious that I have fallen far short of what he merits, for in him I have always recognized the true type of the Kentucky gentleman of that class of farmers who have given Kentucky the name she bears. The modern idea, as sought to be given in newspapers and novels, that the typical Kentuckian is a drinking, card playing, roystering fellow, who spends his time at the race tracks and his money in riotous living, is a libel on the true Kentucky farmer. It is the outgrowth of a narrow vision limited to the observation of those who give their attention chiefly to horses and are rather city men with city habits than farmers proper.

Asa Payne was the typical Kentucky farmer, an early riser who retired at an early hour, a temperate man who always had refreshment for his guests but rarely indulged himself, a frugal but a liberal citizen in all matters of public interest or of charity, God fearing, but not bigoted, a good neighbor, a hospitable friend, an enlightened farmer who rotated his crops judiciously, kept up his fences, cut his weeds faithfully and lived beloved of his family and friends to leave an example worthy of imitation by the generations to come.

Sept. 20, 1894.

THE POGUES.

Portland, Oregon., Dec. 10, 1907.
Editor The Register:

In the very interesting article on "The Old Fort," by Mr. W. W. Stephenson, in the September issue of The Register, I notice a slight error. William Poage was not the first but the second husband of Ann (Kennedy) Wilson Poage Lindsay McGinty. She probably was—surely ought to have been—the sweetheart of William Poage at that time, but the casual reader might infer that they had not yet been married when William Poage made for her the chair mentioned as having been made in the fort in 1776. They had in fact then been married about 13 years and had five children. A few facts concerning William Poage and his wife, Ann, may be of interest in this connection.

William Poage came with his parents, Robert and Elizabeth Poage from Ireland and settled near Staunton, Va., about 1737. The name Poage or Pogue was in Scotland spelled Pollok. It is the same name in origin as Polk, and the Robert Poage who settled in Augusta county, Va., was a nephew or grandnephew of the Robert Pollok or Polk who came from Ireland about fifty years sooner, settled in Maryland and founded the Polk family of America. A few of the descendents of Robert Polk in the direct male line of descent now spell their name Pogue and Poage. William Poage's sister, Martha, married Andrew Woods of Abermarle county and William also lived in that county for a time. While there he served in the Albermarle company of Militia, in actual service for the protection of the frontier against the Indians. (Hening's Statutes, VII, 233.) This was in 1758. Soon after this date he married Ann Wilson, a widow, whose maiden name was Kennedy. Ann's first husband was John Wilson who lived but a short time. He and Ann had one daughter named Martha. William and Ann Poage lived a number of years in Rockbridge county, Virginia, and about 1771 moved to the vicinity of Abington where William was appointed "county sergeant" of militia. In 1774, as stated in Summers History of Southwest Virginia, he was in charge of Fort Russell on the Long Hunters' Road, while Lieutenant Daniel Boone was in charge of Fort Moore, four miles west of Fort Russell. In 1775, the whole family moved to Kentucky. The first child of William and Ann Poage was a daughter, Elizabeth, who was eleven years old at the time of the migration. The Draper Collection of Kentucky manuscripts, owned by the Wisconsin Historical Society, contains her own written statement of migration. It has been published in Bulbert's Historic Highways, Vol. 6, pps. 117 and 118. Although Elizabeth's grandfather, Robert Poage, was by profession a schoolteacher before he came to America, she lived in her childhood on the extreme frontier where the opportunities for a girl to get an education were most meager and her occasional errors in spelling and use of capitals and failure to use points of punctuation may well be excused. Moreover, she was not far removed from the time when even eminent scholars felt no obligation to always spell the same word the same way. Elizabeth's statement, to the publication of which I infer the Wisconsin Historical Society will not object, follows:

"I was born in Virginia on the 4th day of Sept 1764 In Rockbridge county near the Natural Bridge (.) my father moved on the North fork of Holston within 4 or 5 miles of Abbingdom & remained there two or three years and in March, 1775 we moved down Holstien near the Big Island where we remained until Sept 1775 when Col Callaway and his company came along going to Kentucky when my father William Pogue packed up and came with him with our family Col Boone and with his wife and family and Col Hugh Mcgarry, Thomas Denton and Richard Hogan were on the road before us and when we arrived at Boonesborough the latter part of September There was only four or six cabbins built along on the Bank of the Kentucky river but not picketted in being open on two sides."

William Poage was shot by Indians between Harrodsburg and Logan's Station Sept. 1, 1778, and died two days later from the effect of the wounds. Afterwards, as stated, his widow married Col. Joseph Lindsay, the "Hero of the Wilderness," described in Mrs. Morton's poem on page 62 of the issue of the Register published September, 1905.

William and Ann Pogue had seven children. Elizabeth, already mentioned, married John Thomas, of Harrodsburg, and is said to have died at that place about 1850. Robert, born in Virginia, October 6, 1766, was colonel of a Kentucky Regiment in the war of 1812 and constructed Fort Amanda in Ohio which he named for his daughter and not his wife as the histories state. He married Jane Hopkins. He named one of his sons William Lindsay after his father and first stepfather. Most of his descendants spell their name Pogue. The third child was Joseph, born in Virginia, May 8, 1770, is said to have married and moved to Missouri. Martha, born in Virginia in 1772, married a Mr. Hamm or Hannah, and probably lived and died at or near Shelbyville, Ky. Mary, also called Polly, was born in Virginia, March 10, 1775. She married Oswald Thomas and their home was in the vicinity of Shelbyville, Ky. She also showed her affectionate remembrance of her first stepfather by naming one of her sons, Lindsay. Ann was born after the migration, and is said to have been the third white child born in Kentucky. The date of her birth was August 26 1777. She married her second cousin, John Poage, of Greenup county, who was, I believe, Colonel of a Kentucky regiment in the war of 1812. The youngest of the family was Amaziah, born on August 17, 1778. He died while a boy.

H. M. WILLIAMSON.

HISTORY OF WILLIAM POAGE AND HIS WIFE, ANN KENNEDY WILSON POAGE LINDSAY McGINTY.

By Mrs. S. V. Nuckols, Lexington, Kentucky.

Ann Kennedy Wilson Poage, the widow of Wilson, was married to William Poage in Augusta County, Virginia, 1760. They lived a number of years near the Natural Bridge in what is now Rockbridge County, Virginia, and then moved to Fincastle, now Washington County, in 1774, not very far from Abingdon, Virginia.

William Poage, as sergeant, had command of Fort Russell in that vicinity with twenty men, while Daniel Boone (Lieutenant) had charge of another fort a few miles away. In 1775 William Poage and family moved to Harrodsburg, Kentucky.

I found the evidence of William Poage's (Poague, Pougue) first services as a soldier in the war with the Indians in the history of Albemarle County, Virginia, which quotes from Henning's Statutes, vol. 7, page 303, names of the officers and soldiers of Albemarle County militia in actual service for the defense and protection of the frontier against the Indians, September, 1758. The Captain of the company was James Neville, and among the soldiers were William Poage and Robert Poage.

History Summaries of Southwest Virginia shows on pages 156 and 157 that Sergeant Poage was in command of Fort Russell in the vicinity of the present city of Abingdon, Virginia, in the fall of 1774, with twenty men, while Lieutenant Daniel Boone was in command of Fort Moore, four miles west, with twenty men.

The manuscript statement of Elizabeth Poage Thomas in possession of the Historical Society, Detroit, Mich., proves this Sergeant Poage was William Poage; there was no other William Poage in that part of the country at that time.

Collins' History, vol. 2, page 616, states that William Poage, or Pougue, cleared ground and raised corn in 1776, at Cove Spring, about two miles northeast of Harrodsburg, Kentucky.

On September 1, 1778, a company of sixteen men going to Logan's Station, near Stanford, ten miles from where Danville is now situated, were fired on by a party of Indians in ambush in a canebrake. William Poage was wounded by them, three balls entering his body. The others made their escape unhurt; the next day two parties were

93

sent out in search of Poage, who had clung to his horse until out of reach of the Indians, then fell and crawled into a canebrake, and hid until he heard his friends passing near. They carried him to Field's cabin, one and one-eighth miles west of Danville. It was an abandoned cabin; they camped there for the night; the Indians tracked them, surrounded the cabin, and waited to attack them in the morning. But the whites discovered them in time, and suddenly sallied out at daybreak, surprised them in ambush and killed four of them, one of whom had William Poage's gun. This they brought to Harrodsburg and gave to his brave little son, Robert, then twelve years old. He was afterward General Robert Poage, of Mayslick, Mason County, Kentucky. William Poage was set upon a horse with William Maddox to hold him on, and thus rode to Fort Harrodsburg, but he did not die until the next day, September 3, 1778. (Collins' History, volume 2.)

It is interesting to know how the first settlers produced the simple implements of husbandry, and the indispensable articles of kitchen and dairy furniture, unused to labor of that sort, they exercised their ingenuity, and did what they could toward providing such conveniences. William Poage was remarkably ingenious, and while he lived in Harrodsburg, from February 1, 1776, to September, 1778, he made the buckets, milk pails, churns, tubs and noggins used by the people in the fort. He made the woodwork of the first plough, made and used the first loom on which weaving was done in Kentucky, by sinking a post in the ground and pieceing beams and slats to them, after which Ann Kennedy Wilson Poage wove into cloth the first linen made in Kentucky from nettle lint; the linsey was made from this same nettle lint and buffalo wool. She brought the first spinning wheel to Kentucky; she also brought with her from Virginia fowls of all kinds.

There is a manuscript of Williom Lindsay Poage that speaks of many things. He was her grandson. After the death of William Poage, Mrs. Poage in the spring of 1781 was married to Col. Joseph Lindsay, one of the illustrious victims of the terrible slaughter at the battle of Blue Licks in August, 1782. We are indebted to his notebook for many interesting things about his wife. Several years later she was married to James McGinty, and is well remembered by persons now living.

Mrs. Ann Kennedy Wilson Poage Lindsay McGinty was a woman of great energy and self-reliance. Her little son shouldered his father's gun to help drive the Indians out, while his mother molded bullets.

The spring at Harrodsburg called Gore's Spring, after Andrew Gore, was purchased by him from William Poage's heirs. There are patents in the family where 640 acres of land on Gilman's Creek or Lick (Collins' History, vol. 2, page 516), belonged to them.

THE PRYOR ANCESTORY

The following interesting letter from Mr. Henry Strother, the distinguished writer and genealogist, explains itself. The Register takes pleasure in publishing anything concerning the late Judge Wm. S. Pryor, whose distinguished services on the bench reflected so much honor on the judiciary of the State, and whose private life afforded so splendid an example of sterling citizenship.

Ft. Smith, Ark., Nov. 30, 1914.
Mrs. Jennie C. Morton, Regent,

Frankfort, Ky.

Dear Mrs. Morton:

I notice that some of the leading journals of Kentucky state that the grandfather of Judge William S. Pryor was named *John* Pryor. This is a grave error. His name was *Samuel,* as shown by the Judge's own statement in a letter to me, a true copy of which I enclose herewith, and the records show the same. I give below his pedigree as shown by the records. His grandfather, Samuel Pryor, was born in Goochland Co., Va., January 12, 1762; married in Lincoln Co., Ky., Sept. 30, 1785 Mary Curd, daughter of John Curd, formerly of Goochland Co., Va. This young couple located at a very early date on the land now in Trimble county, near Bedford, and known for the past one hundred years as the Capt. Jack Pryor farm (their eldest son.) Here they lived and died and were buried on the place. Samuel Pryor died in latter part of Dec. 1812. His original will is on file in the Henry County Clerk's Office, and is of date Dec. 21, 1812, and proven at the February Term of the Henry County Court, 1813. Appoints his "wife Polly Pryor and my son Jack Pryor executrix and Extor." Will is recorded in Will Book 2, pp. 23, 24 and 25.

The original will of Judge Pryor's father, Samuel Pryor, is on file in same office, and is of date February 27, 1833. Probated at May Term, 1833, recorded in Will Book 5, at p. 236; names his wife, *Nancy* and children, *Wm. S.,* Ann Eliza, James R., and Mary Catherine. Appoints his *"brother Jack Pryor"* and Will H. Allen, Executors. Capt. Jack Pryor, the eldest brother of this Samuel, was born in 1790 and died in 1858. He married Sally Duncan, sister of my grandmother, Mary (Duncan) Strother, wife of Rev. George Strother, of Trimble county. I well remember seeing Old Uncle Jack Pryor at his home when I was a small boy, and years afterward I was introduced to his brother Judge James Pryor, of Covington, Ky., by his nephew, Judge Wm. S. Pryor. I have known Judge Pryor all of my life. My brother, Judge John Pryor Strother, studied law under him in 1856 and

1857, and I studied law under his half brother, the late Judge Joseph Barbour.

My father, Rev. John F. Strother, died in New Castle, July 21, 1879. Judge Pryor visited him the day before his death and he was one of the pall-bearers. Thirty-three long years passed before I saw him again, which was in Aug. 1912, when I visited him at his home in New Castle. We asked after members of each family and talked over many interesting incidents of long ago. I asked him about his parents and of his *grandparents* and of the old Pryor home and graveyard near Bedford. I asked him where his grandfather lived and was buried, and he replied "Right where old Uncle Jack Pryor lived near Bedford." The Judge mentioned some incidents in my father's life I had not heard before. I repeated the kindly words of his letter—that my father was one of the best men he ever knew, and he said with emphasis: "Henry, your father was the best man I ever knew."

It is interesting to know that this old Pryor home has been in the following four counties, being in one until the next was formed from it, viz.:

Jefferson, formed in 1780, Shelby formed in 1792, Henry formed in 1798 and Trimble formed in 1836.

Even the Henry County Local of the 20th inst, quoting from the Courier-Journal of 17th, publishes the error herein noted. I feel that the *Register* is the proper publication to call attention to this error and to correct same, and I have given you the positive proof.

Words fail me to properly express my great esteem and love for Judge Pryor and my high appreciation of the noble character and pure life of that grand and good man. My father held him up to me as my model in life. I have lost an elder brother, the greatest kinsman I had left. My heart is sad, for his place cannot be filled.

Sincerely yours,
HENRY STROTHER.

Judge William Samuel Pryor's Pedigree.

1. Col. Samuel Pryor m. Prudence Thornton, in Virginia. She was b. Mch. 31, 1699.

2. Samuel Pryor, of Amelia Co., Va., m. Mrs. Frances (Morton) Meriwether, Aug. 27, 1760, in Goochland Co., Va.

3. Samuel Pryor, b. in Goochland Co., Va., Jan'y 12, 1762; m. in Lincoln Co., Ky., Sept. 30, 1785, Mary Curd, daughter of John Curd, of Goochland Co., Va., and Lincoln Co., Ky.

4. Samuel Pryor, b. in Ky., m. in Henry Co., Ky., June 22, 1824, Ann (Nancy) Samuel, daughter of William Samuel.

5. Judge William Samuel Pryor, b. in Henry Co., Ky., April 1, 1825, d. Nov. 16, 1914. Twice married and issue by both wives.

(Copy of letter from Judge William S. Pryor to Henry Strother.)

"New Castle, Ky.,
Nov. 11th, 1910.
"Henry Strother, Esq.

"Dear Cousin:—Your very kind and instructive letter reached me some days since, and I see from its contents that you were certainly in and about our little town during the war. Am gratified to know that you are all doing well, and enjoying life.

"Your father was one of the best men I ever knew and I have no doubt is now reaping the reward for his many good deeds when in our midst.

"The Strothers were a remarkable family, as all of them by reason of their native intellect were enabled to fill any position in life.

"I see no change to be made in the history of the Pryor family, and thank you much for permitting me to share in the results of your labor, without any trouble to myself. My grandfather was Samuel Pryor (also the name of my father) and from him I get the name of Samuel.

"Our relation is traced through the Thorntons and is rightfully stated in your letter. I wish much that Arthur could learn more of the Spilman family, and have had Mrs. Barbour who was Sallie Webb to write him.

"I fully appreciate your interest in our family and have retained the copy sent me and will have it encased in an elegant frame. When you have the time give me more of your own history. How many children have you? Has your brother John any children living?

"Remember me with much love to all of your family.

"Yours sincerely,
(Signed) "WILL S. PRYOR."

"Excuse my bad writing—will be 86 years old in April and write a little nervous. W. S. P."

(The foregoing is a true copy of the original. Dec. 1, 1914.)
HENRY STROTHER.

RAILEY-RANDOLPH HISTORY AND GENEALOGY*

John Railey, b. Dec., 1721; m. (Nov. 1750) Elizabeth Randolph, b. 1727.

A RECORD OF THEIR DESCENDANTS:

Railey Coat-of-Arms:

or, a band vair between nine crosses, crosslet qu crest a lion vamp ppr.

JOHN RAILEY-ELIZABETH RANDOLPH.

A review of the tables submitted shows that the Raileys intermarried with the Randolphs, Woodsons, Mayos, Pleasants, Keiths and Strothers of Virginia. John Railey, the progenitor of the Virginia and Kentucky families of that name was an Englishman who delighted in fine horses and rural life, and his estate "Stonehenge," in Chesterfield county, Va., thirteen miles from Richmond, was noted for its fine stock, and very many of his descendants to this period have followed his example. He was bitterly opposed to English sovereignty over the colonies, while the Randolphs were just as intense Royalists, filling very many of the commanding positions of trust in the colonies by grace of the ruling authorities in England, and when John Railey won the heart of Elizabeth Randolph and asked for her hand in marriage the family objected on account of his views touching the obligations of the colonies to the mother country. In order to break off the engagement Elizabeth Randolph was sent to "Shadwell," the home of her sister, Mrs. Peter Jefferson, with instructions to prevent an elopement and to close all avenues of communication, which as usual was not successfully carried out. Soon thereafter by pre-arrangement a meeting took place at the home of Major Hughes, a mutual friend who lived on the opposite side of the river from "Shadwell," Elizabeth persuading the negro ferryman "Scipio" to row her across the river. From the home of Major Hughes they eloped to North Carolina where they married in 1750. Soon thereafter a reconciliation was brought about. Captain Isham Randolph, the elder brother of Elizabeth, then an officer in the Navy, being the medium, but John Railey never surrendered his convictions on the question of the freedom of the colonies and lived until the American Revolution had accomplished what he had so long hoped for, but the death of his son John at the battle of Norfolk and the loss of his wife in 1782 hastened his death in 1783. The descendants of his ten children who married and raised families are now scattered from the Atlan-

*These sketches by William E. Railey were apparently published in book form in 1933. Pages 98-108, this volume, originally appeared on pp. 71-81 of the May 1911 issue of *The Register of the Kentucky Historical Society*. They were reproduced in their entirety, along with supplementary material, in the September 1911 issue of that periodical, as noted in the table of contents to this volume.

tic to the Pacific and from the Gulf to the Great Lakes. I find that some members of all of these branches have kept a record that passed down to them, and for that reason my work has mainly been handicapped in an effort to locate these people and get them sufficiently interested to reply to my inquiries. John Railey and his wife, Elizabeth Randolph, and Col. John Woodson and his wife, Dorothy Randolph, thoroughly acquainted their children with the historical facts touching their family connections and they have been handed down from generation to generation. In fact a family tree started by John Railey and his wife is now in possession of the Rev. Fleming G. Railey, a Presbyterian minister of Selma, Alabama. Though I have never seen it, or had any assistance from it in my work, I am told that it brings the descendants down to about 1850 with much historical information, and traditions of colonial days touching all of the families connected with the Raileys by marriage. The Rev. Fleming G. Railey has lead me to believe for many years that he intended to publish a history of these families and for that reason the family tree has given me no aid in my work. While I am sure that his intentions have been good all these years, I am doubtful if he ever takes time from his ministerial duties, exacting as I know they are, to carry out his purpose to publish a history.

Having made notes of conversations between my mother and some of the older relatives when I was a mere boy, I decided more than twenty years ago to make as complete a record of these people as possible. In doing so I have spent much money, devoted much time that ordinarily would be given to pleasure and recreation, encountered much necessary delay in prosecuting the work on account of either tardiness or indifference upon the part of so many of the relatives who couldn't appreciate my anxiety to complete the work, and the worry that must ensue from trying to keep all of the correspondence and the disconnected and incomplete replies they would send me in mind, but I feel more than repaid when I recall so many nice letters received from many relatives that I have never had the pleasure of knowing personally. As I said earlier in this brief sketch many of John Railey's descendants followed his example in choosing rural life where they take much pride in fine stock, but the majority of them have pursued mercantile channels, while a number have been lawyers, doctors, bankers and preachers, but none of them have ever been conspicuous in the political arena, I am glad to say, yet they are almost universally Thomas Jefferson Democrats politically, and Presbyterians and Methodists in religion, but largely the former. My correspondence with all of these people leads me to say that all of them take great pride in good citizenship and conduct themselves in such a manner as to command the highest esteem in their respective localities. Those who have borne arms in war have been without exception very young men and for that reason few have reached higher rank than Colonel, but all of them have been to the forefront in civic righteousness. It is unusual, but it is true, that none of these people *have ever been drunkards or gamblers*. In fact I have never heard of one that was not a member of some church. The leading traits that have characterized these people are self-reliance, self-respect and a sense of right as a guide to their opinions and actions, then a total disregard of the blame or approval of the world around them. I attribute these virtues, so universally characteristic of the various branches of John Railey's family, to the fact that his children were thoroughly conversant with the history of their ancestors and have sacredly, but modestly, passed it down to succeeding generations as a guide to good citizenship. Hence I am a believer in the study of genealogy, believing it altogether worthy and commendable, and the man who says nay will stake his money every time on a pedigreed horse and assume much dignity in discussing the pedigree of animals. He thus ranks the animal above the man. The ultimate course of such people is toward the haunts of vice, while men and women who take pride in the noble attributes of their forefathers will, as a rule, be found leading movements for the betterment of the moral conditions around them. Family genealogies and traditions ought to have a higher place in the social and religious world. While it may build up vanity or a false pride among a few, it will give stamina and manhood to the greater number, and in doing the proper and sensible thing ourselves we produce higher ideals in those around us, and by handing those traits down to future generations we are making the world better.

JOHN RAILEY-ELIZABETH RANDOLPH.

Their descendants:

John Railey, Jr., [2] born 1752. Enlisted in the Revolution and was killed at the battle of Norfolk. He was the first born of John Railey and Elizabeth Randolph.

Thomas Railey, [2] born Sept. 22, 1754, died 1822.

Married Martha Woodson, Dec. 21, 1786.

Thomas Railey, Jr., [3] born 1787, died 1821.

Married Sarah Railey, 1820.

William Randolph Railey, [4] born 1821, died 1840.

George Woodson Railey, [3] born 1789, died 1846.

First married Maria Bullock, 1822.

Second Annie Marshall.

Elizabeth Woodson Railey, born 1823, died 1839.

Georgie Ellen Railey, [4] born —, died young.

P. I. Railey, [3] born March 16, 1793, died July 1, 1832.

Married Judith Woodson Railey, Aug. 21, 1817.

Martha Woodson Railey, [4] born Feb. 10, 1820, died March 19, 1837.

Richard Henry Railey, [4] born April 26, 1823, died Oct. 3, 1888.

Married Catherine Keith Hawkins, Feb. 25, 1852.
William Edward Railey, [5] born Dec. 25, 1852.
Married Annie H. Owsley, May 26, 1886.
Jennie Farris Railey, [6] born June 28, 1887.
Bertha Hontas Railey, [5] born April 26, 1854.
Married 1st Charles Randolph Darnell, 1882, no issue.
Married 2nd, P. D. McBride, 1892, no issue.
P. Woodson Railey, [5] born July 24, 1864.
P. I. Railey, Jr., [4] born Aug. 25, 1829.
Married 1st Sarah E. Frazier, Oct. 22, 1851.
Married 2nd Rebecca Gough, 1861, no issue.
Married 3rd Seville Church, 1898, no issue.
Josephine Railey, [5] born Sept. 22, 1852.
Married Robert Ward Macey, Nov. 21, 1872.
Pattie Railey Macey, [6] born Mar. 24, 1876.
Sadie Macey, [6] born June 7, 1877.
Robert Ward Macey, Jr., [6] born Oct. 8, 1879.
Railey Woodson Macey, [6] born Aug. 30, 1881.
Thomas Jefferson Railey, [4] born Jan. 10, 1831, died Aug. 18, 1851.
Laura Railey, [4] born Aug. 20, 1832, died Aug. 24, 1849.
Mary Railey, [3] born 1795, died May, 1817.
Married Phillip Woodson.
Mary Woodson. [4]
Married Augustine Withers.
Augustine Withers, Jr. [5]
Mary Woodson Withers, [5] died July 13, 1883.
Married H. P. Huff, 1873.
Susan Withers Huff. [6]
Married E. H. Foster, April 3, 1901.
Susan Railey Withers. [5]
Married James B. White.
Lawson White. [6]
Ellen White. [6]
Married W. W. Newman.
Susan Withers Newman. [7]
Margaret White Newman. [7]
Augustine White. [6]
Maria Withers. [5]
Married Sandy White.
Jane Railey, [3] born 1794, died Nov. 28, 1865.
Married John Berryman, Aug. 9, 1819.
Mary Elizabeth Berryman, [4] born June 5, 1820, died June 4, 1905.
Married George Hamet Cary, Sept. 1, 1840.
Alice Cary, [5] born May 20, 1843, died Mar. 29, 1899.
Married Daniel B. Price, Oct. 17, 1867.
Jennie Cary Price, [6] born Aug. 16, 1868.
Married W. L. Smith, May 20, 1890.
Mary Louise Price, [6] born April 2, 1870.
Married Preston H. Williams, Dec. 27, 1888.
Daniel B. Price, [6] born Feb. 7, 1872.
Married Ada Alice Ingles, June 3, 1909.
Alice Cary Price, [6] born Sept. 14, 1875.

Married John Faulkner, June 27, 1907.

Arthur Cary,[5] born Oct. 1, 1841. Married 1st Fanny Graddy, Dec. 6, 1876.

Married 2nd, Sidney Sayre Bell, Feb. 12, 1895.

Graddy Cary,[6] born April 6, 1878.

Married Marie Burnett, Jan. 17, 1907.

John B. Cary,[5] born Sept. 18, 1846.

Jane Railey Cary,[5] born Nov. 1, 1849.

Married Charles S. Tabb, Dec. 20, 1876.

George Cary Tabb,[6] born Feb. 5, 1880.

Arthur Tabb,[6] born Oct. 20, 1881.

Mary Clifton Tabb,[6] born Sept. 19, 1891.

George Hamet Cary, Jr.,[5] born Nov. 12, 1850; died April 16, 1895.

Married Mary White, May 19, 1887.

James Cary,[6] born April 18, 1888.

Mary Cary,[6] born Aug. 8, 1890.

Mattie Cary,[6] born Sept. 6, 1891.

Elizabeth Cary,[6] born May 20, 1893.

Edward Humphrey Cary,[5] born Nov. 7, 1853.

Married Rebecca Hunter Wickliffe, Dec. 18, 1879.

Hallie Cary,[6] born May 12, 1882.

Logan Wickliffe Cary,[6] born June 24, 1884.

Rhoda Cary,[6] born July 1, 1887.

Married Edwin C. Stevens, Oct. 14, 1909.

Martha Woodson Cary,[5] born Oct., 1855.

Married Newton G. Crawford, 1884.

Mary Clifton Cary,[5] born Dec. 18, 1862.

Married Brown Craig Crawford, Sept. 30, 1886.

George Cary Crawford,[6] born July 4, 1888.

Robert Irvin Crawford,[6] born Aug. 21, 1889.

James T. Berryman,[4] born April 22, 1822; died June 4, 1879.

Married 1st Theresa Willis, Jan., 1845.

2nd Sallie Steele Church, Oct. 8, 1858.

John W. Berryman,[5] born Nov. 19, 1845.

Married Louise Price, June 5, 1867.

Price Berryman,[6] born June 3, 1868.

Married Minnie Hemphill, Nov. 24, 1894.

Theresa Willis Berryman,[6] born Aug. 2, 1872.

Married Oliver H. Farra, Oct. 18, 1906.

Robert S. Berryman,[6] born April 4, 1880.

Married Ruth Gay, May 11, 1904.

James Sthreshley Berryman,[5] born Jan. 9, 1848; died Jan. 1, 1910.

Married Mary Wright, Nov. 7, 1871.

Kate Theresa Berryman,[6] born Aug. 8, 1872.

Married Howard Sanders, May 4, 1899.

Henry Berryman Sanders,[7] born June 10, 1903.

Mary A. Berryman, [6] born Dec. 4, 1874.
Married H. J. Mead, Sept. 24, 1895.
Mary Belle Mead, [7] born Oct. 28, 1897.
Dorothy Randolph Mead, [7] born Jan 20, 1899.
Lalla Mead, [7] born Mar. 8, 1908.
Stuart Robinson Berryman, [6] born July 18, 1876.
Married Eunice Wright, Oct. 18, 1908.
Stuart Robinson Berryman, [7] born July 11, 1909.
James T. Berryman, [6] born July 17, 1878.
Sue M. Berryman, [6] born Jan. 17, 1881.
Mollie Berryman, [5] born May 21, 1850.
Annie Berryman, [5] born Dec. 26, 1852.
Married W. Horace Posey, June 21, 1883.
Genevieve Posey. [6]
Edith Posey. [6]
Cary M. Berryman, [5] born July 22, 1859.
Married Emma Portwood, Nov. 21, 1888.
Church Berryman, [5] born April 2, 1862.
Claude Berryman, [5] born May 5, 1865.
Married Evangeline Leeds.
Clifford Berryman, [5] born April 2, 1869.
Married Kate Durfee.
Hervey Berryman, [5] born May 12, 1870.
Robt. H. Berryman, [4] born April 17, 1824; died April 4, 1878.
Married Maria L. Whittington, June, 1846.

Emma Woodson Berryman, [5] born April 27, 1847.
Married Marvin D. Averill, June 23, 1869.
Robert Averill, [6] born March 23, 1871.
Married Anna Rupp, Aug., 1907.
William Averill, [3] born Feb. 2, 1873.
Married Cammilla Baskett, Jan. 6, 1897.
Christine Averill, [7] born Dec. 25, 1897.
Mary Virginia Averill, [7] born July 10, 1902.
Alice B. Averill, [7] born April 12, 1906.
Louise Averill, [6] born Nov. 5, 1877.
Married Eugene D. Woods, April 11, 1900.
Marvin Averill Woods, [7] born Jan. 18, 1901.
Francis D. Woods, [7] born Jan. 10, 1903.
Robt. Harvie Woods, [7] born Jan. 11, 1905.
Emily Eugenia Woods, [7] born July 30, 1909.
Cornelia Berryman, [5] born Jan. 8, 1851; died Feb. 9, 1890.
Married Clifton Kennedy, 1869.
Willie Marcia Kennedy, [6] born Dec. 12, 1871.
Married Dr. Albert Posey, Dec. 29, 1896.
Robert Handy Berryman, [5] born Nov. 29, 1854.
Married Nellie Jones, Nov. 29, 1877.
Bessie Berryman, [6] born Oct. 19, 1878.
Married Walter D. Franklin, June 12, 1901.

Ellen Buford Franklin, [7] born Aug. 27, 1902.

Catharine Franklin, [7] born June 14, 1905.

Robert B. Franklin, [7] born Nov. 24, 1909.

Lela Berryman, [6] born Feb. 10, 1888.

Buford Berryman, [6] born Mar. 12, 1896.

Mary Virginia Berryman, [5] born Feb. 24, 1856.

Married John W. Crosthwaite, 1887.

Aileen Crosthwaite, [6] born July 16, 1888.

Mary Virginia Crosthwaite, [6] born June 2, 1890.

Married John C. Kreiger, June, 1907.

Jane Railey Berryman, [5] born April 1, 1861.

Married 1st Ed. Reese, 1883.

Married 2nd Edward T. Stanton, 1896.

Cornelia Reece, [6] born Oct. 21, 1887.

Henry T. Stanton, [6] 1897.

Mattie Berryman, [5] born Nov. 4, 1867.

Married Dwight McAfee, July 20, 1887.

Irene McAfee, [6] born June 3, 1888.

Married Adams Carithers McMakin, Nov. 10, 1909.

Henry McAfee, [6] born July 29, 1890.

Clinton McAfee, [6] born Aug. 20, 1898.

Walter Berryman, [5] born April 3, 1880.

Edw. H. Berryman, [4] born Mar. 14, 1826; died Dec. 26, 1896.

Married Sallie Willis, May 27, 1852.

Willis N. Berryman, [5] born April 11, 1853; died Aug. 22, 1881.

Married Elizabeth Scearce, Oct. 5, 1876.

Julia Berryman, [6] born April 17, 1880.

Theresa Woodson Berryman, [5] born June 15, 1854.

Married William S. Barbour, June 15, 1882.

Robert Berryman, [5] born Oct. 6, 1862; died May 12, 1903.

Married Belle Portwood, 1890.

Barbour Berryman, [6] born May 20, 1893.

Mattie Woodson Berryman, [4] born April 24, 1836; died —

Married Robert Fry Montgomery, June 10, 1856.

George Berryman Montgomery, [5] born June 10, 1866.

Married Lucy Mahin O'Neal, Nov. 28, 1895.

Jane Railey Montgomery, [5] born Oct. 2, 1868; died April 26, 1897.

Married Robert G. Lowry, Jan. 1, 1890.

Mary Montgomery, [5] born May 11, 1871.

Married G. Y. Reynolds, Feb. 15, 1902.

Mattie Woodson Montgomery, [5] born May 11, 1871.

Married Jordan Scott Lowry, Dec. 19, 1890.

Jno. B. Montgomery, [5] born June 20, 1874.

Married Irene Holloway, Aug. 25, 1898.

Robt. Montgomery, [5] born June 1, 1878.

George Railey Berryman, [4] born 1838; died 1882.

Frank P. Berryman, [4] born 1842.
Married Susan Hassinger, 1866.
John Berryman, [5] born 1867.
Married Annie Harris.
Kate Berryman, [5] born 1869; died 1887.
Newton Berryman, [5] born 1871; died 1897.
Wilhelmina Berryman, [5] born 1873.
Married Rev. Alexander Henry, Oct. 8, 1890.
Catharine Clifton Henry, [6] born Oct. 7, 1891.
Married Alfred Mosby, Oct. 8, 1909.
Frank Berryman Henry, [6] born Nov. 24, 1892.
Emma Yeaman Henry, [6] born Nov. 29, 1893.
Alexander Henry, Jr., [6] born Jan. 8, 1901.
Sidney Robertson Berryman, [5] born 1875.
Frank P. Berryman, Jr., [5] born 1877; died 1907.
Lucy Railey, [3] born Aug. 5, 1796; died Sept., 1852.
Married 1st John D. Kinkead, no issue.
Married 2nd Rev. William M. King, 1832.
Rev. Samuel A. King, [4] born Oct. 14, 1834.
Married Anna King, Jan. 19, 1860.
Lucy Woodson King, [5] born Oct. 16, 1860; died Sept. 22, 1869.
Jennie Catherine King, [5] born April 25, 1862.
Married A. M. Gribble, Nov. 29, 1882.
Chas. King Gribble, [6] born Sept. 11, 1883.

Andrew W. Gribble, [6] born Jan. 18, 1885.
Anna Gribble, [3] born Nov. 2, 1886.
Jennie Gribble, [6] born Oct. 16, 1888.
A. M. Gribble, Jr., [6] born Mar. 2, 1891.
Samuel Gribble, [6] born July 12, 1893.
Elizabeth Randolph Gribble, [6] born May 22, 1897.
Dr. Walter Blackburn King, [5] born May 14, 1864; died Dec. 11, 1889.
Married Minnie Carroll, Oct. 19, 1887.
Walter Blackburn King, Jr., [6] born Nov. 6, 1889.
Hattie King, [5] born May 20, 1867; died March, 1896.
Married Dr. Ralph Conger, Mar. 12, 1891, no issue.
Samuel Arthur King, [5] born Sept. 20, 1869.
Married Lucy Newman, 1896.
Walter King, [6] born Mar. 16, 1897.
Elizabeth Woodson King, [3] born May 31, 1899.
Ellen King, [6] born June 16, 1905.
Samuel Arthur King, Jr., [6] born July 31, 1907.
Hugh King, [6] born June 17, 1909.
Maggie D. King, [5] born Dec. 2, 1872.
Married Rev. P. H. Burney, Oct. 6, 1892.
Margaret Burney, [6] born Dec. 8, 1893.
Harriet Burney, [6] born June 11, 1896.
Philo Burney, [6] born June 21, 1904.

Anna Railey Burney,[6] born April 24, 1907.

Pattie Markham King,[5] born May 30, 1875.
Married Rev. F. A. Barnes, May 28, 1908.

Ella C. King,[5] born Sept. 14, 1877.
Married Harry A. Wilson, Sept. 26, 1895.

Harry Allen Wilson,[6] born Feb. 26, 1897.

William M. King, Jr.,[4] born June 22, 1833; died, 1864.
Married Hattie King, Jan., 1864.

Willie King,[5] born 1864.
Married J. E. Daniel, June 8, 1893.

Willie Sue Daniel,[3] born June 14, 1895.

Joseph Daniel,[6] born Aug. 5, 1897.

Susanna Railey,[3] born Jan. 15, 1801; died May 1, 1872.
Married William Fleming Markham, July 19, 1825.

Dr. George W. Markham,[4] born July, 1826; died Dec. 24, 1853.

Rev. Thos. Railey Markham,[4] born Dec. 2, 1828; died Mar. 12, 1894.
Married Mary Searles, Nov. 30, 1858, no issue.

Martha Woodson Markham,[4] born July 14, 1832; died Feb., 1910.
Married Fabius M. Sleeper, 1850.

Susan Margaret Sleeper,[5] born July 10, 1851.

Lucy Fleming Sleeper,[5] born April 13, 1853.
Married Robert Fonda Gribble, Feb. 21, 1884.

Elizabeth Gribble,[6] born June 2, 1885.

Robt. Fonda Gribble, Jr.,[6] born June 2, 1890.

Theodore Gribble,[6] born April 10, 1894.

Wm. Markham Sleeper,[5] born Oct. 9, 1859.
Married Laura Risher, April 26, 1892.

Benjamine P. Sleeper,[6] born Dec. 11, 1895.

Martha Margaret Sleeper,[6] born June 17, 1896.

Alethea Halbert Sleeper,[6] born Nov. 24, 1898.

William Markham Sleeper, Jr.,[6] born Oct. 31, 1900.

Francis D. Sleeper,[6] born April 5, 1902.

Thos. Markham Sleeper,[5] born April 29, 1866.
Married Carrie Lockert, Oct. 23, 1890.

Lockert Sleeper,[6] born July 29, 1893.

Markham Sleeper,[6] born Dec. 5, 1895.

Mary Woodson Sleeper,[6] born June 28, 1898.

William R. Sleeper,[6] born July 17, 1900.

Lucy Fleming Markham,[4] born 1836; died 1894.
Married Edward A. Jones, Jan. 1864.

Bessie Cary Jones,[5] born Nov., 1862.
Married Robt. Grier Patton, Feb., 1888.

Robt. Grier Patton, Jr.,[6] born April, 1889.

Edward Jones Patton,[6] born Nov., 1890.

Elizabeth Randolph Patton,[6] born Oct., 1893.

Desha Patton,[6] born 1901.

Susan Markham Jones, [5] born Feb. 14, 1866.

George Woodson Jones, [5] born Dec. 23, 1869.

Mattie Estelle Jones, [5] born Oct. 3, 1871.

William Fleming Markham, [4] born 1842, killed at the battle of Atlanta as a gallant young Confederate officer.

Thomas Railey was the 2nd born of John Railey and Elizabeth Randolph. He was born on the estate of his father, "Stonehenge," in Chesterfield county, Va., twelve miles from Richmond, A. D., 1754, about 1780 and settled upon a farm He came to Woodford county, Ky., that he called "Clifton," a beautiful site overlooking the Kentucky River and the village that sprang up in the valley below took its name from the farm that overlooked the village. He returned to Virginia in 1786 and married Martha Woodson, 9th born of Col. John Woodson and Dorothy Randolph. Besides raising a large and interesting family he exercised a fatherly interest in his four brothers who settled in the same county and always advised with him on matters of business. He died on his estate about 1822. His wife's death occurred in 1834. The home passed into the hands of his daughter, Jane Berryman, and remained in possession of her son, George Railey Berryman, until his death in 1882. His eldest son, Thos. Railey, Jr., married Sarah Railey in 1820, and died within a year after his marriage. His son, George Woodson Railey, married his cousin, Maria Bullock, and moved to Monticello, Mo., about 1825, where he was postmaster until his death in 1846. His son, P. I. Railey, Sr., married Judith Woodson Railey and lived on a farm near Versailles, Ky., where he died in 1832. Mary Railey, the 4th born, married her cousin, Phillip Woodson, and they settled at Tuscaloosa, Ala. I have not been able to learn anything of their descendants except what I learned through my kinswoman, Mrs. Pattie Markham Sleeper. Jane Railey, the 5th born, married John Berryman. Their descendants have generally domiciled themselves within the borders of Kentucky, and they are quite numerous as the record will show. Lucy Railey the 6th born married first John D. Kinkead, of Versailles, Ky. He died within a year and his widow afterwards married the Rev. William M. King, a Presbyterian minister, and they moved to Texas where their descendants live today. Their son, the Rev. Samuel A. King, was pastor of the Presbyterian Church at Waco, Texas, for forty years and only resigned a few years ago to take charge of the Theological Seminary at Austin, Tex. There have been quite a number of preachers in this line. Susanna Railey, 7th born, married William Fleming Markham, of Versailles, Ky., in 1825. They moved to New Orleans soon after their marriage. Their first born, Dr. Geo. W. Markham, practiced medicine in New Orleans for a few years and would have become eminent in his profession had not the seal of death closed his career in young

107

manhood. Their second born was Rev. Thomas Railey Markham, a Presbyterian minister. He preached for forty years for one congregation in New Orleans, having a supply for him while he was a Chaplain in the Confederate army for four years. Martha Woodson Markham, affectionately known among her kinspeople as Pattie Markham. was the 3rd born. She married Fabius M. Sleeper, a lawyer of Mississippi. After the Civil War they moved to Waco, Texas, where Mr. Sleeper and his brother-in-law, Edward A. Jones, constituted a law firm that had a large clientage. Lucy Fleming Markham, the 4th born married Edward A. Jones, a lawyer of Maryland and they moved to Waco, Texas. William Fleming Markham was the 5th born, entered the Confederate army before he had reached his majority and was killed at the battle of Atlanta, a gallant young officer.

The compiler of these notes is descended from the line of P. I. Railey, Sr., the 3rd born, and his wife Judith Woodson Railey.

William Randolph, [1] born 1651; died April 11, 1711.
Married Mary Isham.
William Randolph, Jr. [2]
Married Miss Elizabeth Beverly.
Thomas Randolph. [2]
Married Judith Fleming.
William Randolph. [3]
Married Maria Judith Page.
Thomas Mann Randolph. [4]
Married Anne Cary.
Judith Randolph. [4]
Married Richard Randolph.
Judith Randolph. [3]
Married Rev. William Stith.
Mary Isham Randolph, [3] born 1718.
Married Rev. James Keith, Mar. 2, 1733.
James Keith, [4] born 1733.
Thomas Randolph Keith, [4] born 1734.
Married Mary Blackwell.
John Keith, [4] born 1735.
Married ——— Doniphan.
Alexander Keith, [4] born 1736.
Captain Isham Keith, [4] born 1737; died July, 1787.
Married Charlotte Ashmore, 1778.
John Keith, [5] born 1779.
Mary Elizabeth Keith, [5] born 1781; died 1803.
Married Randolph Railey, 1800.
Isham Keith Railey, [6] born 1801; died 1803.
Charlotte Ashmore Keith, [5] born 1782.
Married James McDonald Briggs.
Catharine Keith, [5] born Sept. 18, 1784; died Feb. 24, 1854.
Married William Strother Hawkins, Oct. 14, 1802.
Catharine Keith Hawkins, [6] born Oct. 18, 1825; died June 22, 1902.
Married Richard Henry Railey, Feb. 25, 1852.
Mary Randolph Keith, [4] born 1738.
Married Col. Thomas Marshall, 1754.
Chief Justice John Marshall, [5] born 1755; died 1835.
Married Mary Willis Ambler, Jan. 3, 1783.
Dr. Louis Marshall, [5] born Oct. 7, 1773; died 1866.

Married Agatha Smith, 1800.
Thos. F. Marshall, [6] born June 7, 1801; died Sept. 22, 1864.
Married Elizabeth Yost.
Edward C. Marshall, [6] born 1821; died June 1893.
Married Josephine Chalfant, 1852.
Louis Marshall, [7] born July 12, 1856.
Married Susan Thorne, Sept. 25, 1883.
Josephine Marshall, [8] born Mar. 4, 1886.
Married Lawrence Amsden Railey, June 2, 1909.
Col. Isham Randolph, [2] born 1690; died 1742.
Married Jane Rogers, 1717.
Capt. Isham Randolph, Jr. [3]
Married Miss Harrison.
Thomas Randolph, Jr. [3]
Married Jane Carey.
William Randolph, Jr. [3]
Married Miss Little.
Jane Randolph, [3] born 1719.
Married Peter Jefferson, 1738.
Mary Randolph. [3]
Married Charles Lewis.
Elizabeth Randolph, [3] born 1727; died Sept. 11, 1782.
Married John Railey, Nov., 1750.
Thomas Railey, [4] born Sept. 22, 1754; died 1822.
Married Martha Woodson, Dec. 21, 1786.
Isham Randolph Railey, [4] born July 15, 1758; died Mar. 14, 1818.
Married Susanna Woodson, April 17 1784.
Anna Railey, [4] born Sept. 16. 1759; died 1826.
Married Mathew Pleasants, Feb., 1784.

William Railey, [4] born Feb. 26, 1760; died Feb. 8, 1818.
Married Judith Woodson, Mar., 1793.
Randolph Railey, [4] born May 14, 1770; died May 28, 1837.
Married 1st Mary Elizabeth Keith, 1801.
Married 2nd Martha Randolph Pleasants, 1819.
Dorothy Randolph. [3]
Married Col. John Woodson, Oct. 28, 1751.
Susanna Woodson, [4] born June 26, 1760; died Dec. 6, 1818.
Married Isham Randolph Railey, Sept. 17, 1784.
Martha Woodson, [4] born July 6, 1764; died 1834.
Married Thomas Railey, Dec. 21, 1786.
Judith Woodson, [4] born Feb. 16, 1767; died Dec. 26, 1818.
Married William Railey, Mar., 1793.
Anna Randolph. [3]
Married 1st Daniel Scott.
Married 2nd John Pleasants.
Married 3rd James Pleasants.
Martha Randolph Pleasants, [4] born Dec. 2, 1779; died July 10, 1849.
Married Randolph Railey, 1819.
Ann Pleasants. [4]
Married Isaac Webster.
Sarah Webster, [5] born April 4, 1809; died Feb. 2, 1899.
Married 1st Dr. Isham Railey, 1835.
Married 2nd Col. John H. Slaughter, July 19, 1849.
Martha Randolph Slaughter, [6] born Sept. 29, 1850; died Dec. 16, 1878.

109

Married Mark Hardin Railey, Jan. 15, 1868.
Gov. James Pleasants. [4]
Married Susan Rose..
Susanna Randolph. [3]
Married Carter Harrison.

Thomas Randolph, of England, married Dorothy Lane and had seven children, of whom Richard and Henry Randolph were two. Henry came to America about 1650 and was clerk of Henrico county, and for many years clerk of the House of Burgesses. His nephew, William Randolph, son of Richard, of "Morton Hall," came to America about 1670, and succeeded his uncle Henry as clerk of Henrico county. He was afterwards Justice, Burgess, Attorney General, Speaker of the House of Burgesses and King's Councillor. He settled on an estate in Virginia that he called "Turkey Island." This estate included a vast domain and was situated on the James River. His entire life was spent upon this estate and he died there during the year 1711. He married Mary Isham, daughter of Henry Isham, and his wife, Catharine, of "Bermunda Hundred," on the opposite side of the James River. They raised nine children, seven sons and two daughters. All of his sons took an active and prominent part in the affairs of their day, holding various positions of trust in the government of the colonies under English regime, but I will only take up the line of two of them, Thomas Randolph, of "Tuckahoe," and Isham Randolph, of "Dungeness," as the Raileys are descended from both of these lines. Thomas Randolph was the second born. He married Judith Fleming, daughter of Col. John Fleming, and Mary Balling, the latter being a descendant of Pocahontas. His descendants, as far as I am informed, haven't any record of his holding any other office than that of Justice. Thomas Randolph and his wife, Judith, lived and died on their magnificent estate, "Tuckahoe," which has never passed out of possession of descendants and is in as good a state of preservation as it was one hundred and fifty years ago, and owned by the Cooliges of Boston at this time. The Cooliges are grandsons of Gov. Thomas Mann Randolph and Martha Jefferson (daughter of Thos. Jefferson), and Gov. Thos. Mann Randolph was a grandson of Thomas Randolph, of "Tuckahoe." Thomas Randolph and Judith Fleming had but three children, William Randolph, who married Maria Judith Page, was the 1st born. He was a member of Burgess. His son, Thos. Mann Randolph, 1st, was a Burgess and member of the Convention of 1775-6. He married Anne Cary. Their son, Thos. Mann Randolph, the 2nd, married his cousin, Martha Jefferson. He was a member of Congress, 1803; Governor of Virginia, 1819-22. His son, Col. Thos. Jefferson Randolph, was a presidential elector, 1845; member of Congress, 1851, and President of the Democratic Convention at Baltimore, 1873.

Mary Isham Randolph, 3rd born, of Thomas Randolph and Judith

Fleming, married Rev. James Keith. Their daughter, Mary Randolph Keith, married Col. Thomas Marshall whose son, John Marshall, became Chief Justice of the United States. Col. Thos. Marshall and his wife, Mary Randolph Keith, were the progenitors of all of the prominent Marshalls of Kentucky and Virginia. A brother of Col. Thomas Marshall's wife, Captain Isham Keith, married Charlotte Ashmore and they were the great grandparents of the compiler of these notes. In this connection I will submit extracts from a letter written by Col. Thomas Marshall Green, who published "The Prominent Families of Kentucky." Col. Green had the honor to be a great grandson of Col. Thomas Marshall:

Maysville, Ky., Nov. 10, 1891.
My Dear William:
Col. Thos. Marshall married Mary Randolph Keith. She was a sister of your great grandfather, Isham Keith. A granddaughter of Thomas Randolph, of "Tuckahoe' and the daughter of Rev. Jas. Keith and his wife, Mary Isham Randolph (here he gives a list or the children of Col. Thos. Marshall, &c., and concludes as follows). You will see by the above that my great grandmother, Mary Randolph Keith, was a sister of your great grandfather, Isham Keith. Thus my grandfather, Capt. Thos. Marshall, was a first cousin of your grandmother, "Kittie" Keith, who married William Strother Hawkins. This made my mother, Mary Keith Marshall, and your mother, Catharine Keith Hawkins, second cousins, and it follows that you and I are third cousins. This is the precise degree of relationship. Through the Randolph women, who married Railey and Woodson, my mother and your father, were fourth cousins and you and I are fifth cousins. If you wish any branch of the Marshalls run out in greater detail, I will do it hereafter.

Very truly yours,
THOS. M. GREEN.
To WM. E. RAILEY,
Midway, Ky.

I remember with much pleasure my kinsman, Thos. F. Marshall, who visited our home prior to 1863 quite frequently. He often ran over the relationships with my mother and I resolved then, as a boy, to make a record of the facts in at least a modest way some day. It was during those visits that I learned that my grandmother, Catharine Keith, was married at "Buckpond," the home of Col. Thos. Marshall, and that her sister, Mary Elizabeth Keith, was married to Randolph Railey at the home of General Humphrey Marshall, near Frankfort. They were each on a visit to their Kentucky relatives at the time. A few years later their uncle, John Keith, settled near Maysville, Ky., to which point Col. Thos. Marshall had moved his residence.

Col. Isham Randolph was the 3rd born of William Randolph and Mary Isham. His estate was known as "Dungeness." He was Colonial Agent at London in 1717 where he met and married Jane Rogers. Was a member of Burgesses, 1740, and Adjutant General of the Colony and Colonel of Militia. His first daughter was Jane Randolph, who married Peter Jefferson. She was the mother of Thomas Jefferson, author of the Declaration of Independence, and President. The third daughter was Elizabeth Randolph, who married John Railey (see letter Col. Thos. M. Green). The fourth daughter married Col. John Woodson, her name being Dorothy Randolph (see letter Col. Thos. M. Green). The fifth daughter was Anna Randolph, who was three times married, the last marriage being to James Pleasants of "Contention," and they were the parents of James Pleasants, who was a United States Senator and Governor of Virginia. They were also the parents of Martha Randolph Pleasants, who married Randolph Railey, the 11th of John Railey and Elizabeth Randolph, whose only two surviving grandchildren are Samuel Wheeler Railey, a lawyer of Washington City, and Mrs. John Calhoun Burnett, of Louisville, Ky. The 6th daughter of Col. Isham Randolph was Susanna, who married Carter Henry Harrison, of Clifton. They had four sons, viz: Robt. Carter Harrison, Peyton Harrison, Randolph Harrison and Carter Henry Harrison who married Sophy Preston, of Kentucky. Robert Carter Harrison, the first son, married Anne Cabell, daughter of Col. Joseph Cabell, and they were the parents of Robert Harrison, of Cooper county, Mo., and the Rev. Cabell Harrison, who frequently visited the home of my grandparents, P. T. Railey, Sr., and his wife, Judith Woodson Railey, both of whom were his second cousins. During one of his visits after the death of P. I. Railey, Sr., the widow, Judith Woodson Railey, presented him with the elk-head cane of her husband made in Virginia before the Revolution and he prized it very highly. It was through the influence of Rev. Cabell Harrison that so many of the Virginia and Kentucky Raileys adopted the Presbyterian faith, John Railey, Sr., being for many years vestryman in the Episcopal church, and his wife, as were all of the Randolphs, being strict members of that faith. The Rev. Cabell Harrison frequently visited the homes of his Railey relatives in Virginia and Kentucky, and they all felt a deep love for him.

Elizabeth Randolph, the 9th born of Wm. Randolph and Mary Isham, married Theoderick Bland and they were the ancestors of General Robert E. Lee in the following line:

Richard Bland, Annie Poythress,
Mary Bland and Henry Lee,
Henry Lee and Lucy Grimes,
Harry Lee and
Robert E. Lee.

Judge James Keith, President of the Supreme Court of Virginia, is the grandson of Thomas R. Keith and Mary Blackwell.

THE WOODSONS AND THEIR RAILEY CONNECTIONS.

Dr. John Woodson. [1]
Married Sarah Woodson.
Robert Woodson. [2]
Married Elizabeth Ferris.
John Woodson. [3]
Married Judith Tarleton.
Josiah Woodson. [4]
Married Mary Royall.
Col. John Woodson, [5] born 1730; died December 2, 1789.
Married Dorothea Randolph, Oct. 28, 1751.
Jane Woodson, [6] born 1752.
Married Archibald Pleasants, July 17, 1775.
Nannie Woodson, [3] born 1754.
Married John Stephen Woodson, Oct. 12, 1777.
Elizabeth Woodson, [6] born Nov., 1756.
Married John Cheadle.
Major Josiah Woodson, [6] born 1758; died Mason county, Ky., 1817.
Married Elizabeth Woodson, Dec. 3, 1778.
Isham Woodson, [6] born 1759; died unmarried.
Susanna Woodson, [6] born June 26, 1760; died in Woodford county, Ky., Dec. 6, 1818.
Married Isham Randolph Railey, Sept. 17, 1784.
Mary Woodson, [6] born 1761.
Married Col. Nathan G. Morris of the British army, Aug. 30, 1778.
John Woodson, [6] born Feb. 28, 1763.
Married Mary Anderson, Mar. 30, 1786.
Martha Woodson, [6] born July 6, 1764; died in Woodford county, Ky., 1834.
Married Thomas Railey, Dec. 21, 1786.
Judith Woodson, [6] born Feb. 16, 1767; died in Woodford county, Ky., Dec. 26, 1831.
Married William Railey, Mar., 1793.
Sarah Woodson, [6] born Nov. 14, 1770.
Married Phillip Woodson, 1790.
Phillip Woodson. [7]
Married Mary Railey.
Lucy Woodson. [6]
Tarleton Woodson. [4]
Married Ursula Fleming.
Susanna Woodson. [5]
Married John Pleasants.
Ursula Pleasants. [6]
Susanna Pleasants. [6]
Mathew Pleasants, [6] born Feb. 16, 1759; died Jan., 1816.
Married Anna Railey, Feb., 1784.
Archibald Pleasants. [6]
Married Jane Woodson, July 17, 1775.
Joseph Pleasants. [6]
Married Elizabeth Jordan.
James Pleasants. [4]
Married Mrs. Anna Pleasants (nee Anna Randolph).
John L. Pleasants. [7]
Martha Randolph Pleasants, [7] born Dec. 2, 1779; died July 10, 1849.
Married Randolph Railey, 1819.
Tarleton Woodson Pleasants. [7]
Ann S. Pleasants. [7]
Married Isaac Webster.
Isaac Webster, Jr. [9]
Sarah Webster, [8] born April 4, 1809; died Feb. 2, 1899.

Married 1st Dr. Isham Railey, 1835; no issue.

Married 2nd Col. John H. Slaughter, July 19, 1849.

Martha Randolph Slaughter, [9] born Sept. 29, 1850; died Dec. 16, 1878.

Married Mark Hardin Railey, Jan. 15, 1868.

Gabriel Webster Slaughter, [9] born Aug. 3, 1852; died Mar. 19, 1874.

Susan Hord Slaughter, [9] born Sept. 13, 1856.

Pauline Pleasants. [7]

Susanna Randolph Pleasants. [7]

Gov. James Pleasants. [7]

Married Susan Rose.

Dr. John Woodson, the first of the name in this country, came to America about 1620 as surgeon to a troop of soldiers under command of Sir John Harvey of the English army. These soldiers were stationed at "Middle Settlement," near Richmond, Va. Dr. John Woodson came from Dorsetshire and he married his wife at Devonshire, England. Tarleton Woodson, the great grandson of Dr. John Woodson, married Ursula Fleming. She was related to the Earles of Wigton in Scotland. They were the ancestors of the Bates, Venables and other prominent Virginia families. Tarleton Woodson's brother, Josiah, married Mary Royall. She was a daughter of Joseph Royall and Elizabeth Kennon. Their son, Col. John Woodson, was sheriff of Goochland county, member House Burgesses, member of the Convention of 1775-76 and member of Committee on Safety. He married Dorothy Randolph, 7th of Col. Isham Randolph and Jane Rogers. Many of their descendants settled in Kentucky and are residents of Woodford county today.

Edward Bates, Attorney General under President Lincoln, was of the Tarleton Woodson-Ursula Fleming line. Inasmuch as all of his relatives were in sympathy with the cause of the South during the Civil War, his action gave great offense to them when he accepted the appointment. The Woodsons, like the Randolphs, have given many distinguished soldiers, lawyers and diplomats to this country. The history being prepared for publication by Mr. H. M. Woodson, of the "Woodson Family," will give an extended account of these people. I will content myself by giving just a few names of the more prominent. Of Virginians are:

Major Frederick Tarleton Woodson.

General Tarleton Woodson.

Col. Charles Woodson.

Judge Creed Taylor.

Hon. Abraham B. Venable.

Hon. Fleming Bates.

Gov. James Pleasants.

John Hampden Pleasants.

Joseph Selden, of Chepultepec fame.

Gov. Frederick Bates, of Missouri.

General Charles Woodson, of Missouri.

Gov. Silas Woodson, of Kentucky and Missouri.

Judge A. M. Woodson, Supreme Court of Missouri.

Gov. Daniel Woodson, of Kansas.
Hon. Abraham N. Venable, of North Carolina.
Hon. James Woodson Bates, of Arkansas.
Gov. Thos. Ligon, of Maryland.
Gov. Henry Allen of Louisiana.

THE PLEASANTS AND THEIR RAILEY CONNECTIONS.

John Pleasants. [1]
Married Jane Tucker.
Joseph Pleasants. [2]
Married Martha Cocke.
John Pleasants. [3]
Married Susanna Woodson.
Ursula Pleasants. [4]
Married 1st George Ellis.
Married 2nd John Brooke.
Susanna Pleasants. [4]
Married Joshua Storres.
Mathew Pleasants. [4]
Married Anna Railey, Feb., 1784.
Archibald Pleasants. [4]
Married Jane Woodson, July 17, 1775.
Joseph Pleasants. [4]
Married Elizabeth Jordan.
James Pleasants. [4]
Married Mrs. Anna Pleasants (nee Anna Randolph).
Martha Pleasants, [5] born Dec. 2, 1779; died July 10, 1849.
Married Randolph Railey, 1819.
Tarleton Woodson Pleasant. [5]
Married Sarah Pleasants.
Ann S. Pleasants. [5]
Married Isaac Webster.
Sarah Webster, [6] born April 4, 1809; died Feb. 2, 1899.
Married 1st Dr. Isham Railey, 1835; no issue.
Married 2nd Col. John H. Slaughter, July 19, 1849.
Martha Randolph Slaughter, [7] born Sept. 29, 1850; died Dec. 16, 1878.
Married Mark Hardin Railey, Jan. 15, 1868.
Gabriel Webster Slaughter, [7] born Aug. 3, 1852; died Mar. 19, 1874.
Susanna Hord Slaughter, [7] born Sept. 3, 1856.
Pauline Pleasants. [5]
Susanna Randolph Pleasants. [5]
Married 1st Graves Storres.
Married 2nd William Trueheart.
Gov. James Pleasants. [5]
Married Susan Rose.

In the home of the Pleasants family at Norwick, England, there was born, in 1643, a son whose name was John Pleasants. After receiving the benefits of a college education in the country of his nativity he sailed for America and landed in Virginia during the year 1668. Impressed with the opportunities that the new country and his surroundings offered he settled at "Curles," in Henrico county, with the determination to give his best efforts in the cause of home and country. Soon thereafter he wooed and won a life partner whose name was Jane Tucker and these two reared an interesting family of children who gave to Virginia many sturdy men and women who did well their duty in the cause of that freedom for which so many patriotic Virginians sacrificed their lives. His grandson, John Pleasants, of

"Pique-Nique," married Susanna Woodson, and their son, James Pleasants, of "Contention," married Anna Randolph. 4th daughter of Col. Isham Randolph, and their son, James Pleasants, was United States Senator and Governor of Virginia. The descendants of John Pleasants and Jane Tucker intermarried with the Jordans, Venables, Randolphs, Woodsons, Mosbys Meads, Adairs, Minors, Flemings and many other Virginia families, and so much in love with the old State with its traditions and history that but few of the names have been adopted by other states. In fact they usually drift back to the old State after a few years domicile elsewhere.

THE MAYOS AND THEIR RAILEY CONNECTIONS.

William Mayo. [1]
Married Joan Mayo.
Joseph Mayo, [2] born Aug. 17, 1656; died Nov. 10, 1691.
Married Elizabeth Hooper.
Major William Mayo. [3] born Nov. 4, 1684: died Oct. 28, 1744.
Married 1st Francis Gould.
Married 2nd Anne Perrott, 1732.
Daniel Mayo, [4] born 1733
Married Thirza Howard, 1753.
Col. William Mayo, [5] born 1754.
Married Catharine Swann, 1772.
Jouette Mayo, [6] born may 24, 1773.
Married Seth Ligon.
Daniel Mayo, [c] born Mar. 12, 1775.
Married 1st Nancy Hamblin.
Married 2nd Elizabeth Judith Crump.
Elizabeth Mayo, [6] born April 10, 1777.
Married Martin Railey, Feb. 27, 1794.
Mary Mayo, [6] born July 12, 1779.
Married Charles Railey, April 4, 1796.
Catharine Swann Mayo, [6] born Aug. 16, 1781.
Married William Mayo.
Nancy Mayo. [6] born 1783.
Married Joseph Randolph Railey, July 13, 1809.
William Mayo, [6] born 1785.
Married Caroline Fleming Pleasants.
Francis Sweeny Mayo, [6] born 1787.
Married William Rodman.
Thirza Howard Mayo, [6] born 1789.
Married John Rowan Steele.
John Mayo. [4]
Married Mary Tabb.
Col. John Mayo. [5]
Married Abigail de Hart.

William Mayo, the first of the name known to the American line, and his wife, Joan, were residents of Bugley, Witshire county, England in the year 1620. Their grandson, Major William Mayo, sailed from his native land for Barbadoes, East India, during the year 1727, where he was engaged in promoting several enterprises in that region for some years with varying success, but finally decided to cast his lot with the American colony that was then struggling with the savage red men in the forests of North America and he and his first wife, Francis Gould, set sail for America about 1733, with a determination to brave the dangers that beset all settlers of the new country. Between the period of his arrival in America, and his death in 1744, he was Major of Virginia militia and surveyed many of the State and county lines of the State. His grandson, Col. William Mayo, who married Catharine Swann, was an officer of the Revolution and a man of considerable wealth and much social and political influence. His home was at Richmond, Va., where three of his daughters were married to three of the Raileys. His uncle, John Mayo, married Mary Tabb. He was a member of Burgesses from 1769 to 1775, member of the State Convention, 1775-6, and his eldest son, Col. John Mayo, was the projector of the celebrated Mayo bridge just below the falls of the James River at Richmond. This bridge was built at his individual expense as the State failed to co-operate with him. He married Abigail de Hart, daughter of one of New Jersey's foremost lawyers and member of the first Continental Congress. The eldest daughter of Col. John Mayo and Abigail de Hart was Marie Mayo, who married General Winfield Scott. She is said to have been a woman of rare beauty and many accomplishments as was her sister, Julia, who married Dr. Robert Henry Cabell, an eminent physician of Virginia. The Powhatan estate in the suburbs of Richmond, one of the most desirable in the State, was in possession of the Mayo's from 1740 until the period of the Civil War. Dr. Robert Mayo, who died in Washington, D. C., during the year 1864, left uncompleted a genealogical history of the Mayo family. Tradition says that Major William Mayo, John Railey and one of the Pleasants family, whose first name I do not recall, were the founders of and planned the laying off of the city of Richmond. The Mayos were intermarried with the Howards, Swanns, Randolphs, Fitzhughs, Scotts, Pleasants, Meads, Woodsons, Flemings and Steeles of Virginia.

ELIZABETH C. RAILEY 3RD

BORN OF JOHN RAILEY AND ELIZABETH RANDOLPH; MARRIED CAPT. JOHN BULLOCK, JR.

THEIR DESCENDANTS.

John Railey-[1]Elizabeth Randolph.

Elizabeth C. Railey, [2] born April 26, 1757.

Married Captain John Bullock, Jr., Sept. 9, 1786.

Jane Railey Bullock, [3] born Aug. 23, 1787; died June 9, 1833.

Married David Anderson, Dec. 5, 1805.

Sarah Elizabeth Anderson, [4] born Oct. 3, 1806; died Dec., 1807

Thomas Lilbourne Anderson, [4] born Dec. 8, 1808; died Mar. 6, 1885.

Married 1st Russella Easton, April 19, 1832.
Married 2nd Fannie Winchell, June 27, 1843.
Rufus Easton Anderson, [5] born Jan. 22, 1833; died 1910.
Married Cornelia Thompson, Jan. 11, 1854.
Edwin Lilbourne Anderson, [6] born Jan. 30, 1855; died 1910.
Married 1st Nannie Harrison, May 15, 1877.
Married 2nd ———.
Edna Francis Anderson, [7] born Aug. 12, 1878.
Tuthill Anderson, [7] born 1881; died 1884.
Russell Easton Anderson, [6] born Oct. 5, 1856; died May 24, 1857.
Margaret Thompson Anderson, [6] born July 28, 1858.
Married Harry Hamilton Markell, Oct. 29, 1879.
Cornelia Thompson Markell, [7] born Jan. 6, 1881.
Married Wm. Logan Owsley, June 7, 1905.
William Logan Owsley, Jr., [8] born Dec. 20, 1908.
Harvey Hamilton Markell, Jr. [7] born Feb. 1, 1883.
Juliet Mitchell Markell, [7] born Nov. 16, 1887.
Married Thad Richardson Smith, Feb. 23, 1909.
Russell Yeatman Markell, [7] born Nov. 11, 1891.
George William Markell, [7] born Feb. 27, 1895.
Juliet Mitchell Anderson, [6] born Feb. 21, 1861.
Married J. Baxter Rightmire, Nov. 13, 1878.
Rufus Anderson Rightmire, [7] born Nov. 11, 1879.

Married Maude Jameison, April 23, 1901.
Marguerite Thompson Rightmire, [7] born Dec. 18, 1887.
Married Alonzo W. Mackey, Nov. 16, 1910.
Cornelia Francis Anderson, [6] born Oct. 14, 1869; died 1909.
Married Albert Raymond Betts, Sept. 21, 1887.
Albert Raymond Betts, Jr., [7] born Dec. 21, 1888.
Rufus Easton Anderson, Jr., [6] born Nov. 28, 1868; died Oct. 10, 1910.
Fannie Corrall Anderson, [6] born April 13, 1871; died Nov. 22, 1880.
Annie Yeatman Anderson, [6] born April 13, 1871; died Dec. 14, 1894.
William Russell Anderson, [5] born Mar. 15, 1835.
Married Annie McPheeters, May 31, 1860.
James McPheeters Anderson, [6] born June 4, 1861.
Married Minnie York, Oct, 1897.
Lucile Anderson, [7] born Aug. 1898.
Thomas Lilbourne Anderson, Jr., [6] born Aug. 23, 1865.
Married Lula F. Albertson, Dec. 3, 1890.
Cyrus Anderson, [7] born Mar. 14, 1895.
Rev. William Russell Anderson, Jr., [6] born Mar. 15, 1868.
Married Susie Effie Gufton, May 2, 1894.
Caroline McPheeters Anderson, [6] born 1870; died Aug., 1882.
Russella Easton Anderson, [6] born Oct. 20, 1872.
Married Rev. Clarence H. Newton, [7] Oct. 20, 1896.

Harriett Ann Newton, [7] born 1898.

Francis May Newton, [7] born 1900.

William Russell Newton, [7] born 1902.

Clare Montgomery Newton, [7] born 1902.

Ann McPheeters Anderson, [6] born Sept. 6, 1875.

Married Dr. Richard Stanley Battersley, June 24, 1909.

Mary Alby Anderson, [6] born April 18, 1878.

Married Otho Floyd Matthews, Dec. 25, 1900.

Samuel Shepherd Anderson, [5] born Feb. 26, 1838; died in the service of the Confederacy, 1865.

Thomas Lilbourne Anderson, Jr., [5] born Aug. 26, 1846: died Feb. 2, 1881.

Married Fannie Senteny, June 15, 1873.

Thomas Lilbourne Anderson, Jr., [6] born Nov. 7, 1874.

Married Gertrude Ballard, April 25, 1905.

Francis Elizabeth Anderson, [7] born April 24, 1909.

Elizabeth Anderson, [6] born Dec. 12, 1876.

Fannie Elizabeth Anderson, [5] born May 25, 1844.

Married Richard Tatlow, April 18, 1866.

R. Harry Tatlow, [6] born Feb. 3, 1867.

Married Letta Crow, Mar. 22, 1899.

Richard H. Tatlow, Jr., [7] born May 27, 1906.

Lawrence Tatlow, [7] born Dec. 9, 1908.

Mary Louise Tatlow, [6] born May 7, 1871.

Fannie Anderson Tatlow, [6] born June 10, 1879.

Married Wylie Morrison Browning, April 18, 1905.

Lee Tatlow Browning, [7] born Mar. 7, 1906.

Robert Vincent Browning, [7] born Aug. 23, 1907.

Genevieve Elizabeth Browning, [7] born Sept. 9, 1908.

Alberta Lee Tatlow, [6] born July 14, 1886.

Jane Randolph Anderson, [5] born Jan. 10, 1849.

Married William H. Claget, Nov. 12, 1872.

I. Anderson Claget, [6] born Aug. 21, 1873.

Married Catharine Watkins, May 10, 1909.

Dudley Malcolm Claget, [6] born Dec. 31, 1875.

Married Nora Robertson, Dec. 29, 1904.

Dudley Malcolm Claget, [7] born July 20, 1906.

John Robertson Claget, [7] born July 18, 1908.

Eleanor Claget, [7] born 1910.

Edith Claget, [6] born Sept. 16, 1882.

Married Wainwright Evans, July 9, 1908.

John Wainwright Evans, [7] born May 14, 1909.

Russella Easton Anderson, [6] born Nov. 3, 1852.

Mary Catharine Anderson, [6] born June 21, 1859.

Married Moses D. Thompson, June 19, 1886.

Alberta Anderson, [6] born July 29, 1862.

Married J. Howard Kelly, Jan., 1888.
Geraldine Kelly, [7] born Mar. 4, 1891.
J. Howard Kelly, Jr., [6] born Sept. 3, 1897.
Joseph Easton Anderson, [5] born Mar. 11, 1861.
Dr. Albert Gallatin Anderson, [4] born April 23, 1811; died 1850.
Married Elizabeth Muldrow.
Walter Anderson, [5] born July 2, 1845.
Married Mrs. Martine S. Green.
Lilbourne Morris Anderson, [5] born Mar. 12, 1879.
Married Willie Strode, Nov. 12, 1904.
Martine Anderson, [7] born 1905.
Albert G. Anderson, [5] born Aug. 17, 1847.
Married Sarah Elizabeth Brown, Feb. 18, 1867.
Lillian Belle Anderson, [6] born Mar. 14, 1869.
Married Walter B. Moore, Jan. 2, 1886.
Georgia Lee Moore, [7] born Sept. 30, 1887.
Clifton Albert Moore. [7]
Roscoe Edward Moore. [7]
Anderson W. Moore. [7]
Fannie Belle Moore. [7]
Sarah Elizabeth Moore. [7]
Lutie Garnett Anderson, [6] born May 12, 1874.
Married Preston V. Matthews, Sept. 30, 1893.
Sarah Lee Matthews, [7] born July 19, 1895.
Elizabeth Maria Anderson, [6] born Mar. 19, 1877.
Married Alfred Bowles, Feb. 28, 1905.

Katharine Bowles, [7] born April 23, 1908.
Mary G. Anderson, [6] born Dec. 25, 1880.
Married James G. Sharp, Sept. 30, 1903.
Walter A. Anderson, [6] born May 8, 1882; died April 19, 1908.
Fannie Anderson, [6] born Dec. 26, 1886.
Married James S. Eaton, Nov. 24, 1909.
Martha Anderson Eaton, [7] born Sept. 20, 1910.
Lillian Anderson, [5] born Dec. 2, 1842.
Married John J. Dimmitt, June 12, 1864.
Rosa Dimmitt, [6] born Feb. 15, 1870.
Married John D. Hughes, June 1, 1893.
John Dimmitt, [6] born July 19, 1876.
Married Pearl Devere, Dec. 20, 1897.
David Thompson Anderson, [4] born Dec. 10, 1813.
Elizabeth Randolph Bullock, [3] born May 20, 1789; died Mar. 27, 1821.
Married Joseph Crockett, Jr., Mar. 25, 1813; no issue.
Maria Patterson Bullock, [3] born Mar. 12, 1791.
Married George Woodson Railey, Dec. 8, 1818.
Elizabeth Woodson Railey, [4] born 1819; died 1835.
Georgie Ellen Railey, [4] born 1821; died young.
Elizabeth C. Railey was born in Chesterfield county, Va., on the "Stonehenge" farm during the year 1757. She was the 3rd born

of John Railey and Elizabeth Randolph. She married Captain John Bullock, Jr., an officer throughout the Revolutionary War, Sept. 9, 1786. Three daughters were born to them while they were residents of Virginia. They came to Kentucky and settled at or near Bowling Green in 1800, or perhaps a few years later. I am sorry not to be able to trace the line of Captain John Bullock, Jr., through the various families of that name in Virginia. Their eldest daughter, Jane Railey Bullock, was married to David Anderson, Dec. 5, 1805, whose death occurred about 1827. Within a short period after his death his widow, with her three children and Elizabeth Bullock, her mother, accompanied by George Woodson Railey and his wife removed to Palmyra, Mo. David Anderson and his two brothers, Thomas and Samuel, were Scotch-Irish. They came with their parents from county Down, Banbridge, Ireland, about 1773, and settled in Albemarle county, Va. They were, as nearly all Scotch-Irish are, Presbyterians. Thos. L. Anderson, born 1808, in Warren county, Ky., eldest son of David Anderson and Jane Railey Bullock, entered the practice of law soon after their arrival at Palmyra, Mo. He was married to Russella Easton, daughter of Missouri's first Attorney General in 1832. During the years 1839 and 1840, he was a member of the State Legislature. In 1845 he was a member of the Constitutional Convention that revised the Constitution of that State. Was a presidential elector for Harrison, Taylor, Scott and Clay. After the disintegration of the Whig party he espoused the cause of the American party and was elected to Congress in 1856. When Congress assembled in 1857 it was found that the American party had only twelve Representatives in Congress, including John J. Crittenden and Humphrey Marshall, of Kentucky, and Thomas L. Anderson, of Missouri. After a conference they decided that it was useless to maintain an organization, so disbanded. A few allied themselves with the Republican party while the remainder, including Thos. L. Anderson, decided to affiliate with the Democrats. Thos. L. Anderson was returned to the National Congress. At the expiration of his four years' service the Civil War had been launched and Thos. L. Anderson decided to retire from political life. He was regarded as one of Missouri's ablest lawyers. An Elder in the Presbyterian Church and an unyielding advocate of temperance. He died in 1885 at Palmyra, Mo., ripe in years and full of honors worthily bestowed. His eldest son, Rufus Easton Anderson, born Jan., 1833, was also a lawyer of ability and Prosecuting Attorney of Marion county, Mo., for many years. He was prominent in Masonic circles, being Grand Master of the Grand Lodge of his State for years. William Russell Anderson, the second son of Thos. L. Anderson, born 1835, is also a prominent lawyer of Palmyra. He graduated at the University of

121

Virginia and served in the Missouri Legislature from 1873 to 1877. Samuel Shepherd Anderson, third son, born 1838, was a lawyer and practiced at Memphis, Tenn., until he cast his lot with the Confederacy in 1861, in which service he gave up his life in 1865. Thos. L. Anderson, Jr., fourth son, born 1846, was a lawyer and practiced at Louisiana, Mo. Quite a number of the grandsons of Thos. L. Anderson, Sr., were also lawyers and one granddaughter, Mary Alby Anderson, who was admitted to the bar at Palmyra, Mo., in 1898, when only twenty years of age. She was City Attorney of Palmyra during 1899, 1900 and 1901. She married Otho F. Matthews, a lawyer of Macon, Mo., Dec., 1902, when she retired from the law and has written several books that have given her an enviable place in the literary world, one of her productions being "Love vs. Law." The grandsons, who are practicing law, are Thos. L. Anderson, born at Louisiana, Mo., 1874. He is practicing law at St. Louis, and is at present City Attorney of that city. Walter Anderson, son of Dr. Albert Gallatin Anderson, practiced law at Hannibal, Mo., where his son, Lilbourne Morris Anderson, is now practicing and is City Attorney. Thos. L. Anderson, born 1865, son of Wm. Russell Anderson, is practicing law at Hannibal, Mo.

Albert Gallatin Anderson, born 1811, was an eminent physician in his day, and practiced medicine at Philadelphia, Mo. His health becoming impaired from exposure he sought a milder climate and in 1849, in company with his father-in-law, Col. Wm. Muldrough, formerly of Kentucky he went to California where he died shortly thereafter. Dr. Richard Stanley Battersby practices medicine at Shelbina, Mo. Wm. H. Clagget is a Presbyterian minister and lives in Pennsylvania. His two sons, Anderson and Dudley Clagget, are Presbyterian ministers, the former living in Arkansas and the latter at St. Joseph, Mo. William Russell Anderson, Jr., born Mar., 1868, is a Presbyterian minister and at present pastor of the church at Shelbyville, Ky. Clarence Hitchcock Newton is a Presbyterian minister and doing work at the station at Kiunchow Hainan, China. The most of the descendants of Capt. John Bullock and Elizabeth Railey live in Missouri. Their second daughter, Elizabeth Randolph Bullock, married Joseph Crockett, Jr., of Kentucky, but left no issue. The third daughter, Maria Patterson Bullock, married her cousin, George Woodson Railey. They had two daughters neither of whom reached womanhood. George Woodson Railey was many years Post Master at Monticello, Mo., where he and his family are buried.

ISHAM RANDOLPH RAILEY 4TH

BORN OF JOHN RAILEY AND ELIZABETH RANDOLPH; MARRIED SUSANNA WOODSON.

THEIR DESCENDANTS.

John Railey [1]-Elizabeth Randolph.

Isham Randolph Railey, [2] born July 15, 1758; died Mar. 14, 1814.
Married Susanna Woodson, Sept. 17, 1784.

John Railey, [3] born July 18, 1785; died Aug. 7, 1844.
Married Elizabeth Railey, June 4, 1807.

John Woodson Railey, [4] born Oct. 4, 1812; died Sept. 30, 1874.
Married Nancy Farris Nunn, Oct. 4, 1832.

Caroline Railey, [5] born Mar. 6, 1835.
Married William Cary, May 18, 1854.

Evaline Cary, [6] born Mar. 13, 1855.

Julia Ann Cary, [6] born Sept. 27, 1856.
Married 1st Allen K. Walker, July 26, 1874.
Married 2nd James S. Copeland, Mar., 1885.

Edna M. Walker, [7] born Dec. 10, 1875.
Married John Chappell, Sept. 20, 1893.

Elmer Louis Chappell, [8] born April 20, 1895.

Dean Jennings Chappell, [8] born Jan. 3, 1897.

Walker Chappell, [8] born Sept. 22, 1899.

James Chappell, [8] born Jan. 2, 1901.

Minnie N. Walker, [7] born Oct. 4, 1877.

Allen J. Walker, [7] born July 24, 1880.
Married Mary Cunningham, April 19, 1906.

Julia E. Walker, [8] born Feb. 3, 1907.

Frank Kendrick Walker, [8] born July 17, 1908.

Hallie N. Walker, [8] born Aug. 15, 1910.

Bessie N. Copeland, [7] born Feb. 6, 1886.

Susie S. Copeland, [7] born Aug. 29, 1888.

Robert W. Copeland, [7] born Sept. 26, 1890.

Ella W. Copeland, [7] born Aug. 2, 1892.

Jesse J. Copeland, [7] born Dec. 30, 1893.

John Herbert Copeland, [7] born Dec. 30, 1893.

Joseph F. Copeland, [7] born April 23, 1895.

Mary E. Cary, [6] born Nov. 12, 1858.
Married E. E. McAfee, July 27, 1884.

Charles Elmore McAfee, [7] born Jan. 9, 1886.
Married Bertha Railey, April 28, 1910.

William Leroy McAfee, [7] born Feb. 13, 1889.

Viola A. McAfee, [7] born Feb. 17, 1891.

Lady Rachael McAfee, [7] born Feb. 3, 1893.

William Woodson Cary,[6] born Nov. 16, 1862.

Susan Ann Railey,[5] born June 9, 1837.

Isham Tarleton Railey,[5] born Dec. 18, 1840.

Married Loretta M. Bailey, Dec. 2, 1869.

Annie Farris Railey,[6] born Sept. 18, 1870.

Married W. L. Herndon, Nov. 24, 1891.

Clara Herndon,[7] born Oct., 1892.

Mary Elizabeth Railey,[6] born Sept. 29, 1872.

Married F. R. Martin, Sept., 1889.

Laura Martin,[7] born July 2, 1890.

Annie Woodson Martin,[7] born Mar. 1, 1894.

Ernest Martin,[7] born Nov. 4, 1898.

N. P. Railey,[6] born Nov. 23, 1875.

John A. Railey,[6] born Mar. 30, 1879.

Married Nannie Griffith, Feb., 1905.

John A. Railey, Jr.,[7] born Jan. 7, 1906.

Robert Woodson Railey,[7] born Sept., 1907.

Aubrey Lee Railey,[7] born Sept., 1909.

Louis Railey,[6] born Oct. 17, 1881.

Married Martha Ecton, June 22, 1909.

W. T. Railey,[6] born May 4, 1884.

Joseph W. Railey,[6] born April 3, 1887.

Edward T. Railey,[6] born Jan. 16, 1890.

Robert L. Railey,[6] born Mar. 2, 1894.

Isabella Railey,[5] born Jan. 4, 1845.

John Randolph Railey,[5] born Mar. 4, 1850.

Married Margaret French, Feb. 23, 1881.

Haydon W. Railey,[6] born Dec. 13, 1881.

Married Lee W. Symms, Oct., 1906.

Bertha Railey,[6] born Feb. 25, 1883.

Married Charles McAfee, April 29, 1910.

Estelle Railey,[6] born July 25, 1886.

Mattie Railey,[6] born July 10, 1889.

Married Rector Herndon, Mar., 1910.

Boone Railey,[5] born Aug. 20, 1852; died Aug. 8, 1871.

Caroline Railey,[4] born Aug., 1815; died 1850.

Married 1st Dr. Joseph Wilson, 1833.

Married 2nd Rev. W. E. Milam, 1837.

Elizabeth McCormick Wilson,[5] born 1834; died 1845.

Tarleton Railey,[3] born Feb., 1787; died June, 1810.

Elizabeth Randolph Railey,[3] born 1792; died 1866.

Married J. B. McCormick, 1812; no issue.

Randolph Railey,[3] born Dec. 19, 1794; died May, 1873.

Married 1st Caroline Crittenden, 1822.

Married 2nd Mary Hunter, 1837.

John Crittenden Railey, [4] born 1823; died on Gulf of Mexico returning from Mexican War.

Margaret Ann Railey, [4] born 1825; died 1839.

Caroline Crittenden Railey, [4] born 1827; died 1839.

Randolph Railey, Jr., [4] born Oct. 11, 1838; died May, 1882.

Married Sallie Thornton, Feb. 13, 1867.

Drake Carter Railey, [5] born 1868; died 1898.

Emma Railey, [4] born Aug. 14, 1841.

Married Rev. Alexander Henry Mar. 26, 1859.

Mary Henry, [5] born Sept. 26, 1862.

Married M. W. Brun, April 25, 1896.

Mary Woodson Brun, [6] born Oct. 13, 1900.

Randolph Henry, [5] born Feb. 3, 1864; died Mar. 8, 1889.

Rev. Alexander Henry, [5] born April 8, 1865.

Married Wilhelmina Berryman, Oct. 8, 1890.

Catharine Clifton Henry, [6] born Oct. 7, 1891.

Married Alfred Mosby, Oct. 8, 1909.

Frank Berryman Henry, [6] born Nov. 24, 1892.

Emma Yeaman Henry, [6] born Nov. 27, 1893.

Alexander Henry, Jr., [6] born Jan. 8, 1901.

James Henry, [5] born Sept. 2, 1866.

Married Nellie D. Ware, June 30, 1901.

Alexander Henry, [6] born July 25, 1905.

Emma Railey Henry, [6] born Aug. 24, 1907.

Margaret Henry, [5] born Nov. 21, 1867.

Married Dr. John Leonard Harris, Feb. 5, 1890.

Alexander Henry Harris, [6] born July 8, 1891.

Emma Railey Harris, [6] born Sept. 21, 1894.

Margaret Leonard Harris, [6] born Dec. 19, 1896.

William Henry, [5] born July, 1869.

Isham Railey, [4] born April 2, 1846; died 1907.

Married Ezza Sanders, May 26, 1869.

Margaret Sanders Railey, [5] born June 2, 1870.

Married Buford Twyman, Aug. 1, 1888.

Ezza Railey Twyman, [6] born April 24, 1889.

Morton Sanders Railey, [5] born Aug. 14, 1871.

Married Ida B. O'Bannon, July 25, 1900.

Isham Railey, [6] born May 7, 1905.

Ida Dixon Railey, [6] born April 17, 1907.

Orville Browning Railey, [6] born Sept. 9, 1909.

Mary Stuart Railey, [5] born June 9, 1873.

Married Ben W. Williams, Nov. 12, 1894.

John Stuart Williams, [6] born July 8, 1895.

Marjorie Williams, [6] born June 13, 1902.

Railey Woodson Williams, [6] born Nov. 29, 1905.

Louise Sharon Railey, [5] born June 21, 1874.
Married John M. McConnell, Nov. 21, 1900.
Sue Tevis Railey, [5] born Aug. 7, 1875.
Edith Hunter Railey, [5] born Dec. 25, 1879.
Lawrence Amsden Railey, [5] born Mar. 1, 1884.
Married Josephine Marshall, June 2, 1909.
Catharine C. Railey, [4] born Jan. 23, 1848.
Married George M. Fishback, June 1, 1869.
Emma Woodson Fishback, [5] born Mar. 3, 1870.
Married Rev. M. V. P. Yeaman, June 19, 1899.
George F. Yeaman, [6] born July 5, 1902.
Jane Lyle Fishback, [5] born April 12, 1872.
Married LeGrand Atwood, Jan. 1, 1903.
George F. Atwood, [6] born Oct. 5, 1903.
Thomas C. Atwood, [6] born Aug. 14, 1905.
Ezza Railey Fishback, [5] born Dec. 11, 1875.
George Taylor Fishback, [5] born June 6, 1877.
Married Elizabeth Bowman, June 12, 1905.
George Taylor Fishback, Jr., [6] born Mar. 18, 1906.
Catharine C. Fishback, [6] born April 12, 1907.
Catharine Mary Fishback, [5] born Mar. 1, 1880.
Married J. T. Stone, Jan. 18, 1905.

Randolph F. Stone, [6] born Jan. 22, 1906.
Randolph Railey Fishback, [5] born Oct. 4, 1887.
Married Cyrene Hunter, Oct. 25, 1909.
William Hunter Fishback, [6] born June 27, 1910.
William Hunter Railey, [4] born April 2, 1850; died Feb. 7, 1891.
Married Martha McConnell, Feb., 1872.
Randolph Woodson Railey, [5] born Dec. 3, 1872.
Robert McConnell Railey, [5] born Feb. 5, 1874.
William Hunter Railey, Jr., [5] born June 1, 1875.
Married Mary Lane, April 2, 1901.
James Railey, [5] born May 22, 1879.
Married Gladys Blair, Sept. 10, 1909.
Mary Railey, [5] born Feb. 13, 1882.
Married R. F. Given, Aug. 30, 1906.
Emma Railey, [5] born May 11, 1884.
Martha Railey, [5] born Sept. 10, 1885.
Caroline Railey, [3] born Feb. 12, 1796; died Mar. 3, 1859.
Married Joseph Frazier, July 29, 1825.
Sarah E. Frazier, [4] born Oct. 5, 1830; died Oct. 25, 1854.
Married P. I. Railey, Jr., Oct. 22, 1851.
Josephine Railey, [5] born Sept. 22, 1852.
Married Robert Ward Macey, Nov. 21, 1872.

Pattie Railey Macey, [6] born Mar. 24, 1876.

Sadie Macey, [6] born June 9, 1877.

Robert Ward Macey, Jr., [6] born Oct. 8, 1879.

Railey Woodson Macey, [6] born Aug. 30, 1881.

Jordan Railey, [3] born Aug. 14, 1797; died Dec. 7, 1816.

Josiah Woodson Railey, [3] born Nov. 18, 1798; died April 5, 1818.

Martha Woodson Railey, [3] born Aug. 15, 1802; died July 17, 1886.

Nancy Railey, [3] born 1803; died Oct. 29, 1821.

Married David Thornton, 1820.

Dr. Isham Railey, [3] born 1805; died Sept. 4, 1845.

Married Sarah Webster, 1835; no issue.

Isham Randolph Railey, the 4th of John Railey and Elizabeth Randolph was born in Virginia on the "Stonehenge" farm near Richmond in 1758. He came to Kentucky with his brother, Thomas Railey about 1780, and settled in Woodford county near Versailles. His estate was known as "Vine Grove" and remained in possession of the Railey descendants until ten years ago it became the property of Samuel Woolridge, Jr. Feeling the need of a companion and housekeeper he returned to Virginia during the year 1784, and married Susanna Woodson the 6th of Col. John Woodson and Dorothy Randolph. They returned to Kentucky accompanied by William Railey, after a perilous journey through the wilderness, inhabited principally by savages, and threatened constantly by vicious wild beasts that roamed the forests. Finally reaching their newly made home in the boundless bluegrass country they entered upon the duties that lay before them with brave hearts and lofty purposes and right well did they succeed. They raised a family of children, each of whom proved a blessing to the home. Their first born, John Railey, married his cousin, Elizabeth Railey, of Virginia, and settled in Cumberland county, Ky., about 1807, where they lived and died. John Woodson Railey, their son, moved from Cumberland county, Ky., to Marshall, Mo., where his descendants live today and they are very numerous.

Randolph Railey, the 4th of Isham R. Railey and Susanna Woodson, married first, Caroline Crittenden, of Frankfort, Ky. They had several children, only one of whom lived to years of maturity, and he enlisted with the Kentucky volunteers to the Mexican War and died upon the Gulf on his return trip. His name was John Crittenden Railey and the older Raileys, who remember him well, speak of him as the handsomest man in all Kentucky. Randolph Railey's second marriage was to Mary Hunter, of Versailles, Ky. There were five children by this marriage. Randolph Railey, who married Sallie Thornton; Isham Railey, who married Ezza Sanders; Emma Railey, who married Rev. Alexander Henry, a Presbyterian minister; Catharine Railey, who married George M. Fishback, and Wm. H. Railey, who married Martha McConnell. The most of their descendants live in Kentucky. Mrs. Robt. Ward Macey, of Versailles, Ky., who is of this line, is a great granddaughter of Thos. Railey, Isham Randolph Railey and William Railey, brothers; and of Martha Woodson, Susanna Woodson and Judith Woodson, sisters.

RAILEY-RANDOLPH (Cont.)

Through the indulgence of the Editor of the "Register," to whom I am so deeply indebted for numerous favors, I want to make a request of the relatives. I have earnestly endeavored in my long and patient effort to get my family record correct in every detail, but I recognize the fact that with such a multitude of notes to run over for verification it is possible that a few minor errors may have crept in. If you find such to be the case I will thank you to advise me of it that I may correct my manuscript, as I shall preserve it. I will also request that you continue the record of names and dates of marriages, births and deaths as they occur in your particular lines so that if at some future period any relative concludes to publish in a more elaborate way a history of these people, the additional data will be more easily obtained. I already have my manuscript prepared with that object in view, giving to each descendant a short sketch. Many of those sketches are already written in my manuscript.

To facilitate the work and relieve me of so much correspondence I urgently request that each relative who subscribed for the Register make me up a list of all descendants of whom they have any knowledge telling me what business each male is engaged in, his religious tenets, political affiliations and other matters of interest. Do likewise as to the husbands of female descendants. In this way I can complete my work in a short while and have it ready for publication on short notice should any of the relatives conclude to publish it. In this way you could also compensate me for my long and expensive labor of love in placing before you your several lines of ancestry covering a period of more than two and a half centuries. I hope that future generations will not lower the standard of veneration to God and respect for manly men set by our ancestors.

In conclusion I will say that the descendants of Thomas Railey and Martha Woodson, Isham Railey and Susanna Woodson and William Railey and Judith Woodson come from Col. John Woodson and Dorothy Randolph, while those of Anna Railey and Mathew Pleasants and Randolph Railey and Martha Randolph Pleasants come from Tarlton Woodson and Ursula Fleming. Tarlton Woodson was the uncle of Col. John Woodson. In order that you may know all about your Woodson relatives I will suggest that you will make no mistake in subscribing for "The Woodson Family" soon to be published by Mr. H. M. Woodson of Memphis, Tenn. He goes into full detail about the Woodsons while I merely bring down the direct line. He has spent twenty years on the work and I am sure it will be worth having. Very truly and affectionately your kinsman,

WM. E. RAILEY.
September 12, 1911.

ANNA RAILEY

Fifth born of John Railey and Elizabeth Randolph. Married Mathew Pleasants. Their descendants:

John Railey [1] -Elizabeth Randolph.

Anna Railey, [2] born September 16, 1759; died 1826.

Married Mathew Pleasants, February, 1784.

Susanna Pleasants, [3] born December 2, 1785; died 1865.

Caroline Fleming Pleasants, [3] born July 27, 1787; died February 21, 1852.

Married William Mayo, 1808.

Dr. Addison F. Mayo, [4] born December 6, 1809; died

Married first Francis St. Clair September 7, 1831; married second Susan M. Wilson, June 19, 1840.

Addison F. Mayo, Jr., [5] born October 18, 1841.

Married Catherine Gertrude Hands, September 30, 1862.

William Frederick Mayo, [6] born June 1, 1865.

Edward Everitt Mayo, [6] born September 24, 1866.

Married Louise Willoughby, June 30, 1908.

Francis Gertrude Mayo, [6] born April 1, 1869.

Married Rufus Edgar Turpin, January 5, 1889.

Catherine Randolph Mayo, [6] born July 28, 1871.

Thomas Jefferson Mayo, [6] born February 4, 1874.

Anna Lillian Mayo, [6] born July 4, 1879.

Married William Henry Tharp, September 4, 1902.

Georgianna Mayo, [4] born April 11, 1813; died October 16, 1840.

Married Dr. William P. Harriman, January 12, 1837.

Dr. William P. Harriman, Jr., [5] born May 28, 1838.

Married Elizabeth Russell, April 5, 1866.

William Peyton Harriman, [6] born December 28, 1866; died May 8, 1883.

Russell Harriman, [6] born March 24, 1868.

Married Josephine Stephens, 1906.

Russell Harriman, Jr.,[7] born January 31, 1907.

Albert C. Harriman,[6] born November 22, 1870.

Married Hortense Adams, April 10, 1900.

Mary Margaret Harriman,[7] born July 3, 1903.

Albert C. Harriman, Jr.,[7] born September 14, 1905.

William Adams Harriman,[7] born April 6, 1909.

Elizabeth Belle Harriman,[6] born January 20, 1872; died May 18, 1908.

Married William C. Ross, June 1, 1892.

Margaret Ross,[7] born September 7, 1903.

Georgianna Harriman,[5] born April 30, 1840; died June 27, 1902.

Married J. F. Rodgers, December 31, 1861.

Frank Rodgers,[6] born February 22, 1869.

Married Emma Thro, November 28, 1893.

Etta Rodgers,[6] born April 7, 1872.

Married A. J. Fluke, January 26, 1899.

George Fluke,[7] born June 16, 1900.

Vivian Fluke,[7] born October 21, 1903.

Frederick E. Mayo,[4] born January 8, 1816; died.

Married first, Mary Rankin; second, Mary McDowell.

F. E. Mayo, Jr.[5]

Peyton Randolph Mayo,[4] born May 9, 1818.

Married, first, Mary James; second, Caroline Prentice.

Caroline L. Mayo,[4] born March 6, 1825; died January 7, 1873.

Married Dr. William P. Harriman, May, 1849. (Her brother-in-law.)

John Hulsey Harriman,[5] born November 25, 1851.

Married Mollie Briggs, May 19, 1874.

Robert S. Harriman,[6] born May 25, 1875.

Married Jennie Stites, June 29, 1904.

Lucile Harriman,[7] born May 31, 1905.

Jennie Harriman,[7] born December 31, 1907.

Joseph Halsey Harriman,[7] born May 14, 1910.

Leslie M. Harriman,[6] born March 25, 1878.

Married Mabel Chamberlain, June 11, 1900.

Briggs Harriman,[6] born September 30, 1886.

Married Iva True, March 28, 1910.

Belle Harriman,[5] born 1853; died 1866.

Jennie Harriman,[5] born February 27, 1854.

Married Joseph A. Thompson, October 19, 1876.

Carolyne Thompson,[6] born January 8, 1879.

Married B. S. Buckridge, October 19, 1901.

Mary Elizabeth Buckridge,[7] born March 4, 1903.

Carolyne Buckridge,[7] born September 19, 1906.

Josephine Thompson,[6] born December 5, 1881.

Married Edward T. McDavid, November 9, 1904.

Emma Catherine McDavid, [7] born April 3, 1907.

Gertrude Thompson, [6] born December 6, 1891.

Robert L. Harriman, [5] born March 12, 1856.

Married Rosa Stephens, February 13, 1883.

Louise Harriman, [6] born June 30, 1884.

Married Wilbur Wallace, March 21, 1906.

Helen Harriman, [6] born July 16, 1890.

Regis A. Harriman, [5] born September 18, 1858.

Married Grace McCutchen, April 24, 1889.

John McCutchen Harriman, [6] born February 11, 1890.

Grace Virginia Harriman, [6] born December 19, 1898.

Caroline Mayo Harriman, [5] born November 22, 1862.

Married John D. McCutchen, November 8, 1885.

Louise McCutchen, [6] born December 1, 1886.

Married Griffin Olson, May 15, 1907.

John Olson, [7] born February 5, 1908.

Isabella McCutchen, [6] born July 23, 1893.

John D. McCutchen, Jr., [7] born August 9, 1898.

George Woodson Pleasants, [3] born July 1, 1789; died 1812.

Peyton Randolph Pleasants, [3] born April 19, 1791; died 1817.

Married Ann Catherine Humphries. (No issue.)

Pauline Pleasants, [3] born July 16, 1793; died 1816.

Married Robert Johnston.

Jane Johnston, [4]

Married, first, William Agin; second, John T. Lyle.

Pauline Lyle, [5] died, aged 14 years.

Annot Mary Lyle, [5] died, aged 16 years.

John Lyle, [5] died young.

Robert Lyle, [5] died, aged 12 years.

Benjamin Franklin Pleasant's, born November 10, 1795; died June 2, 1879.

Married Isabella McCalla Adair, February, 1817.

Pauline Pleasants, [4] born December 13, 1817; died, June 23, 1829.

Ann Catherine Pleasants, [4] born May 22, 1820; died, September 5, 1880.

Married Rev. Mason Noble, 1836.

Rev. Joseph Franklin Noble, [5] born August 25, 1837.

Married Emma M. Prime, June 4, 1862.

Mary Noble, [6] born September 22, 1863.

Married Frederick R. Dudley, June 8, 1892.

Margaret Adair Dudley, [7] born April 23, 1895.

Isabella Pleasants Noble, [6] born December 22, 1864.

Married Henry McKeag, August 16, 1893.

Catherine McKeag, [7] born July 21, 1894.

Catherine Pauline Noble, [6] born July 5, 1872; died January 23, 1878.

Henry Prime Noble, [6] born May 27, 1874.
Married Letitia M. Demarest, October 12, 1905.
Henry Prime Noble, Jr., [7] born January 30, 1907.
Bertha Demarest Noble, [7] born January 19, 1909.
Alice Noble, [6] born May 24, 1878.
Married Francis M. Ball, November 28, 1906.
Francis M. Ball, Jr., [7] born August 29, 1907.
Rev. Mason Noble, [5] born September 12, 1842.
Married Mary E. Adams, September 12, 1867.
George Adams Noble, [6] born June 23, 1868.
Katherine Pleasants Noble, [6] born February 2, 1870.
Rose Noble, [6] born September 6, 1872.
Mason Noble, [6] born October 16, 1874.
Married Minnie Carter, 1906.
Mary Elizabeth Noble, [7] born August 31, 1907.
Mason Noble, Jr., [7] born May 9, 1909.
John Adair Noble, [6] born December 30, 1879.
Carl Noble, [6] born December 26, 1881.
Joseph Franklin Noble, [6] born August 20, 1885; died August 22, 1887.
Rev. George Pleasants Noble, [5] born January 4, 1844.
Married Elizabeth T. Ketcham, September 15, 1868.
Dr. Henry T. Noble, [6] born January 27, 1870.
Married Caroline Leslie Place, December 30, 1896.

George Pleasants Noble, [7] born November 4, 1897.
Rosalind Noble, [7] born March 17, 1900.
Franklin Pleasants Noble, [6] born March 25, 1872.
Married Jennie Francis Backhoven, June 18, 1898.
Jean Noble, [7] born April 23, 1899.
Enid Noble, [7] born June 30, 1901.
Elizabeth Noble, [7] born April 2, 1906.
Fannie Ketcham Noble, [6] born October 10, 1873.
Charles Noble, [6] born January 8, 1877.
Married Grace Charlick, October 22, 1902.
Manly C. Noble, [7] born April 25, 1907.
George Pleasants Noble, [6] born May 29, 1881.
Rev. Charles Noble, [5] born December 3, 1847.
Married first Alice Thomas, January 24, 1874, no issue; married second Mary S. Carlisle, June 16, 1886.
Judge George W. Pleasants, [4] born November 24, 1823, died October 22, 1902.
Married Sarah Bulkley, January 30, 1850,
Adair Pleasants, [5] born April 8, 1850.
Married Sarah Mary Crawford, May 2, 1888.
Dorothy Pleasants, [6] born March 18, 1889.
Mathew Pleasants, [6] born February 21, 1892.
Nannie Buell Pleasants, [5] born January 8, 1858.

Married Samuel A. Lynde, August 27, 1879.
Cornelius Lynde,[6] born February 20, 1881.
Married Bertha L. Pollock, November 25, 1908.
Margaret Emily Lynde,[7] born September 13, 1909.
Isabel Adair Lynde,[6] born October 9, 1883.
Married John Francis Dammann, Jr., November 16, 1909.
George Pleasants Lynde,[6] born March 13, 1887.
Isabel Adair Pleasants,[5] born April 13, 1860.
Married Benjamine Ford Orton, April 10, 1888.
Elen Adair Orton,[6] born December 12, 1890.
George B. Pleasants,[5] born June 26, 1867.
John Adair Pleasants,[4] born May 17, 1826, died November 19, 1893.
Married Virginia Cary Mosby, May 6, 1852.
Mary Webster Pleasants,[5] born February 21, 1853, died March 13, 1854.
Louise McLain Pleasants,[5] born October 24, 1855.
Catharine Noble Pleasants,[5] born April 8, 1857.
Married Judge Edmund Christian Minor, April 18, 1877.
Louise McLain Minor,[6] born March 3, 1878, died May 27, 1880.
Catharine Pleasants Minor,[6] born November 5, 1879, died September 30, 1887.
Virginia Adair Minor,[6] born July 19, 1882.
Married Edward Gilchrist, September 8, 1907.
Catharine Gilchrist,[7] born.
Edmund Christian Minor,[6] born January 10, 1885, died October 22, 1890.
Caroline Minor,[6] born August 19, 1887.
Anna Hyde Minor,[6] born December 3, 1890.
Lydia Mosby Pleasants,[5] born May 14, 1860.
Married Benjamine Ladd Purcell, April 14, 1893.
Martha Webb Purcell,[6] born March 26, 1894.
John Adair Purcell,[6] born May 13, 1900.
Lydia Mosby Purcell,[6] born May 9, 1902.
Benjamine Ladd Purcell, Jr.,[6] born July, 1903.
Rosaline Harrison Pleasants,[5] born September 6, 1864.
Married William Wharton Archer, May 24, 1893.
Adair Pleasants Archer,[6] born August 31, 1894.
Sheppard Archer,[6] born January 19, 1898.
William Wharton Archer, Jr.,[6] born June 13, 1902.
Edmund Minor Archer,[6] born September 28, 1904.
Mathew Franklin Pleasants,[4] born September 17, 1829; died November 2, 1906.
Married Lydia Mosby, October 6, 1852.
Isabella Adair Pleasants,[5] born October 21, 1853.
Married Reginald Gilham, October 16, 1888, no issue.
Virginia Mosby Pleasants,[5] born January 10, 1856.
L. McLain Pleasants,[5] born June 21, 1860; died June 29, 1903.

Married Hester Roberta Kyle, April 12, 1893.

Mathew Franklin Pleasants, [6] born March 4, 1894.

Roberta Kyle Pleasants, [6] born November 30, 1896.

Catherine Cellers Pleasants, [6] born September 25, 1898.

Mathew Pleasants, [5] born July 22, 1865; died September 24, 1867.

John Adair Pleasants, [5] born May 14, 1870; died January 7, 1904.

Elizabeth Randolph Pleasants, [3] born January 9, 1796; died December, 1881.

Married Douglass Young, 1835.

Susanna Railey Young, [4] born March 31, 1836.

Married Dr. T. K. Layton, December 2, 1856.

Jennie Layton, [5] born August 27, 1857.

Married Andrew Wallace, July 19, 1888. (No issue.)

Elizabeth Layton, [5] born September 16, 1859.

Married John M. Garth, January 28, 1879.

Jefferson Garth, [6] born February 15, 1880.

Mattie Garth, [6] born June 28, 1882.

Belle Garth, [6] born December 3, 1884.

Susanna Garth, [6] born February 3, 1887.

David W. Layton, [5] born June 14, 1861.

Married Maude Vance, May 25, 1892.

Kelby Vance Layton, [6] born March 3, 1893.

Barbara Layton, [6] born February 15, 1896.

Francis Layton, [6] born January 2, 1899.

David W. Layton, Jr., [6] born February 7, 1903.

Annie Layton, [6] born February 14, 1906.

Edward S. Layton, [6] born February 16, 1908.

Whitney Layton, [5] born May 9, 1864; died April 27, 1907.

Married Ida Yeaman, February 26, 1890.

Douglass Young Layton, [5] born October 27, 1866.

Married, Zadah McCulloch April 12, 1894.

Benjamine Pleasants Layton, [6] born May 20, 1896.

Douglass Young Layton, Jr., [6] born August 4, 1900.

Thomas K. Layton, Jr., [5] born February 28, 1869; died July 5, 1902.

Nannie Layton, [5] born September 18, 1871.

Married Charles J. Crabb, April 27, 1893.

Charles Layton Crabb, [6] born March 3, 1894.

Elizabeth Crabb, [6] born January 9, 1897.

Susan L. Layton, [5] born March 20, 1874.

Married Marshall B. Reid, August 7, 1895.

Marshall B. Reid, Jr., [6] born August 21, 1897.

Oscar L. Reid, [6] born February 12, 1900.

Hugh P. Layton, [5] born January 18, 1877.

Ambrose Young Layton, [5] born May 8, 1880.

Thomas Jefferson Pleasants, [3] born March 6, 1798; died 1817.

Mathew Pleasants,[3] born February 14, 1800; died 1818.

Anna Railey was the fifth born of John Railey and Elizabeth Randolph born on "Stonehenge" farm in 1759. She married Mathew Pleasants, third of John Pleasants of "Pique-nique" and Susanna Woodson. Mathew Pleasants was an uncle of Gov. Pleasants, of Virginia, and of Martha Randolph Pleasants, who married Randolph Railey, hence Anna Railey became by marriage the aunt of her brother Randolph Railey, and Mathew Pleasants, by marriage was the brother-in-law of his neice Martha Randolph Pleasants. Beside this, Anna Railey and Martha Randolph Pleasants were first cousins, their mothers being daughters of Col. Isham Randolph of "Dungeness," Va.

Susanna Woodson, the mother of Mathew Pleasants, was a daughter of Tarleton Woodson and Ursula Fleming from whom the Venables, Bates and many other prominent Virginia families sprung, and she was a first cousin of Col. John Woodson, who married Dorothy Randolph, another daughter of Col. Isham Randolph. The three Woodson girls who married three of the brothers of Anna Railey were daughters of Col. John Woodson and Dorothy Randolph, and hence the three Woodson girls married their first cousins, and it follows that they were second cousins and sisters-in-law to Mathew Pleasants, and first cousins and sisters-in-law of Mathew Pleasants' wife, Anna Railey.

Mathew Pleasants and his wife came to Kentucky from Virginia, about 1800 and settled in Woodford county, in the old Railey neighborhood where he died in 1816. His daughter Caroline Fleming Pleasants married William Mayo, the seventh son of Col. William Mayo and Catherine Swann of Richmond, Va., This couple moved to Cooper county, Mo., about 1846. Their son, Dr. Addison F. Mayo practiced medicine for many years in Kentucky. His descendants are now residents of Colorado.

George Anna Mayo, sister of Dr. Addison F. Mayo, married Dr. William P. Harriman. Their son Dr. Wm. P. Harriman, Jr., is interested in the banking business in Missouri, but has a winter residence in San Antonio, Texas, where he and his wife, who is related to the Throckmortons of Kentucky and Virginia, spend much of their time. Quite a number of this line are in the banking business in Missouri and Oklahoma.

Peyton Randolph Pleasants, fourth of Mathew Pleasants and Anna Railey married Ann Catharine Humphries. He died a few years after his marriage. If they had children I have not been able to get a line on them. His widow afterwards became Mrs. Knight, of Louisville, Ky.

Benjamine F. Pleasants, the sixth of Mathew Pleasants and Anna Railey married Isabella

Adair, daughter of General John Adair who served a term as Governor of Kentucky. Benjamine F. Pleasants lived at Harrodsburg, Ky., for many years after his marriage and was appointed to a position in the Treasury Department of the United States about 1830 under President Jackson's administration and moved his family to Washington City, where he made his home until his death in 1879. Many Kentuckians and Virginians who visited the Capital City prior to the Civil War made his hospitable home headquarters. Benjamine Pleasants and Isabella Adair had four children, one daughter and three sons who married and reared families. The three sons all adopted the profession of law and were successful lawyers. The daughter, Ann Catherine Pleasants, born at Harrodsburg, Ky., in 1820, married Rev. Mason Noble, a Presbyterian minister, in the City of Washington in 1836. He was a chaplain in the United States Navy for many years. Four children were born of this union all of whom, like the father, studied for the ministry. Joseph Franklin Noble, Mason Noble, Jr., and Charles Noble, being of the Congregational persuasion, and George Pleasants Noble adopted the Presbyterian faith. The Rev. Charles Noble is President of the Iowa College at Grinnell, Iowa. Carl Noble, son of the Rev. Mason Noble, Jr., is a lawyer at Jacksonville, Fla.

George W. Pleasants, third of Benjamine F. and Isabella, married Sarah Bulkley and settled in Illinois where he was elevated to a seat on the Supreme Court Bench and served consecutively for thirty years. His son, Adair Pleasants is now practicing law at Rock Island, Ill., and Nannie Buell Pleasants, daughter of Judge George W. Pleasants married Samuel A. Lynde, a lawyer of Chicago. They have two sons who are lawyers in Chicago.

John Adair Pleasants, fourth of Benjamine F. and Isabella, married his cousin, Virginia Cary Mosby, a descendant of Tarleton Woodson and Ursula Fleming. They settled at Richmond, Va., where he practiced law until his death in 1893. Their daughter Catharine Noble Pleasants married Judge Edmund Christian Minor, of Richmond, Va., where she and her sisters now reside.

Mathew F. Pleasants, fifth of Benjamine F. and Isabella, married his cousin, Lydia Mosby, sister of the wife of his brother John Adair Pleasants. He, too, settled at Richmond, Va., where he also practiced law until his death in 1906. To their daughter, Virginia Mosby Pleasants, I am very much indebted for assistance in tracing the line of her grandfather, Benjamine F. Pleasants. She and her sisters and brothers are residents of Richmond, Va.

Elizabeth Randolph Pleasants, the seventh of Mathew Pleasants and Anna Railey, was born at Richmond, Va., in 1796. She came with her parents to Kentucky when a mere child. She married Douglass Young in 1835 at Versailles, Ky., and resided on the old Jackson farm near Versailles, Ky., until they reached an advanced age. Only one child blessed this union whose name was Susan Railey Young. She married Dr. T. K. Layton and they raised a large family of children who have done well their part in life. Mrs. Andrew Wallace, of Versailles, Ky., is the only one of this line left in Kentucky, her brothers and sisters being residents of St. Louis, Mo., and neighboring towns.

Mrs. Elizabeth Randolph Young was an interesting old lady with a thorough knowledge of family history and traditions, and as a boy I learned much from her conversations that has been of great assistance to me in this work.

WILLIAM RAILEY

Sixth born of John Railey and Elizabeth Randolph. Married Judith Woodson. Their descendants:

John Railey, [1] Elizabeth Randolph.

William Railey, [2] born February 26, 1760; died February 8, 1818.

Married Judith Woodson, March, 1793.

William Randolph Railey, [3] born February 4, 1794; killed at the battle of the "River Raision."

Sarah Railey, [3] born March, 1796; died August, 1862.

Married, first, Thomas Railey, Jr., 1820; second, Parham Walhn, 1829.

William Randolph Railey, [4] born 1821; died 1840.

Judith Ann Walhn, [4] born June, 1830; died August, 1862.

Married Dr. William Steele White, March 18, 1853.

Dr. Thomas Phillip White, [5] born June, 1855; died 1902.

Married Eugene Dillman. (No issue.)

Judith Woodson Railey, [3] born March 15, 1799; died October 31, 1842.

Married P. I. Railey, August 21, 1817.

Martha Woodson Railey, [4] born February 10, 1820; died March 18, 1837.

Richard Henry Railey, [4] born April 26, 1823; died October 3, 1888.

Married Catherine Keith Hawkins, February 25, 1852.

William Edward Railey, [5] born December 25, 1852.

Married Annie H. Owsley, May 26, 1886.

Jennie Farris Railey, [6] born June 28, 1887.

Bertha Hontas Railey, [5] born April 26, 1854.

Married, first, Chas. Randolph Darnell, 1882; second, P. D. McBride, 1892.

P. Woodson Railey, [5] born July 24, 1864.

P. I. Railey, Jr., [4] born August 25, 1829.

Married, first, Sarah E. Frazier, October 22, 1851; second, Rebecca Gough, 1861; third, Seville Church, 1898.

Josephine Railey, born September 22, 1852.

Married Robert Ward Macey, November 21, 1872.

Pattie Railey Macey,⁶ born March 24, 1876.

Sadie Macey,⁶ born June 9, 1877.

Robert Ward Macey, Jr.,⁶ born October 8, 1879.

Railey Woodson Macey,⁶ born August 30, 1881. .

Thomas Jefferson Railey,⁴ born August 10, 1831; died August 18, 1851.

Laura L. Railey,⁴ born August 20, 1832; died August 24, 1847.

William Railey, the sixth born of John Railey and Elizabeth Randolph, was born at "Stonehenge," Chesterfield county, Virginia, February 26th, 1760. He came to Kentucky about 1784 and settled on a farm near Versailles, Ky., that he called "Liberty Hall." Railey's Station on the Louisville Southern Railway is located on the border of this farm. He built one of the first brick houses erected in Woodford county and it is standing today, more than one hundred and ten years after its completion. After getting everything in shape for a useful, busy and prosperous life he returned to Virginia, where in 1793 he married Judith Woodson, tenth born of Col. John Woodson and Dorothy Randolph. He raised but three children, one son and two daughters. His son William enlisted in the War of 1812 and was killed in battle at "The River Raision." He never recovered from this shock and died from grief a few years later. His descendants are but few and the most of them reside in Kentucky. There has been but one professional man in this line, Dr. Thomas Phillip White who was educated in Paris, France. He located at Cincinnati, Ohio, where he built up a lucrative practice, but death ensued when his usefulness was at its meridian height.

P. I. Railey, Jr., is the only living grandchild of William Railey and Judith Woodson and he has passed his eightieth birthday. His brother Richard Henry Railey died in 1888 and the tribute of the late Daniel M. Bowmar, Sr., in the columns of the "Woodford Sun" of that year is worth more than a towering shaft of marble. It is reproduced here:

"RICHARD H. RAILEY."

" 'Alas, poor Yorick, I knew him well.' The trite quotation is not unmeaning, for we did know him well, and he was, as Yorick was, a 'fellow of infinite jest.'

"Richard H. Railey was the son of P. I. Railey, Sr., and his wife Judith Woodson Railey, of whose children, P. I. Railey, Jr., is now the only survivor. Richard was born April 26, 1823, on land settled by his maternal grandfather, adjoining the farm now owned by Logan Railey. He died at Rich Hill, Mo., on October 3, 1888, and was buried in Versailles, Ky., on the fifth inst. His wife and three children, Wm. E. Railey, Bertha Railey and Woodson Railey survive him.

"A kinder heart than Dick Railey's never animated a human breast. A sunnier nature never brightened the rugged pathway of life. Gifted with a superb physique, reared amid plenty, if not luxury, a descendant of the Raileys, Randolphs and Woodsons of Virginia, a kinsman of Jefferson, he was a gentleman by instinct, and his joyous laugh was as natural as the song of a bird. He married one of Kentucky's uncrowned queens, Miss .Catherine Hawkins, a lady who would adorn a palace or a thatched cottage with equal grace.

"Fortune smiled upon him more than once, not with her 'winsome smile,' but rather as if in mockery. At once generous and improvident, money was to him contemptible dross. Judged by the world's standards he was not a successful man, but if to illumine his own home with sunshine, to scatter gladness wherever he went, to inspire his children to noble aims be success, then the beautiful flowers which decorated his grave were laurels fairly won. His closing years were brightened by a steadfast faith in the promises of God."

"D. M. B."

No one knew Richard Henry Railey better than did Daniel M. Bowmar, Sr., as they had been friends for a lifetime. The wife of Richard H. Railey is complimented by Mr. Bowmar also. Catharine Keith Hawkins was the great granddaughter of the Rev. James Keith and Mary Isham Randolph, hence she was a fourth cousin of her husband, both of his great grandmothers being daughters of Colonel Isham Randolph. Richard H. Railey's eldest son, Wm. Edward Railey, was one of the very few Raileys so foolish as to engage in the undesirable game of politics. Soon after reaching his majority he was elected Sergeant-at-Arms of the Kentucky House of Representatives in which capacity he served for about ten years, then accepted a position in the National House of Representatives at Washington. Afterwards he served four years in the Internal Revenue service and was four years postmaster at Midway, Ky. By Kentucky's big-hearted and whole-souled Gov. Luke P. Blackburn, he was honored with a commission as Colonel on his staff. Realizing after thirty years of loyalty to his friends and unwavering service to his party that there was more bitterness than pleasure or profit in politics he abandoned that enticing game and is devoting his time to other pursuits.

William Railey's two brothers, Charles and Randolph, and his sister, Jane, accompanied him and his wife to Kentucky in 1793. "Liberty Hall," their home, was always open to relatives and friends.

JAMES RAILEY

Seventh born of John Railey and Elizabeth Randolph. Married Nancy Watkins. Their descendants:

John Railey, [1] Elizabeth Randolph.

James Railey, [2] born April 16, 1762.
Married Nancy Watkins, May, 1791.
Joseph Randolph Railey, [3] born February 14, 1792; died July 18, 1824.
Married Nancy Mayo, July 13, 1809.
Amanda Malvina Railey, [4] born July 22, 1810; died January 12, 1888.
Married James Mount, August 30, 1847.
Joseph Railey Mount, [5] born December 22, 1849.
Married, first, Carrie Alsop, September 1, 1871; second, Annie McRoberts, November 1, 1876.
Bessie Mount, [6] born June 16, 1872.
Married Shelby L. Allen, April 20, 1898.
Caroline Hobson Allen, [7] born August 12, 1899.
Shelby L. Allen, Jr., [7] born November 26, 1903.
Dorothy Railey Allen, [7] born November 26, 1903.
John McRoberts Mount, [6] born August 14, 1877.
Married Jean Lynn, June 12, 1907.
Margaret Mount, [6] born December 31, 1882.
Jo Ann Mount, [6] born June 14, 1884.
John James Mount, [5] born June 20, 1852.
Married Ruth Morris, January 8, 1878.
Robert Morris Mount, [6] born December 4, 1878.
Married Bessie Berry, June 29, 1903.
Ruth Berry Mount, [7] born October 2, 1904.
Alice Holmes Mount, [7] born September 26, 1906.
Mary Maude Mount, [6] born February 20, 1881.
Charlotte Amanda Mount, [6] born May 31, 1889.
Ella Morris Mount, [6] born December 3, 1903.
Sara Railey Mount, [6] born October 5, 1906.
Lavinia Harrison Railey, [4] born July 4, 1813; died September 18, 1899.
Married Camden Montague Ballard, March 29, 1831.
Joseph James Ballard, [5] born December 25, 1831; died December 23, 1861.
Married Sallie Hillyar, June 29, 1857.
Emma Louise Ballard, [6] born October 22, 1858.
Married George S. Graves, September 15, 1881.
Ruth Graves, [7] born March 24, 1885.
Edna Elizabeth Graves, [7] born December 20, 1888.
Julia Graves, [7] born October 5, 1895.
John Thomas Ballard, [5] born January 6, 1834.
Married Effie Winlock, September 7, 1854.
Camden Winlock Ballard, [6] born December 31, 1856.
Married, first, Susan Reynolds, November 4, 1878; second, Varnette Gregg Reynolds, December 16, 1899.
Fielding Edward Ballard, [7] born October 20, 1881.

Married Hattie Thompson Weakley, December 30, 1903.
Victoria Reynolds Ballard, [8] born October 30, 1904.
Susan Mary Ballard, [8] born January 15, 1908.
Camden Winlock Ballard, [8] born August 6, 1909.
Nancy Peyton Ballard, [6] born January 25, 1859.
Lavinia Harrison Ballard, [6] born December 3, 1860.
Married George Robert Blakemore, May 25, 1887.
Effie Carrie Blakemore, [7] born August 20, 1888.
Thomas Ballard Blakemore, [7] born September 12, 1890.
Fielding Winlock Blakemore, [7] born June 8, 1896.
Edmonia Blakemore, [7] born December 30, 1897.
George Robert Blakemore, Jr., [7] born October 11, 1900.
Fielding Montague Ballard, [6] born August 31, 1862.
Married Grace Winnall, October 23, 1901.
Mary Peyton Ballard, [7] born August 10, 1902.
Nancy Winlock Ballard, [7] born October 27, 1907.
Florence Effie Ballard, [6] born January 1, 1865.
Addison C. Ballard, [5] born May 8, 1840.
Married Helen M. Varry, June 28, 1860.
Lavinia Ballard, [6] born April 9, 1861.
Married James Robert Clark, April 9, 1878.
Mildred Campbell Clark, [7] born January 10, 1879.

Married James Dudley Russell, November 16, 1898.
Mary Clark Russell, [8] born June 20, 1902.
Stuart Heth Clark, [7] born February 29, 1881.
Joe Ballard Clark, [7] born September 5, 1882.
James Robert Clark, Jr., [7] born December 16, 1889.
Anna Belle Ballard, [6] born October 11, 1862.
Married Kirby Smith Collier, July 12, 1888.
Clarence Calvert Collier, [7] born December 15, 1894.
Helen Elizabeth Collier, [7] born December 11, 1898.
Joseph James Ballard, [6] born March 16, 1864.
Married Anna Lee Hogsett, October 24, 1895.
Anna Lee Ballard, [7] born September 5, 1898.
Jonathon Young Ballard, [7] born March 7, 1901.
Joseph James Ballard, Jr., [7] born August 7, 1908.
Effie Winlock Ballard, [6] born November 12, 1866.
Married Samuel Simms Wilhoyte, December 19, 1888.
Allen Sims Wilhoyte, [7] born June 18, 1892.
Norval Joseph Wilhoyte, [7] born October 12, 1901.
Anna Florence Wilhoyte, [7] born January 29, 1909.
Margaret Ballard, [6] born July 16, 1870.
Married Jeptha Montgomery Tharp, December 7, 1888.
Ballard Montgomery Tharp, [7] born February 7, 1891.

William Ely Tharp,[7] born September 26, 1892.

Graham Ely Tharp,[7] born September 1, 1895.

Rachael Mayo Tharp,[7] born November 3, 1898.

Elizabeth M. Ballard,[6] born October 15, 1872.

Married, first, Robert Emmet Blakemore, September 4, 1895; second, John William Paulger, November 15, 1904.

Robert Emmet Blakemore, Jr.,[7] born February 15, 1896.

Helen Verry Paulger,[7] born February 22, 1908.

John Norvil Ballard,[6] born November 5, 1875.

Caroline Varry Ballard,[6] born May 6, 1878.

Married Samuel Franklin Sibert, October 1, 1898.

Samuel Franklin Sibert, Jr.,[7] born July 29, 1899.

Elizabeth Armstrong Ballard,[6] born February 9, 1886.

Married Julius Morris, July 5, 1903.

Margaret Reid Morris,[7] born November 8, 1905.

Ballard Emmanuel Morris,[7] born January 17, 1907.

Frank Sidney Morris,[7] born June 17, 1909.

William Jordan Ballard,[5] born July 22, 1845.

Married Mary B. Moody, December 13, 1865.

Curtis Warren Ballard,[6] born October 13, 1868.

Married Fannie L. Williamson, July 15, 1911.

John Allen Ballard,[6] born February 17, 1870.

William James Railey,[4] born September 14, 1816; died April 18, 1863.

Married, first, Edna C. Blakemore, November 22, 1848; second, Sarah Ann Verry, July 21, 1859.

Sina Keene Railey,[5] born April 1, 1851; died August 6, 1896.

Charles Randolph Railey,[5] born November 9, 1852.

Married Elizabeth Belle Bailey, December 19, 1878.

Cecil Railey,[6] born March 9, 1880.

Loula Railey,[6] born March 30, 1885.

Joseph Lewis Railey,[5] born August 28, 1854; died March 2, 1890.

Sarah Catharine Railey,[5] born September 22, 1861.

Married William Ford, 1910.

Ann Catharine Railey,[4] born March 7, 1819; died February 10, 1883.

Married Thomas S. Blakemore, February 21, 1837.

Henrietta Blakemore,[5] born July 4, 1838; died December 2, 1855.

Joseph William Blakemore,[5] born March 6, 1840; died December 28, 1905.

James Marcus Blakemore,[5] born October 3, 1842.

Married Elizabeth Taylor Armstrong, March 30, 1869.

William Thomas Blakemore,[6] born August 12, 1872.

Robert Emmet Blakemore,[6] born August 12, 1872.

Married Elizabeth Ballard, April 14, 1895.

Robert Emmet Blakemore, Jr.,[7] born February 15, 1896.

Annabine Blakemore,[6] born December 28, 1874.

Married Frederick M. Craven, June 20, 1906.

Virginia Hill Blakemore,[6] born May 31, 1877.

Married Garnett S. Morris, November 27, 1895.

Garnet Elizabeth Morris,[7] born September 1, 1896.

Margaret Nelson Morris,[7] born December 1, 1898.

James Scearce Morris,[7] born January 26, 1903.

Marcus Blakemore Morris,[7] born January 12, 1907.

William Emmet Morris,[7] born September 1, 1908.

Edmonia Blakemore,[5] born December 20, 1844; died July 2, 1878.

Married George W. Sparks, November 3, 1864. (No issue.)

George Robert Blakemore,[5] born March 5, 1852.

Married Lavinia Harrison Ballard, May 25, 1887.

Effie Carrie Blakemore,[6] born August 20, 1888.

Thomas Ballard Blakemore,[6] born September 12, 1890.

Fielding Winlock Blakemore,[6] born June 8, 1896.

Edmonia Blakemore,[6] born December 30, 1897.

George Robert Blakemore, Jr.,[6] born October 11, 1900.

Joseph Jordan Railey,[4] born January 12, 1812; died May 16, 1898.

Married Anna E. Barnes, September 29, 1849.

Oretta Virginia Railey,[5] born May 14, 1853.

Married Dr. Charles A. Riley, February 18, 1869.

Clarence A. Riley,[6] born February 21, 1870.

Married Elvie C. Hampton, December 1, 1890.

Kenneth Riley,[7] born August 4, 1896.

Ben Carleton Riley,[7] born August 25, 1906.

Courtland Riley,[6] born April 16, 1873.

Married September 18, 1895.

Gipson Railey Riley,[7] born December, 1891.

John Gipson Railey,[5] born December 25, 1854.

Married Julia Garner, October 18, 1886.

Joseph Jordan Railey,[6] born October 14, 1888.

Married Nellie Wagner, December, 1909.

J. Garner Railey,[6] born June 28, 1891.

George Alfred Railey,[6] born August 5, 1893.

Janette Railey,[6] born August 28, 1902.

Anna Barnes Railey,[5] born February 19, 1857.

Married J. O. Barbour, May 12, 1881.

Joseph Railey Barbour,[6] born August 21, 1882.

Peachey Lee Railey,[5] born April 20, 1860.

Married A. P. Wilson, May 14, 1884. (No issue.)

Elizabeth Railey,[3] born June, 1793; died January 28, 1853.

Married John Railey, June 4, 1807.

John Woodson Railey, [4] born October 4, 1812; died September 30, 1874.
Married Nancy Farris Nunn, October 4, 1832.
Caroline Railey, [5] born March 6, 1835.
Married William Cary, May 18, 1854.
Evaline Cary, [6] born March 13, 1855.
Julia Ann Cary, [6] born September 27, 1856.
Married, first, Allen Kendrick Walker, July 26, 1874; second, James S. Copeland, March, 1885.
Edna M. Walker, [7] born December 10, 1875.
Married John Chappell, September 20, 1893.
Elmer Louis Chappell, [8] born April 20, 1895.
Dean Jennings Chappell, [8] born January 3, 1897.
Walker Chappell, [8] born September 22, 1899.
James Chappell, [8] born January 2, 1901.
Minnie N. Walker, [7] born October 4, 1877.
Allen J. Walker, [7] born July 24, 1880.
Married Mary Cunningham, April 19, 1906.
Julia E. Walker, [8] born February 3, 1907.
Frank Kendrick Walker, [8] born July 17, 1908.
Hallie N. Walker, [8] born August 15, 1910.
Bessie N. Copeland, [7] born February 6, 1886.
Susie S. Copeland, [7] born August 29, 1888.
Robert W. Copeland, [7] born September 26, 1890.
Ella W. Copeland, [7] born August 2, 1892.
Jesse J. Copeland, [7] born December 30, 1893.
John Herbert Copeland, [7] born December 30, 1893.
Joseph F. Copeland, [7] born April 23, 1895.
Mary E. Cary, [6] born November 12, 1858.
E. Elmore McAfee, [7] July 27, 1884.
Charles Elmore McAfee, [7] born January 9, 1886.
Married Bertha Railey, April 28, 1910.
William Leroy McAfee, [7] born February 13, 1889.
Viola A. McAfee, [7] born February 17, 1891.
Lady Rachael McAfee, [7] born February 3, 1893.
William Woodson Cary, [6] born November 16, 1862.
Susan Ann Railey, [5] born June 9, 1837; died February 9, 1839.
Isham Tarleton Railey, [5] born December 18, 1840.
Married Loretta M. Bailey, December 2, 1869.
Annie Farris Railey, [6] born September 18, 1870.
Married W. L. Herndon, November 24, 1891.
Clara Herndon, [7] born October, 1892.
Mary Elizabeth Railey, [6] born September 29, 1872.
Married F. R. Martin, September, 1889.
Laura Martin, [7] born July 2, 1890.

Annie Woodson Martin, [7] born March 1, 1894.

Ernest Martin, [7] born November 4, 1898.

N. P. Railey, [6] born March 23, 1875.

John A. Railey, [6] born March 30, 1879.

Married Nannie Griffith, February, 1905.

John A. Railey, Jr., [7] born January 7, 1906.

Robert Woodson Railey, [7] born September, 1907.

Aubrey Lee Railey, [7] born September, 1909.

Louis Railey, [6] born October 17, 1881.

Married Martha Ecton, January 22, 1909.

Woodson Tarleton Railey, [6] born May 4, 1884.

Joseph W. Railey, [6] born April 3, 1887.

Edward T. Railey, [6] born January 16, 1890.

Robert L. Railey, [6] born March 2, 1894.

Isabella Railey, [5] born August 4, 1845.

John Randolph Railey, [5] born March 4, 1850.

Married Margaret French, February 23, 1881.

Haydon W. Railey, [6] born December 13, 1881.

Married Lee W. Symms, October, 1906.

Bertha Railey, [6] born February 25, 1883.

Married Charles Elmore McAfee, April 29, 1910.

Estelle Railey, [6] born July 25, 1886.

Mattie Railey, [6] born July 10, 1889.

Married Rector Herndon, March, 1910.

Boone Railey, [5] born August 20, 1852, died August 8, 1871.

Caroline Railey, [4] born August, 1815, died, 1850.

Married first Dr. Joseph Wilson, 1833; married second Rev. W. E. Milam, 1837.

Elizabeth McCormick Wilson, [5] born 1834, died 1845.

James Railey, 7th of John Railey, and Elizabeth Randolph, remained in Va., and married Nancy Watkins in 1791. The date of his birth was April 16, 1762, and he died about 1795. A few years after his marriage, his eldest son, Joseph Randolph Railey, came to Kentucky about 1812, and settled on a farm near Lagrange, Oldham county, where he died in 1824. Before he left his native State, and while yet a youth he married Nancy Mayo, 6th of Col. William Mayo and Catharine Swann. She was a younger sister of the two Mayo girls who married Martin and Charles Railey, uncles of Joseph Randolph Railey, and also a sister of William Mayo, 7th of Col. William Mayo and Catharine Swann, who married Caroline Fleming Pleasants, a first cousin of Joseph Randolph Railey, hence Joseph R. Railey was a brother-in-law to two of his uncles and also to his first cousin. His oldest daughter, Amanda Railey, married James Mount in 1847, and their son, Joseph Railey Mount, represented Oldham County in the Legislature during the memorable session of 1900, the exciting incidents of which brought about the assassination of Governor Goebel. The large families of Ballards, Blakemores and Raileys of Oldham, Trimble and Shelby Counties descend from Joseph Randolph Railey and Nancy Mayo. His son, Joseph Jordan Railey, married Miss Anna Barnes, and for many years was engaged in business in Louisville, Ky., and St. Louis, Mo., raised a family of children, who are residents of Missouri. Some years ago he retired from active business, after which he resided with his son-in-law, A. P. Wilson, a banker of Sweet Springs, Mo. At the home of Joseph Randolph Railey the latchstring was always on the outside and during the early part of the last century the home was noted for the number of social gatherings and the hospitality and cordiality dispensed; and those characteristics seem to have been a part of the inheritance that has come down to each generation. I know of no branch of the Raileys who are more cordial and hospitable. Elizabeth Railey, the second daughter of James Railey and Nancy Watkins, married her cousin, John Railey, and their descendants were sketched under Isham Randolph Railey, fourth of John Railey and Elizabeth Randolph. I know of but two professional men, Dr. Charles A. Railey, of Missouri, and Jo Ballard Clark, a lawyer of LaGrange, Ky., in the line of James Railey and Nancy Watkins. There may be others. Curtis Warren Ballard resides at Jeffersonville, Ind. He was elected to the Legislature as a Democrat in 1904 and before his term expired was elected circuit clerk. Was elected again in 1910—the only man ever re-elected to that office in Clark County, Indiana.

JANE RAILEY

Eighth born of John Railey and Elizabeth Randolph. Married Aaron Darnell. Their descendants:

John Railey [1]-Elizabeth Randolph.

Jane Railey, [2] born August 9, 1763; died July 16, 1824.

Married Aaron Darnell, January 21, 1797.

Elizabeth Pope Darnell, [3] born April 30, 1798.

Married Aaron Mershon, May 30, 1820.

Jane Railey Mershon. [4]

Married Randolph Darnell Mershon. [4]

Lavinia Mershon. [4]

Married Ross Reed.

Mattie Reed. [5]

Fannie Reed. [5]

Ella Reed. [5]

Benjamin Mershon, [4] killed at the battle of Rome, Georgia.

Virginia Mershon. [4]

Married Orlander Mershon.

Minerva Mershon. [4]

Married James Booker.

Elemander Mershon. [4]

Randolph Railey Darnell, [3] born February 12, 1800; died December 29, 1860.

Married Attalanta Whittington, October 9, 1827.

Aaron Darnell,[4] born September 23, 1828.
Married, first, Catharine Hawkins, November 7, 1850; second, Sarah E. Pepper, 1857.
Judge Isham Randolph Darnell,[5] born August 26, 1851.
Married Macie Carter, August 25, 1887.
Catharine Darnell,[6] born January 2, 1892.
Shapley Darnell,[6] born April 23, 1903.
Ruth Elizabeth Darnell,[6] born October 19, 1907.
Samuel Pepper Darnell.[5]
Married Ruth Chandler, November 25, 1885.
Mayme Darnell,[5] born November 2, 1887.
Married J. R. DeRoulac, November, 1908.
Mahala Darnell.[5]
John Robb Darnell.[5]
Married Bessie Davidson.
John R. Darnell, Jr.[5]
Sarah E. Darnell.[5]
Aaron H. Darnell.[5]
Married Nellie Northop.
W. W. Darnell,[4] born March 19, 1830.
Married Sarah Taylor.
James S. Darnell.[5]
John Darnell.[5]
Randolph Darnell.[5]
John R. Darnell,[4] born March 2, 1832.
Married Susan Cotton.
Ann Elizabeth Darnell.[5]
Southey Darnell.[5]
Charles Darnell.[5]
Dunlap C. Darnell.[5]
Married Mrs. Mary E. Lucas, May 5, 1910.

Dr. Mathew Cotton Darnell.[5]
Married Ermina Jett, April 27, 1910.
Southy W. Darnell,[4] born August 31, 1839; died September 4, 1890.
Married Harvey Randolph Darnell.[5]
George Lewis Darnell.[5]
Varsalina Darnell.[5]
Virginia Darnell,[4] born June 20, 1841.
Married Thomas J. Jett.
Attalanta Darnell,[4] born April 9, 1843.
Married Thomas W. Edwards.
Charles Eugene Edwards.[5]
Virginia Pearl Edwards.[5]
George Randolph Edwards.[5]
Wiley Edwards.[5]
Charles Randolph Darnell,[?] born September 26, 1845.
Married B. H. Railey.
Virginia Darnell,[3] born August 26, 1845.
Married John Markley.
Maria Louise Markley,[4] born 1838.
Married F. C. Blankenship, 1858.
Caroline Blankenship.[5]
Ferdie C. Blankenship.[5]
Married Robinson L. Ireland, 1885.
Ann Randolph Markley,[4] born 1840.
Married William A. Givens, 1865.
Agnes Givens,[5] born 1866.
Married Edward J. Meyers, 1901.
Virginia Givens,[5] died 1905.
Jane Railey was the 8th born f John Railey and Elizabeth Randolph. Born in Virginia at the

old homestead "Stonehenge" in 1763. She came to Kentucky with her brothers Charles and Randolph Railey about 1793. Enroute they were joined by Aaron Darnell, a Virginian, who was making his way to Kentucky alone. Aaron Darnell had served through the Revolution as a drummer boy and was used to such hardships and dangers that one must of necessity encounter in overland travel in those days.

The destination of the Raileys was Versailles, Ky., and as Mr. Darnell had no particular point in view he remained with the party until they reached Woodford county, where he, too, settled. In the course of the long journey he made himself very agreeable and companionable, telling many thrilling incidents of the Revolution. For several years after reaching Kentucky he made it a point to see Jane Railey, notwithstanding the protests of her brothers, and finally in 1797 they were married and became residents of Woodford county. He practiced medicine. The most of their descendants have been engaged in agricultural pursuits. They are residents of Kentucky and Missouri. I only know of two professional men in this line, Judge Isham Randolph Darnell is a lawyer and resides in Nebraska. Dr. Mathew C. Darnell is a resident of Woodford county, Kentucky.

I am sorry not to give more dates and information concerning these people, which I would have gladly done if I could have gotten them sufficiently interested. I hope that some one among these families will yet secure the missing dates and send them to me that I may complete my manuscript which I propose to hold for future generations to have access to.

MARTIN RAILEY

Ninth born of John Railey and Elizabeth Randolph. Married Elizabeth Mayo. Their descendants:

John Railey [1]-Elizabeth Randolph.

Martin Railey, [2] born October 27, 1764; died December 28, 1810. Married Elizabeth Mayo, February 27, 1794.

Daniel Mayo Railey, [3] born October 20, 1796; died March 23, 1858. Married Jane Elizabeth Watson, November 26, 1816.

John Martin Railey, [4] born November 29, 1821; died May 21, 1902. Married Elizabeth Jane Steele, October 6, 1842.

Sadie Railey, [5] born October 27, 1847. Married H. C. Cockrill, October 6, 1870.

Rev. Egbert Railey Cockrill, [6] born April 2, 1872. Married Dura Brokaw, May, 1897.

Dura Louise Cockrill, [7] born September 30, 1905.

Louise Mayo Cockrill, [6] born November 19, 1873; died 1893. Married G. B. Richardson, June 7, 1891.

Beverly Randolph Richardson, [7] born July 14, 1894.

Henry Clifton Cockrill,[6] born November 30, 1884; died 1899.

Pocahontas Cockrill,[6] born August 19, 1886.

Married J. A. Hedger, June 3, 1907.

Harry Hedger,[7] born November 22, 1908.

Hampden Pleasants Railey,[5] born February 3, 1850.

Married Katharine Payne, April, 1875.

Elizabeth Railey,[6] born October 1, 1877.

Married Luke Cowan, August 1903.

Jennie Railey,[6] born 1882.

Erastus Williams, August, 1905.

Eva Williams,[7] born August, 1907.

Ella Railey,[6] born January, 1884.

Married Charles King, September, 1908.

John Martin Railey,[6] born August 14, 1886.

Married 1906.

Martin Railey,[7] born August, 1907.

Sadie Railey,[6] born November 21, 1888.

Hampden Pleasants Railey, Jr.,[6] born October 6, 1890.

John Watson Railey,[5] born February 22, 1852.

Married Anna Turner, October 6, 1875.

Arthur Railey,[6] born August, 1876.

Martin Railey,[6] born August, 1880.

Oliver Daniel Railey,[5] born June, 1857.

Married Emma Matthews, 1881.

Oliver Railey,[6] born December, 1882.

Charles Railey,[6] born February, 1885.

Jerry Railey,[6] born November, 1887.

Married Elizabeth Stewart, January, 1910.

Pocahontas Railey,[5] born March 1, 1860.

Married Richard Jacquimin, October 6, 1878. (No issue.)

Eva Railey,[5] born October 27, 1863.

Married E. A. King, January, 1888. (No issue.)

Pocahontas Railey,[4] born September 10, 1824; died June 3, 1882.

Married Joseph V. Parrott, November 4, 1846.

Ella Parrott,[5] born 1850; died 1873.

Elizabeth Jane Railey,[4] born December 25, 1827; died June 30, 1902.

Married T. D. S. McDowell, May 26, 1853.

Alexander Railey McDowell,[5] born December 2, 1856.

Jane Randolph McDowell,[5] born September 13. 1866.

Egbert Railey,[4] born June 6, 1830.

Married Mary E. McAdon, September 5, 1854.

Bertie Railey,[5] born November 18, 1858.

Married John Hardesty, February 17, 1881.

Egbert Hardesty,[6] born December 3, 1881.

Married Minnie Allison, June 20, 1906.

Frank Hardesty.[7]

Bert Hardesty.[7]

Louis Hardesty. [7]
Shortridge Hardesty, [6] born April 13, 1884.
Married Della Terrill, September, 1910.
Mayo Hardesty, [6] born September 15, 1891.
John Hardesty, [6] born April 9, 1896.
Dixie Railey, [5] born March 15, 1861.
Married Joseph E. Mayo, 1881.
Railey Mayo, [6] born August 12, 1882.
Married Maude Newman, September 21, 1905.
Daniel Railey, [5] born December 16, 1863.
Married Anna Alderson, March 17, 1887.
James Railey, [6] born December 29, 1887.
Egbert W. Railey, [6] born July 5, 1889.
Annabell Railey, [4] born June 28, 1833.
Emma Railey, [4] born May 20, 1836.
Henry Heath Railey, [4] born July 17, 1838; died November 1, 1861.
Beverly Randolph Railey, [4] born February 25, 1843; died December 5, 1864.
Catharine Railey, [3] born May 7, 1798; died February 27, 1881.
Married Anderson Shefflett.
Mary Jane Shefflett. [4]
Married Benjamin Sneed.
Edward Sneed. [5]
John A. Sneed, [5] died July 27, 1885.
Married Jane Price Railey, December 15, 1874.

Lula Gordon Sneed, born July 24, 1876.
Cary Anderson Sneed, born August 3, 1878; died November 27, 1900.
John Price Sneed, born August 19, 1883.
Married Nellie Fitzhugh, January 20, 1906.
Louise Price Sneed, born August 4, 1907.
Charles Sneed. [5]
Alice Sneed. [5]
Horace Sneed. [5]
Noble Sneed. [5]
Lilburn Shefflett. [4]
Married Lavinia Gentry.
John Martin Railey, [3] born November 27, 1800; died January 13, 1835.
Married Mary Watson, 1825.
Carter Henry Railey, [4] born February 3, 1826; died October 12, 1884.
Married Mary Jane Tanner, November 9, 1849.
Branch Railey, [5] born July 24, 1850.
Married Caroline Frick, June 9, 1880.
Randolph Railey, [6] born April 6, 1881; died unmarried.
Branch Railey, Jr., [6] born May 1, 1883.
Pocahontas Railey, [5] born June 23, 1852.
Grace Churchill Railey, [5] born November 18, 1854.
John Randolph Railey, [5] born September 4, 1856; died November 1, 1900.
Carter Harrison Railey, [5] born July 2, 1859; died June 7, 1887.
Married Ida Blanche Keith, January, 1881.

Charles Keith Railey, [6] born December 11, 1882.

James Faulkner Railey, [6] born February 28, 1884.

Edwin Railey, [6] born January, 1887.

Sterling Price Railey, [5] born October 1, 1860.

Married Cecelia Jane Parker, December 26, 1887.

Sterling Anglairs Railey, [6] born November 3, 1893.

Mary Cecelia Railey, [6] born February 28, 1896.

Earl Bacon Railey, [6] born May 12, 1903.

John Randolph Railey, [6] born June 10, 1906.

Cabell Breckinridge Railey, [5] born July 2, 1862.

Married Emma Percival, September 2, 1886.

Cabell Percival Railey, [6] born March 6, 1890.

William Montgomery Railey, [4] born June 1, 1828; died July 28, 1909.

Mary Elizabeth Railey, [4] born September 8, 1830; died July 28, 1904.

Martha Virginia Railey, [4] born August, 1832.

Married M. A. Moseby.

Arthur Moseby. [5]

Lilburn Rogers Railey, [3] born April 26, 1804.

Married Lucy Jane Burks, January 28, 1825.

Elizabeth Railey, [4] born April 12, 1826.

Married Thomas Bowman, October 11, 1854.

Lucy Railey Bowman, [5] born October 21, 1862.

Lilburn Edward Bowman, [5] born December 5, 1856.

James Pleasants Railey, [4] born August 28, 1827; died July 21, 1908.

Married Cornelia Burnley, December, 1864.

Carrie Pleasants Railey, [5] born November 13, 1865.

Married William A. Beale, December 5, 1885.

Cornelius William Beale. [6]

Married Mary Elizabeth Graham.

Ruth Burnley Beale. [7]

William Stuart Beale. [7]

Lilburn Burnley Railey, [5] born June 4, 1870.

Married Edna Elizabeth Lewis, October, 1895.

Grace B. Railey, [5] born February 28, 1872.

Isabella Watson Railey, [4] born December 13, 1831; died 1908.

Married William Henderson.

Andrew Henderson. [5]

Col. John Daniel Railey, [4] born October 14, 1833; died July 27, 1899.

Married Ellen Miller, August 12, 1855.

Charles Lilburn Railey, [5] born August 27, 1856; died February 16, 1886.

Married Jessie Merchison, March 16, 1881.

Elizabeth Belle Railey, [5] born March 12, 1862.

Married, first, Ben T. Duvall, May 5, 1880; second, A. V. Harris, March 29, 1910.

Edward Hood Railey, [5] born May 17, 1864.

Married Catharine Riley, 1884.

Walter Railey,[6] born July 18, 1885.

Wesley Railey,[6] born August 8, 1887.

Randolph Stroud Railey,[6] born November 23, 1889.

Vivian Railey,[6] born October 22, 1892.

John Randolph Railey,[5] born October 31, 1867.

Married Minnie Collins, October 15, 1890.

Collins Daniel Railey, born September 22, 1891.

Emma Catharine Railey,[4] born September 22, 1835.

Married William H. Inloe. (No issue.)

Mary Ellen Railey,[4] born February 12, 1838; died February 26, 1880.

Married James Warmouth. (No issue.)

William Baxter Railey,[4] born December 21, 1841; died February, 1910.

Married Cornelia Maupin, July, 1864.

Linwood Walker Railey,[5] born October 26, 1866.

Elizabeth Belle Railey,[5] born March 6, 1870.

Married Arthur Stephens, June 29, 1898.

Logan J. Railey,[5] born March 3, 1872; died unmarried.

Mary Lucy Railey,[5] born June 4, 1873.

Married P. Stanley Stevens, April 6, 1910.

Willie Virginia Railey,[5] born July 27, 1875.

Married Grayson Wood, January 20, 1900.

Rose Malvern Railey,[5] born April 2, 1877; died August 5, 1897.

Emma Inloe Railey,[5] born April 20, 1879.

Merritt Maupin Railey,[5] born March 18, 1881.

Married Cecil Johnson, September 14, 1910.

Cornelia Jane Railey,[5] born January 20, 1884.

Married Hugh Simms, December 29, 1909.

Ann Maria Railey,[4] born December 22, 1843.

Lilburn Randolph Railey,[4] born March 16, 1846.

Married Mollie Gordon, February 27, 1872.

Charles Gordon Railey,[5] born December 20, 1872.

Married Marie Josephine Livandais, August 26, 1901.

Rev. Fleming G. Railey,[4] born July 20, 1848.

Married Sallie Goodloe Barclay, September 25, 1879.

John Barclay Railey,[5] born January 20, 1881; died October 16, 1898.

Lilburn Rogers Railey, Jr.,[5] born April 4, 1882.

Married Tillie Wiggington, April 4, 1910.

Fleming G. Railey, Jr.,[5] born May 31, 1884.

Married Alpha S. Wiggington, September 18, 1907.

Howard Williams Railey,[5] born April 28, 1886.

Married Lunonta Battaille Blackerby, January 27, 1909.

Randolph Burks Railey,[5] born May 25, 1888.

Lucy Belle Railey,[5] born October 24, 1892.

Jane Price Railey, [4] born November 11, 1852.
Married John A. Sneed, December 15, 1874.
Lula Gordon Sneed, [5] born January 24, 1876.
Cary Anderson Sneed, [5] born August 3, 1878; died November 27, 1900.
John Price Sneed, [5] born August 19, 1883.
Married Nellie Fitzhugh, June 20, 1906.
Louise Price Sneed, [5] born August 4, 1907.

Martin Railey, ninth of John Railey and Elizabeth Randolph, was born near Richmond, Virginia, on the "Stonehenge" farm during the year 1764. Like his brother James he lived and died in Virginia, near the place of his birth, the scenes of his childhood, and amid the associations of his young manhood. February 24, 1794, he married Elizabeth Mayo, third born of Col. William Mayo, of Richmond, Va., and his wife Catharine Swann. They raised three sons and one daughter all of whom married, lived and died in Virginia.

Daniel Mayo Railey, their first born, married Jane Elizabeth Watson in 1816. Two of the sons of this couple, John Martin Railey, Jr., who married Elizabeth Jane Steele in 1842, and Egbert Railey, who married Mary E. McAdon in 1854, migrated to Missouri about 1866 and settled at Weston where they engaged in the banking business as Railey and Railey. John Martin Railey, Jr., died in 1902. His daughter Sadie Railey married H. C. Cockrill, a lawyer, and they are now residents of San Jose, California, and her sister, Pocahontas Railey, married Richard Jacquimine a merchant of Kansas City, Mo., who retired from business a few years ago in affluence.

Egbert Railey is still at the head of the banking firm at Weston, Mo., and his three children, Mrs. Bertie Railey Hardesty, Mrs. Dixie Railey Mayo and Daniel Railey reside there.

Elizabeth Jane Railey, daughter of Daniel Mayo Railey and Jane Elizabeth Watson, married in Virginia, in 1853, T. D. S. Macdonell. Their two children, Alexander Railey Macdonell and Jane Randolph Macdonell, are now residents of Sault St. Marie, Mich.

John Martin Railey, Sr., third born of Martin Railey and Elizabeth Mayo, married Mary Watson in Virginia, in 1826. He was born in 1800. His grandson, Branch Railey, is in business in Chicago. Another grandson, Carter Harrison Railey, was in business at Covington, Ky., where he died a few years ago leaving three sons; and another grandson, Sterling Price Railey is a lawyer of Covington, Ky., where he resides, while still another grandson, Cabell Breckinridge Railey was in business in Cincinnati where he died a few years ago.

Lilburn Rogers Railey was the 4th born of Martin Railey and Elizabeth Mayo. He was born in Virginia in 1804 and married Lucy Jane Burks in 1825. He lived and died in the vicinity of the old "Stonehenge" farm. He raised a large family of children the most of whom are at present residents of Virginia. His son Col. John Daniel Railey served throughout the Civil War in behalf of the Confederate cause. After the war he settled at Waco, Texas, where he died during the year 1899. His children and grandchildren are residents of that state. Lilburn Randolph Railey, son of Lilburn Rogers Railey, married Mollie Gordon in 1871 and they have a son, Charles Gordon Railey, in business in New Orleans.

The Rev. Fleming G. Railey was another son of Lilburn Rogers Railey. He was born in 1848 and married Sallie Goodloe Barclay in 1879. He was prepared for the law and practiced some years but his convictions finally lead him into the ministry since which time he has devoted all of his time to work in the Presbyterian church. He is at present located at Selma, Alabama, and has in his possession the Family Tree started by John Railey and Elizabeth Randolph. At the age of fifteen years, while a fierce battle was raging on his father's farm during 1863, he joined the cause of the Confederacy and fought valiantly until General Lee surrendered. An incident in his life that had both a serious and an amusing side occurred while he was pastor of the church at Glasgow, Ky. The young men of that town had organized, or rather raised a company of State Guards. No one in the company was sufficiently acquainted with military tactics to drill the men and they finally persuaded the Rev. F. G. Railey to accept the captaincy until some one of the company qualified. However, was was declared with Spain in a few weeks after his election as Captain and under the advice of the Rev. Dr. Witherspoon, of Louisville, Ky., he went forward as both captain and chaplain of his company. Mrs. John A. Sneed and her sister Ann Maria Railey, daughters of Lilburn Rogers Railey, are residents of Charlottesville, Va. The children of James Pleasants Railey, who married Cornelia Burnley are residents of Albermarle and Fauquier counties in Virginia.

Martin Railey became the possessor of the "Stonehenge" estate after the death of his father, John Railey, in 1783 and he lived on the estate until 1806, when he purchased "Buck Island," (afterward known as "Buena Vista") the old home of President Monroe in Albermarle county, where he lived the remainder of his life and reared his family. At his death "Stonehenge" was transferred to his son, Lilburn Rogers Railey, in whose possession it remained until about the period of the Civil War when it was sold to a syndicate of capitalists of Pittsburg for coal mining purposes. The old house was destroyed during the Civil War. The house was of the colonial type built about 1750. It was a large square house, built of stone with large columns in front. In or about 1770, owing to the increase in the family, John Railey built an addition of brick in the rear. It was situated on the Midlothian road near Chesterfield Court House.

CHARLES RAILEY,

Tenth born of John Railey and Elizabeth Randolph. Married Mary Mayo. Their descendants follow:

John Railey, [1] Elizabeth Randolph.

Charles Railey, [2] born October 26, 1766, died October 27, 1837.

Married Mary Mayo, April 4, 1796.

James Railey, [3] born March 11, 1797, died September 2, 1860.

Married Matilda S. Green, December 14, 1820.

Mary Elizabeth Railey, [4] born January 5, 1824, died April 28, 1910.

Rev. Frederick W. Boyd, 1844.

James Railey Boyd, [5] born August 13, 1846, died May 17, 1901.

Frederick William Boyd, [5] born November 4, 1848, died November 3, 1871.

Married Lutie Temple, 1871.

Walter Stuart Boyd, [5] born November 9, 1859.

Loyd Tilghman Boyd, [5] born December 19, 1861.

Married Susan A. Patterson, 1895.

Katherine Patterson Boyd, [6] born April 14, 1896.

Mary Railey Boyd, [6] born May 5, 1900.

Charles Mayo Boyd, [5] born December 15, 1866, died February 1, 1904.

James Green Railey, [4] born September 30, 1826, died February 27, 1854.

Married Annie Hoop, 1851.

Ernest H. Railey, [5] born January 31, 1852.

Charles Randolph Railey, [4] born May 24, 1833.

Married Emma Laws, October 22, 1860.

Chapman Railey, [5] born August 1, 1862, died unmarried.

Caroline Green Railey, [4] born May 24, 1835, died June 20, 1855.

Madie Matilda Railey, [4] born March 24, 1837, died March 25, 1856.

Hervie Otie Railey, [4] born August 27, 1841.

Married Irene W. Green, 1863.

Frank Railey, [5] born February 6, 1864, died 1907.

Charles Railey, Jr., [3] born August 3, 1798, died.

Married Jane Reames, July 26, 1819.

Charles Randolph Railey, [4] born August 4, 1820, died February 6, 1889.

Married Ann Elizabeth Helm, January 18, 1849.

Ann Maria Railey, [5] born January 6, 1850, died July 14, 1900.

Married Dr. W. W. Black, October 31, 1883.

Charles Railey Black, [6] born August 13, 1884.

Benjamine Wyly Black, [6] born March 12, 1886.

Mavo Walton Black, [6] born May 11, 1888.

Jennie Railey, [5] born March 30, 1851.

Married Andrew Alfred Woods, May 22, 1873.

Charles Railey Woods, [6] born October 8, 1874.

Andrew Alfred Woods, Jr., [6] born March 22, 1876.

C. Clarence Woods, [6] born September 8, 1877.

Elizabeth Helm Woods, [6] born December 31, 1878.

Henry Newton Woods, [6] born July 4, 1880.

James Brison Woods, [6] born March 22, 1882.

William Railey Woods, [6] born November 22, 1885.

William Mayo Railey, [5] born March 8, 1861.

Married Lina L. Howell, April 21, 1887.

Mary L. Railey, [6] born August 3, 1888.

William Mayo Railey, [6] born March 17, 1890.

Hilton Howell Railey, [6] born August 1, 1895.

Charles Randolph Railey, [6] born August 1, 1895.

James Alexander Railey, [4] born June 22, 1822, died January 24, 1892.

Married Mary Barry, 1844.

Augustus Randolph Railey, [5] born.

Married Mary J. Dorden.

Laura Railey, [5] born.

Thomas Railey, [5] born.

Joseph Railey, [5] born.

Charles Railey. [5]

Richard Railey, [4] born June 4, 1824, died 1840.

Lewis Clark Railey, [4] born September 25, 1827, died November 15, 1876.

Margaret Jane Railey, [4] born October 25, 1829, died December 27, 1837.

Alexander Railey, [4] born December 2, 1831.

Edwin Railey, [4] born December 20, 1833, died 1837.

Ellen Railey [4] born January 8, 1836, died November 18, 1841.

Catharine Swann Railey, [3] born January 2, 1800, died January 29, 1872.

Married John Steele, January 18, 1816.

Agnes Winfield Steele, [4] born April 19, 1817, died July 28, 1837.

Married Thomas F. Thornton, January 15, 1835.

Susan Catharine Thornton, [5] born September 6, 1836.

Married Sandy Brown, December 22, 1856.

Charles Rowland Brown, [6] born October 8, 1857.

Married, first Mamie Edwards, May 4, 1886, niece of Mrs. Abe Lincoln; second Grace M. Hatch.

R. Alexander Brown, [7] born April 5, 1888.

Agnes Steele Brown, [6] born July 31, 1860.

George Adams Brown, [6] born November 16, 1861.

Robert Alexander Brown, [6] born November 2, 1864.

Married Catharine Everhart, November 22, 1893.

Catharine Louise Brown, [7] born December 16, 1897.

Thornton Lee Brown, [6] born March 16, 1870.

Married Laura M. Spicer, August 23, 1894.

Dorothy Thornton Brown, [7] born April 1, 1896.

Helen Margaret Brown, [7] born June 7, 1899.

Nancy Scott Railey, [3] born September 29, 1801, died September, 1875.

Married Allen Rowland, December 23, 1828.

Margaret Rowland, [4] born October 7, 1829, died 1887.

Married, first Robert A. Bass, 1854, no issue; married, second Joel I. Lyle, November, 1886, no issue.

Charles Wesley Rowland, [4] born November 17, 1831.

Married Virginia Green, 1854.

Samuel Railey, [3] born June 11, 1803, died October 27, 1884.

Married, first Martha Rowland, February 28, 1825; married, second Sarah Tucker, December 4, 1850.

Mary Railey, [4] born April 4, 1826, died August 27, 1898.

Married Dr. Burr Harrison Cox, October 7, 1845.

Mary Jane Cox, [5] born October 13, 1846.

Married R. H. Gunn, October 10, 1871, no issue.

Samuel Turner Cox, [5] born September 20, 1850.

Ora Cox, [5] born September 2, 1887.

Married Rev. Cyrus N. Broadhurst, March 2, 1887.

Cyrus N. Broadhurst, Jr.,[6] born July 24, 1888.

Wesley Harris Railey, [4] born June 24, 1827, died in California, 1883.

Ruth Ann Railey, [4] born July 27, 1830.

Married, first George Edgar Moore, September 25, 1855, in Versailles, Ky.; married second William A. Jack, in Cass Co., Mo.

John Hubbard Railey, [4] born August 1, 1832, died 1845.

Matilda Green Railey, [4] born March 8, 1834.

Married James Sanford Payne, 1855, in Missouri.

William Vernon Payne, [5] born September 6, 1856.

Married Elizabeth Applegate, March 6, 1884, in Missouri.

William A. Payne, [6] born 1886.

Hazel Oro Payne, [6] born March 26, 1889.

Ralph Glenn Payne, [6] born March 21, 1896.

Charles Wesley Payne, [5] born January 29, 1861.

Married Mary E. Sandusky, March 14, 1888.

Ruby Payne, [6] born July 20, 1889.

Maggie Payne, [6] born October 14, 1891.

William Payne, [6] born September 26, 1893.

Lucy Payne, [6] born March 8, 1895.

Albert Payne, [6] born September 16, 1897.

Catharine Payne, [6] born July 12, 1900.

Della Payne, [6] born April 13, 1908.

Emily Railey, [4] born December 2, 1828, died November 11, 1853.

Married Joel I. Lyle, December 4, 1849, in Versailles, Ky.

Marion T. Lyle, [5] born August 5, 1851.

Married Mary Anderson Thornton, May 3, 1882.

Samuel Lindsey Railey, [4] born October 23, 1835, died in youth.

Francis Railey, [4] born November 21, 1837.

Married Edward T. Payne, 1855 in Missouri.

M. Douglas Payne, [5] born April 12, 1856.

Married Lola Higgins.

Nathan Payne. [6]
Fannie Payne. [6]
Annie Payne. [6]
Sallie Payne. [6]
Lee Payne. [6]
Edward Payne. [6]
Mary Payne. [6]

Martha Ann Payne, [5] born April 9, 1861, died 1878.

Married Campbell Williams.

Nathan Payne, [5] born April 9, 1861.

Married Mary Weyman, no issue.

Watson Railey, [4] born September 11, 1839.

Thornton Railey, [4] born August 6, 1841, died unmarried.

Henry Newell Railey, [4] born October 26, 1851.

Married Delia Edith Courtney, September 22, 1890.

Cornelia Railey, [5] born April 14, 1892.

Samuel Railey, [5] born July 25, 1896.

John Railey, [5] born September 19, 1906.

Margaret Kavanaugh Railey, [4] born December 13, 1853.

Charlotte Railey, [3] born March 29, 1905; died January 31, 1882.

Married Davy Thornton, June 3, 1823, at Versailles, Ky.

Mary Eleanor Thornton, [4] born August 10, 1824.

Married David I. Porter, June 15, 1841, at Versailles, Ky.

Alice Porter, [5] born September 26, 1842.

Married James M. Preston, August 23, 1864, at Versailles, Ky.

Mary Louise Preston, [6] born July 11, 1865.

Married Rev. Charles N. Goulder, June 17, 1890, in California.

Alice Goulder, [7] born August 31, 1891.

Ruth Goulder, [7] born July 27, 1896.

Ernest Preston Goulder, [7] born April 22, 1901.

James William Goulder, [7] born April 22, 1901.

Hontas Preston, [6] born March 13, 1868.

Married William Shearer, July 11, 1888, in California.

Gertrude Alice Shearer, [7] born June 11, 1889.

Mellville Preston Shearer, [7] born December 23, 1891.

Leonora Shearer, [7] born June 15, 1900.

Charlotte Preston, [6] born August 24, 1870.

Robert Irvine Preston, [6] born November 28, 1872.

Thornton Porter Preston, [6] born December 10, 1874.

Married Mrs. Ida Wood, October 25, 1897.

James Oak Preston, [6] born September 30, 1877.

Married Helen Campbell, October 19, 1900.

Woodford Campbell Preston, [7] born August 30, 1901.

Martha Elowise Preston, [7] born July 20, 1903.

Alice Preston, [6] born May 24, 1881, died January 19, 1886.

Eleanor Preston, [6] born February 6, 1884.

Thornton Porter,[5] born July 13, 1845, killed at the battle of Vicksburg under command of General Sterling Price, June 24, 1863.

Edward Lacey Porter,[5] born November 20, 1847.

Married Sallie Boulden, September 28, 1870, in Pettius Co., Mo.

David Irvine Porter,[6] born August 8, 1871.

Married Jennie McFarland, December, 1900.

Edwin Clark Porter,[6] born May 28, 1873.

Married Susan Sparks.

Thornton Porter,[6] born January 25, 1875.

Charles Porter,[6] born August 24, 1877.

Bettie Porter,[6] born May 20, 1879.

Woodford Porter,[6] born July 9, 1881, died December 8, 1901.

Mary Porter,[5] born November 13, 1849.

Married Daniel Cooper, May 22, 1867, at Versailles, Ky.

Thornton Cooper,[6] born March 12, 1869.

Married Mary Louise King, December 11, 1902.

Mary Eleanor Cooper,[7] born July 1, 1905, died September 13, 1909.

John Daniel Cooper,[7] born April 30, 1907.

Charles Randolph Porter,[5] born October 18, 1852, died May 23, 1876.

Married Elizabeth Bennett, January 7, 1875, at San Antonio, Tex.

Elfreda Oak Porter,[5] born December 26, 1854.

Married Frederick Madeira, December 22, 1880, at Versailles, Ky.

Pauline Madeira,[6] born May 7, 1883.

Married Dr. Andrew D. Hoidale, December 27, 1905, at Kansas City, Mo.

Porter Madeira Hoidale,[7] born January 16, 1910.

Louise Madeira,[6] born November 26, 1887.

Married Herman Raymond Seiter, May 2, 1907, at Kansas City, Mo.

Herman Ridgely Seiter,[7] born March 9, 1909.

Pauline Porter,[5] born August 15, 1861, died May 5, 1892.

Married James Montgomery, October 14, 1886, in Missouri.

Oak Montgomery,[6] born April 5, 1889.

Married Granville Blackburn, March 22, 1909, in Missouri.

Paul Montgomery,[6] born December 5, 1890.

Elizabeth Thornton,[4] born September 19, 1827.

Married Ulysses Turner, May 24, 1849, at Versailles, Ky.

Charlotte Turner,[5] born October 25, 1851.

Married Joseph Marshall Bowmar, June 15, 1876, at Versailles, Ky.

Charlotte Thornton Bowmar,[6] born July 19, 1877.

Married Whitley Sessions, June 8, 1904.

Charlotte Whitley Sessions,[7] born February 22, 1905.

Fannie Adams Bowmar,[6] born March 21, 1880.

Married Herman Bowmar, September 9, 1903.

Elizabeth Bowmar,[6] born December 9, 1881.
Married George Taylor Fishback, June 12, 1906.
George Taylor Fishback, Jr.,[7] born March 18, 1907.
Catharine C. Fishback,[7] born April 12, 1908.
Catharine Hunter Bowmar,[6] born April 2, 1884.
Lester Turner,[5] born July 23, 1853.
Married Annie Roe, June 1, 1876, in Brooklyn, N. Y.
Charles Edwin Turner,[6] born March 8, 1877, died April 23, 1896.
Anna Turner,[6] born May 12, 1878.
Lester N. Turner,[6] born March 26, 1881.
Ella Steele Turner,[5] born May 15, 1855.
Hontas Virginia Turner,[5] born February 16, 1857.
Edwin Thornton Turner,[5] born December 28, 1858, died March 6, 1885.
Fannie Turner,[5] born October 16, 1860.
Mary Logan Turner,[5] born October 10, 1863.
Married William O. Davis, February 22, 1887, in Versailles, Ky.
Charlotte Railey Davis,[6] born December 12, 1887.
Ulysses Turner, Jr.,[5] born April 24, 1866.
Married, first Genevieve McDougal, July, 1894; married second Annabel Scearse, June 18, 1908.
Harry McDougal Turner,[6] born January 3, 1899.

James T. Thornton,[4] born June 29, 1834.
Married Mary Simpson, October 2, 1855.
Elizabeth Thornton,[5] born August 19, 1856.
Married John James Stevens, December 3, 1879, in San Antonio, Texas.
Mary Stevens,[6] born December 1880.
Married Claude Spingall, in San Antonio, Texas.
Mary Thornton Spingall.[7]
Thornton Stevens,[6] born July 31, 1882.
Married Mae Douglass, in San Antonio, Texas.
John James Stevens, Jr.,[6] born November 19, 1883.
Married Katharine Douglas, in San Antonio, Texas.
John James Stevens, III.[7]
Douglas Stevens.[7]
Bettie Stevens,[6] born July 16, 1887.
Married Raymond Keller, in San Antonio, Texas.
Raymond Keller, Jr.[7]
Eleanor Stevens,[6] born December 15, 1892.
James Simpson Thornton,[5] born April 2, 1861.
Married Catharine Foster, December 20, 1882, in San Antonio, Texas.
Minnie Thornton.[6]
Charlotte Thornton.[6]
Charlotte Thornton,[5] born April 10, 1865.
Mary Thornton,[5] born August 3, 1871.
Eleanor Thornton,[5] born April 22, 1876.

Hontas Thornton,[4] born September 14, 1837.

Married Edwin S. Craig, November 18, 1873, in Versailles, Ky., no issue.

Edwin Kavanaugh Thornton,[4] born November 4, 1840.

Married Lucrecia L. Hobbs, May 2, 1861.

Wilbur Hobbs Thornton,[5] born March 12, 1862.

Married Laura Hiter, 1884, at Versailles, Ky.

David Thornton,[5] born March 28, 1864.

Married Catharine Haley, January 21, 1885, at Kansas City, Mo.

Mabel Thornton,[6] born February 11, 1886.

Married William Clay Arnold, December 19, 1906.

Stanley Thornton,[5] born September 27, 1867, died January 23, 1894.

Married Virginia Woodson, October 3, 1888, at Kansas City, Mo.

Woodson Stanley Thornton,[6] born October 15, 1890.

James Thornton,[5] born July 2, 1870.

Edwin Thornton,[5] born February 16, 1876.

Woodford Railey Thornton,[4] born August 19, 1844.

Married Lucy Dupuy Bailey, May 22, 1866.

Charles Randolph Thornton,[4] born July 11, 1847, died unmarried.

Margaret Crittenden Railey,[3] born January 5, 1807, died October 7, 1863.

Married, first William Green, December 8, 1825, of Mississippi; married, second Bishop H. H. Kavanaugh, July 24, 1828.

Charles William Kavanaugh,[4] died young.

David Ella Kavanaugh,[4] died young.

Benjamine Taylor Kavanaugh,[4] died young.

John Hubbard Kavanaugh,[4] died young.

Lewis Clark Railey,[3] born December 27, 1808; died September 29, 1891.

Married Susan Mary Hardin, August 16, 1830, at Harrodsburg, Ky.

Martin H. Steele Railey,[4] born June 19, 1831, died February 13, 1888.

Married Maggie Templeton, November 3, 1875, at Pueblo, Colorado.

Mary Hardin Railey,[5] born November 10, 1877.

Married Irving Bliss Esmay, November 1, 1905.

Susan Emory Railey,[4] born September 15, 1832, died September 8, 1876.

Elizabeth White Railey,[4] born November 9, 1833, died young.

Lewis Clark Railey,[3] born February 27, 1835.

Married Maggie Lee Patton, December 31, 1873, at Pueblo, Colo.

Bertie Hardin Railey,[5] born May 6, 1875.

Josephine Railey,[4] born August 21, 1837.

Mark Hardin Railey,[4] born December 17, 1839.

Married, first Martha Randolph Slaughter, January 15, 1868, in

Texas; married, second Clemintine Brown, 1880.

Mary Slaughter Railey, [5] born February 16, 1869. Married George Freeman Schroeter, February 16, 1893, of Texas.

Pattie Schroeter, [6] born February 3, 1894, died young.

William Freeman Schroeter, [6] born February 3, 1896.

Mark Lewis Schroeter, [6] born September 26, 1897.

Lula Agnes Schroeter, [6] born October 11, 1899.

Susie Mae Schroeter, [6] born April 15, 1902.

Hallie Emory Schroeter, [6] born May 3, 1904.

George Railey Schroeter, [6] born December 18, 1905.

John Slaughter Railey, [5] born February 13, 1871, died October 14, 1876.

Martin Hardin Railey, Jr., [5] born April 1, 1872. Married Daisy Speilman, September 29, '1894.

Mary Agnes Railey, [6] born January 12, 1896.

Bonnie B. Railey. [6]

Gabriel Webster Railey, [5] born May 31, 1874. Married Beatricia Barton, January 1, 1896.

Roy Railey, [6] born 1901.

Sarah Pleasants Railey, [5] born September 23, 1876. Married William Pope LeMaster, Oct 18, 1905, at Denver, Colo.

Nathaniel Field LeMaster, [6] born April 22, 1909.

Tarleton Railey, [3] born September 1, 1810, died August 21, 1879. Married, first Sarah McBrayer, October 27, 1835, at Lawrenceburg, Ky.; married second Mary W. Blackwell, August 15, 1839, Lawrenceburg, Ky.

Mary Ann Railey, [4] born February 17, 1838, died April 9, 1887. Married Dr. Alfred Baxter Sloan, December 20, 1855, at Harrisonville, Mo.

Charles Clarence Sloan, [5] born October 18, 1856. Married, first Mary Townsend Addams, November 27, 1878, in Missouri; married second Helen Gordon Brown, June, 1908, in Mo.

Edith Terrill Sloan, [6] born, 1879. Married Charles Gregory Hutcheson, January 5, 1902, in Missouri.

Elizabeth Hutcheson, [7] born September 12, 1903.

Charles Gregory Hucheson, Jr., [7] born May 31, 1907.

Martha Brown Sloan, [6] born October 16, 1909.

Sarah Lee Sloan, [5] born April 3, 1859. Married William Rankin Hogsett, May 11, 1881, in Missouri.

William Sloan Hogsett, [6] born September 29, 1883. Married Sadie Estelle Cook, March 11, 1908, in Missouri.

Dr. Robert Tarleton Sloan, [5] born March 30, 1861. Married Carrie Roberta Parks, May 25, 1887, in Kansas City, Mo.

Mary Roberta Sloan, [6] born May 17, 1888.

Helen Ewing Sloan, [6] born April 18, 1897.

Roberta Tarleton Sloan, [6] born March 10, 1901.

Rowland Boggess Sloan, [5] born December 29, 1866.

Alfred McCready Sloan, [5] born July 10, 1870.

Married Edith Maude Bascom, 1902, in Missouri.

Olive J. Sloan, [6] born October 18, 1903.

Edith Bascom Sloan, [6] born December 4, 1904.

Roberta Lee Sloan, [6] born May 7, 1907.

Alice Patton Sloan, [5] born December 3, 1875.

Married William Sheldon Smallwood, October 26, 1905, in Missouri.

Sarah Elizabeth Railey, [4] born May 14, 1840, died December 19, 1903. Married Richard Oates Boggess, January 20, 1860, in Cass Co., Mo.

Earle Montrose Boggess. [5]

Married Hattie Gough.

Leonidas Clay Railey, [4] born February 6, 1843, died July 26, 1871.

Robert Tarleton Railey, [4] born January 19, 1850.

Married Martha Stuart Beatty, September 3, 1874, in Harrisonville, Mo.

Thomas Tarleton Railey, [5] born February, 1885.

Catharine Steele Railey, [4] born February 6, 1853.

Married James E. Hocker, February 25, 1873, in Cass Co., Mo.

Leonidas Oates Hocker, [5] born November 21, 1873.

Married Mary Norris Berry, June 15, 1904.

Edward Berry Hocker, [6] born November 19, 1908.

Lon O. Hocker, [6] born May 20, 1910.

Logan Railey, [3] born February 17, 1813, died October 28, 1891.

Married Harriet M. Rowland, June 19, 1836, in Versailles, Ky.

Belle Railey, [4] born December 17, 1840, died April 28, 1884.

Married William G. Stone, May 21, 1861, at Versailles, Ky.

William Haydon Stone, [5] born 1862.

Mary Hadley Stone. [5]

Charles Logan Stone. [5]

Married Reba Athey, November 26, 1890, at Covington, Ky.

Reba Athey Stone. [6]

Charles Logan Stone. [6]

Cornelia Lyle Stone.

Cornelia Railey, [4] born March 15, 1843, died October 31, 1881.

Married Joel Irvine Lyle, February 8, 1869.

J. Irvine Lyle, [5] born February 14, 1874.

Married Elizabeth Biggarstaff, December 23, 1901.

Cornelia Elizabeth Lyle, [6] born September 22, 1902.

Joel Irvine Lyle, Jr., [6] born May 3, 1906.

Ernest Thornton Lyle, [5] born December 6, 1879.

Married Grace Boynton, April 18, 1906.

Cornelius Railey Lyle, [5] born October 10, 1881.

Married Marie Leslie Brower, June 2, 1908.

Charles Logan Railey, [4] born April 17, 1844.

Married Ada Pepper, November 4, 1868.

Charles Elmer Railey, [5] born August 18, 1869.

Married, first Mary Belle Bradley, November 29, 1894; married, second Elise Kane Castleman, April 20, 1904.

Bradley Stone Railey, [6] born October 4, 1897.

Charles Logan Railey, Jr., [6] born June 21, 1905.

Elise Railey, [6] born May 17, 1909.

Ada Railey, [5] born May 19, 1871.

Married David Castleman, December 23, 1902.

Ada Mayo Castleman, [6] born March 20, 1905.

Annette Railey, [5] born, 1875.

Married Dr. Charles Stuart Elliott, March 17, 1898.

E. Bayard Railey, [5] born September 20, 1882.

Married Sue Metcalfe, July 19, 1904.

Russell Railey, [4] born February 6, 1850, died September 1, 1911.

Married Elizabeth Walker, December 24, 1903.

Irvine Railey, [4] born June 24, 1853.

Married Mrs. Victor Gray, (Nee Morancey), January 2, 1900.

Agnes Morancey Railey, [5] born January 24, 1906.

Hattie Railey, [4] born July 1, 1855.

Married Edward Ward, May, 1881.

Roberta Ward, [5] born September 18, 1882.

Married W. Lacey Kirtley, September 28, 1904.

Elizabeth Railey Kirtley, born June 28, 1905.

Roberta Ward Kirtley, born September 27, 1907.

Logan Railey Ward, [5] born September 29, 1884.

Married Katharine Weisenbach, 1908.

Logan Ward, born July, 4, 1909.

Anna Davis Ward, [5] born September 19, 1888.

Married E. E. Hughes, November 11, 1904.

Edward Ward Hughes, born August 22, 1905.

Margaret Ward Hughes, born December 26, 1907.

Thomas Elliott Hughes, born May 7, 1911.

Martin Railey, [3] born January 18, 1815, died September 23, 1837.

Francis Sweeney Railey, [3] born November 17, 1816, died August 19, 1843.

Charles Railey, tenth of John Railey and Elizabeth Randolph, was born on "Stonehenge" farm, near Richmond, Va., in 1766. He and his brother, Randolph Railey, came to Kentucky about 1793, and he located near Versailles, Ky., on a farm adjoining the farm of his brother William Railey. After making all necessary preparations for a comfortable future, he returned to Virginia, in 1796 to marry the girl who had looked upon him with favor before he left the old Virginia home. This lady was Mary Mayo, fourth of Col. William Mayo and Catharine Swann, of Richmond. Although his brother Martin Railey had married her sister two years before without parental objection it was not so in the case of Charles Railey, as the family frowned upon the thought of their daughter, Mary, being taken over the mountains to the wilderness beyond, as Kentucky was called at that period by all Virginians east of the "Blue Ridge." They dreaded the dangers one must encounter owing to the numerous tribes of savages that had been driven to the interior as a result of the Revolution. So determined was this opposition to their daughter going to Kentucky, that an elopement was planned to take place from a ball given by the young men of Richmond, Va., on a night in April, 1796. Their plans were well executed and as a result the marriage occurred on the fourth day of April, 1796. They came to Kentucky during the following summer and entered upon life's duties on "Buck Run" farm in the old Railey neighborhood, near Versailles, where they spent a long, useful and happy life, rearing a large family of children to bless their old age. Russell Railey is the present owner of "Buck Run" estate which passed to him through his father Logan Railey, tenth of Charles Railey and Mary Mayo.

Charles Railey served a term in the Kentucky Legislature as the representative of Woodford county, during the 40's, but he positively refused ever afterward to run for office. Their eldest son, James Railey cast his lot in Mississippi at an early age where he married Matilda S. Green, the daughter of a wealthy planter of that State. Mary Eliza Railey, the eldest born of this couple, married the Rev. Frederick W. Boyd, a minister of the Episcopal church, in 1844. This couple raised four sons, one of whom Loyd Tilghman Boyd is the present publisher of the Milwaukee Journal, at Milwaukee, Wisconsin.

Charles Railey, Jr., the 2nd of Chas. Railey and Mary Mayo, settled in New Orleans at the age of eighteen years where he married Jane Reams soon thereafter. The eldest son of this couple, Charles Randolph Railey, married Elizabeth Helm, of Natchez, Miss., and their three children, Ann Maria Railey who married Dr. W. W. Black, Jennie Railey who married Andrew A. Woods, and William Mayo Railey who married Lina Howell, are residents of New Orleans. William Mayo Railey is at the head of a large marine and fire insurance business that takes in several states along the Gulf Coast. Other children and grandchildren of Charles Railey, Jr., and Mary Reams live in Louisiana, Mississippi and Texas.

Catharine Swann Railey, the 3rd of Charles Railey and Mary Mayo was born near Versailles, Ky., in 1800, and married John Steele, of Versailles, Ky., in 1816. Their daughter, Agnes Winfield Steele, who was the only child, was born in Woodford County, Ky., in 1817 and married Thomas F. Thornton, of Versailles, in 1835, and their daughter, an only child,

Susan Catharine Thornton, was born in 1836. She married Sandy Brown, of Versailles, Ky., in 1856. They lived in St. Louis, Mo., for many years, where Mr. Brown was in business, but the family now reside at Joplin, Mo. Mrs. Brown has quite a good deal of family data and is a most estimable woman.

Nancy Scott Railey, 4th of Charles Railey and Mary Mayo, was born in Woodford county, Ky., in 1801, and married Allen Rowland, of that county, in 1828. Their son, Charles Wesley Rowland, married Virginia Green and was one of Cincinnati's business men for many years.

Samuel Railey, 5th of Charles Railey and Mary Mayo, married first Martha Rowland at Versailles, Ky., and second, Sallie Tucker, of Paris, Ky. Their descendants all live in Missouri and possess much data relative to their ancestors.

Charlotte Railey, 6th of Charles Railey and Mary Mayo, was born in Woodford county, in 1805 and married David Thornton in 1823. David Thornton was a banker at Versailles, Ky., for many years and served Woodford county in both branches of the Kentucky Legislature. Their eldest daughter, Eleanor Thornton, married David I. Porter, of Versailles, Ky., in 1841. She is still living at the advanced age of eighty-six years, with her daughter, Mrs. Daniel Cooper, at Sedalia, Mo., and although quite old her mind is wonderfully clear and much of the data concerning the Randolphs, Mayos and Raileys was furnished by her as she received it from her grandparents and others of the old Raileys in person. All of her Kentucky relatives remember her as a woman of many lovable traits of character. Her descendants are in Missouri, Texas and California. Elizabeth Thornton was the second of David Thornton and Charlotte Railey. She married Ulysses Turner, a lawyer of Versailles, Ky., in 1849. The most of their descendants live at Versailles, Ky. Their daughter, Mary Logan Turner, married William O. Davis, an attorney of Versailles, Ky. Hontas Thornton, fourth of David Thornton and Charlotte Railey, married Edwin S. Craig, an attorney at Versailles, Ky.

Edwin Kavanaugh Thornton and Woodford Railey Thornton, sons of David and Charlotte Thornton, were for many years bankers at Kansas City, Mo., where their sons are now connected with banking institutions.

Margaret Crittenden Railey was the 7th of Charles Railey and Mary Mayo. She married Bishop H. H. Kavanaugh, of the Methodist Church, at Versailles, Ky., in 1828.

Lewis Clark Railey was the 8th of Charles Railey and Mary Mayo. He married Susan Mary Hardin, of Harrodsburg, Ky., in 1830. His descendants live in Colorado, New Mexico and Texas.

Tarleton Railey was the 9th of Charles Railey and Mary Mayo. He was twice married, first to Sarah McBrayer, of Lawrenceburg, Ky., and second to Mary W. Blackwell, of the same town, his second wife being a neice of his first wife. He located at Harrisonville, Mo., before the Civil War where he raised an interesting family. His daughter, Mary Ann Railey, married Dr. Alfred Baxter Sloan at Harrisonville, Mo., in 1855, and their son, Dr. Robert Tarleton Sloan, is one of the leading physicians of Kansas City, where he married Carrie Roberta Parks in 1882. William Sloan Hogsett, a lawyer of Kansas City, is a grandson of Dr. Alfred Baxter Sloan and Mary Ann Railey.

Robert Tarleton Railey, son of Tarleton Railey and Mary Blackwell, married Mary Stuart Beatty, daughter of Dr. Thomas Stuart Beatty, in 1874. He is a lawyer and is the general attorney of the Missouri Pacific and Iron Mountain railroads with headquarters at St. Louis. His son, Thomas Tarlton Railey, is also a lawyer. Having known Robert Tarleton Railey from childhood I must say that he is universally esteemed for his manliness and high character.

Catharine Steele Railey was the youngest of the children of Tarleton Railey and Mary Blackwell. She married James E. Hocker at Harrisonville, Mo., in 1873, and their only son, Leonidas Oates Hocker, is one of the leading lawyers of St. Louis. He married Mary Norris Berry in 1904.

Logan Railey was the 10th of Charles Railey and Mary Mayo. He married Harriet M. Rowland in Versailles, in 1836. He lived, until his death, on "Buck Run" farm, the old home of his father and his son Russell Railey is the present owner of the estate.

Now to make plain the relationship of the Raileys to the Mayos you must understand that Martin and Charles Railey, two sons of John Railey and Elizabeth Randolph, married Elizabeth and Mary Mayo, daughters of Col. William Mayo and Catharine Swann, of Richmond, Va. Joseph Randolph Railey, nephew of Martin and Charles Railey, married Nancy Mayo who was a sister of Elizabeth and Mary Mayo. William Mayo, Jr., who was a brother of these three girls married Caroline Fleming Pleasants, daughter of Mathew Pleasants and Anna Railey.

RANDOLPH RAILEY

Eleventh born of John Railey and Elizabeth Randolph. Married, first, Mary Elizabeth Keith; second, Martha Pleasants. Their descendants:

John Railey [1] Elizabeth Randolph.

Randolph Railey, [2] born May 14, 1770; died May 28, 1837.

Married, first, Elizabeth Keith, 1800; second, Martha Pleasants, 1819.

Isham Keith Railey, [3] born 1801; died 1803.

Boone Railey, [3] born October 26, 1820; died March 28, 1869.

Married Elizabeth Wheeler, June 14, 1853.

Randolph Railey, [4] born 1854; died 1860.

Samuel Wheeler Railey, [4] born February 16, 1856.

Anna Railey, [4] born April 29, 1860.

Married John Calhoun Burnett, November 16, 1883.

Gilbert Burnett, [5] born October 8, 1887.

Theodore L. Burnett, [5] born January 1, 1890.

The posterity of Randolph Railey, the 11th born of John Railey and Elizabeth Randolph, occupies less space than is required for each of his brothers and sisters. He was born on the "Stonehenge" farm in Chesterfield county, Virginia, and educated at Richmond. The date of his birth was 1770. He accompanied his brother Charles Railey, who came to Kentucky about 1793, and they both settled in Woodford county on farms adjacent to their brother William. The home of Randolph Railey was known as "Canebreak." This farm passed out of the hands of the family about ten years after the Civil War. Randolph Railey first married his cousin Mary Elizabeth Keith, second born of Captain Isham Keith and Charlotte Ashmore. The marriage ceremony was performed at the home of General Humphrey Marshall, whose wife was her first cousin. Only one child blessed this union. Both mother and child died within a short period after the birth of the latter. Randolph Railey's second marriage was to his cousin Martha Randolph Pleasants. She was also a cousin to his first wife. Martha Randolph Pleasants was the 2nd born of James Pleasants and Anna Randolph and hence a sister of Gov. James Pleasants, of Virginia. Many of the older descendants of the Raileys now living remember Randolph Railey and his wife Pattie, as she was familiarly known, with much pleasure. Many have written of the hospitable old home and speak of the old couple in affectionate terms. Their grandson, Samuel Wheeler Railey, is an attorney-at-law and has been connected with the legal department of the United States Treasury at Washington City since 1886. His motto is liberty, and hence he has never married. He spends his vacations in traveling and has made several trips abroad besides taking in many of the interesting points in America. His presence would assure you that he knew the most fashionable tailor in the community, and the writer knows that he is familiar with the best hostelries. His sister, Anna Railey, married Mr. John Calhoun Burnett, a lawyer of Louisville, Ky., and has several interesting children. Charles and Randolph Railey accompanied their brother William Railey and his wife, Judith Woodson, to Kentucky. In the company was also their sister Jane. Several other Virginians whose names I do not recall were in the company and all settled in Kentucky.

Now to sum up the Randolph relationship you will understand that the mother of these eleven children was Elizabeth Randolph. Thomas, William and Isham Railey married three of the daughters of Col. John Woodson and his wife Dorothy Randolph. Randolph Railey's first wife was a granddaughter of Mary Isham Randolph and the Rev. James Keith. His second wife was a daughter of Anna Randolph and James Pleasants, of "Contention" and a sister of Governor James Pleasants of Virginia. Elizabeth, Dorothy and Anna Randolph were daughters of Col. Isham Randolph and Jane Rogers, and hence sisters of Thomas Jefferson's mother, Jane Randolph. Mary Isham Randolph was a daughter of Thomas Randolph and Judith Fleming. The writer of these notes is descended from Elizabeth and Dorothy and also from Mary Isham Randolph. Samuel Wheeler Railey is descended from Elizabeth and Anna Randolph.

The Strothers and their Railey connections:

William Strother, [1] died 1702.
Married Dorothy (Strother).
Jeremiah Strother, [2] died 1741.
Married Eleanor (Strother).
Francis Strother, [3] of "St. Marks Parrish."
Married Susanna Dabney.
William Strother, [4] of "Orange" born 1728; died 1808.
Married, first, Sarah Pannill, 1751 (widow of Wm. Pannill); second, Anna Kavanaugh. (No issue.) (Widow of Philemon Kavanaugh).

William Dabney Strother, [5] an officer in Revolution killed at battle of Guilford C. H.
Susanna Strother. [5]
Married, first, Capt. Moses Hawkins; second, Thomas Coleman.
William Strother Hawkins, [6] born June 1, 1772, died October 6, 1858.
Married Catharine Keith, October 14, 1802.
Catharine Keith Hawkins, [7] born October 18, 1825, died June 22, 1902.
Married Richard Henry Railey, February 25, 1852.
William Edward Railey, [8] born December 25, 1852.
Married Annie H. Owsley, May 26, 1886.
Jennie Farris Railey, [9] born June 28, 1887.
Sarah Strother. [5]
Married Col. Richard Taylor.
General Zachary Taylor, [6] President, 1848.
Married Margaret Smith.

William Strother, the progenitor of this line, is supposed to have died about 1702. He was of Northumberland county, Virginia, where he settled on the Rappahannock river near Fredricksburg about 1650. He had several brothers of whose descendants I have no record. He and his wife, Dorothy, reared six children. His will is of record in Richmond county, afterward King George county, and is dated 1700, his estate being devised to his wife Dorothy for life and then to his sons, William, James, Jeremiah, Robert, Benjamine and Joseph. The above Jeremiah married Eleanor—He lived in that part of Orange county that afterwards became Culpepper, where he died in 1741. His will was proven by J. Slaughter, John Catlett and Wm. Lighffoot and his estate was devised to his wife Eleanor for life. They reared eight children whose names were James, William of "Stafford," Francis of "St. Marks," Jeremiah, Jr., Christopher, Catharine, Elizabeth and ―――――. His two eldest sons, James and William, of "Stafford," (so-called afterward to distinguish him from his nephew William, of "Orange,") were the executors of his will. Many distinguished people were descended from these eight children. James married Margaret French; William, of "Stafford," married Margaret Watts and they were blessed with thirteen daughters whose descendants added much to Virginia's social and political lustre.

Francis, of "St. Marks," married Susanna Dabney, and Jeremiah, Jr., married Catharine Kimberly.

Frances, of St. Marks, who married Susanna Dabney, daughter of John Dabney and Sarah Jennings, was the proud parent of ten children. The first was John who married Mary Wade. They were the ancestors of John Strother Pendleton, congressman and foreign minister.

Anthony, the second, married first Behethland Storke and second Mary James. From the first marriage came Col. John Strother, of the War of 1812, and his son General David Hunter Strother, of "Port Crayon" fame.

George, the third son, married Mollie Kimberly and by this union came General William Preston, of Lexington, and General Albert Sidney Johnston, who was killed at Shiloh.

William, of "Orange," fourth, married, first, Sarah Pannill, widow of William Pannill; second, Anna Kavanaugh, widow of Philemon Kavanaugh. By the last marriage no issue. The first born was William Dabney Strother, who was an officer in Col. Richard Taylor's command, who was his brother-in-law. He was killed in the engagement at Guilford C. H. Susanna Strother was the second born of William, of Orange, and Sarah Pannill. She married Captain Moses Hawkins who was killed in battle at Germantown, 1777. Captain Moses Hawkins and Susanna Strother were the great grand parents of the compiler of the Railey-Randolph notes. A few years after the death of Capt. Moses Hawkins his widow married Thomas Coleman of Culpepper. Thomas Coleman was a corporal in Captain Hawkins' company. Sarah Strother, the third of William, of Orange, and Sarah Pannill married Col. Richard Taylor and they were the parents of General Zachary Taylor who became President in 1848.

In 1787 William Strother, of Orange, in company with Thomas Coleman and wife and her four Hawkins children moved to Kentucky and settled in Woodford county near Versailles. His will is of record in the clerk's office at Versailles in Will Book C, Page 165. His son-in-law, Col. Richard Taylor, and grandson, Hancock Taylor, are named as executors.

I have a great deal of data concerning the Strothers and their kin that is interesting. They were intermarried with very many of the prominent families of Virginia and held an enviable position in the early history of that state.

NOTE.

Recently I have received quite a number of letters from relatives inquiring why I hadn't given an account of the ancestors of John Railey. To them I will say that I have no data except some memoranda I made when a boy from conversations between relatives long since dead, and from these notes I was not able to trace the exact line, hence left it out entirely. Had I been able to visit England and spend some time poring over old records I have no doubt but that my efforts would have been successful in running John Railey's line back several generations. I hope some relative, taking what I give him or her here, will hereafter do that. In the meantime we must rest contented with this brief statement I made from data in my possession.

When John Railey landed in America about 1740, his name was John Raleigh. Court records in Virginia, if not destroyed during the Civil War, will show that his name was changed from John Raleigh to John Railey, which was the pronunciation given Raleigh by his Virginia neighbors at that time. A few of my old relatives thought probably he was a grandson of Sir Walter Raleigh, but the most of those who discussed it were positive that he was a great nephew of the man who lost his head by disobeying orders at the Battle of Ft. Thomas, Brazil, S. A. However, that may be, it was known by all of the older set that "Stonehenge" farm in Chesterfield county, Virginia, owned by John Railey, was a part of the land grant to Sir Walter Raleigh by the crown of England. It was further known to them that John Railey was born and reared on a part of the possessions of Sir Walter Raleigh in England, and when he settled on the farm in Virginia he called it "Stonehenge" on account of the stately oaks that surrounded the house, as they so much reminded him of the same species of oak that surrounded the home of the "Druid Priests" in England, called "Stonehenge." The home of these Druid Priests, I think, was adjacent to the large estate of Sir Walter Raleigh. These large oaks on the "Stonehenge" farm in Virginia were still standing in 1863 and were spoken of as monarchs of the forest.

I am very glad that so many of the relatives have manifested such a decided interest in acquiring greater knowledge of John Railey's ancestors and it will give me much pleasure if some one of the relation will take up this question and add the links necessary to run his line back several generations. I would have done so myself but for lack of time and money.

That John Railey's grandfather was a brother of Sir Walter Raleigh I feel satisfied, as that was the impression of the old Raileys who lived in the early half of the last century. Through the same source I learned that John Railey was a colonel of militia and active in raising volunteers for the Revolution, but I was unable to prove it by any record and I didn't mention that in the record, yet I am certain of it, and his relatives all speak of him as Col. John Railey who served in the Revolution. I do not believe that his neighbors and relatives called him Colonel because of "his anagosity and general understanding in the neighborhood," as that method of dubbing one colonel has come in vogue the last fifty years. lution. I do not believe that his neighbors and relatives called him Colonel because of "his anosity and general understanding in the neighborhood," as that method of dubbing one colonel has come in vogue the last fifty years.

Now, in accounting for John Railey's action in changing his name from Raleigh to Railey I only know of two reasons, one of which is certainly correct. In the first place, the early colonists soon abandoned many of the customs of their English cousins, and there was a distinct departure in the manner of pronunciation—giving for instance to *a* the same sound in Raleigh that would be given in Railey. This may have actuated John Railey in his act, but I think it most likely it was the result of a sense of mortification, felt by all of his relatives, over the untimely and sad death of Sir Walter Raleigh. John Railey was much embittered against the English crown to the day of his death. What gives me an additional reason for taking the last view as the most reasonable is the fact that many of Sir Walter's relatives in England have for two centuries spelled the name Rayleigh and Rayley.

Trusting that in this brief statement I may arouse enough interest in this subject to cause some one to take it up and carry it to a satisfactory conclusion.*

I am,
Very truly,
WM. E. RAILEY.

*Omissions from p. 151, this volume:
Cornelius Wm. Beale,[6] born September 17, 1886. Married Mary Elizabeth Graham September 11, 1907.
Ruth Burnley Beale.[7]
William Stuart Beale.[7]
Carrie Marie Beale,[6] born May 31, 1889. Married Thomas Willis Lewis November 28, 1911.
Byron Sunderland Beale,[6] born January 26, 1892. Married Rosa Ann Londes, October 18, 1911.
Earle Gordan Beale,[6] born October 28, 1894.
Edna Elizabeth Beale,[6] born June 15, 1899.

BRIEF SKETCHES OF THE RANDOLPHS AND THEIR CONNECTIONS; ALSO A BRIEF SKETCH OF THE OWSLEYS AND WHITLEYS.*

By William Edward Railey.

TABLE 1.

Generation
1st. William Randolph married Mary Isham.
2d. Col. Isham Randolph married Jane Rogers.
3d. Elizabeth Randolph married Col. John Railey.
4th. Thomas Railey married Martha Woodson.
5th. Peter I. Railey married Judith Woodson Railey.
6th. Richard Henry Railey married Katherine Keith Hawkins.
7th. William Edward Railey married Annie Harper Owsley.
8th. Jennie Farris Railey married Douglas Wheeler King.

The name of William Randolph is prominently mentioned in several of the early histories of Virginia relating to its political, social and religious status. He was one of the sons of Richard Randolph of "Morton Hall" in England, and emigrated to America about 1669, when he succeeded his uncle, Henry Randolph, who preceded him to this continent, as clerk of the Colony of Virginia. His country seat was "Turkey Island," which vast estate fringed the James river for many miles. He married Mary Isham, daughter of Henry and Katherine Banks Isham of "Burmuda-Hundred" on the opposite side of the river. He held many offices of public trust that carried much responsibility, as did also each of his sons.

Henry Isham, father of Mary, has an ascending family history that touches royalty in several lines, as is amply attested by English historians. His wife's maiden name was Katherine Banks who, before his death, was the wife of Joseph Royall.

Col. Isham Randolph who, as shown in the table, married Jane Rogers, in London, England, had a daughter Jane who married Peter Jefferson of Virginia, and they were the parents of President Thomas Jefferson. Another daughter, Elizabeth, married Col. John Railey, and still another daughter, Dorothea, married Col. John Woodson. These two girls, Elizabeth and Dorothea, were paternal great grandmothers of Wm. Edward Railey the author of this sketch, as shown in Tables 1 and 2. Col. John Woodson will be sketched under Table 2. Col. John Railey's country seat was "Stonehenge" in Chesterfield Co., Va. He married Elizabeth Randolph in 1750. They reared a large family in their Virginia home and he died there 1783. Five of his

*The Register of the Kentucky Historical Society carried this article in May 1918 instead of a third installment of William Railey's article on the Strothers, which appears on pp. 369-396, this volume.

sons migrated to Kentucky, 1784-93, and settled on neighboring farms in Woodford county near Versailles. It passed down from these brothers, among many other interesting reminiscences of that period the statement that their father manifested his interest in the revolution by preparing the militia for active participation as did Col. John Woodson, both having the rank of Colonel, but when I attempted to verify the statements by the records, Goochland county's records were all right, but Chesterfield's records, like those of many other counties, were in such a state of preservation as to render no service in procuring information of the Revolutionary period, but there never was a doubt among his descendants of his service as Colonel of militia before and during the Revolution. His eldest son John was killed at the battle of Norfolk. His second son Thomas Railey was one of the five who came to Kentucky and was ever the companion and counsellor of the brothers. He dubbed his country seat "Clifton" in honor of his uncle, Carter Harrison, whose country seat was "Clifton," Va. He returned to Virginia during the year 1786 and married his cousin Martha Woodson. They raised a large family on the Clifton farm and their remains were interred there. The old home remained in possession of descendants for many years after the Civil War.

TABLE 2.

Generation.
1st. William Randolph married Mary Isham.
2d. Col. Isham Randolph married Jane Rogers.
3d. Dorothea Randolph married Col. John Woodson.
4th. Judith Woodson married William Railey.
5th. Judith Woodson Railey married Peter I. Railey.
6th. Richard Henry Railey married Katherine Keith Hawkins.
7th. William Edward Railey married Annie Harper Owsley.
8th. Jennie Farris Railey married Douglas Wheeler King.

The country seat of Col. Isham Randolph, whose name also appears in Table 1, was "Dungeness," a part of the original estate of his father known as "Turkey Island." While representing the Colonies at the British Court as its Colonial Agent at London he married Jane Rogers of Shadwell street, that city. It is my impression that their daughter Jane, who married Peter Jefferson of Virginia, was born in London, but I think he returned to America before the birth of any other of the children. At various times he was an officer of the Colonies serving as Adjutant General, member House of Burgesses and Colonel of State militia. His daughter, Dorothea, whose name appears in above table and who was briefly mentioned in sketch under Table 1, married Col. John Woodson, whose country seat was "Dover," Goochland Co., Va. Col. Woodson was sheriff of his county, member conventions 1774-75 and 76, member House of Burgesses and Colonel of militia. He was a strict member of the Episcopal church and one of their vestrymen. In his will his palatial residence (photographed in the book of "The Woodsons") and the Dover estate passed to his son Major Josiah Woodson, a gallant soldier of the Revolution, who remained upon it until 1804 when he came to Maysville, Ky., to reside where several of his children had preceded him. He died there during the year 1817. His granddaughter, Elizabeth Moss, daughter of Dr. Moss, who had moved with his family to Missouri, married General William H. Ashley, who represented that state in Congress. After General Ashley's death she married Hon. John J. Crittenden of Frankfort who served Kentucky as Governor and then in the U. S. Senate. She was a second cousin of Randolph Railey, Jr., of Woodford county, who married Caroline Crittenden, sister of Hon. John J. Crittenden.

A more extended account of Col. John Woodson and his kin, both ascending and descending may be found in the book of the "Woodsons and their connections." His daughter, Judith Woodson, married her cousin William Railey as the table above shows. Two others of his daughters, Martha and Susanna, married Raileys. William Railey and his wife Judith Woodson were great-grandparents of the author of this sketch. They came to Kentucky about 1793, where he had already prepared his domicile He built one of the first two and one-half story brick houses built in Woodford county. The material was of such good quality that the building is still in fair condition although it has been out of the possession of descendants for fifty years. His country seat was known as "Liberty Hall." During the period of the lives of William and Judith Woodson Railey, and for many years after their home was known as a home of unstinted hospitality. Their remains, with those of all of their deceased descendants, repose in the Versailles cemetery.

TABLE 3.

Generation.
1st. William Randolph married Mary Isham.
2d. "Tuckahoe" Thomas Randolph married Judith Churchill.
3d. Mary Isham Randolph married Rev. James Keith.
4th. Captain Isham Keith married Charlotte Ashmore.
5th. Katherine Keith married William Strother Hawkins.
6th. Katherine Keith Hawkins married Richard Henry Railey.
7th. William Edward Railey married Annie Harper Railey.
8th. Jennie Farris Railey married Douglas Wheeler King.

The "Turkey Island" estate contained thousands of acres and as the children of William Randolph married they were settled upon subdivisions of the estate. Thomas Randolph who married Judith Churchill called his country seat "Tuckahoe." He seemed to aspire to official life with much more modesty than his seven brothers, as I am unable to refer to any other office than Justice that he held, but his rulings were fair, as no dissensions were manifest. For many years there has been a division of opinion as to whom he married,* his great nephew, John Randolph, of "Roanoke," and others of that line contending that he married Judith Fleming, while descendants of Gov. Thomas Mann Randolph and his wife, Martha Jefferson, insist that his wife's maiden name was Judith Churchill. The old Raileys thought John Randolph was right, but from information I have had the last two years I am convinced that his wife was Judith Churchill. Gov. Thos. Mann Randolph was born and reared in the "Tuckahoe" mansion as was his father, Col. Thomas Mann Randolph, and his grandfather, William Randolph, son of Thomas at "Tuckahoe," and they all had access to the family Bibles and family records and their statements should satisfy any one, and beside, Martha Jefferson bore the same relationship to Thomas of "Tuckahoe" as did John Randolph of "Roanoke." Although formerly using the name of Judith Fleming I now place the name of Judith Churchill in the table opposite that of Thomas of "Tuckahoe." At any rate Thomas of "Tuckahoe" had three children, viz.: William Randolph III., Mary Isham Randolph and Judith Randolph. William Randolph III. married Maria Judith Page and inherited the "Tuckahoe" estate, which in turn was inherited by his son, Col. Thomas Mann Randolph, and then by his grandson, Gov. Thomas Mann Randolph. Col. Thomas Mann Randolph was first married to Anne Cary and afterward to a daughter of Gabriel Jones and his wife Miss Strother. By the first marriage was Gov. Thomas Mann Randolph, who married his cousin, Martha Jefferson, daughter of the President. Mary Isham Randolph, second of Thomas and Judith Churchill, married the Rev. James Keith, familiarly known as "Parson" Keith, and they were the parents of Mary Randolph Keith who married Col. Thomas Marshall, and of Captain Isham Keith who married Charlotte Ashmore and was an officer in Col. Marshall's Virginia regiment. Col. Marshall and his wife, Mary Randolph Keith were the parents of Chief Justice John Marshall and all of the prominent Marshalls of Virginia and Kentucky.

Captain Isham Keith as shown in the table above married Charlotte Ashmore, who was of a wealthy and prominent old Virginia family, whose brothers were all bachelors and sisters spinsters, hence the name is extinct so far as her line is concerned. Capt. Keith was severely wounded during the Revolution. After the war he served in the Virginia legislature. Before his death his daughters Mary Elizabeth and Katherine Keith visited their Marshall kin at Frankfort and Versailles, Ky., where Mary Elizabeth became the first wife of her cousin Randolph Railey, Sr., and Katherine Keith married William Strother Hawkins, whose name appears in the above table.

Judith Randolph, third of Thomas and Judith Churchill Randolph, married her cousin, Rev. William Stith, son of Captain Wm. Stith and Mary Randolph. His

*See pp. 189-200, this volume.

pastoral services were rendered in Henrico county mainly and he was known as one of Virginia's historians as well as President of William and Mary's College for many years. My notes do not say whether this line of the family was extended or not.

Rev. James Keith whose name appears in the above table, although much written of, will receive but brief mention here as my Keith notes are in Tennessee. The encyclopedia of England claims the "House of Keith" to be one of the most ancient and prominent in Europe. We only know that James Keith and his uncle Bishop Robt. Keith were residents of Scotland just before a Scotch rebellion. He and his two cousins, George Keith, tenth and last Earl, and James Francis Edward Keith, of Prussia, attended Aberdeen College, and while yet in his teens this James Keith was an active participant in an unsuccessful rebellion that so compromised him that he was forced to flee the country and took refuge in America, landing on the shores of Virginia. Soon thereafter he entered the ministry of the Episcopal church and married Mary Isham Randolph. He brought to America a history of his ancestry, but a kinsman whose mother was in possession of this ancestral history wrote that it was destroyed during the Revolution. Much of a legendary nature has been written about the Keiths. However, suffice it to say, that the Rev. James Keith and Mary Isham gave to the nation some brilliant men and women.

TABLE 4.

Generation.
1st. Dr. John Woodson married Sarah Winston.
2d. Robert Woodson married Elizabeth Ferris.
3d. John Woodson married Judith Tarleton.
4th. Josiah Woodson married Mary Royall.
5th. Col. John Woodson married Dorothea Randolph.
6th. Sisters, Martha Woodson married Thomas Railey; Judith Woodson married William Railey.
7th. Peter I. Railey, son of Martha, married Judith Woodson Railey, daughter of Judith.
8th. Richard Henry Railey married Katherine Keith Hawkins.
9th. William Edward Railey married Annie Harper Owsley.
10th. Jennie Farris Railey married Douglas Wheeler King.

Dr. John Woodson came to America about 1620, as a surgeon to a troop of English soldiers under command of Sir John Harvie and located at "Middle Settlement" near Richmond, Va. He was from Dorsetshire and she from Devonshire, England. His great grandson, Tarleton Woodson, brother of Josiah in the above table, married Ursula Fleming, daughter of Charles Fleming of New Kent Co., Va., who was a descendant of Sir Tarleton Fleming second son of Sir Thomas Fleming, Earl of Wigton, Scotland. Sir Thomas Fleming married Miss Tarleton and emigrated to America, landing at Jamestown, Va., the year 1616. His son Tarleton married Miss Bates and they were the parents of Tarleton Fleming who married Mary Randolph, the only daughter of William Randolph and Maria Judith Page, mentioned in sketch under Table 3, and of course a sister of Col. Thos. Mann Randolph and first cousin of Capt. Isham Keith of Table 3.

Tarleton Woodson and his wife, Ursula Fleming, were the parents of Caroline and Susannah Woodson. Susannah married John Pleasants of "Piquenique," Va., and they were the grandparents of Martha Pleasants who married her cousin, Randolph Railey, Sr., of Versailles, Ky.. and of Gov. James Pleasants of Virginia, sketched more extensively under descendants of Anna Randolph and James Pleasants of "Contention" under "Some other Sketches of Isham Randolph's children." Caroline Woodson, the other daughter of Tarleton and Ursula married her cousin, Thomas Fleming Bates, and their children in part were Gov. Frederick Bates of Missouri and Hon. Edward Bates of the same state who was appointed by Mr. Lincoln Attorney General of the United States, and Gov. James Woodson Bates who was active in the political affairs of Arkansas about the period of the Civil War.

Josiah Woodson was a brother of this Tarleton Woodson and his name appears in the above table as having married Mary Royall. Mary Royall was a daughter of Capt. Joseph Royall and Elizabeth Kennon, two of the Kennons having been Admirals in the navy. Josiah Woodson inherited the "Dover" estate of his father upon which he and his wife lived and died, rearing a large family as well as an interesting one. In his will he mentions, among other items, a note due his estate by Col. Thomas Mann Randolph which shows that they were not only of the same period and neighborhood but friends as well. In his will he bequeathed the "Dover" estate to his son, Col. John Woodson, who was born in Goochland Co., Va., in this palatial home in 1730, and married Dorothea Randolph, daughter of Col. Isham Randolph and Jane Rogers, October 28, 1751. Col. John Woodson was briefly sketched under Table 2. Two of his daughters, as shown in the above table, Martha and Judith, were great-grandparents of the author of this sketch. Of the prominent descendants of Dr. John Woodson and Sarah Winston that occur to me as I write of Virginians: Major Frederick Tarleton Woodson, Gen. Tarleton Woodson, Col. Charles Woodson, Gov. James Pleasants and Hon. Hampden Pleasants. Of Missourians were Gov. Frederick Bates, Hon. Edward Bates, General Charles Woodson, Governor Silas Woodson, and Judge A. M. Woodson, who has been for many years Judge of the Missouri Supreme Court, and Judge Robert Tarleton Railey is also associated with the Supreme Court of that state. Of Arkansas is the Hon. James Woodson Bates. Of Kansas, Gov. Daniel Woodson. Several of the Woodsons were prominent legislators and jurists in central Kentucky prior to the Civil War and the Hon. Urey Woodson of Owensboro, Ky., has been a prominent figure in State and National politics for twenty or more years. I might add that Gov. Silas Woodson was a product of Kentucky and served in the Constitutional Convention of 1849 before adopting Kentucky as his home.

TABLE 5.

Generation.

1st. William Strother married Dorothy ———.
2d. William Strother, Jr., married Margaret Thornton.
3d. St. Marks. Francis Strother married Susanna Dabney.
4th. Of Orange. William Strother married Mrs. Sarah Bailey Pannill.
5th. Susanna Strother married Captain Moses Hawkins.
6th. William Strother Hawkins married Katherine Keith.
7th. Katherine Keith Hawkins married Richard Henry Railey.
8th. William Edward Railey married Annie Harper Owsley.
9th. Jennie Farris Railey married Douglas Wheeler King.

William Strother, the immigrant, came to America from Northumberland, England, about 1650. The descendants have been men of courage and talent and the women have universally possessed many charms of character and person. They married into many of the leading families of Virginia and have rendered s rvice in the halls of legislation, both State and National, on the judiciary, pleaders at the bar of justice and in the military department of the government. The church records of King George, Stafford and Culpeper counties, Va., make it plain that they were devout Episcopalians. I have never been able to learn the full maiden name of his wife who is placed in the table as Dorothy. Margaret Thornton, the wife of his son, William Strother, Jr., was a daughter of Francis Thornton and his wife Alice Savage, who was a daughter of Anthony Savage, a justice of Rappahannock County, about 1673. William Strother, Jr., inherited his father's mansion, which was consumed by fire some years after, together with all of the family relics, manuscripts and fine library. The estate that he inherited from his father he bequeathed to his son, William Strother, of "Stafford," who married Margaret Watts, and tradition says from this union came "thirteen blooming daughters," a story pure and simple. They had six daughters whose descendants married into the families of Madison, Jones, Tyler, Norton, Lewis, Marshall, Preston, McDowell, Payton, Blairs, Randolph, Pope and Dabney. Francis Strother, another son of William, Jr., and Margaret Thornton Strother, married Susanna Dabney as shown in the table above. His residence was "St. Mark's Parish," where he and his wife lived many years and reared a large family who intermarried with the Pendletons, Menifees, Stuarts, Brownings, Gaines, Covingtons, Baileys and Wades, of Virginia.

William Strother of "Orange," whose name appears in the table above was one of the sons of Francis

Strother of "St. Mark's Parish" and Susanna Dabney. He was twice married, his first wife being the widow Pannill, whose maiden name was Sarah Bailey, a relative of the Banks and Dabney families. Those who knew her said that she possessed unusual intellectual powers and many other charms that gave her a commanding position among her friends and acquaintances. By this marriage were three children, viz.: William Dabney Strother, Susanna Strother and Sarah Strother. William Dabney Strother was a young man of splendid intellectual attainments who cast his lot with the Revolutionary forces and became an officer in the regiment commanded by his brother-in-law, Col. Richard Taylor, and lost his life at the battle of Guilfords Court House. His sister, Susanna Strother, married Captain Moses Hawkins, March 3, 1770, who lost his life at the battle of Germantown, October 4, 1777. Their names appear in the table above and they were the great-grandparents of Wm. Edward Railey. Sarah Strother, sister of Susanna and youngest of the children of William Strother of "Orange" and Sarah Bailey Pannill, married Col. Richard Taylor of the 9th Virginia regiment and they were the parents of General Zachary Taylor, who became President, 1849. General Zach Taylor had a son who was famous in the cause of the Confederacy and wrote a history of the Civil War that was very popular. He also had a daughter who was the first wife of Jefferson Davis, President of the Confederacy. Col Richard Taylor and his son, Hancock, were the executors of the will of William Strother of "Orange," who died on his farm in Woodford Co., Ky., and his will is of record in the county clerk's office at Versailles. He came to Kentucky to reside about 1800 or soon thereafter, in the company of his second wife, Anna Kavanaugh and his daughter, Susanna, with her four Hawkins children.

As the given names of so many of the Strothers were the same, for the purpose of distinguishing them, especially as regards business relations, they were designated as William of "Stafford," William of "Orange," Francis of "St. Marks," &c., giving their county or country seat as the case may be. William of "Stafford" was a brother of Francis of "St. Marks," who was the father of William of "Orange," &c.

In the previous sketches I have only written of two of the children of Col. Isham Randolph and Jane Rogers and their descendants. They were Elizabeth and Dorothea, both of whom were my paternal ancestors. I will here briefly sketch the lives of the other six children. The eldest was Jane Randolph. I think she was born in London, England, during the incumbency of her father as Colonial Agent at that port. She married Peter Jefferson and had several children. One of their sons was Thomas Jefferson, who shaped the federal constitution under which we enjoy the liberties of freemen and the protection of a strong arm. He served as Secretary of State under President Washington, as Ambassador to France during the Revolutionary period of that country, where he learned much about democracy that made him the father of that creed in America. He also served the country as President. So much has been written about him in the current literature as well as the more enduring history, I will merely mention the fact here that his daughter, Martha, married her cousin Thomas Mann Randolph, Jr., who was a great-grandson of Thomas and Judith Churchill Randolph of Tuckahoe, his wife being a great-granddaughter of Col. Isham of "Dungeness." This Thos. Mann Randolph served Virginia as Governor, United States Senator and in other distinguished capacities. His son, Col. Thomas Jefferson Randolph of Virginia, represented that state in the Electoral College of 1845, was a member of Congress 1851, and President of the Democratic National Convention that assembled in Baltimore in 1872.

Mr. Coolige of Boston, who is owner of the Tuckahoe estate today, is a grandson of Thomas Mann and Martha Jefferson Randolph. The Cooliges have been prominent in business, political and social circles, as have many of this line of the Randolphs who reside in the east from New England to Florida. Samuel Wheeler Railey visited the Tuckahoe property a few years ago and reported that the old home was kept in splendid condition. Their line has been a distinguished one and runs as follows: Wm. Randolph-Mary Isham. Thomas Randolph-Judith Churchill. Wm. Randolph-Maria Judith Page. Col. Thos. Mann Randolph-Anne Cary (daughter of Col. Archibald Cary and Mary Randolph of "Curles Neck"). Gov. Thomas Mann Randolph and Martha Jefferson. Mary Randolph was another daughter of Col. Isham Randolph and Jane Rogers. She married Captain Charles Lewis, Jr., and had Charles Lilburne Lewis, who married his cousin Lucy Jefferson (daughter of Peter and Jane), and Francis Lewis who married Capt. John Thomas, who were the parents of Judge John Lilburne Thomas, who served Missouri in the legislature, as circuit court judge and judge of the Supreme Court of that state, and who about 1893, became Assistant Attorney General of the United States in the Cabinet of President Cleveland. He now resides in Washington City where his son practices law. Captain John Thomas and his wife, Frances Lewis, were the grandparents of Virginia Mitchell, who married the Hon. Richard Bland, better known about 1884 as Silver Dick" Bland, who so ably and so long represented Missouri in the Congress. Their son, Ewing Bland, is now Judge of the Municipal Court of Kansas City.

Anna Randolph, also a daughter of Col. Isham Randolph and Jane Rogers, was three times married, the last marriage to James Pleasants of "Contention," Virginia. They were the parents of Martha Pleasants who became the second wife of her cousin Randolph Railey, Sr., of Woodford Co., Ky., and of Gov. James Pleasants, who, besides the Governorship, served Virginia as United States Senator and in other capacities. James Pleasants of "Contention" had a brother Mathew Pleasants and they were the sons of John Pleasants of "Pique-Nique," Va., and Susanna Woodson, daughter of Tarleton Woodson and Ursula Fleming, mentioned under Table 4. Mathew Pleasants married Anna Railey, daughter of Col. John Railey and Elizabeth Randolph, and their son Benjamin F. Pleasants married Isabella Adair, daughter of General John Adair, who was one of the early Governors of Kentucky. Benjamin was appointed to a position in the United States Treasury by President Jackson and spent the remainder of his life in official capacity in Washington. He was a resident of Harrodsburg, Ky., when appointed. His son, George W. Pleasants, served as Circuit Judge and as Supreme Court Judge in Illinois for thirty years, and his son Adair Pleasants is an attorney at law today in Rock Island, Ill.

John Adair Pleasants and Mathew F. Pleasants were two other sons of Benjamin F. and Isabella Adair Pleasants, who were prominent lawyers at the Richmond, Va., bar and their sister, Nannie Buell Pleasants, married Samuel A. Lynde, a prominent lawyer of Chicago, and they have two sons now practicing at the same bar. But I have digressed a little. Randolph Railey, Sr., who married his cousin Martha Pleasants, was the youngest of the eleven children of Col. John Railey and Elizabeth Randolph. Boone Railey was their only child. He married Elizabeth Wheeler and had two children, Samuel Wheeler Railey, who is a lawyer of Washington City, and Anna Railey, who married John Calhoun Burnett, a lawyer of Louisville, Ky. They have several children.

Susanna Randolph was the youngest of the children of Col. Isham Randolph and Jane Rogers. She married Carter Henry Harrison of "Clifton," Va. Their son, Robert Carter Harrison, had a son Carter H. Harrison, who married Miss Russell, and their son Carter Henry Harrison married Sophronisba Preston of Kentucky. He was assassinated during one of his many terms as Mayor of Chicago, and their son Carter H. Harrison has since served many terms as Mayor of that city. Carter Henry Harrison who married Susanna Randolph was a brother of Benjamin Harrison, who was one of the signers of the Declaration of Independence and I believe Governor of Virginia. He was the ancestor of William Henry Harrison and Benjamin Harrison, both of whom attained to the presidency. The Rev. Cabell Harrison, who was either a son or a grandson of Carter H. Harrison and Susanna Randolph, used to visit his Kentucky relations and it was through his influence that so many of the Raileys became Presbyterians, all of their ancestors being allied with the Episcopal church. I think the mother of the Rev. Cabell Harrison was Anne Cabell, daughter of Col. Joseph Cabell. Beside these six daughters, Jane Jefferson, Mary Lewis, Elizabeth Railey, Dorothea Woodson, Anna Pleasants and Susanna Harrison, Col. Isham Randolph and Jane Rogers had two sons, William and Captain Thomas Isham Randolph. William married Miss Little, but if they had children I have no record of it and I incline to think nothing in the Railey family tree, that is in possession of the family of the Rev. Fleming G.

Railey of Selma, Alabama, indicates any children for them. Captain Thomas Isham Randolph, the other son, who was serving in the navy, married Jane Cary who was, I think, related to Col. Archibald Cary who married Mary Randolph of "Curles Neck," as they had a son whose name was Archibald Cary Randolph and he was the father of Dr. Robert Carter Randolph whose son Isham Randolph is now a resident of Chicago. He is an expert civil engineer and did the engineering work in the construction of the Chicago Canal, besides rendering valuable service in connection with the construction of the Panama Canal and the canals in connection with the drainage of the Florida Everglades. The old Raileys, who migrated to Kentucky, always referred to their uncles, Thomas Isham Randolph and Carter Harrison, in term most complimentary and affectionate, so I judge they were "good men and true."

In closing these brief sketches of the Randolphs and their connections I would not feel satisfied if I did not give a brief sketch of each of the children of William Randolph and Mary Isham, at least of their official status. This William Randolph settled on an estate he called "Turkey Island," about 1660. At any rate he succeeded his uncle Henry as Clerk of the Colony of the James river Anno Domini 1669, and was afterward member House of Burgesses and King's Councilman. I will indicate his children with numerals.

1. William Randolph, Jr., who married Miss Beverly. He was a member of the Council and Treasurer of the Colony. I think Beverly Randolph, who was a member of the Assembly and Governor of Virginia, was a descendant of his, if not then of his brother Sir John Randolph.

2. Thomas Randolph who married Judith Churchill has been sketched as has No. 3, Col. Isham Randolph, who married Jane Rogers.

4. Richard Randolph who married Jane Bolling. He was a member House of Burgesses and succeeded his brother William as Treasurer of the Colony. Their son, John Randolph, who married Miss Bland, was a member of Congress, and their son John Randolph of "Roanake" was classed as statesman, orator and diplomat, and Richard the brother of John of "Roanake" married his cousin, Judith Randolph, daughter of Col. Thos. Mann and Anne Cary. Jane Bolling, wife of Richard, Sr., was a descendant of Pocahontas.

5. Sir John Randolph, who married Miss Beverly, a sister of his brother William's wife. He was Knighted and was the King's Attorney General. He disinherited his son Edmund on account of his democratic views touching the affairs of the Colony, but Edmund was liberally rewarded by the Patriots as he was Attorney General in President Washington's Cabinet, was Governor of Virginia, and I think was Secretary of State.

6. Henry Randolph, who perhaps died early as I have nothing as to his ever marrying or participating in any of the affairs of the Colony.

7. Captain Edmund Randolph,

who married a Miss Groves of England, was in the marine service and his family divided their time, even their residence, between the Colonies and England.

8. Elizabeth Randolph, who married Richard Bland, and they were the ancestors of the prominent Lees and Blands. One of their lines is as follows: Their daughter, Mary Bland married Henry Lee, and their son, Henry Lee, Jr., married Lucy Grimes, and their son, "Light Horse Harry" Lee, married Anne Carter, and their son, Robert E. Lee, of Confederate fame, married Mary Randolph Custis, who was a great-granddaughter of the widow Custis, who married President George Washington.

9. Mary Randolph, who married Captain William Stith, and they were the parents of the Rev. William Stith who married his cousin Judith Randolph, daughter of (2) Thomas Randolph and Judith Churchill. The Rev. William Stith had charge of a church in Henrico county for many years, wrote a very popular history of Virginia, and was President of William and Mary's College. I have been unable to find any notes in my papers giving a continuance of this Stith line. If I had any such notes they have been misplaced or lost, so it may be that the Rev. William was the last of the name.

As you have doubtless observed the Randolphs did a great deal of marrying that did not change the name and it seemed to become contagious as nearly every family of other names who intermarried with them continued the habit of marrying cousins to a great extent. (On the following page I will briefly write of the Owsley families and follow them with a brief sketch of the Whitleys.)

TABLE 6.

Generation.

1st. Captain Thomas Owsley married Ann ———.
2d. Thomas Owsley married Ann West.
3d. Thomas Owsley married Mary Middleton.
4th. Henry Owsley married Martha Bayne.
5th. John Owsley married, 1st. Nancy Whitley; 2d. Jane Shanks.
6th. Henry Ebsworth Owsley married Barbara Ann Harper.
7th. Annie Harper Owsley married William Edward Railey.
8th. Jennie Farris Railey married Douglas Wheeler King.

The American branch begins with Capt. Thomas Owsley and his wife, Ann, whom he married either in Jamaica, to which island he first emigrated from England, or in Virginia, where he afterward resided. Her full maiden name is not known. His descendants are residents in many states as indicated in the "Owsley Family," a book gotten up by Mr. Harry Bryan Owsley of Chicago. Beginning with Thomas Owsley who married Mary Middleton of the third generation, as you will see in the table, I will write a brief sketch of their descendants. He was born in Virginia, 1731, married Mary Middleton in Virginia, 1746. Moved to Kentucky, 1783, and died in Lincoln county, 1796. Mary Middleton was born in Virginia, 1730, and died in Lincoln county, September 16, 1808. Their children were Ann Bayne Owsley, William Owsley, Henry Owsley and Anthony Owsley. Ann Bayne Owsley married, first, Thomas Chilton, second, John Williams. She remained in Virginia when her father migrated to Kentucky with his family. By the first marriage was the Rev. Thomas Chilton who was the father of Thomas Chilton, Jr., the celebrated lawyer and politician who served with distinction in Congress. By the second marriage was Lydia Williams who married William Groves, and they were the parents of William Jordan Groves, who was a very noted man of his day in Virginia. He was elected to Congress in 1831, and his celebrated duel with his friend, Congressman Cilley of Maine, was for many months the sensation of the times. William Owsley, the second of Thomas and Mary Middleton Owsley, married Catherine Bolin and their son William Owsley served in both branches of the legislature, was appointed a member of the Supreme Court by Gov. Scott, and reappointed by Gov. Shelby, and finally was elected the 14th Governor of Kentucky. His brother, Major Johnathan Owsley, distinguished himself at the battle of New Orleans when he went to the assistance of General Jackson at a critical moment that resulted in the repulse of General Packenham's army. Henry Owsley, another of the sons of Thomas and Mary Middleton Owsley, married first Winifred Taylor, daughter of General Taylor of New York, and had Thomas Taylor Owsley and Ellen Owsley. By the second marriage to Martha Bayne of Maryland, were Henry Hawkins Owsley, who married MaryFinley and they were the parents of John Ebsworth Owsley the wealthy Chicagoan whose son Henry Bryan Owsley, at much expense, labor and time, compiled the history of the "Owsley Family."

John Owsley, another son of Henry Owsley and Martha Bayne, married, first, Nancy Whitley and then Jane Shanks. Nancy Whitley was a daughter of Col. William C. Whitley and Esther Fuller. They had no children. By the marriage to Jane Shanks was Henry Ebsworth Owsley who married Barbara Ann Harper of Woodford Co., Ky., a granddaughter of Col. William C. Whitley and Esther Fuller. They were the parents of Annie Harper Owsley who married William Edward Railey, author of this sketch. John Owsley and Jane Shanks were also the ancestors of the McAlisters, Evans, Whitley and Farris families of Boyle county. His first cousin, Gov. William Owsley, also has a number of descendants in Boyle Co., Ky.

Anthony Owsley, the third son of Thomas and Mary Middleton Owsley, married Hannah Young and they had Bryan Young Owsley, who resided at Columbia, Adair County, Ky., and who was an able lawyer. He was a Presidential Elector in 1840, member of Congress 1841-43, Register of the State Land Office 1844-48, and died at Frankfort, Ky., 1849. I think Judge Mike Owsley, who was on the circuit bench for a number of years and who sought the gubernatorial nomination unsuccessfully some years ago, was of this line. I remember him with pleasure as he was a most estimable gentleman. I am not sure which of the three brothers, sons of Thomas and Mary Middleton Owsley, the present Governor of Kentucky, Augustus Owsley Stanley comes from, but from one of them I know.

The first Owsley we have any record of was the Rev. John Owsley who was rector of Glooston, Parish, Leicester Co., England. He married Dorothy Poyntz and they were the parents of Thos. Owsley, who married Ann ———, whose name appears first in above table. The Rev. John Owsley, and his son William Owsley, and his grandson, John Owsley, and his great-grandson John Owsley, all in turn, for a lifetime, were rectors of the above Parish. Mr. Harry Bryan Owsley visited this old church 1890, and states that all of the above named preachers are buried there and that the old church and the tombs of the old Owsleys were well preserved.

TABLE 7.

Generation.
1st. Solomon Whitley married Elizabeth Barnett.
2d. Col. William C. Whitley married Esther Fuller.
3d. Ann Whitley married William Harper.
4th. Barbara Ann Harper married Henry Ebsworth Owsley.
5th. Annie Harper Owsley married William Edward Railey.
6th. Jennie Farris Railey married Douglas Wheeler King.

Col. William C. Whitley was of Irish extraction, his father, Solomon Whitley, being the first recorded in the country that is known. He and his wife, Elizabeth Barnett, were resident of Augusta Co., Va., some years before the Revolution, where they had three children, viz.: William C., Thomas, and a daughter. I have not been able to get a line on Thomas and his sister and don't know whether they left posterity or not, but about 1772 Col. Wm. C. Whitley and his kinsman, General George Rogers Clark, came to Kentucky, where they camped with the Boones for a time. Col. Whitley had his family with him beside a small company of friends, and history and tradition unite in painting their hardships and privations while repelling the Indians and Britons. Col. Whitley built perhaps the first brickhouse erected in Kentucky near Crab Orchard Springs and it stands today as a monument to the splendid workmanship of that period. In this large home and fort the early pioneers, including Boone, met frequently in a war council and many successful campaigns were planned in this hospitable domicile. He was known as a brave and fearless man and quite frequently led scouting parties. After many battles with the red men and Englishmen through Kentucky, Indiana and the northwest he laid down his life in a preliminary engagement at the "battle of the Thames" in a charge upon the enemy by the "Forlorn Hope," of which Col. Whitley was in charge. It was on the 5th of October, 1814, when he gave his men his last command of "liberty or death, boys." He was born August 14, 1749, hence was 65 years of age. Richard Spurr of Fayette Co., Ky., was one of this band who were sent in this engagement to locate the enemy, and the only survivor. He gave a written statement to Hon.

R. J. Spurr of Lexington, Ky., in which he said that in the melee he saw Col. Whitley and a stalwart Indian fire at one another at close range simultaneously and both fell dead near to where he was. He further says that when the skirmish was over he carried Col. Whitley's and the Indian's remains into camp and that General Harrison recognized the Indian as Tecumseh the Indian Chief. This information was conveyed in a letter written by Mrs. Ruth Spurr of Lexington, to Col. J. Stoddard Johnson of Frankfort, Ky., and I think read by him before the Filson Club of Louisville, February, 1901. I think that Mrs. A. Addams of Frankfort or Mrs. John Haldeman of Louisville have a copy of this letter, both of whom are descendants of Col. William Whitley. I have a copy of the Louisville Times, dated October 26, 1893, which carries a photograph of the Whitley home, together with a sketch of the hardships suffered by Col. Whitley and General Clark during the pioneer period. The story that Col. Richard M. Johnson killed Tecumseh elected him to the Vice Presidency, but he never claimed the deed although he was known to have killed an Indian at the battle of the Thames.

Ann Whitley was the youngest of the eleven children of Col. Whitley and Esther Fuller. She married William Harper of Woodford county and was the grandmother of Mrs. Wm. Edward Railey, whose name appears in the above table and whose husband is the author of this sketch. The Harpers were prominent horsemen and farmers, owning many thousands of acres of Woodford county land.

CORRECTION BY THE AUTHOR.*

Capt. Isham Keith, whose name appears in Table 3. Tarleton Woodson and his wife, Ursula Fleming, were the parents of Caroline Woodson who married her cousin, Thomas Fleming Bates, and their children in part were Gov. Frederick Bates of Missouri, and Hon. Edward Bates of the same state, who became Attorney General in the Cabinet of President Lincoln, and Hon. James Woodson Bates who was prominent in the affairs of the State of Arkansas. Josiah Woodson (brother of Tarleton, who married Ursula Fleming) married Mary Royall, daughter of Capt. Joseph Royall and Elizabeth Kennon. He mentions in his will, among other items, an amount of money due his estate by Col. Thomas Mann Randolph. Col. John, son of Josiah Woodson and Mary Royall, was born in Goochland Co., Va., 1730, and married Dorothy Randolph, daughter of Col. Isham Randolph of "Dungeness," October 28, 1751. Col. John's line is sketched under Table No. 2. Two of his daughters, Martha and Judith Woodson, as the above table shows, were the paternal great-grandmothers of Wm. E. Railey, author of this sketch. Of the prominent descendants of Dr. John Woodson and his wife, Sarah Winston, that occur to me at the moment of writing are of Virginians: Major Frederick Tarleton Woodson, General Tarleton Woodson, Col. Charles Woodson and Gov. James

*See pp. 178 & 179, this volume.

Pleasants. Of Missourians are Gov. Federick Bates, Hon. Edward Bates, General Charles Woodson, Gov. Silas Woodson, and Judge A. M. Woodson, who is at present, 1917, and has been for many years, a member of the State Supreme Court, and Hon. James Woodson Bates for many years prominent in the state affairs of Arkansas. Several of the Woodsons were prominent legislators and jurists in central Kentucky prior to the Civil War, and Urey Woodson of Owensboro, Ky., has been prominent in both State and National politics for a number of years. I might add that Gov. Silas Woodson was a native Kentuckian and served in the Kentucky Constitutional Convention before migrating to Missouri.

Feb. 15, 1918.
Mr. W. E. Railey,
Danville, Ky.
Dear Mr. Railey:—

I have read with much pleasure your carefully prepared and interesting genealogical articles of "The Strothers" in the Kentucky Historical Society Register for September and January. I noticed one omission and what I believe to be one error to which I beg to call your attention.

You give the residence of Judge P. W. Strother as Petersburg, Va.* Unless he has removed to Petersburg in the last three or four months, his residence is and has been for years near Pearisburg, Giles county, Va. He lives on a farm about two and one-half miles from that town. I had the pleasure a few years ago of spending a week in his home on the farm near Pearisburg, and he has twice visited me here.

You very kindly mentioned me and three of my children, but omitted the name of my youngest son, Ralph G. Strother, who is First Lieutenant of Battery B, 138th Field Artillery, stationed at Camp Shelby, Miss. I will be glad especially to have the omission corrected.

The Strother family owe you a debt of gratitude for your patience and labor in the preparation of the two articles mentioned, and one which I understand is to follow.

Yours very truly,
JOHN C. STROTHER.

---
*See p. 373, this volume.

Lawton, Okla., June 24, 1918.
My Dear Mrs. Morton:—
I thank you for sending me Mr. Stanard's note correcting my Randolph notes in the May Register, insofar as it related to the wife of Thomas Randolph of Tuckahoe. It gave me an opportunity to take the question up with one of the best authorities on Isham and Randolph history in America. She is descended from Anne Isham, sister of Mary, who married Wm. Randolph at Turkey Island. She is a member of the Virginia Historical Society, knows Mr. Stanard, who has acknowledged her one of the best posted family historians within his acquaintance. I have had much correspondence with her since I wrote the sketches you published in the May issue of the Register and I find that she is an encyclopedia on Virginia families, as she is now engaged in preparing a history of the descendants of Henry and Katherine Isham. I refer to Mrs. Smithwick, of Memphis, Tenn., I am enclosing her letter and that of Mr. Stanard, and would thank you to publish both in full as Mrs. Smithwick's letter settles a question in dispute for a hundred years. Thanking you again, I am,
Very truly,
WM. E. RAILEY.

Richmond, Va., June 4, 1918
Mrs. Jennie C. Morton,
Frankfort, Ky.
Dear Madame:—
I inclose note in correction of article on Randolph and Strother.
The Register of St. Peter's Parish, New Kent County, contains a record of the marriage, on Oct. 16, 1712, of Thomas Randolph, of Henrico Co. (which then included Goochland Co.) and Judith Fleming. She married secondly in 1733. John and Tarleton Fleming, her brothers, were trustees in the marriage contract. There is no doubt, whatever, that Thomas Randolph, of Tuckahoe, married Judith Fleming.
W. G. STANARD.

887 Washington Avenue,
Memphis, Tenn.,
June 20, 1918.
Mr. William E. Railey,
Lawton, Okla.
Dear Cousin:—
Since your letter of the 12th inst., requesting my help in solving the identity of the wife of Thomas Randolph of "Tuckahoe," I have made every effort to arrive at a definite conclusion in the matter, and trust you will be satisfied with the results. Be sure I have left no stone unturned in my effort to aid you.

The seeker after truth who goes into the library of any large city and consults the various volumes bearing upon Virginia genealogy, will find that fully ninety per cent of those authorities give the name of the wife of Thomas Randolph of "Tuckahoe" as Judith Churchill; and the other ten per cent will declare that her name was Judith Fleming. I have consulted all of them, and nowhere do I find any authority who suggests a second marriage for Thomas Randolph of "Tuckahoe." Those who contend that his wife was Judith Churchill do not mention the name of Judith Fleming; and those who contend that she was Judith Fleming, do not mention the name of Judith Churchill. Never have I found even a suggestion that Thomas Randolph married both of these women, and yet, that is just what he did.

The Churchill advocates claim that Judith Churchill was the mother of the three children of Thomas Randolph: William, Judith and Mary, while the Fleming advocates claim that Judith Fleming was the mother of these three children.

Thomas Randolph of "Tuckahoe," married Judith Churchill, of Middlex Co., Va., in 1710, and on Oct. 16, 1712, he married Judith Fleming, of New Kent Co., Va. In December, 1733, Judith (Fleming) Randolph married Nicholas Davies of Goochland Co., and that second marriage of the second wife will account for the fact that she is not buried at "Tuckahoe."

Judith Churchill died in 1712 (probably in the early part of that year), and her son William Randolph was born in that year, the inference being that she died at his birth; and as her husband married Judith Fleming in October of the same year, it is certain that the year 1712 was a most eventful one to Thomas Randolph of "Tuckahoe." Since I have spent so much time in digging among musty tomes of the past, I have learned that Virginia gentlemen of Colonial times married early and often; also that they had short lives (and let us hope merry ones), and that large families were the rule in those old times. A man was old at 50, aged at 60, and a curiosity at 70, in spite of the fact that so many of us are wont to believe that more people lived to ripe ages in those days than now.

As a recapitulation: Thomas Randolph of "Tuckahoe" married (1) Judith Churchill of Middlesex Co., Va., in 1710; (2) Judith Fleming of New Kent Co., Va., on Oct. 16, 1712.

Issue Thomas Randolph and Judith Churchill:

1. William Randolph b. 1712, m. Maria Judith Page.

Issue Thomas Randolph and Judith Fleming:

2. Judith Randolph b. 1724, m. Rev. William Stith.

3. Mary Isham Randolph, b. 1726, m. Rev. James Keith.

In one of your previous letters, you showed the belief that you descend from Pocahontas; but this is not the case. Judith Fleming was a daughter of Charles Fleming, of New Kent Co., Va., and that you may better understand the matter, I will state this Judith Fleming had a brother John Fleming who married Mary Bolling, so that while the descendants of her brother John Fleming were descended from Pocahontas, John's sister Judith was not so descended, as you can see. She had a niece, Judith Fleming, who of course was Pocahontas' descendant, but not herself, and so please relieve your mind of that impression.

The lady who wrote you from Richmond that she descends from Thomas Mann Randolph, Jr. (No. 1) and Martha Jefferson, and who claims to descend from Judith Churchill, was entirely correct in her claim, though, as my recent investigations convince me, you are descended from Judith Fleming, the second wife of Thomas Randolph.

To settle any question as to the identity of Thomas Randolph as the husband of both women, there is on file in Goochland County a deed from John Fleming to Thomas Randolph, in which he describes Thomas as "my brother-in-law, Thomas Randolph of 'Tuckahoe.'"

Now, trusting that I have to your satisfaction, as well as to the satisfaction of all others who may be concerned, really laid the Randolph-Churchill-Fleming ghost, as I promised to do, I am,

Sincerely your friend and cousin,
MARTHA C. D. SMITHWICK

Pueblo, Colo., June 10, 1918.
Mr. W. E. Railey,
Danville, Kentucky.
Dear Mr. Railey:—

We wish to thank you very very kindly for the great pleasure you gave us in your genealogical articles in the May number of the Register of the Kentucky State Historical Society—especially the Woodsons. Your first two ancestors, Dr. John

Woodson and Robert Woodson, are our ancestors also—in the next generation Richard Woodson and Ann Smith makes our third line. We have known that the name of Dr. John Woodson's wife was Sarah, but from your article we learn for the first time that Sarah Woodson's maiden name was Sarah Winston. Thank you very kindly for this information.

From Wm. and Mary College Quarterly, Volume XI, Page 54, note at bottom of page:

"John Woodson came to Virginia in the *George,* which left England, Jan. 29, 1619, bearing the new Governor, Sir George Yeardley, and about one hundred passengers. This ship brought the orders of the company for a free government in Virginia. See Hotten's *Emigrants to America* and Brown's *First Republic.*"—Editor.

April 17, 1619, Sir George Yeardley arrived at Jamestown as Governor and Captain General to put the new system into operation.

We are very much interested in family history and are writing to you with the hope that we may learn something that will help us to trace back further on our Clark line and also perhaps be able to learn something along the Winslow line as to how the Clarks are connected with them. These Clarks are connected with the Sneads, Gathrights, Jones, etc.

The most remote (Clark or Clarke) of which we have record is John Clark, who was in Kentucky at least in 1789, and perhaps earlier. His son, John B. Clark, born June 13, 1773, married Mary (Polly) Hall about 1792. This John Clark had a daughter Prudence, who married John Metcalfe, and another daughter Ann, who married James Hill. We think this John Clark also had a son, Jesse Clark.

This John B. Clark named his sons: Asa Winslow, Levi, Israel. The names of the daughters were Sarah, Prudence, Spicy, Cynthia, Eliza.

Asa W. Clark married Lavinia Winn Snead, daughter of Patrick Snead. Levi Clark married Koziah Jones, daughter of Major Israel Jones. Sarah Clark married Elijah Maddox. Prudence Clark married Wilson Maddox. Cynthia Clark married Andrew Shuck. Israel Clark married Sarah Owen.

These Clarks lived in Madison County, Shelby County, Henry County, Oldham County; at least the first Clarks owned land in these different counties.

The name of the wife of John Clark, father of John B. Clark, was Obedience. This John Clark bought land of Wm. Dowsing of Lunenburg Co., Virginia, 1790. This land was located in Kentucky. From information we have we believe that John Clark had a brother by the name of Godfrey Clark. The heirs of Godfrey Clark were: Mary his wife, William Clark, Bannister Clark, Garner Clark, Absolum Clark, Nancy Clark, who married James Chastain, and William Brown. We have seen the statement that Godfrey Clark had nine heirs, but we have not as yet learned the names of the other two.

As you live at the old historic place of Danville it is very likely that you can put us in touch with some Clark information. It is very likely that they visited Danville in the good old pioneer days. The smallest item will be very gratefully received.

If we have any information of the Woodsons that you would like we would be glad to exchange information with you.

Thanking you in advance for your kindness to write to us, we are,

Very sincerely,
Mr. and Mrs. J. A. Clark.
John Asa.

RANDOLPH NOTES—A CORRECTION
By Wm. E. Railey

In 1911-12, and again in 1917-18 notes that I had prepared on the Randolph and Keith families appeared in the Register.* Mr. Jefferson Randolph Anderson, a lawyer of Savannah, Georgia, who is a member of "The Monticello Association", and its president—sometimes known as the "Jefferson Clan"—has spent many years looking up the history of these two families. He had occasion to look over what I had written of them in the Register and wrote me that I was mistaken in a few statements. As I am satisfied that he is right I am asking the Register to allow me space to note the corrections.**

In one instance I said that the Rev. James Keith was the pastor of "old St. John's Church" in Henrico Parish. Mr. Anderson says that he was Rector of the "old Curls Church" from 1730-33, which was the principal church in Henrico Parish, and that he resigned and moved to Maryland in 1735, but returned in 1736 when he became Rector of Hamilton Parish and died there about 1754. He was never Rector of "old St. John's".

Under Thomas Randolph of "Tuckahoe" I said that Mary Isham Randolph was the older of his two daughters, and Judith the younger. Mr. Anderson says that the reverse is true and gives the dates of the birth of each to prove it. Judith b. —— and Mary Isham b. 1726.

I also said under the same head that if Judith Randolph and her husband, the Rev. William Stith, the historian, had children I was not aware of it. Mr. Anderson informs me that they had three daughters. That Judith the first, and Mary the third, never married. That Elizabeth, the second daughter, married Dr. William Pasteur, but died in 1792 without surviving issue.

In another paragraph I said in relation to the lineage of Thomas Jefferson, that he was the great-grand son of Field Jefferson of Lunenburg. Mr. Anderson tells me that this was a mistake as Field Jefferson was the uncle of Thomas Jefferson, that Thomas Jefferson, the first of record, had a plantation in Henrico County in 1677 where he died in 1698. He married Martha Branch and had a son Capt. Thomas Jefferson who resided in Chesterfield County and married Mary Field 1698 and had three sons, Thomas, Field and Peter. The latter married Jane Randolph, and they were the parents of Thomas Jefferson the President. The first Thomas Jefferson above was either the son or grandson of John Jefferson who came from Wales to Virginia 1615 and was a member of Burgesses in 1619. Mr. Anderson is descended from Peter Jefferson and Jane Randolph.

*See pp. 98-172 and 173-188, this volume.
**See also Jefferson Randolph Anderson's article on the Tuckahoe Randolphs, pp. 204-234, this volume.

Frankfort, Ky., May 19, 1936.

Editor of The Register—

In 1911-12 my notes on *The Raileys and Kindred Families* appeared in The Register and I took the position that Thomas Randolph of "Tuckahoe" married Judith Fleming, and that they were the parents of William Randolph who married Judith Page, Judith Randolph who married Rev. William Stith and Mary Isham Randolph who married the Rev. James Keith.[*]

Many of the Virginia descendants of William Randolph and Judith Page— very prominent socially and politically—wrote me that I was mistaken in the name of the wife of Thomas Randolph. That he married *Judith Churchill* instead of Judith Fleming. As my Keith and Randolph notes which had been gathered from various reliable family sources had all agreed that Thomas Randolph married Judith Fleming, and as these were my three-times great-grand parents, I was interested in having the record correct. I therefore wrote to Mrs. Martha Smithwick, of Memphis, Tennessee, who had made an extensive if not exhaustive study of Randolph and Isham families, and asked her advice. Her reply was, that Thomas Randolph had married *both* women, Judith Churchill in 1710 and Judith Fleming in 1712, and that the former was the mother of William Randolph who married Judith Page and the latter the mother of Judith Randolph who married Rev. William Stith and of Mary Isham Randolph who married the Rev. James Keith.

Although Mr. Stannard insisted that Thomas Randolph was only married once and that to Judith Fleming, I changed my record in accordance with the statement of Mrs. Smithwick and the "correction" appeared in The Register in the "Notes" I published in September, 1918 (pp. 47-49).[**]

Some days ago I received the inclosed letter from Mr. Jefferson Randolph Anderson, a prominent lawyer of Savannah, Georgia, with whom I have exchanged several letters in the last few years. Mr. Anderson has spent many years in an effort to solve the question as to who was the mother of his ancestor, William Randolph who married Judith Page. His letter is most interesting and should silence those relatives who have so persistently affirmed that Thomas Randolph married Judith Churchill. I will thank you for space in The Register for his letter as it settles a contention of many years standing.

Yours very truly,

WILLIAM E. RAILEY.

---

[*] See pp. 175-177, this volume.
[**] Pages 189-191, this volume.

Copies of Mr. Anderson's letters to Mr. Railey and to Judge Charles F. Parsons, of the Supreme Court of the Territory of Hawaii, follow:

Savannah, Georgia, May 4, 1936.

Hon. Wm. E. Railey,
c/o Kentucky Historical Society,
Frankfort, Kentucky.

My dear Mr. Railey:

It has been a couple of years at least since we have had any correspondence, but I sincerely hope that you are still enjoying good health and taking an active interest in affairs as you have always done. I am writing now to tell you that I have completed the investigations which I have been making for three or four years past into the history of Tuckahoe and into the genealogy of the Tuckahoe branch of the Randolph family.

The result of these investigations has convinced me that I must give up my family tradition that Thomas Randolph of Tuckahoe was married to Judith Churchill, and that I must also give up the suggestion I was inclined to accept from you that he had been married twice, the first time to Judith Churchill of Middlesex, and the second time to Judith Fleming of New Kent County. You based your suggestion, you remember, on a letter written you by Mrs. Smithwick of Memphis, and you sent me a copy of her letter, but her letter did not quote any authority for her conclusion. I wrote to her and begged her to look up her records and let me know what her authority was for the statement she had made in her letter to you, but she wrote back that her health was so bad she could not do it. Then I wrote her asking if she could not employ someone at my expense to go through her notes and papers, but, unfortunately, she took offense at that for some reason and then when I again wrote trying to explain that no offense was intended, I received a postal card from a lady friend of hers saying that Mrs. Smithwick was too ill to write. I have never heard anything further from Memphis, and therefore, I feared she must have passed away.

Now, however, I have made, and caused to be made, the most exhaustive search and investigations into County records and Parish records of every County and Parish with which the Randolphs were connected, and I have found positive official records showing that there could not have been any such person in 1710 as Judith Churchill, daughter of Col. William Churchill; also the record of Thomas Randolph's marriage to Judith Fleming; also various County records which contain the positive recitals that Judith Fleming, the wife of Thomas Randolph of Tuckahoe, was the mother of William Randolph, and that she was the grandmother of Thomas Mann Randolph 1st. I am accordingly enclosing to you copy of letter I have written to Hon. Chas. F. Parsons, one of the descendants, who is Judge of the Supreme Court of Hawaii, in which I gave him the result of my investigations and refer him to the official records themselves. I think these records are conclusive and that it must be recognized from them that the question as to the identity of the wife of Thomas Randolph of Tuckahoe and the mother of his three children is definitely and finally settled, and I am accepting the fact that my family tradition is wrong and that the name of my ancestress was Judith Fleming and not Judith Churchill.

There is one question I would like to ask you in relation to the descendants of Rev. James Keith and Mary Isham Randolph. In your book, "The Raileys and Kindred Families", you give on page 11, a list of their children, showing 6 children, but you do not mention anywhere in your book that they had a 7th child, Elizabeth Keith, who married Edward Ford of Fairfax County, Virginia, and moved to Bourbon County, Kentucky, where they had a family of 13 children. Please let me know whether the omission of this family from your book was intentional or accidental. My attention was called to it by a letter to me from Mrs. Geo. R. Mastin, (Grace Murray Mastin), the wife of a Clergyman whose address is, The Rectory, Standardsville, Virginia. She is a descendant of this Elizabeth Keith and Edward Ford and she sent me copy of a letter to her from Thomas Marshall Green, showing that he knew all about this branch of the family.

With cordial regards and best wishes, believe me,

Very sincerely yours,

JEFF RANDOLPH ANDERSON.

April 23, 1936.

Hon. Chas. F. Parsons,
Supreme Court,
Territory of Hawaii,
Honolulu, H. I.

My dear Judge:

Just about three years ago I had some correspondence with you in regard to the Tuckahoe Family Bible and an investigation I was making into the genealogy of our Tuckahoe branch of the Randolph family, and with particular reference to the name of the wife of Thomas Randolph of Tuckahoe, whether it was Judith Churchill as our family tradition has always had it, or whether it was Judith Fleming.

I have now completed my investigations into the history of Tuckahoe itself and into the genealogy of that branch of our family. I succeeded in locating the old Tuckahoe family Bible, which I wrote you about in my letter of March 25, 1933, and which was referred to in your letter to me of April 15, 1933. Unfortunately, however, that Bible began with the generation of Thomas Mann Randolph (1st) so I can get no help from it as to the two first generations of the Tuckahoe family.

The result of my investigations have satisfied me, and I think have conclusively proved that the name of our ancestress, wife of Thomas Randolph of Tuckahoe, was Judith Fleming and not Judith Churchill, and that there really never was any such person as Judith Churchill at that time. I expect to prepare a full sketch showing the results of my investigations and I hope to have it published in the Virginia Historical Magazine, but I know you will be interested in learning now the high points on which my conclusions were based, so I will give you a skeleton outline.

1. The Parish Register of St. Peters' Parish, New Kent County, shows that Thomas Randolph of Henrico County was married to Judith Fleming, October 16, 1712. Goochland was then part of Henrico.

2. She outlived him and was married for a second time December 24, 1733, to Nicholas Davies. Her marriage bond was recorded in Goochland County, and shows that her maiden name was Judith Fleming; that she was the widow of Thomas Randolph of Tuckahoe; and the sureties on the marriage bond were her two brothers, Tarleton Fleming and John Fleming.

3. The records of Middlesex County show that Colonel William Churchill was not married until 1703, and that he then married Elizabeth Wormley, widow of Ralph Wormley. His will gives the names of all of his children and does not include the name of any daughter named Judith. (See P. S. infra.) In his will certain property was entailed to his eldest son. There is an official record of litigation in the Churchill family to set aside this entail. All of his children, or descendants of deceased children, were joined and had to be joined in this litigation and there was no daughter named Judith, and no descendant of any such daughter. There was, therefore, no such person as Judith Churchill, daughter of William Churchill, who could have married Thomas Randolph in 1710, as our tradition has it.

4. Thomas Randolph had a son, William, and two daughters, Judith, who married Stith, and Mary Isham, who married Rev. James Keith. The will of William Randolph, son of Thomas R. is on record in Goochland County and contains an item in which he provides that in the event of failure of his direct heirs, his property should go to the children of "my sister, Judith Stith".

5. William Randolph had one son, Thomas Mann Randolph, (1st). In a deed dated August 6, 1774, and recorded in Cumberland County in Deed Book 5, page 353, 4, 5, signed by him, he expressly recites that he inherited the land from his grandmother, Judith Fleming Randolph, who afterwards married Nicholas Davies. Deed dated August 26, 1774, and recorded in Cumberland County in Deed Book 5, pp. 353-4-5.

6. Likewise, in a deed dated December 2, 1774, recorded in Cumberland County, Deed Book 6, pages 124-126, Thomas Mann Randolph, (1st) quit claimed certain lands to H. L. Davies, son of Nicholas Davies, by his second marriage,

and in this quit claim deed Thomas Mann Randolph, (1st) recites that he inherited this land "from my grandmother, Judith Fleming Davies, formerly Judith Fleming Randolph". Deed dated December 2, 1774, and recorded in Cumberland County in Deed Book 6, pp. 124-126.

These official records seem to be absolutely conclusive and I am therefore now accepting the fact that my ancestress was named Judith Fleming in spite of the family tradition that her name was Judith Churchill.

It is very unfortunate that our cousin, Miss Frances Margaret Dickins, about the year 1890, had a marble tablet placed in the wall of the Tuckahoe Cemetery in which she inscribed the name Judith Churchill of Middlesex as being the wife of Thomas Randolph. This is all the more surprising to me because I have just gone through family papers lent me by our cousin, Mrs. Theodora Keim of Fredericksburg, which papers she is supposed to have inherited from her Aunt, Miss Fanny M. Dickins, and in those papers I found a copy of the marriage bond of Nicholas Davies to Judith Fleming Randolph, widow of Thomas Randolph of Tuckahoe. This, of course, ought to have put Miss Dickins on inquiry, at least, as to the correctness about the tradition about Judith Churchill, but perhaps she found the record of this marriage bond after she had repaired the cemetery. This may have happened because I also found among her papers a letter written to her in 1897 by Capt. Wilson M. Cary, in which he told her that this tradition about Judith Churchill was based on a diary kept by Richard Randolph, the antiquarian, brother of John Randolph of Roanoke, and that he, Cary, had for many years accepted the tradition on that authority, but that a few years before the date of his letter, he had discovered the Parish record of the marriage of Thomas R. to Judith Fleming in 1712, and that he had, therefore, abandoned the tradition.

I have told Theodora Keim of my conclusion and suggested that perhaps something should be done to put a new tablet in the cemetery wall so that our ancestress might even at this late date be given the credit and standing her memory is legitimately entitled to as being the wife of Thomas Randolph of Tuckahoe. Mrs. Keim, however, says the question of the two Judiths has for many, many years been a fascinating mystery and for her part she would like to leave it at that.

With cordial regards, believe me,

Very sincerely yours,

JEFF RANDOLPH ANDERSON.

P. S.—It is a curious co-incidence that the widow Wormley had a daughter, Judith Wormley, who grew up in the Churchill household as one of the Churchill family. She married Mann Page and their daughter, Mary Judith Page married William Randolph, father of Thos. Mann R. (1st). Thus the paternal grandmother of Thos. M. R. (1) was Judith Fleming and his maternal grandmother was Judith Wormley, the step-daughter of Col. Wm. Churchill. Our family traditions seems to have mixed up these two "Judith" grandmothers and changed William Churchill's step-daughter into his daughter.

THE FLEMINGS OF VIRGINIA

Sir Thomas Fleming, b. 1593 (m) Miss Tarleton. He was the 5th Lord, and 1st Earl, of Wigton Scotland. He was a son of John Fleming, and came to Virginia, 1616, and settled at Jamestown. He died in New Kent Co., Va. His sons were 1st John Fleming, b. ─────, d. Aug. 27, 1686 (m) Judith Tarleton, and they had Col. Charles Fleming, b, 1660, d. 1720, (m) Susannah Tarleton, daughter of Stephen Tarleton, and d, about 1678. He and his wife attended the wedding of their daughter Elizabeth who married Samuel Jordan Nov. 10, 1703. He patented land in New Kent County, Va., 1701. Their children were John, Charles, Tarleton, Ursula, Susannah, Elizabeth, Judith, William and Robert. The oldest son Col. John (m) Mary Bolling. He was b, 1688, d, 1720. Tarleton was b, 1705, d, 1750. Ursula (m) Tarleton Woodson. Susanna (m) John Bates, Elizabeth (m) Samuel Jordan, Judith (m) Thos. Randolph of "Tuckahoe".

2nd Charles.

3rd Thomas.

As you will see by reference to "Raileys and Kindred Families", I, Wm. E. Railey, descend from Thomas Randolph and Judith Fleming on my maternal side.*

WM. E. RAILEY.

---

*Page 108, this volume.

The Keiths.

By Mrs Annie H. Miles.

Among the earliest settlers of Virginia was William Randolph, who, by grant, purchase and marriage, acquired on the James river a domain extensive enough to be subdivided into the family estates of Tuckahoe, Dungeness, Chatsworth, Wilton, Varina, Curls, Bremo and Turkey Island. He married Mary Isham, daughter of Henry and Katherine Isham, of Bermuda Hundred.

Of the Isham and Randolph families, Mrs. Pryor thus writes, in her paper on the ancestry of General Lee—Frank Leslie's, February, 1896:

"By Henry Lee's marriage with Mary Bland, very distinguished families are included in the ancestry of General Lee. Mary Bland was the daughter of Richard Bland. Richard Bland's mother was Elizabeth Randolph, daughter of William Randolph of Turkey Island, and Mary Isham, his wife. William Randolph was burgess and king's councilman, a man of great wealth and influence, and progenitor of the Randolph family, of Thomas Jefferson and Chief Justice Marshall. He descended, says Randall, from the Earls Murray—nay, from royalty itself. Mary Isham came from a long and noble line in England —through the De Vere, Greene and Dayton families, including several chief justices, the Earls of Oxford and Lords of Adington Baron; and back to the Dukes of Normandy (Longue Epee and Sanspeur, Hugh Capet, of France), and the Saxon kings. England has known no grander family than that of De Vere. Hard pressed in one of the battles of the Crusade, a De Vere saw in a vision a star fall from heaven and alight upon his shield. Ever after they bore a lone star only, and never was its lustre dimmed!"

Some of their descendants might, were it not for the predominance of *reductio ad absurdum* evidence, tempt one to believe "the source of genius is in ancestry, the blood of descent, the prophecy of destiny." Robert E. Lee, Thomas Jefferson, Chief Justice Marshall and Jack Randolph, of Roanoke, are only the greatest among many distinguished names. Bishop Meade, vol. 1, pages 138-139.

Thomas Randolph, son of William and Mary Isham, married a Miss Fleming, descendant of Pocahontas. Their daughter, Mary Isham Randolph, was the wife of "Parson" James Keith.

We have, from patriotic and chronological motives, given precedence to the Randolphs and Ishams, as they were the first settled in America. The Herald's College, however, ranks few the equals of the Keiths.

The Keiths of Scotland claim descent from the German tribe of Chattie or

Catti, who defied the Senate, foiled the second Caesar and, disdaining to submit to the overpowering force of Germanicus, escaped first to Holland, and, later, by chance and tempest, were driven to Scotland. This claim —legend, certainly; possibly fable— has never been waived by the family, and, in the sixteenth century, George, fifth Earl Marischal, was received by the Landgrove of Hesse, chief of the tribe of Chattie, as a kinsman. It was this George who founded the Marischal College of Aberdeen, where, more than a century later, our ancestor, "Parson" James Keith, was educated with his two cousins, George Keith, tenth and last Earl Marischal, and James Francis Edward Keith, Marischal of Prussia, and, according to Macaulay, the only man Frederick the Great ever really loved.

But, to return from fable and digression to history, as registered in the English edition of the Encyclopedia Brittanica, "The family of Keith, one of the most ancient in Europe." In 1010 the Scots gained a complete victory over the Danes at Camustown, in Angus. King Malcolm II, as a reward for the signal bravery of a certain young nobleman, who pursued and killed Camus, the Danish general, bestowed upon him several lands, particularly the barony of Keith, in East Lothian, from which his posterity assumed their surname. The king also appointed him hereditary great Marischal of Scotland, which high office continued in his family till the year 1715, when the last earl engaged in the rebellion and forfeited his estates and honors, and thus ended the family of Marischal, after serving their country in a distinguished capacity above 700 years. The coat of arms of the Keiths' three pallet quiles on a chief and with the words "Veritas vincit," commemorate this triumph. In the latter half of the fourteenth century, Sir William Keith married Margaret Frazier, grandchild of Alexander Frazier, and Mary, sister of Robert Bruce, their grandson by James II of Scotland, was created Earl Marischal, 1457. The third Earl Marischal married Elizabeth, daughter of Alexander, first Earl of Huntly, and from Alexander their fourth son was descended Bishop Robert Keith and his nephew, "Parson" James Keith. "The Scotch Nation," by William Anderson, vol. 2, pages 586-593; vol. 3, page 104. "Buchane Historical and Authentic Account of the Ancient and Noble Family of Keith." Vindication of Mr. Robert Keith and his young grand-nephew, Alexander Keith, to the honours of a lineal descent from the noble house of the Earl Merischal." This last book contradicts Mr. Tom Green's assertion that it is impossible to trace the relationship between "Parson" James Keith and the Earl Marischal, as does also a letter from Mr. Isham Keith, of Warrenton, Va., a brother of Judge James Keith, presiding judge of Court of Appeals of that State, which I shall read at the close of this paper.

James Keith, compromised by the intrigues which followed the rebellion of 1715, took refuge in Virginia and married, as we have said, Mary Isham Randolph. Among their eight children was Isham, a lieutenant in the Revolutionary army, who married

Charlotte Ashmore. Their daughter, Katherine Keith, married William Strother Hawkins; their oldest son, Isham Keith Hawkins, was my father. Mary Keith married Col. Thomas Marshell and was the mother of Chief Justice Marshall; Elizabeth Keith married Edward Ford, and was the mother of the late William Edward Ashmore, of Versailles, Woodford county.

TUCKAHOE AND THE TUCKAHOE RANDOLPHS[*]

By

JEFFERSON RANDOLPH ANDERSON

of Savannah, Georgia

The early history of this ancient Virginia estate, and of the branch of the Randolph family which founded it and is designated by its name, has been in many particulars a matter of argument and even of controversy for many years; due largely to lack of, or to imperfection of, the very early records.

Even such records as existed have only in recent years become really accessible and available. Goochland County, where the estate is located, was not laid off until 1728, and its records only run from that time. Prior to that time, it was geographically included in Henrico County, which stretched indefinitely to the mountains, but actually it was a very sparsely inhabited frontier region. Dover Church, the nearest Church to Tuckahoe, was not built until 1720-1724. The parish of St. James, to which it belonged, was not established until 1720, and had no permanent resident minister there until 1750, when the Rev. William Douglass was installed; but no parish register or records was begun to be kept until the year 1756. (See Douglass Register.)

"In September, 1744, St. James Parish was subdivided into three; St. James Northam, St. James Southam, and St. Anne." Tuckahoe is in Northam.

With the view of endeavoring to settle all controversial points as far as possible, the author, during the past four years, has made, or caused to be made, an exhaustive investigation into all extant records of which he could find trace or reference; not only those at the State Capitol in Richmond, but also all county and parish or other records which it might be supposed could relate to this place or family. The result of this investigation is given here and it is confidently submitted that it is as accurate and authentic an account as it is possible to make at this late date; more than two hundred years after the founding of Tuckahoe.

All records and all authorities agree that Thomas Randolph was the founder of Tuckahoe, but there have been many widely divergent and conflicting statements as to when it was founded and as to when and how he became its owner. The first error requiring correction is a statement appearing on page 125 of the book "Homes and Gardens in Old Virginia", Garden Club of Virginia Edition 1932; where the writer of the article on Tuckahoe states that Thomas Randolph was the *third* son of William and Mary Randolph of Turkey Island. The fact is that he was their *second* son and their *third* son was Isham Randolph of Dungeness. That Isham was the *third* son is expressly stated in the inscription on his

[*]This article, in a slightly altered format, also appeared in *The Virginia Magazine of History and Biography*, Vol. XLV (1937), pp. 55-86. The reprinted version of that article, with corrections and additions from a subsequent issue of *The Virginia Magazine of History and Biography*, can be found in *Genealogies of Virginia Families* (Genealogical Publishing Co., Inc., 1981), Vol. V, 1-46.

tomb, which is still standing in the family graveyard at Turkey Island; This inscription was copied by me on June 1st, 1933, when I visited Turkey Island.

The question as to when Tuckahoe was founded is also one that has given rise to many conflicting opinions. In the above mentioned book "Homes and Gardens in Old Virginia", it is stated on p. 125, "Tuckahoe has been given a widely varying birthday, ranging from 1674 to 1725 x x x. The combined weight of authority however, seems to point conclusively to its having been built prior to 1700, by or for Thomas Randolph": and again on p. 129 of the same book, it is stated "Thomas Randolph, the founder, whether he moved there in 1690 or earlier" etc. In the book "Virginia Beautiful", published by Wallace Nutting in 1930, it is stated on page 221; "Tuckahoe—The date of this house, like that of most others, can be fixed only approximately. Perhaps 1690 would be as correct a date as it is possible now to fix". Other writers, even some members of the family, have said that William Randolph of Turkey Island gave the land to his son, Thomas, about or prior to 1690, and sent him there at that time to take possession and build a home for himself. The fallacy of all these claims and statements becomes apparent when two established facts are taken into consideration. The first is that all genealogical writers and records agree that Thomas Randolph of Tuckahoe was born in June, 1683. He was therefore only 7 years old in 1690, and even as late as 1700, he was only 17 years old. Manifestly no boy of 7 or lad of 17 would be sent into a wilderness, then still, in part, inhabited by roving Indians, to take up land and build a "family home". The second fact is that William Randolph of Turkey Island did not himself acquire the land on which the Tuckahoe House now stands until 1695, and that Thomas Randolph did not acquire the land until in 1714; as is shown below.

All these divergent ideas and publications as to the original acquisition and ownership of Tuckahoe seem to have grown out of a tradition that has been widely accepted throughout Virginia that William Randolph of Turkey Island either gave the Tuckahoe plantation to his son, Thomas, or devised it to him in his will. This is not the fact. The early records of grants and of land titles are still accessible and are practically complete; and an investigation of these records shows that the actual facts are as set out below. The earliest surveys of the region West of the falls of James River showed an island located near the North bank, opposite the mouth of Tuckahoe Creek, and extending above and below that point. The channel between the island and the north bank was spoken of as the upper and lower branches of Tuckahoe Creek, and the island, after 1695, was known as Randolph's Island.

On April 21, 1695, William Randolph of Turkey Island obtained a grant, or Patent as it was called, from Sir Edward Andros, Lieut-Governor, conveying to him 1221 acres of land on the north side of James River above Westham Creek "beginning at ye mouth of Western Creek and ye mouth of a branch of Tuckahoe

Creek" (Grant Book 8 p. 408). This patent included the Island and a strip of land along the north bank of the river containing the site on which the Tuckahoe House is located.

William Randolph also obtained from or through Edmund Jennings, a tract of 3256 acres lying east of Tuckahoe Creek. The exact date of this conveyance is not known as no record of it has been found, but the fact is mentioned in William Randolph's Will; and in Henrico Deed Book 5, p. 371, is recorded a deed, dated Dec. 1, 1692, from Jno. Pleasants to William Randolph, conveying one or more islands in the James River on the north side and reciting that they contain 165 acres "next the land which ye said William Randolph purchased from Edmund Jennings". The above tract of 3256 acres is exactly one half of a tract of 6513 acres patented by Edmund Jennings October 20th, 1689, (Grant Book 8, p. 2) and it seems possible that he was acting jointly for himself and Randolph. In fact, the Will of John Pleasants, 25 Sept. 1690, devises some land to his son, Joseph, and says that one section "borders on the land taken up by Edmund (Edward) Jennings and William Randolph" (Henrico Co., Wills & Deeds, Book 5, p. 149). This tract of land is mentioned here because this and the Randolph Island grant covered most of the lands above the falls devised by William Randolph of Turkey Island to five of his seven sons.

William Randolph of Turkey Island died in 1711. His Will, dated March 6, 1711, and proved June 5, 1713, did not devise the site of Tuckahoe to his son, Thomas. (See Records Henrico County Court, Part I, 1710-1714, pp. 215-218). On the contrary, the Will states an express desire that his son Thomas, or son Henry, should take charge of a plantation of 1100 acres at Pigeon Swamp in Surrey County to work off an indebtedness to Micajah Perry & Company of London; and provided that if either son would do so, then, when the debt was paid, this property was to belong to such son in fee. As to the lands above the falls of James River, the Will recited that he had already given the lower part of this (Jennings) land to his (eldest) son William, and the Will then directed that the remaining land be equally divided between five of his sons as follows:—"My son Isham to have the lower part, adjoining to my son William; my son Thomas to joyne upon Isham; my son Richard to joyne upon Thomas; my son John to joyne upon Richard; and my son Edward to joyne upon John, being the upper part of the said land," It is to be noted that this provision of the Will does not even give to Thomas the part of the Jennings land nearest to Tuckahoe, as would be natural if it was intended or even expected that he was to have Tuckahoe.

As to the "upper island" property, which actually included the site of the Tuckahoe House, and was covered by the Randolph Island Grant of 1695, the Will provided that this property was to be divided into three equal parts, "my son John to have the upper part, Thomas the middle part and Richard the lower part". These were devises in fee simple, and, under this provision of the Will,

Thomas was definitely excluded from that part (the upper part) of the land afterward forming that portion of the Tuckahoe plantation, on which the House is located.

Thomas Randolph therefore, did not acquire the site of Tuckahoe House either as a gift from his father, or under his father's Will. He obtained the river bank and the island part of it by purchase from his brother John, under a deed dated September 4, 1714, and to the property thus conveyed to him plus the middle third devised to him by his father, Thomas Randolph, gave the name "Tuckahoe" by which it has ever since been known. The above deed conveyed, in consideration of ninety pounds sterling, a tract of land devised to the said John Randolph in fee simple by the last Will and Testament of his deceased father, situate, lying and being in the County and parish of Henrico on the north side of James River at the upper end of Randolph Island, etc. (Deed Book Henrico County, 1710-1714 p. 287).

There is no actual record of the exact date when the present Tuckaho House was erected by Thomas Randolph. His father died in 1711, he was married in 1712, and he probably started building the house shortly after his purchase of the land from his brother, John, in 1714. We know he was living there in 1723, because on Sept. 5, 1723, he enlarged the estate by obtaining a grant of 734 acres on the north side of James River, "lying along the South side of the River Road, West of Tuckahoe Creek and *back of a survey* formerly made by William Randolph; and on which the said Randolph now lives." (Book of Grants No. 11, p. 734; State Capitol) This Grant was over ten years after the death of William Randolph, so this last clause clearly refers to Thomas Randolph himself, as the one then living there. It can be definitely stated therefore that the Tuckahoe House was built between 1714 and 1723. This confirms the statement made on page 116, of the "Manors of Virginia in Colonial Times" published by Edith Tunis Sale in 1909. It was probably completed by or before 1720 for in that year we find that Thomas Randolph undertook the contract for building Dover Church, the first church in that part of Henrico, for the consideration of 54990 pounds of tobacco. (Douglass Register, new ed., p. 5) It may be noted here that the Tuckahoe estate was later further enlarged by Thomas Mann Randolph (1st), the grandson of the founder, who in 1772 purchased from Stephen Woodson 363 adjoining acres along the River Road (Deed Book 12, p. 60 G. C. C.) and in 1775 he purchased from John Martin 343 acres lying between the above tract and the James River and adjoining Tuckahoe on the west (Deed Book 11, p. 111, G.C.C.). A portion of this last tract, designated as "Middle Quarter" was devised by said Thomas Mann Randolph (1st) to his son, Dr. John Randolph; great grandfather of this present writer, who is also a great great grandson of Thomas Mann Randolph (2nd), the founder of Edgehill in Albemarle County.

One of the most controversial questions that has agitated the genealogists of

Virginia is the question, who was the wife of Thomas Randolph, the founder of Tuckahoe? It has been termed "the fascinating mystery of the two Judiths". Was she Judith Churchill or Judith Fleming, or did he marry both of these women, as is stated by Mr. Wm. E. Railey, Curator, Kentucky Historical Society, in his book "The Raileys and Kindred Families".* Except for him those genealogists who say she was Churchill do not mention the name Fleming, and those who say she was Fleming, do not mention the name Churchill. The great majority of the earlier writers, in fact nearly all of them, prior to 1900, said she was Judith Churchill and only a comparative few could be found to the contrary. The unbroken family tradition prior to 1895 both at "Edgehill" and at "Tuckahoe" has been that she was Judith Churchill. It should be remembered that after the time of the first Thomas Mann Randolph (b. 1741 d. 1793) the Tuckahoe branch of the Randolphs became separated into two distinct families, caused by his having married first, Ann Cary, November 18, 1761, and, after her death, he was married secondly to Gabriella Harvie, Sept. 15, 1790; and that by each of these wives he had a son to whom was given the name Thomas Mann Randolph.

The eldest son, Thomas Mann Randolph (2nd) inherited the lands belonging to his father in Albemarle County, where after his marriage to Martha Jefferson, eldest daughter of President Thomas Jefferson, he built his home at "Edgehill" about the year of his father's death, 1793. To the younger son, Thomas Mann Randolph (3rd) was devised the greater part of the "Tuckahoe" estate, including the mansion; the portion known as "Middle Quarter" being given to another son, Dr. John Randolph. Thus the "Edgehill" family thereafter was the Senior line, while the "Tuckahoe" family became the Junior line of the Tuckahoe Randolphs; and as we have said above, the accepted tradition in both these families was that their ancestress, the wife of Thomas Randolph of Tuckahoe, was Judith Churchill. So firmly was this tradition established at Edgehill that the author's father, prior to the year 1870, and with the assistance of all the then family elders, prepared a family roll which we know as the Edgehill Roll of the Randolphs of Virginia. On this Roll all the various branches of the family and their descendants are shown from the first William Randolph of Turkey Island down to the close of the Civil War; and on this Roll the name of the wife of Thomas Randolph of Tuckahoe is given as Judith Churchill. So, likewise, in the Tuckahoe family, this tradition was so firmly fixed that Miss Frances Margaret Dickins, a descendant, in repairing the old wall of the family graveyard at Tuckahoe about the year 1892, caused a marble tablet to be inserted in the wall with an inscription showing, inter alia, that the wife of Thomas Randolph of Tuckahoe was Judith Churchill of Middlesex.

Although this Churchill tradition was thus firmly fixed and accepted by both the Edgehill family and the Tuckahoe family, yet it is to be noted that the Flem-

---

*See footnote on p. 98, this volume.

ing tradition obtained among many other descendants. Strangely enough, the Churchill tradition seems to have prevailed among those descended from Thomas of Tuckahoe through his son, William, while the Fleming tradition seems to have prevailed among those descended from him through his daughter Mary, who married Rev. James Keith, and most of whom live in Kentucky. In the five published volumes of the Compendium of American Genealogy, (The Virkus Co., Chicago) there are published the lineages of sixteen families, in different parts of the United States, who descend from Thomas Randolph of Tuckahoe. From an analysis of these sixteen lineages, the author found that eight traced their descent through his only son, William, and eight traced back through his daughter, Mary Isham Keith. Of the eight tracing back through the son, William, seven give Judith Churchill as the name of William's mother, and only one (1) gives Judith Fleming. Of the eight lineages tracing back through his daughter, Mary, five give Judith Fleming as the name of her mother, one (1) gives Judith Churchill, one (1) gives no name, and one (1), Mr. Wm. E. Railey says, as stated above, that Thomas R. of Tuckahoe was married twice; 1st to Judith Churchill and 2nd, to Judith Fleming.

It is also a curious and interesting fact about these two conflicting family traditions that Richard Randolph of Bizarre, and his brother John Randolph of Roanoke, whose mother, Judith Randolph of Tuckahoe, was a daughter of Thomas Mann Randolph (1st), should each have left a memorandum or genealogical family sketch; and that Richard Randolph, an acknowledged antiquarian, should have therein stated that the wife of their ancestor, Thomas Randolph of Tuckahoe, was Judith Churchill, while John Randolph of Roanoke in his memorandum stated she was Judith Fleming. She was their great great grandmother, so it is evident that the question as to her identity and name had become a matter of tradition, and that these two conflicting traditions about her antedated even their generation. The facts as to these two memoranda are stated in a letter written to my great aunt, Mrs. Ellen Wayles Harrison, at Edgehill in 1883, by Capt. Wilson M. Cary, who was himself a descendant and a recognized authority on the family history. In this letter, he stated that he accepted Richard Randolph's statement of the Churchill tradition rather than that of John R. of Roanoke of the Fleming tradition. A copy of this letter is in my possession; and substantially the same letter was written by him under date of March 8th, 1883, to Dr. R. C. M. Page, and was published in 1893 in his book, "Genealogy of the Page Family in Virginia".

The author, having spent a great part of his childhood at Edgehill, and practically having had his home there from 1876 into 1885, while he was attending school and the university, naturally believed in and accepted the Churchill tradition held by the Edgehill family and did not know until about five years ago that it was then being seriously questioned. This is primarily the reason he began four years ago to make this investigation to see if the correctness of the family tradition could be established by record evidence; and in the hope and expectation that this might be possible, even at this late day. The result of the investigation, however, has shown the following facts:

1. *The old Parish Register of St. Peter's Parish* in New Kent County had been found in the 1890's and deposited in the library of the Virginia Theological Seminary at Alexandria. It contains the following entry in its record of marriages:

> "Thomas Randolph of Henrico and *Judith Fleming* was (sic) married Octo ye 16th, 1712"

Henrico County at that time included the territory that is now in Goochland, which was not laid off until 1728. The presumption therefore immediately arises that this was the Thomas Randolph later known as Thomas Randolph of Tuckahoe. This presumption becomes conclusive, when it is noted from other official records shown below that after his death in 1730, his *widow* was married December 24, 1733, to Nicholas Davies. It was largely the discovery of this entry that caused Capt. W. M. Cary, in answer to an inquiry from her, to write Miss Frances M. Dickens under date of July 28, 1897, that he had abandoned the Churchill tradition and had accepted the Fleming tradition. This original letter was found by the author among the family papers of Miss Dickins, lent him by her niece, Mrs. Theodora Keim of Federal Hill, Fredericksburg, Virginia; and a copy of the letter placed in the author's files. This letter, however, was received by Miss Dickins over five years after she had placed the inscription in the Tuckahoe graveyard showing the wife of Thomas Randolph of Tuckahoe as Judith Churchill of Middlesex.

2. *Extract from Marriage Settlement* between Nicholas Davies and Judith (Fleming) Randolph; made with her two brothers. Recorded in Goochland County records, Book 5, page 148:

> "This deed made this 24th day of December, 1733, between Nicholas Davies of the County of Henrico, Merchant, of the one part, and John Fleming and Tarleton Fleming, Gentlemen, of the other part; Witnesseth that in consideration of a marriage shortly to be had and solemnized between the said Nicholas Davies and Judith Randolph, late wife of Colonel Thomas Randolph, deceased;" etc.

The marriage bond of Nicholas Davies and Judith Randolph is on record in Goochland County. It is dated December 19th, 1733, with Middleton Shaw as surety. This confirms the statement in "The Cabells and their Kin", page 245, that Nicholas Davies in 1733 married Judith Randolph, *nee* Fleming, the widow of Col. Thomas Randolph of Tuckahoe.

3. *Will of William Randolph of Tuckahoe.* It is known from a release signed by his executors (William Randolph, John Fleming and Richard Ran-

dolph) that Thomas Randolph of Tuckahoe left a will, but no record of it has ever been found. The will of his son, William, however, is of record in Goochland County. It is dated March 2, 1743 (N. S.), and is recorded in Deed and Will Book 5, page 75, and contains the following provision:

> "And my will also is that in case all my children before mentioned do die before they arrive to the age of twenty-one years or (before they) do marry, then all my estate, both real and personal shall be equally divided between the children of the Rev'd William Stith (of Henrico) by his present wife, Judith, my beloved sister and their heirs forever."

This shows that Mrs. Judith (Randolph) Stith was his sister, and that they were children of the same mother (Judith Fleming Randolph). This is important because several of the early genealogists and the Page family book give the date of William's birth as 1712, which rather lent color to the theory that his father, Thomas R. of Tuckahoe, may have been married twice and that his own mother may have been the Judith Churchill of the tradition.

4. *Tripartite Deed; Randolph-Davies-Logwood;* dated August 26th, 1774, recorded in Circuit Court Clerk's office Cumberland County, Virginia, in Deed Book No. 5, pages 353-4-5, conveys 1,144 acres on lower side of Muddy Creek in said county in consideration of 600 pounds current money of Virginia. The following extract is taken from this deed:

> "This Indenture Tripartite made this twenty-sixth day of August in the year of our Lord Christ One Thousand seven hundred and seventy-four Between Thomas Mann Randolph and Ann, his wife, which said Thomas Mann Randolph is son and heir at law of **William Randolph deceased, who was son and heir-at-law of Judith Davies** deceased; late wife of Nicholas Davies of the County of Goochland, of the first part;" etc.

The foregoing recital speaks for itself and is a positive statement by Thomas Mann Randolph (1st) that his father, William Randolph of Tuckahoe, was the son of Judith Fleming (Randolph) Davies.

5. *Quit-Claim Deed; Randolph-Davies;* dated December 2nd, 1774, and recorded in Circuit Court Clerk's office, Cumberland County, Virginia, in Deed Book No. 6, pages 124, 125, 126. The following extract is taken from this deed:

> "This Indenture made the second day of December in the year of Christ One Thousand seven hundred and seventy-four Between Thomas Mann Randolph of the County of Goochland of the one part and Henry Landon Davies of the County of Amherst of the other part:
>
> Whereas Nicholas Davies of the County of Bedford, father of the said Henry Landon Davies, in and by certain articles of agreement bearing date the twenty fourth day of December in the year of Christ one thousand seven hundred and thirty three made x x between the said Nicholas Davies, by the name of Nicholas Davies of the County of Henrico, Merchant, of the one part, and John Fleming and Tarleton Fleming, gentlemen, of the other part, in consideration of a marriage then shortly to be had an solemnized between the said Nicholas Davies and Judith Randolph then late wife of Col. Thomas Randolph, deceased, **and the grandmother of the said Thomas M. Randolph,** did among other things covenant", etc.

The foregoing recitals also speak for themselves and constitute a definite and official record that Judith Fleming was the widow of Thomas Randolph of Tuckahoe and after his death had married Nicholas Davies and that she was the grandmother of Thomas Mann Randolph (1st) of Tuckahoe; and therefore that she was the mother of his father, William Randolph of Tuckahoe.

6. *Middlesex and Churchill Records.* A most careful investigation of the records of Middlesex County and of Christ Church Parish shows no mention of Col. Wm. Churchill's ever having been married but once, or of his ever having had a daughter named Judith. William Churchill (1649–1711) came to Virginia from England in 1669 and settled at "Bushy Park" in Middlesex County, and was a Warden and Vestryman of Christ Church Parish there. He married October 5, 1703, Elizabeth (Armistead) Wormeley, daughter of Col. John Armistead, and the widow of Hon. Ralph Wormeley (Parish Register, p. 63). His will, dated November 18, 1710, and proved March 10, 1711, gives the names of all his children and does not include any daughter named Judith. Under his will certain property was entailed to his son. There is an official record of legislation for the Churchill family in April, 1757, to set aside this entail. (Hen. VII, p. 157). All of his children were joined and had to be joined or made parties in a petition to the Virginia Assembly for power to break this entail and sell the land, but there is no mention of any Judith being among them, or referred to in any way. It is reasonable to conclude, therefore, that he had no such daughter Judith; and certainly no daughter of his marriage in 1703 could have answered to the tradition of having married Thomas Randolph of Tuckahoe in 1710.

The facts and circumstances shown from the official records referred to in the preceding six numbered paragraphs are absolutely conclusive and definitely establish that the family tradition about Judith Churchill is wrong and that the ancestress of the Tuckahoe Randolphs was Judith Fleming. She was a daughter of Charles Fleming and Susanna Tarleton of New Kent County. The first of her family in Virginia was Thomas Fleming, who married Miss Tarleton of England (of the same family as Col. Banastre Tarleton, the noted British cavalry officer of the time of the American Revolution), and emigrated to Virginia in 1616. He left three sons and several daughters. The sons were Tarleton, John, and Charles; this last being the father of Judith Fleming, who was married to Thomas Randolph of Tuckahoe October 16th, 1712, and had by him three children, William, Judith, and Mary Isham. After his death, about 1730, she was married again about December 24th, 1733, to Nicholas Davies, who was a large landed proprietor and originally came from Wales.

One of the authorities most generally quoted for the Judith Churchill tradition is the book "Virginia Genealogies", published in 1891 by Rev. Horace Edwin Hayden, where on page 253 he says that Col. William Churchill settled in Middlesex County about 1672, and married Hannah Harrison; that his second child, Judith, born about 1690, married about 1710 Thomas Randolph, and had William,

b. 1712. Hayden cites as his authority The Richmond Critic II, 1. The trouble with Mr. Hayden's above account is that the actual records show that he has confused Col. William Churchill with his son, Armistead Churchill. It was the son Armistead, and not the father, who married Hannah Harrison, and as Armistead was not born until 1704, no daughter of his could have married Thomas Randolph in 1710. We have seen also from the records referred to above that Col. William Churchill himself married the widow Wormeley October 5, 1703, and had no daughter named Judith; and no daughter of that marriage could have been more than seven years old in 1710, the year when Hayden says that Judith Churchill married Thomas Randolph.

In view of all the facts shown above the question may well be asked, what explanation can be given for the Judith Churchill tradition. It is said that every tradition has some basis of truth. In this instance the curious co-incidence and basis for the tradition exists that there was a Judith and she was a member of the household of Col. William Churchill, and she was the grandmother of Thomas Mann Randolph (1st) of Tuckahoe; but she was the step-daughter instead of the daughter of William Churchill, her name was Judith Wormeley instead of Judith Churchill. She married Hon. Mann Page of Rosewell instead of Thomas Randolph of Tuckahoe, and it was her daughter, Maria Judith Page, who married William, only son of the above Thomas Randolph of Tuckahoe, and father of Thomas Mann Randolph (1st). Thus the latter had for his paternal grandmother Judith Fleming and for his maternal grandmother, Judith Wormeley, the step-daughter of William Churchill. The Randolph family tradition seems simply to have mixed up these two "Judith" grandmothers and changed William Churchill's step-daughter into his daughter.

In connection with the foregoing account of the Tuckahoe Randolphs, it seems very desirable to append at least an outline sketch of the ancient and illustrious family of which they are a branch. It may be safely stated that few, if any, families in this country have been more prominent and more influential in the history and in the making of State and the Union than has this Randolph family of Virginia, and its blood descendants, bearing other names. For example, the mother of Thomas Jefferson was Jane Randolph of Dungeness, and her first cousin, Mary Isham Randolph of Tuckahoe was the grandmother of Chief Justice John Marshall. Thus both these commanding figures in American history trace back to the same Randolph ancestor, William Randolph of Turkey Island, the founder of the family in Virginia, and he was likewise the ancestor of General Robert E. Lee.

President Thomas Jefferson, in his Memoirs, says that his mother's family trace their ancestry back into the early mists of Scottish and English history. Jefferson himself apparently took very little interest in such matters, but the family traditions to which he refers go back in Scotland to Thomas Randolph, the Earl of Moray, who became the Lord Regent of Scotland. He was a nephew of Robert Bruce, Earl of Carrick, and later King of Scotland. He makes his first appearance in history at the fatal battle of Methven, and later in 1312 he surprised and took by a desperate assault Edinburg Castle, which was supposed to be impregnable. The next year he was advanced to the command of the center of the Scottish army at the decisive battle of Bannockburn, and greatly distinguished himself by the defeat of Sir Robert Clifford, who had been detached by the English King to turn the flank of the Scottish army and relieve the siege of Stirling Castle, which if successful, would have put an end to the war.

Another noted member of the family in the Scotland of those days was Agnes Randolph, Countess of Dunbar. She was a great niece to Robert Bruce and the wife of the 9th Earl of Dunbar; and was known in legend and history as "Black Agnes of Dunbar" from her famous defense of Dunbar Castle against the English in 1337 during the absence of her husband.

In England, it is recorded in "Domesday Book" that Thomas Randolph of Wiltshire was ordered in the year 1294 to render military service in person against the King of France. A John Randolph was a Burgess from Southampton in the year 1300 and in 1301 was ordered to muster troops at Berwick on Tweed. Richard Randolph was a Burgess from Liecester in 1305. John Randolph was an eminent Judge, and was an official in the English Exchequer in 1385. (App. Cyc. Am. Biog., Vol. V, p. 172.) Sir Thomas Randolph, son of Avery Randolph, a Kentish gentleman, was principal of Pembroke College, Oxford, in 1549, then called Broadgates Hall. From 1560 to 1585 he served as the confidential diplomatic agent of Queen Elizabeth at the Scottish Court, and also on various diplomatic missions to Russia and elsewhere; and he was the Chancellor of the Exchequer in England for four years from 1586 until his death in 1590. (Ency. Brit. 14th Ed., Vol. 18, p. 972.) Thomas Randolph, the poet and dramatist, was born in Northamptonshire June 15, 1605, and died March 12, 1635. (Ency. Brit., 14th Ed., Vol. 18, p. 972.) He was half brother to Henry Randolph and uncle to William Randolph, the two first members of the family to migrate to Virginia.

In the history of Bristol Parish, a footnote on page 213 states: "There was found among the papers of Sir John Randolph of Virginia 'an old antique black-letter pedigree' which thus deduced the descent of William Randolph of Turkey Island". The statement following confirms in the main the account published in the Richmond Critic of September 3rd, 1888, as follows: Robert Randolph of Hams, in Sussex, married Rosa Roberts, daughter of Thomas Roberts of Hawkhurst, Kent, and had William of Harris, near Lewes, Sussex. He married Elizabeth, daughter of Thomas Smith of Newnham, Northamptonshire, and had (1) Thomas, the poet and dramatist, born at Newnham June 15, 1605, fellow of Trinity College, Cambridge, died March 12, 1635; (2) Robert, B. A., of Christ

Church, Oxford, Vicar of Barnetly, and afterwards of Donnington, Lincolnshire, published his brother's poems 1640, died at Donnington July 7, 1671; (3) William, who by his fourth wife, Dorothy, daughter of Richard Law, had William. The Critic article assumes this William to have been the immigrant to Virginia, but the note in the History of Bristol Parish says this William was born November 27, 1623. William Randolph and Dorothy Law had several children, among whom were (1) Henry, the emigrant, (2) Richard, the father of William Randolph of Turkey Island, and (3) William (of the Critic article). Henry Randolph, the uncle of William R. of Turkey Island, came to Virginia about 1650. He was clerk of Henrico County in 1656 and Clerk of the House of Burgesses from 1660 until his death in 1673. He married Judith Soane, daughter of Henry Soane, Speaker of the House of Burgesses, and left one child, a son, Henry (1665–1693) who married Sarah Swann, daughter of Col. Thomas Swann of Swann's Point. The author is not advised whether any members of the Randolph name of this family are still living. Representatives of this family were Judge Peter Randolph of the Virginia General Court (1812–1821), Joseph W. Randolph, the well known publisher in Richmond, and his son, Major Norman V. Randolph. (The Richmond Critic, 1888, Vol. 2, p. 2.)

William Randolph, the progenitor of our family line, came to Virginia about 1672, and was known as William Randolph of "Turkey Island", from the name of his estate. Tradition says he was born in 1651 either in Yorkshire or at or near the village of Moreton Morrell in Warwickshire, in England, but the author has not yet verified this tradition. The History of Bristol Parish says "Yorkshire", but the inscription on his tomb says "of Warwickshire but late of Virginia". His immediate ancestry was as follows: Robert Randolph of Hams, in Sussex, married Rose Roberts, daughter of Thomas Roberts of Hawkhurst, Kent; their son, William Randolph, married Elizabeth Smith, daughter of Thomas Smith of Northamptonshire; and their third son, William Randolph, married Dorothy Law, a daughter of Richard Law, and widow of Thomas West, and had several children of whom Richard Randolph of Moreton Morrell and Henry Randolph, the above mentioned emigrant, were two. This Richard Randolph married Elizabeth Ryland and one of their sons was our William Randolph of "Turkey Island", who came to Virginia about 1672 and succeeded his Uncle Henry as Clerk of Henrico County in 1673. He purchased a large tract of land on the north side of the James River, about fifteen miles or so below the falls, which was called Turkey Island. There, tradition says, he built an imposing mansion of brick imported from England, and with a high cupola; and there he lived until his death, April 11th, 1711 (the date inscribed on his tomb). He was for many years a member of the House of Burgesses and was Speaker of the House in 1698; Attorney General of the Colony 1694–98; member of the Council of the Colony, and one of the founders and trustees of William and Mary

College. Arms: "gu upon a cross or, 5 mullets gu", with two mottoes; "Nil Admirari" above and "Fari quae Sentiat" below. He married in 1680 Mary Isham, a daughter of Henry Isham, "of the antient and eminent family of Ishams of Northamptonshire", and his wife, Katherine Banks of Bermuda Hundred, on the south side of James River.

William Randolph and Mary Isham, his wife, of Turkey Island, the founders of the family, and sometimes termed, from the great number of their descendants, the Adam and Eve of Virginia, had seven sons and two daughters: (1) William, Jr., of "Turkey Island"; (2) Thomas of "Tuckahoe"; (3) Isham of "Dungeness"; (4) Richard of "Curles"; (5) Henry of "Longfield"; (6) Captain Edward, the Mariner; (7) Mary, married William Stith; (8) Sir John of "Tazewell Hall", Williamsburg; (9) Elizabeth, married Richard Bland. This is not the order in which these children are listed in some genealogies, but after a careful comparison of records and dates, we consider the foregoing order to be the correct one.

All of the sons took active and prominent part in the affairs of the Colony, and each received a large patrimony in the distribution of the great estate of their father. Most of them built fine houses and became known by the names of their estates. It is only possible here to make brief references to these various children and their descendants, as at least five of the sons became founders of the several distinct branches of this widespread Virginia family. The facts here stated in regard to them we believe to be thoroughly accurate as they are based on a re-examination of county and parish records, inscriptions and family papers, or taken from well recognized genealogical books and authorities; and a serious attempt has been made here to correct all the various errors that have been discovered in previous genealogies.

I. *"Turkey Island"*, *"Chatsworth"* and *"Wilton"* Branch.

William Randolph (2nd) of Turkey Island, the eldest son of the original William Randolph of that place, was born there in November, 1681, and died October 19th, 1742, aged 61 years. (Inscription on tomb). He was known as *"Councillor"* Randolph; was Clerk of Henrico Court 1714, member of the Council 1727-28, and Treasurer of the Colony; he married June 22, 1709, Elizabeth Beverley (b. Jan. 1, 1691, d. Dec. 26, 1723), daughter of Colonel Peter Beverley of Gloucester County, and had five children: (1) Beverley, (2) Peter, (3) William, (4) Mary, (5) Elizabeth. (History of Bristol Parish.) The above dates as to Elizabeth Beverley were, some years ago, on an ancient monument at Turkey Island.

1. The first son, Beverley Randolph; Justice of Henrico from 1740, Burgess for the College (W. & M.) 1748–1751, was born at Turkey Island 1710,

and resided there. He married Miss Lightfoot, a daughter of Francis Lightfoot of "Sandy Point", and died without issue.

2. The second son of "Councillor" Randolph was Peter Randolph of "Chatsworth"; Justice of Henrico from 1741, Clerk of House of Burgesses, Attorney General of Virginia, Treasurer of the Colony, Burgess 1751, member of the Council 1764, Surveyor General of Customs for Middle District of North America, was born about 1713, and died in 1764. He founded the estate of "Chatsworth" in Henrico and removed there and was known by its name. He married, 1733, Lucy Bolling, daughter of Robert Bolling of Bollingbrook, and had three sons and one daughter. (a) Robert Randolph married Elizabeth Carter, daughter of Charles Carter of Shirley; (b) Beverley Randolph, the second son, b. Sept. 11, 1753, member Virginia Assembly during the Revolution; president Executive Council of Virginia 1787, succeeded Edmund Randolph as Governor of Virginia December 1st, 1788, and served three years. He was born at Chatsworth in 1753 and removed to "Green Creek", Cumberland County, where he died in 1797. He married Feby. 14, 1775, Martha Cocke and left issue; (c) William Randolph, the third son of Peter and Lucy Bolling Randolph, married Mary Skipworth, daughter of Sir William Skipworth and had issue; (d) daughter Ann Randolph, married William Fitzhugh of Ravensworth.

3. William Randolph, third son of "Councillor" William Randolph; was Burgess for Goochland, 1745-6, and was Burgess for Henrico 1758-1761. He was born at Turkey Island about 1719 but removed to "Wilton" where he built a fine colonial residence that is still extant and has recently been removed for preservation, from its original site to Richmond, by the Virginia Society of the Colonial Dames of America. He married about 1735 Anne Harrison, daughter of Benjamin and Anne Carter Harrison of Berkeley; and died at Wilton in 1761, leaving eight children: William, Peter, Harrison, Benjamin, Peyton, Anne, Elizabeth, and Lucy. (1) William Randolph, the eldest son, was born about 1736, and died young; (2) Peter Randolph, born in 1738, married first Mary Spottswood, daughter of Governor Alexander Spottswood, and second, Mary Page of North End but had no issue by either; (3) Harrison Randolph, third son of William Randolph (1st) of Wilton was State Auditor in 1784; (4) Benjamin Randolph, fourth son of William of Wilton (History of Bristol Parish, p. 216); (5) Peyton Randolph of Wilton, fifth son of William (1st) of Wilton married Lucy Harrison of Berkeley and left issue; (a) William (2nd) of Wilton married Miss Andrews (b) Richard Kidder Randolph married Anne Lyman (c) Peyton Randolph of Hampden Sidney College married Anne Innes (d) Elizabeth Randolph married William Berkeley, State Treasurer; (6) Anne Randolph, sixth child and eldest daughter of William (1st) of Wilton, born 1740, married about 1760 Benjamin Harrison of Brandon and died without issue; (7) Elizabeth Randolph, born 1742, married about 1762, Philip Grymes of

Brandon, Middlesex and left no issue; (8) Lucy Randolph, born 1744, married about 1764 Lewis Burwell of Kings Mill, York County.

4. Mary Randolph, born about 1718, fourth child of "Councillor" William Randolph, married John Price, a native of Wales, and had issue.

5. Elizabeth Randolph, fifth child of "Councillor" William Randolph, born in 1720, married Col. John Chiswell, Burgess for Hanover 1744-1758. They had four daughters but no son; (a) Susanna married first "Speaker" John Robinson, second Wm. Griffin; (b) Mary married Warner Lewis of Warner Hall; (c) Elizabeth married Charles Carter of Ludlow; (d) Lucy married Col. William Nelson of The Dorrill. (The History of Bristol Parish, p. 215, says it was Mary who married Chiswell and Elizabeth who married Price.) The name Chiswell was pronounced "Chizzle" and is believed to have been originally "De Choiseul"

II. *"Tuckahoe"-"Edgehill"* Branch.

Thomas Randolph of "Tuckahoe", second son of the original William Randolph of Turkey Island was born there in June, 1683. He settled on land about fifteen miles above the falls of James River and built between 1714 and 1720 the noted old residence, still existing. He named his estate "Tuckahoe", from the Indian name of the Creek flowing through it, and resided there until his death in 1730. Goochland County, where the estate is located, was created in 1728, and he became the presiding Justice and the Lieutenant of the County. He married October 16th, 1712, Judith Fleming, daughter of Charles Fleming and Susanna Tarleton of New Kent County, and left three children: William, Judith and Mary Isham. There is some suggestion that there may possibly have been another daughter, but, if so, she does not appear on the records.

(1) William Randolph, eldest child, and only son of Thomas of Tuckahoe, was born in 1713, and died there in 1745; Burgess for Goochland, he patented a tract of 2400 acres in what afterward became Albemarle County adjacent to 2000 acres patented by his intimate friend Peter Jefferson, and he was the first Clerk of that County when it was created from Goochland in 1744. Prior to that time he was Clerk and later one of the Justices of Goochland County. He married in 1735 Maria (called Mary) Judith Page, second child and only daughter of Hon. Mann Page of Rosewell and Judith Wormeley, his first wife. William Randolph and Mary Page had four children (a) Maria Judith Randolph, born 1736, married about 1756, Edmund Berkeley, Jr. (his first wife) of Barn Elms, Middlesex County, eldest son of Col. Edmund Berkeley of that place and Mary Nelson, a daughter of "Scotch" Tom Nelson of Yorktown. They had one child, a daughter, Anne Berkeley, who married Joseph Clayton, (b) Mary Randolph, born at Tuckahoe 1738, married July 18, 1763 (Doug. Reg., p. 141) Tarleton Fleming of Rock Castel in Goochland and had issue, (c) Thomas Mann

Randolph (1st) of Tuckahoe, born there 1741 and died November 19, 1793. He was Vestryman for Northam Parish, Burgess for Goochland 1772, member of Convention 1776, and of Colonial Committee of Safety, Delegate 1784-1788; Member of Virginia Assembly 1769-76 and Colonel in the American Revolution. He is referred to again below.

(2) Judith Randolph, second child of Thomas Randolph of Tuckahoe and Judith Fleming, was born there about 1716 and married July 13, 1738, Rev. William Stith, (b.   d. 1755), Minister of Henrico Parish 1736-1752, President of William and Mary College 1752 to 1755, and author of History of Virginia. He was a son of William Stith of Charles City County and Mary Randolph, daughter of the original William of Turkey Island, the Aunt to his wife. Issue; (a) Judith Stith, died single in 1773; (b) Elizabeth, married Dr. William Pasteur of Williamsburg, and died in 1792, without surviving issue; (c) Mary Stith, who died in 1816, never married.

(3) Mary Isham Randolph, grandmother of Chief Justice John Marshall, was the youngest daughter of Thomas Randolph of Tuckahoe. She was born there about 1718-1720 and married about 1740 to Rev. James Keith. He was born in Scotland 1696, took part in the rebellion of 1715 and fled to Virginia with his Uncle, Bishop Keith. He returned to England and took holy orders, received the King's Bounty for his trip to Virginia on March 4, 1728/1729, and was minister to Curles Church, Varina, 1730-1733, when he went to Maryland. He returned in 1736 and served at Hamilton Parish, Prince William County, (now in Fauquier), where he died in 1754. Issue; seven children; (1) James Keith, Clerk of Frederick County; (2) John Keith, married Miss Doniphan; (3) Thomas Keith; (4) Alexander Keith; (5) Isham Keith, Lieutenant in Third Virginia Regiment in the Revolution, married in 1778 Charlotte Ashmore; (6) Mary Randolph Keith, married Col. Thomas Marshall, and was the mother of Chief Justice John Marshall; (7) Elizabeth Keith, married Edward Ford of Fairfax County and removed with him to Bourbon County, Kentucky. (The Richmond Critic, Notes to Genealogical Letter XV).

The above mentioned Thomas Mann Randolph (1st) of Tuckahoe was born there 1741 and died November 20, 1793. (Doug. Reg. p. 343). He married twice; first on November 18, 1761, to Anne Cary (1745-1789), oldest child of Col. Archibald Cary of Ampthill; and secondly, on September 15, 1790, to Gabriella Harvie, daughter of the prominent lawyer, John Harvie. By each of these wives he had a son to whom the name of Thomas Mann Randolph was given and this fact of there being three Thomas Mann Randolphs in life in one family about the same time has caused considerable confusion to genealogists. The two marriages also had the result, as we have seen above, of separating the Tuckahoe Branch of Randolphs into two distinct families; the Senior line being thereafter located at Edgehill in Albemarle County, and the Junior line continuing in occupancy and ownership of the Tuckahoe House. By his first wife, Anne Cary, Thomas Mann Randolph (1st), had thirteen children, as follows:

(A) Mary Randolph, born August 9, 1762, died January 23, 1828, married Dec. 9, 1780, David Meade Randolph of Presque Isle on James River. She was buried at Arlington.

(B) Henry Cary Randolph, born Jan. 8, 1764, died March 13, 1765.

(C) Elizabeth Randolph, born June 19, 1765, married 1785, Robert Pleasants of Tilman.

(D) Thomas Mann Randolph (2nd), born October 1, 1768, removed to and founded "Edgehill" in Albemarle County, died at Monticello June 20, 1828. See below.

(E) William Randolph of Chellowe, Cumberland Co., born January 16, 1770, died May 5, 1848, married 1794 Lucy Bolling Randolph, b. Nov. 7th, 1775, (Doug. Reg.) daughter of Beverley Randolph, a son of Peter Randolph of "Chatsworth". They had two sons (a) William Fitzhugh Randolph who married Jane Cary Harrison of Clifton and (b) Thomas Beverly Randolph who married May 31st, 1814, Miss Mayer of Pennsylvania and died leaving twelve children of whom one son, William Mayer Randolph, b. May 24th, 1815, and removed to St. Louis, Mo.

(F) Archibald Cary Randolph, born August 24th, 1771, died October 3rd, same year.

(G) Judith Randolph, born November 24th, 1772, married 1793, her cousin Richard Randolph of "Bizarre", brother of John Randolph of Roanoke.

(H) Anne Cary Randolph, (b. Sept. 16, 1774; d. May 28, 1837), married May 28, 1795, Gouveneur Morris of Morrisania, New York, U. S. Minister to France.

(I) Jane Cary Randolph (b. Dec. 17th, 1776; d. March 2nd, 1832) married 1797 Thomas Eston Randolph of Bristol, who inherited Dungeness, four of her children settled in Florida.

(J) Dr. John Randolph of "Middle Quarter" (b. Sept. 11, 1779; d. August 19, 1834) married 1804 Judith Lewis of Amelia County, daughter of Col. William Lewis (born in Ireland 1724; died 1811;) an officer in the Colonial forces in the French and Indian Wars and a Colonel in the American Army in the Revolution;

(K) George Washington Randolph (b. Dec. 19, 1781; d. July 2, 1783).

(L) Harriet Randolph (b. Nov. 24th, 1783; d. Dec. 1, 1839) married December 19, 1805, Richard S. Hackley of New York, U. S. Consul at Cadiz.

(M) Virginia Randolph (b. January 31, 1786; d. May 2nd, 1852) married August 28th, 1805, Wilson Jefferson Cary of "Carysbrook" a great nephew of

President Jefferson. Among her children was Capt. Wilson Miles Cary, the historian and genealogist.

> NOTE: The above dates for this family are taken from the old Tuckahoe Family Bible, which originally belonged to Ann Cary, first wife of Thomas Mann Randolph (1st). After his death in 1793, it passed to his daughter Ann Cary Randolph, who married Gouverneur Morris of New York in 1795. She bequeathed it, and also the old Family Prayer Book, to Ann Cary (Randolph) Jones, wife of William Strother Jones. She gave the Bible to their son Francis Buckner Jones and it then passed to his son, Randolph Jones, who sold it in 1898 to Mr. Harold Jefferson Coolidge, after his purchase of Tuckahoe; and so the old Book found itself back at its original home.

Section A. Tuckahoe Randolphs—Senior Line—Edgehill Family.

Of the above children of Thomas Mann Randolph (1st) and Anne Cary; the eldest son, Thomas Mann Randolph (2nd) inherited a large part of his father's estate including the 2400 acres in Albemarle County patented by his grandfather, William Randolph of Tuckahoe. He was member of Congress 1803-1807; Colonel 20th Infantry 1813; Governor of Virginia 1819-1821, and a Presidential Elector in 1825. He married February 23, 1790, Martha Jefferson (b. 1772; d. 1836), eldest child of President Thomas Jefferson. They settled first at Tufton, one of Mr. Jefferson's farms near Monticello, but about 1793 built the first house on the Albemarle lands, and named their estate "Edgehill" after the battlefield in England. They had twelve children:

(A) Anne Cary Randolph (b. January 23, 1791; d. Feby. 7, 1826), married Charles Bankhead. Issue (a) Daughter, married John Carter (b) Thomas M. R. Bankhead died in Arkansas without issue (c) John Bankhead settled in Missouri and left issue (d) William Bankhead removed to Alabama.

(B) Thomas Jefferson Randolph, eldest son, born Sept. 12, 1792, died at Edgehill October 7, 1875; married 1815 Jane Hollins Nicholas; (See Below).

(C) Ellen Randolph, born 1795, died an infant.

(D) Ellen Wayles Randolph born Oct. 1796, married 1824 Joseph Coolidge of Boston and left issue (a) Joseph R. Coolidge, married Julia Gardiner (b) Ellen R. Coolidge, married Edmund Dwight (c) Lieut. Sidney Coolidge, U. S. A., killed in Battle at Chattanooga 1864 (d) Algernon Coolidge, twin to Sidney, married Mary Lowell (e) Thomas Jefferson Coolidge, Minister to France, married Mehitabel (Hattie) Appleton.

(E) Cornelia Jefferson Randolph, born July 26, 1799, died single.

(F) Virginia Randolph, born August 30, 1801, married 1821, N. P. Trist who effected the treaty of Hidalgo Guadaloupe, after the Mexican War, in 1848. They had issue (a) Thomas Jefferson Trist; deaf mute, no issue (b) Martha Jefferson Trist, married John Burke of Alexandria, being his second wife and had seven children (c) Dr. H. B. Trist, married Anna Waring of Savannah, Ga., and also had seven children.

(G) Mary Randolph, born November 3rd, 1803, died single.

(H) James Madison Randolph, born at the "White House" in Washington, D. C., January 16, 1806, died single January 1834.

(I) Benjamin Franklin Randolph, born July 14, 1808, married Sarah Carter. Issue (a) Isaetta Carter Randolph b. 1835, d. 1888, married James L. Hubard and left eight children (b) Lewis Carter Randolph, b. 1838, d. 1887, married Jany. 29, 1867, Louisa Hubard, only daughter of Robert Thruston Hubard of Chellowe, Buckingham Co. and left eight children (c) Robert Mann Randolph, b. 1849, married about 1885 Margaret Calhoun Harris, no issue.

(J) Meriwether Lewis Randolph, Secretary of the Territory of Arkansas 1835-6, born January 10th, 1810, died 1837, married in 1835 Elizabeth Martin, a step niece of President Andrew Jackson, and had one son, Lewis Jackson Randolph, who died young.

(K) Septimia Ann Randolph, the seventh daughter and eleventh child, born Jany. 3, 1814, died Sept. 14, 1887, married Dr. David Scott Meikleham, a first cousin of Sir Walter Scott, and had (a) William Meikleham, b. 1839, d. 1889. married first 1865 Fanny Cassidy and had four children; married second 1887 Isabella Parlby Cuthbert, no issue (b) Thomas Mann Randolph Meikleham b. 1840 died single 1922 (c) Esther, died in infancy (d) Esther Alice Meikleham born in Glasgow, Scotland, 1843; died single 1927, (e) Ellen Wayles Meikleham b. 1846, d. 1913, never married.

(L) George Wythe Randolph born March 10, 1818, married 1852 Mary E. Adams (the widow Pope) died without issue. He was a Brigadier General in the Confederate States Army and Secretary of War of the Southern Confederacy. He died April 4, 1867. (The above dates for this family taken from the old Tuckahoe Family Bible).

The above Thomas Jefferson Randolph of "Edgehill", eldest son and second child of Governor Thomas Mann Randolph (2nd) of "Edgehill" and Martha Jefferson, was born September 12, 1792 and died at Edgehill October 7, 1875, and was buried at Monticello. In 1828, he moved the old frame house built by his father and erected the well known brick mansion on its site. He was Presidential Elector in 1845 and President of the National Democratic Convention in Baltimore in 1873. He married March 10 1815 Jane Hollins Nicholas (b. 1798, d. 1871) daughter of Governor Wilson Cary Nicholas of "Warren", Albemarle County and had thirteen children, two of whom died in childhood, the others were:

(A) Margaret Smith Randolph, born 1816, died 1843, married her second cousin, William Mann Randolph, son of Dr. John Randolph of "Middle Quarter" part of the Tuckahoe estate, and had (a) Jane Margaret Randolph (b. May 7, 1840, d. June 27, 1914) married November 8, 1860, Edward Clifford Anderson, Jr., of Savannah, Ga., the father of this author. They left four surviving children. (b) William Lewis Randolph (b. 1842, d. 1892) married first Agnes Dillon of Savannah, Ga., and had five children, married second Margaret R. Taylor of "Lego", Albemarle County, Va. No issue.

(B) Martha Jefferson (Patsy) Randolph (b. 1817, d. 1857) married 1838 John C. R. Taylor of Albemarle and had (a) Col. Bennett Taylor (1836-1898) married 1866 Lucy Colston and had six children. (b) Jane Randolph Taylor (1837-1917) single (c) Susan Beverly Taylor (1839-1890) married John S. Blackburn of Alexandria and had two children (d) Jefferson Randolph Taylor (b. 1843, d) Clergyman, married Mary Bruce and had two children (e) Margaret Randolph Taylor, b. 1844, married William Lewis Randolph of Dunlora, his second wife, no issue. (f) Charlotte Taylor, died in infancy (g) Stevens Mason Taylor (1847-1917) married Mary Mann Page and had three daughters. (h) Cornelia Jefferson Taylor, born 1849. Unmarried (i) Moncure Robinson Taylor, born 1851, married Lucy Willis and had one son (j) Edmund Randolph Taylor, born 1853, married Julia Kennedy, and had four children.

(C) Cary Anne Nicholas Randolph (1820-1857), married 1840, Frank Gildart Ruffin of Valley Farm, Albemarle, and had eight children (a) Jefferson Randolph Ruffin (1842-1908), died unmarried, (b) William Roane Ruffin (b. d. 1899) married 1868 Sally Walthall McIlwaine of Petersburg and had eight children (c) Wilson Cary Nicholas Ruffin of Danville, married 1870 Mary Harvie and had seven children (d) George Randolph Ruffin, removed to Texas, married Amarilla Bell and had two children (e) Frank Gildart Ruffin, Jr., removed to Mobile, Ala. He married Margaret Ellen Henry and had seven children (f) Eliza McDonald Ruffin (1853-1904) lived at Edgehill after her mother's death, and died unmarried (g) Cary Randolph Ruffin (1857-1910) lived at Edgehill, after his mother's death and inherited it. Changed his name to Cary Ruffin Randolph, married Ethel Patterson and died without issue.

(D) Mary Randolph, died an infant.

(E) Mary Buchanan Randolph (1822-1884) was Principal of the well known Edgehill School for Girls. Never married.

(F) Ellen Wayles Randolph (1825-1896) married 1859, William B. Harrison of Upper Brandon, his second wife. Issue (a) Jane Nicholas Harrison (1862-1926) married Alexander B. Randall of Baltimore and had one son (b) Jefferson Randolph Harrison (1868-1931) never married.

(G) Maria Jefferson Carr Randolph (1826-1902) married 1848 Charles Mason of King George County, and had (a) Jefferson Randolph Mason (1850-1888) removed to Texas, died unmarried (b) Lucy Wiley Mason (1852-1922) married Edward Jaqueline Smith and had two children (c) John Enoch Mason

(1854-1910) married Kate Kearney and had three children (d) Wilson Cary Nicholas Mason (1858-1866).

(H) Caroline Ramsay Randolph (1828-1902) Never married. Managed the Edgehill estate after her father's death.

(I) Thomas Jefferson Randolph, Jr. (1829-1872) Married first 1854 Mary Walker Meriwether, who died 1863 leaving six children (a) Francis Meriwether Randolph (1854-1922) married Charlotte Nelson Macon and had four children (b) Thomas Jefferson Randolph (3rd) (1855-1884) never married (c) Margaret Douglass Randolph (1857-1880) never married (d) Francis Nelson Randolph (1858-1880) single (e) Jane Hollins Randolph (1861-1862) (f) George Geiger Randolph (1863-1893) single. T. J. Randolph (2nd) married secondly in 1865 Charlotte Nelson Meriwether and had one child, Mary Walker Randolph, born 1866, married 1894, her cousin William Mann Randolph, son of William Lewis Randolph and Agnes Dillon, and had eight children.

(J) Jane Nicholas Randolph (1831-1868) married May 24, 1854, Robert Garlick Hill Kean of Lynchburg and had four children; (a) Lancelot Minor Kean (1856-1931) married first May 11, 1880, Elizabeth Tucker Prescott and had three sons, who died infants, and three daughters. He married secondly, October 3, 1911, Martha Foster Murphy and had one son, Louis Randolph Kean, b. May 17, 1913. (b) Martha (Pattie) Cary Kean b. April 11, 1858, married April 27, 1882, John Speed Morris (1858-1929) and had two sons and four daughters (c) General Jefferson Randolph Kean, U. S. A. Medical Corps, b. 1860, married first Louise Hurlbut Young and had one daughter and 1 son. He married 2nd, March 24, 1919, Cornelia Knox. No issue. (d) Robert Garlick Hill Kean, Jr., b. 1862, died 1883. Single.

(K) Dr. Wilson Cary Nicholas Randolph (1834-1907) married first Nannie Holladay and had four children (a) Virginia Minor Randolph, born 1859, married 1884, George Scott Shackelford of Orange and had four children (b) Wilson Cary Nicholas Randolph, Jr. (1861-1923) removed to Lynchburg, married Margaret Hager and left one child, John Hager Randolph (c) Mary Buchanan Randolph (1865-1900) never married (d) Julia Minor Randolph, b. 1866, married 1891, William Porterfield and had four children.

Dr. W. C. N. Randolph Sr., married secondly, Mary McIntire of Charlottesville by whom he had a daughter, Elizabeth McIntire Randolph, b. 1893, married 1917, Capt. Thos. Jeffries Betts, U. S. A.

(L) Meriwether Lewis Randolph (1837-1871); Captain C. S. A.; married Anna Daniel and had one child, Meriwether Lewis Randolph, Jr., b. 1870, d. 1876.

(M) Sarah Nicholas Randolph, b. Oct. 10, 1839, died unmarried April 25, 1892. Teacher and Author. Principal Patapsco Institute, Ellicott City, Md.; and of Miss Randolph's School for Girls, Eutaw Place, Baltimore.

Section B—Tuckahoe Randolphs—Junior Line—Tuckahoe House Family.

The above named Thomas Mann Randolph (1st) of Tuckahoe, after the death of his first wife, Anne Cary, Mar. 6, 1789 (Doug. Reg. p. 343), married secondly, Sept. 15, 1790, a young girl of 18, Gabriella Harvie, daughter of Col. John Harvie of "Belvedere", now Hollywood Cemetery at Richmond. He was member of Congress in 1778 and Register of the Land Office. By this marriage he had one son, Thomas Mann Randolph (3rd) and one daughter, Mary Jane Randolph, who died in infancy. Both of his sons, one by each wife, thus bore the same name. He died 1793, and she later married **Dr. John Brockenborough** of Richmond. No descendants.

His son by this second marriage, Thomas Mann Randolph (3rd) born at Tuckahoe 1791, died 1851, was also married twice. He married first Harriott Wilson (d. Jan. 22, 1822) a daughter of Thomas and Elizabeth (Vaughn) Wilson of West Lawn, Richmond, and had six children, viz.:

1. Mary Gabriella Randolph (b.   d.   ) married John Biddle Chapman of Philadelphia, (son of Dr. Nathaniel and Rebecca Biddle Chapman), and had two daughters.

(A) Mary Gabriella Chapman, married Barnard Luis de Potestad-Fornari, and had seven children: (1) Luis Emilio de Potestad, married Maria Cespedes, and had two sons; (2) Emily Mildred de Potestad married Carso S. Caro, Count de Caltavoturo, and had two children. (3) Manuel Henry de P. died single. (4) John Henry de P., died single, (5) Robert E. Lee de Potestad, married Alice Lee George and had one daughter. (6) Mary Gabriella de Potestad married Richard Tilghman of Philadelphia and had two children, (7) Marie Eugenie de Potestad, died unmarried.

(B) Emily Louise Chapman married Prince Joseph Pignatelli d'Aragon, son of the Count Fuentes y Egmont. No children.

2. Margaret Harvie Randolph (b.——, d. 1891), married in 1830 Francis Asbury Dickins (1804–1879) of Washington and "Ossian Hall" in Fairfax County, Va., son of Asbury Dickins, Secretary of U. S. Senate 1836–1861, and Lilas Arnot, daughter of Hugo Arnot of Scotland. They had nine children.

(A) Mary Randolph Dickins, b. 1840, d. 1849.

(B) Francis Asbury Dickins, Jr., married Medora Braxton Garlick, daughter of Braxton and Mary C. (Webb) Garlick of "Waterloo", New Kent Co. Va., and had a daughter, Medora Braxton Dickins, who married Benj. Watkins Lacy, Jr.

(C) Frances Margaret Dickins, died unmarried.

(D) Harriot Wilson Dickins married Henry Theodore Wight, son of Dr. Wight of Goochland County, and had (1) Hattie Randolph Wight, b. 1867,

d. 1869; (2) H. Theodora Wight, married John May Keim, son of George de Benneville Keim of Philadelphia, now of "Federal Hill" Fredericksburg, Va.

(E) Lilas Arnot Dickins, b. 1845, d. 1846.

(F) Ellen Arnot Dickins, b. 1847, d. 1855.

(G) Emily Dickins, b. 1852, d. 1852.

(H) (Thomas Mann) Randolph Dickins, Col. U. S. Marine Corps, married Minnie Viola Stinson.

(I) Albert White Dickins, 1855–1913, married 1887 Virginia Tucker Webb (born 1864), daughter of Captain William Augustine Webb (U. S. and Confederate States Navies), and his wife, Elizabeth Anne Fleming of "Mannsville", Goochland County, Va., and had (1) Randolph Dickins, born St. Louis, Mo., in 1890, Captain 7th U. S. Cavalry, 1919, retired; married Zoya Klementynowska of Warsaw, Poland; (2) Francis Asbury Dickins of Brooklyn, born St. Louis, Mo., 1892, married Hesseltine Marshall Moore (the widow Gayle); (3) Virginia Fleming Dickins, born 1893, now residing in Washington, D. C.

3 John Brockenburough Randolph, Lieutenant U. S. Navy; married Margaret Timberlake of Washington, D. C., and had two children.

(A) John Brockenborough Randolph, Jr., married his first cousin, Gabriella Randolph White, daughter of Senator A. S. White, and had (a) Louise Randolph, married Harrison Osborne of New York; (b) Frances Howell Randolph married Richard Percy Hines of Mobile, Ala., and had two children.

(B) Mary Gabriella Randolph married, first, Col. Myron H. Beaumont of New York, and had a son, Myron Holley Beaumont, who married Eva Kamera of Iowa.

Mary Gabriella (Randolph) Beaumont married secondly Smith D. Fry of Iowa, and had a daughter, Mary Dunbar Fry, who married, first, James Reed, and secondly, Joseph Hartson.

4 Harriet Wilson Randolph (1822–1893) married Albert Smith White, U. S. Senator from Indiana (1839–1845); U. S. District Judge 1864; and had four children.

(A) Albert S. White, Jr., married Julia Cox, daughter of Joseph Cox, of Indianapolis, and had two children, (a) Albert S. White, who married Ethel Webb, of New Jersey, and had two children; (b) Arthur Cox White, married Sue Perine, and had two children.

(B) Randolph White married Nellie Rowe, daughter of Dr. Rowe of Illinois, and had four children, (a) Randolph White, Jr., unmarried; (b) Harriot White, married Royal Grosenbaugh, and had two children; (c) Charles Russell White married Blanche Jamison, and had three children; (d) Herbert White married Pearl ——— and had a son.

(C) Frances Howell White (1849–1895) married, 1869, Silenus de Witt Parsons of Minnesota and had two surviving children. (a) Charles Francis Parsons, born January 18, 1872, Justice U. S. Supreme Court of Hawaii, retired and resides in Honolulu, and unmarried; (b) John Randolph Parsons, born May 24, 1892, married May 16, 1915, Mary Sinclair Battey, daughter of Dr. Henry Halsey Battey of Rome, Ga., and has two sons, (1) John Randolph Parsons; (2) Robert Battey Parsons.

(D) Mary Gabriella White married her first cousin, John Brockenborough Randolph, Jr., q. v. supra, for their descendants.

5 and 6. Elizabeth Wilson Randolph and Harriet Hackley Randolph both died in infancy.

Thomas Mann Randolph (3rd) of Tuckahoe, after the death of his first wife, Harriot Wilson, married secondly, Lucinda Anne Patterson of New York, and had eight children.

1. Thomas Mann Randolph (4th) died in childhood.

2. Henry Patterson Randolph married first, Louise Dempsey of New York, who died without issue, and he married secondly, Ellen Wierman, by whom he had a son, Paul Randolph, who married first, Gertrude Beale Reed (no children).

3. Allan Randolph died unmarried in St. Louis.

4 and 5. Louisa Gabriella Randolph and Robert Livingston Randolph both died in infancy.

6. Clara Haxall Randolph married William Key Howard of Baltimore, son of Dr. William Howard, and had three children.

(A) William Key Howard, Jr., married Florence Lamar Moore of Georgia, and had (a) John Lamar Howard, married May ———, and had two children, (b) Clark Howard married Ross Hill and had two children, (c) Francis Key Howard, (d) Betsy Howard.

(B) Allan Randolph Howard married Fannie Lightfoot Smith, daughter of William Augustine and Mittie Robb Smith, and had two children, (a) Frances Randolph Howard, married her cousin, Robert G. Robb, of "Gaymont", Caroline Co., Va., and had two children, (b) William Key Howard. The above Allan Randolph Howard married secondly Margaret Frost (no children).

(C) Clarence Randolph Howard married Mary French.

7. Mary Louisa Randolph married George Washington Mayo of Richmond, son of Edward C. Mayo, and had five children.

(A) George D. Mayo married Laura Rutherfoord, daughter of Thomas Rutherfoord, and had two children, (a) Laura Rutherfoord Mayo, (b) Thomas Mann Randolph Mayo.

(B) Louise Mayo married H. Burton Gay and had two children, (a) Louise Gay, married Leonard Moore, (b) H. Burton Gay, Jr.

(C) Arthur Randolph Mayo married Kitty Wilson of New York, and has a son, Randolph Mayo.

(D) Adeline Livingston Mayo married Frederick Pomeroy Palen, and has a son, Frederick Pomeroy Palen, Jr.

(E) Lewis Randolph Mayo, unmarried.

8. Arthur Randolph married in Scotland, where he was educated, and moved to New Zealand; had two daughters, one of whom, Clara Randolph, married Alfred Bailey, and has a son.

9. Jane DeHart Randolph married Robert Carter Harrison, and had two children, (a) Randolph Harrison, (b) Howard Harrison.

Thomas Mann Randolph (3rd) was the last of the name to own Tuckahoe. He fell into financial difficulties and sold the place in 1830 to Hezekiah Wight, who sold it in 1850 to Joseph Allen. It remained in the Allen family till 1898, when it was sold for debt and was bought in by Joseph Randolph Coolidge of Boston, Mass., the great-great-grandson of the first Thomas Randolph of Tuckahoe, through the marriage of Ellen Wayles Randolph in 1824 to Joseph Coolidge. The Coolidge family held the property until the death of Mr. Harold Jefferson Coolidge in 1934; and in the distribution of his estate, Tuckahoe was again sold September 30, 1935, to John Hopkins Baker, Jessie Gresham Baker and Isabelle Ball Baker by deed recorded in Goochland County records in Deed Book 66, page 298, et seq.

III. *"Dungeness"* Branch.

Isham Randolph of "Dungeness", in Goochland County, was born at "Turkey Island" in January, 1685. The inscription on this tomb says he was the third son of William and Mary (Isham) Randolph of that place, and that he died in November, 1742, aged 57 years. In his early manhood he was for several years after 1708 the Colonial Agent for Virginia in England. He married in London in 1717 or 1718 Jane Rogers, a daughter of Charles Rogers and Jane Lilburne, of the same family as the noted John Lilburne of the Bishopric of Durham. After his final return to Virginia he settled in Goochland, on the James River, and built an imposing mansion on what was then virtually the frontier of the Colony, and named his place "Dungeness". He took an active and prominent part in Virginia affairs; was a Justice for his County, a member of the House of Burgesses, Adjutant General and then Lieutenant General of the Colony. He left six daughters and three sons:

1. Jane Randolph, born in London about 1720, was married in 1739 to Peter Jefferson of Henrico County. Their marriage bond is dated October 3rd,

1739. and is recorded in Goochland County. They had eight children: (1) Jane (1740–1765), died unmarried; (2) Mary (   ), married Col. John Bolling of Chesterfield and left issue; (3) Thomas Jefferson (1743–1826), author of the Declaration of American Independence, and third President of the United States, married January 1, 1772, Martha (Wayles) Skelton, daughter of John Wayles, and widow of Bathurst Skelton, and had (a) Martha Jefferson (1772–1836), married 1790, Thomas Mann Randolph II, Governor of Virginia, and left issue, (b) Maria Jefferson (1778–1804), married John Wayles Eppes and left issue; (4) Elizabeth Jefferson (1744–1773), died single; (5) Martha Jefferson (1746–1811), married Dabney Carr and left issue; (6) Lucy Jefferson (   ), married Charles Lewis, Jr., and left issue; (7) Anna Scott Jefferson (   ), married Hastings Marks and left issue; (8) Randolph Jefferson (1755–1815), married first Anna Lewis, and had five sons and one daughter.

2. Mary Randolph, born about 1723, married in 1746 Charles Lewis of "Buck Island", and left issue. Their marriage bond is dated July 15, 1746. Their daughter, Ann, married Randolph Jefferson (his first wife), the brother of President Jefferson; and their son, Charles, Jr., married Lucy Jefferson.

3. Isham Randolph, born about 1725, married in Pennsylvania, but died without issue (Edgehill roll). Several genealogies give his name as Thomas Isham and omit the fact that he had a brother Thomas. The will of Jane (Rogers) Randolph, dated December 5, 1760, and probated in Goochland County July 21, 1761 (Cabells and their Kin, p. 239), shows that she had three sons, Isham, William and Thomas, for the will devised Dungeness to each of them successively in turn in case either died without male issue. (See also, History of Bristol Parish, p. 216.)

4. William Randolph, born about 1727; removed to Bristol, England, where he married a Miss Elizabeth Little, and resided there. Left issue. Their son, Thomas Esten Randolph, married Jane Randolph of Tuckahoe, q. v.

5. Thomas Randolph, born about 1728, married 1768 Jane Cary. (See Douglass Register, p. 216, and History of Bristol Parish.) She was a daughter of Col. Archibald Cary of Ampthill, and Mary Randolph, his wife, daughter of Richard Randolph of Curles. They had four children, (1) Archibald Cary Randolph, Captain 12th U. S. Infantry, 1812, born about 1769, married Lucy Burwell, a daughter of Col. Nathanael Burwell of Clarke County, and had six children; (2) and (3) Isham Randolph and Thomas Randolph, twins. The Douglass Register, p. 283, says these twins were born March 27, 1771, and baptized April 15, 1771. Isham removed to Richmond and married Nancy Coupland, by whom he had four children. Thomas, the other twin, married first Miss Mary Skipworth, and had one daughter, Elizabeth, who married E. S. Symington of Indianapolis. He married second Miss Catherine Lawrence, and

left a daughter, Mary, who married William Sheets of Indiana, and left issue. Thomas Randolph was killed in the battle of Tippecanoe Nov. 5, 1811. (4) Mary Randolph, born Feby. 1, 1773, married March 20, 1790, her cousin, Randolph Harrison of Clifton, Cumberland County, and had fourteen children.

6. Elizabeth Randolph, born about 1730, married about 1750, John Railey of Chesterfield County, and removed with him to Kentucky. See Douglass Register, p. 282, for a list of their nine children with names and dates.

7. Dorothea Randolph, born 1732, married October 14, 1751 (Douglass Register, p. 51), John Woodson, member of House of Burgesses from Goochland County. Their marriage bond is dated October 8th, 1751, and the granting of the license is consented to for her by her guardian, Peter Jefferson, and consented to for the groom, though over 21 years of age, by his mother, then Mrs. Mary Farrar. Dorothea (Randolph) Woodson died Feby. 2nd, 1794 (Doug. Reg., p. 346). Left issue.

8. Anne Randolph, born about 1735, was married three times, (1) on November 28, 1751, to Daniel Scott, by whom she had no issue (Doug. Reg.). Their marriage bond is dated November 26, ·1751; (2) to Johnathan Pleasants on June 14, 1759 (Doug. Reg.), by whom she had two children, Samuel and Jane; (3) to James Pleasants, by whom she also had two children, (a) James Pleasants, Governor of Virginia, and (b) Susan Pleasants, who married George Webster.

9. Susanna Randolph, born September 25th, 1738 (Doug. Reg., p. 282), married November 9th, 1760 (Doug. Reg.), Carter Henry Harrison of Clifton, Cumberland County, a grandson of "King" Carter. Their marriage bond is dated November 7, 1760. They had six children, one of whom, Robert Harrison, removed to Kentucky and married Ann Cabell and left issue. They were the grandparents of the late Carter H. Harrison, the well known Mayor of Chicago.

IV. *"Curles"* or *"Curls Neck"* Branch.

Richard Randolph of "Curles", or "Curls Neck", fourth son of William Randolph (1) of "Turkey Island", was born there about May, 1686, and died in England December 17, 1748. (See Brock's Notes to Vestry Book, Henrico County.) He settled on part of the Curles plantation left him by his father, and also inherited an additional part from his brother, Henry. He was a member of the House of Burgesses and succeeded his brother, William, as Treasurer of the Colony. He married about 1714, Jane Bolling (1704-1760), a daughter of John and Mary (Kennon) Bolling of "Cobbs". His wife was the fourth generation in direct descent from Pocahontas. They had seven children:

1. Richard Randolph, Jr., one of the Justices of Henrico, and a member of the House of Burgesses, was born at Curles in 1715 and died June 6, 1786,

age 71. He married about 1750 Anne Meade of Nansemond County, born 1731, died December 9, 1814, age 83. Left issue: (1) Richard Randolph, md. Maria Beverley of Blandfield; (2) David Meade Randolph, md. Mary Randolph of Tuckahoe; (3) Brett Randolph, md. Lucy Beverley of Blandfield; (4) Ryland Randolph, md. Elizabeth Frazier; (5) Susan Randolph, md. Benjamin Harrison of Berkeley; (6) Jane Randolph, md. Archibald Bolling; (7) Ann Randolph, md. Brett Randolph, Jr.; (8) Elizabeth Randolph, md. David Meade; (9) Mary Randolph, md. William Bolling of Bolling Hall; (10) Sarah Randolph, md. William Newburn.

2. Mary Randolph, born 1727, died November 25, 1781 (Hist. Bristol Parish, p. 216); married May 31, 1744, Col. Archibald Cary of Ampthill, Chesterfield County, the distinguished Revolutionary patriot. They had eight children, (a) Anne Cary, b. 1745, married Nov. 18, 1761, Thomas Mann Randolph (I) of Tuckahoe; (b) Mary Cary, b. 1747, d. 1748; (c) Jane Cary, b. Feby. 12, 1751, married 1768, Thomas Randolph of Dungeness; (d) Sarah Cary, b. Feby. 23, 1753, married 1773, —— Bolling; (e) Eliza Cary, b. April 9, 1755, d. Aug. 2, 1775, single; (f) Henry Cary, only son, b. March 2, 1756, d. May 17, 1758; (g) Mary Cary (II), b. Dec. 4, 1766 married Major Carter Page of The Fork (his first wife); (h) Elizabeth Cary, b. 1770, married July, 1787, Robert Kincaid.

3. Jane Randolph, born about 1729, married about 1750, Anthony Walke of "Fairfield", Princess Anne County, and left issue. One of their children was the Rev. Anthony Walke.

4. Brett Randolph, born about 1732, died 1759. Settled in Gloucestershire, England, and married Mary Scott of London. Left issue.

5. John Randolph of "Mattoax", born 1739, died October 28, 1775, married 1769, Frances Bland, daughter of Col. Theoderic Bland of "Cawsons". Removed to Roanoke in Charlotte County, and left issue; (1) Richard Randolph of "Bizarre", born 1770, married 1790, his cousin, Judith Randolph, a daughter of Thomas Mann Randolph (I) of Tuckahoe, and left issue; (2) Theoderic Bland Randolph, born 1771, died 1792, unmarried; (3) John Randolph of Roanoke, born June 3, 1773, died unmarried in Philadelphia May 24th, 1833, after a brilliant career in the United States Congress and Senate; (4) Jane Randolph.

6. Elizabeth Randolph (   ), married Col. Richard Kidder Meade of "Coggins Point", a distinguished Revolutionary officer, who by his second marriage was the father of Bishop Meade.

7. Ryland Randolph, a Justice of Henrico. He purchased the old original family homestead at Turkey Island, and died unmarried.

V. *Henry Randolph of Longfield,* part of Curles, fifth son of William

Randolph (1st), of Turkey Island born about October, 1687. He was a Vestryman and Warden of Bristol Parish in 1720, and died unmarried in England. He devised his part of the Curles estate, received under his father's will, to his brother, Richard of Curles.

VI. *Captain Edward Randolph*, sixth son of William Randolph (1st), of Turkey Island, was born there in 1690, and married about 1717 or 1718 Miss Groves of Bristol, England, reputed to be an heiress. He was in the Marine service, and his family divided both their time and their residence between the Colony and England. (The Richmond Critic, 1888, Vol. I, p. 2). Issue, (1) Joseph Randolph, died unmarried; (2) Edward Randolph, married Lucy, daughter of Benjamin Harrison of Berkeley; (3) Elizabeth Randolph, married Rev. William Yates, President of William and Mary College; (4) Mary Randolph, married Reverend Robert Yates. Their daughter, Catherine, married Dr. Robert Wellford, a surgeon in the British Army, who settled in Fredericksburg.

VII. *Mary Randolph*, seventh child and oldest daughter of William Randolph (1st) of Turkey Island, was born there about 1692, and married about 1712 Captain William Stith of Charles City County, a son of Captain John Stith, who was disfranchised by the Bacon General Assembly of 1676 on the charge of being one of the chief causes of all their grievances. Issue, (a) Rev. William Stith, who married his first cousin, Judith Randolph of Tuckahoe; (b) John Stith of Charles; (c) Mary Stith married Rev. William Dawson, D. D., President of William and Mary College; Commissary for the Bishop of London in Virginia, and member of the Council.

VIII. *Williamsburg—"Tazewell Hall"* Branch.

Sir John Randolph (Knight), eighth child of William Randolph (1st) of Turkey Island, was born there in April, 1693, and died March 5th, 1737, leaving four children. (Obituary in Virginia Gazette of March 11th, 1737). He removed to Williamsburg, where he built his well known mansion of "Tazewell Hall", which is still existing. On a mural tablet to his memory in William and Mary College, which was destroyed by fire in 1859, he was termed "Johannes Randolph, Eques". It is therefore proper to call him Sir John. He was the King's Attorney General for the Colony, Speaker of the House of Burgesses, and also was Treasurer of the Colony. He was buried in the crypt of the Chapel of William and Mary College. He married about 1718 Susanna Beverley, daughter of Peter Beverley of Gloucester County, and sister of Elizabeth, his brother William's wife. He left the following children:

1. John Randolph, born at Williamsburg, 1727, and was Attorney General of the Colony. He married about 1752 Ariana Jennings, daughter of Edmund

Jennings of Annapolis, Maryland, who was Attorney General for both Maryland and Virginia.

The children of John and Arianna (Jennings) Randolph were: (A) Edmund Jennings Randolph, born August 10th, 1753, died September 12th, 1813. He was personal aide de camp to General Washington in 1775; Governor of Virginia, 1786–1788; first Attorney General of the United States, 1789–1790; Secretary of State of the United States, 1794–1795. He married August 29th, 1776, Elizabeth Nicholas ( ), daughter of Robert Carter Nicholas, Speaker of the House of Burgesses and Treasurer of Virginia. They had one son and three daughters, (1) Peyton Randolph, born ——, died December 26, 1828; removed to Richmond and was clerk of the Virginia Supreme Court until his death. He married Maria Ward, daughter of Benjamin Ward, Jr., of Chesterfield, and left issue; (2) Susan Randolph ( ), married J. Bennett Taylor of Albemarle County, and left issue; (3) Edmonia Randolph ( ), married John L. Preston of Rockbridge, and left issue; (4) Lucy Randolph (1790–1847), married Judge Peter Vivian Daniel of Stafford County, U. S. Judge in Richmond, and left issue.

(B) Susan Randolph ( ), married John Randolph Grymes and left issue.

(C) Arianna Randolph ( ), married in England Captain James Wormeley, and was the mother of Rear Admiral Ralph Randolph Wormeley of the British Navy, and had three daughters, each of whom married in this country.

2. Peyton Randolph, second son of "Sir John", was born in 1722, and died in Philadelphia October 22nd, 1775, while a member of the U. S. Congress. He was Attorney General of Virginia 1748, Speaker Virginia House of Burgesses 1766, Chairman of the Virginia Committee on Correspondence 1773; elected to the Congress of the United States 1774, and was unanimously elected President of the first American Congress, which framed the Constitution of the United States; President of the Virginia Convention of 1775, and re-elected to the United States Congress in that year. He married ( ), Elvira Harrison, daughter of Benjamin Harrison of Berkeley, but left no issue.

3. Beverley Randolph, third son of "Sir John" ( ), married Miss .... Wormley of Middlesex County.

4. Mary Randolph, fourth child of "Sir John" ( ), married about 1743 Philip Grymes of Brandon, Middlesex County, and left four children: (A) Philip Grymes, Jr. ( ), married about 1762 Elizabeth Randolph (b. 1742,), a daughter of William Randolph (I) of Wilton, and left issue; (B) Lucy Grymes ( ), married 1761 Governor Thomas Nelson of Yorktown, and left issue; (C) Susan Grymes ( ), married Nathaniel Burwell of "The Grove", York County, and had issue; (D) Mary Grymes ( ), married about

1777 Robert Nelson of "Malvern Hill", Charles City County, a brother of her sister Lucy's husband, and left issue.

IX. *Elizabeth Randolph,* youngest child of William Randolph of Turkey Island, was born there about 1695, and died January 22, 1720. She married about 1711 Richard Bland of Jordan's Point on James River; and she was the great-great-grandmother of General Robert E. Lee. Among her children were (1) Mary Bland, b. 1712, md. 1728, Henry Lee of Lee Hall; (2) Richard Bland, Jr., of Jordan's Point; member of the Virginia House of Burgesses, of the Virginia Convention of 1775, and of the First American Congress at Philadelphia; (3) Theoderic Bland, b. 1720. All her children left issue.

THE FAMILY AND FORTUNE OF GENERAL JAMES RAY, PIONEER OF FORT HARROD

By KATHRYN HARROD MASON

In Kentucky's pioneer history the name of General James Ray of Mercer County is one of the most loved and respected. While today's historians may know him principally as a brave and enterprising boy whose heroic exploits embroider the legends surrounding Fort Harrod,[1] it is fitting that some attention be given to other aspects of his life, particularly to his family and business affairs.

General Ray came to Fort Harrod in 1775 at the age of 14 or 15 with his Mother, step-father, Hugh McGary, and his two brothers, William and John, after a long journey from North Carolina in the party headed by Daniel Boone. The chronicle of his long, useful life in the first years of Kentucky's history, is a heart-warming exception to those of other pioneers, less fortunate than he, less qualified to deal with the constant danger and strife that they found in the wilderness, and still less equipped to make the transition from Indian fighter to peace-time citizen. From the day he made his spectacular race with Blackfish's Indian warriors to sound a warning of danger that for seven years gave the settlers no peace of mind or body, James Ray led a charmed life, as it seemed to his fellow-frontiersmen—a life which ended in peace and material comfort in his fine home on the brow of the hill only a short distance from the scene of that first race to the fort, fifty-eight years before.

This boy, who could not read or write, taught himself these essential arts, and prepared for a time when his physical talents would be the lesser of his assets. In the course of his life which was spent in Kentucky, General Ray achieved an unpretentious economic security. Among the many documents concerned with various aspects of his career, perhaps the most interesting are to be found in early court records in Mercer and Lincoln Counties. A study of his will, and the appraisement of his estate, afford us a picture of Ray, the gentleman farmer, as well as a view of the last years of his life in this prosperous central Kentucky community.

Before examining these documents in detail, it might be well to go back many years, to the time of his arrival in Kentucky. Unfortunately practically nothing is known of his life in North Carolina, not even his father's name, nor the place of his birth. His mother, who was Mary Buntin before her first marriage, had three sons, James, William, and John.[2] Shortly before the family

---
[1] For an extended discussion of his adventures and military services, as well as his contributions of a civic nature in the legislature and in Mercer county, see *The Filson Club History Quarterly*, 1945, "The Career of General James Ray, Kentucky Pioneer," by Kathryn Harrod Mason.
[2] Draper Mss., 12C17.

moved to Kentucky from the Yadkin River country, not far from Daniel Boone's home in North Carolina, the "Widow Ray," as she was called, married Hugh McGary, whose brave deeds and civic contributions are blotted out in the memory of his tragic part in the disaster at Blue Licks. But the rigorous life on the new frontier proved too much for the frail woman, and when her son William was killed by Indians that fateful March 6, 1777, she "took to her bed" with a long and serious illness which ended in her death in 1780.

It was the next year that James married Amelia Yocum, a daughter of Matthias Yocum who came to Kentucky in the fall of 1779 from Bottetourt County in Virginia.[3] The young couple had two sons, William and Jesse. 'Milly' died in 1783 on the first day of December. The young widower remarried in 1785—the fifteen-year old Elizabeth Talbot, who bore eleven children. In 1810 Ray was once more a widower, but did not marry again.

For several months before his death in 1835, the General was confined to his bed, carefully watched over by his devoted family and friends. Colonel Thompson, his neighbor, remained at his bedside a large part of the time, while the faithful chronicler of that pioneer period, Dr. Christopher C. Graham,[4] was in constant attendance. The will, which was dictated to Colonel Thompson a few days before Ray's death, is found in *Will Book*, No. 9, in the Mercer County records:

> "I James Ray of the County of Mercer and State of Kentucky make this writing my last will and testament to have full force and effect as such.
>
> "I give to my daughter Mary Duncan a negro girl named Joanne, this in addition to what I have heretofore given her, and which she has received. The negro girl or woman Johanna, with her future increase is given for the use of said Mary Duncan during her natural life. And at her death to go equally to the children of Said Mary Duncan.
>
> I have heretofore conveyed for the use of my Daughter Catherine Keller, by two deeds of Trust, the trustee in one being Benjamin F. Pleasant and in the other Joel P. Williams, certain property named in said deed. Now I hereby ratify and confirm the conveyance aforesaid, and at the death of my said Daughter Catherine my will is that the property thus placed in Trust, Shall belong in absolute right to such of the children of said Catherine as may then be living—
>
> "I give to my Daughter Jane Wilson two negroes now in her possession, the one a woman named Martha Ann the other a girl named Sally, the Daughter of Martha Ann with the future increase of said negroes. Also twenty acres of land on which said Jane now lives, lying on the west side of the Shawnee run, to be laid off to include the Dwelling house and be bounded by the road on one side and the land of John Dean on the other, to her and her heirs—I give to my Daughter Martha Alfred during her natural life the use of two negro girls named Mary and Amanda—the former now in possession of said Martha Alfred, the other, Amanda, to be delivered at the end of one year from the time of my death, in the mean time to be kept at my home place—And at the death of my said Daughter

---
[3] For a list of Matthias Yocum's children and information concerning the family, see Draper Mss., 12CC136-137.
[4] For documents see article on Ray's career, Mason, op. cit. See Altsheler, Brent, "C. C. Graham, M. D., 1784-1885" in the *Filson Club History Quarterly*, Vol. 7, No. 2..

Martha Alfred, these two negroes and their increase to go to her lawful heirs—I give to my Daughter Lucinda Frost, one negro Woman, which she has now in possession named Margaret, Also my two hundred acres of land lying in Henderson's Tract in Henderson County to her and her heirs—

"I give to my son Harry Ray to him and his heirs, one hundred acres of Land to include his Spring and the house in which he now lives, and to be laid off to adjoin the land of John Dean and the land called the White House tract, lately purchased by Mr. Snail—This bequest is not to take effect till the expiration of one year from my death, then the right to be conveyed by my Executors or such of them as may qualify, in the mean time. I lend to my said Son Harvey the use of said hundred acres of land. I also lend to my Said Son Harvey for one year from my Death—the use of a negro man named Abraham. And at the end of said year to be the property of Said Harvey in absolute right.

"I give to my son James Ray my watch.

"I give to my son Jefferson Ray to him and his heirs the residues of the tract of land on which I live be the same, more or less—Also I give to Jefferson my negro man Washington and my negro woman Sally—to Said Jefferson I also lend for the term of two years from my death the use of my negro man Jim and the negro woman Lucy, to be kept on the plantation where I live, and at the end of the two years my will is that said Jim and Lucy be free. And I hereby emancipate them accordingly, their freedom thence to commence—

"Mr. Samuel Keller owes me three hundred Dollars, due about a year hence. This debt I give to be equally divided when collected between my three sons William Ray Jesse Ray and John Ray—

"My will is that my Executors pay all my just debts and funeral expenses, and to raise funds for this purpose, they are hereby authorized and directed to sell as much of my live Stock as will answer the purpose, upon such credits as they think proper and suitable—The balance of my Stock of every kind and all my Household & Kitchen furniture, and farming utencils, I give to my said Son Jefferson. This Son will have my home Place and the means in his hands to extend the kindness of a Brother to any of his Sisters who may happen to be in distress, And I confidently trust in his generosity and affection to do so —

"I hereby appoint my Friend George C. Thompson, and my son in law Samuel Keller Executors of this my will and hereby direct that when Mr. Keller qualify as such, no security be required of him.

"In Testimony whereof I have hereunto set my hand and Seal this 7th day of May 1835.

witnesses   JAMES RAY   (seal)
BENJAMIN DAVIS
JOHN H. THAYER
GEORGE C. THOMPSON   Mercer county Sct.
                                                      County Court 1835

"The foregoing last will and testament of James Ray Decd. was this day produced into Court and proved by the oath of John H. Thayer and George C. Thompson two subscribing witnesses thereto and ordered to be Recorded.
May 11th, 1835.

                                                                                  Attst. Tho Allin"[5]

---

[5] Mercer County Court House, *Will Book*, No. 9, pp. 544- 45, 46. James Ray's signature is on the margin of the first page.

The references in the will to earlier land transfers may be traced through the Deed books in the Mercer County court house. On page thirty-six, *Deed Book* No. 1, June 26, 1787, is a record of the deed for land sold to Ray by his step-father, Hugh McGary, who, smarting under the continued attacks of his neighbors, decided to leave the State.[6] At that time, McGary and his wife, Catherine,[7] for "the sum of fifty pounds current Money of Virginia . . . sold and conveyed to James Ray one certain Parcel of Land containing one Hundred Acres lying on the Waters of Shawnee Run adjoining McGary's Settlement Survey."

On page sixty-seven of the same record-book, there is an entry for July 22, 1788, showing that for the consideration of fifty pounds paid by John Thompson, Ray and his wife transferred to Thompson a two hundred acre tract on Shawnee Run.

Ray, having been in Harrodsburg since the arrival of the first families, and having raised a "crop of corn" in 1776,[8] was entitled to two hundred acres adjoining his step-father's property on Shawnee. He also claimed land in the Green River tract.[9] In the *Deed Book* No. 12, pages 214 and 215, there is a record of an indenture, "Dated September 4, 1821, between James Ray and William Martin, for the sum of $350 paid by Martin, conveyed by Ray a parcel of land on Chapline's fork of Salt river." The acreage is not listed. The indenture made in 1826, on March 27th, showed that Ray was beginning to parcel out his holdings among his children. The transfer was a "tract of land lying in Mercer on Salt river being where Mary now lives and containing one hundred and two acres and three fourths. . . ."[10]

While these holdings at no time represented the extremes in size, it must be pointed out that Shawnee Run contains some of the richest acreage in central Kentucky. Never in its history has this part of the State been the poor man's frontier.[11] From early times its value has been high, in marked contrast to the land in the Green River tract. From the air above the Harrodsburg area can be seen a lush green strip following the Shawnee springs district, running through the Blue Grass country like a fine velvet ribbon—directly on the land that once belonged to General Ray. In his later years he devoted much time to the development of his small but rich holdings. Today this land sells for as much as $313 an acre, while even in the depression the price did not fall below $250 an acre.[12] In 1827 Ray sold to John McAfee, for $927, a piece of land on

---

[6] Draper Mss. 36J7. He died about 1808 in Indiana, and was buried just south of Princeton in Gibson County, according to this document.

[7] Draper Mss., 12CC136-137, lists McGary as the husband of Catherine Yocum, sister to Millie, Ray's first wife.

[8] Draper Mss., 59J387.

[9] See Mason, *op. cit.*

[10] Mercer County Court House, *Deed Book*, No. 14, page 247.

[11] Draper Mss., 18J38, 39.

[12] According to George Chinn of Harrodsburg in conversation with writer on August 26, 1944, in Washington, D. C.

Salt river estimated at 103 acres,[13] while in 1830, he sold a 102 acre tract to John L. Lillard, for $2,000.[14]

It is interesting to study the county tax books. In the records of 1935, on page sixty-four[15] Ray is listed as paying assessments on three hundred acres of first class land on Shawnee run, one-hundred and twenty-nine acres of second class land on Salt river, and two hundred acres of third class land in the Henderson's tract on Green river. This gives us an interesting comparison of soil fertility.

The inventory of Ray's estate is found in the Mercer County Court House, *Will Book 10*, on pages 313, 314, and 315.

"Appraisement of the Personal estate of James Ray Decd.

1 Yoke oxen	$25.00
5 stears 3 & 4 years old	40.00
2 Stears 2 years old	11.00
6 cows & calves and 2 dry cow	59.00
3 Heifers 2 yrs. old	12.00
2 Heifers 1 yr. old	6.00
1 Old black horse	40.00
1 Sorrel horse, Blaze face	45.00
1 Sorrel mare & colt	60.00
another Sorrel mare & colt	$85.00
another Sorrel mare & colt	80.00
1 Bay filly 2 yrs old	55.00
2 Sorrel horses, 2 yrs. old	80.00
1 Sorrel horse	50.00
1 Sorrel mare Blaze face	30.00
60 head of sheep	45.00
20 Grown hogs	50.00
15 Shoats	4.00
11 Hives of Bees	33.00
1 Wagon	35.00
2 large ploughs	6.50
2 Shovel ploughs	3.00
4 Hoes	1.50
3 axes	2.00
3 augers	2.00
Handsaw, chisel and drawing knife	1.50
About 20 pounds Wool	5.00
1 Keg powder about 15 lbs.	5.62½
1 pr. Steelyard	2.00
1 Press	12.00
1 Bureau	10.00
1 Mantle Clock	15.00
Amount brought forward	$913.12½

---

[13] *Deed Book* No. 15, Mercer County Court House, pp. 151-152.
[14] Ray filed suit for damages and non-payment of debt against Lillard on June 17th, 1830. He asked $1,500, was awarded $281.95 in gold or silver. The record refers to this land as the tract where William Ray lived (evidently his oldest son) *Ray vs. Lillard*, Judgments Packet *R 25*, Mercer Circuit Court Records. See Filson Club *Quarterly, op. cit.*
[15] Kentucky State Historical Society Collection, Frankfort.

1 Sugar chest	5.00
1 Dining table	8.00
1 Small square table	1.25
1 Rifle gun and shot pouch	12.00
1 Small looking Glass	.50
1 Bureau and book case	10.00
another Dining Table	3.00
6 Windsor chairs	6.00
1 Curtain Bedstead, curtains, bed and furniture	20.00
1 Fancy Bedstead, Bed and furniture	18.00
1 Common Bedstead, bed and furniture	15.00
1 Common Bedstead, bed and furniture	14.00
2 Extra coverlids	4.00
1 Watch	25.00
26 Volumes of Old Books	2.50
1 Family Bible	2.00
1 Dictionary, 2 vols. History of the Revolution, of acts of congress....	1.50
1 vol. Life of Christ	3.00
1 Vol. Guthries Geography and two vols. 2.50 Journals of Legislature..	12.75
articles of table furniture	10.00
articles of kitchen furniture	4.00
1 Loom	.75
1 Coffee mill	.25
1 Grind stone	20.00
1 Mans saddle	31.52
About 394 lbs. Hemp	

"The undersigned having been appointed by the county court of Mercer for that purpose have proceeded to appraise the personal estate of James Ray, dec'd. and being duly sworn respectfully report the above to the Court as a full and true-appraisement of the Same, so far as it has been presented to us. Given under our hands this 6th day of June, 1835.

John Basey, George W. Clay, H. P. Horine.

The foregoing list of property with the addition of the following, the undersigned respectfully return to the court as a full and perfect inventory of the estate of James Ray, dec'd. as it has come into our hands, viz.

A note given by Noah G. Hayden payable 1st Sept. next	$12.00
A note given by Robert Jones payable 11th April, 1834	10.00
A note given by Sam'l. Keller payable 5th May, 1836	300.00
Cash	40.00

GEO. C. THOMPSON
SAM'L. D. KELLER
Executors

Mercer Count Sct July County Court 1835

The foregoing Inventory and appraisement of the estate of James Ray dec'd. was this day produced into court and ordered to be recorded.

Attest   THO. ALLIN C. C."

While this list would appear quaint and perhaps meagre to owners of Mercer County land today, we must recall the fact that farming machinery had not reached a high degree of efficiency in the early nineteenth century. Furthermore, the great difficulty of transportation from New England manufacturing centers precluded the wide use of advanced types of equipment in Kentucky. Nearly all they had was made nearby with the tools that were available in this isolated district.

As was pointed out earlier in this paper, little is known of Ray's background. The only clue we have at this time is a letter written by Elijah Calloway, Walnut Grove, N. C., in which a brother of James Ray's father is mentioned. In reply to an inquiry from Dr. Lyman C. Draper of Madison, Wisconsin, Calloway stated that although there were many Ray families from that same branch of the family in the district of Walnut Grove, none of them seemed to know where Ray was born. The writer stated that they had come to Surry County, North Carolina from Augusta County Virginia, "originally." He added that Jesse Ray, the uncle of James, was "every a way a gentleman of truth."[16]

Following the Act by Congress which liberalized the pension laws for service in the War of the Revolution, the General applied and received a sizable yearly allowance.[17] Among the papers on file in the National Archives Pension Records Office in Washington, D. C., are affidavits of Catherine Keller, John Slavens, and Benjamin Wilson, supporting Mrs. Keller's claim for reconsideration of her father's pension grant. While there is no record to show that the petition was granted, there is an appended list of James Ray's children as she gave it in 1852:

"William Ray (since dead)
Jesse Ray, since dead
Polly Duncan Ray
John Ray
Catherine Keller Late Ray
Jane Wilson Late Ray since dead
Patsy Alfred late Ray
Jefferson Ray
Harvey Ray
Lucinda Frost, late Ray since dead."[18]

In comparing these names with those found in the will, we see that Catherine's list is not complete. For instance the names of James Ray, Jr., and

---

[16] Written on June 10, 1845, Draper Mss., 5DD19-20. The date of Ray's birth is not established. While in his pension declaration made in July 7, 1832, he said that he was in "the 72d year of my age", he could have meant that he was seventy-one at that time. He was but twenty years of age at the time of the Battle of Blue Licks, according to Bowmar, Draper Mss., 12C39. His son, Dr. John Ray, wrote that his father was "about 14 years of age" when he came to Kentucky in 1775, adding in the same letter that he was sixty years old in 1812, when he served under Hopkins (he undobtedly meant fifty). The nearest to a definite date we are able to give, based on this data, is that Ray was born in 1760 or 1761; Draper Mss., 12C16.

[17] For a discussion of this subject see Mason, op. cit.

[18] National Archives, Pension Records, S. 31314.

Henry Ray, which appear in Ray's will, are omitted. Polly, evidently was a nickname for Mary Ray Duncan. The same is probably true of Patsy Alfred, who was referred to as Martha Alfred, by her father. Altogether, twelve names appear in these lists, with the thirteenth child's name undisclosed. Dr. John Ray, one of the sons, stated positively in a letter to Draper that his mother had eleven children.[19] There is good evidence that Amelia had but two. Considering the high infant mortality rate in those days, it would not be surprising if one of the eleven children died in infancy.

What became of this large family? While it is not possible to account for all of them, or for that matter, to give a complete chronicle of any one, some interesting facts have been unearthed.

Taking them in order as named in Catherine's list, William was the oldest, the first son of Amelia and James Ray. It is possible that he was named after that chubby, ill-fated brother of the General. Dr. John Ray, his brother, wrote that William died in 1841 in the State of Illinois, where he made his home; that he had raised a large family. The same correspondent stated that Jess, the younger of Amelia's children, was still living not far from Madisonville, Kentucky, in 1843. Nathaniel Hart recalled that William once tried to shoot his father—that the General bore the scar in his face the rest of his life.[20]

The vicinity of Fort Harrod is rich in tradition about Mary Duncan or Polly Ray as her sister refers to her. A few years ago, Miss Neva Williams, a member of the staff of the *Harrodsburg Herald*, found occasion to gather some data on Mary Ray Duncan, largely from the lips of one of her descendants. In quoting from her manuscript we learn that

> "Even to this day there are traditions of her beauty and loveliness of character. Early in 1800 . . . there came to Harrodsburg from Maryland a young man—Martin Duncan. From early fragments of his history one gleans that he must have had learning above the average for those days . . . being the possessor of books—that seems to have set people apart in those early days . . . being a noted 'fiddler.' This pronounced talent marked many of his descendants."

They were married and lived on the land deeded to Mary by the General—a farm located on the State road known as the Frankfort-Louisville pike. The house, still standing when Miss Williams wrote her article, was known in later days as the 'Harvey Woods place.' The children of this marriage were listed as:

Asa—died of cholera in Mercer, 1833, burial unknown.
Daniel—moved to Texas, married there.
Abner—moved to Iowa.
Martin, Jr.—unmarried. Very handsome, reputed to be handsomest man of his day. Died of typhus.
James—married in Kentucky. Moved west.

---

[19] Draper Mss., 12C17; see also, statements by Mr. and Mrs. Benjamin Wilson, Draper Mss., 18J36.
[20] Dr. John Ray to Lyman C. Draper, Draper Mss., 12C17; Col. Nat. Hart to Draper, Draper Mss., 14CC192

Madden—married Sarah Wade Davis; no children; raised a niece, Mrs. N. H. Skiles, Lansing, Ohio.

Green—very fleet of foot.

Talbott—moved to Anderson County, Kentucky. Married; had son, Asa.

Elizabeth (Patsy)—Married Henry Britton.

Mary Ray Duncan—married Burton. Buried in Martin (or Talbot) burying ground. Very fleet of foot. Died of typhus as young woman.

John Ray Duncan—married Eliza Graham, lived and died in Mercer; was in the Civil War, a Major. Prominent in affairs at Duncansville in Mercer. His parents lived with him in their last days and were buried in the Grapevine (Christian) Church cemetery.

Children—Dr. Charles Talbott Duncan, no children; Mrs. Emma Duncan Gray, Harrodsburg and Miami Florida, 2 daughters.

Dr. John Ray was a physician. In the marriage records of Mercer County, 1785-1830, there is an item: "Ray, John, Hickley, Sarah, September 12, 1815." Farther down the page, we find: "Ray, John, Bunton, Mary, January 10, 1790."[21] In his three long letters to Dr. Draper, the devoted son gives no information about himself, confining his remarks to legends and facts concerning his distinguished parent.[22] Since the letters are headed Madisonville, Kentucky, we may assume that he practiced medicine in that locality. The letters are written in a fluent style, with an amusing degree of under-statement, a fine objectivity, and sincerity. At one juncture, the insistent Draper called attention to what he considered an error in his statements; Ray, indignant over a shadow on his reputation, answered promptly that: "I now recollect that . . . you intimated that there might possibly be some clashing with my statement . . . in regard to William McBride and the Blue Lick battle. This is a matter about which you had it amply in your power to settle whilst in Kentucky last summer as to the facts . . . as detailed by me, there cannot be a shadow of doubt . . ."[23] At another point he remarked, "My father was a man of stern integrity and all matters emenating from him was considered unexceptionable."[24]

Another entry as copied by the D. A. R. historian, concerned Harvey T. Ray and Eliza A. W. Cozine, who were married September 21, 1830.[25]

Martha, or Patsy, evidently married a physician, since her husband is referred to as "Dr. Alford" in Miss Williams' manuscript. The informant also said that Ray had four daughters, which would mean that the missing name is that of a boy.

James Ray, Jr., was licensed to practice law in 1810,[26] while the two youngest sons, Jefferson and Harvey, lived on the farms given to them by their father.

---

[21] McAdams, Mrs Harry Kennett, *Kentucky Pioneer and Court Records*, Lexington, 1929, p. 136. See also, *Kentucky Mercer County, Marriages 1785-1830*, as copied by Jane McAfee Chapter of the D. A. R., Harrodsburg, Kentucky, p. 58

[22] Draper Mss, 12C16, 12C17, and 12C18-19; see Mason, *op. cit.*

[23] Draper Mss., 12C17. See also, Mason, *op. cit.*

[24] Draper Mss., 12C16.

[25] *Kentucky Mercer County*, Marriages 1785-1830, *op cit.* p. 58.

[26] Kentucky Historical Society, *Register*, Vol. 8, p. 30.

In view of the singular distinction attained by General James Ray, it is surprising that no more is known about his descendants. The little that has been established, however, helps to round out a reassuring picture. Certain we may be that this young boy, born and raised in the American wilderness, hoped for no more than he was able to provide his children—a secure and happy home with ample physical comfort, an opportunity for education and public usefulness, community respect—a just and satisfying heritage for which his Scotch-Irish ancestors had fought tenaciously over two hundred years, from Scotland to Ireland, to Virginia, to Carolina, and, finally, to Kentucky.

The Rennicks.

Alexander Rennick, of Virginia, married Jane McKamie of the Eastern shore of Maryland, the niece of the Rev. Francis McKamie, and went immediately to the home he had prepared for her, adjoining Mercersburg, Penn. They had one daughter and five sons; the daughter was a remarkably beautiful and talented girl; she had every advantage bestowed upon her that could be procured by money and station in life. She was the pride and darling of her parents and brothers; she had just graduated, in a noted high school, with the highest honors, when she eloped with an Irish tinker, named Hamilton, whom she met on the street on her way to and from school. He was very handsome and full of Irish wit, a smooth tongue and plenty of assurance. He was poor and perfectly trifling and her family was rich; it would be a good scheme, but alas, for human hopes, her mother never forgave her, and after the birth of the first child, they drifted to Washington county and settled there; they had several other children when he died and left his family in the deepest poverty and none of the children old enough to be of any help to the mother.

She was still young and beautiful, and the bravery with which she took up the burden of supporting her family attracted the notice and admiration of a rich old bachelor, who married her and raised the children, raised them well too, for every one of them was a credit and comfort to her. He settled them all round him on farms or as merchants.

She was again left a widow, and all her children being married and settled in homes of their own she was so lonely in her home, at their earnest request, broke up house keeping and lived round among her children. All vied with one another who should make her happiest and who should keep her longest.

At the marriage of her oldest great granddaughter, as the family were about separating, the discussion arose as to whose time it was to have the dear grandmother. During the rather heated contest, several friends approached to hear the conclusion of the matter; among them was a very pleasant looking old gentleman who seemed to be intensely amused at the warfare of words, and laughingly said, "Mrs. B., I would go with no set of people who quarreled about me that way; come and live with me; I need you more than they do, who have all large families, and I have no one; my children have all gone and left me, I am alone" she turned to him in her quick, bright way and said, " I will," he stepped up, shook hands with her and said "It is a bargain, I will see you to-morrow," bowed and left. Next day the old gentleman was over bright and early, made satisfactory arrangements and in less than a week, she was installed in her new home as Mrs. G. He was seventy-five and she seventy-three.

Long years before, the great grandmother had made a second marriage to a Mr. Clarke; she died on the place to which she was brought as a bride in her early youth, at the advanced age of ninety-six.

This is as far as there is any record of the past of the Rennick family, for the Scotch and Scotch Irish had suffered so much in the old countries where titles and hereditaments signified so much, they cherished a contempt for any thing like genealogy or family history, but I suppose the Rennick family suffered as much for the "faith" as any in Scotland.

Miss Ann Nicol told me of a pathetic incident which happened during the last persecutions of the Covenantors. She said her mother used to tell it to her children, and even to this day it was told to the children of the vicinity in which it took place.

Joseph Rennick, a brave man, who stood up for his faith and church, was dragged from his home and young wife and little children, and was taken to England and cast into prison and remained a prisoner until past middle life; his people could hear nothing from him; after many years they gave him up as dead. Even the authorities forgot him, and he just was left there, because he did not know of peace being established, and he was known in prison only as a No., and when after these long years he was released, his wife was dead, his children scattered, no one knew where; his property confiscated, his contemporaries all dead or gone to America, the very face of the country changed; he was a stranger to that generation; he was cared for by his native town, but lived only a few months.

John Rennick, son of Alexander Rennick, came to Kentucky about the year 1787, married Mary Hueston, of Fayette county, went to Mercer county to live, where his son Alexander was born 25th of August, 1791, moved to Frankfort when the child was two months old, and died in 1814.

John Rennick was a quiet, unobtrusive man, public spirited and highly respected for his sterling qualities by his fellow citizens; he was a handsome fine looking man, and was cut off in the prime of life, and vigorous manhood, having given promise of much usefulness both in church and State. His wife, Mary Hueston, was a sweet faced woman, not a beauty, but so lovable and attractive, and gentle in her manners. She had soft brown eyes, rosy cheeks, brown hair; she always wore a lace cap, and kerchief.

She was a notable housekeeper, a true friend, and a veritable Lady Bountiful; she never turned a needy one from her door without a substantial gift. She died in 1827, aged 47 years.

Alexander H. Rennick was the only child of his parents, John and Mary Rennick. He was born in Mercer county, Ky., August 25, 1791; married Letitia Atwell Lee, 1817.

He participated in the War of 1812, in the battle of the river Raisin, under Colonel Paschal Hickman; entered the clerk's office as deputy under Major Willis Lee, in 1817, and at Major Lee's death, in 1824, was appointed clerk, which he held until 1870. He died December, 1871.

The children of this marriage were Mary Willis, who married first, Thomas J. Todd, second, Richard Kiddar Woodson; Eliza, who died unmarried at the age of nineteen; Catherine Martyn, married Rev. John Montgomery, of Harrodsburg; Alisonia Bibb, who married James Madison Todd; Louisa, Workham, married William E. Milton, of Lexington; Willis Lee, John Alexander, Thomas Todd, all of whom died unmarried; Henry Swigert married Miss Julia Birney, of Texas, and Atwell.

They commenced their married life, at Glen Willis, where six of the children were born, moved to Frankfort in 1832, where the other children were born.

Mr. Rennick was a remarkably handsome man, black hair and eyes, six feet two inches in height, brunette complextion, and finely proportioned, was educated in Frankfort.

Mrs. Rennick had every advantage that Frankfort and vicinity could afford; from her eighth to her fourteenth year she went to school to a Mrs. Keats, which had quite a reputation, throughout the State, as a young ladies seminary, about four miles from town. It was afterwards purchased by the Rev. Phillip S. Fall who taught for many years, a flourishing "Female Academy." She was then sent to Fayette county, until she was eighteen, to Parson Moore, the founder of Christ's Episcopal church in Lexington, Ky. He taught a mixed school male and female, and in after years could count as his pupils some of the brightest men and women of that generation; she had graceful carriage, and easy manners, was five feet six inches in height, grey eyes, blond complexion, rather light hair, worn in Grecian coil at the back and three curls on each side of her face. She had fine musical talents, excelled on the piano and played very well on the guitar, and could paint fairly well in water colors, and withal, she was one of the wittiest and most agreeable women of her day, so entertaining to all; old and young enjoyed her society; her children knew no greater pleasure than on a rainy day for her to go into the parlor with them and play the piano, or tell them stories of her school days. The stories were always new to them, although told over and over again.

Thomas J. Todd and Mary Willis Rennick were married April 23, 1838. They had issue, Mary Lee, Alexander Rennick, Letitia, Louis Franklin, William Montague, Thomas Jay.

John Montgomery and Catherine Rennick were married May 2, 1844. Their children were Thomas, Letitia, Kate died in fancy, Lilian, John, Mary, James Todd, Alexander Rennick, Kate, Edith.

James Madison Todd and Alisonia Rennick were married, May 25, 1847. Their children were Alexander Thomas. Lucy Payne, Letitia Lee, Anne Maria, William Johnston, Alisonia, James Madison.

William Milton and Louisa Rennick were married, January 10, 1849. Their children were Mary Willis, William E. Kittie.

Henry Rennick married Julia Birney, of Texas; they had one child, Julia.

Thomas Montgomery married Miss Nellie Lewis; John Montgomery married Miss Blackburn; Lettie married Mr. S. G. Hanly; Lillian married Mr. James Hopkins; Mary married Mr. Zoll; James married Miss Porter.

Alexander Todd married Miss Alice Gay; Lettie Lee married Mr. R. A. Peter; James M. married Miss Nettie Ross; Julia Rennick, daughter of Henry Rennick, married Mr. Montgomery, of Mexia, Texas.

Louis Franklin Todd, son of T. J. and M. W Todd, was born, June 28, 1844, enlisted in the Fifteenth Ky. U. S. Infantry, in November, 1862, was struck in the head with a piece of shell while holding up the colors of his regiment, at the battle of Perryville, two color bearers having already been shot down, and as he fell, received a ball in his right elbow, was captured and arm amputated by a Confederate surgeon and was paroled. When exchanged, returned to the regiment as first lieutenant of his company; and was acting as adjutant of his regiment at the battle of Stone River. when the back of his head was crushed in by a shell; he fell into the hands of the Confederates, who stripped him of his clothing, and left him upon the field, almost dead from loss of blood and exposure.

As brave a lad as ever shouldered a musket or drew a sword. (This extract was taken from the History and Genealogy of Peter Montague.)

"Lieutenant Frank Todd, late of the Fifteenth Kentucky Infantry, was buried here to-day, with military honors. He lost his right arm at the battle of Perryville, where he was orderly sergeant. He was promoted, and at the battle of Stone River, Tenn., lost his life. He was a young man universally respected, and loved by all who knew him. He was tenderly raised, and unused to the hardships of camp life, of delicate frame and features that might become a girl. There burned in his bosom a fire that would not be controlled. No braver spirit ascended from its clayey tenement, upon the bloody field of Stone River than his. He received his death wound in rescuing his captain, who was surrounded by Rebels; taking his sword in his left hand he said, "Come on, boys" the boys did follow; they brought back their captain, but lost their beloved lieutenant. He lived a virtuous life, and died a glorious death. May the turf rest lightly on his youthful and manly head."—(Frankfort correspondent of Courier-Journal.)

"Died. At the residence of his uncle, Mr. William M. Todd, near Versailles, Ky., Nov. 3, 1860, William M. Todd, Jr., aged fourteen years. He was the son of the late Thomas J. and Mary Willis Todd, of Frankfort, Ky. The mother survives and mourns the loss of her son. Thus has fallen, one just blossoming into manhood, and one whom to know, was to esteem. His love of right and hatred of wrong secured for him the warm attachment of all who knew him. As a pupil he was loved by his classmates and teachers, his conduct and habits of study being ever worthy of imitation. His mind was quick and comprehensive and gave clear indication of the future scholar. Let each one of his schoolmates make the solemn inquiry, "Why was he taken and I left?" But Willie is gone, he will never again come to us, but we can go to him. Be ye also ready, for in such an hour as ye think not the Son of Man cometh."—(J. H. M.)

Todd.—Children of A. T. and Alice Todd, Lillian and Alexander.

Children of R. A. and Lettie Lee Peter, Virginia Cary, Alisonia, Robert Arthur, Jr., James Todd, and Lettie Lee.

James Madison, Jr., infant of James M. and Nettie Todd.

Milton.—Children of Deidtrich and Mary W. Wintter, Deidtrich, William E.

RICHARDSONS IN KENTUCKY.

The Richardsons who were numerous in Kentucky at an early day, came from Maryland and Virginia. The ancestors were William, of Maryland, who came to America we learn, with Lord Baltimore. John and Nathaniel Richardson came to Virginia from England about 1640.

William Richardson of Maryland, Burgess, 1676-83. The imigrant, so called, settled in Ann Arundel County, Maryland. He married Elizabeth Ewen Talbott, widow of Richard Talbott of Baltimore, died December 1697, will probated May, 1698. See Will in Annapolis, Md. His sons were: Thos., William, Joseph and Samuel.

1—Joseph married Sarah Thomas, daughter of Samuel Thomas and Elizabeth Hutchins his wife of Calvert County, Maryland. Children: Joseph, Richard, William.

2—Samuel married Mary ———, of Richmond, Virginia.

3—William married Margaret Smith, July 15, 1689. His children were, as given in his will, probated 1744. William, Elizabeth, Samuel, Sophia, Sarah, Joseph, Daniel, Richard, Nathaniel, Thomas.

Of these sons and daughters, there were a number of descendants scattered throughout the South, namely: Richard Richardson, grandson of William Richardson, 2d., who was a Revolutionary soldier, married Sarah Gaines, daughter of Daniel Gaines of Culpepper County, Virginia. His children were: John Richardson, noted among the early lot owners in Lexington, Kentucky. (Collins' History of Kentucky, Vol. 2, page 173.)

Also he made many purchases of land in and around the city. This John Richardson, son of Richard Richardson and his wife, Sarah Gaines, had brothers, William, Daniel and Elijah Richardson, eldest brothers.

It is noted in the records of the Fayette County Court that John and William Richardson are the only men of that name who have not an initial in their names.

Elijah Richardson lived at Marble Creek, near Lexington for many years. After the death of his aged mother, Sarah Gaines Richardson, he moved to Missouri and there died, leaving descendants.

John Richardson married three times: First, Dicie Wainscot. Second, Ophelia Plummer, of Georgetown, Kentucky. Third, a widow, Mrs. Ewing, of Alabama, where at Richardson's Landing, on the Tombigbee River, John Richardson died.

His children were by his first marriage to Dicie Wainscot: David, Mary Ann and Thomas.

By the second marriage to Ophelia Plummer, of Georgetown, Kentucky, he had one child, Ophelia Virginia. By the third marriage to Mrs. Ewing of

Coffeeville, Ala., he had four children: Victoria, John, Alice and William.

John Richardson has often been confused with his cousin, John Croley Richardson, who also came to Lexington, Kentucky at an early day.

Richard Richardson, father of Richard Richardson, the Revolutionary soldier, whose will is before us, mentions the following, daughters: Sophia, Mathews, Margaret, Lucretia and Milcah. These are mentioned as living. Sons: Samuel Richardson, Richard Richardson, Thomas Richardson, John and William Richardson.

Samuel Richardson and Richard Thomas, called in the will his cousins, are the Executors. Will dated 1761. Register of Wills. Frederick, Maryland.

William Richardson, third son of Joseph Richardson and his wife, Sarah Thomas, (and grandson and namesake of William Richardson, Burgess from 1676 to 1683, in House of Burgesses, Maryland) a transcript of whose will is before us, from the Orphan's Court, Maryland, mentions in his will filed 1769; sons: John Croley Richardson, Samuel Calmire (Calmes) Richardson and William Richardson.

In the Genealogical clippings of the Historical and Genealogical Album of the Kentucky State Historical Society, we find the following notice of the marriage of this "William Richardson, Jr." He married Isabel De La Calmes, third child and oldest daughter of the Marquis De La Calmes, a French Huguenot nobleman, born 1705 and died 1751. Came to Williamsburg, James City County, Virginia and married Winifred Waller, &c &c." (See Hist. in May Register 1906.)

The children of William Richardson and his wife Isabel Calmes, were:

Elizabeth, married Col. Samuel Price, of Virginia.

Miriam, born December 27, 1748, married John Buck, of Virginia.

Sarah, born July 25, 1750, married Benjamin Combs, of Virginia.

Mary, born August 31, 1752, married Charles Buck, of Virginia.

John Croley, born March 12, 1754, married Sarah Bainbridge Hall.

Ann, Born October 10, 1756, married Thomas Buck, of Virginia.

Samuel Marquis Calmes, born February 1, 1760, married Catherine Bainbridge Hall.

William, born August 16—married Miss Pugh.

Marquis, born September 21, 1768, married Henrietta Catlett.

The children of this William Richardson, Jr., came to Kentucky, and the names given are familiar to the people of Central Kentucky, where the descendants live. We have tried to secure every name of people who contributed to the settlement of Kentucky from its founding as a State, and have been conspicuous in its upbuilding and its progress. As a rule the descendants of these people, who have passed to their reward in a better world we hope, yet here are almost forgotten, the descendants are anxious to obtain the names of these pioneers on the State and County records.

We deplore the fact, that so many of our early records have been lost by fire or destroyed by vandals. Again and again we have written to different county courts for names and the reply has been, "Our early records are gone" or "The records were lost when our court house was burned" or "We have no records that antedate 1800." Hence we must go to Maryland, Virginia, North and South Carolina, Georgia and Mississippi, to find the names of ancestors of so many Kentuckians, whose descendants scattered from Kentucky to these States many years ago.

The tradgedy connected with Col. Samuel Q. Richardson, in the streets of Frankfort, created a wide-spread interest in this distinguished family, connected with many of the noblest people of America. Our next chapter will give the history of the Richardson-Waring tragedy.

(Richardsons Continued.)

RICHARDSONS IN KENTUCKY.

The cause which led to the difficulty which resulted in the death of Samuel Q. Richardson, from a pistol fired at his breast by John U. Waring has not been given in the accounts of the tragedy.

From the family we learn the trouble began over land titles. It is supposed this led to rash and insulting charges, and language that became unendurable. Both men were high spirited and irascible.

Samuel Q. Richardson was a noted lawyer, a man of brilliant attainments, and an ornament to the Bar of the State. At the time of his death we learn that he lived in Frankfort. The tragedy took place on the steps of the old Mansion House, the noted Hotel of that day. John U. Waring was standing, it is said, at the door of the office of the Hotel, when he saw Richardson approach. Instantly an altercation took place, a few words passed, and Samuel Q. Richardson fell back on the pavement mortally shot. His death created great excitement, and profound sorrow throughout the State.

Some years afterward John U. Waring was shot, and mortally wounded from an upper wnidow of the Shelton Hotel in Versailles, Kentucky. (See Collins Hist. of Ky. Vol. 1.) No arrests were made, and Waring never knew the unknown hand that killed him.

Samuel Q. Richardson was a son of Captain John Corly Richardson, (See Register January, 1909.) and his wife, Sarah Bainbridge Hall, who was a sister of Catherine B. Hall, who married Samuel Marquis Calmes Richardson, son of Isabella De La Calmes, who married William Richardson, Jr. She was the daughter of the Marquis De La Calmes, a French Huguenot nobleman, born 1705, and died 1751, one of the first settlers in the Valley of Virginia.

Samuel Q. Ricardson was born in Lexington, Kentucky, February 1791, killed at Frankfort, Kentucky, February, 1835. He was educated at Transylvania University, and easily took rank among the foremost young lawyers of the Bar. His brother, Dr. William Hall Richardson was one of the most eminent physicians and surgeons in Kentucky. He was one of the founders of that famous University, and was Professor for many years in that institution.

Both men bore the marks, and talent in physique and polish, of their grand French and Revolutionary ancestry.

We have confined our sketches of this family, chiefly to those members of it, that came to Kentucky, and became identified with the interests and upbuilding of the State at an early period of its history.

Samuel Richardson, born in Maryland, supposed son of William Richardson, Burgess for Ann Arundel County, Maryland, 1676-1683, moved to Fairfax County, Virginia.

Samuel Richardson, Jr., born in Fairfax County, Virginia, came to Fayette County, Kentucky.

Thomas Richardson, lived in Culpeper County, Virginia, married Elizabeth Maxey. His son Felix Allen Richardson, was born in Estill County, Kentucky, married young and died in Fayette County, Kentucky. After his death, his widow remarried, name of second husband not given. His children were, Hon. Felix R. Richardson, Librarian of the Supreme Court of Denver, Colorado.

Col. Richardson, of Glasgow, Kentucky.

Mrs. Elizabeth Richardson Porter, Omaha, Nebraska.

The parents of John Richardson came from England to America and settled in Louisa County, Virginia. John Richardson was prominent in that part of Virginia, as a man of influence and large property. He married Martha De Priest, of Hanover County, whose parents came from France, and settled in Hanover County, Virginia.

The children of John Richardson and Martha De Priest were:

1. Polly, married M. Timberlake of Louisa County, Virginia. Had two daughters, names unknown.

2. Samuel Richardson, married Miss Winston of Mississippi. Had three children. Daughter—Martha married M. C. Moorehouse, of Mississippi.

3. Martha Richardson, married Major John Broaddus, U. S. A. Their daughter, Martha, married Col. Jeff. Thompson of Missouri. Had one son.

4. Thomas Richardson married Miss Pollard of Richmond, Virginia. Children were: 1st. John R. 2nd. Robert R. 3rd. Benjamin R. 4th. George Richardson. One daughter, who married Togerton R. Taylor of Richmond, Virginia.

5. William Richardson married Harriet Robinson. Children: Daniel Couch, Harriet, Martha, Eliza, who married Mr. Lane of Texas.

Charles Bruce Richardson married Sarah E. Bosworth, of Lexington. 1 child:

Emma, who married Joseph Lewellyn of Texas.

John Samuel Richardson.

Caroline married Henry of Virginia, Margaret marrist 1st Lewis and 2nd, Daniel of Virginia. David Porter Richardson married Ellen Bosworth, of Nashville, Tenn. Had two sons: Charles and Felix.

6. Robert T. Richardson married Sarah Willis, sister of the Poet N. P. Willis. Their children were, Martha De Priest who married first: Lewis; second, Bishop H. H. Kavanaugh, of Kentucky. Robert Richardson married Miss Wall.

7. Sallie Richardson married Mr. Couch.

8. David Richardson ,lived in Louisa County, Virginia.

9. Judith Richardson, married Mr. Smith of New Kent County, Virginia. No children.

(Published by Request.)
WILLIAM RICHARDSON, JR.—ANNE ARUNDEL COUNTY, MARYLAND.

William Richardson, born August 26th, 1668, married Margaret Smith, died July 13th, 1744.

He was son of William Richardson 1st, who came to Maryland with Lord Baltimore about 1650. Was Burgess from 1676-1683—and held many offices of honor and profit, and was one of the most prominent men of his day. He died November 2nd, 1697. Will probated in ye May, 1698. He married Elizabeth Ewing Talbott, widow of Richard Talbott of Baltimore.

(See Anne Arundel Records, Annapolis, Maryland.)

William Richardson Jr., son of William Richardson 1st., whose will follows, was a man of large estates, and wealth, and held high positions in his State.

(See Thomas' History of Maryland.)

WILL.

I William Richardson, Jr., of Anne Arundel County, Maryland.

Item. To my wife, Margaret, the use of my now dwelling plantation and all the lands I now hold to the east of the Branch of Bever's Dam's, during her widowhood, and no longer, always provided she suffer my son Daniel Richardson, to seat, build and live upon any one part thereof.

Item. I give to my son, Joseph Richardson all my lands lying on the southwest of the aforesaid Beaver Dam's, except 120 acres on the north end, and I reserve 2 Tobacco Houses that I have now upon the land—I give also one negro woman to my son Joseph.

Item. I give and bequeath to my son Daniel Richardson the above excepted 120 acres of land and the 2 Tbacco Houses, as also after the expiration of my wife's natural life or widowhood which first happens, my now dwelling plantation, and all the aforesaid lands, that I have given my wife the use of, I now give the said Daniel and his heirs forever. I also give the said Daniel one feather bed and furnature of ten pounds sterling value. Six high leather chairs, two pewter dishes and 6 plates, one ten gallon Iron pot, all to be new, one third part of my stock, of horses, cattle, hogs and sheep, as also one third part of all my corn, wheat, tobacco, etc., that may be growing or belonging to me at the time of my decease. I also leave him a negro woman, and a negro boy, instead of a debt which I owe him of twenty odd pounds sterling, if he will accept the same in payment of such debt.

Item. I give and bequeath to my son Richard Richardson all my lands in Baltimore County which I bought of Richard Owings and Charles Dorsey —said lands being known by the name of "Owings Adventure" and "Owings Addition" 450 acres, but it is my will and mind that my son Richard pay to my son Thomas Richardson as soon as he can conveniently the sum of 20 pounds in currency for the improvement my son Thomas made on part of the said lands. I also give to my son Richard 2 negro girls.

Item. I give and beqeauth to my son Nathan Richardson one tract of

255

land lying in Baltimore County, which I bought of Dr. Samuel Chew, known by name of "Ventured Friendship" 340 acres—also a negro boy.

Item. I give and bequeath to my son Thomas Richardson all my part of a tract of land lying in Cecil County, and known by the name of "High Spaniolo," being by estimation 558 acres, to him and his heirs forever, I also give him one Iron pot, ten Gallons, and one young negro.

Item. I give and bequeath unto my two grandsons, sons of my son Joseph Richardson, William and Richard, one young negro man now in their father's possession in Lieu of a debt I owe to them upon acct. of their uncle Wm. Richardson's estate amounting to as I supose 16 or 18 pounds.

Item. I bequeath to my dau. Sarah Hill a negro woman Lucy, issue of said wench already bequeathed to be equally divided between her children, Henry and Margaret Hill.

Item. I give and bequeath to Samuel Thompson, the son of Amgt. Thompson and Elizabeth, his wife, one young negro man.

Item. I give and bequeath to my kinswoman, Elizabeth Richardson, daughter of my Brother Joseph Richardson, one cow and calf. I give and bequeath to Joseph Gallaway the sum of 4 pounds to be applied to the use of the people of West River, called Quakers.

Item. I bequeath to my brother Joseph Richardson all my wearing apparel of every sort.

Item. I give and bequeath the use of all the remainder of my personal estate to my loving wife, Margaret, during her natural life, unless she marry again, then to be equally divided between my children, vi.: Joseph, Daniel, Richard, Nathan and Thomas Richardson, Sophia Gallaway and Sarah Hill. I nominate and appoint my loving wife Margaret and son Daniel Richardson Exc. In witness whereof I have hereunto set my hand and seal this 18, of mo. called November, 1741.

WILLIAM RICHARDSON.

Witness:
NICHOLAS WATKINS,
JOHN ROSS,
Thomas Sprigg.
Pro. II, Sept. 1744.

John Richardson of Georgetown, Kentucky, married Ophelia V. Plummer, and their only daughter, Ophelia Virginia Richardson, married at Coffeeville, Alabama, in 1848, Albert Dunlap Lister.

Albert Dunlap Lister was the 3rd son of Judge Josiah Dunlap Lister and Sarah Elizabeth Johnston. Judge Lister raised a company which bore his name and served as Captain in the war of 1812-14. The issue of the marriage of Ophelia Virginia and Albert Dunlap Lister was three daughters, Sarah Virginia Florence and Laura Elizabeth and son, Albert Garland Lister.

Sarah Virginia married Judge Alfred D. Laud of the Supreme Court of Louisiana and had issue, Florence Laura, Alfred Vivian, and Jennie May.

Albert Garland Lister and Florence Lister died in infancy at Marshall, Texas, whither their parents had removed from Alabama, after their marriage Laura Elizabeth Lister married

Taliaferro Alexander and had issue. Percy Alexander, Lister Alexander, Lucille Laura Estelle, Albert Lister Alexander and Taliaferro. Of these children only Percy Alexander who graduated at the West Point Military Academy in June, 1907, and Albert Lister Alexander who received the degree of Bachelor of Laws at the University of Virginia in June 1907 alone survive. Their great grandmother was a Miss Eliza Williamson of Versailles, Kentucky who married their great-grandfather, Judge James Gorin Taliaferro, of the Supreme Court of Louisiana, and came to Harrison leaving Catalinea Point at an early date.

THE ROGERS FAMILY*

JULIA S. ARDERY

The object of this sketch is to treat briefly of the founding of a distinguished family in a New World and more especially to record the contribution made by the Bourbon County branch of this family to the religious and cultural life of the Cane Ridge Church and neighborhood located in the blue grass region of Kentucky. After one hundred and sixty four years the name Cane Ridge has become almost inseparable with that of Rogers, as there are those of the name yet living in ancestral homes in this locality.

At this time when the preservation of the old Cane Ridge Meeting House has become a nation-wide project, the personal journals kept by William Rogers during the latter part of his life and the book "The Cane Ridge Meeting House" written by his grandson, Captain James R. Rogers, are of great historical value.

Directed by Daniel Boone to the rich land on cane ridge, Presbyterians in 1791, under the leadership of Robert W. Finley built here their Church of ash logs which stands today in all its primitive ruggedness. It was here in 1801 approximately twenty-five to thirty thousand souls came to renew their faith at the greatest union camp meeting revival ever held on American soil. Ministers of leading denominations preached in the Church yard for six days and nights which resulted in over 3,000 conversions. Within the meeting house in 1804, the first united appeal was made for Christian Union and a return to the simple apostolic order. The largest indigenous American church resulted, the Disciples of Christ (Christian Church).

William Rogers, first clerk of Cane Ridge Meeting House under Barton W. Stone, was born in Campbell County, Virginia, July 7, 1784. In his fourteenth year he moved with his father, Nathaniel Rogers, to Bourbon County, arriving at their cabin home April 20, 1798, the journey through Cumberland Gap requiring thirty-seven days. He has been described by his grandson, James R. Rogers, as "of elegant and soldierly stature, of extreme height, impressive dignity and affability, companionable with his sons, and the most considerate, affectionate man to the ladies of his household I have ever known." In June 1807, he was the first layman immersed by authority of the mother church, having made his confession along with his wife, Anne Cornick Rogers, before Barton W. Stone and David Purviance; Purviance having been the first and Reuben Dooley the second; the former an elder of Cane Ridge Church and the latter a minister of the gospel. The baptism took place in Stoner Creek, seven miles from the church near the bridge now dedicated to Michael Stoner. "From this eventful era in his career he became a devoted student of the Bible, and his long after-life illustrated an unfaltering

---
*Excerpted from "The Rogers Family and Old Cane Ridge," by Julia S. Ardery, *The Register of the Kentucky Historical Society*, Vol. 53 (July 1955), 234-246.

allegiance to its sublime teaching . . . Exceeding fifty years he was an official of his church, alternating his position from the first clerkship to that of elder, at the will of the brethren. A man of splendid business qualifications, he early in life secured a competency, rearing about him a home of comfort and hospitality, which he called The Old Castle . . . here was assured a hearty greeting to the minister, layman and every caller. Christmas Day every member of his family was an expected guest under the old rooftree until the death of his (2nd) wife and the infirmities of age determined him to live among his sons."

The making of a man is an extended and marvelous process Garfield said . . . "no power of analysis can exhibit all the latent forces enfolded in the spirit of a new-born child, which derive their origin from the thoughts and deeds of remote ancestors, and, enveloped in the awful mystery of life, have been transmitted from generation to generation across forgotten centuries. Each new life is thus the heir to all the ages.' It seems in this connection it would be of interest to give briefly something of the ancestry of Williams Rogers "whose name in matters of importance relating to the church was always mentioned first by minister or brethren." He was a God-fearing man of prayer, at both church and home; a lover of peace and arbitrator; a courteous man loved and admired in every circle in which he mingled. All of these facts and more are manifest in his journals from which a few excerpts will later appear in the sketch.

LINEAGE

I   JOHN ROGERS (c. 1500-1555) of London, Prebendary of St. Paul's, Vicar of St. Sepulchre's, Reader of Divinity, was educated at Cambridge and was the first of the martyrs who suffered at Smithfield, Feb. 14, 1555, in the reign of Queen Mary. He was the Editor of the English Bible known as Matthew's. This volume, however, was not translated . . . by Thomas Matthew but was a compilation from the translations of Tyndale and Cloverdale, made under the editorship of Rogers, who revised them to some extent before sending them to press. The wife of John Rogers was Adriana Pratt. They were the parents of ten children. According to proven records the family of Rogers of Cane Ridge, Bourbon County, Kentucky, is directly descended from the aforesaid John Rogers of London.[1]

II JOHN ROGERS (s. of John and Adriana Pratt Rogers) was born Sept. 10, 1548; died 1601 (will); married 1st Agnes Carter, 2nd Mary (family name unknown) b.c. 1550; died 1579.[2]

III REV. JOHN ROGERS (s. of John Rogers II by Mary, his wife) was born at Moulsham, Chelmsford, England, 1571; died Oct. 18, 1639. He was a distinguished Puritan and Reader of God's Word who preached at Dedham, England. He married Elizabeth (Gold) Hawes.[3]

IV REV. NATHANIEL ROGERS (s. of Rev. John III and wife, Elizabeth (Gold) Hawes Rogers) established the family in America, arriving in Boston, Massachusetts, 1636. He was born at Haverhill, England, 1598 and graduated from Cambridge, A.B. 1617; settled at Ipswich, Massachusetts; colleague pastor with Rev. Nathaniel Ward and was active in the founding of the Colony. He died July 3, 1655. His wife was Margaret, daughter of Robert Crane, born at Coggershall, England, c. 1600; died at Ipswich, Jan. 23, 1676.[4]

V REV. DR. JOHN ROGERS of Ipswich (s. of Rev. Nathaniel and Margaret Crane Rogers) was born at Assington, England, Jan. 23, 1630; died July 2, 1684. He was a physician and minister of the Gospel who in June 1676 was elected President of Harvard College but declined. However, in April 1682, he was again elected and on August 12th, 1683 he was installed as the fifth president of this institution from which he had graduated. He married Elizabeth, daughter of Daniel and Patience (Dudley) Denison who was born April 10, 1642. Daniel Denison served as Acting Secretary of the Massachusetts Colony; Justice of the Court, applied to revise and codify the laws; Commr. United Colonies 1654-57; 1659-62; Major General 1655-60; Deputy-General Court; Speaker of the House. Her mother was a daughter of Thomas Dudley, seven years the governor of Massachusetts and the founder of Harvard 1637, who married 2nd Dorothy Yorke.[5]

VI REV. JOHN ROGERS (s. of Rev. Dr. John and Elizabeth Denison Rogers) was born at Ipswich, Massachusetts, July 7, 1666; died December 28, 1745. He was minister of the Church at Ipswich and married March 4, 1691, 2nd, Martha, daughter of William and Mary (Lawrence) Whittingham, who died March 9, 1759.[6]

VII WILLIAM ROGERS (s. of Rev. John and Wife, Martha Whittingham Rogers) was born in Mass. July 19, 1697; moved to Albemarle County, Virginia, where he married Margaret Caldwell, daughter of John and Margaret (Phillips) Caldwell. John Caldwell was the leader of a large emigration of Scotch Irish Presbyterians to the section of Virginia commonly called "Southside." Through his influence settlements were made and churches were built at Cub Creek in Charlotte County; Buffaloe and Walkers in the present Prince Edward and Hot Creek and Concord in present Campbell. At the time of organization Cub Creek was in Lunenburg and Buffaloe Creek was in Amelia County. William Rogers died leaving will in Lunenburg County, Virginia, written Oct. 15, 1750 and recorded April 3, 1751, in which he appointed David Caldwell, Thomas Rogers and his wife Margaret to divide and title his land among his children at their discretion and to sell and title any part thereof that they judged convenient for the maintenance and support of his family. After his death, his wife married second, in 1752, James Mitchell. She had five children by each husband. Two of the daughters died in Virginia and others moved to Kentucky.[7]

VIII THOMAS ROGERS (s. of William and Margaret Caldwell Rogers) was born 1725 and died in Charlotte County, Virginia 1786. He married Elizabeth Ann Carr. In his will he mentioned wife and children and appointed his "three eldest sons Executors" (Thomas Rogers qualified); witnesses were: John Rogers, Benjamin Rogers, Nathaniel Rogers, Andrew Rogers and John Roberson. The will was written Jan. 25, 1785 and recorded Sept. 4, 1786.[8]

IX NATHANIEL ROGERS (s. of Thomas and Elizabeth Ann Carr Rogers) was born in Albemarle County, Virginia; served in the Revolutionary War and in 1798 removed from Campbell County, Virginia, to Cane Ridge, Bourbon County, Kentucky. He married 1st August 14, 1783 Frances Cobbs, daughter of Captain Charles and Ann (Walton) Cobbs, who bore him three children—William, Elizabeth and Ann Walton Rogers. After the death of his wife in Virginia, Nathaniel Rogers married a second time, there being no issue. Nathaniel Rogers was the first person baptized by Barton W. Stone in 1803, while he labored under the commission of the presbytery with a proviso, the staunch supporter of his minister as he had been of his country's cause. He died in Bourbon County and was buried in the Cane Ridge Meeting-house graveyard. The handsome stone erected by his son, William Rogers bears the following inscription: "Here lies Nathaniel Rogers who was born July 23, 1755. He was a member of the Convention that framed the Constitution of Kentucky, 1799. What is of far more consequence, he was a member of the Church of Christ in the bosom of which he died, Dec. 22, 1804, at the age of 49 and reposes in the midst of his friends he loved so well. His only son (William Rogers) from a sentiment of filial respect consecrates this stone as a memento to his memory."[9]

X WILLIAM ROGERS (s. of Nathaniel and Frances Cobbs Rogers) whose journals inspired this record, was born on the 7th of July 1784 in Campbell County, Virginia. He married 1st July 8th, 1806, Anna Cornick (Cornock) who was born 1790 and died Dec. 16, 1816, daughter of Richard and Olivette (Phelps) Cornick, the latter's parents, John and Mary Williams Phelps having come to Cane Ridge from Bedford County, Virginia. To this union four sons were born:

(I) NATHANIEL Purviance Rogers (1807-1863) married, 1st, Nancy A. Moran and 2nd Mary Evaline Bayles. His home known as "LaGrange" was located near the Cane Ridge Meeting-house as the boundary of his land at one point adjoined that of the church. By his first wife he had four sons and two daughters; there was no issue by his second wife.[10]

(II) Warren Brown Rogers (1810-1864) married 1838 Marie Louise Lindsay (1822-1906) daughter of Colonel Nimrod Long and Luvina (Grimes) Lindsay. Warren Rogers became a convert at the great revival at North Middletown, Bourbon County, in 1838, joining Cane Ridge Church and soon thereafter was ordained a deacon. His wife, Marie Lindsay Rogers was President of the Ladies' Aid Society of Cane Ridge under whose auspices the church was put in perfect condition in 1882. In an old letter written by the Hon. Garrett Davis, United States Senator, dated 1864, he refers to Warren Rogers as "one of nature's noblemen." "Glenwood," the home of Warren and Marie Louise Rogers was built (1839-40) immediately in front of their earlier home. Joel T. Hart, at that time a stonemason who later became Kentucky's greatest sculptor, built at "Glenwood" the stone fence, foundation, chimneys and steps to the mansion as well as the springhouse. Much of his work is yet to be found in the Cane Ridge neighborhood. Warren B. Rogers and wife had three children: Louise Rogers, James R. Rogers, the last clerk of Cane Ridge Church, author of the Cane Ridge Meeting-House who served as a Captain in the Confederacy and Alice Rogers who married Robert Stoner, a Colonel in the Southern Army on the staff of General John Hunt Morgan; these last were the parents of May Lindsay Stoner who married Sidney Green Clay and who is the present owner of "Glenwood." She with her cousins, Harvey and William Rogers were three of a committee of seven in charge of the restoration of the Cane Ridge Meeting House in 1932.

III Harvey Addison Rogers (1812-1866) married 1st (1832) Sarah Neal and 2nd (1838) Elizabeth Jane Moran. These "built their home, Mt. Auburn, immediately back of their first home near the cabins," the contract was let Friday, 13, 1855, according to William Rogers's journal. Soon after Harvey Rogers united with the Cane Ridge Church, he was ordained a deacon, "filling this position most creditably until his final summons." By his first wife he had two daughters, also a son who died unmarried; by his second marriage he had five sons and four daughters. Through one of these sons, Warren Moran Rogers "Mt. Auburn" came to the present owner, William Rogers.

(IV) Benjamin F. Rogers, born 1815, married 1st Mary Elizabeth Spears and second Elizabeth "Betty" Jameson. By his first wife he had two sons and two daughters, one of whom, Annie Cornick married a grandson of Barton W. Stone; by his second wife he had a son, Richard Reid Rogers. Benjamin F. Rogers succeeded his father as clerk of Cane Ridge. His home

"Sunny Side" was the most permanent residence of William Rogers after he left "The Old Castle" to live among his children. Sunny Side was built about 1853-5 in front of a much older log structure which was retained and incorporated in the completed handsome dwelling.

X WILLIAM ROGERS SR. (1784-1862) married 2nd, July 24, 1817) Katherine Skillman, daughter of Christopher and Henrietta (Payne) Skillman, the Rev. Barton W. Stone performing the ceremony. By this wife he had four children who reached maturity:

(V) William Skillman Rogers, born 1819, married Henrietta Roseberry and lived at "New Forest." These were the parents of one daughter and five sons; the daughter, Mary, "Mollie," Katherine Rogers married Samuel Clay, Jr. She was the family genealogist and author of "The Clay Family."
(VI) Hugh Brent Rogers

(VII) Charles Christopher Rogers, born 1829, died 1880, married Louise Scott and built "Woodlawn" where they lived until it was sold to Edwin Bedford. These had a son, Lindsay Rogers. In his journal, William Rogers referred to his son, Christopher as "my youngest son and dearly beloved."

(VIII) Anna Elizabeth Rogers, born 1832, married Captain James M. Thomas. To this daughter William Rogers, Sr. gave the old home place of James Houston on Cane Ridge. Later they built a large brick residence on South Main in Paris.

NOTES

1, 2, 3—(English Ancestry):
New England Hist. and Gen. Reg. Vol. 1, p. 245; Genealogies of New England vol. 1, by Wm. Richard Cutter (1914) N. Y.—Lewis Hist. Pub. Co.; Monumental Stone, Aldens Epitaphs. Encyclopaedia Britannica, IX Edition, vol. XX, p. 620, Vol. VIII, p. 386, World Nobility and Peerage Vol. 87, p. 514. Moses and the Prophets, Christ and the Apostles, Fathers and Martyrs by J. E. Stebbins, 1866, p. 565.

4—ibid; Hist. Ipswich, Felt; Hist. Collections, Ipswich.

5-6 ibid; Josiah Quincey's Hist. of Harvard p. 38; Alden's Coll. V 11, pp. 67, 75, V. R. Ipswich; App. Encyclopaedia V p. 309; Benj. Pierce's Hist. Harvard p. 49, Memoirs of Nathaniel Rogers.

7—ibid; established records in Daughters of the Barons of Runnemede, Magna Charta Dames, and Colonial Dames of America in the Commonwealth of Kentucky; court records of Lunenburg County, Virginia. Will Book 1, pps. 35-36; Virginia Magazine V IX, p. 93.

8—ibid; Charlotte County, Va. Will Book 1 p. 385; "Heads of families in and around Cub Creek"; deeds in Lunenburg Co., Va.; old family letters.

9—Johnson's History of Kentucky V 11, pps. 883-4; Kentucky Court and Other Records V 11 p. 227; History of The Cane Ridge Meeting-House by J. R. Rogers; Voices from Cane Ridge by Rhodes Thompson.

10—ibid; journals of William Rogers of Bourbon County, Kentucky; the 1853 journal refers to his grandfather Thomas Rogers.

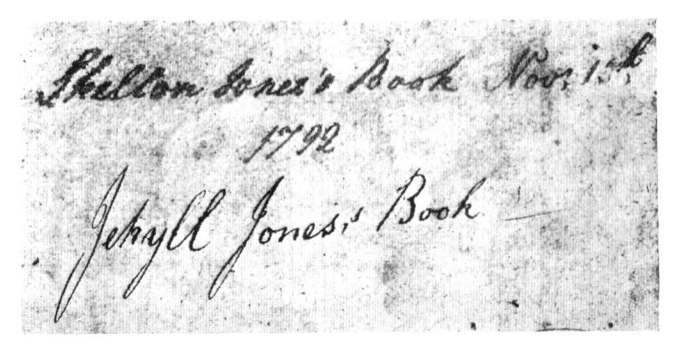

Handwriting of Skelton Jones on the first front flyleaf of the book Siege of Gibraltar by Ancell, referred to in this article. Underneath, supposed to be the writing of his brother Jekyll.

Name written on the inside of the left back of the book, Siege of Gibraltar, etc., referred to in this article.

SKELTON

By Judge Lewis H. Jones, Louisville, Ky.

It is being contended with some insistence that there were no people in Virginia as early, say as 1735, named Skelton—that they were all Sheltons; that Skelton Jones was really named Shelton Jones; that the James Skelton who figured in Virginia about this time and later was really James Shelton.

We present a facsimile of a bond executed by James Skelton in 1735, having his signature attached, the original of which is with the Jones papers in the Library of Congress, donated to the library by the heirs of Thomas ap Thomas Jones, of Clark county, Kentucky. Mrs. Jane Skelton, the wife of James Skelton, for whose benefit, in part, the bond was executed, was a daughter of Francis Meriwether, first clerk of Essex county, Virginia, whose wife was Mary Bathurst daughter of Lancelot Bathurst fifth son of Sir Edward Bathurst, baronet. Francis Smith whose name appears in the bond married Lucy, another daughter of Francis Meriwether and Mary Bathurst. They were the parents of Meriwether Smith a man of ability and prominence, first represesentative in Congress from his district, 1778-82, who was the father of George William Smith, at one time Governor of Virginia, who lost his life in the lamentable burning of the Richmond theater in 1811. Frances Meriwether, another daughter, married Theodoric Bland from whom descended the Revolutionary patriot Colonel Theodoric Bland. Mary, another daughter of Francis Meriwether and Mary Bathurst, married William Colston; married, 2nd, in 1723-4, Thomas Wright Belfield, doubtless the T. W. Belfield whose name appears as a witness to the bond. James Skelton died in 1753 or 4, his wife in January, 1751. (Wm. and Mary Quarterly).

The daughter Sally Skelton mentioned in the bond, for whose benefit, jointly with her mother, the bond was executed, became the wife of Thomas Jones of Northumberland county, Virginia. They raised a large and interesting family of six sons and four daughters. Of the daughters, Elizabeth married Gawin Corbin, of "Yew Spring," Caroline county; Mary married Lancelot Lee, of Berkeley; Jane married Judge John Monroe, of "Coane Place," Westmoreland county, a near relative of the president; Sally married Capt. Nathaniel Henderson.

One of the sons was named Skelton in honor of his mother's family. On a front fly-leaf of an old book in the possession of the heirs of the late Mr. Joseph F. Jones, of Clark county, entitled "The Siege of Gibraltar, from Sept. 12th, 1779, to Feb. 3rd, 1783, by Samuel Ancell, Clerk of the 58th Regiment, in a series of letters wrote on the spot," the following appears in the handwriting of Skelton Jones: "Skelton Jones' Book Nov. 15th, 1792;" and opposite, on the inside of the left back

Bond dated 1735, executed by James Skelton, referred to in this article.

of the book, the name "Skelton Jones, 1794," is written with such a profusion of scrolls and whirligigs as to suggest strongly the penmanship of his brother Bathurst. Underneath Skelton Jones' writing are the words "Jekyll Jones' Book," supposed to be the writing of his brother Jekyll. Facsimiles of the writing accompany this article.

They lived for many years at "Spring Garden" in Hanover county, a valuable and beautiful estate, or seat, which the wife received under the will of her brother Meriwether Skelton, who died a bachelor. She had also a brother Reuben Skelton and a brother Bathurst. Reuben Skelton married, Elizabeth, daughter of Lunsford Lomax, Esq., and died without issue. After Reuben's death she married John Wayles, Esq., of Charles City county, Virginia. Bathurst Skelton married, in 1766, Martha (Patty) Wayles, daughter of the Mr. Wayles we have just mentioned, and died leaving one child, a son John who died without issue. His widow, as Mrs. Martha Skelton, became the wife of Thomas Jefferson. Mrs. Jones had a sister, Lucy Skelton, who married a Mr. Gilliam. There were no other children.

The heirs of the late Mr. Roger Jones, of Clark county, have in their possession a family Bible in two large volumes, in each of which is the same armorial bookplate, displaying the Skelton arms, under one of which is written the name Meriwether Skelton and under the other the name Reuben Skelton. In the book "Capt. Roger Jones of London and Virginia, some of his Antecedents," etc., page 156, there is an exact reproduction of Meriwether Skelton's bookplate and signature, and we here present a facsimile of Reuben Skelton's bookplate and signature.

In the Richmond (Va.) Standard of Sept. 25th, 1880, the editor Dr. R. A. Brock, says: "We have the bookplate of Reuben Skelton and have seen the letter of Meriwether Skelton ordering one similar to be engraved in England in 1770. The arms are: *Az. a fesse or betw. three fleur de lis or.* Crest: *A peacock's head erased ppr. in the beak an acorn or stalked and leaved vert.* These agree with these of Skelton, Armathwaite Castle, county Cumberland, originally of Skelton (one of the family represented Cumberland in Parliament *temp.* Edward 1.), except that the last bears on the fesse a Cornish chough sa beaked and legged gu." (See also Burke's General Armory.)

The words "originally of Skelton" probably refer to Skelton Castle in Yorkshire. In the Century Dictionary, under "Laurence Sterne," he is mentioned as associated with "John Hall Stephenson, of Skelton Castle, Yorkshire."

A younger branch of Skelton of Armathwaite Castle was Skelton of Branthwaite, Co. Cumberland, *temp.* Henry V, the last male heir of which, it is stated, was General Skelton who died in 1757 (Burke's General Armory, 3d edition, 1844).

The arms of the Virginia family are identical with the arms of Skelton of Osmondthorpe, England, who do not use the Cornish chough for difference (see Papworth).

It does not follow however that merely because their name is Skelton they are

Reuben Skelton's bookplate in the Skelton Bible, referred to in this article, displaying the Skelton arms, viz.: Azure, a fesse between three fleur de lis or. Crest: A Peacock's head erased proper, in the beak an acorn or stalked and leaved vert.

entitled to bear the arms of some Skelton family. Similarity of names does not necessarily imply similarity of origin. Families having similar names, or the same name for that matter, may be as diverse in origin and family prestige as any having names the most dissimilar although there are people who will never seem to realize this.

In written matter the name Skelton is sometimes mistaken by copyists for Shelton and so finds its way into print. The copyist is familiar with the name Shelton and it is present in mind, while the name Skelton is quite out of mind and it may be, never heard of by the copyist—so, in doubt, he reads it Shelton. There is no affinity or connection whatever between the letters h and k. These letters have always been distinct and independent characters from the beginning of our language and have always served to make a distinction or difference between things.

While the name Skelton has been mistaken for Shelton, the writer has never known an instance where the name Shelton has been copied or printed Skelton. The reason is not far to seek; in writing a muddled letter k may easily look like an h, but an h could hardly be muddled into looking like a k.

In the issue of the Richmond Standard from which I have quoted, Dr. Brock continues: "We find of record in the Virginia Land Registry Office the following grants: James Skelton grants of 1,200, 400, 400, and 400 acres, all in Henrico county, and dated February 20, 1743, book No. 11, pp. 338, 339; James Skelton, 'of King William county,' two grants of 1,600 acres each and one of 750 acres in Henrico county, January 14, 1726, Book No. 13, pp. 14, 15."

The Slaughter Genealogy*

Col. Robert Slaughter, married Frances Anne Jones, a daughter of Col. Cadwallader Jones, son of Richard Jones, of Devon, England. Col. Slaughter commanded in the French and Indian Wars, and Col. Cadwallader Jones was of the British Army in Virginia. To this marriage we know of but three brothers, Robert the second, Thomas and Francis. Robert and Francis were chosen vestrymen and first church wardens of St. Mark's, at the January meeting, 1731. Thomas, the other brother's family has been located recently. Robert second married Mary, daughter of Capt. Augustine Smith (1723), a son of Col. Laurence Smith, who was one of the most distinguished Virginians of his day. Capt. Smith was civil engineer and surveyor in the company of fifty, under Governor Spottswood, 1716, styled "the cocked hat gentry," of the old Dominion, to whom it is accredited, went to lift the blue veil, which once hid from the eyes of the white man the fair face of nature in the Valley of Virginia. The children by this marriage are:

²Robert (¹Col. Robert) married Mary Smith in 1723. Children—
1. Robert³ married Susannah Harrison.
2. William married Miss Zimmerman; settled in Jefferson county, Ky.
3. Thomas married Miss Robinson.
4. Francis married Miss Luggett.
5. Colonel James married Susan, daughter of Major Philip Clayton.
6. St. Lawrence married a daughter of Col. John Field.
7. Colonel George married a daughter of Colonel John Field.
8. Elizabeth married Major Lightfoot.
9. Martha Jones married ¹Captain Gabriel Jones, ²Major William Broaddus.

³Robert (²Robert, ¹Col. Robert) married Susannah Harrison in 1750. Children—
1. James married Miss Hampton.
2. Charles married Miss Poindexter, of Louisa.
3. Governor Gabriel married ¹Miss Slaughter, of Caroline, ²Miss Hoard, of Virginia.
4. Jesse married Miss Slaughter, of Caroline.
5. Augustine, S. married Miss Susannah Fisher.
6. Daughter married ⁴Robert, (³John, ²Francis, ¹Colonel Robert.)

The family of ³Robert moved to Kentucky about 1785, except Charles, who remained in Virginia.

Of the Slaughter family of Culpeper, Va., there were seven officers of the Revolution: Col Jas. third, and Col. John, third, sons of Robert, second and Francis, second, were members of the committee of safety of Culpeper. Robert, Francis, Col. Robert, Col. James, Thomas, Robert, Jr., Lawrence Cadwallader, Samuel, Wm. B. and Philip, Jr., were vestrymen of St. Mark's Parish.

The Slaughter name appears on record in land entries by John Slaughter, 1620; Richard, 1652; George, 1710, and including numerous other entries and records.

The family's chief seats in England, were Lincolnshire, Gloucester and Worcester.

*Excerpted from "Colonel B. G. Slaughter," by Jennie C. Morton, *The Register of the Kentucky Historical Society*, Vol. 2 (Jan. 1904), 89-97.

Gabriel Stout Slaughter married Eliza Drake November 16, 1831, daughter of Col. A. S. Drake and Hannah Prall, of Lexington, Ky. Their children were—
1. Mrs. B. W. (Mary E.) Gaines married Benjamin W. Gaines.
2. James A. Slaughter married Ada P. Stout, daughter John Stout and Susan Bohannon.
3. Simeon Slaughter died, aged three years.
4. Simeon D. Slaughter married Olivet Stout, daughter of John Stout and Susan Bohannon.

Benjamin Gabriel Slaughter, born March 8, 1845; married Sept. 3, 1867, Lucy Osborne, daughter of Capt. Gabriel Glenn Osborne and Nancy Jones Osborne, whose father, Phillip Osborne, was a soldier in the Revolutionary War.

Pride in Family History.

(From the "Veteran.")

Comrade Benjamin Gabriel Slaughter, of Winchester, Tenn., had a hard lot in the war. He is colonel as the official commissary on the Staff of Maj. Gen. George W. Gordon, commanding the Tennessee Division, U. C. V. In the history of the Slaughter family by Dr. Philip Slaughter, of St. Mark's Parish, Culpeper county, Va., it is recorded that the Slaughters emigrated from Lincolnshire, Gloucester, and Worcester, England, prior to 1620, and made valuable land entries up to 1732 in Virginia. The history dwells upon the name of Col. Robert Slaughter, famous in the French and Indian wars, and his wife, Francis Anne Jones, daughter of Col. Cadwallader, of honored lineage.

It will be seen from this correct genealogical table, by Col. B. G. Slaughter, Governor Gabriel Slaughter, was a son of Robert Slaughter, third, and brother of Austin Smith Slaughter, whose name appears on the Fisher family tree, as if his father.

5. Augustine Smith Slaughter married Susannah Fisher in 1801. She was the daughter of Stephen Fisher (Baron Von Fisher) and Mary Magdalene Garr, of Culpeper county, Va. Their children were: Stephen, who married Annie Sloan; Gabriel Stout, who married Eliza Drake; Robert V. first, second, Nancy Kendrick; third, Mary Jane Poore.

Mrs. Lucinda Majors; Mrs. Eliza Nelson, second, married Bradshaw; Mrs. Mary Barrows, second, married Bell; Mrs. Susannah H. Hawkins.

Col. Robert Slaughter's sons—
1. Robert Slaughter.
2. Lieut. Lawrence Slaughter of the Virginia State line.
3. Francis Slaughter.

Lawrence Slaughter, son of Col. Robert Slaughter, Lieut. in the Virginia State line, married Susannah Field, daughter of Col. John Field, killed in the battle of Pt. Pleasant, during the Revolutionary War.

Children—
1. John Field Slaughter.
2. Anne.
3. Mildred.
4. Robert F.
5. Matilda.
6. George S.
7. Lawrence.
8. Francis.

Francis Slaughter (son of Col. Robert Slaughter) in 1729, married in Culpeper Co., Va., Annie Lightfoot, and had—
1. Francis.
2. John.
3. Reuben.
4. Cadwallader.
5. Frances, who married Capt. Wm. Ball.
6. Mrs. Edward Thomas.

The Slaughter Family.
By W. A. Slaughter.

When Gabriel Slaughter and several members of his immediate family migrated from Virginia to Kentucky about the year, 1785, there was one of his brothers, Charles Slaughter, who remained in Virginia. This Charles Slaughter settled in Campbell county, his wife was Miss Elizabeth Poindexter, of Louisa county, to whom he was married on February 3, 1780 she was the daughter of John Poindexter, Jr., and Sarah Poindexter, his wife. The children of Charles and Elizabeth were:

Nancy P., born June 17, 1782; married Glover Davenport in 1801.

John P., born March 27, 1784; married (1) Miss Patsy Armistead; (2) Miss Agnes Cobb, of Bedford county.

Mary Smith, born January 2, 1786, died in infancy.

Robert Harrison, born October 6, 1786; married (1) Miss Anderson; no issue; (2) Miss Mary Rice Garland.

Elizabeth, born July 22, 1796; married John Bullock.

Charles Slaughter ran away from boarding school to join the Revolutionary Army and was a private in Captain Alexander Spotswood Dandridge's troop of light dragoons, from July 19, 1776, to December 1, 1778; commanded by Colonel Theodore Bland. His two sons were both physicians; Robert Harrison Slaughter attended the University of Pennsylvania in 1810, later he attended the University of Edinburgh.

Dr. John Poindexter Slaughter married (1) Miss Patsy Armistead, of Charlotte county in the year 1805; they had three children who were:

Charles, who married Juliet Clemens and had two sons, Dr. John and Henry Clay; the latter was a lawyer and married Ann Mayo Read, December 18, 1858. They had four children, Edmonia, of Danville, Va.; S. Jackson, who married Miss Carter, Nicolas Cabell (died in infancy) and Henry Clay, Junior.

Sarah, married Josiah Hunter and had three children; Dr. Josiah E. Hunter, Robert and Jane.

Pauline, married Robert Hunter and had two children; Selina, who married Rev. Mr. Dinwiddie and Rev. Joshua Hunter.

Dr. John Poindexter Slaughter married (2) Miss Agnes Cobb, of Bedford county, by whom he had one daughter, Susan Agnes.

Dr. Robert Harrison Slaughter married (1) Miss Anderson in 1812; he married (2) July 15, 1818, Miss Mary Rice Garland, daughter of Rice Garland of Albemarle county; they had eight children, who were:

Charles Rice, born September 29, 1819; married Catherine M. Garland, August 22, 1846.

Elizabeth A., born May 30, 1821; died May 7, 1841, unmarried.

Robert Burr, born March 11, 1823; died June 30, 1840, unmarried.

Mary James, born March 13, 1825; died January 11, 1878 unmarried.

Dr. Samuel Maurice, born September 20, 1826; married Miss Elizabeth Henderson.

John Flavel, born February 23, 1828; died January 23, 1893; married Miss Mary Harker.

Celeste Pauling, born May 15, 1850; died January 23, 1881; married J. M. Cobbs; no issue.

Austina, W. S. F. married Robert Withers Brodnax, two children.

The seven children of Charles Rice Slaughter and Catherine were:

Mary E., married Judge J. Singleton Digges, of Lynchburg, Va.; their two children are: Catherine and Dudley.

Charles Alexander, married Bettie Garland; they have one daughter, Althea.

Catherine Lightfoot (unmarried) of Lynchburg, Va. Robert G., Althea, James P. Garland, S. Garland, died in infancy.

The only child of Dr. Samuel Maurice Slaughter and his wife, Elizabeth, was a daughter, Mary Roberta, who married Charles Matson Harker, Jr., of Mount Holly, N. J. Their four children are: Edith Ridgway, Elizabeth Walker, Charles M., Jr., Mary.

The two children of Austina and Robert Withers Brodnax were:

John Slaughter (died in infancy) and a daughter, Mary, who married George Cameron, of Petersburg, Va.; they had three children: Helen, Brodnax and Gabrielle.

Charles Rice Slaughter was an M. A. of the University of Virginia; member of the State Committee, 1860; drew up the articles of the Secession of Virginia. He died February 10, 1862.

The ten children of John Flavel Slaughter and Mary were:

(1) Miss Mary Duke, of Albemarle county, one daughter, Mary.

Dr. Charles married (2) Miss Hattie Gray, of Richmond; two children, Charles and Susan.

John Flavel, Jr., of Lynchburg, Va. (unmarried).

Robert, married Miss Augusta Banister, of Alabama; two children, Robert and Monroe.

Dr. Samuel G., married Miss Mayme Richardson; three children, Rosalie, Willis and Sam. Augustus, Susie, Mary, died in infancy.

Edith Ridgway, married Judge R. T. W. Duke, Jr., of Charlottesville, Va., five children: Mary, R. T. W. Duke, John S., Eskridge, Helen.

Dr. B. Rosalie, of Washington, D. C. (unmarried).

William Austin, lawyer, married Miss Florence Lewis, daughter of Rev. Jno. K. Lewis.

John Flavel Slaughter was an alumnus of the University of Virginia and a lawyer by profession, being a member of the firm of Garland & Slaughter, of Lynchburg, Va.; he was one of the "Committee of Nine," who interviewed General Grant in Washington at the close of the Civil war and helped to secure an early readmission of Virginia into the Union. He was president of the First National Bank of Lynchburg, 1876-1892. He married Mary Haines Harker, of Mount Holly, N. J., December 15, 1853. She was a daughter of Charles M. Harker, Sr.

273

Three of the sons of John Flavel Slaughter, viz., Charles, Samuel Garland, and William are alumni of the University of Virginia. Rosalie is an alumna of the Philadelphia Women's Medical College.

"1754 Thomas Slaughter, Hogg's Company, served under Colonel George Washington in the French and Indian wars. This fact is noted in a roll of the officers and soldiers who engaged in the service of the colony before the battle of the Meadows in 1754, according to a return made at Will's Creek, July 9, 1754." (Virginia Historical Magazine, Vol. I., No. 3, p. 282.)

"In an old act of the Assembly of Virginia, dated 1758, the following items appear:

```
To William Slaughter for 54 days @ 3
  shillings ........................ £ 8
Thomas Slaughter and others 54 shill-
  ings each.
Lieut. William Slaughter from May 15
  to last of August inclusive, 109 days,
  3 shillings @.................... £ 16 7s
Col. Robert Slaughter and pay of the
  men (40) sent by order of President
  Blair to garrison Fort Pattersing the
  same time, 109 days............... £ 218
The account was passed September 14, 1758.
```

"The Virginia Land Registry shows the following names among those who received county lands from the State: Lieutenant Wm. Slaughter, Lieutenant John S. Slaughter, Lieutenant Thomas Slaughter (twice), Lieutenant Robert Slaughter, Ensign Wm. Slaughter, Surgeon Augustine Slaughter, of the Seventh Regiment, Private Nathaniel Slaughter and Private Francis Lightfoot Slaughter."

If this Thomas Slaughter was the same individual who was with the Boones, Henderson and others at Boonesborough on May 23, 1775 (see query in my last letter) we might suppose that he was an influence that most induced Governor Gabriel Slaughter to migrate from Virginia to Kentucky about the year 1785. This subject of Thomas Slaughter has always interested me, particularly as his existence seems to have been ignored by some of the older genealogists and to reinforce my idea that there must in early days have been a family rallying point in Carolina, I cite the following alliances that were formed there: Governor Gabriel Slaughter married Miss Susan Slaughter of Caroline county and later he married Miss Hord of the same county; Jesse Slaughter likewise married a Miss Slaughter from there and Francis Slaughter's wife, Miss Halloway, was from the same place. Francis Slaughter and Thomas K. Slaughter, sons of John Slaughter, married wives from Caroline county and Gabriel Slaughter, son of William, married Miss Elizabeth Terrell from the same county, thus forming quite a Caroline county motif in our family history.

In reference to Thomas Slaughter it has occurred to me that possibly he might have been the uncle of Governor Gabriel Slaughter. I understand that the governor's first wife was his cousin, Miss Susan Slaughter, daughter of Thomas Slaughter, of Caroline county, Virginia. This Thomas Slaughter was a brother of Robert Slaughter and Francis (the church wardens). Concerning Thomas Slaughter I have the following notes "1753-1757 the names of the following persons appear in a record as having served in a compaign against the French and Indians about this time. Colonel Robert Slaughter, Lieutenant William Slaughter and Thomas Slaughter." (History of Saint Mark's Parish.)

With regard to the antiquity of the Slaughter line, it is, we think, safe to say, one of the oldest in England, and its history worthy of preservation by the American descendants.

Looking up the family motto—"Movictac Fidelitatis Procrimny," is, we understand, the same as that of the city of Hereford. At upper Slaughter manor, Berton-on-water, in Gloucester county, England, occurs the coat of arms, of James, carved over the doorway of the old manor. Miss Rosalie Slaughter of Washington City, visited the old manor house in 1899, and brought home with her a picture of it. The original spelling of the name as far back as 1130, was Slou-tre (Anglo-Saxon) "home lover."

Mr. Edwin A. Abbey, the eminent English artist, who now lives near the place, says that "the ancient doorway is greatly admired and is much copied by architects as a pure example of the early style."

Like other old manors, it has been added to at various times, but the result is even now very attractive, particularly the addition made in the time of Queen Elizabeth.

There are many brasses and documents in the manor chapel with the names of the Slaughters upon them.

From the notes of W. A. Slaughter, of Mount Holly, New Jersey, it is learned that Martin Slaughter, of England, was the author of the play, "Hercules," noted during the reign of Elizabeth.

Walter Slaughter, of England, wrote the music for the celebrated pantomine of "Babes in the Woods," a few years ago.

Slaughter & May is the firm of lawyers of distinction in London.

Mrs. Conan Doyle, wife of the famous novelist, was a Miss Slaughter.

Thus we find representatives of the old stock still at the front in the mother country and we, their American cousins, are anxious to connect the lineal lines.

Are there readers of "The Register," who will lend a helping hand? We wish to secure the ancestry and history of Colonel Robert Slaughter, who served in the French and Indian wars.

B. G. S.

In the sketch of Governor Gabriel Slaughter, J. C. M. does not mention the third marriage of the governor. Can you tell us the name of his third wife? S. S.

Answer: She was Elizabeth Rhodes, the widow of Waller Rhodes, her cousin, of Madison county, Kentucky. Her maiden name was Elizabeth Thomson. She survived Governor Slaughter many years. There were no children by this third marriage.

She was a daughter of William Thomson and his wife, Anna Rhodes, who were married in Virginia, 1750.

B. G. S.

Sir Richard Steele and Descendants

in America and Kentucky.

By Mrs. Many Willis Woodson.

The Steele family is of Irish descent, the first one of which we have record, was Sir Richard Steele,* a native of Dublin; he was born in 1671, was secretary of the Lord Lieutenant of Ireland; dramatist and essayist.

He was a man of great versatility of talent; was the author of several treatises and comedies, was a chum of Addison's, and was connected with the Spectator, Tatler and Guardian, extending from the year 1709 to 1714.

He wrote a poem on the death of Queen Mary, and dedicated it to Lord Cutts, a Colonel in the Guards, who was so pleased with his talents and wit that he procured him a captaincy in the Fusiliers and his name was presented to the king for promotion, but the king died before any thing could be done. Steele probably owed the king's favor really to honest admiration of the excellent principles in the "Christian Hero," his first prose production, published in 1701. Steele complained of the reception of his book among his comrades, for they would try him by his own standard, and the least levity he displayed, they would annoy and chaff him so, that he said he thought he would have to redeem and enliven his character, and wrote a comedy, and called it "The Funeral,"

Through the influence of the Lord Lieutenant his eldest son was placed in the "Charter House school," London.

He was married twice, both times to heiresses. At the death of Queen Anne, he was inspector of the royal seals and was knighted by George I. He was also, at one time a member of parliament; but notwithstanding all those advantages and emoluments he was a great spendthrift, wasted two large fortunes, it is reported, and afterwards, retired to a small estate he owned in Wales, called Llangunnon, and died there, in September, 1729.

Richard Steele, the grandson of the above, was the ancestor of the Ameri-

NOTE.—In a history of Ireland, published in 1852, we learn that Richard Steele, Esq., resided in his castle at Ballyedmund, to the left of Rathdowney, a small town near the source of the Erkin, on the road from Dublin to Thurles. This was his residence when he was the leading literateur of Ireland. He died in Wales, many years after, in 1729.

can branch of the family; nothing has been written of his father, and in fact, very little about himself, beyond that he was a grandson of Sir Richard Steele, and emigrated to America, and had obtained a grant of a thousand acres of land, from the King of England. This land was in Pennsylvania and he located his claim around about where the town of Mercersburg is now and he settled there.

Richard Steele, married in Ireland, wife's name unknown. He had eight children, that he raised in Mercersburg, where he lived and died.

When Kentucky was an unbroken wilderness three of his children, namely, Richard Steele, Jr., and family, Mrs. Jane Hueston, husband and family, and Mrs. Mary Lytle, husband and family, left Mercersburg and came to the far west, as Kentucky was then called, for the purpose of making their homes here. They were Presbyterians, and left good homes, good churches, and good schools, to locate here. These families moved down the Ohio in flat boats, and were in constant fear of the Indians. They landed on Corn Island near the falls of the Ohio, built a fort, and there remained two years, at the end of which time, they with other families, who had joined them, went on Beargrass creek, and built a fort at Spring Station, and was there until the Indians were driven back toward the lakes.

In order to demonstrate the unflinching courage and self sacrificing spirit of the women of those days, an incident is mentioned in a manuscript still preserved in the family.

The fort was a very desirable locality, a fine strategic point, and the Indians were disposed to contest their right to it with great determination; hostilities were imminent, and it was determined to move the women and children to Floyd Station, about five miles distant, where they would be in comparative safety, while all the males that could bear arms, or be otherwise useful, remained to meet the foe. In a short time a skirmish ensued, in which Mr. Steele was shot through his left shoulder and left hand; his wife soon heard of it, and determined to go to him. It was of course at the peril of her life for she had to go through an Indian settlement, a thick woods and it was a dark night; Mr. Lytle, her brother-in-law, protested vehemently against her going and exposing herself to almost certain death, but she persisted and went, arrived safe and attended her husband until he could return with her.

Some years after these events Richard Steele and company moved to Fayette county, near Lexington,* and settled upon a farm, known afterwards as the Nat Hart farm. He was the first elder from Kentucky to the general assembly of the Presbyterian church, that year held in New York City. He went on horse back, over the mountains in company with his minister, the Rev. Mr. Cameron, and that was considered, in those days, a greater trip than to go round the world is now; he lived and died on that farm in 1808; his brothers-

---

NOTE.—It is claimed that Richard Steele was drawn to Lexington and its vicinity by Andrew Steele, his cousin, who had helped to settle that part of the State, and had located in the county on his land grant, after the close of the Revolutionary War.

in-law, Messrs. Hueston and Lytle, lived on adjoining farms.

Mary Lytle's daughter Nancy, who afterwards married Judge Rowan, was a child seven years of age when they lived at Spring Station, and could distinctly remember her fort life, and often gave her older children and niece, Mrs. Martha Mendenhall Baxter, reminiscences of that life, which she (Mrs. Baxter) has written down. Jane Hueston (nee Steele) had eight children, Nancy, married George Graham, of Pennsylvania; Sarah, married Benjamin Woods, of New Jersey; Robert, married Mary Bartholomew Bodley, sister of General Thomas Bodley, of Fayette county, Ky.; Susan, married James January, of Maysville, Ky.; Jane, married James M. Nair of Pennsylvania; Mary, married John Rennick, of Pennsylvania; Elizabeth, married Robert Perry, of Virginia; William died unmarried.

Mary Lytle was the grandmother of the Rowans of Kentucky and the Lytles of Ohio, she was the great grandmother of General William Lytle* who fell at the battle of Corinth, Miss.

During the prevalence of the effort to exclude the Duke of York from the succession, because of his being a Papist, there was a bitter conflict between Papacy and Prelacy, which afforded some temporary relief to the Protestants, and many of the Covenanters embraced with thankful hearts the opportunity providentially given to them of leaving their old Scotch homes and coming to America, which was then opening her arms to all those who sought relief from troubles in the old country. By far, the greatest proportion of them that came that year seemed to have been drawn as with a loadstone, to the eastern shore of Maryland, and as they increased in numbers moved into the Valley of Virginia and Pennsylvania. The McKamies, Rennicks, McAfees, Montgomerys, Campbells and McCouns, settled for some time on the Eastern shore and some of the descendants are still there,

NOTE.—This General Lytle wrote the poem, "I am dying, Egypt, dying."

Captain Andrew Steele,

A Revolutionary Soldier; a Descendant of Sir Richard Steele of Ireland.

By Mrs. Jennie C. Morton.

During that terrible period in Kentucky, when as a frontier county of Virginia, it was exposed to the raids and barbarities of the savages, and to attacks of the British troops and Indians combined, Andrew Steele came from Pennsylvania, to what is now Fayette county, Kentucky, to cast in his lot among the noble pioneers and Revolutionary soldiers who had preceded him, to this defenceless paradise of Boone. We learn he had been educated at the University of Dublin, and was intended by his father for a minister of the Presbyterian church. He, however, became imbued with the spirit of the liberty-loving people of Londonderry who were flocking then to America, and joined a party bound for the new land across the sea. He settled first in Pennsylvania near Mercerburg among his kindred of noble descent. There he met and married his cousin, Jane Lindsay.

In 1776 (Collins' Hist. of Ky., pp. 550-764, Vol. 11), he came to Kentucky with a company of seven men. He bought lots in Lexington in 1783. As soon as possible he brought his family to Kentucky; then armed himself to defend them from harm, and aid by every means, in his power, in defense of the life and liberty of the citizens and homes then established. He was consulted upon all important measures for the welfare of the imperiled little Commonwealth, left to the exigencies of the awful border warfare, which culminated in the battles, of "Bryan's Station," and "Blue Licks," in both of which Andrew Steele was a soldier.

Mr. Steele was empowered to write the most urgent letters to Governor Harrison, descriptive of the peril and dangers to which Kentuckians were exposed. In Calendar Vol. III. of Va. State Papers, will be found these eloquent and thrilling letters of Andrew Steele, to the Governor of Virginia descriptive of these battles and the suffering and sorrow resultant therefrom. His eloquent petitions for aid from His Excellency, Governor Harrison, are regarded as among the finest specimens of writings of his day. In recognition of his services in the "rear guard of the Revolution" as Kentucky border warfare is styled, he was given large grants of land in Kentucky. The patents may be found in the Land Office in Frankfort, one of the largest being in a body of 1,000 acres, in Fayette county, Ky. (book 1, p. 244). Another in Franklin county he gave his daughter, Mrs. Clement Bell, and it has been known ever since as "Bell's Grove." The name of Andrew Steele, may be found on the rosters of the soldiers of the "Battles of Blue Licks and "Bryan's Station." (History of battle of Blue Licks by Colonel Bennett H. Young). He lived to see Kentucky an honored State in the Union, of that immortal circle, of thirteen Colonies. About 1807, his wife died. He returned to Ireland, and there married his second wife, Ann Carr. On his return to America, he was taken ill, and died on the Atlantic Ocean. His children by his first wife were, Margaret, who married Clement Bell, a pioneer from Salisbury, Maryland (grandfather of the writer), Annie, who married her cousin, Col. Jno. Steele of Woodford county; Jane ("pretty Jane,") she is called in Perrin's History of Kentucky), who married, Abraham S. Vandegraff, (son of Governor Wm. Vandegraff, of Ceylon), 1801; Priscilla, who married Verpyle Paine; Elizabeth William Steele, who never married, and John Steele, who married his cousin, Jane Patterson, a daughter of Col. Robert Patterson, of Lexington, Ky., said to be the founder of the three cities, Lexington, Cincinnati and Dayton, Ohio. (See history of Robert Patterson, in "Our Forefathers.") Andrew Steele was descended from William, a son of Sir. Richard Steele, Secretary to Lord Lieutenant, of Ireland, and Inspector of Royal Seas, of King George I., by which king he was knighted. In a history of Ireland, we learn "the castle in which Sir Richard Steele, the most eminent man of letters and affairs, in Ireland, in his day, resided," is shown at Ballyedmund on the left of the road to Hathdowney, a small town near the source of the Erkin on the road from Dublin to Thurles. Our ancestor was born in Limavady, Londonderry county, Ireland, a small town now of importance in the beautiful vale of Roe; Newton-Limavady it is called. In its vicinity is the wonderful mountain, Ben Yoenagh, whose verdant summit reaches the clouds, and is more than a thousand feet above the sea. The scenery is sublime in the region of Limavady. We learn every man in this historical region is duly proud of his birthplace, as the siege of Londonderry makes it one of the most celebrated in history.

Andrew Steele never lost his love for his native land, the Emerald Isle, and thought with the poet,

"Immortal little Island,
 No other land or clime
Has placed more deathless heroes
 In the Pantheon of time."

Yet oppression, and tyranny will drive a proud spirit from earth's fairest paradises, to seek liberty, justice, and happiness in a less favored spot of earth. Andrew Steele believed in American independence, he fought for it, worked for it, in Kentucky, and evidently found his reward, and became a man of high position and influence. He is styled "Captain Andrew Steele" in Perrin's History of Kentucky; perhaps the title was given by courtesy as we have been unable to verify his claim to it, on any record in the Land Office in Frankfort. However, these military and treasury warrants are not conclusive evidence of a soldier's rank in the Revolutionary War.

It was in 1796, his eldest daughter Margaret Steele (grandmother of the writer), married Clement Bell, Esq., a notable pioneer at Frankfort, Ky., 1790. Her father gave her as before stated in this sketch, the estate lying on the uplands of North Elkhorn, about five miles east of Frankfort; a part of a Revolutionary grant, the patent to which, signed by Gov. Patrick Henry, was given as a souvenir to a grandson of Clement Bell, Lewis B. Ely, of Carrollton, Missouri, a widely known Christian philanthropist during his life.

Andrew Steele had many other valuable tracts of land in the counties of Bourbon, Mason, Fayette, Scott, Woodford and Franklin, but his residence was in Fayette county, near Lexington, Ky.

As we may understand from the locality of his birth. Newton-Limavady, he was Scotch-Irish, and in coming to Kentucky, he settled among his kindred. His brothers-in-law were those noted pioneers, Robert Patterson, Joseph and James Lindsay; the two last, lost their lives in the battles of Boonesboro and Bryan's Station, (Collins' History of Kentucky, Vol. 11.) His cousins, Richard Steele, Adam and Robert Steele, also settled near him, and in early days we learn, there was the most affectionate relationship between the families, now scattered far apart, with branches in almost every State in the Union, unknown to their kindred by name in Kentucky.

The list of the descendants of the Londonderry Scotch-Irish is an honorable one. They were never appealed to in vain by colonist or pioneer. Their help with purse or rifle was always at command. They were distinguished for their courage, their endurance and their well-known ability, whether in the Revolution at the front or as civil officers, or as the rear guard of the Revolution in the terrible border warfare, along the Ohio river, on the south shore line of Pennsylvania, Virginia and Kentucky.

Bancroft, the historian, pays the Scotch-Irish of America this compliment: "We shall find the first voice publicly raised in America to dissolve all connection with Great Britain came not from the Puritan of New England, or the Dutch of New York, or the planters of Virginia, but from the Scotch-Irish Presbyterians." The Steeles were of this order. They made no concessions to wrong and maintained the right with their own right arms and rifles.

In Kentucky we find them good citizens. Born to wealth in the old country, they acquired it here by industry and intelligence and quietly enjoyed their independence and prosperity. They had lots in Lexington and Frankfort, and in looking up old papers in the county court in this city, Frankfort, we find Steele street, one of the handsomest avenues of Frankfort, was called for William Steele, a cousin of Andrew and Thomas Steele. He drew the plat of South Frankfort in 1796. He was noted as a skilled draughtsman.

The writer will be pleased to have an "addenda" to this brief sketch of her great grandfather, Andrew Steele, from other descendants who may have interesting facts concerning this forefather with descriptions of visits to Newton-Limavady, and Dublin, and so enhance this limited history, of the oldest branch of the Steele family in Kentucky.

Note.—The writer has collected these facts concerning her great grandfather, Andrew Steele, from Public Records, from letters of the late Hon. Andrew Steele, of Fayette county, Ky., and family records.

Thomas Steele, Pioneer.

In response to the request made of descendants of Andrew Steele, I received the letter given below, from my cousin, Hon. Jno. A. Steele, banker, Midway, Ky. He is the only son of the late Dr. Theo. Steele, of Midway, Ky., and his wife, Caroline Dupre Worthy, deceased, of Georgia, and grandson of Major John Steele, of Woodford county, Ky., and his wife, Annie Steele, both deceased, and a great grandson of Thomas Steele, pioneer, and his wife, Eleanor Moore, of Newton-Limavady, on the banks of the Roe Londonderry county, Ireland.

Thomas Steele was a younger brother of Andrew Steele, the Revolutionary soldier, my great grandfather and also the great grandfather of Hon. Jno. A. Steele, his grandmother, Annie Steele, being the daughter of Andrew Steele, above mentioned and first cousin of her husband, Captain, afterwards Major John Steele, of the Kentucky Militia (1823).—Ed. The Register.

Midway, Aug. 25, 1903.

My Dear Cousin:

Your biographical sketch of our great grandfather, Andrew Steele, was read with deep interest. I had written what I knew of him, but as much of it was the same as that you have written, I shall only present such additional facts and corroborating matter as has come within my knowledge, and if it will be of interest, you can weave it with yours, perhaps it may lend additional value to your sketch.

As you have already shown, our ancestors came from Newton-Limavady, Londonderry county, Ireland, and were Scotch-Irish Presbyterians. Andrew Steele emigrated to this country first, and the facts you set forth, correspond with my information, in regard to him, his character and his advent in Kentucky. My information is (further) that after the Revolutionary War and matters became settled somewhat, he located on a farm about six miles from Lexington, on the old Frankfort and Lexington road, and on a tributary of South Elkhorn, known to-day, as Steele's Run, and there a branch of his posterity reside at this time.

His younger brother, Thomas Steele, emigrated to America and came to Kentucky some years after, joining his brother Andrew here about the year 1787-8. He, Thomas, located in Woodford county on land near the old Presbyterian church, and this farm is now a part of the Alexander tract of land which it adjoined. He built there one of the first brick houses in the county, which is in a good state of preservation at the present time. He was a high spirited, quick tempered man, but his heart was so full of kindness and charity, he was greatly beloved by his relatives and neighbors. He was married in Ireland to Eleanor Moore, where my grandfather, their only child, John Steele, was born in 1784. As to how many brothers and sisters, our great grandfathers had I do not know. I know there was a sister Anne, as I have a letter from her to my grandfather, from Ireland.

In talking once with an old Irish friend, some years ago, I spoke of our ancestral home of Newton-Limavady, he said he knew the place well. I asked him what sort of place it was? He said it was not a town, but a narrow valley between mountainous crags, and in the distance looking up the valley, it seemed as if the crags met overhead. He said the English meaning of the word is "The Dog's Leap." It took its name from a tradition that an Irish chieftain was out enjoying a chase when the stag, being hard pressed, leaped across the chasm. One of his favorite dogs followed after and caught him; hence the name of Limavady—"(In Frazier's guide book through Ireland we find the following, pp. 535-6. "From Dungiven to Newton-Limavady a road runs on both banks of the Roe. On the east side of the beautiful vale, which that river refreshes with its pure stream rises Benbreda and Donald's hill and in the west the lesser heights spring, which belong to the richer and more distant hills of Legavannon. A few miles distant is Ben Yevenagh, whose verdant summit is 1,260 feet above the sea. From it and even from many of the lower prominent parts of its beautiful cliffy sides under favorable circumstances, we are told the traveler will learn more of this mountainous district and its shores from Fair Head to Quishowen Head than from any of the most minute description. In addition, this region is rich in objects of natural science."

Thus we learn our ancestors came from one of the most celebrated districts of Ireland, where Nature was and is to-day prodigal in objects of transcendant beauty and sublimity. They were born to the worship of the beauty in nature as well as to the religion of the Presbyterian church. Hence on coming to America, it was but natural that they should select Kentucky, the virginal paradise in America as their home.

I regret that I can not go further back than the lines of the two men already written of. Sir Richard Steele, was as you know, one of the most eminent men of his time. He was a soldier and statesman, and as a man of letters ranked even above his friend, Addison. He fought under the Duke of Ormonde and William of Orange, with whom he was a great favorite. He was a distinguished member of Parliament, and held many important civil offices, but it was as a writer he acquired his greatest distinction. His versatile pen was wielded with equal effect whether his subject was serious, philosophic, humorous or sarcastic. He will always be prominent in English literature.

This is all that I can recall at present, of our people, that is of interest to us or to them.

I remain, sincerely, your cousin,

JNO. A. STEELE.

Major John Steele
Of the War 1812-15.
Grandfather of Hon. John A. Steele, Midway, Ky.

The children of Major John Steele, whose picture accompanies this sketch, were, namely: Judge William Steele, who married Mary Winston of Alabama; Andrew Steele, who married Keturah Metcalfe, daughter of Governor Metcalfe; Thomas Steele, who married Eliza Wilson, daughter of Captain Isaac Wilson, of Franklin county, Ky.; Dr. Theophilus Steele, who married Caroline Worthy, of Georgia, and Jane Steele, who died young, unmarried.

We reprint this notice of other Steeles in Kentucky related to each other:

380.—Steele.—The will of Richard Steele was probated in county court of Fayette, at Lexington, Ky., November 15, 1808. Mentions wife, Martha, sons Adam and Richard, Joseph, John, and Robert M. Beall, and daughters, Esther, Nancy Pollock, Polly Sutherland and Patsy Beall.

345.—Steele.—Adam Steele, born December 4, 1770, died July 15, 1824, at Shelbyville, Ky., was twice married, first, December 9, 1799, to Betsy Brooke Beall, had seven children, two of whom left descendants, namely: Patsy Somers, married William Gibson Luckett, and Betsy Brooke, married Michael Graham Bright, older brother of Senator Jesse D. Bright, of Indiana. December 2, 1815, Adam Steele married Hannah Graham; Amantha married Samuel Womack; and Minerva Fleming, married George Moore Bright, younger brother of Senator Bright. Adam Steele was president of the Farmers' and Merchants' Bank at Shelbyville. He had brothers, Richard, William and Robert. The two latter had mercantile houses at Wheeling, Cincinnati and Louisville. Adam Steele was related to the Steeles of Lexington, who were original lot owners of that town. Would be pleased to have what A. A. B. knows of the Steele family.—(Courier Journal—Ed. The Register.)

Supplement to the
"STEELE GENEALOGY"

In January Number of the Register, 1904.

By Miss Idelle Keyes, Boston, Mass

Referring to page 83, Register of Kentucky State Historical Society, the following may be of interest to that branch of the Steele family in Kentucky. (Page 285, this volume.)

Richard[2] Steele, one of the eight children of Richard[1] Steele and his wife, Rebecca Makemie (the emigrant to Mercersburg, Pa.), married Martha Makemie, daughter of a Breckinridge of Kentucky and —— Makemie, a niece of Bishop Francis Makemie.

The children of Richard[2] Steele (born 1748) and Martha Breckinridge Makemie were as follows:

1. Adam[3] Steele, born Sept. 4, 1770; married (1) Brooke Bealle, daughter of Lieut. Robert Bealle of the 8th Virginia (Continental Army) and his wife Elizabeth (Summers) Stephenson, a widow. He married (2) Hannah Graham at Fincastle, Botetourte Co., Va.
2. Richard[3] Steele, born Sept. 20, 1775; married Amelia Neville, daughter of General Joseph Neville, of Moorfield, Hardy Co., Va. (see his will in same county) and is ancestor of the Steeles, of Louisville and Jefferson Co., Ky.
3. Joseph[3] Steele, born July 7, 1779; married Miriam, daughter of George Boone.
4. Jane[3] Steele, born August 8, 1781; died *sine prole*.
5. John[3] Rowan Steele, born June 16, 1783; married Thurza Howard Mayo
6. Mary[3] Steele, born May 22, 1795; married John Sutherland.
7. Martha[3] Breckinridge Steele, born June 23, 1786; married (1) Robert Bealle, brother to Brooke; married (2) John Mendenhall, M. D.
8. William[3] Steele, born Jan. 1, 1788; married Mary Rowan, daughter of John Rowan and Anne Lytle.
9. Robert[3] Makemie Steele, born Sept. 14, 1790; married Ellen Joel Lewis, daughter of Major Howell Lewis (son of Fielding and Betty Washington Lewis).
10. Esther[3] Steele, born July 14, 1792; married (1) Wm. Kirkpatrick; (2) John Edwards, of Kentucky.
11. Nancy[3] Polk Steele, born Feb. 7, 1795; married John M. Talbot, M. D., of Louisville, Ky.

Mary[2] Steele born August 5, 1736, married October 27, 1761, William Lytle (General), son of John and Jane Lytle of Pennsylvania. He was born October 15, 1728 and died August 14, 1779. Mary Steele was daughter of Richard[1] Steele and Rebecca Makemie, Children were:

286

1. Jane Lytle, born 1762; married Robert Todd, of Kentucky.
2. Mary Lytle, born 1764; married Robert Blanchard.
3. John Lytle, born 1766; married Dorcas Waring, of Kentucky.
4. Sarah Lytle, born 1768; no further record.
5. William Lytle, born Sept. 1, 1770; married Feb. 28, 1798, Elizabeth Noel Stahl, of Philadelphia, ancestors of General Robert Todd Lytle and William Haines Lytle.
6. Anne Lytle, born 1772; married John Rowan (Judge, United States Senator, &c.) of Kentucky. It was at the home of Judge Rowan, "Federal Hill," Bardstown, Ky., that Stephen Collins Foster wrote "My Old Kentucky Home.'
7. Elizabeth Lytle died, *sine prole*.
8. Joseph Lytle died, *sine prole*.

IDELLE KEYES.

382 Newbury St., Boston, Mass.

MRS. MARTHA McKAMIE STEELE.

The McKamie family (or clan Mc-Kamie) was a power in the north of Scotland, and not unknown to heraldry. They were Presbyterians, consequently subjected to petty annoyances. It was a liberty-loving family, and not one to humble itself before any human power; especially so were the branches that emigrated to the north of Ireland and to the eastern shores of Maryland, thence into the valleys of Virginia, Pennsylvania and Kentucky. They loved an untrammeled, free and pure life, and were willing to sacrifice temporary comfort and undergo hardships and dangers for its possession; and it was no mean wage when won, and bore with the accomplishment distinction and honor. In this connection we mention Richard Steele[2], and his good wife, Martha McKamie Steele[2], and their kindred, who came to the "dark and bloody ground" Kentucky, when it was an unbroken wilderness, teeming with many dangers and much promise.

The McKamies and Steeles were of well-known and high families in the old and new worlds, born to comfort and cultivation, reading Latin and Greek with as much ease and pleasure as we of to-day read our magazines; having the ambition to be men of learning and of lands, a credit to the country and an influence and aid to the people among whom they lived. The Mc-Kamies and Steeles were of those Scotch-Irish Presbyterians who first set forth the idea of independence for this country and helped to carry the belief into effect and to a triumphal culmination.

"More human, more divine than we—
In truth, half human, half divine—
Is woman, when good stars agree
To temper with their beams benign
The hour of her nativity."

Surely all of the good stars were in accord and beamed on the nativity of Martha McKamie,[2] for her whole life glowed with an effulgence and radiance to those who knew her in life, and has not been dimmed even to this day with those in whose memory she lives still with a good and strengthening influence. Who is it that can say good deeds ever die, or that a beautiful life, no matter how long severed with this world, ever loses its imprint for good made to follow generation after generation? She was as pure as light, and as beautiful as morning.

In her day she was known far and near for her goodness, beauty of form, face and character. Martha McKamie was a daughter of Robert and Martha Breckinridge McKamie.[1] She was a niece of Rev. Francis McKamie, famous,

MRS. MARTHA McKAMIE STEELE.

Copy of portrait painted by Jouett about 1820, when this lady was seventy-two years of age, with scarcely a wrinkle showing on her beautiful face.

to Presbyterianism, and of Revolutionary fame. He saw much service during the Revolutionary War, fighting during the week with the soldiers whenever it was to be done, and preaching to them on Sundays. It was he who founded the school that is now known to the civilized world as "Princeton." There are several Presbyterian churches in the United States named for him, notably one in New York City, called the "Francis McKamie Memorial Church." Her mother's maiden name was Breckinridge, related to the Breckinridges of Maryland and Kentucky. From Martha Breckinridge down to the present generation there have been five Marthas in direct line of descent, viz.: Martha Breckinridge[1], Martha (McKamie) Steele[2], Martha Breckinridge (Steele) Mendenhall[3]. Martha (Mendenhall) Baxter[4], Martha Antoinette Baxter.[5]

Richard Steele[1] (who was a grandson of Sir Richard Steele, of Ireland) and his wife, Jane (McKamie) Steele[1], married in 1745, emigrated to this country from Londonderry county, Ireland, landing on the eastern shore of Maryland. He had a land grant of 1,000 acres, by the crown, for military services, which he located in the beautiful country near Mercersburg. Pa. He and his wife raised there a family of eight children.

Richard Steele[2], their oldest son, married Martha McKamie[2], the subject of this sketch, in 1769. A Steele Bible, printed in Edinburg in 1735, by Alexander Kinkaid, His Majesty's printer, was brought over by Richard Steele[1] and now is in the possession of our oldest sister. Unfortunately, a page of record was torn out by children at play, but on the remaining page is a record of the births and marriages of the children of Richard[2] and Martha McKamie Steele.*

The Steeles lived on their lands near Mercersburg until after the death of Richard Steele[1].

Richard Steele[2] saw service during the Revolutionary War, as also did many of his and his wife's kinsmen, notably Gen. John Steele. a member of Washington's family and field officer of the day at "Yorktown."† The country was in need of brave and tried men on the frontier, and selected and offered men large land grants in the western counties of Virginia (Kentucky being then a county of Virginia) to go and protect her borders from the ravages of the Indians and British.

Richard Steele[2] was one of the above. From Boone, his people had heard of the beautiful Ohio river and the incomparable Kentucky country. He submitted his plans to his wife, as he did all of his undertakings, and his good and brave wife answered and said she would go with him when and wherever his judgment led. The handful of brave souls was made up, consisting of the widowed mother—Jane Steele,[1] Richard Steele[2] and wife, Martha McKamie Steele[2]; his sisters, Mary Lytle[2] and Jane Hueston[2], and their husbands, and a number of other trusted ones. They travelled on flat-boats down the Ohio river, and were in constant dan-

* This list appears on page 51, May, 1904 number of The Register of the Kentucky Historical Society. Other interesting Steele history appears in the January, 1904 number of the Register.

† The American Historical Register, February, 1896, p. 644.

ger. Three children had then been born to Martha McKamie Steele and husband, the youngest at that time being Joseph, aged nine months. This was in the spring of the year 1780. They left good churches, schools, civilization, and good homes, and after a hazardous trip, landed on Corn Island at the falls of the Ohio. Here they were compelled to stay for a number of months on account of the Indians. The father of U. S. Senator John Rowan, who was the head of the Kentucky bar when legal giants pleaded before her tribunals, was one of the company of pioneers. Corn Island afterwards became a part of the Rowan estate. In time the pioneers moved over to the main land and built a stockade and fortress on Beargrass creek (present site of Louisville) and called it Spring Station, they being in reality the founders of Louisville. Each fall the Indians would come to Kentucky on annual hunting trips, and would cause much suffering and hardship to this little band of pioneers at Spring Station by their forages and attacks. One combined attack of extermination was planned by the Indians. A friendly Indian warned the pioneers. The children and women, among whom was Martha McKamie Steele, were sent for safety to Floyd's stockade, seven miles away. The fight began, as was anticipated, before daylight, and was continued during the day and into the night. The Indians were repulsed, but did not leave the vicinity immediately. During the fight and a sortie by the pioneers, their commander, Richard Steele[2], was shot above the heart and in the left hand. Col. Wm. Lytle, a brother-in-law, at midnight carried the news of the victory to the women and children, who were in anxiety waiting at "Floyd's." Martha McKamie Steele. hearing of her husband's terrible wounds and condition, could not and would not be persuaded of the almost certain death she would court by venturing to her husband's side and aid. She made them bring her a horse, mounted it with a nursing babe in her arms, and rode out into the night, in a wilderness, past the Indians, safely through the quickly opened and closed heavy gate at the stockade, and nursed her husband to life and health.

It was this brave band of pioneers who helped to maintain the western line of defense during the Revolutionary War, and the organized resistance to the British with their Canadian and Indian allies along the Kentucky shore. "This," says Col. J. Stoddard Johnson, in his admirable address on the "Life of Gen. George Rogers Clark," proved an important factor in the struggle. Had this line been broken by these incursions, as was that in Western Virginia in the early part of the French and Indian War, when the settlers were driven back to the Blue Ridge, Washington's eastern line would have been taken in the rear at a critical period of the war. Kentucky would have been relegated to the wilderness state, and the struggle for independence might have had a different termination.

"When peace came to the Atlantic States by the treaty which closed the war, it was long only nominal in the West. Indian hostilities, encouraged from the British posts, continued there for more than ten years later, from which the Kentucky pioneers suffered, her soldiers proving also the chief defense for the Northwestern frontier until the treaty of peace at Greenville. Ohio, in 1795. This is a feature of the history of the West in its contribution to the struggle for independence and the preservation, as well as extension, of our national boundaries, for which due credit has never been awarded."

Jane Steele[3] was born to Richard and Martha McKamie Steele while on Corn Island, and John Rowan Steele[3] was born to them while in the fort at Spring Station. Nancy Lytle. daughter of Mary (Steele) Lytle[2], was a child about nine years of age during the stockade life at Spring Station. She married United States Senator John Rowan, of "Federal Hill," Bardstown, and she often told her children and our mother of the Indians and of her fort life. About the year 1784, Richard Steele[2] and family moved to their plantation near Lexington, for in March, 1785, we find (Davidson's History) Richard Steele represented Mt. Zion church (Lexington) at the first "general meeting" for conference, five Presbyterian churches being represented. He was one of the organizers of the Presbytery of Transylvania, at Danville, on March 17, 1786, "and a member of this august and honorable body, the first Presbytery of Kentucky." A few years later, Richard Steele[2] was appointed a delegate to the General Assembly, which met in New York in May. He consulted his wife, Martha, about the trip, and its hardships and dangers. She heard, with silence and a strange respectfulness, the revelations of his plans, then answered that it was for, and in, a good cause, and that he would be blessed on his trip, and safely returned. She, by instinct or the grace of Heaven, had, in early girlhood, given herself to God, and during a life of saintly purity had the convictions and good that come from faith. She was a woman of superior motives and heart, as shown by her loyalty to God, to her husband and to duty. In those days when most needed there were many brave and good women of the same spirit as Martha McKamie Steele; we can not show too much reverence for them. Much has been said and written of the good wives and mothers who really were the moulders of greatness in times of emergency and need.

She had a love ineffable for strength and tenderness for her husband and children. She bade him good-bye, then came long days of waiting, with morning and evening family prayers for the safe return of the husband and father, then the bedtime "bairnies cuddle doon" song from the hopeful mother of Scotch descent, then many dreamless and wakeful nights until her husband's return.

Richard Steele was accompanied on this journey by Rev. Archibald Cameron, and the trip to and from New York was on horseback, through wilderness, across streams, over mountains, the entire journey consuming about two months in time. The danger from Indians and ambuscade were many, and the hardships of the trip were innumerable. It was promised by the "Steele folks" to let the countryside know of the safe arrival home of Richard Steele and the Rev. Archibald Cameron, by a certain signal from the huge dinner horn used by the strong-lunged negro cook to call the blacks from the fields to refreshment.

One day, in the latter part of June, "the delegates" were espied by the one on watch, coming over a distant hill. Immediately the signal was given, and taken up and reverberated by many horns from the different plantations for miles; then the inpouring of the good neighbors commenced and assembled to welcome the travelers home. The best cooks were commissioned, and the day and night turned into one of feasting and joy. In this journey of danger and hardship, and the abnegation of Martha McKamie Steele, was the Christian faith of Richard Steele and his good wife exemplified. She gazed upon him on his return with eyes that beamed with love ineffable, and a glow of pride which the gravity and well-bred poise could not disguise; but she was besides other things a good hostess. She and others were the women who enveloped this plain prosaic world of ours in an ideal atmosphere.

Six children were born to Richard[2] and Martha Steele while on their plantation, making in all eleven children, among whom was our good grandmother, Martha Breckinridge Steele (born June 23, 1786), and of whom we hope to write later, her history being a part of the early Kentucky life. She married John Mendenhall, M. D., surgeon in the War of 1812, on the 14th of February, 1826, and from this marriage came our good mother, Mrs. Martha Mendenhall Baxter. Martha McKamie's[2] sister, Jane McKamie, married Alexander Renick; another sister married Captain McAfee.

The flitting forms of dusky savages at twilight did not always disturb the dreams of Richard and Martha McKamie Steele, but hopes sprang to meet the light of dawn, and the days that followed were many days of peace and contentment, spent by them on their plantation in Fayette county, Ky., surrounded by kindred and friends. Any descendant of these good souls, in Kentucky or on the frontier, can safely say, "My name is McKamie, and my foot is upon its native heath."

At Frankfort, in the land office, can be found records of land grants to Richard Steele[2] (for military service), located in the counties of Jefferson, Oldham, Shelby, Henry, Carroll, Owen, Gallatin, Boone, Woodford, Franklin, and notably the home plantation near Lexington, consisting of 1,000 acres. Other land grants to him by Virginia were located near Charleston, West Virginia, and are on record at Richmond, Virginia.

Richard Steele[2] died at the age of sixty-two, and was buried at Bethel church, near Lexington. His will was probated in the Fayette county court in May, 1809. Martha McKamie Steele[2] after her husband's death, made her home with her oldest son, Adam Steele (Shelbyville), who was the organizer and president of the first bank in Shelby county. Her husband and children had her constant love, unlimited save by the bounds of mortal tenderness. At the age of seventy-two her portrait was painted by Jouett, her face at that age scarcely showing the ravages of time, being placid and benign. She died at 8 o'clock on the morning of September 22, 1822, at the home of Adam Steele. A daughter, Esther (Steele) Edwards, died the same day and date, at 8 o'clock in the evening, at the Edwards place, four miles east of Louisville, on the Ohio.

Martha McKamie Steele was a good woman, "who, with insight keen, had wrought a scheme of life, and measured well her womanhood; had spread before her feet a fine philosophy to guide her steps; had won a faith to which her life was brought in strict adjustment—brain and heart meanwhile working in conscious harmony and rhythm with the great scheme of God's great universe, on toward her being's end."

Standing by the mound that has long covered her earthly mold, the words come unbidden—

"Grateful for all her tender ministry
In life and death, I bring these leaves, entwined
With her own roses, dewy with my tears,
And lay them as a tribute of my love
Upon the grave that holds her sacred dust."

WM. EDWARDS BAXTER.
Frankfort, Ky., November 9, 1904.

Errata for sketch of life of Martha McKamie Steele in January number of Kentucky Historical Register.*

On page 70, 1st column, 1st line, Revolutionary should read Colonial, and 3d line, Revolutionary War should read Colonial Wars. Same page and same column, the date relating to marriage of Richard[1] Steele and Jane Mc-(Kamie) Steele, should read 1835 instead of 1845.

On page 71, 1st column, and in 5th line, the date 1780 should read 1778, and after the word stockade in 19th line the date 1780 should appear.

On page 74, 1st column, 2d line, morning should read evening, and September 22d should read September 18th; and same column 5th line, evening should read morning.

WM. EDWARDS BAXTER.

*For pp. 70, 71 & 74 see pp. 290, 291 & 294.

STEPHENSON—LEE—LOGAN—GILMORE FAMILY RECORDS.

Papers contributed by MR. L. O. STEPHENSON, Mayfield, Ky.

Somerset, Pulaski County, Ky.

My Grandfather, Silas Lee, born in Virginia about 1800, died in Pulaski County in 1885.

His wife was Miss Rhoda Holmes, born ——— in Belfast, Ireland, died at New Madrid, Missouri in 1850.

Their children were:

1—Silah B. Lee, Jr.—b. ——— at New Madrid, Mo.—d. near Fort Worth, Texas in 1880.
2—Frederick Lee—b. ——— at New Madrid, Mo.—d. ——— in Montana—
3—Rhodett Lee—(b. May 5th, 1836, at New Madrid, Mo.—d. May 2, 1890, at Union City, Tenn. m. ——— Lindsay Vardaman Stephenson—)
4—Amanda Lee—b. ——— at New Madrid, Mo.
5—Faunt Lee—b. ——— at New Madrid, Mo.

William Lee—b. ——— in Virginia
His children:
1—Lizzie Lee—b. ——— 1815 in Virginia, died ——— 1905, in Pulaski Co., Ky., aged 90 years.
2—Frankie Lee (Miss)—b. ——— 1818—d. ———.
3—Socrates Lee—b. 1825 in Virginia—d. ——— 1903, Pulaski Co.
4—Joseph Lee—b. ——— 1826 in Virginia—d. ——— Pulaski Co.
5—William Lee—b. ——— 1827—d. ——— in the Gold Rush at Fort Lorma (Laramie?) Kansas—
6—Martha Lee—b. ——— 1829—d. ——— 1879.

Socrates Lee's children (born in Pulaski Co., Ky.):
1—William R. Lee—born April 17, 1866.
2—Ezekell Tom Lee—born ——— 1868.
3—Dewitt Clinton Lee—b. July 10, 1870.

WILLIAM R. LEE'S BIBLE

William R. Lee's Bible, owned by William R. Lee
Somerset, Ky., Pulaski County, June 12, 1930

William R. Lee, son of Socrates Lee was born April 17—1866 was united in marriage to Addie Hudson, daughter of Daniel Hudson on March 22—1899, to this union was born 3 children—they are
1. Fitzhugh L. Lee, born April 24—1901.
2. Nancy Eiien Lee, born July 4—1902.
3. Walter M. Lee, born Sept. 24—1904.

His wife born Sept. 30—1876, Pulaski County, Somerset, Ky.

Ezekiel Thomas Lee is the son of Socrates E. Lee, born Feb. 14—1868, in Pulaski County, Ky. His wife Miss Addie L. Cowan, who was born Nov. 11—1876. She is the daughter of George S. Cowan and Elizabeth.

Ezekiel Thomas Lee, Somerset, Ky., above mentioned gave this information to Mr. Stephenson.

Copied from the Dewit-Clinton Lee Bible.

Dewitt Clinton Lee, b. July 10—1870 in Pulaski County, Ky. m. Miss Sue Will ——Cowin in 1899, at Somerset, Ky., to them was born one child, Ata Leighton Lee, born Jan. 10—1901.

William R. Lee
Ezekiel Thomas Lee
Dewit Clinton Lee
    are brothers.

                Somerset, Pulaski County, Kentucky—

The Schedule and affidavit of *James Lee*, an applicant for a pension verified by his oath, signed and ordered to be recorded, and same follows in these words, towit:—

State of Kentucky, 12 Judicial District, Set.—

On the second day of November A. D. 1820, in open court before the Circuit Court for the County of Pulaski, in the State and District aforesaid, the said court being a court of record established by Act of Assembly and proceeding according to the course of Common Law, personally appeared *James Lee, a pensioner* who produced his certificate dated the *14th day of December, 1819,* and who being duly and legally sworn declared upon his oath that on the 7th day of June A. D. 1777 he enlisted in the regular service of the United States in the Revolutionary War for & during the term of three years in the company of Strother Jones, in the regiment commanded by Colonel Grason, and in the Brigade of General Charles Scott being a part of the Virginia Line in the Continental establishment, he states that he continued in the regular service of the United States for the said term of three years and received his discharge at Richmond in the State of Virginia, signed by Colonel Nathaniel Gist, which discharge, on his way home, he lost, or got it destroyed, he states that he is 67 years of age & that he is unable to Labour, he states that he is a tiller of the ground, and the said James Lee upon his oath aforesaid further states that he was a resident citizen of the United States on the 18th day of March A. D. 1818, and that he was not since that time, by gift, sale or otherwise disposed of his property or any part thereof with intent thereby to diminish it so as to bring himself within the provisions of the Act of Congress entitled an Act to provide for certain persons engaged in the land and naval service of the United States in the Revolutionary War passed on the 18th day of March, 1818, and that he has not nor has any person in trust for him any property or securities, contracts or debts due to him nor has he any income other than what is contained in the Schedule below signed by him, towit:—

2 cowes & 2 calves of the value of $20.00

9 hogs of the value of $15.00

12 geese of the value of $6.00

12 sheep of the value of $12.00

$6.00 worth of pot metal, nothing owing to him, and owes about $35.00.

He states that he has eleven children being viz.:

William, about 23 years of age lives apart to himself;

Lewis, about 21 years of age lives apart to himself;

Betsy about 19 years old, married and lives apart to herself;

Willis Green about 15 years old lives with his father and able to support himself;

Sally about 25 years old lives with him and able to support herself;

John about 12 years old lives with his father and not able to support himself;

Charles about 8 years old, lives with his father, not able to support himself;

Bethel, about 6 years of age lives with his father not able to support himself;

Polly, about 5 years of age lives with her father, unable to support herself;

Drewry, about 3 years of age lives with his father not able to support himself;

Anny, about 2 years of age lives with her father and unable to support herself;

Signed—James Lee—

Sworn to & subscribed in open Court before me, John L. Bridges a Circuit Judge in and for the Commonwealth of Ky., & 12th Judicial District and presiding Judge of the Pulaski Circuit Court, given under my hand this 2nd day of November, 1820. Signed—John L. Bridges.

And Daniel Smith an acquaintance of the said James Lee states upon his oath that he believes the schedule of the said James Lee to be correct, that he is a very poor man, and William Fox made oath that he believes the said James Lee to be a man of fair character, and the court upon considering the affidavit and schedule of the said James Lee, and the evidence of Daniel Smith and William Fox aforesaid is of opinion that the said schedule and statements of the said James Lee are true and correct. Wherefore the same with the opinion of the Court expressed is ordered to be certified to the Secretary of War of the United States.   Signed—John L. Bridges.

State of Kentucky
    County of Pulaski, Sct.—

I, C. I. Ross, Clerk of the Pulaski Circuit Court, and custodian of its records, do hereby certify that the foregoing is a true correct and exact copy of an entry in Order Book No. 5, pages 69, 70 and 71, of the records of said Court; I do further certify that the said Pulaski Circuit Court is now embraced in the 28th Judicial District of the Commonwealth of Kentucky, and presided over by Honorable R. C. Tarter, Somerset, Kentucky.

In testimony whereof, I have hereunto subscribed by name and affixed my official Seal, in the City of Somerset, Pulaski County, Ky., this June 12th, 1930—
            Signed—C. I. Ross, Clerk Pulaski Circuit Court, Ky.
            By—C. Hamilton, Deputy Circuit Clerk.

The above affidavit is a copy of one contributed to the Historical Society by Mr. L. O. Stephenson, Mayfield, Ky., in connection with Stephenson, Lee, and other genealogical material which he has generously furnished with permission to copy, Aug. 7, 1930.

Somerset, Kentucky—

This day Silas Lee appeared before me the undersigned Justice of the Peace for Pulaski County, Ky., and made oath that he brought a negro Girl from Virginia by the name of Mary & he purchased said Girl for his own use. Sworn to before me this the 27th day of March, 1825.
                        Signed—Ralph Williams—J. P.

Kentucky, Pulaski County, Sct.—

I William Fox, Clerk of the County Court Holder for the County aforesaid do hereby certify that the within certificate from Ralph William Esq. to Silas Lee was produced to me in my office on the 4th day of April 1825 and the same hath been duly recorded in my office.
                        Attest—Will Fox, Co. Clerk.

A Copy—Attest—Orie P. Hamilton,
        Clerk Pulaski County Court, Kentucky.

Dewey Lee—Pltf.
    against
George Smith & Philip A. Sublette—Defts.
Infase (No date Given)

On the motion of the Plaintiff, by his Attorney, and the said plaintiff having made oath as the law directs. It is ordered by the Court, that the Sheriff take bail on the Defendant Smith, in the sum of Thirty pounds—

State of Kentucky,
County of Pulaski, Sct.—

I, C. I. Ross, Clerk of Pulaski Circuit Court, and as such custodian of its records, do hereby certify that the above is a true, correct and exact copy of an entry that appears on Page 184 of an un-numbered Order Book of said Court, under date of June 27th, 1803, of the records of said Court. I do further certify that said Court is now embraced in the 28th Judicial District, now presided over by Honorable R. C. Tarter, of Somerset, Kentucky.

In Testimony whereof, I have hereunto subscribed my name and set my Official Seal, in Somerset, Pulaski County, Kentucky, on this 12th, day of June, 1930.

        Signed—C. I. Ross,
         Clerk Pulaski Circuit Court, Kentucky.
        By C. Hamilton—D. C. C. C.
              Aug. 7—1930

JAMES LEE—REVOLUTIONARY SOLDIER

Copy of letter from *Bureau of Pensions*, Washington, D. C. to L. O. Stephenson, Mayfield, Ky.

                     Sept. 6, 1930.

Mr. L. O. Stephenson,
 Mayfield, Ky.,
Dear Sir:

You are advised that it appears from the papers in the Revolutionary War pension claim R. 6250, that *James Lee* enlisted in Fauquier County, Virginia, June 7, 1777, and was a private in Captain Strother Jones' Company, Colonel Grayson's Regiment and was discharged in Richmond, Virginia, by Colonel Nathaniel Gist, having served three years. There is no specific date of discharge given. He stated that his discharge was lost.

He was allowed pension on his application executed October 30, 1818, at which time he was living in Pulaski County, Kentucky, and stated that he was aged about fifty-seven years.

In 1821, he stated that he was sixty-seven years of age.

The soldier married in 1790 or 1791 in Madison County, Kentucky, Keziah Mobeley or Mobely. She was about forty-five years of age in 1821.

He died December 25, 1836, in Pulaski County, Kentucky, and she died April 12, 1844, in said Pulaski County.

They had eleven children—William, Lewis, Elizabeth married Daniel

Smith, Willis or Willis Green, Benjamin, John, Charles B. or Charles Bethal, James B., Mary who married John Godby or Gadby, Drury, Anne or Anna who married Gabriel Godby or Gadby.

Very truly yours,
E. W. Morgan
Acting Commissioner

WAR DEPARTMENT
The Adjutant General's Office.
Washington

August 19—1930

In Reply
Refer to ORD.
FJM:isi. ·
Respectfully returned to
L. O. Stephenson,
    212 North 7th Street,
        Mayfield, Kentucky.

James Lee served in the Revolutionary War as private, Captain Heabeard Smallwood's Company, Colonel William Grayson's Regiment, Continental Troops.

His name first appears on the company muster roll for July, 1777, which roll does not show the date of enlistment. The company payroll to September 1-1777 shows commencement of pay April 6-1777, and time of service 4 months and 25 days. On some later rolls he is shown to have enlisted June 7-1777 for three years; was transferred about May, 1778, to Captain Strother Jones' Company same regiment. This regiment was consolidated with Colonel Gist's Regiment, Continental Troops about April-1779, and his name last appears on the muster roll of Captain Strother Jones' Company of that regiment for November-1779.

The collection of Revolutionary War records in this office is far from complete, and it is suggested as a possibility that additional information may be obtained from the Librarian, Virginia State Library, Richmond, or the Commissioner of Pensions, Washington, D. C.

Harvey W. Miller
Colonel A. G. D.,
Acting the Adjutant General.
by FJM

Given by Mr. L. O. Stephenson, Mayfield, Ky.
Copied by the Kentucky Historical Society, Aug. 7—1930.

Logan Record

Mrs. Malinda Logan died August 1832 and John Logan died March 1846, Having the following named children:

Mary Logan m. John Haydon
David Stephenson Logan m.
James B. Logan m.
Elizabeth Logan m. A. T. Larel
William C. Logan m.
Thomas Logan m.
Margaret A. Logan m.

James B. Logan the second son of John and Malinda Logan was b. in Lincoln County, August 11—1832, on Logans Creek. He moved to Jessamine County on 220 Acres called "Sunny Side", on the banks of Hickmans Creek. He married May 17—1849, Lucy, the daughter of Maria (Tapp) Arnold and David Arnold. Their children are:

Anna M. Arnold m. John G. Masters
William A. Arnold m.
John L. Arnold m.
Mary K. Arnold m. John Bronaugh
Randie E. Arnold

John Logan was lieut. in Capt. Owsley's Company of Lincoln County in the War of 1812 and took part in the battle of New Orleans.

Ephraim Pennington Dawes—born at Walnut Flat, Lincoln Co., Ky. 1853—
Married *Maggie J. Crawford,* in Fulton County, Kentucky in 1892.
Their children were:
1—John Andrew Dawes—b. in Fulton Co., Ky.—1893
2—Frances Mariah Dawes—b. in Fulton Co., Ky.—1895
3—James Stephenson Dawes—b. in Fulton Co., Ky.—1897
4—Ephraim Pennington Dawes, Jr.—b. in Fulton Co., Ky.—1899.

Marriages—

John Andrew Dawes c. Rubena Atkinson, of Lynn Grove, Ky., in 1923—
Frances Mariah Dawes m. N. E. Thomas, of Wingo, Ky., in 1923—
James Stephenson Dawes m. Leola Bailey of Benton, Ky., in 1928—
Ephraim Pennington Dawes, Jr. m. Lola Anderson, of Paducah, Kentucky, in 1925.

(Copy of letter from Robert Gilmore, an Union Soldier, to his "wife and friends", dated from Chattanooga, Tenn., Sept. 24, 1863. The letter was loaned to the Historical Society, with permission to copy, by Mr. L. O. Stephenson, of Mayfield, Kentucky). (Nov. 11, 1930)

Chatanooga, Ten.
September 24—1863

Dear wife & Friends—

I am well & harta at this time & I hope & I hope when these fiew lines come to hand tha may find you and all the rest of the friends in Good helth.

wea took Chatanooga on the 9 instant with the Loss of only one man the rebels Retreated back towords rome Jorga. wea foload thame a bout 12 miles to Lees & Gordens mile (mill?) on the Chickmauga Creek in Georgia & thair Brag took a stand Hea was large rean forgt? From Lee & Johnston the Fite commenct on frida the 18 & ended on Sunday the 20th one of the most terific late Batels of the war our los is vera heva in ciled wounted & mising after 3 days hard fitinG wea was compelled to fol back on ChatnooGa Brags forces was 10050 thousand our strength was 75000 I past thrue the hcal fite without a cratch my close was Hat & torn buy bulits my hide not tuched we air in ChatnooGa to day hard at work fortifian the place the rebels cloas buy us in site.

The re(b) els had the AdvantaGe of us tha the woods to Shelter thame & wea the open land to fite in but now we will Whip thame wors then tha Ever was whipt sence the Wor beGun for we air in a fortifide place i lost one man ciled that i no Silas wrainwater his father lives cloas to horigon (?) I have several a mison i hop ant ciled ner cap (t) tered our loss is between 10 & 15 000 thousand the rebel loss is reported 20 000.

I sent you a Present the last leter in my likeness tak out the picter in the box you will find the present.

Give my respects to all of my friends i must close for this time tell uncal Jon trimbell tomy is well & harta sam & wess Tartar air both well you shil her from mea a Gain soon ef I live rite soon the bois is Generla well.

Robert Gilmore to Elizabeth E. Gilmore friends our loss in ciled & wounded & missing is 150 no more at present.

WILL OF JAMES GILMORE, PULASKI CO., KY.

In the name of God, Amen, I, James Gilmore of the county of Pulaski and State of Kentucky, being weak and feeble of body but of sound mind and memory do make ordain and publish this as my last Will and Testament—hereby revoking all former Wills made by me. That is to say—

I will that all my just debts be paid out of the proceeds of the debts owing to me and my loose property which loose property consists of all my Horses, Cattle, Hogs and other live stock and perishable property not herein after bequeathed and the debts owing to me after paying my debts out of the same, I will and bequeath it to James Gilmore, son of Robert Gilmore, Mary Martha Gilmore daughter of Jefferson Gilmore, Martha Lee, James G. Lee and

Pauline Lee, children of David & Ann Lee to be equally divided between them.

I will devise and bequeath to my sister Patsy Carson, to he absolutely without any condition, all my Interest in a negro boy slave named Shelton, and my waggon and Oxen and all my farming tools and utensils to her for her lifetime and then go to Cyrenius Gilmore hereinafter named.

I will and devise my home plantation consisting of all the 20 acre Tract Patented in my father's name which I have let my brother Jefferson Gilmore have and a small Tract of thirty odd acres also Patented in my Father's name and both said tracts are Deeded to me by the heirs of my Father. The said thirty odd acres Tract and balance of the 200 acre tract ly together and form my home place, which I will and devise to my Sister Patsy Carson for and during her lifetime, then to go to my nephew Cyrenius Gilmore during his natural life with the remainder in fee to the heirs of his body if he should have any if he should have none then the remainder in fee is hereby devised to Anderson Smith Gilmore, Robert Gilmore and James Gilmore, children of my brother John Gilmore, James Gilmore Son of my brother Robt. Gilmore, Mary Martha Gilmore daughter of my brother Jeeffrson Gilmore, Martha Lee, James G. Lee and Pauline Lee, children of David Lee and my Sister Ann Lee, to be equally divided among them to them and their heirs or assigns forever.

I nominate and appoint Anderson Gilmore my Executor of this my last will and testament.

In testimony whereof I hereunto affix my name and seal at home in Pulaski County this 22nd day of September, A. D. 1841.

Signed sealed & ack.   (Signed) James Gilmore
as the last will and Testament   (Seal)
James Gilmore and witnessed in
his presence By
    A. J. James
    Samuel Evans

                                      A Copy—
                                      Teste—A. Williams, D. C.
                                         for Will Fox—C. P. C.

Agreement between William M. Weaver and W. H. Logan of one part and W. R. Lee, Socrates E. Lee, Fountain Gossett, Bourn G. Ford, John S. Ford and Shelby Barker of Wayne County, Kentucky—

We the undersigned William M. Weaver, and W. H. Logan of the one part, and W. R. Lee, Socrates E. Lee, Fountain Gossett, Bourn G. Ford, John S. Ford and Shelby Barker (of Wayne) of the other part, All of the County of Pulaski and State of Ky. do hereby agree to form a partnership for the purpose of obtaining Gold at the California mines on the following terms, Towit—W. M. Weaver and W. H. Logan agree on their part to furnish four hundred dollars in money or in a Suitable Waggon and oxen for the trip; that is Weaver two hundred & Logan two hundred in Due time for the first trains from this to California. And the second named party W. R. Lee, S. E. Lee, F. Gossett, J. S. Ford, Bourne G. Ford and S. Baker agree on their part to furnish all other necessaries for the outfit covering their clothing the whole time engaged thare in business and proper tools & impliments for obtaining gold from the mines and one months provisions after reaching the mines; keeping a proper account of the Items and amts. so expended, So as to compair with Weavers & Logans four hundred dollars vested.

They also bind themselves to prosecute the trip to the mines, and form themselves into a common bo*dd*y, and make a fair & reasonable trial to obtain Gold or money as they best can making a Common and equal interest of the whole Joint opperation, so as to make equal proffets dividing luck & labor, and make a true return to Weaver & Logan of the whole matter.

Now whereas it is customary for hands to give half their earnings or profits for their transportation to the mines we do seveally and jointly bind ourselves to give Weaver and Logan a part of our profits in proportion to the amt. necessary for the outfit and expenses before alluded to compared to Weavers & Logans $400, as the whole is worth half so half expense is worth a fourth all necessary expense deducted before division.

It is understood there is no responsibility for unavoidable accidents.

Given under our hands this 21st day of Feb. 1850.

Test—   (Signed) W. M. Weaver
  Robert Gilmore   W. H. Logan
  J. M. Logan   W. R. Lee
                                            S. E. Lee
                                            Fountain Gossett
                                            Bourn G. Ford
                                            J. S. Ford
                                            Shelby Barker

(Letter from Socrates E. Lee to his Mother and Sisters.)

Eldorado Co. California
Aprile the 23, 1851

Dear Mother & Sisters—

I again take my pen in hand to drop you a few lines altho I have no nuse of importance.

Times hear at this time is very dull and I cannot tell whether they will

Change for the better or not we have been working hard for the last month and have not more than cleaned our teeth the water has been so high we hope when the water gets down that we can do better.

We are all in good health at this time California seems to agree with me first rate. I am as hevy this Spring as I ever was in the winter at home my wate the last time I waid was 160. Tel Mrs. Gossett that fountain is harty & lively. I want you all to enjoy yourselves the best you can. do not work out if you want anything Sell anything about the place no matter what.

I have Staid hear this long I have Stood this country pretty well and I think it expedient to try it till fall and then I will be a Striking for home. you needs not think Strange if you do not get no more letters from me for I seldom get a Chance to mail them and when they are started thare is no Sirtenty in their going. as for gold hear it is very plenty but it is very hard it Seames for me to get much at a time though I will keep in Spirits as long as I can have my helth and I have hopes that my helth will continue good I cannot it Seames get a letter from home I would be verry glad to hear from you all but I hope that you are as well as if I was with you.

Give my respects to all my friends. I have no more to write at present of importance

But Remain Yours

(Signed) S. E. Lee

L. O. Stephenson's ancestors' war record:

Great, great grandfather;

James Lee, born in Richmond, Virginia 1752. Served through the Revolutionary War.

Great Uncle Thomas Logan Stephenson, born in Harrodsburg, Ky., served through the War of 1812-1813.

My uncles and cousins served through the Civil War as Confederate soldiers.

My brother, Dr. Samuel Logan Stephenson of Corinth, Miss. served through the Spanish War and the British Boer War in the company of the Imperial Light Calvary under Lord Kitchner. Also served through the World War as Lieutenant and Captain on the medical staff.

GILMOORE FAMILY

Family record presented to Mr. L. O. Stephenson of Mayfield, Kentucky, by DeWitt Clinton Lee, of Fishing Creek, Pulaski Co., Kentucky, Nov. 28, 1930.

Many of the persons here recorded are buried in the old Gilmoore family burying-ground, in Pulaski County.

Martha Gilmour was Bornd Oct. 19, 1782
John Gilmoore was Bornd Nov. 25th, 1784
Robt. Gilmoore was Bornd Jan. the 10, 1787

Anny Gilmoore was Bornd June the 13, 1789
James Gilmoore was Bornd Jan. 24, 1792
William Gilmoore was Bornd Jan. the 13th, 1794
David Gilmoore was Bornd May 12, 1796.
Winston Gilmoore was Bornd Jan. the 13th, 1798
Jefferson Gilmoore was Bornd Jan. the 3 (?) 1800
Samuel Gilmoore was Bornd April 10, 1802

Copied from the Bible owned by Stevie Logan Stephenson, 719—24th St., Louisville, Ky., through the courtesy of Mr. L. O. Stephenson, Mayfield, Ky. Bible published by the National Publishing Co., Ziegler & McCurdy, 1870.

Opposite title page in pencil is written "Presented by Bettie Stephenson, her father's Bible."

Marriages.

Thomas D. Hill & Lucy Ann Bingaman was married August the 17th, 1837.
T. D. Hill and Eliza Shipley was married January the 14—1858.
Samuel D. Pollock and Mary Ann Hill was married May the 26th, 1864.
Thomas J. Tucker and Martha Susan Hill was married May the 25th, 187—
 (last number not legible—scratched out—in original).
Wm. P. Stephenson and Bettie K. Hill was married June the 11th, 1872.
 (above all in same handwriting)
Samuel Henry Hill and Mary Prudence Hall was married in Bowling Green, Ky. Sept. 24th, 1874.
Sue Tucker and A. Steinbergen married Dec. 20—1883.
Logan Stephenson and Mary Gaines, Oct. 4—1916.

Births.

Thomas D. Hill was born Dec. 21st, 1812.
Lucy Ann Hill was born Dec. 27th, 1813.
Eliza Shipley was born July the 2nd, 1813.
Rebecca Jane Hill was born May the 14th, 1838.
Samuel Henry Hill was born Aug. the 10th, 1840.
Mary Ann Hill was born Nov. the 16th, 1842.
Margaret C. Hill was born Jan. the 21st, 1846.
Martha Susan Hill was born March 5th, 1849.
Wm. Thomas Hill was born March the 5th, 1849.
Permelia H. Hill was born Jan. the 10th, 1851.
Bettie K. Hill was born Dec. the 28th, 1852.
 (above all in same handwriting)

STEVIE LOGAN STEPHENSON BIBLE

Stella A. Stephenson was born Mar. 17th, 1873.
Mary E. Stephenson was born Nov. 10th, 1874.

James W. Stephenson was born June 1st, 1877.
William T. Stephenson was born June 16th, 1882.
Mamie Steinbergen, born July 2, 1885.
Lee Steinbergen, born Dec. 31, 1888.
Stevy L. Stephenson was born Feb. 29th, 1889.
Stuart Hill Stephenson born Dec. 11, 1917.
Wm. Gaines Stephenson born Feb. 28, 1920.
Martha Elizabeth Stephenson born Feb. 11, 1922.
Marion Virginia Stephenson born Dec. 31, 1924.

Deaths.

Lucy Ann Hill died Jan. 1st, 1857, aged 43 years and three days.
Mary Ann Pollock departed this life January 30th, 1867, æ 24 years, 2 months, and 14 days.
Rebecca Jane Hill departed this life July 21, 1871, æ 32 years.
Maggie C. Hill died October the 1st, 1874, aged 28 years, 8 months, and 9 days.
(above all in same handwriting)
Mary Prudence Hill wife of Samuel Henry Hill departed this life in Bowling Green, Ky., April 2nd, 1887. Aged 36 years, 8 months and 29 days.
Eliza Hill (wife of T. D. Hill) died July 1, 1892.
T. D. Hill died March 20, 1893.
Stella Stephenson died July the 9th, '88.
Bettie Hill Stephenson died April 17, 1922.
W. P. Stephenson died January 28, 1923.
Marion Virginia Stephenson, Oct 27, 1925.

* * *

Stevie Logan Stephenson, son of William Pitts Stephenson, born February 29, 1888, in Campbellsville, Ky., Taylor Co.
His wife Miss Mary Martha Gaines, born Aug. 3, 1898, Fairfield, Ky., Spencer County. On June 20, 1930 living 719 24th St., Louisville, Ky.

Children

Stuart Hill Stephenson, born Dec. 11, 1917.
William Gaines Stephenson born Feb. 28, 1920.
Martha Elizabeth Stephenson born Feb. 11, 1922.
Marion Virginia Stephenson born Dec. 3, 1924, died Oct. 27, 1925.

Mrs. Sue Haydon,   Shelbyville, Ky.
Harrodsburg, Ky.   Dec. 6—1927.

Dear Cousin "Sudie":

I am addressing you as I used to hear my dear old Daddy call you "Sudie". I wrote you some seven years ago about our Stephenson line of ancestry and in looking over some files, I came across your letter in answer to my inquiry.

In it you state that your grandfather, David Stephenson's mother was Malinda Logan. Do you know whether or not his father's name was Thomas Stephenson and if this Thomas Married Malinda Logan?

If that is a fact, then your grandfather David and my great-great grandmother, Isabelle Stevenson (or Steph) were brother and sister, as Isabelle married in Stanford 1784, Moses Hall. Their oldest child's name was Elizabeth Logan Hall, and one son, Benjamin Logan Hall.

He came to Shelby County about 1792.

Lincoln County, Ky.
D. of Thomas
Moses Hall m. Sept. 4—1784, Isabelle Stevenson, b   1765
   b. Apr. 24—1756   d. Apr. 24—1841
   d. Sept. 4—1829

Children

1. Elizabeth Logan Hall, b. 1786—m. 1815 Col. Mark Hardin.
2. Moses Hall, Jr. b. 1788—m. 1809 Elizabeth Page Crawford.
3. John Hall, b. 1791—m. 1815 Sallie Lane Knight.
4. Woodford Hall, b. 1793—never married d. 1875.
5. Maria Isabella Hall, b.   —d. at 25 years of age.
6. David Stevenson Hall b.   1799 m. Juliet Owen.
7. Allen Hall, b. 1795—m. Eliza Craig.
8. Benjamin Logan Hall, b. 1806 m. 1831 Evelyn Pickerill.

Since writing you I have found this article:

"One of the pioneers of Kentucky was David Logan, b. and reared in Va. and accompanied his uncle, Benjamin Logan, on his second visit to Kentucky.

He settled in Lincoln County and took part in building Logan Fort. David Logan m. Mary Perry of Va., they had seven children:

1. Hugh Logan
2. Betsy Logan m. Ruben Emerson
3. Polly Logan m. James Forsythe
4. Margaret Logan m. Samuel Robinson
5. John Logan
6. David Logan
7. George Logan

John Logan 5th child was born in Lincoln County, May 4—1790, m. Malinda Stephenson d. of David Stephenson & Mary Logan & grand niece of Benjamin Logan.

(David Stephenson m. Mary Logan)

I find in Lincoln County Records that:
David Stephenson m. April 9——1791—d. of Thomas & Elizabeth Logan
Mathew Logan m. 1790—Dicey Thurmond
David Logan m. 1790—Nancy Thurmond
Moses Hall m. Sept. 4-1784—Isabelle Stevenson d. of Thomas Stevenson
Joan Stephenson m. 1787, d. of Thomas Stevenson—Robert Reburn.

 I wonder if you know of any one to whom I might write for further information about the Stephensons and Logans of Lincoln County? Are there any Bible Records or graveyards which might give us a clew? If David Stephenson's children still live on the old homestead there would likely be an old graveyard on the place.

L. O. STEPHENSON.

STEPHENSON FAMILY RECORDS
Contributed by L. O. Stephenson, Mayfield, Ky.

STEPHENSON BIBLE

(This copy of the John Franklin Stephenson Bible, owned by Mrs. Sallie Stephenson of Stanford, Ky., Route 1, presented to the Kentucky Historical Society by Mr. L. O. Stephenson, Mayfield, Ky.)

Rebecca McRoberts was born December 25-1783, died November 11-1862. Age 78 years, 10 months, 16 days.

Charles C. McRoberts was born ——— 17, died May 30-1833

Margaret Stephenson died July 29-1897, Age 72 years, 5 months, 20 days.

Will Tom Stephenson died November 9-1901. Age 80 years, 8 months, 6 days.

Alexander Stephenson, died February 9-1901, Age 48 years, 5 days.

John F. Stephenson, died September 13-1926, Age 81 years, 1 month, 1 day.

William T. Stephenson and Margaret McRoberts were married October 3-1844.

John F. Stephenson and Sallie Martin were married September 8-1874.

J. Alexander Stephenson and Sallie Tanner were married September 4-1885.

William Thomas Stephenson was born March 3-1821.

Margaret Taylor McRoberts was born February 9-1825.

John Franklin Stephenson was born August 12-1845.

Charlie McRoberts Stephenson was born September 7-1847.

Charlie McRoberts Stephenson, died Dec. 9-1848, Age 1 year, 3 months, 10 days.

Anna V. Stephenson died August 28-1865, Age 7 years, 10 months, 10 days.

Rebecca W. Stephenson died October 19-1879, Age 23 years, 1 day.

Sallie Stephenson wife of J. A. Stephenson died September 7-1885, Age 28 years.

Dr. Ephriam Thomas Stephenson died February 22-1890, Stanford, Age 35 years, 8 months.

George Lindsey Stephenson was born January 24-1863.

Lindsey Stephenson Sr. was born March 22-1792, died December 10-1870, Age 77 years, 10 months, 18 days.

Willie Stephenson was born Sept. 4-1885, son of J. A. and Sallie Stephenson.

Mary G. Stephenson, died September 8-1885, daughter of John and Sallie Stephenson, Age 4 years.

William Lincoln Stephenson was born September 25-1849, died Oct. 26-1878.

Alexander Stephenson was born February 4-1852.

Dr. Ephriam Stephenson was born June 15-1854.

Rebecca White and Anna Vardiman Stephenson were born October 18-1856 (twins).

Dr. William Lincoln Stephenson died November 4-1879, Age 30 years, 1 month, 8 days.

Margaret Lincoln Stephenson born September 6-1877.

Rebecca McRoberts Stephenson born October 14-1879.

BIBLE OWNED BY MRS. DUDLEY HOLMES, BETWEEN CRAB ORCHARD AND STANFORD.

MARRIAGES.

Morgan Vardeman and Mary Trousdale were married Jan. 24-1792.

Elizabeth married Ephriam Pennington Sept. 20-1812.

Ann married Lindsay Stephenson Sept. 12-1815.

Jane married P. W. Stephenson May 10-1820.

Jeremiah married Polly Coffee March 11-1828.

Polly married Garland Smith Aug. 2-1826; also married William Farris, Oct. 13-1838.

Patsy married John Welch Feb. 23-1843.

Eliza Emily married Samuel Holmes Sept. 2-1840.

BIRTHS.

Elizabeth Vardeman born Nov. 10-1792, died Mar. 17-1845.

Ann Vardeman born Dec. 10-1794, died Oct. 14-1830.

Jeremiah Vardeman born May 10-1797, died Mar. 28-1854.

John T. Vardeman born Mar. 13-1800.

Jane Vardeman born April 23-1802.

Polly Vardeman born Sept. 18-1805, died June 17-1845.

William Vardeman born June 9-1807, died July 12-1846.

Martha Vardeman born April 14-1810, died Apr. 21-1852.

Eliza Emily Vardeman born Oct. 10-1812, died Jan. 28-1878.

Lindsay Vardeman Stephenson born Oct. 14-1830 (Grandson of Ann.)

Morgan Vardeman born Dec. 16-1766.

Mary Vardeman born April 1-1721.

Jane Clemons, 1804 (the adopted daughter also married Ephriam Pennington May 19-1846).

John S. Higgins born Dec. 29-1789 also married E. L. Pennington Jan. 13-1840.

John Welch born Mar. 8-1775.

DEATHS.

Morgan Vardeman died July 30-1847.

Mary Vardeman died Oct. 1-1844.

Jane Clemons Pennington died Jan. 6-1883.
Eliza Emily Holmes died Jan. 28-1878.
Samuel Holmes born Aug. 26-1814, died Aug. 4-1872.
Dudley V. Holmes born Aug. 29-1845, died Jan. 22-1926.
John W. Holmes born Jan. 30-1848, died Jan. 11-1923.
Samuel M. Holmes born July 21-1851, died Dec. 9-1925.

FAMILY RECORD.

Morgan Vardeman grandchildren.
Elizabeth Pennington children
Polly born 16, Sept. 1813,
Kity Ann born May 6-1815,
E. Lewis b. July 17-1817,
Elizabeth Vardeman born Feb. 15-1820, died April 25-1838,
Lindsay Ephrum born March 18-1822, died July 14-1828,
Tom M. born Aug. 10-1824,
Eph. R. born April 14-1827,
Eph. D. born Feb. 16-1831,
Saley E. born Nov. 6-1835.
Annie Vardeman Stephenson children:
1. Mary Edith born Dec. 17-1816,
2. Dave Morgan born April 5-1819,
3. William Thomas Stephenson born March 3-1821,
4. James Alexander Stephenson born 1822—decd. 1908,
5. Malindy Jane Oct. 2nd-1825,
6. Patsy Ann b. — d. July 15-1824,
7. Dr. Samuel Logan Stephenson 1826,
8. Lindsay Vardeman born Oct. 14-1830, died July 24-1890.
Jane Stephenson's children:
1. George Morgan b. Aug. 13-1824,
2. Mary Stephenson born Nov. 13-1826,
3. Robert Stephenson born July 24-1828,
4. Martha Stephenson born March 16-1830,
5. Elizabeth Jane Stephenson born Feb. 26-1833.

TOMBSTONE INSCRIPTIONS FROM STEPHENSON-VARDEMAN-HOLMES BURYING GROUNDS ON CEDAR CREEK 3½ MILES FROM CRAB ORCHARD, LINCOLN COUNTY, KY.

Hannah B. Stephenson
Sept. 20-1841
Dec. 22-1865

Eliza E. Stephenson
Born Oct. 15-1839
Died May 16-1862

Dave Morgan Stephenson
Born April 5-1819
Died April 24-1863

Our Father Lindsay Stephenson
Born Mar. 25-1792
Died Feb. 10-1870

Willie F. son of T. J. & M. E. Christerson
Born Oct. 29-1872
Died Mar. 29-1873

Morgan Vardeman
Born Dec. 16-1767
Died July 30-1847

William Vardeman
Born June 9-1807
Died July 12-1846

Polly Vardeman
Born April 25-1808

Married to Jeremiah Vardeman
March 12-1829
Died May 30-1842

First Daughter of Jessie and Elizabeth Coffee

Holmes
Second son of Samuel & Eliza Holmes
Born July 28-1843
Died Aug. 11-1843

Ephriam Pennington Holmes
Born June 24-1841
Died Sept. 3-1852

Samuel Holmes
Born Aug. 26-1814
Died Aug. 4-1872

John Christopher
Second son of Polly Vardeman
Born April 8-1833
Died Oct. 16-1849

Hannah Stephenson
Born Mar. 24-1835
Died Feb. 13-1837

Infant daughter of L. & E. Stephenson
Born without life 1837

Ann E. Stephenson
Born Dec. 28-1810
Died March 20-1846

Martha A. Stephenson
Born 7-6-1828
Died July 15-1844

Stephenson
Born May 6-1841
Died Sept. 1841

STEPHENSON MARRIAGES IN LINCOLN COUNTY, KENTUCKY

(Copied from data in the Library of the Kentucky State Historical Society, Frankfort). *See Register K. S. H. S.*—1914.

Moses Hall married Isabell, dau. of Thomas Stevenson, Sept. 4, 1784.

Thomas Stephenson married Hannah McNeilly—Jan. 7-1789.

David Stephenson married Edeth, dau. of Thomas & Elizabeth Logan—April 9-1791.

Mills Stephenson married Jenny Kilpatrick Sept. 21-1791—consent of Peter Jump—guardian of Jenny.

Robert Stephenson married Elizabeth Whitley — 1793.

STEPHENSON FAMILY

Copied from Lindsay Vardaman Stephenson, Senior's, Bible.

Mayfield, Kentucky.

Lindsay Vardaman Stephenson, son of Lindsay Stephenson, Senior, and Annie Vardaman, was born in Lincoln County, October 14, 1830. Died in Union City, Tennessee, July 24, 1890. Married Miss Rhodaett Lee, who was born in New Madrid, Missouri, May 5, 1836. Died in Union City, Tennessee, May 2, 1890. Their children as follows:

First: Jennie Pennington Stephenson, born May 19, 1861, Bradfordville, Marion County, Kentucky.

Second: William Alexander Stephenson, born December 31, 1863, in Pulaski County, Kentucky. Died in Fulton, Kentucky, January 16, 1897.

Third: Morgan Vardaman Stephenson, born July 31, 1866, in Pulaski County, Kentucky. Died in Mayfield, Kentucky, September 24, 1904. Married Miss Agness Rightenour of Illinois, 1895. To them was born Violett Lee Stephenson, who now lives in Evergreen, Alabama.

Fourth: Silas Lee Stephenson, born in Lincoln County, October 15, 1868. Died in Mayfield, Kentucky, August 24, 1898.

Fifth: Lindsay Orell Stephenson, born in Lincoln County, September 3, 1871. Married Miss Elizabeth Adaline Bierley, who was born in Louisville, Kentucky, February 22, 1876. Died in San Antonio, Texas, January 31, 1928. She was buried in Maplewood Cemetery, Mayfield, Kentucky. A child was born to them, Lindsay Orell Stephenson, Junior, March 5, 1905. Died March 5, 1905.

Sixth: Lola Annie Stephenson, born April 23, 1874, in Lincoln County, Kentucky. Married Trimble Benson Robertson July 3, 1898. Their children: Lindsay Vardaman Robertson, born August 9, 1905, in Gulfport, Mississippi. Helen Virginia Robertson, born in Mississippi City, Mississippi, November, 1907.

Seventh: Ollie May Stephenson, born in Christian County, Kentucky, February 22, 1878. Died in New Orleans, Louisiana, December 29, 1918. Half brother, Fountain Eli Dogan, born in Pulaski County, Kentucky, 1853. Died in Belmont, Missouri, December 24, 1900. He was buried in Fairview Cemetery, Fulton, Kentucky. All of Lindsay Vardaman Stephenson's family that are dead are buried in Fairview Cemetery, Fulton, Kentucky.

Eighth: Dr. Samuel Logan Stephenson, born in Christian County, Kentucky, September 17, 1880. Married Addie Dunlap Harris of Okolona, Mississippi, 1911. She was born in Corinth, Mississippi, 1892.

Their children: Sam Logan Stephenson, Junior, born July —, 1914. Jane Antoinette Stephenson, born December 23, 1925. Lindsay Harris Stephenson, born December 23, 1925. This family lives in Corinth, Mississippi.

Dr. Samuel Logan Stephenson, served through the Spanish American War and the British Boer War in South Africa, a member of Light-horse cavalry under Lord Kitchener. Also served through the World War as Lieutenant and Captain on the medical staff, U. S. A.

A STUDY OF SOME STEWART AND ALLIED FAMILIES

PART I

By William C. Stewart

THREE OR MORE brothers Stewart, who appear to have been allied to a noble Stewart house of Scotland, although they probably were not close blood relatives, were "gentlemen of no estate" when they came to seek their fortunes in the new lands (America about 1740-1745. They were born in Scotland or Ireland, perhaps on the Island of Bute or Arran,[1] according to what evidence is available, but for a time they lived in—and embarked for America from—Ulster, Ireland. One brother—Major Robert Stuart —served as adjutant to George Washington in the French and Indian Wars; and among the other brothers' descendants in Kentucky, the Rev. Robert Stuart was a beloved Presbyterian preacher and an early professor of Transylvania College; his son John Todd Stuart encouraged Abraham Lincoln to enter the law and was his first partner in Springfield, Illinois; and still another descendant is Jesse Stuart, a noted poet of today. The brothers were Robert and John Stuart of what is now Rockbridge County, Virginia; James Stuart of what is now Bath County, Virginia; and perhaps— proof is lacking—William Stuart of Bath, now Highland County.

[1] The Stewarts—variously spelled Stuart, Steuart and Steward—may have been of native stock of Norman, but the first authentic ancestor was Walter, son of Alan, who was High Steward of Scotland under Kings David I and Malcolm IV and who founded Paisley Abbey in 1164. His duties included management of the royal household, collection of the national revenue and command of the king's army. Walter died 1264 and was succeeded by his son Alexander who married Jean, heiress of James, Lord of Bute, and in her name seized the islands of Bute and Arran. The best known member of the house of Bute was John Stuart Bute, third Earl of Bute, born 1713, died 1792, a prime minister of England under King George III. Sources for the data in this study, submitted by the writer, have had to be omitted because of space limitations; the writer has consented to supply citations to interested researchers who send stamped reply envelopes. Primary records in the United States, Jamaica and England have been consulted. Much help was given by George Edson of Olathe, Kansas, who has for forty years published the Stewart Clan Magazine, and is a recognized authority on the family.

In the period from 1717 to the beginning of the American Revolution, a great wave of Scotch-Irish emigrated from the North of Ireland to escape economic, political and religious oppression. The famines of 1727 and 1740 swelled the exodus from Ulster and the ship-agents greedy for bound servants in the overseas plantations played their part in enlarging and shaping the emigration. Most of them entered through ports on the Deleware River; usually they remained for a time in Pennsylvania or perhaps New Jersey, and after 1736, a majority pushed on into Virginia, making Augusta and Rockbridge Counties the strongest Scotch-Irish entrenchments in the United States, then and today. From Virginia farms and small business enterprises in the towns, they or their sons moved southward in the Valley of Virginia, some eventually to Kentucky, others into the Carolinas and Georgia and thence westward. With this rolling tide from Ulster, bringing their household goods, the tools of their trades and such little money as they could gather, came the Stewarts who had removed earlier from Scotland. While the family name derives from the office of steward of the royal household, there were among these emigrants few intimates of kings or nobles. Most of these Stewarts were farmers, small merchants, weavers, stone masons—craftsmen whose skills would be welcome on the frontier. They became noted Indian fighters, fierce partisans against King George, sturdy pioneers in the burgeoning west.

Of the Stewarts considered in this paper, most are related and all may be. In general, they left few records at the places of original settlement; their position in the economic scheme, their fondness for the same given names—John, James, William, Robert, etc.—and their usual exclusion from the better kept vestry records, make it difficult to trace some of them with any degree of certainty. When all the families under consideration arrived in this country is uncertain, but it appears likely they were among the large group of emigrants about 1740 as stated in family tradition. By 1747, several families of Stewarts were firmly established in Augusta County, including the area now embraced by Bath, Highland and Rockbridge Counties. The brothers apparently came first to Borden's Tract (Rockbridge County); John remained there; Robert became a professional soldier and James moved to the Cowpasture when those lands were opened for settlement. There have been surmises that this family was related to the better-known families of Archibald Stuart and his kin in Augusta County, but no evidence of this has been found, nor are other Virginia Stuarts known to be related.

For the purposes of easier narration, Major Robert will be considered before his older brother, John Stuart.

MAJOR ROBERT (4) STUART of Rockbridge County, Va.

Robert was born about 1710-1712, probably in Scotland. He was younger than his brother John and older than James and William Stuart. In a letter to George Washington Sept. 28, 1759, he spoke of himself as "already an old fellow" whose hopes of advancement in the army had not been fulfilled.[2] The rather large Stuart-Washington correspondence gives grounds for assuming that Robert was allied with the Stuarts of Bute; among other instances, when he went to London in 1763, he was expecting Lord Bute, the Prime Minister, to help him obtain an army command. It is not likely that an otherwise rather obscure colonial soldier would expect to gain the attention of the Prime Minister of Great Britain unless he had some claim on him, such as that of a poor and distant kinsman or one who looked to the Butes as hereditary chieftians. On Jan. 25, 1769, Robert wrote Washington from Jamaica, where he was serving as Comptroller of Customs, that he had been advised by his doctor to seek a colder climate. "I have hopes given me that *my native air,* exercise and a proper regimen will in time effect the reestablishment of my health. Whenever I get my affairs settled in London, I propose to return either to the Highlands of Scotland or the South of France as the Physicians shall direct." This is one among several indications that he was born in the British Isles; his brother John's son John was almost certainly born in Ireland about 1740. John's descendants stated the family came to Pennsylvania about 1740, remained awhile and then removed to Virginia, where John and probably Robert purchased land from

---

[2]The large correspondence between George Washington and Robert Stuart may be found in S. M. Hamilton, Letters to Washington and Accompanying Papers, 1899; and Worthington Chauncey Ford, Writings of George Washington, 1889.

Benjamin Borden, Sr. Robert may have tarried awhile in Albemarle County, Va.[3]

It is probable, however, that Robert was in Augusta (now Rockbridge) County before the conveyance of land to him in 1750. William Edmiston, deposing April 18, 1806 in Washington County, Va., in one of the numerous suits over Borden's land, stated that he lived there from 1740 to 1745, the Edmiston land being bounded by that of Robert Stuart, Robert and Joseph Coulton and John Buchanan. John Stuart's land was purchased from Benjamin Borden Sr., before the formation of Augusta from Orange County. On Feb. 25, 1750, 200 acres on Hays Creek, adjoining John Stuart, was conveyed by Borden's executors to Robert Stuart. Many Borden conveyances were made years after purchased.

Robert appears to have preferred a military life to that of a farmer; for years before his death his farm was operated by James Stuart, his heir-at-law, a son or more likely a nephew, as will appear. When Gov. Dinwiddie sent Col. George Washington with a regiment of provincials over the mountains in the spring of 1754, Robert Stuart went along as captain of a company of men from the border counties. He was wounded in a battle with the French at the Great Meadows, in Fayette County, Pa. (then considered part of Virginia) on July 9, 1754. Washington's ledger showed a list of officers with claims under Dinwiddie's Proclamation of 1754, and later Robert for his service was granted land in what is now Wood County, W. Va., which he never claimed, apparently because he was not in this country. Robert accompanied Washington on the March to Fort Duquesne the following year, 1755, Capt. Robert

[3]One Robert Stewart was among those calling the Rev. Samuel Black to a Presbyterian Church near Woods Gap in Albemarle County, Va., March 29, 1747. A native of Ireland, Black came to Pennsylvania in 1743. He was married to Catherine Shaw and their son Samuel had a daughter Dorcas. Benjamin Borden began disposing of his land in 1737 and entries were made in 1738-1739 by Thomas Armstrong, who married the widow of James (4) Stuart, and others who appear in this chronicle. Early purchasers included John Edmiston, John and Charles Hays and Samuel Walker. Deeds recorded in Orange County before the formation of Augusta County included those for Joseph and Robert Culton, John Matthews, John Lowery, John Buchanan and Alexander, James and John Walker. The first Timber Ridge Church, built 1746, and the New Providence Church, built for the settlers on Hays and Walkers Creeks 1747-1748, called Rev. John Brown in 1753. John Stuart signed the call and among his neighbors were Andrew and Samuel Steele, Alexander and John Walker, Francis Beattie, William Hamilton, James Montgomery, Samuel Hay and James Greenlee.

and Lt. Walter Stuart being under the command of Col. Charles Lewis, and he was at Braddock's defeat. When claims were being adjudicated in 1780, John Jameson's statement in Greenbriar County Court that he was a soldier in Capt. Robert Stuart's Company in the First Virginia Regiment was proved by John Estill.

In the winter of 1756-1757, the Indians tried fiercely to drive the English-speaking settlers from the mountain valleys, and in one of their forays they killed Robert's brother, James Stuart. In the summer of 1757, the Indians were moving up from the south and Washington was stationed at Fort Loudoun near Winchester, Va. On Nov. 9, 1757, Robert wrote Gov. Dinwiddie from that fort that Washington had been ill for three months, was getting worse and that Stuart himself needed a leave of absence. Serving as Washington's adjutant, he wrote five days later that Washington had been compelled to go home. Stuart's subsequent letters to his commander gave a graphic picture of the militia, some of them "destitute of every necessity." He was in command at Fort Loudoun when he left Oct. 17, 1758 to join General Bouquet, "Stalnaker having brought up some food and Col. Byrd having procur'd some Forrage." When the First Virginia Regiment was disbanded, Stuart was allowed compensation for special services rendered as a brigade major. He was unable to obtain regular military rank, however, and Washington offered to loan him money to buy a regiment, as was customary in the British Army of that day. He served at many frontier posts, in Byrd's Cherokee expedition and at all times kept Washington informed of events. He stayed for awhile with his "friend, Dr. Walker" in Albemarle County, suffering from rheumatism, then rejoined the army at Fort Lewis on the Cowpasture (the seat of Col. Charles Lewis, not to be confused with Fort Lewis on the Roanoke). Following a visit with Washington at Mount Vernon in the Spring of 1762, he planned a trip to London to attempt to advance his military fortunes, was hopeful the Earls Bute and Loudoun would help him, and looked forward to "going home." Before he could sail, peace between England and France was established, but taking with him a loan of L300 from Washington, he continued on to London, writing Jan. 14, 1764 that he had arrived and was included among a group who with Lord Egremont planned to inaugurate a settlement in Newfoundland. Apparently nothing came of this and on March 10, 1768, Stuart wrote Washington from Kingston, Jamaica that he had been appointed Comptroller of Customs there. The cost of living in the island was very high,

Stuart wrote, adding that the rather small income he enjoyed "would in some Countries do very well for *a bachelor in my way*, but in this extravagant and very expensive place . . . barely sufficient to support me in a decent manner"; however, he was able to repay Washington's loan. Apparently late in 1769, Stuart returned to London and in 1775 Washington, reporting he had recently received no letters from "my old friend, Colo. Stewart," asked George Mercer, representative of the Ohio Company in London, and whose brother John Fenton Mercer had served under Stuart, to seek him out and "give him my warmest wishes."

In his letters to Washington, Stuart indicated his concern over the growing discord between England and the Colonies, and there is no evidence he ever returned to America; he once said he was land hungry, but he never claimed his Virginia military land grant, and he does not appear in the Rockbridge County records again until Oct. 20, 1782, when he was dead. His heir-at-law, James Stuart, and the latter's wife Margaret, of Montgomery County, Va., sold to John Carrick of Rockbridge County, the 200-acre farm which Robert purchased from Borden in 1750, adjoining the plantations of John Stuart and Samuel Steele. Depositions in Borden controversies show that this land had been known locally as James Stuart's, indicating James had been working the farm. On the basis of data available, it cannot be said with certainty whether Stuart's reference to himself as "a bachelor in my way" actually meant he had never married, or that he was then living as a bachelor, perhaps following the death of a wife. The deed disposing of his land speaks of James Stuart as his heir-at-law, not as his son, although this, too, may not be conclusive. There is no reference in his correspondence with Washington to a family, although he frequently spoke of Washington's wife. The writer surmises that the James Stuart who sold Robert's land, and the Robert Stuart who witnessed the deed may have been sons of John (4) Stuart and thus nephews of Robert Stuart.

JOHN (4) STUART, of Rockbridge County, Va.

John is believed to have been born about 1708 and he probably married, about 1728-1729, a first wife whose name is unknown, and again, about 1738, in Ireland, Mary Shaw, according to descendants. A grandson, the Rev. Robert Stuart of Kentucky, said he was told by his grandmother Mary Stuart that his father, John (5) Stuart, was born in Ireland, and that the family came to the United States in the spring of the year following the winter of the black frost (1739-1740), spent some time in Pennsylvania and then removed to Augusta (Rockbridge) County, Va. Mary also said she and John (4) had only one other child, a son who was born in this country and died in infancy. While doubtless true, this does not exclude a first marriage for John (4) and considerable circumstantial evidence indicates he had two or more children by a first marriage.

In 1742, John Stuart arranged to buy 313 acres of land from Benjamin Borden Sr. and this and other purchases were conveyed by deed May 20, 1752, by Benjamin Borden Jr., the land adjoining Stewart's old survey, on Hays Creek, which joins Walker Creek and flows into the Maury or North River of the James. In December, 1742, John Stuart was among the 30-odd men in Capt. John McDowell's company who responded to the call of Col. James Patton to repel an Indian raid. John and his brother Robert Stuart of Hays Creek lived in the vicinity of Timber Ridge, not far from the old Timber Ridge Church; by 1767, when Robert was abroad, only John and James Stuart were listed in the Augusta County fee book as living in Borden's Tract, James apparently being Robert's heir-at-law of 1782, who was then operating Robert's farm. When some of the Edmiston family left in 1765 for the Holston River country (Washington County), John purchased their adjoining land. He was freed of the tax levy in 1768-1769 and was probably aged 60 by then. He died c1782 and his widow Mary, "Widow Stuart of Borden's", died after 1788. The family thereafter was represented in Rockbridge County by their son John (5) Stuart.

JOHN (5) STUART of Rockbridge County, Virginia.

John was born about 1739-1740 in Ireland and came to Rockbridge County with his parents by 1742. He was married about 1760-1762 to Elizabeth, daughter of James Walker of Walkers Creek, a neighbor,[4] and spent all his life on the farm. He was a

[4]Edson, Stewart Clan Magazine, Tome D, p. 148. John Walker arrived in Maryland in 1726, moved to Pennsylvania. His son Alexander died in Rockbridge County, Va., 1784 and his widow Jane (Hummer or Hammer) Walker in Woodford County, Ky., 1798. Alexander's son John Walker married 1771 Margaret Hutson and in 1783 Margaret Kelso. He had daughters who married Alexander and Hugh, sons of John (5) Stuart, who himself married Elizabeth, daughter of Capt. James Walker. The latter also had daughters Mary, married Hugh Kelso; and Jean, married John Moore.

Revolutionary soldier. The will of his wife, Elizabeth, was probated Dec. 5, 1825; he died April 8, 1831, and his will was probated Sept. 5, 1831. Their children were:

1. James (6) Stuart, born 1761-1763 in Rockbridge County, served at the Battle of Yorktown, moved to Orangeburg County, S.C., before 1800, and married a widow nee Ann Sabb. His daughter Ann E. married William Lynn Lewis, great grandson of John Lewis of Augusta County.

2. Mary (6) Stuart, born 1763-1766, was married to William Walker, son of John and Mary (Culton) Walker of Rockbridge County, July 31, 1783.

3. John (6) Stuart, born c1768, married April 1, 1790, Virginia (Jenny) Wardlaw. They removed to St. Charles County, Mo., and he died about 1831. They had children: James, Mary, John Hopkins, Walker, Jane, and perhaps three other children shown in census enumerations but not named in John's will.

4. Walker (6) Stuart, born c1770, married before 1810, Mary, daughter of Malcolm McClure. Their children, some of whom removed to Monroe County, Mo., were John Alexander, Samuel, Mary, Joseph, James, William, Robert and Walker.

5. Rev. Robert (6) Stuart, who removed to Kentucky. (See below.)

6. Joseph (6) Stuart, died before 1825 in Charleston, S.C.; unmarried.

7. Hugh (6) Stuart, born c1776, died Dec. 2, 1824. He married April 8, 1813, Elizabeth, daughter of John and Margaret (Kelso) Walker, born Nov. 11, 1787, died on Walkers creek, Sept. 30, 1838. They had children: John, James, Margaret and Mary.

8. Alexander (6) Stuart, born c1778, died Aug. 13, 1837. He married Dec. 14, 1809, Mary, daughter of John and Margaret (Hutson) Walker, who was born June 21, 1778, and died March 21, 1838. They had no children.

REV. ROBERT (6) STUART, son of John (5) Stuart of
Rockbridge County.

Robert was born Aug. 4, 1772 at the family farm on Hays creek in Rockbridge County. He was educated at Liberty Hall Academy (now Washington and Lee University) and became a Presbyterian minister. After preaching for a time in Virginia, he removed to Fayette County, Ky., in 1798 to become one of the first three professors in Transylvania University. In 1803, he became pastor of Walnut Hill Church and served until his retirement in 1842. His pastorate there has been described by the Rev. Robert Stuart Sanders in The Register.[5] Robert married, first, in Woodford County, Ky., Frances Hawkins, who died Oct. 30, 1800. In 1802, Robert married Hannah, daughter of Gen. Levi and Jane (Briggs) Todd of Fayette County. Robert and his first wife had a son James Hawkins Stuart who died in infancy, and by his second wife a son Levi Todd Stuart, who was killed in boyhood by a fall from a horse. Surviving children of Robert and Hannah Stuart were: 1. Mary Jane, born March 16, 1804, married Major Daniel B. Price, died June 3, 1889; 2. Eliza Ann, born Nov. 17, 1805, married Nov. 16, 1843, a widower, Rev. Samuel Steele, pastor of Hillsboro, Ohio, Presbyterian Church, died Aug. 11, 1884; 3. John Todd, born Nov. 10, 1807, see below; 4. Judge Robert Todd, born April 10, 1810, married Nov. 27, 1838 in Saline County, Mo., Jane Gaines Miller, daughter of Gen. William and Jane (Gaines) Miller, from Danville, Ky., died in Marshall, Mo., Sept. 23, 1880; 5. David Todd, born June 23, 1812, married Oct. 28, 1836, Olivia Winchester Hall of Louisville, was a Presbyterian minister and president of Shelbyville Female College, died Sept. 26, 1868; his grandson Rev. Robert Sanders is a Presbyterian minister; 6. Rev. Samuel Davies Stuart, born Feb. 15, 1815, died June 19, 1895, married Cornelia St. Clair Waddell, daughter of Dr. Addison Waddell of Staunton, Va., served as Presbyterian minister in Kentucky and Virginia, as a Confederate chaplain and with several colleges, including the Stonewall Jackson Female Institute in Abingdon, Va., which he founded in 1868; 7. Margaret, born Sept. 20, 1817, married Nov. 27, 1845, Joshua Woodrow in Hillsboro, Ohio, died March 23, 1916 in Woodford County, Ky. The Rev. Robert Stuart's wife Hannah died March 21, 1834 and he died at Nicholasville, Ky., Aug. 5, 1856.

John Todd (7) Stuart, son of Rev. Robert Stuart, was born Nov. 10, 1807, seven miles east of Lexington, Ky., was educated at Centre College, studied law with Judge Daniel Breck in Richmond, Ky., and arrived in Springfield, Ill., where he became a noted lawyer, on Oct. 28, 1828, after a 10-day horseback ride from his Kentucky home. A Whig of the old school, he was only 25 when he was elected to the Illinois State Legislature, and he later served in

[5] *Register*, v. 54, pp. 113-124 and 221-236, April and July, 1956. The Rev. Mr. Sanders also published, 1962, The Reverend Robert Stuart, D.D.

Congress. He and his wife, Mary Virginia, daughter of Gen. Frank Nash, had children: 1. Bettie J., who married Christopher C. Brown; 2. John T.; 3. Frank N.; 4. Virginia L.; 5. Hannah; and 6. Robert L.; a son Edward died in infancy. John Todd (7) Stuart's mother, Hannah Todd, was a sister of Robert Smith Todd. The latter had four daughters: Elizabeth P., who married Ninian W. Edwards, son of Gov. Ninian Edwards; Frances, who married Dr. William S. Wallace; Mary, who married (President) Abraham Lincoln; and Anna Marie, who married C. M. Smith of Springfield, Ill. Lincoln, as a volunteer in the Black Hawk War, met Major John Todd Stuart in April, 1832, and was encouraged to enter the law. He borrowed law books from Stuart for study and in 1837 they entered partnership, which was dissolved in 1841.

JAMES (5) STUART, perhaps son of John (4) Stuart of Rockbridge County.

A study of all the James Stuarts in this family indicates that the James with wife Margaret who was heir-at-law of Major Robert Stuart in 1782 was either a son of the Major himself, in spite of his somewhat vague characterization of himself as a bachelor (perhaps a widower), or of his brother, John (4) Stuart by a first wife. There is considerable circumstantial evidence that John was married before he wed Mary Shaw at the age of 30 or older. If James were a son of John, Robert's older brother, the Major's land may well have passed to him in conformity with laws and customs of the day. The name of James (5) first appears in the records with certainty in 1767, when he would have been aged 30 to 37 years. However, he probably was the James listed with other Rockbridge County members of the militia serving in September, 1754. His residence in Borden's Tract was noted in the Augusta County fee book in 1767, and land he was farming adjoined that of Samuel Buchanan in 1770. He moved to Montgomery County before 1782, perhaps leaving a younger brother Robert to run the farm on Hays Creek. There is some reason to believe that he was the James Stuart who entered land in 1775 on the New River with Andrew Reid (of Rockbridge County, son-in-law of Samuel McDowell of Jessamine County, Ky.) near where Ralph Stuart later lived.[6] It has been surmised, without proof, that this

[6]Andrew Reid, clerk of Rockbridge County, also had a land partnership with Col. John Stuart of Greenbriar County, W. Va., who was not of the families being considered here. There were several Andrew Reids with Stewart connections.

was the James Stuart with wife Margaret who died in Knox County, Tenn., in 1815. In his will, he named his children Jane Moore, Margaret Moore, Robert, John, James, Andrew and Joseph. The son Andrew's will was probated in Lincoln County, Tenn., in 1817, leaving his estate to his brother Joseph except "the cost of a silk dress to my cousin Darkis (Dorcas) Shaw."[7] Robert Stuart, who witnessed the sale of Major Robert's land and who is presumed to be a brother of the heir-at-law, James, has not been traced; there were four Roberts in this general area from 1774 to 1800. James may also have had other brothers: a William Stuart was in Rockbridge County in 1773 and in 1779 sold 210 acres in Rockbridge County to Mary Greenlee, was on the 1782 tax list and he or another William was delinquent in his taxes in 1796; and other Williams were in Montgomery and Washington Counties, Va. An Alexander (5) Stewart in Botetourt County, Va., who was not Alexander, son of Archibald (3) Stuart of Augusta County, has not been traced; but Alexander (6) who may be of this family, has been charted. In applying for a Revolutionary War pension, he said he was born in Augusta (Botetourt) County Nov. 25, 1761. On Dec. 13, 1785, in Botetourt County, he married Dorothy McGee, who was born in 1768. She was the daughter of James McGee who was allied with the McAfees and McCouns, among the group that went from Botetourt County to Kentucky in 1779. The will of James McGee of Mercer County, Ky., dated July 8, 1818, and proved in August of that year, named his wife Molly and five children including Dolly Stewart. Betty McGee—not named in the will but evidently a daughter—married Mr. Blythe and the birth

[7]There are several Stewart-Shaw connections, not fully traced. John (4) Stuart of Middle River, Augusta County, had a sister Mary who married an Andrew Shaw. A Shaw family lived near James and William Stuart in Bath County. Another Shaw family lived in Rockbridge County near John (4) Stuart who is said to have married Mary Shaw in Ireland. William (5) Stuart, probably son of Hugh Stuart, both of whom went from Chester County, S.C., to Christian County, Ky., married Jane, daughter of William Shaw. In Caldwell County, Ky., the will of Abner Shaw, Aug. 16, 1816, named his children Mary Ann Dodd, Dorcas Shaw and John Shaw, with Samuel Black and Dorcas Shaw as executors, and Hugh Kincaid, Samuel Black and Katurah Black as witnesses. Rev. Samuel Black of Albemarle County, Va., had wife Catherine Shaw and grandchild Dorcas Black. James Stewart of Christian County, Ky., married Susan Colvin from Chester County, S. C., where the Colvins were allied with the Cornwells and the Stewarts who may stem from James (4) Stuart of Bath County, Va.

of their son James Blythe is recorded in Alexander Stewart's Bible, as of Oct. 25, 1806. Stewart gave consent to Blythe's marriage to Mary Young in Clark County, Ky., in 1827; he evidently had lived with the Stewarts after the death of his mother prior to 1818.

Alexander and Dolly removed to Kentucky about 1786, settling in Madison County, and then moved to Bourbon County, where in 1818 they deeded land to John Stewart of Bourbon County. Alexander was living in Bath County, Ky. (formed from Montgomery County) where other Stuarts of this family are found, when he died about June 24, 1836. He named in his will his wife Dorothy; the children of Jane Gilbert, deceased, Isaac, Emily and Ezekiel Gilbert; and James and John Stewart, James Blythe and Elizabeth Call. Dorothy was living in Bath County July 17, 1840, aged 72, when she applied for a pension. Their children were: 1. James, born Jan. 6, 1787; 2. John, born Feb. 28, 1789; 3. Robert, born Aug. 16, 1792; 4. Janet, born Oct. 7, 1796, married Aquilla Gilbert; 5. Elizabeth, born May 6, 1802, married Jan. 6, 1821, Hamilton Call. John (7), son of Alexander, married Oct. 25, 1809, Polly Gilbert, in Madison County. Isaac Gilbert, father of the bride, gave his consent, and in 1827 named her in his will. His son, Aquilla Gilbert, married April 1, 1810, Jane, daughter of Alexander Stewart.

The theory of some genealogists that William (4) Stewart of Highland County, Va., was a brother of James (4) of Bath County appears to be based chiefly on the fact that William appeared in the neighborhood at about the same time as James; no evidence has been found to connect them. William appeared in the Bath (Highland) County records in 1755. He married Margaret, daughter of Edward Ushur, and settled at the mouth of Shaw's Fork of the Cowpasture, some distance north of James Stuart's home. He was born about 1732 probably in County Down, Ulster, Ireland, and died in 1797. Most of his descendants moved to West Virginia and Missouri, some to Kentucky. His children were: 1. James, born 1757, died 1841; 2. Edward, born 1759, married Mary Callahan; 3. John, born 1761, married Hannah Hicklin; 4. Mary, born c1762, married Charles Callahan; 5. Jane, born c1764, married Capt. James Hicklin; 6. William R., born c1767, married successively Jane Hicklin, Jane Stewart, Elizabeth Kincaid and Margaret Gwin; 7. Ushur, born 1769, never married.

JAMES (4) STUART of Cowpasture, Bath County, Va.

James Stuart and his brother-in-law Ralph Lafferty lived on Stuart's Run of the Cowpasture River near Millboro in the part of Augusta County, Va., that became Bath County in 1791, where they farmed and kept a small store. To the south was the settlement of Adam Dickenson who came by 1744 by way of Hanover, N.J., and Lancaster County, Penn. Others on Stuart's Run were Thomas and Hugh Gillespie, James McKay, Sampson and George Matthews. To the north was the Fort Lewis settlement, the Cartmells and Hugarts. Many families familiar in early Kentucky history lived along the Cowpasture: Kelso, Kincaid, Sitlington, etc. James Stuart's farm was some 13 miles by crow flight from the farms of John and Robert Stuart in Rockbridge County.

James Stuart is believed to have been born in Ulster, Ireland, c1719-1723. He married Mary Ann, sister of Ralph Lafferty, probably about 1738. Although he probably was there earlier, he first appeared in the Augusta County records March 18, 1747, when the County Court ordered a road built from the Stuart's Run area to Carter's Mill on the Calfpasture River leading to the more settled part of the county. Those named to work on the road besides Stuart, Lafferty and Dickenson were John Cartmell, William Dougherty, William Muldrough, Hugh Coffey, John Donnally, Alexander and James McKay, John Mitchell, John Moore, James Hughes and James Huey. Stuart was granted a patent for 300 acres on Stuart Creek (Stuart's Run) adjoining Lafferty, where he had been living for several years, June 1, 1750, and the land was held in the family until 1800, when it was sold by James' son Robert Stuart to Richard Matthews and by him to James Kincaid in 1802.

James and Ann had at least four sons by 1748—Robert, born 1740-1743; James, born c1744; Ralph, born c1747; and John, born c1748. James' sister Mary married John Hamilton in 1748.[8] In 1755, when land was processioned, James Stuart was in Capt. Dickenson's militia company; ten years later the processioners found James' son Robert on the Stuart's Run farm.

[8]John and Mary Hamilton's grandson Archibald Hamilton later lived in Montgomery and Bath Counties, Ky., according to Oren Morton, *History of Bath County, Va.*

Lafferty[9] built a small fort as the Indians sought to drive the English-speaking settlers out of the mountain valleys. In February, 1757, on one of their forays, James Stuart was killed and his son James was captured, along with two of the Cartmell children. Many of the settlers fled; one who remained, John Moore, was killed and his wife and five children captured May 16. Young James Stuart escaped, but how and when he returned home is not known. Of the various members of this family said to have been captured by Indians, his is the only case authenticated.

Ann (Lafferty) Stuart made bond as administratrix of James' estate Nov. 17, 1757, with John Dickenson and George Wilson as bondsmen. James' estate was appraised March 14, 1758. Robert, the eldest son, took over the Cowpasture farm, while the widow

[9]Ralph Lafferty (or Laverty) lived on Stuart's Run of the Cowpasture as early as 1746, was a militia soldier in 1758 and furnished supplies for the army during the Revolution. His first wife is believed to have been Miss Steele. He married, second, Nov. 20, 1764 (bond) Jane Graham, daughter of Thomas Hicklin and widow of Robert Graham, son of Christopher Graham. Lafferty's children were: 1. William Stuart Lafferty, to whom Ralph and Jane Lafferty conveyed 224 acres of land adjoining Adam Dickenson June 15, 1770, probably about the time he married Jane _____. They moved to the New River, where he and his brother Steele Lafferty and William Meek (perhaps the Meek who married Martha Lafferty) entered land at the mouth of Indian Creek of New River in Monroe County, W. Va., in 1774 when it was part of Botetourt County. Col. Samuel Estill, James Ellis and John Bradshaw left Cook's Fort on Indian River and scouted the mountains between William Lafferty's plantation and Laurel Creek in 1779, Bradshaw said in his Revolutionary pension application. William Lafferty died in 1818. He had 14 children: William, John, Steele, James, Alexander, Robert, Nancy, Clara, Mattie, Polly, Elizabeth, Jane, Ralph and Rebecca. His son Ralph Lafferty joined Ralph Stuart in Logan County, W. Va., by 1830. 2. Steele Lafferty was killed by Indians at his home on Indian Creek in 1780 as was Mrs. Bradshaw; his neighbor William Meek described the raid. Meek, his wife and an infant child were killed the following March in another raid; two other of his children were captured but recovered. 3. Elizabeth Lafferty, married James Hamilton. 4. Agnes Lafferty, married William Haddon. 5. Sarah Lafferty, married Allen Clark of Greenbriar (Monroe) County. 6. Martha Lafferty, married (William?) Meek. 7. Rebecca Lafferty, married John Hamilton in Augusta County, Va., Aug. 10, 1786. Ralph and Jane Lafferty in their old age conveyed half their possessions to Rebecca. The Laffertys and Brattons of Bath County, Va., were connected in some way; Ralph and Jane Lafferty and Robert and Ann Bratton sold land owned jointly to William Givens Aug. 16, 1769, and to Bratton's son Adam Jan. 24, 1770.

Ann soon after married a widower, Thomas Armstrong[10] of Jennings Branch of Middle (or Cathey) River. Robert, about this time, married Elizabeth, daughter of Henry Cartmell,[11] who with Ralph Lafferty and James McKay, appraised James' estate. There appears to have been a family discussion of finances in 1762 for on Feb. 17, John Stuart, orphan of James, was ordered bound out, although there is no record that he actually was; and he and his brothers, James and Ralph, chose guardians. James, aged 18, chose John Hamilton, husband of his aunt Mary, with his elder brother Robert as surety. Ralph, aged 15, chose his brother Robert with Hamilton as surety. John, aged 14, chose Henry Murray, husband of Thomas Armstrong's daughter Rosanna, with Armstrong himself as surety.

[10]Thomas Armstrong obtained 100 acres from Benjamin Borden Sr., Feb. 21, 1738. James Bell had made an entry with Borden previously. None of these early settlers received deeds and Bell sued Benjamin Borden Jr. Bell on May 21, 1747, sold to Armstrong 400 acres on Jennings Branch of Middle River, Augusta County, half of which Armstrong conveyed to his son William Armstrong Nov. 21, 1759, and left the other half, on which he lived, to his son Abel in his will, dated April 29, 1776, and probated Aug. 20, 1776, with his wife Ann (Stuart) Armstrong and his son William as executors. He also named his son Abel and his daughters: Jane, who married Robert McKittrick; Sarah, who married Edward Rutledge; and Rosanna, who married Henry Murray. Robert Armstrong, perhaps a brother, was a witness to the will. Abel Armstrong married Mary, daughter of Margaret (-Wanless) Carlile, widow of John Carlile, who died c1796 and some of whose family went to Green County, Ky. Abel was living in Augusta County, Va., as late as 1816 and his wife was dead by 1821. He had sons Thomas and John. Armstrongs in early Mercer, Franklin and Caldwell Counties, Ky., appear related to this branch of the family.

[11]Henry Cartmell's will, probated Feb. 13, 1787, in Botetourt County, Va., named among others Robert Stewart who married his daughter and their son Henry Stewart. Robert Stuart and wife Elizabeth sold July 21, 1800, to Richard Matthews land on Stuart's Run in Bath County, Va., granted 1750 to his father, James (4) Stuart. It is assumed his wife was Elizabeth Cartmell, as he is not known to have married more than once. Cartmell did not give his daughter's name in his will, and the clerk did not note the name of the bride when Robert married. Cartmell moved from Pennsylvania c1757-1758 to Augusta (Bath) County in 1768 to Botetourt County, where he purchased land on Purgatory Creek. His son Henry said in his 1832 application for a Revolutionary War pension that he was born in Chester County, Pa. Richard Armstrong was in Cartmell's militia company in Botetourt. Ralph Lafferty and Robert (5) Stuart witnessed a deed for land sold to Samuel Cartmell in Monroe County, W. Va. The Cartmell family was in Kentucky as early as 1790 and in Montgomery County, Ky., in 1800. In the 1810 Montgomery County census William, Samuel, John and Andrew Cartmell were neighbors of James Stewart and Archibald Hamilton (from Bath County, Va.).

The purpose of these proceedings may have been to safeguard the boys' portion of the estate; there evidently was some family trouble, became Thomas and Ann Armstrong was called into court to make an accounting on Sept. 24, 1763, but this was settled in 1765. The legal age for choice of one's own guardian was 14 and if James and Ann Stuart had children who were unmarried or under 21 other than the four known boys, they would have been under 14 in 1762 and thus not involved in these proceedings. Large families were the fashion in those days and there is no reason to believe there were no children after the birth of John in 1748; other possible children are listed below. Thomas Armstrong died between April 29 and August 20, 1776, and was survived by his wife, Ann, the date of whose death is not known. She is not mentioned in Armstrong records and probably went to live with one of her children after her husband's death.

Children of James (4) and Mary Ann (Lafferty) Stuart:
1. Robert, born 1739-1740, see below.
2. James, born c1744, see below.
3. Ralph, born c1747, will be discussed in a second article.
4. John, born c1748, see below.
5. (?) Elizabeth Stuart made a purchase at the sale of personal property of Thomas Armstrong; she may have been a daughter of James (4) or perhaps the wife of Robert (5) Stuart or John (5) Stuart.
6. (?) Mary Stuart, perhaps a daughter of James (4) is said in family tradition to have married Col. Richard Elliott, who died in Montgomery County, Ky., in 1799. Ralph Stuart's first wife was Mary Elliott.
7. (?) William Stuart. This name appears frequently in the families descended from James (4) and there is some evidence he had a son William. There have been several surmises as to his identity. The man who appears most nearly to fit the requirements—proof is missing—was born, probably in Virginia, c1750-1755 and so would have been too young to select a guardian in 1762. This William lived, it appears, for a time in Southside Virginia and in the Surry County, N.C., area before going to Pendleton District, S.C. c1790. About 1800 he sold his farm in what is now Oconee County and moved to Jackson County, Ga., and in 1810 to Morgan County, Ga., where in 1811 he purchased land in Jasper County, Ga. In the period 1815-1817, he moved to Walker County, Ala., where he died in 1828. He and his wife (Mary Elizabeth?)

had at least five children: 1. James, born c1774, married Olive ———, died before 1830; 2. William, born c1775; 3. Absalom, born 1776 in Virginia, married 1806 in Jackson County, Ga., Betsy, daughter of Elijah Cornwell, died in DeKalb County, Ga., after 1850; 4. John, born 1783 in Virginia, married 1813 in Jackson County, Sarah, daughter of John Woods, who removed with the rest of his family to Logan (now Simpson) County, Ky. About 1827, the Woods family moved to Morgan County, Ill., where they helped found a town named Simpson in honor of their former home and later called Franklin. John Stuart moved to Walker County, Ala.; 5. Mary, born c1784, may have married William Vickery of Jackson County, Ga.

ROBERT (5) STUART, son of James (4) Stuart of Cowpasture.

Robert was born about 1739-1740, perhaps in Ireland (where his cousin, John (5) Stuart, son of John (4) Stuart, was born about the same date) or in Pennsylvania or Virginia. He was aged about 16-18 when his father James was killed by Indians in 1757; he was old enough to serve in the militia company of his neighbor, Capt. John Dickenson, in the 1758 campaign against the Indians. He was paid L4.5.0 for this service and—on May 18, 1780—he was allowed in Augusta County Court, 50 acres of land. After his mother married Thomas Armstrong, Robert took over management of the family estate. In September, 1761, Robert furnished supplies for the militia at Fort Lewis, and he, Lafferty and John Dickenson furnished beef for the troops in the Revolution. On Feb. 17, 1762, Robert was chosen as guardian for his brother Ralph and bondsmen for the guardian of his brother James. Robert probably was the man of that name who married Aug. 18, 1762 (no record was kept of the bride's name); she was a daughter of Henry Cartmell, probably named Elizabeth. Cartmell, who soon moved to Botetourt County, in his will probated Feb. 13, 1787, named his son-in-law Robert Stuart and the latter's son Henry. In the 1782 Augusta County tax list, Robert was shown in Capt. John Brown's list. Bath County was set off from Augusta in 1791 and on the first tax list, in Assessor Samuel Vance's district, were Robert Stuart and his son James, and Ralph Lafferty, as well as the William Stewart family further up the Cowpasture. In the second district, that of John Oliver, was Robert's son Henry Stuart. In 1792, either Robert Stuart or—less likely—his son Robert married Polly Armstrong, daughter of Robert Armstrong who was probably a brother or other relative of Thomas Armstrong.[12] In 1800, Robert Stuart sold the 300 acres that had been patented to his father James and court action concerning this land indicates Robert was alive in 1809. Either he or his son Robert may have been the man aged 45 or more enumerated in the 1810 Bath County census. He may have moved to Giles County, Va., near the home of his brother Ralph. A marriage license for one of Ralph's daughters is signed by "Uncle Robert", although this does not appear conclusive; the signer may have been his son Robert (6).

Children, probably among others, of Robert (5) Stuart were:

1. JANNETT (6) STUART, was married in Bath County, June 20, 1796, to Samuel McMullen, by Rev. John Montgomery. Robert Stuart Jr. (her brother) was bondsman.

2. HENRY (6) STUART, son of Robert (5) Stuart. Born c1766 in Augusta (now Bath) County, Va., Henry was living on his own farm in 1791, and on Dec. 19, 1791, he was married (perhaps for the second time) to Sarah Moore by the Rev. John Montgomery.

---

[12]The marriage license of Robert Stuart and Polly Armstrong was signed by Robert Stuart with another Robert Stuart as surety April 13, 1792, in Augusta County, and the ceremony was performed the following day by the Rev. John McCue. It has not been possible to determine whether it was Robert (5) or his son Robert (6) who married Polly. The writer surmises it was Robert (5), who would have been aged about 52, who was the bridegroom. Polly was the daughter of a clothier and fuller, Robert Armstrong; he was perhaps the Robert Armstrong who witnessed the will of Thomas Armstrong in 1776. Robert Armstrong's will, dated June 27, 1782, named his wife Elizabeth; and his children: Samuel, Mary (unmarried), Nancy (unmarried) and Jane Shields. The will was witnessed by Alexander Long and William Davit. It was proved by Long Sep. 20, 1788; and by Davit, in a deposition requested by Robert Stuart, which was signed in Union County, S.C., Nov. 18, 1793. The daughter Nancy married Hugh Means Oct. 26, 1785, and was preparing July 1, 1795, to move to South Carolina. Jane was the wife of John Shields. Samuel Armstrong, who was executor for his father's will, died by July 16, 1788, his will naming his mother and sisters but no wife. The will of Samuel's mother, Elizabeth Armstrong, dated Aug. 19, 1790, and proved in July, 1795, conveyed to her daughter Mary, 30 acres left her by her son Samuel. John Shields was witness to the will. Robert Armstrong's son William was left nothing in the 1782 will, and he sued Robert and Mary Stuart in Augusta County Court of Chancery, April 10, 1795. The outcome of the suit is not shown in Lyman Chalkley's *Chronicles of the Scotch-Irish Settlement in Virginia*, and the original papers cannot be found in their proper place, Augusta County File 909.

She was doubtless related to Nancy Moore,[13] who married his brother James in 1794. Henry married again, Elizabeth Kelly, in Bath County, Feb. 25, 1799. He may have moved prior to 1810 to Monroe County, (West) Va., where his cousin, Ralph Stuart Lafferty, had settled as early as 1774.[14] By 1820, Henry was again living in Bath County, and died there 1833. He had eleven children, among them Andrew, James, Henry, Matilda, Eliza, Patsy (and Robert?).

3. JAMES (6) STUART, son of Robert (5) Stuart, was born between 1763 and 1765 and was in the 1791 tax list, identified as son of Robert. He may have been married before he was wed to Nancy Moore in Bath County, Oct. 20, 1794, by the Rev. James Montgomery. James and his wife Nancy in 1810 sold 100 acres on Stuart's Run to Elisha Williams. The 1810 Bath census showed James and his wife aged 45 or more, another woman 26-44, a boy 10-15, two boys under 10, a girl 10-15 and two girls under 10. He was not enumerated by name in the 1820 census; the appraisement of his personal estate was recorded in Bath County August 25, 1821.

4. ROBERT (6) STUART, son of Robert (5) Stuart, was born between 1764 and 1778, probably about 1766. He may have married Polly Armstrong in 1792; if not, he was surety for his father's marriage to her. He was married, Jan. 16, 1798, in Bath County, to Catherine Aleshire, daughter of Benedict Aleshire, by the Rev. James Wood. They had two children, Elizabeth born 1799-1800 and William, born c1802. Catherine died and the children went to live with their grandparents, the Aleshires, in

---

[13]Samuel Moore, perhaps father or brother of Sarah Moore, signed her marriage bond to Henry Stuart in 1791. The 1794 bond for marriage of Henry's brother James Stuart to Nancy Moore identified her as the daughter of Margaret Moore, whose signature also appears on the 1791 bond but without a statement of relationship. It is surmised they were of the family of John Moore of the Cowpasture.

[14]There were two Henry Stuarts in Monroe County (W) Va. in 1810, only one in 1820. The latter, a younger man, could not have been a son of Henry and Sarah Stuart unless Henry married before 1791; he may have been a nephew. The Henry who remained in Monroe County was born about 1784 and served in the War of 1812. When he applied for a pension June 12, 1871, he was living in Douglas County, Ill. His post office was across the line in Champaign County where George C. Stewart from Henry County, Ky., lived after 1856, although this may not have any significance.

Mason County (West) Virginia.[15] It is uncertain whether Robert married again and whether it was he or his father who was enumerated in the 1810 Bath County census, aged 45 or older, a woman the same age, a boy 16-25 and a girl 10-15. He does not appear by name in the 1820 Bath census and may have been the Robert enumerated that year in Giles County, Va., aged 26-44, a wife the same age, a boy under 10 and two girls under 10.

5. (?) RALPH (6) STUART was born in Maryland and moved with his parents to Virginia when he was a small boy, according to a county history which contains a number of errors; he may have been born in Virginia and there is a possibility—proof is lacking—that he belonged to the family under discussion. He was born in 1782 and was married three times: in Franklin County, Ky., (bond) Feb. 20, 1809, to Prudence, daughter of Richard Armstrong, with John Armstrong as bondsman; in Woodford County, Ky., June 4, 1814, to Sally, widow of John Usselton; also in Woodford County, Oct. 23, 1817, to Agnes Hugh (Campbell) Kirkham. Ralph moved to Henry County, Ky., where he died Aug. 31, 1834. His son, George C., and family, and the widow Agnes, moved to Champaign County, Ill., about 1856.[16]

[15]Benedict Aleshire, probably the man of that name in Frederick County, Va., in the early 1780s, was living in Point Pleasant, Mason County (W.) Va. in 1810. His will, dated Dec. 4, 1819 and probated March 21, 1820, named his wife Elizabeth, his son Jacob, his married daughters, and Betsy and William Stewart (his grandchildren). Elizabeth Stuart married John Eckard (or Ecard, Accord). They were enumerated in the 1850 Mason County census as was William Stuart, born c1802, died July 10, 1889, married Martha Van Sickle.

[16]Ralph Stuart's will, probated in Henry County, Ky., December, 1834, named his three youngest children, Nancy, Sarah Jane and George; daughter Prudence King; stepdaughter Phoebe Dawson. Prudence Armstrong appears to have been of a Mercer County, Ky., family from Virginia. Agnes Hugh (Campbell) Kirkham apparently was a widow. She told the compiler of Chapman's History of Champaign County, Ill., that her Campbell family was related to Alexander Campbell, founder of the Christian Church or Disciples of Christ (Campbellites). She was born in Virginia c1781. Known children of Ralph Stuart were: 1. Prudence, born c1811, married Dec. 6, 1832, Addison King; 2. John, died or left home before 1830; and (by Agnes) 3. George C., born Nov. 15, 1818, in Woodford County, Ky., married Sept. 30, 1847, Elizabeth, daughter of John and Eliza (Ellis) Bridges, in Henry County, moved c1856 to Champaign County, Ill., died Aug. 19, 1894, leaving seven children: Samuel Campbell, Leslie C., John B., Ralph, George E., Agnes E. and Lucy E.; 4. Nancy M., born May 22, 1820, died Sept. 19, 1840; 5. Sarah Jane, born July 7, 1821, died Aug. 29, 1840.

JAMES (5) STUART, son of James (4) Stuart of Cowpasture.
James was born about 1744, perhaps in Rockbridge County or in what is now Bath County, Va., as was his brother Ralph three years later. He and two of the Cartmell children were taken captive by the Indians who killed his father, James, in 1757. After he escaped or was released he returned to the family farm on Stuart's Run. He married, Aug. 20, 1766, Isabella ————————. In 1772, he moved to what is now Randolph County, W. Va., clearing a farm which remained in the family for the next 20 years, and which was operated successively by himself and his brothers John and Ralph, on Stuart's Run of Tygart's Valley River, a branch of the Monongahela. The farm was successively in Augusta, Monongalia, Harrison and Randolph counties. An abortive attempt to establish settlements there had been broken up by the Indians in 1753 and it was not until 1772 that permanent settlements were established by the Stuarts, Darby Connelly, John Haddon, the Warwicks, Westfalls, Riffles, Nelsons, Stalnakers and Whitemans. While serving in the militia, James was killed by Indians almost as soon as he had built his new home. His widow, Isabella, was appointed administratrix of his estate Aug. 18, 1772. She married, probably soon after, —————— Barker. She, William Westfall, Henry Delay, John Hamilton and Ralph Stuart sold the farm Aug. 28, 1792, to Daniel McClain, who had moved to Fayette County, Ky., in the 1780s. Richard Elliott acted as attorney for Isabella Barker and Ralph Stuart, indicating both were absent. Ralph Stuart was then living in Montgomery County, Va., and the Barkers may have gone to Washington County, Va. Ralph Stuart's first wife was a sister of Richard Elliott; John Hamilton had married Ralph's aunt. The Westfall and Delay connections are not known.[17] The border warfare chronicles do not reveal whether James and Isabella had any children, but it seems probable they did. The four discussed below—Robert, John, James and Mary—are assigned to James largely on the basis of surmise, but there is some evidence they belong to this family group.

1. ROBERT (6) STUART, perhaps son of James (5) Stuart, was born c1766. He may have been the James who married Mary

[17] The John Hamilton who acted as agent for the sale of Randolph County land in 1792 may have been the John who married Mary Stuart, or his son John. Their descendants and also the unusual name Delay were found later in Montgomery County, Ky.

Colton (Coulton)[18] in Washington County, Va., in August 1787, and the Robert who was acting as administrator for the estate of a Mary Stuart in Augusta County Sept. 23, 1799.

Robert Stuart of Waynesboro, Augusta County, and later of Botetourt County, where he died 1819, is first definitely identified Sept. 20, 1792, when he bought of John Hager[19] 113 acres of land adjoining John Berry. He was married, almost certainly for the second time, to Jane (perhaps Steele) by July 24, 1799, when she witnessed the will of Catherine Merritt.[20] Robert Stuart had been surety on the marriage bond of James McLaughlin who was married in Augusta County May 30, 1787, to Mary Stuart—perhaps Robert's sister—by the Rev. Samuel Shannon. When the Staunton Fire Department was organized Jan. 9, 1790, among those participating were Robert Stuart, James McLaughlin, Jacob Peck, John Gordon and Alexander St. Clair. The land purchased from Hager was sold by Robert and wife Jane to Jacob Peck March 23, 1807. Robert bought Nov. 23, 1807, of Claudius Buster and Jacob Baumgartner a lot in Waynesboro laid off by Samuel Estill. In the Augusta County 1810 census (p. 409) Robert Stuart was shown as aged 45 or more, his wife 26-44 and two sons (Samuel and Hugh) born in or subsequent to 1800, matching his marriage assumed to have been 1799. Robert and Jane sold the Waynesboro lot to John Reed March 14, 1815, and on Oct. 19,1818, he purchased of John and Peggy Hamilton 200 acres on Catawba River at Hall's Bottom, four miles north of Fincastle, Botetourt County, adjoining Joseph Peck and Peter Noftsinger. Robert died in 1819 and on Nov. 4 the inventory of his estate was taken by Robert Kyle, Joseph Peck and

[18]William Edmiston, whose family was allied with John (6) Stuart, probably the brother of the Robert here considered, deposed in Washington County April 18, 1806, that he previously had lived in Rockbridge County on land bounded by that of Joseph Coulton, (Major) Robert Stuart and John Buchanan during the early days of Borden's Tract.

[19]John Hager married Mary Ann Shroader and George Hager married Ann Stroader in Augusta County, Va., in 1785. John Hager Sr. was born in Hesse Cassel, Germany, Dec. 26, 1759, served in the Revolutionary War on the American side, moved from Virginia to Kentucky in 1806, settling in Floyd County, subsequently Johnson County, with his sons Joseph and Daniel, and died 1819. Rachel Hager of this family married Absalom Stuart, a grandson of Ralph (5) Stuart, whose family settled in Lawrence County, Ky.

[20]Robert and Jenny Stuart and Samuel Steele witnessed in Augusta County the will of John Steele, probated in 1804. Jenny Stewart, Alexander St. Clair and Jacob Swoope witnessed the will July 24, 1799, of Catherine Merritt, wife of Samuel Merritt and widow of Valentine Cloninger.

Joseph Powers; the widow Jane was administratrix. She was shown in the 1820 Botetourt census with her five sons and in 1830 with four of them, Samuel having set up his own home. Jane died in 1836 and an inventory of her estate was taken July 9 by Joseph Peck, Andrew McCartney and William Peck. The children of Robert and Jane Stuart were: (a) Samuel (7) born c1800, died 1850, married in Botetourt County Oct. 27, 1823, Priscilla, daughter of Nathan and E. Switzer; Thomas Switzer, securety. Her death in 1853, aged 54, was reported by her brother George. They had several children, among them Priscilla; Elizabeth; and Samuel L., born 1841, who was married in Montgomery County, Va., March 24, 1870, to Mary St. Clair. (b) Hugh (7) born 1801-1810, went to Arkansas in 1833. (c) Robert (7) born c1810. (d) John B. (7) born 1811-1815, was perhaps the John B. who married Ellin C. Cecil in Pulaski County, Va., Nov. 6, 1843, and was shown in 1850 census, aged 34. (e) David L. (7) born 1811-1815.[21]

2. JOHN (6) STUART, perhaps son of James (5) Stuart, was born 1765-1768 and first appeared in Washington County, Va., records when he was married to Rosannah, daughter of Francis Beattie, Feb. 24, 1789, by the Rev. Charles Cummins. The Beatties[22] arrived in Augusta County in the 1740s, by 1750 were living on Kerr Creek in now Rockbridge County and removed to the Middle Fork of Holston in 1772. John Stuart's will dated May 18, 1818, and probated Dec. 20, 1825, named his wife Rosannah; his son Robert; his daughter Betsy (wife of Gen. William Campbell

---

[21] Robert and Jane Stuart definitely had a son David L. Whether he was the David L. who married in Botetourt County, April 9, 1839, Eliza, daughter of James Pullen, is uncertain. One source—a county history—says the David who married Eliza was a son of Joseph and Adaline (Blucher) Stewart; that Joseph was a Scot who manufactured dental instruments and that his son David was a dentist who moved from Fincastle, Va., to Rush County, Ind. The 1850 census of Franklin County, adjoining Rush County, shows a David Stewart, 35, dentist, with wife Elizabeth, 37, both born in Virginia, and children Mary, James, Robert, Sarah, Elizabeth and Virginia, all born in Iowa between 1839 or 1840 and 1849.

[22] Francis Beattie named his daughter Rosannah Stuart in his will, probated February, 1791, giving her the 209 acres later passed on to her son Robert Stuart. Beattie's daughter Jane married Mr. Bustard (Buster). A nephew of Beattie was killed while serving under Capt. James Dysart at the Battle of King's Mountain; one of his fellow soldiers was Samuel Stewart, whose antecedents are unknown.

Edmiston) and her son John S. Edmiston; and Robert Lowery.[23] In both the 1810 and 1820 Washington County census, John was shown as 45 or older. On Jan. 2, 1826, the widow Rosannah conveyed to her son Robert the 209-acre home farm in an agreement under which he would support her for life; she also conveyed to Robert and her daughter, Mrs. Edmiston, four slaves.

ROBERT (7) STUART, son of John (6) Stuart, was born c1791-1797 and married in Washington County, Va., September 1819, Martha D. Kincannon. She died (dates cannot be read on her tombstone) and Robert married, perhaps, Mary Fleming (born 1805, died June 28, 1830) in September 1828, and again, July 1831, Martha S. Glenn. On May 8, 1840, Robert conveyed the 209-acre farm he had received from his mother to his children: Rosannah M., James A. M., Elizabeth A., John F., Sarah Jane, Mary S., Absalom B. and Ann S. Stuart. He had a son William T. S., born c1840, in Virginia, and son Charles B., born c1844 in Maryland. On July 21, 1848, Robert, his wife and younger children were living in Fountain County, Ind., when he sold 630 acres of the old Beattie land adjoining the site of Emory and Henry College east of Abingdon, Va., and the family was enumerated in the 1850 census of Fountain County.

3. JAMES (6) STUART, perhaps son of James (5) Stuart. Born c1770, he was perhaps the James Stewart, orphan child of Elizabeth (Isabella?) Barker, ordered bound in Washington County, Va., May 2, 1783, to John Greenaway "to learn the art and mystery of Black Smith and Cutlar" for seven years. While this remains a tentative identification, it seems unlikely many Mrs. Barkers had sons named James Stuart.

The portion of Montgomery County, Ky. (formed 1796 from Clark County) that was set off in 1811 to establish Bath County, was settled largely by families from Bath County, Va. The 1810 census of Montgomery County sounds like an earlier Bath County, Va., tax list: Stuart, Hamilton, Lafferty, Barker, Cartmell, Bratton,

[23] John Stuart bequeathed some books to Robert Lowery, who may have been a friend or may have married a daughter of Stuart's who died before the will was written. John Lowery purchased from Borden land on Moffetts Creek in Rockbridge County, adjoining the land of John (4) and Major Robert Stuart. Lowery left this land to his sons William and Robert, who sold it in 1771 and moved to Washington County, where Robert died in 1780. It is assumed Robert Lowery of Stuart's will is of this family. The younger Robert was aged 26-44 in 1820, and had a wife and four children.

Kincaid, Delay, Dunlap, Hugart, Kelso, Hicklin, Feemster, Elliott, Armstrong.

James Stuart married Ann, daughter of William Elliott[24] and in Montgomery County in 1799 he was made attorney by Ann's brother Robert Elliott to sell land in Fayette County, Ky. This Elliott family is said to have been related to Richard Elliott, whose sister Mary married Ralph (5) Stuart and the Richard Elliott who married Mary Stuart. James Stuart, the Elliotts, and Archibald Hamilton, grandson of John Hamilton and his wife Mary (Stuart) Hamilton of Bath County, Va., lived on Flat Creek, now in Bath County, Ky. James Stuart bought of Mark Mitchell of Hawkins County, Tenn., Jan. 16, 1801, 225 acres of land on the waters of Flat creek which he sold during the years 1803-1807. On Sept. 12, 1808, James Stuart and wife Ann of Montgomery County, Ky., and Robert Elliott and wife Susannah of Natchez District, Miss., deeded to John Henry their right in a tract of land near Coon's Station in Fayette County that had belonged to "William Elliott, father of Robert Elliott and Ann Stewart".[25] In the 1810 census of Montgomery County (p. 193) James Stuart was shown aged 26-44 (born 1766/84) with a wife the same age, a boy 16-25, four boys 10-15, two boys under 10 and two girls under 10. His near neighbors included Thomas Barker, Archibald Hamilton and William Cartmell, as well as others of the Hamilton family. Thomas Cartmell and other Bath County, Va., settlers had arrived as early as 1793. John Hamilton was appointed coroner in 1796 and the 1797 tax list contained the names of James Stuart, Richard Elliott, Ralph Elliott, Archibald Hamilton and others of these families.

James Stuart moved after 1810 to Lexington, Ky., where he engaged in the grocery business with Joseph Barbee on Water Street. He died in 1823 and the widow Ann (called Nancy) was made administratrix of the estate Dec. 8, 1823, with James McCauley as her bondsman. Her son, Robert, of Pulaski County, Ky., relinquished to her his interest in his father's estate and on March 1,

[24]Edson, Tome D, p. 322; Tome F, pp. 104-5.

[25]Archibald Hamilton, grandson of John and Mary (Stuart) Hamilton, purchased land on Flat Creek, adjoining James Stewart, on Jan. 2, 1804, from James Stuart Elliott, representing the estate of John Elliott. The latter purchased the land Jan. 15, 1801, the day before James Stewart bought adjoining property, and died before November, 1801. John Elliott's widow, Elizabeth, married Abner Hamilton of Barren County, Ky. Stewart already had a tract in the vicinity before 1801 and in the 1810 census was enumerated two farms from Hamilton.

1828, Ann made a prenuptial agreement with Dr. Henry Morehead, and was married to him in Jessamine County, Ky., March 6, 1828.

JOHN (5) STUART, son of James (4) Stuart of Cowpasture.

John was born c1748 on Stuart's Run of Cowpasture in Augusta (Bath) County, Va. He was 14 when he chose on Feb. 17, 1762, as his guardian, Henry Murray, son-in-law of Thomas Armstrong, who married his mother, Ann (Lafferty) Stuart, widow of James (4) Stuart, who was killed in 1757. In 1768 John was farming the home place with his older brother, Robert. John and his brother Ralph Stuart served under Col. Charles Lewis at the Battle of Point Pleasant in 1774. Sometime in this period he married Miss ------ Hamilton, doubtless a kinswoman of John Hamilton who had married Mary Stuart. In 1774, John and Ralph both were living on Stuart's Run of Tygart's Valley in now Randolph County, W.Va., where their brother James had been killed by Indians in 1772. On Dec. 17, 1777, during an unexpected snow storm, twenty Indians penetrated the Tygart's settlements and attacked Darby Connell's house, killing him, his wife and several of his children, taking three others as prisoners. They then proceeded a short distance down the river to the next cabin, that of John Stuart. They killed John, "his wife and child, and took Miss Hamilton, his wife's sister, prisoner."[26] John Haddon (from Bath County, Va.), discovered the bodies the following day and notified Capt. Benjamin Wilson; a group of settlers pursued the raiders but lost their trail. Administration of John Stuart's estate was granted March 17, 1778 to William Hamilton.[27] It is assumed that no child of John's survived the attack. No representative of his branch of the family was listed when the farm was sold in 1792.

(To be concluded)

[26] The sister may have been named Mary Hamilton. J. Lewis Peyton, *History of Augusta County, Va.*, says Jacob Warwick returned Mary to the settlements along with other Indian prisoners and he probably was referring to this incident, although the matter directly preceding refers to an earlier Kerr Creek raid in Rockbridge County; another Mary Hamilton was killed on Kerr Creek.

[27] William Hamilton probably was the father or brother of John Stuart's wife. William and John Hamilton and John Warwick appraised the estate of Darby Connolly who was killed the same day as Stuart. The first Jacob Warwick was a surveyor and the family moved from Augusta (Bath) County to Greenbriar County and was active throughout the area.

A STUDY OF SOME STEWART AND ALLIED FAMILIES

Part II

By WILLIAM C. STEWART

WEST OF THE settled frontier of Virginia, the rivers flowed toward the wonderful new land of Kentucky. The sparcely occupied Big Sandy Valley promised peace and prosperity for the family of Capt. Ralph Stuart who had grown up in the midst of two wars and innumerable Indian raids during which his father and two of his brothers had been killed. Ralph had been an outstanding example of the restless breed that was continually pushing the frontier westward. A characteristic of at least three generations of this family was its custom of seeking land on the outer edge of the frontier, always subject to forays by Indians angered at the encroachments of the white man; borders for which England and France had fought for years before the Revolution. Ralph's sons followed the Indian trails to the Guyandotte River and thus to Kanawha County (now Wayne and Cabell Counties) W. Va., and then across the Big Sandy to Greenup (now Lawrence) County, Ky. Ralph himself joined them there for a time and then returned to his farm in what is now Wyoming County, W. Va., to live out his last days.

Ralph (5) Stuart was born in Augusta (now Bath) County, Va., in 1747 or 1748[1] at the home of his father, James (4) Stuart, on Stuart's Run of the Cowpasture River, and was named for his mother's brother, Ralph Lafferty. After the death of James Stuart

---

[1] Pension application W-6168; Augusta County, Va., Order Book 1, p. 156; Will Book 3, p. 244. Ralph's gravestone in Wyoming County, W. Va., states he was aged 86 years, 10 months on the day of his death, Nov. 17, 1835, but it seems likely the age of 15 given when he chose a guardian in 1762 may be more nearly correct. Sources for most of the data in this study, submitted by the writer, have had to be omitted because of space limitations; the writer has consented to supply citations to interested researchers who send stamped reply envelopes.

in an Indian raid in 1757, Ralph's elder brother Robert continued to operate the family farm while the widow, Mary Ann (Lafferty) Stuart, married Thomas Armstrong. On Feb. 17, 1762, Ralph chose his brother Robert as guardian, with John Hamilton—who had married his aunt Mary—as Robert's bondsman.

By 1772, in that somewhat remote part of Augusta County, during the quiet before the storm that was to break as the Revolution, Ralph and his brothers, James and John, decided to go west. Undeterred by the memory of the death of their father, they purchased land along Tygart's Valley River of the Monongahela, unsettled since the Indians almost twenty years before had broken the first effort of English-speaking farmers to open up the wilderness in what is now Randolph County, W. Va. James, the older of the three brothers, took charge of the farm on a branch still called Stuart's Run in memory of their Bath County home. Hardly had he moved into his cabin before the Indians raided the tiny settlement and killed him. But this time, his fellow frontiersmen stuck it out—the first permanent settlement had been achieved. The farm was taken over by John Stuart who ran it until he, too, was killed by Indians in 1777 with occasional help from Ralph, who was almost continuously in the armed forces from 1773 to the end of the Revolution. After that, Ralph was to move down to Montgomery County, Va., living along the New River in what is now Giles County, and later in Mercer County before he took land in Logan (later Wyoming) County, W. Va.

In 1773, Ralph was commissioned by Lord Dunmore, Governor of Virginia, as captain of a company of Rangers raised to protect the defenseless frontier of Virginia. In his application for a Revolutionary War pension, Ralph stated he marched to the headwaters of the Monongahela River and then to Tygart's Valley, where his company was stationed for a short time prior to the Battle of Point Pleasant (October, 1774) at which place they joined the army under Col. Charles Lewis, commander at Fort Lewis on the Cowpasture, and participated in the battle. He remained on guard in Tygart's Valley until 1778, when his commission was renewed by Gov. Patrick Henry and he joined the army under Gen. Nathaniel Greene. Although he was undoubtedly there earlier, the first reference found to Ralph in what is now Randolph County was in an Augusta County court order March 17, 1774, that Ralph Stuart, Richard Elliott (his brother-in-law) and Jacob and John Warwick were to view a road from Joseph Gregory's to William Hamilton's farm on the Monongahela of which Tygart's Valley

River is a tributary. Ralph Stuart and Elliott were exempted from working on the road until it was completed, probably because of militia duties. This was one of a network of new roads to connect the Monongahela and Greenbriar settlements with the Cowpasture, Staunton and Borden's Tract.

In Green's army, under Col. Robert McCrary[2] and Major Smith, Ralph participated in the Battles of Guilford Courthouse (March 15, 1781), Hotwater, Groundsquirrel Ridge and Charlottesville. He was severely wounded in the right arm by a cut from a sabre in the hands of a British cavalryman and after recuperating at home, rejoined his regiment and proceeded to the Siege of Yorktown. After the surrender of Cornwallis, he aided in marching British prisoners to Winchester Barracks, where he was discharged, his certificate being signed by an aide of Gen. LaFayette. He refused to take his pay in depreciated Continental currency and received nothing for his service until he was given a small pension by the Commonwealth of Virginia in 1823. He stated in his pension application to the Federal Government in 1834 that he had been personally acquainted with Generals George Washington, LaFayette, Wayne and Scott.

Ralph Stuart appears in the records of the portion of Augusta County that became Randolph County from 1774 to 1782, when he began to scout for new land further west. He looked over the New River country where Ralph Lafferty's sons had settled in 1774, and on June 28, 1785, he surveyed 100 acres on the north side of New River, joining Mitchell Clay's lines. Ralph's wife Mary, sister of Richard Elliott, had died during or soon after the

---

[2]The McCrary and Bratton families of Bath County, Va., were related in some way to the Stuart and Lafferty families. John and Robert McCrary lived just north of Stuart's Run in 1767-1768 near Thomas Feemster. John McCrary died in 1768, leaving among others his son Robert, a militia captain in 1777, who was succeeded Nov. 21, 1780 by John Cartmell and thereafter served as a colonel. Adam Bratton also was in his troop. Nancy, daughter of William Thompson and granddaughter of Col. James Patton, married Henson Gardner of Walkers Creek of New River. They were dead by 1804, leaving children Patton Gardner and Cynthia Gardner, who married David Stuart McCrary. Henson's son and son-in-law, and Samuel C. Gardner, a party with them to a suit over the Gardner-Patton land (Sheffy vs. Cloyd, Augusta County, Va.) were living in Jackson County, Ga., by 1803, neighbors of William Stuart who may have been a son of James (4) father of Ralph (5) Stuart.

Revolution,[3] and on June 25, 1788, he married Mary Clay in Montgomery County, Va. She was a daughter of Mitchell Clay[4] and Phoebe (Belcher) Clay. William Tracy was bondsman and Richard Elliott witness on the marriage bond. Ralph was now about 41 and Mary Clay inherited a family of some six children, born from 1770 on. Ralph on April 1, 1791, bought of Henry Farley 100 acres on New River, at the mouth of Wolf Creek (in present Giles County) and on August 26, 1799, of John William Howe[5] 125 acres on Brush creek of Bluestone River in Montgomery (Mercer) County. Ralph and Mary sold their New River land Feb. 3, 1806, and moved to a part of Giles County that became Logan and then Wyoming County, W. Va. During the late 1820's, Ralph moved temporarily to Lawrence County, Ky., leaving some of his children to run the Wyoming County farm. He was enumerated in the 1830 census of Lawrence County but had returned to his (West) Virginia home by Jan. 10, 1834, when he applied for his Revolutionary pension. He died Nov. 17, 1835; his widow was still alive Dec. 17, 1846.

Ralph married Mary Elliott c1769 and had children Absalom, Charles, Ralph, Mary, Richard and James; by Mary Clay whom he married in 1788, he had Robert, Catherine, Phoebe, (perhaps) Anna, Mitchell, Rebecca, Sarah, William, Margaret, Henry, Amy, John and (according to family tradition) Ora.

1. ABSALOM (6) STUART, son of Ralph (5) Stuart.

Absalom was born 1770 in Augusta County, and is said in an unconfirmed story to have been stolen by Indians when he was a boy and held captive for seven years. Absalom appears to have been married in 1790 or 1791 perhaps to a Miss Wilson, but he first enters known records with his marriage (bond) July 30, 1793,

[3] One unconfirmed account says Ralph's wife Mary Elliott died while they were on a trip to Kentucky during the Revolution. So far as is known, Ralph maintained his residence in Randolph County, W. Va., until 1782; his share of the Stuart's Run of Tygart's Valley River farm was sold Aug. 28, 1792.

[4] Mitchell Clay was living in Bedford (now Franklin) County, Va., in 1760 when he married Phoebe Belcher. His settlement in 1775 in what is now Mercer County, W. Va., was the second in that area; in 1783 some members of his family were victims of an Indian raid. Among his children were Mary, born 1772, and Patience, who married George Chapman and stated in Ralph Stuart's pension application she had known him since 1778. Numerous members of the Clay, Belcher and Chapman families removed to Kentucky, among them George Chapman, of Lawrence County.

[5] John William Howe was a Revolutionary War pensioner who moved from Montgomery County, Va., to Greenup County, Ky., in 1806.

in Montgomery County, Va., to Susannah, daughter of Isaac Smith, who was bondsman, with Nimrod Smith[6] and Mitchell Clay as witnesses. Absalom married, perhaps for the third time, May 26, 1798, Tabitha Clay, in Montgomery County (by publication). She may have been a daughter of David Clay and almost certainly was related to Mitchell Clay. On May 1, 1800, Absalom bought of Jesse Willson[7] 17 acres on Brush Creek of Bluestone, then in Montgomery County and now in Mercer County, W. Va., adjoining John William Howe's survey near where his father Ralph had purchased land from Howe in 1799. Absalom was not in the 1810 Giles County, Va., census and there is some evidence he already had gone to Kanawha (later Cabell, now Wayne) County, W. Va., by 1808. He purchased March 31, 1812, from Henry Hayney 100 acres on Buffalo Creek and Duvall's line, now in Wayne County. The sons of Ralph Stuart began to move over into Kentucky as early as 1810 but Absalom remained in Virginia until after the 1820 census. The first land grant of record in Lawrence County (formed 1821 from Greenup County) to the Stuarts was 100 acres for Absalom on the Big Sandy Sept. 12, 1822, followed the next day by grants for his brothers Ralph and James, and on Sept. 14 for his brother Mitchell and his son Andrew. This 100 acre tract was conveyed to his son-in-law, James Prichard, July 30, 1827. Absalom died between Sept. 28, 1828, when he dated his will and April 13, 1829, when it was probated. He named his wife Tabitha and his 13 children: Andrew, William, Elizabeth, Prichard, Nancy Campbell, Rebecca Rice, Charles, Eleanor, Mary, Emily, James, Hiram, Melinda and Johnson. His remaining property was left to his wife, the land to go after her death to his four younger sons and the personal property to his four younger daughters. Tabitha relinquished her dower rights March 12, 1834, and may have died before 1840. Absalom's children:

1. ANDREW (7) STUART, born 1791-1792, was granted three 50 acre tracts on Bear Creek which he sold between 1825 and 1838 to John Ridge, Richard Evans and Harvey Stuart. In

---

[6]Nimrod Smith probably was the man of that name in the 1810 Giles County census. He or another Nimrod surveyed land March 31, 1829 in Clay County, Ky. A number of Stewarts in Clay County had names similar to members of Ralph's family but this county has not been researched by the writer.

[7]Jesse Willson surveyed the land in 1788; in 1802 it was conveyed to Richard Blankenship. A James Stewart, unplaced, entered land on the North Fork of Holston in 1782 as assignee of James Wilson.

1848, William Holiday and wife Nancy, John Ridge, Andrew Stuart, Mary Jane Stuart, Amelia L. Stuart and Henry R. Stuart were parties to a suit brought by Absalom Stuart, apparently their cousin, the son of Charles (6) Stuart, son of Ralph (5) Stuart, concerning land granted to Andrew in 1823 (1822?). Mary Jane appears to have been Andrew's second wife. He apparently died between 1848 and 1850 and in the 1850 census of Lawrence County (No. 557) were Mary J. Stuart, 35, born in Virginia; Henry R. 7, and Amelia Ann, 5, both born in Kentucky.[8]

2. WILLIAM (7) STUART was born June 17, 1793, in Rockbridge County, Va., according to descendants. This is possible although it is more likely he was born in the New River country. In 1850 he gave his age as 55 and in 1871 in his application for a pension, he gave his birth date as 1793. He was drafted in Cabell (Wayne) County in September, 1814, for service as a boatman in the War of 1812. He said he married Eleanor Walker Jan. 16, 1817, at the home of Charles Walker (her father), lived in Greenup County, Ky., about 1815-1820 and after that in Wayne County, W. Va. William died there, July 27, 1880, and his widow Eleanor died June 28, 1882. Their children were: 1. Elizabeth, born 1819, unmarried in 1870; 2. William, born 1821, married Caroline ——— and had in 1860 children Benjamin F., John or James C., Mary E., Luther C. and William T.; 3. Sarah A., born 1827, no data; 4. Albert, born 1820-1826, said to have gone to Colorado; 5. Charles C. or A., born 1830, said to have moved to Kentucky after 1850; 6. Henry Washington, born 1832, died 1912 in Huntington, W. Va., was married to Mary A. ——— and in 1870 had children James W., Charles K., George E. and Edwin; 7. James M., born c1834, married Sarah A. Riggs on Nov. 19, 1857, and in 1860 had son James T.; 8. Harrison Daniel, born c1836, married Martha Belle Hull and in 1870 had children Adia M., Thomas H., William M., John and Anna M.; 9. Martha E., born c1839, no data; 10. Thomas Harvey, born c1843, said to have been killed in the Civil War.

3. CHARLES (7) STUART, born c1795-1797, was living in Greenup County, Ky., in 1820, probably in what became Lawrence County. He married 1815-1816, Cynthia, daughter of Benjamin and Elizabeth (Brown) Mead, who were married in Bedford

---

[8]That the Andrew Stuart of Lawrence County who apparently died 1848-1850 was a son of Absalom (6) Stuart is based on evidence other than direct identification. The Andrew Stuart of Carter County, Ky., born c1795-1797, who married (second) Rachel Cook in 1838, appears to have been a son of Ralph (6), brother of Absalom (6).

County, Va., Dec. 29, 1796; they were one of numerous families who removed from Bedford and Franklin Counties, Va., to Kentucky.[9] Charles died before 1840, when the Greenup County census showed Cynthia as a widow. They had children: 1. George Washington, born Sept. 10, 1816; 2. Sanford Mead, born April 15, 1818, married Louisa ------ before 1850, when they had a daughter Cynthia A; 3. John Marshall, born Feb. 13, 1820; 4. James, born 1826-1830, living with brother Sanford M. in 1850; 5. Sophia Elizabeth, born 1831, married William F. Riggs, perhaps a relative of the Miss Riggs who married James M., son of William (7) Stuart. Various census enumerations indicate Charles had other children.

4. ELIZABETH (7) STUART, was born in Giles County, Va., July 26, 1802, according to family records, but probably earlier, and married in Cabell County, Dec. 10, 1818, James Prichard.[10] They lived in Cabell County for a time and then moved to Lawrence County, Ky., where her father conveyed to them July 30, 1827, 100 acres of land on Bear creek at Sandy River. They had moved by 1860 to Boyd County, Ky.

5. NANCY (7) STUART, born perhaps c1797, was married before 1828 to Mr. Campbell.

6. REBECCA (7) STUART, was married in Lawrence County, June 11, 1822, to James Rice.[11]

[9]Benjamin (son of Robert) Mead and his wife Elizabeth (daughter of Daniel Brown) sold their farm in Bedford County in 1811 and moved to Cabell (Wayne) County, W. Va., and later to Greenup County, Ky., where Benjamin died 1821 and Elizabeth 1851. Their daughter Cynthia was born June 25, 1799 (A. M. Prichard, Mead Relations, p. 34). Some of the Meads preceded Benjamin to Kentucky, settling first in Floyd County. The Browns and Tolers were among related families who came from Bedford County to Kentucky.

[10]The Prichard family lived in Bedford and nearby Henry County, Va. Some members, including William Prichard, moved to Russell County, Va., and then to Greenup County, Ky. William's son James Prichard, who married Elizabeth Stuart, was born May 3, 1796, died in Boyd County, Ky., Sept. 21, 1877. Among others from Bedford County was Euclid Wills, who married Betsy Stewart, daughter of Elizabeth Smith, April 3, 1780 in Bedford County and later settled in Montgomery County, Ky., where his will was probated March 12, 1799. Betsy has not been identified.

[11]William Ely, The Big Sandy Valley, 1887, p. 55, said the Rice family came from east of the Blue Ridge (Bedford County?) to Cabell County, W. Va., where James M. Rice, a noted lawyer of Lawrence County, Ky., was born 1802, and married (second) (Mary) Matilda Brown (March 19, 1840 in Lawrence County). It is assumed that Rebecca Stuart, who married a James Rice June 11, 1822 in Lawrence County, was the first wife of Judge Rice. James Elliott (8) Stuart studied with James M. Rice. Eleanor, Rebecca's younger sister, may have been the girl who married William Messer in 1829. Their sister Mary may have married William Evans in 1830.

7. ELEANOR (7) STUART, evidently was not married when Absalom wrote his will in 1828.

8. MARY (7) STUART, no data.

9. EMILY (7) STUART, no data.

10. JAMES (7) STUART, born between 1799 and 1806, appears to have been the James Stewart, born between Nov. 1, 1799, and 1801, who was married to Jemima Goode, daughter of John Goode, in Halifax County, Va., Oct. 11, 1821. Her sister, Susannah, married Johnson Stewart in Trigg County, Ky., in 1827, and another sister married Anderson Sizemore.[12] These and other allied families, including the Ladds, are found variously in Southside Virginia, Stokes County, N. C., Campbell County, Ga., Wyoming County, W. Va., and in Kentucky, particularly in Trigg County, as will appear. Trigg County was formed Jan. 27, 1820, from Christian and Caldwell Counties, and among its citizens when the county was established were Benjamin Goode, his father John, and the Ladds and Sizemores. Some members of the Goode family had been in the vicinity as early as 1809. James and Jemima Stuart (Stewart) perhaps moved to Kentucky shortly after their marriage although James does not appear in available Trigg County records until 1826. John Goode, father of Jemima, died in 1814. Susannah and perhaps some of the other children either went with the Stuarts to Kentucky or joined them there later. James Stewart died Feb. 2, 1872, aged 72 years, four months, two days,[13] and is

[12]John Goode, son of William Goode and wife Mary, daughter of Nash Glidewell of Halifax County, Va., married (second) Elizabeth Cole in 1809 and died in 1814. Settlement of the estate June 3, 1818 mentioned John's widow Elizabeth; Daniel C. Goode, guardian of John's children William H., John, Mary, Nancy, Susannah and Jemima (the last two married Johnson and James Stuart, lived in Trigg County, Ky.) and Richard Tuck, who was guardian of Lucinda and Daniel C. Goode, also children of John Goode. His daughter Sarah married Anderson Sizemore. John's widow Elizabeth married Thomas Evans before 1831. It has not been concretely proved that James and Johnson Stuart of Trigg County were sons of Absalom (6) Stuart, although they fit the known facts in every respect. The exact relationship of the above Goodes and Benjamin Goode, who was living in Kentucky before Trigg County was formed, is not known. Benjamin, son of John Collier and Elizabeth J. (Hawkins) Goode of an Amelia County, Va., family (G. Brown Goode, Virginia Cousins, 1887) was born in North Carolina, probably Stokes County, where a number of Ralph Stuart's neighbors in Wyoming County, W. Va., lived earlier.

[13]His gravestone indicates James was born in November, 1799. Other evidence, including the 1850 and 1860 census, indicates he was born closer to 1801. Eurie Pearl Wilford Neel, Statistical Handbook of Trigg County, 1961, is a necessity for Trigg County research.

buried at Montgomery, Ky., by the side of Jemima, who was born Jan. 2, 1800, died Oct. 4, 1876. Their children were Dabney, William, Cassandra, Wilson J., John, Fielding, Wiley, Anderson and James M.[14]

11. HIRAM (7) STUART, born c1802, probably was the Hiram shown in the 1830 and 1840 census of Greenup County.[15]

12. MELINDA (7) STUART probably was born c1803 and perhaps was the Melinda who was married Feb. 3, 1837, in Lawrence County to Henry Mead, and the widow Malinda Mead in the 1850 census shown, perhaps incorrectly, as aged 38.

13. JOHNSON (7) STUART appears to have been the man of that name related to James Stuart, in Trigg County, who was

[14]Children of James Stuart were: 1. Dabney, born in Virginia 1823-1824, married in Trigg County, May 26, 1845, Elizabeth Anne Guthrie. In the 1850 census they had children Francis M. and Irby W. (Irby Guthrie, born in Virginia c1812, lived near Dabney Stuart in 1850. The name Irby is reminiscent of Halifax County, Va.). 2. William, born 1825 in Kentucky (1850 census), married Nancy Annis Ladd in Trigg County, Dec. 18, 1843, and in 1860 had children William H., Jemima, John J., Thomas M., Benjamin F. and George J. 3. Cassandra, born Feb. 17, 1827, died Aug. 29, 1860, and is buried at Montgomery, Ky., next to her husband, Charles H. Robertson, whom she married in Trigg County, Oct. 7, 1850; Robertson married (second) Mary J. Wood (who appears to have been a daughter of Harrison (7) Stuart. In the 1860 census of Trigg County, she was in his home and William Wood was in the home of James (7) Stuart). 4. Wilson J., born June 7, 1829, in Kentucky, married in Trigg County, March 4, 1850, Elizabeth Ann Sizemore, died May 21, 1888. 5. John, born in Kentucky c1831-1832, married in Trigg County, Sept. 27, 1852, Margaret L. Russell, in 1880 (census) had a daughter Mollie. Next door to John and Margaret (Russell) Stuart in 1880 was T. R. Russell, 72, born in Kentucky, and wife Arrey. 6. Fielding, born c1834, lived with father in 1850, was not found in 1860 census. 7. Wiley, born c1836, married in Trigg County, Jan. 11, 1860, Mary A. Stewart, who probably was the daughter of Daniel C. Stewart, shown with him in the 1850 census of Campbell County, Ga. The relationship of Daniel C. Stewart, if any, to the family being studied, is not proven, but it appears he may have been a son of Charles (6) Stuart, son of Ralph (5) Stuart. In the 1880 Trigg census, they had children Armena, Sarah C. and Larra B.; Wiley's nephews Frank 22, and Charles Stewart, 18, worked on his farm. 8. Anderson, born Sept. 8, 1837, married Lucy A. ———— by 1861, died Nov. 15, 1898. In the 1880 census they had children John J., Virginia, M. (Emmy?) Lou, and Mack. 9. James M. (Madison) born c1839-1840.

[15]No record of Hiram was found in Greenup County other than the 1830 and 1840 census. Possibly his widow was the unplaced Sarah Stewart, 46, born in Virginia, with Margaret, 20, and James A., 17, both born in Kentucky, in the 1850 census. The younger Hiram Stuart of Carter County was not this man, although probably related. The Hiram of Knox County, Ky., probably was not related.

born Oct. 15, 1804, and died April 10, 1883. He married Dec. 17, 1827, in Trigg County Susannah Goode, sister of James Stuart's wife Jemima. He was in Trigg County by 1826, probably earlier. His children: 1. Johnson, born c1829, shown in 1850 census and records of the 1860's; 2. Harrison B., born 1831-1834, married Dec. 18, 1854, Martha Stuart, perhaps daughter of his cousin Harrison (7) Stuart; married (second) Dec. 21, 1861, Frances Stuart, probably sister of his first wife; and (third) July 6, 1880, Drucilla Redd; in 1880 he had daughters C. I., Cora and Oda T., son Curtis H., probably others; 3. Martha A., born c1834-1835, married Dec. 2, 1850, Wilson Stuart, probably son of Harrison (7) Stuart, had children Martin, Adaline, Henry B., Sidney, Robert, Sue; 4. James, born c1848; 5. Leroy, born c1841; 6. Thomas Riley, born c1846, married Dec. 18, 1866, Virginia Price and (second) April 3, 1876, Eliza J. Warren; 7. Mitchell, born 1847, died 1902, married Belle ———.

2. CHARLES (6) STUART, son of Ralph (5) Stuart.

Charles, second son of Ralph, was born 1771[16] and having gone probably by 1808 to what is now Wayne County, W. Va., crossed the Big Sandy and by 1810 was enumerated in the Greenup County, Ky., census, along with some other Stewarts of apparently unrelated families. He is the first Stuart of this family definitely proved to be in Kentucky, where Edward Burgess and other friends from Giles County, Va., already had found homes. Shortly after the formation of Lawrence County, Ky., Charles in 1822 with some of his brothers received land grants on Bear Creek and in 1836 he and his son Absalom were granted additional land. He sold one 50 acre grant to Simon Chafin[17] and the other 50 acres he con-

---

[16]Charles (6) Stuart stated in the 1850 Lawrence County, Ky., census that he was born in Tennessee, although he was almost certainly born in Virginia. He may have lived in Tennessee in his early years, before going to Kentucky, probably not before 1808. A man whose antecedents is unknown was in the 1850 Greenup County census: Robert Stewart, 42, born (c1808) in Tennessee, with wife Margaret and children E. A. (feminine), Mary J., William, Nancy F., Sarah and Hiram, the children having been born in Kentucky between c1835 and 1848. Charles is believed to have had a son Robert, who has not been located.

[17]Simon Chafin was a member of another of the families from Bedford County, Va., who settled in Lawrence County, Ky., a number of them stopping for a time in Russell County, Va., on the way. The Short family was in Halifax County, Va., as early as 1752 and is found in Bedford, Henry and Franklin Counties, nearby. William Stewart, who is unidentified, married Catherine, daughter of Winifred Short, Sept. 3, 1806 in Franklin County, Va., formed from Bedford and Henry Counties. Elisha Short was born in Bedford

veyed Jan. 7, 1827, to his son Absalom who agreed to support his father for life. In 1850 (census, Number 172) Charles was living with his son Absalom and next door to his son Charles. He apparently died before 1860; the name of his wife, dead by 1850, is not known. He is believed to have had fifteen children, of whom only Absalom, Charles and Mitchell may be listed with certainty; the others are allotted to him on the basis of family tradition and circumstantial evidence. The fact that Ralph (5) Stuart's sons by his first wife were siring children with the same given names at the same time that he himself was having sons by his second wife makes it impossible to be entirely certain on some points. Charles' children are believed to have been: Mitchell, Robert, Harrison, George W., Absalom, Charles, Thomas H., Wilson, William, Wiley, and perhaps Julina, Rebecca, Margaret and Daniel C.[18]

County, Va., in 1778 and died in Lawrence County, Ky., March 21, 1855. His death certificate as printed in *The Register* stated he was the son of "Lemon" and A. E. Chafon. This name should be Simon Chafin, who evidently married the Widow (Ann?) Short. Simon is found in the Bedford County records, and a younger Simon Chafin, born in Virginia 1798, lived in Lawrence County, and probably is the one who purchased the Stuart land. Thomas Short, aged 78, son of Thomas and Nancy Short, born in Russell County, Va., died in Lawrence County, Ky., Aug. 15, 1853. Thomas Short who married Jemima Chapman in Floyd County, Ky., July 12, 1809, was shown in the 1850 Lawrence County census.

[18]The children of Charles (6) Stuart:

Almost nothing is known of 1. Mitchell (7) born c1795-1802 (Greenup County 1820 census) or of 2. Robert (7) who was perhaps the Robert in Giles County, Va., or in Logan County, W. Va., in 1830. Of the others:

3. Harrison (7) Stuart, believed (but not proven) to be a son of Charles (6) was born 1803 in Virginia and was married, about 1822, probably in Halifax County, Va., to Elizabeth (perhaps Goode). He moved to Campbell County, Ga., by 1840 and in 1850 was living next to Daniel C. Stewart. His neighbors in 1840 included Daniel C. Goode, Sr., aged 70-80 (see Note No. 12) and Reuben J. Goode, aged 40-50. About 1852, Harrison moved to Trigg County, Ky. (as did the Barefields and various other families) to join his kinsmen who had been there a generation. He had children William H., Mary, Wilson, James, John F., Martha C., G. Jefferson, Frances, Lewis J., Susan A., Dabney W., Reuben J. and Clementine. The children before 1837 were born in Virginia and the death certificate of James shows he was born in Halifax County c1831. Martha C. married Harrison, son of Johnson (7) Stuart as did her sister, Frances.

4. George W. (7) Stuart, believed to be a son of Charles (6), was born c1804-1813 and married Narcissa Goode Dec. 27, 1832 in Trigg County. He had children George W., William and Wiley and died 1840-1850.

5. Absalom (7) Stuart, son of Charles (6), was born c1805 in Virginia, married Rachel Hager before 1830. Living with him in Lawrence County

in 1850 were his wife, born c1808 in Virginia, children Elizabeth and David, and his father, Charles (6).

6. Charles (7) Stuart, son of Charles (6), was born in Virginia c1807, and married in Lawrence County, June 30, 1833, Sarah Grubb, of a family that appears to have gone to Kentucky from Bedford County, Va., by way of North Carolina. Charles was living in 1850 next door to his brother, Absalom, with children Wesley, Nancy, Sarah G., Mary J., Rachel, Martha and George P.

7. Thomas Harvey (7) Stuart, believed to be son of Charles (6), was born 1810-1813 and married, apparently for the second time, Julia Ann Grubb in Lawrence County, May 14, 1853. He had a daughter Minerva, who married in 1859 William E. Dean, with whom Thomas H. was living in 1860; and by his second wife, Julia, he had children Adam, George and William R.

8. Wilson (7) Stuart, believed to be son of Charles (6), was born May 9, 1811 in Virginia, and married in Christian County, Ky., Dec. 24, 1832, Lucinda Adams from North Carolina. He may have gone after 1880 to Missouri to live with one of his children. They were: Eustatia A., Elizabeth, Serena H., Sarah, Johnson D., Lucinda, Thomas M., James Henry. Johnson D., born Feb. 1, c1843, moved to Bates County, Mo., and left family papers stating his father Wilson was related to James, Harrison, Johnson, William, George, Wiley, Dabney, "Nancy who married Mr. Warren, and Polly who married Mr. Ferrell," in Trigg County. Also apparently related was Mason Stewart, who died in Trigg County before April 11, 1840.

9. William (7) Stuart, believed to be son of Charles (6), was born c1812 in Virginia, married in Trigg County, April 18, 1831, Mary P. Wash and had children: George W., Melissa A., Nancy, James W., Henry Clay, John M. and Amelia Elizabeth.

10. Daniel C. (7) Stewart doubtless was related to the other Stewarts/Stuarts in Trigg County, but whether he was a son of Charles (6) is not known. He was born c1813 in Virginia, married by 1836, probably in Georgia, Nancy A. _____, lived next door to Harrison Stewart/Stuart in Campbell County, Ga., 1850. Children shown in 1850: Mary A. (married Wiley, son of James (7) Stuart of Trigg County), William G., John D., Eliza Jane, Marthena, Parthena, Nancy and Isaac N.

11. Wiley (7) Stuart, whose exact relationship is not certain, was born in Virginia c1816, married Frances ——— and was living in Christian County, Ky., in 1850-1860. He had children William Martin, James J., Benjamin F. and H. H. With him in 1850 was Charles T. Stewart, born c1810 in Kentucky, relationship unknown.

12. Rebecca (7) Stuart, believed to be daughter of Charles (6), was born c1813-1817 in Virginia, married in Lawrence County, Ky., April 14, 1838, Isaac Grubb, evidently his second wife. Isaac was born in North Carolina c1800, son of George and Sarah Grubb, and died in Lawrence County, Oct. 11, 1855.

Said by the family to be related to the other Stewarts in Trigg County were Nancy Stewart, who married William H. Warren Dec. 25, 1838; and Mary Stewart, who married William Ferril Jan. 6, 1841. In Lawrence County, the following may be related: Ruth A. Stewart married James Price, Dec. 21, 1827; Julina (or Malinda) Stewart married Madison Bromfield April 18, 1837, and among other children had son Absalom; Margaret Stewart married Edward Roach May 19, 1838. Charles (6) had at least three daughters—or other kin—shown in census who have not been identified.

3. RALPH (6) STUART, son of Ralph (5) Stuart.

Born c1772, Ralph was married to Elizabeth ——— by 1807 but probably at least 10 years earlier. In 1808, Ralph Stuart Jr. of Tazewell County, Va., was granted 25 acres on Guyandotte River in an area that may have been anywhere from present Cabell to Wyoming County, W. Va., (the 1810 Tazewell and Cabell census enumerations are not extant.) The death certificate of Ralph's son John states the latter was born 1808 in Lawrence County, Ky., but he probably was born in Virginia. However, by 1820 (Greenup County census) Ralph Jr. was living in what is now Lawrence County with three boys and four girls in his family. He appears to have had at least eleven and probably other children, of whom only John and Elliott may be assigned with certainty. He died after 1860. Several families in Carter County, Ky., may have been of this group.[19]

[19]On the basis of census, tradition and some rather fragmentary records, the following are believed to be children of Ralph (5) Stuart: 1. Polly, born 1802 in Virginia, married in Lawrence County, Ky., Feb. 22, 1829, Daniel White (son of Soloman and Barbary White) who was born in Lawrence County c1804 and died there Dec. 31, 1854. 2. John, born 1808, died Aug. 17, 1856 in Lawrence County, where he had married June 29, 1834, Lucinda Evans. They were shown in the 1850 census with children Eliza, Richard, Andrew, Sidney, Elizabeth and William. Eliza may be the girl who married in Lawrence County Aug. 22, 1855, Wiley Branham. John and William Branham were in Henry County, Va., 1782-1787, and in 1794, John Branham and his wife Martha were living in adjoining Bedford County, Va., but moved shortly thereafter to Montgomery County, Va., and by 1810 was living in Floyd County, Ky. John Branham's daughter Rebecca was born in Bedford County in 1794 and married in Floyd County, June 4, 1812, Zachariah Hale (son of Peter and Sarah Hale) who was born in Franklin (formed from Bedford and Henry) County, Va., in 1792. Palina Branham was born in Montgomery County c1795 and married ——— Hale. Both Rebecca and Palina died in Lawrence County Dec. 5, 1857. Zachariah Hale married (second) Margaret Dean, born in Rockingham County, Va., who was 58 when they were married May 29, 1858. Zachariah died Feb. 1, 1860. Wiley Branham married in Lawrence County, May 7, 1845, Rachel Fannin, who bore him a son Joseph. By his second wife, Eliza Stuart, Wiley had children Riley, Elvira, Elizabeth, Laura A., perhaps others. 3. Nancy, born 1810, who married Mr. Balmore, died by 1840, and married (second) June 6, 1852, Mr. F. Smith. This name has also been rendered as Balmone, Bellmore and Bellomy. 4. Charles. The Charles Stuart who was born c1804 in Virginia, married Nancy Cook, had children George W. and Charles F., and lived in Wyoming County, W. Va., is said in family tradition to have been the son of Ralph (5) Stuart, but it would appear that he may have been a son of Robert or Richard, sons of Ralph (5) Stuart; and that Ralph (6) Stuart's son Charles may have been the Charles H. Stewart, born 1810-1812 in Kentucky (?), lived in Carter County, Ky., with wife Jane, and by 1860

had these children: Albert, Landon, Braxton, Benjamin F., Martha, Daniel, Elizabeth N., Cynthia A. and Araminta (see other Carter County families below). 5. Andrew, born c1797, lived in Carter County 1838-1860, married (second) Rachel Cook in Carter County, Dec. 25, 1838, and had by 1860 children Missouri, Henry, Alfred, James and Greenville. 6. Hiram T. Stewart of Carter County was born c1823 in Kentucky, married in Carter County, June 17, 1847, Arminta Blankenship, and by 1860 had children Albert W., Harriet S., Eliza J. and Cynthia. 7. Malinda Stewart, born c1822, married in Carter County, Oct. 11, 1840, Hampton Toliver. 8. Johnson Stewart, born c1825, who was living in 1850 with the Tolivers and in 1860 with Hiram T. Stewart. Perhaps related to Hiram T. Stewart was James R. Stewart, born 1816-1818, who married Nancy A. Thompson in Carter County, Nov. 20, 1843, and by 1860 had children George W., James N., Elmira, Hiram T. and Rebecca. It should be remembered that Absalom (6) Stuart named in his will a son Hiram (older than Hiram T. above). 9. Elliott Stuart, born c1825, was living in 1850 in the home of Ralph (6) Stuart. 10. Ora, who married Charles Clay, said in family tradition to be daughter of Ralph (5) may have been a daughter of Ralph (6) Stuart; and the same may be true of the daughter Anna, about whom nothing is known. A Cynthia Ann Stewart, born c1825, married in Carter County Jan. 25, 1844, Andrew M. Savage. Polly Stewart, born c1831, married in Lawrence County, Oct. 15, 1852, Andrew J. Savage of Carter County.

A man whose antecedents are not known with any certainty was James Madison Stewart, born in Kentucky in 1822, who in 1850 was living in Lawrence County, Ky., next door to the widow of Henry Mead—Malinda, daughter of Absalom (6) Stuart—and two doors from Ralph (6) Stuart. Descendants have stated James Madison Stewart was the son of Eli Cadwallader Stewart, a cabinet maker who lived in Kentucky, Ohio, Indiana, Iowa and Missouri, and had also children John, William, Charles Eli, Cordelia Adelaide, Ruth Ann, Samuel, Henry, Francis Marion and Alice Minnettie. James M. Stewart and his wife Rebecca had in 1850 children Granville, Nancy and Marinda. He is said to have married four times, to have had a son Warren, and to have died Feb. 11, 1893 in Daviess County, Mo.

Some others who may have been related to the Ralph Stuart family were: 1. James Stewart, born 1803, married in Greenup County, Ky., Feb. 2, 1832, Edy Skidmore, and they were living in Carter County in 1850-1860, with children Emily, Joicy, Harriet, Elmira or Elmina, James, Joseph, Phoebe, Charles, Mary, William and Martha J. 2. Lewis Stewart surveyed 50 acres in Lawrence County in 1843. His land, on Bear creek, where the Ralph Stuart families lived, was sold to William Fulkerson in 1846; he is perhaps the same Lewis Stewart who married in Greenup County, Jan. 3, 1850, Jane Ruggles. (Elizabeth Stewart married Robert Ruggles in Lawrence County, Jan. 5, 1855). In 1850, Lewis, born c1819 in Ohio, and wife Jane were living in Carter County. His full name may have been Charles Lewis Stewart—after Charles Lewis of Bath County, Va., who was killed at Point Pleasant—a name found several times in Ralph Stuart's family. 3. William Stewart, born c1824 in Kentucky, was living in Carter County in 1850 with wife Louisa and children Thomas, James and John.

In Greenup County, Ky., Sept. 14, 1849, an Absalom Stewart married (bond) Jane, daughter of Elizabeth Hoop, with William Lowery as bondsman. He was almost certainly a descendant of James (4) Stuart, perhaps was a son of Ralph (6) Stuart, but is unplaced and was not found in the 1850 census of any of the counties in which the family was known to be living at that time. The fact that his bondsman was named Lowery may indicate some connection with the Robert Lowery who was left some books in the will of John (6) Stuart of Washington County, Va., in 1825. Some of the Washington County Stuarts removed to Indiana and perhaps others went to Kentucky.

4. MARY (6) STUART, daughter of Ralph (5) Stuart.

Mary, born c1773, apparently was named for her mother Mary, sister of Richard Elliott. She was married to William Walker in Montgomery County, Va., Nov. 15, 1791. He was in Giles County in 1810 and was related to Charles Walker of Giles County, whose daughter Eleanor married William, son of Absalom (6) Stuart in Cabell County. Whether they were related to the Walkers of Rockbridge County, Va., is not known.

5. RICHARD (6) STUART, son of Ralph (5) Stuart.

Other than meager family tradition, nothing is known of Richard, probably named for Richard Elliott. He may have moved to Indiana or Ohio.

6. JAMES ELLIOTT (6) STUART, son of Ralph (5) Stuart.

Born in what is now Randolph County, W. Va., in 1775, James E. was married in Montgomery County, Va., to Nancy Ann, daughter of Edward Burgess,[20] by publication June 7, 1798, the ceremony being in the Aug. 28 return of the Rev. Alexander Ross, who also officiated at the marriage of James' sister, Mary. James was in Cabell (now Wayne) County, W. Va., as early as 1812, and lived on a farm at Buffalo Shoals of Buffalo creek. He moved to Greenup (now Lawrence) County, Ky., before 1820, living on a Bear creek farm adjoining those of his brothers Mitchell and

---

[20]Edward Burgess was a Revolutionary War pensioner (S-35806) who was born in Virginia about 1744 and met Ralph (5) Stuart during the French and Indian wars. Burgess lived in what is now Tazewell County during the Revolution and bought land May 9, 1790 on Wolf creek of New River, now in Giles County, where Ralph purchased land the following year. He removed to Floyd County, Ky., by 1806, with his wife Nancy and some of his children; his son Edward had sons George, Edward and Gordon; his son William had sons George R., Edward, Reuben, Strother and John. Edward Sr. moved to Lawrence County, Ky., by 1822 where he was a justice of the first court. He probably was related to the Burgess families of Bedford and Pittsylvania Counties, Va., and may have had Culpeper County, Va., antecedents. He served during the Revolution under Col. Abram Buford of Culpeper and some of the Strother family removed from Culpeper to Giles County.

Charles. He died in 1835;[21] Nancy after 1850. Their children were: Col. Ralph, Levicy or Lucy, Mary, William, Absalom, Robert, Elizabeth, Eliza, Burgess, James, Henry Francis, John and perhaps as many as six others.[22]

[21] The headstone on James E. Stuart's Bear creek grave says he was born in 1769, but this was erected fairly recently by a descendant and the date is admittedly a guess; the evidence indicates he was born in 1775.

[22] The children of James E. Stuart were:

1. Col. Ralph, born 1799, married in Lawrence County, July, 1829, America, daughter of Reuben Canterberry, who with two brothers, came to the area about 1800, according to the historian Ely. The family was in Augusta County, Va., by 1767 and in Bourbon County, Ky., by 1800. James E. Stuart's sister Amy married John Canterberry in Giles County, where the family probably lived before moving to Kentucky. Ralph (7) had children: (a) Judge James Elliott Stuart, born Oct. 1, 1832, read law with Judge James M. Rice, removed to Paintsville, Johnson County, Ky., where he married Cynthia F., daughter of Lewis Mayo, Jan. 11, 1860; in 1868 he was elected Commonwealth Attorney for a district of seven counties and in 1876, judge of the criminal court; later removed to Louisa, Ky. (b) Elizabeth, born 1834, perhaps the one who married Moses Newman in Lawrence County, Feb. 21, 1854, less likely the Elizabeth who married Robert Ruggles, Jan. 5, 1855. (c) Lafayette, born c1836. (d) Jeremiah F., born c1839. (e) Albert H., born c1841. (f) Nancy A. or Frances, born c1843. (g) Gerard M., born 1846. (h) Anna or Emma, born c1849. (i) Milton M., born c1851. (j) America, born c1853.

2. Levicy or Lucy, born c1800, married Feb. 4/March 6, 1818 in Cabell County, W. Va., Jacob Peterman, who was probably related to the man of the same name who moved from Botetourt County, Va., to Highland County, Ohio. Jacob and Lucy removed to Lawrence County, Ky., before 1830.

3. Mary, born c1802, married David Kenner about 1820, lived on Bear creek in Lawrence County. The Kenners came from Southwest Virginia. (In Rockbridge County, Va., an unidentified Andrew Stewart married March 20, 1794, Hannah, daughter of Andrew Kinnear, which may be the same family). In 1850, Mary's mother Nancy (Burgess) Stuart was living with her; David died between 1850 and 1860. They had children Granville, Hansford, David, Henry, Lafayette, Mary F., Margaret, Louisa, perhaps others.

4. William, born c1805, is said to have married Polly Holiday, in Lawrence County, May 27, 1828, and to have removed to Indiana about 1840.

5. Absalom, born c1807, married July 10, 1828 _____ _____ and (second) Dec. 18, 1838, Amy Fannon (Fannin) in Lawrence County. He had children John M. (married Martha Merritt, Nov. 1, 1870, in Cabell County), William R., Isaac, Kesiah, Leander, James H., A. E. (feminine) and Almrah K., probably others. Amy is said to have been related to Isaac Newton Fannin, Big Sandy Valley circuit rider from Virginia, who is said to have married (second) Mary Stuart, who seems not to have been related to the family under study.

6. Robert, born c1809, probably was married three times, judging by the ages of his children. Compiling data on this Robert is made more difficult by the fact that at last one of the children of Robert of Wyoming County, W. Va., eventually moved to Cabell County, where this Robert lived.

It is not certain whether he was the Robert B. Stuart who surveyed land in Lawrence County, Ky., in 1836, but in any event, by 1841 he was teaching school in Cabell County, W. Va., where he spent at least most of the rest of his life, and where he died. He married, probably second, Tabitha Hudson, July 29, 1844 in Cabell County, and Tabitha having died, he married again, about 1845, Martha Ann _____. He died about 1880 and Martha Ann died Nov. 24, 1885. In 1875, Robert owed money to P. C. Buffington, and in the latter's home in the 1860 census was one Henry Stuart, aged 11, born in Texas as nearly as the census can be read. The Buffington connection is obscure; was Martha Ann a Buffington? Robert's children, from family tradition, and census records, appear to have been: Druzilla C., Ann C., James A., Martha J., Mary F., Emma, Ella F. (shown in 1850-1870 census) and (according to family records) Hezekiah Burgess, John, Charles, Allan and Henry (perhaps the boy in the Buffington home in 1860, a year in which Robert was not found in the Cabell census). Also see Robert (6) son of Ralph (5) Stuart, below.

7. Elizabeth, born 1811, married Colbury (rendered in one census as Calvery) Carter, in Lawrence County, April 18, 1838, and he was enumerated in the Boyd County, Ky., 1860 census as Calvin. Children included John H., Mary E., Octavia and Eliza J.

8. Eliza. A Lawrence County death certificate showed "Eliza Mannon, age 48, parents, James and Nancy Stewart; born Cabell County and died March 27, 1860 in Lawrence County". Nothing else is known. She may be the daughter said in family tradition to have married "Mr. Bowman." A Mannon family is found in Giles County, Va., and Lawrence County, Ky.

9. Burgess, born c1817, married Marie Ann Wigner or Wagner Aug. 13, 1845 in Cabell County, where he died before 1870. They had children Hamilton H., Mary, Daniel E., Viola A., Fletcher and Sarah B.

10. James, born May 21, 1818, married in Lawrence County, March 1, 1839, Sarah Jane Lakin, said to have been the daughter of Joseph Lakin or Leaken, born in Ohio in 1798. Sarah was born 1822, died 1909; James died March 3, 1876. They lived in Cabell County and had children: Isaac Foster; Hansford H., Confederate cavalryman killed in battle in 1863; Joseph Sylvester, physician and Confederate soldier; Columbia A.; James Boyd; and Henry Harrison.

11. Henry Francis, born 1819, died in Bloomington, Ill., in 1888, married in Cabell County in 1842, Rebecca Jane Mays, who had a brother named Elisha. Henry took his family to Osage, Mo., in a wagon, Rebecca died there and he married Sarah Chism or Chisholm, and moved to Illinois. Children shown in the family Bible were: Thomas Jefferson, America, Francis Henry, Lemuel, William Riley, Lafayette, Theresa, Edna, Martha, Emmen, James Elliott, Alonzo David, John Erastus, Mary Ann and Albert Gallatin. (The name William Riley is found many times in families descending from Ralph (5) Stuart; its significance is unknown).

12. John, born c1823, married Miss Burgess, according to the Big Sandy historian, Ely; this may be true or Ely may have confused John with his father, James, who married Nancy Burgess. John's first wife is not otherwise identified; he married, (second) in Lawrence County, Nov. 19, 1843, America Sperry of a family that came from Virginia to Kentucky before 1810. John had children Serapta and Sylvester in 1850 and before 1860 had moved to Kansas.

Five boys and a girl shown in James' home in 1820-1830 have not been identified; they may have been children or cousins.

7. ROBERT (6) STUART, son of Ralph (5) Stuart.

Family tradition states merely that Ralph had a son Robert, who married Miss Ball. Robert was born c1776-1789, apparently the first child of Ralph and Mary (Clay) Stuart, but perhaps son of Mary (Elliott) Stuart. He had children George P. and Robert, and it may have been Robert the son who married Miss Ball, rather than Robert (6).[23]

8. CATHERINE (6) STUART, daughter of Ralph (5) Stuart.

Catherine was born c1790, married in Giles County, Va., Aug. 15, 1806, William Cook. They lived in Wyoming County, W. Va.

9. PHOEBE (6) STUART, daughter of Ralph (5) Stuart.

She was born c1790, married in Tazewell County, Va., June 3, 1806, Samuel Morgan. They were living in Giles County in 1810.

10. ANNA (6) STUART

Anna is said in family tradition to have been a child of Ralph (5) Stuart, but it is possible she was a grandchild.

11. MITCHELL (6) STUART, son of Ralph (5) Stuart.

Mitchell—named for Ralph's father-in-law, Mitchell Clay—was born in Montgomery (now Giles) County, Va., c1792, and removed to Greenup (now Lawrence) County, Ky., between 1810 and 1822, when he served as road surveyor from the Greenup County line to the farm of his brother, Ralph (6) Stuart on Bear Creek in newly formed Lawrence County. His brother Charles Stuart was surveyor from Ralph's farm to "where the East Fork intersects the river road." This probably was the East Fork of Little Sandy. Mitchell was granted 50 acres on Bear Creek Sept. 14, 1822, adjoining farms granted on Sept. 12, 13 and 14 to his brothers

---

[23]Children of Robert (6) Stuart, who bought land in Kanawha (now Boone) County, W. Va., March 25, 1826, included: (a) George P., born c1811, married Margaret (perhaps Johnson), lived in Wyoming County, W. Va., and had children John, Nancy, Jane, Charles, Polly, Henry, Margaret, Andrew, Robert and William; and (b) Robert, born c1814, who appears to have married Malinda (perhaps Ball) in Kentucky about 1835 and (second) Martha J. _____ by 1850, when he was living in Wyoming County, W. Va. (Four other Roberts of the Ralph (5) Stuart families had wives named Martha, all about the same age, which does not make it easy to trace them as they move from county to county). Robert appears to have had children: 1. Charlotte (born c1836 and living in 1850 with James Ball's family in Lawrence County, Ky.); 2. Henry F. and 3. James H., born in Kentucky c1837 and c1838; and these born in (West) Virginia: 4. William H., 5. Julia Ann and 6. Malinda. Henry F., "son of Robert and Melinda Stuart", moved to Cabell County, where he married Elizabeth Pauley Dec. 24, 1863.

Absalom, Ralph and James.[24] He was granted another 50 acres in 1836 and he conveyed 100 acres April 14, 1841, to his son Clay Stuart. Mitchell married Frances _____ by 1817, perhaps in Giles County, Va., or Cabell County, (West) Va. Both died subsequent to 1860. All of his children have not been definitely established by name; some, including Clay, spent some time in Arkansas and perhaps Missouri. Mitchell appears to have had a daughter born between 1815 and 1820; a son, George P. born c1823; son William Riley born c1824; a daughter born 1826-1830; daughter Rebecca born c1829; son Robert born c1830; daughter

[24]Two Mitchell Stuarts are shown in the 1820 census, one in Giles County, Va., and one in Greenup (now Lawrence) County, Ky. One was the son of Ralph (5) Stuart and the other the son of Charles (6), son of Ralph (5) Stuart. It has proved impossible to separate the record of one from the other except by circumstantial evidence. Family tradition is uncertain whether the Mitchell who was born c1832-1834 and who married Cynthia Mead was the son of Mitchell (6) or of Mitchell (7) son of Charles (6). However, the Mitchell in Lawrence County from 1822 and shown in the Lawrence County census in 1850 and 1860 as born c1791-1792 is almost certainly Mitchell (6) son of Ralph (5) and the weight of the evidence is heavily that he was father of Mitchell who married Cynthia Mead. What became of Mitchell, son of Charles (6) is not known. A peculiarity of this family, proven in several instances in this: The dozens of children all had the same or similar given names and there seems to have been an agreement that the elder would choose, in any given community, the name he wished to use in everyday business. For instance, if a man named Henry Harrison Stuart living in Doe County was joined there by a cousin also named Henry Harrison, the elder of the two might elect to be known as Harrison, while the younger then was known as Henry, although he may have been known in his previous residence in another county as Harrison. This has understandably made for difficulties in this search. Members of this family made numerous changes of residence, back and forth between Kentucky and West Virginia, and appear to have pursued a not uncommon custom of the children of one family helping out on the farm of a brother or cousin, so that youngsters listed in census enumerations must be checked carefully with other data. For reasons of time and expense, it has not been possible for the writer to check the records of every county in a dozen states for data on the scores of members of this family. The chief purpose of this compilation has been to furnish a reasonably accurate outline of the family up to 1850 and in some cases later, with a view to helping others interested in the family. So little has been known and published about the family that an imperfect start seems better than a vain pursuit for perfection; as it is, the study of this family has required the equivalent of four years of research.

Mary born c1831-1832; son Albert R. born c1833;[25] and son Mitchell (7).

Mitchell (7) was born in Lawrence County, Ky., between 1832 and 1834. He was not shown in the 1850 census of Lawrence County, perhaps being with his brother William Riley in Arkansas or Missouri. He returned to Kentucky and married in Lawrence County April 20, 1859, Cynthia Mead.[26] He was shown in the 1860 Lawrence County census aged 27, with a farm worth $300, his wife "Sintha" aged 18, and a son James, aged 1, all born in Kentucky. In 1896, he removed to the Plum Grove community in Greenup County, but later returned to Lawrence County and died in Boyd County, Ky., Jan. 21, 1916. His children in addition to James, included Marion (probably Francis Marion) who lived in Wayne County, W. Va., and Mitchell (8) who was born in Lawrence County in 1880 and died in 1945.

Mitchell (8) married Martha Hylton (born Aug. 1, 1882, died May 11, 1951), daughter of Nathan and Violet (Pennington) Hylton.[27] They had children: Sophia, Jesse, Herbert, Mary, James,

[25]Clay Stuart was born c1818 and married March 21, 1841 Mary Ferguson, and the following year was granted 60 acres of land in Cabell (now Wayne) County, W. Va. Not long after, he appears to have moved to Arkansas, where his son William R. was born c1846. He returned to Kentucky and then moved to Wayne County, where he married (second) Polly Litt, Sept. 11, 1859. He had children Kelly, William Riley, Hiley Ann/Mary, James, Levicy and Mitchell.
Other children of Mitchell (6) included: (c) George P. (middle initial may have been S. or L.) born c1823, married Sarah or Sarelda _____ had children James H., Laverna, Araminta, Robert M. and others. (d) William Riley, born c1824, married Frances _____ (born in Arkansas), lived in Missouri c1852, returned c1853 to Lawrence County, Ky., had children: Columbus, Mitchell, Cornala, Jeremiah, Sophia and perhaps others. (e) daughter who may have been the Cynthia Ann Stuart who married Isaac M. Savage in Carter County, Ky., Jan. 25, 1844. (f) Rebecca, born c1829. (g) Robert, born c1832, died in Greenup County, Aug. 10, 1911. (h) Daughter, perhaps Mary of Lawrence County who married Andrew J. Savage of Carter County, Oct. 15, 1852. (i) Albert R., born c1833, married Ellender _____, had children Elizabeth, Marion F., Edward and probably others.
[26]Cynthia Mead was doubtless of the Greenup County family from Bedford County, Va., but the exact relationship is unknown. Charles (7) son of Absalom (6) Stuart married an older Cynthia Mead. Mitchell (7) is said by the family to have married (second) Emma Sprouse and to have had at least 12 children.
[27]Jesse Hilton (also Helton or Hylton) was born c1755 and married c1775 Juda Wright in Bedford County, Va. Jesse and his father John moved to Kentucky. Jesse had a son Benjamin, born March 13, 1786, died June 4, 1856, leaving son Eliphaz (born Feb. 28, 1820, died February, 1896) who

Martin and Glannis. Jesse, born in 1907, and named for an uncle, Jesse Hylton, is the noted poet of Greenup County.

12. REBECCA (6) STUART, daughter of Ralph (5) Stuart.

Born c1793-1794, Rebecca married in Giles County, Va., Aug. 15, 1811, Isaac Chapman, and they removed to Lawrence County, Ky., by 1830.[28]

13. SARAH (6) STUART, daughter of Ralph (5) Stuart.

Born c1795-1799, Sarah married in Giles County, Nov. 1, 1815, Daniel Gunnoe or Gonoe. They appear to have died or removed from Logan/Wyoming County, W. Va., after 1830.

14. WILLIAM (6) STUART, son of Ralph (5) Stuart.

Born 1801, William married Jan. 6, 1824, Eleanor Canterberry, in Giles Co., Va., where both were born. They were still living in Wyoming County, W. Va., in 1870. Their children included Ralph, Caroline, William C., James H. and Nancy.

15. MARGARET (6) STUART, daughter of Ralph (5) Stuart.

Born 1802-1803 in Giles County, she married Francis Hendricks there March 29, 1820.

16. HENRY C. (6) STUART, son of Ralph (5) Stuart.

Henry C. (probably C. for Cartmell) was born c1804-1805 in Giles County, Va., and between 1835 and 1838 moved to Indiana, where he opened a store at Russiaville, then in Carroll later in Howard County, trading with the Indians and as far away as Chicago. After 1850 he moved back to Wyoming County, W. Va., while some of his children remained in Indiana. He may have returned to Indiana, as he was not found in the census of 1860 in Wyoming County. His wife was Jane Taylor, born in England, and children included: Harrison H., Catherine (married William Sarver, Wyoming County court clerk) David, Henry B., George P., Charles Lewis and Perry. Harrison, a deputy sheriff, was shot by a horse thief who called himself John Thrall and who killed a clergyman before he was downed by a shot from the pistol of

---

had son Nathan Hylton, born Oct. 29, 1851, died aged 91. Nathan married in Carter County, Ky., May 4, 1873, Violet Pennington (born April 30, 1855) and they were the parents of Martha Hylton, who married Mitchell (8) Stuart.

[28]The Stuarts and Chapmans appear to have been neighbors as early as 1796 on New River in Virginia. The Chapmans came to Kentucky from Giles County, Va., in 1806. George Chapman, one of the first settlers in the Big Sandy Valley, married Patience, daughter of Mitchell Clay.

"Henry B., son of the coroner, John Stewart."[29] Harrison recruited the last company raised for the Union Army in Howard County. Robert T. Stewart, of Howard County, a soldier in the U. S. 126th Regiment, who died at Louisville, Ky., Feb. 6, 1865, may have been a relative.

17. AMY (6) STUART, daughter of Ralph (5) Stuart.

Born c1805 in Giles County, Va., Amy married there June 22, 1820, John Canterberry, who died before 1870. Their children included Ralph and Henry Canterberry.

18. JOHN (6) STUART, son of Ralph (5) Stuart.

It has been said in family tradition that John was born about 1770-1776, and it is true that a John appears in Cabell County deeds in 1815, but the family of Col. John Stuart of Greenbrier had land on the Guyandotte River, and it appears more likely that Ralph's son John was the John H. Stuart born about 1808 who was living in Wyoming County in 1860 with wife Elizabeth and children James C., Lucinda, John, Rhoda J., Elizabeth and William L. John may have moved to Indiana after 1860.[30]

19. ORA (6) STUART, daughter of Ralph (5) Stuart.

She is said to have married Charles L. Clay in Giles County in 1806(?).

---

[29] John Stewart the coroner would appear too old to have been a son of Henry (6), was more likely Henry's brother. Whether Henry and John both had sons, Henry B., is uncertain; the historian, Jackson Morrow, History of Howard County, Ind., c1886, v. 1, pps. 203, 289, may have been confused.

[30] John (6) was born in 1769, according to at least one county history, but all evidence found by the writer indicates he has been confused with John, brother of Ralph (5), and that Ralph's son John was not born until c1808. However, no one can afford to be dogmatic about a man called John Stuart—his name was legion.

The Strother Family.

Some claim that the family was of Scotch origin, and that it had the prefix "Mac."

Judge C. W. Strother, of Giles county, Va., says Gen. Dick Taylor told him he had visited the old burial ground of the family in the Isle of Thanet, the county of Kent, England, and there had seen the name in its various transitions from its original form, "Straathor," to its present orthography. He saw these tombstones over a thousand years old. The family belonged to the priesthood in the worship of the Saxon god "Thor," from whom our Thursday is named; hence, also, the Straa-thor. Chaucer mentions the name in "Canterbury Tales," showing its existence in its present form in the fourteenth century.

There were Strothers in Ireland, who went there with William III in his war with James II, and were rewarded with lands and estates. Some say the race is of Scandinavian origin, as in the only European countries in which it exists to-day, and in which it is spelled as we do, is in Sweden and Denmark, and they suppose it was planted in Northumberland by the Danish vikings in the eighth, ninth and tenth centuries. Others think it came in the Norman invasion with William the Conqueror in the eleventh century. The name there appears on the land books with the French prefixes, "De," "Del." From the records it appears that the Strothers figured as great landed gentry during the thirteenth, fourteenth and fifteenth centuries, holding many high offices and baronial titles from the crown of England.

A few years ago, several of the American branch of the family spent some time in England, and while there met a family of Anstrothers, and by them were induced to believe that was the original name, and that the family on coming to America dropped the first two letters.

The records of offices and estates held by them in those early days are too numerous to mention in this paper. One, Alen del Strother, died in 1381, leaving to his children ten extensive and rich manors. William del Strother married Jean del Wallington, and their son, William, lived at Castle Strother, in Glendale, Northumberland, in 1426. William del Strother, five hundred years ago, was entered in the register of that place as "a good borderer and a trew man." Twenty generations after, we find his descendants in Virginia taking an active part in the Revolutionary War.

One descendant says, that in the Revolution of 1776 our ancestry, in their war against British supremacy and British institutions, rid themselves of much that was superannuated, useless and oppressive, but they also cast overboard some dignified and respectable hobbies which we have cause to regret. One was respect for ancestry and family tradition. Macaulay says, "A people which take no pride in the noble achievement of remote ancestry will never achieve anything worthy to be remembered by remote descendants."

The coat of arms is registered in the College of Heraldry, in London, but it was valued highly and carefully preserved in the Manor House, below Fredericksburg, Va. The house was accidentally burned over a hundred years ago. The crest of the coat of arms is a greyhound, the shield red, across it a silver bend on which are three blue eagles. The first of the name we find in Virginia was William Strother, who died in 1702. He was said to have been one of the body guards of King William. He was in Virginia prior to 1673, before William and Mary reigned. He lived on the Rappahannock, and devised his lands to his wife, Dorothy, for life. His sons were William, James, Jeremiah, Robert, Benjamin and Joseph.

There are many public records of the Strother family intermarried with the Lewis, Randolph, Marshall, Harvie, Hawkins, Preston, Taylor, James, Blair and Jones families, and really too many others of prominence to mention, so I will confine myself to a few of the descendants of William, James, Francis and Jeremiah.

William Strother and his wife, Margaret Watts, were blessed with thirteen daughters. The oldest married Thomas Lewis, son of the brave pioneer Irishman, John Lewis, and his wife, who was descended from the Laird of Loch Lynn. Three of their sons were officers in the Revolutionary army, and a daughter was the mother of Gov. Gilmer, of Georgia. Agatha Strother married John Madison, a cousin of the president. She was the mother of Bishop Madison; and a son, General Thomas Madison, married Susanna, the sister of Patrick Henry. Margaret Strother married, first, George Morton, who soon after was accidentally killed, leaving her a large fortune. She then married the talented Welshman, Gabriel Jones, who was afterwards known as the "Valley lawyer." He was a relative and executor of Lord Fairfax, and was the most distinguished lawyer of new Virginia. She lived to be ninety-eight years old, and was much beloved. A great granddaughter, writing of her, says there are two portraits of her in the family. At middle age they represent her as a noble-looking woman, and must have been, in youth, extremely handsome. She must have had a hard time with her irascible husband, the severity of whose temper has passed into a proverb. A granddaughter married Charles, the son of Col. Thomas Marshall and Mary Randolph Keith. A daughter married Col. John Harvie, and their daughter, Gabrella, was noted for her beauty, grace and accomplishments. She was spoken of for many years as the "Fair Gabrella." One of her daughters, a noted belle, married a son of the celebrated Dr. Chapman, of Philadelphia, a granddaughter married a Mr. Podesta, for many years secretary of the Spanish legation at Washington.

There were many prominent men of the Strother, Jones and Harvie descent, influential in both State and National affairs; also some in the Confederate service. One was secretary to President Jefferson Davis, another Inspector General of Northern Virginia on the staff of Gen. Joseph E. Johnston. General Jaquelin B. Harvie served with distinction with Decatur in the Tripolitan war, and married Mary, the only daughter of Chief Justice Marshall. James Strother married Margaret French. He died in 1761. Their son, French Strother, died in 1800, after having been for thirty years consecutively in the House of Burgesses, Convention of 1788, which adopted the Constitution of the United States. He belonged to the House of Delegates and State Senate; held many important offices, and his descendants intermarried with prominent families, and many were officers in the Confederate army. His seventh child, George French Strother, married, first, a daughter of Gen. James Williams. Their grandson, Judge Philip W. Strother, was senator from Giles county, Virginia, and has done much to keep a clear record of the Strother ancestry. George F. Strother's second wife was Theodosia Hunt, of Lexington, Ky. Their gifted and accomplished daughter, Sarah, married the wealthy Baron de Fahnarburg. He left his immense estate to his wife, and she willed it to her Strother kin, but I believe it is yet held by the courts. David Hunter Strother, known in the world of letters as "Porte Crayon," was the son of John, and grandson of Anthony Strother. He entered the U. S. Army, July 6, 1861; colonel of 3d Virginia cavalry and Brevet General; was Adjutant General in Virginia 1865-66; was consul to Mexico 1879-85. His daughter married John B. Walker, of Colorado. On a visit to England, he went to the College of Heraldry and sketched the Strother coat of arms; around the shield he beautifully draped the American flag, he said, to distinguish the American branch of the family.

Francis, the nephew of Jeremiah, was of St. Mark's Parish, and died in 1752. He married Susan Dabney, who was a daughter of John Dabney and an English lady, Sarah Jennings. She should have inherited a large fortune, coming to her from England, but has not yet succeeded in obtaining it. Among their descendants are many prominent people, Hon. John S. Pendleton, Gen. Edmund Pendleton Gaines, Gen. William Preston and Henrietta, the wife of Gen. Albert Sidney Johnston.

William Strother, son of Francis, of St. Marks, married Mrs. Sarah Pannill (nee Bailey). Her will, proven 1774, shows her to be a woman of intellect, strength and decision of character. Their children were William Dabney, Frances, Gerard Banks, Sarah and Susanna. William Dabney died in the army during the Revolution. He was considered quite a good poet. The descendants of Frances Banks became prominent residents of the Carolinas. Sarah married Col. Richard Taylor, and was the mother of General President Zachary Taylor, his daughter, Sarah, was the first wife of President Jefferson Davis. His son, Richard, was Lieutenant-General in the Confederate army, and was the author of Destruction and Reconstruction," one of the very finest books of the late war. The funeral of Mrs. Sarah Taylor was preached by our late beloved Philip S. Fall. Susanna, the second daughter of William and Sarah Strother, married, first, Captain Moses Hawkins, who was killed at Germantown in the Revolutionary War. He left four children—Sarah Hawkins, who married James Thornton; William Strother Hawkins, who married Katherine Keith; Lucy Hawkins, who married William George, who was killed in the War of 1812, and Moses Hawkins, who married Sarah Castleman.

Susanna Strother married, second, Thomas Coleman, who was also an officer in the Revolutionary army, and the guardian of her Hawkins children. They had five children—Nancy Coleman, married Joseph George, who was killed in the War of 1812; Strother and Ambrose Coleman died single and John was killed in the Indian War. Susan, the youngest, married Lewis Sublett, whose great grandfather was one of the Huguenot refugees to Virginia in 1700. He was also in the War of 1812. Susanna Strother Hawkins Coleman was remembered by her grandchildren as very fair and beautiful, even in old age. Many of her descendants were in the Mexican and Civil Wars; others are successful business men in the South and West. A great granddaughter, Mrs. Lucy Thornton Key (the wife of Bishop Key, of Texas), is president of one of the largest and most flourishing institutions of learning in the Southwest. The oldest son, William Strother Hawkins, married Katherine Keith, the youngest daughter of Lieutenant Isham Keith, of the Revolutionary Army. They had twelve children, only two now living— William Strother Hawkins, of Woodford county, and Katherine Keith Railey, of Oklahoma. The oldest son (my father), Isham Keith Hawkins, died four years ago, in his eighty-eighth year.

General David Hunter Strother says: "As a race, there is uniformity in their leading traits of character. They were men and women of great self-reliance and integrity; unostentatious, without social ambition, as if the sturdy, personal independence disdained the support of social prestige, and their own self-respect and sense of right being a guide to their opinions and actions; they took no heed to the blame or approval around them; such men, immovable in politics, rarely ever mentioned in the newspapers, seldom grow rich, but are highly esteemed, and their true worth recognized by their neighbors.

Read by Annie Hawkins Miles before the Historical Society of Colonial Daughters, Frankfort, Ky., February 6, 1896.

THE STROTHERS.

By William E. Railey.

Author of The Randolph-Railey Genealogy.

Through the generosity of one of our most valued members and contributors, Mr. Railey, we are indebted for the genealogy and history of one of the most historic and widely known families of America, the Strothers. The name is found in every State in the Union, it is said, but the largest number of the name is found in Kentucky and Virginia.

This history will probably run through three editions of the Register—September, 1917, and January and May, 1918.*

We make this announcement that this noted people throughout the Union, and in Kentucky and Virginia especially, may secure copies of this valuable family history, which has been pronounced by the most critical genealogists and invaluable historical genealogy—(Ed. The Registrer.)

The Strother family is a very ancient one and supposed to be of Scandinavian origin. It exists in Sweden and Denmark to the present day. The supposition is that it was introduced into England by the Vikings as the bearers of it are mentioned in the Annals of Great Britain about that time.

The Strothers first took possession of the Island of Thanet, at the mouth of the Thames, in the fifth century, and General Richard Taylor, son of President Zach Taylor, visited the island and saw the family burying ground.

It was early in Northumberland where the name is found during the reign of Henry III, and for centuries the name has figured among the landed gentry of that part of England, members of the family being in high esteem by Royalty, and they were intermarried with the most influential and powerful families of Northern England. Wm. del Strother, brother of Alan Strother, Jr., was Mayor of New Castle on the Tyne 1352, and subsequently represented that city in Parliament. The descendants of Henry Strother resided at Castle Strother, Glendale, who owned it 1460. In 1639 Wm. Strother matriculated at Oxford. Thomas Orde of Talkington married Mary, sister of Sir Strother of Towerly Tower and had a son John, who lived to an advanced age and died 1789.

From the family of Northumberland the family of Strothers of Virginia claim descent through Wm. Strother. The coat of arms as shown by Hodgson, Burke and other authorities is a shield gules

---

*The Register of the Kentucky Historical Society carried only two installments on the Strother family by William E. Railey—in September 1917 and January 1918 (pp. 369-394, this volume). The May 1918 issue of the periodical did include an article by Railey entitled "Brief Sketches of the Randolphs and Their Connections; Also a Brief Sketch of the Owsleys and Whitleys," containing additional information on the Strother family. This article appears on pp. 173-188 of this volume.

displayed crest, greyhound segant. General David Hunter Strother (Porte Crayon) wrote a letter, a copy of which I have, in which he says: "Fifty years ago I had a silver watch stolen from me which had been brought from England by a great-grand uncle, and descended to me through my father and grandfather. On the inside case of this double case watch were engraved the armorial bearings described above."

It is not known exactly when the first of the family came to America, but Gov. Gilmer, of Georgia, whose grandmother was a Miss Strother, thinks as early as 1650. In his book on Georgians, 1855, he states that the Strothers emigrated from England to Virginia in the early days of the colony. They were connected by blood and marriage with many of the most respectable families in Virginia, and have been distinguished by courage and talents, members of the Legislatures, officers of the army and members of both branches of Congress. The first person who died in Georgia for the cause of liberty was Wm. D. Strother, who was a captain in a Georgia regiment.

The Strother family were devout Episcopalians and the transfer to American soil made no difference in their church relations for many years, as they remained staunch and active churchmen, as attested by the old church records of King George, Stafford and Culpeper counties. Bishop Meade, in his "Old Churches and Families" says: "I cannot take leave of old St. Mark's parish and vestry without a brief reference to those who once composed them. The Spotswoods, Slaughters, Pendletons, Fields, Greens, Strothers, Williams and others who, amidst all of the adversities of the church, have been faithful to her."

Family tradition, history and public records, however, show that Wm. Strother was the first of the name in Virginia, where he appeared July 12, 1673, to designate the mark of his cattle in the court of old Rappahannock county, existing in 1692, with Richmond, where his will is recorded, on the north and Essex on the south of the Rappahannock River. In this vicinity he farmed. He settled on an estate adjoining that of Francis Thornton and Anthony Savage, who were justices of Rappahannock and Richmond counties, respectively. Littleburne parish, on the Rappahannock River, near the present Port Conway, now in King George county, where there is a creek called Strother, is where he died in 1702. His wife's maiden name is not known, but she is called Dorothy in his will. His estate, at that early date, was upon the outer border of civilization and he was greeted with a welcome from his red brother similar to that received by the Western pioneers a century later. Among other neighbors of Wm. Strother were Cadwallader Jones and John Bodie, who, during March, 1676, in behalf of the people, submitted their grievances in court as follows: "On ye 25th Jany, 1675, there were 36 persons taken prisoners and killed in ye distance of about ten miles by ye barborous Indians.

We were in these upper parts of ye Parish of Cittinburne, 71 plantations on ye 25th Jany as above said and by ye 10th Feby were reduced to 11." This quotation from the record is given to show the dangerous locality in which Wm. Strother cast his lot.

Francis Thornton, in his deposition given in the dispute between the Crown and Lord Fairfax, stated there were two settlements above Snow creek not far above Ft. Conway and the falls of the Rappahannock, about the year 1700, and John Talliaferro, in his deposition, confirms it, about which time the Indians destroyed the buildings on Cal Carter's plantation, a few miles above the falls.

November 20, 1678, Anthony Savage, of upper precinct of Cittinburne parish, conveys to Francis Thornton and Alice Savage Thornton, his wife, 300 acres to be divided from the tract he then lived on of 1,000 acres, called Mongoheocala, with division to granddaughter, Margaret Thornton, who afterward married Wm. Strother, Jr., son of the first William and his wife Dorothy. In 1727, Wm. Strother, Jr., and his wife, Margaret Thornton, conveyed this land to their son, Wm. Strother, of "Stafford" (who married Margaret Watts), and in turn Wm. Strother of Stafford sold the property to John Skinker, together with so much of his own patrimony not previously disposed of. I produce the above notes here because they are from court records and if borne in mind will be appreciated more fully further along in this record.

The will of Wm. Strother the imigrant is dated Dec. 20, 1700, and probated in Richmond county, Va., Nov. 8, 1702. His wife Dorothy is named as executrix and his son, James Strother, as executor, while James Phillips, Edward Langley and Wm. Smith were witnesses, with James Sherlock, court clerk. He devised one-half of the land upon which he lived, together with the mansion, to his elder son, Wm. Strother, Jr., after the death of his wife Dorothy, and the other half to his son, James Strother, after the death of Dorothy, and the remainder of his lands to his sons, Robert and Benjamine Strother. After providing for the education of his youngest son, Joseph, and a special bequest to his grandson, Wm. Strother (of Stafford), who married Margaret Watts, the remainder of his estate, consisting of goods and chattels, with all of corn, tobacco, servants and other personalty, revert to his loving wife Dorothy during the time of her widowhood; "but if my life shall otherwise dispose of herself as to marry again, my will is that my son, James Strother, do order an account to be taken of my personal estate and that it may be equally divided between my wife and my sons, James, Jeremiah, Robert, Benjamine and Joseph." She had not otherwise disposed of herself in 1716, when she witnessed the will of her son James, who never married, but willed his property to his younger brother, Joseph.

Following you will find a list of the children of Wm. Strother the 1st and his wife Dorothy, as nearly in the order of their births as a careful research can make. Also opposite their names will be found the names of their wives before marriage:

Wm. Strother, Jr. — Margaret Thornton.

James Strother—Died unmarried 1716.

Jeremiah Strother—Eleanor ——

Robert Strother—Elizabeth Berry.

Benjamine Strother—Mary Waffendell.

Joseph Strother—Margaret Berry.

Wm. Strother, Jr., as you will see by reference to the above table, was the eldest son of Wm. Strother, the imigrant, and Dorothy. He married Margaret Thornton, daughter of Francis Thornton and Alice Savage. He was a planter and lived in the mansion inherited from his father. In 1722, he gave this property by deed to his eldest son, Wm. Strother, who married Margaret Watts, and was afterward known as Wm. Strother of "Stafford," to distinguish him from his nephew, Wm. Strother, son of his brother, Francis Strother, of St. Mark's parish, and Susannah Dabney, and this nephew was afterward known as Wm. Strother of "Orange." This method of distinguishing them was adopted in order to avoid the confusion of mistaking the one for the other in business affairs as neither had a middle name.

This Wm. Strother, Jr., who married Margaret Thornton and deeded his home to his son, Wm. Strother of "Stafford," was a vestryman of Hanover parish and sheriff of King George county; died in 1726. His will was admitted to probate by his widow, who qualified as his executrix. His children were:

Wm. Strother of Stafford—Margaret Watts.

Francis Strother of St. Marks—Susannah Dabney.

Anthony Strother—1, Bethethland Storke; 2, Mary James.

Benjamine Strother—Mrs. Mary Fitzhugh.

Wm. Strother of "Stafford," first of the above children of Wm. Strother, Jr., and Margaret Thornton, married Margaret Watts. They lived in the original Strother mansion deeded to him in 1822 by his father, until its destruction by fire, which carried with it the historical records and ancestral relics near Port Conway. After the destruction of the home he sold the estate, purchasing another on the river opposite Fredericksburg in 1727, where he died in 1732, aged about 35 years. In his will he directed the sale of his lands in King George and Prince William counties, and appointed his wife, Margaret Watts Strother, who afterward married John Grant, executrix. His Fredericksburg property was sold by his executrix November, 1738, to Augustus Washington, father of the President, who owned and occupied it until his death in 1743. Mr. Washington devised this estate to his son, George Washington, and it has ever since been known as the Washington farm, where grew the historic cherry tree, which likely was set and nurtured by instructions of Wm. Strother of "Stafford." There, too, to the shores of this estate, Burnside, in

December, 1812, lashed his pontoons in violation of those principles of self-government for which Washington pledged his life, his fortune, and his sacred honor. The dwelling house was a large frame building painted red.

Tradition says that Wm. Strother of "Stafford" and Margaret Watts had "thirteen blooming daughters," and General David Hunter Strother, in his notes, gives credence to this idle story, but the records of the Virginia courts prove it to be a myth and it is hard to understand how it originaed. Data in my possession clearly shows that many of the early Strothers had as many as thirteen children in the family, but none of them had thirteen blooming daughters. It is possible that Margaret Watts Strother, after her marriage to John Grant, had seven daughters, making a total for her of thirteen, but I have no information concerning the children as the result of her marriage to Mr. Grant. General David Strother's notes are defective in several instances, as proven by court and church records. Judge Phillip W. Strother, of Petersburg, Va., and Mr. Henry Strother, of Ft. Smith, Ark., have made quite an exhaustive search into these records in those counties in Virginia where the Strothers were residents, and have in their possession copies of all of their wills, deeds, etc. Now, to disabuse the minds of those who believe that Wm. Strother of "Stafford" and Margaret Watts had thirteen daughters, let me submit this court record: "In March, 1737, Mrs. Margaret Strother asked for an appraisement of the estate of her late husband, just one year before it was sold to Augustine Washington; and Hancock Lee, Abram Kenyon and John Grant (whom she afterward married) were appointed to make the appraisement and to set aside one-seventh of the estate for the widow, which indicates six children, instead of thirteen, as generally believed. On Nov. 3, 1738, Anthony Strother, who was the uncle of the girls, qualified as guardian of Elizabeth, Agatha, Margaret, Ann and Jane, giving bond to pay five-sevenths of the debts of the said Wm. Strother of Stafford, thus indicating six children, five of whom are named above. The eldest daughter was Alice Strother, and she had married Henry Tyler, clerk of Stafford county, and for that reason was not included in the list under the guardianship of Anthony Strother.

This Wm. Strother of Stafford, as was his father before him, was vestryman, sheriff and justice of King George county. I give below a list of the children of Wm. Strother and Margaret Watts and the names of their husbands:

Alice Strother—Henry Tyler.
Elizabeth Strother—John Frogg.
Agatha Strother—John Madison.
Margaret Strother—1, George Morton; 2, Gabriel Jones.
Anne Strother—Francis Tyler.
Jane Strother—Thomas Lewis.

The two Tylers who married Alice and Anne Strother were brothers. Of their families my notes give but little information. Thos. G. Strother Tyler succeeded his father, Henry Tyler, as clerk of Stafford county, and was married to Edith Taylor. Other children of

Henry and Alice Strother Tyler, as shown by the church record, were: John Tyler, born April, 1743; Anne Tyler, born January, 1749; Mary Tyler, born March, 1751.

Elizabeth Strother, second daughter of Wm. Strother and Margaret Watts, married November, 1738, John Frogg, of Prince Edward county. Subsequently they moved to the Valley of Virginia. Their son, John Frogg, Jr., married Agatha Lewis, daughter of Thomas Lewis and Jane Strother. He was killed at the battle of Point Pleasant, October 10, 1774, leaving one daughter. His widow married Col. John Stewart, of Greenbrier, in 1778. Col. Stewart was distinguished as a civilian and Indian fighter, leaving an honorable posterity, one of whom married Hon. Samuel Price, Lieutenant Governor of Virginia, and also a U. S. Senator from West Virginia.

Agatha Strother, daughter of Wm. Strother and Margaret Watts, Married John Madison in 1745. He was the first clerk of Augusta county, and a near relative of President Madison. He was a member of the vestry and repeatedly elected to the House of Burgesses and Delegates. He died on his estate, "Visses," in Boutetourt county, March, 1784, Their children were:

Wm. Strother Madison—Elizabeth Preston.
Gaul Thos. Madison—Susanna Henry.
Rowland Madison— —— Lewis.
James Madison— —— Catesby.
George Madison—Jane Smith.
Margaret Madison—Judge Wm. McDowell.

Wm. Strother Madison lived in Boutetourt county, and died in 1782. His wife, Elizabeth Preston, was a daughter of the first Wm. Preston, of Virginia. They had two daughters, Susanne and Agatha Madison. Susanne married John Howe Peyton, who was a distinguished member of the Staunton bar. Eight children resulted from this union. Agatha Madison married Garnett Peyton, an officer of General Wayne's army, and they were blessed with five children.

General Thos. Madison married Susanna Henry, sister of Patrick Henry, the great orator. He was a lawyer. The Bowyers and Lewises of Boutetourt county are their descendants.

Rowland Madison married a daughter of General Andrew Lewis and moved to Kentucky. The date of his birth was in 1759, and he died in 1845.

James Madison, who married Miss Catesby, was born near Port Republic August, 1749, and died March, 1812, leaving two children, James C. Madison, of Roanoke, and Mrs. Robert G. Scott, of Richmond, Va., whose husband was a lawyer of prominence and served as Consul to Rio Janeiro. This James Madison, who married Miss Catesby, was a man of accomplishments, being educated at William and Mary College, where he took the Boutetourt gold medal, the highest honor in the college. In 1771 he studied law, but soon abandoned it for the ministry. In 1773 he was a professor of Mathematics in that college, and in 1777 become its president. In May, 1785, he presided over the first Episcopal convention and was an ardent patriot during the Revolution.

George Madison, who married Jane Smith, commanded a battalion in the campaign against the British and Indians in the War of 1812, and was distinguished for bravery and skill. His wife was a daughter of Major Francis Smith, and a niece of Col. Wm. Preston. After the war he came to Kentucky, where he was elected Governor. Their daughter, Myra Madison, married ———— Alexander, of Woodford county, and they had a daughter, Apoline, who married General Frank P. Blair, of Missouri. After the death of General Blair she married Franklin Dick. Her brother, Andrew J. Alexander, was a brigadier general of volunteers and major in the United States Army.

Margaret Madison married Judge Wm. McDowell, of Kentucky, who was a son of Judge Samuel McDowell. This family has left the impress of its genius and valor upon the institutions of the country. Lucinda McDowell, a daughter, married General Merrill. Mary McDowell, another daughter, married George C. Thompson, of Mercer county, Ky., who was a man of influence and wealth. Agatha McDowell, still another daughter, married James G. Birney, who was the Abolition candidate for President. Their sons, Col. Jas. G. Birney, Jr., General Wm. M. Birney, and General David B. Birney, served with distinction in the U. S. Army during the Civil War, as they did before and have done since in private life. The other children of Judge Wm. McDowell and Margaret Madison were Mrs. Nathaniel Rochester, Wm. M. McDowell, Jr., and Samuel McDowell.

Margaret Strother, daughter of Wm. Strother of "Stafford" and Margaret Watts, was born in King George county, Va., 1726. She married, first, George Morton, April 26, 1744. He was accidentally killed soon after the marriage, leaving his widow a large fortune. On October 6, 1749, she married Gabriel Jones, son of John and Elizabeth Jones. He was prepared for the legal profession of London, Eng., and became a lawyer of great ability and integrity, but was classed as irascible in temperament. He was denominated the "Valley lawyer," and represented Frederick and Augusta counties in House of Burgesses and served in the convention of 1778, as did his brother-in-law, Thomas Lewis. He was the friend, counsellor and executor of Lord Fairfax. He died near Point Republic October, 1806. His home was in the valley of Virginia, on the Shenandoah River, and his farm was of great fertility and extent and adjoined the farms of his brothers-in-law, Thos. Lewis, John Frogg, John Madison, and his friend, Peachy R. Gilmer. Mrs. Jones is described as a woman of eminent Christian character and a most exemplary woman in all relations of life. She possessed a fine mind, was well informed, benevolent and serious. Bishop Meade says: "I also knew that venerable old lady, Mrs. Gabriel Jones. The first visit I ever paid that county (Rockingham) was with her grandson, Strother Jones, of Frederick, when we saw her in her old age rejoicing in the prospect of the resuscitation of the church of her love." She also died near Port Republic in 1822, in her 97th year. Their children were:

Margaret Jones—Col. John Harvie.

Gabriella Jones—1, Col. Thomas Mann Randolph; 2, Dr. —— Brockenbrough.

Elizabeth Jones—John Lewis.

Strother Jones—Fannie Thornton.

Anna Jones—John Hawkins.

Col. John Harvie, who married Margaret Jones, lived in Albemarle county, and in early life became a very successful lawyer. He was a delegate in the House of Burgesses as early as 1765, was appointed jointly with John Walker to treat with the Indians at Ft. Pitt. He was a member of the convention of 1776, a member of Congress and one of the signers of the "Articles of Confederation," after which he was Register of the Virginia Land Office. Subsequently he was elected by the city of Richmond to the House of Delegates, where he served only a few years, and retired to private life. He died at his country seat, "Belvidere," in the year 1807, leaving a large family of children; but Mrs. Harvie survived her husband many years. John Harvie, Jr., son of Col. John and Margaret, married his cousin, Margaret Hawkins, f Kentucky. They moved to Frankfort, Ky., and had Gabriella Harvie, who married James Breathitt; Lewis Harvie, who was private secretary to President Jefferson; Edwin J. Harvie, who married Pattie Hathaway, and lost his life in the fire that consumed the Richmond theater in 1811. This couple had two sons—Lewis Edwin Harvie, who married Sarah Blair, and was for thirty years prominent in the Legislature and State affairs; one of their sons was an officer in the Confederate army and was killed in battle in West Virginia, and another, Edwin J. Harvie, was Inspector General on the Staff of General Jo. E. Johnson. This line figured extensively in the service of the Confederacy.

General Jacqueline B. Harvie, another son of Col. John and Margaret Jones, was at one time in the Navy and served with distinction under Decatur in the Tripolitan War. He subsequently resigned and represented the city of Richmond, Va., in both branches of the Legislature for many years. He married Mary Marshall, the only daughter of Chief Justice John Marshall. Their daughter, Virginia Harvie, married Gov. Spicer Patrick, of West Virginia, and their son, Lewis E. Harvie, of Amelia county, was one of the most prominent politicians in Virginia, and held many positions of honor and trust. Judge Wm. Pape Dabney wrote of him as follows: "When a student at Hampton-Sidney College I was present one day in the gallery of the House of Delegates and saw James French Strother, a Whig, and Lewis E. Harvie, a Democrat, form a combination between the Whigs and the Calhoun or Chivalry wing of the Democratic party, and elect Robt. M. T. Hunter and James M. Mason to the U. S. Senate, notwithstanding the old Hinker Democracy had a decided majority." His son, Col. Edwin J. Harvie, of Washington, D. C., was an officer in the U. S. Army, but cast his lot with the South in the war between the States and served on the staff of both R. E. Lee and Joseph E. Johnson.

Gabriella Jones, daughter of Gabriel Jones and Margaret Strother, married first Col. Thos. Mann Randolph, father of Gov. Thos. Mann Randolph, of Virginia, who married Thos. Jefferson's daughter. Gabriella Jones' second marriage was to Dr. John Brockenbrough, a prominent citizen of Richmond. She was frequently spoken of as a woman of grace and beauty—talented and accomplished. She was known in Richmond as the "Fair Gabriella." By the first marriage was one son, who was twice married and had two children by each marriage. Dr. Brockenbrough and his wife built the Jeff Davis Mansion at Richmond.

Elizabeth Jones, daughter of Gabriella Jones and Margaret Strother, married John Lewis, son of Fielding Lewis and Catherine Washington. He was a prominent lawyer of Fredericksburg, but moved to Kentucky. Their son, Gabriel Lewis, married a daughter of Judge George M. Bibb, of Frankfort, Ky.

Anna Jones, daughter of Gabriel Jones and Margaret Strother, married John Hawkins, adjutant in Col. Thos. Marshall's regiment, and they located in Kentucky. Col. O. E. Butler, of Carrollton, was a grandson.

Strother Jones, son of Gabriel and Margaret, was born March 21, 1756, and as early as 1767 his name was on the catalogue of William and Mary College. He was a captain in Grayson's regiment May 11, 1777, and transferred in 1779 to Gists' regiment in the Continental line, and resigned in 1781. Afterward he was colonel of militia. He married Fannie Thornton, daughter of Francis Thornton, of the Falls, and his wife, Ann Thompson, who was a daughter of the Rev. John Thompson, of Culpeper. Fannie Thornton, the wife of Strother Jones, was a descendant of Francis Thornton and Alice Savage, mentioned early in this record. Strother Jones was an accomplished gentleman, but had much of the temper of his father. His residence was at Vancluse, Frederick county, Va., where he died in 1788, aged 32 years. His wife survived him and their only child was Wm. Strother Jones, born Oct. 7, 1783, who also resided at Vancluse, and on January 3, 1806, married, first, Ann Maria Marshall, daughter of Charles Marshall, and grandniece of Chief Justice John Marshall. He was married, second, to Ann Cary Randolph, and had, first, Wm. Strother Jones, Jr., born 1817, who married Miss —— Taylor; second, James F. Jones, who married Ann Lewis Marshall, granddaughter of Chief Justice John Marshall; third, Francis B. Jones, lieutenant colonel 2nd Virginia Regiment Infantry, and was killed at Malvern Hill; fourth, Mrs. Banton, mother of R. T. Banton, of Winchester, Va., who was the author of Banton's Practice.

Anne Strother, another daughter of Wm. of "Stafford" and Margaret Watts, married Francis Tyler May 17, 1744. They lived in Culpepper at one time, but in 1761 were residents of Augusta, when the five sisters became neighbors.

Jane Strother, daughter of Wm. of "Stafford" and Margaret Watts, was born 1732 and died in 1820. She married January 17, 1749, Thomas Lewis, the eldest of the distinguished sons of Col. John Lewis and Margaret Lynn. His habits were studious and his library large, filled with classical books selected by Gabriel Jones in England. He was a man of excellent talents and great probity, as shown by the frequent expressions of approval at the polls by his constituents at a period when fraud and bribery, such frequent appliances of the present day, were not resorted to to thwart the will of the people. He was the colonial surveyor of Augusta county, which he also represented in the House of Burgesses and of Delegates, and was a member of the convention of 1776. He was also one of the earliest advocates of American Independence. Upon the formation of Rockingham county, his home, near Port Republic, the scene of the battle between Jackson and Shields, was thrown into that county, which he represented in the Legislative convention of 1788, in which he voted for the ratification of the Constitution of the United States. In 1849, he was a commissioner to survey the line for Lord Fairfax between the head Springs of the Potomac and Rappahannock. In 1779, he was a commissioner to treat with the Indians. He died in 1790, leaving a family consisting of thirteen children. His sons, John, Andrew and Thomas Lewis, were officers of the army during the Revolution, John and Andrew being with Washington at Valley Forge and during the New Jersey campaign against the Indians, and John and Thomas were at the surrender of Cornwallis, while Andrew was an officer under General Wayne in his expedition against the Western Indians in 1795, when he lost an arm in one of the engagements.

When Thomas Lewis died in 1790 he devised most of his large estate to his sons, Charles and Wm. B. Strother Lewis, who being Federalists, were excluded from office. Lighthorse Harry Lee was accustomed to visiting the Lewises, who were his personal and political friends, for the sake of social enjoyment, as well as to seek relief from the importunities of his creditors. Charles Lewis married a Miss Yancey, of Rockingham county, and they were the parents of General Daniel Lewis, who for years was president of Rockingham court. General Daniel Lewis married, first, his cousin, Ann Lewis, daughter of John Lewis, of Bath, and granddaughter of Col. Charles Lewis, who was killed at Point Pleasant. He married, second, a daughter of Judge John T. Lomax; and Judge L. L. Lewis, of the Virginia Court of Appeals, was a son of the last marriage. Among the children of the first marriage to Ann Lewis were Col. Charles H. Lewis, Secretary of Virginia and Minister to Portugal; John F. Lewis, who was a U. S. marshal of Virginia, and a member of the Virginia secession convention. He was for a preservation of the union of the States and adhered to his views with the firmness and courage characteristic of the family. He was twice elected Lieutenant Governor of the State and also served his State in the U. S. Senate. He married a daughter of the distinguished lawyer and Congressman Daniel Sheffy, and died in 1896. Dr. Sheffy Lewis, who filled the office of U. S. District Attorney, and Mrs. John Ambler Smith, whose husband was a member of Congress, were among their children. Judge L. L. Lewis, son of General Daniel Lewis and Miss Lomax, was for twelve years president of the Virginia Court of Appeals, prior to which time he was attorney for Culpeper county, and district attorney for the Eastern District of Virginia. In 1897 he made the race for Congress on the Republican ticket and was defeated. He was twice married; first to a daughter of John M. Batts and second to Jane Looney, of Memphis, Tenn.

Two daughters of Thomas Lewis and Jane Strother were Margaret and Agatha Lewis. Margaret married Capt. McClanahan and Agatha married her cousin, Capt. John Frogg, son of John Frogg and Elizabeth Strother. Capt. John Frogg and Capt. McClanahan were killed at the battle of Pt. Pleasant, October, 1774. Three other daughters of Thomas Lewis and Jane Strother were Mrs. Jane Hughes, Mrs. Mary McElhany, and Mrs. Fanny Yancy. The husbands of these three women were in the Continental Army. Still another daughter, Elizabeth Lewis, married Thos. M. Gilmer and moved to Georgia, where their son, George R. Gilmer, was twice elected Governor of the State and three times elected to Congress, while a brother of the Governor, Wm. Benjamine Strother Gilmer, was noted in that State for his wealth and generosity. It is supposed that they were grandsons of Peachy M. Gilmer, spoken of elsewhere as the friend and neighbor of Gabriel Jones and Thomas Lewis. The descendants of Thomas M. Gilmer and Elizabeth Lewis in the South are worthy scions of a distinguished ancestry. Ann Lewis was a daughter of Thomas Lewis and Jane Strother that I overlooked. She married, first, a Mr. Douthatt, and, second, Mr. —— French, of Kentucky. The youngest daughter was Sophia Lewis and I do not know whether she was ever married or not.

The foregoing concludes the line of Wm. Strother of "Stafford" and Margaret Watts. You will bear in mind that this Wm. Strother was the eldest son of Wm. Strother, Jr., and Margaret Thornton, and the grandson of Wm. Strother the imigrant. I will now take up the line of Francis Strother of St. Mark's Parish, who was the second son of Wm. Strother, Jr., and Margaret Thornton. His first residence was in St. Martin's Parish, Hanover county. He was a brother of Wm. Strother of "Stafford," whose descendants, in part, I have just concluded. By General David Hunter Strother and others who have made notes on the Strothers, he is confounded with a son of the first Jeremiah Strother, who bore the same given name, and in that way I was led into error in some notes prepared and published in the Kentucky Historical Journal in January, 1912. Mr. Henry Strother, of Ft. Smith, Ark., who, with Judge P. W. Strother, of Petersburg, Va., Mrs. Meaken, of Georgia, and others, have gone through the court and church records of Virginia, and know all of the facts, called my attention to the errors and furnished the missing data that makes this record accurate. Jeremiah Strother was the uncle of Wm. of "Stafford" and Francis of "St. Marks," as you will see by reference to tables submitted earlier in this record. Here I will insert a few court records in order that we may have a clearer understanding of these relationships. On November 20, 1678, Anthony Savage, of upper precinct of Crittinburne Parish, conveys to Francis Thornton and his wife, Alice Savage, who was his daughter, 300 acres divided from the tract he then lived on of 1,000 acres, called Mongoheocala, with division to granddaughter, Margaret Thornton, who married Wm. Strother, Jr., the eldest son of the imigrant. On August 1, 1727, Margaret Thornton Strother, widow of Wm. Strother, Jr., conveyed to her son, Wm. Strother of "Stafford," 300 acres on the Rappahannock River, given by her grandfather, Anthony Savage, except one-half acre for burying ground, including graves thereon (Wm. Strother of "Stafford" sold this land to John Skinker, together with so much of his own patrimony not previously disposed of). On the same day, August 1, 1727, Margaret Thornton Strother deeded to her son, Francis Strother, who then resided in "St. Martins Parish," Hanover county, certain slaves with reversion to her grandson, Wm. Strother, who afterward was known as "Wm. of Orange," to distinguish him from his uncle, "Wm. of Stafford." On January 27, 1735, Wm. Coleman conveys to Francis Strother of St. Martins Parish, Hanover county, a tract of 583 1-3 acres in St. Marks Parish, in Orange county, being one-third of 1,750 acres, known as "Delmere."

THE STROTHERS.

By Wm. E. Railey.

CORRECTION.*

Editor's Note: The author of the Strother history desires the following correction made in his paper in the September Register, page 96, when the table should have read:

Margaret Jones married Col. John Harvie.
Anna Gabriella Jones married John Hawkins.
Elizabeth Jones married John Lewis.
Strother Jones married Fannie Thornton.

Delmere—This is near the county seat of the present county of Rappahannock, where he, Francis Strother, settled, and he was ever afterward known as Francis of "St. Marks Parish." The estate of his eldest son, Capt. John Strother, who married Mary Wade, adjoined the estate. On this estate Francis Strother died in 1752. His will was probated in Culpeper county and his wife, Susannah Dabney Strother, is made executrix. He enforces his wife to execute deeds to John Minor to part of tract upon which he lives, and his son, John Strother, to unite in said deeds; also another tract adjoining, but for which he had not yet obtained deed from ye Lord Fairfax office. Devises to son George Strother, one tract lying at Little Pine Mountain. To son Francis one survey at the bluff end of Pignuts Ridge, and to wife residence of the home place during her life and then to son Robert. Slaves and personalty to wife during widowhood. If she marries to be equally divided between his children, Anthony, George, Francis, Robert, Mary, Behethdad, Elizabeth and Susannah. It is known that he had a son William and a daughter, Margaret, who are not mentioned in his will. The absence of the name of Wm. Strother of "Orange," may be accounted for by reason of the fact heretofore stated that his grandmother, Margaret Thornton Strother, devised slaves to her son, Francis Strother, with reversion to her grandson, Wm. Strother, but I am unable to account for the absence of the name of his daughter, Margaret, and presume that she was either dead at the time of the will or was already provided for, as was Captain John Strother, who was not mentioned in the will except to participate with his mother in certain deeds. The data in my possession gives the name of one of his daughters as

*See p. 376, this volume.

Behethdad, which I think is a mistake. Her uncle, Anthony Strother, married first Behethland Storke, and I think it likely she was named for this aunt. Francis Strother says further in his will: It is my will that my sons Anthony and George be at liberty at my death and if my wife marries my sons Francis and Robert shall be of age at 16 years.

The maiden name of Francis Strother's wife was Susanna Dabney and she was his executrix. It is supposed that she was a relative of John and Cornelius Dabney, who were Huguenots from France and settled near old Hanover town, where Francis Strother resided when he married.

The children of Frances Strother and Susanna Dabney were:

Captain John Strother—Mary Wade.

Margaret Strother—Robert Covington.

Wm. Strother (of Orange)—1, Sarah Bailey Paumile; 2, Anna Kavanaugh.

George Strother—Mary Kinnerly.

Anthony Strother — Frances Eastham.

Francis Strother—Anna Furgeson.

Robert Strother—Elizabeth Dillard.

Mary Strother—1, Robert Deatherage; 2, George Calvert.

Behethdad Strother—Oliver Wallis.

Eliabeth Strother — James Gaines.

Susanna Strother — Thomas Gaines.

Captain John Strother was the eldest of this family. He was born in Hanover in 1721 **and married** Mary Wade, after which he moved to Culpeper county, near where Little Washington now is, where he died April 1795. His residence was known as Wadefield, which has passed down the generations and is now in possession of a lineal descendant. Between 1755 and 1759 he served in a campaign against the Indians as captain of his company. He was a strong churchman and built and supported an Episcopal church near his residence. He served his county as sheriff and as a justice and was noted for his decision of character and perseverance in business affairs, as a result of which he accumulated a large fortune. He and his wife, Mary Wade, were blessed with the following children:

Joseph Strother—Nancy Stuart.

John Strother, Jr.—Helen Piper.

Susanna Strother—1, John Lawler; 2, James Hughlett.

Mollie Strother—Charles Browning.

Sarah Strother—Wm. Hughes.

Elizabeth Strother—Capt. John Browning.

Lucy Strother—Francis Covington.

Mildred Strother—Wm. Covington.

Ann Strother—John Strother.

Joseph Strother, first of the above, married Nancy Stuart. On Dec. 16, 1784, a patent was issued to him for 1,000 acres of land on Prather's Creek, in Jefferson county, Ky. He occupied several positions of trust in Virginia, but in 1800 he moved to Kentucky, with several of his younger children. His son, Wm. Strother, married Mildred Medley in Culpeper in 1790 and their daughter, Harriet Strother, married Rev. Horace Stringfellow, whose son and grandson pursued the same vocation. Another son, Chas. S. Stringfellow, was a lawyer at Richmond, Va. James Wade Strother, son of Wm. and Mildred Strother, was born 1797. After practicing law for thirty years, he became a Presbyterian minister, and died July 20, 1867, at Brownsville, Tenn. He married Susan McConchie, granddaughter of Capt. Phillip Slaughter and Margaret Strother. (This Margaret Strother was a daughter of French Strother and Lucy Coleman.) Jas. Wade Strother and Susan McConchie had a son, James Robert Strother, who was a lawyer at Vicksburg, Miss., and his son, James Thomas Strother, is now practicing law in that city. Benjamin Strother, second son of Joseph Strother and Nancy Stuart, was an officer under General Wayne. John Strother, third son of Joseph Strother and Nancy Stuart, married a daughter of Captain Edwards, of Jefferson county, Ky., and they had a son, Pendleton Strother. Joseph Strother, fourth of Joseph and Nancy, was a lawyer of Navostak, Va.; fifth, Mary Strother, married Wm. Menifee, and Howard R. Bayne, a lawyer of New York City, is their descendant. Lucy Strother, sixth of Joseph and Nancy, married Francis Wyatt Green (son of Wm. Green and grandson of Robert Green and Eleanor Dunn, who settled in Culpeper), and Dr. Norvin Green, President of the Western Union Telegraph Co., was their grandson. Sarah Strother, daughter of Joseph and Nancy, married first, Edward Pendleton, son of Col. Henry Pendleton; she married, second, John Strother, grandson of Jeremiah 1st.

John Strother, Jr., son of Capt. John and Mary Wade, married Helen Piper, who was an aunt of Col. James Piper, who, when a student at Washington College, climbed the Natural Bridge and inscribed his name at a greater height than was that of General Washington. This John Strother inherited Wadefield, the home of his father, and died Sept. 22, 1814. His children were: 1st, Nancy Strother, born Nov. 20, 1784, married June 1799, Wm. Pendleton, son of James Pendleton, a descendant of Henry Pendleton and Mary Taylor, who was a daughter of Col. James Taylor, whose wife was a daughter of General Brown, of Maryland. Wm. Pendleton was also a nephew of Nathaniel and Judge Edward Pendleton. Among the children of Wm. Pendleton and Nancy Strother were John Strother Pendleton, born March 1, 1802, and died at his residence, "Redwood," in Culpeper, Oct., 1868. He was a distinguished lawyer and a man of genius and an orator. He served in the State Legislature, in Congress and was seven years in the diplomatic service, being appointed Foreign Minister by President Tyler. His wife was Lucy Ann Williams. His brother, Albert G. Pendleton, was no less distinguished for natural ability and was a prominent member of the Virginia bar. He filled many positions of trust in civil life and was repeatedly in the Virginia House of Delegates and a member of the Virginia Constitutional Convention of 1850-51. He married Elvira Chapman and they were the parents of

383

tion of 1850-51 to revise the Constitution. He m. Elizabeth Roberts, dau. of Maj. John Roberts, of Culpeper, an officer in the Revolution. Issue: Geo. French Strother, late superintendent of the Penitentiary; Capt. John Strother, member of the Assembly for many years. He m. a dau. of Dr. Payne; Phil W. Strother, Judge and Representative of Giles Co., Va., m. a dau. of Albert Pendleton. Issue: James F. Strother, Elvira Strother.

After the death of the 1st Wm. Pannill, his widow nee Sarah Bayley (or Bailey) m. Wm. Strother, of Orange Co., Va., (not the Wm. S. of Stafford) and had children: 1. Wm. Dabney Strother. 2. Sarah S. m. Lieut.-Col. Richard Taylor. 3. Susannah S. m. Moses Hawkins. (Note—Mrs. Sarah B. P. Strother dying, her 2nd husband Wm S. m. 2nd, Mrs. Ann Kavanaugh, the mother of Philemon K., who died in Orange Co. in 1784 and appointed his stepfather, Wm. Strother, executor of his estate.)

In 1758 Wm. S. gives negroes to his dau. Susannah and son "Dabnaugh." In 17— Wm. S. conveys land in Orange adjoining Susan Hawkins. In 1774 Mrs. Sarah P. B. Strother made will leaving her son Wm. Dabney Strother, her dau. Frances Banks (dau. by 1st husband) and friend, Chas. Bruce, executors. She directs her lands to be sold, gives 20 pounds to gr.-dau., Sarah Bailey Morton Pannill, dau. of Wm., 20 pounds to her gr.-son, Wm. R. Pannill, son of David. 20 pounds to Gerard Banks, son of Frances Banks, a dau., 20 pounds to Sarah Bailey Hawkins (dau. of Susannah Strother Hawkins), 20 pounds to Sarah Runnolds, dau, of Tabitha Runnolds (was she a sister of Moses Hawkins?), the remainder of her estate to be divided between her son Wm. Dabney Strother, dau. Frances Banks and dau. Sara Strother (Note—Was the name of Susannah Strother Hawkins left out of the will?)

Land Office Military Warrant No. 3326 was issued to Wm. Strother Hawkins, heir at law to Moses Hawkins.

Wm. Strother (son of Jeremiah) m. Mrs. Sarah Pannill nee Bailey. The will of Sarah S. (widow of Wm. S.) proven in 1774, bequeathed to her children, Wm. Dabney S., Mrs. Frances Banks (Nee Pannill), and Sarah S. In 1758 Wm. S. of Orange, made a deed to his dau. Susannah and son Wm. Dabney S. As far as ascertained these are their children: Wm. Dabney Strother died in the Army during the Revolution. He is said to have written very pretty poetry; Francis Banks; Susannah m. Moses Hawkins. Issue: Wm. Strother Hawkins, Moses Hawkins and 2 daughters, Sally and Lucy. They lived in Woodford Co., Ky.; Sally Strother b. Dec. 11, 1760, d. Dec. 13, 1829, m. Aug 20, 1779, Col. Richard Taylor, b. April 3, 1741, d. Jan. 19, 1829. They had six sons and three daughters.

Francis Strother of St. Mark's Parish, and son of Jeremiah, died in 1752. Date of will, April 17th, 1751; entered of record, April 16th, 1752. He appointed his wife, Susan, Executrix. He m. Miss Susan Dabney (dau. of John Dabney and Sarah Jennings). His children were: John, Anthony, William, George,

tors and her daughter, Francis Pannill Banks, was executrix. In her will she mentions no bequests to her Pannill children except Francis Banks, but remembers one child of her son, David Pannill, one daughter of her son, Wm. Pannill, one son of her daughter Francis Banks, and one child of her son Joseph Pannill. Neither did she make a bequest to her daughter, Susannah Strother, who married Capt. Moses Hawkins, March 3, 1770, but remembers their daughter, Sarah Bailey Hawkins. The last item of the will includes the names of Wm. Dabney Strother, Francis Banks and Sarah Strother, the infant heir, as beneficiaries to share equally in the remainder of realty and personal estate. The presumption is that the Pannill children and Susannah Strother had received their share of the estate before their mother's death as they were all married and had children. However, Susannah had been deeded property.

A few years after the death of his wife Wm. Strother was married to Anna Kavanaugh, widow of Philemon Kavanaugh of Orange county, but no children resulted from this union.

Susannah Strother, daughter of Wm. and Sarah, married Capt. Moses Hawkins March 3, 1770. He joined the Revolutionary Army early in the struggle and was captain of a company in the 14th Virginia Regiment, being killed at the battle of Germantown Oct. 4, 1777. Their children were Sarah Bailey Hawkins, Wm. Strother Hawkins, Lucy Hawkins, and Moses Hawkins. After the Revolutionary War Susannah Strother Hawkins, widow of Capt. Moses Hawkins, married Thomas Coleman, a friend of her former husband, and a corporal in his company, when his friend and neighbor was killed. A few years after the latter marriage, Thomas Coleman and his wife, Susannah, in company with the four Hawkins children and their grandfather, Wm. Strother of "Orange," and his wife, Anna Kavanaugh Strother, came to Kentucky to live and settled on a large estate near Mortonsville, in Woodford county, where they all lived and died. When I was a boy I was shown the burying ground that was then in bad shape and it is doubtful if any marks remain to indicate the graves of each. Wm. Strother of "Orange," was born about 1728 and died in 1808, his will being of record in the county clerk's office at Versailles, Ky., in Will Book C, page 105. His son-in-law, Col. Richard Taylor, and grandson, Hancock Taylor, are named as executors. He was the grandfather of General Zachary Taylor, who became President in 1849.

Of the Hawkins children, Sarah Bailey Hawkins married James Thornton, of Woodford county, and had a large family, many of whose descendants still live in the county, James T. Wilhoit, who has served as judge and sheriff of Woodford county, being one of them.

Wm. Strother Hawkins was the second child. His birth was June 1, 1772, his death Oct. 26, 1858. He married Catherine Keith, Oct. 14, 1802, who was a daughter of Captain Isham Keith and Charlotte Ashmore, and a granddaughter of Rev. James Keith and Mary Isham Randolph. Wm. Strother Hawkins and Catherine Keith raised a large family of children, Isham Keith Hawkins, who married, first, Lucy Majors, and, second, Sarah Hall, being one of them, and Catherine Keith Hawkins, who married Richard Henry Railey, being another. Their son, Wm. E. Railey, is the compiler of these notes. Lucy Hawkins, the third child, married Wm. George, of Woodford county, and they have many descendants. Moses Hawkins, Jr., was the fourth. He married Sarah Castleman and moved to Missouri, where their descendants are numerous.

Wm. Dabney Strother, second of Wm. Strother of "Orange" and Sarah Pannill, was an officer in the regiment of his brother-in-law, Col. Richard Taylor, and was killed during the battle of Guilford's Courthouse. He was of a literary tendency, his parents sparing nothing that would aid him in acquiring a first rate education, and had it not been for his sacrifice in a duty he felt he owed his country, he would likely have attained great distinction.

Sarah Strother was the third and last of the children of Wm. Strother of "Orange," and Sarah Pannill. Her birth was in 1760 and she was only fourteen years of age when her mother died. She married Col. Richard Taylor, who was a son of Zachary Taylor, Sr., and Elizabeth Lee, and Zachary Taylor, Sr., was a son of Col. James Taylor, who came to Virginia in 1658.

Col. Richard Taylor was a gentleman of culture and colonel of the 9th Virginia Regiment during the Revolution. Soon after the termination of hostilities he moved from Virginia to Jefferson county, Ky., with his family. They had several children. Their son, Zachary Taylor, Jr., was born in Orange county, Virginia, in 1786, and was an officer in the U. S. Army, distinguishing himself during the struggle with Mexico, which service made him available to the Presidency, to which position he was elected, but the duties of the office were so taxing that he died before the expiration of his term. He married Margaret Smith and their son, Richard Taylor, was a lieutenant general in the Confederacy, and skillfully and ably distinguished himself during the Rebellion. Other children of Col. Richard Taylor and Sarah Strother were Hancock, Wm. Dabney, George, Richard, Joseph P., Elizabeth, Sarah and Emily, all of whom have many descendants in Kentucky and other Southern states, who are prominent in social, political and business circles. This ends the line of Wm. Strother of "Orange" and Sarah Pannill.

George Strother, as you will see by the table, was a son of Francis Strother and Susannah Dabney. He married Mary Kinnerly, who was a daughter of Capt. James Kinnerly, and a niece of Catherine Kinnerly, who married Jeremiah Strother, Jr., son of Jeremiah Strother, Sr., son of Wm. Strother the Imigrant (see first table). George Strother's will is dated June 20, 1767, during which year he died. His wife, Mary Kinnerly, survived him and lived to quite an advanced age, dying in 1830. Their children were:

John Strother.
George Strother.
Margaret Strother—George Hancock.

Elizabeth Strother.

John and George moved to Tennessee. They were both officers in the army, the former serving on the staff of General **Andrew Jackson** during the Seminole or Creek War, and at the Seven Islands is a Fort Strother, named as a compliment to him, and he was expressly complimented in General Jackson's reports, in which he is spoken of as Major John Strother. His sister, Margaret Strother, born Sept., 1763, and died Oct., 1834, was married Sept., 1781, to Col. George Hancock, of Botecourt county, Va., who was defeated for re-election to Congress in 1799, after serving his district for four years. His defeat was particularly regretted by General Washington, as set forth in a letter by him to Chief Justice John Marshall. The children of Col. George Hancock and Margaret Strother were:

George Hancock—............ Croghan.
Jno. Strother Hancock.
Caroline Hancock—Major Wm. Preston.
Mary Hancock—George Griffin.
Julia Hancock—Gov. Wm. Clark.

George Hancock married a daughter of Major Croghan. Caroline Hancock married Major Wm. Preston, of the U. S. Army, and a son of the first Wm. Preston of Virginia. Major Wm. Preston and his family moved to Louisville, Ky. Their **daughter, Henrietta** Preston, was the first wife of General Albert Sidney Johnston, of Confederate fame, who lost his life at the battle of Shiloh, in which the South sustained an irreparable loss. They were blessed with two children— 1, Wm. Preston Johnston; 2, Hen**rietta Johnston.** The late General Wm. Preston, of Lexington, Ky., was a son of Major Wm. Preston and Caroline Hancock. He married Margaret Wickliffe and their daughter, Mary Preston, married Col. John Mason Brown, of Frankfort, Ky., while another daughter, Caroline Preston, married Robert A. Thornton, a lawyer of Lexington, Ky. General Wm. Preston was a member of Congress, Minister to Mexico, and Major General in the Confederate Army.

Maria Preston, daughter of Major Wm. Preston and Caroline Hancock, married John Pope, of Louisville, Ky. Caroline Preston, another daughter, married Col. Abraham Woolley, of the army, while still another daughter, Josephine Preston, married Capt. Jason Rogers, of the army. The Preston descendants are numerous in Kentucky and through the South.

Mary Hancock, daughter of George Hancock and Margaret Strother, married George Griffin, and their daughter, Elizabeth Griffin, was the second wife of General Albert Sidney Johnston.

Julia Hancock, daughter of George Hancock and Margaret Strother, married Gov. Wm. Clark, of Missouri, who was with Meriwether Lewis in his expedition to the Pacific Ocean. This ends the line of George Strother, fourth son of Francis Strother and Susannah Dabney.

We will now take up the line of Anthony Strother, another son, as you will see by referring to the table, but my data gives but little information of this line. He married Francis Eastham and was the guardian of the daughters of his brother, Wm. Strother of "Stafford." Their children were: Wm., Robert, John, Francis, Benjamine, Phillip, Mary, Nancy, Susannah, and Catherine. My notes do not indicate to whom any of these children were married, merely stating that Phillip was a minister of the Methodist church and that some of the descendants live in Carter county, Ky., one of them having been County Judge of that county. My notes are also short on Francis Strother, the son of Francis of St. Marks Parish and Susanna Dabney. He married Ann Furgeson, and perhaps was also married to Miss Graves. He died in Culpeper in 1777. His executors were John Strother and James and Wm. Pendleton. The children of this Francis were: Samuel, George, John, and Francis. Samuel and George died young, and John died on a trip to England. Francis removed with his uncle, Col. John Graves, to Georgia in 1823, where he married and had a son, Charles R. Strother, who was a lawyer and served with credit in the Legislature and in the Secession Convention of 1861. This completes, as far as my notes go, the line of Francis Strother of St. Marks and Susannah Dabney.

I will now take up the line of Anthony Strother, third of Wm. Strother, Jr., and Margaret Thornton. He was a brother of Wm. of Stafford and Francis of St. Marks, whose lives we have just closed. He was the ancestor of Gen. David Hunter Strother, who, in his notes on the Strothers, claimed descent from another Anthony. Anthony Strother, Sr., was born Aug., 1710, and died Dec., 1765. His will was probated Oct., 1766. He married, first, Behethland Storke, Aug., 1733; second, Mary James, 1754. In 1739, Wm. Thornton conveys to Anthony Strother 250 acres below the Falls of the Rappahannock, in King George county, and after the death of Augustine Washington, in 1743, Lawrence Washington and Nathaniel Chapman, his executors, conveyed to Anthony Strother 150 acres adjoining the land below Clairbornes Branch, and these two tracts became "Albion," the Strother farm, which adjoined the Washington farm, and also "Travelers' Rest," the home of Col. Burgers Ball, a few miles below Fredericksburg, where his son, Anthony, lived and which remained in possession of descendants until the misfortunes of war ruined so many. Anthony Strother, Sr., was a merchant at Fredericksburg, and in 1757 Gov. Dinwiddie, who had appointed James Patton, Joshua Fry and Linsford Lomay commissioners to meet the Indians at Logstown on Dec. 13th of that year, wrote Col. Patton to proceed immediately to Fredericksburg, and there receive from Mr. Strother the goods sent as a present by his majesty to the Indians.

Anthony Strother provides in his will that his property remain as a whole for ten years, then be sold and the proceeds be equally divided between his widow, Mary James Strother, and his children. Of the first marriage were:

Anthony Strother, Jr.—Miss Kenyon.

Benjamine Strother—Kitty Price.

Anthony Strother, Jr., in 1772 was sheriff and justice in King George county, which offices he held until change in county boundary lines put him into Stafford county.

His son George married Sallie Kenyon and inherited Albion Farm, while his son Anthony married Miss Newton and moved to the valley. Benjamine Strother, second of Anthony and Behethland, was born June, 1750, and died 1805. He entered the Virginia navy in 1776, where he served with credit for three years, when he was promoted to be lieutenant. After the navy was abandoned, he entered the land service, where he remained until the end of the war. He married Kitty Price in 1778 and settled in Berkely county (now Jefferson) and built Park Forrest, near Charlestown, on land purchased from Burchard Washington and Lighthorse Harry Lee. His children were Mrs. Benjamine Pendleton, Mrs. J. M. Crane, Mrs. Cato Moore, Mrs. Richard Duffield and Col. John Strother. Col. John Strother was born Nov., 1782, and married Sept., 1815, Elizabeth Pendleton Hunter, sister of Andrew Hunter, a distinguished lawyer, whose home was burned by General Daniel Hunter, of the U. S. Army, and whose mother was the aunt of R. M. L. Hunter, U. S. Senator from Virginia; of Anthony Kennedy, U. S. Senator from Maryland, and of John Pendleton Kennedy, member of Congress and Secretary of the U. S. Navy. This John Strother, the son of Benjamine and Kitty Price, served in the war with England, was clerk of Berkeley county, and a man of sterling qualities and great force of character. His independence led to an unjust imprisonment by the Confederate authorities and that is said to have determined the course of his son, General David Hunter Strother, in entering the service of the Union Army during the Rebellion, for he wrote a friend the following lines: "My relations on my mother's side are Hunters, Kennerlys, Pendletons, Dandridges and Tuckers, all well known names in Virginia, but I always liked my father's name and character better as he was one of the most sincere, upright, high-toned and fearless men I ever knew, and I have always considered that others of the name whom I have met have more or less of the same substantial qualities, however little they may have had of the external paint and gilding of society." His father, Col. John Strother, took an active part against secession and died Jan. 20, 1862, before the questions raised by the South had been decided by the arbitrament of arms. He left ten children, two of whom were General David Hunter Strother ("Port Grayson") and Emily Strother. General D. H. Strother was born at Martinsburg, Pa., Sept., 1816, while his father, Col. John Strother, was in the War of 1812-16. He was educated in New York and later went abroad and was a student four years in Rome. Upon his return to this country he became very popular as a contributor to Harper's Magazine and other periodicals sketching Southern life by original and unique illustrations. These writings made him a reputation rarely attained. During the Civil War he remained loyal to the Union, served on the staff of General Banks and other commanding officers, was colonel 32nd West Virginia Cavalry and breveted brigadier general in 1865. After the war he was appointed Adjutant General of Virginia and was appointed by President Hays Consul General to Mexico. He married, first, Mrs. Anne Bayne Wolff, May, 1849. By this marriage was a daughter, Emily Strother, who married Gen. John Brislan Walker, of Denver, Colo., and they have six sons. Gen. Strother's second marriage was to Mary Elliott Hunter, who with her son, John Strother, survives him.

Emily Strother, daughter of Col. John Strother and Eliabeth Pendleton Hunter, was born April, 1820. She married James Lingon Randolph, who was chief engineer of the Baltimore & Ohio Railroad. They have two sons, Beverly Strother Randolph and Lingon Randolph, who are civil engineers. This ends the line of Anthony Strother and Behethland Storke.

I will now briefly write of the line of Anthony Strother and Mary James, his second wife. Their children were:

Mollie Strother—Charles Ficklin.

James Strother—Elizabeth B. Morton.

George Strother.

Elizabeth Strother.

James Strother, born Nov., 1755, married Elizabeth B. Morton, and lived in Farqueir county, but about 1807 moved to Russell county. He was a non-commissioned officer in the War for Independence. Their children were James Payne Strother, Nancy and Jane Strother. James Payne Strother was born Nov., 1799, married Eliza Cummins Nov., 1827, and had eight children, one of whom was Mary Strother, who married J. P. Moore, a wealthy merchant of New Orleans. Mr. and Mrs. Moore, in company with Mrs. Moore's youngest sister, Elizabeth Strother, went to Europe at the conclusion of the war between the States and remained about two years.

James Payne Strother died about 1870, and was regarded as a worthy, high-toned gentleman in Washington county, Va. After the death of Anthony Strother, Sr., his widow, Mary James Strother, married Col. Henry Smith, of Tennessee, who surveyed with Walker the Tennessee and Virginia line and moved to Russell county, Va.

I will now take up the line of Benjamine Strother, who was a son of Wm. Strother, Jr., and Margaret Thornton, and of course a brother of Wm. of "Stafford," Francis of "St. Marks" Parish, and Anthony, of whose descendants I have written quite at length. As the table shows, he married Mrs. Mary Fitzhugh, whose maiden name was Mary Mason. Jan. 8, 1834, Margaret Watts Strother, widow of Wm. of "Stafford," gives power of attorney to loving brother, Benjamine Strother, to convey dower. His daughter, Alice Strother, married Robert Washington, Dec., 1756. Benjamine Strother was a vestryman of old Acquia Church in 1756, when old Mr. Moncure, the ancestor of the venerable Judge R. C. L. Moncure, of Virginia Court of Appeals, was rector of Stafford. The court records disclose very little as to him. Thos. Hunt conveyed to Benjamine Strother. In 1760 a deed from Benjamine Strother to his daughter, Anne, conveyed several slaves, and in 1790 John James, his administrator, asked for commissioners to settle. His wife was an aunt of George Mason of "Gunston Hall." Their children were:

Mary Strother, who married Col. Wm. Bronaugh, of London; Alice Strother, who married Robert Washington. Their son, Lund Washington, born Sept., 1767, was the father of Peter G. Washington, who was Asst. Sec'y U. S. Tr., and Col. L. Q. Washington, the venerable newspaper correspondent of Washington City, whose spicy letters to the Louisville Courier-Journal several decades ago were read with interest by Kentuckians. Ann Strother married John James, who was administrator of her father's estate, and they had a large family and their son, Benjamine James, was a lawyer at Laurens, South Carolina, and served in the Legislature of that state, and his granddaughter, Marie Garlington, married R. W. Simpson, of Pendleton, S. C., who was a lawyer and member of the Legislature, and a cousin of Gov. Simpson, of that state. The children of John James and Anne Strother were: Nancy, George, Mollie, Alice, John, Jr., Wm. and Benjamine James. Thus ends the chapter relating to the descendants of Wm. Strother, Jr., and Margaret Thornton.

I will now devote my time to a brief record of the descendants of Jeremiah Strother, who was the third son of Wm. Strother the Imigrant and Dorothy, his wife.

Jeremiah Strother, who was the third son of the first Wm. Strother and his wife Dorothy, lived in that part of Orange county that was afterwards known as Culpeper. Many of Virginia's most distinguished citizens came from this line. His wife was Eleanor Strother, whose maiden name is not given by any authority that I have consulted. Jeremiah Strother died in 1741, his will being proven by J. Slaughter, John Catlett and Wm. Lightfoot. By his appointment his sons, Wm. and James Strother, were executors of his estate, which he left to his wife Eleanor for life. Their children were:

James Strother — Margaret French.
Wm. Strother.
Francis Strother.
Jeremiah Strother, Jr.—Catherine Kinnerly.
Christopher Strother.
Catherine Strother.
Elizabeth Strother.

James Strother married Margaret French, of King George county, who was a daughter of Daniel French. His death occurred in the year 1761. Their children were:

French Strother—Lucy Coleman.
James Strother.
Mary Strother—George Gray.

French Strother, who married Lucy Coleman, died in 1800, after having served thirty years consecutively in the House of Burgesses, in the convention of 1776, which adopted the first state constitution, in the convention of 1788, which adopted the Constitution of the United States, in House of Delegates and Senate. He intended being a candidate for Congress against Mr. Madison at the first election under the Constitution, but yielded to Mr. Monroe, who afterward became President. French Strother and Lucy Coleman had seven children, one of whom, Margaret Strother, married Capt. Phillip Slaughter. Another daughter married Col. John Evans. A son, George French Strother, married, first, Sarah Williams, daughter of Gen. James Williams, and granddaughter of General Moses Green; second, Theodosia Hunt.

Lucy Slaughter, daughter of Capt. Phillip Slaughter and Margaret Strother, married Isaac Williams, an eminent lawyer of Virginia, and their daughter, P. French Williams, married John M. Patton, who was acknowledged the ablest lawyer at the Virginia bar at that day. He was a member of Congress for eight years, and their son, John M. Patton, Jr., who married Miss Taylor, was colonel of the 21st Va. Infantry and commanded a brigade at the battle of Winchester in 1862, which he continued to the close of the valley campaign under "Stonewall" Jackson, and his brother, Isaac Patton, who married Miss Merritt, was colonel of a Louisiana regiment in the Confederacy, and afterward commanded one of the forts in Mobile Bay. Another brother, George S. Patton, was colonel 22nd Va. Infantry, C. S. A. He was killed by a shell while commanding a brigade at Winchester in 1864. Another brother, W. Tazewell Patton, was colonel 7th Va. Infantry, and was killed while leading that regiment in the charge of Pickett's division on the heights of Gettysburg in 1863. Still another brother, James F. Patton, who married Miss Caperton, was a lieutenant in the Confederacy, and was wounded at the battle of Cold Harbor; and still another, Hugh M. Patton, who married Miss Bull, of Orange, was a lieutenant in the Confederacy, being wounded at the second battle of Manasses.

Ophelia Williams, daughter of Isaac Williams and Lucy Slaughter, married the Rev. George A. Smith. Their son, Isaac Smith, was a captain of engineers in the Confederate Army, and of two other sons, George Hugh Smith was a colonel and Henry Smith a captain in the Confederate service.

John James Williams, son of Isaac Williams and Lucy Slaughter, married Miss Thompson, and was one of the leading lawyers of California.

Susan Slaughter, daughter of Capt. Phillip Slaughter and Margaret Strother, married Dr. McConchie, and they had a daughter, who married James Wade Strother, who was a great-great-grandson of Francis Strother and Susannah Dabney. (5, Jas. Wade; 4, Wm.; 3, Joseph; 2, Capt. John; 1, Francis.)

Sallie Slaughter, daughter of Capt. Phillip and Margaret, married her cousin, Phillip Slaughter, son of Judge Slaughter, of Kentucky, and their son, Dr. D. F. Slaughter, practiced medicine at Shelbyville, Ky.

Daniel French Slaughter, son of Capt. Phillip and Margaret, married, first, Letitia Madison, daughter of General Madison, and they had General James E. Slaughter and Major Phillip Slaughter. His second marriage was to Mary Winston.

George French Strother, son of French Strother and Lucy Coleman, was a lawyer and served in the Legislature of Virginia, elected twice to Congress from that state, but resigned before the expiration of the second term to accept the receivership of public moneys at St. Louis, Mo. His first marriage was to Sarah Williams, daughter of

Gen. James Williams and granddaughter of Gen. Moses Green; and second to Theodosia Hunt, daughter of John Hunt, of Lexington, Ky. By the first marriage was James French Strother, who served in the Virginia Legislature, was speaker of the House of Delegates, member of Congress 1850-51 to revise the Constitution. He married Elizabeth Roberts, daughter of Major John Roberts, a citizen of Culpeper and officer in Revolution. They had first George French Strother, who for many years had the management of the state prison; second, Capt. John Strother, who married a daughter of Dr. Payne, and was a member of the General Assembly for years; third, Judge Phillip W. Strother, of Petersburg, Va., who married Elvira Pendleton, granddaughter of Wm. Pendleton and Nancy Strother, and Nancy Strother was a great-granddaughter of Francis Strother and Susannah Dabney. (4, Nancy; 3, John; 2, Capt. John; 1, Francis.)

Judge Phillip W. Strother served in the State Senate and was circuit judge of his district. He has spent much time in searching through the court and church records of Virginia for Strother data and is in possession of much valuable history relating to them. Their children are: James, Elvira, Elizabeth, Pendleton, and Sallie Strother.

George French Strother's second marriage to Theodosia Hunt resulted in the birth of John Hunt Strother, who died in Europe in 1863, and Sallie Strother, who married Baron de Fahnenburg. The Baron died and left the widow much wealth, which, at her death, reverted to her Lexington, Ky., relatives. This ends the line of James Strother and Margaret French, and I will take up his brother, Jeremiah, Jr.

Jeremiah Strother, Jr., was a son of Jeremiah Strother and his wife Eleanor. He married Catherine Kinnerly, who was the aunt of Mary Kinnerly, who married George Strother, son of Francis of St. Marks and Susannah Dabney. The above Jeremiah Strother left Culpeper county and settled on Saluda river, in South Carolina, where he died. A deed in 1746 is of record in which Jeremiah is joined by his wife Catherine in conveying 210 acres of land on Cannons river, near the Rock Hills in Rappahannock county, to John Batts. This is probably about the period of his removal to South Carolina. They had a son, George Strother, who reared a family in South Carolina, and died there, and another, Solomon Strother, who married Nancy Lawler, daughter of John Lawler and Susannah Strother, of Virginia. They had John and Samuel Strother. Shortly after the birth of the latter, Solomon Strother moved his family to Grassy Island, on the Pedee, in North Carolina, where he died. After his death his widow, Nancy Lawler Strother, married a lawyer by the name of Crawford, who removed the family to Nashville, Tenn. John Strother, son of Jeremiah and Catharine, and brother of the above Solomon, came back to Virginia and married Ann Strother, daughter of Capt. John Strother and Mary Wade, and their children were:

Jeremiah Strother—1, Martha Payne; 2, Nancy Clayton.

Rev. George Strother—Mary Duncan.

John Strother — Mrs. Sallie Strother Pendleton.
Catharine Strother.
Mary Strother.
Jeremiah Strother first married Martha Payne, and had Dr. Archer Strother and George Woodson Strother. The latter died on the Green river in Kentucky, and Dr. Archer Strother married Miss Fry, but left no children. Jeremiah Strother's second marriage was to Nancy Clayton, and they had four children, one of whom, Elizabeth Strother, married Hamilton Hansbrough. She inherited the estate of her uncle John at his death. Hamilton Hansbrough died at the residence of his son, Col. George Woodson Hansbrough, near Salem, Va. Another son was Rev. John Strother Hansbrough, an Episcopalian minister.

Rev. George Strother, son of John and Ann, was born Feb., 1776, and died July, 1864. He lost his parents in youth, after which he resided with his grandparents, Capt. John Strother and Mary Wade Strother, until at the age of 18 years he enlisted as a soldier to suppress the insurrection of Western Pennsylvania. On the 18th of Feb., 1796, he married Mary Duncan, and in May following moved to Bourbon county, Ky., and in 1802 removed to Trimble county, Ky., where he spent the remainder of his life. He was a Methodist minister. Of their eight children the Rev. John Fletcher was one. He married Lavinia Bruce and they had a son, Henry Strother, who married Sallie White, and lives at Ft. Smith, Ark. He has made several visits to Virginia, as did his grandfather, the Rev. George Strother, in quest of information about the Strothers, and he has a rich store which he may put into print some day, as he has all of the dates of family, courts and church records. Another son of the Rev. George Strother and Mary Duncan was French Strother, who reared a large family. He married Lucinda Maddox. The Hon. John C. Strother, a lawyer of Louisville, Ky., is a son. He married Mary F. Greenwood. They have Catharine Pryor Strother, Shelby French Strother, and Eugene T. Strother.

John Strother, another son of John and Ann, and a brother of Rev. George, married Mrs. Edward Pendleton, whose maiden name was Sallie Strother, daughter of Joseph Strother and Nancy Stuart. When he died he willed his property to his niece, Mrs. Hamilton Hansbrough, and the supposition is that his wife preceded him in death.

CORRECTIONS OF STROTHER NOTES.*

No. 45, Vol. 15, page 89, Col. 2: Sir Lancelot Strother of Towberry Towers.

Page 90, Col. 2: Use Sittenbourne Parrish instead of Littleburn and Cittenburne where they appear.

Page 91, Col. 1: Should be Colonel Carter's plantation.

Page 92, Col. 2: 1822 should be 1722. Augustine Washington instead of Augustus.

Page 94, Col. 1: Should read first clerk of Augusta County and uncle of President Madison.

Page 94: Madison Table should read General Thomas Madison, not Gaul Thomas.

Page 96, Jones Table: Erase names of Gabriella Jones, Col. Thos. Mason Randolph and Dr. Brockenbrough. The last line in the table should read Anna Gabriella Jones married John Hawkins.

Page 97, Col. 1: Should read, Gabriella Harvie, daughter of Col. John Harvie and Margaret Jones, married, first Col. Thomas Mann Randolph; second, Dr. John Brokenbrough. Also Anna Gabriella Jones married John Hawkins.

Page 98, Col. 2; Substitute 1769 for 1849.

No. 46, Vol. 16, page 93, Col. 3: Use Behethland here and elsewhere for Behethdod.

Page 94, Strother Table: William Strother married Sarah Bailey Pannill. The name Kinnerly here and elsewhere should be Kennerly.

No. 46, Vol. 16, Page 95, Col. 2: Erase from William Pendleton, &c., down to and including Judge Edmund Pendleton and insert the following: Nancy Strother married William Pendleton, who was one of the sons of Col. James Pendleton and Elizabeth, and he a son of Henry Pendleton and Mary Taylor, and she a daughter of Col. James Taylor and Mary Gregory. Col. James Pendleton was a brother of Captain Nathaniel Pendleton of the Continental line and also of Judge Edmund Pendleton.

Page 96, Col. 1: Should read Nancy Pendleton married Judge P. W. Strother of Pearisburg, Va.

Page 98, Col. 1: After the sentence, raised a large family of children, insert the following: Isham Keith Hawkins, who married first, Lucy Major; second, Sarah Hall; Charlotte Ashmore Hawkins, who married James Vaughan; Lucy Hawkins, who married Thomas McGinniss; Susan Strother Hawkins, who married Thos. S. Edwards; Bejamine Dabney Hawkins, who married Jane Watts; Moses Hawkins, who married Mary Sublette; William Strother Hawkins, who married Mrs. Elizabeth S. Gough; James K. Hawkins, who married Anne Sublette, and Katherine Keith Hawkins, who married R. H. Railey.

Page 99, Col. 1: Erase Elizabeth Strother.

Page 99, Col. 2: Erase—and was the guardian of the daughters of his brother, William of Stafford. See Vol. 15, No. 45, page 93, Col. 2, Par. 1.

Page 100, Col. 1: Col. John Groves married a sister of Ann Fargeson.

No. 46, Vol. 16, page 100, Col. 2:

*For Vol. 45, pp. 89, 90, 91, 92, 94, 96, 97 & 98 see pp. 369, 370, 371, 372, 374, 376, 377 & 378, this volume. For Vol. 46, pp. 93, 94, 95, 96, 98, 99, 100, 101, 102 & 105 see pp. 381, 382, 383, 384, 386, 387, 388, 389, 390 & 393, this volume.

Anthony Strother married Francis Elizabeth Kenyon.

Page 101, Col. 1: Should be Bushrod Washington.

Page 101, Col. 2: Should be Hunter's, Kennedy's, &c., instead of Kennerly's. Substitute Porte Crayon for Grayson.

Page 102, Col. 1, Par. 2: After Behethland Storke add the following: Benjamine Pendleton, who was a descendant of Henry Pendleton and Mary Taylor, married Elizabeth Strother, daughter of Benjamine Strother and Kitty Price, and their daughter, Catherine Thornton Pendleton, married John Bailey Nicklin, whose son, J. B. Nicklin, Jr., married Elizabeth Pringle Kaylor, one of the sons of this last couple. Col. Benj. Patten Nicklin is an officer in the U. S. army and is doing duty in France. He is also the hereditary representative of Captain Benjamine Strother in the Virginia society of the Cincinnati. His brother, Lieutenant J. B. Nicklin III., is also in France doing duty.

Page 105, Col. 2: Should be John Minor Botts, not Batts.

Page 102, Col. 2: Should read Anne Doyne Wolff and John Brisban Walker.

In writing of the Strothers in 1917-18 I said that Gabriella Harvie married Col. Thomas Mann Randolph, the father of Gov. Thomas Mann Randolph who married Martha Jefferson, daughter of the President. Mr. Anderson tells me that Col. Thomas Mann Randolph was twice married, first to Ann Cary, daughter of Archibald Cary, and that his second marriage was to Gabriella Harvie. That there were children by each marriage and each wife named a son Thomas Mann Randolph. It was Thomas Mann Randolph by the first wife who became Governor of Virginia and married his cousin Martha Jefferson. The half-brother Thomas Mann Randolph by the second wife inherited the "Tuckahoe" estate including the mansion with all of its contents—family relics and portraits.

THE STROTHER FAMILY

Compiled by the late John Chaplin Strother, of Louisville; the late Henry Strother, of Ft. Worth, Texas, and the late Mrs. Susan T. Green, and Presented by Miss Katherine P. Strother, of Louisville, Ky.

Some think this family of Scotch origin and that it had then the prefix of Mac. Others insist that it is Saxon. Gen. Dick Taylor, son of the President, whose mother was a Strother, says, as we learn from Judge Strother of Giles Court House, Va., that he had visited the old burial ground of the family, in the Isle of Thanet, County of Kent, Eng., and there had seen the name in its various transitions from its original form, Straather, to its present orthography. He saw there tombstones over a thousand years old. The family belonged to the priesthood in the worship of the Saxon god, "Thor," from whom our Thursday is named; hence, also the name Straather. Anstrother is said to be one of the original forms of the name, also Anstruther.

There are Strothers in Ireland, who went there with William III, in his war with James II and were rewarded with lands and estates. The coat of arms is a yellow greyhound, the shield red, with a silver band across, and three blue eagles on the band.

The earliest date to which we have traced the family in Va., is 1734, when Anthony Strother patented a tract of land under the double mountain in what was then St. Mark's Parish, and is now Bromfield, in Madison. According to Rev. Geo. Strother of Trimble Co., Ky., a pious and very intelligent minister of the Methodist Church, who was born in Va. in 1776, and lived until 1864, the first of the name who came to America was Wm. Strother, who is said to have been one of the bodyguard of William III. Other tradition says, (according to Judge Strother of Giles) that three brothers came together to Fredricksburg. Certain it is there was a Wm. Strother, who lived opposite Fredricksburg, adjoining the farm of Gen. Washington's father. He m. Margaret Watts and had 13 daughters, the eldest of whom, Jane m. in 1769, Thomas Lewis, ancestor of John F. Lewis, late U. S. Senator from Va. The next, Margaret, m. Mr. Morton who died soon after, when she m. Gabriel Jones, "The Valley Lawyer." Another daughter m. John Madison, the father of Bishop Madison. Another m. John Frog. Another a Washington, from whom are descended Peter G. Washington at one time Asst. Sec. of State and L. J. Washington, correspondent of Louisville Courier Journal.

Benj. Strother died in Culpeper in 1759. Nothing is known of him, except the report of the appraisers of his estate.

Jeremiah Strother died in 1741 leaving his property to his wife Eleanor and appointing his sons James and Wm. his executors. These are probably the three brothers: Wm., Benj., and Jeremiah, who may have been sons of a former William of the bodyguard; but there is no authority for such statement, nor is the relation between these three distinctly known.

The first record—William died in Richmond Co., Va. (now King Geo.), in 1702, date of his will 1700. He lived on the Rappahannock and devised his lands to his wife, Dorothea, for life and two sons, William and James. His other children were: Jeremy (Jeremiah), Robert, Benjamin, Joseph. James died without issue devising his land to his brother Joseph. Jeremiah was a land owner in Westmorland and came to Orange where he died in 1741; children: Wm., James Lawrence, Christopher, Jeremiah, Francis. William died 1727, having m. Margaret, dau. of Francis Thornton; ch., Wm., Francis, Anthony, and possibly others.

William Strother, of Stafford, m. Margaret Watts. Their first daughter, Jane, m. Thomas Lewis and had 13 children. Their three eldest sons, John, Andrew and Thomas were officers in the Revolutionary War. John and Andrew were with Washington at Valley Forge and thruout the Jersey campaign; John and Thomas Lewis were at the surrender of Cornwallis. Andrew Lewis was an officer under Gen. Wayne in his expeditions against the western Indians in 1795 and lost his arm. The two youngest sons, Charles and Benjamin Lewis, inherited the most of Thomas Lewis' large estates.

Gen. Samuel Lewis, the son of Col. Charles, m. 1st his cousin, a dau. of John Lewis of Bath, 2nd, the dau. of Judge Lomax and 3rd, Mrs. Fry. He had a large family. One of his sons m. a dau. of Daniel Sheffey.

Col. Charles Lewis had other sons, Charles and Thomas, and daughters, Jane and Margaret.

Margaret Lewis, the oldest dau. of Thomas Lewis, m. 1st, Capt. McClannahan, who was afterwards killed at the battle of the Point. Her 2nd husband was Col. Bowyer. Agatha, the second dau., m. 1st Capt. Frog, and 2nd Capt. John Stuart. Her daughter, Miss Frog, m. Mr. Estill and their dau. m. Mr. Erskine. Her son, Lewis Stuart, was for a long time clerk of Greenbrier Co. He m. Miss Lewis of Bath.

Charles Stuart, her second son, was Pres. of the Board of Public Works of Va. Her dau., Miss Stuart, m. Col. Crockett, of Wythe, Va.

Jane, the third dau. of Thomas Lewis, m. Capt. Hughs, of the Continental Army. They removed to Kentucky. She left only one son who died young.

Mary, the fourth dau., m. Capt. McElhany of the Continental Army, Elizabeth the fifth, m. Thomas M. Gilmer, the son of Peachy B. Gilmer. They emigrated to Broad River, Ga., where she had nine children and lived past her 89th year. Her oldest son, Peachy Ridgeway Gilmer m. 1st, Mary Boutwell, the daughter of Daniel Harvie, and 2nd, Caroline Thomas.

Mary Merriweather, the oldest dau. of Thomas Gilmer, m. 1st, Warner Taliaferro, and 2nd, Nicholas Powers. She had 10 children, four by her first husband and six by her last.

Thomas, second son of Thomas Gilmer, m. 1st, Nancy Harvie and 2nd, Mrs. Anne Harper. He had 6 children.

George B., third son, m. Eliza Frances Grattan, no issue. He was several times elected to Congress and twice elected Governor of Georgia.

John, fourth son, m. 1st, Lucy Johnston, and 2nd, Mrs. Susan Gresham, dau. of Joel Barnett. Three children by his first marriage and four by his second.

William Benjamin Strother, fifth son of Thomas Gilmer and Elizabeth, his wife, m. Elizabeth Marks, dau. of Merriweather Marks and grand-dau. of Gov. Matthews.

Charles L., sixth son, m. 1st, Nancy Marks and 2nd, Mrs. Matilda Kyle. Six sons and one daughter by his first wife and two by his last.

James Jackson, seventh son of Thomas Gilmer, m. Elizabeth Jourdan. They had five children.

Ann, the sixth dau. of Thomas Lewis and Jane, his wife, m. 1st Mr. Douthatt and 2nd Mr. French. They removed to Kentucky.

Fanny, 7th dau. of Thomas, m. Col. Layton Yancey of the American Army during the Revolution.

Sophia, the eighth and youngest dau. of Thomas Lewis, m. John Carthral, their dau. Mary, m. Col. Bankhead.

Margaret, second dau. of Wm. Strother and Margaret Watts, m. 1st, Henry Morton, who was accidentally killed soon after, leaving her a large fortune and no children. She m. 2nd, John Gabriel Jones, a well educated Welshman, the friend, kinsman and executor of Lord Fairfax. His residence was in the valley of Va. on the Shenandoah River, upon a farm of great fertility and extent, adjoining the farms of his three brothers-in-law, Thomas Lewis, John Madison and John Frog and his friend, Peachey R. Gilmer. He was the most distinguished lawyer of New Virginia. He left a large estate to his descendants. Mrs. Jones lived to the extended age of 97 years, much loved and respected. Bishop Meade says in "Old Churches and Families of Va.," Vol 2, page 325, "I also knew that venerable old lady, Mrs. Gabriel Jones. The first visit ever paid to that parish was in company with her grandson, Mr. Strother Jones, of Fredrick, when we saw her in her old age, rejoicing in the prospect of the resuscitation of the church of her love. Her large old prayer book is in the hands of one of her descendants. Her husband, Mr. Gabriel Jones, was for a long time so prominent in the valley that he was called 'the Lawyer.' His name is on the vestry book of Frederick parish as counsel for the Church in one of her suits."

Margaret, dau. of Gabriel Jones, m. Col. John Harvie, Register of the Land Office of Va.

Gabriella, eldest dau. of Col. John Harvie, m. 1st Col. Tom Mann Randolph and 2nd, Dr. Brockenbrough, for years one of the most prominent citizens of Richmond. She is said to have been a lady of rare grace, beauty, talent and accomplishments, was known and is spoken of to this day by old persons who knew her as the "fair Gabriella." By Mr. Randolph she had but one child:

Thomas Mann Randolph's first wife was Miss Harriet Willson of Va., his 2nd was Miss Patterson of New Jersey. His children were: John Randolph;

Mary Randolph, a famous belle, m. John Chapman, son of the celebrated physician, Dr. Chapman of Phila. They had two children: Ella, m. Mr. Podesta, for many years Secretary of the Spanish Legation at Washington. They had one child, Emily Chapman; Margaret Randolph, m. Mr. Asberry Dickens, a lawyer of Washington City. Their Children: Fanny, Harriet and Frank Dickens; Harriet Randolph m, Mr. White at one time U. S. Senator from Indiana. They reside in Lafayette, Ind.; Allen Randolph is only one of the children of Thomas Mann Randolph's second marriage whose name is known. John and Mary Brockenbrough both died young; are the children of Gabriella's second marriage.

John Harvie m. his cousin Margaretta Hawkins, dau. of John Hawkins and Anna Gabriella, his wife, of Scott Co., Ky. They had nine children. Gabriella Augusta m. James Breathitt, had one child, Harvie Whitlock Breathitt who never married, but was drowned from a steamer on the Illinois River in his 22nd year.

Mary Whitlock Harvie died young, also Katherine Ellen Harvie, and Lewis Edwin Harvie, who had been private Secretary of Pres. Jefferson. John Strother and Llewellyn Jones died unmarried.

Edwin J. Harvie m. Miss Pattie Hardaway. He was burned in the Richmond Theater about 1811. They had two children: Lewis Edwin Harvie m. Miss Sarah Blair. He lives in Amelia Co., Va., and has been for 30 years prominent and influential in the Legislature and affairs of State. Their children are: Irving Harvie, an officer in the Confederate Army was killed in one of the battles in Western Va., towards the close of the War.

Edwin J. Harvie was Inspector General of the Army of Northern Va. on Staff of Gen. Joseph E. Johnston. He m. Miss Edmonia Meade. Names of children unknown.

John B. Harvie, also an officer in Confederacy, m. Miss Anderson of Southwestern Va.; Pattie Harvie, m. Mr. Taylor of Va.; Wm. Old Harvie, officer in C. A., m. Miss Jefferson; Courtney Harvie m. Mr. Taylor of Va.; Seddon Harvie in C. S. A.; Lewis E., and Charles Harvie.

Dr. Brockenbrough Harvie, son of Edwin J. and Pattie, his wife, is an influential citizen of Powhatan Co., Va., and for many years its County Judge. He m. Miss Mary Blair, a sister of his brother's (Lewis) wife, Sarah Blair. They had 8 children: Sarah m. Lieut. Chaffin of C. S. A., Lewis E. was an officer in C. S. A., and is now a practicing Physician. He is married; James m. Miss Melehoir; Mary m. Nicholas Ruffin; Eliza; Blair; Martha and Fanny Harvie.

Jacqueline B. Harvie was at one time in the navy and served with distinction under Decatur in the Tripolitan War. He resigned on account of the death of his father to take care of his mother and their large estate and became a leading citizen of Richmond, representing the city for many years in both branches of the State Legislature. He m. Mary, only dau. of Chief Justice John Marshall of

Va. Their children were: Mary, who was a confirmed invalid and died some years ago; John was an officer in the U. S. Army (a graduate of West Point) on staff of Gen. Worth and died of yellow fever in Fla. during the Seminole War; Ellen m. Col. Frank Ruffin of Richmond, Va. No children; Virginia m. Gov. Spicer Patrick of West Va.; Susan m. Mr. Wade, an Episcopal clergyman; Wm. Wallace was an officer on the staff of Gen. Beverley Robertson and died unmarried in Arkansas; Anna Harvie; Lewis Edwin was accidentally killed while gunning, a mere lad in 1846; and Emily Harvie.

Julianna Harvie, 2nd dau. of 1st John and Margaretta Harvie, never married and was burned in the Richmond Theater with her brother, Edwin J., and her niece, Mary Whitlock.

Emily Harvie, 3rd dau. of 1st John, 1st m. Mr. Whitlock by whom she had one child. After his death she m. Mr. McGrau of Va. They had no child. Mrs. John Harvie survived her husband many years.

Elizabeth, 2nd dau. of Gabriel Jones, m. John Lewis, a distinguished lawyer of Fredericksburg, whose brother m. Betty, the sister of Gen. Washington, and had so many children that she said she counted them every night when she put them to bed to be certain that the bears had eaten none during the day. They numbered 15.

Anna Gabriella, dau. of Gabriel Jones, m. John Hawkins. They removed to Ky. One of their dau. m. her cousin, John Harvie.

Strother Jones, only son of Gabriel and Margaret, was an officer in the Rev. Army. He died young leaving one son (name unknown) who m. Miss Marshall, a niece of Chief Justice Marshall.

Agatha Strother, dau. of Wm. and Margaret Strother m. John Madison, who held the Clerkship of Augusta Co., Va. Their son, James Madison, was for a long time Pres. of Wm. and Mary College. He was appointed Bishop of Va. Wm. I. Madison, another son, m. Elizabeth Preston. They had two daughters. Susanna Madison m. John Howe Peyton. Had one son, Wm. Madison Peyton, m. Sally Taylor of Bottetourt Co., Va. Their children were: Elizabeth, died unmarried; Susan M., m. 1st Joseph H. White and 2nd, Col. Washington of N. C. No issue; Sally T., m. 1st Thomas Reed and 2nd, Dr. James White, one child, Bettie Reed; Agatha Garnett Peyton m. Walter Preston, issue: Sally Y., Ellen, Elizabeth, Susan, John; Wm. Madison Peyton; Juliet Peyton died unmarried; Allen Y. Peyton died unmarried; Bernardine Peyton.

Agatha Strother Madison, 2nd dau. of Wm. and Elizabeth Madison, m. Garnett Peyton, brother of John H. Peyton, and an officer in Wayne's campaign against the Indians. Children: Benj. H. m. Mrs. Ellis, dau. of Col. Wm. Momford, no child; James Peyton, died unmarried; John Bowse Peyton m. Miss White, no child; Wm. Preston Peyton m. Miss Momford and resides in Missouri. Children not known; Ann Frances Peyton.

George Madison, son of John and Agatha Madison, m. Jane Smith, niece of Mrs. Wm. Madison, nee Preston. He commanded a battalion in the campaign against the British and Indians in the war of 1812. When Winchester was defeated, he and his battalion stood their ground long after the others had surrendered or been dispersed. He was afterwards Gov. of Ky. He had only one dau., Myra Madison m. Andrew Alexander of Woodford Co., Ky., her children were: Apolline Alexander, m. Frances P. Blair, issue: Andrew Blair, Christine Blair, James Blair, Geo. M. Blair, Francis P. Blair, Cary M. Blair, Myra Alexander m. Franklin Dick, issue: Wm. A. Evans, and Franklin Dick; Geo. M. Alexander m. Mary Campbell. No child; Andrew J. Alexander, Brigadier Gen. of Vol. and Major of Regular Army, m. Evalina Martin, issue: Emily Alexander.

Gen. Thomas Madison, son of John and Agatha Madison, m. Miss Susanna Henry, dau. of the great orator, Patrick Henry. The Bowyers and Lewises of Botetourt Co., Va., are descendants.

Roland Madison, another son, m. the dau. of Gen. Andrew Lewis and was the father of Capt. Madison of the United States Army.

The other daughter of Wm. Strother we have been unable to trace. One of them married Capt. John Frog and one of her sons, Capt. John Frog, married his cousin Agatha Lewis. He was killed by the Indians at the battle of the Point on the 10th of Oct., 1774. His daughter m. Mr. Estill and her daughter married Mr. Erskine. Another daughter (of Wm. Strother) m. a Washington and another is said to have married another Lewis.

FAMILY OF JEREMIAH STROTHER

Jeremiah Strother died in what was then Orange Co., Va., (Culpeper not being yet formed) in 1741. His will was proven by J. Slaughter, John Catlett and Wm. Lightfoot. He devised his estate to his wife, Elinor, for life. Executors: his sons James and Wm. His children were: James, William, Francis, Jeremiah, Lawrence, Christopher, Catherine, and Elizabeth. James died in 1761. He m. Margaret French, dau. of Daniel French of King George Co., Va. His children were: French, James, and Mary who m. Geo. Gray.

French S., (son of James) died in 1800, after having been for 30 years, consecutively, in the House of Burgesses, —convention of 1776, which adopted the first State Constitution,—convention of 1788, which adopted the Constitution of the United States,—House of Delegates and State Senate. He was near being a candidate for Congress against Mr. Madison at the first election under the Constitution, but yielded to Mr. Monroe, afterwards President. He m. Lucy Coleman of Culpeper and had children: Daniel French S., m. a Miss Thompson, went to Louisville, Ky., and left 3 sons, names unknown; a dau. of French S. m. Capt. Phillip Slaughter, children: Lucy m. Isaac H. Williams, a lawyer, issue: Phelia W. m. Rev. Geo. A. Smith, issue: Isaac Smith, Capt. of Engineers in the (Civil War); Geo. Hugh Smith, Col. C. S. A.; Henry Smith, Capt. C. S. A.; A dau. m. Dunbar Brooke; Eliza Smith m. Corse; Eleanor Smith, deceased, and Belle Smith.

P. French Williams m. John M. Patton, acknowledged as the head of the bar in his day, and member of Congress for eight years. Children: Robert W. Patton, died recently. John M. Patton m. Miss Taylor. He was Col. of the 21st Va. Infantry, and commanded a brigade from the time of the battle of Winchester in 1862 to the close of the valley campaign under Stonewall Jackson. Isaac W. Patton m. Miss Merritt. He was Col. of a Louisiana regiment, was made prisoner at the fall of Vicksburg and afterwards commanded one of the Forts in Mobile Bay to the end of the War. Geo. S. Patton m. Miss Glassell. Was Col. of the 22nd Va. Infantry, was killed by a shell while commanding a brigade at the battle of Winchester in 1864. W. Tazewell Patton, Col. of 7th Va. Inf., killed while leading that regiment in the charge of Pickett's division on the heights of Gettysburg in 1863. Hugh M. Patton m. Miss Bull of Orange, was a Lieut C. S. A. He was wounded at the second battle of Manassas. James F. Patton m. Miss Caperton, dau. of Sen. Caperton. He was a Lieut. C. S. A. Wounded at Cold Harbor; Wm. M. Patton m. Miss Jordan, of Rockbridge; Eliza W. Patton m. John Gilmer, of Pittsylvania Co.

Eleanor Williams m. Dr. Hite of Amherst Co., Va. Children: Isaac, Edmund, Fontaine and Eliza. Eliza Williams, 4th child of Isaac H. and Lucy Williams, died in girlhood. Lucy Anu Williams, unmarried. John James Williams m. Miss Thompson.

Susan, 2nd dau. of Capt. Phil Slaughter and Margaret Strother m. Dr. Maconichie and is the mother of Mrs. Strother of Tenn.

The 3rd dau. of Capt. P. Slaughter m. Frank Conway, issue: Dr. Philip C., Dr. Albert, a dau. m. Robert Shepherd and a dau. m. P. Clayton.

Eliza Slaughter m. J. B. Dade. Issue: Capt. Townshend, Philip and a dau. m. Edward Smith.

Sally Slaughter m. Philip son of Judge Slaughter of Ky. Issue: Dr. D. F. Slaughter of Shelbyville, Ky.

Daniel French Slaughter (late Senator) m. 1st, Letitia, dau. of Gen. Wm. Madison. Issue: Gen. James E. S., and Major P. Slaughter; D. F. Slaughter m. 2nd, Mary Winston, issue: Mary, Eliza, Caroline, John and Daniel.

The third child and 2nd dau. of French and Lucy Strother m. Col. John Evans.

The 4th child and 3rd dau. of French Strother m. Daniel Gray.

Elizabeth French Strother was the 5th child and 4th daughter; Lucy Strother was the 6th and Geo. French Strother was the 7th. He died about 1840 in St. Louis, Mo. His 1st wife was Sarah dau. of Gen. James Williams and grand dau. of Moses Green, uncle of the General, by whom he had one child, James French Strother. His 2nd wife was Theodosia, dau. of John Hunt of Lexington, Ky., by whom he had John Hunt Strother who died in Europe in 1853 and Sallie Strother, who m. Baron Fahnenburg. She died April 12, 1885, leaving a large fortune.

James .French Strother, son of George French Strother, died in 1860. He served in the Legislature, was Speaker of the House of Delegates, member of Reform Conven-

Elvira Pendleton, who married Judge P. W. Strother, of Petersburg, Va., who has made a thorough search in Virginia for Strother history. The children of Judge Phillip W. Strother and Elvira Pendleton are James French, Elvira, Elizabeth, Pendleton and Sallie. Mildred Strother, second of John Strother and Helen Piper, married Bailey Buckner in 1814. Their son, Judge Aylette Harvey Buckner, moved to Missouri, where he was elected judge and served that state many years in Congress. He was also a member of the peace conference in 1861. Lucy Strother, third of John Strother and Helen Piper, married Nov., 1805, Wm. Ashby, son of Gen. Turner Ashby, and they had a number of children. Sarah Ann Strother, fourth of John and Helen, married Dr. Thomas Barbour and moved to Missouri. Elizabeth Strother, fifth of John and Helen, married, 1814, Wm. F. Thompson, and their son, Phillip R. Thompson, was a member of Congress from Virginia. Polly Strother, sixth of John and Helen, married, 1805, Col. Wm. Ward, and they had a son who practiced law in Illinois and died in that state. Captain French Strother, son of John and Helen, married his cousin, Mary Ann Pendleton Browning, daughter of Charles E. Browning and Miss Pendleton, and Charles E. Browning was a son of Charles Browning and Mollie Strother. They moved to Calloway county, Mo., where they raised a large family.

Wm. Strother "of Orange" was the second son of Francis Strother and Susan Dabney. In 1751 he married Sarah Bailey Pannill, widow of Wm. Pannill, who died in 1749. His wife's maiden name was Sarah Bailey, a lady of unusual intelligence and many other charms. She had several children by the first marriage. Feb. 20, 1752, she was assigned dower in the estate of her late husband, Wm. Pannill and Wm. Strother was appointed guardian of her children. By the marriage to Wm. Strother "of Orange" were the following children:

Susannah Strother—Capt. Moses Hawkins.

Wm. Dabney Strother — killed battle Guilford Courthouse.

Sarah Strother—Col. Richard Taylor.

In 1749 there was a patent issued to Wm. Strother of "Orange," son of Francis Strother and Susan Dabney, of 400 acres of land in Orange county, and another in 1761. In 1768 he conveyed the 400 acres to John Strother, presumed to be his eldest brother. The records of Culpeper, Va., Oct. 19, 1752, show a deed of Courtney Norman to Wm. Strother of "Orange" of 100 acres of land. Another deed, 1758, of Wm. Strother of "Orange" to his daughter, Susannah Strother, and son, Wm. Dabney Strother, who were then mere children. He was a large land proprietor in both Orange and Culpeper counties as the record shows. On August 1, 1727, Margaret Thornton Strother, his grandmother, conveyed to his father, Francis Strother, certain slaves with reversion to his son, Wm. of "Orange," and that property came to him not later than 1752, when his father died. His wife, Sarah (B. P.) Strother, died in 1774, and during that year her will was probated. Her son, Wm. Dabney Strother, and friend, Charles Bruce, were execu-

Francis, Robert, Mary (m. Deatherage), Behathalind, Elizabeth (m. Thomas Gaines) and Susannah (m. James Gaines,) —ch. Gen. Gaines. Nothing is known of his son Robert. daughter named Pigg m. a Covington, and Hester m. a Wallace and one a Tyler. From James Gaines, Gen. Edmund Pendleton Gaines is descended; the Deatherage still remain in Rappahannock Co., Va., and through Pres. Tyler this Tyler, County Clerk of Stafford, was connected with the Strother family.

The history of the other children of Francis of St. Mark's Parish is better known. John, 1st son of Francis of St. Mark's was born in 1721 and died in 1795. Made will, Mar. 29th, 1795, entered April 17th, 1795. Bequeaths to his wife, Mary, for life, to Geo. and John Strother, sons of his dau. Anne,—to Michael Lawler, son of his daughter Susannah, to his dau., Mary Browning, (wife of Chas Browning), to Sarah Hughes, to Lucy Covington, to Elizabeth Browning, and to Mildred Covington. His ch. were Joseph Strother who went to Ky.; Anne S., who died in 1788; Susannah Lawler, who afterwards m. James Hulett in S. C.; Mary Browning; Sarah Hughes; Lucy Covington; Elizabeth Browning; Mildred Covington, and John Strother (who died in 1818).

The first John Strother m. Mary Willis Wade, who had a sister married to Parson Fontaine, and they had a son Capt. Fontain, who moved to Ky. near Louisville and had three daughters, one m. Thomas Prather, one m. John Jeremiah Jacob (called John I. Jacob), and one m. Fortunatus Cosby, all of Louisville. Mary Wade is said to have been a very amiable woman. John S. was born in Va., (perhaps Hanover Co.) in 1721; shortly after his marriage came to Culpeper, the upper end of the County, 7 miles east of Thorton's Gap, immediately on the road leading from said Gap to Fredricksburg and Falmouth. Here he lived until his death, April, 1795. He was a man remarkable for decision of character and perseverance in business. His eldest and youngest children were sons, Joseph and John; he had 7 daughters.

In 1795, John Strother and Mary, his wife, made a deed to James Hulett. In 1802, Mary Strother, widow of John, made a deed to James Hulett and Susannah, his wife, (her dau.), all her interest in the estate of her brother, James Wade of Anson Co., N. C.

Joseph Strother, son of John, m. Nancy Stewart, dau. of Mary and Robert Stewart of Culpeper Co., Va., said to have been a very beautiful woman, and they had 12 children, four sons, William, Benjamin, John and Joseph, and 8 daughters, Mary, Lucy, Sally, Elizabeth, Nancy, Milly, Peggy and Senaca. He was deputy sheriff in Culpeper and there are in Hennings Statutes special acts in regard to him. He went to Ky. in 1800. Some of his children went with him and others remained in Va.; children Benjamin Strother, eldest son of Joseph, was an officer in Wayne's army. He died at Hot Springs in Va., and had never married. Wm. S. the 2nd son of Joseph, m. Miss Milly Medley and had 5 ch.: Harriet Strother, m. Charles Giles; Louisa

405

Strother, m. Rev. Horace Stringfellow, an Episcopal minister. They had several daughter married in Petersburg; one is m. to LaFayette Watkins, Esq., of Petersburg, Va. Chas. F. Stringfellow, a lawyer in P—, Va. Rev. Horace J. Stringfellow, an Episcopal minister of Montgomery, Ala., who has a son; Rev. James Stringfellow, minister; Chas. Strother, m. Miss Yoolley (or Jorley) and his ch. are: William, Joseph, Charles, Mary, Archer and Abby, who m. her cousin, Dr. Henry, son of James Strother; Reuben Strother m. Miss Giles and had 5 ch. One of his sons left a dau., Mary Ann S., who was assistant teacher to French Strother, Jr., in Mo.

James Strother m. Miss McConitry. He was an Episcopal minister and lived near Memphis, Tenn., where he died several years ago. His son Dr. Henry S. m. Abby Strother.

John S., 3rd son of Joseph, m. 1st a daughter. of Capt. Edwards on the muddy forks of Beargrass in Jefferson Co. Ky., had a son named Pendleton Strother; John S's 2nd wife was Miss Clopton from near Winchester, Va., by whom he had several children. One lived in Illinois. His daughter Florida S. m. Mr. Garnes, of St. Louis; Joseph m. Miss Finley in the same neighborhood in Jefferson Co., Ky. She died and he returned to Va., and m. Miss Davenport of Jefferson Co. Va. He settled in Woodstock, where he spent the rest of his life in the practice of law. Left no Children.

Mary S., eldest dau. of Joseph m. Wm. Menefee, leaving one son Benjamin Menefee and three dau., Nancy, who m. Thompson Ashley of Fauquier Co. and an uncle to Gen. Ashley. They have these daughters; —— Ashley m. Mr. Bane. —— Ashley m. Mr. Miller. —— Ashley m. Mr. Bane; Milly Menefee m. Dr. Yutt; Sally Menefee.

Wm. Menefee lived in what is now Rappahanock Co., on what is known as the old "Duncan place," now owned by Lafayette Browning.

Lucy, 2nd dau. of Joseph S., m. Francis Wyatt Green of Culpeper Co., Va. They moved to Ky. with her father in 1800, lived in Jefferson Co., Ky., m., and died in Breckenridge Co. about the year 1824. They had 18 children, most of whom did not reach maturity. The 1st, Robert Green, was a soldier in the war of 1812 and was present at the battle of New Orleans. After the war was over he remained there. Of him we have no record; William Green was drowned in the Miss. River. He never married; Betsey Green; Nancy Green m. Mr. Bostwick; Lucy Green; Joseph Green was also at the battle of N. O. a youth of 18. Married in 1817 Susan Martha Ball, a much beloved and honored lady, a descendant of the Balls of Va. She became totally deaf about 3 years after her marriage, but her lovely disposition won her many friends. She died July 8, 1849; her husband died in 1851. They had 7 sons; only three of them lived to maturity. The oldest, Dr. Norvin Green, was born April 17, 1818. He m. Martha A. English, dau. of Capt. James W. English, in Carrollton, Carroll Co., Ky., in April 1840. He has been several times elected to the Legislature of Ky. and was once a prominent candidate for the U. S. Senate. But the chief work of his life has been the management and control of the Telegraph lines of this country. He was president of the Western Union Tel. Co. from 1868 until his death Feb. 12, 1893. He has 6 children living and one dead; Susannah Thornton Green; Dr. James Olive Green m. Amy Hewitt; Pinckney Frank Green, m. Carrie Conant of Louisville. Their children are: Gertrude d. in infancy. Cora d. in infancy. Nester C., Ada, Norwin English, and Frank W. Green; John English Green m. Annie Lindenberger, had 4 girls; Ethel, Mabel Martha and Mildred Green. Warren Green m. Blanche Smith. Norva Green died young. Grace N. Green, no record. Neville Green, 2nd son of Joseph Green, m. Mary Jane Morris and left no child. He went to Mexico in 1848 and fought thru the war. After peace was declared he returned as far as N. O., when he disappeared and was never heard of more. John Ball Green, 3rd son of Joseph, d. in infancy.

Lawrence Green d. at 13 years of age.

Thornton Green, m. Matilda Stewart. Ch.: Daniel S. Green, m. Minnie Todd; Joseph M. Green, m. Sallie Gwinn; Norvin Green, m. Ida Stratton; Mollie Green, m. Wm. Erwin; James Green, m. Ella Maddox; Rennie Green; Annie Green; and Jennie Green, m. Elmer Rice.

Warren, son of Joseph Green died at 13 years of age. Benjamin Franklin Green, d. an infant. Thompson Green, son of Francis W. Green, m. Betsey Askins. He has lived to a great age in Breckenridge Co., Ky., and has no children; Francis Green; John Green, m. Mary Holt, issue: Wm., Keeziah, Martha, John, Clemmie, James and Norvin.

Austin Green married and lived in Perry Co., Ind. Had 2 children. Strother Green died single. Other sons and daughters died young.

Sally Strother, 3rd dau. of Joseph Strother m. 1st, Edward Pendleton, son of Capt. Harry Pendleton of Culpeper by whom she had one dau. who died in 1836. She m. 2nd her cousin, John Strother.

Elizabeth Strother, m. Robert Hughes, moved to Jefferson Co., Ky., where they lived until her death. They had a large family.

Nancy Strother, m. Mr. Prince. They moved to Jefferson Co., Ky., afterward to Indiana.

Milly Strother, m. Wm. Yolley.

Peggy Strother, m. Wm. Ward, of Va., being his 3rd wife. Two children: Mildred Ward, m. Dr. Briggs.

Senaca Strother, m. Wm. Sebastian, son of Judge Sebastian of the Court of Appeals of Kentucky.

Susan Strother, dau. of John and Mary Wade, m. 1st John Lawler. They had 6 children, 5 girls and one son. After his death she moved to N. C. where she m. 2nd James Hulett. Children: Michael Lawler, m. Miss Williams; Nancy Lawler, m. Solomon Strother, son of 2nd Jeremiah. Mollie Lawler, m. Geo. Humphrey, who moved to N. C., then to Tenn.; Sallie Lawler, m. Geo. Bigbee and moved to N. C., then to Tenn.; Caty Lawler, and Susan removed, single, with their mother, to N. C.

Nancy or Anne Strother, dau. of John, m. John Strother, son of 2nd Jeremiah.

Anne outlived her husband and died in 1788. Made will Sept. 24th, 1787, entered Oct. 20, 1788. Appoints her honored father, John S. Sr., and her brother, John S., Jr., executors. Witnesses to will: Wm. Hughes, Tho. Hughes, and Chas. Browning. Her ch. were: Jeremiah, George, John, Caty, Mary. Jeremiah was twice married. His first wife was Martha Payne, by whom he had 3 children. Second wife was Nancy Clayton by whom he had 2 sons and 2 daughters. Issue: Dr. Archer Strother, m. Miss Fry, of Bath, and settled near Warm Springs, Bath Co., Va. No child. Geo. Woodson Strother came to the west on business for his father and died on Green River, Ky.; Martha Strother, unmarried; Jeremiah Strother, unmarried. Elizabeth, m. Hamilton Hansbrough, to whom John S., son of Anne, left his property when he died in 1832. Mr. Hansbrough died at the residence of his son, Col. Geo. Woodson Hansbrough near Salem, Va., who is a lawyer and was a Col. during the war. Rev. John S. Hansbrough is an Episcopal minister.

Philip Strother went to Alabama and died.

Sarah Strother, m. Mr. Logan of Goochland Co. They lived in Salem, Va.

Rev. Geo. Strother was born Feb. 14, 1776, and died July 30, 1864. While young he lost his father, and his mother died when he was 12 years old. A part of his youth he spent with grandfather, who died in 1795. When 18 years of age he volunteered as a soldier to suppress the insurrection in Western Pennsylvania. On the 18th of Feb., 1796, he m. Miss Mary, dau. of James and Seeny Duncan, and in May following, with his father-in-law and family, emigrated to Bourbon Co., Ky. In 1802 he moved to what is now Trimble Co. He was of the delegation to the Capital to procure the formation of a new county, and by request he gave a name to the county, selecting the name of Judge Trimble. He was much beloved, especially by his relations, among whom he visited a great deal and he was thoroughly familiar with them both in Va. and Ky. Before his death, seeing that oral tradition would not preserve the records of the family, he left a clear and vivid history of his branch of the Strother family. They spent the latter part of their lives about five miles from the present city of Madison, Ind., where he was for many years a local preacher in the M. E. Church. Children: Nancy Strother, d. in 1817. Polly Strother, m. James W. Talbott, Apr. 27, 1824. Issue: Helen, Mary, James, Nancy, George, Isham, Seeny, Sarah.

Jeremiah Strother, m. first, Fanny W. Pryor, Aug. 31, 1828, m. 2nd, Sallie Peniston, 3rd Sarah McClellan. Issue: Sam Pryor Strother, Richard Henry Strother, Oliver Peniston Strother, Frank Taylor Strother, Fanny Morton Strother, Ben Herbert Strother, James McClellan Strother, Wm. Walker Strother, Mary Allen Strother, Lizzie Strother, Alonzo Bascom Strother, Jeremiah Pierce Strother, Charles Wesley Strother.

John Fletcher Strother, m. Lavinia Bruce, Jan. 21, 1830. Issue: Geo. Wm. Strother, m. Amanda Owens; Ch.: Sanford S., m. Mattie Gray. Ch.: Geo. Mm.

Strother, Lula Strother; Sarah C. Strother, m. Wm. N. Shelton. Ch.: James R. Shelton, John Thomas Shelton, Frank Shelton, Emma Lavinia Shelton, William Shelton, George Shelton.

John Pryor Strother, m. Mildred E. Lewis. Ch.: Chas. Lewis Strother, Albert Randolph Strother, John Pryor Strother, Sydney Strother, Henry Strother, Perla Strother, Wallace Strother.

Emma Strother, m. Thomas J. Hutchison. Ch.: Chas. E. Hutchison, Geo. Wm. Hutchison, Henry Strother Hutchison, Emma Belle Hutchison.

Robert Bruce Strother, m. Anna Spillman. Ch.: Arthur Strother and Mary Lavinia S.

Geo. Duncan Strother, d. Aug. 29, 1842, m. Nancy Lockhart. Ch.: John French Strother, Mary Elizabeth Strother.

French Strother, m. Lucinda Owsley Maddox in 1842, and d. Oct. 10, 1870. Ch.: Geo. Strother, John Chaplin Strother (the compiler of these notes), m. Mary F. Greenwood. Issue: Kate Pryor Strother, Shelby French Strother, Eugene Thomas Strother, Ralph G.

James Strother, m. Fanny Pryor; Alice Cathrine Strother; Chas. Strother, m. Sarah J. Hill; Irvin Strother, Mary Emily Strother; Sarah French Strother.

Oliver C. Strother, m. America Owens. Issue: Wm., Geo., Joseph, Edwin, Philip, and Mary Maria Strother.

Sarah Catherine Kennerly Strother, m. Wm. B. Duncan. Issue: One ch. died in infancy.

John, son of Anne and John Strother, was twice married. His 1st wife was the widow Pendleton, whose name was Sally Strother. His 2nd wife's name is not recollected. He left his property to Hamilton Hansbrough and wife, his niece, when he died in 1832; he had no child.

Catherine S. died single, 22 years of age.

Mary S., m. Ralls Calvert, and they had 12 children: Jerry Calvert, m. Miss Smither, went to Ala. and then to Tex. He had a large family. One of his dau. m. McCullough, the Texas Ranger; Nancy Calvert, m. 1st Mr. Smith and 2nd Henry Spiller. By the 1st marriage she had 2 sons and 2 dau.; by the last, one son and 2 dau.; Geo. Calvert, m. Miss Carr and raised a large family in Loudon Co., Va.; Kitty Calvert, m. Mr. Hollingsworth. She had one child; Virginia H., m. Mr. Finx and lives near Staunton, Va.; Lucy Calvert m. Mr. Powers. No child. Lidia Calvert never married; Betsy Calvert never married; John S. Calvert was for a number of years Treasurer of the State of Va., and died from injuries received when the gallery of the capitol building of Richmond fell; Edward Calvert, (twin of John S.) m. Miss Jenkins and moved to Ky. and d. in Carrollton, Ky., where he was teaching school; Balls Calvert died young.

Molly Strother, 3rd dau. of John, m. Chas. Browning. Had 13 children: John, Francis, Wm., Elizabeth, Joseph, Chas., Lucy, Nancy, Polly, Sally, Loyd, Cassia and Willis. John Browning, m. a dau. of Capt. Harry Pendleton. Their only dau. was six months old when he died. Afterward his widow m. Col. Ward, and she d. when her dau. was 4 years old. Mary Ann Pendleton Browning was baptized by old Mr. Woodville. She m. a cousin, Capt. French Strother, and the old couple now (1868) reside in Mo., aged 86 and 79. Issue: Henry Strother, m. Miss White. He died and left one son, Willis Strother; Chas. Oscar Strother; Wade Dabney Strother, m. Miss Hull. He lives in Marion, Smith Co. Has been Commonwealth's Atty. for years; French Strother has been professor for many years in Mo. He m. Miss Petty and had 3 dau. and one son; Harriet Strother, m. John H. Bibb. They live in Charlottesville, Va. Issue: Pendleton Bibb, Helen Bibb, Kate Bibb; Helen Strother m. Edward Wood. She has 5 sons and 2 dau., Eddie, Blanche, Adele, Roger, French, Ware Dabney, Chalmers Bourbon.

Kate Strother, m. Mr. McClanahan. No child; Anna Strother, m. Robertson Woodson; ch.: Wm. French Woodson, Chas Oscar Woodson, Albert Robertson Woodson, Edgar Woodson; Susan Strother, m. Dr. Weems; Bettie and Willis Strother.

Francis Browning, m. Polly Yates, removed to Ky. and settled in Adair Co.; Wm. Browning, m. Lucy McClanahan. Issue: John, Wm., Chas., Lucy, James; Elizabeth Browning, m. Geo. Yates and moved to Adair Co., Ky.; Joseph Browning, m., moved to Ky. and settled on Salt River in Spencer Co., Ky.; Chas. Browning; Lucy Browning; Nancy Browning, m. Mr. Ashby and moved to the Green River Co., Ky.; Polly Browning, m. Mr. Yates and came West; Sally Browning, m. a Scotch merchant named Morrison; Lloyd Browning, m. a cousin, dau. of Shadrach Browning; Cassia; Willis Browning lived on the old Chas. Browning (paternal) farm.

Sally Strother, 4th dau. and 5th child of John, m. Wm. Hughes. Issue: Thomas Hughes, m. Miss Smith. James Hughes remained unmarried. Betsey Hughes, m. Mr. Gaines, moved to Ky. John Hughes, m. Miss Brown and went to Bath Co. to live. Milly Hughes remained unmarried.

Betty Strother, 5th dau. of John, m. John Browning, brother of Chas. Browning aforesaid. They had 14 or 15 children; the following only recollected: Molly Browning m. Mr. Yates. Lucy Browning, m. Nimrod Duncan, moved 1st to Madison Co., Ky., and then to Green River; Fanny, Nancy, Milly, Betsey; George, m. Gilla Covington and moved to Green River; John Browning, m. and lived and died on the paternal farm; Wm. Browning, m. and moved to Ohio.

Lucy Strother, 6th child of John, m. Francis Covington. Issue: Peggy C., m. Daniel Brown. No issue. Polly C., m. Wm. Deatherage, first cousin to her father and mother. Robert Covington and John C., m. and remained in Va.

Milly Strother, 7th dau. of John, m. Wm. Covington, a first cousin. Issue: Wm. Strother, Nancy, Susan, Peggy.

John Strother, youngest son of John, who died in 1795, died Sept. 22, 1818. He m. Helen Piper when he was 18 and she 14. Issue: John, French, Nancy, Polly, Lucy, Sally, Betsey, Milly. John Strother was bred to the law, settled at Culpeper Court House, commenced practising and died unmarried. Nancy S. m. Wm. Pendleton, son of Col. James Pendleton. Issue: John S. Pendleton.

He was twice a foreign minister and twice elected to Congress; he m. Lucy Ann Williams; Albert G. Pendleton, m. Elvira Chapman. Issue 3 daughters. One m. Philip W. Strother of Giles C. H., Va. Issue: James French Strother, Elvira Strother, Elizabeth Strother, Pendleton Strother, Sallie Strother. One m. Wm. Taliferro, one m. Mr. Crockett; James French Pendleton, m. Narcissa P. Cecil. He lives at Marion, Smith Co., Va. Issue: Albert G. Pendleton, John S. Pendleton, James F. Pendleton, William C. Pendleton, Edmund Pendleton.

Wm. Pendleton d. young and unmarried.

French Pendleton d. young and unmarried.

Polly Strother, 2nd dau. of John, was the 2nd wife of Col. Wm. Ward, aforesaid. Issue: John Ward, became a Methodist preacher, went to Illinois and married; Daniel French Ward, d. unmarried in Ill.

Lucy Strother, m. Wm. Ashby (uncle to Gen. Ashby). Issue: John Ashby, m. Miss Buckner; Dr. Wm. Ashby, m. Miss Dickerson; Ann Ashby, m. Mr. Jones; Elizabeth Ashby, m. Mr. Meade; Martha Ashby, m. Richard Buckner; Mary Wade Ashby, m. Rev. Warden.

Sally Strother d. young.

Betsey Strother, m. Wm. F. Thompson. They lived some years in Washington City and then removed to Boro, Ind., where she died, leaving one dau. in her minority.

Milly Strother, m. Mr. Baly Buckner and lived on the old paternal farm. Issue: A dau. m. Mr. Taliaferro. A dau. m. Mr. Birke; Judge Aylette Buckner, is now in Congress from Mo.; John Buckner, m. Miss Gibson; Dr. Sam Buckner, m. ———; Richard Buckner, m. Sarah Ashby; Calhoun Buckner, m. Miss Dickerson.

Sarah Ann Strother, youngest dau. of John, m. Dr. Thomas Barbour, son of Philip, and went to Mo. She has 2 sons. Her only dau. Fanny Barbour, m. Mr. Gray and lives in Louisville, Ky. Thomas Barbour, m. Miss Gamble. Dr. John Barbour.

Capt. French Strother, now living in Calloway Co., Mo., m. a dau. of John Browning, who was Chas and Molly Browning's eldest son. Issue: Henry Strother, m. Miss White. Issue: Willis Strother; Chas. Oscar Strother; Wade Dabney Strother, m. Miss Hull; French Strother, m. Miss Petty. Issue: Harriet S., m. John M. Bibb; issue: Pendleton Bibb; Helen Bibb; Kate Bibb.

Helen Strother, m. Edward Wood, Issue: Eddie Wood, Blanche, Adele, Roger, French, Wade Dabney, Chalmers, Barbour.

Kate S., m. Mr. McClanahan; Anna S., m. Robertson Woodson. Issue: Wm. French Woodson, Chas. Oscar Woodson, Albert R. Woodson, Edgar Woodson; Susan S., m. Dr. Weems. No child; Bettie Willis Strother.

THE RICHMOND STROTHERS.

Anthony Strother, son of Francis and Susan, was b. 1710, d. 1765, m. Bethaland Stroke, Aug. 25, 1733. Issue (she d. in 1753): Wm., b. Aug. 29, 1734; Anthony, b. May 10, 1736; Elizabeth, b. Sept. 23, 1738; Margaret, b. Sept, 23, 1740; John b. Feb., 11, 1742; Francis, b. Nov., 23, 1743; Alice, b. Jan. 18, 1745; Wm., the 2nd, b. April 30, 1746; Betty,

b. Aug. 8, 1747; Benjamin, b. June 22, 1750; Stroke, b. April 12, 1753. He m. 2nd in 1754, Mary James. Issue: James, b. Nov. 19, 1755; Mary, b. June 2, 1757; Geo., b. Sept. 1, 1760; Betty, b. July 20, 1763.

Benjamin S., son of Anthony, entered the Va. Navy, on the ship Tempest, as Midshipman, with Capt. Celies Saunders; served 3 years with credit, and when the Va. Navy was extinct entered the land service. He m. Kitty Price in 1778 and settled in Berkeley Co., Va. (now Jefferson) about 1787, built "Park Forest," near Charleston, on lands purchased from Bushrod Washington and Light Horse Harry Lee. He died in 1805. Issue: Elizabeth, b. Dec. 23, 1783, m. Benj. Pendleton, Oct., 31, 1805, d. Nov. 1822. Kitty, b. Feb. 24, 1786, d. June 2, 1847, m. Jan. 8, 1807, to Joseph Minor Crane. Margaret, b. Aug., 13, 1788, d. —, m. April 26, 1814, — Moore. Mary Stroke, b. Sept. 24, 1790, d. Aug. 27, 1856, m. June 7, 1814, Richard Duffield. John, b. —, d. Jan. 16, 1862, m. Sept. 7, 1815, Elizabeth Pendleton Hunter. Issue: David Hunter Strother, b. Martinsburg, Va., Sept. 26, 1816, m. May 15, 1849, Anne Doyne Wolff. Emily, b. April 8, 1820, m. James Lingan Randolph and Strother Randolph. Emily, dau. of David and Anne Wolff Strother, was b. Mar. 21, 1850, m. April 17, 1871, J. Brisben Walker, had 6 sons. David H. Strother, m. 2nd, May 6, 1861, Mary Elliott Hunter. Issue (he d. Aug. 15, 1871): David Hunter S., b. Dec. 24, 1866, d. Aug. 25, 1871. John S., b. March 13, 1868.

John, son of Anthony, m. Catherine Fox Price, their son, Wm. Porter S., m. Elizabeth Kendal Hewlitt. Issue, 5 sons and one dau. William A., m. 1st, Sallie Mitchell, had 2 sons, Wm. and Robert; m. 2nd, Jennie Langhorne, who had one son, Sidney. (2) Richard Hewlitt Strother, m. Sarah Selden, and d. leaving 2 children. (a) Thomas Nelson S., m. Emily Viele, dau. of Gen. Viele. One child. (b) Elizabeth Hewlitt S., m. John Wright, a San Francisco lawyer. (3) John Meredith S., m. Elizabeth Whiting Powell; he was at the time of the breaking out of the war Adjunct Professor of Math. at the U. Va. and afterward founded the University for boys in Richmond. Five children (4) Robert Quarles S., m. Mary Cameron Ross. Had one child, May, who m. Fredrick R. Scott and has one child, Sidney Buford Scott. (5) Sidney, the youngest son, was killed at Cold Harbor during the war; he never married. (6) Margaret, the only dau., m. Samuel B. Smith. Had 5 children. Three are dead. Wm. S. Smith is a naval officer, m. and has one child. Richard Hewlitt Smith, m. Mary Burton. Had several children.

Extracts from a letter from Judge P. W. Strother to J. M. Bourne.

"There are three different crests to the Coat of Arms, showing three different branches. From the one we have, I think our branch came from Northumberland, Eng., and, to England, I suspect, with the other "Danish Robbers."

The first one whom I can find anything of in America was Wm. Strother, who died in Richmond Co., Va. (now King George) in 1702, date of will 1700. I have heard it stated, or suspected, he was King William's bodyguard. However, I never cared, having very little respect for English royalty. He lived on the Rappahanock, and devised his lands to his wife, Dorothea, for life, and to sons, 2, William 3, James. His other children were: 4, Jeremiah, 5, Robert, 6, Benjamin, and 7, Joseph, 3, James devising his to his brother, Joseph.

2, William d. 1727, having m. Margaret, dau. of Francis Thornton; he had as I gather, 8, William, 9, Francis, 10, Anthony, and probably others.

4, Jeremiah was a landowner in Westmoreland and came to Orange where he died in 1741; children, 11, William, 12, James, 13, Lawrence, 14, Christopher, 15, Jeremiah, 16, Francis.

I suspect that Wm. was the father of Mrs. Gabriel Jones, Mrs. Lewis and Mrs. John Madison (he was a brother of 9, Francis and 10, Anthony.)

9, Francis, m. Miss Dabney, had 17, Wm., 18, John, 19, Anthony, 20, Geeorge, 21, Francis, d. in Ga., 22, Robert. His son, 17, William, m. Mrs. Pannill, was grandfather of Gen. Taylor and moved to Woodford Co., Ky. His son, 18, John, was a large landed proprietor in Culpeper, and by the union of his dau. Anne with John (?), grandson of Jeremiah —. Two daughters of Francis, m. Gaines, one was mother of Gen. Gaines. Mr. Thomas Gaines of Culpeper C. H. may give you some information. Anthony, son of William, m. 1st Miss Stroke, 2nd Mary James, by whom he had three children. She (Mary James) m. 2nd Henry Smith of Fredricksburg and moved to Russell Co. This Anthony was gr.-grandfather of "Porte Crayon."

Jeremiah's son, William, I think, died in Westmoreland, leaving a large estate. His son James m. Miss French, by whom he had 3 children: French, James, died in 1864, and Mary, wife of Geo. Gray. Her descendants, or some of them, now live in Louisville, Ky. French, m. Miss Coleman. Issue: Daniel F., m. Miss Thompson and died in Louisville. Mrs. Phil Slaughter, Mrs. John Evans, Mrs. Dave Gray, Elizabeth F., Lucy C., and Geo. F. Strother.

15, Jeremiah, Jr., son of Jeremiah (4), went to S. C., where he died.

14, Christopher, lived in Carolina.
P. W. Strother."

TANDY

Compiled by Henry T. Allen, Major General, U. S. Army.

The Tandy family has been noted in Irish history for its patriotism and political activity. It is said there was a Tandy connected with the Gunpowder Plot.

In the song, "The Wearing of the Green," mention is made of a Napper or Nappa Tandy; he was an actual character and political refugee in Paris.

> "I met with Napper Tandy and he tuk me by the hand
> And he said, 'How's poor ould Ireland, and does she stand?'
> She's the most distressful country that ever you have seen,
> They are hanging men and women for the wearing of the green."

It is believed that the progenitors of the families in Virginia came from Armagh, Ireland.

According to George Cabell Greer's "Early Virginia Immigrants," there were two immigrants.

One, William Tandy, settled in Warwick County, Va., in 1643. He was a headright of Thomas Taylor.

Another William Tandey arrived in 1650. He was a headright of William Clapham. The place of his settlement is not stated but it was probably in that part of old Rappahannock County that is now Essex County.

There is nothing to indicate the degree of kinship between these two men.

It is possible, however, that the Tandy family is of English origin. There is in New Hampshire a Tandy-Allen line that furnishes a curious parallel with the Virginia family.

Richard Tandy, a native of Worcestershire, England, probably born about 1690, was impressed on board a British man-of-war, but managed to make his ecsape when the ship reached Boston. He found refuge at the home of a Mr. Allen in Dorchester, Massachusetts. He subsequently married Mr. Allen's daughter, Mary, and settled probably in Kingston, in what is now New Hampshire. Their descendants still reside in New England, honored and respected.

(History of Hancock, N. H., By Rev. W. W. Hayward.)

1st Generation.

William Tandey, son of ———, was born ———.

According to George Cabell Greer's "Early Virginia Immigrants" he was an immigrant to Virginia in 1650, being a headright of William Clapham. The place of his settlement is not stated but it was probably in that part of old Rappahannock County, that is now Essex County.

He married ———. He is the progenitor of our branch of the Tandy family in America.

Issue: Henry Tandy.

2d Generation.

Henry Tandy, son of William, was born in Old Rappahannock County, Va. Married ———.

Oct. 24, 1672, patent was granted by Governor Sir William Berkeley to Henry Tandy for 868 acres in the county of Rappahannock on the south side of the river in the Parish of Farnham. (Book 6, page 437, Virginia Land Grants.)

This land fell in Essex County on the creation of that county in 1692.

March 13, 1676, Henry Tandy was one of the signers of the Grievances of the County of Rappahannock, presented to the General Assembly, protesting against the quality of the ministers sent to the colony; praying for an honorable peace with the Indians or else that the war be prosecuted effectually; demanding that the uses of the tax money be investigated and that some particular person be forced to reimburse the county; no man should hold more land than that for which he pays quit rent; that none of the aiders and abettors of Bacon's damnable conspiracy should be permitted to sit as judges; all offices of public trust should be filled by discreet and knowing gentlemen; all ships arriving in the country should pay fort and castle dues; that the meeting place of the Assembly should be in the centre of the country; and that the courts should be held in convenient and accessible localities. (Journals of the House of Burgesses.)

An interesting and illuminating petition.

In 1677, he witnessed the will of Lawrence Washington in old Rappahannock County, Sept. 27, 1677. (Crozier)

In 1683, he witnessed the will of Elizabeth Crask in old Rappahannock County. (Crozier)

Issue: Henry Tandy, of whom later.

3d Generation.

Henry Tandy, son of Henry, was born ———, married ———.

April 16, 1684, Henry Tandy, Jr., received pay for ten days' services in old Rappanhannock County by Act of the General Assembly begun at James City April 16, 1684. (Journals of the House of Burgesses.)

Removed from Essex County to King and Queen County where he died intestate in 1705. Administration was granted by the King and Queen County court to James Taylor and George Clough.

Inventory of estate in Essex County was made by Edmund Pagett, Robert Mills, and Henry Byrom. The inventory disclosed only a few head of cattle and other items of small value. (Deed book 12, page 98, Essex County.)

Issue: Henry Tandy, John Tandy, Roger Tandy.

4TH GENERATION.

Henry Tandy, son of Henry, was born in South Farnham Parish, Essex County, Va. Married Frances (probably daughter of Henry Crittenden.)

He died in 1741. His will dated Sept. 2, 1741, proved Oct. 20, 1741, named his devisees: daughter Ann Waller; grandson William Waller; daughter Martha Tandy; daughter Frances Tandy, son Silvanus Tandy, "that land that belonged to my father and one hundred acres additional that I bought of Paget." Son Silvanus Tandy and son in law, Edward Waller to be executors. (Will book 6, page 343, Essex County.)

Ann Tandy. Married Edward Waller. Issue: William Waller. Martha Tandy. Silvanus Tandy. Died intestate, 1761. (Liber 11, page 291, Essex County). Frances Tandy. Married Thomas Burris.

John Tandy, son of Henry was born ———. Married ———.

No definite information as to his place of birth, residence, or name of wife or of their deaths can be found.

It is probable that he lived in King and Queen or Caroline County; the early records of both these counties were destroyed during the Civil War.

It is known by descendants of William Tandy that his father's name was John, and that John and Roger Tandy were brothers. (Rev. A. W. Tandy, Fulton, Mo.)

ISSUE: William Tandy. Married Jane ———.

3816 Jenifer Street, Chevy Chase.
Washington, August 18, 1927.

The County Clerk,
King and Queen County,
Virginia.

Sir:—

I am trying to locate the will of Roger Tandy who in 1727 while in King and Queen County had a grant of land in Spotsylvania. His will is not in Spotsylvania.

Will you please tell me whether or not it is on record in your office? Are there any other Tandys recorded there?

Thanking you in advance for any information, I am,

Very respectfully,

(signed) S. A. McCarthy.

(Stamped on bottom of letter: All Records Prior to 1865 Destroyed by Fire, H. C. Hall, Clerk, King & Queen County.)

3816 Jenifer Street, Chevy Chase,
Washington, August 18, 1927.

The County Clerk,
Bowling Green,
Caroline County, Va.
Sir:

I am trying to locate the will of William Tandy who was living in Caroline County in 1759.

Will you please tell me whether or not his will is on record in your office. Also any other Tandys?

Thanking you in advance for any information, I am

Very respectfully,

(signed) S. A. McCarthy.

Do not find the name Tandy among the record of wills. Early records destroyed.

E. S. Coghill.

Bowling Green, Va.
August 19th, 1927.

William Tandy, son of ———, was born ———.

According to George Cabell Greer's "Early Virginia Immigrants," he settled in Warwick County, Va., in 1643. He was a headright of Thomas Taylor.

He married ———.

"William Tantey died 1677." (Bruton Parish Register.)

He owned 375 acres in St. Peter's Parish, New Kent County, adjoining Richard Allen. By deed he gave 100 acres to John Moss and the remainder to his son, Thomas Tandy, who left daughters Agnes and Ann. (This fact is recited in deed of John Bird and Elizabeth, his wife, of St. Peter's Parish, New Kent, dated 1739, to John Dennett of the Parish of St. Paul's. The deed is in the possession of the Virginia Historical Society, Richmond.)

The records of New Kent were destroyed in 1865.

ISSUE: William Tandy. d. s. p. before 1691. (York County records Book 9, page 157). Thomas Tandy. John Tandy.

Thomas Tandy, son of William, was born in Warwick County, Va., Married Jone ———. Was domiciled in Bruton Parish, York County, Va.

In a deed dated 1739, from John Bird and Elizabeth, his wife, of St. Peter's Parish, New Kent County, to John Bennett of the Parish of St. Paul's, it was recited that William Tandy, late of Warwick County had 375 acres in St. Peter's Parish adjoining Richard Allen, and by his deed gave 100 acres to John Moss and the remainder to his son, Thomas Tandy, who left daughters Agnes and Ann. This deed is now in the possession of the Virginia Historical Society.

Thomas Tandy died before 1693.

Deed of gift of Alexander Mackenny, for love and good will, to Agnes Tandy and to Ann Tandy, daughter of Thomas Tandy, deceased, 75 acres each on the north side of the James River near the falls in Henrico County. Deeds dated the twentieth day of the tenth month, 1693. (Deed book 5, pages 455 and 456, Henrico County.)

"Jone Tandy, wife of Thomas Tandy, died 1701." (Bruton Parish Register.)

ISSUE: Agnes Tandy. Ann Tandy.

John Tandy, son of William was born in Warwick County, Va., Married ———. Was domiciled in Bruton Parish, York County, Va.

March 18, 169–, he instituted a suit against William Jackson for the detention of a negro given him by the will of his father, William Tandy. (Book 9, page 113, York County.)

The decision of the court was that the bequest being conditional on the life of another son, William Tandy, who having died the negro belonged lawfully to William Jackson.

ISSUE: (Probably) Henry Tandy, who removed to Henrico County and thence to Goochland County.

Ann Tandy, daughter of Thomas and Jone was born in Bruton Parish, York County, Oct. 24, 1701, she was charged with the murder of her bastard male child, and held in gaol for the action of the Attorney General, to whom all the papers in the case were sent. (Book 12, page —, York County.)

Henry Tandy, son of John, was born in York County, Va., Lived in Henrico County before 1737. Married ———.

1737. William Woodson made a deed to Henry Tandy for land in Henrico County. (William and Mary Quarterly, X, 89.)

1737. Henry Tandy of Henrico County bought of William Woodson part of 1500 acres in Goochland County which had been granted April 11, 1732, to William Woodson and his brothers. (Woodson Genealogy.)

Frances Tandy, daughter of Henry and ———, was born in Farnham, Essex County, Va. She married Thomas Burris. He was a soldier of Braddock's War and the Revolutionary War.

ISSUE: Jane Burris. Married James Quisenberry Dec. 4, 1776. He was a son of Aaron and Joyce Quisenberry of Spotsylvania County. He was born July 5, 1759. In 1783, they removed to Kentucky. For descendants see Memorials of the Quisenberry Family, by A. C. Quisenberry, 1900.

Henry Tandy, son of Roger and Sarah (Quarles) Tandy, was born in Orange County, Va. in 1741. He married Ann Mills, July 18, 1762. In 1782, he had 12 whites in family; and in 1783, 13 whites. There were 17 blacks owned by him. (Heads of Families, 1st Census of the U. S.).

He died in 1809. The will of Henry Tandy, Sr., of Orange County, Va., dated July 6, 1807, proved Aug. 8, 1809, made devise as follows: To son Roger, the land on which he lives and land in Madison County, Ky., (£120); son Henry, the land on which he lives (£400); son William, the land on which he lives (£350); son Mills, £100 and livestock; son Ralph £100 and livestock; son Jackson, £100 and livestock; son Nathaniel, slaves, and the home plantation after the death of my wife; daughter Mollie, slaves, and if she marry again they are to go to her six children—Elijah, Nancy, John, Henry, George and Charles; daughter Nancy, slaves and £50, etc.; daughter Sally, slaves, etc.; wife Ann, my estate for life; my tract of land in Spotsylvania County near Oliver's tavern adjoining the lands of Booker Walter and Dr. French to be sold. Sons Roger and Henry to be executors. John Pendleton, Mordecai Cooke, and Nathaniel Mills, Sr., witnesses. (Will book 4, page 331, Orange County.) The personal estate was appraised at $6624.

ISSUE: Roger Tandy. Married Mary Adams in Orange County, 1795. Henry Tandy. Married Betsy Adams in Orange County, 1796. William Tandy. Mills Tandy. Married Amelia Graves of Louisa County. Ralph Tandy. Jackson Tandy. Married Sarah Mills, March 29, 1809.

Nathaniel Tandy. Died intestate; inventory made Feb. 24, 1824. (Will book 7, page 424, Orange County, Va.)

Mollie Tandy. Married John Morton, April 24, 1788.

Nancy Tandy. Married James Perry, 1791; Joseph Mason, 2d.

Sally Tandy. Married Claibourne Graves.

Jackson Thompson Tandy, son of Henry Jackson and Narcissa Bowdry (Peery) Tandy, was born in ———.

He married Martha Elizabeth Keyes, they had five children.

ISSUE: Rev. A. W. Tandy, D. D., of Fulton, Mo. has a picture of his great-grandfather Henry Tandy of Orange County, Va.

Ford Tandy, son of ——— was born ———.

He was appointed a processioner in Fredericksville Parish, Louisa County, in 1764.

William Tandy, son of John and ——— was born ———. He married Jane ———. Before 1759, he was domiciled in Caroline County.

July 24, 1759, deed of Joseph Pulliam and Jerusha, his wife, of the county of Louisa, to William Tandy of the county of Caroline, conveyed for £110 the land the said Pulliam now lives, 300 acres, lying on the branches of Gold Mine Creek. Abram Venable and John Ashburn, witnesses. (Deed book B, page 317, Louisa County.)

William Tandy's settlement was in Fredericksville Parish in Louisa County. He took an active part in the affairs of the Parish.

The following notes are taken from the Vestry Book of Fredericksville Parish, Louisa County, Va.

Oct. 24, 1759. Vestry meeting. William Tandy appointed a processioner.

March 29, 1760. William A. Lewis reported to the vestry; "We have processioned all the lands within our bounds from the Secretary's Ford to the county line except a line of Mr. Car's and some of the lines of Mr. William Tandy's land which we cannot get shewed to us. The rest of our bounds is processioned by Joseph Martin and John Hammock through a mistake."

March 27, 1762. Vestry meeting held for the election of vestrymen for the reorganized Fredericksville Parish in Albermarle County.

1764. The line of William Tandy was processioned by Thomas Smith and Nicholas Lewis.

Nov. 25, 1767. Vestry meeting. Ford Tandy appointed a processioner. William Tandy and Curice Lee ordered to procession the lands from the top of the mountains to the river south of the old county line. William Simms and Richard Allen to procession all the lands between Pretty's Creek, the river, and the Piney Mountains and to across to Sumpter's Mill.

Nov. 14, 1774. William Tandy was one of the processioners to procession the lands from Martin Key's north line, the top of the mountains, and the river. David Allen also a processioner.

In 1783, William Tandy mentioned as present at a processioning.

1783, William Tandy ordered to make a procession.

———day of ——— 1760, deed of John Clark and Ann, his wife, to William Tandy for £300 conveys 410 acres, being part of a larger tract taken up by Jonathan Clark, Joseph Smith, Edwin Hickman, and Thomas Graves, containing 3277 acres under patent, located on the Rivanni River or north Fork of the James River. (Deed book 5, page 22, Albemarle County.) on this tract, George Rogers Clark, "the Hannibal of the West" was born, Nov. 1752. (Cabells and their kin)

In 1762, John Carr and Barbara, his wife, of the Parish of St. Martin, County of Louisa, lease to William Tandy of the Parish of Trinity, county of Louisa, a tract of land for ten years beginning Oct. 1, 1762, for £10 per annum. (Deed book 3, page 513, Albemarle County.)

During the Revolutionary War, in 1779, William Tandy, Sr., and John Tandy his son of Albemarle County took the oath of allegiance to the Commonwealth of Virginia (Virginia Historical Collections, VI, 137.)

March 11, 1773, deed of William Tandy to Martin Key for £170 conveys part of a tract granted to Joseph Smith by letters patent dated 1734. (Deed book 6, page 87, Albemarle County.)

In 1783, deed of William Tandy and Jane, his wife, conveyed to Martin

Key 409 acres in Albemarle County whereon said Tandy now lives on the Rivanna River. (Deed book 8, page 114, Albemarle County.)

In 1784, William Tandy, settled in Kentucky near Lexington on the old Mason County Road, with his family, consisting of his wife Jane and seven children, together with 40 slaves.

ISSUE: John Tandy. Married Judith ——. William Tandy. Married ——. Living in Albemarle County 1784. Achilles Tandy. Married Nancy Ferguson. Gabriel Tandy. Married Miss Castleman. Lucy Quarles Tandy. Married Major Thomas Hughes. She died 1809. Moses Tandy. Married —— Lipscomb. Frances Tandy. Married —— Lipscomb. Sally Tandy. Married Moses Bledsoe. Jane Tandy Married Judge John Allen. Milly Tandy. Married, 1st —— Chinn; 2d, Major Thomas Hughes.

WILL OF WILLIAM TANDY.

Will Book B, page 417—

In the name of God Amen My Will and desire is that all that track or parcel of land whareon I now live be devided in the following maner Viz. I give to my son John Tandy one fourth part of my said land, including his plantation whareon he now lives yet not to come nearer to my plantation than a line run by Mr. John Bradford, and in case that should not include his quantity he shall make it up on the south joining the lines of Owens and Rogers, to him and his heirs forever. Item I give and bequeath to my son Archillis Tandy one forth my said land to include his plantation whareon he now lives, and joining the line between me and him and Beckleys line to him and his heirs forever.

Item I give and bequeath to my son Gabriel Tandy one forth part of my said track of land including the plantation I now live, and the improvements made by John Allen* to him and his heirs forever . . . Yet so that John Allen have the use of his improvement Gratis till my son Gabriel comes to the age of Twenty one years—Item I give and bequeath to my loving wife Jane Tandy and my daughter Lucy Tandy one forth part of my said track of land adjoining Prestons, to be equaly devided between them to them and their heirs forever. In case my son Gabriel Tandy or my daughter Lucy Q. Tandy shoud die before the age of twenty one years that then all his or her part of the estate shall be equally divided among all my surviving sons and daughter, in Kentucky, them and their heirs forever. Item I give and bequeath to my loving Jane Tandy, the one half of what lands is hereby will to Gabriel Tandy, including the house and plantation, whareon I now live together with the following Negroes towit Nolly, Booker or old Winny, Nan Sollomon, Mile and all her children together with all my stock of horses, cattle hoges and sheep and with all the house hold and kitchen furniture—To hold dureing her life—

Item I give and bequeth to my loving wife Jane Tandy, one negroe lad

---
*Great-grandfather of Henry T. Allen.

named Lewis, and one negroe woman named Winny and all her increase to her and her heirs forever.

Item I give and bequeath to my son John Tandy two negroes, Reuben and David which he has already received to him and his heirs forever. Item I give and bequeth to my son Acchillis Tandy a negroe women named Grace and all her increase and negroe man named Sollomon after my wifes death, to him and his heirs forever.

Item I give and bequeath to my son Moses Tandy a negroe man named Phill and eighty pounds cash or the residue in land conveniently situated in the County of Fayette, or Bourbon which cash is in the hands of Mr. John Allen, to him and his heirs forever.

Item I give and bequeath to my son Gabriel Tandy one negroe woman named Mile and all her increase after the death of my wife to him and his heirs forever I give and bequeath to my daughter Francis Lipscomb Milley and all her increase.

Item I give and bequeth to my daughter Sally B. Bledsoe, one negroe woman named Tiller and her increase sca Item I give and bequeath to my daughter Jane Aleen one negro woman named Tiller and her increase sca—

Item I give and bequeath to my daughter Lucy Tandy (married Major Thomas Hughes of Bourbon) one negroe woman named Dicy also a horse and saddle worth £15 and a good feather bed &c And my ferther will and desire is that after the death of my wife the rest and residue of all my estate shall be equelly devided between my children now living in Kentucky, ferther I give and bequeath the ballance of cash in John Allens hand after paying my son Moses Tandy legacy of £50 to my wife Jane Tandy, to and her heirs forever, and that said John Allen pay only principle and no intrust, ferther my will and desire is that a negro man named Nolly, cld Winny and Nan be emancipated, and no longer live in slavery after my wife death—

My ferther will and desire is that loving wife Jane Tandy, Acchillez Tandy Moses Tandy and Moses Bledso be and hereby are appointed my Executors to this my last will and testament and do hereby revoke all former wills by me heretofore made.

In testimony this 2d day of May 1792.

William Tandy

Coppye, Witnesses: Jno. Mason, Wm. Bush, Jno. Arnoll, G. M. Tompkins, Jno. Corncello.

This copy was produced in Court at the Oct. Term of the Fayette County Ct. Kentucky in the year One Thousand Eight Hundred and Twelve and proven to be a true copy of the Original Will by the oath of John Mason one of the subscribing witnesses and ordered to be recorded—

Att John D. Young Clk

And appoint this my last will and testament in manner following that is to say first of all *I my soul* to God who gave it to me and my body to be buried and what worldly goods it has pleased God to bless me with I bestow in the following manner viz

My will and desire is that all that tract or parcel of land whereon I now live be divided in manner following that is to say I give to my son John Tandy ——fourth part of my said land including his plantation, whereon he now lives yet not to come near my plantation, than a line run by Mr. John Bradford and in case that line should not include his quantity he shall make it up on the south joining the lines of —sings and Rogers, to him and his heirs forever.

Item I give and bequeath to my son Achillis Tandy —— fourth part of my said Tract of land to include his ———— whereon he now lives and adjoining the line ——— him and Beckley Line to him and his heirs forever ....
....improvement gratez till my son Gabriel age of twenty one years.

Item I give and bequeath to my loving wife Jane Tandy and my daughter Lucy Q. Tandy one fourth part of my said tract of land, adjoining Prestons Garvey to be equally divided between them to them and their heirs forever. In case my son Gabriel Tandy or my daughter Lucy Q. Tandy should die before they arrive to the age of Twenty one years, that then all his or her part of my estate shall be equally divided among my surviving sons and daughters, in Kentucky, to them and their heirs forever:

Item I give bequeath to my loving wife Jane Tandy the one half of what lands is hereby willed to Gabriel Tandy including the houses and plantation whereon I now live together with the following negroes viz. Notly, Booker, Winnie, Nan, Solomon Mi................ all her children together with all my ....
&c with ....
............Winnie and all her increase to her and.........................forever.

I give and bequeath to my son John Tandy.......................es Reubin and David which he has already received to him and his heirs forever.

I give and bequeath to my son Achillis Tandy a negroe woman named Grace and all her increase and a negro man named Solomon after my wifes death to him and his heirs forever —

Item I give and bequeath to my son Moses Tandy a negroe man named Phill and Eighty pounds cash, on the ....it is land conveniently situated in the County of Fayette or Bourbon, which cash is in the hands of Mr. John.................. len to him and his heirs forever.

I give and bequeath to my son Gabriel Tandy a negroe woman named Mill & all her increase after the death of my wife to him and his heirs forever—

I give and bequeath to my daughter Frances L................ woman named Milly and all her increase...................her heirs forever .... and bequeath to my daughter J...................woman named Tiller and all her increase .... and heirs forever—

Item I give and bequeath unto my daughter Lucy Tandy a negroe woman named Dicy & all her increase to her and her heirs forever, also a horse and saddle worth L. a good feather bed and furniture. And my further will is that after the death of my .... the rest and residue of all my estate shall be equally divided between John Tandy, Archillis Tandy, Sally Bledsoe, Jane Allen, Lucy Tandy, Gabriel Tandy, & Milley Chinn, to them and their heirs forever—and I further give and bequeath the balance of .... in John Allens hands after paying my son Moses Tandys legacy of £80 to my wife Jane Tandy to her and heirs forever, and that said John Allen, shall pay only the principal and no interest—Further my will and desire is that a negroe man named Notly, Old Winnie and now be imancipated, and no longer held in slavery, after my wifes death .... further will and desire is that .... revoke, all former wills by .... In Testimony whereof I have this day .... seal and subscribed the same in the presence .... under written witnesses this 2nd day of ma............ One thousand seven hundred and ninety two.

William Tandy (LS)

Teste: John Mason, William Bush, John Amott, Guinn Tompkins.

FAYETTE COUNTY MARCH COURT 1794

This last will and testament of William Tandy was produced in Court, proved by the oaths of John Mason, Guinn Tompkins subscribing witnesses thereto and ordered to be recorded.

Teste Levi Todd C. C.

I certify that the foregoing is as fully extracted from the record of wills in my office, which was partly consumed by fire when the office was burnt as is possible.

Levi Todd Clerk
May 20th, 1807

Fayette County Court   October Court 1812

This extract of the will of William Tandy deceased was produced in Court and ordered to be recorded.

Att John D. Young clk.

STATE OF KENTUCKY,
COUNTY OF FAYETTE.   Sct.

I, Theo. Lewis, Clerk of the County Court of Fayette County, State of Kentucky, and as the custodian of the seal and all records of or appertaining to said court, do hereby certify the foregoing to be a true and accurate copy of the last will and testament of William Tandy, as the same appears of record in my office.

IN TESTIMONY WHEREOF, Witness my hand, the seal of said court this 21st day of May 1913.

Theo Lewis

(SEAL)   Clerk Fayette County Court.

SAMUEL W. HUGHES,
Real Estate, Loans and Insurance,
512 VICTORIA BUILDING

St. Louis, Dec. 16, 1910.

Major Henry Allen,
Washington, D. C.

Dear Sir:—

I am very much interested in collecting the history of the Tandy Family, with the intention of ultimately publishing it, and have been referred to you for information as being a great-grandson of Maj. John Allen who married Jane Tandy. My great-grandfather Maj. Thomas Hughes of Bourbon Co., Ky., married Lucy Tandy the sister of Mrs. Allen, and after her death he married another sister, Mrs. Chinn. They were the daughters of Gabriel (William)* Tandy, who I understand removed from Albermarle Co. Va. to Kentucky.

Do you know whom Gabriel Tandy married? Do you know the names of all of his children? I think there was another sister than those mentioned above, probably Mrs. Elliott. I would appreciate very much anything you could tell me about the early Tandys in Kentucky, and the children and descendants of Judge John Allen and Jane Tandy. I have heard my aunt (now deceased) speak of visiting in Kentucky when she was a little girl, a "Cousin Julia Ann Grishon (Grosjean)." Am spelling it as it sounded and the last name may not be correct. Was this lady a daughter of Judge John Allen?

I assure you that any information you give me will not be wasted or thrown away as I intend to put these records together with many more which I already have, where they cannot be destroyed and will always be at the service of those interested.

My grandfather Elliott Hughes was the son of Thomas Hughes' first wife Lucy Tandy who died 1809. Then his stepmother was his mother's sister. His father died 1826 and he came to Missouri. My father Elliott Hughes, Jr., was for 18 years a Circuit Judge in this state and received a stroke of apoplexy while on the Bench in Mexico, Mo., 1903.

Very truly yours,
(signed) Samuel W. Hughes.

TANDYS.

Jane Tandy wife of John Allen. Her father was William Tandy of Albemarle Co. His father was Gabriel Tandy of James City Co. Jane Tandy Allen had two sisters—Milly and Lucy—who married a second time Major Thomas Hughes. Major Hughes' first wife was a sister (Milly?) to his second wife. Gabriel Tandy came over from Ireland and settled in James City Co. Va. One son Schilles Tandy served seven years in Revolutionary War. He (William)

*They were the daughters of William Tandy and he was the son of Gabriel Tandy.

moved out to Fayette Co. Ky. in 1784 and married Nancy Ferguson. Another son was Gabriel.

John, William, David, Samuel and Robert were living in Bourbon Co. in 1810 and each over 45 years of age.

SAMUEL W. HUGHES,
Real Estate, Loans and Insurance
512 VICTORIA BUILDING

St. Louis, January 17, 1911.

Maj. Henry T. Allen,
Washington, D. C.
Dear Sir:—

I appreciated very much your sending me the clipping from the Eastern papers regarding Senator Charles Hughes. The papers here did not contain so much.

I have never met Mr. Hughes, though I corresponded with him at one time. My grandfather's brother William married Mr. Hughes' father's sister Margaret Hughes. They were first cousins, and had only one son Gabriel Tandy Hughes. Last week I received an invitation to the weding of Miss Mary Menefee Hughes of Richmond, Mo., to a Mr. Jones of this city. The lady is a niece of Senator Charles Hughes' wife, who was Miss Menefee. I presume she is also a niece of Senator Hughes, as her name and coming from Richmond would indicate. My invitation came through the family of Mr. Jones, and as I will meet her when she comes here to live, I can find out all about it.

I think there is no doubt in the world that your ancestress, Jane Allen (wife of John Allen) was the granddaughter of Gabriel Tandy of James City Co. Virginia, probably the first to come over, but from the notes I am sending you, you will observe that there was a Henry Tandy, Jr. in Virginia in 1677, associated with the Washington family. In those days people married pretty much in the same class, and it is interesting to note that Mary Washington, the mother of George, had a sister Esther (Ball) who married Raleigh Chinn, and they were the grandparents of the Mr. Chinn who married Milly Tandy, sister of Jane Allen and Lucy Hughes and who afterward became the second wife of Maj. Thos. Hughes.

If I learn more of the early Tandys will send it to you. I know the best way would be for me to go to Kentucky and Virginia and look it up, and I will some time, but it is impossible for me to do so now. Perhaps I may do so in the summer.

Thanking you again for the interest you have taken, I am,

Very truly yours,
(signed) Samuel W. Hughes.

Mrs. L. B. Tandy:

"There is a tradition in the Tandy family that there were three brothers, John, Gabriel, and Roger who came over from Ireland and settled in Virginia." She is descendant of Roger Tandy.

Rappahannock Co. Wills:

Will of Lawrence Washington (brother to the grandfather of Genl. Washington) dated 1677, witnessed by Henry Tandy Jr., who testifies that he is 17 years of age.

Records of Spotsylvania Co.:

Patent granted to Roger Tandy Oct 13, 1727. Deed Nov. 6, 1733. Roger Tandy of St. Stephens Parish, King and Queen County to Wm. Dyer of Spots. Co. 100 acres of land in Spots. Co.

Albemarle Co.:

Declaration of Independence signed by citizens of Albemarle Co. among others were Wm. Tandy Sr. and John Tandy 1779.

T. M. Green:

"Judge John Allen of Bourbon was one of the purest men and ablest lawyers of that day and District. He was born in James City Co. Va. 1749. Entering the patriot army at the beginning of the Revolution he rose to the rank of Major. He was well educated and a well trained lawyer. Marrying Miss Jane Tandy of a respectable family of Albemarle Co. he came to Ky. prior to 1788 and located in Fayette. Upon the organization of Bourbon he settled in Paris. He was the first Judge of the District Court of Bourbon and afterward the Circuit Court. In point of personal worth and integrity of character, Judge Allen was not inferior to any man in Kentucky of his time, and to but few in point of intelligence and ability. His descendants, many of whom live in Bourbon, Nicholas and Bath, have just cause of pride in such an ancestor."

Bryant & Rose:

"Major Thomas Hughes, of Bourbon County married Miss Lucy Tandy, and had William, Gabriel, Thomas, Henry Clay, Elliott McNiel, Susan and Jane. The Major's first wife died 1809, and he subsequently married her sister, who was a widow. Major Hughes held the position of Justice of the Peace for forty years and all of his decisions were sustained by the higher courts. He was also Senator and Representative for Bourbon County in the Kentucky Legislature. He died 1826.

His eldest son William married his cousin Margaret Hughes (aunt of Sen. Chas. J. Hughes Jr.) and settled in Boone Co. Mo.

Elliott M. (my grandfather) received a classical education, came to Missouri when a young man, taught school in and near Danville several years. He married Jane Sandidge McConnell and died in Danville 1862. He exercised a large influence in his community and was a general favorite with all. He was fond of practical jokes, full of wit and humor and a prominent member of the Evenix Society of Danville.''

The Children of Maj. Thos. Hughes:
1. William married his cousin Margaret and had one son Gabriel Tandy Hughes.
2. Gabriel died young.
3. Thomas married Margaret Bledsoe.
4. Henry Clay died single.
5. Elliott M. married Jane McConnell.
6. Susan married Hiram Bledsoe and came to Mo. and was the mother of Col. Hiram Bledsoe of Cass Co. and Judge Joseph Bledsoe, also several others.
7. Jane married Mr. Bolin and afterward Mr. Pritchard.

From Mrs. Leila Tandy Reynolds:
"Gabriel Tandy came from Ireland and settled in Virginia, near Jamestown, James City Co. on the James River.

Achillas Tandy, his son, was born near Jamestown Virginia. He served seven years in the Revolutionary War. He emigrated to Fayette Co. Ky. in 1784 and was married to Nancy Ferguson. To them were born fourteen children:

Mary, Capt Willis, Lenton, Edward, Gabriel, Lucy, Jane, Scott, George, Thomas, Martha, Millie, Sarah and Robert.

Willis the son of Achillas was born Nov. 1, 1788. He served through the war of 1812, was wounded and lost an eye and taken prisoner by the Indians. The old squaw having lost a son adopted him as her son and had him painted and dressed as an Indian but after a time he made known to the soldiers that he was a prisoner and he was taken from the Indians.''

"He was married to Martha Reed Oct. 31, 1822 and died 1849. To them were born twelve children:

"Mary, Andrew Jackson, Annis, Sarah, Stephen, Edward, George, Walter, Willis, Martha, Charles and Henry Clay. All lived to grow up except Charles Scott and Martha H. He moved to Illinois 1834 and lived near Jacksonville.''

Letter of A. J. Tandy to S. W. Hughes 1898:
"I knew your grandfather Hughes very well and was present at his wedding. He married Miss Jane McConnell and the first child was named Blanche.''

"I wish to correct a wrong impression that you have. Lucy Tandy, the wife of Thomas Hughes was not my father's sister. She and my father were first cousins, her father was an uncle to my father and a brother to my grandfather Tandy. I never knew his name. I always understood that my great-grandfather Tandy had a large family of boys and girls. I only knew the names of two of his family, Achilles and Gabriel. I am quite certain that my great-grandfather's name was Gabriel. My great-grandfather Tandy was Elliott Hughes' great-grandfather."

"I cannot give you any information about Lucy Tandy's brothers and sisters. What I know about Lucy is what I learned from my father and your grandfather Hughes. The summer and fall before he was married he spent a good part of his time with my father and I have often heard him speak of his mother."

Letter of Mrs. Laura Sickles (aunt of Sen. C. J. Hughes, Jr. 1898 of Col.):

"My father moved to Missouri in the fall of 1825. Your grandfather Hughes, Elliott, came to my father's I think the same fall that Uncle Thomas Hughes died and spent the winter. I was too small to remember much of him. Your great-grandfather Thomas Hughes married Miss Lucy Tandy. I remember my mother talking so much of her, she thought so much of her. She died when Clay was a baby. Uncle then married Mrs. Chinn. I know nothing of the Tandy family myself, though I know they stood high and were among the first people of Bourbon Co. Cousin Bela Hughes of Denver married a Miss Tandy. My mother left nine children. All gone but me, and I am in my 78th year.

916 College Hill
CAPE GIRARDEAU, MISSOURI

The John Tandy branch I am so interested in: In your Tandy data have you any record of who the wife of John Tandy I is?

I do not understand from your letter whether you are descendant of Judge John Allen or interested from the standpoint genealogist. In either event, I would like to keep in touch with you.

Most sincerely
Mrs. Frederick A. Groves.*

6TH GENERATION.

John Tandy, son of William and Jane (   ) Tandy, was born in Caroline County, Va., Dec. 9, 1751. He married Judith ———.

In 1778, John Tandy bought 198 acres from Alexander Henderson and 4981½ acres from Thomas Wherry. (Deed book 7, pages 43 and 270, Albemarle County.)

She is a daughter of Great Aunt Julia Allen Grosjean, a daughter of Judge John Allen, both of whom died and are buried in Paris, Kentucky.—H. T. A.

During the Revolutionary War, in 1779, William Tandy, Dr., and John Tandy took the oath of allegiance to the Commonwealth of Virginia. (Virginia Historical Collection, VI, 137.)

In 1780, John Tandy and Judith, his wife, sold the 198 acres tract to John More, (deed book 7, page 457, Albemarle County) and Aug. 1, 1784, he sold the 498½ acre tract to William Tandy, Jr., (Deed book 9, page 538, Albemarle County)

William Tandy, son of William and Jane (   ) Tandy, was born ———. Married ?

Aug. 1, 1784, he bought of John Tandy and Judith, his wife, for £100 498½ acres on the Great Mountains on the old gap which John and Judith Tandy purchased of Thomas and Rosann Wherry near the Wherry Mountain place. (Deed book 9, page 537, Albemarle County.)

Achilles Tandy was a witness to the deed.

Achilles Tandy, son of William and Jane (   ) Tandy, was born ———. Married ?

Aug. 1, 1784, witnessed a deed of John Tandy and Judith, his wife, to William Tandy, Jr. (Deed book 9, page 537, Albemarle County.)

Gabriel Tandy, son of William and Jane (   ) Tandy, was born in ———. He married a Miss Castleman.

In 1804, he had a survey for 400 acres in Logan County, Ky. (Finnell's History of Russellville and Logan County.)

ISSUE: Dr. David Tandy.

Moses Tandy, son of William and Jane (   ) Tandy, was born ———.

About 1800, Samuel Pryor of Virginia moved to Trimble County, Ky. His daughter married Moses Tandy. (Va. Mag. Hist.)

Moses Tandy was granted £11 for services performed by him in the commercial department during the late war. Act of the Virginia Assembly, Nov. 22, 1792. (Hening's Statutes, XIII, 622.)

Sallie B. Tandy, daughter of William and Jane (   ) Tandy, was born ———. She married Moses Bledsoe. He was a famous Baptist preacher.

ISSUE: Jesse I. Bledsoe.

Roger Tandy, son of Henry, was born ———. Married Sarah Quarles (in Orange County, Va., ?)

Oct. 13, 1727, patent by William Gooch, Governor of Virginia, to Roger

Tandy of King and Queen County, for 520 acres upon the branches of Eastnorth East in St. George's Parish, Spotsylvania County, bounded by Robert Baylor, Captain John Camm, Samuel Smith, and Harry Beverly. (Vol. 13, page 169, Land Patents of Virginia, Richmond, Va.)

Nov. 6, 1733, Roger Tandy of St. George's Parish, King and Queen County, sold to William Dyer of St. George's Parish, Spotsylvania County, 100 acres in the latter Parish for £10, currency. George Smith, Talliferro Cragg, and Philip Bush witnesses. (Deed book B, page — Spotsylvania County.)

Nov. 4, 1734, Roger Tandy witnessed a deed of John Madison of Drysdale Parish King and Queen County, in Spotsylvania County. (Deed Book C, page — Spotsylvania County.)

Roger Tandy and John Tandy are said to have been brothers, who immigrated from Ireland early in 1700. Proof wanted. (Rev. A. W. Tandy, Fulton, Mo.)

ISSUE: Henry Tandy. Married Ann Mills.

Dr. David Castleman Tandy, son of Gabriel and ———— (Castleman) Tandy was born ————. He married Anna Cabell Castleman. Studied medicine in Italy; after graduation settled in Lebanon, Ky. Their descendants are carried out in "Cabells and their Kin," page 527.

Jesse I. Bledsoe, son of Rev. Moses and Sallie B. (Tandy) Bledsoe, was born ————.

He was Secretary of State of Kentucky in 1808; Professor of Law in Transylvania College, Lexington, Ky.; U. S. Senator 1813-14; State Senator 1816-1820.

He married Sarah Gist, daughter of Colonel Nathaniel Gist. A sister of Sarah Gist married Colonel Nathaniel Hart, a brother of Mrs. Henry Clay.

Of Jesse I. Bledsoe, Henry Clay said that he was the most eloquent man he ever heard. In his later life, he abandoned law and became a Baptist preacher.

Henry Tandy, son of Henry and Ann (Mills) Tandy, was born in Orange County, Va.

In 1796, he married Betsy Adams in Orange County, Va.

In 1795 he bought from William Quisenberry land in Kentucky. They were both residents of Orange County at the time.

Mills Tandy, son of Henry and Ann (Mills) Tandy, was born in Orange County, Va.

He married Amelia Graves, daughter of William Graves of Louisa County, Va.

Removed to Kentucky, where he settled in Christian County.

Oct. 17, 1818, Mills Tandy and Amelia Tandy, his wife, of Christian County Ky., appointed William P. Graves of the same county and State, to represent them in all matters pertaining to the will of William Graves of Louisa County, father of said Amelia Tandy. (Deed Book O, page 110, Louisa County, Va.)
ISSUE: William Henry Tandy.

Jackson Tandy, son of Henry and Ann (Mills) Tandy, was born in Orange County, Va.
March 29, 1809, he married Sarah Mills in Orange County.
ISSUE: Henry Jackson Tandy. Married Narcissa Bowdry Peery.

8TH GENERATION
William Henry Tandy, son of Mills and Amelia (Graves) Tandy, was born in Christian County, Ky., Sept. 24, 1806.
Dec. 7, 1826, at Pembroke, Ky., he married Alice Wolfolk. She was born in Spotsylvania County, Va., Aug. 15, 1806, daughter of Elizabeth Lewis and John Wolfolk, and granddaughter of Waller and Sarah Lewis.
(Lewis and kindred, by McAllister and Tandy, 1906.)

Mary Tandy, daughter of Henry and Ann (Mills) Tandy, was born in Orange County, Va.
She married John Morton. (Marriage license, Orange County, Va., April 24, 1788. He was son of Elijah and Elizabeth (Hawkins) Morton, of Spotsylvania County, Va.
Her father's will dated July 6, 1807, names her children:
Elijah Morton, Nancy Morton, John Morton, Henry Morton, George Morton, Married Edmund (?) Terrill. Charles Morton. (Mortons and their kin; Daniel Morton—MS. in Congressional Library.)
Sally Tandy, daughter of Henry and Ann (Mills) Tandy, was born in Orange County, Va.,
She married Claiborne Graves.
Mr. Graves died in 1839. His will dated Nov. 29, 1839, proved Dec. 23, 1839, made devises to sons Clairborne G. Graves, Albert G. Graves, Isaac F. Graves, and Charles T. Graves, and daughter Elizabeth Brockman (wife of William L. Brockman), Frances N. Brockman (wife of Samuel Brockman) and Virginia White (wife of John White), and to wife Sarah Graves. (Will book 9, page 71, Orange County, Va.)

Charles Tandy Graves, son of Clairbourne and Sally (Tandy) Graves, was born in Orange County, Va., Oct. 10, 1799.
Sept. 18, 1821, he married Anne Rogers Webb, daughter of Augustine and

Lucy (Crittenden) Webb. She was born near Somerset, Orange County, Va., in 1802.

They are buried in the family graveyard once belonging to Augustine Webb near Somerset, Orange County, Va., with the following tombstone inscriptions:

"In memory of Ann R. Graves who departed this life on the 23d day of May, 1834 in the 32d year of her age."

"In memory of Chas. Tandy Graves, born Oct. 10, 1799; died Oct. 22, 1878."

(William and Mary Quarterly, V second series, page 173.)

9TH GENERATION.

Henry Jackson Tandy, son of Jackson and Sarah (Mills) Tandy, was born in ———. He married Narcissa Bowdry Peery.

ISSUE: Jackson Thompson Tandy. Married Martha Elizabeth Keyes.

Smyth Tandy, son of ——— was born ———. Married Feb. 15, 1776, he witnessed the lease of Alexander Spotswood, Esq., to James Lewis. (Deed book J, page —, Spotsylvania County.)

Smyth Tandy was living in Amherst County in 1783; five whites in family and six blacks. (Heads of Families, 1st Census of the U. S.)

The town of Cabellsburg was established on the land of Smyth Tandy at a place now known as New Glasgow in Amherst County and trustees were designated for the sale of lots. Act of the Virginia Assembly, Oct., 1785. (Hening's Statutes, XII, 229.)

Smyth Tandy had a bleaching mill near Staunton, in Augusta County, Va. Trustees were appointed to conduct a lottery for the purpose of raising $4,000 to be applied to the expense of repairing and completing the bleachery. Act of the Virginia Assembly, Oct., 1791. (Hening's Statutes, XIII, 316.)

He was appointed as a justice of the County Court of Augusta County, Va., 1778-1779; dropped as a nonresident, 1779. (Chalkley's Abstracts of Augusta County Records, I, 202 and 211.)

Holman, Tandy, son of ——— Holman, was born ———. Married ———. Was living in Albemarle County, 1760. (Virginia Magazine, X, 390.)

In 1781, 1st Lieut., Goochland militia.

In 1782, Captain, Goochland militia. (Virginia Magazine, XXII, 83.)

BLEDSOE–TANDY

From April, 1930, Register, P. 162 "Sally Tandy, daughter of William Tandy and his wife Jane ———, who settled in 1784 near Lexington, Ky., married Moses Bledsoe." P. 171 "Moses Bledsoe was a famous Baptist preacher. Issue: Jesse J. Bledsoe." From old family Bible records of Moses Bledsoe Smart, of Calloway County, Mo. "Rev. Moses Bledsoe (1705-1809) married Lucy Ann Jameson. They had three daughters: Lucy Virginia, married Albert Harrison (Missouri), Congressman 1835; Pamela Audress, born Sept. 28, 1801, married Nov. 5, 1818, David P. Smart; Dulcena M. Bledsoe married Micajah Volney Harrison of Montgomery Co., Ky. Mrs. Lucy Jameson Bledsoe married 2nd Asa Porter of Va. who had a son John Porter by his first wife."

MRS. ARTHUR FERGUSON, Fulton Mo.

REMINISCENCES OF JAMES BLEDSOE TANDY[*]

I, James B. Tandy, have this day undertaken to write a short Biographical sketch of my family so far as my memory will serve me and, what I have retained in mind that I learned from my Father and Mother and the rest of the older relations, thinking that in after years it may be of some interest to some of our decendents to trace our decent. I was born on the Ohio River about one mile below the town of Ghent, [Carroll Co.] Kentucky, the 10th day of April, 1812. Consequently, at this writing, November, 1886, I am past 74 years old. I shall commence the sketch I propose writing on the following pages, which will be done at my leisure if I am spared long enough.

The Tandys came to Kentucky from Fluvannah County, Virginia. My Grandfather, John Tandy, was born December 9th, 1751. My Great Grandfather, William Tandy, settled near Lexington on the Mason County road, coming to the territory from Old Virginia in the year 1784 with his entire family which (besides 40 blacks) [consisted of] 3 sons and 4 daughters. The oldest son was name Akillis, the second John (my Father's Father). The daughters I have not at this time a clear remembrence of there given names, but remember three of them perfectly well. They intermarried with: one a Mr. or Judge Chinn; the second married Huse; the third married Judge Allen; fourth married Moses Bledsoe who become a famous Baptist Preacher in his day. Jessie Bledsoe, son of Moses Bledsoe, [was] Secretary of State of Ky. [1808-1812] Aunt Ellen, Aunt Huse, and Chinn visited at my fathers in my boy days often, tho living some distense away. My recollection does not serve me so well in regard to the sons, but I know, and remember well, Gabriel married a Miss Castleman, by whom he had one son

[*]James Bledsoe Tandy, 1812-1895, was the maternal grandfather of the late James Tandy Ellis, of Ghent, Kentucky, Adjutant General of Kentucky, 1915-1919, and the author of a number of books of fiction and poetry. The diary is owned by Mrs. Justine Tandy Campbell, of Ghent, granddaughter of the writer, and was lent to Dr. Willard Rouse Jillson, Vice President of the Society, for publication in The Register. It is reproduced here as written, with editing only in some instances where it seemed necessary to make the meaning clear.

James Bledsoe Tandy

name David. He studied Medicin and went to Itily, and graduated there, and settled in Lebanon, Ky. Aunt Allen had a son named Tandy Allen who started south with a flat boat with many Negros on [it] and stuck on Holts Barr. The negros raised and murdered him, and Brackenridge County had to stand the entire expense of the prosecution and price of the slaves executed which bankrupted the County. This has gone into Ky. history. My Grandfather, John Tandy, second son of William Tandy, moved to this State at the time his Father come in 1784 and settled near Lexington. He had 5 children at the time he left Virginia, William, Jane, and my Father John Tandy. My Grandfather married in Fluvannah County, Virginia, a Miss Judith Martion, [Martin] in 1770, the daughter of Henry Martion. His wifes maden name was Judith Guelph, Sister of George the Third King of England (and sister of the duke of Glousester). They also moved to Ky. and settled in Jefferson County near Louisville, having first settled in Fluvannah County, Virginia when they emigrated to the United States before the Revolutionary War. I am not cleare in my mind that my Great Grand Mothers Name was Judith, yeas I am, but of that, should anyone be inquisit enough to desire to kno, they may satisfy themselves by consulting the History of England. My father was born in Virginia, September 21st, 1777, and was 7 years old when his Father moved to Ky. As I have stated, my Grandfather had 5 children when he come, and three others by his said wife after he moved to Ky., Moses Tandy, born in Virginia, Henry born 1778, Died December 25, 1811, age 33, Roger born in 1788 in Fayett County surely. Henry who was thrown from a horse and killed. My Grandfather came to this county in 1802 and settled in what is called Whites Run neighborhood, and Died there about the year 1815 leaving a Second Wife by whom he had 8 children, as near as I recollect. The Children of my Father's Mother, and Heirs of her Mother, Judith Martin, having been notifyed that there was a large (Henry Tandy died December 25th, 1811, thrown from a horse and killed, he was thirty-three years old) legacy awaiting there identifying themselves in England, met at My Fathers about the year 1821, and made and executed a power of Attorney to Wesley Martin, the youngest son of my Great Grand Mother; and he started to England to collect the said legacy. Nothing was ever heard of him afterward and as there was but little Communication between the Countrys at that time, the Heirs concluded that he had drawn the Money and Settled there, and the matter passes quietly from there minds. But, since then, about the year 1850, I met with a Claim Agent, who was engaged largely in collecting such Claims for Citizens of this Country, [who] told me that he had seen the bequest on the Books of the Lord of the Manor often and that no application had ever been mad for it; so I am constrained to believe that Wesley Martin was lost on the Ocean, and that he and the Papers of Identity all wer sunk in Oblivion.

The genealogy of My Grand Fathers Children I will give here before trasing my Fathers, which would naturally come in Second. The oldest son, William, married a Miss Nancy Parlou; they settled in Whites Run, and lived and died there. They had seven sons, John, William, Paschal, David, Henry, Jeptha and Sprat, and two daughters Jennie and Elizabeth. Moses married a Miss Farley by whom he had 3 children, Permelia, Daniel, and Nancy. His wife dieing, he afterwards married a Mrs. Catharin Duncan she was formerly a Miss C. Pryor, by whom he had 2 sons, Granville, and Milton. Jennie married Reubin Scantlin, a Methodist Preacher, by whom she had 2 sons, Moses and Reubin and 2 daughters, Elizabeth and Polly. They kept the Methodist Church at ther house during her widowed life, which was a long while.

Roger married a Miss Sally Wayland, whose farm joined his Fathers, and opened himself a farm in the same Neighborhood. By this same Marriage he had six children, 3 boys and 3 girls: Scott, Russel, and Samuel, Katharine, Nancy and Marthy. His said wife dieing, he contracted a Marriage again with his first wife's sister, Catharine Wayland, by whome he had 5 children, Boon, Wayland, Robert, and Mary, and Senit.

I now come to My Father, John Tandy's genealogy, which I feel I can give with precision. My Father, John Tandy, and Mother, Sally Bledsoe, wer married at the fork of Elcorn, [Elkhorn] Creeks in Franklin County, Ky., the fourth day of June, 1801, he being 22 years, eight mo. and 13 days old, and she 15 years and 4 days old. They moved to what is now Carroll County; they lived togeather 48 years; had, and raised, 13 children, 5 boys and eight daughters. My Father died November 1st, 1848, being seventy years, one month and ten days old.

My Mother, Sally Bledsoe, came to this Country when but a little Girl when the Indians infested this State. Her parents settled in Franklin County. She was born in Culpeper County, Virginia. Her Mothers Maiden Name was Judith Ward. She and my Grandfather, James Bledsoe, was raised in the same County. My Grandfather died before my remembrance leaving but one child, my Mother. My Grandmother married a second husband, William Forsee, who had a large Family of Children and many Blacks. My Grandmother had no children by this second marriage. She lived at the forks of Elkhorn, Franklin County, until her last husband died. After that I moved her down to my Fathers where she lived until she died (My Grandmother Judith Bledsoe, nie Ward, and afterwards Forsee, was born March 20th, 1764) which occured August the 4th, 1847, being 83 years, 4 months and 14 days old. She was stricken with paulsey many years before her death while on a visit to my mothers and, after some time, recovered sufficient to return home, but never fully recovered from the effect. My Mother was one of the most thorour business women I ever saw.

My Great Grandfather Bledsoe settled in Mason County, Ky.; they wer from

Virginia, but the Bledsoes wer originally from Holland. He had a numerous family.

I knew many of my Mothers uncles who settled in this County. William settled back of Warsaw; Joseph settled above Ghent; Abraham settled also above Ghent, the places now owned by Froman; Isaac below Ghent, the place now owned by Walton Craig; Jacob settled the place now owned by Scott Tandy, and James, whom I never knew.

My Grandfather settled, as heretofore stated, on North Elkhorn. John, the oldest uncle, remained in Mason County. My Grandfather Bledsoe left to My Mother by Will, 1,000 acres of Land in Mason County, and, as land at that time was not considered worth looking after, it was settled by Squatters and through the lapse of years they held it by possession. My eldest Brother, after he became grown up, went there to look after it; but there possession had run 30 years, and the impression was that My Mothers' title was effectually bared. The land, when My Brother went to see it, was worth $30.00 per acre. It would now, perhaps, bring $100.000.

The Tandy Family was originally from Ireland. Knaper Tand[y?] came to this country long years before the Revolutionary War from which we all sprang, he being the parent stock, and of historic fame and settl[ed] in Va.

I now return to My Father's family. I have already told you that there was thirteen of us. Willis, the first, born April 23, 1803. He was married on the 26th day of August, 1826, to Miss Elizabeth Blanton, whose mother owned and lived on the farm now owned by D. P. Craig. He died there the 25th day of August, 1827, in his 25th year of his life, leaving one child, James W. Tandy, who is now living. His widow never married again. His son has a numerous Family and, as I do not propose to follow the branches further in ther desent, I return to the next. The second child, Lucinda, was born the 29th day of May, 1805; and was married the 30th day of August, 1821 to Hardin Davis. They raised a numerous family. She departed this life about the year 1884 full of years and good works.

The 3rd child, Eliza Ann, was born August 28th, 1807; and was married December the 15th, 1824, to A. R. Forsee, by whom she has 6 children, John William, Mary, James Nichlaus, Emily, Granville and Sallie. She departed this life 6th of July, 1870. She was full of Good Works, having taken Several Orphan Boys and raised them to be usefull Citizens. She died suddenly in Ghent, Ky. of apoplexy, haveing come to town trading, and was stricken as soon as she got off her horse, and expired that eavening at the house of James Sarlls died August 12th, 1888. [?]

The 4th, Judith, was born February the 10th, 1810; and was married to William P. Dean, the 14th February, 1839. They had six children, five of whome is now living. My sister is still living at this writing, her husband having died some 4 or 5 years ago. They settled on Eagle Creek, this County.

J. B. Tandy, the 5th child, will reserve for the Conclusion of this Biography.

Sary Jane, the 6th child, was born February 8th, 1814; and was married to William Vinson the 4th day of October, 1830. They had 5 Children, Elijah, Sally, Georg, John, and William. They settled first on a Farm given him near the Kentucky River on what is called the Muddy fork of White's Runn. They Sold that and there slaves, and mooved out on the State road 9 miles back of Madison, Indiana, where they lived until there children wer pretty well raised. They then sold out and mooved near Carrollton, Missouri where my Sister Died. After her death Vinson contracted a secon Mariag by whom he had Several Children, tho I never met with any of them. Georg and William are still living near Carrollton, Mo. John mooved to Oragon shortly after the close of the rebelion, he having been a union soldier during the war, and was with Sherman on his March through the South, and was disbanded at Richmond, Virginia. His brother George was in the same service to the close.

Emily, the 7th child, was Born on the 14th day of October, 1816, and was married on the 6th of October, 1836 to Joseph Craig, by whom She had two Children, Edward and Lewis. The oldest now lives in Carrollton, Ky., and Lewis in Maryville, Missouri. There mother died September the 5th, 1846. They wer left orphants. There father Married a Second time, a Mrs. Southers, by whome he had a numerous family. Not having the date of My Sister Emily's death at hand, I here leave this Space in Case I come across it, but memory is that it occured about 1846. (She died September 5th, 1846.)

Drusilla, the 8th child, was born the 25th of June, 1819. She was married to Granvill Tandy, her Cousin, Son of Moses Tandy, the 12th day of October, 1837. They had five children that I now remember. The oldest, Emer, married Martin Smith. She has been dead several years. Catharine married Jas. Diuguid, James and Sally Mote. These three are still living, one dieing before she was grown.

Lutitia, the 9th child, was born the 1st day of November, 1821; was married to Lewis Craig (who was born July 26th, 1819) September the 17th, 1840. They had eight children, seven of whome are now living, Sally, John S., Lutitia, Perlinia, Dr. James T., Lewis, and William. They are all residing in Missouri. Ther Father died in the State of Arkansas, January 25th, 1867, leaving My Sister without any Means to return back to Mo. to there Farm. Her Brothers, learning of her destitution, sent her $500.00 by brother William who met her at St. Louis, and accompanyed them to her farm, and saw them comfortable domiciled. One year thereafter she notifyed her brother there was a mortgage upon her said Farm of 400 acres that had ben executed by her said husband,.and that the entire premice had been Sold to satisfy it, amounting to $3851.80, which took her said brothers with Surprize. Nevertheless they raised Said amount, the writer furnishing $2000.00 and the other 3 living Brothers the remainder. And the writer of this went out to Missouri and redeemed the said farm and quieted the title.

Sometime thereafter our Sister Married again, a Mr. Richard Popplewill. Some [time] thereafter She and her Children proposed for us to take 240 acres of Said farm and deed the remainder, 160 acres, to her and her Children (she having no children by her last Marriag), which we did in order to secure her a permanent Home. We never having recieved anything in the way of Interest or rents, we then left our part in there hands to Manage the product there off, which a little over paid the taxes. We have since sold our part, after holding for 16 or 17 years, for about $4180. Nearly half is still unpaid. We feel we don a good deed not looking to our own agrandisement. Our said brother-in-law, like many in life, involved himself going to Arkansas to Make a Fortune raising Cotton after the War, lost his life with Typhoid fever and bankruped his family, his Children, all being Small, Neading his protection more than at any time. Ambitious to be rich pearses many throug with Sorrow, a lession but few learn untill it is too late. Our sister Lutitia (since writing this) departed this life April 3rd, 1887.

Edward J., the 10th child, was born the 3rd day of January, 1824. He was married to Mrs. Martha Forsee (widdow of John Forsee Dec. She was Daughter of Roger M. Tandy, consequently his cousin) September the 27th, 1859. They had two children, Charles and Scott. His said wife died last August, three years ago, and he has contracted a Secon Marriage with a Miss Annie Klasettler, by whome he has one son name John, his first wife dieing suddenly with apoplexy.

Nancy C., the 11th child, was born the 8th of February, 1826, and was married to Scott Tandy, oldest Child of R. M. Tandy, her Cousin; they having 5 living Children, Willis, Sally, Nancy, Junius C., and Catharine. None Married except Willis who is now located at Lynvill, Tennasee, professor of a colledge. His wife was a Miss Lew Hawkins.

John Q. A., the 12th child, was born the 28th, October, 1828; and was in business with the writer in Ghent, engaged in the mercantile business at the time he was Married. He Married a Miss Emer Mcluer. Some time after he sold out and returned to his farm, and remained there untill some time after the War of the Rebellion. He returned back to Ghent and entered into the same buisness with Bro. William, and is still engaged in that buisness, making it a Complete Success. They have three living Children, Mary T., Magga, and Jessie Emer. None of them are Married. They had one son they called Edward; it died befor it was a year old.

William H. Tandy, the 13th and last child, was born July the 25th, 1831. I took him in to my Store at the age of fourteen years. He was a bright boy and learned the buisness very rapidly, and become a Successful Merchant. He was in partnership with the writer after the withdrawal of J. Q. Tandy, and remained So untill I sold out my interest in the Store about the year 1853 to Scott Tandy, they continueing in buisness until 1860. On the breaking out of the war they Closed there buisness, and he returned to his farm. Some time after the Close of Hostilities between the States, on an invitation from the writer, he come back to Ghent and again entered into buisness in partnership with me, [under] the firm name J.B. and W.H. Tandy, which was conducted verry Successfully for several years. My brother J. Q. Tandy, desireing again to engage in buisness, William and L desolver partnership, and he and J.Q. formed a copartnership under the firm name of J.Q. and W.H. Tandy which continued up to his death. He was Married the   day of to a Mrs. Magga B. Teats, widdow of John P. Teats Dec., and departed this life on the   at Cincinnati while he and his wife wer there buying goods; dieing verry Suddenly, falling dead without a moments warning while buying goods; was brought home and burried in Odd Fellows Cemetery with the honors of the Order.

I now return to my personal history. As I have already told you, I was the 5 in decent of My Father's family, was born the 10th of April, 1812. I was here when this section was regarded as the frontear, and when My Father mooved from the River to Whites Runn Section it was a Wilderness of timber. I was 5, going on 6; he moved in the fall. I well remember seeing deer and turkeys runn across the trace as we wer going along. There was no rode at that time, wer following the old Indian trace across and along the ridge from the now Wise place to where we stoped. My Father, before mooving, had put up a round log cabin with a partition in one end for meat and other supplies, one room for all, whites and black. The next day after we arrived, they cut down trees and built a negro cabin close by in which the cooking was done that winter. My Father then went to felling white ash trees, and put up the house that now remains on the place. This was in the winter 1817 and 18. It was one and one half stories high, with three rooms below, and three above. After it was raised he hired a black man, uncle Hut, that belonged to my Grand Father's estate, to hew it down inside and outside. He done it of nights by the lights made from the scoring chips, and completed it [in a] much shorter time than one would think.

I well remember that it took two hold days to raise the House. The People came from fare and near, some to cut the logs, and the teams hauled those that wer too fare to pack. After it was ready for the roof it was covered with Board Ridge polls and wait polls.. The floors wer laid in part of it loos, so that it could be occupied, the cracks chinked and daubed. During all this time clearing was going on to provid land to make our bread.

The next summer he employed two young Carpenters from where New Liberty now stands. One of them was named Tune, the Father of the late Dr. Tune, who done all the Carpenter work on the first Story. It remained that way untill the next Season when he had shingles made, and Hired Old John Husten, a sorter of Carpenter, who put up rafters, and shingled the house, and laid all of the upper floors, runn up Stars and etc.

We wer, all who wer old enough, going to School. My Father made that a special point; we wer either at work hunting, or going to school. He would alwas have the Teacher to Board with him, and all he ever charged was the tuition of his Children, deeming it of great benefit to have the Teacher with us. I well remember that our advantages over other patrons of the School wer regarded as superior to theres, and our family usially stood head in there classes in there Studdes. At least it give to My Self a great degree of Self Confidence and Self Sufficiency.

I well remember the first time I ever saw dates written. My Teacher, Wm. B. Forsee, wrote 1821 on My Copy Book. I thought it was wonderful without understanding what it indicated; nor did I comprehend its meaning for several years thereafter, being then nine years old. But our Father kept us at School during the winter months at lest. As the dripping of water gradually makes impression on rock, so my Mind gradually expanded, and I received a Smattering Knowledge of the branches of an English education. In Arithmetic we, or I, myself, was taught and drilled in the English system, Pound, Shilling and Pence, old Arithmetic. But in after years I procured an Arithmetic of federal system, Professor Walshes, the first that made its appearance in the U.S., which I geathered much usefull and Practical information which, in after life, I persued Mathematics with as a science with much interest.

I worked on the Farm through the Sumer, fall and Spring months clearing land, splitting rails, and plowing, going to School during the Winter months, untill the fall after I was seventeen years old. My father then Permitted me to accept a position in a Dry Goods Store in Ghent with Samuel Sanders and Jonathan Ramey who had Commenced buisness then. I regarded this Change wonderfull for Me, and tho I found, to My Surprise My great inefaciency, I said nothing, but set myself dillagently to work, learning many things I did not know and correcting many that I had learned amiss, and realized then and now that year in ther store was worth more to me than all the years I had gone to school. It would be a great mistake at this time for Parrents to send there Children to Such Schools when there is institutions where the foundation can be properly laid to build upon, but that was the best to be done in Our Pionier days. I have seen the necessity and have practised in the educating of those left to my care, of laying the foundation and bases correct, and the super structure will stand sure, and there will be progression, no going back to dig up the foundation to be laid by a Master workman.

After this I took a position in Fisher's store one winter, as a salesman which improved my ability to attend to busness very much; and in the interiam between this time and my becoming of age, I staid in his Store while he went to New York and Philadelphia to buy Goods which useally [took] six weeks; much of the trip was then made by Steamboat, Canal, and Stage.

When I arrived at the age of twenty-one years I felt completly at a loss to know what to do with myself and under this dilemma I called to mind what I had heard old men say "if a man had nothing to do let him marry a wife." So my mind was fixed on not being idle and as it was considered in those days a great disgrace for a young man to marry and have no place or home to take a wife too, I set to work to build me a house on a piece of Land My Father had given and deeded to me. Tho used to handling an axe, but for the past three years not useing one much, my hands wer all blistered and in a strutt. But, nothing daunted, I stuck to the work through the Spring and Summer untill I had my house completed. The hardest work that I ever remember of doing was whipsawing, cutting out the joist. I hired William Spicir, an experienced Sawyer, and I, who had never sawed any in that line, cut out over 400 feet of Joist in one day.

When all was ready I went for my bird. I and Susanna A. Vinson wer married December the 11th, 1834. She was raised on the Kentucky River, her parents wer named Eli and Cumfort Vinson, they wer originally from Maryland. My said wife give birth to a daughter on the 22nd day, August, 1836, and departed this life fifteen days thereafter. I succeeded in getting a home for my infant child with my sister Eliza Ann Forsee who give birth to a daughter on the same day. I called my daughter Drusilla T. My Sister kep her one year, and after that her Grand Mother Took her and kep her untill she was large enoughf to go to School.

During the interval from the time I lost My Wife untill my said daughter was five years old I spent rather as a wanderer. The year 1837 I spent in Carrollton selling goods for a Mr. Philip Senour. He borded me and give me $25.00 per month. From there I returned to My Fathers, assisted them on the Farm during the Spring and Summer, and the fall and winter went South with produce on flat boats. I made two trips to Natcheze and while there in the winter of 1838, loaded a part of my Cargo on a Steam Boat and went up the Red River as fare as Natchatosches. Not likeing the prospects of trade there, I droped back to Alexandre. The night after I arrived there I was taken very sick, and had quite a long spell, and was removed from my boarding place to a hotell where I was well cared for. The Land Lord was an Irishman; his wife took as good Care of me as it was posseble for any one to do. When I recovered sufficiently to get out I opened out my produc[e] for sale (which was stored in a warehouse) and the Citizens partly I took it seamed to Vie with each other which would exceed each other in giv[ing] me the biggest price for what I had so that I done well.

I then took the Boat for Natcheze and when I arrived there my partner, Scott Tandy, did not recognize me untill I spoke to him, I was so emaciated. We finished closeing out our load and was ready to start for home having as we Suposed made some money. Much of the money in Circulation was what we now call Wild Cat money. I well remember a little circumstance that ocured soon after we landed at Natcheze which serves to show how demoralized the banking institutions wer in the Southern Country at that time. A French man came to me with a ten dollar bill of the Cotten Press Co., an institution of the City of Natcheze, and pointed out to me the Vignet on the bill, a Cotten plant, and said, "You see that Cotten plant?" I said, "yes." He said, "He no picked!" I said, "yes." He said, "By gar, you no pick him either!"—Which served as a warning to me, tho at par then, before we left it was down to ten cents to the dollar. But we had taken considerable money of the real est Bank of Arkansas wihch we discounted before we left which afterwards come down to nothing. But we held and brought home $200.00 of the Union Bank of Tennessee which had runn down to eighty cents to the dollar. Everybody, Bankers, and those we had confidence in, advised us to hold it, that it was bound to be good—which we did. And the next Season, when we went back, we wer glad to get it off at eight cents to the dollar. But, full of energy and ambition, we made up a load of pork, apples, potatoes, etc. and fifty barrels of Whiskey. And when we reached Memphis we learned that pork was flat on the lower Missipia and at New Orleans not selling for more than what we paid at home for it. We determined to leave the Missipia River below Helena and go into the Yazoo pass, and traverse that Country. This was in the fall of 1839, the year after General Jackson had issued his famous Order moving the Talehasee, Yellow, Bushey, Yazoo, and Pearl River Indians North of the Missippia River. A great many of the straglers of the different tribes remained in the country with whome we had a good trade.

We reached Yazoo Citty early in the winter, remained and traded there untill Spring, selling out our entire load at remunerative prices except the whiskey, which did not bring us but 25 cents per gallon by the barrell, the price we had paid for it the Spring before loosing freight, Schrinkage, leadadge, etc., which I regarded then, and ever since, as one of the very best investments I ever made for I never delt in it again and have adopted the Motto, Tutch not, hande not, the accursed thing which has made Coutnless Thousand Morne.

We, from Yazoo City, took our emty Boat and drifted down to Vixburg where we sold it and returned home, my Partner and I having about $1,000. a pease. We, in the Spring of 1841, engaged in the Goods buisness in the town of Ghent, Ky.; he investing $800. in the buisness and I borrowing $600. I investing $1,600, making a capitol of $2,500. We continued the buisness for eighteen months or a little over under the firm name of J. B. and S. Tandy, he being entitled to one third of the profits, and I two thirds, acording to the capitol put in. At the end of said time, during the fall of 1842, we found our buisness very much hampered and involved in debt having sold principally on a Credit of twelve months and in order to pay our debts, we were under the necesity, during the winter of 1843, of closing our store and Boxing up our Goods, and turning our debts into produce, and going South on flat Boats to make the money to meet our debts, which our Creditors willingly conceaded too. Early in the fall we loaded one boat with apples, potatoes, oats, and dried fruits; paying for apples 37½ cents per barrel delivered to our Boat, 10 cts. per bushel for potatoes, and 12 cents for oats. We started this boat South with my partner, it costing us $300.00 at the landing, all paid for with the accounts and notes. I then went to work and secured another Boat and loaded it with pork, apples, potatoes and flour, costing $1,800, the pork costing us $2.00 per hundred, and started out and fell in with my partner at Rodney Missippi where I had directed him to wait for me, he having been to New Orleans and come up that fare to wait my coming, he having realized net $300.00 for the load—just what it cost at home. We went from there to Natcheze and remained during the winter selling all the pork we could at $2.50 per hundred, hams, after smoking at 5 cents, and lard at 5 cts. per pound. With the remainder of our load we started on the Coast the 1st of April and Coasted all the way to New Orleans, having filled up our Boat with Flour before starting at $3.00 per barrel which as luck would have it advanced shortly after our purchase $1.00 per barrel.

We were one month on the Coast tradeing for Shugar and Molasses, paying for Molasses 10 cents per gallon we furnishing our own barrel which we provided before starting from Natcheze. When we landed at New Orleans we closed out what pork we had at $2.25 per hundred and our potatoes at fifty cents per barrel, sold our Boat and shiped for home, shiping our Shugar and Molasses home (having about $1,000. worth), clearing about $400. on this load. On reaching home our first act was, after hauling up our groceries which consisted of sugar, molasses and Coffee bought at New Orleans at 6%, we went to Cincinnati and paid off every debt that we owed. They, our creditors, complimented us and said, Well done, now we want to sell you all the goods you want on such terms as you may desire. We said no, we had graduated, that we felt under many obligations to them for there kind forbearence, but would never buy another piece of Goods or article on a credit to sell. And as for the futur, our minds wer made up and wherever we could buy for cash on the best terms we intended to buy—not confining ourselves to any special house.

On our return home my partner was inclined to go out of the buisness and I bought him out in the fall, giving him $1,200. for his interest, and continued the buisness continuing untill the fall of 1845 when I invoiced and sold out to John C. Lindsay. My brother William having been taken into the store at the age of 14, I transfered him over with my store to J. C. Lindsay. I bought me a boat and loaded it with bulk pork, apples, etc., paying $3.50 per hundred, and went South. Was gone about four months on which I cleared $1,000. which set me on my feet and then I felt I could stand alone fully. I remained out of buisness untill the fall of 1846 when I again formed a partnership with J. A. Gex which continued about one year. We cleared about $2,500. that year on Goods and trading South. My said partner, having a chance to buy the Leroy Yager Farm the same he now resides upon for $30 per acre, sold his interest in the Store to Walton Craig, making our firm Tandy and Craig. We continued the buisness for 3 years, he paying me, or the firm, $300. per annum to attend to the buisness. I made one trip South with a produce boat during our copartnership. At the end of our partnership we divided our stock, I taking my Brother, W. H. Tandy, in with me. After running the buisness a short time, sold out to him and Scott Tandy determining never again to engage in the Mercantile buisness unless I married a second time, which seemed hardly probble at that time.

I was engaged in traiding in mules and other stock up to the Spring of 1855 when I from association and much attention on both sides become greatly enamored with Miss Harriet A. Schenck of Vevay, Ind., she being 18 years my Junior. It was mutial attachment and devotion that brought us togeather. We wer married on the 6th day of June, 1855 by the Rev. Stewart, Minister of the Baptist Church. We come Home on the next day and, after the usual dinners and Congratulations of friends, having a respetion given us at my Mothers, we assumed housekeeping in a much more congenial form than I had conducted it previously; making me feel that the 18 years I had lived a widdower and had kept house and Boarded, etc., had been spent to but little purpose and, it seamed to me, had been thrown away. We lived hapyly togeather and felt that we wer in a little world of our own. In the latter part of August of the following fall we went to Niagara and New York on a bridal tower, reaching N. York about the 1st of September. We spent some time there and, as I now began to realize that it was important that I should now have some settled buisness, while there I purchased a Stock of Goods and, When we returned to Ghent, I opened out my stock of goods in one of the rooms of the Odd Fellows building, continuing the buisness from that on untill 1884. Of this union there was born unto us three Children. Carroll S. Tandy was born May 30th, 1856, John J. Tandy, June 13th, 1858, and

Justine A. Tandy, the 23rd March, 1860. My buisness prospering, I took into partnership my brother J. Q. Tandy, and we succeeded beyond our expectations which we continued verry pleasantly togeather untill he married on the 15th of March, 1860. My Brother W. H. Tandy and Scott Tandy being in buisness in Ghent at the same time I having sold out to them some years previous, My Brother being desireous to return to his farm, and the buisness outlook being rather gloomy, I bought his Interest in the Goods. Having built the New Store House on the Oposit side of the Aley the fall before, we had them moved into it. I continued the buisness right along alone throug[h] all the national troubles while all the other Merchants closed up there affairs and went out of buisness. While altho I settled down a Stanch Union Man and realized in my heart without a Stanch Goverment we could have nothing. And tho one might accumolate property without a Goverment that was competant to protect him, his transmissions to his posterity would amount to but little.

o o o o

After the lapse of many years, this 28th day of February, 1891, I take up my Pen to continue a Pen picture of the vicitude that one passes through if he lives long in this life.

In August 4th, 1864, my wife, Harriet A. Tandy, departed life leaving me broken hearted, sad, disconsolate and loan—yet not aloan with three healpless Children to care for which were doubly endeared to me by there motherless condition, which I endeavored with all my energy, determined to fill the place of Father and Mother in there little hearts. But who can fill the place of a Mother? Now I am fully assured but feel assured a devoted Father, in a great measure, may heal and, by little kindnesses, asuage there little hearts as well as it is possible for a man to do in this life—but who can supply the aching void that is felt by one who has once known a Mother in this life? But my Children aloan know how neare I have come to supply in the place of Mother and Father and, if entitle[d] to any credit, will fully award it.

Feeling my insufficiency to raise them without the refining influence of one to stand in the place of Mother to them, to assist me in bringing them up in the fear and admonition of the Lord, I contracted a third marriage, after waiting four years, with Mrs. Caroline Teats, which marriage took place February 11th, 1869, a sister of there Grandfathers and, to my mind, come as neare filling the place of Mother to them as it was possible for any mortal to do, they being the judges thereoff.

My said Children growing up and becoming of age to go from home to school, I sent Carroll to the State University of Indiana to study Law. At the commehcement, or neare the close of the second year, returning home for Christmas vacation on a visit, his brother John was taken sick on the night he arrived and after suffering three days died. My son, John J. Tandy, departed this life December 21st, 1871, leaving me heart broken, dispondent, from which I have never recovered; but, feeling my mission in this world was not with the dead but with the living, I there for, have endeavored to fill that mission as well as I could mechanically tho I confess without heart in it.

I then divided my Property between my three children, Drucilla, Carroll, and Justine Stating to my friends and relations that I wanted to see what they would do with it, giving each over $15,000. a piece. My daughter Drucilla died the 16th of June, 1884, leaving three boys and a husband incompetant, and children raised to do nothing; he dieing February 14th, 1891. I have lived to see what has become of the part given to my daughter Drusilla T. Ellis or in other words to see it or the greater part thereof to melt away as a May snow. My son Carroll is a good Financier and up to this time has managed his part well. Justine married a Mr. Charles C. Cook of Canton, Ohio, October 19th, 1882, having three children. The oldest was (George Tandy Cook) was seven years 19th January, 1891. Justine S. Cook was born January 9 . . . . . Merriam L. Cook was born . . . . .

o o o o

April the 10th, 1893, I spent this day, my anniversary 81st, with my son Carroll S. Tandy and his wife and his 3 children. The day was plesent and we had a royall day, and one of the long remembered days of my long life. I have not written in this diary for many years and thought within myself I would not write more but the vividness of the enjoyment of this day made such an impression could not refrain from speaking of it here.   J. B. Tandy.

o o o o

December 14th, we spent the day in Vevay at Carrolls, went over in company with Hon. W. B. Lindsay to attend the Farmers institute in which Carroll was asked to deliver a paper or speach on free roads. He being confined to his bed with lagripe, Hon. Marian Griffith volunteered to present it to the institute which he did in an effective manner which carried conviction to evry interested listener of the important commercial value and feasibility of free Roads to Citizens. And I trust we may soon be in the enjoment of them in evry State; and that toll roads may be a thing of the past.

(End of Diary.)

Note: James Bledsoe Tandy died January 15, 1895.

Four generations of John Taylor's descendants: his youngest daughter, Sally Taylor Smith, b. 1807; her second son, John Taylor Smith, b. 1825; his only son, Fred E. Smith, b. 1853; his only son, Vincent Smith, b. 1881.

TAYLOR LINE

John Taylor married Alice Gaskins; 5 children
"of Wicomico" (Gascoigne)
died 1702 died 1702
    I—John Taylor married Ann Vesey; 5 children
        died 1714/1717
    II—Thomas Taylor married Elizabeth Therriat; 6 children
        died 1717
    III—Lazarus Taylor married Mary Vesey; 6 children
        circa 1667–1726
        1—William Taylor
        2—Argyle Taylor married Judith ——; 1 daughter
            died 1758
        3—Aaron Taylor married Betty Wilde [Wilder?]; 5 children
            died before 1751
            A—Elizabeth Taylor married —— Wornum
            B—Suckey Taylor married —— Hurst
            C—Lazarus Taylor married Hannah Bradford; 8 children
              born 1718
              a-Argyle Taylor married Mary (Tibbs) Ashby; 8 children
                1750–1825
              b-Leanna Taylor married Peter Lehugh; children
                born 1751
              c-JOHN TAYLOR married Elizabeth Kavanaugh; 9 children
                1752–1835
                (1) Benjamin Taylor, born 1784; married (1) Theodocia Payne, 5 children; (2) Elizabeth ——
                (2) Joseph Taylor, 1786–1845; married Mary Fogg, 7 children
                (3) Nancy Taylor, 1788–1847, married (1) John D. Gray, 3 children; (2) Thomas L. Tate, 1 son
                (4) Polly Taylor, 1792–1879, married William French, 11 children
                (5) Jane Taylor, born 1795, married (1) William Plummer, 1 daughter; (2) James Elliott, 4 children
                (6) John Wickliffe Taylor, born 1798, married Jemima Gray, 5 children
                (7) Cave Taylor, 1800–1810
                (8) Eliza Taylor, 1803/1803
                (9) Sally Taylor, 1807–1895, married Joseph Smith; 6 children
              d-Thomas Taylor, unmarried
              e-Bradford Taylor, unmarried
              f-Wilder Taylor; 1 daughter
              g-Susannah Taylor married —— Hughes
              h-Joseph Taylor
              i-Jane Taylor, died 1841, married Jeconias Singleton; 2 sons
            D—William Taylor, circa 1730–1760, married Sarah Bradford; 2 children
            E—Joseph Taylor, unmarried, circa 1732–1782
        4—John Taylor, died 1751, married Margaret ——; no children
        5—Margaret Taylor married —— Winter
        6 —— Taylor married George Dameron
    IV—Mary Taylor married —— Everett
    V— —— Taylor married Edmond Basye

ANCESTORS AND DESCENDANTS OF THE REV. JOHN TAYLOR (1752–1835)

By DOROTHY BROWN THOMPSON

John Taylor of the Ten Churches, whose contribution to frontier Kentucky was discussed in an earlier article, seems to have been in his ancestry about half Scottish and half French. He was the son of Lazarus Taylor and his wife Hannah (or Anna) Bradford, of Fauquier County, Virginia. The emigrant ancestor John Taylor, from Scotland, married Alice Gaskins, originally Gascoigne. Their son Lazarus Taylor married Mary Vesey (variously spelled Vezy, Vezey, Vese) the daughter of George Vesey. The Gascoignes and Veseys appear to have been of Norman-French descent, of families long resident in England. In the Bradford line of John Taylor's mother, the French connection is more immediate. Hannah Bradford's mother was Mary Marr, probably born in France. She was the daughter of John Marr, very likely Jean Baptiste de la Marre originally, a Huguenot who left France some time before the revocation of the Edict of Nantes brought so many French refugees to America. And John Bradford, Hannah's father, was again Scottish. In my grandmother's family when anyone showed temper or strong emotion of any kind, my aunts would shake their heads with tolerant smiles, and murmur, "That's your Taylor blood." With that ancestral background, a certain ebullience might be expected.

As in most families, records vary in extent and in accuracy, depending on the percentage of genealogical patience (and of fires) in the several branches. John Taylor's own Bible record was included in the earlier articles. Two other Bible records bear testimony to Taylor forebears: those of Benjamin Taylor, John's oldest son, and of Joseph Smith, who married John's youngest daughter Sally. The record of his wife's ancestry was written by Joseph Smith into his mother's Bible; his mother had been Lydia Lane before her marriage to Temple Smith. In "Lidia Smith's Book" then, is added to records already there, her son Joseph Smith's entry:

Sarah Smith, daughter of John Taylor, was born 22nd Nov. 1807
John Taylor, her father, 27th Dec. 1752
Lazarus Taylor, G. father born
Aaron Taylor G. G. father born
John Taylor G. G. G. with his two brothers Argle [Argyle] and William landed from the ship Amsterdam at the head of Fleet's Bay in Virginia in the year 1650
Aaron Taylor's wife was Betty Wilde
Lazarus Taylor's wife was Hannah Bradford, her mother Mary Marr from France, her father from Scotland
Sarah Smith's mother, Elizabeth Kavenaugh, b. June, 1761

Phillip Kavenaugh, grandfather an Irishman, born 1732 [Philemon]
Nancy Cave, grandmother, born 1734

Benjamin Taylor's Bible may still be extant, but I have not been able to find out its whereabouts. I do have a statement by his grand-daughter, Lucie Cabell Castleman:

> John Taylor landed with his two brothers, William and Argyle and their families at the head of Fleet's Bay, Virginia, in 1650 from the ship Amsterdam. 1st John Taylor was the great great grandfather of 2nd John Taylor, his wife's name not given. Aaron Taylor, the son of John, married Betty Wilde, and their son Lazarus Taylor born 1718 married Hannah Bradford, her father from Scotland, and her mother, Mary Marr, of France.
>
> John Taylor, son of Lazarus Taylor, born in Fauquier County, Virginia, 1752, was a Baptist minister. He emigrated from Virginia to Kentucky in 1783, settled in Woodford County, and died near Frankfort, Kentucky, in 1835. His wife, Elizabeth Kavanaugh, born 1761, daughter of Philemon Kavanaugh, an Irishman, born 1732, and his wife Ann Cave, born 1734, daughter of Benjamin Cave and his wife Hannah Bledsoe, daughter of William Bledsoe. Benjamin Cave was vestryman of St. Mark's Parish, Spottsylvania County, from 1731 to 1740 and of St. Thomas Parish from 1740 to his death in 1762. Benjamin Cave represented Orange County in the House of Burgesses 1752 to 1755, and 1756 to 1758. All this has been sworn to by Alexander Brown of Virginia. The family tree was copied from my grandfather's Bible.

The grandfather was Benjamin Taylor, son of the Rev. John Taylor; the Alexander Brown referred to is probably the author of *The Genesis of the United States,* since he also wrote a family genealogy, *The Cabells and Their Kin,* in which he refers briefly to the Rev. John Taylor. So much for the family record. These two agree exactly in tracing the line, and probably stemmed from the same source. But that source, probably due to confusion from two Lazarus Taylors, seems to have telescoped the two earliest generations and left out Lazarus Taylor who married Mary Vesey, the son of the immigrant John.

In an article in the *Virginia Historical Magazine,* volumes 35, 36, and 47, Mrs. L. C. Anderson of Bainbridge, Ohio, writes of *The Taylor Family of Northumberland and Lancaster Counties, Virginia.* In this, she cites convincing evidence for the inclusion of this earlier Lazarus. She has found records of a William Taylor at the same time and place as the immigrant John, but no record of a brother Argyle, and no proof that William was the brother of John. There are many records in Northumberland of Taylors named John, William, Thomas, and Argyle, and several of the name of Lazarus. There is room for much research to be done to unravel the resulting confusions. Some items are definitely identifiable. There were several Taylor families certainly not related in any way. One

John Taylor of Northumberland, easily confused with John "of Wicomico," the immigrant in our line, had a wife Elizabeth who, after her husband's death in 1652, married Tobias Horton. Still another John died in Northumberland in 1667, probably the same one who made a gift to his son William in 1665. The immigrant in our line lived in Wicomico Parish, which comprised part of Northumberland and part of Lancaster counties. He owned large tracts of land bordering on the streams Wicomico and Corotoman, and the inlets of the Bay.

John Taylor the immigrant was probably twenty-three years old in 1650, when he arrived on the *Amsterdam* "at the head of Fleet's Bay." He made a deposition in 1657 stating that he was then thirty years of age,[1] which would place his birth in 1627. If he came with "his family," and was already married, probably the Gaskins family came about the same time. This family were in Lower Norfolk quite early, going from there to Northumberland. The presumption is that Thomas Gaskins (Gascoigne) had two daughters, who married James Jones and John Taylor, since he seems to have deeded land to the two jointly, on at least two occasions. In the Northumberland County Order Book 1658–1662:

> Thomas Gaskins deeds 200 A. to James Jones and John Taylor—land patented in Northampton County, deed made in year 1662.

and in the record book of 1666-1672:

> James Jones and John Taylour 1000 A. situated between Wicomico branches and the branches of Corotoman River in Lancaster Co.,: land being formerly granted to John Hughlett, and by sd Hughlett sold to Thomas Gaskins, May 28, 1658, and by the sd Gaskins assigned over to James Jones and John Taylour Oct. 24, 1659, granted by William Berkley, June 22, 1664.
> James Jones deeds all patents, rights, etc. to land (described above) to John Taylour, Nov. 16, 1668. Leonard Howson, James Poper, Henry Hudson, witnesses.

In the Richmond Land Office, these records:

> John Ellis, James Jones, & John Taylor, 500 A., 1648, Northampton County.
> John Taylour, 100 A., pat. 1652, gr. 1662
> John Taylour, 400 A., pat. 1652, gr. 1662 } All three grants situated on
> John Taylour, 450 A., pat. 1652, gr. 1662 Creeks Bay, Lancaster Co.

Northern Neck Grants:

> John Taylor, 600 A., 1666, Wicomico.

Many early records of Northumberland have been destroyed by fire. John Taylor's will is missing, but land records, deeds and depositions of other members of the family show that he was in Wicomico Parish from at least 1652, that he had sons John, Thomas, and Lazarus, and daughters Mrs. Edmond Baysey [Basye] and Mrs. Mary Everett, and probably other daughters; and that he died in 1702. The earliest date named in connection with him is 1648 (above) in the record of 500 acres belonging to him with John Ellis and James Jones. Northampton records show that James Jones was one of those transported into this county March 23, 1640. John Taylor may not have been in the country at the time of the

---

[1] Virginia Magazine, v. 36, p. 383.

1648 entry. In 1651, his name appears in Northampton County among those promising to be true to the King. He is described as "of Northampton County" in a deed:

> John Taylor of Northampton County deeds 250 A. to John Parremore, land lying upon south side of Occahannock Creek, it being half of a Devident, granted by patent unto John Ellis, James Jones and ye sd John Taylor, Sept. 30, 1654. Again recorded April 20, 1658.

Occahannock Creek is in the extreme northern part of the county, forming the boundary line between Northampton and Accomac counties. The above deed is also recorded at Accomac, Accomac Co., April 28, 1658, the original deed having been made Sept. 30, 1654. [One William Taylor owned large tracts of land on Occahannock Creek, in both counties, Northampton and Accomac. His will, pr. Accomac Co. June 21, 1687, names sons William and Elias and two daughters—no proof of relationship to John Taylor of Wicomico.] In 1659, Dec. 1, James Jones deeded two tracts of land, one of 300 acres, the other of 250 acres to Thomas Leatherby, the latter tract having formerly belonged to James Jones, John Ellis, and John Taylor, the latter two having assigned over their rights to James Jones, Northampton County. It was in connection with a business transaction with James Jones, March 1, 1657, that John Taylor made deposition he was then thirty years of age.

John Taylor died at the age of seventy-five, early in the year 1702. His wife Alice and his son John were executors, but Alice died that same year. In the Order Books of Northumberland County 1699-1713 is the record:

> On motion of Alice and John Taylor, they are made executors of the will of John Taylor, deceased, April 15, 1702. John Howson a witness.

That Alice Taylor had died by October is evidenced by this entry:

> Oct. 25, 1702. Mrs. Mary Everett, daughter of Alice Taylor, deceased, late widow of John Taylor, deceased, brings suit vs. John Taylor to get something from her mother's estate.

Also in that same year Edmond Basye brought suit against John Taylor, Jr., for a share of land, which was laid off accordingly. Alice Taylor was apparently in sufficiently good health in April to have been appointed executor, and by October her son John is in sole charge and at least two other children suing for a share; so she must have died intestate, perhaps suddenly.

Children of John and Alice (Gaskins) Taylor [order uncertain]:

I. John Taylor, married Ann Vezey, daughter of George and Joan Vezey He was a merchant, justice, vestryman of Wicomico Church, described in records as "Gent." He died between 1714 and 1717; had sons John, Moses, Thomas, James, Benjamin.

II. Thomas Taylor, married Elizabeth Therriat, daughter of William Therriat. Thomas is described as planter; will dated 1717; had son Thomas to whom he left the plantation, son Therriat, daughters Martha, Elizabeth, Ana and Sarah.

III. Lazarus Taylor, married Mary Vezey, sister of Ann above [see later.]
IV. Mary Taylor, married —— Everett. Sued brother John 1702 for share of estate.
V. —— Taylor, married Edmond Basye. His will, Oct. 2, 1714, named brothers John and Thomas Taylor.

SECOND GENERATION

Lazarus Taylor, born about 1667; died 1726 or later [date of codicil to will written in 1711, when he deposed he was forty-four years of age.] He was born in Virginia, probably in Wicomico Parish, Northumberland County, son of John Taylor the immigrant of this line and his wife Alice Gaskins (Gascoigne). He must have grown up in a group of neighbors predominantly French, as his mother was. He and his brother John married daughters of George Vezey, and his brother Thomas married Elizabeth Therriat.

The Vezey (Vesey, Vese) family appear in Lancaster County, Virginia, records from 1655. In 1659 George Vezey and Nathaniel Brown were administrators of the estate of James Nicholson, deceased, at James City County. It is possible that Nicholson was the father of their wives. Certainly George Vezey was very close to Nathaniel Brown, whom he names as a guardian for his children, Ann and Mary. The older Ann married John Taylor, older brother of Lazarus, who married the younger daughter Mary. George Vezey died in 1665, and Stephen Tomlin and Nathaniel Brown were named the children's guardians. Both girls were still under age September 9, 1669 when the property of Richard Crouch, deceased, was ordered appraised, Thomas Banks, administrator:

> The said Richard Crouch having married Joan, mother of the Vezey orphans, widow of George Vezey, deceased. Nathaniel Brown and Stephen Tomlin, guardians of sd. orphans, Mary being the younger.

George Vezey's will was probated in Lancaster County, March 14, 1665, and administration granted to "Joan, widow and relict of George Vezey." The will was not found in the record books of Lancaster County, but was in a package of old wills. It mentions a son Thomas besides the two daughters; evidently he died young, as appears from this record in Lancaster County, Book 7, p. 21:

> Taylor to Taylor, deed Nov. 13, 1689. Lazarus Taylor of Wicomico Parish, Northumberland Co., planter, and Mary his wife to John Taylor, Jr., land in Parish of White Chapel, Lancaster Co., granted by patent unto George Vezey Sept. 2, 1663, one tract. Other tract pat. by George Vezey Sept. 18, 1665. Sd land was given by will of George Vezey to only son Thomas Vezey, who deceased without will or issue, so land descended unto Ann, wife of John Taylor, and Mary, wife of Lazarus Taylor, in co-partnership; and sd Ann and Mary being sisters of the whole blood unto the sd Thomas Vezey deceased. Edwin Conway, Sarah Conway, witnesses.

Lazarus and Mary (Vezey) Taylor had five sons: William, Argyle, Lazarus, Aaron, and John; and at least two daughters, Margaret Winter and Mrs. George Dameron. In 1711, Lazarus Taylor deposed that he was forty-four years of age.

On February 2, 1711, the same year, he made his will. In it he named his eldest son William and brother John Taylor; sons Argyle, Lazarus, Aaron, and younger son John; daughters mentioned but not named; son-in-law George Dameron and brother John Taylor named as executors. On January fourth, 1726, he added a codicil which named sons William, Argyle, Lazarus, Aaron and John, and daughter Margaret Winter; son William sole executor; beloved friends William Coppedge and Capt. John Howson. Witnesses were James Taylor, John Coppedge, and John Hill. He would have been, according to his earlier deposition, fifty-nine years old at this time. His brother who had first been named executor had died earlier.

Mary Vezey Taylor was not mentioned in her husband's will of 1711, when he was forty-four. She must have died before that date, and after the Taylor to Taylor deed of 1689. Since they had at least one married daughter by 1711, but no son old enough to act as executor, the probabilities are that Lazarus and Mary were married not long before the Taylor to Taylor deed. Since they had six children at least, Mary must have lived till near the time that Lazarus made his will. It seems not unlikely that her death suggested to him the advisability of making provision for his children.

Children of Lazarus and Mary (Vezey) Taylor [order not known except for William]:

    I. William Taylor, named in will as oldest son, father's executor. Born c. 1690.

   II. Argyle Taylor (called Captain) vestryman or church warden of Wiconico Church from 1739 to 1754; married Judith —— who survived him; had daughter Mary, who was under 21 at his death in 1758. Will names wife and daughter; nephews William and Lazarus Taylor [sons of his brother Aaron] and Joseph; nieces Betty Wornum, Peggy Yerby and Susannah Taylor; Judith Coppedge daughter of Charles; Betty and Judith Gibbons; and Edwin Fielding son of Edwin who was clerk at Wicomico Church. Judith Taylor, his widow, married Argyle's cousin Richard Taylor [son of Benjamin, son of John II, son of John the immigrant]. Richard Taylor died 1774; left four children and step-daughter "Nancy" Taylor [Mary?].

  III. Aaron Taylor born Northumberland County, Virginia; married Betty Wilde [Wilder?]; died before 1751, when named as deceased in brother's will; had at least 5 children. [See later.]

  IV. John Taylor, died 1751; married Margaret ——; apparently no children. Will names wife Margaret, nephew Joseph Taylor son of Aaron Taylor deceased, cousin Elizabeth Wornum [daughter of Aaron Taylor], sister Margaret Winter, and godson John Hornsby; executors Charles Coppedge and brother Argyle Taylor.

V. Margaret Taylor, married —— Winter.
VI. [Daughter] married George Dameron. Probably the oldest child, since George Dameron "son-in-law" was named as executor of Lazarus's will in 1711. He was not named in the codicil in 1726, so we may guess that he had remarried in that interval. Since Lazarus Taylor mentioned daughters but did not name them, and in the codicil named Margaret Winter as a daughter, the supposition is that this older daughter was still living in 1711, or else that there was another daughter.

THIRD GENERATION

Aaron Taylor, son of Lazarus Taylor and his wife Mary Vezey, was born in Wicomico Parish, Northumberland County, Virginia, probably in the 1690s; died before 1751, when he was named as deceased in the will of his brother John. His wife is named as Betty Wilde in family records of two children of the Rev. John Taylor. Nothing so far can be found about her. The fact that one of her sons named a son Wilder, and another had a child whose name is recorded variously as Willey or Wildey, it seems at least a possibility that Betty's name was Wilder, though that is pure conjecture on my part. It affords at least a lively clue to further research.

Aaron seems to have left no will but the will of his bachelor son Joseph Taylor gives the names of brothers and sisters, and enables us to list the children of Aaron and Betty Taylor, though not in certain order:

I. Elizabeth Taylor, married —— Wornum.
II. Suckey Taylor [Susan?], married —— Hurst.
III. Lazarus Taylor, born 1718; married c. 1748-9 to Hannah Bradford, daughter of John and Mary (Marr) Bradford; died probably Kentucky. [See later.]
IV. William Taylor, born c. 1730; died 1760; married Sarah Bradford, sister of Hannah above. In 1774, Mary Marr Bradford's will mentions this daughter as Sarah Rose; she had married secondly Hosea Rose, and had several children by this second marriage. William and Sarah (Bradford) Taylor had at least two children: Leroy born 1758 [given a shilling in his uncle Joseph's will] and Parmenas. They used their step-father's name, Rose, but served in the Revolution under their own name Taylor, both becoming Colonels. Parmenas, the older, was born 1753, married Betty White, had eleven children. Leroy married twice (1) Susan Sherrill (2) Mary Bradford a "second cousin" [exact relationship unknown]; had twenty-four children by the two marriages.

V. Joseph Taylor, unmarried, died 1782 "then about sixty years old." This was the uncle mentioned, though not named, by the Rev. John Taylor in his *History of Ten Churches*. He was a tutor in the household of Robert Carter of Nomini Hall, and made John Taylor his heir [discussed in earlier article, *The Register*, July, 1948]* Joseph Taylor's will [see photostat from Northumberland County Record Book 1780–1782] follows:

In the name of God Amen I Joseph Taylor of the County of Northumberland and Wicomico Parish Being in Good Sounding Sences and understanding and memory do make ordain and Constitute this to be my Last Will and Testament Revoking and Annuling all other will or Wills heretofore made by me Either by word or writing and this to be taken for my Last will and Testament and none Other—Item I give my Soul unto Almighty God that Gave it unto me and my body to the Earth to be buryed in a Christian manner at the Discretion of my Executors hereafter mensioned—Item I give and bequeath my Temporal Estate that my Blessed God and father gave unto me in manner and form as followeth—Item I give and bequeath unto my sister Elizabeth Wornum one Shilling Sterling and no more to her and her heirs forever—Item I give and bequeath unto—nephew Leroy Taylor the Son of my Brother William Taylor Decesd One Shilling Sterling and no more to him and his heirs forever—Item I give and bequeath unto my sister Suckey Hurst One—Shilling Sterling and no more to her and her heirs forever—Item I Lend unto my Brother Lazarus Taylor Enduring his natural Life one young Negro man Ephriam and at my Brother's death Then—Item I give and bequeath Ephriam with Seven other negroes as followeth—Item I give and bequeath unto my Nephew John Taylor the Son of my Brother Lazarus Taylor Eight negroes—Vizt Jack Ephraim Moll Nann Jemima Letty May and Asa They and their increase to him and his heirs forever—Item I give and bequeath unto my nephew John Taylor my Land with all the apurtenances thereto with all my Stock of all kinds. Viz. horses Cattle Sheep hogs my household furniture of all kinds Crops in the houses and Crops in the fields to him and his heirs forever—Item I give and bequeath unto my nephew John Taylor the part of Dower that falleth unto me at the death of my Uncle Argile Taylor's Widow with what Debts is justly due unto me to him and his heirs forever—my desire is that my Cousin John pay off my just Accounts if any—I appoint my three loving and Trusty friends my whole executors—John Taylor, Alexander Hunton and Lewis Luneford—As witness my hand and Seal the 27th day of may 1778—And in the Second year of our Commonwealth—Test Charles Prichard   Joseph Taylor

Wm. Parrett
Richard Howson Payne
Joseph Swain
William Lizenby

At a court held for Northumberland County the 14th day of October 1782— This last will and Testament of Joseph Taylor Decd. was presented in court by John Taylor one of the Executors therein named who made Oath thereto According to Law and the Same being Proved by the Oaths of Joseph Swain and William Lizenby Two of the Witnesses thereto was admitted to record and on the motion of the said Executor Giving Security a Certificate is Granted for obtaining a Probate thereof in due form—Teste

                              Catesby Jones Ct. Cur.

FOURTH GENERATION

Lazarus Taylor, son of Aaron Taylor and his wife Betty [Wilde or Wilder], was born in Wicomico Parish in Northumberland County, Virginia, in 1718. He married about 1748-9, Hannah Bradford, whose sister Sarah Bradford had mar-

*See "John Taylor of the Ten Churches," by Dorothy Brown Thompson, in *The Register of the Kentucky Historical Society*, Vol. 46 (July 1948), 541-572.

ried his brother William Taylor. Hannah and Sarah were the daughters of John Bradford[2] of Prince William and Fauquier Counties, and his wife Mary Marr, daughter of John Marr.[3] They were living in Fauquier County in 1752, when their son John Taylor was born. In 1767, Lazarus Taylor and his wife Hannah were in Frederick County. In 1785, with a family of four persons, they had crossed the Blue Ridge and were living in Shenandoah County. Their names appear in the records, as do the names of their sons John, Argyle, and Bradford Taylor. There were nine children in the family. After John Taylor became a Baptist minister and went out to Kentucky in 1783, several of his family followed him, and apparently his parents moved later to Woodford County, and probably died there.

Children of Lazarus and Hannah (Bradford) Taylor:

I. Argyle Taylor, born May 25, 1750; died Jan. 8, 1825; married Mary (Tibbs) Ashby, widow of William Ashby. She was probably the daughter of Foushee Tibbs, at one time Burgess of Prince William County. She was born May 30, 1750; died Jan. 4, 1829. Their children:
   1. Artemisia born June 17, 1774, Shenandoah Co. Va.; m Stephen Furr.
   2. John F. born July 6, 1776; died Oct. 19, 1802; m Ellen ———.
      Children: Lazarus, Harriet, Grayson Bradford Taylor.
   3. Catherine born Oct. 6, 1778.
   4. Lucretia born Sept. 11, 1781; died April 8, 1815; m William Warren, Jr.
   5. Meredith Fleet born Feb. 27, 1784; died August 1793.
   6. Foushee T. born Sept. 17, 1785; married Mary C. Warren; ch.
   7. Willey [Wildey, perhaps Wilder?] born July 9, 1788; died Aug. 1, 1793.
   8. James W. died in 25th year at Mattazas, Cuba.
II. Leanna Taylor, born 1751; married Peter Lehugh; lived Front Royal, Va.; had several children.
III. John Taylor born Oct. 27, 1752; died 1835, near Frankfort, Kentucky; married (1) Elizabeth Kavanaugh, nine children (2) Mary Nash, no children. Baptist minister; author *History of Ten Churches* [see biographical article in *The Register*, vol. 46, *John Taylor of the Ten Churches* by Dorothy Brown Thompson.] *
IV. Thomas Taylor, unmarried
V. Bradford Taylor, unmarried

---

[2] See TYLER'S QUARTERLY, vol. 27, no. 2, p. 114 et seq. *The Bradford Family of Fauquier County, Virginia* by Mrs. Philip Wallace Hiden.
[3] See TYLER'S QUARTERLY, vol. 26, no. 4, p. 286, et seq. *John Marr of Stafford County* by M. W. Hiden.
*See the footnote on page 459.

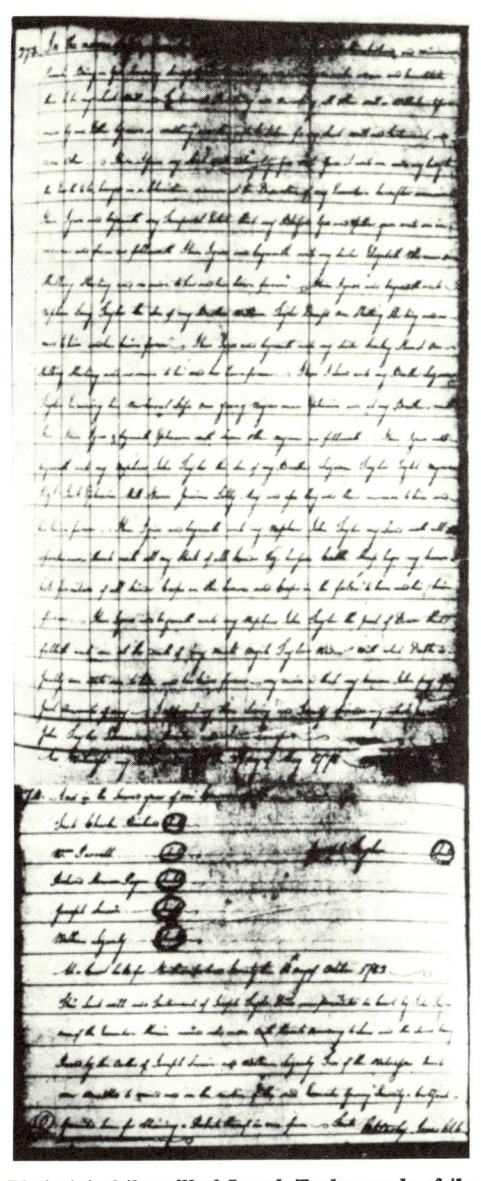

Photostat of the will of Joseph Taylor, uncle of the Rev. John Taylor, making John his principal heir. From Record Book of Northumberland County, Virginia, 1780-1782.

VI. Wilder Taylor, married (wife's name unknown) and had an only daughter Sally; lived "in the Dunkard's Bottom of Cheat River" [West Virginia].

VII. Susannah Taylor, married —— Hughes and "lived on the Cowpasture River in the Western part of Virginia."

VIII. Joseph Taylor, not known whether he was older or younger than his brother John, with whom he seems to have appeared older. He is the brother mistaken by the congregation for the preacher, in John's account in the *History of Ten Churches:* "by the wishful look of the people on him, with his fine black cloth and clean neck band, he soon discovered their mistake, and though a wild ratling man, he perhaps put on more solemn looks than he would have done; and when the preacher was done, an opening was immediately made between him and the pulpit, while I had to scramble through and over the people, to get to the place."

IX. Jane Taylor, born in Virginia, came out to Kentucky with her brother John when he had gone to Virginia on a visit—she was then about sixteen. Married Jeconias Singleton in Woodford County; he died 1836; she died 1841. He was the son of Manoah Singleton and Sarah Craig (daughter Toliver Craig and Mary Hawkins). Jeconias and his brother Mason were both Captains in the War of 1812. Jeconias and Jane (Taylor) Singleton had sons John and William. John Singleton was used as a model for the character of Mr. Middleton in the novel *Tempest and Sunshine,* by Mary Jane Holmes, a frequent visitor in the Singleton family. John's two daughters became the models for the title characters, Susan for "Sunshine" and Betty for "Tempest." William Singleton, the other son, was born 1798 and married Jan. 6, 1846 in Woodford County to Lucinda Carroll. Their son Samuel Singleton married Susan Mary Sparrow, and had a daughter Mary Ruth Singleton, later to be the mother of Bayless E. Hardin, secretary of the Kentucky Historical Society.

FIFTH GENERATION

This brings us to the generation of the Rev. John Taylor who married Elizabeth Kavanaugh. His biography has been given in some detail in the earlier article; but some mention should be made of his wife's family. Considerably more is known of these lines, particularly the Cave family. Elizabeth Kavanaugh was the daughter of Philemon Kavanaugh (1732–1764) who married in Culpepper County, Virginia, Ann Cave, b. 1734, daughter of Benjamin Cave and his wife Hannah Bledsoe. Probably it was these grandparents of his bride's which John Taylor had especially in mind when he said she was "a girl of good family." Benjamin Cave had been vestryman, justice, sheriff, and was a Burgess from Orange County; his wife was the daughter of William Bledsoe, first sheriff of

Spotsylvania County. The Cave family came from England. Benjamin Cave, the immigrant ancestor of this line, was born at Windsor between 1684 and 1691, where his father, the Rev. William Cave, was Canon; his mother was Anna Stonehouse, daughter of the Rev. Walter Stonehouse.

The Kavanaugh line (written variously Cavanaugh, Cavenaugh) is said to have come from Ireland. The immigrant was Elizabeth's grandfather, Philemon Cavanaugh, recorded "from Great Britain" in a list of importations dated 1736. A deed in Spotsylvania dated 1724 shows that he was in Virginia at least that early. He married Sarah Ann Williams, daughter of William and Jael (Harrison) Williams, and they had seven daughters and two sons, including Philemon who was under age when his father died in 1744. The younger Philemon was the father of Elizabeth Kavanaugh Taylor; and there was still a third Philemon, Elizabeth's brother. These three generations of the same name have resulted in the loss of a generation in some accounts of this family.

Ann (Cave) Kavanaugh, Elizabeth Taylor's mother, widowed in 1764, married secondly in 1775, William Strother, a large landholder of Orange and Culpeper Counties, who was known as "William Strother of Orange" to distinguish him from his uncle "William Strother of Stafford."[4] He married Ann Cave Kavanaugh June 9, 1775.[5] They went to Kentucky and settled in Woodford County, near Mortonsville, where he died in 1808, his wife surviving him. His first wife was Mrs. Sarah (Bayly) Pannill, widow of William Pannill; she died in 1774, leaving three children. The youngest of these, Sarah Strother, married Col. Richard Taylor; they were the parents of Zachary Taylor, President of the United States. This Sarah Strother Taylor, step-sister of Elizabeth Kavanaugh Taylor, has caused some confusion to family historians, who were quite sure there was a relationship to the Zachary Taylor family. There was no blood relationship between the two Taylors, though the families of Col. Richard Taylor and the Rev. John Taylor were very close in their affections, and the youngest daughter of the Rev. John Taylor and his wife Elizabeth Kavanaugh was named Sally for Sarah Strother Taylor.

DESCENDANTS OF JOHN TAYLOR AND HIS WIFE ELIZABETH KAVANAUGH

I. Benjamin Taylor

This oldest of the nine children of John and Elizabeth (Kavanaugh) Taylor was born February 22, 1784, at Gilbert's Creek, Craig's Station, Lincoln County, Kentucky. The date of his death is unknown. He attended Transylvania University 1807-8. He was married [probably about 1815] to Theodosia Payne, daughter of Judge Henry Payne and his wife Anne Lane (daughter of James and Lydia Hardage Lane). Theodosia (Payne) Taylor is the subject of a me-

---
[4] Wm. E. Railey. *History of Woodford County*, p. 145.
[5] Recorded in back of Deed Book 17, Orange County, Virginia.

morial sketch written by her husband and included in his father's *History of Ten Churches*. She died November 29, probably 1826, since John Taylor says she died "very lately" and the book was published in 1827. She was in her thirty-fourth year, and "had been delivered of a female child, from which she never recovered." Her husband's sketch says she had been ill ten months, while John Taylor says she died "of consumption," leaving "five children and an aged father." I have been unable to find information on any of these five except

Mary Jane Taylor [dates unknown] who married Philander L. Cable of Rock Island, a man of much importance in railroad history. They had one daughter, Lucy Reed Cable who married George A. Castleman, no ch.

In L. F. Johnson's *History of Franklin County, Kentucky* [p. 69] a Benjamin Taylor is listed as a member of the State Legislature in 1821.

Benjamin Taylor evidently had a second wife before 1835, when he sold a share of his father's estate, and his wife Elizabeth signed with him, in Fayette County.

Certainly there must be other descendants of Benjamin Taylor, and it was hoped that some of them might be heard from, following the publication of the biographical article on John Taylor. Failing that, this report of his line remains incomplete.

Ancestry of Theodosia Payne who Married Benjamin Taylor

Theodosia Payne was the daughter of Judge Henry Payne and his wife Anne Lane. Her father Henry Payne was born January 26th, 1753; died 1828; married March 5, 1775 to Anne Lane, and they moved to Kentucky in 1786. The Payne family was English; Judge Henry Payne was a great great grandson of Sir John Payne, who was knighted by James I, and who established Payne Manor in the Northern Neck of Virginia. Henry Payne's uncle was the "little man" who is said to have felled George Washington in a political quarrel, and to whom Washington apologized the following day. Judge Henry Payne was the son of Edward Payne and his wife Ann Holland Conyers.

Anne Lane, mother of Theodosia (Payne) Taylor, was born Aug. 24, 1753, daughter of James Lane and his wife Lydia Hardage; she died October 1821. Children of Henry and Anne (Lane) Payne: 1. Nathan Payne, 2.Henry Conyers Payne, 3. Nancy Payne, 4. Betsey Payne, 5. Lydia Payne, 6. Theodosia Payne married Benjamin Taylor, 7. Ann Payne.

The Lane family is English, thought to be from Staffordshire. The tradition is that the family came from the Lanes of Bromley Hall, whose Colonel John Lane and sister Jane assisted Charles II to escape after the battle of Worcester, 1651, when Jane rode pillion behind Charles disguised as her servant. For this service the family were permitted to add to their coat of arms a quartering of three lions of England on the shield, and to assume as a crest a horse bearing the regal crown between his forehoofs, with the motto, "Gerdes le Roy." This crest appears, according to family tradition, on the silver spoons used in the family of Col. Joseph Lane, son of William Lane of Westmoreland, and it has been thought that through the Irish branch of the Staffordshire family, the Virginia and Maryland Lanes are descended. This is important only because the tradition seems to have been preserved in considerable detail, and so may be a clue to provable facts. So far, it remains a family story.

The first proved records in this line are in 1740, when a William and a James Lane, brothers, moved from Westmoreland to Prince William County, Virginia, to lease adjoining tracts of land from George Turberville, agent of Lord Fairfax. This was the form of conveyance in use at that time—a quit-rent was paid to Turberville, who in turn guaranteed quit-rents to Lord Fairfax. The two brothers had married sisters, William to Sarah, James to Lydia Hardage, daughters of James Hardage (1686–1749) and his wife Elizabeth ———. The lease describes the two brothers as coopers. William lived only about two years after the leases were signed; his widow married secondly Col. Francis Summers. Children of William and Sarah (Hardage) Lane were 1. John (later Dr.) who married Catherine (Newton) Jett, 2. James Hardage Lane (1735–1787) who married Mary Jane Smith, 3. William Lane who married Nancy Bellfield (who married (2) Enoch Smith), and 4. Anny (or Amy) Lane.

James Lane who married Lydia Hardage had nine children, of whom Anne, mother of Theodosia (Payne) Taylor, was the youngest. Three of Anne's sisters married three Smith brothers, and of these, Temple Smith and his wife Lydia Lane were the parents of Joseph Smith, who married Sally Taylor, youngest daughter of the Rev. John Taylor. Children of James and Lydia (Hardage) Lane:

I. Aaron Lane born Nov. 7, 1735, married Eleanor Green (dau Robert and Mary (Ball) Green) settled Culpeper County. Son William Armistead Lane.

II. Betty Lane born June 25, 1738; died before 1790; married Jacob Remy; ch: Lydia Remy married James Wilson, Anna Remy married Tasley(?) Willson, James Remy, Sanford Remy, Samuel Remy, John Remy. [Amy Clagott, grchild of James, must have been either Betty Remy's dau, or James Jr.'s.]

III. William Lane born Aug. 30, 1740; died March 16, 1808; married Sarah Lane (daughter of William Carr Lane and Ann Wilson his wife) on April 15, 1779. Sarah was born Dec. 8, 1740.

IV. James Lane, Jr. born January 14th (or 17th) 1743; died 1788 [estate settled Feb. 15, 1803] married (1) Elizabeth ——— ; children Hannah, Moses, perhaps others; married (2) Sarah ———, who survived him, no children [her father-in-law, James Lane, Sr. willed her a slave in appreciation of her generosity in turning over to her husband's children by his first marriage, her entire share in his estate.]

V. Kerrenhappuch Lane, born Feb. 8, 1744. Her Scriptural but unusual name has been a great trial to copyists. It seems to have been written sometimes Kerren Happuch, and has been variously guessed as Kearn H. Lane, Heath H. Lane, Kenenhuppuck, etc. Her father's will says Keron. She married George Smith, twin of Withers who married her sister Jane. The twins were halfbrothers of Temple Smith who married her sister Lydia Lane. George Smith and Kerrenhappuch had eight children: 1. Weathers (Withers) Smith, in Montgomery Co. Ky. 1794; 2. James Smith; 3. Samuel Smith; 4. Temple Smith; 5. Lane Smith; 6. Nancy Smith, married —— Whaley; 7. Sally Smith married —— Thrift, 3 ch.; 8. William Smith [died before Oct. 6, 1821] son Geo. D. Smith. All except Withers probably remained in Virginia. "Extra Billy" Smith, General C.S.A.M.C. and Governor of Virginia, is said to have been a descendant of Kerrenhappuch and George, but I have been unable to find any statement of the line.

VI. Hardage Lane, born January 1746; died Jan. 21, 1803; married (1) Rachel Beall, daughter of Ninian Beall (son of Ninian Beall); married (2) Mary Greenfield; lived Montgomery Co. Md.; Gentleman Justice of Loudoun Co. and member of the county Committee of Safety. Children of first marriage: 1. Dr. Hardage Lane; 2. James Beall Lane; 3. Elvira Lane, married Gov. Ninian Edwards of Illinois, son of Benjamin Edwards and Margaret Beall (sister of Rachel who married Hardage Lane); Gov. Edwards and Elvira Lane were first cousins; 4. Lydia Lane married Wm. Coleman; 5. Julia Lane married Thomas van Swearengen; 6. Harvey Lane; 7. Keturah Lane married John Keene; 8. Henry Lane; 9. Andrew Lane married Ann Carr Lane (b. 1781, dau of Wm. Lane and Sarah Lane, dau of Wm. Carr Lane and Ann Wilson) children William Hardage Lane and Samuel Lane.

VII. Jane Lane born Dec. 30, 1748 married Withers Smith, twin of George; she died June 15, 1825; he died before 1814. Children: 1. Hardage Smith, unmarried; 2. Charles Smith married Polly Allen 1803, Bourbon County; 3. George Alexander Smith; 4. Anne Smith married Charles Rogers; 5. Margaret Smith married Benjamin Thomas [grandson, Gov. Claude Mathews of Indiana]; 6. Susannah Smith married Charles Rogers [?]; 7. Lydia Smith married Temple Smith; 8. James W. Smith [probably should be earlier in list]. Withers and Jane Smith are buried on the "George A. Smith Place" in Bourbon County, Kentucky.

VIII. Lydia Lane born June 28, 1751, married Temple Smith, half-brother of twins George and Withers. [See section on Ancestry of Joseph Smith who married Sally Taylor.]

IX. Anne Lane, who married Judge Henry Payne, mentioned earlier in this section, mother of Theodosia (Payne) Taylor.

II. Joseph Taylor

Joseph Taylor, John Taylor's second son, followed him into the Baptist ministry. Joseph was born August 17, 1786, at Clear Creek, Woodford County, Kentucky. He was probably named for his father's uncle Joseph, who had made John Taylor his heir. The first son had been named Benjamin, rather significantly in a day when it was almost a tradition to name the first son for the father's father. There was evidently not too much sympathy between John Taylor and his father Lazarus Taylor, in spite of the fact that John had lived at home till he was thirty years old and he says his father had provided him "some broken land" where he raised a crop to feed his horse for his itinerant preaching. John Taylor mentions his parents' dismay at his affiliation with the Baptists, and the fact that his uncle Joseph was the only member of his family who saw religious matters as he did. And he also mentioned that "through the intemperate use of spirits . . . my poor father had so far consumed his living that hard labour was my inevitable lot in raising." None of his four sons was named Lazarus; but Benjamin was certainly named for Benjamin Cave, his wife's grandfather, justice, vestryman, and Burgess, the progenitor to whom the family might point with pride. And then came Joseph, named for the uncle who had been closest to John Taylor of any member of his own family. Joseph was a student at Transylvania University in 1807-8, with his older brother Benjamin. Although he became a preacher, he was evidently a long time making up his mind to that calling, for he was not baptised until 1827, at the Buck Run Church, when he was forty years old. He was ordained about two years later, preached in Franklin and surrounding counties, and moved to Illinois in 1834, where he lived in Clinton County. He returned to Lexington on a visit in 1845, and died there in September of typhoid fever, at the home of E. W. Craig; buried in the family cemetery in Franklin County.[6] The well-known colored preacher, G. W. Dupee, was born his slave. His wife seems to have been Mary M. Fogg, daughter of James Fogg and his wife Elizabeth Dupuy (who married secondly George Smith). The Dupuy family were descended from the Huguenot refugee, Count Bartholomew Dupuy. Children of Joseph and Mary Fogg Taylor were: John, Elizabeth, Benjamin, Joel, Dione, Lucy, and Joseph. [Ermina Jett Darnell, in *Forks of Elkhorn Church*.

III. Nancy Taylor

This oldest daughter was born December 14, 1788, at Clear Creek in Woodford County. Here the tradition was followed "oldest daughter for the mother's mother," and Nancy was named for her maternal grandmother, Ann (Cave) Kavanaugh, who had been called Nancy. Nancy married twice. Her first husband was John D. Gray; the time and place of their marriage is not known, nor the date of his death. They had three children:

---

[6] OBSERVER AND REPORTER, Lexington, Kentucky, newspaper for Sept. 27, 1845.

1. Mary Jane Gray, who married Rice Smith, 1831, in Franklin Co., Ky.
2. Elizabeth T. Gray, who married in 1832 in Franklin County, Peter Forsee, son of William Forsee and wife Mary Ann Smith.
3. Sally Ann Gray, married Peter Forsee in 1835, after her sister's death.

Nancy's second marriage was June 15, 1829, to Col. Thomas L. Tate, a soldier of the War of 1812, whose father James Tate had fought in the Revolution. By this marriage one son was born May 2, 1831, James W. Tate; died about 1890; married June 3, 1856 to Lucy J. Hawkins, daughter of W. W. Hawkins of Woodford County, had one daughter Edmonia. James W. Tate was a merchant, Assistant Secretary of State, and for eighteen years the Treasurer of the State of Kentucky. January 1887, he was impeached because of a deficit in his accounts. He left the country, supposedly for South America, and his later whereabouts are unknown. A suit brought by his daughter against a life insurance company for the amount of a policy, stated that he had not been heard from for seven years, and that at her last knowledge of him, he had been in California. So far as any one knew, he appeared to have taken little with him, and not to have profited personally. It was said that he had been overindulgent to an extravagant daughter. He had long been known as "Honest Dick Tate," and was highly regarded in the community. Probably no one will ever know what actually occurred.[7] His mother, Nancy Taylor Gray Tate, had fortunately died long before this, in 1847.

IV. POLLY TAYLOR

Polly Taylor was born at Clear Creek, in Woodford County, Kentucky, June 17, 1792; died January 7, 1879; married in 1805 William French, later a Captain in the War of 1812. He was the son of James French II (1765–1835) who had come from Virginia to Lincoln County, Kentucky after serving in the Revolution, and was married at Boonesboro June 19, 1783, to Keziah Calloway, daughter of Col. Richard Calloway. She was "pretty Kizzie Calloway," younger sister of the two girls who, with Daniel Boone's daughter, were captured by Indians and rescued three days later near Mount Sterling. According to tradition, she was too young to be allowed to go with them, and so escaped that terrifying adventure. She was married in a dress of her own weaving. James and Keziah French had two sons and four daughters, William, Richard, Catherine Farrow, Susanna Farrow, Theodora Hood, Lina Smith, Captain William being the oldest. Will of James French II is in Will Bk. D, p. 515, Montgomery Co., Ky. William and Polly (Taylor) French went to housekeeping in a brick house built for them by her father, the Rev. John Taylor, on their farm on the Georgetown turnpike. There they are said to have "dispensed an elegant hospitality." Handsome family silver of theirs, still extant, testifies in some degree to that

---

[7] Darnell, FORKS OF ELKHORN CHURCH, p. 138; Johnson, *History of Franklin County*, pp. 146, 209 et seq.; Centennial Edition of Frankfort newspaper, 1886.

"elegance." They were members of the Buck Run Baptist Church, for which her father wrote the constitution. William French died in 1863, his wife sixteen years later. They are buried on what was probably their farm, in Franklin County on the Georgetown road, about ten miles from Frankfort. I am indebted to Miss Hattie Scott of Frankfort for this information, and for copying the marking of the graves.

William French b. March 1, 1785, died March 16, 1863

Polly French, wife of Wm. French (dau of Rev. John Taylor) born June 17, 1792, d. Jan. 7, 1879 (d. at residence of son John W. French)

William and Polly French had eleven children. His will, in Franklin County, is in Will Book 3, p. 92; dated Jan. 19, 1863; proved April 2, 1863; executors B. T. Quinn, Joseph L. French, J. Wickliffe French.

Children of William and Polly (Taylor) French:

I. William French—b. 1806; m. Martha Wingate (dau. of Isaac Wingate of Frankfort, Ky.) and had:
   1. Sallie French—m. W. L. Pence, and had—
      Luther Pence—m. —— Fincel, had 2 ch.
      Sallie French Pence—m. Thos. Jesse, no ch.
   2. Sidney French—m. Helen Richard, Springfield, Ills. and had:
      Florence French—m. J. Craik Jackson, Frankfort, Ky., had dau.
         Helen Page Jackson—m. Chas. J. Cooper, has son
            Chas. J. Cooper, Jr., student at Georgia Tech.
      Jennie French—d. young, unmarried
      Anne French—m. Rob Farmer, has son
         Sidney French Farmer—m. Beverly Meyer in 1948.
   3. Isaac French—m. Elizabeth Richard, had children:
      Jay French, Susan French and Clara French, Springfield, Ills.
   4. Susan French—m. Logan McKee, Frankfort, Ky., no ch.
   5. William French—d. unmarried, Frankfort, Ky.
   6. Laura French—d. unmarried, 1947, Frankfort, Ky.

Martha Wingate French is said to have died at the age of 92, but the date is unknown. Repeated attempts have been made to obtain information on this line, but such descendants as have been reached have not been disposed to answer letters.

II. James French
III. Joseph French, died after 1863, when he served as father's executor (said to have dropped dead on Elkhorn Creek bank). Married Emma ——; no children.

IV. Sidney French
V. Stephen French
VI. Richard C. French
VII. Benjamin French
VIII. Catherine French; married —— Ford
IX. Jane French; married LeGrand Buford, 1828 Franklin Co., Ky.
X. Sarah Ann French, born Franklin County, Kentucky; married the Rev. B. T. Quinn of Georgetown, son of Richard and Cynthia (Nall) Quinn. He was born in Scott County, Sept. 15, 1825, educated Georgetown College 1842-4, then began teaching and preaching. He had charge of several churches, one at Big Spring, Woodford County. After the death of Sallie (French) Quinn, the Rev. B. T. Quinn married (2) Cerella Stapp of Madison County, Indiana; and (3) a Miss Wingate of Franklin County, daughter of Isaac and Jane (Snead) Wingate. Perrin's *History of Bourbon, Scott, Harrison and Nicholas Counties* says he was a Baptist, a Democrat, and a Granger, and that he "has two children," but does not name them or say by which marriage.
XI. John Wickliffe French, born June 5, 1823; died January 31, 1896; married Amanda Chinn (born 1831; died April 24, 1895) on January 27, 1851. She was the daughter of Franklin and Mary (Scott) Chinn. John Wickliffe and Amanda (Chinn) French lived near the mouth of Elkhorn Creek; there most of their children were born. Later they moved to North Fork, a small settlement in Franklin County now called Switzer. They lived in a small cabin near the front gate of the property until the large house could be built; it is still there and occupied by a grandson.

Children of John Wickliffe French and his wife Amanda Chinn:
1. Joseph French, born Nov. 2, 1851; died Oct. 29, 1852.
2. Mary Katherine French, born March 14, 1854; died July 12, 1918; married James William Jones February 16, 1882; they had nine children; lived on a farm adjoining that of her father. James Jones died Feb. 7, 1945, aged 91. Children:
    a. Mary Alice Jones born Sept. 19, 1883; died Sept. 26, 1885.
    b. James Sidney Jones born July 27, 1885; married Bonnie Smith Mitchell; no ch.
    c. William French Jones born March 21, 1887.
    d. Thomas Dawson Jones born Feb. 5, 1889; married Lurlene Newton; one daughter Ann Thomas Jones.
    e. Russell Jones, born March 17, 1891; married Sarah Claxon; two children: William Russell Jones, and Sarah Katherine Jones who married Sherwood Bennett.

- f. Amanda Elizabeth Jones, born May 11, 1894.
- g. Edward Jones born May 7, 1897; married Margaret Moorman, one daughter Mary Jones.
- h. Howard Jones born Jan. 21, 1899; married Christine Poe; children: Howard Phillip, Vivian Amanda, and Florence.
- i. Louis Jones born Dec. 8, 1901.

3. William French, born Jan. 19, 1856 (another record says August); died unmarried April 8, 1926.
4. Franklin French, born Dec. 4, 1857; died Jan. 6, 1943.
5. Alice French, living 1948, Franklin County, Kentucky.
6. Wickliffe French born July 4, 1861; died infancy.
7. Robert Lee French born July 27, 1863; married Sarah Head Pryor (daughter of Dr. Green Lewis Pryor and wife Martha Ann Head in Monterey, Kentucky, October 12, 1892. Had two daughters:
   - a. Harriet Pryor French married William Whitley Moore, their daughter Sarah French Moore[8] married Pershing Wilson Clough; children:
     Susan Harriet Clough
     James Lee Whitley Clough
   - b. Alice Lee French married James Lister Darlington.

   Robert Lee French died May 13, 1934.
8. Dr. Richard Calloway French born Aug. 18, 1865; died Nov. 1900; graduated from Louisville School of medicine, practiced in Midway, Kentucky.
9. Benjamin Quinn French born Feb. 12, 1866; died Aug. 9, 1945.
10. Elizabeth French born Sept. 19, 1872; died Dec. 18, 1894; married the Rev. Fred W. Eberhardt of Bourbon County, Ky.

V. Jane Taylor

Jane Taylor was born June 21, 1795, at Bullittsburg, in Boone County, Kentucky. She was married twice: first to William Plummer, son of William and Rachel (Hobbs) Plummer, and by this marriage had one daughter Ophelia, whose birth is recorded in her grandfather's Bible (the Rev. John Taylor), October 14, 1816. Ophelia Plummer was married in 1836 to George W. Triplett, son of Thomas and Rebecca Wagner Triplett. She had one daughter Ophelia Triplett who married Dr. Samuel. Jane Taylor Plummer married second James Elliott in 1827, in Franklin County, Kentucky. According to one record, he had been married in 1812 to Sarah G. Peart, date of her death not given.

[8] I am indebted to Mrs. Clough for family records on the French family, especially John Wickliffe French's line.

James Elliott was the son of the Rev. James Elliott and his wife Mary, who had come to Woodford County from Virginia. Jane had four children by the Elliott marriage, three born in Kentucky. They moved about 1836 to Sangamon County Illinois, living at Richland. A letter from Jane's younger sister, Sally (Taylor) Smith, to Sally's daughter Eliza, written probably about 1843, shows that Eliza had gone to Kentucky to visit with her Aunt Jane and that they were visiting the French family. She asks that "dear little Ophy" add a postscript, which must refer to Ophelia Triplett, Jane's grand-daughter, who was born about 1837, and must have been at least six years old to be of writing age. In this letter she says, "Tell sister Mr. Elliott looks disconsolate; Jimmy says he sits on the style looking toward Kentucky a good part of his time. We try to comfort him in the way of bread and pies but that is not Jane." James Elliott died in June, 1856, in Sangamon County, Illinois. His wife survived him some years. The date of her death is not known, but she was still living about 1877.

Children of James and Jane (Taylor) Elliott:
   I. John James Elliott, born 1828, Franklin County, Kentucky; died 1861 Springfield, Illinois.
   II. William B. Elliott, born 1830; married Jacksonport, Arkansas, to Ellen Tussell, who was born there; had two sons:
      1. Tom Elliott
      2. Mormon Elliott
   William R. Elliott died at Jacksonport 1864, and his wife remarried.
   III. Temple Elliott, born Dec. 9, 1835, Franklin County, Kentucky; married Oct. 8, 1862 at Elkhart, Illinois, to Mary Constant; lived in Springfield, Illinois, and later his mother, Jane Taylor Elliott, made her home with them. Temple Elliott was deputy sheriff 1870-2, and later was with a Springfield newspaper, the *State Register*. Children of Temple and Mary (Constant) Elliott
      1. Hallie Elliott married Franklin Ridgeley; children: Temple, Mary Jane, and Nicholas.
      2. Archie Elliott.
      3. Rita Elliott.
      4. Harry Elliott.
      5. Griffith Elliott.
   IV. Lewis Elliott [?]

VI. John Wickliffe Taylor

It would be interesting to know the origin of the name Wickliffe in this family. This is the first time it appears. Both Polly and Sally Taylor named sons Wickliffe, whether for this brother or for some earlier source from which his own name comes, does not appear.

John Wickliffe Taylor was born at Bullitsburg, Boone County, Kentucky, April 21, 1798. He married Jemima Gray (1804–1874) called "Mimy," in Trimble County, June 1, 1820. Her parentage is not known; possibly she was of the same family as Nancy Taylor's first husband. She died near Wheatfield; and after her death in 1874, John Wickliffe Taylor (Uncle Wick in the family) lived with his sister Mrs. Joseph Smith (Sally Taylor) at Bates, Sangamon County, Illinois. He served from 1852–1856 as Judge of the Sangamon County Court. Presumably he died in Illinois, but the date is not known.

Children of John Wickliffe Taylor and his wife Jemima Gray:

I. John P. Taylor, born April 10, 1821, in Kentucky; died there July 19, 1832.
II. Benjamin P. Taylor, born Sangamon County, Illinois; died there at three years old.
III. William H. Taylor, born Aug. 2, 1838, Sangamon County, Illinois. Lived for a time in Colorado, later at Wheatfield, Illinois. Not known whether he left descendants.
IV. Sallie Jane Taylor, born Aug. 12, 1843; died April 18, 1858.
V. Matilda Taylor (Matty) married Benjamin Gray; had one daughter Annie M. Gray who married Joseph Sidney Smith (son of Joseph Smith and Sally Taylor); no children.

Unless the third son, William, left descendants, there are none from this family of five children.

VII. CAVE TAYLOR

The youngest son of John and Elizabeth Taylor was named for the family of his mother's mother. He was born September 3, 1800, at Bullittsburg (nearly opposite Lawrenceville, Indiana). He was drowned at ten years old, August 11, 1810, while the family were living at Mount Byrd, in what is now Trimble County, Kentucky, then Henry County. His death, following that of his baby sister next younger, and other calamities from fire, caused his father John Taylor to compare himself to Job in the time of his affliction, and to feel that "the author of this fire" which had started from lightning "would have me leave this place."

VIII. ELIZA TAYLOR

Born June 11, 1803; died August 7, 1803, at Mount Byrd.

IX. SALLY TAYLOR

Sally Taylor, the youngest child, was born November 22, 1807, at Mount Byrd; died in her eighty-eighth year April 21, 1895, at "Elmbrook," east of Springfield, Illinois, the home of her daughter Mrs. David Allen Brown (Eliza Jane Smith). Sally Taylor was married at Frankfort, Kentucky, April 9, 1822, to Joseph Smith. She was fifteen years old; he was thirty. The Taylor family had come to Frankfort in January of 1816, and John Taylor preached in the Senate Chamber, Court House, or wherever the little Baptist congregation could find a meeting-place. After two years, he helped to found the Buck Run Church "within the forks of the Elkhorn" where they built "a snug little brick meeting house, forty feet by thirty." It was probably in this church or in her father's home that Sally was married, the Rev. William Hickman officiating. The bridegroom was injured the day after his marriage, on his way to the "infare," by his horse falling on him, and was always slightly lame thereafter. In 1828, Joseph and Sally Smith moved to a farm six miles east of Frankfort on the Georgetown Pike, where John Taylor had built a stone house for his daughter Sally, as he had done earlier for his daughter Polly when she married William French. By that time, Joseph and Sally (Taylor) Smith had three sons; and they owned farms in Montgomery, Bath, and Owen counties. In January 1823, their oldest son Temple, then ten years old, was drowned in Elkhorn Creek, by his horse falling while fording the stream. The next year, Joseph and Sally Taylor Smith moved to Illinois. The stone house, where they had lived only six years, was sold to Mr. John Lewis, poet, novelist, and celebrated teacher, and there he established a school. He called it "Llangollen" after his former home in Virginia, which had also been a school. It became a landmark in the neighborhood until early in the present century, when it was torn down. The only one of the Smith children born at "Llangollen" was their only daughter Eliza Jane, January 21, 1830. [See frontispiece in *The Register* for July, 1948.]

Joseph Smith bought two sections of land in Sangamon County, Illinois, seven miles west of Springfield at Richland, in what is now Cartwright township. Two more sons were born at Richland: in 1840 Bradford Temple Smith, who died in infancy, and Micajah Wickliffe Dewitt Smith in 1844. In July of 1841, Joseph and Sally Smith were baptised at Richland, (the exact place described in detail in Joseph's Bible entry, quoted later) by William M. Brown, great-grandson of the Rev. William Hickman who had married them in Kentucky. How this event had been so long deferred, under the vigor of the Rev. John Taylor's preaching, is not explained. It seems probable that the Rev. William Brown may have been of the despised "Campbellites" against whom John Taylor had written a pamphlet. Certainly, Sally Smith was a member of that church in her later years. Her father had died six years before in 1835.

Joseph Smith, like the Taylors, had come from Virginia. He was born in Loudoun County, October 29, 1792, tenth child of Temple Smith and his wife Lydia Lane. About 1800, when he was seven or eight years old, his family moved to Kentucky. When he was fifteen, he went into a store in Paris as a clerk, and at twenty-one had his own business in Frankfort. In 1845, eleven years after moving to Illinois, Joseph Smith formed a partnership in the general merchandise business with a remote cousin, James M. Bradford. Under the firm name of Bradford and Smith, they continued in business in Springfield until 1849. He also continued to manage his farm; and served for a time in the State Legislature representing Sangamon County. He died August 2, 1853, at the farm, about six months after the marriage of his only daughter Eliza, to David Allen Brown. A letter written to his wife from Leesburg, Kentucky, dated Jan. 31, 1853, has been preserved—it may have been his last letter home, almost certainly on his last journey. The reason for it appears when he says "the sale of the land comes off on the 14th of Feby and if 1 am not compelled to buy it I will return as soon as the sale is over." There is nothing to indicate whose land it was, but it may have been a part of the estate of Micajah Smith, a brother who died unmarried in 1847 and named Joseph Smith as an executor. Joseph said in the letter that his health was unaltered "but my disease has made me very uncomfortable for a long cold spell of weather" and "it is probable that I shall not see Mary Cable or your other relations as the roads are so bad it is almost equal to death for me to travel over them."

After the death of Joseph Smith, his widow lived for a time at Bates, Illinois, with her son Joseph Sidney Smith (Jay), and later with her daughter Eliza, Mrs. David Allen Brown. She lived to see, in her eight-eighth year, an established community where her sons occupied positions of leadership and usefulness, and where her daughter carried her own qualities into the next generation—best expressed by a friend of Eliza Brown as "that charming faculty of making everyone in her presence comfortable." She died at her daughter's home April 22, 1895.

Children of Joseph and Sally (Taylor) Smith:

  I. Temple Smith, born Jan. 18, 1823; drowned Jan. 2, 1833, at Church's ford on the Main Elkhorn, Franklin County, Kentucky.
  II. John Taylor Smith, born March 6, 1825, Franklin County, Kentucky; died Springfield, Illinois, Jan. 25, 1892; married March 27, 1850 in Springfield, Illinois, to Sophia N. Ridgely. He was a merchant in Springfield from 1844–1874, when he retired; dealt in lands and stocks; director Ridgely National Bank. They had four children, one of whom died in infancy; the others were:
   1. Julia V. Smith, born 1851; died 1873.
   2. Fred E. Smith, born July 18, 1853; graduated June 1876, from West Point; in 1876 was lieut. Co. D, 13th U. S. Inf. stationed at New Orleans; married Mabel Oldham of New York City, had one son, Vincent Smith, born July 9, 1881; lived in Colorado; died in early manhood in California.

3. Jessie Taylor Smith, born Nov. 13, 1864; married John Howe Brown 1891; no children.

III. Joseph Sidney Smith (called Jay) born July 21, 1827, Franklin County, Kentucky; died April 9, 1902, in Santa Rosa Hospital, San Antonio, Texas, where he had gone for his health. He was a Major in the Union Army, serving for three years until wounded and mustered out. Then he crossed the plains with wagons, camped all winter in Nevada, reaching Sacramento in the spring; he came back to Illinois through Panama, spent some time in the cattle trade in Texas and Dodge City and later took up ranching in Montana. The historic winter of 1886-7 destroyed most of his herd, but he built up another fortune from the remnants of the old.[9] When in Illinois, he spent much time with his sister's family, where "Uncle Jay" was much loved. He had no children of his own. His brief marriage to Annie M. Gray proved a tragedy; he discovered the day of his marriage that his bride was insane, and she died soon after. From then on, he devoted himself to his many enterprises, and distributed his affections, and ultimately his property, to his nieces and nephews. Two of those nephews cared for him in his last illness.

IV. Eliza Jane Smith (called "Puss") the only daughter, was born at "Llangollen" in Franklin County, Kentucky, January 21, 1830; moved to Illinois with parents 1834; married at Richland, Illinois, December 8, 1852, to David Allen Brown; had two sons and four daughters; died at the family home "Elmbrook" near Springfield, Illinois, October 1, 1901. David Allen Brown and his twin brother Daniel Calvin Brown, were the first-born of William Bartlett Brown and his wife Harriet Lowry Allen, September 27, 1824, in Green County, Kentucky. The Browns were a Covenanter family, descended from John Brown of Muirkirk in Ayrshire, Scotland (of whom Scott writes in his *Tales of a Grandfather*), shot for his faith by Graham of Claverhouse, in 1685. His widow Isabel took her children to Ireland, and the two sons came to America together in 1720, John and James, with their young families.[10] John Brown and his wife Hannah settled in Paxtang township, Lancaster County, Pennsylvania (now Dauphin County); their son James Brown born 1724 moved west to Carlisle in Cumberland County, which he represented in the Pennsylvania Constitutional Convention 1776, later in the General Assembly. He enlisted in his fifties as a private in the Revolution after the death of his young brother Matthew in service; and died April 17, 1780 while on furlough. By his second wife Mary McClelland, James Brown

---

[9] See RIP VAN WINKLE RETURNS TO THE RANGE, a pamphlet by John Clay, published by Clay, Robinson & Company, Live Stock Commission, printed by James H. Rook Co., Chicago, 1914, for some of Major Smith's range experiences.
[10] Pennsylvania Hist. Register, v. II, no. 1, ser. 3, 1884, p. 47 et seq.

had a son Daniel Brown, born 1799, who moved with the frontier into Kentucky with his young wife Theresa Bartlett from a Beverly, Massachusetts, family. They settled in Green County, where Daniel was a merchant, and a ruling elder until his death in 1846. His son William Bartlett Brown, born 1802, was a pioneer in Illinois, dying there 1852. It was his son David Allen Brown who married Eliza Jane Smith. David grew up in Athens, Illinois, and he and his twin brother were sent to school in Springfield, where they earned their first money sawing laths for the State House now the Sangamon County Court House. Young David was reading law with Col. E. D. Baker at the outbreak of the Mexican War; at Col. Baker's suggestion he began organizing a company, later consolidated with a Logan County detachment, and he became a second Lieutenant. He was at the bombardment of Vera Cruz, and the battle of Cerro Gordo in 1847, mentioned in dispatches for bravery in action and promoted to aide de camp on the regimental staff. After his regiment was ordered home, he resumed his law studies, this time in the office of Lincoln and Herndon. After his admission to the bar, he served for six years as circuit clerk of Menard County, and later was in partnership with his brother Christopher in law practice in Springfield. After his marriage to Eliza Smith, they moved in Springfield; in 1860 built a home at Bates; and in 1893 bought "Elmbrook" east of Springfield; here David Brown died Feb. 25, 1895. It remained the family home until the death of Eliza Smith Brown, October 1, 1901. Children of David and Eliza Brown:

1. Sallie Clara Brown, born August 14, 1856; died Dec. 9, 1932, unmarried. She is the member of the family chiefly responsible for assembling these and other records, and took great interest in the work of the Illinois Historical Society. She was educated under private teachers and in Monticello Seminary.
2. William Joseph Brown born January 18, 1859; died March 31, 1911, Kansas City, Missouri; married October 22, 1894 to Harriet May Gardner (daughter of Hiram Edwin and Harriet Eliza (Bradford) Gardner); educated under private teachers and at the military school at Champaign, Illinois; with his uncle Joseph Sidney Smith in the cattle business in Montana; lived in Springfield, Illinois; El Dorado, Kansas; Spokane, Washington; Denver, Colorado; Paolo, Kansas; before moving to Kansas City, Missouri. One daughter, Dorothy Allen Brown, born May 14, 1896; married Dale Moore Thompson July 2, 1921; son William Brown Thompson born April 6, 1922, Kansas City, Missouri.
3. Harriet Lowry Brown (Harriet Jane in father's Bible) born at Bates September 19, 1861; died Springfield Hospital June 21,

1839; educated at home and at Monticello Seminary; married April 5, 1894 to the Rev. William A. Galt at "Elmbrook" her parents' home near Springfield. The young minister was a home missionary to the Omaha Indians in Nebraska, and he took his bride there. Later he held other pastorates under the Home Mission board of the Presbyterian Church in various parts of the country, finally retiring to live in Decatur, Illinois. After his death in 1926, she came to Springfield, living near, and later with, her three sisters. The Galts had no children.

4. Mary Elizabeth Brown, born at Bates, May 27, 1864; educated at home and at Monticello; died August 2, 1939, unmarried.

5. Jay Taylor Brown, born at Bates, October 6, 1870; died there May 22, 1877, of an infected knee from a fall.

6. Carolyn Allen Brown, born at Bates, March 7, 1873; died in her home on South Second Street, Springfield, Illinois, June 8, 1940; married June 4, 1902 to Harrison Edward Foster, who died January 17, 1905. Their only child Eliza Brown Foster (named for her Grandmother, and like her called "Puss") was born November 10, 1903; married January 4, 1941 to Thomas Lorton Pankey, who had been a classmate at the University of Illinois. By a former marriage he had a daughter, Jane. They live in Milwaukee, Wisconsin.

V. Bradford Temple Smith, born January 8, 1840; died May 21, 1840 of whooping-cough; buried near the home of James Elliott, at Richland, Sangamon County, Illinois.

VI. Micajah Wickliffe DeWitt Smith (later called DeWitt Wickliffe) born December 13, 1844 at Richland, Illinois; died Springfield, Illinois, 192–; married (1) Adelia McConnell, September 1, 1864 (daughter of Andrew and Augusta (Rogers) McConnell) had four children all born at Bates, Illinois:

1. Sidney Andrew Smith, born 1866; married Gertrude Lapsley of Kansas City, Missouri, 1894; no children.

2. Eliza Adelia Smith (called Lyle) born 1867; married 1890 Harry M. Pindell of Peoria, Illinois, editor of the Peoria newspaper. Children:

 a. Frances Adelia Pindell married Carl Slane
 son Harry Pindell Slane

 b. Elizabeth Augusta Pindell married the Rev. Howard Talbot
 daughter Betty Talbot

3. Temple Smith born 1870; died 1893, unmarried.

4. Augusta Smith, born 1875; married 1899 Charles VanBergen Carroll

daughter Edith Lyle Carroll married George Luthy, president of bank in Peoria, Illinois; daughter Carroll Luthy and son George Luthy

Augusta (Smith) Carroll married (2) John G. Oglesby of Springfield, son of Gov. Oglesby of Illinois.

DeWitt Wickliffe Smith married (2) Gertrude Moore, in 1895; had three children, all born in Springfield, Illinois.

5. Mary Temple Smith married Stuart Broadwell
6. William Lane Smith (called Pete)
7. Elizabeth Wilde Smith married Emmerson Anthony of Peoria, Illinois.

Sally Smith's will, dated May 19, 1894, proved May 21, 1895, Sangamon County, Illinois leaves all her property in equal parts to her daughter Eliza Jane Brown and to her son DeWitt W. Smith. She adds: "I make no provision for my son Joseph S. Smith for the reason that he requests me not to do so, neither do I make any provision for the heirs of my deceased son John Taylor Smith for the reason that he requested me not to do so for him when he was living, and for the further reason that his heirs are already amply provided for." DeWitt W. Smith was made executor; Joel B. Brown and Edwards Brown, witnesses.

Copy of the Family Record in the Bible of Joseph Smith, publication date 1812:

MARRIAGES

Joseph Smith and Sarah Taylor m. by the Rev. William Hickman Sr., on the ninth day of April 1822 in Franklin County, Ky.

Joseph Smith and Sarah Smith were baptised in Richland below Harrison's Mill being in the section 36 Town 17 Range 7 of the 3rd Principal Menden west on Friday July 10, 1841 by William H. Brown, great grandson of the above named Hickman.

BIRTHS

Temple Smith was born 4th April 1744.

Lydia Lane his consort was born June 28th 1751.

John Taylor was born 27th Oct. 1752 who was married Sept. 1782 to Elizabeth Kavanaugh born 18th June 1761.

Joseph Smith was born 29th Oct. 1792.

Sarah Taylor was born 22nd Nov. 1807.

To whom were born

Temple Smith was born 18th Jany. 1823
John Taylor Smith was born 11 o'clock on Sunday evening 6th March 1825
Joseph Sidney Smith was born 21st July 1827 about 3 o'clock A. M.
Elizabeth Jane Smith was born on 21st Jan. 1830 about 2 o'clock Ante Meridian
Bradford Temple Smith was born 8th Jan. 1840
Micajah Wickliffe Dewitt Smith was born 13th Dec. 1844.

DEATHS

Temple Smith was drowned at Church's Ford on Main Elkhorn on Wednesday 2nd Jan. 1833.

Bradford Temple Smith died with whooping cough on 21st May 1840; buried near the residence of James Elliott, at Richland, Sangamon County.

ANCESTRY OF JOSEPH SMITH WHO MARRIED SALLY TAYLOR

This line has not been traced with certainty, beyond Joseph Smith's grandfather. Joseph was the son of Temple Smith, whose father was Nathaniel. The family Bible was lost when Temple's family moved from Virginia to Kentucky; and Smith is not an easy name to trace. Nathaniel Smith was born probably between 1690 and 1700, and died 1762 in Stafford County, Virginia, where his inventory is of record in Deed Book, Liber O, 1748–63. He lived in Overwharton Parish, where the baptisms of his sons George, Withers, and Temple, are recorded, and the death of his wife Elizabeth, April 25, 1752. She is said to have been Elizabeth Temple, but no proof of this has been found. George and Withers were twins, and according to family traditions were half-brothers of Temple, their mother a Miss Withers. That also remains unproved. A Nathaniel Smith of Orange County married a Nancy Withers; but he is definitely not our Nathaniel. George, Withers, and Temple Smith married three sisters, daughters of James and Lydia (Hardage) Lane, and this memorable item of three brothers marrying three sisters is preserved in all branches of the family, and is of real help in tracing the line. Withers married Jane; George married Karenhappuch (named for a daughter of Job); Temple married Lydia. A deed of gift dated Dec. 20, 1752, from Nathaniel Smith to his children [Liber C, No. 1, p. 386] shows that he had children much older than these three, possibly by a still earlier marriage, living in Fairfax County: Clator, Nathaniel, Benjamin, and Susannah (wife of John Cotton), also daughters Sarah and Jemima, living in Stafford. Evidence seems to point to Joseph Smith of Westmoreland County (1651–1718) as the father of Nathaniel, but proof is still lacking. It has been suggested that the name Clator (Clater, Claytor) among Nathaniel's older children, might give a clue to his first wife's maiden name, but that is conjecture only. Clator appears to have been Nathaniel's oldest son; he was appointed guardian of his young brother or half-brother, Temple Smith, May 11, 1762, with Charles Tyler, Jr., and John Peak, named as his securities for his bond [Loudoun OB 1, p. 584].

Temple Smith was born April 21, 1745, and married about 1769. He had moved to Kentucky by 1797; and died in Harrison County near Leesburg, February 3, 1818. His wife Lydia Lane was born June 28, 1751; died in Leesburg, Kentucky, August 8, 1841. Children of Temple and Lydia Smith were: 1. Amelia (Milly) Smith married William Stowers, 2. Jane Smith married Archibald Perrin, 3. Nancy Smith married Major Thomas R. Magee, 4. Annie Smith married Archibald Shanks, 5. Betsey Smith, unmarried, 6. Micajah Smith, unmarried, 7. Hannah Hardage Smith married Col. (later Major General) William Elliott Boswell, 8. Joseph Smith married Sally Taylor (dau Rev. John Taylor), 9. Gustavus Smith, unmarried.

A descendant of George Smith (the twin who remained in Virginia), Mr. A. Lawrence Leigh of Vienna, Virginia, has written me that George had seven children: Temple II (died 1829 unmarried), Wethers, Ann, Samuel, William, Lane, and Sally. He is descended from Samuel, who married Eliza Offutt, and they had a son Temple III who married Sarah Elizabeth Oliver. A cousin of Mr. Leigh, Mrs. Gene Shelly Thatcher of Washington, has written me:

> My grandfather Temple Smith's grandfather was George who married one of the Lane sisters. *His mother was a Withers* as you already have the record. My grandmother Sarah Oliver Smith, widow of Temple, had volumes of letters over two hundred years old and when she came to live with us she rented the old Temple Smith homestead. They neglected to move the letters and a tenant took liberty to make a bonfire of the entire contents which was four large bags dating back to their first voyage to this country. But as a little girl I remember my grandmother telling me the Smith family was connected with George Washington. I do remember she spoke of the Lewises, Douglasses and Washingtons in a line of my mother's direct ancestors. That has been over fifty years ago so you can imagine how faint in my memory it could be . . . I do know they came up from Northumberland County and on to Fairfax County. The site of our home was built on George Fairfax's, when he either moved or died the latter part of sixteen hundred or early seventeen hundred. There is also a family connection. The records of Fairfax Court House were burned during the Revolutionary War so it is impossible to trace from there, but Prince William court house has records of some of the original Smith family that I have not had time to go into. The Smith family in Maryland are of the same line, as both Offutts (my grandfather's mother's) line and the Smiths settled there in early seventeen hundred. That is just across the river from Virginia. My mother was Sally Temple Smith named after her father and his sister. My great aunts were Sally

back three generations. The family were great land owners and donated land for Andrew Chapel church where many descendants are buried.

Withers Smith (often called Wethers or Weathers) appears in Fairfax and Loudoun records, and in June 1780 the Loudoun court recommended Wethers Smith for a commission as 2d Lieut. This item, as well as the 1752 deed of gift, were sent to me by Col. Arthur C. Rogers of Alexandria, Virginia, who says he has found no record of Withers Smith's appointment of service, but that his name appears on a tablet in Paris, Kentucky, erected in memory of Revolutionary soldiers who died citizens of Bourbon County, and that an application for the Children of the American Revolution says he was second lieutenant to Captain William Lane. Col. Rogers adds:

> About the turn of the century, Withers Smith and family migrated to Kentucky, where he took up thousands of acres of bluegrass land, and where he signed himself "Weathers Smith, Gent." He and his wife Jane Lane were buried in the family graveyard of his son George Alexander Smith, on the Bourbon County farm which, when I saw the graves in 1897, was still known as the George A. Smith place, though George A., an 1812 soldier, had died in 1854.

According to Perrin's *History of Bourbon, Scott, Harrison and Nicolas Counties* (p. 448) Withers Smith had seven children: 1. Charles Smith, 2. George A. Smith, 3. Hardridge [Hardage] Smith, 4. James Smith, 5. Margaret Smith, 6. Susan Smith, 7. Lydia Smith.

Obviously, the descendants of John Taylor must be more numerous than this article shows. All that are known to me have been included. In the interests of an accurate record, it is again urged that those who have further information sent it either to me (Mrs. Dale M. Thompson, 6435 Pennsylvania Avenue, Kansas City 5, Missouri) or to the Kentucky Historical Society. Also, where data given here is at variance with other records, I shall be grateful for that information. In addition to the sources cited, I am greatly indebted to the Society's tireless secretary, Mr. Bayless Hardin, not only for searching out material but for recognizing pertinent items in unlikely places and passing them on to me. Material concerning Taylor descendants in Illinois is drawn in part from Powers' *Early Settlers of Sangamon County*, and largely from papers of my aunt, Sallie C. Brown, whose painstaking effort over many years assembled from living memory, from old letters and records, and from voluminous correspondence, family history which otherwise would have been lost.

ADDITIONAL NOTES ON THE JOHN TAYLOR FAMILY

BY

DOROTHY BROWN THOMPSON

Taylor Graves

John Taylor's grave, with five others of his family, was found in a small private cemetery formerly on their own farm by Sarah (French) Clough, a descendent of John Taylor's daughter, Polly (Taylor) French, in August, 1950. The cemetery is a part of the Bedford Macklin farm, one-half mile from Forks of Elkhorn on the Georgetown Pike. [See also KY. REG. vol. 6, pp 66-67, Sept. 1908, *Chronicles of the Old Neighborhood by Mrs. Jennie C. Morton.*] Other graves of the Macklin family were moved to Frankfort. The six stones remaining are all upright and facing east, toward a cliff above Elkhorn Creek. In order from north to south, the inscriptions are:

Rev. John Taylor Born October 27 1752 Died April 12th 1835	Elizabeth Taylor Born June 18th 1765 Died December 24th 1832	Rev. Joseph Taylor Born Aug 17 1786 Died Sep 23 1845
Elizabeth T. Forsee was born June 23 1811 and died August 6 1833	Nancy wife of Col. Thomas L. Tate Born Dec. 14 1788 Died Sep 24 1847	Col Thomas L Tate Born Aug 14 1787 Died Nov 7 1852 Soldier of War of 1812

Mrs. Clough had received a clue to the location of the grave from Mrs. Ermina Darnell, author of FORKS OF ELKHORN CHURCH; and had phoned Mrs. Macklin, asking permission to come to the farm. A letter from Mrs. Clough to Dorothy Brown Thompson, written in September 1950, describes their visit, and Mrs. Macklin, their charming hostess who spoke warmly of the long-time friendship between the French and Macklin families:

> No words can give an idea of the beauty of the bluegrass pastures, or the black Angus cattle. I could almost visualize the old road . . . we drove through the gate that did lead to the mansion and stopped; we could see the depression where the gray stone building stood; the rest was rank with

weeds, grass and trees in stately ruin. The house burnt about 1919, but I could see it as she descibed it with the precise flower-beds, neatly cut lawn, and handsome trees. Above all, the ever-changing and beautiful view of Elkhorn Creek. About one hundred yards beyond this, and through a devastating thicket, we found the burial place. Only six graves remained . . . Ten paces east would have you against a big tree or hanging on a barb-wire fence. That was all between you and a cliff sheer down to the creek. North and south was open field, I suppose, but waist-high in iron-weed and other hay-fever producers. West was the same—no fence, no boundary, no nothing. There were four other places that may be graves, only rocks set upright in the ground. Mrs. Macklin says negroes were also buried near there. I got down in the burrs and read the inscriptions . . . some hard to read, had to have paper laid over them and rubbed with a pencil . . . The acreage Rev. Taylor owned was immense. The present Macklin farm is worthy of the name "estate." The farms he gave Polly and Sally were mere drops in the bucket and were more than a mile from his own house, clear across the creek. He wasn't very far from the site of Buck Run Church (then) as the crow flies, but there is at least a mile of winding road out of the farm to the pike from where the old house stood . . . Look at the map in the front of Mrs. Darnell's book FORKS OF ELKHORN CHURCH. Find Forks of Elkhorn and the name G. Smith. That little dot is the site of the old house and the burial place of the Rev. Taylor. See how far Llangollen is? Mrs. Macklin said Rev. Taylor built the old house.

Elizabeth (Kavenaugh) Taylor, wife of the Rev. John Taylor, was evidently the first to be buried here; her death-date is 1832. Elizabeth Forsee's is 1833, grand-daughter of the first Elizabeth, and no doubt her name-sake. She was the daughter of Nancy Taylor by her first marriage to John D. Gray. Nancy had also another daughter, Sally Ann, by her Gray marriage, and both Gray girls married Peter Forsee. Peter and his second wife evidently are not buried here, unless theirs are the unmarked graves, which is unlikely. The next grave to be added to the family plot was that of the Rev. John Taylor in 1835; then the Rev. Joseph Taylor's ten years later, 1845. Joseph Taylor was living in Illinois at that time, but died while visiting in Kentucky. The next date is Nancy Taylor Gray Tate, wife of Col. Thomas L. Tate, in 1847. Col. Tate's in 1852 is the last.

The French family of John Taylor's oldest daughter Polly, had their own burial place on their farm. See the inscriptions from this family cemetery in the KENTUCKY REGISTER for April, 1950. These also were copied by Sarah French Clough (Mrs. P. W. Clough) of Paris, Kentucky.

John Wickliffe Taylor, Jane Taylor Elliott, and Sally Taylor Smith, all children of John Taylor, had moved to llinois. Where Benjamin Taylor's family is buried is not known. This family, of John Taylor's oldest son, remains untraced, and the writer still hopes to hear from some descendant.

Nancy Taylor's Marriage to John D. Gray

Mrs. Darnell is also responsible for clearing up the uncertainity about the parentage of Nancy Taylor's first husband, John D. Gray. She found this item in the Acts of the Kentucky Legislature, dated Dec. 10, 1822:

> John D. Gray died October 1, 1822, leaving 400 acres in Gallatin. Commissioners appointed were Presley Gray (his father); Benjamin and William Gray (his brothers); John Taylor (his wife's father); and John W. Taylor (his wife's brother). John D. Gray sold to Benjamin Taylor of Franklin County ten acres on the Ohio River.

This last item may indicate that Benjamin Taylor's family should be looked for in Gallatin, but Benjamin and Elizabeth Taylor [2d wife] were living in Fayette County when they sold his share of his father's estate in 1835:

> Deed to Addison Lewis 1835 from the children of John Taylor: Benjamin and Elizabeth Taylor of Fayette; John W. and Mary Taylor; Thomas L. and Nancy Tate; William and Polly French; James and Jane Elliott; Joseph and Sally Smith.

The identification of Presley Gray as John D. Gray's father has its background story in John Taylor's HISTORY OF TEN CHURCHES, pp. 132-133, 135, 137, when John Taylor tells of his trip from Bullittsburg in Boone County, to Gallatin, in 1800, to survey the land he had bought there. He was entertained by Captain Gray on Corn Creek, later Colonel Presley Gray. They became close friends, and he describes in some detail the religious experience of Captain Gray and his wife, and their baptism at Corn Creek by John Taylor. Probably the Jemima Gray who later married John Wickliffe Taylor, was of the same family. The deed above names John W. Taylor's wife as Mary, while Joseph Taylor, who had a wife Mary, is not named among the children. This looks like a telescoping of the two names, and probably indicates miscopying somewhere down the line.

In connection with the account of the Grays, we find John Taylor's only attempt at verse-making which has so far come to light. While it cannot be called inspired poetry, at least it does rhyme and scan with absolute correctness. John Taylor had stopped at Corn Creek on a pastoral tour he was taking with William Cave in 1800. They found Mrs. Gray in great distress of mind (this was just before their decision to be baptized) and also she was disturbed that her husband was away from home. He had gone after runaway horses and was not expected to return before the time they must leave. Since John Taylor did not expect to see Captain Gray, he wrote him a letter, which he said was meant to express "all the friendship and tenderness that one man could to another, but finding I came very short of the feelings of my heart, I now recollect I closed with a single verse following:

> Now to conclude, my dear friend Gray,
> It is but little I can say—
> But 'tis a truth, I wish you well,
> More than my pen or tongue can tell."

Captain Gray did return before their departure, and the letter, or subsequent discussions, evidently helped to resolve his difficulties. Taylor says, "Sometime after this I baptized both Gray and his wife, but not at the same time. They were among the first fruits at Corn-creek."

Correction of the list of children of Lazarus Taylor and his wife Mary Vesey

This Lazarus Taylor died c. 1726, and was the son of the immigrant John Taylor and his wife Alice Gaskins (Gascoigne), and the father of Aaron Taylor with wife Betty Wildey. In the earlier article [p. 28,* vol. 47, KENTUCKY REGISTER] two daughters were listed for Lazarus and Mary (Vesey) Taylor. There should have been one daughter only, in two marriages. Their daughter Margaret Taylor married (1) George Dameron, (2) Thomas Winter. Her first husband George Dameron (d.1720) was the son of George Dameron and his wife Elizabeth [perhaps Garlington?] widow of John Dennis. The elder George Dameron (d. 1698) was the son of Lawrence and Dorothy Dameron.

By her first marriage, Margaret (Taylor) Dameron had at least two daughters, one of whom married John Waddy; also a son of George Dameron. Evidently Margaret had no children by her marriage to Thomas Winter (d. 1763), whose will names various members of his own and his wife's family, including his godson Thomas, son of John and Elizabeth Waddy.

Further Data on Aaron Taylor and his wife Betty Wilde (Wildey, Wildy)

At the time the article was written for the KENTUCKY REGISTER on *Ancestors and Descendants of the Rev. John Taylor*, [January 1949, vol. 47],** no will of Aaron Taylor had been found, and the family group had been pieced together from other records, chiefly the will of Aaron's bachelor son, Joseph Taylor, who had been tutor to the family of Counselor Carter of Nomini Hall. It now develops that Aaron Taylor did leave a will, which had been overlooked in indexing, possibly because the name is written *Aron*. It is dated Feb. 25, 1734/s; proved December 10, 1746, inventory filed January 11, 1747, estate account recorded March 9, 1752; which would indicate that he probably died late in 1746 or early in 1747. He does not name his wife, so she must have died before 1734/5s. The will follows, Northumberland Co. Rec. Bk. 1743-1749, p. 167a

---
*Page 456, this volume.
**Pages 451-482, this volume.

[I am indebted to Dr. John E. Manahan of Radford, Virginia, for the discovery of this will]:

> In the Name of God Amen I Aron Taylor of the County Northumberland Wiccocomoco parish being Sick and weak but of perfect mind and memory Do make this my last Will and Testament and first and princeibly I give and bequeath my Soul to god that give it and my Body to Earth from whence it Came Trusting in the Merritts of my Blessed Jesus that my Parden is Sealed in heaven before I goe hence and be no more seen as as Tuching my worldly Estate wherewith it hath pleased Almighty God to bless me with in this Life I give Devise and Dispose of it in the following manner and forme, Item I give and bequeath unto my Son Wm. Taylor all my land house and plantation to him and his heirs for ever,—Item I give and bequeath unto my son Joseph Taylor my Negro man named Jemey to him and his heirs for Ever, Item I give and bequeath unto my Daughter Elizabeth Taylor one Gold Ring, Item I give and bequeath all the Remainder of my moveable Estate which I have not above mentioned unto my Son Lazarus Taylor and my Daughter Elizabeth Taylor to be Equally Divided between them and my will is that my Estate Should not be appraised after my Death and my Will is that my three Loveing Brothers Argail Taylor Lazerus Taylor and John Taylor be whole & Sole Executors of this my last will & Testament Rattifying & Confirming this and no other to be my last will & Testament whereunto I do Sett my hand and Seal this twenty fifth Day of February in the year anno: one thousand Seven hundred thirty-four five
>
> Aron Taylor (L I)

Signed Sealed in the presents of us—

John Hornsby   Northum.^d at a court Continued and held for
     her   northumberland County the 10th Day of December 1746
Sarah + Moahan
  mark

This last will and Testament of Aron Taylor Dec.^d was proved in Court by the Oath of John Hornsby a witness thereto and ordered to be Recorded—
—Teste—Billy Clairborne Ct:Cur:

In spite of Aaron Taylor's express wish that his estate be not appraised, it was appraised. Probably this was because of his guardianship of William Butcher, since there is a record of settlement of Wm. Butcher's estate out of Aaron Taylor's dated March 10, 1747, and signed by John Nutt, Josias Basye, and Charles Copedge. The Virginia State Library at Richmond has the record in Northumberland Co.Rec.Bk. 1747-1749, p. 16, Jan.15, 1747. Argail Taylor was executor. The inventory was not impressive—household goods chiefly; one crop of tobacco (but no farm implements); a case of pistols and sword; "one Fine Hatt"; ten books; one negro man. One assumes he had divided his possessions among his children after his wife's death; the only items at all reminiscent of her are "one old wheel and cards & some trifles" and "one old Side Saddle." The inventory was recorded 11th Jany. 1747.

Argail Taylor's memorandum of debts paid out of the estate was recorded March 9, 1752 in Northumberland County. This included items to John Taylor Guardian of Wm. Butcher, to John Knight on his estates account, to Mr. John Graham Crop Tobo, to Mr. Gordon, to Thomas Palmer, to Henry Mayes, to Joseph Taylor, to Joseph Nutt, to Mr. Clairborne, to Mr. James McCall, to Richd. Marsh, to Mr. David Galloway crop tobo, to Mr. David Galloway for Rum for ye funeral, to Mrs. Eliza. Nutt, to Capt. Geo. Conway, to Edwin Fielding, to John Dunaway, to Mr. Francis Brown, to Mr. John Nutt for brandy and cyder at Pagmy [?], to Mr. Thomas Edwards, Senr., by William Galloway, by Robert Nash, by Joseph Webb, by Charles Pritchard, Test Thos. Jones, Jr. Cl. C.

Aaron Taylor's name appears in Northumberland records in 1739 as an appraiser, with William James and John Nutt, of the estate of Richard Helms, Henry Mayes Administrator [North.Co.Rec.Bk. 1738-1743, p. 42]. On the same page, under date of April 9, 1739, the settlement of a difference between Aaron Taylor, administrator of Thomas Butcher deceased, and Michael Tobin, was decided in favor of Taylor on June 11th. Later records [p. 178] show that Aaron Taylor was guardian of William Butcher son of Thomas, and served till his death. His brother John took over the guardianship and served till May of 1751, when he turned over the guardianship to John Knight. Probably this was because of John Taylor's failing health, since he died in October of that year. Wm. Butcher's own will was dated 1757, pr. 1768. The will was proved by the oath of John Knight, his final guardian. He named a wife Hannah and two daughters, and he named in the event of their death, the children of John and William Nutt. What the relationship or friendship may have been between these several families has not yet been determined.

It now seems certain that Aaron Taylor's wife was Betty Wildey, also spelled Wilde and Wildy. The name appears frequently as a given name, as does the feminine name Leanna, which was a favorite in the Wildey family. The Rev. John Taylor, grandson of Aaron Taylor and Betty Wildey, had a sister Leanna, who married Peter Lehugh and lived at Front Royal, Virginia, and a brother Wildey who lived in Preston Co. West Virginia [see **HISTORY OF PRESTON COUNTY**, vol.1, pp. 60, 61, 93, 398, 541]; and his oldest brother Argyle had a son Wildey who died in childhood. The Wildey family were in Virginia early, but Betty's exact connection is still to be learned.

Aaron Taylor's daughter Susanna, listed as "Sukey" in the earlier article, was born Dec. 10, 1738; died 1815; married (1) Kemp Hurst (2) Onisephorus Harvey. She had eight children by her first marriage, six living at the time Kemp Hurst made his will, 1782. [See TYLER'S QUARTERLY, vol.31, Jan. 1950]. Her second husband probably was the grandson of the early Onisephorus Harvey, Quaker, who married Dorothy Gaskins [a further evidence of the connection of the early Taylor and Gaskins families.]

TAYLOR AND MORRIS FAMILIES.

By Mrs. Henry D. McHenry.

Mrs. Henry D. McHenry, of Hartford, Ohio county, Ky., contributes a brief genealogy of her people. It is authentic as far as it goes. It is hoped readers of the Register who may be members of these Taylor and Morris families will add their information to Mrs. McHenry's, and thus complete the genealogy, which embraces the States of North Carolina, Virginia and Kentucky. Mrs. McHenry is the "sweet singer" of the old Louisville Journal, who, we read, delighted George D. Prentice with her lovely poems under the *nom de plume* of Rosine.

Thos. Taylor Family.

Thomas Taylor, son of Edward Taylor, was born March 15, 1738.

Mariam White, daughter of William and Margaret White, was born September 17, 1745, and died February 6, 1800.

James Taylor, their son, was born in Leureitrich county, North Carolina, April 1, and died March 22, 1867.

The children of Thomas Taylor and Mariam White were Lemuel, Lovey, Edward, William, Jessie, Mariam, Nancy, Elizabeth, and James, my father.

The children of James Taylor and Sarah Morris are Diedamia, Elizabeth, Godfrey, Mariam White, James William and Martha Jane—myself, though I have always been called Jennie.

I was married to Henry D. McHenry, son of John Hardin McHenry and Hannah Davis, January 29, 1856, and our children are Hannah, Morton D., Mary Taylor, Henry D., John James, Isabella Howe and Lemuel Hardin.

There could be much honorable mention of the Hardin and McHenry families, who are well known in Kentucky. You see we cling to family names on both sides of our old families.

All that I Know of the Godfrey and Morris Families.

THE GODFREY BRANCH.

Mathew and Frederick Godfrey came from England in the early colonial days and settled in Princess Anne county, Va.

Mathew Godfrey and Sarah Valentine, his wife, were the parents of Sarah Godfrey.

Sarah Godfrey was married to William Morris, son of William Morris, Sr., and Isabelle Howe.

THE MORRIS BRANCH.

William Morris, son of William Morris and Isabelle Howe, of England, was born November 15, and died October 16, 1838.

Sarah Godfrey, his wife, daughter of Mathew Godfrey and Sarah Valentine, was born February 11, 1760, and died March 26, 1817.

Sarah Morris, daughter of William

Morris and Sarah Godfrey, was born December 18, 1794, and died May 22, 1883.

There were, doubtless, other members of both families, but no records have been kept of them. Had I known when younger the pleasure these names would have been to me, I should certainly have tried to rescue them from oblivion.

THROCKMORTON AND WARNER AND DESCENDANTS
SIR JOHN THROCKMORTON.

Sir John Throckmorton married Eleanor, daughter and co-heiress of Sir Guy de Spinets (Lord of Coughton, County Warwick and acquired that estate, which has ever since been the principal seat of the family). He died April 23, 1445, leaving:

Thomas Throckmorton, high chief of Warwick and Leicester, in the reign of King Henry IV., married Margaret (daughter and co-heiress of Sir Robert Olney, Kn't of Weslin, Co. Buckingham) by whom he left:

The Right Hon. Robert Throckmorton (his heir), who married Elizabeth Baynham. He attempted a trip beyond the seas at an advanced age, and died there, leaving:

Sir George Throckmorton (his heir, and high sheriff for the county of Warwick, Leicester, in the eighteen and thirty-five years of King Henry VIII.), married Katherine, daughter of Nicholas, Lord Vaux of Harrowden, and left:

Sir Robert Throckmorton, high sheriff of Warwick and Leicester County, in the first year of Queen Mary, married Muriel (daughter of Thomas, Lord Berkley), and left:

Thomas Throckmorton, his successor, married Margaret (daughter and co-heiress of William Whorwood, Attorney General to King Henry VIII.), and left:

John Throckmorton, who married Agnes (daughter of Thomas Wilford, son of Sir James Wilford, Knt., of New Hall, Essex, died March 13, 1614, during his father's lifetime), and left:

Sir Robert Throckmorton (1st Baronet of Coughton, Co. Warwick, created a Baronet Sept. 1, 1642. He married, first, Dorothy (daughter of Sir John Fortescue, K. B., of Salden Bucks; she died without issue Nov. 14, 1617). He married, second, Mary (daughter of Sir Francis Smith, Knt. of Ashley Folville, Co. Leicester), by whom he had:

Gabriel Throckmorton, son and heir of Robert Throckmorton, married Alice, daughter of Wm. Bradle, of Bedfordshire, England, by whom he left:

Gabriel Throckmorton, who married Frances, daughter of Mordica Cooke, by whom he left:

Robert Throckmorton, who married Mary, daughter of John Lewis, by whom he left:

Robert Throckmorton, who married Lucy, daughter of Mordica Throckmorton, left:

Mary Throckmorton, who married Major Wm. Moore.

CAPTAIN AUGUSTINE WARNER.

Born 1610, in England, and died in Virginia on Dec. 24, 1674. In 1635, Warner patented 250 acres of land in Elizabeth City County. He also took up land on the Pianketank, which the Cheesecake Indians had owned. The patent dated 1666 reads: 1,224 acres in Abingdon Parish. In 1653, another land grant. His wife's name was Mary. Among his children was Sarah, who married Lawrence Townley. Another daughter, who married Major David Cant, a son, Augustine. Captain Warner was a member of the House of Burgesses in 1652—and again from Gloucester County in 1658-59, and also a member of the Royal Council in 1659-60.

Colonel Augustine Warner.

Col. Augustine Warner, son of Capt. Augustine Warner (the emigrant) was born in Virginia in 1642. Educated at the Merchant Tailors' School, in London, and at Cambridge. He was a member of the House of Burgesses in 1666, and speaker of the House in 1672. He died in (Gloucester Co.) Virginia June 19, 1681. He married Mildred Read, daughter of George Read; his children were George and Robert (sons), both died unmarried. His daughters: Mildred Warner married Lawrence Washington (grandparents of the President). Mary Warner married Col. John Smith. Elizabeth Warner married John Lewis (son of John Lewis and Isabella Warner). His portrait is in the State Library at Richmond, Va. Mary Lewis, daughter of Elizabeth Warner and John Lewis, married Robert Throckmorton. She died 1748, and was buried in Gloucester Co., Va. She left children: John Throckmorton, who married, first, Elizabeth (daughter of John Cooke), and, second, Rebecca (daughter of Wm. Richardson). Second, Major Robert Throckmorton, who married Lucy Throckmorton, daughter of Mordica Throckmorton. Third, Frances, who married Wm. Debnam. Fourth, Elizabeth, who married Davis, and Mary married Thomas Throckmorton. Robert married second time, Sarah, daughter of Austin Smith, of "Shorter's Hall," and had Mordica, Warner and Sarah.

Mary Throckmorton, daughter of Major Robert Throckmorton and Lucy Throckmorton, and granddaughter of Col. Robert Throckmorton and Mary Lewis, married Major Wm. Moore.

Rebecca Moore, daughter of Mary Throckmorton and Major Wm. Moore, married Capt. Reuben Taylor.

Lucy Taylor, daughter of Rebecca Moore and Capt. Reuben Taylor, married Benjamin Alsop.

James Alsop, son of Lucy Taylor and Benj. Alsop, married Mary A. Very.

Lewis.

John Lewis, son of Colonel Robert Lewis, married Isabella Warner (probably a daughter of Col. Augustine Warner, the emigrant), and left:

John Lewis, who married Elizabeth Warner, daughter of Colonel Augustine Warner, and his wife, Mildred Read, and left:

Mary Lewis, who married Col. Robert Throckmorton, and left:

Robert Throckmorton, who married Lucy, daughter of Mordica Throckmorton, and left:

Mary Throckmorton, who married William Moore, and left:

Rebecca Moore, who married Capt Taylor.

MEMORABILIA OF THE TRABUE FAMILY.
By MRS. Z. F. SMITH.

The name of Trabue indicates a French origin. The reminiscent records of the family and its ancestry, both traditional and historic bear testimony to the fact that the Trabues in America are descendants of the French Huguenots who were of that numerous body of Protestant Reformers who for conscience sake, suffered persecutions even unto death, or exile under the cruel reign of Louis XIV., and many thousands of whom fled for refuge to Holland, to England and to America, near the close of the seventeenth century, thus impoverishing of the best blood, and brawn, and brain of France, only to enrich that of rival Nations.

The name Trabue is well distributed in a number of States of this Union; especially in the Ohio Valley, and west of the Mississippi river from Missouri to Texas. The descendants by marriage of other names, are yet more numerous. There is an interesting tradition held in the family, and worthy of record, that the Trabues were of an Ancestry, of honorable lineage, the name spelled Strabo.

The Editor, of St. Louis, in "The Americans of gentle birth, and their Ancestry," has to say "That at the time of the persecution they were seated at Montanban, France, and were prominent among the defenders of the faith which they had espoused." This is confirmed by an old church letter still preserved by descendants as a valuable relic, which was brought to this country by the son and heir of Pierre Trabue or Strabo. When the storm broke forth following the Revocation of the Edict of Nantes in 1685, Antoine determined to leave France. He with a companion in 1867, youths of nineteen years of age, went under the disguise of wine merchants, with their cart and casks of wine, toward the frontier, selling by the way. Their route took them to Switzerland, and at Lausanne, Antoine found his old pastor of the church of Languedoc, who gave him the following letter in antique French, much worn, yellow with age, and scarcely legible, written on vellum or parchment, made of sheep skin.

"A RARE RELIC."
Translated.
Old Huguenot Church letter.

"We the undersigned certify that Antoine Trabue, native of the city of Montanban, nineteen years of age, dark chestnut hair, has always professed the Reform religion just as his parents before him without his committing any offense, that has ever come to our knowledge, other than that which the violence of the late persecutions in France has caused him to commit, and which God has given him grace to abandon, and for which he has made reparation.

"We commend him to the divine Providence, and to the cordial love of our brethren." Done at Lausanne the 15th day of September, 1687.

Signatures.

Vertiers, formerly minister of the church at Dittenade, and that of Montanban, Balli, pastor...... in Languedoc, and five deacons. Lausanne and Der Berne, Switzerland, indicating the route of Antoine's retreat, and escape down the Rhine, and into Holland.

Antoine born 1666, and married about 1990, and died 1724, remained in Holland several years, Antoine was the son of Messeur Pierre Trabue, a man of estate, fine appearance and address. While in Holland he married Magdalene Verrueil, daughter of Magdalene Prodhomme, who married Moise (Moses) Verrueil, a wealthy merchant of the Canton of Berne, and came over to America with the Trabues, Dupuys, Flournoys, Chastains, Fontains, and other Huguenot exiles. Antoine came to England, and with the above mentioned persons embarked on a vessel September 1700—in command of Captain Perreau (Pero), and settled in Virginia in Mannakintown, eighteen miles above Richmond, on James river, on land set apart for them by the English King. The incident is related that the clerk of the ship that left England for America, in registering the passengers, by some oversight left off the first letter S, and wrote the name Trabo instead of Strabo.

Thus it came to be Americanized Trabu or Trabue. In the new world of English speaking people, this altering of French names to English paraphrase being not uncommon. The family name in France was Strabo, and no Trabues have been found in that country since. We have the will of Magdelene Prodhomme Trabue, who after the death of her husband Antoine, married again Pierre Chastain. It is dated June 2nd, 1729, King William Parish, Henrico County, Virginia, and in it she distributed many pieces of apparel, of jewelry, and articles of *virtu,* to her daughters Magdalene and Judith, leaving her farm, stock, negroes, etc., to her sons, showing a display of opulence beyond the ordinary. Her father was a wealthy merchant of France, her mother a Prodhomme, a family then, and to-day distinguished in letters and art, in France and whose works are found in the art galleries of that country. The talent and taste for fine art is a marked characteristic of her descendants in this country, and they hold in reverance and pride the name of this noble maternal ancestress, who has bequeathed to them something even more valuable than the jewels and silks mentioned in her will.

Antoine and Magdalene Prodhomme Verrueil Trabue and five children, Anthony, Jacob, Magdalene, Judith and John James Trabue. Anthony married Miss ——— Clark, two children, John and Caroline of whom he speaks in his will, in which he bequeathes certain lands, and money to his son, John, and daughter, Caroline. And to his beloved wife, Clark Trabue, the land they dwelled upon, three hundred and twenty-three acres, during her natural life, after her death, "I give to my daughter Caroline." If she die without heirs to return to my son John Trabue, and in case of his dying without heirs, to my brother John James Trabue, and to his heirs forever, and constituted and appointed his beloved wife, Clark Trabue his sole and whole executrix of this his last will and testament, February 2nd, 174.. Signed, his name,

ANTHONY TRABUE, JR.

Of the Parish of King William, of the County of Goochland, who lived a Christian, &c.

2. Jacob Trabue, married Marie, ...

3. Magdallene Trabue, married Peter Guerrant.

Their daughter Judith, married George Smith.

Their daughter Esther, married James Martin (A Baptist minister.)

Their son, William Holman, married Susannah Hall.

Their daughter, Caroline Jane Martin married Warren Viley, and their daughter Martinette Viley, married Mr. Lister Witherspoon—three children, Ellen, Ethel and Warren W. Viley. Ethel Witherspoon married Mr. Alexander, and they live in Woodford county, Kentucky.

Judith Trabue married Stephen Watkins.

5. John James Trabue married Olymphia Dupuy, a grand daughter of Captain Bartholomew Dupuy, the famous officer of the body guard of Louis XIV., and high in favor of the King, who a Huguenot, yet more loyal to his God, chose to exile himself from France, rather than recant his religion, or suffer persecution.

Rev. B. W. Dupuy (Beverly W.) of Virginia in his recent book, —— "The Huguenot, Bartholomew Dupuy, and his Descendants" gives a thrilling account of the romantic flight to Germany of this renowned officer of his Majesty the King, with his beautiful bride, the Countess Susanna La Villain, disguised in the garb of a page; of his tragic rencounters, and of his final escape across the border. Miss Eliza Dupuy, the distinguished authoress, and a direct descendant, in her historic novel, entitled, "The Huguenot," ——had woven into an interesting story, the heroic and gallant deeds, of the Cavalier.

That tri-angular sword, famously wielded in the invincible hands of the brave old soldier ancestor, has done valiant service since in the hands of his posterity, in the War for Independence, in the second War with England, and in the later war of "The Lost Cause." The sword was lost in a raid of Federal troops, near Petersburg, Va., during the Civil War, either burned with the residence of Mrs. Julian Ruffin, mother-in-law of Dr. J. L. Dupuy, of the C. S. A., who had left it there, or carried off by the Federal soldiers. The sword was of French rapier pattern. The blade was straight, about three feet in length and triangular in shape, somewhat like a bayonet. It combined lightness with great strength and made the weapon very effective in the hands of a skilled swordsman.

The old progenitor had two daughters and two sons, Peter Dupuy married Judith Le Fayre.

John James Dupuy and wife had children; Olymphia Dupuy, who married John James Trabue, from the will signed and sealed, by the old soldier, March 7th, 1742, and recorded in the office of Goochland County, Virginia, May 7th, 1743.

2. Bartholomew Dupuy, married Mary Motley.

3. Susanna Dupuy married James Lockett.

4. Rev. John Dupuy married Elizabeth Minter.

5. Mary Dupuy married Ben Hatcher.

6. Elizabeth Dupuy married Thomas Atkinson.

7. Rev. James Dupuy married Ann Stark, a daughter of Maj. John Stark, of Virginia.

8. Martha Dupuy married James Foster.

We have also a copy of the will of John James Dupuy, son of Captain Bartholomew Dupuy, signed and sealed February 9th, 1775, and recorded in the Office of Cumberland County, Virginia, February 27th, 1775. He was many years a Vestryman of his Parish, and a man of large estate and influence.

He divided among his heirs by his will, 2,380 acres of land, and not less than 35 negroes, besides much personality mentioned.

Revs. John and James Dupuy were ministers of the Baptist Church in Powhatan county, Virginia. Rev. John Dupuy moved to Woodford County, Ky., and later to Shelbyville, Ky., where he died in 1831. Rev. James Dupuy moved to Clear Creek, Oldham County, in 1786, and after united to constitute Buck Run church, both in Shelby County. Rev. Stark Dupuy, son of Rev. James and Ann Stark Dupuy, was brought to Kentucky with his parents in 1786. In 1812 he edited, ——, "The Kentucky Missionary and Theologian," at Frankfort, the first religious periodical west of the Alleghenies, and was the compiler of Dupuy's hymns, which attained great popularity in Kentucky and Tennessee, and throughout the South, more than one hundred thousand copies were put into circulation. He was greatly respected by Baptists and other Christians. Of the remaining five children of John James Dupuy, we have not much information of interest here, excepting as to their son, Bartholomew, who married Mary Motley, and who moved to Kentucky from Amelia County, Virginia, about the year 1785, and settled in Woodford County. His will giving names of his children, of date, June 5th, 1790, is preserved as recorded in that County. The decendants of Bartholomew, Jr., and Mary Motley Dupuy, are numerous and well known especially in Central Kentucky.

They are recorded nowhere so fully and accurately, as is in that recent valuable book of Rev. B. H. Dupuy, "The Huguenot Bartholomew Dupuy and his descendants."

The issue of their marriage:
1. Achsa Dupuy married Ben Davis. Both died of cholera in 1882.
2. Susanne Dupuy.——
3. Joel Dupuy married Lucy Craig, and died at his farm home, in Woodford County, two miles out from Versailles, Louisville pike.
4. Elizabeth Dupuy married Mr. —————— Fogg, Woodford Co. issue, Mary Fogg married Rev. Joseph Taylor, John, Elizabeth, Benjamin, Joel, Dione, Lucy and Joseph.
5. John Dupuy enlisted at eighteen as a Revolutionary soldier, and served five years.
6. Judith Dupuy married William Samuel,—issue; Washington married Miss Gray, their children Eleanor, Benjamin, Edward and Richard Gray.
Mary Motley Samuel married David Castleman Suggett. Their children: Lucy, Judith, Benjamin, Samuel, Sophronia.
7. James Dupuy.
8. Nancy Dupuy married Abram McClure. Their children: Achsah, Mary, Alexander, Samuel, Abram, William. Bartlett married Ann Ashby, moved to Texas, where his wife killed three Indians in defense of herself and children.
9. Martha Dupuy married Col. Abram Owen, of New Castle, Henry County. Born in Prince Edward County, Virginia, 1769, killed at the battle of Tippecannoe, November 7th, 1811. He came to Kentucky with his family in 1785, and helped to build Owen's Station, near Shelbyville. He served in the Indian wars with General Wilkinson, on the Wabash; with Col. Hardin and General St. Clair. He commanded the first Shelby County Company in Wayne's Expedition. He served in the Legislature in the Senate and in the Constitutional Convention of 1800. He fell upon the field of Tippecanoe as Aide to General Harrison. No man was more beloved or lamented in Kentucky. Owen County was named for him.

To Abram and Martha Dupuy Owen were born James Dupuy Owen, killed in 1836, at the battle of San Jacinto, Texas, under General Houston; Col. Clark Lewis Owen fought Indians upon the frontiers of Texas and was killed in the C. S. Army, at the battle of Shiloh, 1863.

Harriet Owen married Thomas Smith, of New Castle, who built the Louisville and Frankfort railroad.

Nancy Owen married Turner Woolfork.

Lucy Wooten Owen married William Smith.

Susan Owen married William Henderson Allen.

Elizabeth Owen married Daniel Brannan. All the above are residents of New Castle. The two sons moving to Texas and enlisting in the Army for Independence. Their descendants have been and are prominent in business and in affairs of church and State.

10. Joseph Dupuy married Nancy Peay, of Jefferson County. He was born in Nottoway County, Virginia, March 8th, 1765, and settled in Henry County. Nancy Peay was born in Virginia. Their children— Bartholomew Dupuy died unmarried; Martha Turner Dupuy mar-

ried Edward Branham; Judith Coleman Dupuy married Dr. Edward C. Drane; His children—Dr. Joseph S. Drane and Judge Canning Drane; Eliza Ann Dupuy married Morton Brinker, the daughter of whom, Mary Coleman Brinker, married Judge William S. Pryor, of New Castle.

Mildred D. Dupuy married Zackariah Smith, to whom was born Zachary F. Smith, of Louisville, Kentucky. Augustine Dupuy married Lucy Jane Thomas; Mary Motley Dupuy, Joseph Dupuy and James died without issue. The children and grand children of Joseph and Nancy Dupuy were natives or citizens of Henry County.

11. Sarah Dupuy married Poindexter Thomasson. His children,— Dr. John James Thomasson married first Sarah E. Coleman; second Elizabeth B. Neighbor.

Joseph Thomasson married Martin Bartlett.

William Poindexter Thomasson was in Congress from the Louisville District, married Charlotte Leonard. Joel Thomasson married Mary Kerby; Nelson Bartholomew Thomasson married Mary Kerby Sneed.

Elias Thomasson married and had children, two daughters, one married and had children, and Mary Thomasson.

We have connection made of the two families above by the marriage of Olymphia Dupuy, grand daughter of the old Huguenot, to John James Trabue, son of Antoine Trabue, Huguenot. John James Trabue was born in King William Parish, Virginia, and died December 23rd, 1803. He was Ensign in the Revolution, received pay and bounty lands under Act of Congress. Children of this marriage were:

1. James Trabue, born January 29th, 1745, married Jane E. Porter, had sons and daughters. They married and lived in Kentucky, and are represented by Dr. Tom A. McGregor's daughters, Chastain and Matilda, both married and have children.

James Trabue was in the Revolutionary war, and Colonel in the Commissary Department; he was taken prisoner and sent to Canada; made his escape and came over and entered the army, and remained to the close, then married in Virginia, came to Kentucky, and settled in Bourbon County, where he died in 1803.

2. Magdalen Trabue married Edward Clay, and had children. They moved to Alabama, represented by Hon. James P. Dameron. The family were French Huguenots and came to this country in the ship with the Dupuys, Trabues and Clays and settled in Virginia.

3. ——— Phoebe, born 1750, died 1767.

4. Jane Trabue, born January 12th, 1852, died 1802. Married Joseph Minter, had children; all but one married and left families in the South and West; represented in Memphis by the Parkers, Raineys, Gregories and Stovalls; Martha Stovall compiled the Dupuy Tree.

5. John Trabue, born march 7th, 1754; in Revolutionary War, married E. Pierce in 1788.

6. William Trabue, born March 13th, 1756, died March 2nd, 1786.

He was Colonel in the Revolutionary war, and joined the regiment of the Colonial line of Virginia, served until the close of the war, and received his bounty land of 200 acres. He was taken prisoner and held in South Carolina for some time, and exchanged. After the war he married Elizabeth Haskins, born November 26th, 1763; married February 12th, 1783, had two daughters; Trabue, born November 24th, 1783; married William Caldwell; had sons and daughters. All married and were prominent in Society and State. Three were gifted lawyers, George Alfred, Congressman; William B. Caldwell was a prominent physician, and married Ann Augusta Guthrie, daughter of Senator Guthrie and Secretary of the Treasury under Franklin Pierce.

The daughters married prominent and prosperous men of Kentucky.

Phoebe Trabue, daughter of William and Elizabeth Haskins Trabue, was born February 21st, 1785; married Isaac Hodgen, born August 8th, 1779, and died 1826. Phoebe died March 12th, 1857. He was a Baptist minister. They had children, represented by Orlando and Hogen Wilson, of Kansas City, and Miss Lena, Miss Mamie and Arthur Wilson, of Louisville, Kentucky; also Mary and Carrie Wilson, and Eugene Wilson and children, of Memphis.

7. Mary Trabue, born February 26th, 1758; married Lewis Sublett.

8. Daniel Trabue, born March 31st, 1760, died 1840; married Mary Haskins, Colonel in the Revolutionary war, of the Commissary Department of Kentucky; represented in Louisville, Kentucky, by Mr. James Trabue, a prominent and wealthy citizen and merchant, and his sons, Richard and William Trabue. The latter married Miss Lizzie Shreve; issue: James Upton, Little and William Trabue.

9. Martha Trabue married Josiah Wooldridge.

10. *Edward Trabue,* born 1764. The tenth child and fifth son. A soldier at sixteen, in the battle at Gilford, at Gates defeat, and in several skirmishes. In one the Tories were victors.

Colonel Forkner ordered the soldiers to retreat and escape as best they could.

11. Stephen Trabue, born 1766, married Jane Haskins, daughter of Col. Robert Haskins; had children; represented by Bettie Gill and Judell Mac Gregor, Stephen Fitz, James Trabue and children, of Frankfort, Kentucky. Edmund married Miss Cochran; one child, Lucinda. Stephen, Willett and Alice Trabue.

12. Elizabeth Trabue, born Sept. 4th, 1768; married Fenelon Wilson.

13. Samuel, born 1770 and died young.

14. Susan, born 1772; married John Major; represented by the Majors of Frankfort.

15. Judith, born 1774; married Thomas Major; descendants in Bloomington, Illinois.

After Edward Trabue returned safe from this defeat, he joined his older brother, Daniel, and traveled and tented together, and were present at the siege and surrender of Yorktown in 1782. Daniel Trabue, after he married, wrote of his life, and his experiences in the Revolutionary war; Mss is in the Library at Madison, Wisconsin, left there by L. C. Draper, L. L. D. historian, of which Alvah L. Terry has a copy, of Louisville, Kentucky. A full history of the Trabue family can also be found in the Genealogical history of Rev B. H. Dupuy, of Beverly, West Virginia, entitled, "The Huguenot, Bartholemew Dupuy and His Descendents," published in 1908.

Virginia was the ancestral home of the Trabues, Dupuys and Haskins, and there were many ministers of the Baptist Church among them, also the Hills, Watkins and Pittmans. They bear arms and are of English descent. The Watkins from Wales, Dupuys and Trabues French Huguenots, fled in 1685-87.

John James Trabue and five sons were Revolutionary soldiers.

1. James married Jane E. Porter.
2. William married Elizabeth Haskins.
3. Daniel married Mary Haskins.
4. John married E. Pierce.
5. Edward married Martha Haskins, and Stephen married Jane Haskins, daughters of Col. Robert Haskins, and descendants of each are represented in Louisville, Kentucky; others are settled over the South and West.

Among Jane Trabue Minter's descendants are Attorney General P. Watt Hardin, Judge Charles Hardin and Ben Hardin, of Harrodsburg; also Mrs. Hugh McElroy, formerly Mary Handy, and her brother, George Handy.

Miss Pauline Gregory, a beautiful Christian character, and an authoress, of Kentucky, and brother, and Nancy Minter married Joseph Watkins; issue, two children, Jacob and Lucy. Ann Watkins married Abelard Temple Smith, had children; one Mary E. married William A. Beavers, had children Herschel, Averill and Lois married John D. Johnson; issue, two sons.

Four Trabue brothers married daughters of Col. Robert Haskins. It was a high tribute paid by the mother of these four happy wives to the noble manhood of their husbands, when she proudly said: "I wish I had another daughter for the other son."

Edward Trabue was born in 1764, in Chesterfield County, Virginia; a Revolutionary soldier, and after the war in 1786, married Martha Haskins, a daughter of Col. Robert Haskins, of Virginia. Martha, from historic accounts, was a member of the Baptist Church, handsome and dressy; and kept pace with the fashions; she was refined and accomplished, and assumed prominence in society. Edward was a typical gentleman of the old school, possessing qualities of mind and character which impressed his personality upon the community. He was public spirited and liberal, and his home was the center of hospitality and social enjoyment. He was diligent in business, and amassed a fortune, and educated his children. Edward was a member of the Baptist Church and raised his children in the same belief. Many of the Dupuys, Trabues and Watkins were ministers, and history speaks of Edward Trabue entertaining them, staying all night and going from there to other points to fill engagements to preach.

Edward Trabue's Home.

He selected a beautiful table land, stretching back from the towering cliffs, but overlooking the Kentucky river, a mile from Sublett's Ferry, and here built a two story brick house, with out-houses of every description. The site is opposite the village of Tyrone, Anderson County, which it overlooks. The fifth Lock and Dam on the river is but a short distance above, while the suspension bridge of the Southern R. R. is in sight below. A pencil sketch of the house and its picturesque surroundings was drawn by the gifted hands of his third daughter, Nancy, who married Asa Pitman, the mother of Mrs. Z. F. Smith, also Anna Pittman that was; Mrs. Pittman would never name any of her sons Asa, saying, "It would be old Asa and young Asa." So Ann was the ninth and youngest child, and friends suggested that she give the little brown eyed baby the name of honor, and they *did*. She was called "Asie" all her school life.

Nancy Haskins Trabue later had her pencil sketch of the Trabue home enlarged and painted in oil, with the attractive features of a beautiful country home in the Blue Grass region. It has long been in the hands of others, and still retains its picturesque beauty—and romantic scenery. They had a park with deer and white rabbits; this home was as beautiful in winter, with its white mantle of snow covering all trees and earth, and the ice bound river, as in the spring time when all nature was covered with verdure.

Edward and Martha Haskins Trabue had children, Mary, Elizabeth, *Nancy* and George.

Nancy Haskins Trabue married Asa Pittman, both from Woodford County, Kentucky; he was the son of Williamson H. Pittman, a Baptist minister from Virginia, of English descent, and Judith Watkins, daughter of Joseph Watkins, of Welch descent, and Mary Lockett, whose mother was a Walthall, both English.

Joseph Watkins was a Revolutionary soldier, under Captain Fleet, in 1782, and was in the Yorktown seige, resided in King and Queen County, Virginia, and at his death his widow, Susan, received a pension.

His second wife:

WATKINS.

James Watkins, from Wales, was in the Virginia Colony with John Smith, the explorer, in 1608. Had a son, Henry.

2. Henry Watkins 1st.

3. Henry Watkins 2nd, his son married Mary Crisp. He was a Burgess and owned Marborne Hills. In his will, 1717, he mentions his sons, Benjamin, Joseph and Stephens.

4. Major Joseph Watkins, married Mary Lockett.

5. Judith Watkins, married Williamson H. Pittman; had two sons, Asa and Williamson P. They lost their mother, Judith, when three and five years of age; their father married a second time.

Their uncle Ben Watkins led two horses to Virginia, and brought the boys to Kentucky, about 1812.

6. Asa Pitman, in the war of 1812 to 1815. Asa became a volunteer from Kentucky in the army of the Northwest, under General William H. Harrison, in the second war with England. Asa Pittman was taken prisoner and sent to Canada, and held till exchanged. After the war he returned home, and went into business. He met and married Nancy H. Trabue. Asa was tall, very erect and fine looking, brown eyes and hair, with the fair, ruddy complexion of the English. He was a gallant young soldier, and a favorite. Nancy was the daughter of a Revolutionary soldier, and an attractive and lovely girl. Her mother died when she was two years of age, and she was raised mostly by her grand-mother, Olymphia Dupuy Trabue; she displayed in childhood a talent for drawing, and when about grown, embroidered a beautiful counterpane from cotton grown, woven and spun on the Trabue home, which Mrs. Z. F. Smith has preserved as a relic and valuable heirloom.

Asa and Nancy Trabue Pittman married and had children, several married. Edward F. Pittman married Anne Harrison, and they had children, Hattie, Edward, George, Ida Mary married, Anne Belle and James Pittman.

Williamson H. Pittman married Hannah Daviess; their children, Nannie M, Arthur Anderson; one child, Jean, died.

William Daviess Pittman married Sally Patterson; have children, Marie, Cora and W. Daviess Pittman, Jr., Asa M. Walker, both deceased; one child, Martha Pittman.

Trabue Pittman married; they live in St. Louis, Mo.

Martha J. Pittman married Jesse Graddy Crutcher; had children; Asa never married and died.

Henry Crutcher married Louise Taylor; had children; all died but J. H. Crutcher, Jr., Earle and Anna Lee, who married Mr. W. H. Wheeler; one child in Texas.

Richard L. Crutcher married Emma Stephens, and have children, boys and girls.

Anna married P. B. Stanley; two girls, both married.

Mary Crutcher married John W. Bateman; children, Dupuy Bateman, who married Lola Bell Harris; issue, two sons, Dupuy, Jr., and another.

Ralph, Claude, John and Bonnie May Bateman.

Jessie died, Mattie Crutcher married Clifford Witherspoon; sons, Ford, Guy, Clifford, Horace Trabue and Anna.

Flora Crtucher married Robert G. Brown; have children, sons and daughters.

Robert and Anna B. married; Eddie and Pittman Crutcher died; others live in Texas, except Richard, who lives in Frankfort.

George Trabue Pittman, one of the three brothers who were wholesale dry goods merchants in St. Louis; other children died; Anna A. Pittman married Hon. Z. F. Smith, the present historian of Kentucky. They live in Louisville.

George W. Trabue married Elizabeth Buford Chambers; their children, Dr. Ben Trabue married Lelia Anderson, daughter of the Rev. Henry T. Anderson, a Christian minister; they had children who married—Helen Trabue married William Terry, and they had children, Bettie, Aloah, Mary, William, Maude and Buford, all married and live in Louisville, Kentucky. Elizabeth Trabue married Mr. Samuel Van Culin, sons and one daughter, all married.

Lillie married Mr. Harper, and lives in Philadelphia; one son lives in the West.

Joseph and George married and had children.

Edward Trabue married second time, Jane Clay, first cousin of Henry Clay; had children.

Charles C. Trabue married Agnes Wood; had sons and daughters; all married except Fannie and Mattie.

Anthony married Christine Manley and had children; all married. He compiled the Trabue Tree, with the assistance of Anna R. Pittman in getting the Kentucky names. The Tree was very large, of which had but small photograph when he died. The house burned, and the Tree and all histories, notes and we have only the small photographs of seven years work in the eighties.

The children of Edward Trabue and Jane Clay all married and had children. They live in Missouri.

Olymphia Dupuy was ninety-three years old when she died at the home of her son, Edward, and was buried at the family grave yard, in Woodford County. Edward died in 1814, and was buried beside his mother, Olymphia, and first wife, Martha Haskins.

Mrs. Jane Clay Trabue lived with one of her daughters, died and was buried there.

THE GENEALOGY AND HISTORY OF THE TRABUE FAMILY

Alice Trabue

COAT OF ARMS OF TRABUE.
Az, 2 Arrows, Arg. Crossed, a star, Or in chief, 2 compasses, as below; Crest: a Unicorn, Rampant.

Among the earliest pioneers and largest land owners in Kentucky, and from whom have sprung some of our ablest citizens, who figured prominently in the public and social affairs of the State, was the French Huguenot family of Trabue. Some of the most notable examples are represented by the names of Trabue, Caldwell, Hardin, Terry and others.

The emigrant Antoine Trabue and Bartholomew duPuy had fled from France during the Huguenot persecutions, and after a sojourn in Holland, Germany and England, had found their way to America in 1700.

In 1685, Louis XIV signed the Revocation of the Edict of Nantes and from 300,000 to 400,000 Huguenots left France. At this time, the family of Trabue had their seat at Montauban on the Tarne, in old Guyenne, France. It was about two years later that the son and heir, Antoine, born 1667, was sent as an exile. He was disguised as a wine merchant, and with a comrade went at night with a cart containing casks of wine. They passed through Switzerland, and at Lausanne, Antoine found his old pastor of the Church of La Ngauedoc, France, who gave him a letter of recommendation. He left Switzerland and went into Holland, where many Huguenots had already settled. A year later, he married (1699) in Holland, Magdelain Flournoy, born 1671, near Montauban, France, died Henrico County, Virginia, November, 1731. She was the daughter of Jacob Flournoy, who had also left France for Holland on account of the persecutions. He died January, 1724, in King William Parish, Virginia.

A translated copy of the certificate that Antoine Trabue brought with him from France:

"Lausanne, France, 15 Sept., A. D., 1687. We, the undersigned, certify that Antoine Trabue is a native of Montauban, age about 19 years, of good size, fine carriage, dark complexion, having a scar under his left eye; has always professed the Reformed Religion in which his parents raised him. He has never committed any offense that has come to our knowledge, otherwise than that the violence of the late horrible persecutions justified, which persecutions God has had the kindness to stop and for which He has given us reparations. We commend him to the care of a kind Providence and to a cordial reception from our brethren. Done at Lausanne, this

TRABUE

15th day of Sept., A. D., 1687." Signed by "T Latur," formerly minister of the Church of Villinds, and also of the Church of Montauban. It was likewise signed by the church pastors of Lansignaque, Languedoc, Dauphiny, Lausanne and Berne, Switzerland, indicating clearly the line of Antoine Trabue's retreat down the Rhine, Germany and Holland.

This ancient letter or certificate was on vellum, written in antique French with blue ink, and much worn. It was stained here and there with dark splotches, possibly blood, but enough was left to decipher or translate. On its back was a well drawn picture of Antoine Trabue done with pen and ink. It was owned by Mr. Anthony E. Trabue, of Hannibal, Mo., it having been sent to him by Mr. Macon Trabue, of Virginia, many years ago.

When Mr. A. E. Trabue's residence was burned in 1889, this letter was destroyed, but fortunately he had taken the impression in gelatine and had presented several copies to his various kinsmen.

About 1700, King William of England had invited the refugees to the colonies, promising a free passage and freedom of religion. Beginning in the spring of 1700, seven hundred French Protestant refugees in four separate fleets, at intervals of several months apart, embarked from England to America with Marquis de la Muse at their head. Accompanying them were three ministers of the gospel, namely, Claude Philippe de Richeboug, Benjamin de Joux and Louis Latane, besides two physicians, Castaing (Chastain) and Lasosee.

From about two hundred of these refugees, a settlement was formed at Manikin Town in King William Parish, then Henrico County, Va., sixteen miles above Richmond, on the south side of the James river. The Parish consisted of ten thousand acres, granted by the Act of the General Assembly, Dec., 1708, to the Huguenot refugees. This land was to be divided among the families into tracts of 133 acres, and a portion of the most valuable was to be set apart for the support of their minister. They built a church, and worshipped twice daily on the Sabbath, where one is still standing on the spot. They also erected a school and educated their children. In the Virginia Land Registry were the following records:

"Anthony Trabue, March 23, 1715, 163 acres south side of James river, Henrico Co., Va."

"Anthony Trabue, March 18, 1717, 522 acres on the Great Fork of Swift Creek."

The old vestry book of King William Parish shows that he was a church warden and Vestryman from 1707 to 1723.

We find in the hands of the Virginia Historical Society the old "French Church Register" of King William Parish. In the death register is the following:

"January 29, 1723, died Sieur Anthony Trabue, aged 56, was buried on the 30th of the same.
          "J. Soblet, Clerk."

After the death of Anthony[1] Trabue, his widow, Magdelaine

(Flournoy) Trabue married Pierre Chastain of Manikintown, Va.

Anthony[1] Trabue and Magdelaine, his wife, had five children, three sons and two daughters:

1. Anthony[2] Trabue, Jr., born about 1702, married a daughter of Moyse Vermeil.

2. Jacob[2] Trabue, born about 1705, married Marie —— in 1730, left many children.

3. Judith Trabue, born about 1712, married Stephen Watkins, left children.

4. Magdelaine Trabue, born about 1715, married Peter Guerrant, who was a son of Daniel Guerrant. Left children.

5. John James[2] Trabue, born at Manikintown, Va., 1722.

Most of the descendants of Anthony[2], Jr., and Jacob[2] Trabue, remained in Virginia while John James[2] Trabue married in 1744, Olympe[3] duPuy and had fifteen children, most of whom eventually drifted to Kentucky. All of their five sons, old enough to bear arms, were officers in the Revolution.

Olympe[3] duPuy was the daughter of John James[2] duPuy and Susanna Levilain, and granddaughter of the immigrant.

After the Revolution was over, Olympe[3] duPuy Trabue removed to the home of her son, Edward[3] Trabue, in Woodford County, Ky., where she died in 1822, aged 93 years, and is buried on the place by her son's side.

It is a rather interesting fact to note that four sons of this family married four daughters of Colonel Robert Haskins and Elizabeth (Hill) Haskins of "The Hills of Surrey." Col. Robert Haskins, born 1732, of Chesterfield County, Va., died 2 December, 1804, aged 72. He was a Colonel in the Revolution. Elizabeth Hill, born 1733, died 13 April, 1817, aged 84, both buried near Haskinsville, Ky., in family graveyard.

Bartholomew[1] DuPuy, the progenitor of the family in Virginia, was born about 1652 in the province of Languedoc, France. He died in King William Parish, Manikintown, Va., 1743.

By virtue of his descent from a family of nobility, he was heir to the title of Count.*

He enlisted in the French Army when eighteen years of age and was appointed Lieutenant, then Captain. He was in fourteen battles in Flanders besides skirmishes and duels; served fourteen years, then retired to private life; bought a vineyard for fifty pounds and married in 1785, the Countess Susanne Levillon.

While an officer of the guards of Louis XIV, he was frequently charged with the performance of duties of such importance that his orders bore the signature and seal of the King himself. The possession of one of these orders aided him, subsequently, in effecting the escape of himself and bride from France. After the Revocation of the Edict of Nantes, finding their flight imminent, a suit of men's clothes was immediately made for the bride, who, impersonating a page, rode by

---

* "The Huguenot, Bartholomew DuPuy and his descendants." P. 90-93.

his side, making their perilous ride of eighteen days to the frontier. He wore his uniform, which assisted him in evading most of the pickets, but one more viligant than the rest, accosted him, whereupon, with one hand, he held out the King's signature and, drawing his sword with the other, he forced an apology for "daring to molest a King's officer," and rode on. After fourteen years in Germany, he arrived in England and joined the Refugees to Virginia, 1700.

For a detailed account of this well known and romantic story, see "The Story of the Sword," which has been republished in "The Huguenot Bartholomew Dupuy and his Descendants," by Rev. B. H. duPuy of Beverly, W. Va.

WILL OF BARTHOLOMEW DUPUY.

He died between 7 March and 17 May, 1743. His wife died between 27 October, 1731, and 13 May, 1737.

"In the name of God, Amen, I, Bartholomew Dupuy of Goochland Co., and in King William Parish, Virginia, being sick in body but of good and perfect memory, thanks be to the Almighty God, and calling to remembrance the uncertain estate of this transitory life, and that all flesh must yield unto death, when it shall please the Almighty God to call, do make, constitute, ordain and declare this to be my last will and testament and none other and in manner and form following, revoking and annuling by these presents all and every testament or testaments, will or wills heretofore by me made or declared, either by word or writing and this only to be taken only for my last will and testament and none other. And first being penitent and sorry from the bottom of my heart for my sins past, most humbly desiring forgiveness for the same, I give and commit my soul unto the Almighty God, my Savior and Redeemer, in whom and by whose merits I trust and believe assuredly to be saved and to have full remission and forgiveness for all my sins past, and that my soul with my body at the general day of Resurrection shall rise again with joy, etc. . . .

"Item. I give and bequeath to my eldest, Peter Dupuy, five pounds Virginia currency to him and his heirs forever.

"Son, John James Dupuy, ten pounds.

"Grandson Bartholomew, son to Peter Dupuy, two pounds.

"To the poor of King William Parish five pounds.

"The remainder of his estate to son-in-law, John Levilain, Junior. Also appointed executor of the same.

"Dated 7th day of March, 1743, proved at a court for Goochland Co., May 17, 1743. Witnessed by John Gordon, Stephen Mallet, Stephen Watkins.

"A copy Testi: Moses T. Monteiro, Clerk."

John James[2] Dupuy was born about 1698. He died between the 9th of February and the 27th of the same, 1775, in Cumberland County, Va. He was for many years a church warden and vestryman of the Parish of King William. He was married about 1729 to Susanna Levilain, probably a daughter of

509

John Levilain, Sr. His estate at his death consisted of 2,380 acres and not less than 35 negroes. His will devising these, household furniture, cattle, etc., to the following:

To son Bartholomew; granddaughter Susanna Dupuy, daughter of my son Bartholomew Dupuy; son John Dupuy; son James Dupuy; daughter Olympe Trabue; grandson Benjamin Hatcher; daughter Mary Hatcher; daughter Elizabeth Dupuy; daughter Martha Foster and grandson George Foster; granddaughter Susanna Foster; grandson John Lockett, son of daughter Susanna Lockett; grandsons James, Joel and Brittaen Lockett, sons of daughter Susanna Lockett; beloved wife; granddaughter Susanna Trabue; granddaughter Susanna Hatcher; granddaughter Mary Foster; son James Dupuy.

Executors, sons Bartholomew and son-in-law Benjamin Hatcher. Made 9 February, 1775, proved 27 February, 1775.

Bondsmen, Samuel Hobson and Thomas Haskins.

Thomas Swann, Clerk.

From the Old Vestry Book Records.

"The 12th of November, 1729, was born Olimpe Dupui, daughter of Jean Jaque Dupui and of Susane Dupui; was baptized by Mr. Swift; had for godfather Jean Levilaine, and for godmother Philippe Dupui and Judith Dupui."

Will of John James Trabue of Chesterfield County, Va., p. 79, Will book No. 3, at Chesterfield Co. Clerk's office, 1777.

In the name of God, Amen, this tenth day of October in the year of our Lord Christ one thousand seven hundred and seventy-five, I, John James[2] Trabue of Chesterfield Co. and Manchester Parish, being weak of body, but of perfect mind and memory do make and ordain this my last will and testament.

Imprimis. I leave for the use of my beloved wife, Olimpe, the upper part of the tract of land I now live on . . . use of 4 negroes, 3 work horses . . . 20 head of cattle and stock of hogs.

Similar bequests he made to the following: To son John James; to son John; to son William; to son Daniel; to son Edward; to son Stephen; to son Samuel; to daughter Magdeline; to daughter Jean (or Jane); to daughter Mary; to daughter Martha; daughters Elizabeth, Judith, Susanna. To daughter Susanna 30 pounds current money, it being the legacy given to her by her grandfather, John James Dupuy, which I have received. I appoint James Dupuy, my wife's brother, my son, William[3] Trabue, and Joseph Watkins, executors . . . signed,

John James[2] Trabue.

In presence of Judith Dupuy, Joseph Watkins, Jacob Ashurst. Examined on inventory of John James[2] Trabue, deceased, taken by James Dupui, executor, Dec. 21st, 1775.

He died between Oct. 10th and Dec. 21st, 1775.

CHILDREN OF JOHN JAMES[2] TRABUE, BORN 1722, DIED 1775, MARRIED 1744, OLYMPE DUPUY, BORN 12 NOV., 1729, DIED 1822.

I. James[3] Trabue, born 29 January, 1745, in Chesterfield County, Va., died 23 December, 1803; married 1782, Jane E. Porter, born in Virginia about 1756, died in Kentucky 17 March, 1833 (daughter of Robert Porter, a Scotchman).

James Trabue served in Lord Dunmore's War as a Lieutenant, according to the statements of Daniel Trabue in his diary:

"In 1774 there was an Indian War against the Shawnees. Governor Dunmore went out against them, also brother James, went with Governor Dunmore as a Liuetenant. He raised some of his men in our country. They had cockades of red riband. . . . When brother James and the soldiers came home, they told us about the battle at the mouth of the Kanawha on the 10th of October (Point Pleasants). They also told us about Kentucky, a newly discovered, wonderful country."

Serving as a Lieutenant in 1778, he and his young brother, Daniel, came at the instigation of Col. George Rogers Clark to Kentucky, and was with Col. Clark at the capture of Kaskaskia and Vincennes. He was captured when Ruddle's Fort was taken by the Indians and British, and imprisoned in Montreal for over a year; finally making his escape, he returned to Kentucky and the Fort. After this he was Commissary General of the Quartermaster's Department.

He became a surveyor under Daniel Boone, and located large tracts of land in Bourbon and Harrison counties, and was one of the largest early land owners in the State. His heirs received about ten thousand acres for his Revolutionary services.

James[3] Trabue, and wife, Jane E. Porter—issue:

1 Judith[4] Trabue, married George Ewing.
2 Mary[4] Trabue, married William T. Scott—issue:
  1 Olympia[5].
  2 John[5].
  3 George[5], M. D.
3 Robert[4] Trabue, born ————, married 1810, Mary Grimes, born 1795, died 1865, left issue:
  1 Edw.[5], born 1816, died 1865.
4 James[4] Trabue, born Charlotte County, Va., April 24, 1791; moved to Kentucky with mother and family 1807. Commanded the militia of Bourbon County, Ky., for many years; died 22 February, 1874; married first, Judith Woolridge; married second, Lucy Dupuy Cosby; issue by both wives.
5 Elizabeth[4] Trabue, born 11 February, 1799, died 9 December, 1849, at "Weehawken," country seat near Frankfort, Ky., married 20 November, 1818, Chastain Haskins Trabue, her first cousin, born 25 November, 1796, died 2 September, 1852, at "Weehawken"—issue:
  1 Stephen Fitz-James[5] Trabue, born Bourbon County, Ky., 19 Sept., 1819, died Louisville, Ky., 13 December, 1898, at the home of his son, E. F. Trabue. He graduated in law at Transylvania University, Lexington, Ky., 1842. Resided at "Weehawken" near Frankfort, Ky. for fifty-seven years, and practiced law in that city about fifty years. He was a "lawyer of fine ability and scholarly attainments, being versed in Latin, Greek and French languages, an earnest, eloquent public speaker." (See personal account, post.)

  Married June 1, 1854, Alice Elizabeth Berry, born 2 November 1835, died 16 August, 1893; daughter of Edmund Taylor Berry, born Newport, Ky., 9 June, 1811, and wife Sarah Frances Taylor, and sister of Surgeon William Berry, U. S. A., 1861; and Rear Admiral Robert Mallory Berry, U. S. N.—issue:

  1 Edmund Francis[6] Trabue, lawyer of Louisville, Ky., of the firm of Trabue, Doolan, Helm & Helm; married Caroline Bullitt Cochran, daughter of Gavin H. Cochran and Lucinda Wilson, his wife—issue:
    1 Lucinda Cochran[7] Trabue, married Dr. John Rowan Morrison, M. D.
  2 Stephen Fitz-James[6] Trabue, Jr., lawyer of Florida, married Annie South, daughter of Samuel South—issue:
    1 Virginia Taylor[7] Trabue.
    2 Marion South[7] Trabue.
  3 Willett C.[6] Trabue, lawyer, resides Philadelphia, Pa., married Mrs. Belle Moore Dabney—no issue.
  4 William Berry[6] Trabue, died aged five months.
  5 Robert Berry[6] Trabue, New Orleans, La., associated with "Mutual Life Insurance Company of New York," married Juliet Maude Barr, daughter James O. Barr of Louisiana—issue:
    1 Stephen Fitz-James[7] Trabue, 3rd.

2 Isaac Haskins[7] Trabue.
6 Alice Elizabeth[7] Trabue, unmarried.
2 Aaron[5] Trabue, born 19 February, 1821, died 2 August, 1823.
3 Marion Frances[5] Trabue, born 21 February, 1823, d.ed 12 February, 1853.
4 Henrietta Jane[5] Trabue, born 24 May, 1826, died 23 November, 1903, married Dr. Milus Cooper Nisbet, issue two daughters and one son, Milus.
5 Isaac Hodgens[5] Trabue, born 23 March, 1829, died 16 July, 1907. Graduated at Transylvania University, Lexington, Ky. Lawyer, Colonel in Union Army, 1861; married 1865 in Savannah, Ga., Virginia Taylor. Removed to Florida.
6 William Chastain[5] Trabue, born 22 May, 1834, died Hawesville, Ky., 12 March, 1875. Fine lawyer, one of the leading chess players in America. Soldier in the C. S. A.
7 Ann Eizabeth[5] Trabue, born 1836, died 7 October, 1905, married Charles W. Gill.
8 Judith Helen[5] ("Judelle") Trabue, born 4 February, 1838, died 22 June, 1900, married Dr. Thomas A. MacGregor—issue:
1 Chastine Elizabeth[6] MacGregor, married Ernest W. Sprague—issue:
1 Chastine MacGregor[7] Sprague.
2 Ernest W.[7] Sprague, Jr.
3 Helen Elizabeth[7] Sprague.
2 Mathilde Lewis[6] MacGregor, married Joseph M. Huston—issue:
1 Judelle MacGregor[7] Huston.
2 Craig[7] Huston.
9 Henry Joseph[5] Trabue, M. D., born 22 February, 1841, died 15 October, 1876, unmarried. Surgeon C. S. A.
6 Martha T.[4] Trabue, married 1822, Dr. Archibald King—issue:
1 Mary Ann[5] King.
2 Eliza Jane[5] King.
3 Susan M.[5] King.
II. Magdelene[3] Trabue, born 1748, died 1815, married Edward Clay, uncle of Henry Clay, moved to North Carolina—issue ten children.
III. Phoebe[3] Trabue, born 1750, died 1767, unmarried.
IV. Jane[3] Trabue, born 12 January, 1752, died 1802, married Rev. Joseph Minter (Baptist), born 19 March, 1754 died 1814—issue:
1 James[4] Minter, died young.
2 Nancy[4] Minter, born 9 January, 1777, married Joseph Watkins, soldier in Revolution—issue nine children.

3 Elizabeth[4] Minter, born 21 July, 1778, married James Major—issue six children.
4 Judith[4] Minter, born 28 September, 1779, married James Gow—issue, Emily.
5 Jane[4] Minter, born 6 March, 1781, married Benjamin Watkins born 1 October, 1775 (son of Joseph Watkins)—issue fourteen children of whom:
7th Caroline W.[5] Watkins, 7th child born 7 May, 1813, married Parker H. Hardin (lawyer)—issue:
1 Judge Charles[6] Hardin, a prominent lawyer and circuit judge of Harrodsburg, Ky., married Jennie McGoffin—three sons:
1 Charles[7] Hardin, Jr., a circuit judge of Harrodsburg, Ky.
2 Parker Watkins[6] Hardin, Lawyer, served as Attorney General of Kentucky for three terms. Democratic nominee for Governor 1895, and widely known publicly, married Mary Sallee—issue six children:
1 John[7], died.
2 Caroline[7] married W. E. Harris of Virginia.
3 Parker[7], Jr., died.
4 Rev. Martin[7], married Miss Stevenson.
5 Jane[7], married.
6 Julia[7], M. D.
6 Sarah[4] Minter, born 13 August, 1782, died October, 1859, married 1810, William H. Cosby—issue seven children.
7 John[4] Trabue Minter, born 16 May, 1784, married Elizabeth Scarse—issue eight children.
8 William[4] Minter, born 16 December, 1785, died about 1863, married Elizabeth Green Waggoner, moved to Tennessee.
9 Martha[4] Minter, born 14 April, 1787, died 11 December, 1860.
10 Joseph[4] Minter, born 17 June, 1789, died 1833, married Elizabeth Ann Cosby—issue.
11 Tabitha[4] Minter, born 9 February, 1791, married William H. Pittman, of Columbia, Ky.—issue.
12 Anthony[4] Minter, married Elizabeth Kerr.
13 James[4] Minter, born 14 March, 1794, married.
14 Jeremiah[4] Minter, born 23 June, 1796, married Sallie McDowell.
V. John[3] Trabue, born 17 March, 1754, died at Logan's Fort, Ky., 1788, married Margaret Pierce.
Colonel Revolutionary War. Original member of the Society of the Cincinnati of Vir-

512

ginia, Deputy Surveyor of Kentucky lands under John May. No issue.

VI. William[3] Trabue, born Chesterfield County, Va., 13 March, 1756, died 2 March, 1786, married 12 February, 1783, Elizabeth Haskins, born 29 September, 1759, died 10 October, 1825 (Daughter Colonel Robert and Elizabeth (Hill) Haskins)—issue:

1 Nancy[4] Trabue, born 24 November, 1783, died 16 February, 1846, married William Caldwell (his second wife), born 10 August, 1777, died 10 January, 1854—issue:
  1 Elizabeth Haskins[5] Caldwell, born 26 November, 1811, died 25 October, 1865, married William Trabue (son of Stephen Trabue and Jane Haskins)—issue:
    1 Laura Alice[6] Trabue, married John D. Wickliff.
    2 Nancy Lucretia[6] Trabue, married F. C. Shearer.
    3 Matilda Jane[6] Trabue, unmarried.
    4 Lucy Ellen[6] Trabue, died unmarried.
    5 Edward Haskins[6] Trabue.
  2 Ann Jane[5] Caldwell, born 9 March, 1813, married John Dudley Winston, M. D. of Nashville, Tenn.—issue ten children of whom:
    1 George Alfred[6] Winston, married Mary Hite—issue:
      1 George Alfred[7] Winston.
      2 Dudley[7] Winston.
      3 Nanny Hite[7] Winston.
  3 George Alfred[5] Caldwell, born Columbia, Adair County, Ky., 8 October, 1814, died September, 1866, in Louisville, Ky. Member of Kentucky Legislature from Adair County, Major of Volunteers in the Mexican War; promoted to Colonel for valuable services rendered the City of Mexico; member of Congress from the Fourth District; head of a prominent law firm in Louisville, Ky., until his death. Considered by some to have been the greatest lawyer in Kentucky of his day, unmarried.
  4 Phoebe Lucretia[5] Caldwell, born 3 July, 1817, died 1893, married William Duvall Helm, M. D., left issue.
  5 William Beverly[5] Caldwell, M. D. of Transylvania University, Lexington, Ky. Practiced medicine in Adair County, Ky. Moved to Louisville, Ky., 1846, where he built up a large and lucrative practice. Director of the L. & N. R. R. and the J. M. & I. R. R. Occupied many positions of prominence in Louisville, Ky. Devoted member of the Baptist Church. He was born Columbia, Adair County, 3 April, 1818, died Louisville, May, 1892, married 1847, Ann Augusta Guthrie, daughter of James Guthrie, Secretary of the Treasury under Franklin Pierce—issue:
    1 Ann Eliza[6] Caldwell, married Ernest Norton—issue:
      1 Caldwell[7] Norton, married Nanny Stephens. Served on Board of Public Works of Louisville, Ky.—issue:
        1 James Stephens[8] Norton, 1st Lieutenant.
        2 Brooke Minor[8] Norton.
      2 Ernest[7] Norton, married Ferda Zorn, dead.
    2 William Beverly[6] Caldwell, married Minnie Norton, no issue.
    3 James Guthrie[6] Caldwell, married Nannie Standiford. Served as President of Farmers' & Drovers' Bank; member of Board of Public Works of Louisville, Ky.—issue:
      1 William Beverly[7] Caldwell.
      2 James Guthrie[7] Caldwell, First Lieutenant.
      3 George Danforth[7] Caldwell, Capt., married Jane Keller.
      4 Junius[7] Caldwell, Serg.
      5 Nancy[7] Caldwell.
    4 Augusta[6] Caldwell, married Horatio Bright—issue:
      1 Augusta[7] Bright.
    5 Junius[6] Caldwell, married Ella Payne—issue:
      1 Julia[7], married Charles Jefferson, M. D.
      2 John P.[7], Corp.
    6 Mary Phoebe[6] Caldwell, married Rev. Rufus P. Johnston, D. D.
  6 Junius[5] Caldwell, born Columbia, Adair County, Ky., 2 March, 1820, died November, 1891, married Henrietta Rochester. No issue. Educated in schools of Adair County and Georgetown College. Succeeded his father as clerk of Adair County, and served twenty years. Practiced law in Columbia for a few years before removing to Louisville, 1865, when he entered into partnership with his elder brother, George Alfred, and younger brother, Isaac.

As a lawyer, he was a thorough, indefatigable worker, never resting until he had exhausted every research in the preparation of his cases. A great student of literature and the sciences.

Loved poetry, history and theological literature, a devout member of the Baptist Church.

7 Isaac[5] Caldwell, born Columbia, Adair County, Ky., 30 January, 1824, died about 1886. Educated at the local schools and at Georgetown College. Practiced law in Columbia several years with Judge Zachariah Wheat; formed partnership with eldest brother, George Alfred, and removed to Louisville, Ky., 1852, where they built up a large and lucrative business. He had already acquired a high reputation at the bar, but after his brother's death, 1866, when he was forced to show the versatility of his talents, this steadily increased until his position at its head was conceded. His methodical business habits, untiring industry and fine analytical mind, in addition to his eloquence before a jury classed him as a great lawyer, considered to have no superior in the State.

It has been said of these three lawyers and one physician brother, that they were probably the four most illustrious brothers ever in the State. He married 20 January, 1857, Catherine (daughter of Daniel and Hettie (Palmer) Smith)—issue:

1 Isaac Palmer[6] Caldwell, married Jane Jacobs.
2 Mary[6] Caldwell, dead, married Philip P. Peace.
3 George Alfred[6] Caldwell.
4 Robin Adair[6] Caldwell, dead.
5 William[6] Caldwell, dead.
6 Catherine[6] Caldwell, married Mr. Patton.
7 Margaret[6] Caldwell.

VII. Mary[3] Trabue, born Chesterfield County, Va., 26 February, 1758, died Woodford County, Ky., 1792, married 5 March, 1779, Lewis Sublett, born Chesterfield County, Va., 1759, died Woodford County, Ky., 1830, soldier in Revolution—issue:

1 William[4] Sublett, born Chesterfield County, Va., 3 March, 1780, died Belleville, Iowa 1840. Served in War of 1812. Married and left issue.
2 James[4] Sublett, born 15 July, 1783, died Clinton, Ky., 9 June, 1860. Served in War of 1812. Married and left issue.
3 Lewis[4] Sublett, born 1787, died Woodford County, Ky., 1827; in War of 1812, married Susan Coleman, born 1793, died Woodford County, Ky., 1834. Eight children.
4 John[4] Sublette, born Woodford County, Ky., killed 1813, serving in War of 1812. Married and left issue.
5 Frances[4] Sublett, married William Vaughan.

VIII. Daniel[3] Trabue, born 31 March, 1760, died 1840, married Mary Haskins (daughter of Col. Robert and Elizabeth (Hill) Haskins). Captain in Revolution. Issuing Commissary under his brother, James Trabue, who was Commissary General. Was at the surrender of Yorktown; served under Col. George Rogers Clark; under Lafayette and Muhlenberg; sheriff and justice of the peace in Kentucky. Settled on Greer's Creek, Fayette County, Ky. Writer of the Diary and Journal held in Archives of Draper Collection, Madison, Wisconsin. Had eight children:

1 Judith[4] Trabue, married S. Scott, left issue.
2 Sallie[4] Trabue, married G. Anderson, issue three children.
3 James[4] Trabue, born —————, died ————— in Louisville, Ky. He was an influential and wealthy merchant of Louisville, of the firm of "Trabue-Davis and Co.," and a most beloved citizen. Was long the Commissioner of the Sinking Fund of Louisville, and a pillar of the First Christian Church. Married Eliza Stites—issue:
  1 Richard[5] Trabue, married 1864, Kate Dougherty.
  2 Corinna[5] Trabue, died 13 years of age.
  3 Sarah[5] Trabue, died unmarried.
  4 James[5] Trabue, died young.
  5 Mary[5] Trabue, married William H. Barksdale—issue:
    1 William[6] Barksdale.
    2 Trabue[6] Barksdale.
  6 William[5] Trabue, married Lizzie Shreve—issue 3.
4 Mary[4] Trabue, married Lewis Sublett—seven children.
5 John[4] Trabue, murdered at the age of twelve years by the notorious Harpers, a gang of highwaymen.
6 Daniel[4] Trabue, Jr., married Mary Paxton of Texas—issue:
  1 Colonel Robert[5] Paxton Trabue, born 1 January, 1824, died 12 February, 1863, in Richmond, Va., of pneumonia. Lawyer and soldier, was Captain in Mexican War; raised the Fourth Kentucky Regiment of the Orphan Brigade, C. S. A., and personally equipped his regiment with blankets the first year from his private resources. He commanded throughout the Battle of

Shiloh and though notified, while ill, of his promotion to Brigadier General, he died before serving as such. He was much beloved by his soldiers and greatly revered for his courage and intrepidity in the midst of battle; for his graceful horsemanship and military tactics. He married Miss Hibernia Inge of Natchez, Miss. No issue.
2 Ann[5] Trabue.
3 Ellen[5] Trabue.
4 William[5] Trabue.
5 George[5] Trabue, were brothers and sisters of Col. Robert P. Trabue.
7 Presley[4] Trabue, died young.
8 Robert[4] Trabue, married Lucy Waggoner in Illinois—issue:
  1 Eliza[5] Trabue.
  2 Sallie[5] Trabue, married George Patterson.
  3 Robert[5] Trabue, married Martha Witherspoon—issue:
    1 Leatitia[6] Trabue.
    2 James[6] Trabue.
  4 Mary[5] Trabue, married Joseph Lester.
  5 Martha[5] Trabue.
  6 John[5] Trabue.
  7 Olympia[5] Trabue, married Hall.
IX. Martha[3] (Patsy) Trabue, 1762, married Josiah Woolridge—issue:
1 Seth[4] Woolridge, married Mary Ewing. Issue six children.
2 Daniel[4] Woolridge, married Lucy Thurman.
3 Samuel[4] Woolridge, married ———. Issue six children.
4 Martha[4] Woolridge, married Mr. Cheatham in Illinois.
5 Mary[4] Woolridge, married Joseph Barton White, born 1780, died M. 1873.
6 Claiborne[4] Woolridge, died March 1838, married Frances Trabue.
7 Stephen[4] Woolridge, married Mary Williams. Issue four children.
8 Josiah[4] Woolridge, married Elizabeth Hill.
9 Judith[4] Woolridge, married James Trabue.
10 Levi[4] Woolridge, married Henrietta Phelps.
11 Livingston[4] Woolridge.
X. Edward[3] Trabue, born Chesterfield County, Va., 1762, died 6 July, 1814. In Revolutionary War at General Gate's Defeat; in battle of Guilford, N. C., 15 March, 1781. Drafted at age of 16 years and became a Colonel. Settled in Woodford County, Ky., married first about 1786, Martha Haskins (daughter of Col. Robert Haskins and Elizabeth Hill). She died about 1794—issue:

1 Mary[4] Trabue, born 1787, married Anselm Clarkson. Issue seven children.
2 Elizabeth[4] Trabue, married Robert Hatcher. Issue five children.
3 Nancy Haskins[4] Trabue, born 8 October, 1791, married 6 November, 1816, Asa Pittman of Chesterfield County, Va., born 1788, died 6 May 1837—issue:
  1 Edward Francis[5] Pittman, married Ann Harrison.
  2 Martha Jane[5] Pittman, married Gesse Grady Crutcher.
  3 William Haskins[5] Pittman.
  4 George Trabue[5] Pittman of St. Louis, Mo.
  5 Anna Asa[5] Pittman, married Zachary Smith.
4 George Washington[4] Trabue, born Woodford County, Ky., 22 February, 1793, died Louisville, Ky., 5 September, 1873, at the home of his daughter, Mrs. William Terry, married 13 January, 1820, Mrs. Elizabeth Buford Chambers, born Woodford County, Ky., 8 December, 1794, died Glasgow, Ky., 30 August 1869, Issue:
  1 Joseph B.[5] Trabue, Glasgow, Ky., born 22 Dec., 1820, died 27 March, 1845, married Judith E. Mullins. One child.
  2 Benjamin Franklin[5] Trabue, M. D., born 6 October, 1882, died 25 November, 1905, married 12 June, 1855, Lelia Anderson. Issue three children.
  3 Judith Helen[5] Trabue, born Glasgow, Ky., 16 November, 1824, died Louisville, Ky., 2 December, 1893, married 8 September, 1842, William Terry, born Todd County, Ky., 6 November, 1816, died Louisville, Ky., 25 April, 1891, as a result of poisoning at a wedding. Issue:
    1 George W.[6] Terry, born 1844, died 1871.
    2 Elizabeth[6] Terry, married Rev. Mortimer Murray Benton, Episcopal Church. Issue two children:
      1 William Terry[7] Benton, married Frances Keller.
      2 Angelyn[7] Benton, unmarried, dead.
    3 Mary C.[6] Terry, unmarried.
    4 William[6] Terry, Jr.
    5 Alvah Lamar[6] Terry, married 15 July, 1880, Elizabeth Loving. One of the most influential and prominent business men of Louisville, having been connected for forty-five years with the largest wholesale dry goods store in the South, J. M. Robinson Norton & Co. Served twenty-five years as a Vestryman of

Calvary Episcopal Church; a most esteemed and beloved citizen. Issue two sons:
1 John Loving[7] Terry.
2 Alvah Lamar[7] Terry, Jr. Capt. of the Motor Transport located in France.
6 Helen[6] Terry, died in infancy.
7 Napoleon Buford[6] Terry, married Mattie Snowdon. He died 1907.
8 Maude Baker[6] Terry, married Henry DeBow. Issue:
1 Helen Terry[7] DeBow.
2 Elizabeth[7] DeBow.
4 Elizabeth Buford Chambers[5] Terry, lived one year.
5 Elizabeth Mary[5] Trabue.
6 Elizabeth Dupuy[5] Trabue, born 31 May, 1835, died Philadelphia, Pa., 15 August, 1909, married 1 December. 1853, Samuel Ware VanCulin, born 29 April, 1824, died Philadelphia 12 October, 1887. Issue:
1 Trabue[6] VanCulin.
2 Lillian Dupuy[6] VanCulin, married first, Rev. Joseph Leslie Richardson of Mt. Eden, Ky., infant died; married second, Thomas Roberts Harper of Pennsylvania. It is to her intelligence and industry that we owe the valuable book, "Colonial Men and Times."
3 Samuel Ware[6] VanCulin, died unmarried.
4 William Townsend[6] VanCulin.
5 DuPuy[6] VanCulin.
7 George Washington[5] Trabue, Jr., born Glasgow, Ky., 21 January, 1839, died 29 April, 1869, married 24 May 1860, Mary T. Wade. Issue:
1 Buford[6] Trabue, married Fanny Murphy.
2 Elizabeth[6] Trabue.
3 Nellie E.[6] Trabue, married Charles Lewis.

(X.) Edward[3] Trabue, born 1762, died 6 July 1814, married second, Jane E. Clay (daughter Rev. Eleazer Clay of Chesterfield Co., Va.), 2 October, 1797. She was born 1 January, 1776, died 8 June, 1845. Issue:
5 Charles Clay[4] Trabue, born Woodford County, Ky., 27 Aug., 1798, served with General Jackson with distinction; married July, 1820, Agnes G. Woods. Removed to Missouri and served one term in the Legislature. Removed to Nashville and was Mayor of that city; died 24 November, 1851. Issue:
1 James Woods Walker[5] Trabue, died young.
2 Martha Ann Sommerville[5] Trabue, born 5 July, 1832, married George T. Thompson, 1845.
3 Anthony Edw. Dupuy[5] Trabue, born 2 April, 1825, married 1864, Christiana Hans Manly. Issue.
4 Joseph Thomas Crutcher[5] Trabue, born 4 February, 1827, died 1880.
5 Jane Woods Clay[5] Trabue, born 24 November, 1828, married John Houston Reynolds of Memphis, 1850.
6 Sarah Elizabeth[5] Trabue, born 29 March, 1830, married first, John B. Stevens; married second, Col. William R. Shivens, C. S. A.
7 Charles Henry Clay[5] Trabue, born 8 September, 1834, died on the battlefield at Sharpsburg, Md., 1862, aged twenty-eight years.
8 Robert Wood Howell[5] Trabue, 9 January, 1837, married Mary Maslin Bibbs. He died 19 November, 1878. Left issue.
9 John George Washington[5] Trabue, born 21 February, 1839, died 1 May, 1884, aged forty-five years, married 18 November, 1868, Ellen Dunn. Issue:
1 William Dunn[6] Trabue, married Lucinda O'Bryan.
2 George W.[6] Trabue.
3 Charles Clay[6] Trabue, prominent lawyer of Nashville, Tenn., married Julia Malone.
6 John E.[4] Trabue, M. D., married Elizabeth Atkinson, left issue.
7 Martha[4] Trabue, born 1803, died 1 July, 1833, married 6 April, 1819, Aaron Trabue, left issue.
8 Jane E.[4] Trabue, twin with Cynthia Trabue, born Woodford County, Ky., 7 November, 1805, died M., 1888, married John White Lewellen.
9 Cynthia Ann[4] Trabue, born 7 November, 1805, died Mo., 1886, married Taylor Jones of Ralls, Mo.
10 Susan[4] Trabue, married Philip Clayton.
11 Matilda O.[4] Trabue, born 6 January, 1808, died 1881, married Amos Sutton.
12 Prince Edw.[4] Trabue, born 9 December, 1812, died 20 October, 1890, married Lydia Neville.

XI. Stephen[3] Trabue, born 2 February, 1766, died 24 November, 1833, married 24 July, 1788, Jane Haskins, born 12 October, 1767, died 15 September, 1833 (daughter of Col. Robert and Elizabeth (Hill) Haskins). Issue:
1 Rebecca[4] Trabue, born 3 August, 1789, died 15 June, 1834, married John Hill.

2 Haskins D.[4] Trabue, born 24 December, 1790, died 13 Feb., 1860, married 20 November, 1816, Olympia Wilson.
3 Aaron[4] Trabue, born 12 January, 1793, died 26 October, 1877, married first Martha Trabue; married second, Martha Cheatham.
4 William[4] Trabue, born 7 March, 1795, married first, 1816, Elizabeth McDowell; married second, Elizabeth Haskins Caldwell. Issue:
1 Emily[5] Trabue, married John Lewis.
2 Elizabeth Ann[5] Trabue, married David Winston.
3 Hannah J.[5] Trabue, married Lindsey Watson.
4 Harriet Olympia[5] Trabue, married Joseph Winston.
5 Benjamin McDowell[5] Trabue, M. D., married Fanny E. Sale of Todd County, Ky., had issue:
1 William H.[6] Trabue, prominent business man in New York City, married Corinne Boyde, issue two children.
2 Leroy P.[6] Trabue, M. D., married Maria Jefferson.
3 Helen M.[6] Trabue, married E. U. Bland.
4 Benjamin McDowell[6] Trabue, married Bessie Morrison.
5 Elizabeth Burns[6] Trabue, unmarried.
6 Annie E.[6] Trabue, married H. P. Gray.
7 Mattie Y.[6] Trabue, unmarried.
8 Etta H.[6] Trabue, unmarried.
(4) William[4] Trabue, married second, Elizabeth Haskins Caldwell. Issue:
1 Laura Alice[5] Trabue, died 1875, married John D. Wickliff.
2 Nancy Lucretia[5] Trabue, died 1892, married F. C. Shearer.
3 Matilda Jane[5] Trabue.
4 Lucy Ellen[5] Trabue.
5 Edward Haskins[5] Trabue.
5 Chastain Haskins[4] Trabue, born 25 November, 1796, died 2 September, 1852, married 20 November, 1818, his first cousin, Elizabeth[4] Trabue (daughter of James[3] Trabue and Jane E. Porter).
6 Edward[4] Trabue, born 1798, married Mary Rogers. Some of his descendants are prominent people of Nashville, Tenn. Among them are Charles[6] Trabue, married Miss Steel; Horace[6] Trabue and Olympe[6] Trabue and several others.
7 Frances[4] Trabue, born 11 August, 1800, married Claiborne Woolridge, died 1838.
8 Elizabeth[4] Trabue, born 7 February, 1804, married William Gill.

9 John James[4] Trabue, born 7 February, 1806, married March, 1808.
XII. Elizabeth[3] Trabue, born 29 February, 1768, died 6 August, 1835, married 14 April, 1794, Fenelson R. Willson, born England, 14 February, 1768, died 1838. Issue:
1 Rev. Slater[4] Willson.
2 Letitia[4] Willson.
3 Olympia[4] Willson.
XIII. Samuel[3] Trabue, born 1770, died 1777.
XIV. Susanna[3] Trabue, born 1772, died 24 January, 1862, married 17 April, 1793, Thomas Major, born 25 December, 1769, died Franklin County, Ky., 6 May, 1846, lived at "Weehawken," near Frankfort, Ky. Issue:
1 Olive Trabue[4] Major.
2 John James[4] Major.
3 Elizabeth Redd[4] Major.
XV. Judith[3] Trabue, born 1774, married John Major. Lived in Illinois. Issue:
1 William T.[4] Major.
2 John[4] Major.
3 Joseph Winter[4] Major.
4 Benjamin[4] Major.
5 Chastain[4] Major.
6 Eliza[4] Major.
There were thirty-two men by the name of Trabue who served in the Confederate Army during the Civil War.

STEPHEN FITZ-JAMES TRABUE.

Probably the best known representative of the name of Trabue in Kentucky was the late Stephen Fitz-James Trabue, born Bourbon County, Ky., 19th September, 1819, died at the home of his son, Edmund F. Trabue, Louisville, Ky., 13th December, 1898. The Biographical Encyclopaedia of Kentucky, published 1878, p. 408, says of him:

"Descended from an old and distinguished family of Huguenots who fled from France during the days of the persecutions of that people. His father, Chastain Haskins Trabue, was a prominent merchant for many years, and at his death was engaged in the banking business in Louisville.

517

"His grandfather (maternal) James Trabue and all of his family, who were able to bear arms, were soldiers in the Revolution, and when the second war with England began, to a man, took up arms in defense of their country. This family of patriots left Virginia about 1783, and coming to Kentucky were among the first land owners in Woodford County. Some members of the family settled in the Green river country, and others in other parts of the State, where they became conspicuous in the affairs of the early settlements and Indian wars, and were ever ready to buckle on their armor in defense of their country.

"His mother was Elizabeth Trabue, daughter of James Trabue and Jane E. Porter.

"James Trabue went as a Lieutenant under Gov. Dunmore against the Shawnees in 1774, raising his company in Chesterfield, his home county in Virginia, and was at the battle of Point Pleasants. Later as a Lieutenant and accompanied by his younger brother Daniel,* who was but eighteen years of age, he came at the instigation of Colonel George Rogers Clark to Kentucky, in 1778. Here he become 'Commissary General under Col. Clark and was present with him at the capture of Kaskaskia and Vincennes. He located large tracts of land in Bourbon and Harrison counties and was one of the wealthiest land owners in the State.'

"Stephen Fitz-James Trabue received a fine education under private tutors and at Adair Academy and Tuscombia, Ala., and, although he removed before graduating, he became a fine scholar and is thoroughly versed in the Latin, Greek and French languages. He chose the law for a profession and entered upon its studies in 1841 at Frankfort in the office of Cates and Lindsey and graduated in the Law Department of Transylvania University the following year, 1842. From early youth, he displayed not only great aptitude in learning, but more than ordinary ability for trade and speculation, and engaged quite successfully before entering upon his professional studies, in dealing in the depreciated paper of the banks of Mississippi and Alabama. Immediately after finishing his legal preparations, he went to Richmond, Va., and Washington city with a view of recovering the bounty lands, amounting to about ten thousand acres due the heirs of his grandfather, for services during the Revolution. This induced him to engage in land speculations in Illinois, Wisconsin, Minnesota, Iowa, Missouri and Kentucky, west of the Tennessee river, which he continued with great success until 1852, accumulating a large fortune, a great deal of which his restless, enterprising spirit led him to sink in the coal banks at Hawesville, Ky., and other points on the Ohio river; and after other considerable losses, brought about by the necessities of his friends, he finally returned in 1854 to Frankfort with a view to settling down upon his farm three

*Note.—Daniel Trabue, Document P. 11, "Colonial Men and Times." By Lillian Dupuy Van Culin Harper.

"WEEHAWKEN".

Built by S. F. J. Trabue in 1860. The Colonial porch added by Mr. S. French Hoge, its present owner.

miles from Frankfort, and entering upon the practice of his profession.

"The first purchase of land in his home place was in 1839, of Dr. Archibald King, who had married his Aunt Martha Trabue. The records show that in 1799 this home was owned by Thomas Major, whose wife, Susanna Trabue, was a great-aunt of Stephen Fitz-James Trabue, hence the place, 'Weehawken,' was owned by three generations of Trabues, and not out of the family until 1897, a period of ninety-eight years, when sold to Mr. Stephen French Hoge, its present owner. Stephen Fitz-James Trabue accumulated land adjoining the original tract, until his homestead consisted at one time of thirteen hundred acres; this he reduced afterwards to four hundred. The original residence was large and of frame, but it having burned in 1860, he immediately thereafter built the present spacious brick home, which is situated upon a knoll with a front lawn covering two or more acres of ground, and surrounded by the picturesque limestone fence characteristic of the bluegrass region.

"'Weehawken' was wide-famed for its hospitality, presided over by the wife of Stephen Fitz-James Trabue, a woman of unusual dignity and fine presence, noted beauty, of strong intellect and character, and of great justice and generosity.

"Although Mr. Trabue took an active interest in political affairs and made some exciting contests, he continuously engaged in the pursuit of his profession, in which he was prominent in many of the leading cases before the courts. He was a lawyer of fine ability and scholarly attainments, an eloquent, earnest public speaker, a man of large views, great administrative ability, conscientious and just in his dealings with men, and was possessed of those traits of character which would bring him to the front in any public emergency. He occupied a high position in some of the social organizations of the day, in which he was a leader, and was one of the most active, energetic and enterprising men of his section.

"He was a member of the Knights Templars and was for twenty-five years Grand Commander of the Frankfort Commandery, which he was principally instrumental in establishing.

"He was a member of the Episcopal Church in Frankfort, Ky.

"He married the 1st of June, 1854, Alice Elizabeth Berry, born 2nd November, 1835, 'Spring Hill,' Oldham County, Ky., daughter of Edmund Taylor Berry, born in Newport, Ky., and wife, Sarah Frances Taylor, and granddaughter of Washington Berry, born in King George County, Va. She died 16th August, 1893.

"Stephen Fitz-James Trabue and wife, Alice E. Trabue, had six children:

"Edmund Francis Trabue, lawyer of Louisville, Ky.

"Stephen Fitz-James Trabue, Jr., lawyer in Florida.

"Willett C. Trabue, lawyer, lives in Philadelphia, Penn.

"William Berry Trabue, died at five months of age.

"Robert Berry Trabue, lives in New Orleans, La.

"Alice E. Trabue, unmarried."

REV. ANDREW TRIBBLE, PIONEER.

By BESS L. HAWTHORNE.

The earliest known member of this family was George Tribble, of Welsh extraction, and a farmer in Caroline County, Virginia.[a] Nothing further is known of him, though there are references to a George Tribble of King and Queen County, who may have been the same person.[b] Of his family we know nothing with the exception of one son, Andrew Tribble. There may have been another son, George,[c] but so far no proof has been found that there was.

Andrew Tribble was born 22 March 1741, and very early became a member of the Baptist Church. Often he was heard to say that he was the 53d Baptist north of the James River.[a] Soon after his conversion he began to preach, and went to Orange and surrounding counties to baptize new converts.[d] Then for a while he was a member of Goldmine Church in Louisa County. From this church he was sent as a messenger to the first meeting of the General Association of Virginia in May, 1771.[a]

In 1777, he became pastor of a little Baptist Church in Albemarle County, variously known as Albemarle, Buck Mountain, and Chestnut Grove. This church was organized in January 1773, being the first Baptist church in Albemarle.[e] It was near "Monticello," the home of Thomas Jefferson. It is said the two men became personal friends and Jefferson often attended the meetings here. Many claim that Jefferson gained his idea of a popular government for this country through watching the business management of this little Baptist church by Rev. Andrew Tribble.[a]

Mr. Tribble purchased a farm of 175 acres not far from this church, which he did not sell until 1785, about two years after he had moved to Kentucky.[e]

In 1768, most probably while he was preaching in Orange County, he was married to Miss Sarah Ann Burris (Burrus), daughter of Thomas Burris (Burrus) of Orange County. (See article on "Thomas Burris, Ancestor of Kentucky Pioneers.") Sarah Ann Burris was born 30 September 1753, it is thought in Orange County, Virginia, and was a red-headed, high spirited woman, from whom all the Tribbles inherit their high tempers. She was a woman of remarkable character and her descendents, even to the fifth and sixth generations, inherit from her certain unmistakable physical and mental characteristics.

Andrew Tribble and his family moved to Kentucky in 1783, and first settled on the Dix River, but soon moved into what is now known as Clark County.[a] In 1785, he had his membership in Providence Church ("the old stone meeting-house") where he and Rev. Robert Elkin were both pastors.[1] In January 1786, he became a member of the Howard Creek church, but during this same year he founded Tate's Creek Church in Madison County and became its pastor. Something over three years later, owing to a personal quarrel between him and the minister at Howard's Creek Church, Tribble and his adherents, about half the congregation, withdrew and established (1790) Unity Church[a] in the eastern part of Clark County.[f] It had a membership list of about 70, including the two ministers, Andrew Tribble and his brother-in-law, James Quisenberry. (See article, "Thomas Burris, Ancestor of Kentucky Pioneers.") Andrew Tribble probably acted as pastor until 1792 when he was succeeded by Rev. Quisenberry. His pastorate was ended because of a law suit with one of the members of the church,[a] in which it would seem that Mr. Tribble was not altogether blameless. Following this he moved to Madison County.[i] Just how long Unity Church remained in existence is not known, but it had only two other pastors, John M. Johnson and David Chenault, a son-in-law of Mr. Tribble's.[e]

He continued in his ministry to Tate's Creek Church however until shortly before his death. This church had been founded by him in 1786 under the name of "Tate's Creek Church of Separate Baptists." In 1790, it united with the "South Kentucky Association," remaining in that association until 1793, when together with four others, they withdrew and formed "Tate's Creek Association of United Baptists".[a]

"Mr. Tribble was a preacher of good ability and of commendable zeal. His early labors were performed in Virginia, where he endured the persecutions that were the common lot of Baptist preachers at that period. Like the Craigs, Shackleford, and a host of others, he endured his term in a Virginia jail for preaching the gospel contrary to law. He was a very active and successful laborer in Kentucky for about 35 years. His son . . . supposes he must have baptised 2000 persons in Kentucky".[a]

His last sickness was long and painful. It was caused by stricture of the bladder and resulted in his death on 22 December 1822[a] (or 30 December 1822[g]). A few hours before he died he said to his son, Peter Burris Tribble, a preacher also, and another young minister, "Boys, you see me here now. In a few days I shall be gone. I give you this charge—play the man for your God."[a] He was buried three and a half miles from the present city of Richmond, Kentucky, on a farm on what is now the Lexington Pike. This farm is owned at present by Mrs. Mary Tribble Neal, a great-grand-daughter of Mr. Tribble.

His wife, Sarah Ann Burris-Tribble, survived him several years, her death occuring on 15 December 1830, when she was past 77. She was probably buried in the same graveyard, as it was the custom in those days for each family to have a private burial ground on their own land.

To Rev. Andrew and Sarah Ann Tribble were born a number of children—

1. Frances Tandy Tribble, b. 3 November, 1769; d. 11 May, 1852; m. Michael Stoner (b. 1748, on the Schuylkill River, near what is now Philadelphia; d. 3 September, 1814, near Monticello, Wayne County, Kentucky).

Stoner was the close friend and comrade of Daniel Boone, and a sketch of his life will be given later.

2. Samuel Tribble, b. 30 or 31 December, 1771; m. Polly Martin, (b. 13 March, 1772).

3. Peter Burris Tribble, b 8 March, 1774, in Va.; d. 18 March, 1849, in Madison Co., Ky.; m. 8 October, 1793, Mary Boone (b. 2 April, 1776; d. 14 September, 1831). She was a daughter of George Boone, brother of Daniel (See the "Boone Family," Hazel A. Spraker, p. 133). Peter Burris Tribble followed in his father's footsteps and became a Baptist preacher too. He and his wife are buried in their old family burying ground, three miles south of Richmond, Ky., on the Big Hill pike. (The land on which it is situated adjoins that owned by Mr. Tom Chenault.)

4. Thomas Tribble, b. 13 June, 1776; m. .... Phelps.

5. Nancy Tribble, b. 6 November, 1778; d. 2 August, 1862; m. 3 April, 1794, David Chenault (b. 30 September, 1771; d. 9 May, 1831). "Their remains are laying near Cane Spring Church," is the inscription taken from the Tribble monument in the Richmond, Ky., cemetery.

6. Sally B. Tribble, b. 9 February, 1781; 2 February, 1810; m. 7 March, 1799, David Crews (d. 1821 in Madison Co., Ky.), who after her death married again.

7. Silas Tribble, b. 3 June, 1783; d. 18 November, 1842; m. 30 October, 1809, Jerusha White.

8. Andrew Tribble, b. 2 December, 1785; d. December, 1869; m. 24 June, 1810 in Madison Co., Ky., Lucy Boone (b. about 1790 or '91; d. August, 1868 or '69), a grand-daughter of George Boone, brother of Daniel. Both died and are buried at the old home place in Shelby Co., Ky. (See the "Boone Family.")

9. Mary Tribble, b. 29 March, 1788; m. 23 December, 1806, Joseph Stephenson (Stevenson)

10. (General) John Tribble, b. 15 August, 1790; m. 1st, 18 September, 1834, Martha A. White (d. 20 June, 1850), and 2nd, 6 May, 1852, Sally Coffey (d. 3 January, 1865).

11. Martha (Patsy) Tribble, b. 7 March, 1794; m. 5 October, 1812, Dr. Jacob White.

12. Dudley Tribble, b. 1 May, 1797; m. 21 January, 1819. Matilda H. Tevis.

(NOTE:—In June 1925 there was living in Richmand, Ky. a grandson of Rev. Andrew Tribble, who was past 90 years of age.)

Notes and References:

(a) Spencer's "History of Kentucky Baptists," Vol. I, p. 128.

(b) Printed Records of Spottsylvania County, Virginia.

P. 90. November 3, 1722, Larkin Chew, Gentleman, of Spottsylvania County to George Tribble of King and Queen County, 228 acres of land in Spottsylvania County, for 5 shillings, sterling, part of said Chew's patent, granted June 4, 1722. In St. George's Parish, Spottsylvania County.

P. 97. April 5, 1725. George Tribble of King and Queen County sold to William Johnson of Spottsylvania County, Virginia, for 12 pounds sterling, 223 (?) acres of land in Spottsylvania County. The said land bought by said Tribble from Larkin Chew, June 4, 1722.

(c) Printed Records of Spottsylvania County, Virginia, give the following article on George Tribble, who may possibly have been a son or grandson of the George Tribble mentioned in the records given above.

P. 529. September 3, 1832. George Tribble of Spottsylvania County, aged 76 years. Enlisted in the army of the United States in 1776 with Captain Vivion Minor of the Virginia line under the following officers: His enlistment was under the said Minor in Colonel Richard Johnson's regiment, as Minute Man, marched to Williamsburg, where he joined the battalion commanded by Major Andrew Buchanan; then marched to Hampton, where he remained until discharged, etc.; served 9 months, etc.; returned home, and was shortly afterwards drafted in the Virginia militia under Captain William Taliaferro and marched to Williamsburg and Jamestown; served 7 different tours, at different times in the Virginia militia during which period he was stationed at Port Royal, Va.; joined LaFayette in Culpepper County and thence marched to Charlottesville, and Yorktown. At the time of Cornwallis' surrender at Yorktown he was in a detachment reconnoitering the adjacent country of Gloucester County, Va.; was in but one engagement, and that was in Gloucester County. Was born in Caroline County in 1757, whence he was called into service, etc.

(d) Records of Spottsylvania County, Virginia.

P. 280. Andrew Tribble was witness to a deed for land October 16, 1770; said land located in Berkley Parish, Spottsylvania County, and apparently Andrew Tribble was living in said county at that time.

(e) "History and Genealogies," W. H. Miller, p. 41.

(f) Spencer's, "History of Kentucky Baptists," Vol. I, p. 206.

(g) "History and Genealogies," Miller, p. 346.

(h) Spencer's, "History of Kentucky Baptists," Vol. I, p. 206.

(i) "Genealogical Memoranda of the Quisenberry Family, and Other Families," Anderson Chenault Quisenberry, p. 55.

THE TURNER FAMILY.

By Jozie Mae Turner Matthews (Mrs. Walter Matthews).

The fact that Maryland was the first of the colonies to allow religious freedom to all who professed the Christian faith, and to allow the people a voice in the laws, caused many to choose it for their homes.

Among the early colonists was Edward Turner. He was of English parentage, and was born about 1631, since on December 3, 1651 "att a Court held at St. Maries," "Edward Turner, aged about 20 years was sworn and examined in open court," as a witness. (Maryland archives.) He is frequently mentioned in the records and apparently there was no other person of the same name at that time in the county.

Having sold tobacco to a Captain Tillman, in 1657, he sued for the payment of same in the Provincial Court at "Putuxent" and won his case. In 1676 he was assessed for 1055 pounds of tobacco taxes. In 1682 his name occurs in connection with the giving of information to the Council against one John Pryor, for trading with the Indians. He most assuredly was a person of much importance, for when in 1696 news reached the colony of a conspiracy in England against William and Mary, his name appears below a loyal address which was drawn up and "signed by the Civill Officers and Magistrates of St. Maries Co."

He owned land which was called Turner's Forest, the first survey of which is dated 1670. He was married twice; the name of the first wife was Elizabeth; she was probably the mother of his children. He married, second, Mary ——, who survived him. His children were: Thomas, Samuel and Elizabeth. He died about 1707. In his will, proved July 27, 1707, he left all his property as follows: Thomas received the plantation whereon Edward Turner had lived, Samuel received the plantation "whereon my quarter is built, called Bow."

Samuel Turner, second son of Edward Turner, was a well to do planter; he had large tracts of land in both St. Mary's and Charles counties; his residence was in Charles county. He married Lydia Dent, daughter of John Dent. Their children were: Edward, John, Samuel, Ruth and Mieba. He died perhaps in 1746, since according to his will, proved October 29, 1746, he made the following bequests: To Edward 200 acres of land on the east side of the Wicomico river, St. Mary's county, in Bastile "manner;" also part of a tract in Charles county called "Turner's Forest." To John was left a part of Turner's Forest, in Charles county. To Samuel was given a part of Turner's Forest, "formerly called Bow."

Just how many acres Turner's Forest comprised is not known. In 1712 450 acres were added to it. According to the foregoing will, it seemed to have been a very large tract.

The testaments and family names reveal the line of descent very clearly. Samuel Turner inherited from his father, Edward Turner, a plantation "called Bow." He, Samuel, in turn bequeathed to his youngest son, Samuel, "part of my land formerly called Bow, now called Turner's Forest."

Edward Turner, eldest son of Samuel Turner and Lydia Dent, like his father, is spoken of as "planter." Like his father, he held large tracts of land in both Charles and St. Mary's counties. His residence was in St. Mary's county. In the records of Trinity Parish, Charles county, dated April 8, 1751, he is mentioned as a church warden. The following entry appears on the Trinity Parish records, Charles county, Maryland." Children of Edward and Eleanor Turner:

John, born February 11, 1729. Died September 5, 1743.
Lydia, born December 13, 1731.
Randal, born September 20, 1739.
Joshua, born July 14, 1741.
Mary, born May 9, 1743.
Charles, born April 21, 1745.
Joseph, born March 1, 1747.
Elizabeth, born November 7, 1748.
Edward, born August 24, 1735. Died September 2, 1743.

Names of other children not recorded on Trinity Parish records are: William, Sally, Susannah, Eleanor and Randolph; the last perhaps is the same as the above Randal. Just why the names of all the children are not upon the record is not known.

Edward Turner's will was proved May 1, 1773. In it he did not mention the daughter, Eleanor. She was perhaps born after his death. Susannah's name is known from her tombstone in the burying ground of Christ's Church, Chaptico, St. Mary's county. The names of Samuel, William, Randolph, Charles, Joshua, Elizabeth, Joseph, Sally and Nelly appear in the will of Edward Turner. The testament, however, alludes to six sons and six daughters.

In Christ's Church, Chaptico, Maryland, there is a stained glass window to the memory of a Samuel Turner. He is perhaps the son of the above mentioned Edward.

Joshua Turner, son of Eleanor and Edward Turner, lived perhaps in St. Mary's county, and was married there. The name of his first wife has not been found. Their children were: John, Joshua, Nellie, Patsy and Clara.

There is in the Maryland Historical Society an original manuscript entitled, "Militia returns for each county 1780." Joshua Turner's name appears on this list, which proves that he aided in the cause of the American Revolution. He was married second on the 3rd day of December, 1792, in Culpeper county, Virginia, by the Rev. John Prickett, to Mary Ann Maddox Corly (widow of Aquilla Corley), daughter of Susannah Burch and Notley Maddox. The Maddox family also had lived in Maryland, but moved to Virginia in 1783, where Notley Maddox had received a land grant for Revolutionary services. The children of Mary Ann and Joshua Turner were:

Notley, Samuel, Mary (Polly) and Joseph Burch, all born in Virginia.

In the spring of 1813 or 1816, Joshua Turner, his wife and children, the children of his wife by her Corley marriage, the Magruder and Maddox families and others, moved to Kentucky, making the trip by flat boat. They brought their negroes, stock, household goods and some crude farming implements. They landed at Port William (now Carrollton) at night. They went to secure lodging and the man to whom they went refused them. They then told him they would sleep in his barn, but he told them he would rather have them in his house than his barn. The chances are they stayed with him. At dawn they started out in search of a place to locate. The Maddox and Magruder families located near where Pleasureville now is. The Turner family decided on a place in Henry county, adjoining the Barker farm. Just whom the land was bought from is not known. It was all in woods and the task of clearing it was stupendous.

The first house was of log, and was built near where the Turner burying ground is. Later another house was built, several hundred yards east of the first site. Some of the settlers brought seeds from Virginia with them; among these were three Catalpa seed. One was planted on the farm of Joshua Turner, and a tree from the seed is still standing. Joshua Turner died March 27, 1825, on the farm where he settled, and was buried in the Turner burying ground. His wife lived to be 93 years of age. She died January 25, 1856, and was buried at the same place.

Notley Turner, oldest son of Joshua and Mary Ann Turner, married and went to Mississippi.

Samuel Turner, second son, married Matilda Bickley, a descendant of Sir William Bickley, Baronet. Their children were: Barton, Samuel and Jane.

Mary Turner, daughter of Joshua and Mary Ann Turner, was born August 18, 1799, died April 3, 1889. She married Thomas Ransdall. Their children were:

(1) Susan, married Captain Smith Chilton. Issue: George T., James F., Alvin O., Mary Susan, William P., John B., Henry S., Millard, Eve and Ransdall.

(2) Joseph Ransdall, married first Eliza Vories. Issue: Fulton and Alice. Married second, Elizabeth Montfort. Issue: Thomas, Joseph and Elizabeth.

(3) B. Franklin Ransdall, married first Adaline Bowen. Issue: George and Lucy. Married second, Martha Vories. Issue: Mary, Wm., Sallie, Carrie and Kate. Married third, Isabel ———. Issue: Jennie, Virginia, John, Lucinda, Martha, Frank, Jasper, Isabel, Smith and Joseph.

(4) Notley Ransdall never married.

(5) Lucy Ransdall married first, Samuel Turner, Jr. Issue: Martha Jane and Thomas Samuel. Married second, Thomas Chilton. Issue: Anne, Notley, Eve and Jeff.

(6) Mary Ransdall married B. F. Chilton. Issue: Dora and Robert.

(7) Martha J. Ransdall married Jacob Hawkins. Issue: Sallie, Joseph, Emma and Steven.

(8) Eveline Ransdall married first James Voires. Issue: Emmett, William,

Willard, Nathaniel and Jefferson. Married second, Thomas Antle. Issue: Harriett and Jacob.

(9) Thomas Randall married Sarah Ringo. Issue: Morgan, Luther, James, Mary and Sallie.

(10) Wm. Ransdall married Letitia Stewart. Issue: Mary, Ann, Nancy, John and Joseph.

Joseph Burch Turner, youngest child of Joshua and Mary Ann Turner, was born in Culpeper county, Virginia, February 3, 1803. As a boy he worked on the farm and there was very little time for him to go to school. However, he realized the importance of an education, and pursued his studies until he was soon able to teach. He was a splendid mathematician. It was from his mother's family, no doubt, that he inherited this accomplishment, for his uncle, John Maddox, was one of the foremost surveyors and mathematicians of his day, having written the arithmetic and geometry he taught in Virginia and Kentucky in the early part of the nineteenth century.

Joseph Burch Turner inherited part of his father's farm, and at various times added to it. One early record shows where he bought 517 acres of land for $500. An indenture made and entered October 27, 1832, reads: "For and in consideration of the sum of $150.00, to me in hand paid by Joseph B. Turner, having bargained and sold and do by these presents bargain and sell unto the said Turner all that piece or parcel of land lying on Mill creek, being part of Peter Shepherd, 1,000 acres survey and bounded as follows, &c. Signed Moses Olds."

He united with the Sulphur Fork Church of Regular Old School Baptists, near Campbellsburg, Kentucky, on the third Sunday in January, 1829, and was baptized by Elder John A. McGuire. He was one of the messengers and bearers of the letter to the Sulphur Fork Association during the split among the Baptists in Kentucky, in 1840, and he brilliantly showed his faith in doctrine and church discipline. In 1842 he was elected clerk of the Mount Pleasant Association of Regular Baptists, and was clerk of that body for twenty-two years. He was Deacon of Sulphur Fork for a number of years. He has been known to ride horseback for seventy-five to one hundred miles to attend an Association.

In early manhood he was Colonel of militia. He never held public office, although he was asked to do so many times. In politics he was a Democrat and never failed to vote the ticket except on the occasion of his voting for Horace Greely. On the 5th of September. 1839, he was united in marriage with Martha Ann Jones, daughter of William Jones and Mary E. Travis, she being a lineal descendant of Sir Francis Mason, one of the Virginia Cavaliers, who settled at Jamestown, Virginia, in 1613, seven years before the landing of the Mayflower at Plymouth. Children of Martha and Joseph Burch Turner:

William Jones Turner, born August 21, 1840.

Joshua Turner, born December 23, 1842.

Joseph Samuel Turner, born July 22, 1844.

James Polk Turner, born September 14, 1846.

Thomas Jefferson Turner, born October 29, 1848.

Of these children, the three oldest in the Civil War joined the Confederate forces, serving in the Fourth Kentucky cavalry, under General Giltner. The life they had lived fitted them for the making of good soldiers, for they had spent most of their time in the open, hunting, riding and working hard on the farm. However, the ordeal proved too much for Joshua Turner, and he was stricken with fever, and gave his life for the cause he believed was right, January 18, 1863. He was buried in the Gillenwater burying ground on the farm of Dr. Gillenwater, near Rogersville, Tenn. The other two boys served until the close of the war, and are still living, proud to know that a united north and south went to war in 1917 for the same principles for which they fought—constitutional liberty.

William Jones Turner, oldest son, was married November 30, 1865, to Frances Montfort. Issue:

Mary Turner, married Dr. W. L. Vories.

Carrie Turner, married Ivan Teague.

Henry Turner, never married.

Fulton Turner, married Minnie Lawrence.

George Turner, married Anna May Meade.

Bettie Turner, married first, Will May; second, William Lindsey.

Lena Turner, married Charles Singleton.

Martha Turner, married Shannon Meade.

Minnie Turner, married Jesse Pyles.

William Turner, married Mamie Jeffries.

Joseph Samuel Turner, third son, married November 9, 1871, Mary Campbell: Issue:

George Campbell Turner, married Florence O'Bannon.

Mary Lula Turner, married George Tingley Browder.

Joseph Chester Turner, married Lula Maddox.

Leonard Turner, married Mamie Wilkerson.

Eda Ruth Turner, married William Newman Clarke.

James Polk Turner, fourth son, married October 12, 1871, Lena Ann Elston. Issue:

Patria Ballard Turner, married Justus Albert Price.

Jozie Mae Turner, married Dr. Walter Matthews.

Thomas Jefferson Turner, fifth son, never married. He died May 17, 1882.

Martha Ann Jones Turner, wife of Joseph Burch Turner, died April 8, 1850. After her death he married, October 7, 1851, Caroline Ringo, daughter of Sarah Bryan and George Ringo. Children by this marriage were:

George R. Turner, born January 9, 1853.

Mary Elizabeth Turner, born June 9, 1854.

Sarah Olive Turner, born December 12, 1855.

John Coblin Turner, born October 18, 1857.

Franklin Turner, born November 16, 1859.

Virginia Turner, born July 18, 1861.

Robert Lee Turner, born August 7, 1863.

Annie L. Turner, born February 10, 1866.

With twelve children in a household one can imagine the good times they must have had, and also can imagine how much work must have been done to have kept them clothed and fed. Nearly everything used was made on the farm. The women, with the assistance of several old negro servants, spun and dyed the yarn and made it into clothes, while the men and boys raised all of the food used, with the exception of the coffee. On one occasion, when more potatoes had been raised than could be used, Joseph Turner rode on horseback to Lane's Landing, near Port Royal. and took a sack of potatoes, for which he received fifteen cents per bushel, the price per bushel paying for one acre of ground.

George R. Turner, oldest child, married first January 13, 1876, Sallie Ransdall. Married second August 26, 1891, Jennie Ransdall. Issue: Joseph Turner (died young). Married third, September, 1900, Sadie Brown.

Mary Elizabeth Turner, second child, married Sept. 11, 1873, Lewis Elston. Issue:

Cora Elston, married William Morris.

William Elston, married Minnie Stigger.

Lee Elston, unmarried.

Roy Elston, died unmarried.

Sarah Olive Turner, third child, married Dec. 4, 1874, Elisha K. Perry. No children.

John Coblin Turner, fourth child, married September 16, 1890, Beatrice Neblett. Issue:

Hassell Turner, married, first, ——— Singleton; second, Margaret Lee.

Elizabeth Turner, married James Kelley.

James Turner, died young, Helen Turner, Franklin Turner, fourth child, married Sept. 9, 1880, Elizabeth Dunaway. Issue

Orva Turner, married Daisy Perry.

Lester Turner, married Annie Leslie.

Virginia Turner, fifth child, married Nov. 16, 1882, John K. Duncan. Issue:

Annie Laurie Duncan, married first, Robert Stark; second, Lee Tyler.

Oscar Duncan, married Lorena Treanor.

Charles Duncan, married Rica Ormes.

Mary Duncan, married first Warren Dunaway; second, George D. Harmon.

Elizabeth Duncan, married first Edgar Hamilton; second, George O. Dodson.

Samuel Duncan, married first, Irine McKinney; second, Evora Folk.

Joseph Duncan, married Ethel Sawyer.

Lorena Duncan.

Robert Lee Turner, sixth child, married May 1, 1890, Bettie F. Laytham. Issue:

Irine Turner.

Frank Laytham Turner.

Annie L. Turner, youngest child, married April 10, 1888, Thomas E. Neblett. Issue:

Robert Neblett, **married Elizabeth** Nash.

Ollie Neblett.

Mary Neblett.

Joseph Burch Turner gave valuable assistance in securing the Short Line Railroad. The first ground broken for it in that section was that on his farm. It was completed April 18, 1869, the total cost, including equipment, being $3,933,401. Later a station was established near his farm, and in appreciation of his efforts it was called Turner Station.

He died November 3, 1898. His second wife, Caroline Ringo Turner, died March 3, 1900. He and both wives are buried in the Turner burying ground at Turner Station, Kentucky.

Authorities: Md. St. Mary's wills, Charles county records, Turner family Bible, Henry county, Ky., records. The writer is indebted to Dr. E. R. Turner, Ann Arbor, Mich., for valuable data, also Mr. Hayes, secretary of the Maryland Historical Society.

TURNER FAMILY

Compiled by SAMUEL STEPHEN SARGENT, CHARLESTON, ILLINOIS

The Turner family with which this is concerned is that of Edward Turner who settled in what is now Madison County, Kentucky, sometime about 1786, when his name is found on the tax records pertaining to Lincoln County. See Kentucky Historical Register.

Information as to the previous residence of this Edward Turner is found in the Coles County, Illinois History, published by LeBaron & Sons, Chicago, Illinois, 1879, page 605, under the biography of Fountain Turner. Fountain Turner was a grandson of Edward Turner and was born in 1795, Madison County, Kentucky, the son of Thomas Turner and Anna Rodes Martin. In this biography he gave to the historian the information that his father (Thomas Turner) came from South Carolina. Meaning that he came to Madison Co., Ky., as that was the location of the family after leaving South Carolina.

Other Turners in what is now Madison County, Kentucky, contemporary with Edward Turner, Sr., were John Turner who married Rebecca Smith and had children—Andrew, Thomas, Edward, John, Cornelius, Anna, Sarah, Charity and by his second marriage to Jane Barnett were: James, Phillip, Barnett, Jesse, Jonathan, William, Mildred, Catherine, Patterson and Eleanor Jane Turner. This John Turner was born 1732 and died 1813 Madison Co., Ky. He lived in Rowan Co., North Carolina previous to removing to Kentucky and served in the Revolutionary War, as did his son Thomas Turner who married Anna Berry. It was thought by W. H. Miller, Richmond, Kentucky, historian, that this John was related to Edward Turner, Sr.

Another Turner was Phillip who removed from Raleigh, North Carolina to what is now Madison Co., Ky., and who was the grandfather of Talton Turner, a prominent man in early Missouri history, who settled in Howard Co., Mo.

Another was Thomas Turner who lived in Madison Co., Ky., where he probably died. He married Catherine Smith and most of his children settled in Boone and Howard Counties, Missouri. He was supposed to have been born in Virginia.

There were other Turner families in Madison County at an early date and it is believed by some that they were related.

EDWARD TURNER, SR.

On the 4th of July 1803, Madison Co., Ky., Jesse Noland, John Turner, and Samuel Davis were appointed Administrators of the estate of Edward Turner, deceased, and they qualified and gave bond with Barney Stagner, Edward

Turner and Richard Callaway as securities of £2000, and Talton Embry, James Berry, Robert Moore and William Martin were appointed guardians to Martin Turner and Elizabeth Turner orphans of Thomas Turner, deceased, son of Edward Turner, deceased, and he gave bond with James Johnson as surety for £300.

The Will of Nancy Turner, wife of Edward Turner, Sr., bears date 1821 probated April 6, 1821, Madison Co., Ky., in which she names her children and grandchildren devises to wit: Sallie Noland, Ellenore Williams, Samuel Turner, Thomas Turner's children, (also named in order of court in the appointment of administrators of Edward Turner's estate, and guardian for said children) and John Turner's children, said John Turner being dead, and Polly Johnson and her children, Sallie Johnson, Polly Johnson, Lucy Johnson and Matilda Johnson.

EDWARD TURNER
Children of Edward and Nancy Turner

I. Vincent Turner—not named in court orders or in the Will of his mother, but supposed to have been dead, without issue, as it seems that the sons and daughters and grandchildren of Edward Turner inherited his estate.
II. Sallie (Sarah) Turner—married Jesse Noland. Lived in Madison Co. for a long time then removed to Estill County, Ky. Had children.
III. Polly (Mary) Turner—married Richard Johnson Aug. 18, 1796—children named in Will of her mother.
IV. Nellie (Elleander) Turner—married Shadrack Williams—had issue.
V. Samuel Turner—died without issue, and perhaps unmarried. Left Will, dated Dec. 31, 1844, probated May 5, 1855. Executors Martin Turner, and James Rice. Gave his property to his nephews and nieces: Martin Turner, Elizabeth Turner wife James Rice, Fountain Turner, children of Thomas
VI. John Turner—married ———? He was dead at time of his father's death. Turner, deceased, and children of John Turner.
Left issue.
VII. Thomas Turner—married Anna Rodes Martin in Amherst Co., Va., 1793. Their record to follow.

There were two old Turner cemeteries on Barnes Mill Pike, a few miles from Richmond, Kentucky. In 1928 this writer visited them in company with Matt Arbuckle, a resident of the community, and related to the Turner family by marriage.

There was no sign visible of the oldest of the two cemeteries, but in one there were a number of tombstones visible and inscriptions.

Thomas Turner, date of birth unknown, son of Edward Turner and Nancy ———? was a slave trader by occupation. His home was in Madison Co., Ky., where he settled soon after his marriage to Anna Rodes Martin, Oct. 5, 1793, Amherst Co., Va. It is believed that they may have lived a short time in Virginia before he took his bride back to Kentucky, where she lived the balance of her life. Anna Rodes Martin was born in Albermarle Co., Va., May 4, 1774 and died in Madison Co., Ky., Feb. 24, 1859. She was the daughter of Azariah Martin, Sr., and Mary Rodes of Albermarle Co., Va. This Martin family were connections with the Garland, White, Meredith families of Albermarle and adjacent Counties, in Virginia.

The Rodes family goes back into the Crawford, Duke, and number of old Virginia families. Thomas Turner disappeared while taking a number of slaves from Virginia to the Carolinas. It was believed that he was killed enroute. There were three children born before his death in 1798. His young widow grieved until her death over his disappearance and fully believed that he would return, eventually.

The children were:

I. Martin Turner—born July 15, 1794, died Oct. 4, 1849, married March 14, 1836, Judith Walker, daughter of Stephen Walker and his 1st wife Mary Williams. Both died resident of Madison Co., Ky., and were buried in above Turner cemetery—left issue.

II. Elizabeth Turner—born 1797, died March 16, 1862, Madison Co., Ky., married in Lincoln Co., Ky., James Rice, born July, 1787, the eldest child of Charles Rice and Sarah Bryant. Both buried in Rice cemetery which is high on a hill above Taylor's Fork of Silver Creek, Madison Co., Ky. Martin Rice, the fourth child of sixteen children, emigrated in 1849 to Coles Co., Ill., and settled near where Comargo, Illinois is now, where he reared a family

III. Fountain Turner—born Madison Co., Ky., Feb. 3, 1795, died Jan. 7, 1884, Ashmore Twp., Coles Co., Illinois. Married Dec. 10, 1818, Madison Co., Ky., Elizabeth Phelps, born Feb. 12, 1803, Madison Co., Ky., died Aug. 4, 1888, Ashmore, Illinois. Both buried Ashmore, Illinois. She was the daughter of Jarret Phelphs, born 1774, and died in Madison Co., Ky., and his wife Mildred (Millie) Duncan. Jarret Phelps was the son of Josiah Phelps and Elizabeth Patterson who removed from Rockingham Co., Va., to Kentucky in 1775 and settled at what became Fort Boonesborough where his wife died after their third child was born. His plantation was near there on the road to where Richmond, Ky., is now. He married several times afterwards. Mildred Duncan was the daughter of Charles Duncan who died Culpeper Co., Va., 1789, leaving his widow with a large family. They migrated to Madison Co., Ky. Her name was Sarah (1742-1824), born in Culpeper Co. Her maiden name is unknown. It is believed it could have been either, Browning, Kavanaugh, or Courtney. She was buried in the Duncan cemetery on Muddy Creek, Madison Co., Ky. Josiah Phelps was a Revolutionary War soldier and helped to defend the Fort during the War against the Indians. His name is inscribed with others on the monument at Fort Boonesborough site, as a defender.

Children of Fountain Turner and Elizabeth Phelps were:

I. Samuel Turner—born Madison Co., Ky., July 12, 1821—died July 13, 1865, Charleston, Illinois. Married Jan. 8, 1846, Coles Co., Illinois, Eliza Jane Wiley—born Sept. 20, 1828, Bracken Co., Ky., and died May 19, 1901, at the Sargent homestead, Hutton Township, Coles Co., Illinois. Both buried Ashmore, Illinois. She was the daughter of Samuel Wiley and his wife Hester Ann Murphy, who removed from Bracken Co., Ky., to Coles Co., Ill., about 1840 where they died and were buried in the Wells cemetery, two miles south of Ashmore, Ill. Samuel Wiley was the son of Eli Wiley and Elizabeth Seals who had fifteen children. He was born 1773 Redstone, Pennsylvania the son of John Wiley and ——— Vernon. Elizabeth Seals was daughter of Mary (McCormick) Seals, whose husband's name is unknown. They came from Maryland, probably to western Penn., then to Bracken Co., Ky.

II. Jarrett Turner—died unmarried Nov. 29, 1875, age 52-2-0.
III. Thomas Turner—born Oct. 29, 1826 Madison Co., Ky., died Nov. 8, 1900, married Maria Ann Wiley, Mar. 12, 1854, she was born Aug. 25, 1830, Bracken Co., Ky., died May 19, 1918, Comargo, Ill. Both buried Westfield, Ill., Maple Hill cem. Had large family.
IV. George A. Turner—died Oct. 26, 1854 unmarried.
V. Mary E. Turner—born July 4, 1836, Coles Co., Ill., died Aug. 9, 1912—married Samuel C. Ashmore. Both buried Ashmore, Ill. Had issue.
VI. Anna Martin Turner—born March 9, 1838 Coles Co., Ill., died April 14, 1918, married James Riley Davis of Coles Co., where they resided all their lives and reared a large family. Both buried Ashmore, Ill.
VII. Mildred A. Turner—died Aug. 26, 1828 in infancy.
VIII. Oliver S. Turner—died Feb. 1, 1853, childhood.
IX. Martin Turner—killed at the Battle of Perryville, Ky., Oct. 8, 1862. Was in Company K. 123rd Illinois Vol. Infantry. Never married.

Children of Samuel Turner and Eliza Jane Wiley

I. Mary Elizabeth Turner—born Oct. 18, 1846, Coles Co., Ill., died Dec. 2, 1913, Paris, Illinois. Married Jan. 16, 1866, Clark Co., Ill., Archibald Easton—born March 30, 1836, Clark Co., Ill., died Aug. 13, 1913, Paris, Illinois, where both are buried. Had children Arthur Z., and DeWorth Easton.
II. Maria Anna Turner—born June 3, 1848, Hutton Twp., Coles Co., Ill., died May 20, 1924, Charleston, Illinois, at the home of her daughter Mrs. Pearl Cox, 803 Monroe Street. She buried Mound Cemetery, Charleston, Ill.
Married March 24, 1870, St. Louis, Mo., to John Stephen Sargent—born March 20, 1846, Hutton Twp., Coles Co., Ill., died Sept. 22, 1932, Esters, Florida, where he was buried. He was a Civil War Veteran. Son of Stephen Sargent, born 1797 Candia, New Hampshire and died 1878, Hutton Twp., Coles Co., Ill., and his wife Nancy Robinson (Chenoweth) Harlan, the parents of two children, the other being Margaret Sargent. Stephen Sargent was the son of Jacob Sargent and Margaret Patten of Candia, N. H. The son of John Sargent and Susannah Harriman, the son of Jacob Sargent and Judith Harvey of Newberryport, Mass., the son of William Sargent and Mary Colby, of Ipswich, Mass., the son of William Sargent and Elizabeth Perkins, emigrants to America in 1633 with the Winthrop Colony. Nancy R. Chenoweth was born 1805 Harrodsburg, Ky., the daughter of John Chenoweth and Rebecca Rose, who settled Clark Co., Ill., where they died after rearing a large family. John Chenoweth was son of Arthur Chenoweth and Elspa Lawrence who emigrated from near Winchester, Va., to Jefferson Co., Ky., where they lived on Floyd's Fork. They both died Columbus, Indiana in 1829—graves lost. He was Revolutionary War Soldier. Rebecca Rose was daughter of Captain Lewis Rose and his 1st wife. They lived at Cane Run or Harrodsburg, where they both died. He was noted as an Indian fighter and was in the famous Battle of Blue Licks, Ky., and was born Bingen on the Rhine in 1749.
III. Sarah Virginia Turner—born Nov. 12, 1849, Coles Co., Ill., died Charleston, Ill., April —, 1942. Married 1st Amos. Erskine and 2nd Franklin Cooper, and had children, all girls: Carrie, Dick, Sue, and Frank Cooper.

IV. Thomas Duncan Turner—born April 6, 1853—died Jan. 8, 1884, **unmarried**.

V. Susan Jane Turner—born May 18, 1858—died in childhood, **buried Oakland, Ill.**

VI. Martin Samuel Turner—born Nov. 26, 1864, died Dec. 20, 1919, Coles Co., Ill. Married Jan. 16, 1900, Coles Co., Ill., Mae Martha Dallas—born Dec. 31, 1882, Coles Co., Ill., still living 1946. Children: Samuel Dallas who married Freda Biggs and Wanda Thelma, born April 12, 1910, Coles Co., Ill., married Richard Irby, who was captured at Corregidor, Philippine Islands, and died a prisoner of the Japanese. They had one daughter, Anna Marie Irby, born Feb. 3, 1930, Fort Riley, Kansas.

VII. Wahala Clement Turner—born May 9, 1866—died Nov. 20, 1903, unmarried, Coles Co., Ill.

Children of Maria Anna Turner and John S. Sargent all born Hutton Twp., Coles Co., Ill.

I. Margaret Pearl Sargent—born Jan. 28, 1871, died Nov. 2, 1940, 2805 Estara Ave., Los Angeles, California. Buried Md. Cem. Charleston, Ill. Married Dec. 24, 1899, Charleston, Ill., Claudius C. Cox of Coles Co., Ill., the son of Adam Cox and Mary Garrison. Children: Palmer Sargent Cox, born Jan. 6, 1907, Coles Co., Ill., married Marian Bull of Tuscola, Ill., and have children: Edward and Mary Sue Cox. Claudius C. Cox died Charleston, Ill., Jan. 22, 1931.

II. Jessie Ruby Sargent—born April 23, 1872, died April, 1926, Coles Co., Ill., married April 2, 1891, Edgar Co., Ill., Frank Brown Lee of Hutton Twp., the son of David Lee & Sarah Thornton. Children: Oural Herman, Vivian Lorraine, Leland Frank, Jennings Bryan, Ruby Monzella, and Ferol Sargent.

III. Ada Opal Sargent—born Sept. 15, 1875, living Charleston, Ill., 1946. Married 1st Azro Cox, brother to above Claudius C. Cox. He born Oct. 28, 1872, died Aug. 12, 1913 Hutton Twp. No issue. She married 2nd Abraham Hodge by whom there were no issue.

IV. Coral Turner Sargent—born Jan. 25, 1878, living 2907 Moss Ave., Los Angeles, California. Married July 6, 1904, Coles Co., Ill. Dr. Arthur Roy Koen, born June 22, 1874, Walshville, Ill. He is living at above address. No issue.

V. Paul Turner Sargent—born July 23, 1880, died Feb. 7, 1946, at his home in Hutton Twp., Coles Co., Ill. Never married. Was an Artist, graduate of Art Institute, Chicago, Ill. Fifty-three years of painting. Member of the Brown Co., Indiana Painters Group. Buried Mound Cemetery, Charleston, Ill.

VI. St. John Sargent—born Mar. 23, 1884, farmer, living Coles Co., Ill., unmarried.

VII. Samuel Stephen Sargent—born Sept. 12, 1892, living Hutton Twp., Coles Co., Ill., farmer. Married Mar. 16, 1943, Fort Worth, Texas, Bertie Irene Thompson, born Feb. 4, 1905, McComb, Mississippi, the daughter of William E. Thompson and Daisey Margaret Bethea. She daughter of Richard W. Bethea and Alice C. Porter of McComb, Miss. He son of Dr. Robert Cochran Bethea and Mary E. Legette, natives of Marion Co., South Carolina. See page 2269, Vol. 3, "Kinsfolks" by William Curry Harllee, 1937.

History of the Upshaws, Lafons, Jacksons and Youngs.
For the "Society of Colonial Daughters," by Miss Sally Jackson.

Colonial and Revolutionary ancestry of Mrs. Virginia Jackson Crittenden and Miss Sally Jackson, sisters.

The four lines traced are Upshaw, Lafon, Jackson, Young.

CHAPTER I.

The earliest and most accurate account I can procure of the Upcher family is from Thos. G. Upshur, of Nassawadox, Va., who has traced them to Essex and Norfolk, England. The descendants of the Upshaws and Upshurs, branches of the same family, are still in England, where they first took root, having fled from France during the terrible times of the massacre of St. Bartholomew (1572). The historian and genealogist further states: "Abel and Arthur Upcher, aged eighteen and sixteen, ran away from their homes in Essex and Norfolk, England (still there, and called 'Sheringham Hall'), it is said, to escape the persecutions of a stepmother, and landed at the capes of Virginia in the year 1640. Their names are entered on Capt. Stone's list of headrights of ship in the year 1640. Capt. Stone paid the passage money of the youths. He (Capt. William Stone) was the first Protestant Governor of Maryland." See Hayden's Genealogy.

The brothers, Abel and Arthur, separated at "The Capes." Abel, our ancestor settled in Essex county, Va. The English ancestors still spell the name Upcher, as it was spelled in France, and it is, therefore, the correct way, and not "Upshaw," "Upshur" and "Upsher." The name spoken to the clerks of courts could easily be spelled as it sounded.

The line runs thus: Abel, William, John. This last is our great grandfather. We are in the sixth generation from the first Upcher who landed in Virginia in 1640.

Our great great grandfather, William Upcher's age is not certainly known, but he died in Essex county, Va., in 1720. His will is in the possession of the writer of this history, and was probated the above date. Our great grandfather, the third from Abel, was born in Essex county, Va., 1715. He married Mary Lafon, from the adjoining county of King and Queen. I remember our grandmother well, being fourteen years old when she died. Our grandmother, who was a daughter of our great grandfather, John Upshaw, did not speak of the personal appearance of her father and mother, but was proud to dwell on the exalted character and high station of her father. The records sustain fully her account of his social and official position. I will copy an extract from the family Bible of John Upshaw's youngest daughter, Mrs. Cordelia Terrell, and also one from the blank leaf of my grandmother's prayer-book.

Extract from family Bible of Mrs.

Cordelia Terrell, copied by her son, Mr. Thos. Terrell, of Paducah, Ky., and sent to me:

"John Upshaw, of Essex county, Va., was a respectable man, of good reputation, and wealthy. He married Mary Lafon. He was 49 years of age, and she about 18. They left living 8 children—3 sons and 5 daughters. He was a member of the Va. House of Burgess before the Revolution in America. He was decidedly in favor of the independence of the United States and took an active part towards effecting it. He was a member of the 'Committee of Safety' in his county and adhered firmly to the principles he professed. He was for some time a member of 'The Senate of Va.' after the establishment of independence. His estate consisted of three large tracts of land in Essex and adjoining counties and 110 slaves, which were divided amongst his children, his land amongst his three sons, Edwin, Horace and William. The names of the daughters were Sally, who first married Warring, and afterwards Bridges; Lucy, married, first Warring, second Major S. Threshley; Maria (our grandmother), married her cousin, Nicholas Lafon; Hannah married Capt. Richard Price; Cordelia married Mr. Chiles Terrell. The last three married and removed to Kentucky prior to 1810.

"Signed, THOS. F. TERRELL.
"Paducah, Ky., March 9, 1875."

Extract from prayer book:

"Died, at his seat in Essex Co., Va., 'White Hall,' July 21st, 1801, John Upshaw, in the 86th year of his age. He was a man of fine parts; his character for probity was preserved unblemished through his long and honored life. He sat for many years in 'The House of Burgesses,' Va., and was a member of 'The Committee of Safety' for his county during the Revo."

Our grandmother, Mrs. Lafon, often spoke of her mother's gentle disposition, combined with great strength of character, shown by the manner in which she reared a large family of children, her sons holding many high positions in the State and army and navy. Dr. William Upshaw, the youngest son, was surgeon on the staff of Gen. Wilkinson, and fought a duel with Gen. Winfield Scott.

The younger brother of Abel Upcher (Arthur) settled at Norfolk, and also became a prominent colonist. Thos. T. Upcher (the genealogist before referred to) is one of his descendants, and writes me: "He (Arthur) owned a large body of land in Accomac county, eastern shore of Virginia, which is still owned by Mr. Upcher Quinby, and known always as 'Upcher Neck,' another descendant of Arthur, in the seventh generation. The home place of this first Arthur was built of materials brought from England, standing now in a fine state of preservation, called 'Warwick,' as is his tombstone thus inscribed: 'In memory of Arthur Upcher, born in ye county of Essex in ye Kingdom of England, who died January 26th, 1709, in ye 85th year of his age.'"

I append here the following extracts from Hayden's Virginia Genealogies, as they so forcibly impressed the writer with the noble and correct sentiments and facts of their distinguished author in regard to the origin of the ancestry of Virginia's early settlers:

"The greatest Virginians of the seventeenth century, George Washington and Richard Lee, with either of whom any man in America might be proud to begin his lawful pedigree, knew nothing save by tradition of their English descent. No lines of royal blood, however concentrated, could add to the kingly character of these heroes, who in all that constitutes nobility of manhood were well nigh peerless.

"The first persons sent to Virginia were English prisoners of war.

"It is well known to readers of English history that the gentle blood of England to-day is not found exclusively among titled families, but among the middle classes or landed gentry, most of whom trace their descent back to the Norman conquest.

"Of the noble families of Great Britain to be found in the latest edition of Burk's Peerage, few can trace their origin beyond the fifteenth century. The history of this middle class is the history of England. To this class largely belongs the Virginia settlers of the seventeenth century. They came here inspired by the same motives which lead men now to emigrate to the Western States of this Union, to make or redeem lost fortunes.

"Every advantage was offered by the Crown to induce emigration to Virginia, while those who came to New England were compelled to buy every foot of soil they owned. The Virginians were given the head right of fifty acres of land for every soul brought into the colony, hence it is that not the nobility, nor landed gentry, but the younger sons and their descendants whom the law of entail cut off, provided a large proportion of the Virginia colonists of the seventeenth century."

Note.—"I think nothing of rank, but I think very much of race, and I do not understand how men who are so careful of the descent of their horses and hounds are so indifferent to the contaminations of their own blood."

CHAPTER II.

(History of the Upshaw, Lafon, Young and Jackson Family—Continued.)

My grandfather, Nicholas Lafon (the early records in Virginia spell the name Le Fon), was of French extraction. His ancestor came to Virginia soon after the revocation of "The Edict of Nantes," in 1685, and settled in King and Queen county. My grandmother, Mrs. Nicholas Lafon, who lived to extreme old age, delighted to entertain the children in the family with accounts given her by her grandfather of "the old Huguenot's" traditions. She said he brought two sons with him to Virginia, his wife having died in France; that he lived on his plantation in rooms apart from the family, in hermit-like seclusion. He usually seemed to be oblivious to those around him, and in summer would sit in the yard, and whenever seen, was pouring over the pages of an old French Bible in absorbed devotion; would greet the children of the family with a gentle smile of welcome, but never sat down under any other roof than his own. His meals were brought to him. The clerk's office of King and Queen county, Va., was destroyed by fire during the late Civil War, so I have been unable to trace from land deeds and marriage registers the names of intermediate generations, nor can I get this information from church registers, as it seems impossible to determine to what church organization the Huguenots attached themselves in this country. We read: " The name was first applied to the followers of both Luther and Calvin in the sixteenth century. The origin of the word even is uncertain, but is stated to be derived from "Eidgenosen," meaning "bound together by an oath," a term borrowed from the Confederate Cantons of Switzerland by certain inhabitants of Geneva, who were among the earliest to introduce reform notions of religion in France." Macaulay says: "Louis XIV had, from an early age, regarded the Calvinists with an aversion at once religious and political. As a zealous Roman Catholic, he detested their theological dogmas. As a prince, fond of arbitrary power, he detested those republican theories which were intermingled with Genevese divinity. He gradually retrenched all the privileges the schismatics enjoyed, since the Edict of Nantes, though practically violated in its most essential provisions, had not been formally rescinded, but the bigots and flatterers who had his ear gave him advice which he was but too willing to take. The final blow was struck. The Edict of Nantes was revoked. The Calvanistic ministers were ordered to leave the kingdom or to abjure their religion. Other professors of the reformed faith were forbidden to leave the kingdom, and the outposts and frontiers were strictly guarded. But in spite of this, it was calculated that in a few months 50,000 families quitted France forever. Nor were they such as a country could well spare; they were persons of intelligent minds, of industrious habits, of austere morals. In the list are found names eminent in war, in science, in literature and art. Some offered their swords to William of Orange and distinguished themselves by the fury with which they fought against their persecutors. A more peaceful class planted vines even to the "Cape of Good Hope," or pursued in distant lands agriculture." This last occupation was adopted by our Huguenot ancestor. My great grandfather was a Baptist preacher, as was his brother Thomas.

This brings me to the pioneer history of my ancestors, the Lafons.

Extract from the family Bible of Captain and Mrs. Nicholas Lafon:

"He was born in King and Queen county, Va., April 6, 1762, and died at his residence, 'Spring Garden,' Woodford county, Kentucky, January 20, 1831.

"This Captain Nicholas Lafon was a great grandson of Lafon the Huguenot, and his wife, Maria Lafon, nee Upshaw, was a great great granddaughter."

Captain Lafon came to Kentucky in

1784 with General James Wilkinson and settled in Fayette county.

He was afterwards induced by General Wilkinson to remove to Frankfort in 1787, and he very generously presented him choice of the most valuable lots in the town in the center, comprising the block frontage on St. Clair street, Main, Washington and Broadway.

Captain Lafon's Revolutionary record is found in "Virginia Baptist ministers" and army records. He was eighteen years old when he enlisted as a private in Green's army; was in the battles of Eutaw Springs and Cowpens.

In the latter part of the century he built what was then considered a handsome home on Washington street. In 1801 my grandfather visited Virginia, and on the 12th of March married his cousin, Maria Upshaw. Immediately afterwards they set out on the then perilous journey over the wagon road through the mountains and across streams of the wilderness to this town. Think of such courage and enterprise in a girl reared amid the pleasures and luxuries of an eastern Virginia plantation in that day, where every wish was gratified by parents grown rich from shipping tobacco down the Rappahannock river to the sea and across to Europe, by return voyages bringing silks and jewelry and all the accessories of an elegant life. My grandfather evidently appreciated the sacrifice when he prepared for her the home above referred to. This period in the history of Frankfort was a very stormy one. Collins (history) says: "Wilkinson, on his arrival in Kentucky, became involved in the fiercest political controversies, and has left his countrymen divided in opinion as to whether he acted from patriotic and honorable motives or was a selfish and abandoned adventurer ready to engage in any project that would advance his interests." My grandfather, who had known General Wilkinson long and intimately, believed him patriotic and honorable, the victim of the plots and the machinations of the Federalist party. As "The Society of Colonial Daughters" had for one of its objects the preservation of the history of the pioneer women as well as the men of this city. I will now write of my grandmother, Maria Upshaw Lafon.

She was of a commanding height, and majestic in appearance—a woman of fine intellect. Governor Charles S. Morehead, who knew her well, said that she had that rare combination—a brilliant mind and sound judgment. She said to me: "If my father's daughters had been given an education at William and Mary College that each of our three brothers received, we would have been their superiors; as it was, we had the ordinary education of that day." That ordinary education, it seemed to me, was all she required; her conversation was fascinating, and her letters—now in my possession—are models of sentiment and expression and elegant English. She retained through life the fashion of dress worn by her when she left Virginia a bride, fifty years before her death (in 1857).

The old Empire style, low neck, short sleeves, with a half square of linen cambric covering her neck, the arms in winter protected with sleeves below the puff.

On State occasions she would take

out of the hair trunk, in which it was brought form Virginia a handsome Irish poplin gown—it was worn over a pink satin petticoat curiously quilted in figures; the skirt of the poplin was open in front to show the elegant underskirt to advantage. The waist of the gown was very short, the front of pink satin covered with a white lace "stomacher." This costume was perfectly preserved when shown me in 1860.

Mrs. James Todd and Mrs. Mary Wills Woodson, now deceased, said they recalled her appearance on one occasion walking on Wapping street, dressed for an evening with the famous Mrs. Love, at the Historic "Love House" on this street, and they thought she was a picture of the French countess. Our grandfather left Frankfort in 1807, removing to a farm in Woodford county. Here our mother, Mrs. Mary Lafon Jackson was born, 14th of February, 1808.

Capt. Lafon afterwards purchased another farm in the same vicinity, to which he removed in 1816; it was called "Spring Garden." It contained 1,000 acres of land.

The house was built by Judge Thomas Todd. Mr. Charles Todd, of Owensboro, writes that it was built in 1793, the year after Judge Todd came to Frankfort as the first clerk of the Court of Appeals.

Judge Todd married (some time prior to 1812) the widow of a namesake and nephew of General Washington, Major George Washington (nee Lucy Payne, a sister of the celebrated Dolly Madison). I have heard that Judge Todd was disappointed in the impression his country home made upon his bride, for she soon became dissatisfied, probably from the contrast to the life she had led when visiting the "White House," where her sister, Mrs. Madison, had surrounded herself with the gayety and elegance of court life. At any rate, Judge Todd, then on the supreme bench of the United States, disposed of the plantation to a Mr. Duncan, and he in a short time sold it to my grandfather, Captain Lafon, who resided here until he died, on January 20, 1831, in the sixty-ninth year of his age.

My grandmother, Maria Upshaw Lafon, resided at "Spring Garden" until 1835, when the estate was divided and sold to my father, Richard G. Jackson. Her son-in-law and she removed to a home near Frankfort, purchased of Kean O'Hara, the famous teacher, and the father of the celebrated poet, Theodore O'Hara.

I have the deed of the transfer of this property to my grandmother. My cousin, Mr. John Upshaw Price, married Mary Helen, daughter of Kean O'Hara, and own sister of Theodore O'Hara.

My mother, Mary Lafon, was a pupil of Kean O'Hara, who was regarded as one of the most distinguished educators of his time; he came to Woodford county shortly after the birth of his celebrated son, Theodore, in Danville, Kentucky, 11th of February, 1820.

As a curio, I append the following list of studies proposed to Captain Lafon and lady for their daughter, Mary Lafon:

"Mr. O'Hara proposes for the course of instruction for Miss Mary Lafon, with the approbation of Captain Lafon and lady, the following:

"1. A hasty recital and review of geography, ancient and modern, illustrated with maps and globes, the latter to be furnished by O'Hara, as well as sheet-maps towards the end of the course.

"2. English grammar; review, exercise in verbs, and parsing.

"3. History in the following order: Grecian, Roman, British, and American.

"4. French, for which will be immediately required a grammar, dictionary and Perrin's fables.

"5. Arithmetic; required, Pike's Arithmetic, slate and pencils.

"6. Paper, ink, etc.

"Respectfully,
"KEAN O'HARA,
"17th August."

CHAPTER III.

THE YOUNG AND JACKSON ANCESTRY OF MRS. VIRGINIA CRITTENDEN AND MISS SALLY JACKSON, SISTERS.

WRITTEN BY SALLY JACKSON.

Our great-grandfather, Col. Richard Young, was born in Fauquier county, Va., about 1745. He emigrated to Kentucky in 1780, having married previous to that time Mary Moore, of Fredricksburg, Va. He settled in Fayette county and it is recorded in deed books in the land office in Frankfort, Ky., that he was the owner of many thousand acres of land in Fayette and adjoining counties; whether all these were Revolutionary grants or by purchase of Treasury warrants is unknown.

The county of Woodford was formed in 1788; the residence of Col. Young was in the new county, near Versailles.

In 1792, he, with John Lee, John Watkins, Case Johnson and Marquis Colmes, founded the town of Versailles and were its first trustees. (Collins' Hist. of Ky., Vol. II., p. 756).

Col. Young was a member of the Convention of 1792 which framed the first Constitution of Kentucky, held in Danville (Collins, 355). He was also elector of the Senate and a member of the first Legislature under the new Constitution, and was re-elected successively from 1792 to 1803. It is a tradition in the family that he was a revolutionary soldier. He died before the pension laws of 1818 were made, hence his name is not recorded.

Col. Young died in his home near Versailles in 1815, leaving three sons, Richard M. Young, Merritt Young and A. G. Young, and four daughters, Mrs. Henry Lee, Mrs. Benj. Vance, Mrs. Francis Johnson and Mrs. Alice Jackson, wife of John Jackson. Our grandparents were married in 1792, license recorded in clerk's office in Versailles. John Jackson was a native of Edinburg, Scotland, and emigrated to Woodford county a few years prior to 1792. When the town was established in 1792 he returned to Edinburg and brought back with him the largest and fullest stock of dry good then imported to any store in the West. Mr. Graves, of Woodford county, who survived his friend many years and lived to extreme age, said he was a gentleman of fine education and good business capacity, and was a very successful merchant. He had four sons and five daughters. Mrs. Douglas Young, Mrs. Dr. Bartlett; America and Eliza both married Martin; Alice married William E. Ashmore; David married Juliet Threshley; John married Lucy Letitia Lafon; William married Lucy Upshaw, of Essex county, Virginia, and Mary Virginia Lafon, our mother married Richard Gilbert Jackson, November, 1825. Our father Richard G. Jackson, was given a fine farm within one mile of Versailles by our grandfather, with a handsome stone house on it. Here the two eldest daughters, Maria and Virginia, were born.

Our parents resided in this home until July, 1836, when our father bought the thirds of our grandmother, Mrs. Maria Lafon and the other heirs of the estate of our grandfather, Nicholas Lafon, halfway between Versailles and Frankfort, seven miles from each place, and removed there. Our father was a scientific farmer, subscribed for all the best farmers' journals. He was an importer at that early day of fine stock, was owner of the famous racer "Monmouth Eclipse," and Durham cattle he imported and dealt largely in.

Our mother, Mrs. Richard Jackson, nee Mary Lafon, was educated principally by the famous teacher, Kean O'Hara, and was a cultured and charming conversationalist and a gifted letter writer. This fact ought to silence any invidious comparisons as to the so-called superior advantages of this day.

Both my father and mother were devoted Presbyterians, both members of the church at Versailles, our father being an elder there until his death in 1852.

In their homes in both places near Versailles and at the latter one, "Spring Garden," our parents dispensed a beautiful hospitality, entertaining alike the famous and distinguished people and the humbler ones who were ever given food and shelter when needed. Here Maria and Virginia were married the same night, May 6th, 1846. Maria married George T. Cotton, Lieutenant-Colonel 6th Kentucky on the Federal side in the late Civil War; and Virginia married Col. John Allen Crittenden, then Marshal of the Louisville Chancery Court. Col. Cotton was killed at Murfreesboro in 1863; Col. Crittenden died in Frankfort, Ky., in 1887. Our mother died October, 1880, at her residence in South Frankfort, Ky. Maria Jackson—Mrs. Geo. T. Cotton—died January 17, 1847, at Spring Garden. Mrs. Virginia Crittenden and myself (Sally Jackson) are now residents of South Frankfort, living in adjoining homes.

We republish the following tribute to the memory of our beloved mother by the late Judge Lysander Hord:

IN MEMORIAM.

On the night of the 28th of October, 1880, in the seventy-third year of her age, quietly and peacefully passed away at her home in South Frankfort, Mrs Mary Virginia Jackson. The deceased was the daughter of Nicholas and Maria Lafon, and the widow of the late Richard G. Jackson, in his day one of the most prominent and highly respected citizens of Woodford county. In education, manners and habits she was a lady of the old Virginia school. In disposition she was mild and gentle to a remarkable degree. Perhaps the most striking feature in her character was the beautiful simplicity of her nature. Pure and natural in all her thoughts and actions, she never suspected a wrong or artifice in others. Charitable and forgiving in all her feelings, she was ever ready to put the most favorable construction upon the conduct of others. In her married life, and long widowhood, she regulated her household with admirable order, neatness and economy; and in her home, first in Woodford, and afterward in South Frankfort, she dispensed a most generous hospitality. With a mind vigorous by nature, and well cultivated by education and reading, she was at all times a most agreeable fireside companion. She had a heart without guile. A devoted wife and mother, a steadfast friend; and above all, a Christian of the purest and gentlest life. Humble and modest in a remarkable degree, relying alone for her future peace upon the promises of the Gospel, and not at all upon any good works of her own. And in her life and conduct she was a beautiful illustration of the religion she professed in the Presbyterian Church, with which she was so long connected.

THE VAN METEREN'S OF HOLLAND AND AMERICA.

By AMELIA CLAY LEWIS VAN METER ROGERS

PREFACE

This paper—a tribute to an honored name—endeavors to present some fragments and parts of history relating to the origin, descent and sundry migrations of a branch of the Van Meteren family from its habitat in Holland to its beginnings in America.

It treats in particular, of the ancestry and descendants of Isaac Van Metre, the founder of "Point Pleasant" in the Valley of Virginia, and who left a numerous and worthy progeny.

Woven into the story is something from the annals of early days—tracing the movements and reciting the experiences, adventures, hardships and perils of an heroic life spent along the border.

The lives of these forefathers are noteworthy for the influence and progressiveness which they exercised in the communities where they dwelt, and upon the conditions of the times in which they lived—which was in that Spartanic formative epoch that has no parallel in the history of any country at any time. And from such as these—whose perseverance, courage and daring contributed much—has been evolved this wonderful American nation.

The compiler has made extensive research among various original and official records, has made free use of various authors and has left for your consideration only such facts as are really believed to be accurate and conclusive.

There is but little available concerning the residences of the Van Meterens in Holland; one sketch, however, has been obtained which refers to the "Huise Van Meteren" situate in the Heerlykleid Metere, in Geldermelsen, as shown in the picture. It was a stately structure, and the home, for many years and generations, of one the branches of the Van Metre family, and subsequently of others. This mansion stood in a beautiful park of magnificent trees, some of which were of great height and dimensions. The house was rebuilt in 1768-9, but it has at last served its day; it was sold in December, 1906, and has since been torn down.

If one examines the map of Holland it will be found that the Rhine, flowing down from Germany, enters the Netherlands; and as it approaches the sea, divides into several branches. Upon one of these is Arnheim, the chief town in Gelderland, some fifteen and odd miles from Amsterdam. Utrecht is on another estuary that empties into the Zuyder Zee. The Waal, the principal branch of the Rhine, takes its course westerly until it unites with the Meuse, and its waters from that point to the sea, are called the River Merwe. On the right bank of the Waal, as it nears the Meuse, is situated the pretty little town of Thiel; one of the fortifications of Holland, twenty-two miles west-southwest of Arnheim, and farther down, on the left bank, where the waters of the two rivers join, is the island of Bommel, on the west side of which stands the castle of Loevenstein made famous in 1619 as the prison of Grotius, the father of international law, and author of "Belli et Pacis," or War and Peace. Thus, within the radius of a few miles, lies the fatherland of the Van Meterens.

Coat-of-Arms

Riestap, in his "Armorial Generale", describes the Cuicks Van Meterens as follows: "The Armorial bearings of the Cuick Van Metere were shield gules, with two fesses argent, accompanied by three marlets of the same, arranged two and one," or, in plain English, the shield has a red ground with two horizontal bands silver and white, and three marlets (in heraldry, a sort of swallow without feet, denoting cadency—a younger son) arranged two and one thus: * *   or   * . The Coat-of-Arms of the Van
                                                                                             *   * *
Meteren family of Holland are "quartered, first and fourth of silver, with a fleur de lis, gules, with second and third of gold with two fesses, gules accompanied with eight martlets of same color arranged in arle." That is to say, around the outer rim of the shield. The crest, a fleur de lis (the royal emblem of France). The title here, "Jr.," is synonymous with Jonkvrouw, young woman, feminine, and Jonkheer, young man, masculine. "Ridderschap" and "Ridderedd" signifies either Nobility or Knighthood.

The first mention of Meteren is in a deed dated September, 1253, in which Otto, Count of Bentheim, transferred to Otto, Count of Gelre, his alodium, malsen, along the Earldom of Bevan Asperen. . . . It belonged to the ancient family and estates of the Cuicks as recited in a certain deed of 1265, etc.

Meeteren, also called Meteren, is a village in the Tielerwaard. It belonged to the community of Geldermalsen, of which it constitutes the southernmost section. Meteren was formerly a manor in the province of Tiesterband, apparently, a possession of the counts who were placed over the section where Meteren was situated . . . and belonged to the estate which family Van Cuick Van Meteren possessed between the Rhine and the Waal.

Almost one and a half centuries elapse before one again finds mention made of Meteren and then it was under the direction of Willem, Duke of Gelre and Cuick. After the death of Jan V, Lord of Cuick, who had been at odds with his father, the succession to Cuick fell to his sister Johanna. In 1394, Johanna became Lady of Cuick and Grave. When she took possession of the manor, or about that time, she was given in marriage to Willem, son of the Duke of

ARMS OF THE VAN METERENS OF HOLLAND

Mechteld. The marriage agreement was concluded at Grave, October 3, 1394, and the wedding held at the same place December 24, 1394.

Johann Van Meteren, at Meteren, appears on the knighthood of 1548, and on the list of 1555 "dead" is written after his name. He and Otto Van Haeften, heirs of Johanna Van Cuick Van Meteren, had a suit against the Count Van Buuren, on account of a flood in the Waal, as appears in letters of the Count of Gelre from 1546 to 1547.

Jasper Van Meteren appears in the "Ridderschap" (book of the knighthood, or nobility) of 1563 and 1578; at the later date the word "dead" is written before his name. In the same list is mentioned Willem Van Metere and Johan Cuick Van Metere; and Aert Van Metere in the Bommelwaard. Jasper Van Metere, in the knighthood of 1570, had five sons and two daughters.

 i. Cornelius Van Meteren, living 1581.
 ii. Jan Van Meteren, living 1613.
 iii. Jr. Jasper Van Meteren, justice at Deijl 1610; "well to do."
 iv. Johan Van Meteren, living 1625.
 v. William Van Meteren-Van Meteren, Lord of Meteren, living 1624.
 vi. Marie Van Meteren.
 vii. Cornelia Van Meteren.

Cornelius Van Meteren, of the Bommelwaard, appears in the Chivalry (Knighthood) of 1578. He had four children: (1) Captain Johan Van Meteren; (2) Roelof; (3) Barbara, and (4) Gertruida Van Meteren, living 1624.

 iv. John Van Cuick Van Meteren and Willem Van Cuick Van Meteren (v) are mentioned in the list of the nobility for the years 1600, 1601—'2, 1605, 1614, 1615-18 and in roll for 1619-21, as "dead". In the records of Deijl, Willem is mentioned as Lord Meteren; justice of 1620. He makes his will dated August 9, 1624, and names the son of his brother Cornelius i., Captain Johan Van Meteren, as heir to the manor of Meteren, with his nephew Roelof and the latter's sister, Marie Barbara and Gertruida joint heirs, otherwise. Exlm. 29 July, 1629. Capt. John Van Cuick Van Meteren also inherits from his uncle, Willem (v), certain legacies as recorded in a deed dated 12 November, 1652, and in it are mentioned Capt. Johan's children A. Melchoir, in Knighthood of 1615-24; B. Anneken, who married Maas Janzoon; C. Balthaser, D. Adriaan; E. Johanna who married Jr. du Bois Van Houten; F. Joan, her Will in 1641; and G. Hendrix Van Cuick Van Meteren, married in 1624.

 A. Among the children of Melchoir, who married Anneken Ariens in 1630, is, Justice 1640 deceased 1650, is eldest son Goosen (Jooste?) Van Meteren Van Cuick. Anna, Melchoir's widow, records deed May 12, 1600; makes her Will September 7, 1656; and names heirs Jans Derick Olie, Gertje Van Beest and Anneken Van Beest. She was a widow when she married Melchoir Van Meteren and the Van Beest children were by her first husband. Goosen and Gertyje were children by Melchoir's first marriage.

1. Captain Johan Van Cuick Van Meteren, son of Cornelius (i) married Diske Van Meteren, and their son Melchoir married Anneken Arience and had a son, Goosen, who was admitted to the "Ridderschap" of Neijmegen, June 26, 1651. The above Melchoir was presented, June 10, 1612, appeared 1615 and admitted—as he had left the military service—and filled the office of Tielerwaard, September, 1630; appears again in 1633 and 1649, signs "Van Meteren" and is called in the Book of Heraldry "Van Meteren Van Cuick".

Among the names noted as inhabitants in the vicinity of Meteren may be mentioned these:

1540. Jacob Van Meteren married with . . . Van Boxmeer.
1541. 10 Dec., Jan Van Meteren, justice at Meteren.
1541. Melchoir Van Meteren, justice in 1560 and 1663.
1544. Gysbert Van Meteren.
1645. Gysbert Van Meteren married Jutten Van Herinjnen.
1565. Willem Van Meteren, justice.
1567. Cornelius Van Meteren at Deijl.
1634. Johan Van Meteren, master of horse at Tielerwaard, etc.

A. D. 1500 Cornelia Van Cruick Van Meteren married to Otto Van Beeste. 7 June 1571, in the General State Archives the seals of Arnt and Jan Van Meteren can be found. A. D. 1600 Waalberg Van Meteren married Otto Van Haeften in the Country of Nymegen. 20 November, 1634, Johann Van Meteren was sergeant-major of Cavalry in the Country of Tiel (Thielerwaardt). 27 December 1646, Michael Jordaen de Cahiliser and Lady Josina Van Cuick Van Meteren were married at Hertogenbosch, the Capitol of the province of North Brabant. 20 October, 1671 Maximilliaen Van Meteren "is considered as absolutely Knightly".

A son of Jan Van Cuick van Meteren, Lord of Meteren and a member of the Riddersedel of 1555, Adriaan by name, became Lord of Meteren and Kerkwick, Colonial governor of Wandricken, and Lovenstein, married, and the wedding was published in the Hague, December 15, 1636, to Emerentia Van Aerssen, daughter of Jacques, Lord of Triangel, president of the Council of Brabant and Marie Van der Vecken. Adriaan was buried at Meteren, with eight quarterings.

Emmanuel Van Meteren

The western world's wonderful progress and its dominant civilization springs, primarily, from its discovery by the Genoese Navigator, Columbus; in 1492, and then after some of the leading powers of the then Europe, stimulated and spurred on by the success of Spain and eager to emulate her enterprise, began to rival each other in exploration and territorial aggrandizement, found compensating rewards in later discoveries, hence we find France, England, Sweden and the Netherlands striving to achieve supremacy in the New World. The Dutch had carefully explored and taken possession of a vast realm; and were rapidly planting her sons upon a province that extended from the Connecticut River on the east, crossed the Delaware, and stopped at the eastern shores of the Chesapeake Bay, before the English were aware of the significance and extent of the Dutch policy of "peaceful penetration." Upon this magnificent territory they bestowed the name of New Netherland in honor of the fatherland. Her great day dawned in 1609 when Captain Henry Hudson, in his famous ship 'The Half-Moon'', ploughed the waters of the North River which now bears his name. From that eventful day down to the present time, the impress of the Dutch influence is ineradicably stamped upon the land and its inhabitants. In this historic event one of its most interesting features is the fact that it was brought about, mainly, through the prestige and influence of the family Van Meteren of Holland. We are told by the late Professor Fiske, in his "Dutch and Quaker Colonies,"[1] that "the moment that history first actually knows him (Henry Hudson) is the first day of May, 1607, when he sailed from Greenwich in command of an Arctic expedition; but we also know that he was a citizen of London; and the Dutch historian Van Meteren, tells us that there was a warm friendship between Henry Hudson, the navigator, and Captain John Smith." Again: in a reference to the Dutch East-India Company, Fiske says: "Their offers were probably made through Henry Hudson's friend, the Dutch consul Van Meteren." Then again: "It was Hudson's friend Van Meteren who declared that English was only 'broken Dutch' "; and still again: "Hudson, in 1608, knew scarcely a word of Dutch." Emmanuel Van Meteren wrote an account of Hudson's Voyage of Discovery.[2]

Let us consider, for a moment, who this potential Emmanuel Van Meteren was. Reliable authorities rank him as one of the most learned and prominent of Hollanders. As a youth starting in life as a student—but all the while being trained in the business house of Sebastian Daukhearts at Antwerp, and passing beyond this—to become a scholar, historian, statesman, and philosopher. These represent some of the degrees of progression in his career. He was the author of "Historie Van de Oorlogen en Geschiedenissen der Nederlanderen" (A History of the Netherlands), a book that has been translated and published in several languages; and all these accomplishments were being acquired while continuing his business, and serving his country as Dutch consul, at London, during the reign of Edward VI and his sister Mary, of England. Emmanuel was born at Antwerp, June 9, 1535, he was the grandson of Cornelius Van Meteren, and the son of Jacob Van Meteren, of Breda—who was a printer, a linguist and a scientist. This Jacob, in association with Miles Coverdale, was the translator, printer and publisher, at Antwerp, of the first English version of the Bible a work that is, today, in its original edition, worth its weight in gold. The mother of Emmanuel,

---
[1] Fiske, "Dutch and Quaker Colonies," Vol. I, p. 82.
[2] Winsor, Justin, "Narrative and Critical History of America," Vol. IV, p. 424.

Jacob's wife, was Ortillia Ortels, or (Ortelius), the daughter of William Ortels of Ausburch (Augsberg), and a granddaughter of Abraham Ortels, the famous geographer. It will thus be readily seen that the lineage of Emmanuel Van Meteren was of the most worthy and auspicious character, which was reflected in the qualities of their gifted son.

The Van Meterens removed to London to reside—to which place he had been appointed Dutch consul.[1] In 1583 he was chosen to be chief of council of the "College of Dutch Merchants" of London; meanwhile carrying on his business and attending to his duties as consul until his death, in his seventy-seventh year, April 8, 1612. He was buried at St. Denis' Church, in London, where a monument was erected.

JAN JOOSTEN VAN METEREN

The branch of the family with whom we are concerned came to America in 1662, as revealed in the papers of the ship "Vos" (Fox), arriving at New Amsterdam on the 12th of September of that year,[1] though there is some evidence that leads us to suppose that the emigrant ancestor was here at least a year before this date.[2]

The coming of the Van Meteren family in the latter part of the seventeenth century to New Netherland was in the period when the colony was progressing under the most favorable conditions and at a time which coincided with the founding of a settlement among the foot-hills of the Catskill Mountains on the west side of the Hudson, in Ulster County, New York, and about sixty miles above the Bay. Here a group of Dutch, and another of French Huguenot emigrants, had obtained patents for lands and were already established and the settlements were constantly being increased by additions from the Bay towns below and in a short time the fertile valleys of the Waalkill and the Esopus sheltered a collection of thrifty little communities, thus, in the twenty-odd years between 1660 and the maturity of the Van Meteren or Van Metre children, about 1680, the settlements known as New Paltz, Wyltwick, Eusopus, Hurley, and Marbletown were founded in close proximity to each other and were finally merged into what has since been called the Kingston County. Behind them rose the bulwark of the Catskills, and beyond these mountains, and out of their western slopes, gushed the head-springs of the Delaware and the Susque-

---

[1] Winsor, Justin "Narrative and Critical History of America," Vol. IV, p. 424, Notes 1 and 2.
  Emanuel Van Meteren, author of "Historie Van de Oorlegen en Geschiedenissen der Nederlanderen" born at Antwerp, 1535, was a grandson of William Ortels, of Augsburg, and first cousin of the historian, Abraham Ortelius. He lived in England as merchant and Dutch consul until 1612, the year of his death. Emanuuel Van Meteren's history was originally published in Latin at Amsterdam, 1597. He translated the work into Flemish, and published it in 1599, then continued it in the same language up to 1612, in which shape it was published after his death at Arnheim in 1614. French editions of the work appeared in 1618 and 1670 and a German one at Frankfort in 1669. "It is a minute description of the discoveries made by Hudson, and his information regarding Hudson's voyage of 1609, we may assume, was derived from Hudson himself on his return to England."
[1] "Documentary History of New York," III, pp. 52, 63.
[3] New Netherland Register, February, 1911, p. 26.

hanna rivers, which, in their respective courses, first provided trails for the native tribes, and by which they had intercourse with their southern contemporaries.

On the east shore of the Delaware, in south Jersey, the Swedes had located early and fortified their holdings. Between Fort Nassau, which was located nearly opposite the site of Philadelphia, down to Fort Elsinborg, on Penn's Neck, which was across the river from Fort Christiana at the mouth of the Brandywine, were several intervening settlements; so we find them colonized on the Racoon, Timber, Cohansey, Salem and Maurice Creeks; and along a trail which the Van Meterens afterward took, leading southward from the bay at New Amsterdam to New-Amstel, or, as it is now, New Castle, in the state of Delaware. The eastern part of this overland path started from Bergen and ran southwesterly, crossing the Passaic and Raritan rivers, and touching the Delaware at "the Falls" now Trenton, New Jersey, and there, by fording the shallow rapids to the west side, passed through the old Swedish plantation on the Pennybeck, and so on to New Castle. At this point, where the Delaware peninsula is the narrowest, another overland trail led to the head of Elk river, in Maryland; and by that tributary entered Chesapeake Bay, and by it and beyond, passed through the mountain gaps of the Potomac, to distant points in the colony of Virginia.

The path from New York to Philadelphia was called "The King's Highway" in 1675, and was then, as it is today, the main artery of travel between the two chief cities of the eastern colonies. Another path followed the eastern shore of the Delaware, intersecting the little Swedish villages that lay along the way between Somerset and Middlesex counties to the province of East Jersey, on down to the vicinity of Fenwick's English colony at Salem, in the province of West Jersey. En route, there was a divergence in the trail which led to Mattinicock Island and Lassa Point, situated about where the city of Burlington now stands. It was by these primitive paths that the various and widely separated settlements in the middle colonies were connected and from which they continually acquired growth from the flow of pioneers, were to pierce the Blue Ridge at the Potomac and absorb the Virginia Valleys beyond.

The foregoing is thus elaborately set forth that we may the more readily trace and understand the migratory movements of the Van Metre or Van Meter forefathers from Ulster County, New York, to their final abiding place in Virginia.

It is well known in Holland the prefix "Van" to a name signifies of "The House of Meteren" and was originally spelled without the capital "V".

The Van Meter family of America as far as I can find out descended from two men; Jan Gysbertsen van Meteren, who married Neltje Van Cleef, and Jan Joost van Meteren both of whom emigrated from the province of Gelderland

Holland. These two names in English would be John Gisbertson of Meteren and Kryn or Krine Jansen Van Meteren. They located in Ultricht, in Kings' County, and afterwards removed to Monmouth County, New Jersey.[1]

Jan Joost Van Meteren

Jan Joost Van Meteren of Thierlewoodt, with his wife and five children, whose ages ranged from two and a half to fifteen years, arrived in the ship "Fox", at New Amsterdam, in New Netherlands on the 12th of April, 1662.[2] He married in 1646 Macyke Hendricksen or (Hendrygksen) of Mappelen, in the province of Dreuth in Holland, the daughter of Hendricks of Laeckervelt and his wife Anne Jan Jans. She is supposed to have been the sister of Femmetjen Hendricksen, who married Jooste Adriensen, of Pynnaker Holland, on the 20th of March, 1663-4. Upon the death of Jooste Ariencesen of "Boswick", upon Long Island circa 1685, Jan Joosten Van Meteren was appointed administrator, tutor of decedent's children, and arbitrator in the proceedings regarding the sale of some land in Hurley which had been sold to Derick Schepmos by Arience during his life time.

Jan Joosten Van Meteren's children were: Jooste Jans, Cathrin, Geertje, Lysbeth, and Gysbert; Jooste Jans, being the eldest son, as appears by the father's records.[3]

In the fall of 1662 Jan Joosten Van Meteren settled in Wildwych (now Kingston, Ulster County, New Jersey) and dwelt many years in that vicinity, which included the towns of Hurley, Marbletown, and Esoppus. He is not noted in the activities of that community until the 7th of June, 1663, the date when the Minnisink Indians made an attack on the village and its vicinity raiding and burning the settlement of Hurley and Kingston and carrying away women and children in captivity. Among the latter were Jan's wife and children, Jooste Jans being one of them as well as Catherine du Bois, the wife of Louis du Bois, and their daughter Sarah; whom Jooste Jans Van Meteren later married. These were taken to the fastnesses of the Catskill Mountains and remained in captivity for months, but were rescued on the eve of torture by du Bois, and Captain Martin Kreiger's company of Manhattan soldiers; the trainband finally rounded up the Indians and defeated them on September 3, 1663. In connection with this tragic experience the following statement is quoted: "About ten weeks after the capture of the women and children, the Indians decided to celebrate their own escape from pursuit by burning some of their victims and the ones selected were Catherine du Bois, and her baby Sara. A cubical pile of logs was arranged and the mother and child placed

---

[1] Bergen's "Annals of King's County, New Jersey," pp. 345, 346.
[2] "Documentary History of New York," III, pp. 53-63. Yearbook Historical Society New York, 1896. "New Netherland Register," February, 1911, p. 26.
[3] Probate Records of Ulster County, New Jersey.

thereon; when the Indians were about to apply the torch, Catherine began to sing the 137th Psalm as a death chant. The Indians withheld the fire and gave her respite while they listened; when she had finished they demanded more, and before she had finished the last one her husband and the Dutch soldier's from New Amsterdam arrived and surrounded the savages, killed and captured some, and otherwise inflicted terrible punishment upon them, and released the prisoners.[1, 2]

Captain Kreiger's Journal which gives a general account of the expedition of rescue, unfortunately does not name him, but it is elsewhere stated that it was due to Jooste Jan's three months' association with the Indians, during his captivity, that gave him the knowledge of their habits, trails, plans and war feuds with other tribes, and so impressed him with a desire for their adventurous life.

In a list of the inhabitants of Ulster County, New York, who subscribed to the oath of allegiance, due to a change in the sovereignty of the country, between the 21st and 26th of October, 1664, the name of Jan Joosten appears among them. After this date frequent notice of him occurs upon the records of Kingston as a farmer, and a man of growing importance in civil and religious matters. In 1665 he was appointed referee in a law suit between two of the citizens, and on August 26, of the same year, he is mentioned as an appraiser of the personal estate of Dr. Gysbert van Inbrock, who was a physician and apothecary of the vicinity. The decedent's inventory included among other valuable books, a copy of Emmanuel Van Meteren's History; and at a sale of the effects, on the 9th of September, following, Jan was a purchaser to the extent of nearly 100 guilders—two of the items he bought were the "Beehive", by the famous Marnix, Lord of St. Aldegonde, and "The Chronicles of the Kings of England", and these books aptly showed the character of Jan Joosten's culture.[3] A further appointment came to Jan a "Scheppen", or to a position synonymous to that of the minor judiciary, which, under the laws of the time, gave him jurisdiction in all civil cases under the sum of 100 guilders; but in cases above that amount such action must be referred to the Director-General and the Council. He could pronounce sentence in criminal actions, subject to appeal, so we may assume that he enjoyed a position but little removed below the highest court in the province.

From about this time Jan Joosten was frequently sought as a witness to various marriages, or as sponsor at the baptisms of children at the homes of relatives and friends. In some instances baptisms were performed "at Jan Joosten's in the presence of the whole consistory," these distinctions were no doubt due to his position in the church, in which he had been elected an elder,

---

[1] Martin Kreiger's Journal.
[2] MacKenzie's "Colonial Families of United States," VII, p. 472.
[3] "New Netherland Register," February, 1911, pp. 25, 26, 27. "Hazzards Annals," I, p. 223.

in 1667, or, as a civil officer in the community. During the trouble in Wyltwick in the same year, caused by the offensiveness of the soldiers of the English garrison, Jan Joosten, with three other citizens, acted as mediators in the dispute and were able to conciliate the inhabitants and thus prevented violence to lives and property.

The first instance of his purchase of land appears in a record which reads: "Jan Joosten had, from Governor Lovelace, a deed for a lot dated March 20th, 1671, in Marbletown," and "on the 11th October following—received confirmation of his 30 acre lot in Marbletown."[1]

Jan Joosten was selected, October 6, 1673, as one of the four magistrates of Hurley and Marbletown—to supervise the merging of the village of Niew-Drop into those of Hurley and Marbletown under the English rule. The other magistrates were Jan Broerson, Louis du Bois, and Roelof Hendricksen. And notwithstanding the change of government, Jan was continued in that civil office until the return of Dutch supremacy, in 1675, when Governor Colve reappointed him to serve for another term.

Jan Joosten is named as justice of the peace for Eusopus and was present at the Court of Azzizes, in New York, on October 4, 5 and 6, 1682.[2]

Macyken, wife of Jan Joosten is named as a beneficiary in the will of Everdt Pary; dated 26th March, 1675.[3]

With the regaining of the Country by the English, the inhabitants were again required to swear allegiance to their new overlords, so it is recorded that Jan Joosten once more performed this act of fealty 1st September, 1689.

We now approach a very interesting phase of Jan Joosten's career, in which he takes on the status of a patroon, or landed proprietor. Aside from what he had acquired in Ulster County—the Wassemaker's land, for instance, and possibly other parcels—he obtained land grants in the province of East Jersey through a period extending from 1689 to the year of his death, in 1706.

In Company with his son-in-law, Jan Hamel, who had married his daughter Geertje Crom (sometimes called "Girty Jans") in 1682[4] Jan Joosten appeared in East Jersey, where they jointly bought on October 18, 1695, from Edward Hunloke, the deputy Governor, of Wingerworth, Burlington County, a plantation of 500 acres located at Lassa, or "Lazy Point" on the Delaware River, opposite the present city of Burlington. Lassa Point lay about twenty-three miles northeast of Philadelphia, and was originally seated by three or four Dutch families "who were there"—said Governor Philip Carteret—"in 1666", and to whom he confirmed patents in 1678. The Mattinicock Island, which lay in the river opposite Burlington and Lassa Point, was subsequently the home of Peter Jegue, a noted Colonial character and trader. The record of this pur-

[1] New York Land Papers, I, pp. 37, 42.
[2] New York Historical Society Collections 1912, pp. 25, 26. 1913, p. 18.
[3] Ulster Co. Probate Records, Vol. —, p. 37.
[4] Col. Arch. New Jersey, 1st Ser., XXI, p. 464.

chase by Joosten and Hamel reads that title was given "to John Joosten and John Hamel, both now or late of Sopus (Eusopus in the Kingston locality) N. Y., yeomen". At the same time Hunloke gave the grantees a bond guaranteeing them undisputed possession of the premises; and on the following day the grantees executed and delivered to Hunloke their bond and mortgage on the 500 acres.[1] Later, Jan Joosten, in his own name, granted two hundred acres of this land at Lassa Point, and the title was confirmed by law in 1697.[2]

Jan Joosten next appears as an individual purchaser of certain lands in Somerset County East Jersey, as may be seen from the record of a deed passing title from Governor Andrew Hamilton and Agnes, his wife, and under date September 13, 1700, to "Jane (Jan) Joosten of Marbletown, New York, Yeoman." There were four parcels of this land, seperately numbered, and designated as unsurveyed and unappropriated lands, lying contiguous on the South Branch of the Raritan River, in the neighborhood of the present city of Somerville, N. J., the County seat of Somerset. As a whole, the plantation aggregated 1,835 acres. It consisted of broad and fertile meadows on the Raritan; and the locality was already partially seated by groups of Dutch and Scotch people from the Kill-Van-Kull and Perth, with a few French from Staten Island, who had come into this region about fifteen or twenty years before. On the above date there is a record of Jan Joosten being at Piscataway (Perth), where he probably went to meet the Governor and obtain his grant.[3] The above seems to be the extent of his purchases. His will was found filed, with an inventory of his personal property, in the Burlington County Surrogate's office. This instrument is endorsed "Will of Jan Joosten of . . . June 13th, 1706," and is further marked "Dutch." His personal estate included six slaves, a negro man, women and four children. The appraisers were Joris Van Neste and Hendrix Runersen; it was sworn to by "John Van Mator." Antedating this document is "a testamentary disposition" signed jointly by Jan Joosten and his wife, Macyke Hendricksen, and dated 16th December, 1681, which reads: Macyke Hendricksen shall retain full possession of the estate. She consents that the survivor shall possess everything, lands, houses, personal property, money, gold, silver—coined or uncoined. After their decease the property is to be inherited by their children—Jooste to have one half the entire estate first. Jooste and Gysbert to have the land at Marbletown—Jooste one-half and then the other half to be divided between them. Geertye to have the land at Wassemaker's land. Children of Lysbeth, deceased, to have their portion in money from the other children.[4]

Jooste Jans was the eldest son—therefore, the heir-at-law and entitled to a double portion. Geertze was the eldest daughter, who, from the additional name

[1] Col. Arch. New Jersey, 1st Ser., XXII, pp. 318, 497, 517.
[2] Index to Spicer and Leaming's Laws of New Jersey, p. 24.
[3] Col. Arch. N. Y., 1st Ser., XXX, p. 480.
[4] Probate Records Ulster Co., New York.

of "Crom," suggests that she had been married before this time, or that she was the daughter of Jan Joosten by a former marriage and carried her mother's name as the custom was in Holland. Lysbeth pre-deceased her father and left children. Another daughter, not named in the will, is supposed to have been Cathrin, and can only be accounted for by her marriage and in having received her portion and so disappears from consideration in the distribution of the property.

Jan Joosten Van Meteren was in every sense, an enterprising and influential citizen; a man of vision, initiative, culture and other fine and useful qualities, and in whom the people placed their matters of trust without fear of being betrayed or exploited. He was indeed, a worthy progenitor of the line of descendants who have distinguished themselves in every sphere of usefulness. He died in 1706, his will dated June 12th of this year being filed among the Dutch wills of New Jersey.

His Colonial Record is "He took the oath of allegiance 1664, was referee in a lawsuit 1665, Schepen 1665 and 1668." In 1673 he was one of the four Magistrates of Hurley and Marbletown and in 1676 petitioned for a minister to governor Andros.[1, 2, 3]

Joost Janse Van Meteren

Joost Jans Van Meteren's (born 1660 died 1700–05 the eldest son of Jan Joosten Van Meteren) early life, aside from his adventures, while yet a small boy, with the Indians in 1663, has not been revealed, but may be assumed to have been pretty much the same as that of other youths, until the time of his engagement to marry was published in the banns of the Reformed Dutch Church at Kingston, on the 18th of November, 1682, and which was followed by his marriage announcement in this wise: "Jooste, Jans, J. M. of Meteren, born in Gelderland, residing in Mormer (Marbletown) and Sara du Bois, J. D. of Kingston, residing in the Nieuw-Pals (New Platz) married in the Pals, 12 December, 1682."[4]

Sara du Bois was the daughter of Louis du Bois (1626–96) The "Patentee" from Artois, France and Cathrine Blanchan, his wife. Sara was baptized at Kingston, September 14, 1664. They had issue:

    i. Jan, bapt. October 14, 1683. Sponsers: Jan Joosten, Macyken Hendricksen.
    ii. Rebekka, bapt. April 26, 1686. Sponsers: Jacob du Bois, Gysbert Crom.
    iii. Lysbeth, bapt. March 3, 1689. Sponsor: Catrynda du Bois.
    iv. Isaac, bapt. circa, 1692. (Record missing.)
    v. Hendrix, bapt. Sept. 1, 1695. Sponsers: David du Bois, Janekken.[5] Molenawi.

---
[1] Rhodes, N. O. "Colonial Families of the United States," Vol. VII, pp. 470, 474.
[2] Smith's "Dulse Shephed, Van Meter Genealogy," pp. 9-27.
[3] Laidley "Van Meter Sketches."
[4] Records Reformed Church at Kingston, New York.
[5] Rhoade's "Colonial Families of the United States", Vol. VII, p. 474.

i. Jan (John) in 1683 who later settled in Berkeley County, Virginia, dying there in 1745, leaving eleven children one of whom, Elizabeth, married Col. Thomas Shepherd and another Soloman Hedges mentioned in Geo. Washington's Journal when surveying beyond the Blue Ridge 1747-48.

ii. Rebecca Van Meter born 1686. Wed-1704, Cornelius Elting, and had ten children.

iii. Lysbeth Van Meter born 1689.

iv. Isaac Van Meter the fourth child of Joost Jan Van Meteren and Sarah du Bois was not baptized at Kingston as far as the records show. . . .

v. Hendrick (Henry) Van Meter born 1695, who married a number of times, and finally settled in Salem County, New Jersey, where he died in 1759, leaving ten children; his last wife was Mary, sister of Erasmus Feltere.

Joost Jan Van Meteren became sufficiently Americanized to spell his name John instead of Jan, and finally dropped the "n" off, thus leaving the name Van Metre. So Joost Jans is the John Van Meter a "Dutchman from the Hudson" who was the noted Indian trader and explorer of the Shenandoah Valley who 'Spied out the land" about the time of Governor Spotswood's Expedition, 1716. He equipped a band of Delaware or Caugh Indians and while on this expedition he explored the country then almost unknown to the white people, the Valley of the South branch of the Potomac (known then by the Indian name of the Wappatomake). On his return he advised his sons to take up the land in "The Wappatomica Valley in the South Branch Bottom above the Trough," as it was the finest land he had discovered in all his travels.[1] By the nature of his life, his habitation was seldom fixed for a definite length of time, but proof exists that he dwelt at different periods in the states of New York, New Jersey, and Pennsylvania.

Isaac Van Metre

A particular instance which involves quite a group of the Van Metre family is found in "An Indenture dated June 19, 1714, between Colonel Daniel Coxe, of Burlington, of the one part, and Jacob du Bois, of the county of Ulster New York, and Sarah du Bois of the county of Salem, and John Van Metre and Isaac Van Metre, of the County and division aforesaid, of the other part," recites that Daniel Coxe purchased Thomas William's land in Salem County—7,000 acres— in consideration of "£750 lawful pounds money of New York, at eight shillings the ounce," and the said Coxe conveys unto the said Jacob du Bois, Sara du Bois, John Van Metre and Isaac Van Metre, 3,000 acres beginning on a branch of the Maurice River, and being part of the 7,000 acres taken up upon the right of the three property purchases of Thomas Williams by Daniel Coxe.[2] Shourds, the Salem county historian, states that "these parties divided their lands by the

[1] Kercheval, Samuel, "History of the Valley," p. 46.
[2] Liber, D. D., p. 316, Salem Deeds.

compass, the du Bois taking theirs on the north side of a line and the Van Metres on the south side. The Van Metres continued to purchase until they owned a very large portion of the land reaching from the Overshot Mill on Upper Alloways Creek, near Daretown, southeasterly to Fork Bridge, about 6,000 acres in all."[3] The grantees thereof were Sarah du Bois, wife or widow, of the elder John Van Metre; her two sons, John and Isaac Van Metre; and her brother, Jacob du Bois. Here Sarah established her son Isaac permanently, as she thought, as by a deed dated 27 May, 1726, reciting "for and in consideration of the love, good will and affection I have and do bear toward my loving and dutiful son Isaac Van Metre of the province aforesaid," the mother transfers to him three hundred and two acres of land lying at Pile's Grove between Nickomus Run and Salem Creek. Possession of this property was taken over by Isaac on the 26th of May, 1726, in the presence of Cornelius Elting Jr.[4] In Salem, prior to 1709, is a record in the "Eare Marke Book" reciting that John and Isaac Van Metre Jr. had recorded cattle and swine.[5]

The ambition, and that restless spirit, inherited from the father with his vision and early advice, inspired the two Van Metre brothers to launch the scheme to colonize their relatives and friends in the Valley of Virginia. Between them John Van Metre and his brother Isaac they obtained from Governor Gooch, of the British Crown and council of Virginia, on the 30th of June 1730, a grant of forty thousand acres of land, unappropriated and unsurveyed, in Spottsylvania county in the Northern Neck of Virginia.

Copy from the Original Van Meter Grants

"At a council held in the capitol the 17th day of June, 1730. Present.—The Governor, Robert Carter, James Blair, William Byrd, John Robinson, John Cart, Rd. Fitzwilliam, John Grymes, Wm. Dandridge, John Curtis,—Esquires. Several petitions being this day offered to the Board for leave to take up land on the River Sherando on the Northwest side of the Great Mountains, Robert Carter, Esq. Agent for the Proprietors of the Northern Neck moved that it might be entered that he on behalf of the sd Proprietors claimed the land on the sd River Sherando as belonging to the sd Proprietors & within the limits of their Grant it belonged sole to the Proprietors to grant the sd lands wch moven at his request is entered and then the Board proceded to the hearing of the sd Petitions. On reading at this Board the Petition of John Van Metre setting forth that he is desirious to take up a Tract of land in this Colony on the West side of the Great Mountains for the settlement of himself and eleven children and also that divers of his Relations and friends living in the Government of New York are also desirous to move their families and effects and Settle in the same place if a

[3] Shourd's "History of Fenwick's Colony," pp. 302-4.
[4] Liber, D., p. 203, Salem Deeds.
[5] Ear Mark Book, Salem Co., N. J.", p. 7.

Sufficient Quantity of land may be assigned them for that purpose and praying that ten thousand acres of land lying in the forks of the Sherando River including the places called by the name of Cedar Litch and Stoney Lick and running up between the branches of the said river to complete that quantity and twenty thousand acres not already taken up by Robert Carter and Mann Page, Esqrs., or any other,—lying in the fork between the sd River Sherando and the River Cohonguroota and extending thence to Operkon and up the South Branch thereof may be assigned for the Habitation of himself and family and friends. The Governor, with the advice of his council is pleased to give leave to the sd John Van Metre to take up the sd first mentioned tract of ten thousand acres for the set'lem't of himself and his family, and that as soon as the Petitioner shall bring on the last mentioned Tract twenty families to Inhabit on that this Board is satisfied so many are to remove thither leave be and it is hereby granted him for surveying the last mentioned tract of twenty thousand acres within the limits above described in so many several dividens as the pet'r and his sd partners shall think fit. And it is furthered ordered that no person is permitted to enter for or take up any part of the afsd Lands in the meantime provided the sd Van Metre and his family and the twenty other families of his Relations and friends do settle thereon within the space of two years according to his proposal."[1]

"Isaac Van Meter of the Province of West Jersey having by petition to this Board set forth that he is desirous to settle himself on the West side of the Great Mountains. He has been to view the land in those parts and has discovered a place where settlement may conveniently be made, not possessed by any one of the English Inhabitants and praying that ten thousand acres of land lying between the lands surveyed for Robt. Carter, Esq., and the forks of the Shenando river and the river Operkon in as many several tracts or Dividends as shall be necessary for the accommodation and settlement of ten families (including his own) who proposes to bring to the said land:

The Governor with the advice of the Council is pleased to order as it is hereby ordered that the said Isaac Van Meter for himself and his partners have leave to take up the said quantity of ten thousand acres of land within the limits above described and that if he bring the above number of families to dwell there within two years; Patent be granted him and them for the same in such several tracts or Dividends as they shall think fit and in the meantime the same be referred free from entry of any other person, Dated at Williamsburg, 17th June, 1730."

The Council sitting at Williamsburg from 1721 to 1734 expressly sets forth in their order dated 17th June, 1730, that Isaac the Petitioner had been to view the lands in those parts—"those parts"—are described in the survey made

---
[1] MSS., Journal of the Governor and Council of Virginia, Session 1721-1734, p. 364.

within the two years—as lying along both sides of the Shenandoah—one to John and one to Isaac. And these surveys embrace forty thousand acres each, and were confirmed to these brothers May 12, 1732.[2, 3]

The Van Metres, within the two years allowed in the grants had transferred land to Jost Hite, their relative in New York, also a Hollander, on August 5, 1731 to begin settlement on the lands.[1] The Van Metres, however, under some mutual arrangement, retained options on certain choice spots in the Valley in the area originally granted them by Governor William Gooch. One of these parcels—there are two—contained one thousand seven hundred and eighty six acres and the other eight hundred and eighty five acres, and both were located on the west side of the Sherando River, in a new country soon to be called Orange. Patents for these tracts were issued on October 3, 1734, the year Orange County was erected and established.[2]

Thus it was that the Van Metre's beheld and explored that "land of Promise" where they envisioned the future as they looked upon the beautiful valley of Virginia sweeping southward, enfolded by the evergreen Blue Ridge, whose western slopes fell gently to the verdant meadows and sheltered limestone bottoms that were washed by the swift waters of the Shenandoah and those of the placid Potomac. This sylvan wilderness of Lord Fairfax, which he called "the Northern Neck" of Virginia was the "land of Goshen" to which the restless pioneers of the east shortly came, and whose first settlement may be traced to the intrepid trader Van Metre; and it actually began with the granting of a vast area to his sons on the 17th of June, 1730. Known as the Shenandoah (Shenendo, Sherando, or Sherundo) Valley of Virginia.

Isaac Van Meter, in conformity with his father's advice came to Virginia about the year 1736 or '37, and made what was called a "Tomakawk Improvement" on these lands, immediately above the trough, where "Fort Pleasant" was afterward erected.[3]

Isaac Van Metre owned tracts of land in Salem County and passed a very active life there. He took a prominent part in the founding of the Pittsgrove (Pikesgrove) Presbyterian Church of Salem County, New Jersey, the covenant of which was signed as no. 1—his wife Hannah, 2—their son Henry, 3—their daughter Sarah, 4—

Isaac Van Metre married about 1717 at Mooreland Manor, Pennsylvania, Anne or Annah (Annetgie) Wynkoop, the daughter of Garritt Wynkoop and his wife Jacomytge Fakker. Unfortunately the records of the Church and the Church were destroyed. In the beginning it was the fatherland religion but was admitted to the Presbytery of Philadelphia, which accounts for the change

---
[2] See old files in State Library, Richmond, Virginia.
[3] Cartwell, "Shenandoah Valley Pioneers and Their Descendants," p. 13. *
[1] West Virginia Historical Magazine, I, pp. 53-54.
[2] Land Records, Richmond, Va., Vol. XV, pp. 323, 327.
[3] Kercheval, Samuel, 'History of the Valley", p. 46.
*For *Cartwell* read *Cartmell*.

to Presbyterianism of Isaac and his family. Their seven children were born in Ulster County, New York, between the years 1694 and 1713.

    i. Henry Van Meter wed March 7, 1741, at the First Presbyterian Church, Philadelphia, Rebecca du Bois, daughter of Isaac and Rebecca (his cousin du Bois).
    ii. Sarah Van Meter baptized February 23, 1722, married January 27, 1741-2, John Richman.
    iii. Rebecca Van Meter, who married Abraham Hite, son of Joost Hite, in 1751.
    iv. Garret Van Meter (b. 1732, d. 1788), of whom later we will deal in full.
    v. Jacob Van Meter, of whom nothing definite is known.
    vi. Catherine Van Meter, who married George McCulloch and died presumably without issue between 1757-68.
    vii. Hilda Van Meter, of whom nothing is known.

These parents and four children took up their permanent abode at "Fort Pleasant" in the Indian Old Fields, now Hardy County, West Virginia, in 1744.

Isaac Van Meter, the founder and owner of "Fort Pleasant" when quite an old man was killed and scalped by the Indians, only a short distance outside of his fort in the year 1757, leaving a widow and four children. His will dated February 15th, 1754, was probated in 1757, and recorded in the old County Clerk's Office at Romney, West Virginia.[4]

Garrett Van Meter

Garrett Van Meter and the son of Isaac Van Meter the founder of "Fort Pleasant" and his wife Anne Wynkoop was born in the State of New York, February, 1734, and came with his parents and the balance of their family to Hardy County, Virginia in 1744. He married Mrs. Ann Sibley, whose maiden name was Ann Markee, in 1756. He inherited from his father's estate "Fort Pleasant", and a large tract of the surrounding lands. He was a Colonel in the Revolutionary War, and commanded a regiment of militia in General Washington's Army.[1, 2] He lived and died in 1788 at old "Fort Pleasant" as full of honor as of years. Their children were:

    i. Isaac, born December 10th, 1757, married Bettie Inskeep. He was in Gen. George Rogers Clark's campaign in 1778 against Vincennes. A Burgess from Frederick County, Virginia.
    ii. Jacob, born May 18, 1764, of whom later—.
    iii. Ann, born April 15th, 1767, married Abel Seymour.

Jacob Van Meter

Jacob Van Meter born May 18th, 1764, married 1791 Tabitha Inskeep the daughter of Joseph Inskeep and his wife Hannah McCullock. He was a Colonel and commanded a regiment in the War Against Great Britain in 1812-13.

---
[4] Cartwell, "History of Frederick County, Virginia," p. 259.*
[1] Kercheval, Samuel, "History of the Valley," pp. 129-30.
[2] Eckeurode, H. J. "Rev. Soldiers of Va." Special Report Archives and His., 1912. **

*For *Cartwell* read *Cartmell*.
**For *Eckeurode* read *Eckenrode*.

He built in the South Branch Valley a flour mill, which was constructed to run by water power. He was an enterprising business man, and for many years a partner with Chief Justice Marshall in the breeding of thoroughbred horses.[3] Colonel Jacob Van Meter's house was headquarters for ministers of the gospel who passed through the Shenendoah Valley, whether Presbyterian or Methodist. He was an elder in the Presbyterian Church.[4] He died in 1825.

Colonel Jacob Van Meter and his wife Tabitha, had born to them the following children.

    i. Hannah, born 8th November, 1791, married John Hopewell.
    ii. Ann, born 1st April, 1793, never married. Died October, 1892.
    iii. Isaac, born 24 September, 1794, of whom later.
    iv. Rebecca, born 2nd May, 1799. Never married.
    v. Susan, born 12th December, 1807. Never married.

Isaac Van Meter

Isaac Van Meter, born 24th September, 1794, in old "Fort Pleasant," Hardy County, in what is now West Virginia. He received a good English education from the best teachers obtained at that time, a thorough training from his father in the best mode of farming and the care and attention of live stock. He supplied the Philadelphia and Baltimore markets with the finest beef and pork.

When Isaac Van Meter was about twenty-three years of age he came to Kentucky; bringing with him about seven thousand dollars worth of property, consisting chiefly of negro slaves, horse stock and money. He was married by the Rev. William W. Martin, on June 17, 1817, to Rebecca, daughter of Captain Isaac Cunningham and his wife, Sarah Harness, who was born in Hardy County, Virginia, October 14, 1800, and removed with her parents to Clark County, Kentucky, in 1802.

Isaac Van Meter and Captain Isaac Cunningham were for many years equal partners in their business affairs. They bred the finest thoroughbred horses for some years; and became quite noted for their famous importation of Shorthorn cattle in 1834. They each owned more than one thousand acres of as valuable lands as were in Kentucky; about four miles northwest of Winchester, on the "Van Meter Pike" which to this day carries that name. He died in 1854.

Isaac Van Meter and his wife Rebecca had fifteen children born to them, and raised ten to be grown. They were:

    i. Solomon was born July 10, 1818, died Sept. 1859. He married 1st Elizabeth Stonestreet, 2nd Lucy Hockaway, 3rd Martha C. Prewitt.
    ii. Isaac was born October 8, 1820, died April 14, 1898. Married Fannie Hull.

---
[3] Cartwell, "Shenandoah Valley Pioneers and Their Descendants," pp. 104, 662.*
[4] Mead, Bishop, "Churches and Families of Virginia." **
*For *Cartwell* read *Cartmell*.
**For *Mead* read *Meade*.

 iii. Jacob was born February 10, 1822, died October 19, 1849. Married Florida E. Miles October 20, 1846.
 iv. Sarah Ann was born October 26, 1825, died 1844. Married Dr. John Hall July 25, 1843.
 v. Susan Tabitha was born August 1, 1827. Married Dr. Algernon Sidney Allan April 15, 1846.
 vi. Benjamin F. Van Meter was born January 30, 1834, died October 1, 1927. Married November 30, 1854, Amelia Clay Lewis, (born 1836, died July 21, 1927), the daughter of Thornton Lewis, and his wife Emma Wright, the grand daughter of Hon. Thomas Lewis, Burgess[1][2] of "Bellefonte", the son of Colonel John Lewis, the founder of Staunton, Augusta County, Virginia.[3]

  Benjamin F. Van Meter (the grandfather of the writer of this paper) resided at "Sycamore" the ancestral home he inherited from his father on the Van Meter pike,[4] where he perpetuated the breeding of thorough-bred horses, and Shorthorn cattle. On two occasions he made trips to England to select his importations— He was the author of "Genealogies and Sketches on some Old Families." For thirty-two years a loyal member and an honored elder of the Presbyterian church. A devoted husband, loving father, faithful friend, wise councillor, leading citizen, devout Christian, a true man.

 vii. Thomas C. was born October 29, 1835. Married Orpha Campbell.
 viii. Eliza Caroline was born September 15, 1837, died 1841.
 ix. Abram was born May 20, 1839. Married October 26, 1859, Anna Elizabeth Kleiser.
 x. Louis Marshall was born February 8, 1841.

The Van Meter Family in Kentucky

I. SOLOMON, the first son of Isaac Van Meter and his wife, Rebecca Cunningham, resided at Duncastle, three miles from Lexington, in Fayette County, Kentucky. As stated, he married first Elizabeth Stonestreet, the daughter of James Stonestreet and his wife, Lucy Fishback. His second wife was Lucy Hockaday, a daughter of Irvine Hockaday and his wife, Emily Mills; they had one daughter, Lucy, who married Dr. Kerr, of Fulton, Missouri. His (Solomon's) third wife was Martha C. Prewitt, daughter of Nelson Prewitt and his wife, Mary Ann Coleman, and from this marriage there were three sons, Isaac (1), Nelson Prewitt (2), and Solomon (3).

II. ISAAC, the second son of Isaac Van Meter and his wife, Rebecca Cunningham, resided in Fayette County, Kentucky. He married Fanny Hull, the daughter of Henry Hull and his wife, Hannah Harness. They had ten children born to them: (1) Charles L., (2) Sallie, (3) Edwin, (4) Scott, (5) J. Brown, (6) Louis M., (7) Benjamin, (8) Jessie, (9) Anna Rebecca, (10) Fannie.

III. JACOB VAN METER, the third son of Isaac Van Meter and his wife, Rebecca Cunningham, married Florida E. Miles and died early, leaving no issue.

---
[1] Standards, "Colonial Virginia Register," p. 201.*
[2] Peyton, J. Lewis, "History of Augusta County, Virginia," p. 333.
[3] Waddell, Joseph A., "Annals of Augusta County, Virginia," Ed. 1902, p. 37.
[4] Records, Clark County Court House, Winchester, Kentucky.

*For *Standards* read *Stanard's*.

IV. SARAH ANN VAN METER, the fourth child of Isaac Van Meter and Rebecca Cunningham, married Dr. John Hall, removed to Illinois and left no issue.
V. SUSAN TABITHA VAN METER, the fifth child of Isaac Van Meter and his wife, Rebecca Cunningham, married Dr. Algernon Allan of Fayette County, Kentucky, and left no issue.
VI. BENJAMIN FRANKLIN VAN METER, the sixth child of Isaac Van Meter and his wife, Rebecca Cunningham, married Amelia Clay Lewis, daughter of Thornton Lewis and his wife, Emma Wright. They had eleven children: (1) Emma, (2) Everitt, (3) Annette, (4) Thomas Wright Lewis, (5) Frank B. M., (6) Mary Belle, (7) Joseph, (8) Dr. Benjamin F., (9) Amelia Ellen, and two infant boys, who died at birth.
VII. THOMAS C., the seventh child of Isaac Van Meter and his wife, Rebecca Cunningham, married Orpha Campbell of Mercer County, the daughter of Whitaker Hill Campbell and his wife, Permelia Perkins. They resided in Eminence, Kentucky, and raised one daughter, Kate Van Meter.
VIII. ELIZA CAROLINE VAN METER, the eighth child of Isaac Van Meter and his wife, Rebecca Cunningham, died at the age of four years.
IX. ABRAM VAN METER, the ninth child of Isaac Van Meter and his wife, Rebecca Cunningham, married Anna Elizabeth Kleiser, daughter of Jonas Marks Kleiser and his wife, Malita Stapp. They resided in Cools County, Texas, and had seven children: (1) Leta Mary, (2) Jonas K., (3) Walter M., (4) Isaac, (5) Elizabeth K., (6) Anna Rebecca, (7) Thomas M.
X. LIEUTENANT LOUIS MARSHALL VAN METER, the tenth child of Isaac Van Meter and his wife, Rebecca Cunningham, married Nannie Moore, the daughter of Thomas R. Moore and his wife, Hannah Ransdall. They resided in Shelby County, Kentucky, and had eight children: (1) Maria B., (2) John D., (3) Louis Marshall, Jr., (4) Evaline B., (5) Thomas Matthew, (6) Nannie, (7) Sallie M., (8) Benjamin.

Thus, from this pioneer Isaac Van Meter, into Kentucky from the Valley of Virginia were scattered numerous descendants into the different counties of Fayette, Shelby, Mercer, Jefferson, Clark and Hardin. Among these descendants were many men of prominence who held responsible positions in their communities and who walked in the footprints of their forefathers in government, religion and war.

The Venables.

BY

MISS MORTON, of Virginia.

Abraham Venable and his brothers.
Joseph Venable, Md.
Wm. Venable, Bucks Co., Penna., came to Va. in 1682.
Abraham Venable married Mildred Lewis, wid. of John Nix.
Abraham Venable, b. 1700; d. 1768; m. 1724 Martha Davis, d. of Robt. Davis, of St. Mary's, and Abadiah Lewis, d. Hugh Lewis, b. 1703.
Abraham Venable was Justice of the Peace, Louisa Co., from first Co. Court, Dec. 13, 1742.
Justice of Peace Hanover Co.
Vestryman of St. Paul's Episcopal Church prior to 1742.
Vestryman Fredericksville Parish from 1742 to 1768.
Vestryman Trinity Parish, 1762 to 1768.
Captain of Colonial Militia.
Member of Va. House of Burgesses, 1748, 1752, 1755.
County Lieutenant of Louisa Co.
Will registered Louisa Co., dated Apr. 6, probated Jan., 1769—
"My friend, Patrick Henry, Trustee."
James Venable, b. about 1734; d. in Ky., 18——; (m. Judith Morton, d. of Joseph Morton and Agnes Woodson.)
Trustee, Visitor and Manager of Hampden-Sidney College, 1775.
Elder Briery Church, Va.
Moved to Shelby County, Ky, in 1796.

Elder Mulberry Presbyterian Ch; buried in Shelby Co., Ky.
Joseph Venable, b. 1761; d. 18—; m. 1791, Eliz. Watkins, (d. Francis Watkins and Agnes Woodson); b. Prince Edward Co., Va., 1769; d. Shelby Co. Ky., 1832.
Elizabeth McRoberts Venable, m. Wm. Quin Morton, s. Quin M. and Mary Anderson. Col. Quin Morton, b. Va.; d. Ky.; m. Elizabeth Logan.
Abraham Venable, m. Eliz. Michaux, d. Jacob Michaux and Judith Woodson.
Children of Abraham Venable:
1. John V., m. Eliz. Raine.
2. Sam'l V., m. Ann Anderson.
3. Jacob V., m. Mary Venable.
4. Abraham V.
5. Nathaniel V., m. Martha Venable.
6. Josiah V.
7. Mary V., m. Chas. Allen.
8. Martha V., m. Jno. Holcombe.
Abraham Venable, m. Mary Morton, d. Sam'l and Sallie Moore. Their children:
1. Sam'l.
2. Hampden.
3. James.
4. Geo., m. Eliz. Hill.
Children of Geo. and Eliz. Hill Venable:
1 Lucy.
2. Caroline, m. Thos. Green. Their d., Lucy Green, m. Randolph Dade.

Hugh Lewis Venable, m. Mary Martin. Their children:
1. Nathaniel.
2. John.
3. Abraham.
4. Martha, m. —— Banks.
5. Judith, m. Moorman.
6. Eliza, m. R. Bragg.
7. Mary, m. John Moorman.

Chas. Venable, m. Eliza. Smith, d. of Robt. Smith, of Port Royal, Va. Children:
1. Robt., m. Sarah Madison.
2. Chas.
3. Mary, m. Robt. Martin.
4. Eliza, m. M. Womack.
5. Sarah, m. Peyton Gleson.
6. Martha, m. Wm. Brown.
7. Ann, m. Dan Glenn.
8. Dorathea, m. Jno. Goode.
9. Agnes.
10. Nancy.

James Venable, m. Eliza. Cowan, d. of John and Mary Craig. Children:
1. Sam'l, m. Louisa Allen.
2. John C., m. Marg. Glass.
3. Jas., m. Mary McDonald.
4. Wm. H.
5. Mary, m. Rev. Jas. Harvey Logan.
6. Sarah, m. Dr. Jos. Allen.
7. Martha, m. Hugh M. Glass.

James Venable served in the war of 1812.

John Cowan Venable, married Margaret Jane, d. of Sarah Paxton Steele and David Glass.

Their children, David Glass Venable, married Katherine Reading, Frankfort, Ky.

William Thompson Venable.

Sarah Steele Venable, married Col. Wickliffe Cooper, Lexington, Ky.

Elizabeth Cowan Venable, married William Thomas Reading, Frankfort, Ky.

Joseph Glass Venable, married Susan Hahn, Danville, Ky.

Mary Eliza Venable, married Samuel T. McElroy, Lebanon, Ky.

John Cowan Venable, married Elizabeth Lee Gibson, Richmond, Va.

Elizabeth Cowan Venable, married William Thomas Reading. The children are:
John Windell Reading.
William Thomas Reading.
Coulter Steele Reading.
Margaret Dryden Reading.
David Glass Venable Reading.

John Windell Reading, married Katherine Claggett Gay, Woodford county, Ky. Their children:
Windell Gay Reading.
James Edward Lee Reading.

Sarah, daughter of James Venable and Elizabeth Cowan, married Dr. Joseph Allen.

Their only child, Sarah, married John Bell, and their only surviving child is Gen. J. Franklin Bell, one of Kentucky's most distinguished sons.

Agnes Venable, m. Rev. Wm. Mahon. Children:
1. Jas.
2. Infant.
3. Wm., m. Miss Ray.
4. Eliza, m. Wm. Harbison.
5. Jane, m. Foster.
6. Jas., m. Matilda Pennick.
7. Archibald, d. age 4 years.
8. Judith, d. age 3 years.
9. Martha, d. age 3 years.
10. Mary, m. Jno. Reed, of Indiana.

Nathaniel Venable, m. Eliz. Woodson, d. Richard and Ann Michaux.

Wm. Venable, m. Ann Clark.

Ann Venable, m. Dr. Geo. Lynn, no children.

Jno. Venable, m. Agnes Moorman.

Mary Venable, m. Nathaniel Price, s. of Wm. and Mary Morton.

Ann Venable, m. Philip King.

Eliza Venable, m. Josiah Woodson, s. of Jos. and Agnes Woodson.

Frances Venable, m. Leonard Robinson.

Ann Robinson, m. Archibald Scott.

Eliza. Venable, d. unmarried.

Jane Venable, d. young.

Martha Venable, m. first, David Harbison; second, Samson Morley

Children of Ann Venable and Philip King:

1 Jas., m. Eliza King.
2. Jennie, m. Finch Offutt.
3. Geo., m. Agnes Harbison.
4. Davis, m. first, Miss Paynes; second, Mrs. Campbell.
5. Baxter, m. Lucy Venable.

6. Pauline Harbison, m. Edward Payne.

Abraham Michaux, s. of ——— Michaux and Saurin, Nismes, France, m. Susannah Rochette, Sedan, France, d. of Moses Rochette, in Holland, had issue:

1. Jacob, m. Judith Woodson, d. of Richard and Ann Smith.
2. Jno.
3. Jas.
4. Paul.
5. Abram.
6. Jane, m. Peter Le Grande.
7. Nannie.
8. Susan.
9. Judith, m. Morgan.
10. Eliza., m. S. Woodson.
11. Anne, m. Richard Woodson, s. of Richard Woodson and Ann Smith.

A book of Common Prayer sent by M. James Saurin, minister of French Church, to Abraham Michaux, his nephew, is in the Episcopal Seminary at Alexandria, Virginia. The old French Bible containing family records is the possession of Mrs. Thos. Graden, Gardenia, Prince Edward Co., Va.

THE VILEY FAMILY.*

This family is said to be of French descent, and there are many evidences which seem to indicate that this is true. The first of the family of whom we have knowledge, were George Viley and his twin sister, Henrietta, wife of Francis Downing. George and Henrietta Viley were born in 1745 and lived in Montgomery County, Maryland, not far from the "Falls of the Potomac." The plantation of George Viley in Maryland was known as "Wolf Cow" and was disposed of shortly after the family emigrated to Kentucky. The wife of George Viley was Martha Ann Jeanes or Janes, a daughter of William and Martha Ann Janes, who were Quakers. The father William Janes, was a surveyor in Montgomery County, Maryland, and was a son of Joseph and Elizabeth Janes of Prince George County, Maryland. In the year 1795 George Viley and Francis Downing and their families, between whom there existed the closest and tenderest relationship, which has extended to their descendants of the present generation, left Maryland for the settlements of Kentucky. They brought with them their string of thorough-bred horses and their servants—one little negro boy who was born on the journey, lived to a great age, is well remembered by the writer as "Old Uncle Buck."

Among the neighboring Maryland families intimate with the Vileys, were the Robinsons, who came to Kentucky at an early period and were probably largely instrumental in inducing the Vileys to settle in the new State. The Robinson emigrants (who were parents of James F. Robinson, Governor of Kentucky) had located in Scott County between Georgetown and Payne's Depot. On Christmas Eve, the Viley emigrant wagons, by means of which they had crossed the mountains and traveled the Wilderness Road, halted near the comfortable house of the Robinsons, and there the reunited friends celebrated the joyous occasion on Christmas day, 1795.

After resting from their long journey with these hospitable friends, both the Vileys and the Downings located permanently in Scott County, near the Stamping Ground. Here the Viley home was built. Six of the children of George and Martha Ann Janes Viley weer born in Maryland, while six more were born in the Kentucky home, and here the six daughters were married. George Viley died in this home, November 1st, 1814, and his wife died here June 13th, 1832. The old Viley home place has never passed out of the hands of the family, but during the occupany by George Viley, a grandson of George and Martha Ann Janes Viley, the house was burned and rebuilt later by him. It is now owned by Dr. Wm. H. Coffman, who married Anne Payne, a great great granddaughter of the original owners. The Blue Grass homes of the Viley de-

*See also the Viley bible record, pp. 737-738, this volume.

scendants were numerous and distinguished for lavish hospitality. Among these may be mentioned the Ward home, still standing near Georgetown, Ky., and another, quite as splendid and famous, was the Minor Williams home near the same place. These places were the summer homes of their owners, whose winters were spent on their southern plantations. The father's love of thorough-bred horses and other fine live stock seemed to have been inherited in the greatest measure by his son, Capt. Willa Viley. The first home of the son, Capt. Willa Viley was located near Paynes Depot, which home he later gave to his son, Andrew Jackson Viley, while he and his wife, Lydia Smith Viley removed to his beautiful farm near Lexington, now known as the Lyle place. Capt. Willa Viley was a notable man of his day. He was characterized by the sterling qualities of firmness and decision, yet of a gentle and affectionate disposition in all his relations. A soldier of the war of 1812, he was distinguished by a military bearing through life, a marked erectness and apparent sternness, but at heart there was gentleness which manifested itself in his tender love towards all children, and his devotion and careful thoughtfulness of his gentle, noble wife.

As a farmer he was one of the best in all the Blue Grass region, but, the feature which marked his career among the foremost men of that day in the development of Kentucky, was his superior judgment as to horses, and in his success in raising them. He was one of the pioneers in rearing and training race-horses, and many of the most notable horses of his day were from his stables, among which were "Dick Singleton," "Alex Churchill," and "Lexington." He was one of the originators of the Lexington Racing Association in 1823, and continued his interest in the course until the Civil War. Just as Capt. Willa Viley inherited his taste for horses from his father, so it seems that these qualities were transmitted to his son, Warren Viley of "Stonewall" near Versailles, in Wodford County. Warren Viley was a splendid type of the Kentuckian at his best. Noble hearted, courageous and upright, of Knightly courtesy, hospitable and generous, simple and kindly. He enjoyed, during his long life, the highest esteem of all who knew him, and the devoted love of his personal friends. He was a noted turfman and was engaged during most of his life in farming and raising thoroughbred horses. One of his most noted horses was "Capitola" by "Vandal," a long distance mare of high merit from whom he developed the celebrated "King Alfonso." He presented Gen. John H. Morgan with "Black Bess" which had a war reputation almost equal to that of her distinguished owner, "Stonewall." Warren Viley's lovely home, has always been the seat of cordial hospitality, and there, have been entertained the most prominent men of the day. Its famous woodland has been the scene of a number of big barbecues which have marked great epochs in Kentucky politics. John C. Breckinridge was here launched upon his public career at a barbecue given in his honor by Warren Viley. The Hon. James B. Beck was the guest of honor at a similar gathering, and in 1874 the Hon. J. C. S. Blackburn was likewise entertained.

The stone fence from which "Stonewall" takes its name was built in 1863, and so excellent was the workmanship that in almost a half century, no repairs have been necessary, and the fence is today in almost perfect condition. "Stonewall" is now the home of Breckinridge Viley, the son of Warren Viley, and just across the roadway are the beautiful woodlands of Loto Wana" and "Glenartney," the estate of Lister Witherspoon and his wife, who is a daughter of Warren Viley.

The children of George[1] and Martha A. Janes[1] Viley were as follows:

I. Elizabeth[2] Viley, b—Feb. 3, 1786, d—Jan. 21, 1820; married General James McConnell.

1. George[3] McConnell, married Margaret Hord.

a. James[4] McConnell married Mrs. Mary (Johnson) Shortridge.

b. Kate H.[4] McConnell.

c. George[4] McConnell married Susie Sessions. One child, Margaret[5].

2. Robert[3] McConnell, married Mary Thompson.

a. Eliza[3] McConnell, married W. H. Cleveland.

Emma[5] Cleveland, Wm. T.[5] Cleveland, married Maria Crutcher; Jas.[5] Cleveland; Kirtley[5] Cleveland; Robert[5] Cleveland.

b. Martha[4] McConnell, married Wm. Railey.

Randolph[5] Railey; James[5] Railey, married Gladys Blair; Hunter[5] Railey, married M. L. Lane; Mary[5] Railey, married R. F. Given; Emma[5] Railey; Martha[5] Railey.

c. Wm. Thompson McConnell, married Nannie Carpenter.

Eliza[5] McConnell; Robert[5] McConnell; Sarah Miller[5] McConnell.

d. Robert[4] McConnell, married Mrs. Glover (nee Lane).

Robin[5] McConnell.

e. James[4] McConnell, married Lizzie Hunter.

Hunter[5] McConnell.

3. Martha[3] McConnell, married Jerry Wilson.

4. Elizabeth[3] McConnell, died young.

5. Wm.[3] McConnell, died in young manhood.

II. Willa Janes[2] Viley; b—Feb. 10, 1788, d—March 28, 1865; married Apr. 6, 1813, Lydia Smith.

Excursus: Smith—Rodes—Thomson—Crawford.

Lydia Smith (Jan. 16, 1794—Jan. 13, 1869), who married Willa J. Viley, was a daughter of Rodes Smith and Eunice Thomson, his wife; both natives of Louisa County, Virginia. Rodes Smith was the son of William Smith and his wife, Mary Rodes. Eunice Thomson was a daughter of William Thomson and his wife, Ann Rodes. Mary Rodes Smith and Ann Rodes Thomson were daughters of John Rodes and his wife, Mary Crawford, of New Kent County, Virginia. Mary Crawford was a daughter of Captain David Crawford and his wife, Elizabeth Smith. Many descendants of these families came to Kentucky in the early days. The Rodes and Thomsons were very largely represented in this State, particularly in the Blue Grass section.

1. Ann E.[3] Viley, b—Apr. 25, 1815; married General George W. Johnson,* August 20, 1833.

   a. Eliza W.[4] Johnson, married Col. J. Stoddard Johnston.

   George W.[5] Johnston, married Mattie Darling; Mary H.[5] Johnston, married Wm. Bell Wisdom; Eliza E.[5] Johnston; Harris[5] Johnston, married Julia Cox; J. Stoddard[5] Johnston, Jr., married Georgie Moore.

   b. Willa V.[4] Johnson, married Lily J. Tilford.

   Emily M.[5] Johnson, married V. W. Allen; George W.[5] Johnson, married Luda Lamb; Mary B.[5] Johnson, married C. C. Menzies; Annie[5] Johnson; Wm. B.[5] Johnson.

   c. Madison Conyers[4] Johnson, married Adele Stokes. These had six children, all of whom died in infancy except George W.[5] Johnson, who died in young manhood, and Eliza C.[5] Johnson.

   d. Martha L.[4] Johnson, married George V. Payne.

   Annie[5] Payne, married Dr. W. H. Coffman; Wm. J.[5] Payne; Margaret A.[5] Payne, died in childhood.

   e. Junius Ward[4] Johnson, married Fannie W. Willis.

   f. Henry V.[4] Johnson, married first Rosa Parrish; second, Mrs. Mary (Berry) Garley. Junius[5] Johnson; Henry V.[5] Johnson; Hamilton[5] Johnson, and others.

   g. Euclid[4] Johnson.

Excursus:—Martin, Hale, Smith, Douglas, Holman, Guerrant, Trabue, Downman, Travers. Catherine Jane Martin, who married Warren Viley, was a daughter of William Holman Martin and his wife, Susanna Smith Hale. William H. Martin was a son of James Martin and his wife, Esther Smith, emigrants from Powhatan County, Virginia, to Woodford County, Kentucky. James Martin was a son of Anthony Martin and Sarah Holman. The parents of Anthony Martin were Pierre Martin and his wife, Mary Ann Rapine, Huguenot refugees from France to Virginia. These came with their parents, John and Margaret Martin and Antoine and Margaret Rapine. Sarah Holman Martin was a daughter of James and Jane Holman, of Cumberland County, Virginia. The father of James Holman was James Holman, Sr. Burgess from Goochland County, Virginia. Esther Smith Martin was a daughter of Rev. George Smith and his wife, Judith Guerrant, emigrants from Powhatan County, Virginia, to Franklin County, Kentucky. Rev. George Smith was a son of Thomas Smith and his wife, Mary Ann (Rapine) Martin. Judith Guerrant Smith was a daughter of Peter Guerrant and his wife, Magdalen Trabue. The father of Peter Guerrant was Daniel Guerrant, a Huguenot emigrant to Manikintown, Virginia, in 1700. Anthony Trabue and Magdalen Verrueil, his wife, the parents of Magdalen Trabue Guerrant, were also Huguenot emigrants to Manikintown, in 1700.

Susannah Smith Hale, wife of William Holman Martin, was a daughter of Smith Hale and his wife Nancy Douglas, emigrants from Fauquier County, Virginia, to Woodford County, Kentucky. Nancy Douglas was a daughter of Colonel William Douglas, emigrant from Ayreshire, Scotland, and his wife, Elizabeth Offutt, widow of Thomas Lewis. The Douglas home in

---

*General George W. Johnson was a son of William Johnson and his wife, Elizabeth Payne; William Johnson was a son of Robert Johnson and his wife, Jemima Suggett, the leader of the heroic band of women at Bryant's Station; Elizabeth Payne was a daughter of Henry Payne and his wife, Ann Lane. George W. Johnson died of wounds received at the battle of Shiloh.

Fauquier County was called "Garralan," from the Douglas family-seat in Scotland.

Smith Hale was a son of George Hale and his wife, Sarah Smith, of Lancaster County, Virginia, late of Fauquier County. (The spelling was changed by the Kentucky branch.) George Heale and his sister, Bettie Heale, wife of Kendall Lee, of "Ditchley," Northumberland County, Virginia, were the only children of William Heale and his wife, Priscilla Downman Heale. William Heale was the posthumous son of George Heale (died 1697), Burgess from Lancaster County, Virginia. Priscilla Downman Heale, who married second Joseph Chinn, was a daughter of William Downman and his wife, Million Travers. Million Travers was a daughter of Colonel Raleigh and Elizabeth Travers of Lancaster. Sarah Smith, wife of George Heale, was a daughter of Capt. Philip Smith and Mary Mathews, his wife, of Northumberland County, Virginia. The father of Mary Mathews's husband was Baldwin Mathews, son of Capt. Francis Mathews, and grandson of Governor Samuel Mathews, of Virginia. Capt. Philip Smith was a son of John Smith and Mary Warner, his wife, of Purton, Gloucester County, Virginia. The father of John Smith, was Major John Smith, of Purton, Gloucester, Speaker of the Virginia House of Burgesses in 1657. The wife of Major John Smith, of Purton, was Anna, daughter of Richard and Anne Corderay Bernard. Mary Warner, wife of John Smith, and mother of Capt. Philip Smith, was a daughter of Augustine Warner and his wife, Mildred Reade, who was a daughter of Col. George Reade, whose wife was Elizabeth Martian, daughter of Capt. Nicholas Martian, of York County, Virginia, and his wife.

2. Warren[3] Viley, married Catherine Jane Martin.

a. George W.[4] Viley, died in young manhood.

b. John Warren[4] Viley, of the "Orphan Brigade," died in Southern Army.

c. Ann E.[4] Viley died in youth.

d. Martha J.[4] Viley died in youth.

e. Stoddard J.[4] Viley died young.

f. Martinette[4] Viley, married Lister Witherspoon.

Warren Viley[5] Witherspoon, married Lilly Herbert Fahs; daughter[5] died in infancy; Ellen Douglas[5] Witherspoon; Lister[5] Witherspoon, Jr.; Ethel[5] Witherspoon.

g. Breckinridge[4] Viley, married first, Flavilla Searles; second Mary Phil Parrish.

Warren[5] Viley; Breckinridge[5] Viley.

h. Lydia May[4] Viley, married, first Lawrence Jones; second James C. McFerran, and third, Paul Lansing.

James C.[5] McFerran, married Georgia Gay; Viley[5] McFerran.

3. Martha A.[3] Viley, married first, Squire Gaines, and had one child, Squire[4] Gaines, Jr., who married Eliza Thomson; Martha A. Viley married second, Lewis T. Payne.

b. Asa[4] Payne, married Rosa McCrackin.

c. Lydia[4] Payne, married George Cogar.

Marion[5] Cogar.

4. Major John Rodes[3] Viley, C. S. A., married Mary S. Johnson (a daughter of Rev. John T. Johnson, brother of Richard Johnson, Vice-President of the United States) and Sophia Lewis, and granddaughter of Col. Robert

---

*Lister Witherspoon, who married Martinette Viley, was a son of Dr. Lewis Johnson Witherspoon and his wife, Martha Lillard. The parents of Dr. Lewis Witherspoon were Robert Witherspoon and his wife, Sallie Johnson, emigrants from Virginia to Franklin County, Kentucky. The parents of Martha Lillard were Ephriam Lillard and his wife, Margaret Prather.

Johnson and Jemima Suggett, his wife.
   a. John T.[4] Viley.
   b. Willa[4] Viley, married first, Sallie Hall; second, Mrs. Mary Brand Avery; no children.

Jno. T.[5] Viley, married Josie McMiehan; George W.[5] Viley, married Mary Brown; Willa S.[5] Viley married ——; Sallie H.[5] Viley, married Francis C. Bell; Fannie P.[5] Viley, married Chas. Redmon James; Jno. Rodes[5] Viley, married Nell Browne.

   c. Betsy[4] Flournoy Viley, married W. B. Hawkins.

Mary[5] Hawkins; Elijah[5] Hawkins, married Marie Harden.

   d. Mary Breckinridge[4] Viley, married Jeff D. Clark.

Mary Elizabeth[5] Clark; John T.[5] Clark; Jeff D.[5] Clark, Jr.; John Rodes[5] Clark, Henry Conyers[5] Clark.

5. Elizabeth[3] Viley, married Thomas. W. Bullock.
   a. Waller[4] Bullock.
   b. Lydia[4] Bullock, married J. W. Utter.
   c. Maria B.[4] Bullock.
   d. Annie[4] Bullock.
   e. John Rodes[4] Bullock.
   f. Desha[4] Bullock.
   g. Elizabeth[4] Bullock, all died in childhood.

6. Andrew Jackson[3] Viley, married Mary L. Peak.
   a. Lydia[4] Viley, married Robert C. Nuckols.

Cecil[5] Nuckols, married Claudine Moses; Louise[5] Nuckols, married Rev. St. Elmo George.

   b. Sallie[4] Viley, married R. A. Bell.
   c. Leland[4] Viley, married Katie Morehead, granddaughter of Gev. Chas. Morehead.

Leland[5] Viley; Charles Morehead[5] Viley; Catherine[5] Viley; Warren[5] Viley.
   d. Willa[4] Viley.
   e. Mary[4] Viley, married ——Peck; died without issue.

7. Maria[3] Viley, married Thomas H. Payne, son of Col. Henry Conyers Payne and his wife, Kitty Lewis. Henry C. Payne was a son of Henry Payne and his wife, Ann Lane.
   a. Henry[4] Conyers Payne, married Elizabeth Bell.

John[5] Payne; Thomas[5] Payne; Janette[5] Payne; Henry[4] Conyers Payne married second Sarah F. Bell, his first wife's sister.

   b. Romulus[4] Payne, married Della McClintock.

Viley[5] Payne; Luella[5] Payne.

   c. Sallie[4] Payne, married Eugene Rucker.

Mary Allison[5] Rucker died in youth; Maria P.[5] Rucker; Katherine P.[5] Rucker.

   d. Elizabeth V.[4] Payne, married Wm. French.
   e. Katherine[4] Payne.

8. Edward[3] Viley died young.
9. Mary A.[3] Viley died young.

III. Samuel[2] Viley, b—Jan. 9, 1790, d—April 7, 1859. Married first, Polly Suggett, Dec. 29, 1816.

1. George[3] Viley, married Willina Green.
. 2. Milton[3] Viley, married Susan Long.
3. Albina[3] Viley, married William Payne.
   a. Robert[4] Payne.
   b. Mary E.[4] Payne.
   c. George V.[4] Payne, married Martha L. Johnson.

d. Eliza R.[4] Payne.

Samuel[2] Viley, married second, Mrs. Maria (Williams) Payne, widow of Robert Payne and sister of Minor Willians who married Cyrene Viley.

IV. Warren[2] Viley, b—Fed. 7, 1792, killed at Battle of Tippecanoe, Nov. 12, 1812.

V. Alethia[2] Viley, b—Nov. 18, 1793, d—Sept. 4, 1838; married Clifton Rodes Burch.

Five children of these died young.

1. Mary Cyrene[3] Burch, married General John C. Breckinridge.
  a. Cabell[4] Breckenridge.
  b. Frances[4] Breckenridge.
  c. Clifton[4] Breckenridge.
  d. Mary[4] Breckenridge.
  e: John Owen[4] Breckenridge.
2. Sarah[3] Burch, married first, David Smith; second, Professor Danford Thomas.
  a. Elizabeth[4] Thomas.
  b. Rodes Burch[4] Thomas, married Alice Witherspoon.

Mary Witherspoon[5] Thomas; Sarah Burch[5] Thomas.

3. Malvina[3] Burch, married Dr. Paul Rankins.
  a. Rodes[4] Rankins, married Elizabeth Kimbrough.

Wagner[5] Rankins; Penelope[5] Rankins.

  b. Malvina[4] Rankins, married E. M. Roberts.

Paul[5] Roberts; E. M.[5] Roberts.

  c. Elizabeth[4] Rankins, married — Green.

Martha[5] Green.

  d. Wm.[4] Rankins, married Laura McMeekin.

Jessie[5] Rankins.

VI. George[2] Viley, b—Nov. 20, 1795; d—Sept. 6, 1797.

VII. John[2] Viley, b—Jan. 1, 1797, married first, —— Eley.

1. Elizabeth[3] Viley, married Wm.[3] Burch.

John[2] Viley, married second, a sister of his first wife.

2. Logan[3] Viley, married Stephen Yancey.
3. George[3] Viley.
4. Willa[3] Viley.
5. John[3] Viley.
6. Keen[3] Viley.
7.

VIII. Martha[2] Viley, b—Dec. 16, 1799; d—Apr. 29, 1881. Married Milton Burch, a brother of Clifton Rodes Burch, who married Alethia[2] Viley.

1. George[3] Burch, married first, Mary McConnell.
  a. Marion[4] Burch, b—1844; d—Jan. 16, 1907. Married first, Ella Curry; 4 children.

George[5] Burch, Jas.[5] Burch, Mary[5] Burch and Martha[5] Burch. Mary[5] married Dr. T. L. Mastin, Alabama. Martha[5] married Jones Nelson, of Alabama.

George[3] Burch married second, Miss Embry.
  b. Milton[4] Burch.

George[3] Burch married third, Anna Smith.
  c. Anna[4] Burch, married Reuben Offutt.

Sue Ford[5] Offutt.
  d. George V.[4] Burch.
2. Sallie[3] Burch, married James Smith.
  a. Milton[4] Smith, married Mary Wells.

576

b. Martha[4] Smith, married first, Mr. Rout; second, Jas. Middleton.
c. Sallie[4] Smith died young.
d. James[4] Smith, married Miss Bryan.
e. Dorothy[4] Smith, married Rev. Mosby Seay, of Suffolk, Va.
f. Julia[4] Smith.
g. William[4] Smith.
h. Warren V.[4] Smith.
3. John[3] Burch, married Martha Smith. Son, Carr[4] Burch.
4. William[3] Burch, married Elizabeth[3] Viley, daughter of John Viley, of Missouri.

IX. Maria[2] Viley, b—June 16, 1801, married General James McConnell, who had previously married her sister, Elizabeth[2] Viley.
1. James[3] McConnell, married Katherine Payne.
a. Payne[4] McConnell and HenryeC
a. Payne[4] McConnell, married Miss Harp.
James[5], Robert[5] and Henry[5] McConnell.
b. Mary[4] McConnell, married J. P. Grey.
William[5] Grey, Katherine[5] Grey and Louise[5] Gray.
2. Henry[3] McConnell, married Mary Moss.
a. Cyrene[4] McConnell, married John D. Emack.
a. Henry[4] McConnell married Elizabeth Avent.
c. James[4] McConnell married Belle Hunter.
d. Elizabeth[4] McConnell married Edgar Avent.
e. Emma[4] McConnell married Powhattan Wooldridge.
f. Belle[4] McConnell.

3. Mary[3] McConnell, married George[3] Burch.
a. Marion[4] Burch, married first, Ella Curry.
George[5] Burch; James[5] Burch, Mary[5] Burch, married Dr. Maston, Ala.; Martha[5] Burch, married Jones Nelson, Ala.
Marion[4] Burch married second, Mrs. Belle Slaughter (Moss) Wooldridge.

X. Cyrene[2] Viley, b—Dec. 10, 1803, d—1892; married Minor Williams.*
1. Dr. James[3] Williams, married Annie Glover.
a. George[4] Williams.
b. Margaret[4] Williams.
2. Elizabeth[3] Williams, married James McHatton.
a. Minor[4] McHatton.
b. Robert[4] McHatton.
c. James[4] McHatton.
d. Charles[4] McHatton.
e. Fannie[4] McHatton.
f. Bettie[4] McHatton, married George[4] McGee.
3. Maria[3] Williams married George Viley[3] Ward.
a. James[4] Ward.
b. Junius[4] Ward.
4. Martha[3] Williams married Charles Musik.
a. Daisy[4] Musik.
b. Edwin[4] Musik.
5. Merrit[3] Williams married Mrs. Irene (Smith) Bullitt.
Charles[4] Williams married Ada Howell.
6. Charles[3] Williams married Annie Brumleigh.
a. Irene[4] Williams married Judge B. F. Roach.
b. Kate[4] Williams.

c. Minor[4] Williams.
d. Caroline[4] Williams.
e. Viley[4] Williams.
f. Ruth[4] Williams.
g. Fannie[4] Bullitt Williams.

XI. Horatio[2] Viley, b. Jan. 13, 1806, died Feb. 3, 1824.

XII. Matilda[2] Viley, b. Sept. 16, 1808, died Oct. 15, 1882. Married Junius Ward, son of Col. William Ward and his wife Sally, daughter of Col. Robert Johnson and Jemima Suggett, his wife.

1. George Viley[3] Ward, married Maria[3] Williams.
2. Elizabeth[3] Ward, married Edward McGee.
  a. Ira[4] McGee.
  b. George[4] McGee married Bettie McHatton.
  c. Robert[4] McGee.
3. Martha[3] Ward married Johnson Erwin.
  a. Ward[4] Erwin.
  b. Victor[4] Erwin.
  c. Elizabeth[4] Erwin.
  d. Dudley[4] Erwin.
4. Junius[3] Ward.

1. Henrietta[1] Viley, twin sister of George[1] Viley of Maryland, married Frances Downing, a native of England. She died near Georgetown, Ky., July 24, 1834, aged 88 years.

*Minor Williams, who married Cyrene Viley, was the son of Benjamin (?) Williams and his wife, Elizabeth Redd, daughter of Mordica Redd and his wife, Agatha Minor, emigrants from Spottsylvania County, Virginia, to Woodford County, Kentucky, in pioneer days. Agatha Minor Redd was the daughter of Thomas and Alice Thomas Minor, of "Locust Hill," Spottsylvania County.

Their children.

I. John[2] Downing married Betsey Roberts.
1. Elvina[3] Downing married John F. Payne.
2. Ellen[3] Downing married John F. Payne.
   George[4] Payne.
3. George[3] Downing married Rachel Cooper—no children.
4. Henrietta[3] Downing died, aged 12 years.
5. Henrietta[3] Downing married —— Bonnell; four[4] children.
6. Ruth[3] Ann Downing married Benj. F. Offutt; one[4] daughter.

II. Mary (Polly)[2] Downing, died unmarried.

III. Betsy[2] Downing married —— Cameron.
1. Polly[3] Cameron married ——
2. Nancy[3] Cameron married ——
3. James[3] Cameron.

IV. William[2] Downing died unmarried.

V. George Viley[2] Downing died unmarried.

VI. Nancy[2] Downing married John Crawford Gibson.
1. Nancy[3] Gibson died unmarried.
2. Betsy[3] Gibson married Isaac Sprake.
   George[4] Sprake married Margaret Graves; Susan[4] Sprake died unmarried.
3. Susan Cotton[3] Gibson died unmarried.
4. Andrew Crawford[3] Gibson died unmarried.
5. Eleanor[3] Gibson born Oct. 22, 1821, married Dr. Frances Whitney.
   Anne Elizabeth[4] Whitney married Warren K. Smith.

a. Eleanor[5] Whitney, married Richard D. Collins.

Elizabeth[6] Collins; Lillian[6] Collins.

b. Fleetwood[5] Smith, married .....

c. Francis Whitney[5] Smith, married Emma Nentley.

Anne Whitney[6] Smith; Laura Gibson[6] Smith.

d. Lillian Berry[5] Smith, married Theophilus Davis.

Eleanor[6] Davis.

e. Jo. Desha[5] Smith.

f. Marie Gibson[5] Smith.

g. Junius Johnson[5] Smith.

VII. Hon. James[2] Downing, married ———.

VIII. Eleanor[2] Downing, married —— Lackland.

MARTINETTE VILEY WITHERSPOON.

THE THURSTON-WADDY FAMILY
OF SHELBY COUNTY, KY.

Plummer (2) Thurston, son of Seth (1) and Mary Thurston, was born February 8th, 1749. He married June 19th, 1777,

Mary Talbot, born June 20th, 1759, daughter of Charles and Drusilla Gwin Talbot.

The children of Plummer (2) and Mary Talbot Thurston were:

1. John (3) Thurston, born June 19th, 1778; died January 17th, 1779.

2. Paulina (3) Thurston, born June 11th, 1780; died November 27th, 1805; married Isaac Watkins, August 10th, 1803.

3.* Robert (3) Thurston, born Campbell County, Va., January 16th, 1783; died Shelby County, Ky., August 16th, 1856; married Maria Searcy, January 23d, 1814.

4. Harvey (3) Thurston, born August 4th, 1785; died 1822; married Sarah Motley, September, 1809.

5. Plummer (3) Thurston, born October 15th, 1787; died December 2d, 1816; unmarried. He was one of the first clerks of the Shelby Circuit Court.

6. Elizabeth (3) Thurston, born January 31st, 1790; died September 4th, 1815; married John Alexander Knight, January 8th, 1814.

7. Lucinda (3) Thurston, born January 30th, 1794; died March 22d, 1846; married Dr. George Watkins Nuckols, January 8th, 1814.

8. Louisiana (3) Thurston, born February 14th, 1804; died January 16th, 1805.

Excursus — Talbot: The first member of this distinguished English family to settle with his family in Virginia was Matthew (1) Talbot. His wife, whom he married in England, was Mary Wiliston. The children of Matthew (1) and Mary Wiliston Talbot were: Charles (2), John (2), Matthew (2), Isham (2), Thomas (2), and two daughters. Charles (2) Talbot, the eldest of these, married Drusilla Gwin. Charles (2) and Drusilla Gwin Talbot had nine children, as follows: Wiliston (3), John Moil (3), David Moil (3), Lucy Moil (3), Providence (3), George (3), Ezekiel (3), Mary (3), who married Plummer (2), son of Seth (1) and Mary Thurston, and Christina (3), who married Ezekiel (2), son of Seth (1) and Mary Thurston.

Excursus—Searcy: Maria Searcy, who married Dr. Robert (3) Thurston, was one of the two children of Edmund and Hannah Miller Searcy who grew to maturity.

Edmund Searcy was born March 25th, 1767.

Hannah Miller, wife of Edmund

---

*For sketch of Capt. Robert (3) Thurston, see "Register" for January, 1910. **
**See footnote on p. 594, this volume.

Searcy, was born December 12th, 1777. Her father died when she was quite young, and her mother subsequently married a Mr. Ruddell, of Ruddells Mills, Bourbon County, Ky.

Edmund Searcy and Hannah Miller were married September 6th, 1796. They lived in Woodford County, Ky., but removed thence to New Castle, Henry County, Ky.

Their children were:

Maria, born May 27th, 1799; wife of Dr. Robert (3) Thurston.

Harriet, born December, 17th, 1806.

Richard, born August 4th, 1814.

Mary Eleanor, born May 19th, 1820; married Joseph Welch Walker, of Louisiana, April 11th, 1839. Joseph Welch and Mary Eleanor Searcy Walker have descendants in the South.

Dr. Robert (3) and Maria Searcy Thurston had only two children who grew to maturity:

Lucinda Elizabeth (4) Thurston, who married Dr. Robert H. Smith, of Shelby County, in 1842.

Maria Louise (4) Thurston, who married William Lewis Waddy, of Waddy, Shelby County, December 16th, 1847.

A daughter of Dr. Robert and Lucinda Thurston (4) Smith married William Bullard, and is living in Shelby County.

The children of William Lewis (5) and Maria Louise (4) Thurston Waddy were:

1. Robert Samuel (5) Waddy, born February 18th, 1850, died April 19th, 1876.

2. George William (5) Waddy, married Mary S. Cardwell, January 17th, 1876.

3. Thomson Miller (5) Waddy married Katie Lee Nash, November 9th, 1882. The children of Thomson (5) M. and Katie Nash Waddy are: Thurston (6), Cecil Clendenin (6); William Landon (6), born September 9th, 1894; died in 1897, and Noble.

4. Maria Louise (5), Waddy, married Landon Thomas Bailey, of Shelby County, Ky., January 23d, 1890.

Maria Louise (4) Thurston Waddy died at Waddy, Shelby County, Ky., December 26th, 1907, aged seventy-five years.

Excursus—Waddy: The name of Waddy in Virginia is associated with the early history of New Kent County, which, in 1654, was formed from York, one of the original counties. Early court records of New Kent have been completely destroyed, but numerous entries concerning the Waddy family are to be found in the invaluable "Register of St. Peter's Parish." *St. Peter's Church, begun in 1701, is still standing in excellent condition, and is one of the most interesting and oldest structures in Virginia.

The earliest Waddy entries in "St. Peter's Register" are as follows: Mary, daughter to Samuel Waddy, was baptized June ye 20th, 1687. Elizabeth, daughter of Samuel Waddy, was baptized October

---

*It was in St. Peter's Church, according to commonly accepted tradition, that General Washington and the Widow Custis were married. The Custis home known as the "White House," was not far distant from St. Peter's Church, New Kent. General Washington was a kinsman of the Waddys of Shelby County, Ky., as will be shown in the Register" for September, 1910.

ye 24th, 1689. Judith, daughter of Samuel Waddy, was baptized January ye 21st, 1701. Mary, ye daughter of Anthony Waddy, was baptized May ye 21st 1711. Anthony, ye son to Anthony Waddy by Sarah, his wife, was born December ye 14th, 1714.

Jane, ye daughter to Samuel Waddy, deceased ye 15th of January, 1687-8.

Samuel, ye son to Samuel Waddy, deceased ye 31st of January, 1687-8.

Sarah, daughter of Anthony Waddy, died December 9th, 1725.

†John, son of Anthony Waddy, born October 28th, 1725.

Frances, daughter of Anthony Waddy, born June 18th, 1729.

St. Peter's parish, originally of very great extent, was divided at various times to form new parishes, and one of these was St. Paul's, Hanover County. Many of the Waddy family were located by this division in the new parish, which was formed in 1704. Unfortunately, "St. Paul's Register" has not been preserved. This Register and the early Hanover County records, had they not been destroyed, must have given much information concerning the Waddys in Hanover. At least one Waddy family remained in New Kent after the last division of St. Peter's parish, as

†Family tradition states that the wife of Anthony Waddy, the emigrant, was Ann Parke. In the first mention of Anthony Waddy above, his wife is given as Sarah. It is possible that Anthony Waddy may have married more than once, and that Anne Parke may have been the mother of John Waddy above, since it is in that line that the tradition is preserved.

almost the last record in "St. Peter's Register" is of the birth of John and Mildred Waddy, children of Anthony and Mary Waddy.

According to family tradition, two Waddy brothers, Samuel (1) and Anthony (1), came to New Kent in the seventeenth century from North England, near the Scotch border.

These church records seem to verify the Waddy family tradition. Elizabeth (2) Waddy, daughter of Samuel (1) Waddy, baptized in St. Peters, ye 24th October, 1689, was an ancestress of a number of families distinguished in Kentucky history. She married Francis Smith, and one of their children, Susanna (3) Smith, married William Preston. William and Susanna (3) Smith Preston were the parents of Gen. Francis (4) Preston, whose wife, Sarah, was a daughter of Gen. William Campbell and his wife, Elizabeth, sister of Gov. Patrick Henry—and Susanna (4) Preston, who married Nathaniel Hart, son of Col. Nathaniel Hart, Sr., the famous Kentucky pioneer. Ann Sophonisba (5), daughter of Gen. Francis Preston, married Rev. Robert J. Breckinridge, and after her death, Dr. Breckinridge married her first cousin, Virginia (5) Hart, daughter of Nathaniel and Susanna (4) Preston Hart, and widow of Alfred Shelby, son of Governor Shelby, of Kentucky.

Anthony (1) Waddy is known to have had at least three sons who grew to maturity, and also several daughters.

It is supposed, and very probable, that one of these daughters married a son of Robert and Judith Thomson, of New Kent, thus connecting for the first time these families, in which thereafter, intermarriages often occurred. This family of Thomsons are known, by way of distinction, as the *Waddy-Thomsons.

The known sons of Anthony (1) Waddy were:

Anthony (2), of New Kent; John (2), of Hanover, and Samuel (2), of Louisa.

Samuel (2) Waddy was the ancestor of the Kentucky family.

John (2) Waddy, born October 25th, 1725, married Rebecca Nelson, and these had two children—a daughter, who married a Thomson, and died shortly after her marriage, and a son, William (3) Waddy, who married Sally, posthumous daughter of John Thomson, of Hanover.

William (3) Waddy and Sally Thomson Waddy had six children:

Elizabeth (4), who married a Mr. Goodwin, and emigrated to Tennessee.

Mildred (4), who married a Mr. Anderson.

John (4).

Anthony (4).

Garland (4), who married first a Miss Chisholm, and second a Miss Pleasants.

William (4), who married Patsy Harris.

William (4) and Patsy Harris Waddy had nine children:

Adromache (5), who married her cousin, the son of William Nelson and his wife, Mary Garland (4) Thomson, only child of Nelson and Ann Waddy (3) Thomson; Sally (5), Mary P. (5), William (5), Nelson (5), Robert Burns (5). who died November 29th, 1867, and John (5), who married his first cousin, Jemima Harris, the children of whom were:

Lucy (6), who married a Mr. Cosby.

Robert Burns (6), a prominent physician of Lexington, Ky.

Samuel (2) Waddy, son of Anthony (1) Waddy, married Sarah Owen, and in 1758 was designated Capt. Samuel Waddy in Louisa County records. He died in 1764, leaving eight surviving children, only two of whom married and left issue. These children were:

John (3), Mary (3), Sarah (3), Owen (3), Frances (3), who died in 1778; Elizabeth (3), Ann (3), and Samuel (3).

Samuel (3) Waddy, son of Samuel (2) Waddy, was a brave soldier of the Revolutionary war. He is designated Captain Waddy, and it is known that he took part in many of the important battles fought for American liberty. During the terrible winter at Valley Forge, Capt. Samuel (3) Waddy suffered a severe attack of smallpox, which, with other hardships endured there, undermined his constitution, and he died shortly after his return to his home in Louisa County.

John (3) Waddy, son of Samuel Waddy, married Jane Cobbs, daughter of Samuel Cobbs, of Louisa, and his wife, Mary Lewis.

*A sketch of the Waddy-Thomsons will be given in the "Register" for September, 1910. (Pages 586-593, this vol.)

Samuel Cobbs, who died in 1758, and his wife, Mary Lewis Cobbs,* had only three children:
Robert, whose family became a distinguished one in the history of Georgia.
Judith, who died young.
Jane, who married John (3) Waddy.

Ann (3) Waddy, daughter of Samuel (2) Waddy, married Nelson Thomson, son of Waddy Thomson and his first wife, Elizabeth, daughter of Nelson Anderson, of Hanover. Nelson and Ann (3) Waddy Thomson had an only child, Mary Garland (4) Thomson, who married William Nelson.

John (3) and Jane Cobbs Waddy had an only child, Samuel (4) Waddy, whose parents died when he was quite young, and who was reared in the household of his maternal grandmother, Mary Lewis Cobbs Thomson. Thus the only descendants of the large family of Samuel (2) Waddy were Samuel (4) Waddy and his first cousin, Mary Garland (4) Thomson. While still little more than a boy, Samuel (4) Waddy came to visit his Thomson cousins in Woodford county, Ky., and here he married on June 1st, 1796, his cousin, Mary Thomson, youngest daughter of *Anthony and Ann Bibb Thomson, emigrants from Louisa County, Va.

Samuel (4) Waddy located in Shelby County, Ky., and became one of the county's most prominent citizens. Shortly after their marriage, his wife, Mary Thomson, died, and he married some years thereafter Sarah, daughter of **James Dupuy and his wife, Ann Starke. James Dupuy was a son of John James and Susanna La Villain Dupuy.

John James Dupuy was a son of Bartholomew and Susanna La Villain Dupuy. Huguenot refugees from France to Virginia in the early Eighteenth century.

The second wife of Samuel (4) Waddy died shortly after marriage. He married for the third time Elizabeth, daughter of Joseph and Ann Manyard Hobbs.†

There are no descendants of Mary Thomson, first wife of Samuel (4) Waddy, or of Sarah Dupuy, his second wife.

The children of Samuel (4) Waddy and his third wife, Elizabeth Hobbs, were:

1. Ann J. (5), born 1804; died 1826; married Nicholas Smith.

---

*Mary Lewis Cobbs was a daughter of Robert Lewis, of "Belvoir," Albemarle, and his wife, Jane, daughter of Nicholas Meriwether. After the death of Samuel Cobbs, his widow, Mary Lewis, married as a second husband Waddy Thomson, of Louisa, but later of Albemarle County, Va.
A fuller account of Mary Lewis Cobbs Thomson and her connection will be given in the September number of the "Register." (See p. 589, this vol.)

*A fuller account of these Thomsons will be given in September "Register."
**For fuller account of the Dupuy family see "Trabue" in "Register" for September, 1909.
†Other children of Joseph and Ann Manyard Hobbs were:
Deborah, who married James Fountain.
Sarah, who married Greenberry Dorsey.
Susan, who married Miller Stone.
Mary, who married Robert Tevis.
Rachel, who married Joshua Hobbs.

2. Joseph Owen (5), born 1806; died 1829.

3. Mary Lewis (5), born 1808; died 1831.

4. Sarah A. (5), born 1811; died 1845; married L. Foree.

5. Frances E. (5), born 1814; died 1845, married first Daniel Wilson, second John Neagle Boyle. She had two children—a daughter, (6), who married a Mr. Dawson, of Mexico, and J. F. (6) Boyle, of Little Rock, Ark.

6. Susan M. (5), born 1816; died 1864; married Ephraim Jessee. Their children were: Samuel Waddy (6), Millard (6), William G. (6), and a daughter, who married a Mr. Elliott.

7. William Lewis (5), born 1819; died 1895; married Maria Louise (4) Thurston.

8. Amanda M. (5), born 1822; married first John N. Boyle, second B. F. Danley.

Compiled by GEORGE C. DOWNING.

NOTES CONCERNING THE WADDY-THOMSON FAMILY.

The Thomsons* are of Scotch origin and are septs or dependents of the Clan Campbell of Argyle. Those bearing the name have emigrated to England, Wales and Ireland, and from thence, or directly from Scotland, they have come at various times to America. The name has been a particularly distinguished one in scientific investigation. Probably the greatest scientist of our own day was William Thomson, Lord Kelvin, a Scotch-Irishman. Scarcely less famous, was Count Rumford, born Benjamin Thompson, and a native of New England.

One of the Scotch-Irish emigrants to the American colonies was Charles Thomson (1729-1824), Secretary of the Continental Congress and, as such, was identified with the struggle for American independence.

It would transcend the limit of this article to give more than a very brief sketch of one branch out of the many Thomsons who came to the colony of Virginia.

It is a matter of record that five Presidents of the United States were Thompson descendants. These were Madison, Taylor, the two Harrisons and Tyler. This family, according to their family record, was long seated in Yorkshire and various members of it emigrated, in the seventeenth century, to Virginia. The first of these was William Thompson, son of Roger Thompson.

This William Thompson's daughter, Martha, became the wife of James Taylor, of Orange county, Virginia, and these latter were the great-grandparents of Presidents Madison and Taylor, and ancestors of many others scarcely less distinguished in their services to their country. The family of Martha (Thompson) Taylor's brother, Roger Thompson* is largely represented in and around Mercer county, Kentucky, where they have been prominent citizens since the establishment of the Commonwealth. Frances Thompson, of this Yorkshire family, married Anthony Armistead and was an ancestress of the two Harrisons and Tyler. Another native Yorkshireman, distinguished in Virginia history, was Stevens Thomson (died 1714), an elder brother of Sir William Thomson‖—one of the really great Eng-

---

*The archaic form of spelling is Tomson. Those careful to preserve their traditions and Scotch origin usually spell it Thomson. The most general spelling outside of Scotland is Thompson.

*The name is invariably spelled Thompson, by descendants, but in the signature of Roger Thompson, above, who was high sheriff of Hanover county, Virginia, as well as in old records, the name is spelled without the "p." For full account of these Thompsons, see H. D. Pitman's "Americans of Gentle Birth and their Ancestors." For descendants of the Thompson-Taylors see Haydon's "Virginia Genealogies," as well as many other works.

‖For account of Sir William Thompson, see William and Mary Quarterly, Vol. III.

lishmen of his day—and for many years Attorney-General of Virginia. Stevens Thomson's daughter, Ann, married Colonel George Mason, of Stafford county, Virginia, and these latter, were the parents of the patriots George and Thomson Mason, and ancestors of many other famous Virginians.

Another prominent Virginia family were descended from Reverend John Thompson, who married the widow of Governor Spottswood.*

The family to which Mary Thomson, cousin and first wife of Samuel Waddy||, belonged has, for two centuries, been known as the Waddy-Thomsons. The two families of Waddy and Thomson were neighbors in New Kent county, Virginia, in the seventeenth century, and it is reasonable to suppose that an early intermarriage introduced the unusual Christian name of Waddy as a mark of distinction in this Thomson family. The compiler of this article, and other descendants, have never been able to verify this reasonable presumption. The lamentable destruction of the early records of New Kent and adjoining counties, renders verification of this connection and other persistent traditions impossible at the present day, unless they may somewhere be preserved in private record. We find, from the "Register of St. Peter's, New Kent," that the first of the family publicly recorded was Robert Thomson, who died April 12th, 1702. His wife was Judith, who died March 14th, 1709. Their children recorded in the Register were, Robert, baptized April 24th, 1687; David, baptized September 4th, 1690; Hannah, baptized February 25th, 1696, and Martha, baptized August 31st, 1701. A division of St. Peter's parish, located this family in St. Paul's, Hanover, whose Register is not preserved, and the record is again rendered incomplete.

The sons, David, Robert and perhaps others, became the ancestors of the so-called Waddy-Thomsons who were very numerous in New Kent, Hanover, Louisa and other Virginia counties.

The tradition of the Waddy-Thomsons, preserved in widely separated branches, claims their descent from Maurice Thomson, a wealthy London merchant. In English pedigrees it is stated that Robert Thomson, great-grandfather of this Maurice Thomson "come out of the North," and settled near London. There are numerous allusions to this family in English history. Various members took great interest in the affairs of the British colonies in America, and played important parts in the management of American affairs. "Maurice Thomson, Gentleman," came to Virginia in 1620. It is further stated that besides Maurice, the eldest of his family, there were at least three brothers and a sister living in Virginia in 1624, in which colony they possessed considerable property. The sister, Mary Thomson (born 1599), was the wife of Captain William Tuck-

---

*For an account of these Thompsons see "History of St. Mark's Parish, Culpeper county, Virginia."

||See Thurston-Waddy family in Register for May, 1910. (Pages 580-585, this vol.)

er (came to Virginia 1610), Commander of the fort at Kiccoughton (now Hampton), 1625, member of the King's Council, and, at various times, member of the House of Burgesses. The brothers of Maurice Thomson who lived in Virginia were, George (born 1603), Paul (born 1611), and William (born 1614). Another brother, Robert, may have lived in Virginia also, but there is no record of it. Maurice Thomson was a man of great business enterprise and much interested in public affairs. He established a fishing station in New England, erected sugar works in the Barbadoes and was Governor of the East India Company in the reign of Charles the First. He sided with Parliament in the Civil War, and, in 1649, was examined by the Committee of Admiralty as to what the interests of the Commonwealth required in Virginia. Maurice Thomson's son, John Thomson, was created Baron Haversham in 1673, Major Robert Thomson. brother of Maurice, owned considerable property in both England and New England. He became "so great with Cromwell that he had nearly married his daughter." He died in 1695. Another brother, William Thomson, after his return from Virginia to England, was knighted and became Governor of the East India Company in the reign of Charles the Second. Colonel George Thomson, another of these brothers, was a member of the Virginia House of Burgesses in 1629 and, in the same year, was also Lieutenant of a force sent out against the Indians.

Colonel George Thomson returned to England and "lost his leg fighting against the king, but got a great estate. * * * When the army had fallen into the posture of a brand-iron, with the Rump in the middle, threatening a battle royal, Haselrigg and Morley to support the Rump and Lambert and his party to pull them down, this Colonel George Thomson was, with some thousands, in St. George's-in-the-Fields, Southwark, and, with Bibles in their hands, and good swords also, they declared, for King Jesus, which signified what they pleased except King Charles."

The coat-of-arms which the Waddy-Thomsons claim together with their descent from the Maurice Thomson family is as follows:

Arms: "Or., on a fesse dancette, *azure*, three estoiles of the field; On a canton of the second, the sun in glory, of the first."

Crest: "An arm erect, vested *gules*, cuffed argent, holding in the hand, proper, five ears of wheat."

Motto: "In lumine lucem."

Of the first known Waddy Thomson, grandson of Robert of New Kent (There is reason to suppose that this Waddy Thomson was the son of David Thomson, previously mentioned), a fairly complete record is obtainable. He was born in Hanover county, Virginia, about 1725 and died in Albemarle county, of the same state, in 1801. His first wife was Elizabeth Anderson, daughter of Nelson Anderson, of Hanover. In the earliest records of Louisa county we find numerous allusions to this Waddy Thomson, who was a Justice of Peace there, and a member of the Louisa Committee of Safety. On the death of his first wife, he married Mary* daughter of Colonel Robert and Jane (Meriwether) Lewis, of "Belvoir," Albemarle county, Virginia, and widow of Samuel Cobbs, of Louisa county.

Waddy[1] and Mary (Lewis) Thomson, with their family removed from Louisa to Albemarle "where he was considered a man of high public esteem and was referred to for his fine judgment and probity, as evinced by the frequency with which his name appears in the family papers of his wide circle of friends and neighbors."** Mary Lewis, wife, first, of Samuel Cobbs and second of Waddy Thomson, died in Albemarle county in 1813. Her Cobbs children were Robert Cobbs, who married Ann Poindexter, descendant of whom were numerous in Virginia and the South; Judith Cobbs, who died young; and Jane Cobbs, wife of John Waddy, the only child of whom was Samuel Waddy, who was reared in the household of his maternal grandmother.

The children of Waddy[1] Thomson and his first wife, Elizabeth Anderson, were:

I. Nelson[2] Thomson married his cousin, Ann Waddy and these left an only child, Mary Garland[3] Thomson, who married William Nelson.

II. David[2] Thomson married his cousin, Eleanor[2], daughter of Anthony[1] and Ann (Bibb) Thomson. Removed to Kentucky.

III. Anderson[2] Thomson.

IV. Garland[2] Thomson.

V. Waddy[2] Thomson. Removed with his family to Rockingham county, Virginia.

VI. Susanna[2] Thomson married first David Rodes, second James Kerr. She died in 1847 in Albemarle.

VII. Lucy[2] Thomson.

VIII. Frances[2] Thomson.

The children of Waddy Thomson and his second wife, Mary Lewis, were:

IX. Ann[2] Thomson married first John Slaughter, second Philip Grafton. She had Mary Lewis[3] Slaughter, Waddy Thomson[3] Slaughter, who married Frances Ballard, and Robert Lewis[3] Slaughter.

---

*Samuel and Mary (Lewis) Cobbs were the parents of Jane, wife of John Waddy and mother of Samuel Waddy of Shelby county, Kentucky (Register for May, 1910). The Lewis family of which Mary Lewis was a member was one of the great families of Virginia. Their descent, in part, was as follows: Robert Reade married Mildred, daughter of Sir Thomas Windebank, and his wife, Frances, daughter of Sir Edward Dymoke, heriditary champion of England. Colonel George Reade, son of Robert and Mildred (Windebank) Reade, came to Virginia in 1637 and married Elizabeth, daughter of Colonel Nicholas Martian of Yorktown. Of the children of these last, Mildred Reade married Colonel Augustine Warner. Their daughter, Isabella Warner, married Major John Lewis, and these were the parents of Colonel Robert Lewis of "Belvoir." Another daughter of Colonel Augustine and Mildred (Reade) Warner, Mildred, married Lawrence Washington, and these were the grandparents of General George Washington, President of the United States.

**For account of the Cobbs family see William and Mary Quarterly for July, 1910. The quotation concerning Waddy Thomson, above, is from a "History of Albemarle County."

X. Susanna[2] Thomson (second daughter of the name) married Jesse Davenport.

XI. Judith[2] Thomson married William Poindexter.

XII. Mary[2] Thomson married James Poindexter.

XIII. Mildred[2] Thomson born Sept. 22d, 1775, died Oct. 9th, 1829, married 1807, Dr. James Scott*.

The children of Dr. James M. and Mildred (Thomson) Scott were:

1. Mary Ann Lewis[3] Scott (1808-1840) married, 1827, Lewis A. Boggs.
2. John Thomson[3] Scott (1810-1862) married, 1832, Huldah Lewis.
3. James McClure[3] Scott 1811-1893) married, 1832, Sarah Travers Lewis.

Another grandson of Robert Thomson, of New Kent, a brother or cousin to Waddy[1] Thomson was Anthony[1] Thomson. Anthony Thomson was a native of St. Paul's Parish, Hanover. He served in Colonel Joseph Fox's Rangers in the French and Indian War. For this and other military service, he obtained land grants. Shortly after the close of the Revolution he emigrated with his entire family, save his oldest son, Robert[2], to one of his numerous land grants in Kentucky, locating in Woodford county, about five miles north of Versailles, where a portion of his Manor house, which was fortified as a safeguard against Indian attacks, may still be seen. He died in Woodford county in 1794, and his will is recorded in the Woodford court†.

Anthony[1] Thomson married Ann, daughter of Henry Bibb*, of Fredericksville Parish, Louisa county, Virginia. She died in Woodford county, Kentucky in 1798.

The children of Anthony and Ann (Bibb) Thomson were:

I. Eleanor[2] Thomson (1759-1820), married her cousin, David[2], son of Waddy[1] and Elizabeth (Anderson) Thomson. These emigrated from Louisa county Virginia,

---

*A full list of the descendants of Dr. James M. Scott and his wife, Mildred Thomson, is to be found in Haydon's "Virginia Genealogies" and elsewhere.

†The copy of Anthony Thompson's will in Will Book I has the signature spelled with a "p." The original signature does not have the "p." This is an example of the way in which the name has been changed in many cases.

*The Bibb family was largely represented in Virginia and elsewhere in the South. They were descendants of Benjamin Bibb, who lived and died in St. John's Parish, King William county, Virginia. He died about 1720, and his will was once on record in King William, but has been destroyed with other old county records. Two of Benjamin Bibb's descendants became Governors of Southern States (see Saunder's "Early Settlers of Alabama"), and many other descendants held positions of honor and trust in their State or the National Government. In Georgia and Alabama there were numerous inter-marriages between the Thomsons and Bibbs. Henry Bibb, above, was one of a number of sons of Benjamin Bibb. The wife of Henry Bibb and mother of Ann (Bibb) Thomson is supposed to have been a member of the Fleming family of New Kent and adjoining counties. The children of Henry Bibb, who married and left issue, were: Robert Fleming Bibb, Benjamin Bibb, Charles Bibb, Thomas Bibb (a lieutenant in the French and Indian War), Elizabeth, wife of Nathaniel Garland; the wife of Joseph Woolfolk; and Ann, wife of Anthony Thomson. Besides these there were sons, John, Henry and David Bibb, who with their father died prior to 1763. Henry Bibb had a brother Benjamin, who also had a large family located in Louisa. ※※

**For additional information on the Bibb family see *Genealogies of Kentucky Families* (Vol. A-M), 46-47.

with her father to Woodford county, Kentucky, where both died.

They had at least eleven children, as follows:

1. Anthony[3] Thomson (1782-1850), married Sarah Thomas. He lived in Greenup county, Kentucky, where his descendants are numerous. The children of Anthony[3] and Sarah (Thomas) Thomson were:

Washington[4] Thomson, who married Paulina, daughter of Nathaniel[2] and Frances (Major) Thomson; Eleanor[4] Thomson, wife of William Cable; Reuben[4] Thomson who married first Ann Scott, second Nellie O'Neal, third Elizabeth Waugh; Cynthia[4] Thomson, wife of Robert Thomas; Louisa[4] Thomson, wife of Jonathan Sanders; Anthony[4] Thomson, who married Mary Fuqua; Ann[4] Thomson, wife of John Leitch; Sarah[4] Thomson, wife of John Bagby; Winifred[4] Thomson, wife of Mathew Thompson; Anderson[4] Thomson, who married Katherine Fuqua; Elizabeth[4] Thomson, wife of John Barnes; Mary[4] Thomson, wife of Robert Thomson; David[4] Thomson, who married Elizabeth Thomas; John Thomas[4] Thomson, who married Anna Hughes.

2. Anderson[3] Thomson (1784-1832).

3. Elizabeth[3] Thomson married Thomas Blanton in 1812.

4. Ann Bibb[3] Thomson (1790-1823), married Robert Adams in 1817. They had Virginia[4] Adams and David Thomson[4] Adams, who married Bettie Johnson. These latter were the parents of Julia[5] Adams, Robert[5] Adams, of Mississippi, and Lennie[5] (Adams) Calhoun, also of Mississippi.

5. Mary[3] Thomson married Edmund Shipp in 1812.

6. Judith[3] Thomson (1794-1823).

7. Sarah[3] Thomson.

8. William[3] Thomson (1797-1869), married Eliza Peters, and these had Mary[4] Thomson, wife of Robert McConnell.

9. David[3] Thomson married Eliza Beatty, and these had Robert Alexander[4] Thomson, who married Lavinia, daughter of Isaac and Jane (Sneed) Wingate.

10. Louisa[3] Thomson married Joel Thomasson in 1812.

11. Waddy[3] Thomson married Cynthia Thomas and these were the parents of David[4] Thomson; Ann[4] Thomson, Parthenia[4] Thomson and Robert Thomas[4] Thomson, who married Mildred Henton, of Woodford county, Kentucky.

II. Judith[2] Thomson married Thomas, son of Thomas and Elizabeth (Weir) Bell.* The children of Thomas and Judith[2] (Thomson) Bell were:

Thomson[3] Bell, Samuel[3] Bell, Thomas[3] Bell; all of whom married members of the Hewlett family; John[3] Bell; Robert[3] Bell, who married Mary Monroe, and Jefferson[3] Bell, who married a Payne.

III. Robert[2] Thomson, lived and died in Louisa county, Virginia, where his descendants still live.

— — —

*Thomas Bell, the elder, was a native of Ireland. Of his nine children, Thomas married Judith Thomson; Ann married Andrew Monroe, and these latter were the parents of Judge Ben Monroe, who married Cynthia Montgomery; Judge Thomas Bell Monroe, who married Eliza, daughter of Governor Adair; James Monroe, who married Tabitha Collins; Mary K. Monroe, wife of Joseph M. Hardin; Elizabeth Monroe, wife of Alexander Adair and Rachael Monroe.

IV. Susanna[2] Thomson, married, November 8th, 1801, Edmund Vaughan, of Franklin county, Kentucky. Their children were:

1. James[3] Vaughan, who married Charlotte Ashmore Hawkins, and their children were Edmund[4] Vaughan, and William[4] Vaughan, who married Mrs. Sarah (Ellison) Crockett.

2. Mary Ann[3] Vaughan (1807-1859), married Dandridge Spottswood Crockett, a prominent citizen of Franklin county, and a son of Colonel Anthony Crockett, of Revolutionary fame. Their children were:

1. George[4] Crockett, who married Sarah Elizabeth Ellison.
2. Susan[4] M. Crockett, who married Dr. John Hickman.
3. Edmund Vaughan[4] Crockett, who married Mary Holton.
4. William Overton[4] Crocket[1], who married Margaret Dillon.
5. James[4] Crockett.
6. Dandridge Spottswood[4] Crockett.
7. Florence[4] Crockett, who married Alfred Stedman.
8. Emma[4] Crockett, who married Dr. Coleman Pattie.

V. Anthony[2] Thomson was twice married: First wife was Ann, daughter of Richard Pemberton, of Franklin county, whom he married in 1797. The children of Anthony[2] Thomson by both marriages were:

1. Richard[3] Thomson emigrated from Kentucky to Missouri.
2. Anthony[3] Thomson. Accidentally killed, while hunting, by his brother-in-law, Francis Black.

Second Marriage:
3. Ann Bibb[3] Thomson married Francis Black, who after her death, married Mrs. Bland, mother of "Silver Dick" Bland, of Missouri.
4. Margaret[3] Thomson married Francis Berryman.
5. Mary[3] Thomson married —— McDonald.
6. Katherine[3] Thomson married William Hines.
7. Henry[3] Thomson married twice. First a Miss Harris, second a Miss Bell.

VI. Nathaniel[2] Thomson married Oct. 27th, 1795, Frances, daughter of John and Elizabeth (Redd) Major*, of "Weehawken," Franklin county, Kentucky. After the death of his parents and unmarried brother and sisters, these lived at the old Thomson home in Woodford county until their death.

VII. Sarah[2] Thomson died unmarried, Woodford county, 1800.

VIII. Elizabeth[2] Thomson, died unmarried, Woodford county, 1798.

IX. Mary[2] Thomson, married, June, 1796, Samuel Waddy, of Shelby county, Kentucky.

X. Henry Bibb[2] Thomson (1781-1810), died unmarried.

There were other grandchildren of Robert and Judith Thomson, of New Kent, living in Virginia in the eighteenth century. One of these was Nathaniel Thomson, of Hanover, who was ensign in the French and Indian War; another was William Thomson, an officer of rank in the French and Indian War. Presumably it was he who married a Miss Mills, of Hanover, and became the ancestor of the celebrated Mills-Thomson family, of Culpeper county, Virginia. Another

*See Register May, 1905, for descendants of Nathaniel and Frances (Major) Thomson, great-grandparents of the compiler.

(*Genealogies of Kentucky Families* (Vol. A-M), 721-728.)

Waddy-Thompson (the family is so designated and the name is invariably so spelled), branch has, for generations, been located in South Carolina and elsewhere in the South. These have been eminent and distinguished in their state and in national affairs. The first of these in South Carolina was Judge Waddy Thompson, first Chancellor of South Carolina,—the highest judicial position in that state—who held office for more than a quarter of a century. He was born in Cumberland county, Virginia, 1769. His son, Waddy Thompson (1798-1868), a very distinguished man of his day, was Minister to Mexico and author of "Recollections of Mexico." A grandson of Judge Waddy Thompson, the late Hugh S. Thompson, was governor of South Carolina.

Still another Waddy-Thomson family was that of Samuel Thomson, of Louisa county, Virginia, who married Ann Jennings and removed to Amelia county, Virginia, where he died in 1783. One of their sons, Waddy Thomson (born Nov. 16, 1777), married Katherine James, and emigrated to Western Kentucky. The daughter, Mary, of these last, was the mother of the late Captain Ed. Porter Thompson, Historian of the famous Orphan Brigade.

Another Thomson family which is intimately associated with the history of Kentucky, and whose connection in Virginia, Kentucky and elsewhere was a very large one, and members of which played important parts in the development of their respective localities, was the so-called Rodes - Thomsons, of Louisa county, Virginia. Their traditions and records do not connect them with the Waddy-Thomson family. According to their record their emigrant ancestor to Virginia was Samuel Thomson, of "Blair Manor," Scotland, the only known son of whom was William Thomson, who married Ann Rodes, and lived and died in Louisa. William and Ann (Rodes) Thomson had a large family. After the death of William Thomson, his wife and many of their children removed to Kentucky. Among these children were Elizabeth, third wife of Governor Gabriel Slaughter, of Kentucky, and General David Thomson, of the War of 1812.

Complied by George C. Downing.

THE ROBERT THURSTON FAMILY*

Robert Thurston, son of Plummer and Mary Talbot Thurston, was born in Campbell county, Va., January 2, 1783. The family of Plummer Thurston, together with the families of his brothers, Walker Thurston and Ezekiel Thurston, emigrated from Virginia to Kentucky at some time near the close of the eighteenth century. They first settled at Bryan's Station, but later removed to Shelby county.

Robert Thurston received a medical education, and, about the year 1810, began the practice of his chosen profession. He married on January 2, 1814, Maria, daughter of Edmond and Hannah Miller Searcy, of Woodford county, Ky. After the marriage of his daughter, Maria, Edmond Searcy moved to New Castle, Henry county, Ky., where Dr. Thurston left his wife in her father's care, when he went on his military expedition to New Orleans. Upon Dr. Thurston's return he resumed the practice of medicine and continued to practice until about the year 1836, when he gave up his practice, because of ill health, to Dr. Robert H. Smith, who married Lucinda E., the elder of Dr. Thurston's two daughters. The only other child of Robert and Maria Searcy Thurston, who grew to maturity, was Maria Louise Miller Thurston, who, in 1847, married William Lewis Waddy. Dr. Robert Thurston was a man of lofty principle and sterling integrity. One of his maxims, often used and well remembered by his friends, was: "If you can not say good never say ill of anybody." He had many warm, personal friends, among whom were Churchill Blackburn, Thomas Joyce, George W. Johnson, Dr. Joseph Venable, James Craig and William Craig. He was a conscientious, consistent member and elder of the Christian church, donating the land upon which was erected "Jeptha Church," one of the first Christian churches built in Shelby county, of which both he and his wife were charter members. Of his seven grandchildren, who reached maturity, six were of the same faith, and five of these were converted at "Jeptha Church." Dr. Thurston died August 16, 1856.

GEORGE C. DOWNING.

*Excerpted from "Captain Robert Thurston," by George C. Downing, *The Register of the Kentucky Historical Society*, Vol. 8 (Jan. 1910), 97-101.

Captain John Wall and Major John Taylor.

Sketch of the Revolutionary Ancestry of
MRS. W. W. LONGMOOR, SR., OF FRANKFORT, KY.

THE WALLS, TAYLORS AND ADDAMS.

Capt. John Wall, an officer in the Revolutionary War, has descendants in this State as well as in Pennsylvania and Virginia. The Walls are among the earliest pioneers in New York. Wall street, New York City, was "laid off" and called for one of the early fathers of that name who had, we learn, large possessions in New Amsterdam. Capt. John Wall served as a commissioned officer in the Pennsylvania organization on the frontier of the State, defending it from the Indians during the Revolutionary War. From the colonial chapter of the Revolutionary heroes, read before the Frankfort Society of Colonial Daughters, 1897, we take the following data, which was furnished the writer by J. Sutton Wall, of the Department of Records, Harrisburg, Pa.

"John Wall settled on Peter's creek, in Washington county, Pa., about the year, 1776. He was captain of a company of militia organized for the protection of the frontier settlements from Indian depredations during the Revolution (see Pennsylvania Archives, vol. 14, p. 750, second series).

At a council of war held at Catfish Camp in the District of West Augusta, January 28, 1777, for the purpose of more fully organizing and devising means for protection and defense against the Indians, who were threatening hostilities in the coming spring, Capt. John Wall is mentioned in the list of the several county listments of the three counties (Monongalia, Yohogannia and Ohio), and thirty-two captains of militia were present at the meeting. In the absence of the Continental troops who were fighting the British in the East, the militia performed important service in protecting the frontier settlements in the then so-called West, from the hostile Indians, and deserve a fair share of the credit therefor.

In the court records of Yohogannia county, under date of May 25, 1778, the name of John Wall is mentioned as one of three persons appointed to view a road from McKee's Ferry on the Monongahelia river (opposite McKeesport) to Pentecost's Mills on charters and make report at the next meeting of court (see History of Washington, p. 218)."

His services were various, and wherever duty led, there he was found, standing firm in defense of the position and his cause.

At the close of the Revolutionary War, John Wall, with many other families in western Pennsylvania, emigrated to Kentucky. About the year 1791 Capt. John Wall, with his wife and family, settled in Harrison county, Kentucky, where he resided the remainder of his life, a highly honored and influential citizen (see Collins' History of Kentucky).

He was born in New Jersey April 27, 1742, and died in Harrison county, Ky., June, 1814. He was twice married. His second wife he married in New Jersey in 1776. She was Hannah Ketcham, daughter of Stephen and Elizabeth Ketcham, who was born February 4, 1750, and died in Cynthiana, Ky., December, 1831.

Capt. John Wall and Hannah Ketcham, his wife, were the parents of Judge Wm. K. Wall, a distinguished lawyer of Harrison county, Ky., who was born May 19, 1786, married Priscilla Taylor, daughter of Septimus Taylor, of same county, and died in Cynthiana, March 22, 1853, aged sixty-seven.

There are descendants scattered throughout this and other States of Capt. John Wall, and in our city (Frankfort, Ky.) there lives a descendant, a great granddaughter, Mrs. Loula B. Longmoor, widow of W. W. Longmoor, Confederate soldier, and clerk of the court of appeals in 1890; died March, 1891.

To the honor of Kentucky we publish the fact that upon the death of this honored Confederate soldier, Mrs. Longmoor was made regent of the court of appeals, her brother, Abram Addams, being elected to conduct the office for her benefit. Mrs. Longmoor is also descended from another officer of the Revolutionary War, Maj. John Taylor, of Virginia, of Col. Hazen's regiment, Continental troops, of which fact there is record in the Pension Office, War Department, Washington, D. C.

Maj. Taylor was also a noted officer previous to his entrance into the Revolutionary War. We have this data from the "Records of Virginia."

On being appointed a major in Col. Hazen's regiment, "Resolved, That a commission be granted him and that the same be dated 15th of November, 1776." Journal of Congress; directed by an act of Congress August 10, 1790. Previous to the above appointment we read that on May 6, 1776, it was "Resolved, That John Taylor be appointed Judge Advocate to the Continental troops in the Colony of Virginia." The will of the above John Taylor, dated 1798, produced and proven 1st day of July, 1805, a copy of which we obtained from the clerk of the county court of Frederick county, Virginia, indicates the high Christian character of this patriot and soldier, John Taylor, who died at his residence in Frederick county, Virginia, 1805. He married Mary McMahon, of Fredericksburg, who survived him some years. His son, Dr. Septimus Taylor, came to Kentucky and settled in Harrison county, whose daughter, Priscilla, married Judge William K. Wall, and whose daughter, Mary Taylor Wall, married Dr. Abram Addams, of Cynthiana, who were the parents of Mrs. Loula B. Longmoor, now a resident and property owner of Frankfort, Ky. Her only child is Mr. W. W. Longmoor, of Frankfort, one of the leading business men of the city, a lawyer and promoter of progressive improvements at the capital.
J. C. M.

THE WARD FAMILY.

This family is represented early in the 17th Century by the notable branches, of John Ward. at Jamestown, Va; William Ward, of Sudbury, Wardville and Worcester, Mass., and Andrew Ward of Fairfield, Conn.

We find the Virginia Wards, many of them emigrated to Kentucky—but both the north and south are represented by Wards now living in different counties of Kentucky. In the beginning of its Statehood we find William Ward, known as General William Ward, in the Convention at Danville, 1787-8. And in 1792, he is a member of the first Legislature convened in Frankfort, the Capital, and he was returned from Mason County, where he located in coming to Kentucky, until 1795. In this year he seems to have removed to Scott County, Kentucky—and retired from public life. In 1795 he married Sallie Johnson, daughter of Col. Robert Johnson and Jemima Suggett Johnson, the splendid heroine of Bryan Station, and brave leader of the women and girls to the famous spring, in view of five hundred Indians, who were at the time investing the historic fort, and preparing to destroy it. The women under the lead of the fearless Jemima Johnson, marched bravely to the Spring, filled their buckets and pails of water, and returned to the fort in safety. This brave act placed these women among the foremost heroines in the history of the world. That any man or woman can claim to be descended from Jemima Johnson, wife of Col. Robert Johnson of Kentucky, gives them a rank and distinction no coat of arms of the royalty of Europe can confer. They need go no further for a patent of nobility. Mrs. William Ward, (Sallie Johnson) is said to have guarded the cradle of her baby brother, the future Vice President, Richard M. Johnson, while her mother went to the spring, with the courageous band of women.

In 1787-9, William Ward was in the Convention at Danville. In 1792, he was in the Legislature and was a member of the General Assembly, until 1795, when he married Sallie Johnson, and settled in Scott County. In 1816, we learn from the inscription on her tombstone in the Great Crossing Burying ground she died—In 1817, William Ward became guardian of his children who were minors, (see records in Scott County Court). Their children were Robert J. Ward, Junius Ward, William and George Ward, Sallie, Malvina, Polly and Elizabeth.

In Collin's History of Kentucky we find frequent notices of these descendants who all or nearly all of them settled in Kentucky. The most conspicuous of them being, Robert J. and Junius Ward, the latter of whom we have written in last year's Register, giving a picture also of his elegant home near Georgetown, Ky. Robert J. Ward, the most widely known and wealthiest of the brothers, was a citizen of Louisville, with large plantations in the South. We learn from a recent history of the family, that he was in the Legislature of Kentucky in 1825 as Speaker of the House. He was in the House of Representatives from Scott County from 1822 to 1831. He was a man of splendid personal appearance—talented and eloquent and very popular. He was the father of the famous American beauty, Sally Ward.

George Ward, another brother, went to Texas to live. The men of the family were all men of force and won and held high positions, of trust and usefulness.

Of William and Mathew Ward we have no data. It is supposed they died young. The daughters married Kentuckians and raised large families, and their descendants may be found throughout the Union today.

Of the family of Joseph Ward of the Seth Ward line in Amelia County, Va., we have in Kentucky the families of William Ward of Lexington, Ky., died, 1804—the late Judge Quincy Ward of Bourbon County; Dr. John Ward, of Louisville, Ky., and Mr. Edwin Ward. of Georgetown, Ky. Still another branch of the Wards is represented in the descendants of Andrew Ward, of Harrison County, Ky., the late Hon. A. Harry Ward, of Cynthiana and his brother, Col. Zebulon Ward, deceased who was at one time Warden of the Kentucky Penitentiary and member of the Kentucky Legislature from Woodford County, from 1861 to 63. Andrew Ward, their father and Col. William Ward, the founder of Urbana, Ohio, were closely related—he, the founder. was a son of Capt. James Ward, killed at Point Pleasant battle, Oct. 10, 1774.

In the east and in Virginia we find the fullest and perhaps most authentic records of the Wards.

Mrs. E. W. Doremus of New York, has an extensive history of the Wards; she is a daughter of George Ward and grand-daughter of Gen William Ward, and her history, she has been collecting for many years. To her generous courtesy we are indebted for much of our information in this brief sketch. Also for permission to publish for benefit of the Ward's of Kentucky and the South, the following carefully prepared manual, of the history and genealogy of the descendants of Seth Ward, who came to Kentucky in the early days of her Statehood, and from Kentucky went West and South where they became prominent citizens wherever they settled.

(Ed. The Register).

THE WARD FAMILY.

This is one of the old Virginia stocks; Seth Ward was granted 350 acres in Henrico County, Va., in 1643, (probably the nucleus of the Sheffield estate in what was subsequently Chesterfield,) and the name of Seth Ward was handed down for five generations as the name of the first-born son in the eldest branch of the family. Tradition tells us that the English ancestor was Seth Ward, a Bishop in the English Church, perhaps Seth Ward, V. R. S., Bishop of Salisbury and Exeter, Savilian Professor of Astronomy and president of Trinity College in the University of Oxford, born in Hertfordshire, in 1617. Colonel Seth Ward, grandson of the first of the name in America, would appear to have at least three children, viz: Seth Ward of Sheffield who married Mary Goode, (see Goode genealogy, No. 89) 2. Benjamin

Ward of "Wintopoke," Chesterfield Co., whose daughter Maria was affianced to Randolph of Roanoke, and who afterwards married Peyton Randolph, (for descendants, see Carter family tree) and 3, Mary Ward, born 1749, died 1787, who married first, William Broadnax, and 2, Richard Gregory, (for descendants, see Richmond Standard, 11, 4, p. 4.) Martha Ward Gregory, daughter of Richard Gregory, married Gen. John Pegram, and was ancestor of many well-known Virginians, (see Slaughters "Bristol Parish," pp. 205-209.)

(For above note, see Va. Cousins, p. 109, "The Whitby Goodes," 233, at bottom of page.)

THE WHITBY GOODES, 233. P. 109.

Seth Ward, of Lynchburg, Va., son of Seth and Mary Goode Ward, No. 89, p. 54, was born at Sheffield, Chesterfield, Co., Va., April 10, 1772, and died in Tennessee, about 1859. Married Feb. 4, 1796, Martha Norvell, daughter of Hon. Wm. Norvell, of Lynchburg. (Note.—The signatures of William Norvell and Robert Carter Nicholas appear on many issues of the Virginia Continental paper currency. For an account of the Norvell family see "Sketches and Recollections of Lynchburg," by Mrs. Cabell, p. 231.)—Children.

725.—Seth Ward, born July 9, 1798, married Miss Hendricks: Issue, 1, Edmond, a wealthy citizen of St. Louis? 2, Georgiana.— 726, Mary, born Oct. 9, 1800. died Nov. 10, 1802. 727.—Benjamin, born Oct. 5, 1802, lived near Flat Rock, Bedford Co., a farmer, married Eliza White, daughter of Col. White of Bedford Co., Issue.—1, Seth. 2, James Pegram, a soldier, C. S. A., and others died young. 728, Martha, born March 29, 1805, died May 10, 1806. 729 William Norvell, born April 19, 1807, died Feb. 25, 1881. 730, Lucy E., born May 12, 1809, married Fielding Williams. 731, George Edward, born April 2, 1811. 732, Nancy Edmonia, born June 24, 1813, married Matthew M. Kerr, 733, Mary Goode, born, Feb. 9, 1916. 734, Samuel Goode, born Aug. 27, 1818. 735, (adopted son) James W. Pegram.

Seth Ward was left early without a father, and was placed under the guardianship of his uncle, Col. Robert Goode, of Whitby, No. 90. He was heir to a large estate, but owing to unfortunate endorsements of papers belonging to his friends, he lost his property and removed to Lynchburg. He was a man of sterling and beautiful character, one of the patriarchs of the Episcopal Church in South-western Virginia, and greatly esteemed by all who knew him. The widow of one of his sons writes. "I always found him a charming companion, usually cheerful, but sometimes sad, when he reverted to his changed circumstances. Pleasant evenings we spent in the piazza at old Brecknock, my husband's home, when he told over incidents of his youth, and of his old friends, John and Edmund Randolph, and many others of their time. He told many interesting anecdotes of the oldest friend of his boyhood, William Henry Harrison, afterwards President of the United States, whom his mother received into her household as a companion for him, and who had the same tutor. He removed to Tennessee with two of his married daughters, and accompanied by his youngest daughter, Mary Goode Ward, to whom he gave, when I was at his house, a beautiful miniature of her mother, Mary Goode, and her diamond ring."

His mother's niece was left a widow with twelve children by the death of her husband, Gen. John. Pegram, and herself died soon after. Their fourth son, James West Pegram, was brought up by Mr. Ward as one of his own sons. He was subsequently General of Virginia troops, and was killed by the explosion of a steamboat in 1844. He married Virginia, daughter of Col. Wm. Ransom Johnson, the "Napoleon of the turf." His children were, 1, Major-General John Pegram, C. S, A., killed in battle, married Hettie, daughter of Wilson Miles Cary, of Baltimore, now wife of Prof. Henry Newell Martin, of Johns Hopkins University. 2, Major James W. Pegram, C. S. A. 3, Virginia, wife of Col. David G. McIntosh, C. S. A. 4, Brig. Gen. Wm. R. J. Pegram, C. S. A., killed at the battle of Five Forks, April, 1865. 5, Mary, wife of Gen. Joseph R. Anderson, of the Tredegar Iron Works, Richmond, Va.

Maria Ward, who was the object of the romantic attachment of John Randolph of Roanoke, and whose loveliness is still a tradition in Virginia, was daughter of Benjamin Ward of "Wintopoke," uncle of Seth Ward, and after her father's death was a member of the household at "Sheffield," where occurred the estrangement which embittered the life of the eccentric Virginia statesman. (See Garland's Life of John Randolph.) 725-667-727 :. 1700-1796-p. 203.

Seth Ward of Lynchburg, Va., son of Seth and Martha Norvell Ward, No. 233, p. 109, was born July 9, 1798, and died about 1830, married Miss Hendrick. Children: 1795, Edmund Ward, born about 1815. 1796, Georgiana, married Mr. Nelson, of Northern Mississippi, an extensive planter on the Mississippi River.

727—Benjamin Ward, of "The Cottage," Campbell Co., Va., son of No. 223, was born Oct. 5, 1802, died 1840-'50. A well-to-do planter, married 1829, Betsy White, (Aunt of Rev. A. White Pitzer, D. D. of Washington, D. C.,) daughter of Col. Samuel White, of "Fort Lewis," Roanoke Co., Va., and his wife, Fannie Penn, grandaughter of William Penn., the founder of the Pennsylvania Colony. Children, all dead but the youngest. 1797, Fanny Ward. 1797 1-3, Paulina Jane, 1767 2-3, Seth. 1798, Matilda. 1798 1-2, Alice. 1799, James Pegram, Soldier, C. S. A., in 1886, engaged in farming near Rome, Ga.

729-PAGE 204.

Rev. Wm. Norvell Ward, of "Bladensfield," Richmond Co., Va., son of Seth and Martha Norvell Ward, No. 233, p. 109. was born in Lynchburg, Va., April 19, 1805, and died Feb. 25, 1881. Married August 9, 1836, Mary, daughter of Sampson and Martha Jones Blincoe, of Leesburg, Loudon Co., Va., born Dec. 18, 1815. Children: 1800, Martha Ward, born June 8, 1837, married James Cary. 1801, Wm. Norvell, born March 3, 1839, died August 29, 1862. Soldier, C. S. A., killed in battle. 1802, Mary Virginia, born Dec. 24, 1840, married A. D. V. Burr. 1803, Edmonia Kerr, born Nov. 6, 1842, died Dec. 8, 1882, married Dr. Pearson Chapman, of Harford Co., Md. 1804, Charles Blincoe, born Feb. 14, 1845, died June 9, 1863. Soldier C. S. A., killed in battle. 1805, Lucy Randolph. 1806, Henry Tayloe, 1807, Estelle, died young, 1808, Evelyn Douglas. 1809, Florence Landon. 1810,

Channing Moore. 1811, Randolph Goode.—

Mr. Ward was appointed to the U. S. Military Academy at West Point, at the age of twenty, and was there a classmate of Gen. Robert E. Lee, with whom, as well as with Jefferson Davis, who was in the class above him, he kept up a lifelong friendship. During his cadetship, he was much impressed by the preaching of Mr. Parks, who visited West Point, and in company with Leonidas K. Polk, afterwards Bishop of Louisiana, and Lieutenant-General, C. S. A., he left the Military Academy to enter the ministry of the Protestant Episcopal Church. He was graduated from the Theological Seminary of Virginia, at Alexandria, Va., in 1834, and for nearly half a century lived the quiet, self-sacrificing life of a country clergyman. He had invitations to city parishes, and to more influential positions in other states, but his love of country life led him to refuse the former, while his devotion to Virginia forbade his removal to another state.

He was successfully rector of parishes in Clarksburgh, and in Spotsylvania Co., and of Cople, Farnham, and Lunenburg parishes in the Northern Neck of Virginia, and in addition to his regular duties, he devoted much time, during the last four years of his life, to unremunerated missionary work in the region so greatly impoverished, and so nearly depopulated, by the war, in the neighborhood of the Wilderness battlefield, often traveling fifty miles in a week to visit churches which had no other provision for pastoral attention.

He owned a plantation, "Bladensfield," near Warsaw, Richmond Co., which was his home for many years before his death.

At the opening of the war, he yielded to the solicitations of Gen. Lee, and other friends, who knew that he had received a military education. He entered the Confederate Army, and was appointed by Gen. Letcher, Major in the 55th Virginia Infantry, in which capacity he served, and as Commandant of Fort Lowery, near Tappahannock, until after two years he was forced by feeble health to resign.

After the death of two sons, a brother and many other relatives near to him and dear, who were killed in battle, he became very much changed. "He was, throughout the remainder of his life," writes a relative, "like one who walked in a dream: His mind was strong and vigorous, when any occasion roused him up, and it was said that one of his most powerful speeches was made in the last Convention before his death. Ordinarily, however, he looked, as if he were living in the far-away past."

He was a man of courtly manners and scholarly tastes, singularly unambitious and unobtrusive, and was greatly beloved by all who knew him.

Sampson Blincoe, father of Mrs. Ward, (born 1779, died 1826) was the son of Thomas Blincoe, a native of Wales, (Brecknockshire?) and grandson of Sir Jeffrey Blincoe.

Martha Jones, (born 1782, died 1824) his mother, was the daughter of Wm. Jones, (born about 1760) and Sarah Edwards. The latter was descended from the Edwards family, of "Northumberland House" in Northumberland County, Va. John Edwards, who in 1653 received a grant of 1050 acres in Lancaster Co., and 300 in Northumberland, and subsequently others in the same region, was her grand-father or great-grandfather. (Va. Land Register, Vol. III, pp. 2, 45, Vol. IV, pp. 178, 194, 299, 489. For this reference, and all others to this Register, I am indebtedness to the kindness of Mr. Brock.) Her father, Mrs. Ward's grandfather, whose name has been lost sight of owing to the destruction of records, was the heir to Northumberland House, long since in ruins, and from him it passed by sale to the Presleys and the Thorntons, when he married the wealthy Miss Smith, his cousin, and removed to Point Lookout, Maryland, where her family had long been established. He owned packets which plied between the Chesapeake Bay and London, and made investments in real estate in New York City, which, it is said, were leased for ninety-nine years, and would have reverted to his heirs, in 1879, but for the loss of their family records. His only son, John Swann Edwards, died unmarried. His nephew, Hon. Ninian Edwards, the first territorial Governor of Illinois and U. S. Senator, born in Northumberland Co., in 1779, was the father of Judge Ninian W. Edwards, whose wife was sister of the wife of President Abraham Lincoln.

The traditions of the family regarding their Jones ancestry, would indicate that they are descendants of Frederick, the elder of the two sons of Captain Roger Jones, a Cavalier, who came to Virginia in 1660, with Lord Culpepper, and commanded a sloop which was stationed in Chesapeake Bay for the suppression of piracy, and who, returning to London, died there about 1700 (Va. Land Register, Vol III, pp. 2, 45. Vol. IV, pp. 178, 194, 299, and 489.)

This Frederick Jones*, who died in North Carolina in 1722, had a daughter Jane, who married Samuel Swann, and their daughter Jane married her cousin, Frederick Jones, and had an only son whose name was changed at the request of a wealthy and childless relative, (uncle, says the Ward tradition,) to John Swann. In some way, through an intermarriage with the Edwards family in all probability, the Swann name and wealth came into the possession of the great-grand parents of Mrs. Wm. N. Ward. I hope that with the assistance of Mr. H. L. Jones, of Winchester, Ky., who has prepared an elaborate history of the descendants of the descendants of Col. Thomas Jones, the younger son, of Capt. Roger Jones, this matter may be made somewhat more clear, and a fuller statement printed in the Appendix to this book. Wm. Jones, the grandfather of Mrs. Ward, was the grandson of one Jones who lived in North Carolina, married a Miss Orr, (so says the Ward tradition,) and had three sons who returned to Virginia. One of these married Mrs. Martha (Gwyther) Burns, half-sister of Elizabeth Waughop, of St. Mary's County, Md.; his eldest son, Philip, died in the first year of the Revolutionary War, his second son, John Swann Jones married Elizabeth Monroe, (aunt of President James Monroe,) his fourth son, Roger Jones, a Tory, died single; his only daughter married Mr. Fields; his fifth son, William, was the grandfather of Mrs. Ward; his sixth, was Ap Catesby Jones; his seventh has descendants now living in St. Mary's County, Maryland.

(*Note.—The arms, as described in a memorandum dated 1728, are Sable, a fesse, or, between three childrens' heads proper, quartered with Hoskins, (Roger Jones' mother being an heiress, as follows: Party per pale azure and gules, a chevron engrailed, or, between three lions rampant, argent.) His wife's arms, those of Walker, of Mansfield, Nottinghamshire, were, Argent, three amulets, between nine cinquefoils sable. The Jones crest was, A child's head proper. These details are inserted for the purpose of calling attention to the fact that Mr. L. H. Jones, of Winchester, Ky., and Mr. F. Binford, of Owensboro, Ky., are anxious to correspond with any one in England who is interested in any of the families concerned.)

The tradition in the Ward family has it that one of their ancestors was the younger son of Robert Catesby, who, after the Gunpowder Plot and the death of his father, was captured by the emissaries of Packingham and sent to Virginia, where he married the daughter of a Welsh planter named Jones, and assumed the family name. Whether this be true or not, the Jones and Catesby families were associated intimately in early days, through the marriage of Col. Thomas Jones, younger son of Capt. Roger Jones already mentioned, to Elizabeth Cocke, niece of Mark Catesby, the English naturalist, who, during his scientific exploration of Virginia and the Carolinas, made his home with her and the other children of his sister, the wife of Dr. Wm. Cocke, Colonial Secretary. The name of Catesby in the younger branches of the Jones family is thus accounted for, but it is difficult to see how it crept into the elder branch, except through the influence of the tradition just referred to.

731—1817-1817—PAGE 207.

731.—Major George Edward Ward, C. S. A., of Lamar, Barton Co., Missouri, son of No. 233, p. 109, was born in Lynchburg, Va., April 2, 1811, and died at Dover Creek, Ark., Oct. 2, 1862, from the effects of wounds received at the battle of Pea Ridge. Married at Harrodsburg, Ky., Dec. 10, 1833, Charity Green, who lives, 1886 at Lamar, a hearty, beautiful old lady of 75 years." Children: 1813, Josephine Ward, born Sept. 8, 1836, died Dec. 29, 1860. married Judge J. C. Parry. 1814, Edward Greene, born Feb. 28, 1839, 1815, Theodosia, born August 29, 1841, died August 8, 1873. Married (I) Dr. Albert Smith, Soldier, C. S. A., killed in battle: (2) Hon. E. M. Hulett. 1816, James T., born June 5, 1844. 1817, Mary, born Nov. 8, 1846, Married Robert J. Tucker.

Major Ward went from Virginia to Kentucky when a young man, and at the age of forty-one removed to Missouri, settling in what was then Jasper County, a vast and beautiful prairie region with few inhabitants. He was the founder of the town of Lamar, which he named for his dear friend, Mirabeau B. Lamar, president of the Texas Republic, and also of Barton County, named for David Barton.

He was a large and strikingly handsome man, six feet and one quarter in height, with dark hair and rosy cheeks.

At the opening of the war, he, with sin sons and his sons-in law, joined with Shelby and Pike in their military operations. Their exploits are frequently referred to by John N. Edwards, in his thrilling narrative of the war in the Southwest, entitled "Shelby and His Men." and I am indebted to Major Edwards, editor of the St. Joseph Democrat, for placing me in communication with the surviving members of the family.

"The brave and devoted Major Ward of Lamar, received his death wound," says Edwards, speaking of Pea Ridge, "and his gallant young son, James, although shot in the ankle, at Cassville, on the retreat, yet went again into the fight with his father, and was wounded severely, the second time in the leg. Another son of the noble old veteran was struck down at his side with a painful wound, and the father and his two boy heroes were torn from the field, the one to die, and the others to strike, afterwards, hard and heavy blows for the Confederacy." (Shelby and His Men; or The War in the West By John N. Edwards.)

"They were from Barton Co., Missouri, and their mother and sister suffered long and weary wants of shameful imprisonment in St. Louis, at the hands of men who had no heart to spare the helpless. The heroineism of Missouri women, during the war, is a book of itself, that abler hands than these will write.

"A beautiful and accomplished sister of the young soldiers. (James and Edward Ward.) Mrs. Theodosia Smith, was a heroine beyond comparison. Elegant, fascinating, and diplomatic as Talleyrand, she made a dozen visits through the lines, braved many dangers with remarkable coolness, avoided numerous grave dangers with great skill, and never failed once in the accomplishment of her mission, and in offering the most complete and valuable information." (p. 411.)

Speaking of the campaigns around St. Louis, Edwards remarks: (P. 409), "There was scarcely a day of the time that Shelby's division operated, that he did not have his soldiers about the very headquarters of the Federals in St. Louis, and in the warriors' camps and forts along the line he was watching. The adroit answer, the self-possession, the coolness and nerve necessary to a man who ventures into places where he faces death any moment, requires that address which few men possess, and in which no soldier ever excelled those of Shelby's command. The hairbreadth escapes and cunning exploits of such men as Brown Williams, Arthur McCoy, Newton, Hockinsmith, (finally taken in Clayton Post, at Pine Bluff, Arkansas.) . . . Sid. Martin, Edward Ward, or any one of a dozen I might name, who were usually detailed for their meanness, would fill a larger volume than this with truths that might appear stranger than fiction.

"Before leaving Pocahontas, Gen. Price had asked for a spy to go into St. Louis, and Shelby gave him private James Ward, a brave and intelligent soldier of the advance under the wounded Thorp, and the daring Williams, and who was afterwards a captain of the Old Brigade, (in Slayback's regiment), and aid to Gen. Slayback, At the battle of West Point, Gen. Price gave him his instructions minutely. He was to visit Gen. Rosecrans' headquarters in St. Louis, learn everything relating to troops and military movements possible, ascertain the sentiments and dispositions of the people towards a general uprising, and report at some point on the Missouri River. Ward started and gained Helena in safety. Leaving his arms and horse near the town, he entered that post afoot. He was quite young, almost a boy, in fact, and was readily permitted to take passage on a steamboat as a fugitive from the conscript law. He went in this way as a cabin passenger, and 'higher civilization' folks from the North only discovering in him a speciment of the green Arkansas 'swamp-rat.' At St. Louis he reported directly to Gen. Rosecrans, had several personal interviews with him, and from him and those around him got the very information he was sent to seek.

He then asked permission to go to Iowa to attend school. This he was permitted to do, taking the cars on the North Missouri Railroad he reached Chillicothe. From there he made his way to a camp of recruits, and with them joined the main force and reported to Gen. Price at Waverly, having accomplished his hazardous undertaking to the day, and to the utmost satisfaction of his officers. This may seem a very simple thing now; but in those days it was no child's play, and the penalty of detection, especially if the papers he had on his person were found, would have been certain death. The military budget brought by young Ward was important, and known only to Gen. Price. This James Ward otherwise greatly distinguished himself, especially in the battle of Westport, and in the defense of the arsenal at Tyler." (See "Shelby and His Men," P. 432.)

"Edward, Ward," says Edwards, "was another member of the advance who allowed no one to 'out-soldier' him, as it was expressed in camp phrase. Like his brother, James, he was frequently employed on secret missions inside the enemy's lines. He was seriously wounded at New Iberia, early in the war; was Lieutenant in McCoy's regiment, and Captain in that commanded by Col. D. A. Williams. He was a young, beardless fellow, brave and high-spirited. (See Appendix for additional notes.)

734.—P. 219.

Samuel Goode Ward, of Texas, son of No. 234, was born August 27, 1818. He was one of the companions of Houston, in the struggle for the independence of Texas, in 1835-1836, and probably participated in the later war between Mexico and the United States. He was an exceedingly handsome man, six and one quarter feet in height, and well-proportioned.

1033-9. Page 275.

Wm. H. Ward, of Tazewell C. H., Va., son of Wm. Ward of Wythe Co., died 1881. Married Jennie C. Daniel, daughter of Hezekiah Goode Daniel, No. 156-6, grand-daughter of William Pride and Ann Goode Daniel, No Ward 72, p. 49. (Mrs. Jennie Daniel Ward, now a resident of Washington, is the only one of the Virginia third-cousins, save Dr. Murrell, whom the writer has been privileged to see.)

1735: 4230-4293. P. 343.

1795. Seth Edmund Ward, of Kansas City, Mo., son of No. 725, p. 203, was born in Campbell Co., Mo., March 4th, 1830. Married Feb. 9th, 1860, Mary F. McCarthy, daughter of John Harris, of Westport, Mo., Children:—

4291, John Edmund, b. June 21, 1861. 4292, Hugh Campbell, born, March 10, 1863. 4293, Mary F., died young.

The following sketch of Mr. Ward is from his biography in the U. S. Biolographical Dictionary, Missouri Volume.

"Being deprived of educational advantages by the early death of his father, he went to Indiana at the age of fourteen, and remained for a time under the charge of Jacob Haas, (See above, No. 179, p. 90) but soon began an independent career. The year 1838 found him in Independence, Mo., where he joined the company of Capt. Lancaster P. Lupton, a fur trader, and shortly afterwards entered service with the fur company of Thompson and Craig, and with them crossed the Rocky mountains on a trading expedition,—one of the earliest ventures in this direction. Among his associates on this trip, was Kit Carson,—the Nestor of the Rocky Mountains,—and his first horse was a gift from Carson, who had won it from an old mountaineer on a wager that a green hand like Ward could not bring down a buffalo at the first dash.—Ward accomplished the feat, though at the cost of painful injuries to himself. In 1839, he went with a party of trappers into the territories of the Navajo and Digger Indians, but the Indians shot many of their horses, and wounded one of the trappers, and the party returned on foot through the wilderness, bringing their companion on a litter to Taos, N. M. For seven years he pursued his adventurous calling in various parts of the Southwest. In 1845, he went with Bent and St. Vrain to Union Fort in New Mexico, (now Colorado), and upon this trip was associated with Francis P. Blair, afterwards Senator, with whom he formed an enduring friendship. In 1845, he had accumulated capital to the extent of $1,000, with which he entered business for himself, as an Indian trader. On one expedition, in 1848, he obtained 6000 buffalo robes. After ten year's profitable occupation i nthis business, he was appointed sutler in the U. S. Army at Fort Laramie, where he continued from 1856 to 1871. During all these years his business was immense; honesty and promptness in meeting all his papers had given him almost unlimited credit, and his increasing trade necessitated the building of large warehouses for its accomodation. In 1873, he was elected president of the Austin Bank, in Kansas City, a position which he still holds, and in which he has been eminently successful. He is a member of the Baptist Church, and of the Odd Fellows' and Masonic Orders.

"His home, near Kansas City, is described as beautiful and well appointed, standing in the midst of grounds 450 acres in extent, such as might be found in the fertile blue-grass region of Kentucky, the greensward dotted with trees and groves. He has been instrumental in introducing the short-horn breed of cattle into western Missouri, and his herd is one of the finest in the State.

"Here he is spending his best days, surrounded with every luxury, blessed with an effectionate family, enjoying the confidence, the respect, and the steadfast friendship of the many to whom his virtues and his manliness have commended him." (P. 469.)

1801-1802. 4311-4317. P. 345.

1801. Capt. Wm. Norvefl Ward, C. S. A., son of No. 729, was born March 3rd, 1839. He entered the University of Virginia in 1857. At the beginning of the war, he enlisted in the 47th Virginia Infantry, and served through the Peninsular campaign in Gen. A. P. Hill's division, receiving a mortal wound at the battle of Gaines' Hill, from the effects of which he died, August 29th, 1862 "A splendid type of Southern manhood," talented, brave, and gentle, he gave promise of a brilliant and useful career. See Johnson's "University Memmorial," P. 755.

1804.—Page 346.

1804. Charles Blincoe Ward, of Richmond Co., Va., son of No. 729, was born Feb. 14th, 1845. At the beginning of the war, just as he was entering the Virginia Military Institute, he was seized by the Federal troops and carried to Washington, where he was imprisoned. Although only 17 years old, his father entered his name on the roll of the 9th Virginia Cavalry, and he was exchanged and entered active service, and was killed in an engagement at Beverley's Ford, Culpeper Co., Va., June 9th, 1863, when only eighteen, having voluntarily left his position in charge of the horses of his company, and gone into battle in the place of an elderly man in his company, whose life he felt would ill be spared by his family.

1806. P. 346.

Henry Tayloe Ward, of "Bladensfield," Richmond Co., Va., son of No. 729, was educated at the Virginia Military Institute. A farmer. Unmarried.

1810. P. 346.

Channing Moore Ward, of Washington, D. C., son of No. 729, was born August 15th, 1857. He was educated at the Alexandria High School, and in 1878 and 1879 was with the U. S. Coast Survey, working on the North Carolina Coast. In 1880, he entered the service of the Baltimore and Ohio Railroad, and in 1887 was resident Engineer at Grafton, W. Va.

1811. P. 346.

Randolph Goode Ward, of Uniontown, Pa., son of No. 729, was born May 24th, 1860. Married Nov. 21st, 1882, Belle Manning Brown, daughter of Wm. Warren and Charlotte Hudson Brown, of Portland, Me.—Children:

4320, Cornelia Channing, born Dec. 20th, 1883. 4231, Charlotte Warner, born July 14th, 1885.

1814. P. 347.

Capt. Edward Greene Ward, of Lamar, Barton Co., Mo., son of No. 731, was born Feb. 28th, 1839. Married Jan. 31st, 1869, Mary V., daughter of Dr. Johnson and Ann Eliza Logan, of Carlinsville, Ill.—Children:

4324. Edward L. Ward, born July 1st, 1870. 4325, Annie, born April 12th, 1872. 4326, William B., born April 26th, 1874. 4327. George E., born July 19th, 1777. 4328, William, born Oct. 6th, 1880. 4329. John, born May 1st, 1883. Capt. Ward served in command of a detached company of picked men, assigned to special duty under Gen. Price, until he surrendered himself and his men at Shreveport. Some of his exploits, as described by Edwards, have already been referred to in the biographical notice of his father, on page 207.

4291. P. 416.

John Edmund Ward, of Kansas City, Mo., son of Seth Edmund Ward, No. 1795, p. 343, was born June 21st, 1861. Educated at William Jewell College. In business with his father in Kansas City. Married Nov. 10th, 1886, Mary Octavia Jones, daughter of Major B. F. Jones, and Mary Ann Nesbit Jones, both descended from old Georgia families.

4292. P. 416.

Hugh Campbell Ward, of Kansas City, Mo., son of No. 1795, was born March 10th, 1863. Graduated from Harvard University in the class of 1886. A student of law in St. Louis since October, 1886.

WATLINGTON

HISTORY AND GENEALOGY FROM AN OLD FAMILY LETTER

By MRS. H. V. McCHESNEY, Sr.

Frankfort, Kentucky

As a descendant of the very old family of Watlingtons, I have, for many years, been collecting much of historical interest in connection with it. The Watlingtons were among the largest landowners of Halifax County, Virginia, and Caswell County, North Carolina. They were prominent in distinguished Colonial service in Virginia. They were among the oldest settlers of Bermuda, and some came to Virginia after 1609. We find the family of Sir Harry Watlington, who was knighted for installing the splendid water system of the islands. The Watlingtons date back to early history in England, where there is a town of the name.

I now have my own lineage from this family complete back to 1637 in Virginia, and back to early history in England through Colonel George Reade who came to Virginia from England and was Colonial Secretary in 1671.

While examining my old genealogical records recently, I found a copy of a unique and interesting old letter written sixty years ago. It was never intended for publication, and I hope I may be pardoned for having it printed at this time.

The letter was written by Mrs. Adaline Bennett Drake, of Auburn, Kentucky, to her brother, Judge Caswell Bennett who lived in a beautiful old white columned house on the outskirts of my old home town of Smithland, Kentucky. The farm and house, recently restored, are now owned by my niece, Mrs. Harry L. Dunn of Smithland. After Judge Bennett was elected to the Kentucky Court of Appeals, he became a resident of Frankfort.

Only a few years ago, I learned that Judge Bennett, whose mother was Frances Donohoe Watlington of Caswell County, North Carolina, and my father, Theodore David Presnell, of Smithland, whose mother was Nancy Ann Watlington of Caswell County, North Carolina, claimed kinship through their related Watlington ancestors. Research has since established this to be true.

Appended to the original letter was this notation by Mrs. Jennie Chinn Morton who for so many years served as Secretary-Treasurer of the Kentucky Historical Society: "This letter is not only interesting but very valuable as genealogical data."

Auburn, Ky.
Nov. 3, 1889

Judge Caswell Bennett,
Frankfort, Ky.

Dear Caddie:

Two days since I received a sweet sensible letter from your wife.

I defer answering her directly, till after relating to you most of the verbal history, I can recollect, of our direct and lineal ancestors.

Our father, Ambrose Lee Bennett, was a man of great learning, dignified, grave, of fine personal appearance and reticent. Under the old Constitution of N.C., he was appointed Magistrate of Caswell County, was chairman of the justices entitled to the title of Judge. He objected to the title and was called Chief Justice of the county till I recollect a new constitution made the office elective—his modesty prevented his asking for office—after places were all filled by election—he was growing old too, had ample means, and preferred a retired life. Pa knew his family history back to Colonial times. He traced the Bennetts back to Bennett who was appointed a Parliamentary Commissioner to settle (with Clairborne and Curtis) the affairs of Maryland. He was elected Governor of Virginia after Berkley returned to England. Most U.S. histories make mention of him.

Pa's father was Major Richard Bennett—he served in the Revolution—he died before my recollection.

Our grandmother was Miss Annie Lee, of the family of Gen. Henry Lee, from whom descended Gen. Robert E. Lee, of Southern Confederacy. Henry Lee is sometimes mentioned as "Light Horse Harry Lee" in history. Pa told much concerning his family that I can recollect, only in outline, not as a whole.

Major Dick Bennett left a vast estate, so great was our father's share (Ambrose Lee), that when he sent fifty negroes south at one time, they could not be missed. You have heard us talk of his selling that fifty to pay for the failure of the Sheriff of Caswell County, whose security he was. Security was our father's one fault, his curse.

Do you remember that I used to try to instill into the minds of the younger members of the family, a hatred of security, to resist it as you would some vicious, personal enemy. I feel the same warmth of opposition today. "Old age ne'er cools the Douglas' blood".

Pa died in 1845, as robust in form and well poised in mind, as most men at forty. He was 76, died of congestion from violent cold, was not bedfast. He had retired and suddenly died during the night. He was buried at Donohoe Place, near Yanceyville, Caswell, N.C.

Our mother was Miss Frances Donohoe Watlington, born 1802 in Halifax, Va., died in Cleburne, Texas, April 1, 1881. She was the daughter of Capt. John

Watlington of Halifax Co., Va., and his wife Elizabeth Donahoe, of North Carolina. John Watlington served as Captain in the Revolution, and he was a life officer in Virginia service, minute men being kept under drill for state service, after close of regular war. When the pensions afterward granted to our grandmothers and their children were collected, I remember the talks about it, but am not certain as to whether the State of Va. paid any part of it. As an evidence of Capt. John Watlington's military services, I refer you to an incident that you have some recollection of, no doubt, namely, in 1850, a Mr. Stovall, Congressman from Halifax, Va., visited our house on the Dan, and brought with him for division among our grandfather's heirs, about $8000.00 cash, and the title to public lands wherever to be found.

Capt. John Watlington left seven heirs. Ma's share of land was 490 acres, I think. Well, Mr. Stovall kept ⅓ or ½ I am not certain which, as his pay for procuring proofs and proving their claim. That allowance by Congress is cited to give "body" to my imperfect sketch.

Our mother's mother was Miss Elizabeth O'Donahoe, by custom Donahoe, of Caswell Co., N.C. You ought to recollect grandma Watlington, tall, thin, straight as an arrow. She lived till 1850. She was then receiving from the government the pay allowed a Captain's widow. I remember that the name Watlington is sometimes shortened to Waddleton in N.C.

Our great-grandfather Donahoe was Major Archie Donohoe, (Note: This name should be Thomas Donohoe) yet when I think of other family Donohoe names, I may possibly mix them. He served in the Revolutionary War. I can give you several evidences to refer to pension records at Washington.

In my childhood, Grandma Donohoe in the '90s still lived on the Donohoe Place. Often, I have played with her little "niggers" around the spring on the place by which a part of Green's army rested when getting away from Cornwallis, before the Battle of Guilford. Grandma valued the place—never suffered woods to be cleared from around it. Major Donohoe was connected with the command.

I was thirteen when she died, quite a hundred. I am not certain if it was not more. At that time, she yearly received a Major's pay for her deceased husband. Our Grandfather Donohoe's grave I have often seen. He died before my recollection. He had the reputation to being a high liver, hale, hearty, generous, of large estate, not recklessly a spendthrift, not that, but generous, with fine business judgement—as an instance, I went to school with grandchildren of the old soldiers, who yearly received their bread from the Donohoe mills. He so devised and his entire estate of lands were entailed till they finally fell into the possession of his grandson Thomas Donohoe, of Milton, N.C., but all the soldier's families who might apply were to have bread as long as the mills should exist. At the same time, he owned much public land west. I never understood what was done with it.

Major Donohoe died with gout, was buried at Donohoe Place, N.C.—I don't know the year.

Grandmother Donohoe was a rare little old lady. She went to church every Sunday in a "gig", a Negro man on horseback, a negro girl behind—her daughter, grandma Watlington with her—both were widows and lived together—both wore straight narrow black satin dresses, walked severely straight, sat together. They were Episcopalians till near death when both joined Baptists. One Sunday grandma pulled me close to her side and opening the morocco reticule, in which I carried Testament and sweet cakes, for Sunday School, she crammed in a bundle and said, "If you open this, or show it to anyone till you reach home and hand it to your mother, I'll find it out". So the two boys and I walked home, you were too young to be along. As we went on out two brothers, Dick and Fayette, coaxed me to let them peep in, but I was afraid of Grandma's piercing steel gray eyes. When we rushed in with the treasure to ma, she opened it, and rolled $500.00 out. Grandma was dividing her yearly pension, for she was too rich to need it.

Now, Caddie, I will mention others, well authenticated by our parents, aunts, uncles and older citizens, for you must bear in mind that family traditions are more indulged in among permanent people than in the west, or in new countries. I do not dislike progress, but why should not coming generations, by some permanent principles or law, if you will, have, enjoy and emulate the private and public virtues of family ancestors? Such an arrangement as will give written records of family history, must have the effect on the young of making better citizens, more patriotic, more aspiring after the noble in life rather than the gaudy transient visions, which most people pursue.

I'll go back now and pick up the Watlingtons. My mother's Paternal grandfather was Col. Armistead Watlington, a pure-blooded Englishman, lived in Pittsylvania Co., Va., or Halifax Co. I suddenly have a doubt which. He often entertained British officers, some of them kin to him. I can't recall if 'twas he or his wife, kin to Pres. Madison. He was a nephew to one of them. Two of that great-grandfather's daughters married two Mr. Barksdales. They produced statesmen and military officers, the latest of whom was Gen. Barksdale, Southern Confederacy.

To North Carolina again. Grandpa Donohoe left three or four sons, one Colonel Saunders Donohoe while stationed, I think, at Pensacola with the army, either during or after the War of 1812. The circumstance is sure, I forget when, but our great uncle, Col. Donohoe was shot by a drunken soldier whose arrest he had ordered.

Dixon Donohoe, Congressman from Caswell, N.C. died young.

Col. Archie Donohoe (Note: Name should be Thomas) who served in N.C., I forget what war, left a family at Milton, N.C. 'Twas his son, who, at Grandma

Donohoe's death inherited Major Archie Donohoe's (name should be Thomas) landed estate. Donohoes, who were Irish, came over before Revolution.

Of Grandma Donohoe's family, she was Miss Keziah Saunders, a Scoth family, vastly rich and stingy, but produced some important characters, notably Romulus Saunders, Congressman since I can recollect, for many terms and minister to several European powers—I think France and Spain. He visited Grandma Donohoe in my childhood. She was his aunt. He completed the claims she had on government as a Major's widow.

You see, by calling on me for tales of ancestry, you let loose a sluice that will well night drown you, but all the same, I am thankful for this privilege.

Yours, Caddie,
(Mrs.) Adaline Drake

Call on me any time. God bless you. I possess slightly the Seer's privileges. He does bless you—have you any conception to what extent? I believe you have.

(Coloney Armistead Watling referred to in this letter, was born in Gloucester County, Virginia, December 27, 1730, and lived later in Halifax County, Virginia, where he died 1803. He was a member of the King's Council of Virginia, 1764. He, with his three sons, Captain John, Captain Paul and Rowland (of the Navy) were soldiers of the Revolution from Halifax County, Virginia. His daughter, referred to in this letter, was Elizabeth (Betsy) Watlington, who was married in 1782 to Peter Barksdale, son of Nathaniel Barksdale, who came from England to Virginia about 1770.)

The Ancestry of Edward West of Lexington, Kentucky, 1757-1827

By Mabel Van Dyke Baer

Important as was Edward West, silversmith and steamboat inventor, of Lexington, Kentucky, it has been printed inaccurately in several important publications that he was the son of the Reverend Dr. William West of Baltimore, Maryland.[1]

To clear the way for a solid foundation in fact there follows a transcript of the family Bible of the Reverend Dr. William West, rector of St. Paul's Episcopal Church in Baltimore, Maryland, from 1779-1791.[2] The Bible was owned by Miss Jean Rumsey, copied by Miss Victoria Gittings and deposited in the library of the Maryland Historical Society, Baltimore, Maryland, in October, 1931, by Dr. J. Hall Pleasants. Additional material which evidently was added to the original record is shown in parentheses.

Family Bible of the Reverend Dr. William West, 1737-1791
Doctor James Walker was born at Peterhead (Scotland), May 11th, Anno 1705, and died near Baltimore Town, January 14th 1759. On the 26th of August 1731, he married Susanna Gardner who was born in Maryland, March 12th 1715.

Hugh West (son of John West and Ann Harris) was born March 18th A. D. 1705, and died Aug. the 25th 1754.
On the 29th of Dec. 1725, he married Sybil Harrison (dau. of Captain Wm. Harrison and Sarah Halley, his wife) who was born the 3rd of Febr'y 1705, and died May 27th 1787, about 4 o'clock on Sunday morning.

---

[1] Lewis Collins, *History of Kentucky* . . . (Louisville: John P. Morton and Co., 1924), I, 620; George W. Ranck, *History of Lexington, Kentucky* (Cincinnati: Robert Clarke and Co., 1872), pp. 145, 184; Letta Brock Stone, *The West Family Register* (Washington, D. C.: W. F. Roberts Co., Inc., 1928), pp. 328-329. Mrs. Stone expressed doubt as to the parentage of Edward West, Jr., in this work and later discovered the true record of Edward West's father and mother.

[2] Frederick Ward Kates, *Bridge Across Four Centuries: The Clergy of St. Paul's Parish, Baltimore, Maryland, 1692-1957* (Baltimore: St. Paul's Parish, 1957.)

William West (the 4th son of Hugh West and Sybil his wife) was born Aug. 17th 1737.

Susanna Walker (the 4th child of James Walker and Susanna, his wife) was born Febr'y 26th 1738.

William West was mar. to Susanna Walker, April 26th 1768.

George William West (the first child of William West and Susanna, his wife) was born Jan. 22nd 1770, in the Parish of St. Andrews, in St. Mary's County, Md.

Margaret West (dau. of Wm. and Susanna West) was born July 9th 1773, in the Parish of St. Margaret's, Westminster, in Anne Arundel County, Md.

Sybil West their daughter was born Aug. 4th 1774 at 1 o'clock P.M. in Harford County, Md.

Susanna West, their daughter, was born Aug. 4th 1774 at 5 o'clock P.M. and died the 20th of the same month.

John West, their son, was born April 24th 1780, and died Aug. 6th following in Baltimore Town.

Susanna West, the valuable and beloved wife of Wm. West, died in Baltimore Town, July 13th 1787, and is buried on the South End of the Chancel of St. Paul's Church.

The Rev. Dr. Wm. West died in Baltimore Town, March 30th, 1791, and is buried in his Vault in St. Paul's Church.

Mr. George William West, son of the Reverend Dr. Wm. West, died August 1st, 1795, in the 26th year of his age, and is buried in the family vault in St. Paul's Church.

Sibyl West, daughter of Hugh West and Elizabeth, his wife, was born October 21st 1762.

John Beale Howard, Junr. and Margaret West were married Sept. 26th 1796.

The parish register of St. Paul's Church, Volume 1, 1710-1808, records the burial rites of the Reverend Doctor William

West, Rector, on March 30, 1791.[3] Dr. West's will, dated March 29, 1791, filed in the City of Baltimore, mentions his children Margaret West and Sibyl West, as well as his son George William West, who was named his executor.[4]

There is no reference in the Bible or the parish register indicating that the Reverend Dr. William West had a son named Edward.

Edward West, Jr., silversmith and inventor, who was born in 1757, and figured so prominently in Lexington, Kentucky, from 1785, was the son of Edward West, Sr., and his wife Elizabeth Mills of Fairfax County, Virginia, whose marriage on October 6, 1752, is recorded in the Overwharton Parish Register, Stafford County, Virginia.[5] Edward West, Sr., gunsmith, left Fredericksburg, Virginia, in 1784, and settled in Georgetown, Kentucky, then in Woodford County.[6] In 1785, a year later, Edward West, Jr., arrived in Lexington, Fayette County, Kentucky, and in 1788 set up a silversmith shop on High Street. By 1793, he had invented his steamboat. In 1799, he and his wife Sarah conveyed a lot in Lexington to the German Lutheran Church for a place of worship and a burying ground.[7]

The will dated December 5, 1791, of Edward West, Sr., of Woodford County, Kentucky, which was then in Virginia, mentions his son Edward West. The entire transcript of the will follows:

---

[3] A copy of this register is in the Maryland Historical Society Library, Baltimore, Maryland.

[4] Baltimore County, Maryland, Will Book No. 4, p. 541.

[5] William F. Boucher, *Overwharton Parish Register, 1720 to 1760: Old Stafford County* (Washington, D. C.: The Saxton Printing Co., 1899), p. 189.

[6] B. O. Gaines, *History of Scott County, Kentucky* [Georgetown, Ky.: B. O. Gaines Printery] 1905, II, 236. Edward West is here described as the uncle of Captain Lynn West, of the War of 1812, who was the son of James West. Note that Woodford County was formed in 1788, from Fayette County, and that Scott County was formed in 1792, from Woodford County.

[7] Charles R. Staples, *History of Pioneer Lexington (Kentucky), 1799-1806* (Lexington, Ky.: Transylvania Press, 1939), pp. 37, 55, 172, 178, 281. (This work includes references to Fayette County, Kentucky, District Court Book B, p. 465; Fielding Bradford's interview with Draper, MSS 13 CC 211.)

Woodford County
Kentucky

Will Book A, pp. 51, 52
December 5, 1791

    I, Edward West of Woodford County and state of Virginia being weak of body but sound in memory and understanding do make this my last Will and testament, First my will and desire is that all my just debts be first paid out of my estate by my Executors which shall be hereafter appointed, Secondly I give to my son and daughter, Edward West and Betsy Gunnins, five shillings each of my personal estate as they have received a proportionable part formerly and each of them an equal part of the said with the other children to them and their heir forever; Thirdly I give and bequeathe to my beloved wife Elizabeth West and my sons William West, John West, Thomas West, Lewis West and James West and my daughters Polly West, Peggy West and Sally West all the rest of my estate both real and personal to be equally divided amongst them to them and their heirs forever, my son William West is to have the lands obtained by a warrant for twelve hundred and nine acres and number 11828 which is in my name but was purchased with said William West money and is now a part of my estate, therefore it is not to be charged in his properties, my son Thomas West hath received of my estate to the amount of seventy pounds, Beside Bond to be collected to a considerable amount and my desire is that my son Thomas West is to be charged with the seventy pounds aforementioned in his proposition of my estate so that he may have an equal part with the others and no more, Also my Son John West hath property in his hand to a considerable amount which is part of my estate which he is to account with my executors for, my desire is that my estate shall be kept together as long as it may be convenient others divided, And lastly I nominate and appoint my son William West and Thomas Martin my executors, In witness whereof I have hereunto set my hand and seal this fifth day of December in the year of our Lord one thousand seven hundred and ninity one.

Signed in the presence of   his
James Martin   Edward x West   (Seal)
Adam Johnston   mark

Woodford County   April Court 1792

The last Will and testament of Edward West deceased was produced in Court proved by the oaths of James Martin and Adam Johnston two subscribing witness thereto and ordered to be recorded. And on the motion of William Wills West and Thomas Martin the executors therein named, who made oath thereto according to law and together with John Grant and James Martin their securities entered into and acknowledged bond in the penalty of eight hundred pounds conditioned as the law directs certificate is granted them for obtaining a probate thereof in due form.

Teste Cave Johnson   CCJ

The will of John West of Stafford County, Virginia, dated November 4, 1774, establishes him as the father of Edward West, Sr., of Fredericksburg, Virginia, and Georgetown, Kentucky, and the grandfather of Edward West, Jr., of Lexington, Kentucky. John West's wife was Dorothy whose maiden name is unknown. The will is recorded on page 411 of Will Book M, 1729-1748, of Stafford County, Virginia, which was lost for many years.

Mr. Charles Arthur Hoppin tells an interesting story about the lost Will Book M.[8] He relates that the book fell into the hands of a Union soldier in 1862, during a Civil War engagement in Stafford County, Virginia, and, probably because it contained two wills of members of the Washington family, those of John Washington and Townshend Washington, was preserved rather than abandoned and scattered as were other early will books of the Stafford Court house taken at this time. Will Book M passed from hand to hand until by 1908 it was in possession of the commanding officer of the Veteran Zouaves of Elizabeth, New Jersey.

By 1926, the book was in the custody of a person "whose identity cannot be disclosed other than by himself and at his own time and pleasure." Mr. Hoppin visited this anonymous person and recommended to him that the volume be restored to the Commonwealth of Virginia. Mr. Hoppin expressed his expectation that the restoration would take place by the end of 1926. This expectation was realized by the return of Will Book M to the Stafford County Court by the Union Historical Society of Elizabeth, New Jersey. A photostatic copy of the book was made on February 28, 1927, and deposited in the Virginia State Library, Richmond, Virginia.[9]

Thus, it is possible to print the following copy of the will of John West of Stafford County, Virginia, dated November 4,

[8] Charles Arthur Hoppin, "The Lost Will Book, 1730-1748, of Stafford County," *Tyler's Quarterly Historical and Genealogical Magazine*, VIII (1926), 111-117.

[9] Mr. John W. Dudley, Assistant Archivist, The Virginia State Library, Richmond, advised the writer on April 9, 1959, that this is the only instance where a volume referred to by "O.G.I." (Old general Index) in Embrey's index to Stafford County records has been found.

1744, as well as its proof by Dorothy West, his widow and executrix, and the inventory of his estate, which are on pages 411, 412 and 425 of "lost" Will Book M.

Stafford County Will Book M, p. 411, 412
Virginia November 4, 1744

In the Name of God Amen I—John West of the County of Stafford being sick and weak in body but of sound & perfect memory thanks be given to God for the same and knowing it is appointed for all men . . . to die Do make and Ordain this my last will and Testament in manner and form following revoking all wills by me at any time heretofore made. Impr my precious and Immortal soul I give & . . . into the hands of God that gave it not doubting but that the merits and passion of my blessed Saviour and Redeemer to meet with joyful resurrection and touching what worldly Estate it hath pleased God of Infinite Mercey & Goodness to bless me withal I give and devise in the following manner.

Item I give and bequeathe unto my Dear and loving wife Dorothy the use of my whole Estate during that in she remains my widow for the support of herself and Children on this restriction and proviso that she pay my Children their respective Legacies not here bequeathed as they retain their respective ages but it is my desire if my said wife should marry then only to be Entitled to the third of my Estate, only my Negro man Harry I give and bequeath to my said wife and to her heirs and assigns forever.

Item I give and bequeath to my four sons Edward John William & James West my Negro woman Jenny and her now and future Increase to be equally divided among them as they respectively Attain their several Ages and so continually in Equal portion afterwards what Increase the said Jenny shall leave to them & their Heirs forever.

Item I give and bequeath two hundred Acres of land lying in Prince William County bought of William Cockrill to my sons Edwd and John West to be Equally divided between them and the Heirs of their bodies Lawfully begotten and for want of such Heirs to my sons William & James and those Heirs of their bodies

Lawfully begotten & for want of Such then to my right Heirs forever.

As to the residue of my Estate of what kind soever I desire that after my wife's decease or Marriage may be Equally divided among my four children above named Edward John William & James West and their Heirs forever and in case of their Deaths then to the Survivour or survivors in Equal portions as near as may be allotted in Quantity and Quality allowing my said Wife the use thereof during her life or widowhood as before exprest & intended under the above & said limitations who I appointing as whole & sole Exr desiring my estate may and be Appraised.

In Witness whereof I have hereunto set my hand and Seal this 4th day of Novr 1744.

His
Signed John (I W) West (Seal)
Mark

Sealed and published as the last will and testament in presence of us

Rogers Will Mills
Thomas West

At a Court for Stafford County Feby. the 12th 1744—The within last will and Testament of John West decd was presented into Court by Dorothy West the Exr therein named who made Oath thereto according to Law and being proved by the Oaths of the witnesses as thereto subscribed is admitted to record and on motion of the sd. Exr and she having complied with what is usual in such Cases Cert. is granted her for obtaining a Probate thereof in due form.

Teste   H. Tyler Cl. Ct.

Many words in the original inventory are illegible and are indicated by "..." in the following transcript.

Stafford County   Will Book M, p. 425
Virginia   April 10, 1745 Court

An Inventory of the Estate which belonged to John West late of Stafford County ordered at the time of his Death as followoth, viz. One Featherbed and furniture. 2 old beds and their furniture. A Gun and box. Iron and heaters ... 12 plates pewter ... 3 Iron potts & potthook, a kettle and a skellott. a pair of ... & crossed legged table ... of coopers tools. carpenters tools and ... 5 flagg chairs. a lott of ... furniture and two other. saddles and outside saddle. A Wine Pipe. 2 hogsheds or water casks & 5 small casks & 2 Bibles & 2 Testaments. 2 Testaments & 2 psalters & one old small Bible and Spire Morter & Pestle. a looking glass, vinegar cruet. a pair of stillards. a white servant Edward two years to serve. a negro woman and negro child about 2 years old. & ... wearing apparrell. 3 cross hogsheds of Tobo. about 850 Tobo, each. 17 barrells Corn. 10 bushels wheat. 2 old horses. 2 young do & 2 young mares. 10 head of sheep. 25 head of cattle. 32 head of hoggs. 10 gees. 300 gallons of cyder. 2 narrow axes. 2 old grubing hoes. 2 old weeding hoes. 2 ploughs old 2 narrow hoes one frying pan a quart tankard 2 house Iron & 2 Potts 2 ton gallon & Do 2 iron candle stands. Hive of bees three sickels & lanthorn. Tin ... and one pewter funnel pair sheep shares. 3 doz bottle. 1 doz. pewter spoons. 6 ... of leather a parsel of piggins. Pails Tubs baskets and other old ...

10 April 1745   Dorothy West   (Seal)

At a court held for Stafford County April the 10th 1745. This inventory of the Estate of John West dec'd being ... is admitted to record.

                                    Test. H. Tyler Clk. Ct.

Edward West, Jr., died August 23, 1827, at 70 years of age, in Lexington, Kentucky. His wife Sarah, daughter of Samuel Brown and Maria Creed, had died three years before him on February 7, 1824, at the age of 63 years. They were first buried in the garden of their home on High Street and then the bodies were removed to the Presbyterian Cemetery in Lexington.[10] They had twelve children:

Jane, married August 25, 1806

John B.

Catherine, married July 11, 1809, Dr. Arthur Campbell

William Edward, born 1788, died 1857, unmarried

Maria Creed, married October 4, 1810, Samuel Price

Edward, died at the age of 19 years

Thomas Lewis, died April 14, 1806, at the age of 10 years

Sarah Brown, married May, 1818, Robert Woods

Hannohretta, married March 1, 1814, Moses Norvell

Eliza Mills, married November 15, 1818, Simon Bradford

Benjamin Franklin, unmarried

Patterson Bain, unmarried

William Edward West, fourth child of Edward West, Jr., became a celebrated painter, famous for his portrait of Lord Byron. Among his portraits was one of his father, Edward West, Jr.

[10] Margaret M. Bridwell, "Edward West, Silversmith and Inventor," *The Filson Club History Quarterly*, XXI (1947), 301 *et seq.;* Dr. W. R. Jillson, "Samuel D. McCullough's Reminiscences of Lexington," *Register of the Kentucky Historical Society*, XXVII (1929), 420-421; *ibid.*, XXXVI (1938), 163-165, 169, 173, 175, contains the record of marriages of a number of Edward West's children, compiled by G. Glenn Clift.

THE WHITTINGTON FAMILY*

By MRS. M. C. DARNELL
Frankfort, Kentucky

William Whittington (1759-1824) and his brothers, Joshua and Littleton Whittington, came from Maryland about 1790 and settled in Woodford County, Kentucky. William was appointed in 1795 as one of the trustees of Versailles, but soon afterward he removed to his farm at Clifton, on the Kentucky River.

In an old leather bound book, which is still treasured by his descendants, he recorded from time to time various accounts and events of interest, and after his death these records were continued by members of his family.

In 1799-1801, inclusive, are recorded the following names of his neighbors in sundry transactions: John Edwards, Jr.; Bela Cropper; Capt. Anthony Thompson; Thomas Hinton, Jr.; Enos Miles; Moses Edwards; Isaac Johnson; William Semple; Isaac Johnson, Jr.; Roderick Perry; Richard Shipp; Rosanna Mitchell; Joshua Tull; John Edwards, Jr.

William Whittington married Lucy Long, one of the heroines who carried water to the men in the fort at Bryan's Station. In the winter of 1806 William and Lucy rode horseback to Maryland, returning in the spring with a new baby—Attalanta. Of this visit he wrote:

"Being with my wife in Somerset County on the Eastern Shore of Maryland in the Winter & Spring of the year 1806, a curiosity which I had a long time prompted me to enquire into the Ancestry and present State of our family as springing from Old Col. William which I found to be as herein arranged—[Chart follows]

"This man was a native of some part of England and came over to America in early times, settled first in [Northampton] County, Virginia, near Cherry Stones, from thence he moved to Indian Town, Worcester County, Maryland, where he ended his days. He had Five wives & Large possessions of land and other property. Remarkable for his stature, being, it is said, seven feet high, and is said to have been so small when he was born that curiosity prompted them to put him in a pottle measure [two-quart] and shut the lid down on him. His Religious profession was presbyterial." (Note: The word *presbyterial* is a form of *presbyterian*, now rare.)

William was in error in stating that Col. William was a native of England, as it was Col. William's father, Captin William Whittington, who was the immigrant. One record says he came from Derbyshire, in which the town of Whittington is located; and another links him with Nottingham. He was in Northampton County, Virginia, in 1640, and held several political offices.

*Excerpted from "William Whittington's Book," by Mrs. M. C. Darnell, *The Register of the Kentucky Historical Society*, Vol. 47 (Oct. 1949), 314-324.

Colonel William divided his time between Virginia and Maryland, being in the Maryland Assembly in 1692, and a Major in Accomac, Virginia, in 1693. He did have five wives; but the task of assigning his children to their various mothers, like proving the family's claim of descent from the famous owner of the cat, is beyond the scope of this writer.

Some time later William wrote in his book:

"Woodford County, State of Kentucky, 19th August, 1808. I, William Whittington, aged 49 years, two months & a few days, and having cause to fear that I am Rather declining than advancing in Religious attainments, and being very uneasy under my present situation in that Respect, have determined to take a serious view of my past life to ascertain, if possible, whether I ever have been in possession of that Inestimable Jewel, the life of God in my soul, and if so to search for and ascertain the causes why I have advanced no further and why I am subject to so many declentions. And may the God of all Grace whose Gracious Mercies I certainly have often experienced assist me in the undertaking and bring me to a Right Conclusion in this great and weighty matter.

"I was born in Somerset County, then the province but now the state of Maryland. My parents as far as I know were at that time possessors of Religion. My mother was Raised in the Established Church, but after marrying with my Father, became, I believe, united with him to Presbyterian Church. I was their second child and first son. My Mother, as I have been informed, took great pains to teach me many things as soon as I was able to speak, all which I remember nothing of. At 6 or 7 years old I was sent to school, which circumstance seems to form the first regular succession of ideas my memory retains, for altho I remember several things prior to this time they seem like points to stand alone— I neither know what went before or followed after. I soon attained Reading and used to wonder much about the Garden of Eden, the land of Canaan & those things related in the beginning of the Bible. Rather concluding they were not of this world, and altho at this time I had some knowledge of God and of Jesus Christ, I know not when or how these ideas took place in my mind. I tho well recollect that about this time or perhaps very shortly after I read a little book which gave an account of a little girl who was much devoted to God and expressed great love to her Saviour. Methought I would desire to be like her, and altho I believe I had similar desires and thoughts of this nature long before this time, I cannot trace them to any particular point. But now they seemed at least to revive and have left, I believe, the first lasting impression now in my recollection. Perhaps it was shortly after this that I heard the first sermon preached that I recollect of. It was the State minister of the parish, Mr. Sloan.

"A young woman, one of my cousins by my Mother, came by my Father's one Sunday morning and took me to church with her. She paid great attention to me and took me into the pew with her, where I paid great attention to all that passed. My mind being also at this time perfectly free from all Religious prejudice and not being able or indeed rather not having anything in me that might incline me to suspect the purity of the motives or sincerity of either minister or people, I thought all I heard and saw was excellent. My mind and feelings went out spontaneously in a manner with all the excellent words that were there spoken or sung."

His spiritual zeal never abated, and in 1832 several of his children and their neighbors in the Clifton area organized a little Presbyterian church, Macedonia, which, though eventually merged with another congregation, continues in service to this day.

Names appearing in 1813 were: Aaron Darnell; Robert D. Gale; John Pattie; John Tull; Littleton Whittington; Thomas Hughes; Jacob Semple; Edward Carr; William Brightwell; Michael Mitchell; Fred Mitchell; a transaction involving Joshua Whittington and his son Thomas; Mr. Vance of Versailles, Mr. Jesse and Reuben Long. In 1817, Benjamin Davis to William Hawkins at Southy and Littleton Whittington's.

After William Whittington's death, some of the family went to Newcastle, Henry County, Kentucky.

In 1826 are mentioned Isaac Miles and Sam C. Whittington; and in 1827 (or 1837), peach seed from R. R. Darnell, and from Newcastle, Versailles and Shelbyville, and "apple seedlings to be graffed" by W. H. Whittington.

Mentioned in 1834–1837, inclusive, are: Joseph Major; George Shealy; Isaac Johnson; Anderson Brown; Villore Gale; Isaac Beauchamp; Andrew Johnson; Andrew Hearn; Samuel Miles; Alex Crockett; R. P. Blackwell; James Samuel; Wm. Boler (Boulware?); I. Hawkins; Thos. Parker; Jno. Lillard; Wm. Harper; F. Edwards; Robt. Gaines; R. P. Gaines; Wm. Mitchell; Barr & Whittington; B. F. Hawkins; B. Giltner; W. Stewart; N. Harris; Patrick Cogghill; Humphrey M. Whittington.

William and Lucy Long Whittington had fifteen children, and their education presented a problem. In 1830 there was a bill from Robert Alexander to Lucy for Henry's schooling, $3.00; "John Coons, do.; Edward Evans and Curran Cox, do." In 1833 she paid James McCasland $7.57 for schooling in Newcastle; in 1835, William King for schooling; in 1839 John L. Moore on account, and J. Murphrey for schooling.

In the following chart the records are presented for the most part as they appear in the book. No attempt has been made to list children in the order of birth, or to carry the lines beyond the sixth generation.

All information outside of family records is marked ( )°.

All surnames are *Whittington* unless given otherwise.
(1. Capt. William Whittington, b 1616 or 1621, d 1659, m first Mary ....;
second Susane ...., by whom he had:
    2a Ursula, m Col. Edmund Scarborough
    Capt. Wm. Whittington m third Elizabeth Weston. Issue:)°
    2b—Col. William Whittington (1650–1720, m first Tabitha Smart; second Esther Littleton; third Attalanta Toft Osborne; fourth Tannah Hopkins; fifth Elizabeth .... Issue:
        3a—Tabitha, m Edmund Custis
        3b—Smart, died young)°
        3c—William (1681 or 1692–1756)° m Elizabeth Taylor
            4a—William m Betty Martin
                5a—William m Mary Henry
                      6a—William m Betty Handy
                      6b—John, died single
            4b—Esther m .... Gibbons
            4c—Southey m Ann Wishart
                5a—Betsy m John Nichols—several children
                5b—Littleton died abroad without issue
                5c—Hannah m George Blake—no children
                5d—George, single as yet
                5e—Gertrude m Thomas Abbott—left some children
                5f—Arthur m ...., has some children
            4d—Betty m .... Draper (Ardis)°
            4e—Joshua m Betty Nairne
                5a—Esther
                5b—William m .... Bowman
                      6a—Matthew
                5c—Betty
                5d—Mary
        3d—Esther m (first William Skirven)° Isaac Morris
        3e—Hannah m .... Huff (Edmond Hough)°
        3f—Atlanta (b 1700)° m Steven White
        3g—Southy, born 1694 (surveyor for Somerset County in 1720)° m Mary Fossett
            4a—William Fitz—died young
            4b—Littleton—died single
            4c—Southy m Esther Nairne
                5a—Mary m Robert Marshall
                      6a—Robert Nairne Marshall
                      6b—Betty Marshall
                      6c—Esther Marshall

            6d—Mary Marshall
        5b—Jeanett—died single (1803)°
        5c—Esther m L. Selby
        5d—Southey m first Mary Turpin
            6a—Maria
            6b—Mary
        5d—Southey m second M. Coulbourn (1804)°
            6c—Southey Fossett (to New Jersey)°
        5e—Sally m A. Gillett
        5f—Betty m E.
        5g—Leah m T. Long
        5h—Katherine m J. Powell
        5i—John m Bettie Drummond
            6a—John Nairne
            6b—Sarah Drummond
            6c—Eliza
4d—Hannah m J. Sterling (m John Cox)°
4e—Mary m .... Brinkley
4f—Esther m A. Sterling
4g—Isaac (b 1730)° m Elizabeth Wishart—both natives of Maryland. Issue:
    5a—Hannah, b 1756, m Henry Handy
        6a—William Handy
        6b—Peggy Handy
        6c—Nancy Handy
        6d—Betty Handy
        6e—Henry Handy
        6f—Charlotte Handy
        6g—James Handy
        6h—Sarah Handy
        6i—Joshua Handy
        6j—John Handy
    5b—Ann m William Cox—no issue
    5c—William, 1759–1824, m Lucy Long in Woodford County, Kentucky, 1791
        6a—Littleton m Frances Glenn, Woodford Co., 1819, and went to Shelby County, Kentucky
        6b—Southey—in Kentucky Legislature, 1830
        6c—Mary m James McCasland, of Henry Co., Ky.
        6d—Elizabeth m Sanford Owen, Henry Co., Ky., 1841

  6e—Anna m Handy T. Davis, 1827, went to Indiana
  6f—John Long 1801-1844
  6g—James, 1802-1833
  6h—Rev. Wm. Handy, 1804-1855, minister Christian Church, m first Adelia Kavanaugh, 1839; second Ann Kavanaugh, 1847. His daughter Mary was Lady Principal at Daughters College, Harrodsburg, Ky.
  6i—Attalanta, 1806-1878, m Randolph Railey Darnell, Woodford Co., 1827. They were ancestors of the Darnell family in Frankfort.
  6j—Isaac Stevenson m Mary Edwards, Woodford Co. 1833
  6k—Hannah Handy m Anderson Brown
  6l—Samuel Shannon, 1812-1840
  6m—Hervey m Ann M. Storey, Clay Co., Mo., 1835. Later was postmaster at Plattsburg, Mo., though the mail came only once a week.
  6n—Jemima m Richard S. H. Taylor, Henry Co., Ky., 1842. They went to Missouri.
  6o—Henry Haynes, 1820-1845
5d—James m Sarah Coulbourn (1799)°
  6a—Mary—died young
  6b—Nancy—died young
  6c—Isaac m Miss Coulbourn—several children
    6d—James—drowned in Green River, Kentucky
  6e—William m Sarah Polk—some children
  6f—Thomas m Rebecca Polk—some children
5e—Thomas Wishart (1763-1818)° m Sarah Conner (in 1789)°
  6a—Joshua
  6b—John
  6c—Elijah
  6d—Betty
  6e—William
  6f—Henry
5f—Joshua (b 1765)° m Mary Marshall, Woodford

Co., Ky., 1791. They probably went to Missouri about 1812.
- 6a—Fanny
- 6b—Thomas (m Lucy Brittenham, Woodford Co., 1819)°
- 6c—Betty
- 6d—Mary
- 6e—Isaac
- 6f—Jane
- 6g—Anna
- 6h—Charlotte (m W. H. Cummins)°
- 6i—Humphrey M., m Elizabeth Burchfield, Franklin County, Kentucky, 1840.
- (6j—Kate m James Dearing)°

5g—Littleton m Sarah Hearn, Woodford Co., Ky., 1795
- 6a—Dr. William Wishart m Ann Handy
- 6b—Isaac m Matilda Perry, Woodford Co., 1828
- 6c—Milcah m James Smith, Woodford Co., 1835
- 6d—Jane m Col Samuel S. Graham
- 6e—Betsy m Warren Hearn, Woodford Co., 1829
- 6f—James m Margaret Lillard, Anderson Co., Ky., 1831
- 6g—Nancy
- 6h—Caroline m Richard S. H. Taylor, Woodford Co. 1833
- 6i—Edna
- 6j—Edward Henry m Sarah Cordelia Hawkins, 1833

4h—Stevenson m Sarah Coulbourn
- 5a—Nancy m .... Holland—one child
- 5b—William m .... Ennolds
- 5c—Sarah m J. Hudson—some children
- 5d—Mary m J. Coulbourn
- 5e—Stevenson—died single

4i—William (d 1819)° m Priscilla Polk (1740-1834)°
- 5a—Betty m (Mitchell)° Russam
- 5b—Mary m first Dr. W. Strawbridge; second W. Allen; third John Porter
- 5c—Isaac m .... Foster
- 5d—William—died single

    5e—Peggy m William Porter (came to Woodford Co., Ky.)°
    5f—Eleanor m J. Harper
    5g—James (m .... Lawson, 11 children)°
  (4j—Tabitha
  4k—Priscilla
  4l—Sarah m Benjamin Polk, born 1738; large family, including
    5+—Sally Polk m John Drummond Whittington
      6a—Southey
      6b—Edward
      6c—Hester)°
(2c—Elizabeth, born 1659, m Thomas Johnson
  3a—Whittington Johnson m Alice Todd)°

BIBLIOGRAPHY

Maryland Calendar of Wills, 8 vols., 1635-1743, Baldwin, 1928
County Court Note Book, 10 vols., 1921-1931, Bethesda, Maryland
Northampton County Records: Vol. I, p. 148; Vol. II, p. 51; Vol. III, p. 89
Ancestral Records & Portraits, a compilation from the Archives of Chapter I, The Colonial Dames of America, Vol. I
Collins' History of Kentucky, 2 volumes
Railey's History of Woodford County
Polk Family, by W. H. Polk, Lexington, Kentucky, 1912
Notes of Henry I. Kirk, Maryland genealogist.

BIOGRAPHICAL SKETCH OF THE WOOD FAMILY

OF MASON COUNTY, KY.

By Lucy Coleman Lee.

George Wood, the progenitor of the family in Mason county, came from Roxborough, or Philadelphia, Pennsylvania. He was the son of Andrew Wood and Elizabeth Keyser. His wife was Elizabeth Whiteman.

The Woods, Whitemans and Keysers all came originally from Amsterdam, Holland, and settled in or near Philadelphia, previous to the year 1700; we do not know the exact date of the settlement of the Woods and Whitemans in that place, but Dirck Keyser came in 1668.

Andrew Wood, of Roxborough, married Elizabeth Keyser, of Germantown, November 16th, 1752. The record says of Philadelphia county.

Their children were:

1. George Wood, born November 29th, 1753. Married May 8th, 1776. Died August 22d, 1832.

Elizabeth Whiteman, born October 10th, 1755; died August 6th, 1807. George Wood married a second time, in 1808, a widow, Ann Corwin.

2. Michael Wood, born October 2d, 1755.

3. Mary Wood, born November 25th, 1757.

4. Andrew Wood, born January 11th, 1760.

5. Elizabeth Wood, born February 12th, 1762.

6. John Wood, born April 12th, 1765.

7. Hannah Wood, born July 16th, 1767. Married, first, a Rittenhouse; second, Lane.

8. Ann Wood, born March 22d, 1772.

Children of George Wood and Elizabeth Whiteman were:

1. Andrew Wood, born March 11th, 1777; died March 2d, 1860; married Matilda Fox, December 16th, 1810.

2. Hester Wood, born November 13th, 1778. Married William Ritchie, October 18th, 1796.

3. Elizabeth Wood, born November 12th, 1780. Married Capt. Benjamin Bayless, September 15th, 1798.

4. Charles Wood, born September 26th, 1782. Married Achsah Taylor, November 27th, 1814.

5. Dolly Wood, born December 14th, 1786. Married Ezekiel Forman, February 18th, 1808.

6. David Wood, born April 13th, 1789. Married, first, Emma Scudder; second, Lucretia Stull.

7. Benjamin W. Wood, born May 18th, 1791. Married Scota Worthington, February 27th, 1816.

8. Catherine Wood, born August 6th, 1793. Married William Little.

9. Ann Wood, born October 18th, 1795. Married Dr. Wilson Coburn.

10. William R. Wood, born March 10th, 1798. Married Mary Coburn, August 7th, 1822.

George Wood was a Matross (artillery man), in Capt. Andrew Summers' company, commanded by Col. John Eyre. He enlisted September 12th, 1777, and this company was mustered into the service of the United States September 15th, 1777. Authority,—13, Pennsylvania archives, second series, page 650. An aunt who is now upwards of eighty, remembers her grandfather, George Wood,confirms the fact of his having served in the American Revolution. She remembers having attended his funeral.

I have, on the authority of one who made a study of genealogy, the origin of names and of people, that the Woods were of English descent; they were originally from London, and were silk merchants, and traded between London and Amsterdam. One of them located there, married a dutch woman, and was the progenitor of the family that afterwards came to Pennsylvania.

The four oldest children of George Wood and Elizabeth Whiteman, Andrew, Hester, Elizabeth and Charles, were born in Pennsylvania.

In 1786, George Wood, and family, emigrated to Kentucky, and located in the town of Washington, there on the 14th of December of that year, Dolly Wood was born. She had the distinction of being the first white child born at that place.

The descendants of George Wood are very numerous, and while not a great many of them have attained great distinction, there have been preachers of note, physicians, lawyers, and many prosperous citizens, beloved and respected.

They are scattered far and wide, and I believe, can be found in every State in the Union,but however far they roam, their hearts still turn to "Old Kentucky Home."

Record of the family of General Benjamin Whiteman, a soldier of the Revolution.

1. Martin Whiteman.
2. Wendell Whiteman.
3. Jacob Whiteman.
4. John Whiteman.

Remained in Pennsylvania; born 1751. Wounded in Battle of Germantown.

5. Benjamin Whiteman, born 1756. Married Catherine Davis, and came to Kentucky.

6. Catherine Whiteman, married Thomas Holloway, and remained in Pennsylvania.

7. Elizabeth Whiteman, born 1755. Married George Wood; came to Washington, Ky.

8. Mary, or Ann, Whiteman. Married Van Pelt; came to Lexington, Ky.

9. Hester Whiteman, married — Ferra, came to Fayette county, Ky.

11. Clarissa Whiteman; married Higbee; came to Lexington, Ky.

The name was Weidman, in Dutch, but, being Anglicised, became Whiteman. They, too, came from Holland,and located in Pennsylvania. We know that there are many descendants of these families in Pennsylvania, but for many years there has been no communication between them and the family in Kentucky. I have been unable to trace the families of Higbee and Van Pelt, but know some of the Farras, of Fayette, and some of the descendants of Catherine Holloway are living in this town, but none of them have given me any assistance in my research. Two nephews of Elizabeth Whiteman Wood, came to Mason county, but afterward located in Cincinnati, where they became prominent citizens. They were Benjamin and Lewis Whiteman. Their descendants are there still, and Benjamin Whiteman died two years ago, having attained a ripe old age.

The Keyser Family of Germantown, Pennsylvania.

Elizabeth Keyser, married Andrew Wood, November 16th, 1752. Her father was Dirck Keyser, born September 26th, 1701, died February 8th, 1756. Married 1725; Alitje (or Alice) DeNeus, born 1702; died October 1st, 1752.

Peter Keyser, of Germantown (Philadelphia), born in Amsterdam, Holland, 1676; died, 1724. Married September 4th, 1700, Margaret Souplis, who was born 1682; was living in 1724.

Dirck Keyser was born in Holland, settled in Germantown, Pennsylvania, in 1668; was married in Holland November 22d, 1668, to Elizabeth ter Wimple.

Dirck Gerritz Keyser, of Amsterdam, Holland, married Cornelia Govertz. Gerritz Keyser was the father of Dirck Gerritz Keyser, of Amsterdam. Dirck Keyser was a silk merchant, doing business in Printz Gracht, opposite Rees street, in Amsterdam. A Menonite, connected by family ties with the leading Menonites of that city, he arrived in Germantown, Pennsylvania, by way of New York, in 1668. Tradition has it, that he was a descendant of that Leonard Keyser, the friend of Martin Luther, who was burned to death at Scharding in 1527.

Long after coming to Germantown he wore a coat made of silk, which was a matter for disapproval, if not a subject for envy. His father was Dirck Gerritz Keyser, a manufacturer of Morocco. His grandfather was Gerritz Keyser. His mother was Cornelia, daughter of Tobias Govertz van den Wyngaert, one of the most noted of the early Menonite preachers, the learned author of a number of theological works, of whom there is a fine portrait by the famous Dutch engraver, A. Bootelingh.

When George Wood came with his family to Mason county, Washington was a small place, having that year been established as a town. There was no accommodations for strangers, but in those pioneer days, hospitality reigned in the breasts of the people, and they were ever ready to offer a shelter and the comforts of life, to the stranger within the gates. Arthur Fox had been married some time, to Mary Young, the daughter of Col. Richard Young, of Woodford county. They had built a home in Washington, quite an imposing residence for a new country. The shell of it is still standing at this writing. They opened their hearts to this homeless family, until a house could be provided for them, and there, on the fourteenth of December, 1786, the first white child was born in Washington (as I before stated), if not the first in Mason county, but this has been contradicted, though I know not upon what grounds. On the twenty-fourth of December, just ten days after the birth of Dolly Wood, Mrs. Fox gave birth to a daughter, the second white child born in Washington, she was Elizabeth Fox, and married Major Richard Graham, (Dolly Wood, was my great aunt, and Elizabeth Fox, my aunt, she was my Father's half sister.) Dolly Wood married Ezekiel Forman, and her descendants are very numerous, two of her sons became very distinguished Presbyterian preachers, one of them a missionary to India, where he accomplished more good than has ever been written or told. Five of his children are carrying on the work that he began in 1848.

As soon as it was feasible George Wood set about building a home. He purchased some ground on the west side of the Town, and built a two-story stone house, which stood near the place where the old Goggin house now stands. I can remember as a child, that it was pointed out to me, as the home of my great-grandfather, it was then in a state of dilapidation, it had a little *cork screw* stair way only wide enough for one person to come down at a time. My great aunt, Mrs. Ann Coburn, has told me that when she was married they had to come down single file, she ran ahead, and called back, come on Wils'e—she was very full of humor and fond of a joke, until the day of her death. They went to Cincinnati on a Bridal journey, on horseback, he carried his clothes in saddle bags, flung across his saddle, and she carried hers in a carpet bag hung on the pommel of her saddle. She lived to be ninety-six years of age, beloved by all who knew her, and a very beautiful old lady.

George Wood established a tan yard in Washington, which he and his sons, Andrew and Charles, carried on for many years. He evidently inherited his taste for the trade from his ancestor, Dirch Gerritz Keyser, whom we have already stated was a manufacturer of Morocco.

The country was still infested by Indians. One summer day when the men were some distance from home, at work in the woods, Andrew, Charles and Betsy (or Elizabeth,) were sent by their mother to take their dinner to them. After reaching a dense part of the forest they discovered a party of Indians following them and of course became very much alarmed, knowing the danger they were in, for the Indians frequently captured the children of settlers and carried them off, or perhaps killed them. Andrew, who was the oldest, a lad perhaps eleven or twelve years of age, displayed great courage and presence of mind, not letting his brother and sister see that he was frightened, constantly urging them on, saying run Betsy, run Charles, and to keep silence. The boys being swifter of foot than the little sister, out ran her; but presently they came to a large tree that had either fallen or been cut down with the foliage very thick and heavy. Betsy finding she could not keep up with with her brothers hid in the branches of the tree. When the boys reached the place where the men were at work, having dodged the Indians, who were nowhere to be seen, nor could they see anything of Betsy. They felt confident that the Indians had captured her. The men at once started in pursuit of them. As they came to the fallen tree, Betsy, who was very securely hidden, peeped through the leaves, and seeing her father followed by the other men, knew she was safe, and stepped from her hiding place. Then there was rejoicing over her safety. This story has been handed down from generation to generation. This same Betsy afterwards married Captain Benjamin Bayless. She was the great-grandmother of the gentleman to whom I am deeply indebted for a great deal of my data, enabling me to write this sketch. He has shown more interest, and treated me more courteously, than any one with whom I have corresponded on this subject. I refer to Mr. S. P. Cochran, of Dallas, Texas. He is a member of the Colonial Society of Pennsylvania, and has made many researches in that State, with the aid of a Genealogist of Philadelphia.

I remember, when a very small child, that I saw a sister of my great-grandfather; her name was Hannah; she married first a Rittenhouse, a member of that prominent family of Philadelphia; afterward she married a man named Lane, (my mother always called her aunt Lane, as did all the family). She was living with her nephew, David Wood, in Washington, and was very old, (when I saw her she was knitting).

From my childish view she seemed very old indeed, but I doubt if she really did attain to the age of some of her nieces.

Andrew Wood, the oldest son of George Wood and Elizabeth Whiteman, married Matilda, the youngest child of Arthur Fox and Mary Young. There is now but one of their children living, Mrs. Anna M. Metcalfe, of Azusa, California. She has in her possession a portrait of George Wood, our great-grandfather, which she inherited from her father.

Of the other children, there are four of David Wood's still living, three sons and a daughter. One of Catherine's, a daughter. Two of William's, a son and daughter, and three daughters of Charles Wood.

Charles Wood married Achsah Taylor. This is the branch of George Wood's family, in which I am especially interested, they being my grandparents.

Achsah Wood was the daughter of Robert Taylor and Jane Downey. Of Jane Downey we know nothing but the name, and that Robert Taylor married her in Philadelphia.

Robert Taylor was a younger son of an Irish nobleman; he with a brother came from their home in County Monahon, Ireland, to seek home and fortune in the new world. They, too, located in Philadelphia; the brother became dissatisfied and started to return to Ireland, but was lost at sea.

Robert Taylor afterward migrated to Kentucky and settled at Maysville, in Mason County. They had a large family of children, and many grand-children, among them some very distinguished people.

Achsah Taylor's relatives came frequently to visit her, after her marriage, which occurred in November, 1814. One of her father's sisters, Martha Taylor, married a nobleman named Moorhead, three of her sons came to America, and lived for a time in Cincinnati; two of them, Dr. John and Dr. Robert Moorhead, became very eminent as physicians in that city. Dr. John afterward inherited his father's title and estates and returned to Ireland. His descendants are still living at the ancestral home of the family, Ana McCarrig Castle in County Monahon.

Dr. Moorhead married a Philadelphia lady of wealth, beauty and position, he took her to Ireland where they lived in splendor.

One of my cousins has a photograph of Sir John Moorhead and wife, taken in London, presented to her by a great niece of Dr. Moorhead, Miss Annie Foster, whose father, Dr. Nat. Foster, was the son of Dr. Moorhead's sister. Dr. Foster was a distinguished physician of Cincinnati; his wife was Miss Josephine Lytle, a sister of General Lytle. Robert Taylor never returned to his native land, but lived and died in Kentucky. He and his wife are buried within twenty miles of Maysville. His older brother was heir to his father's title and estates, and his descendants are living there now, so far as we know. The Taylors were of English extraction, descended from Walter Tyler, or Watt the Tyler, who lived in the reign of Richard the Second, and was a leader of the Commons against the oppression of the nobles. He was murdered by one of the King's Esquires (Ralph Standish) who pretended to believe that Tyler had threatened the life of the King. The name is from the Norman French, De Teleres, or le Telier. During the religious persecutions in England the Taylor's, who were Protestants, fled to Ireland, where they had large possessions, and thus it was they became identified with the Irish people, and my great grandfather was known as an Irishman. My mother was the second daughter of Charles Wood and Achsah Taylor. She married Edward P. Lee, youngest son of General Henry Lee and Mary Young, of whom I have written a sketch, which has been published in the Register.

NOTE.

If there are any descendants of the family of Wood, Whiteman or Keyser living in Pennsylvania, who can give me any further information about any of them, I would be glad to have them correspond with me on the subject. I should like also to know more of the Taylors. It has been claimed by some members of the family that George Taylor, who was one of the signers of the Declaration of Independence, was of the same family, but I am confident that it is a mistake; he belonged to a different family, but their ancestry may have been the same.

THE WOOD FAMILY OF WOODLAWN, KENTUCKY

By EVELYN CRADY ADAMS

Jonathan Wood, progenitor of the Kentucky branch of his family, migrated from Frederick County, Maryland, to Nelson County, Kentucky, in 1796, in his fiftieth year. He, with his wife, Catherine Williams Wood, and eigth of their children, located on a plantation about four miles east of Bardstown. The land remained in the family for more than a century and a quarter, and estates in the vicinity are still owned and occupied by descendants. The village of Woodlawn commemorating the family name was founded in 1887 by Dr. Jonathan Clinton Wood and his wife, Ann Ferguson Wood, both of whom were Jonathan Wood's grandchildren.

This chronicle begins in 1735 when the 155-acre tract of land called Brotherhood was laid out in St. Mary's County, Maryland, for Jonathan Wood's father, Joseph Wood,[1] who is said to have been of Welsh descent. Joseph Wood may have been an immigrant and he may have been related to some of the forty-six members of the Wood family listed from 1633 as early Maryland settlers. The Wood name is among those appearing most frequently on the list. Many of their numerous land patents bore their name, such as, Wood's Addition, Wood's Conveniency, Wood's Discovery, Wood's Joy, Wood's Landing, Wood's Pleasure, Wood's Chance, Woods Design, Woods Gain and Woodland. When Brotherhood was resurveyed for Joseph Wood in 1742 the name was changed to Wood's Inclosure with one hundred and eighty-nine acres added. The location described as east of Gum Branch and north of the road from All Faith Church to Cool Springs would be in the present neighborhood of Mechanicsville and Charlotte Hall, the latter of which was first known as Ye Cool Springs of St. Mary's.[2]

Following the northwesterly tide of migration after Frederick Town was laid out, Joseph Wood moved over the Old Annapolis Road in 1746 to that part of Prince George's County which two years later became a portion of Frederick County. The picturesque rugged terrain of the section awaiting cultivation was referred to as "wild country". But Joseph Wood met adversities with courage and lived to see the French and Indian War and the Revolution. He, a yeoman, sought farming land near streams. In the spring of 1747 he acquired Wood's Lott, or Wood's Inclosure, of 126 acres in Conococheague Manor lying along the North Branch of the Linganore slightly east of present Unionville. Within a year his holdings exceeded fifteen hundred acres of rich creek bottom land and he continued to add other tracts one of which was Pollicy. From 1750 to

---
[1] Land Records, Annapolis, Md. LG, E, p. 335.
[2] Ibid. LG, B, p. 707.

1754 he sold more than a thousand acres some of which may have contained deposits of copper or iron commonly found in the section.[3]

The approximate location of Wood's Lott to the east of Unionville and north of the Liberty Road leading to Baltimore has been arrived at through the painstaking research of Dr. H. Hanford Hopkins, of Baltimore, in tracing the early landholdings of his ancestor, Charles Wood, Sr. Sketches accompanying the Resurvey of The Grove in 1772 for Charles Wood, Sr., and the Resurvey of Wood's Lott for Joseph Wood in 1750 show the northern boundary of the former to be identical with the southern boundary of the latter.[4] Two very old homes standing just north of this common boundary may have once been occupied by members of Joseph Wood's family. The 179-acre tract sold two years after Joseph's death, to John Stevenson by Joseph Wood, Jr., and Jonathan Wood for 1254 pounds and 6 shillings,[5] must have been improved, for the price was high for the times. This tract may have been the site of the paternal homestead.

Seven of the children of Joseph Wood (1705?–1793) and Mary Wood (1710?–1776?) were John, Lucy (1733–1823), Sarah, Jonathan (1747–1837), James, Joseph, Jr., and Thomas. There may have been others. Joseph's wife, Mary, subscribed her consent to his land sales prior to 1777. From 1777 to 1781 Joseph gave farms of a hundred acres or more to each of six children, receiving in return small sums ranging from six pence to five pounds and five shillings. In 1777, John was deeded 155 acres; in 1778, Lucy, the wife of Daniel James, and Sarah, the wife of Edward Evans, were deeded 100 acres each; in 1780, Jonathan was deeded 153 acres, and in 1781 James and Joseph, Jr., were deeded slightly more than 100 acres each.[6]

Record of Joseph Wood's sons John and James disclose only that they received sizeable farms from their father; of the daughter Sarah only that she and her husband received a hundred acres of land from her father in 1778 for five pounds and five shillings and sold it the following year for eight hundred pounds, and of the son Thomas only that he was provided for in 1817 in the will of his brother Joseph, Jr.[7]

Lucy Wood (11-3-1733:1-1-1827), daughter of Joseph and Mary Wood, married Daniel James (1734–1793), the son of John James (1700–1750). Daniel James, a man of means, bequeathed slaves, mills, money and large tracts of land to his sons John, Daniel and Joseph; his daughters Elizabeth, Susanna, Achshah, Margaret and Rebecca, and his grand daughter Drusilla James. To his "beloved wife Lucy" he left the home place. She and her son John were named

---

[3] Ibid. TI, 1, p. 39; EI, 3, p. 466, & 4, p. 362; BT&BY, 3, p. 231; BY&GS, 1, p. 655, & 2, p. 382; BC&GS, 2, p. 428, & 4, p. 386.
[4] Ibid. BC&GS, 48, p. 398, & 50, p. 164; BY&GS, 1, p. 655, & 2, p. 382.
[5] Land Records, Frederick Co., Md. WR, 13, p. 489.
[6] Ibid. RP, 1, p. 265; WR, 1, p. 17, p. 19; 2, p. 643, p. 1027, p. 1078.
[7] Ibid. WR, 1, p. 395; Will Book HS, 2, p. 72.

administrators. The James will was written October 17, 1793, and probated nine days later.[8]

For thirty years Daniel James had shared family responsibilities with his "beloved wife Lucy" in their pretentious 10-room two story stone house. The date 1763 is clearly chiseled at the entrance of this well preserved Frederick County landmark standing four miles south of Unionville on the Old Annapolis Road. A Frederick County map of 1808 represents it as one of the mansions of the period. It is two rooms deep and extending lengthwise are the main rooms alongside the central halls, with a kitchen dropped a half story on a natural slope from which there is an entrance to two large utility cellar rooms. The enormous fireplace in the living room is flanked by the original cupboards enclosed by beautifully designed elliptical-headed double doors of symmetrical panels. Fondly remembered is the library of choice books that once lined the walls of the front room in the upper hall. Clustered about the home are stone barns, cribs, stables, a meat house, a hen house, and a circular walled cooling chamber with a conical roof, all of which served so well in times past and are still in use. The slave quarters, symbol of former wealth, fell in ruins a generation ago. The many gurgling millraces of the nearby Linganore continue to rush madly along but now in futile haste. The Wood-James homestead remained in the family for about a hundred and seventy-five years.

Major Daniel James (1763–1838), son of Lucy Wood and Daniel James, married Margaret Clemson. Three of their children, Sidney Ann (1800?–1848), Zealand (1808–1818) and Major Sir Pratby James (1809–1850) are buried in the family plot near the Wood-James home. Sidney Ann's rare beauty, which is apparent in her daguerreotype and portrait owned by Mary Morgan Kimmel of Baltimore, so impressed General Anthony Kimmel when he saw her at a social function that he asked to be presented. Soon he won her heart, and in the autumn of 1822, her hand.

General Kimmel was the son of Anthony Kimmel who was born in Manheim, Germany, in 1746 and migrated by way of Pennsylvania to Baltimore where he was a successful hardware merchant and banker. General Kimmel, too, was successful and was one of the most prominent citizens of Frederick County. He was a skilled agriculturist, active in military affairs and in politics, and was at one time a State senator. A devout Episcopalian, he built a small chapel on the Old Annapolis Road in memory of his wife, whose name it bore. He traveled far and wide on the Continent and entertained in great style, being numbered among the American hosts of Lafayette.[9] Betsy Patterson of Baltimore who married Napoleon Bonaparte's youngest brother, Jerome, was one of the family's friends. The handsome built-in floor clock, secretary, Sheraton sideboard and table, rosewood cellarette, canopied beds and the lovely spinet which once

---

[8] Will Book, Fred. Co., Md. GM, 2, p. 498.
[9] T. J. C. Williams, *History of Frederick County, Maryland*, p. 846ff.

graced the Wood-James home were inherited by a member of the present generation. The spinet built by Joseph Hisky, renowned piano builder of Baltimore from 1820 to 1845, was in the Chestertown Room of the Baltimore Museum of Art until 1942 when it was permanently transferred to the Hammond-Harwood House in Annapolis.[10]

Colonel Anthony Z. Kimmel (1836-1896) was the only one of General Kimmel's and Sidney Ann's six children to reach maturity. He, of brilliant mind, was a student at Princeton College and the University of Virginia, and a graduate of Harvard Law School. Born with a golden spoon in his mouth he inherited the paternal estate and in addition the Wood-James home together with fourteen hundred acres of land and other possessions left him by his maternal uncle Major Sir Pratby James. During the Civil War he owned a hundred slaves. Unlike his father he managed his estate poorly and at the time of his death his wealth had greatly dwindled. Colonel Kimmel married Mary Morgan, daughter of Mary Rollington and Thomas Morgan. They lived in the Wood-James mansion which was the birthplace of their children, Pratby James, Anthony Z., Mary, Thomas Morgan, Michael and Ellen. The daughter Ellen married Joseph Kent Hill, great grandson of Governor Joseph Kent of Maryland, and their children were William Kimmel, Fred J. and Mary Ellen.

Pratby James Kimmel, oldest son of Colonel Kimmel, married Nannie Pottinger Gibson, daughter of Susan and Dr. Gregg Gibson. Five of their children, Pratby, Agnes Gibson, Gregg, Anthony Z., and William W., are deceased. Two daughters, Miss Mary Morgan Kimmel, a registered nurse, and Miss Elizabeth Marshall Kimmel, who is in government service, reside in Baltimore with their mother. Another daughter, Eleanor James Hall, lives in Philadelphia. Eleanor's daughter, Ann Gibson, is a graduate of the University of Michigan, and her son, Nicholas Snowden Hall, was an aviator in World War II. Pratby James Kimmel regained through his able management a portion of the ancestral estate previously disposed of by his father but after his death in 1933 the title of the Wood-James homestead that had been owned and occupied by descendants through six generations passed to an outsider.

Of Lucy Wood's and Daniel James' son Joseph (1765-1850) we know only that he bore the rank of colonel, and of the daughter Rebecca that she married a Mr. Bennett. Margaret, another daughter, married Henry Poole (1764-1822) and lived in a large two story stone home near the Wood-James homestead. The Poole residence has withstood the ravages of time and it, too, is a Frederick County landmark. The only headstones in the family plot are those of Henry Poole and Wesley Howard Jones (1830-1831). The eight children of Margaret James and Henry Poole were Daniel, Margaret, Lucy, Matilda, Bushrod, a physician; Joseph James, Henry and Thornton. Thornton Poole married Rachel Ruth, the daughter of Dr. Beall Owings, and lived in the Poole homestead

---

[10] See: *The Baltimore Sun*, April 6, 1930, pp. 14-15; *The Evening Sun*, June 30, 1939, p. 24.

where their nine children were born. They were Narcissa, Lucy, Edward, Margaret, Cordelia, Emma, Claire, Henry Thornton and Charles Edgar. The last two sons were college graduates. Charles Edgar Poole married Harriet, the daughter of John Downey.[11]

Lucy Wood James died on New Year's Day, 1827 in her 94th year and is buried in the family plot near the Wood-James home. In the plot rest her husband, Daniel James; her father-in-law, John James; two sons, Major Daniel James and Colonel Joseph James; and three grand children, Sidney Ann Kimmel, Zealand James and Major Sir Pratby James. A number of plain slabs may be the marking of the burial places of slaves. The oblong cemetery atop a slight knoll is two hundred years old. It is shaded by old trees apparently planted in a pattern, and is completely protected by a strong stone wall that has no gateway.

Joseph and Mary Wood's son, Joseph, Jr., named in his will in 1817, two sons Jonathan and Aaron; a daughter Mary Poole; and Diana Sewell and her three sons, Basil, James and John Wood. Jonathan, the son of Joseph, Jr., named in his will in 1846, a son Thomas. Aaron, the son of Joseph Wood, Jr., named in his will in 1820 Sarah, the widow of Basil Poole, and a sister Mary, the widow of Frederick Poole, and her three daughters Lydia, Sarah and Achshah. Mary Wood, daughter of Joseph Wood, Jr., married Frederick Poole December 9, 1806.[12] The foregoing descendants of Joseph Wood, Sr. and Mary Wood lived in Frederick County, Maryland.

The military service of Joseph Wood's sons is obscure. Only that of Jonathan who went to Kentucky is certain. The names of John, James, Joseph, Jr., William, Thomas Wood and others appear in Maryland military records, some of them more than once, but it is impossible to identify them since there were at least two other contemporary pioneer Wood families in Frederick County, those of Colonel Joseph Wood and Charles Wood, Sr., Colonel Joseph Wood, descendant of Robert Wood of Cecil County, Maryland, was the founder of Woodsboro eleven miles north of Frederick. Various accounts of his prominent family, who were affiliated with the Episcopal Church, fill many pages of Maryland history. The family history of Charles Wood, Sr., "A Frederick County Saga; the Wood and Related Families" was compiled by Dr. H. Hanford Hopkins, of Baltimore, a descendant. Charles Wood, Sr., and Joseph Wood may have been related although proof is lacking. Both settled in the 1740's along the North Branch of the Linganore on adjoining properties which, combined, exceeded twenty-five hundred acres. These two early families were Methodists. It is claimed that Wesleyan Methodism was first propounded in America in the 1760's in Frederick County.[13] It immediately took root and still flourishes in the section.

[11] Williams, *op. cit.* p. 1073.
[12] Will Books, Fred. Co., Md. HS, 2, p. 72, p. 407; GME, 3, p. 167; See: Marriage records, Fred. Co., Md.
[13] Williams, *op. cit.* p. 11, p. 457.

Joseph Wood died intestate. In the final accounting of his estate May 11, 1793, by his son Joseph, Jr., the administrator, the personal property was valued at one hundred and seventy-seven pounds, nineteen shillings and eleven pence, and John Norris was paid two pounds, sixteen shillings for the coffin.[14] Mary Wood's death is approximated in 1776 from the omission of her signature from her husband's land sales in 1777. Two years after Joseph's death, Jonathan began to prepare for his migration to Kentucky and within a year he was on his way.

* * * * * *

Jonathan Wood (1-21-1747: 4-13-1837), son of Joseph and Mary Wood, was born near Frederick, Maryland, and died in Nelson County, Kentucky. From 1775 to 1776 he served in the Revolution as a private in a company of expert riflemen from Frederick County under the command of the renowned General Otho Holland Williams. General Williams was then a lieutenant but took command of the company during the prolonged illness of Captain Thomas Price.[15]

On March 27, 1777, Jonathan Wood married Catherine Williams (2-4-1757: 1-15-1815), the daughter of John Williams, yeoman of Frederick County. They lived on the farm presented to Jonathan by his father to which Jonathan added through purchase for four hundred and fifty pounds in 1794 the hundred acres his father had given Lucy Wood James. The following spring he sold his land and in the autumn he appointed his father-in-law, John Williams, to manage his affairs after his departure "for the State of Kentucky or the Western Country". The western journey was made in 1796.[16]

Jonathan Wood's name appears on the Nelson County tax list of 1797 and on March 13, 1798, he bought a plantation of 375 acres from David and Nancy Glenn for 187 pounds on the headwaters of Stewart's Creek, a branch of Beech Fork.[17] On this land Jonathan spent the remainder of his life. A remnant of his log home now serves as the master bedroom in the modern residence of Mrs. V. Boblett, the present owner of the farm. The inscription on Jonathan's headstone in the nearby family plot states that he came to Kentucky in 1796. Close by are the headstones of Catherine, his wife; Mary Catherine Cox-Ball and Susanna Wilson, his daughters; Susanna's husband, Joseph Glass Wilson, and Joseph Wilson's second wife, Elizabeth Allen Wilson.

The hardships attending the new settlement of the Maryland family in that "Western Country" must not have been too severe. Nevertheless the fertile rolling bluegrass acres could not have wholly dimmed occasional wistfulness on the part of Jonathan and Catherine and their older Maryland-born children for

---

[14] Will Book, Fred. Co., Md. GM, 1, p. 464.
[15] U. S. Pension Office, Certificate No. 3219; See: *Records Survey Project, Maryland Historical Society*, Nov. 1940, "Calendar of General Otho Holland Williams Papers" Doc. 3, p. 1; Doc. 7, p. 2.
[16] Land Records, Fred. Co., Md. WR, 13, p. 489, p. 584.
[17] Deed Book, Nelson Co., Ky. 5, p. 372.

another lingering view of the colorful haze overhanging the foothills of their native Blue Ridge Mountains, and the longing to see once more their kindred in the handsome homes of stone along the shores of the Linganore.

Nelson County in 1796 was no longer on the frontier. Since the founding of Cox's Station in 1780 it had developed rapidly and was well populated. An Indian had not been seen for a decade. Bardstown was one of the most important centers in Kentucky but Botland two miles south of the Wood plantation, on the stage coach line between Bardstown and Springfield, was the neighborhood village. Mill Creek Baptist Church, established in 1793, was within two miles, and Ferguson's Chapel was built in 1792 by the famous Methodist minister, Joseph Ferguson, on his own land close by the Wood estate. The Fergusons, the Crumes and the Coxes were among pioneer neighbors destined to provide romantic interest for Jonathan Wood's growing daughters.

Other land was added to the original purchase, but Jonathan Wood, forthright and pious and a good provider for his large family, was not wealthy. Eight of his children, John, Susanna, Ann, Joseph, Mary Catherine (Polly), Elizabeth, Otho and Daniel were born in Maryland; and two of them, William and Catherine Williams, were born in Kentucky. The Wood life span was long. Two sons and a daughter as well as a number in succeeding generations were octogenarians. When Jonathan died at more than ninety years of age, only his wife, Catherine, and his daughter Susanna had gone before him.[18] John, Ann, Polly, Elizabeth and Catherine were married and prospering in homes quite near. Joseph was well along in the acquisition of fertile land in Illinois, and perhaps William had already gone to Mississippi. Daniel and Otho, with his young family, lived in the homestead and these two sons managed the farm. The history of each of the ten children follows:

1. John (Jack) Wood (1778–1853) married Susanna Halbert (1782–1854), the daughter of Thomas Halbert, Sr., August 26, 1807. They resided on a farm on Simpson's Creek bequeathed by John's father. The ten children of John and Susanna Wood were Thomas, who married Caroline Moore of England; Mac, who married in Illinois; Nathaniel; Lydia, who married a Mr. Burdell; Catherine (1817–1894), who married Isaac Hall; Sarah; Joseph; William; Elizabeth; and John, who died in the Confederate Army.[19] The oldest son, Thomas, served as administrator of his parents' estates.[20] He himself owned some fifteen hundred acres of land and was a county official. His descendants, Wood Barnes and Joseph P. Crume, reside in Louisville. Mrs. Frank J. Brown, Bloomfield, Kentucky, is a descendant of Catherine Wood and Isaac Hall.

2. Susanna Wood (10-21-1779: 2-12-1810) married Joseph Glass Wilson (12-4-1772: 11-24-1851) September 9, 1799. Joseph Wilson came to Kentucky from Winchester, Virginia, in 1784, and prospered as a farmer. After a brief ten

---
[18] Will Book, Nelson Co., Ky. 2, p. 205.
[19] Nelson County Census 1850; information given by Wood Barnes, Louisville, Ky.
[20] Will Book, Nelson Co., Ky. 8, pp. 84-85.

years of marriage Susanna died, leaving four small children, Upton, Rhoda, Presty and Jonathan Wood Wilson. Joseph Wilson's children by his second marriage to Elizabeth Allen (1776–1831) were Martha Moriah, who married Green Duncan, a man of prominence; and Sarah Ann, who married a Mr. Lewis. Apparently only two of Joseph Wilson's children survived him, Wood Wilson by Susanna Wood, and Martha Duncan by Elizabeth Allen. The Wilson estate consisting of silver, linens, slaves, money, and land was equally divided among Wood Wilson, administrator; Martha Duncan; and the children of Rhoda Bukley and Sarah Ann Lewis. The slaves were appraised at $8,000 and notes at nearly $10,000.[21]

Jonathan Wood Wilson (1808–1864), son of Susanna Wood and Joseph Wilson, married Elizabeth Muir February 25, 1831. Elizabeth was the daughter of Isabel Brown and Jasper Muir, and the sister of Peter Brown Muir, distinguished attorney and jurist of Louisville. Wood Wilson was well educated and achieved success in the business world. He served as administrator of many Wood estates and is said to have built a fine home in Bardstown. About 1855 he moved to Louisville where he was the head of a wholesale grocery firm with a home in the suburbs. In his will recorded in Jefferson County March 21, 1864, he left $10,000 to his widow, Elizabeth; $2,000 to each of his sons, Jasper Muir Wilson and Joseph Glass Wilson; and the same amount to "each other child" whose names are omitted. In 1869 Elizabeth Wilson moved from the family residence at Eighth and Jefferson Streets to 322 First Street. At the time of Wood Wilson's death his son, Jasper Muir, was practicing medicine in Louisville. His son, Joseph Glass Wilson, had opened a law office three years previously. The latter died in his suburban home in 1879. Named as heirs in his will were his wife, Priscilla, and infant children. His law library was appraised at five hundred dollars and his bank deposits were considerable.[22]

3. Ann Wood (2-4-1772:?) married James McCown, March 27, 1807. They are buried beside Joseph Wood in the Spangler Cemetery in Indiana, twenty-five miles east of Metcalf, Ill. The McCown family was prominent. James' father, Alexander McCown (1755-1835), came from Pennsylvania to Kentucky in 1780. He held public office and was one of the intimate friends of the inventor, John Fitch, whom he often befriended and whose will he witnessed. James' brother, Burr McCown (1806–1881), was a clergyman and educator of note, having held the chair of Latin and Greek for eleven years at Augusta College, the first Methodist college in the west, after which he accepted a similar post at Transylvania College.[23] Later he founded a boys' school at Anchorage where he taught until a short time before his death.

Dr. Harrison Wood McCown (1809–1869), son of Ann Wood and James McCown, married Elizabeth M. Doom (1820–1892), December 30, 1836. Eliza-

---
[21] *Ibid.* 6, p. 598.
[22] Will Books, Jefferson Co., Ky. 6, p. 176; 38, pp. 627–30; 39, p. 263; Louisville, Ky. Directories 1855–1869.
[23] W. E. Arnold, *History of Methodism in Kentucky*, pp. 121–23.

beth was the daughter of Cassandra Phillips and Colonel Ben Doom, who was an early settler in Kentucky from Culpeper County, Virginia. Colonel Doom amassed a fortune in the tanning industry and his family lived in elegant style. He built two magnificent Georgian homes in Bardstown before building the suburban residence, Culpeper, in which he spent his declining years. Colonel Doom's fine carriage and piano were among the first, if not the very first, in the community. The story has been handed down of pranksters tacking on to the family carriage the sign "Who would have thought it? Wet leather bought it." The lovely old rosewood piano with much of its beauty retained is temporarily housed in the Filson Club, Louisville, Kentucky. It was purchased in Philadelphia about 1830 and has descended through Elizabeth Doom McCown to her great grand daughter, May Wood Wigginton, head librarian of the Denver Public Library, Denver, Colorado. Among cherished family heirlooms are a silver soup ladle, egg cups, a silver comb, a snuff box, and the mortar and pestle from Dr. McCown's office, now owned by Elizabeth Brown and Mrs. Charles Ball of Louisville.

Dr. Harrison Wood McCown and his family resided in the stately Georgian home in Bardstown bequeathed to his wife by her father. The 14-room residence was built in the early 1800's for Colonel Doom by Dr. McCown's father, James McCown. Skilled slave labor fired the brick. The McCown house still stands resplendent in its quiet granduer at 212 East Stephen Foster Avenue, as the home of Mr. and Mrs. W. J. Smith and family, who take especial pride in preserving the original design and ornamentation.

The six children of Dr. McCown were Emaline (1839–1894); James, a major in the United States Army; Sarah Jane (1842–1918), who married John Thomas Miller (1838–1905); William; Laura Doom, who married Charles C. Brown; and Annie, who married Christopher Columbus Figg. Among descendants are Laura Miller, granddaughter, and May Wood Wigginton, great granddaughter, of Denver, Colorado; Helen Louise (Mrs. Walter) Beecher, great grand daughter, Anchorage, Kentucky; Elizabeth Brown, Ann Figg (Mrs. Charles) Ball, granddaughters, and Charlie Wood Brown, grandson, Louisville, and Mamie Figg (Mrs. P. Burr) Crume, grand daughter, Bardstown.

4. Joseph Wood (7-17:1784:8-26-1869) was the first member of Jonathan Wood's family to leave Kentucky. Lured by the fertile soil of Illinois he went to Edgar County in 1832, where in time his dreams of success came true. By 1852 he owned more than a thousand acres of rich prairie land bought at five or ten dollars per acre and presently valued at three hundred dollars per acre. About 1855 his brother Daniel and nephew, John Benton Wood, joined him. Sometime later Catherine Cox Brown and her family, and James McCown settled in Edgar County. In Joseph's will written on Christmas Day, 1864, when he was well past eighty years of age, he requested burial in Spangler Graveyard and the equal division of his estate among his nine brothers and

Mary Catherine (Polly) Wood Cox-Ball. Sketched from Original by Douglas Gore.

sisters or their heirs. He died five years later and his brother Daniel purchased the bulk of his land.[24]

5. Mary Catherine (Polly) Wood (11-13-1787: 9-24-1857) married (1) Isaac Russell Cox (7-29-1792:12-2-1823) November 4, 1813, and (2) James Hilary Ball, March 10, 1829. There were no children by the second marriage. Major Isaac Russell Cox was the son of Brigadier General James Cox and Mary Cox, who were born in Virginia. Isaac's ancestors came to Cox's Creek in 1776, built Cox's Station the first settlement in Nelson County in 1780, and took up some 75,000 acres of land in Kentucky alone. The Cox family was one of refinement and wealth, and enjoyed a high degree of prestige in community building, political organization, and military service.[25]

Two aged letters owned by the author throw light on Polly Wood's courtship and marriage. In a letter written March 6, 1813, Isaac Cox ardently implores her to name an earlier wedding date and closes by saying, "I shall attend at the appointed time when I expect to have the exquisite pleasure of receiving a satisfactory answer". In a post script he begs for an answer by the bearer should Polly deem it proper. But Polly, being five years older than Isaac, was perhaps more restrained. At any rate the wedding did not take place until November. In the other old letter written December 9, 1820, to Major Isaac Russell Cox of Breckinridge County, his father, General James Cox, sends the following words of admonition:

> I expect you have certainly got your new house raised and fit to live in by this time and removed your wife and children out of your old wigwam. You are young and in the prime of life. Spend no more time foolishly but in the necessary industry to provide a future support for one of the best wives and a rising family of children.

Two and a half years later Isaac died, leaving his widow Polly with five children ranging from nine years of age to less than a year and a half. Polly and her children lived with her father for five years and then she married James Hilary Ball, who, as was implied by the oldest child, Fannie Cox, the author's grandmother, was not too solicitous concerning the family's welfare.

The five children of Polly Wood and Isaac Cox were Fannie Moriah, Frank, Jonathan Wood, James and Mary Catherine. Fannie Moriah Hull Cox (8-18-1814: 6-1-1900) was named for Captain Isaac Hull, commander of *The Constitution* which so brilliantly defeated the British ship, *Guerriere*, in August, 1812. On November 22, 1834, Fannie Cox, barely turned twenty, married John Brown (4-1-1808: 2-10-1865) of Pennsylvania, who was a widower with two small children, Charles and Barbara Lucretia. Fannie and John Brown's nine children were George (1836–19....); Mary Catherine (1838–1864), who married Charles Dewell; Elizabeth (1840–1865), who married John Poland Moses Linton Isaac Howard Fox; Laura Loretta, (1843–1926) who married the husband of her

---
[24] Will Book, Edgar Co., Ill. 3, p. 258; See: Land Records, Edgar Co., Ill. 1832–1852.
[25] Evelyn C. Adams, *The Filson Club History Quarterly*, "The Coxes of Cox's Creek, Kentucky," Vol. 22, No. 2, April 1948.

deceased sister Elizabeth; Cora Johnson (8-16-1846:10-30-1934), who married William Henry Crady (12-18-1845:10-26-1915), a merchant at Nelsonville, Kentucky; James Isaac (1849–1886); Martha Jane (1852–1939), who married Wilson B. Miller; Malachi Styron (1854–1937), who married Lena Smock (1858–1920); and Norton Jonathan (1856–1889).

John Brown, devoted husband and father, died in the late winter of 1865 and his widow Fannie Cox Brown valiantly and efficiently assumed the family responsibilities during the remaining thirty-five years of her life. She continued the management of two farms and the careful education of her children. Besides, she opened her home to her brother James, who served in both the Union and the Confederate Armies, and her nephew Isaac, the son of Jonathan. Her epitaph "She shines in endless day" pays due tribute in the family cemetery a few hundred yards from her homestead near Younger's Creek in Hardin County where many members of her family are buried. Among numerous descendants are Rodney Miller, railway official, Chicago; Merle Miller, with the United Nations abroad; the late Craig Miller, Purdue student, instructor in the British Royal Air Force and aviator in the American Air Force in World War II; Mrs. John Parrish and Miss Mabel Miller, Louisville; Mrs. Effie Sutherland, Mrs. Sallie Greenwell and Mrs. Vergil Troutman, Bardstown; the late Wood Crady, who gained international recognition in the fertilizer industry; B. A. Crady of Mississippi; and M. N. Crady of California in the chemical industry; Evelyn Crady (Mrs. Sydney S.) Handy, official in the field of merchandising, Baltimore; and the author of this history.

Frank Cox, oldest son of Polly Wood and Isaac Cox, died soon after the Civil War in which he served on the Union side. His widow, Sallie Hughes Cox, with her four small children, sought refuge with the Shakers and later established her home in Lebanon where a few descendants still reside. Polly and Isaac Cox's second son, Jonathan Wood Cox (1818–1851), married Louisa Taylor, December 3, 1842. Louisa died when her two sons, Isaac and David, were infants, and Jonathan died when they were 8 and 5 years of age. The orphaned lads made their homes with relatives.

Mary Catherine (1822–1911), the youngest child of Polly and Isaac Cox, married George Washington Brown (1818–1907), December 27, 1849. Washington Brown spent his early years as a flat boatman running to New Orleans, and was later a merchant in Bardstown. The family, consisting of three daughters, Marcia; Sallie, who married Charles Morris; and Mary, who married Dr. D. D. Roberts, one time coroner of Edgar County, established their permanent home in Illinois near other members of the Wood family. Dr. Roberts' son Russell died in Germany during World War I and is buried in Arlington Cemetery. A daughter, Irene Roberts, and a son, William Edward Roberts, live in Paris, Illinois.

6. Elizabeth Wood (5-20-1789: 9-11-1876), daughter of Jonathan Wood,

married John Crume (11-26-1776: 12-8-1865) October 5, 1824. John Crume, member of a prominent pioneer family, was a widower of means and a neighbor.[26] The two children were Joseph Wood and Daniel Burr Crume. Joseph Wood Crume (12-27-1827: 1-15-1894) married Susan M. Thomas January 28, 1850, and their seven children were Elizabeth Ellen; Mildred Emily (1853-1883); Benjamin, who married Rose Mock and lives in Chicago; Anna; John William; Mary, who married Arch Weathers; and Mundy. Their fifth child, John William Crume, is a retired railway official living in Florida. He married (1) Kate Barnes, his cousin, and (2) Ada Johnson Crane of Manchester, England. The three sons by the first marriage were Jackie, who died in infancy; Benjamin Wood Crume of Cleveland whose two sons, Benjamin and Thomas, are graduates of the University of Louisville; and Joseph P. Crume of Louisville, whose two daughters married officers of the U. S. Army, and whose son, John Bruce Crume, a graduate of Harvard University and a career diplomat, is stationed with his wife, Agnes Snyder, journalist, at Teheran, Iran.

Daniel Burr Crume, the second son of Elizabeth Wood and John Crume, married Fannie Eddleman, a descendant of the Daniel Boone family. Their eight children were Emma; Lelia, who married Frank Sprague and whose son is a graduate engineer of the University of Cincinnati; Anise; Woodie, who married Hugh D. Stiles; Jones, who married Ora Troutman; Dr. William Ernest Crume, who married Effie Kimberlin, and whose son William Ernest is a graduate of the University of Alabama; Philip Burr Crume, who married Mamie Figg Muir; and Jonathan Robert Crume, pharmacist in Bardstown, who married Beatrice Lawson. Robert and Beatrice Crume's son Keith practices medicine in Bardstown; their son John Robert is a graduate of West Point Military Academy and a colonel in the U. S. Army, and their daughter Elise studied music in Rome, Italy.

7. Otho Williams Wood (6-27-1792: 12-21-1854) was named for General Otho Holland Williams of Maryland under whom Jonathan Wood served in the Revolution. On September 25, 1834, Otho Wood married Elizabeth Crume (10-30-1816:4-15-1841), the daughter of John Crume by his first wife Elizabeth Cotton. Otho and his bride lived in his father's home where their three sons, Jonathan Clinton, John Benton and Joseph Putnam were born. Elizabeth died six years after marriage, and Otho reared the children with the help of slaves. The three sons, aged 19, 17, and 15 years when Otho died,[27] were educated at Hanover College, Indiana, under the guardianship of Wood Wilson, and each lived to be 88 years of age rounding out full eventful lives crowned with success.

Dr. Jonathan Clinton Wood (1835–1923) received his diploma from the Kentucky School of Medicine, Louisville, in 1866 and retired from practice in 1909. He married his first cousin, Ann McCown Ferguson (1833–1915), and

---

[26] Will Book, Nelson Co., Ky. 13, p. 194, p. 253.
[27] Ibid. 7, p. 478, p. 536, p. 543.

they resided in the neighboring spacious Ferguson homestead which burned a few years ago. The modern residence built near the old site belongs to a daughter, Ada (Mrs. Fletcher) Dodson of Lexington. Other children were Adra (Mrs. J. P.) Dodson, now of Bloomfield, and Kate and Otho, who are deceased. Dr. Jonathan Clinton Wood and his wife Ann sold land to the Louisville and Nashville Railroad when it was extended to Springfield in 1887 and gave the name of Woodlawn to the station near their home.[28]

John Benton Wood (1837–1925), Otho's second son, went to Illinois in the 1850's with his uncle Daniel to join Daniel's brother Joseph who had become a wealthy land owner. Daniel was forty-three years old and living in his father's home when John Benton was born there and they were not separated except during the few years his nephew attended Hanover College. Daniel expressed his life long devotion to John Benton by naming him his sole heir to his extensive holdings. John Benton spent three score years and ten in Illinois. He served a term as treasurer of Edgar County but was primarily concerned with the management of his large estate. His special interest was large scale marketing of hogs and cattle and the breeding of fine horses. His trotters, Laury M. Stranger, and Sallie Howard, and his pacers, Big Annie and Foxey, were fast in their day and brought fancy prices. John Benton bequeathed his estate valued at nearly a half million dollars almost entirely to his nieces, nephews and one surviving brother in Nelson County, Kentucky.[29] The more than fifteen hundred acres of land that he owned at the time of his death have currently doubled in value.

Joseph Putnam Wood (1839–1928), Otho's youngest son, attended Hanover College and read law in Bardstown for a short period. After a brief stay with his kin in Illinois he returned to Nelson County and married Lizzie Doom (1848–1884), the daughter of Miriam Samuels and William Doom, and the grand daughter of Colonel Ben Doom. They lived directly opposite the Doom homestead, Culpeper, in the commodious home, Willow Valley, now owned and occupied by their daughter, Miriam (Mrs. H. H.) Mashburn. The farm was an original part of the John Rowan estate and still adjoins the property of the Old Kentucky Home.

Joseph Putnam Wood's eight children were Miriam, widow of the Reverend H. H. Mashburn, Bardstown; Joseph (1871–1884); Glenn, a pharmacist in Louisville; Mary Lily (1874–1931); Daniel Benton, who attended Valparaiso College, Indiana, and resides in Bowling Green; John McLeod (1879–1880); Edwin, a retired farmer, Bowling Green; and Jennie (1883–1948), who married Orville Morris. Miriam was a student at the Conservatory of Music, Cincinnati, Ohio, and was a successful teacher for many years. Mary Lily, also a successful teacher, was at one time a candidate for the office of superintendent of schools,

---
[28] Files of the L. & N. R. R., Louisville, Ky. Deeds No. 2211, No. 2265.
[29] Will Book, Edgar Co., Ill. 11, p. 434.

the first woman to campaign in this field in Nelson County. At the time of her death she owned Culpeper Place and other land.

8. Daniel D. Wood (9-19-1794:3-27-1880) was a man of exemplary habits. He divided his eighty-six years equally between residence on his father's farm in Nelson County, Kentucky, and on his own land and that of his brother Joseph in Edgar County, Illinois. A skilled and successful farmer he left his nephew John Benton Wood an estate of nearly a thousand acres.[30] His grave is on the Wood plot in Edgar Cemetery, Paris, Illinois, where many other members of the Wood family are interred.

9. William Wood (1796/98:1863?) went to Mississippi but just where he located is not known. The author's mother often spoke of visits to Kentucky by a member of his family. Mr. Charles G. Wood of Hattiesburg, Mississippi, son of William Kilcrease Wood (1850–1924) and Arabella Gartman, a cousin of President Martin Van Buren, writes that his grandparents, whose names he does not know, died near Port Gibson. They had lost their land and slaves during the Civil War and their three children, John, William Kilcrease, and Sallie, were reared by relatives. The dates are reconcilable and Christian names are duplicated but there is no proof of relationship to William Wood of Kentucky.

10. On March 27, 1827, Catherine Williams Wood (3-22-1800:1-16-1871), the youngest child of Jonathan Wood, married her neighbor, William S. Ferguson (11-29-1796:8-18-1844), son of the Reverend Joseph Ferguson (1759–1828). Joseph Ferguson, one of the earliest Methodist ministers in Kentucky, came from Fairfax, Virginia, in 1784, and about 1792 he built historic Ferguson's Chapel, said to have been the second Methodist house of worship in the State. The little one-room chapel of round logs and clapboard roof which stood near the Ferguson home was replaced in 1822 by a hewed log building some fifty yards to the west. The third structure, known as the Poplar Flat Methodist Church, was erected of brick in 1844 about fifty yards beyond the second,[31] and in recent years when modern highways left the grounds remote, the meeting house was removed to Woodlawn about a mile distant. The old cemetery has spread over the tree-covered knoll where the pioneers worshipped, until it now includes the early Ferguson burial plot which was adjacent to the early chapel. Tended with loving care, it still serves the congregation.

The five children of Catherine Wood and William Ferguson were Van B. (1829–1857), a school teacher; Ann (1833–1915), who married her cousin Dr. Jonathan Clinton Wood; Sarah (1836–1878), who married Benjamin Lee Duncan (1836–1919); Catherine (1839–1870); and William H. (1841–1844).[32] The family is buried in Poplar Flat Cemetery on a plot next to Joseph Fergu-

---
[30] *Ibid.* 4, p. 136.
[31] W. E. Arnold, *op. cit.* p. 69, p. 71, pp. 177–79; A. H. Redford, *Methodism in Kentucky,* pp. 25–26, p. 285.
[32] Nelson Co. Census 1850; Will Book, Nelson Co., Ky. 4, p. 256; 15, pp. 307–10.

son's. The only surviving grand children are Ada (Mrs. Fletcher) Dodson, and Adra (Mrs. J. P.) Dodson, the twin daughters of Ann Ferguson and Dr. Jonathan Clinton Wood. Mrs. Fletcher Dodson still owns the original Ferguson land.

The Wood family name is borne by an ever decreasing number. Its popularity over the years as a Christian name is evidenced by the following: Wood Wilson, Harrison Wood McCown, Jonathan Wood Cox, Joseph Wood Crume, Benjamin Wood Crume, Isaac Wood Miller, Sara Wood Whitesides, Wood Barnes, Charlie Wood Brown, Woodie Crume Stiles, Wood Crady, May Wood Wigginton and Mary Wood Crady.

In far flung homes throughout eight or more generations of Wood progeny there have been successful physicians, pharmacists, attorneys, engineers, educators, librarians, authors, statesmen, large-scale farmers and industrialists. A gratifying number has rendered armed service in America's defense. Among those engaged in World War II alone, were Captain Joseph Miller, Lieutenant Joseph Llyod Miller, Lieutenants Robert and Charles Ball, Captain William Miller Whitesides, Captain Joseph Alexander Miller, John Thomas Miller Olson, Robert Olson, Lieutenant Benjamin Crume, Thomas Crume, Colonel John Robert Crume, John Bruce Crume of Intelligence Service, Aviator Craig Miller and Ray Troutman. There are the many who have paid loving tribute to their forefathers in varied endeavors to extend the bounds of social disciplines on which the advancement and security of a modern world rest. They in advancing these new frontiers are perpetuating ancestral traditions. They, too, are pioneers.

THE AUTHOR

Mrs. Evelyn Crady Adams, descendant of Jonathan Wood, was born and reared in Nelson County, Kentucky. She holds degrees from Miami University, the University of Cincinnati, and Columbia University; is the author of *American Indian Education* and contributes to various journals and periodicals. Mrs. Adams is a member of the Kentucky Historical Society and the Maryland Historical Society.

WOODSONS AND WATKINS,

BY

MISS MORTON.

THE WOODSONS.*

I. Jno. Woodson, Dorsetshire, England (wife Sara, from Dorsetshire) came to Va. in the good ship "George," in 1619, settled at Fleur de Hundred. Physician.

II. Robt. Woodson, b. Va.; m. Eliza Faris, dr. Richard Faris, of "Curls," Henrico Co., Va. II John Woodson. m. Mary Tucker.

III. Jno. Woodson, m. Judith Tarleton, dr. Stephen Tarleton. Their children:

IV. 1. Tarleton, m. Ursula Fleming.
2. Jno., m. Susan Fleming Bates.
3. Jacob.
4. Josiah, m. Mary Royall.
5. Robt., m. Sarah Womack.
6. Stephen.

III. Richard Woodson, m. Anne Smith. Seven children.

Children of Richard Woodson and Anne Smith:
1. Richard Woodson, of "Poplar Hill," m. Anne Michaux.
2. Obadiah Woodson, m. Constance Watkins.
3. John Woodson, m. M. Anderson., dau. Col. Thos. Anderson, of Henrico Co.
4. Elizabeth Woodson, m. (1) Thomas Morton, (2) Edward Goode.
5. Judith Woodson, m. Jacob Michaux.
6. Mary Woodson, m. Rich'd Truman.
7. Agnes Woodson, b. 1711, d. 1802, m. Joseph Morton, b. 1709, d. 1782.

III. Robt. Woodson, m. first Sarah Lewis; second, Rachel Watkins.

Children of first wife:
1. Stephen.
2. Joseph, m. Eliza Mattox.
3. Robt.
4. Eliza, m. Jno. Povall.
5. Sara, m. Jos. Parsons.
6. Mary.

Children of second wife:
1. Jonathan.
2. Eliza, m. Jno. Knight.
3. Judith, m. Jno. Cooke.

III. Joseph Woodson, m. Mary Woodson, dr. Jno. and Mary Tucker Woodson.

Their children:
1. Tucker, m. first, Sara Hughes; second, Mary Netherbud.
2. Mary, m. Stephen Woodson.
3. Judith, m. Chas. Chrisman.
4. Martha, m. Jno. Cannon.

III. Benjamin Woodson, m. Sara Porter. Their children:
1. Wm., m. Sara Allen.
2. Benj., m. Eliza Watkins.
3. Jos., m. Susan Watkins.
4. Jno., m. Mary Miller.
5. Robt., m. Rebecca Pryor.
6. Eliza, m. Jno. Daniel.
7. Sara, m. Jno. Allen.

III. Elizabeth Woodson, m. Wm. Lewis. No children.

III. Mary Woodson, m. Geo. Payne, sheriff of Goochland.

---

*For additional information on the Woodson family see pp. 113-115, this volume.

III. Judith Woodson, m. Wm. Cannon.

IV. Richard Woodson, oldest son of Rich'd Woodson and Anne Smith, "Poplar Hill," Pr. Edward Co., Va., m. Anne Michaux, dr. Abram Michaux and Susannah Rochette, dr. Moses Rochette, Sedan, France. Huguenots.

IV. Obadiah Woodson, 2d son of same, m. Constance Watkins, dr. Jno. Watkins.

IV. Jno. Woodson 3d, m. Mary Anderson, dr. Thos. Anderson, Henrico Co., Va.

IV. Eliza Woodson, dr. same, m. first, Thos. Morton; second, Ed. Goode.

IV. Judith Woodson, dr. same, m. Jacob Michaux, s. Abram Michaux and Susannah Rochette.

IV. Mary Woodson, dr. same, m. Richard Truman.

IV. Agnes Woodson, dr. same, b. Feb. 27, 1711; d. Mch. 10, 1802; m. Jos. Morton.

V. Eliza Woodson, dr. Richard Woodson and Ann Michaux, b. 1730; d. 1811; m. Nathaniel Venable, b. 1732; d. 1804; s. Abram Venable and Martha Davis Venable.

V. Agnes Woodson, m. Francis Watkins, s. Thos. and Fanny Anderson, Clerk Pr. Edward Co., Mem. Com. of Safety, Trustee, Manager, Visitor, Hampden-Sidney Coll., died. 1826; buried at "Poplar Hill."

Children of Eliza Woodson and N. Venable:

VI. 1. Samuel W., m. Mary Covington.
2. Abraham, burned at the Richmond Theatre.
3. Rich'd M., m. Mary Morton.
4. Nathaniel.
5. Wm., m. ——— Nantz.
6. Thos.
7. Betty, m. Thos. Watkins.
8. Martha, m. Nathaniel Venable.
9. Eliza, m. Col. (?).

THE WATKINS FAMILY.

I. Thomas Watkins married Fanny Anderson.

II. Francis Watkins (Clerk Pr. Ed. Co.—Mem. Com. Safety Pr. Ed. Co. Trustee, Manager, Visitor Hampden Sidney College.) d. 1826.

III. Richard Watkins m. Mrs. Catherine Chappel Jones. Tenn.

IV. Their child, Agnes Watkins, m. Dr. Wm. Sayle.

III. Elizabeth Watkins, b. Pr. Edward Co., Va., Dec. 6, 1769; d. Shelby Co., Ky., Apr. 23, 1832, m. Jos. Venable, b. 6-8-1761, Charlotte Co., Va. Grad. Hampden-Sidney; in law, Nassau Hall (Princeton), N. J., Commonwealth's Atty., Pr. Edward and Charlotte Cos. Under age, but acted as aid to Gen. Lawson and carried dispatches to LaFayette in Rev. War. Moved to Shelby Co., Ky., 1810; Judge of Shelby Co., Trustee Hampden-Sidney Coll., 1796, Elder Mulberry Pres. Ch., Shelby Co., Ky. Buried at "Poplar Hill," Pr. Ed. Co., Va. Died (?).

III. Agnes Watkins, m. Dr. David Flournoy.

III. Francis Watkins, m. Ann Haskins, dr. Thos. Haskins and Parmelia Penn.

III. Benj. Watkins, m (?).

III. Henry Watkins, m. Agnes Venable, dr. Col. Sam'l and Mary Carrington.

IV. Their children:
1. Francis N., m. Mary Scott.
2. Henry E.
3. Mary C.
4. Rev. S. W., m. 1852, Alice Horsley.
5. Agnes.
6. Lizzie Ann.
7. Richard V.
8. Margaret C.
9. Henrietta.
10. Catherine.
11. Frances S.

III. Jos. Watkins, m. Ruth Hunt.
IV. Children:
1. Josephine, m. Dr. Joel Watkins.
2. Susan, m. Wm. Robards.
3. Dr. F. B., m. Mary Elfreth.
4. Betty Jane, m. Col. Horace Robards.

III. Selina A. Watkins, m. Col. S. L. Lockett, s. Stephen and Mary Clay Lockett. Their children:
1. Frances Lockett, m. Albert Jones, s. Col. Thos. and Mary Crenshaw Jones.
2. Mary Lockett, m. Napoleon Lockett.
3. Selina Lockett, m. Horace Robards.
4. Lucius Lockett, m. Emma Fowlkes.
5. Henry Lockett.
6. Virginia Lockett, m. Jos. H. Speed.

III. Frances Watkins, m. Jas. D. Wood.
IV. Their children:
1. Agnes, m. R. G. Branch.
2. Dr. Henry A. Wood.
3. Eliza W.
4. Francis P.
5. Susan M., m. Rev. Moses Hoge.
6. S. Chesley.
7. Frances.
8. Selina.
9. Cora. V.
10. Josephine.

WRIGHT—HAMILTON FAMILIES

Copy of old record in the possession of Mr. Wm. Clark, Paris, Ky., 1926. Copied and presented by Mrs. W. B. Ardery.

Some account of my Paternal and Maternal ancestors and other relatives arranged and compiled in the year 1863 from material obtained by recollection and record.

William Wright,
Bourbon Co. Ky.

My Great Grandfather, Adam Wright, was a citizen of the New Eugland States. His son, Peter Wright, was my grandfather. He emigrated to Bottetourt Co. Virginia at a very early period in the settlement of that part of Virginia. He married Jane Hughart and settled on Jackson's river, between the mouth of Dunlap's and Potts creeks. They had thirteen children, eight daughters and five sons. Their names are as follows, though not in the order of their births. Sarah, Thomas, James, William, Peter, Martha, Rachel, Jane, Nancy, Rebecca, John, Elizabeth, one name not recollected.

Sarah married Palser Kimberlin. Rebecca married Kinkead. One whose name I do not recollect married Smith, all of Virginia. Martha married James Estill, Rachel married William Estill both of whom removed at an early period to Kentucky. James Estill was killed by the Indians. William Estill died and Rachel, his widow afterwards married Mr. Proctor of Kentucky. Jane married Wallace Estill. Nancy married Christopher Clark. Elizabeth married John Sprowl, Wallace Estill and Dr. Christopher Clark removed to Kentucky in 1794 and setted in Madison Co. afterward Wallace Estill removed to Tennessee and there died. Thomas Wright married Sarah Henderson, settled in Greenbrier Co. Virginia.

James married Martha Hamilton, settled on Pott's creek, Bottetourt Co. Virginia, he and Thomas Wright removed to Kentucky in 1794 and settled in Bourbon Co., and there died. William married Rachel Sawyers, settled on Pott's creek near the mouth, removed some time between 1794 and 1800 to Tennessee and settled a few miles from Nashville. Thence (years afterwards) removed to Missouri, where he died. John Wright married in Virginia, removed to Kentucky, thence westwardly, I know not where. Peter Wright, Jr. married in Virginia, had a large family of daughters, removed to Missouri and there died.

James Wright (son of Peter Wright and Jane Hughart) married Martha Hamilton. They resided in Bottetourt Co. Va. until the 6th. of May 1794, when they set out for Kentucky and arrived at their house on Houston creek, two miles southwest of Paris, Bourbon Co. Ky. on the 7th. day of June of same year. They had eleven children as follows:

Sarah born January, 29th. 1777.
Jane, born September, 26th. 1778.
Andrew H. born July, 9th. 1780.
Mary born February, 4th. 1782.
William born Dec. 15th. 1783.
John born March, 26th. 1786.
Martha born September, 25th. 1787.
Isaac born August, 10th. 1791.
Rebecca born December, 6th. 1793.
James R. born October, 16th. 1796.

An infant born in Virginia died a few days after birth. I think it ought to be placed between Martha and Isaac.

Sarah Wright married William Mitchell. They had six children, Martha, Thomas, James, William, Hamilton, Sarah and Ruth, the last two being twins.

Jane Wright married Andrew Hodge. They had two children, Paulina and Andrew, both of whom died before they were grown. Mrs. Hodge afterward married David Lowry of Ohio. They had four children, Martha S., David Wright, Robert Mitchell and Rebecca.

Andrew H. Wright married Ruth Hamilton, daughter of William Hamilton of Greenbrier Co. Va. (she was his cousin) she died in less than a year after they were married. He remained a widower until he died, which was on the 19th. of May, 1857.

Mary Wright married Isaac Allen. They had eight or nine sons and two daughters, Eliza and Sallie Jane. Eliza married Robert Turner and Sally Jane married George Shirley.

William Wright married Eliza Ann Jackson. They had seven children, two sons and five daughters, their birth being as follows:

Edwin Wright born Nov. 6, 1815.
Rebecca Wright born May 1, 1817.
Margaret Jane born April, 27, 1819.
Sarah born February 13, 1821.
William Wright Jr. born February, 25, 1822.
Martha Ann born April, 1, 1824.
Mary born August, 5, 1829.

Edwin Wright, son of William Wright Sr. married Sarah Gay. They had six children, James Gay, William McIlvain, John Wason, Mary Annie and an infant that died quite young.

Rebecca Wright married John W. McIlvain. They had one daughter Annie Wright McIlvain.

Margaret Wright married Thomas Wason, had no children. William Wright Jr. married Georgien Rion. They have one child Annie McIlvain Wright.

John Wright, son of James Wright Sr. married Martha Kelley, had four sons and five daughters. James Wilson, Andrew William, Isaac Kelley, John Alexander, Amanda, Martha Hamilton, Mary Ann, Rebecca and Ruth.

James Wilson married Harriet Thomas, had five children, Laura, Isaac, William Lindsay, two died in infancy, after her death he married Cynthia Jones, who had three children, Martha Wilsie, James Wilson and Clarence Jones.

Andrew William married Naomi Ruth Ward. They had four children, Maria Belle, John Ward, Sallie Keziah and William Volney.

Amanda Wright married Morris Thomas. They had six children, Margaret, Martha Rebecca, John, James, Jennie and Morris Jr.

Ruth Wright married James Robnett. They raised three children, John, Alice and Annie Lee.

The other children of John Wright senior did not marry.

Martha Wright, daughter of Jennie Wright Sr. married Robert Barnett. He died in a short time after they were married. Afterwards she married James Ward of Harrison Co. Ky. They had six children, James Hervey, Rebecca, Ruth, Martha Jane, William Russell and Mary Margaret.

Rebecca married Benjamin Williams of Ohio. Martha Jane married B. B. Marsh. Ruth married Robert Clark. Mary Margaret married William Posey of Ill.

Isaac Wright, son of James Wright Sr. married Maria W. Varnon. They had no children.

James R. Wright, son of James Wright Sr. married Mrs. Mary Ann Curl. They had one child Laura. She died young, after his wife Mary Ann died, he married Jane Godden.

Maternal Ancestors

My Maternal Grandfather was Andrew Hamilton. Some say he was born in Terrone Ireland near Blissits Hill and others say he was born in Pennsylvania (I know not which) I cannot tell who my Grandmother Hamilton was previous to her marriage, neither do I know the dates of their births. She was born in County of Derry Ireland. They resided in Augusta Va. Grandfather Hamilton had eight children, three sons and five daughters. Their names are as follows:

Andrew Hamilton
John Hamilton, was killed by Indians.
William Hamilton
Sarah Hamilton

Jane Hamilton
Mary Hamilton
Martha Hamilton
Margaret Hamilton.
I do not know that this is order of their births.

Andrew Hamilton married Elizabeth (or Isabel) Kinkead. They moved to Woodford Co. Ky. at an early period in the settlement of that state.

William Hamilton married Miss Clemans. They resided in Greenbrier Co. Va. and there died. They had a numerous family of children, some of whom died young. Some removed to Ohio and others remained in Virginia.

Sarah Hamilton married Major William Renick. They resided in Greenbrier Co. Va. and there died. They had no children.

Jane Hamilton married John Hodge. They resided in Augusta Co. Va. They had several children.

Mary Hamilton married James Hodge. They resided in Rockbridge, Co. Va. Had one daughter and several sons.

Martha Hamilton married James Wright, as before stated, and moved to Kentucky.

James Wright Sr. was born in Bottetourt Co. Va. about 1754.

Martha Hamilton Wright, his consort, was born in Augusta County, Va., in 1755.

James Wright Sr. and Martha Hamilton were married Feb. 29th. 1776.
James Wright Sr. died June, 24, 1825.
Martha Wright died April, 22, 1827.
Sarah Wright Mitchell died Feb. 23, 1808.
Rebecca Wright died Oct. 12, 1813.
John Wright died October, 25, 1849.
Andrew H. Wright died May, 19, 1857.
Martha Wright Ward died Jan. 18, 1854.
Mary Wright Allen died Dec. 4, 1854.
James R. Wright died May, 9, 1856.
William Wright Sr. died June, 11, 1880.

SOME DESCENDANTS OF THE WASHINGTON FAMILY IN JEFFERSON COUNTY, KENTUCKY

STRATTON O. HAMMON

Before I relate these things concerning the local posterity of the Washington bloodline, I will explain briefly that General George Washington had no children and hence no one who can claim him personally as an ancestor. Fortunately he did have a great-aunt Anne (Washington) Wright, a great-uncle Captain John Washington, four half sisters and brothers, and five full sisters and brothers from most of whom descendants, now numbering in the thousands, carry in their veins the blood of this illustrious family which numbers the Father of our Country as one of its great sons.

"A hundred writers have written a hundred books containing material about George Washington. The history of this great man, and of the affairs in which he played a part, has enriched the world. Comparatively, almost nothing has been brought out concerning his background save a skeleton pedigree. The mystery as to his antecedents long enhanced the romance of it all; now the revelations have begun to exceed in romance the mystery. What lies behind George Washington is as important as it is interesting—unknown though it has remained for generations. He did not, like Pallas, spring forth full armed from the head of Jove. He sprang from forebears who, in their day and place, were almost as important, in some cases even more important, than he was in his time. He repeated what, in other ways, had been achieved by the blood he inherited, and what may be, by that strain, repeated again. He was a lineal descendant of the aristocracy, of the nobility, and even of the royalty of England. He was a lineal descendant of six kings and six queens of England who resigned after the Norman Conquest—of a long line of kings and queens of Scotland, of monarchs of Flanders, of France, and of Spain, and of monarachs of Saxon England, extending back in long lines of both French and Saxon blood until the generations become dim in the vista of antiquity. He was a lineal descendant of Alfred the Great, of England, by two lines. He was lineally descended form Hugh Capet and forty other continental monarchs; likewise from King John, the grantor of Magna Charta, and from baronial sureties for that famous document, namely, Richard de Clare, Earl of Hertford, Gilbert de Clare, Earl of Hertford, John de Lacie, Lord of Pontefract, Saire de Quincy, Earl of Winchetser, Roger and Hugh Bigod, Earls of Norfolk, William de Albini, Baron of Belvoir, and Robert de Roos, Baron of Hamlake. He was a lineal descendant of the great emperor Charlemagne.

"What of it? Thousands of living Americans, in all walks of life, had similar or the same ancestors. This is not stated as an exclusive fact of history, but as proof that many other American families are of a similar derivation, though not all of them know of it. The upshot of George Washington's ancestry is that it was his ancestry, and that the majority of his fellow countrymen did not so descend. Hence the question: Would he have been what he was had his ancestry been of the low and humble for a thousand years? Genealogy has revealed families that have continued in obscurity for nigh a thousand years; and it has disclosed others that, time and time again, have risen to eminence, and remained in an elevated status for a period equally long. Indeed, 'What has been will be.' Genealogy indicates that what has been *is*—that what was, *abides* in some form.

"Following the many monarchs of the earth, from whom descended George Washington, he derives through earls, baronets, lords, knights, gentlemen, and ladies of England—of the best blood, so to speak, of that nation, socially, politically, and intellectually. Our first president did not know this as a fact of history. He could not have known it unless a record of his ancestry had been prepared and bequeathed to him, nor could he have caused to be discovered what has since been revealed, because, in his day, the British archives were largely a sealed book—not arranged in a condition enabling an investigator adequately to search them. But he did know that the Washingtons were aristocratic and not democratic, as the terms were understood in his time. He maintained that social distinction throughout his own life. He knew that he was never to forget the pride of his birth, the responsibility of power, and the dignity of authority; nor did he forget or allow others to forget. His writings reveal that he had the belief that he was of no common, obscure, or unennobled stock; that he knew enough of his forebears to feel that he was born to rule by virtue of inherited capacity and by his right of self-assertion and application. Had George Washington had spread before him the evidence of his ancestry, we believe that he would have acknowledged it as something to be viewed with respect, and to be reflected upon, but not to be by himself or by others considered as entitling him to any additional esteem or recognition over any other honorable living man however humble."[1]

Those who wish to investigate in detail the Washington lineage, given here in broad outline, are recommended to "The Washington Ancestry," a very scientific genealogical work by Charles A. Hoppin. The founders of the family in Virginia were Colonel John Washington[2] who was born in England in 1632, arrived in this country 1656, and died in Westmoreland County, Virginia 1677, and his wife Anne Pope,[3] daughter of Lieutenant Colonel Nathaniel Pope.

Three of the five children of this couple lived to maturity. Of these Captain Lawrence Washington[4] was the grandfather of General George Washington; Captain John Washington[5] married Ann Wickliffe and had three sons; and the only daughter Anne Washington[6] married Major Francis Wright[7] and had a son and a daughter born to her.

It is possible that Jefferson County may be the residence of descendants of several of the Washington branches but this article will deal only with those coming down from the last named union of Anne Washington and Major Francis Wright. The first was their son John Wright,[8] gentleman, justice, sheriff's deputy, surveyor, and vestryman, born circa 1682 in Westmoreland County, Virginia and died 1732 in Prince William County. His wife Dorothy Awbrey,[9] married circa 1706, had died by 1739 in Prince William County, Virginia.

Their son John Wright,[10] gentleman, justice, sheriff, captain, and vestryman, born 1707 in Westmoreland County and died 1791 in Prince William County, Virginia. "John Wright was the first male member of the family of Richard Wright of Northumberland in America to live beyond middle age. . . . He was the eighth justice, the seventh military officer, the second sheriff, and the eighth 'gentleman', successively, in the American history of his ancestry. Well may we recount, at this moment, that his great-great-grandfathers were Lieutenant Colonel Nathaniel Pope, gentleman and justice, and Colonel John Mottrom, gentleman, justice and burgess of the Colony of Virginia; his great-grandfathers were Colonel John Washington, gentleman, justice and burgess, Captain Henry Awbrey, gentleman, justice and burgess, and Captain Richard Wright, gentleman and justice; he was second cousin (a generation older) of General George Washington, first President of the United States; his grandfather, Major Francis Wright, was a justice and sheriff; while his father, John, was the seventh successive justice, in Westmoreland, and a prospective founder of the county of Prince William. That John Wright should maintain the social position of his family is to be expected."[11] His wife was Elizabeth Darnall,[12] married circa 1729, died after 1785.

Their son William Wright,[13] born circa 1735 in Prince William County, Virginia captain in both the French and Indian and Revolutionary Wars, died 1806 in Fauquier County. His first wife Mary ————, or more probably his second wife Elizabeth—————.[14]

Their son John Wright,[15] born circa 1760 in Fauquier County, Virginia, and his wife Ann Mason. The marriage of this couple is recorded in Fauquier County, Virginia, as of 3 November 1790.[16] Through a printing error the "Washington Ancestry" gives this date as 1780.[17] The writer examined the original document at Warrenton, Virginia and with it was the following consent by the bride's mother; "I do hereby certify that John Wright has my consent to marry my daughter Ann Mason. Given under my hand this 3rd day of November 1790. Signed Margaret Mason. Witness Richard Picrel, Frances Brooke, Clerk."

John Wright completed his service in the Revolutionary War[18] and had made, according to tradition, three previous journeys to the Falls of the Ohio before returning to Virginia to marry his young bride. This tradition is supported by the fact that John entered 50 acres upon a Military Warrant in Jefferson County in 1780,[19] that 100 acres were issued to him in 1783 "in consideration of his services for three years a soldier in the Virginia Continental Line,"[20] and that he or his father purchased 333 acres on Floyd's Fork in Jefferson County 14 March 1787 in the name of Elizabeth Wright.[21]

Now it is not certain whether this Elizabeth was John's mother or stepmother. His father married first Mary ———— who was living in 1762[22] but left a will[23] naming wife Elizabeth and mentioning fourteen children but did not enlighten us as to all their names or maternal side. That John named one daughter Elizabeth and none Mary seems to indicate that Elizabeth might have been his mother but this is speculation.

John and Ann remained in Fauquier County, Virginia two and a half years and during this time two children were born to them, a son named Reuben and a daughter Margaret, named for her maternal grandmother Margaret Mason.

Those who intended to migrate from Fauquier County, Virginia to Jefferson County, Kentucky in 1793 had an equal choice of routes. They could go far out of their way toward the southwest, enter Kentucky at the Cumberland Gap and follow the Wilderness Road overland or they could go equally far out of their way to the northwest, take a flat boat at Pittsburgh and float down the Ohio. John and Ann chose the latter route. Possibly they were influenced in their choice because ten years before Daniel Brodhead had begun the regular transportation of goods of all kinds from Philadelphia to Pittsburgh by wagon and thence down the Ohio to Louisville by flat boat.[24] Such regularity of transportation would naturally increase the safety of other travelers.

However, some trouble was encountered on the trip down the Ohio as they were fired upon by Indians.[25] Upon arrival at Louisville, whose population was numbered then only in the hundreds, they settled on Elizabeth Wright's 333 acres on Floyd's Fork. Sometime before 1810 John was, according to tradition, killed by Indians. He was, whatever the cause, no longer living by this date. Before his death, five more children were born. The following is a list of the seven children as proven by Jefferson County, Kentucky marriage licenses, marriage bonds, suits and wills:

1. Margaret Wright, born in Fauquier County, Virginia, 1791, brought to Jefferson County, Kentucky by her parents in 1793, married Jonathan Paget 9 June 1810, and died in Jefferson County 11 June 1842–of whom more below in detail.

2. Reuben Wright, born in Fauquier County, Virginia, 1792, brought to Jefferson County, Kentucky by his parents in 1793, married Mary Ward, sister of John Ward, 29 Dec. 1812[26] and left within several days to join the Kentucky volunteers in the second war against England.[27] In his will,[28] he names children Joseph F. Wright and daughter Elizabeth Ann

who married David A. Ward in Jefferson County in 1835.[29] Jefferson County records contain many deeds, suits, etc., establishing the relationship between Reuben, his children, his sisters and brothers, and his in-laws. This Reuben Wright is not to be confused with the Reuben Wright who married Kezziah Jackson in 1817[30] in Jefferson County for he was still married to Mary Ward when he died in 1855.

3. Elizabeth Wright, born circa 1794 in Jefferson County, married Samuel Cox in 1815[31] and by him had children, John, Samuel, and Martha Cox. Married second Hiram Clarkson in 1831[32] and by him, or the following husband, had son James Clarkson. Married Thomas Clarkson in 1832,[33] and fourth and last married John H. Long sometime before 1848.[34]

4. John Wright, born circa 1795 in Jefferson County, married Frances Barbee 1819 in Shelby County, Kentucky[35] and had daughters Ann who married Hiram Washburn in 1834,[36] Elmira who married William Dohoney,[37] and a son Samuel.[38]

5. Gabriella Wright, born circa 1795 in Jefferson County, married first John Cranford in 1816[39] and second Daniel B. Doiser,[40] date unknown. If she had children by either of these marriages, it does not appear in the records searched.

6. Mildred Wright, born circa 1796 in Jefferson County, married William Douglass in 1819[41] and had two children William and Jane.

7. Martha Wright, born circa 1801 in Jefferson County, married first Eliel Forsythe in 1821[42] and second English O. Smith in 1838[43] leaving no children. She died in 1842 and in her will[44] left $500.00 each to her niece and nephew Jane and William Douglass. All the balance of her estate, including valuable real estate on LaFayette Street in Louisville, she bequeathed to her husband but since she had placed it in trust with her nephew Joseph F. Wright before her marraige to Smith, all her sisters and brothers and their children made claim and through this suit[45] we are able to identify all then living.

Care must be taken not to confuse John Wright and his wife Ann of Shelby County with our Jefferson Countians of exactly the same names who, to make matters worse, lived only a few miles away on the other side of the county boundary line. John of Shelby was born 1753 and died 1823 leaving a will.[46] His wife Ann died 1844. Their children were: John who married Nancy Taylor 1818; Thomas who married Fanny Taylor 1809; Frances; George; Richard (there was also a Richard, son of Samuel Wright); Lorenzo D.; William; Elizabeth who married ------ Payne; Susanna who married ------ Ratcliff; Rebecca; Sarah; Polly; and Mildred Ann. We have no interest in this family except to identify them with the purpose of keeping them from becoming entangled with our Wright family by later generations.

We will leave these multiplying families and return to the first born Margaret. She first appears in the public records when a license is taken out for her marriage in Jefferson County. "Jonathan Paget to Peggy Right dau. Annie Right c.p. (consent proven) by Richard Right June 9, 1810."[47] The marriage bond adds to our information; "Jonathan Paget, son of Theophilus Paget, consent proven, to Peggy Right daughter of Anne Right, consent proven. Bondsman Reubin Right. License and bond June 9, 1810. Married June 9, 1810 by Nathan H. Hall."[48] This license and bond establishes the identity of Margaret's mother and Jonathan's father. "Peggy Right" is, of course, Margaret Wright. "Reubin" is Reuben her brother and "Richard" is the son of Samuel Wright[49] and probably a cousin.

While this article traces the descent from Colonel John Washington, who founded the family in Virginia, to some of his present living posterity, the work of gathering the data necessarily progressed in just the opposite direction. It was not enough that by common knowledge in the Wright family it was known that Margaret Wright Paget was the daughter of John Wright—legal proof had to be found. Months of research produced the proof in a roundabout way that resembled an algebraic equation. The essentials were that a suit in the Jefferson County Circuit Court[50] contained the information that Margaret and Mildred Wright were sisters. Working from this, Mildred's marriage license; "William Douglass to Mildred Right daughter of John and Ann Right, mother's consent proven Sept. 2, 1819"[51] made it evident that John was also Margaret's father since he and Ann were married as far back as 1790. The mother's consent was given because the father was dead.

Jonathan Paget, who married Margaret Wright, was of one of the oldest families in America and one of the first to arrive in Jefferson County. Paget is thought to be a contraction of the cognomen "Plantagenet." Though still a very rare name, as it was centuries ago, some of its owners have always been prominent in the past and are prominent today in England and America. William Paget was Sergeant at Mace of the City of London in 1350;[52] Sir William Paget was one of the two leading organizers of the original Virginia Company in 1618;[53] the present Sir Richard Paget has kindly assisted the writer in ascertaining the forebears of the American branch; Major General Bernard Charles Tolver Paget, son of the late Bishop of Oxford was a hero in both World Wars; and Lady Elizabeth Paget carried the train of Queen Elizabeth at her coronation. The first, of the branch of the family with which this account is concerned, to come to America was Edmund Paget who was born in England in 1646 and arrived in Old Rappahannock County, Virginia in 1665.[54] He had son Francis of Essex County, Virginia;[55] who had son Reuben of Shenandoah County, Virginia;[56] who had son Theophilus[57] who came by the river route to Jefferson County,

Kentucky, while it was yet "territory of the United States south of the Ohio River."[58]

Jonathan Paget conducted a mercantile establishment in Louisville on Market Street between Floyd and Preston[59] from shortly after his marriage to Margaret Wright until his death. He and Margaret had six children:[60]

1. Matilda Paget, born circa 1812, bought and sold much real estate in Louisville. She married Robert Moody in 1847[61] but died in 1849 leaving a will in which James Speed performed his last act of a lifelong friendship to Matilda by acting as witness.[62] There were no children.
2. Joshua Paget, sometimes called Joseph, born circa 1815, died unmarried in Jefferson County before 1848.[63] He was named for Joshua Jennert of Fauquier County, Virginia, uncle of his mother.
3. Benjamin Bryan Paget, born circa 1817 in Jefferson County, died a bachelor before 1843.[64]
4. William Paget, born circa 1822 in Jefferson County, Kentucky,[65] married Rebecca Mills in Owen County, Indiana,[66] and later moved to Greene County, Indiana.
5. Martha Ann Paget, born circa 1827[67] in Jefferson County, Kentucky in 1841, married Judge Jesse Franklin Hammon, son of John Hammon, Revolutionary soldier and pioneer Kentuckian.[68] Ultimate heir of her mother and sister Matilda, Martha Ann died in Louisville in 1877 leaving three children.
6. Pamela Paget, born 13 June 1830 in Jefferson County, married ------ Thomas[69] and moved first to Chilicothe, Missouri and later to Wheeling, Missouri where she was visited in later years by her niece Frances, daughter of Martha Ann Paget Hammon.

The Paget family had fought their way westward, generation after generation, from Tidewater Virginia to the Piedmont, then to the Shenandoah Valley, and on to Kentucky, to Indiana, Illinois, Missouri, and on to the coast. In each place small units of the family remained to take root while the rest went on. For awhile these units kept in touch with each other and it was during one of these visits to the Pagets of Owen County, Indiana that Jonathan Paget died, sometime prior to 1842.

In 1837 his wife Margaret Wright Paget inherited a considerable estate from her Washington-Wright family in Virginia and among other things decided to erect a fine house. At that time the present "Point", which is now possibly the least desirable location for residential purposes in the city, was fashionable and the most desirable. The "Point" of that day was something of a mile further west, including land now under the second street bridge, and was so called because Beargrass Creek, still in its original bed, swung in a long S curve downstream and emptied into the Ohio between Third and Wall (now Fourth) Streets, forming a long "point" of land on the river side of the creek. A bridge crossed this creek near its mouth at Second Street, just under the present bridge, and from it a 12 foot plank road traversed the point, more or less following the route of the present River Road until it reached Adams Street where it followed Fulton Street on to the eastward. Beyond Adams Street, the present River Road was the alley to the lots facing Fulton Street and the River.[70] A ferry carrying passengers to and from Indiana landed between Adams and Wayne Streets.[71]

A newspaper article described the scene very well, "The location on Fulton Street on 'the Point' was at that time (1838) considered the most promising part of the city. Tow Head Island had not yet been formed and the most elaborate passenger craft on the Ohio found moorings on the 'Point'. A hotel celebrated for its cuisine stood at the fork of Fulton Street and (what is now) the River Road.

"All the houses along Fulton Street, including the 'Mansion House' (Paget house), were provided with balconies to enable the owners to keep a comfortable eye on their boats. It was here that the prosperous settled. They landscaped the grounds, planted trees, shrubbery, flowers and vines, for the influence was that of New Orleans whence many of the boats came and went. 'Mansion House' was designed by a New Orleans architect.

"Of course, the subsequent fate of the once-lovely 'Point' is well known. A barge was sunk and there followed the formation of Tow Head Island which ruined the whole neighborhood by preventing large steamboats from landing. Later, repeated floods made necessary the building of a levee which despoiled the site by covering the sloping lawns and smothering the trees."[72]

Fulton Street was once known as Frenchmen's Row for many of the "prosperous" who settled there were residents of New Orleans who journeyed up the river each year to spend the summer here and escape the yellow fever. In addition to the reasons given by the newspaper, the Point section began to decline when in 1854[73] the present artificial channel was dug which caused Beargrass Creek to empty into the Ohio above the Point instead of below. This not only caused deposits of sand and silt to accumulate faster than usual but as the town grew the creek became more and more a sewer. When the "cut-off" was made there was no longer a "Point" remaining but the name persisted. However, strangely enough the location designated by the word "Point" shifted from the real point near Third Street to its present location almost a mile up-river.

But all these faults of higher civilization were scores of years off the future when in 1837 Mrs. Margaret Wright Paget set out to find a spot on which to build her fine house. Even though the population of Louisville was then just over 10,000, empty lots were not available in this section so she purchased a house and lot from Lloyd and Lydia White "on the south side of Fulton Street and being the western or lower 65 feet of lot No. 8 in Geiger's[74] addition to Louisville and extends the same width southwardly 210 feet to an alley."[75] This alley is the present River Road.

The White home was not destroyed but was kept as the rear wing of the new house. Today the original house is plainly evident because of its entirely different and earlier architecture. Its date can be placed as being between 1790 and 1800, one of the oldest, if not the oldest, house remaining in Louisville and in almost perfect condition due to the excellent care it has received throughout the years. It was already so old in 1838 that it was necessary to replaster the ceilings.[76]

A combination contract-specification, now in the possession of the writer, which was signed 8 May 1838 between Jeremiah Hollinsead, the builder, and "Margaret Pagget" calls for mouldings "not inferior to Dan'l Smith's house on Fifth Street . . . . wooden lintils and sills as good as in the Kentucky Engine House" and is, all in all, a surprisingly complete specification for that time. The house was constructed in such a fine manner that it withstood almost complete submersion in the great flood of 1937 without suffering any serious damage while half the other houses in the neighborhood were washed away or turned over.

After the building was completed, Margaret was faced with the necessity of adding to her domestics. She was evidently fastidious as to the type of slave she purchased for she went to Federal Hill, better known as My Old Kentucky Home, and purchased two negro women named Aggy and Phebe from John Rowan, Esq.[77] When all was complete, the house, furnishings, staff, and landscaping, Margaret had the finest place in Louisville. An 1842 deposition still existing states that it was always known as "The Mansion House."[78]

Unfortunately, Margaret was to enjoy her new home for only a short while as she died suddenly on the 11th of June 1842.[79] Her eldest daughter, Matilda Moody, succeeded by means of the courts in obtaining the largest share of the estate but in her own will in 1849 suffered remorse and returned the part rightfully belonging to Pamela and Martha Ann Hammon with this statement, "this bequest is made to my two sisters because it never has been my intention to take from them any portion of my mother's estate."[80]

Of the six children of Jonathan Paget and Margaret Wright, only Martha Ann Hammon raised a family in Jefferson County. Pamela Thomas brought her family up in Missouri as we have said and William Paget probably had a family in Indiana. The others died childless.

Martha Ann and Jesse Franklin Hammon had three children: Edward Hammon, who engaged in the steamboat business and never married; Frances Hammon, who married Peter Thomas and had eighteen children, many of whom are still living; and Charles Franklin Hammon, who married Barbara,[81] daughter of

Matthew Miller (an early Louisville merchant), and raised seven children to maturity, two of whom are still living in Louisville.

So today in Jefferson County, Kentucky some of the families named Wright, Thomas, Ward, Hammon, Cox, Clarkson, Washburn, Rudy, Fisher, Howell, Douglass, and Robertson carry as much of the Washington blood in their veins as any person alive. "The outstanding fact to be noted . . . . is that there is something vital and far-reaching in heredity; that the Reverend Lawrence Washington's loyalty to church and state recalls the remarkable royal and noble ancestry of his mother, Margaret (Butler) Washington; that the great leadership and eminent citizenship displayed by the Washingtons and by some of their descendants in America was long in the making; that when made such qualities often stay made, even through periods of great stress and fortitude; that the American who imagines that the great success of his country, as well as his own, is an exotic mushroom, grown up from nothing, owing nothing to a past, is shortsighted."[82]

FOOTNOTES

[1]Washington Ancestry by Charles Arthur Hoppin, Privately Printed, Greenfield, Ohio, 1932, Vol. 1, Page 1-2.
[2]Ibid. Vol. 1, Page 139.
[3]Ibid. Vol. 1, Page 248.
[4]Ibid. Vol. 1, Page 212.
[5]Ibid. Vol. 1, Page 213.
[6]Ibid. Vol. 1, Page 211.
[7]Ibid. Vol. 1, Page 338.
[8]Ibid. Vol. 1, Page 363.
[9]Ibid. Vol. 1, Page 366.
[10]Ibid. Vol. 1, Page 394.
[11]Ibid. Vol. 1, Page 405.
[12]Ibid. Vol. 1, Page 401.
[13]Ibid. Vol. 1, Page 423.
[14]Ibid. Vol. 1, Page 423.
[15]Ibid. Vol. 1, Page 424.
[16]Fauquier County, Virginia, Marriage Book 5, 304.
[17]Washington Ancestry, Vol. 1, Page 424.
[18]John Wright is among the 139 men listed "In Memory of Revolutionary Soldiers Buried in Jefferson County, Kentucky," Filson Club Quarterly, Vol. 15, Page 48.
[19]Jefferson County, Kentucky, Entry Book A, Page 182.
[20]Kentucky Land Office, Warrant 2090.
[21]Jefferson County, Kentucky, Deed Book 1, Page 363.
[22]Washington Ancestry, Vol. 1, Page 424.
[23]Ibid.
[24]History of Kentucky by Lewis Collins, Revised by Richard H. Collins. Published by Richard H. Collins, Louisville, Kentucky, 1877, Page 372.
[25]Ibid.
[26]Jefferson County, Kentucky, Marriage Book 1, Page 74.
[27]Kentucky Roster; War 1812 by Hill, Page 27.

[28]Jefferson County, Kentucky, Will Book 5, Page 10.
[29]Jefferson County, Kentucky, Marriage Book 2, Page 157.
[30]Jefferson County, Kentucky, Marriage Book 1, Page 95.
[31]Jefferson County, Kentucky, Marriage Book 3, Page 190.
[32]Jefferson County, Kentucky, Marriage Book 2, Page 75.
[33]Jefferson County, Kentucky, Marriage Book 2, Page 80.
[34]Jefferson County, Kentucky, Old Circuit & Common Law Court, Case 38498.
[35]Shelby County, Kentucky, Marriage Book 1819.
[36]Jefferson County, Kentucky, Marriage Book 2, Page 123.
[37]Jefferson County, Kentucky, Deed Book 81, Page 430.
[38]Jefferson County, Kentucky, Old Circuit & Common Law Court, Case 38498.
[39]Jefferson County, Kentucky, Marriage Book 1, Page 86.
[40]Jefferson County, Kentucky, Old Circuit & Common Law Court, Case 38498.
[41]Jefferson County, Kentucky, Marriage Book 1, Page 108.
[42]Jefferson County, Kentucky, Marriage Book 1, Page 126.
[43]Jefferson County, Kentucky, Marriage Book 3, Page 57.
[44]Jefferson County, Kentucky, Will Book 3, Page 296.
[45]Jefferson County, Kentucky, Old Circuit & Common Law Court, Case 38498.
[46]Shelby County, Kentucky, Will Book 6, Page 179.
[47]Jefferson County, Kentucky, Marriage Book 1, Page 67.
[48]Jefferson County, Kentucky, Marriage Bonds, Filson Club, Book 1, Page 67.
[49]Jefferson County, Kentucky, Will Book 1, Page 245.
[50]Jefferson County, Kentucky, Old Circuit & Common Law Court, Case 38498.
[51]Jefferson County, Kentucky, Marriage Book 1, Page 108.
[52]Castles and Halls of England by Rev. F. O. Morris, Page 4.
[53]Records of the Virginia Company, Edited by Susan M. Kingsbury, Government Printing Office, Washington, D. C., 1906, Vol. 3, Page 86, 525, 528.
[54]Cavaliers and Pioneers, Abstracts of Virginia Patents and Grants, by Neel M. Nugent, Dietz Printing Company, Richmond, Virginia, 1934, Page 567.
[55]Essex County Virginia, Deed Book 13, Page 252, Date 1709.
[56]Shenandoah County, Virginia, Will Book C, Page 23.
[57]Shenandoah County, Virginia, Deed Book A, Page 336.
[58]Shenandoah County, Virginia, Deed Book 1, Page 364.
[59]Louisville Directory for 1832, Published by Richard W. Otis, James Virden, Printer, Page 63.
[60]Jefferson County, Kentucky, Deed Book 59, Page 504.
[61]Jefferson County, Kentucky, Marriage Book 4, Page 169.
[62]Jefferson County, Kentucky, Will Book 4, Page 201.
[63]Louisville Chancery Court, Case 4210, Date 1843.
[64]Ibid.
[65]Ibid.
[66]Owen County, Indiana, Marriage Book C, Page 31.
[67]Louisville Chancery Court, Case 4210, Date 1843.
[68]Filson Club Historical Quarterly, Vol. 23, Page 202, July 1949.
[69]Louisville Chancery Court, Case 4210, Date 1843.
[70]Map, Louisville and Environs, E. D. Hobbs, Date 1831.
[71]Jefferson County, Kentucky, Deed Book KK, Page 393, Date 1833.
[72]Courier-Journal, 18 September 1940.
[73]Historical Quarterly, Filson Club, Vol. 2, Page 20.

[74] Jacob Geiger, founder of Huntingburg, Indiana (History of Dubois County, Indiana, by George Robert Wilson, Printed by the author in Jasper, Indiana, 1910), son of Captain Fred Geiger who was wounded in Battle of Tippecanoe (Battle of Tippecanoe, Alfred Pirtle, J. P. Morton & Company, 1900, Page 36).

[75] Jefferson County, Kentucky, Deed Book UU, Page 471.

[76] Louisville Chancery Court, Case 4210.

[77] Louisville Chancery Court, Case 3767.

[78] Ibid.

[79] Ibid.

[80] Jefferson County, Kentucky, Will Book 4, Page 201.

[81] Jefferson County, Kentucky, Marriage Book 10, Page 284.

[82] Charles Hoppin in the Washington Ancestry, Vol. 1, Page 141.

YOUNG FAMILY

Compiled by Asa D. Young in 1925. Dates and names added since his death are in Italic type. Submitted by Mrs. Vincent R. Jones.

JOHN CHILDERS AND RACHEL PERKINS FAMILY

John Childress was born in Goochland County Va., in 1730. He served in the Revolutionary War in the second Virginia Regiment. Married Rachel Perkins of Albemarle County, Va., in 1753. He died in August 1797. They had four sons and two daughters, John born 1754, Henry born 1757, Robert born 1760, died 1855, Abram, Rachel and Sarah.

John Childress son of the above John and Rachel Childress was the grandfather of President James K. Polk's wife. Her name was Sarah and her fathers name was Joel Childress.

ROBERT CHILDRESS AND RACHEL EASTRIDGE FAMILY

Robert Childress son of John and Rachel Perkins was born in 1760, married Rachel Eastridge of Goochland County, Va., in 1786. He died in 1855. 5 children, William born 1787 died 1865, Henry born Dec. 10, 1788, died October 4, 1873, Robert born 1789, Abram and Nancy.

ISAAH GREER AND RHODA DIVERS FAMILY

Isaah Greer was born 1758; Rhoda Divers was born 1760, they were married in 1785; their daughter Sarah Greer was born October 24, 1788, died July 28, 1873. She married Henry Childress.

HENRY CHILDRESS AND SARAH GREER FAMILY

Henry Childress, born December 10, 1788, died October 4, 1873. He married Sarah Greer November 4, 1816, moved with their family to Kentucky in 1836 and settled near Dry Fork, Kentucky, where they lived and died. They were buried at the Ellis grave yard. They had the following children:

Cynthia F. Childress born November 1, 1817, died January 19, 1894, married D. G. Ferguson.

Ampsa P. Childress born December 3, 1818, died February 14, 1898, married Varlinda J. Ellis.

Jane G. Childress born April 8, 1822, died December 25, 1876, married Milton Berry.

Rachel Childress born Mar. 28, 1824, died September 13, 1906, married Sam Tolle.

Caswell J. R. Childress born December 16, 1826, died August 18, 1900, married Julia A. P. Ellis.

John A. Childress born May 14, 1829, died August 18, 1846, died single.

DOUGAL G. FERGUSON AND CYNTHIA F. CHILDRESS FAMILY

Dougal G. Ferguson born September 25, 1814, died August 6, 1900, came from Virginia. He married Cynthia F. Childress in 1838. They lived fifteen miles south of Glasgow, Kentucky and were buried at the Ellis grave yard. They had the following children:

Henry E. Ferguson, born April 30, 1839, died November 30, 1901, married Amanda Dillon.

Sallie A. Ferguson born October 1, 1840, died September 16, 1916, married George C. Young.

George Ferguson born February 14, 1844, died October 29, 1893, married Bettie Beheler.

Mary Ferguson born April 24, 1846, died March 22, 1914, married John B. Austin.

Julia A. Ferguson born April 11, 1849, died November 18, 1882, married Marcellus Matthews.

Abraham Ferguson, born February 1, 1851, died January 10, 1866, single.

Thomas C. Ferguson born August 28, 1853, died *May 29, 1931*, married Rachel Thomerson.

Morris Ferguson born August 15, 1856, died March 3, 1914, married A. J. Thomerson.
Yetmon Ferguson born June 11, 1858, died *November 15, 1930,* married Irene Parrish.

The above Dougal G. Ferguson was a son of Thomas Ferguson, who married Agnes Chambers. They lived in Franklin County Virginia and were buried there.

GEORGE BUSH AND ARMINE PHILBERT FAMILY

A Miss Stone married a Mr. Redford and he died; she next married a Mr. Philbert, she having two sets of children.

Their daughter Armine Philbert married George Bush, he died in 1826; she died first. They died in Southern Barren County Kentucky, near Caney Fork Creek, and were buried there. They had the following children:

Armine Bush born April 7, 1790, died in 1831, married Asa Ellis.

Walter Bush born in 1792, died in 1834; first wife Lucy Grubbs, second wife Cynthia Whitney.

William Bush born February 24, 1795, died in 1831, married Jennie Hagan.

George Bush born December 7, 1797, died in —— married Catherine ——.

Jane Bush born April 10(9) 1799, died July 2, 1852, married Loamy Whitney.

Archie Bush born December 7, 1802 died —— married ——.

Josiah Bush born December 25, 1804 died May 20, 1863; first wife Sarah J. Hughes, second wife Jane H. Button.

Isaac Bush born September 14, 1806, died in 1848, married Matilda Parker.

Rebecca Bush born in 1810, died in 1830, married Fleming Bibb.

Peter Bush born in 1812, died 1848, married Lucy Franklin. Charles Bush born June 15, 1808, died 1873, married Jemima Herndon.

ASA ELLIS AND ARMINE BUSH FAMILY

Asa Ellis, who married Armine Bush March 23, 1804 came from South Carolina about 1800 and settled near Pleasant Hill church in southern Barren County where they are buried. He was born August 2, 1777, died in 1853. They had the following children:

John Ellis born August 8, 1806, died March 23, 1807.

Mary Ellis born April 14, 1808, died January 10, 1895. married Asa Young.

George Ellis born October 11, 1809, died May 9, 1874, married Fannie Wheeler.

Martha Ellis born July 13, 1811, died January 31, ·1812.

Jane Ellis born December 7, 1812 died ——, first married John Wheeler, second O. H. Morrow.

Katherine Ellis born January 1, 1817 died ——, married Fleming Bibb.

Alfred Ellis born August 8, 1821, died August 7, 1904, married Mary Dickerson.

Asa Ellis born January 5, 1823, died November 18, 1885, married Sallie Lyons.

Armine Ellis born January 28, 1825 died ——.

Josiah B. Ellis born November 10, 1826, died in 1847, single.

William Ellis born September 20, 1828, died in 1848, single.

Isaac Ellis born January 31, 1832, died January 16, 1857, married Salemna Lyons.

James C. Ellis born April 22, 1836, died January 1904, married Mollie Boyd.

GEORGE CHAPMAN AND DIANA DERRITT FAMILY

George Chapman was born December 25, 1736 and died on the way from North Carolina to Kentucky in 1781 and was buried at Beans Station, Tennessee, which is about forty-five miles northeast of Knoxville. He married Diana Derritt in 1758, who was born in 1737 and died June 27, 1800 in Fayette County Kentucky where she had settled with her children as follows:

Frances D. Chapman born October 10, 1759, died June 3, 1832, married James Young.
Elizabeth Chapman born March 27, 1761, died July 1840, married John Ellis.
Nancy Chapman born May 7, 1763, married a Thomas and moved to Illinois.
Margaret Chapman born February 16, 1766, married Aaron Higgins, moved away.
George Chapman born Dec. 14, 1770.
Polly Chapman born July 26, 1775.
Asa Chapman born July 2, 1779, married and had five children and moved away.

CHURCH CERTIFICATE OF JAMES YOUNG

Dundee Scotland May 25, 1774.

That the bearer James Young a young unmarried man has resided three years in this place under a fair character and now removed free of all public scandal ground of church censure so that there is nothing known to us that may hinder his reception into any christian congregation or family where Divine providence may order his lott is attested date and place aforesaid.

By James Blinshall Min.
John Small cl.

See Ky. Baptist History vol. 2 page 447.

JAMES YOUNG AND FRANCES CHAPMAN FAMILY.

James Young came from Dundee, Scotland to the British colonies in 1774 and resided at Yorktown, Virginia. He came to Fayette County Kentucky and married Frances Chapman May 23, 1792. They moved to Cumberland County in 1801 but on account of the Indians they moved to Barren County on Peters Creek fifteen miles south of Glasgow where he died August 13, 1821 and she died June 3, 1832 and they were buried on the home place. They had the following children:

George Young born January 5, 1794, died October 15, 1821, single.
Asa Young born May 13, 1795, died January 13, 1865, married Mary Ellis.
Mollie Young born February 7, 1799, died in 1881, married William Boyd.
Jades Young born July 23, 1801, died June 4, 1853, married Martha Depp, second wife Julia ——.
William Young born March 15, 1805, died May 4, 1830, single.

ASA YOUNG AND MARY ELLIS FAMILY

Asa Young and his wife Mary Ellis, born April 14, 1808, died January 10, 1895, were buried on the James Young farm fifteen miles south of Glasgow Kentucky. They were married October 2, 1823, and had the following children:

George C. Young born September 19, 1824, died June 18, 1896, married Sallie A Ferguson.
Amanda J. Young born January 21, 1826, died August 23, 1897, married Samuel T. Davis.
Mary F. Young born February 24, 1835, died March 24, 1848, single.
Asa E. Young born October 14 1836, died March 31, 1918, first wife Eliza J. Dillian, second wife Ellie Smith.
James M. Young born April 5, 1839, died August 17, 1843.
Armine Catherine Young born February 21, 1841, died October 11, 1894, married Thomas H. King.

GEORGE C. YOUNG AND SALLIE A. FERGUSON FAMILY

George C. Young and his wife Sallie A. Ferguson, born October 1, 1840, died September 16, 1916, were buried on the James Young farm. They were married March, 14, 1860 and had the following children:

James W. E. Young born July 27, 1863 died December 25, 1865.
Lola A. Young born April 29, 1867, died *Aug. 4, 1938*, married Virgil L. Mansfield.
Asa D. Young born January 5, 1869, died *June 6, 1939, single.*__
Samuel T. Young born February 25, 1871, died *Dec. 5, 1934* first wife Pearle Hancock, second Melva McBride.
Ampsa P. Young born May 7, 1876 died *Sept. 9, 1946*, married Claudie White.
Eugene Yetmon Young born August 1, 1870, *died July 22, 1935* married Bernice Smith, *2nd wife Madge Myers, who were married Aug. 31, 1929.*

VIRGIL L. MANSFIELD AND LOLA YOUNG FAMILY

Virgil L. Mansfield born August 27, 1863 died June 11, 1897. His wife was Lola A. Young. They were married June 12, 1895 and had one child, Virgil L. Mansfield, born June 18, 1897, died September 21, 1918, single.

SAMUEL T. YOUNG AND PEARL HANCOCK FAMILY

Samuel T. Young married Pearle Hancock, born December 15, 1874, died February 14, 1919. They were married June 2, 1897 and had one child, Horace C. Young, born October 10, 1898, died ——. He married Lula McGrath. Sam T's. second wife Melva McBride, born Jan. 6, 1901 died ——. They were married June 3, 1925.

EUGENE YETMON YOUNG AND BERNICE SMITH FAMILY

Eugent Yetmon Young married 1st Bernice Smith born April 11, 1881. died——. They were married April 21, 1903 and had one child, Asa D. Young, born April 20, 1904 died ——. Married *Sarah Conner Apr. 30, 1934*. His second wife Madge Myers born June 27, 1891 died——. m. Aug. 31, 1929.

AMPSA P. YOUNG AND CLAUDIE WHITE FAMILY

Ampsa P. Young married Claudie A. White born may 21, 1881, died ——. They were married November 22, 1898 and had the following children:
Amanda Young born November 30, 1899, died ——, married F. Dooley.
Son born and died August 28, 1901.
Paul L. Young born February 9, 1903, died ——, married Leone Pardue.
George C. Young born October 25, 1905, died ——.
Sarah E. Young born June 3, 1908, died July 11, 1913.
Virginia M. Young born July 16, 1910, died ——.
Mary White Young born April 4, 1913, died ——. married W. T. Riherd.
L. Frances Young born November 10, 1915, died —— *married Howard Malcolm Jones*.
Catherine B. Young born Sept. 10, 1917 died ——. *Married Ed Peterson*.
Ampsa P. Young Jr. born November 1, 1920, died ——.

FITZHUGH DOOLY AND AMANDA YOUNG FAMILY

Fitzhugh Dooly born February 6, 1898 died —— his wife was Amanda Young. They were married March 23, 1921 and had the following children:
Eloise born March 27, 1922 died ——.
Elizabeth Anne Dooly.
Martha Neal Dooly.
Irene Dooly.

HORACE C. YOUNG AND LULA McGRATH FAMILY

Horace Chapman Young born October 10, 1898, died *May 1944*. His wife Lula McGrath born ——, died ——. They were married February 9, 1925.

WILLIAM BOYD AND MOLLIE YOUNG FAMILY

William Boyd who married Mollie Young January 16, 1820 and settled on a farm near Antioch Church, died May 20, 1870. They were buried on their farm. Their oldest child John Boyd was killed by an Indian in California in 1864, their second child Fannie Boyd died about 1890, their youngest child Mollie was born January 4, 1840 and died July 18, 1915. She married James C. Ellis January 5, 1860 but they had no children. J. C. Ellis was born April 22, 1836, died 25, 1904. J. C. Ellis and his wife were buried at Cave City Kentucky.

JAMES YOUNG AND MARTHA DEPP FAMILY

James Young married Martha Depp December 14, 1826 and moved to Mississippi County, Arkansas. She was born April 27, 1803, died April 26, 1846. They had one child, a daughter Fannie J., who married a Mr. Buckner and they had several children.

James Young's second wife was Julia A. ---. No children.

SAMUEL TURNER DAVIS AND AMANDA JANE YOUNG FAMILY

Samuel Turner Davis who married Amanda Jane Young was born August 24, 1813, died June 9, 1880. They were married October 6, 1842 and had two children:

Elizabeth Davis born June 28, 1844, died May 6, 1897, married L. Caldwell.

Hardin Davis born June 6, 1847, died January 31, --- married F. Curd.

THOMAS H. KING AND ARMINE CATHERINE YOUNG FAMILY

Thomas H. King who married Armine Catherine Young was born January 7, 1831, died January 15, 1899. They were married October 15, 1860 and had four children, viz;

Asa King born August 17,1861 died ---.

Mary E. King born October 30, 1863, died ---, maried B. L. Wilson, September 29, 1887.

Ella King, single.

George King born --- died ---. married Lelia Sink.

ASA E. YOUNG AND ELIZA J. DILLON FAMILY

Asa E. Young married first May 15, 1867 to Eliza J. Dillon, born November 23, 1847, died March 5, 1883 and had the following children:

James W. Young born May 1, 1868 died ---. Married first Myrna Bixenstein, second L. B. Crabtree.

George D. Young born October 25, 1869 died --- married Verda Childress.

Edgar Young born October 25, 1871, died November 3rd 1883, died single.

Minnie Young born March 24, 1874 died --- married S. F. Smith.

Ellis Young born November 13, 1875 died --- First wife Vickie Smith, second wife Donie Smith.

Hardin Young born July 14, 1881, died *July 12, 1928.*

Oscar Young born March 19, 1878 died *March 14, 1933.*

ASA E. YOUNG AND M. ELLIE SMITH FAMILY

Asa E. Young married second October 13, 1885 M. Ellie Smith, born April 15(?) 1858. They had the following children:

Mary J. Young born, ---, died --- died single.

Annie Lillian Young born September 16, 1886 died --- married Herbert Bowles.

John S. Young born July 5, 1888 died --- married Constance Breight.

JOHN ELLIS AND ELIZABETH CHAPMAN FAMILY

John Ellis who married Elizabeth Chapman was a son of William Ellis who came from Virginia and settled with others at the fort on Elkhorn Creek near Lexington Kentucky. They were not related to the Ellis'. who came from South Carolina. John married Elizabeth Chapman March 6, 1794 and moved to Barren County Kentucky in 1804. She died in 1840 and he died in 1849 and they were buried at the Ellis grave yard on their farm, They had five children, viz.:

William Ellis who married Elizabeth Hughes and were the parents of George A. M. Ellis and others.

George Ellis married Kittie Gillock and were the parents of James M. M. Ellis and Mrs. Verlinda Childress and others.

Catherine Ellis married D. Wilson.

Elizabeth Ellis married George Darnaby.

Betty Ellis married J. Depp.

AMPSA P. YOUNG & CLAUDIA AMELIA WHITE FAMILY

Paul L. Young m. Leone Pardue, two daughters Anne & Eleanor.

Gaeorge C. Young m. Edwina Curtis two children, Jane & George Chapman Jr.

Virginia M. Young m. Joe Van Zant, one daughter Amelia.

Mary White Young, m. W. T. Riherd, two sons Joe and Frank.

Lillian Frances Young m. Howard M. Jones, Aug. 4, 1941, two dau. Jean Luckett b, Sept 24, 1943, Frances Malcolm b, Feb. 18, 1947.

Catherine B. Young m. Ed Peterson, no issue.

Ampsa P. Young m. Jean —, two daughters, Verlinda Jean and Susan Frances.

APPENDIX A

BIBLE RECORDS

KENTUCKY BIBLE RECORDS

The following records taken from old Family Bibles have been contributed by members and friends of the Historical Society and by members of the various D. A. R. Chapters throughout the State who have most generously furnished them to the Society and to the State Chairman of Genealogical Research of the D. A. R. in 1927-1928.

Among the Bible Records herewith presented are the following:

Adams-Hampton.
Alexander
Bacon
Bibb, Richard
Bibb, T. P. Atticus
Cannon
Cox
Crutchfield
Elley
Everett
Garrard
Haggard
Harlin
Harlow
Higdon
Howard
Jacobs
Lancaster
Littlepage
Neale
Park
Pedego
Peyton
Redford
Richardson
Robertson
Scott
Searcy-Smith-Thurston-Waddy
Smith, Basil Gaither
Smith, Benedict
Snoddy
Stinson (Stevenson)
Trumbo
Twyman
Waddy
Wilson-Brinegar
Woodruff
Young-Proctor

ADAMS-HAMPTON BIBLE RECORDS

(Copied by Mrs. Robert R. Gum from Bible of Mary Jane Adams, who married second Dudley Richardson. They were the grand-parents of Robert Richardson Gum, Frankfort, Ky.)

John Adams, Sr., born April 4, 1758, married Elizabeth ———— born June 25, 1768.

ISSUE

1. Traves Adams, born May 2, 1786.
2. Francis Adams, born Mar. 15, 1788.
3. Mary Adams, born Jan. 26, 1792.
4. John Adams, Jr., born Feb. 22, 1795, d. Oct. 23, 1856.
5. Elizabeth Adams, born June 29, 1798.
6. Nancy Adams, born Sept. 26, 1799.
7. Jane Adams, born Nov. —, 1801.
8. Wm. Adams, born Jan. 7, 1804.
9. Sidney Adams, born Nov. 4, 1806.
10. Lowry Adams, born Jan. 7, 1808.
11. Dolly Adams, born Nov. 30, 1809.

John Adams, Jr. (b. Feb. 22, 1795), m. June 22, 1820, Elizabeth Hampton (b Mar. 4, 1793).

ISSUE

1. Mary Jane Adams, born June 20, 1821, d. Jan. 15, 1901.
2. Elizabeth Nancy Adams, b. Feb. 1, 1823, d. June 13, 1843.
3. David Hampton Adams, b. Aug. 10, 1825, d. Jan. 10, 1856.

David Hampton was born June 1, 1764, d. Jan. 26, 1842, married Mary Johnson, born Aug. 1, 1771, d. Sept. 4, 1818.

Issue
1. John Hampton, b. July 23, 1788.
2. Sarah Hampton, b. Oct. 17, 1790.
3. Elizabeth Hampton, b. Mar. 4, 1793, m. John Adams, Jr.
4. David Hampton, Jr., b. Aug. 15, 1795.
5. Cynthy Hampton, b. Feb. 8, 1798.
6. Mary Hampton, b. July 19, 1800.
7. Nancy Hampton, b. Mar. 8, 1803.
8. Wade B. Hampton, b. May 30, 1805.
9. Alfred Howard Hampton, b. Feb. 28, 1808.
10. David Reed Hampton, b. May 22, 1810.
11. Geo. Washington, b. Sept. 9, 1812.
12. John Andrew Jackson Hampton, b. April 17, 1815.

ALEXANDER BIBLE

(Contributed by Mrs. J. K. Polk South, Jr., Franklin County, Kentucky, member of the Susannah Hart Shelby Chapter.)

Record copied from old Bible brought from Virginia to Woodford County, Kentucky, by William Alexander, and beginning with the births of his children.

BIRTHS

John Regis Alexander, born 13 November, 1793, Henrico Co.

Andrew Jonathan Alexander, born 19 March, 1769, Calfpasture.

Charles Alexander, born 21 July, 1798, Calfpasture.

Mariamne Alexander, born 30, Decr., 1800, Calfpasture.

James Robert Alexander, born 22, September, 1803, Calfpasture.

Apolline Alexander, born 15th October, 1807, Calfpasture.

William Alexander, son of John R. & Marian F. Alexander, was born 17th April, 1820, Woodford Co., Ky.

James Robert Alexander was born 12 August, 1822.

Frances Agatha Alexander was born July 12th, 1824.

Thomas Biddle Alexander, born April 5th, 1827.

John Regis Alexander, born Aug. 2nd, 1829.

DEATHS

Pierre Victoir Delaporte, died 30 July, 1796, aged 17 years.

Made. Mariamne Delaporte, aged 65 yrs., died at Rockcastle, 7 August, 1811.

William Alexander, son of Robt. & Eliza Alexander, died August 1816.

James Robert Alexander, died Oct. 8th, 1817.

Marie Agatha Henriette Sophie Alexander, wife of William Alexander, died Oct. 17th, 1817.

William Alexander, aged 90 died in Woodford Co., Kentucky, 10th January, 1819.

Mariamne Alexander, died April 28th, 1819, aged 18.

Andrew J. Alexander, was killed by the machinery of a steam saw-mill, December, 1833.

Jane Alexander, daughter of A. J. & Mira Alexander, died Oct., 1832.

Eliza Jane Alexander, wife of John Regis Alexander & daughter of Elizabeth Brooks, June 6, 1901, deceased aged 89, twenty-five days of being 90.

John Regis Alexander, husband of Eliza Jane Brooks, died 18th of Oct., 1883, age 89, twenty-five days of being 90.

M. F. Alexander, died Aug., 1843.

MARRIAGES

William Alexander to Marie Agatha Henriette Sophie De laporte, married 12 Novr. 1792.

Robert Alexander to Eliza Richison Weiseger, married October 2, 1814.

John R. Alexander to Marion Francis Campbell, married 14th May, 1818.

Charles Alexander to Martha M. Madison, married December 4th, 1821.

John Regis Alexander to Eliza Jane Van De Graphe, nee Brooks, 18449.

J. R. A. & E. J. V., married on 6th Nov., 1848.

BIRTHS

William Alexander, son of Eliza & Robert Alexander, was born August 6th at Frankfort, Kentucky.

Robert Andrew Alexander, son of J. Regis and Marian F. Alexander, was born 21st

October at Roslin, Woodford County, Kentucky (1833).

Charles Williams Alexander, son of J. R. Alexander & Marian F. Alexander, was born the 8th of Sept., 1837.

John Campbell Alexander, son of J. Regis & E. J. Alexander, 20th of April, 1852

Alice Seeley Alexander, daughter of John Campbell Alexander Born 19th March, 1898.

EDITORS NOTE—The Bible from which the above Alexander records were copied, (February 6th, 1928) by Mrs. Jouett Taylor Cannon, State Chairman of Genealogical Research for Kentucky, was printed at Philadelphia by Mathew Carey, No. 122 Market St., 1809. The bible is now owned, and in possession of Mrs. J. K. Polk South, Jr., nee Alice Seeley Alexander, above.

BACON BIBLE RECORD

(Copy of record in old Bible now 1927) in possession of Mr. J. Swigert Taylor, Frankfort, Kentucky, having been left to his late wife, Mrs. Sadie Bacon Crittenden Taylor, by her great-aunt, Miss Sarah Ware Bacon, of Frankfort, daughter of John Bacon and his second wife, Elizabeth Ware of Franklin County, Kentucky. John Bacon, and his brothers, recorded below, were all born in New Kent County, Virginia. Their father being Captain Lyddall Bacon, of the Revolution, and their mother Ann Apperson.)

The entries below are in two sections as follows:

Page 393—
John Bacon, son of Lyddall and Ann was born the 10th March, 1767.

Lyddall Bacon, son of Lyddall and Ann, was born the 29th August, 1775.

Langston Bacon, son of Lyddall and Ann was born the 20th February, 1777.

Edmund Bacon son of Lyddall and Ann was born the 26th August, 1780.

Page 677—
John Bacon and his wife, Anna Bacon, was married the 13th November, 1794.

John Bacon and his wife, Elizabeth Bacon, was married the 31st May, 1799.

Anne A. Bacon, daughter of John and and Elizabeth was born March 25, 1800.

Sally W. Bacon, daughter of John and Elizabeth, was born March 24th, 1802.

Williamson Bacon, son of John and Elizabeth, was born March 7th, 1804.

James W. Bacon, son of John and Elizabeth was born March 22nd, 1807.

Elizabeth P. Bacon was married to B. H. Bryan Dec. 31, 1839.

Anne A. Bacon was married to Philip S. Fall May 1st, 1821.

Charles P. Bacon was married to Caroline Castleman, May 18, 1821.

Williamson W. Bacon was married to Anne Maria Noel November 3rd, 1824.

John M. Bacon was married to Sarah Jane Haggin on the 29th day of March, 1835.

Richard A. Bacon was married to Elizabeth E. Terrill on the 15th of April, 1830.

Richard Apperson Bacon, son of John and Elizabeth, was born July 2, 1809.

James W. Bacon was married to Alice Riggs on the 24th of March, 1836.

Page 678—
Charles P. Bacon, son of John and Anna, was born 26th Sep., 1795.

James Bacon, son of John and Anna, was born the 9th July, 1797.

John Mosby Bacon, son of John and Elizabeth was born 31st October, 1811.

Amanda Bacon, daughter of Benedict and Susan, was born the 7th November, 1812.

Elizabeth P. Bacon, daughter of John and Elizabeth, was born 7th of May, 1814.

Albert Gallatin Bacon, son of John and Elizabeth, was born 8th of December, 1816.

Page 679—
Maria L. Rouzee, the daughter of Philemon and Agnes, was born Sept 1808.

The children of W. W. Bacon:
Maria, April 11, 1826.
Anna, May 1, 1828.
Sarah Cordelia, Nov. —, 1830.
Laura, Feb. —, 1834.
Alice, August 12, 1836.
Williamson, Feb. 3rd, 1844.

James Slater Fall, son of Philip S. & Anne Apperson Fall, was born April 4th, 1822.

John Bacon, son of Charles P. and Caroline M. Bacon, was born 15th of March, 1822.

James Haggin Albert Bacon, son of John M. & Sarah J. Bacon, was born January the 30th 1836, died August 30th, 1837.

Romulus Riggs Bacon, son of James W. & Alice, b. Dec. 31, 1836.

Alice E. Bacon, daughter of James W. & Alice, was married to B. H. Blanton Jan. 15th, 1868.

James W. Bacon Blanton, her son, was born the 2nd of Jan., 1869.

Page 680—

Anne Bacon, wife of John Bacon, departed this life the 15th of July, 1797, aged 24 years, two months and a few days.

James Bacon, son of John and Anne, departed this life the 19th July, 1797 aged 11 days.

Susan Bacon, wife of Benedict Bacon, departed this life the 30th March, 1813.

John Bacon departed this life May the 9th, 1817, aged 50 years and two months.

John M., son of John & Elizabeth, died the 16th of September, 1843.

Williamson, son of John & Elizabeth died the 17th of March, 1845.

Elizabeth, wife of John Bacon, died July 30th, 1849.

Elizabeth (Bryan), daughter of John and Elizabeth Bacon died Oct. 15, 1850.

Charles P. Bacon, son of John and Anna, died Sept. 17th, 1854.

Albert Bacon, son of John and Elizabeth, was killed in battle Dec. 28, 1861.

James W. Bacon, son of John and Elizabeth, died Oct. —, 1863.

Richard A. Bacon, son of John and Elizabeth, died Oct. —, 1865.

John Bacon, son of Charles, died Sept. 26, 1854.

R. R. Bacon, son of James and Alice, died Sept. —, 1868.

Howard Bryan, son of Elizabeth, died August 30th, 1849.

(NOTE BY COPYIST—As a direct descendant of John Bacon and his second wife, Elizabeth, through their daughter Anne Apperson Bacon and her husband Philip S. Fall, and their daughter Elizabeth Fall and her husband Edmund H. Taylor, Sr., I will add to the above Bible record the following data from statements made to me by my mother and her parents, who could remember most of the persons whose names are recorded in the Bible, or had received the data from those who knew them:

John Bacon and his brothers Lyddall, Langston, and Edmund were the sons of Captain Lyddall Bacon, of New Kent County, Virginia, and his first wife Anne Apperson, sister to Captain Richard Apperperson, of the Revolutionary Army; the name of her father is not definitely known. Benedict Bacon, the death of whose wife Susan and daughter Amanda, is recorded, was the son of Capt. Lyddall Bacon by his second marriage to Mrs. Crump, of Virginia, nee ————. John Bacon moved from Virginia to Kentucky prior to 1794, and married Anna Patterson, niece of Col. Robert Patterson, and daughter of Charles Patterson. She died in 1797, and John Bacon married second Elizabeth Ware, daughter of William Ware and his wife Sarah Samuel, both of Woodford County, Kentucky.)

The above record and note contributed by

JOUETT TAYLOR CANNON,

Susannah Hart Shelby Chapter,
Frankfort, Kentucky,
March 9, 1927.

BIBB BIBLE RECORDS
(Virginia and Kentucky)

BIBLE PUBLISHED AT PHILADELPHIA
BY MATHEW CARY, 1812

Inscription of fly-leaf "Richard Bibb, Sr., January 29th, 1813."

"And the children of Reuben and the children of Gad called the alter Ed, for it shall be a witness between us that the Lord is God—Joshua XXII, XXXII."

"Jeremiah, 31st Chapter, Verse 13th: "Ahaz King of Judah has the brazen altar moved to the north side of the altar."

MARRIAGES

Richard Bibb to Lucy Booker, Sept. 28th, 1775.

Geo. M. Bibb to Martha T. Scott, May —, 1799.

Lucy B. Bibb to Tho. S. Slaughter, April 6, 1802.

Mary Bibb to Gab. Lewis, Nov. 24, 1807.

Richd. Bibb to Eliz. Roberts, Nov. 14th, 1811.

Susanna Elizabeth Bibb to Doct. Boanerges Roberts, Nov. 28, 1816.

Richd. Bibb, Senr., to Mary Ann Jackson, Dec. 25, 1817, 2nd wife.

John B. Bibb to Sarah P. Horseley, daughter of Jno. Sam'l Hopkins, Aug. 22, 1831.

Eugene B. Bibb (son of R. Bibb, Jr.,) to Mary Jane Burgess, Oct. —, 1848.

Richd. Bibb, Jr., to Mrs. Elizabeth Bacon, 1829, his second wife. Two children, Dr. G. R. Bibb & Florence King.

BIRTHS

State of Virginia:

Richard Bibb, Apl. 15, 1752. Wife, Lucy Bibb, Sept. 16, 1758.

*Geo. M. Bibb, son of the above, Oct. 30, 1776.

**Richd. Bibb, January 11, 1780.

Mary Bibb, November 24, 1782.

Lucy Booker Bibb, March 13, 1786.

John B. Bibb, October 27, 1789.

Edwd. C. Bibb, March 17, 1792.

Thomas Bibb, July 17, 1795.

Susa. Eliza Bibb, April 3, 1800.

Kentucky—

Edward Booker Bibb, son of Geo. M. Bibb, Dec. 11, 1801.

Mary Ann Bibb, Jany. 30, 1777, was born of the Spirit Feb. 14, 1824. (She was R. Bibb, Jr.'s, second wife.)

*Geo. M. Bibb was U. S. Senator, Chief Justice of Ky., Sec'y of the Treasury of the U. S. & Chancellor of Ky., &c.

**Richard Bibb was a successful merchant & stood high as an honorable man. He was President of the Branch Bank of Kentucky at Russellville.

Jno. Bibb, father of Richd. Bibb, 1703, Susanna Bibb his wife, 1711.

Susanna Bibb of the above, 1737.

†William Bibb of the above, 1739.

Eliza Bibb, Feb. 28, 1741.

John Bibb, Sept. 10, 1743.

James Bibb, Dec. 28, 1745.

Thomas Bibb, March 29, 1749.

Richard Bibb, April 15, 1752.

Notes—(Presumably in the handwriting of John B. Bibb to whom this Bible descended, and who died in Frankfort, Ky. in 1884):

Richard Bibb was a Captain in the Revolutionary War, & Member of the Legislature of Virginia & of Kentucky.

William Bibb moved to Georgia from Virginia & was the Father of William & Thos. Bibb. William was Senator of U. S. from Georgia and afterwards Governor of Alabama.

Thos. was also Governor of Alabama.

†John B. Bibb was a Major in the War of 1812, Representative & Senator in the Ky. Legislature from the County of Logan in the years 1828, '29, '31, '32, '33, '35.

R. Bibb (Richard, Senior, 1752) was an educated man & a successful farmer and business man. He was a local Preacher in the Methodist Church and strongly advocated in several pamphlets & newspapers, in his latter days, a reform in Church government, so as to have a Lay delegation. This has since been effected.

The descendants of Jas. Bibb & John Bibb are scattered about the U. States—some in Kentucky.

DEATHS

Thos. Bibb, July 1766, aged 17 years.

John Bibb, father of the above and of R. Bibb, June 1, 1769, aged 66 years.

William Bigger, Sr., June 22, 1770, aged 86 years.

Susanna Bibb, Dec. 22, 1786.

Edward C. Bibb, Sept. 2, 1794 (Son of Richd. & Lucy Bibb).

Thomas Bibb, Son of Richard & Lucy Bibb, Dec. 2, 1795.

Lucy Bibb, Wife of R. Bibb, Sr., Aug. 21, 1815, almost 57 years old.

An infant son of Rd. & Lucy Bibb, about 1784, aged abt. 2 weeks.

Mary Lewis, Aug. 10th, 1819, aged 36 years, 8 mos., 16 days.

Susanna Elizab. Roberts, Sept. 13, 1825, aged 25 years 5 months, 8 days.

Richd. Bibb, Junior, 22nd June, 1839, aged 59 years 5 mos. 11 days.

Lucy B. Slaughter, Jan'y 14, 1848.

Thos. S. Slaughter, her husband in the year (Sept.) 1838.

Mrs. Elizabeth Clark (Mother of Jno. W. Scott), 6 July, 1836.

Edward Booker Bibb, son of Geo. M. Bibb, Jan'y 27, 1827, in Florence, Alabama, aged 26 years, 1½ months.

Elizabeth Bibb, wife of Richd. Bibb, Jr., March 1, 1827, in the 38th year of her age.

Susanna Elizabeth Roberts, daughter of Boanerges and Susanna Elizabeth Roberts, Sept. 21, 1827, 5 years, 8 months and 28 days old.

James Bibb, brother of Richd. Bibb, Sr., Nov. 1820, aged 75 years near, lacking about one month.

Martha T. Bibb, spouse of Geo. M. Bibb, April 12th 1829.

Elizabeth Bibb, second wife of Richd. Bibb, Jr., Feb. 25, 1878, aged 71.

Mary Ann Bibb, Spouse of Rr. Bibb, Sr., March 20, 1831, aged 54 years, 1 month and 20 days (11 o'clock morning).

Elizabeth Farrar, abt. May 1828, aged 87 years & about 3 months (born Feb. 28, 1741).

Richd. Bibb, Sr., 25th Jan'y, 1839, aged nearly 87 years.

Eugene B. Bibb (son of R. Bibb, Jr.), Sept. 20, 1852.

Geo. M. Bibb, 13th March, 1859.

Sarah P. Bibb, wife of John B. Bibb, April 7, 1869.

John B. Bibb, died Easter morning, April 13th, 1884. (The words in black face are written in feminine hand differing from other entries.)

T. P. ATTICUS BIBB'S FAMILY RECORD
(Copied by Mrs. Jouett Taylor Cannon, Susannah Hart Shelby Chapter, N. S. D. A. R., Frankfort, Ky., from papers found in the effects of Miss Patsy Bibb, late of Frankfort, grand-daughter of T. P. Atticus Bibb.)

BIRTHS

Titus Pomponius Atticus Bibb, son to George M. & Martha Tabb Bibb, was born on the 3rd day of July, 1814 (Eighteen hundred & fourteen).

Mary Scott Bibb, wife of T. P. A. Bibb and daughter of John Smith Snead and Martha Ann Snead, was born on Sunday, the seventeenth day of February, 1822 (Eighteen & twenty-two).

The mother of T. P. A. Bibb was a daughter of Gen'l Charles Scott, and Mrs. Bibb's mother was a grand-daughter, being the daughter of John Postlewaite and Polly his wife who was Polly Scott.

DEATHS (In different hand-writting.)

T. P. Atticus Bibb son, of George M. & Martha Tabb Bibb, died March 4, 1872 (Eighteen hundred seventy-two), Frankfort, Kentucky.

Charles Scott Bibb, son of T. P. A. Bibb and Mary Scott Bibb, died on the 18th of November 1884 at 12:10 O'clock, aged 29 & 8 mos. & two days (Eighteen hundred eight-four), at Samuel P. Snead's, 614 First St., Louisville, Ky., buried at Frankfort, Ky., Nov. 20th, 1884.

MARRIAGES

T. P. Atticus Bibb and Mary Scott Snead were married on the 26th of September, 1851.

George M. Bibb and Martha Tabb Scott, daughter of Maj. Gen'l Charles Scott, were married in 1799 (Seventeen Hundred and ninety-nine).

My Mother had twelve children, two of whom are now living, Frances Ann Burnley and myself. My brother John has a child in Georgetown, D. C., Burnley Bibb.

684

Mrs. Burnley has three daughters living, one married Robt. H. Crittenden. These are all the descendants of my mother, who died in 1829, in March. (Feb., 1868.)

My grandfather Charles Scott was a Virginian, a General of the Revolution, came to Kentucky very early and was elected Governor in 1808 over Col. John Allen, the Federal candidate.

My grandfather Richard Bibb was also a Virginian and was educated for the ministry in the Episcopal Church. On coming to Kentucky and finding few or no churches and the ministry in the State abandoning the church, one by fighting a duel, the other by corruption and bribery, he joined the Methodist Church and entered the pulpit. He died a Methodist at the age of 86 (Eighty-six). He was a man of fortune. He emancipated all his slaves, and gave them lands in Ky. and Illinois.

(In different hand-writing)—

Geo. N. Bibb and Mary E. Thompson were married December 5th, 1881, at Marshall, Texas.

George Burnley Breckenridge, son of T. P. A. Bibb and Mary S. Bibb, was born on the 11th day of July, 1852, in Trimble Co., Ky.

Patsy Bibb, daughter to T. P. A. & Mary S. Bibb, was born on the 16th (sixteenth) day of September, 1853, in the city of Covington, Kenton County, Ky.

Charles Scott Bibb, son of Mary S. & T. P. A. Bibb was born on the 16th (sixteenth) day of April, 1855, at the city of Frankfort, Ky.

George Nehemiah, son to T. P. A. & Mary S. Bibb, was born on the 18th day of January, 1857, at the city of Frankfort, Ky.

Harriet Crittenden, daughter to T. P. A. & Mary S. Bibb, was born on the 1st (first) August, 1858, at city of Frankfort, Ky.

(Different hand-writing)—

Joseph H. T. Bibb, son of George N. & Mary E. T. Bibb, was born on the 29th day of October, 1883, in Texas, baptised on the 15th day of April, 1885, by Rev. E. A. Penick (of Frankfort, Ky.).

Charles Scott Bibb, son of George N. Bibb & Mary E. Bibb was born on the 23 day of August, 1885, in Texas.

Robert Crittenden Bibb, son to Mary E. T. Bibb and George N. Bibb, was born on the 10th of October, 1893.

DEATHS

George Burnley Breckenridge Bibb, son of T. P. A. & Mary S. Bibb, died on the 25th of July, 1852.

Mary Scott Bibb wife of T. P. A Bibb, departed this life at Frankfort, Ky., on the sixth day of August, A. D. 1858, aged 36 & 3 mos. & 19 days.

Harriet Critenden Bibb, daughter of T. P. A. & M. S. Bibb, died the 9th day of August, 1858, aged 2 mos. (?) & nine days.

The day of Mrs. Bibb's funeral the Public Offices at Frankfort were all closed by the order of the Governor out of respect to her and myself, then Assistant Secretary of State.

My father, Geo. M. Bibb, died in Washington City, D. C., April 1859, aged 83 (Eighty-three). He came to Kentucky 1798, a graduate of two colleges Hamden—Sydney and William & Mary, and Licensed Lawyer. He was four times on the Bench of the Court of Appeals, twice as Chief Justice. He was Senator in Congress in 1812 and resigned and was again elected in 1829. In 1835 he was made Chancellor and in 1844 Pres. Tyler made him Secretary of the Treasury. Few men have exerted so much influence in life. His legal knowledge was profound and his general knowledge various, accurate and extensive.

My two boys and myself, George & Scott left Kentucky in March, 1861 and joined the Confederacy at Montgomery, Ala. I was in civil service C. S. A. until close of War, returning to Ky. June 1866, the Yankees would not allow me to come sooner although I was paroled as Captain 4th Va. Vols.

(Signed) T. P. Aticus Bibb.

BOONE—GRANT—LEMOND RECORD

(Copied from old manuscript owned by Mrs. Louise Norwood Walker, Lexington, June 11, 1927.)

Squire Boone was born in 1696, in Manchester, England. Died January the 1, 1765, in Carolina.

Sarah Morgan, afterwards Sarah Boone, was born 1701, of Welch parents. Died January the 1, 1777, in Carolina. Born in Pennsylvania.

William Grant, son of William Grant & Margery ———, was born February the 22, 1726, in Virginia. Died June the 22, in Kentucky.

Elizabeth Boone, afterwards Elizabeth Grant, was born February the 5, 1733, in Pennsylvania. Died February 24, in Kentucky, 1814.

Daniel Boone, was born in 1735, in Pennsylvania, died in Missouri, October, 1820.

James Lemond was born August the 10, 1768, in Pennsylvania. Died December 5, 1820, in Kentucky.

Eliza Boone Lemond, daughter of J. & R. Lemond, was born November the 29th, 1795, in Fayette, Kentucky.

Frances Augusta Lemond, Daughter of J. & R. Lemond, was born January the 10, 1798, in Fayette, Kentucky. Married (possibly married in Campbell) December 3, 1818. (Name of husband not given.) Died September 17, 1825, in Campbell Co., Ky.

Mary Grant Lemond was born January the 17, 1800, in Campbell Co. Married December 23, 1824. Died May 24, 1841, in Madison, Indianna.

Sarah Grant Lemond was born October the 3, 1801 in Fayette, Ky. Married May, 1821 in Campbell.

Augustus William Lemond was born December the 1, 1803, in Fayette, Kentuck. Died November the 4, 1828, in Natchez, Louisiana.

Rebecca Knox Lemond was born in Fayette, October the 4, 1807. Married in June. (Date and name of husband not given.)

Agness Vernor Lemond was born in Fayette, in October the 31, 1809. Married. (No further data.)

John James Lemond was born in Fayette in January the 16, 1813.

(NOTE—James Lemond above, married Rebecca Grant, the daughter of William & Elizabeth Boone Grant. They were parents of the 8 Lemonds in the above list.

J. T. CANNON.)

CANNON BIBLE RECORDS

(Copied from Bible published in 1813, and owned in 1928 by William Lindsey Cannon, of Midway, Kentucky, son of John W. Cannon. Copied by Mrs. Jouett Taylor Cannon.)

MARRIAGES

John H. Cannon & Ann Coston was married the 16th of Feby., 1813.

Alex C. Lindsey & Mary G. Cannon was married August 8th, 1834.

James Brown and Ann Cannon, his wife, was married March 20th, 1837.

Phil. E. Ayers and Adelaide C. Brown was married March 28, 1859.

John D. Powell and Louisa Lucretia Cannon was married Jan'y 4th, 1842.

John W. Cannon was married Aug. 31, 1854 (to Louisa Stout).

Henry Costen and Ann, his wife, was married December 13th, 1803.

Joseph B. Oglesby and Rosey Ann Coston was married Apl. 12, 182—.

BIRTHS

Rosanna Coston was born September 13, 1803.

Sarah H. Coston was born October 4th, 1807.

Joseph Cannon was born Nov. 11, 1806.

Elijah Cannon was born March 11, 1808.

Betsy Cannon was born Jan'y 7, 1810.

Burton Cannon, Jr., was born April 12th, 1812.

William Cannon was born Nov. 19, 1813.

Ann Cannon was born March 24, 1815.

Mary Cannon was born August 20th, 1816.

*John W. Cannon was born June 17th, 1820.

Louisa Lucretia Cannon was born June 4th, 1824.

Catherine B. Cannon was born June 24, 1826.

Children of James and Ann (Cannon) Brown:

Adelaide C. Brown was born April 10th, 1840.

James William Brown was born April 9, 1842.

John Richard Longest was born August 28, 1850.

William Powell Longest was born June 29, 1853.

Ann Elizabeth Ayres was born February 19, 1860.

DEATHS

Joseph Cannon died March 1st, 1829, at St. Thomas (illegible).

William Cannon died Friday, the 18th of September, 1835.

Ann Cannon died June 1, 1843.

Catherine B. Cannon died September the 3rd, 1843.

John D. Powell died July the 1st, 1845.

John H. Cannon died the 9th of June, 1846.

James William Brown died Oct. 28, 1845.

James Longest died December 23, 1854.

Mary G. Lindsey died Aug. 27th, 1864, in her 48th year. She is gone but not forgotten.

James S. Carlton died June 22nd, 1868, in his 50th year.

Ann Longest died Sept. 8, 1871, in the 56th year of her age.

Rosanna Oglesby died Aug. 6, 1878 in the 72nd year of her age.

John W. Cannon died April 18, 1882, in the 62 year of his age, in Frankfort, Ky.

Louisa Lucretia Carlton died July 2nd, 1899, in Breckenridge Co., Ky.

---

*Owner and captain of the famous steamboat, "R. E. Lee." The Cannons were among the early settlers of Breckinridge County, Ky.

COX FAMILY BIBLE

Copied by Mrs. Wm. T. Fowler, Aug. 16, 1926.

Minton, Howe, Carden, Shreve, Cowherd, Patterson, Halsell, Buckner, Cabell families and White.

John P. Cox and Elizabeth H. White were married February 12, 1795.

Jackson G. Minton and Nancy Cox were married Dec. 23, 1819.

Archibald Cox and Sallie W. Howe were married May 2, 1822.

Samuel Cox and Anna Carden were married Dec. 21, 1824.

John Shreve and Elizabeth B. Cox were married July 20, 1826.

Francis Cowherd and Judith G. Cox were married Jan. 6, 1829.

John P. Cox, Jr., and Regina D. Patterson were married May 2, 1833.

Fredrick Cox and Precious L. Halsell were married August 14, 1834.

Archibald Cox and Harriet Buckner were married Jan. 14, 1835.

Thomas J. Cabell and Lucie Ann Cox were married April 6, 1837.

The last named were the parents of Mrs. Erma Catherine Cabell Brownfield, of Bowling Green, John Cabell, Prof. Frank Cabell, of Bowling Green; and Martha Cabell Chef, of Harrodsburg.

The Cox family lived in Taylor County, Ky.

CRUTCHFIELD

(Record from Bible of John C. Crutchfield, published by Jasper Harding, No. 57 South Third St., Philadelphia, 1814; J. Harding, Printer. Now owned by John D. Twyman, 229 Moundale Ave., Winchester, Ky.)

John C. Crutchfield was borned April the 12, 1802.

Janet Crutchfield was borned December the 4, 1808.

Huldah Crutchfield was borned Nov. 30, 1827.

Sally Crutchfield was borned Sept. 16, 1829.
Amanda Crutchfield was borned Feb. 25, 1831.
Harriet Crutchfield was borned Dec. the 18, 1832.
Ann E. Crutchfield was borned Dec. 13, 1834.
George N. Crutchfield was borned Dec. 4, 1836.
Hester C. Crutchfield was borned Dec. 13, 1838.
Delfina Crutchfield was borned April 12, 1841.
William W. Crutchfield was borned June the 4, 1843.
John R. Crutchfield was borned July 25, 1845.
Tacy F. Crutchfield was borned Sept. the 5, 1848.
Mary E. Crutchfield was borned Oct. 29, 1850.

John C. Crutchfield & Jenet Cummings was married Jan. the 8, 1827.
Ann E. Crutchfield and Pleasant H. Twyman was married Oct. 13, 1861.
Harriet Crutchfield and William R. Sharpe was married Oct. 7, 1862.

John C. Crutchfield Dec'd July the 22, 1864.
Hulda Crutchfield Dec'd April 16th, 1851.
Amanda Crutchfield Dec'd January 25th, 1854.
Wm. W. Crutchfield Dec'd May the 23rd, 1865.
Tacy F. Crutchfield Dec'd Jan. 13th, 1876.
Jenette Crutchfield died June 22, 1885.
Hester Crutchfield died —
Sally W. Crutchfield died October 5, 1899.
Mary C. Crutchfield died October 27, 1905.
Delfina Crutchfield died November 18th, 1905.
George N. Crutchfield died Sept. 1st, 1915.
Harriet Sharp died Nov. 27, 1920.
John R. Crutchfield died Dec. 1st, 1921.

(John C. Crutchfield lived all his life in Clark County, Ky.)

(Copied by Miss Ruth Beall, Hart Chapter, N. S. D. A. R., Winchester, Kentucky, March —, 1928.)

DILLINGHAM

(Records taken from Bible of Mrs. Sallie Dillingham Colyer, of Richmond, Ky.)

Charity Park, b. Dec. 22, 1793, d. May 5, 1831, m. Sept. 24, 1812 to Henry H. Dillingham, b. July 7, 1791, d. Mar. 7, 1857.
1. John P. Dillingham b. July 25, 1813.
2. Paulina Dillingham b. Jan. 27, 1815.
3. Elizabeth Dillingham b. Dec. 1, 1816.
4. William Dillingham b. Feb. 28, 1819, d. Aug. 13, 1844.
5. Joshua Dillingham b. May 25, 1821, d. Nov. 15, 1841.
6. Henry B. Dillingham b. Sept. 17, 1823.
7. Amanda F. Dillingham b. Dec. 1, 1824.
8. Solomon Dillingham b. Mar. 13, 1826, d. July 7, 1829.
9. Vachel Dilingham b. Feb. 4, 1828, d. May 15, 1831.
10. Elihu Dillingham b. Apr. 16, 1830.

ELLEY

(Copied by Mrs. Jouett Taylor Cannon, Susannah Hart Shelby Chapter, N. S. D. A. R., Frankfort, Kentucky, from Sale of Mrs. Sallie Johnson Burgin, Scott County, Kentucky, Oct. 10, 1927. Bible dated MDCCXCI.)

Henry Elley, son of Henry & Esther, was born April 2, 1746. Married Sarah Burbridge Oct. 30, 1763 (daughter of Thomas & Sarah Burbridge) which was born Sept., 1748.

CHILDREN

Elizabeth Elley born Oct. 30, 1764.
Thomas Elley born May 25, 1766.
Nancy Elley born Oct. 27, 1767.
Edward Elley born April 16, 1769.
Henry Elley born Dec. 15, 1770.
Sally Elley born Sept. 5, 1772.
Polly Herndon Elley born July 16, 1775, died 1776.
George Elley born Aug. 17, 1778.
Polly Elley born Aug. 2, 1788 (or 1780).
Sarah, wife of Henry Elley, died June 12, 1812.

George Elley died Aug. 16, 1864.

Sally Shipp, wife of Colby Shipp, died Sept. 17, 1817.

Nancy Welch, wife of James Welch, died Aug. 7, 1857.

Edward Elley, son of Henry Elley, died Oct. 21, 1837.

NOTE—The Bible from which the above record was copied was purchased by Mrs. Cannon, and is now (1928) in the Library of the Kentucky State Historical Society.

SAMUEL EVERETT'S BIBLE

(Contributed by Mrs. W. Basil Smith, Edmund Rogers Chapter, D. A. R., Glasgow, Ky.)

Wm. N. Everett, born Nov. 10, 1811.

Zion R. Huggins, born Oct. 15 (?), 1808.

Elizabeth Ann Huggins, born Nov. 22, 1814.

Nancy Everett, born Aug. 10, 1773.

Samuel Everett, born Apr. 3, 1782.

Lizzie Lawrence Huggins, born Apr. 3, 1869.

Clement Williams Huggins, born Sep. 19, 1871.

Bettie R. Huggins, born Sep. 20, 1889.

Sarah J. Huggins, born June 5, 1832.

William Edmund Huggins, born June 1, 1834.

Ann Mary Huggins, born Sep. 12, 1836.

James Pendleton Huggins, born June 4, 1842.

Elizabeth Huggins, born Oct. 14, 1839.

Howard (Malcolm) Huggins, born March 14, 1845.

Samuel W. A. Huggins, born March, 1848.

John T. Huggins, born Jan. 10, 1851.

Ellen J. (Nellie) Huggins, born Nov. 13, 1854.

Rosa Huggins, born May 19, 1858.

John W. Shirley, born Nov. 25, 1854.

Ann Mary Shirley, born July 17, 1856.

Ann Laura Huggins, born Sep. 24, 1858.

Harry Munford Huggins, born Oct. 3, 1859.

Eugenia B. Huggins, born March 18, 1861.

DEATHS

Wm. N. Everett, died Sep. 29, 1834.

Sarah Jane Huggins, died March 10, 1836.

Nancy Everett, died Jan. 17, 1853.

John Thomas Huggins, died Nov. 5, 1854.

Ann Mary (Huggins) Shirley, died Aug. 11, 1856.

Rosa Huggins, died April 15, 1859.

Harry Munford Huggins, died Dec. 18, 1860.

Clemmy Depp Huggins, died March 2, 1863.

Samuel Everett, died June 22, 1864.

Lizzie Huggins, died July 17, 1864.

Howard Malcolm Huggins, died Aug. 15, 1871.

Zion R. Huggins, died Sep. 29, 1872.

Elizabeth Ann Huggins, died Sep. 6, 1880.

Wm. Ed. Huggins, died Oct. 20, 1884.

Elizabeth Huggins, died July 17, 1864.

GARRARD

(Copied from Garrard Family Bible owned by Mrs. William Talbot Lindsey, Frankfort, Kentucky, 1928.)

MARRIAGES

James Garrard & Elizabeth Mountjoy was married Dec. 20, 1769.

James Garrard, Junior, and Nancy Lewis was married Dec. 10th, 1793.

John Edward, Senr., and Mary Garrard was married July 6th, 1794.

Isham Talbot and Peggy Garrard was married January 24th, 1804.

John Garrard and Sarah Shipp was married May 25th, 1805.

Daniel Garrard and Lucy Toulmin was married February 20th, 1808.

Thomas W. Hawkins and Ann Ellinor Garrard was married March 20, 1808.

James A. Brooks and Elizabeth Mountjoy Garrard was married May 9, 1810.

Peter Dudley and Maria Garrard was married November 15th, 1815.

William Garrard and Susannah Pears was married January 20, 1818.

BIRTHS

James Garrard, son of William Garrard and Mary, his wife, was born January 14th, 1749.

Elizabeth Garrard, daughter of William Mountjoy and Phyllis, his wife, was born May 2nd, 1751.

William Garrard, son of James and Elizabeth, his wife, born April 20th, 1771.

James Garrard, son of James and Elizabeth, his wife was born January 31, 1773.

John Garrard, son of James and Elizabeth, his wife, was born September 28th, 1774, and departed this life July 28th, 1776.

Mary Garrard, daughter of James and Elizabeth, his wife, was born September 17th, 1776.

John Garrard, son of James and Elizabeth, his wife, was born November 26th 1778.

Daniel Garrard, son of James and Elizabeth, his wife, was born November 10th, 1780.

Elizabeth Mountjoy Garrard, daughter of James and Elizabeth, his wife, was born March 6th, 1783.

Nancy Garrard, daughter of James and Elizabeth, his wife, was born January 14th, 1785, and departed this life September 9th, 1785.

Ann Elinor Garrard, daughter of James and Elizabeth, his wife, was born July 3rd, 1786.

Peggy Garrard, daughter of James and Elizabeth, his wife, was born July 31, 1788.

Maria Garrard, daughter of James and Elizabeth, his wife, was born December 22, 1790.

Sarah Garrard was born February 22, 1793, and departed this life August 18th, 1793.

Eliza Garard Talbot, grand-daughter of James and Elizabeth Garrard, was born August 27th, 1806.

(Copied from Garrard Bible by Mrs. Jouett Taylor Cannon, Susannah Hart Shelby Chapter, Frankfort, Ky., and Miss Genevieve Lindsey, Frankfort, Ky., March, 1928.)

GOODWIN—DOBSON—MEUX

Copied from old Bible owned by Mrs. Milton Elliott, Bridgeport, Franklin Co., Ky.

John Goodwin departed this life on Thursday, the 22 day of March, 1759.

Frances Dobson departed this life on Sunday, the 15th of November, 1768.

John Anderson died December 2, 1760.

John Goodwin departed this life Oct. 28, 1762, on this day.

Mary Horsley departed this life 10th May, 1773.

Ann Burrus departed this life the 22 day of February, 1840.

James S. Littlepage departed this life March 30th, 1864. John & Frances Meux was married 23rd Feb., 1764.

Richard Meux, son to John & Frances, born 1st January, 1765.

Frances Meux, born 20th October, 1767.

John G. Meux, born 20th November, 1769.

Ann Meux, born 10th September, 1771.

James Meux, born 7th January, 1773.

James Meux departed this life on Sunday, 15th Aug., 1773.

GRIFFITH BIBLE RECORD

The following Record was copied from an old Bible which has long been in the Library of the Kentucky State Historical Society. The Bible was published and sold by Daniel D. Smith, 190 Greenwich St., New York, in 1824."

On the inside the cover the name "—— Griffith" is faintly written in pencil. Several of the names appear to have been retraced over the fading ink of the original entry.

BIRTHS

Clemons Griffiths, April the 17, 1797.
Marinda Griffiths, Sept. the 2, 1807.
John M. Griffith, Feb. the 20, 1824.
Spenser Griffith, May the 7, 1826.
Calvin Griffith, June the 5, 1828.
Samuel a Griffith, Aug. the 17, 1831.

Mary Griffith, Oct. 2, 1834.
Marinday Griffith, May the 8, 1837.
Clemons Griffith, Jr., Dec. the 18, 1841.
Charles Griffith, June the 9, 1844.
Elenore E. Griffith, Dec. the 16, 1847.

DEATHS

Samuel A. Griffith died April the 29, 1835.
Calvin Griffith died Dec. the 11, 1849.
Mary Griffith died Sept. the 28, 1853.

HAGGARD

(The Bible with records of Pleasant Haggard, of Allensville, Kentucky, was publish in 1836 by Fessenden and Co., Brattleboro, Vermont, and is now (1928) in the possession of Miss Ruth Beall, Winchester, Kentucky.)

Pleasant Haggard, born Jan. 30, 1777, died Jan. 27, 1869.
Elizabeth Watts, born April 27, 1787, died July (?) 17, 1830.
Above two married Aug. 5, 1802.
Matilda Haggard, born Aug. 17, 1803.
Milly Haggard, born Feb. 23, 1805.
Franky Haggard, born Feb. 26, 1807.
David D. Haggard, born Apl. 17, 1808.
John T. Haggard, born Dec. 28, 1810.
Mary Haggard, born Dec. 25, 1812.
Nancy Haggard, born Jan. 25, 1814.
Lewis Haggard, born Oct. 23, 1816.
Pleasant Haggard, born July 31, 1818, died Apl. 6, 1835.
Sarah Haggard, born Sept. 20, 1820.
Elizabeth Haggard, born Oct. 22, 1822.
Martin Haggard, born Aug. 13, 1824.
Garrett Haggard, born Aug. 23, 1826.
James Haggard, born Sept. 27, 1828, died Apl. 5, 1920.
Lizzie Wills, wife of James Haggard, born Apl. 3, 1847, di. Feb. 27, 1924.
Mary Igo, born Jan. 11, 1789, died Aug. 24, 1854, married to Pleasant Haggard Sept. —, 1832.
Frank S. Allen, born Apl. 19, 1821, died July 5, 1882.
Elizabeth Allan, born Oct. 17, 1822, died Dec. 20, 1893.

Pleasant Haggard was born in Clark County, Ky., and lived in the same county all his life.

HARLIN BIBLE

(Contributed by Mrs. W. Basil Smith, Edmund Rogers Chapter, D. A. R., Glasgow, Ky.)

BIRTHS

S. C. Harlin, borned Nov. 25, 1843.
Phebe D. Harlin, borned Sept. 12, 1845.
A. D. Harlin, borned Feb. 11, 1870.
Lola Harlin, borned Apr. 7, 1872
I. C. Harlin, borned June 24, 1874.
Sarah L. Harlin, borned Sept. 8, 1876.
William R. Harlin, borned Dec. 17, 1878.
John B. Harlin, borned June 26, 1881.
Phebe E. Harlin, borned Jan. 7, 1883.
Grover Harlin, born Jan. 28, 1888.
E. Paul Webb, born Sep. 13, 1908, Roseville, Ky.
Joe Harlin Webb, born Apr. 14, 1910, Cave City, Ky.
Infant son of Phebe Edna & Andrew Webb, born March 28, 1915, departed life on same day, Horse Cave, Ky.
Andrew Depp Harlin, Jr., son of Andrew Depp and Esther Elizabeth Harlin, born March 18, 1919.
Phebe E. Harlin, daughter of John B. & Nellie W. Harlin, born March 6, 1921.
Mary Ann, daughter of Grover & Renie T. Harlin, born Aug. 10, 1918, Barren Co., Ky.
Ralph Travis, son of Grover & Rine Harlin, born July 3, 1921, Barren Co., Ky.
Maud Carter, born Jan. 20, 1899, at Rock Bridge, Monroe Co., Ky.
Jewell Carter, born Sep. 29, 1900, Rock Bridge, Monroe Co., Ky.
Lucile Carter, born Sulphur Lick, Monroe Co., Ky., Oct. 2, 1903.
Samuel Seay Harlin, born March 28, 1906, Laverty, Okla.
Samuel Quintus Hays, born March 3, 1920, Sulphur Lick, Ky.
Robert Clay Harlin, born March 28, 1906, Laverty, Okla., son of Clay and Mary Harlin.

DEATHS

Phebe Depp Harlin, departed this life Jan. 12, 1912.
  Phebe Edna Webb, died May 20, 1920.
  Sarah Lela Harlin, died Aug. 11, 1920.
  Lula Overton Harlan, died Dallas, Texas.
  Andrew Depp Harlin, died Monroe La., Dec. 27, 1922.

MARRIAGES

S. C. Harlin & Phebe D. Depp married 2 March, 1859.
A. D. Harlin & Lula Overton married 1 Sept., 1903.
Lola Harlin & S. H. Carter married March, I. C. Harlin & Mary Seay married 11 Oct., 1904.
  Phebe Edna Harlin & J. A. Webb married 27 Nov., 1907.
W. R. Harlin & Peffie Stubblefield married 15 April, 1908.
J. B. Harlin & Nellie Williams married Mar. 4, 1909.
Grover Harlin & Rine Travis married 23 Oct., 1917.
Maud Carter & Ned Harper married 27 Oct., 1918, LaFayette, Tenn.
Jewell Carter & Creed Howard married 23 May, 1922, at Summer Shade, Metcalf, Co., Ky.
S. C. Harlin & Mrs. N. E. Gray, of Hopkinsville, Ky., married 20 Oct., 1914.

HARLOW BIBLE

(Contributed by Mrs. W. Basil Smith, Edmund Rogers Chapter, D. A. R., Glasgow, Ky.)
This bible was the property of William D. Harlow, born 1785, and his wife Fannie Hall Harlow, born 1789. Contains the Old Testament, New Testament, and the Apocrypha. Published at Philadelphia, by McCarty & Davis, 171 Market St., 1828.
William D. Harlow married Fannie Hall Feb. 21, 1808.
John H. Harlow married Frances Ford Feb. 24, 1835.
Kathrine Harlow married John Ford June 23, 1842.
James L. Harlow & Clara McFerren married Nov. 7, 1850.
William E. Harlow married Susan Hudson March 27, 1851.
B. F. Harlow married Martha Anderson Jan. 13, 1853.
Amanda J. Harlow married M. T. Wright Jan. 29, 1861.
William D. Harlow, born Feb. 4, 1785.
Fannie H. Harlow, born May 13, 1789.
John H. Harlow, born Jan. 21, 1809.
Jane Eliza Harlow, born Aug. 27, 1810.
Harriet Byron Harlow, born Nov. 12, 1812.
James L. Harlow, born Dec. 2, 1814.
William E. Harlow, born April 18, 1817.
Kathrine Harlow, born July 16, 1819.
Martha Ann Harlow, born Sep. 21, 1821.
Benjamin F. Harlow, born Aug. 1, 1823.
Alexander P. Harlow, born Sep. 3, 1825.
Mary F. Harlow, born Oct. 30, 1827.
Amanda J. Harlow, born May 5, 1830.
Emely F. Harlow, born March 31, 1832.

DEATHS

W. D. Harlow departed this life Apr. 13, 1863.
Fannie H. Harlow died Oct. 22, 1858, aged 69 years, 5 mos., 9 days.
Jane Eliza Harlow, died July 3, 1829.
Harriet Byron Harlow, died July 12, 1829.
Martha Ann Harlow, died Sept., 1823.
Mary F. Harlow, died Feb. 27, 1829.
Emely F. Harlow, died Feb. 28, 1866.
Alexander P. Harlow, died Mar. 30, 1865. Aged 39 yrs., 6 m., 27 ds.
B. F. Harlow, died July 25, 1878, aged 55 years.
John H. Harlow, died Jan. 8, 1883, aged 74 years.
Mrs. B. F. Harlow, died Dec. 7, 1873.
Jane Dodd, died Nov. 10, 1857, aged 79 years.
Frances M. Harlow, died April 3, 1877.
Amanda J. Wright, died Feb. 13, 1891.
James L. Harlow, died Jan. 3, 1892.
M. T. Wright, died Feb. 17, 1893.
John Ford Sr., died Apr. 10, 1871, aged 66 years, 6 months, 5 days.
Frances M. Harlow, wife of John H. Harlow, died Apr. 3, 1877.

Katherine Ford, wife of John Ford, died Nov. 27, 1888, aged 69 years and 4 months.

Susan Harlow, wife of W. E. Harlow, died Nov. 13, 1899, aged 73 years.

William E. Harlow was burned to death March 30, 1903, aged 85 years, 11 mo., 12 days. He was burned at 3 A. M. and died at 12 o'clock.

ISHMAEL HIGDON'S BIBLE

(Contributed by Mrs. W. Basil Smith, Edmund Rogers Chapter, D. A. R., Glasgow, Ky.)

William Betersworth and Posey(?) his wife, married 18 Aug., 1806.

Ishmael Higdon, son of Joseph Higdon and Margaret his wife, born Dec. 14, 1798.

Martha Wilson, now wife of I. Higdon, born 17 May, 1813.

Joshua W. Higdon, son of I. Higdon and Martha, his wife, was born April—

Isaac A. Higdon, son of I. Higdon and Martha his wife, born 13 March, 1846.

Ozirres L. Higdon, born 29 Sept., 1848.

Rachel R. S. Higdon, born 10 May, 1851.

William Betersworth, born 20, April 1735.

Pasy (?) Betersworth, his wife, born 27 March 1739(?).

Almorium(?), dau. of William Betersworth born 3 July, 1807.

Armerie Betersworth, daughter of William Betersworth, born 16 Aug., 1810.

Argalus Jefferson Betersworth, son of William Betersworth, born June 26, 1812.

Arominto Coly Betersworth, daughter of William Betersworth, born Dec. 6, 1813.

Alen O. H. Jerry (?), son of Wm. Betersworth, born Sept. 18, 1816.

Ann Flo, daughter of William Betersworth, born April 7, 1819.

Arthur W. Bettersworth, born Sep. 5, 1821.

Adonis, son of Wiliam Bettersworth, born Jan. 21, 1824.

DEATHS

Argalus Betersworth, son of W. Bettersworth, departed this life July 29 1812.

Ishmael Higdon, died Nov. 2, 1887.

Ishmael Higdon and Ann A. Higdon, his wife, were married Dec. 15, 1828.

Ishmael Higdon and Martha, his wife, married March 22, 1843.

Mary Elizabeth Hunt, born March 5, 1820.

Martha Jane Higdon, daughter of Ishmael Higdon and Ann A. Higdon his wife, born Dec. 1, 1829.

Margaret Anna Higdon, born Mar. 30, 1832.

William Jasper Higdon, born May 18, 1834.

Susan Mariah Higdon, born March 13, 1836.

James Newton Higdon, born Dec. 6, 1837.

Joseph Allen Higdon, born Nov. 25, 1841.

Sarah Thompson Higdon, born April 6, 1833.

DEATHS

Sarah Thompson Higdon, daughter of Ishmael and Ann A. Higdon his wife, departed this life August 6, 1833.

Ann A. Higdon, wife of Ishmael Higdon, died Dec. 14, 1841.

Joseph A. Higdon, son of Ishmael and Ann A. his wife, deceased Feb. 12, 1842.

Martha Jane Higdon, daughter of Ishmael Higdon and Ann A. his wife, deceased Oct. 6, 1854.

Ozias H. Higdon, son of Ishmael Higdon and Martha, his wife, deceased Nov. 19, 1849.

Sarah T. Higdon, died Feb. 11, 1885.

HOWARD BIBLE

(Copied from the family Bible of Benjamin Howard, Sr., of Fredrick County, Maryland, and contributed by Mrs. Mary Neale Thompson, of Richmond, Kentucky.)

Benjamin Howard, Senior, was born September 6th, 1755.

Benjamin Howard, Sr., died April 15th, 1835, aged 79 years, 7 months and 9 days.

Benjamin Howard, Sr., was married in 1792 to Rebecca Turney, who was born May 1st, 1762. She died March 11th, 1837. Their children were:

Matthew, Benjamin, Thomas, Mary, Rebecca, Eleanor, Lavinia, Catherine Elizabeth and Nancy.

Benjamin Howard, Jr., was born May 31st, 1796. He died March 8th, 1880, aged 83 years, 9 months and 8 days.

Benjamin Howard, Jr., and Sarah Riley were married December the 2nd, 1824.

Sarah Riley (wife of Benjamin Howard, Jr.), was born March 10th, 1764. She died June 8th, 1871. (?)

Zerelda Howard, daughter of Benjamin Howard, Jr., and Sarah Riley, was born October 30th, 1825. She died Feb. 4th, 1858.

Zerelda Howard married William Lewis Neale the 5th day of October, 1843.

Benjamin Howard Neale, son of William Lewis Neale and Zerelda Howard, his wife, was born Sept. 1st, 1844, died July 6th, 1909. Married Miss Margaret Jones, November 19th, 1868.

Margaret Jones Neale, wife of Benjamin Howard Neale, was born October the 3rd, 1850. She died June the 18th, 1922.

JACOBS BIBLE RECORDS

(Copied by Mrs. Robert R. Gum, Frankfort, Ky.)

Nathan Jacobs, Sr., son of Benj. Jacobs, b. June 26, 1762, d. May 18, 1846. Married in 1787.

Sarah Clark (dau. of John Clark, of S. Hadley, Mass.), b. July 17, 1766, d. Aug. 22, 1843. Issue:

1. Achsah Jacobs, b. Feb. 23, 1788, m. Dec. 27, 1820, Nathan Gould.

2. Ferrand Jacobs, b. Oct. 27, 1789, d. May 22, 1841.

3. Nathan Jacobs, b. Dec. 25, 1791, d. June 15, 1795.

4. Sarah Jacobs, b. Dec. 24, 1793, m. May 9, 1839, Calvin Ellinwood.

5. Samantha Jacobs, b. Feb. 3, 1796, m. Mar. 18, 1808, (?) to Jonathan Howard.

6. Nathan Jacobs, b. May 1, 1798, m. Berilla Whitney, July 8, 1823.

7. Clark Jacobs, b. May 28, 1800, d. **Sept. 3, 1801.**

8. Clark Jacobs, b. Aug. 11, 1802, m. Apl. 21, 1839, Clarissa Dunkley.

9. Benjamin Franklin Jacobs, b. Jan. 15, 1805, d. Aug. 26, 1854.

10. William Loring Jacobs, b. Mar. 21, 1807.

11. Enoch Jacobs, b. June 30, 1809, m. Electra Whitney, June 22, 1831.

12. Edwin Arnold Jacobs, b. Dec. 8, 1811.

(The above record given by Enoch Jacobs (Consul to Montevideo under A. Lincoln), to Henry Whitney Jacobs.)

Nathan Jacobs, Jr., b. May 1, 1798, d. Nov. 8, 1881, m. July 8, 1823.

Berilla Whitney, b. Mar. 7, 1804, d. July 11, 1898.

ISSUE:

1. Caroline Hoyt Jacobs, b. Dec. 21, 1824, d. Dec. 29, 1908, married Will Mize.

2. Sarah Clark Jacobs, b. Oct. 1, 1826, d. Dec. —, 1891, married Montgomery Howard.

(3) Henry Whitney Jacobs, b. Aug. 11, 1828, Brooklyn, N. Y., d. Apl. 13, 1912, married Matilda Richardson.

4. Benjamin Franklin Jacobs, b. Aug. 1, 1830, d. Sept. 30, 1830.

5. Geo. Washington Jacobs, b. Apl. 4, 1832, d. Oct. 9, 1911, m. Paulina Hamilton.

6. Emeline Jacobs, b. Aug. 11, 1835, d. Feb. 17, 1836.

7. Isaac Newton Jacobs, b. Apl. 26, 1837, d. Oct. 17, 1862, m. Mollie Fletcher.

8. Emiline Amelia Jacobs, b. Nov. 24, 1839, m. Hart Witt.

9. Benjamin Franklin Jacobs, b. May 20, 1842, m. Bettie Sholl.

10. Francis Clark Jacobs, b. May 26, 1845.

(3) Henry Whitney Jacobs, b. Aug. 11, 1828, d. Apl. 13, 1912 at Irvine, Kentucky, m. July 7, 1852, Matilda Richardson, b. Aug. 25, 1828, d. Nov. 14, 1907.

ISSUE:

1. Mary Berilla Jacobs, b. June 26, 1853, m. Sept. 30, 1874, Robt. W. McAfee (b. Mar. 13, 1853, d. Dec. 9, 1881) had:

    a. Kate J. McAfee, b. Sept. 29, 1875, m. Oct. 19, 1899 to Sam Owens (b. Feb. 16, 1865) had:

        1. Mary Evelyn Owens.

    b. Henry Whitney McAfee, b. Aug. 25, 1877, m. Apl. 30, 1901 to Fannie Smith (b. Aug. 11, 1877).

c. Sallie E. McAfee, b. Dec. 23, 1880, m. Wm. Frank Parson, and had: Mary McAfee Parson, b. Apl. 29, 1920.

(Copied from the Bible of Mrs. Robt. McAfee, 635 Central Ave., Lexington, Ky.)

LANCASTER—FLETCHER—WEST

Records from Family Bible of Joseph Lancaster.

(Copied by Mrs. Margaret Davies, Bethel, Bath Co., Ky., and presented to the Historical Society by Mr. Lucien Beckner, Winchester, Ky., March 2, 1926.)

(Joseph Lancaster, b. April 31 (?), 1772. His wife Rachel Fletcher, b. ————,1783.)

I haven't the date of their marriage. They had eight children, will give their names below:

Mary Lancaster, b. May 1799, m. David Davis, 1815, went to Ind. Her children all dead but one, she is frail.

Nancy Lancaster, b. March, 1801, m. Jacob L. Beckner, Jany. 20, 1820.

Rebecca Lancaster, b. March 1803, m. Samuel Rogers, March 29, 1829. Was a fine man. Went to Ills. near Springfield.

Catherine Lancaster, b. Dec., 1804, m. Charles McAlister Jan. 15, 1829. He died with small pox. She m. 2nd, James Whaley.

America Lancaster, b. Nov., 1806, d. Aug. 20, 1858, never married, fine woman.

Thomas Lancaster, b. Oct. 8, 1808. Had he lived would have married soon; was buried in his wedding suit; good man.

Samuel S. Lancaster, b. June 11, 1811, m. Harriet Davis Feb. 13, 1840.

Joseph Manerva Lancaster, b. Sept. 15, 1813, m. Herod Patrick Jan. 6, 1836; she was not only a beautiful woman, but a grand woman, I don't suppose there was ever a finer family than the Lancasters. When I was 20 years old I met a Merchant that paid Grandmother many nice compliments. She was left with her family and Slaves, had a hard time to get along.

Joseph Lancaster died April 14, 1814. His wife, Rachel Lancaster, died Dec. 19, 1828.

Their children's deaths—

Rebecca Rogers d. Feb., 1835.
Thomas Fletcher d. Sept. 25, 1835.
Joseph Manerva Patrick d. Feb. —, 1837.
America Lancaster d. Aug. 20, 1858.
Mary Davis d. in the 18-Sixties.
Nancy Beckner d. 1864.
Catherine Whaley d. Jany. 14, 1884.
Samuel Lancaster d. June 7, 1889. His wife, Harriet Davis Lancaster, d. April 29, 1879.

Nancy West was a sister of Benjamin West, the Artist, who was for many years President of the Royal Academy in England.

His sister, Nancy West, lived in Delaware, married a man by the name of Samuel Sorency. They had three boys, David, Jacob & Samuel. Her husband was killed in the Revolutionary War. She with her three boys and old Aunt Hettie, the colored woman came to Bourbon County near Paris, Kentucky, and lived several years. The Wests from whom we are descended were related to the Maryland Wests, Lord Delaware's family name was West, and we are of the same tribe. One of our ancestors was an Aunt of William Penn. So you see we are of considerable Quaker stock.

Thomas Fletcher was Colonel in the Revolutionary Army. His father (Gen. Robert) was killed at Bunker's Hill. The Fletchers came from England to Nova Scotia. Through New England into Virginia. Thomas Fletcher came from Lynchburg, Virginia, to Kentucky and located at a Stone house between Paris and Millersburg, Bourbon County.

Col. Thomas Fletcher and the widow Nancy West Sorency married in Bourbon County, Ky., they with her three boys and old Aunt Hettie moved to Bath County, Kentucky, on a farm near Flat Creek; died and buried on the farm. After their death the farm passes into Mr. Johnson Young's hands. Grandfather and Grandmother Lancaster are buried on the same farm.

Benjamin West visited his sister in Kentucky and wore his Quaker costume. He died in 1820.

Thomas and Nancy Fletcher had seven children. Will give their names and marriages—

*1. Rachel Fletcher m. Joseph Lancaster. Lived & died in Kentucky.

2. Mary Fletcher m. Quinton Moore, went to Missouri, the friends lost sight of them after a long time.

3. Rebecca Fletcher m. Ely Hazelrigg, lived in Kentucky.

4. Anna Fletcher, never married, buried at Old Bethel.

5. Catherine Fletcher m. Augustus Byram.

6. Rutha Fletcher m. Valentine Byram.

7. Thomas Fletcher's first wife was Miss McIlhaney. Second wife Mrs. Howe. These are Grandmother Lancaster's Sisters and Brother. He was General in the War of 1812, wounded at Fort Erie, had a fine home East of Sharpsburg, Ky. Was buried on the farm.

*According to Mr. Lucien Beckner, Rachel Fletcher was born in 1783. Mrs. Davies' statement that her parents, Thomas Fletcher and Nancy West were married in Bourbon County is therefore evidently an error, as Bourbon was not formed until 1785. The marriage was probably recorded in Fayette Co. Joseph Lancaster, father of Rachel, was son of Major John L., Penn. Line, killed at Brandywine.

LITTLEPAGE

(Copied from old Oxford Bible owned by Mrs. Milton Elliott, Bridgeport, Franklin Co., Ky.)

(Date of Bible MDCCXLVII.)

(At top of record, written in pencil, "Mollie Towles Armstrong's Great Aunts & Grandfather.")

John M. Littlepage was born the 30th day of August, 1788.

Frances S. Littlepage was born the 15th day of April, 1791.

James S. Littlepage was born the 29th day of April, 1793.

Robert B. Littlepage was born the 31st day of August, 1795.

Mariah M. I. Littlepage was born the 19th day of March, 1798.

Richard W. C. Littlepage was born the 24th day of August, 1800.

The above are the children of Richard and Ann Littlepage.

Mary S. Littlepage was born the 6th day of August, 1822.

Richard Littlepage was born the 17th day of January 1824.

Frances A. Littlepage was born the 25th day of August, 1825.

James S. Littlepage was born the 3rd day of September, 1827.

The above are the children of James S. & Dorothea W. Littlepage.

Mary L. Towels, who was Mary S. Littlepage, departed this life the 20th of September, 1859.

Dorothea W. Littlepage departed this life the 2nd day of November, 1859.

James S. Littlepage, Jr., departed this life October 12th, 1864.

Children of Mary Littlepage and Rawleigh D. Towles:

Mary Frances Towles, born 1860, Oct. 18.

Price Curd Towles.

Elizabeth Ann Towles,

Mary F. Towles married Rawleigh D. Armstrong, a first cousin. By the marriage was mabel F., Ruby D. & Rawleigh D., Jr. Mabel married William Roland Magoffin, of Harrodsburg, Ky.

Elizabeth Ann Towles married John ——. By their marriage was two children:

Mary Frances, m. A. B. Hackley,

Maude Lee, m. James Searcy.

NEALE BIBLE

(Contributed by Mrs. Mary Neale Thompson, Richmond, Kentucky.)

Copied from family Bible of James Neale, born in Northumberland County, Virginia.

James Neale was born the 10th of February, 1788.

James Neale died the 10th day of November, 1829.

James Neale and Anna Rainey were married on the 28th day of November 1816.

William Lewis Neale, their son, was born October the 5th 1817. He died Sept. 25th, 1893.

James Neale, their son, was born August 3rd, 1819.

James Neale, Jr., was born July 3rd, 1821.

Eliza Anne Neale was born April 3rd, 1825. Died Sept. 8th, 1900.

James M. Neale, Jr. (brother of Wiliam L. Neale) departed this life the 20th day of May, 1849 (In the War of 1812, never married).

Anne Rainey Neale was born Dec. 26th, 1802. Died Nov. 27th, 1874.

William Lewis Neale and Zerelda Howard married the 5th of October, 1843.

William Lewis Neale was married the second time to Miss Carrie Goodloe, daughter of Judge William Goodloe, Nov. 20th, 1865.

PARK

(Copied by Mrs. Robert Gum, Frankfort, Ky.)

Data taken from Bible belonging to Mrs. Amanda Park Chandler, of Liberty, Mo.

Simpson Park b. Apr. 25, 1813, d. 1897, m. May. 23 1837 to Rebecca Jane White, b. June 11, 1821, d. 1853.

1. John Wesley Park, b. Feb. 20, 1838, d. Jan. 13, 1901, m. Mar. 28, 1867 to Anna Bronaugh b. Oct. 21, 1844, d. Dec. 21 1876, m. 2 June 30, 1880, Sarah Eliza Jacobs.

2. Mary E. Park, b. Oct. 21, 1839, d. Mar. 17, 1859, m. Jan. 10, 1859 to Alfred W. Allen.

3. Geo. Clark Park, b. Feb. 8, 1842, d. June 1, 1842.

4. Matilda Park, b. Dec. 24, 1844, d. Feb. 11, 1848.

5. and 6. Twin daughters, b. Sept. 17, 1845, d. Sept. 18, 1845 and Oct. 15, 1845.

7. Joe Park b. May 25, 1847, d. Jan. 30, 1848.

8. Elihu Park, b. Apr. 21, 1849, m. Laura Ragan.

9. Amanda Jane Park, b. Apr. 4, 1852, m. May 26, 1870 to Dr. Edward Henry McDonald.

1. Mattie McDonald, b. Oct. 14, 1871, d. Oct. 14, 1871.

2. Mary McDonald, b. Aug. 12, 1873, d. Aug. 19, 1874.

3. Bertha McDonald, b. Mar. 27, 1875.

4. Lilian McDonald, b. Jan. 14, 1878, d. Apr. 14, 1886.

5. Douglas De La Gal McDonald, b. June 14, 1884, m. July 11, 1908, Etta Hunter.

a. Mary McDonald, b. Nov. 28, 1911.

6. Norman Simpson McDonald, b. May 16, 1883, m. July 10, 1911 to Mable Dysart.

a. Edward Dysart McDonald, b. May 28, 1915.

b. Norman Simpson McDonald, b. Oct. 27, 1917.

7. Edward Henry McDonald, b. June 23, 1885, m. Amanda Jane Park McDonald, m. 2 Apr. 28, 1896, Maj. John Temple Chandler.

1. John Temple Chandler, Jr., b. April 18, 1898, m. July 24, 1923 to Dorothy Petty.

Simpson Park m. 2 Jan. 3, 1856, Julia White Fields Malone, b. May 13, 1822, d July 18, 1860.

1. Eliza Fillmore Park, b. Nov. 11, 1856, d May 5, 1918, m. June 15, 1876, Garrard Chesnut.

Simpson Park, m. 3, July 1, 1862, Martha Peters.

(Copied from Bible of Nell Park Gum. Frankfort, Ky.)

John Wesley Park, b. Feb. 20, 1838, d. Jan. 13, 1901, m. 1, Mar. 28, 1867 to Anna Bronaugh, b. Oct. 21, 1844, d. Dec. 21, 1876.

1. John Simpson Park, b. Nov. 2, 1869.

2. Francis Bronaugh Park, b. June 8, 1871.

3. Robert White Park, b. Nov. 30, 1872, m. Nov. 9, 1904, Chicago, to Ella Georgia Steck, b. Dec. 22, 1880.

a. Ann Bronaugh Park, b. Apr. 25, 1907.

b. Harry Morton Park, b. Mar. 19, 1909.

4. Edward McDonald Park, b. Aug. 19, 1874, d. Mar. 30, 1898.

John Wesley Park, m. 2, June 30, 1880, Sarah Eliza Jacobs, b. Oct. 21, 1855.

1. Charlie Whitney Park, b. May 1881, d. June 1881.

2. Fannie Waugh Park, b. Nov. 4, 1882, m. Sept. 24, 1902, Liberty, Mo., William Steele Piper, b. Mar. 17, 1878.

 a. Helen Frances Piper, b. 7/17/1907.
 b. Virginia Park Piper, b. 9/29/1909.
 3. Elihu Scott Park, b. Oct. 11, 1886, m. Nov. 1, 1913, K. C., Kan., to Bess Barr Armstrong, b. Oct. 9, 1895.
  a. John Wesley Park, b. Apr. 5, 1916.
 4. Matilda Park, b. Oct. 26, 1888, m. Oct. 25, 1911, Fredrick Earl Cooley, b. Feb. 6, 1876, m. at Liberty, Mo.
  a. Sarah Margaret Cooley b. Sept. 6, 1914.
  b. Mildred Cooley, b. July 31, 1918.
 5. Nell Marshall Park b. Aug. 3, 1891, m. Feb. 10, 1914, Liberty, Mo., to Robert Richardson Gum, b. Oct. 10, 1880.
  a. Robert Park Gum., b. May 19, 1917
 6. Mary Park, b. July 16, 1895, d. Oct. 17, 1918.

WILLIAM PEDEGO'S BIBLE

(Contributed by Mrs. W. Basil Smith, Edmund Rogers Chapter, D. A. R., Glasgow, Ky.)

William Pedego, born Aug. 13, 1814.
Perlina Dale, born June 20, 1817.
William Pedego and Perlina Dale were married Dec. 18th, 1834.
Amanda Pedego was married Jan 8th, 1860.
H. M. Pedego was married March 7, 1865.
John M. Pedego was married Feb. 10, 1870.
Isaac Alonza Pedego and Sallie Bryant were married April 3, 1884.

BIRTHS

Sarah E. Pedego, born May 22, 1836.
Mary A. Pedego, born Nov. 27, 1838.
Henry M. Pedego, born March 27, 1838.
George T. Pedego, born March 29, 1842.
James G. Pedego, born April 29, 1844.
John W. Pedego, born May 3, 1845.
Joseph Pedego, born Jan. 16, 1847.
Sarah L. Pedego, born July 3, 1848.
Martha J. Pedego, born Dec. 5, 1850.
Elizabeth S. Pedego, born Nov. 22, 1856.
Isaac Alonza Pedego, born Aug. 24, 1858.

DEATHS

Sarah E. Pedego, died Feby. 2nd, 1838.
Jas. G. Pedego, died Aug. 5, 1844.
Elizabeth S. Pedego, died Jan 30, 1858.
George T. Pedego, died Jan. 15, 1862.
William Pedego, died Feb. 23, 1862.
Joseph Pedego, died June 21, 1863.
Martha J. Pedego, died March 16, 1868.
Sarah L. Pedego, died March 20, 1870.
Mary A. West, died Jan. 13, 1875.
H. M. Pedego, died Aug. 4. 1897.
Ellen D(epp) Pedego, died Feb., 1906.
John W. Pedego, died Dec. 6, 1906.
Perlina Pedego, died Aug. 24, 1908.

PEYTON BIBLE

(Contributed by Mrs. Mary Neale Thompson, Richmond, Kentucky.)

Yelverton Peyton was born in Stafford County, Va., Nov. 20th, 1755. Yelverton Peyton died Jan. 23rd, 1849.
Anne Guffey Peyton, his wife, was born March 1st, 1762. Died Dec. 15th, 1848.
Yelverton Peyton, Jr., was born Dec. 17th, 1793.
Yelverton Peyton died Jan. 23, 1849.
Yelverton Peyton, Jr., married Sallie Ann Garvin, Oct. 11th, 1836.
Craven Peyton, (son of Yelverton) was born Jan. 2nd, 1799. Died Sept. 13th, 1876.
Margaret Moore Peyton his wife was born Nov. 26th. Died April 23rd, 1873.
Mary Jane Peyton, daughter of Craven Peyton and Margaret Peyton, was born Jan. 28th, A. D. 1830. Died Sept. 18th, 1901. Married Newland Jones, Dec. 18th, 1849.

REDFORD BIBLE

(Contributed by Mrs. W. Basil Smith, Edmund Rogers Chapter, D. A. R., Glasgow, Ky.)

This book was purchased April 15, Anno Domini 1803, by James Shelburn.
James Shelburn married Anna Pettus, 22 Sept. 1765.
P. H. Redford married M. R. Pace, Dec. 7, 1864.
Silas Shelbourn married Mary H. Stone, Nov. 17, 1814.

Susanna Shelbourn, daughter of James Shelbourn and Anna his wife, born Nov. 13, 1766.

James Shelbourn & Anne his wife was born Feb. 4, 1739.

Salla Shelbourn, daughter of James Shelbourn and Anne his wife, born March 20,

Polly Shelburn, dau. of James Shelbourn and Anne his wife, born June 15, 1783.

Pettus Shelbourn, son of James Shelbourn & Anne his wife, born July 21, 1787.

Silas Shelbourn, son of James Shelbourn & Anne his wife, born June 4, 1790.

(Tom) Redford, son of P. H. Redford & M. R. Redford, born Sep. 20, 1865.

William Durward Redford, son of the same, born March 25, 1867.

Hawood Leslie Redford, son of P. H. & M. R. Redford, born May 22, 1873.

Francis Redford, born April 11, 1790.
Eliza A. Redford, born Aug. 10, 1817.
Mary Redford, born April 10, 1818.
William P. Redford, born Nov. 21 1821.
Emely Susan Redford, born J. 29, 1823.
Jam(?) Robert Redford, born Sept. 20, —.
John Edward Redford, born Aug. 14, 1828.
Caroline Rebekher Redford, born May, 1831.

Mucther (?) Frances Redford, born April 4, 1833.

William Shelbourn, son of Silas Shelbourn & Mary, born, Nov. 18, 1815.

Sephus Shelbourn, son of Silas Shelbourn & Mary his wife, Feb. 10, 1817.

James Shelbourn son of Silas Shelbourn & Mary his wife, born Dec. 4, 1813.

Sally A. Redford, born April 23, 1835.
Thomas William Redford, born Apr. 23, 1837.
Frank Redford, born July 18, 1839.

James Shelbourn departed this life Mar. 6, 1829.

Anna Shelbourn, departed this life March 9, 1831.

Emely S. Redford, died Nov. 2, 1853.
Frances Redford, died Oct. 5, 1859.
P. H. Redford, died March 15, 1885.
Margarette Ruth Redford, died Jan. 12, 1918.

B. F. Redford, died July 16, 1917.
Bessie Redford, died Feb. 16, 1915.

James Shelbourn married Anna Pettus Sept. 22, 1765.

H. L. Redford & Emma Kidd were married March 8, 1904.

Margaret E. Redford & James Hedpeth married Jan. 26, 1914.

Henry Redford &

Mary Redford & J. C. Hamilton married June 1, 1920.

Robert Redford & Alice Key married July 5, 1921.

Ruth Redford & Henry Amos married Dec. 25, 1921.

RICHARDSON

Copied from an old law book of John Park, Sr., by H. W. Jacobs.
(Given by Nell Park Gum, Frankfort, Ky.)
John Richardson, b. June 9, 1792, m. Barbara Park June 11, 1816, in Estill Co., Ky., b. July 27, 1799.

1. Woodson P. Richardson, b. Nov. 22, 1816.
2. Mary Ann Richardson, b. Dec. 12, 1819.
3. Dudley Richardson, b. Oct. 3, 1821.
4. Elizabeth Richardson, b. Apr. 27, 1823.
5. Shelton Richardson, b. June 25, 1825.
6. Matilda Richardson, b. Aug. 25, 1828.
7. Paulina Richardson, b. Oct. 24, 1830.
8. Wm. M. Richardson, b. Jan. 30, 1833.
9. Simpson P. Richardson, b. Aug. 10, 1835.
10 Ann Eliza Richardson, b. Jan. 26, 1838.

(Record taken from the old family "New Testament" of Mrs. Belle Griffith, of Clarksville, Texas. The Bible was given to her grandmother, Mariam Park Richardson, dau of Susan Park and Asa Park, on her wedding day by Miriam's gr. grandfather.)

Barbara Park, b. July 27, 1799, d. May 9, 1873, m. Jan. 11, 1816 to John Richardson, Jr., b. June 9, 1792, d. Dec. 18, 1875.

1. Woodson P. Richardson b. Nov. 22, 1816, d. Nov. 7, 1900, m. Mariam Park, b. Jan. 27, 1815.

a. John Richardson, b. May 6, 1838, d. Jan. 7, 1870, m. July 29, 1859 to Margaret F. Person, b. Apr. 2, 1838, d. Feb. 4, 1870.
  1. Woodson P. Richardson, b. Oct. 11, 1860.
  2. Mara E. Richardson, b, July 12, 1861.
  3. Wm. S. Richardson, b. Oct. 14, 1862.
  4. Elizabeth M. Richardson, b. Dec. 15, 1864.
  5. Eli Richardson, b. Apr. 8, 1866, d. Aug. 27, 1866.
b. Mary E. Richardson, b. Oct. 31, 1839, d. May 6, 1858.
c. Barbara A. Richardson, b. May, 26, 1842, m. Feb. 3, 1860 to D. Z. M. Parks, b. Apr. 18, 1838, d. Dec. 2, 1868.
  1. Mary Belle Parks, b. Dec. 6, 1860.
  2. John Price Parks b. Aug. 26, 1866, d. Nov. 12, 1915.
d. Susan Frances Richardson, b. Jan. 20, 1844, d. Oct. 2, 1923, m. Jan. 31, 1869, Chesterfield Cox, b. Oct. 10, 1841.
  1. Geo. H. Cox, b. Nov. 22, 1869.
e. Paulina Richardson, b. Dec. 15, 1846, m. May 4, 1865.
James K. Robertson, b. Jan. 1837, d. Apr. 7, 1870.
  1. Wm. David Robertson, b, Sept. 14, 1866.
  2. Wade H. Robertson, b. June 28, 1868.
  3. Susanna Robertson, b. Sept. 22, 1870.
f. Sarah Richardson, b. June 13, 1848, m. Sept. 6, 1866 to Philip Hobacker, d. Jan. 24, 1870.
  1. Robert Hobacker, b. Nov. 4, 1867.
g. Martha Richardson, b. May 28, 1852.
Names and dates as found in Bible, re-arranged for convenience.

Nell Park Gum
Frankfort, Ky.

ROBERTSON FAMILY BIBLE

Copied from Bible printed and published by M. Carey, 121 Chesnut St., Philadelphia, 1816, and presented to the Kentucky State Historical Society by Mr. William R. Buford, Chatanooga, Tenn., grandson of Judge Robertson, in 1923.

Enclosed with the Bible was a memorandum which had been compiled by Mr. Buford from the "Life & Times of George Robertson" (the distinguished Kentucky Jurist) in whose hand-writing all the entries in the Bible, with the exception of the record of his own death, were made.

The memorandum is as follows:
"Alexander and Margaret R. Robertson arrived at Gordon's Station, about four miles from Harrodsburg, December 24, 1779. He was Sheriff of Mercer County in 1792. He died Aug. 15, 1802 and his widow, Margaret R. Robertson married in 1805, Job Johnson and moved to Lancaster in 1806.

"Margaret R. died in Frankfort, Jan. 13, 1846.

"The children of Alexander and Margaret R. Robertson were:

"Elizabeth, Margaret, Jane, Martha, James 3rd, Alexander, George and Charlotte.

"George, born Nov. 18, 1790, married at Lexington, Ky., Nov. 28, 1809, Eleanor James McIntosh Bainbridge.

"Charlotte (daughter of Alexander & Margaret Robertson) married Robert Perkins Letcher, and died at Frankfort, Ky., Oct. 29, 1879.

"Charlotte Corday Robertson, daughter of George and Eleanor Robertson, married in Lancaster, Ky., June 5, 1834, Dr. David Bell, of Fayette, Co., Ky."

MARRIAGES

George Robertson and Eleanor Bainbridge were married on the 28th day of November, 1809.

Our oldest daughter Margaret Eliza was married to Wm. Buford April 17th, 1828.

The second daughter Eleanor McIntosh Robertson was married to Dr. Samuel M. Letcher, February 21st, 1833.

The third daughter Charlotte Corday Robertson was married to David Bell, June 5th, 1834.

Alexander H. Robertson was married to Eliza Dunlap of Jacksonville, (Illinois) 13th September, 1853.

James B. Robertson was married to Annie M. McGrath, of Louislle, (Ky.) 18th October, 1853.

BIRTHS

George Robertson was born in Mercer County, Kentucky, on the 18th day of November, 1790.

Eleanor Bainbridge, now Eleanor Robertson, was born in the State of New York, on the 27th day of April, 1794.

Margaret Eliza Robertson the first child of the sd. George and Eleanor, was born near Lancaster, Garrard County, Kentucky, on the 25th day of January, 1811, about sunrise.

Eleanor McIntosh Robertson was born in Lancaster, Ky., on the 28th of January, 1813, about the dawn of day.

Mary Oden Robertson was born Friday, the 5th day of May, 1815, about 4 o'clock P. M.

Charlotte Corday Robertson was born on the night of the 14th day of June 1817, about 12 o'clock P. M. in Lancaster.

Alexander Hamilton Robertson, the first son of the sd. George & Eleanor, was born in Lancaster on the 17th day of March, 1820, about 12 o'clock in the day.

Bainbridge Robertson, the second son and sixth child of George and Eleanor, was born 13th Dec. 1822, about 9 o'clock A. M.

Martha Jane Robertson was born on the 24th of July, 1824, about one o'clock p. m. Lancaster.

George Samuel McKee Robertson, our third son, was born the 2nd of November, 1827, about 8 A. M. He was named after myself and my benefactor and best friend the late Samuel McKee.

James Bainbridge Robertson was born October the 4th, 1831, at 5 o'clock P. M.

George Robertson (the last child of George & Eleanor) was born May the 12th, 1838, about 1 o'clock A. M. in Lexington, Kentucky.

DEATHS

Bainbridge Robertson, the second son of George and Eleanor, departed this life on the 9th day of February, 1823, about 8 A. M., disease supposed to be erysiplas. He was a very large promising child.

Martha Jane Robertson died on the 17th of May, 1826, about 4 o'clock P. M., aged 22 months, disease the influenza and hooping cough. She was a most beautiful and highly gifted child. She was the idol of the family and the admiration of all who knew her.

George S. McKee Robertson, died about 3 o'clock P. M., Dec. 12, 1837, of scarlet fever, aged 5 years, 1 month and 10 days, an uncommonly promising boy in every respect, amiable, intellectual and handsome. He was the favorite of every member of the family.

Mary Oden Epes Robertson died of cholera on the 20th of June, 1833. She was 18 years old and of fine person and mind.

George Robertson, Jr., died about 5 o'clock A. M. 12th of Dec., 1856. Although healthy, ruddy and robust from his birth, having caught cold about the 1st of Jan'y, 1856 he had symptoms of bronchitis tending to consumption, and on the night of his death having played on the violin better than usual, he went to bed and coughing up a little blood about half after 4 o'clock he requested his mother to "send for the Doctor" and while she was calling a servant, he sitting in the bed, said to his father "I can't get my breath" and instantly sank into his father's arms and expired. The shock was tremendous and even now nearly two years after his death his parents are almost as gloomy and disconsolable as on the day of his death.

Eleanor J. Robertson, wife of George Robertson, after living most happily with him for more than 55 years, died at 15 minutes before 2 o'clock on the morning of January the 13th, 1865, leaving him and her long happy home desolate and hopeless and producing a social void that nothing earthly can ever fill; a neater, modester, or juster woman, a better wife, mother and mistress never lived. She was the Soul and Idol of her family circle, whose fatal bereavement is irreparable and crushes the heart of the devoted husband. May all who knew her reverence her memory and profit by the beautiful example of her model life.

Note in different handwritting:

The hand that wrote the foregoing brief memorials of love and death is cold. The heart that never ceased in life to melt at the recital is still. The eldest in time of all whose names are inscribed on these pages is now the youngest of them in eternity.

After a long career of usefulness and honor and after a protracted ilness, which he bore with Christian fortitude, George Robertson on the 16th day of May, 1874, at 10 o'clock P. M., departed from the earth. How well he performed his duties as a citizen, with what affection and self denial he discharged all domestic offices his country and his children atest.

The important and final question recurs: "If a man die shall he live again?" To the eye and ear of faith the answer comes: "There is but one thing needful," and among the many which ennobled the life of George Robertson, those who loved him remember with most satisfaction that 'he chose that good part," because hope finished the sentence with the words "which shall never be taken from him."

DATA FROM THE SCOTT FAMILY BIBLE

(In possession of family of Mr. Levi H. Scott, formerly of Henry County, Kentucky.)

Presented by Miss Hattie Scott, Susannah Hart Shelby Chapter, D. A. R., Frankfort, Ky.

BIRTHS

Levi H. Scott was born June 22nd, 1827. Died Dec. 19, 1908.

Louisa M. Duvall, wife of Levi H. Scott, was born Oct. 25, 1825. Died Nov. 19, 1906.

Alexander C. Scott was born Oct. 27, 1856.

Mary A. Scott was born Dec. 28th, 1857. Died May 8th, 1859.

John H. Scott was born Nov. 17th, 1859.

Lewis M. Scott was born Jan. 19, 1862.

Walter L. Scott was born Oct. 9, 1863.

Fannie E. Scott was born Oct. 12, 1865. Died April 30, 1880.

Alonzo Scott was born Nov. 11th, 1867. Died June 16th, 1869.

Henry Clay Scott was born Feb. 13, 1871.

Susannah Scott was born April 30th, 1873.

Leslie Thomas Scott was born Aug. 12th, 1877.

Laura J. Scott was born May 5, 1879.

Daniel Scott, father of Levi H. Scott, was born Jan. 30th, 1797. He died 1830.

Susannah (Witherspoon) Scott (mother of Levi H. Scott) was born Feb. 15th, 1799, died Sept. 12, 1838.

John A. Scott was born March 14th, 1819. Died July 25, 1848.

William Lloyd Scott was born Sept. 25th, 1820, died Oct. 23, 1875.

Nancy Jane Scott was born Sept. 3rd, 1822, died Aug. 28, 1900.

Lewis Witherspoon Scott was born Dec. 8th, 1824, died Aug. 1855.

James Scott, was born July 4th, 1829, died Sept. 1852.

Sarah Witherspoon, wife of Robert Witherspoon, was born 1775, died Oct. 16, 1851.

Lewis J. Witherspoon was born Nov. 22, 1801, died May 25, 1852. (Son of Robert and Sarah (Johnson) Witherspoon.)

Fannie Witherspoon, daughter of Robert and Sallie Witherspoon, born March 27, 1805.

Nancy Witherspoon, daughter of Robert and Sallie Witherspoon, born Apr. 27, 1803, died March 5, 1852.

John Witherspoon, born Jan. 26, 1807.

Johnson Witherspoon, born Oct. 19th, 1813.

Lot Duvall, father of Louisa Duvall Scott, born Jan. 3rd, 1799, died Nov. 20, 1881.

Lucy Duvall, wife of Lot Duvall, and daughter of Thos. and Acton Marshall, was born Jan. 19th, 1802, died Sept. 1, 1845.

Levi H. Scott and Louisa M. Duvall were married Jan. 17th, 1856.

SEARCY BIBLE RECORDS

(Contributed by Mrs. E. B. Smith, Isaac Shelby Chapter, D. A. R., Shelbyville, Ky.)

Bible owned by Mrs. Charles Weakly, Shelby County, Ky.

Printed and sold by John Holbrook
1816—

Richard Searcy was born Aug. 21, 1738.
Edmund Searcy was born Mar. 25, 1767 (son of the above).
Hanna Searcy, his wife, was born Dec. 12, 1777.
Harriet Searcy, daughter of Edmund and Hanna, was born Dec. 17, 1806.
Richard Edmund Plummer, son of same, was born Aug. 4th, 1817.
Mary Ellenor Sarah, daughter of same was born Mar. 19th, 1820.
Edmund Searcy died 15th day of October, 1825.
Hannah Searcy departed this life the 19th day Sept., 1834.
Harriett Searcy, daughter of the above, died 1st day Feb., 1810.
Richard Edmund Plummer, son of same, died Sept. 15, 1824.
Maria Searcy, born May 27, 1799, wife of Robert Thurston.

MARRIAGES

Edmund Searcy and Hanna Miller was married Sept. 6th, 1796.
Robert Thurston and Maria Searcy was married the second day of January, 1814.
Robert Thurston was born 16 January, 1783.
Maria Thurston was born 27th of May, 1799.

BIRTHS

Mary Plummer Thurston, daut. of Robert and Maria, was born 20 Oct., 1814.
Edmund Plummer Thurston, son of same, was born Nov. 22nd, 1816.
2nd daut. of same was born 25 Apr. 1818.
Lucinda Elizabeth Thurston, daughter of same, was born 23 Jan., 1826.
Maria Louise Miller Thurston, daut. of same, was born 3rd day of May, 1832.
Sophia Bailer Walker, daughter of Joseph and Mary Ellenor, was born Nov. 6th, 1840.
Robert Samuel Waddy, son of William L. Waddy and Maria was b. 18 Feb., 1850.

DEATHS

Mary Plummer Thurston died November 1815.
Edmund Plummer Thurston died December 27, 1816.
Babe died 16 May, 1818.
William Lewis Waddy born March 31st, 1819.
William Lewis Waddy died Sept. 11, 1895.
Maria Louise Miller Waddy died Dec. 26, 1907, age 75 yrs., 6 months, 23 days.
Joseph Welch Walker and Mary Ellenor Searcy was married the 11th day of April, 1839.
William L. Waddy and Maria L. Thurston was married the 16 December, 1847, age 15 yrs., 7 mo., 13 days.
Lucinda E. Thurston and Robert H. Smith married Feb. 23, 1842. 16 yrs., 1 month old when she married.
Robert Thurston and Maria Searcy were married 2nd. of Jan., 1814.

BIRTHS

Anna Maria Stevenson, daut. of R. H. and L. E. Smith, was born 8 Dec. 1842.
Robert Thurston Knight Smith, son of same, born Oct. 31, 1844.
Lucinda Elizabeth Smith, daut. of same born Mar. 14, 1846.
Infant Smith, son of same, born 2, May, 1848.
Sarah Louise, daut. of same, born.
Maria Louise, daut. of W. L. & M. L. Waddy, was born July 23, 1861.
Maria Louise, daut. of same (Smith), born Apr. 27, 1852.
George William Thurston, son of W. L. & M. L. Waddy, was born Dec. 28, 1855.
Geo. William Thurston, son of W. L. & M. L. Waddy, was born July 26, 1852.
Thomson Miller, son of W. L. & M. L. Waddy was born Dec. 28, 1855.
Lucinda Ida, daughter of W. L. Waddy & M. L. Waddy, was born July 6, 1858, Tuesday.

DEATHS

Infant son of R. H. & L. E. Smith, died July 7, 1848, age 2 mo. 5 days.
Sarah Louise daut of same died.

Lucinda Elizabeth Smith wife of R. H. Smith, died May 12, 1852, age 26 yrs., 3 mo. & 19 days.

Robert Thurston died Aug. 16, 1856, age 73.

Maria Thurston, wife of Robert Thurston, died May 18th, 1866, age 66 yrs., 11 months, 21 days.

Robert H. Smith died Sept. 2nd, 1890.

Lucy E. Smith died Mar. 11th, 1895.

Lucinda Ida Waddy died Nov. 28, 1891.

Thomson Miller Waddy died Sept. 25, 1911.

BASIL GAITHER SMITH'S BIBLE

(Contributed by Mrs. W. Basil Smith, Edmund Rogers Chapter, D. A. R., Glasgow, Ky.)

Basil Gaither Smith, born April 3 1806.

Nancy Nuckols, born Oct. 10, 1808.

Hezekiah P. Smith, son of Basil G. Smith and Nancy his wife, born June 28, 1831.

Marcellus Smith, son of Basil G. Smith and Nancy his wife, born April 17, 1832.

Isaac A. Smith son of Basil G. Smith and Nancy his wife, born Oct. 6, 1833.

Julian Smith, son of Basil G. Smith and Nancy his wife, born March 10, 1835.

Quintus M. Smith, son of Basil G. Smith and Nancy his wife, born Nov. 2, 1836.

Bazilia Smith, son of Basil G. Smith and Nancy his wife, born July 18, 1842.

Leonidas Smith, son of Basil G. Smith and Nancy, his wife, born March 7, 1845.

Martha S. and Susan M. daughters of Basil G. Smith and Nancy his wife, were born Mar. 24, 1846.

Mary E. Luckett, born June 19, 1819.

Maria M. Smith, daughter of Basil G. Smith and Mary his wife, born Sep. 10, 1852.

Benjamin Luckett Smith son of Basil G. Smith and Mary his wife, born March 18, 1855.

Doctor Smith was born April 12, 1840.

Llewelyn Holten Smith, son of Basil G. Smith and Mary his wife, born Feb. 21, 1857.

William Basil Smith, son of Basil Gaither Smith and Mary his wife, born Oct. 25, 1861.

Kate Q(?). Smith, daughter of Basil G. Smith and Mary his wife born Oct. 24, 1861.

Humphrey Marshall Smith, son of Basil G. Smith and Mary his wife, born Oct. 25, 1862.

MARRIAGES

Basil Gaither Smith was married to Nancy Nuckols Apr. 29, 1830.

Basil Gaither Smith married Mary E. Luckett June 10, 1851.

Hezekiah P. Smith Married Miss Richmond in Miss.

Isaac A. Smith married.

Julian Smith married Mary E. Smith 1879.

Susan M. Smith married John Kincheloe.

Martha S. Smith married ———Spencer.

Maria M. Smith Married Samuel Pedan 1869.

Benjamin Luckett Smith married Sallie Ritter.

Llewellyn Holton Smith married Bina Wichard.

Humphrey Marshall Smith married Louise Neiddefer———.

DEATHS

Marcellus Smith died Oct. 19, 1833.

Quintus M. Smith died Sept. 7, 1854.

Doctor Smith was killed in battle at Chickamauga.

Leonidas Smith died June 6, 1845.

Isaac A. Smith died ———

Nancy Nuckols Smith died April 10, 1849.

Kate Q. Smith died Oct. 31, 1861.

Basil Gaither Smith died Aug. 15, 1889, aged 83 yrs.

Mary E. Luckett Smith died July 13, 1895, aged 76 yrs.

Humphrey Marshall Smith died ———.

SMITH

(Benedict Smith's Bible Records, Danville, Mercer Co., Ky., April 7, 1810, owned by Mrs. Nannie B. Tichenor, given to her by cousin Julia Sloan Spalding 16, Mar., 1918. Now in possession of Mrs. Henry Sayles, Shelbyville, Ky., 1927)

Benedict Smith

Mary Gardner, m. 8 Feb., 1795

John R. Bean
Maria Smith m. 4, Feb., 1823.

Edward B. Smith
Annie Lancaster m. 28, Nov., 1826.

Henry A. Reid
Ann T. Smith, m. 2, Sept., 1828.

Charles Haydon
Matilda B. Smith, m. 31, Aug., 1830.

John Smith Bean.
Emeline Cameron.

Mary M. Bean
Charles Tichenor, 21, Nov., 1878.

Minnie Bean
Charles Tichenor, 21, Mar., 1878.

SNODDY

(Records from the Bible of Samuel Snoddy, son of John Snoddy, of Madison County. The Bible is now the property of Mrs. Robert R. Burnam, of Richmond, a direct descendant of the pioneer, John Snoddy. Copied by Mrs. Robert Gum, Aug. 1st, 1927.)

MARRIAGES

Samuel Snoddy and Jane, his wife, was married on the 26th of July, 1798.

Jefferson Williams and Cynthia Snoddy were married August 5th, 1824.

John Parke and Nancy Snoddy were married October 11, 1827.

Margaret Jane Parkes and Charles S. Wilmore were married Nov. 20, 1851.

Elizabeth Ann Parkes and William B. Smith were married Aug. 11, 1854.

BIRTHS

Samuel Snoddy was born Aug. the 23rd, 1776.

Jane Snoddy, his wife, was born 12th June, 1774.

Their children's births are as follows:

1st., born on 18th of April 1799.

Second, who is named Patsy, was born May 3rd, 1800.

Third Peggy was born on the 20th of June, 1802.

Fourth Cynthia was born June, 1805.

Fifth, Nancy, January 21, 1808.

Sixth, Betsy, March 14th, 1810.

Seventh, John Kincaid, was born 6th, Feb., 1812.

Eighth, Jane Ann, on 14th Jan., 1814. The last.

(Records from the Bible once owned by John Kincade Snoddy, now owned by Mrs. Robert R. Burnam, Summit Ave., Richmond, Ky. The Bible was printed by special command of King James, First, of England, in the year 1811.)

(Copied by Mrs. Robert Gum.)

Jefferson Williams and Cynthia Snoddy were married Aug. 5th, 1824.

Samuel Snoddy was born Aug. 23rd, 1776.

Ann Snoddy was born Oct. 19, 1776.

John Snoddy was born Oct. 18th, 1780.

Isabell Snoddy was born Apr. 8th, 1782.

Joseph was born Aug. 29th, 1784.

Margaret Snoddy was born Sept. 8th, 1788.

(Next name was so faded it was not legible.)

Nancy Snoddy was born June 8th, 1788.

Betsy Snoddy was born Oct. 28, 1790.

Joseph W. Snoddy was born June 29th, 1793.

James Snoddy was born Oct. 18th, 1796.

John M. Reid was born 5th of Sept. 1838.

William S. Reid was born Apr. the 6th, 1843.

Anderson Woods Reid was born Nov. 8th, 1848.

Jefferson Williams was born Oct. 22, 1801.

John Parke was born Dec. 17th, 1802.

Samuel Snoddy Parke was born Oct. 10, 1829.

Margaret Jane Parkes was born Aug. 20, 1831.

Elizabeth Ann Parkes was born July 8th 1833.

Nancy Snoddy Smith was born Dec. 9th, 1855.

John Williams Wilmore was born 25, Sept. 1852.

Elizabeth Wilmore was born Dec. 27, 1856.

Maria Brown Smith was born Oct. 13, 1857, Platte City, Mo.

Cynthia Williams Smith was born Jan. 5th, 1860. Platte City, Mo.

Margaret Wilmore Smith was born Nov. 26, 1861. Platte City, Mo.

DEATHS.

The first born as in the foregoing never was named. Died 28 of April, 1799.

Patsy also died 20 Aug., 1804.

Peggy died likewise 10th July, 1804.

Samuel Snoddy departed this life Wednesday morning, Dec. 18th, 1833, ten minutes before six o'clock.

Nancy Parkes departed this life Wednesday, ½ past 10 P. M., March 12, 1832. Only sick 2½ hours.

Jane Ann Robinson died.

Jane Snoddy of Samuel Snoddy, decd, died 28, Feb., 1852. Saturday night 8 o'clock P. M.

Elizabeth Reid, wife of A. W. Reid, decd., died 25th Feb., 1852.

Cynthia Williams died Nov. 13th, 1866, Tuesday, 5 o'clock 50 minutes P. M.

Jefferson Williams died Jan. 4th, 1879, at the home of W. B. and E. A. Smith and was buried in Richmond Cemetery on Tuesday, the 7th day of January, 1879. He was buried with Masonic Honors and a large crowd was at his burial.

STINSON (STEVENSON)

(Contributed by Miss Ruth Beall, Hart Chapter, N. S. D. A. R., Winchester, Kentucky.)

Record from Bible of John Stinson (Stevenson). Now owned by Waller Rupard, Clark County, Ky.

John Stevin was maryed to his wife Margaret Majors In the year of our Lord one thousand seven hundred and Eighty-two May the twenty second day.

James Mason Stevinson was born in the year of our Lord one thousand seven hundred Eighty three, November the thirteenth day.

William Stevinson was born in the year of our Lord one thousand seven hundred and eighty six April they third day.

John tomson Stevinson was born in the year of our Lord one thousand seven hundred and eighty eight, January the fifth day.

Thomas Stevinson was born in the year of our Lord one thousand seven hundred and ninety January they twentieth day.

Leucinday Stevinson was born in they — of our Lord one thousand sevin hundred and ninety three fabruary they twentieth day.

Williamson Stevinson was born in the year of our Lord one thousand sevin hundred and ninety five fabruary they eighteen day.

Mary Stevinson was born in the year of our Lord one thousand seven hundred and ninety seven fabruary they third.

Samuel Stevinson was born in the year of our Lord one thousand seven hundred and ninety nine January the twenti Eight day.

Josiah Stevinson was born in the year of our Lord one thousand Eight hundred and one November the fourteenth day.

Augustus Vernon Stevinson, son of Josiah Stevinson and Alice his wife was born Friday 27th of February 1826.

Margaret Majors Stevinson daughter of Josiah Stevenson and Alice his wife was born Friday 8th of April 1831.

Mary Jane Stevenson daughter of Josiah Stevinson and Alice his wife was born Monday (9 o'clock in the evening) October the 7, 1833.

Mary E. Stevinson was born December the 25th, 1858.

Will Stevinson departed this life In the year of our Lord one thousand seven hundred and Eighty Seven June the first day.

Thomas Stevinson Departed this life In the year of our Lord one thousand seven hundred and eighty nine September the thirtyeth day.

John Stevinson Departed this life In the year of our Lord one thousand eight hundred and seventeen October the fifteenth Day.

Margaret Stevinson departed this life on the twenty third day of March in the year of our Lord eighteen hundred and thirty one aged sixty nine.

Mary Ellen Stevinson was born the 25th of De in the year 1838.

John Stinson or Stevinson was born in 1755 in Buck's Co., Pa.; removed to Md. about nine years afterwards; to Va. in 1783 and to Clark Co., Ky. in 1793. Was in the War of the Revolution, Battle of Germantown. Rank—Private and Ensign—(From Bureau of Pensions).

(The last paragraph of the record above was probably added by the copyist.)

TRUMBO BIBLE RECORDS

(Exact copy of records taken from the Bible of John Trumbo, now 1927) owned by his grandson, Jake A. Trumbo, Camp Dick Robinson, Bryantsville, Garrard Co., Ky.

Jake A Trumbo served in the Confederate Army under Morgan, was also one of the personal bodyguard of Jeff Davis. On account of the ink being faded one half page of the records could not be read.

MRS. ROBERT GUM,
Frankfort, Ky.

Jake A. Trumbo and Mary E. Bradshaw were married Dec. 23, 1869.

Adam L. Trumbo and Lucy J. Jacobs were married Jan. 20 1897.

A. L. Trumbo was b. Jan. 20, 1871.

Lucy J. Trumbo was born Dec. 17, 1897.

Henry Whitney Trumbo was born Apr. 23, 1901.

Andrew Trumbo was born Nov. 11, 1903.

Frank Trumbo was born Feb. 12, 1906.

James Allen was born the 15th day of Jan. in the year of our Lord 1794.

Jake A. Trumbo was born Oct. 24, 1845.

Mary E. Trumbo was born Apl. 6, 1849.

Adam A. Trumbo, son of Jake and Mary E. Trumbo, was born Jan. 20, 1871.

Sallie A. Trumbo was born July 24, 1873.

James F. Trumbo was born May 9, 1875.

Maggie L. Trumbo was born Nov. 30, 1878.

Jimmy was born 15th day of April 1845.

Betsy was born 20th day of Apl. 1847.

Mary E. Trumbo, wife of J. A. Trumbo, died March 24, 1883, aged 32 years, thirteen days.

John Trumbo and Sarah Atchison married Oct. 29, 1795.

Adam Trumbo and Hannah Allen married Apl. 12th, 1840.

John A Trumbo and Orra Emmons married June 19, 1863.

John Trumbo, born Oct. 12, 1776.

Sarah Trumbo, born July 15, 1778.

Isaac Trumbo, born Sept. 6, 1796.

Elizabeth Trumbo born July 2, 1798.

Nancy Trumbo, born Aug. 10, 1800.

Sarah Trumbo, born Mar. 24, 1803.

Margaret Trumbo, born Oct. 8, 1805.

Doratha Trumbo, born Dec. 22, 1808.

Deborah Trumbo, born Feb. 24, 1811.

Ruthann Trumbo, born Mar. 30, 1813.

Rachel Trumbo, born 21, 1815.

Adam Trumbo, born Aug. 17, 1820.

John A. Trumbo was born Feb. 4th, (Friday) 1841.

James B. Trumbo was born Tues. Sept. 26, 1843.

Jacob A. Trumbo was born Oct. 24, 1845.

Sarah Eliz. Trumbo was born Tues., ——— 18, 1848.

Clay Trumbo was born Sun., Jan. 13, (or 15) 1851.

Nancy Trumbo was born on Tuesday, 1st of Sept. 1853.

Lucy E. Trumbo was born Sat., 16th of Mar. 1861.

Ella Lee Trumbo was born May, Sun. 8th, 1864.

Nannie Trumbo was born Mar., Wed. 7th, 1866.

DEATHS

Nancy Warner, late Nancy Trumbo, departed this life Sept. 15, 1826.

James B. Trumbo, son of Adam and Hannah Trumbo, departed this life on the 13th of Aug. 1851, at 9 o'clock in the morning.

Clay Trumbo, son of Adam and Hannah Trumbo departed this life on the 30th of May, 1852 at one o'clock in the morning.

Departed this life in the 78th year of her age, Mrs. Sarah Trumbo, on the 23rd day of Oct. at 7 o'clock and 15 min. p. m. 1853.

John Trumbo departed this life Mar. 30th, 1856, 79 yrs., 5 mos., 18 da.

Margaret Snedaker departed this life Aug. 4th, 1870.

Adam A. Trumbo died Mar. 18th, 1:18 p. m. 1896.

Hannah S. Trumbo died June 18, 1887.

On the fly-leaf of John Trumbo's Bible was a record of the birth of his slaves:

Maria Jane, born Jan. 15, 1834.

Her son, George Washington born 17th Aug. 1852.

Her son, James born May 3, 1854.

Her daughter Alferret born Mar. 1st, 1856.

Tom, born Mar. 1st, 1840.

Lue, born Sept. 1, 1852, died Sept. 1st, 1852.

TWYMAN

(Records from Bible of David R. Twyman, published by McCarty & Davis, No. 171 Market St., Philadelphia, 1834. I. Asmead & Co., Printers. Bible now owned by John D. Twyman, 229 Moundale Ave., Winchester, Ky.)

David R. Twyman was born June 24th, 1795.

Matilda Twyman was born August 17th, 1803.

Lucy R. Twyman was born December 22nd, 1821.

Pleasant H. Twyman was born November 5th, 1823.

Franky Ann Twyman was born Feb. 7th, 1828.

Elizabeth Watts Twyman was born July 8th, 1830.

Martha A. Twyman was born October 27th, 1832.

George Allin Twyman was born July 22nd, 1835.

John Garrett Twyman born 17th August, 1837.

Sarah Ann Twyman born 13th January 1841.

David Lewis Twyman born 10th April, 1844.

David R. Twyman died May the 31, 1858.

Matilda Twyman died July the 27th 1896.

Pleasant H. Twyman died March 14th, 1908, age 85 years, 4 months, 9 days.

Franky Ann Wills died March fourth, 1881.

Mary S. Beall died April 25th, 1875.

Elizabeth W. Twyman died August the 13th, 1862.

Martha A. Parris died July 15th, 1865.

George Allin Twyman died 14th November, 1835.

John Garrett Twyman died April 21, 1877.

Sarah Ann Twyman died 24th December, 1848.

David Lewis Twyman died 22nd December, 1848.

Lucy R. Wills died August the 6th, 1880, aged 58 years, 8 mo., 15 days.

Matilda Twyman died July 27, 1896.

(David R. Twyman was born in Albemarle Co., Va. Early in life he came to Ky. and died in Clark Co., Ky., where he lived most of his life).

David R. Twyman and Matilda Haggard was married in the year of our Lord Novmb. 30, 1820.

Mary Shepherd Bell and Othy Bell maried in the year of our Lord August 28th, 1856.

Franky A. Twyman and Sympson Wills, was married March the 4, 1858.

Pleasant H. Twyman and An E. Crutchfield maried in the year of our lord October 13, 1861.

John G. Twyman and Gusta Ann Todd was married September the 25th, 1862.

Martha A. Twyman and Thomas Parris was married May the 30th, 1865.

Lucy R. Twyman and Elijah Wills was married June 26th, 1867.

(Twyman record copied by Miss Ruth Beall, Hart Chapter, N. S. D. A. R., Winchester, Ky., March —, 1928).

SAMUEL WADDY'S BIBLE

(Copied by Mrs. E. B. Smith, Shelbyville, Ky. Bible owned by Mrs. Cecil Waddy Weakly, Shelby Co., Ky.)

Published by John Grigg, No. 9 North Fourth Street.
1829

MARRIAGES

Samuel Waddy and Elizabeth Hobbs was married 9th January, 1804.

Lud Fore and Adoline Waddy was married 27th July, 1830.

Nicholas Smith and Nancy Jane Waddy was married Jan., 1823.

Daniel E. Wilson and Frances Eliza Waddy was married 22 Jan., 1835.

M. N. Boyle was married to Frances Eliza Wilson (late Waddy) the 30th April, 1839.

Ephriam G. Jefsy and Susan M. Waddy was married the 19th Aug., 1841.

Jno. N. Boyle and Amanda Malvina Waddy were married the 30th Sept. 1847.

William Lewis Waddy and Maria L. M. Thurston were married the 16th of Dec., 1847.

Ben F. Danley and Amanda M. Boyle were married the 15th March, A. D. 1855.

Thomas B. Moore and Helen W. Wilson were married Dec. 26, 1853.

John F. Boyle and Matilda Dorsey were married May 10, 1873.

BIRTHS

Jane Cobbs was born 1753, 27th April.
Robert Cobbs was born 23rd of Nov., 1754.
Judith Cobbs was born 5th, Apr. 1757.
Samuel Waddy was born May 2nd, 1771.
Elizabeth Hobbs was born 25 Dec., 1780.
Nancy Jane Waddy was born 25 Oct., 1804.
Joseph Owen Waddy was born Sept. 24, 1806.
Mary Lewis Waddy was born Oct. 11th, 1808.
Sarah Adaline Waddy was born 28th Mar., 1811.
Frances Eliza Waddy was born 5th Feb. 1814.
Susan Mildred Waddy was born 28th June 1816.
William Lewis Waddy was born 30 Mar., 1819.
Amanda M. Waddy was born 7 June, 1822.
Mary Elizabeth Smith was born 18th Sept., 1825.
Mary Jane Fore was born 10th June, 1831.
Samuel Fore was born 5th July 1832.
Helen Vaughan Wilson was born 10th Dec., 1836.
Samuel Waddy Jefse (Jesse) was born 30 June, 1843.
Sarah Adaline Jesse was born July 28, 1845.
John Francis Boyle was born July 14, 1845.
Mary Eliza Boyle was born July 17, 1848.
Mary Eliza Jefse was born Apr. 21, 1849.
Thomas Edward Moore was born June 30, 1855.
Samuel Waddy Donly was born 22 Dec. 1853.
Albert Samuel Waddy was born Feb. 18th, 1850.
George William Waddy was born 26 July, 1852.
Thomas Miller Waddy was born 28 Dec., 1855.
Lucinda Ida Waddy was born July 6, 1858.
Maria Louise Waddy daughter of W. L. Waddy & M. L. Waddy was born July 23, 1861.
M. F. Jesse, son of Ephriam Jesse & Susan M. Jesse, was born Nov. 13th, 1851.
William G. Jesse, son of Ephriam & Susan M. Jesse, was born Oct. 14, 1857.

DEATHS

Nancy Jane Smith departed this life 27 Dec., 1826.

Joseph Owen Waddy departed this life 17th Sept., 1829.

Mary Lewis Waddy departed this life 26th Jan. 1831.

Mary Jane Fore departed this life 10th Aug. 1831.

Samuel Fore departed this life 15th Sept. 1832.

Daniel E. Wilson departed this life Jan. 22nd, 1837.

Mary Elizabeth Smith departed this life 25th July, 1837.

Nicholas Smith, departed this life Oct. 18th, 1833 (?).
Sarah Adoline Fore departed this life Jan. 22nd, 1836.
Elizabeth Waddy departed this life 20th Sept, 1857.
Frances Eliza Boyle departed this life 26 July, 1845.
John N. Boyle departed this life Sept 21, 1848.
Mary Eliza Boyle departed this life Oct. 11, 1855.
Samuel Waddy Donley departed this life 28 Oct., 1855.

WARE FAMILY RECORD

(From data compiled by the late Philip Fall Taylor, of Frankfort, Kentucky, and now in possession of his sister Mrs. Jouett Taylor Cannon.)

1. James Ware, Sr., born November 15, 1714; resided in Gloucester (?) County, Virginia, died ———; married ——— Agnes, born Dec. 20th, 1714. (His will recorded Franklin County, Kentucky, Will Book No. 1, dated Sept. 25, 1790, probated April 19, 1796, made by "James Ware, of Woodford County, Ky., P. F. T." His will names son John; son Nicholas, deceased, and his heirs; son James; daughter Clary; son William; son Edmund.)

Children:

John Ware, b. December 12, 1736.
Nicholas Ware, b. August 12, 1739.
James (Doctor), b. March 13, 1741, 42.
Richard, b. May 18, 1745.
Clara, b. December 11, 1747.
William Ware, b. March 29, 1750.
Edmund Ware, b. April 25, 1753.

William Ware, (son of James, Senior, and Agnes) born in Gloucester County, Virginia, March 1750, d. in Franklin County, Ky., ——— m. ——— Sarah Samuel, (daughter of Wiliam Samuel) and had:

Elizabeth Ware, b. about 1776/78, died July 30, 1849, m. May 31, 1799, John Bacon (b. March 10, 1767, d. May 9, 1817).
James, b. May 12, 1780.

Agnes, b. May 17, 1783, m. 1st, Philemon Rouzee, m. 2nd, William Porter.
Rebessa, b. ——— m. Jan. 1, 1812, Willis Blanton.
Sarah, b. ——— m. William Porter, Jr.
Samuel, b. ——— m. Mrs. Elizabeth ( ) Redd.

RECORDS FOUND IN THE FAMILY BIBLE OF

WILLIAM WILSON (1785-) AND MATILDA BRINEGAR, NEE BOONE

(Furnished by Mrs. Smith D. Hogan, of Frankfort, nee Catherine Wakefield.)

MARRIAGES

William Wilson, Snr., was married to Matilda Brinegar, October the 1, 1816.
Lydia G. Wilson was married to Philip P. Robinson, June 9, 1836.
William B. Wilson was married to Elizabeth Ann Offutt, July 12th, 1842.
Nancy G. Wilson was married to Thomas G. Crutcher April 18th, 1849.
Matilda B. Wilson was married to G. W. Moore, December 12th, 1855. (Mrs. Hogan informs us that "G" in above initials stands for "George.")
On July 3rd, 1860, by Rev. Thomas Daniels, Mattie Wilson to Walker Daniels. T. G. Crutcher.

BIRTHS

T. G. Crutcher, born 27 Dec., 1817; died Oct. 31, 1891, age 74 yrs. & 10 months.
Nancy G. Crutcher, born May 22nd, 1827; died Oct. 24th, 1900, age 73 yrs. & 5 months.
George Brinegar was born June the 15 day, 1815.
Lydia Garner Wilson was born September the 5 day, 1817.
William Boon Wilson was born October the 18 day, 1820.
Joel Hampton Wilson was born July the 5 day, 1824.
Nancy Grubs Wilson, born May 22, 1827.
Abner Wilson, born January 10, 1830.

710

Matilda Boon Wilson, Born September 7, 1832.

Mary Elizabeth Wilson, Born May 7, 1835.

Martha Louisy Wilson, Born August 17th, 1837.

Mattie Lou Wilson, born August 17th, 1837.

Colored Slaves—

Emma Brown Johnson was born March 26th, 1854.

Alice B. Johnson, born March 18th, 1871.

Aletha Johnson was born February 9th, 1874.

William Wilson, son of Abner & Lydia Wilson, was born August the 20 day, 1785.

Matilda Wilson, daughter of William & Nancy Boon, was born December the 1 day, 1795.

Laura B. Crutcher, born Oct. 15th, 1856. (The "B" stands for Boon.)

Evelina Watts Moore, Born November 26th, 1856.

William Daniel Wakefield, Feb. 10th, 1878, at the residence of his father on Smithfield Pike.

James Marcus Wakefield, April 5th, 1884; Carlisle, Ark.

DEATHS

Deceased an infant son of William & Matilda Wilson, June 25th, 1849.

Died at New Orleans on the 15th December, 1851, George B. Brinegar, son of George & Matilda Brinegar, aged 36 years, 6 months.

Died at the residence of her husband on the 16th of November, 1852, Mrs. Matilda Wilson in her 57th year.

Died on the 3rd of August, 1855, Mary E. Wilson.

Died on the 10th of June, 1871, our Father, William Wilson, in the 86 year of his age.

Died at the residence of her Father, T. G. Crutcher, Sept. 13th, 1878, at ½ past 7 o'clock, A. M., Mary D. Crutcher, aged just 17 years.

Died at the residence of her husband, G. W. Moore, on the 4th of July, 1879, Matilda B. Moore, in the 47 year of her age.

Deceased this life daughter of William & Matilda Wilson, November 3, 1819.

Also deceased another daughter of William & Matilda Wilson, April 26, 1823.

Deceased by untimely birth two sons of William & Matilda Wilson, May 17, 1826.

Abner Wilson, son of Wm. & Matilda Wilson, Deceased this life October 18, 1831, age 1 year, 9 months.

Deceased by untimely birth, a son, 25 June, 1840 (2?).

Joel H. Wilson deceas'd January 31, 1842, aged 11 years, 6 months.

Criss, deceased this life August 1, 1823, aged 6 years.

Emily, deceased this life Sept. 1, 1823, age one year.

Anthony, deceased this life November 1, 1824, age forty-five years.

George deceased this life July 7, 1825, age six years.

Martha, deceased this life February 2, 1834, 2 years of age.

Julia, Robert and Annie also died March.

Martha, Deceased this life February 2, 1834, 2 years of age.

The majority of these people lived and died in Shelby County, Kentucky.

JOHN WOODRUFF LINE

(Bible records of late Gideon King, Eminence, Ky.)

(Contributed by Mrs. E. L. Sloan, Historian, Bland Ballard Chapter, Eminence.)

John Woodruff I, came over to America in Gov. Winthrop's train, from England, in the year 1638.

John Woodruff, b. England 1604, d. U. S. A. 1670, married Ann ———.

Their son—

John Woodruff II, b. 1637, d. 1691, married Mary (Mercy) Carle. He was one of the founders of Elizabeth, N. J.

Their son—

John Woodruff III, b. 1662, (First white child born in Elizabeth, New Jersey.) married Sarah Cooper, daughter of Timothy Cooper, of Springfield, Mass., b. 1665, d. 1727.

Their son—Timothy Woodruff, b. 1682, d. 1766, married, May 12, 1709, Mary Baker.

Their son—

Timothy Woodruff II, b. 1716, d. 1798, married Elizabeth Parsons, b. 1712, d. 1762.

Their son—

Enos Woodruff, b. 1750, d. 1821, (Soldier of Revolution and line proven.) married Charity Ogden Aug. 19th, b. 1753, d. 1828.

Their son—

Ezra Woodruff, b. 1787, d. 1842, married Aug. 8, 1822, Maria Parson, b. about 1800, d. about 1829. Marriage record in Cincinnati, Ohio.

Their daughters—

Almira Woodruff, born about 1824, died early.

Sophia Woodruff, b. June 5, 1826, d. Mar. 26, 1899, married Jan. 22, 1856, Gideon King, b. Nov. 15, 1817, d. Nov. 29, 1889.

Their daughters—

Mary P. King, b. Nov. 30, 1856, married Sept., 28, 1875, Winfield P. McCorkle, b. Oct. 20, 1850, Tenn., d. Dec. 28, 1921, Ky.

Allie F. King b. Oct. 7, 1859, Henry Co., now live in Wichita, Kan., married Nov. 30, 1881, Jesse N. Haymaker.

YOUNG-PROCTOR BIBLE RECORD

This Bible "Stereotyped by E. and J. White for The American Bible Society, 1829" bears on the title page the following inscription: Willoughby T. Young's, bought at the Eagle Book Store, Maysville, Ky., price $2.25, presented to my sister Margaret Cook this 12th decr. 1838.

(Signed) W. T. Young.

Besides the family record which is written on the flyleaf at the beginning of the New Testament, Willoughby T. Young wrote his will and a codicil, and he also wrote on the front fly-leaf, a letter to his sister.

The Bible was evidently presented to the Historical Society by Prof. John R. Procter, of Maysville.

The will and codicil follow:

In the name of God, I Willoughby T. Young, a citizen of Mason County, Kentucky, being confined at the Hospital at Lexington, being in possession of a disposing memory do make this my last Will and Testament, this Eleventh day of December in the year of Our Lord 1838.

Item—All the property it has pleased God to bless me with I give to my Mother Judith Young and Sister Margaret Cooke, during their natural lives, after paying my just debts, the balance to pass by law of Decents. My Daughter Anne Maria to be decently clothed and supported until she marrys or arrives at the age of twenty-one years, then to inherit what may be left, subject however to the control of my Exrs.

Item—My Will and desire is that is that the Quarter section of land in Davies County Indiana Patented to Presley Day be sold and the tract west of the Flemmingsburg road I bought of E. S. Pepper being by survey made to contain twenty-seven acres one half and twenty poles Also my two tracts in Campbell one on Pond Creek, the other being my interest in Robert Young's Pre-emption or so much as will pay my just debts the large tract covering Moe Gills to be investigated, the land on Mill Creek to be rented out, the claim on Genl. Government to be investigated so soon as the papers are obtained from N. D. Coleman, the servants to which I am entitled now in possession of my Mother to be liberated as soon as they clear fifty acres of land on the West Fork of White River Indiana for my Daughter, for doing of which I request my daughter to give them the wood to enable them to purchase land for themselves. lastly I do appoint my friends George Chinn (?) and Peter Lashbrooke my Executors of this my last Will and testament.

Given under my hand the day first written.

(Signed) Willoughby T. Young
(Seal)

See Codecil or Supplement—

Supplement or Codecil—

The tract on Pond Creek was given by Squire Grat to satisfy an Execution in my favor contains three hundred acres, in the name of White &c. Grant's title being doubtful a motion was before the Campbell Circuit Court to set the sale aside, the result I have not been apprised of, my exc. was older than Kirtley's under which Grant's home farm was sold.

The Quarter Section in Daviess County, Ind. Seth B. Shackleford has a Mortgage to secure the payment of a small sum which I wish paid immediately he holding my note of hand for the same, what I am indebted to my sister Cook, if the land I bought of E. S. Peper suits her, she shall have to release me from the Mortgage of my brother Robert's interest in the servants conveyed to me, at what the land may be worth believing Pepper to be paid, when back rents are taken out and what I paid him before he forced (?) the possession.

My books I give to Lettie (?) Cooke.

(Signed) Willoughby T. Young.

Letter:

Hospital at Lexington, Ky.
19th April, 1839

My dear Sister,

I am very tired of staying here and wish to be imployed at something profitable. Since I returned the last time I have taken six pills and one or two doses of Salt & water.

You will find my Will about the first of the New Testament—If the Hords (?) and Judge Read are satisfied I ought to be. I have a great deal of business to settle but give it up. I am trying to finish my course with joy. If I should not be spared to see You again in this world I hope I shall meet you where parting is not known. My love to Mother and Giles. I hope you will see Anne Maria often tell her to write me a letter. Agreeable to my view of right she ought to wrote before this time.

Your brother,
(Signed) Willoughby T. Young.

Family Record

Willoughby T. Young, born Decr. 8th, A. D. 1790. Married fourth day of February A. D. 1821 to Lucy Shackleford, by which mariage Anne Maria was born twelfth March One Thousand Eight hundred and twenty-two—Let no man deceive you, we still may be happy.

Lucy Young Daughter of Geo. and Elizabeth Shackelford, born 1796, departed this life 20th day of April, 1826.

Robert Young departed this life 4th May, 1790, being the Ancestor of Willoughby T. Young.

Thomas Young, Robt. Young's oldest child, was born 2 day of May A. D. 1782.

Robt. Young, born on the 19th day of January A. D. 1784.

Saml. H. T. Young, born on the 9th January, A. D. 1786.

Margaret Young, late Margaret Cook, born on the 1st August A. D. 1788.

George M. Procter, Married to Anne Maria Young, January 28th, 1839.

Lucy Procter, daughter of Geo. M. & Anne Maria Proctor, born 5th March, A. D. 1842.

John Robert Proctor, son of Geo. M. & Anne Maria Proctor, born the 16th March, A. D. 1844.

KENTUCKY BIBLE RECORDS—MERCER COUNTY

Copied from original records by Lockette Smith, August, 1933.

Armstrong and McAfee

(From Bible owned by John Lapsley Armstrong and Alabama McAfee and now in the possession of Miss Jennie Sharp, Mercer County, Kentucky.)

McAfee, Samuel—born Sept. 19th, 1773. Died 1825.
Cardwell, Mary—born Dec. 12th, 1778. Died 1850, and were married April 5th, 1796.

Anne—born July 26th, 1797. Died Aug. 1797.
Robert—born Aug. 1st, 1798. Died Feb. 1860.
John J.—born Dec. 22nd, 1800. Died Mar. 1861.
Samuel W.—Born Nov. 12th, 1802.
William C.—born Feb. 3rd, 1805. Died 1879.
Rice—born Jan. 3rd, 1807. Died 1871.
Indiana—born Sept. 24th, 1809. Died 1846.
Alabama—born Mar. 2nd, 1811. Died Nov. 6th, 1892.
Polly—born Mar. 27th, 1813. Died April 18th, 1895.
Samuel—born Mar. 23rd, 1815. Died 1865.
James M.—born May 20th, 1817. Died 1839.
Margaret W.—born June 8th, 1819. Died 1871.
Elizabeth J.—born Feb. 18th, 1822.

Armstrong, John L.—born Aug. 15th, 1801. Died April 6th, 1877.

Bayse

("The William Bayse Bible" now the property of Miss Cora Bohon of Harrodsburg, Mercer Co., Kentucky.)

Bayse, William and *Jane Logan*, were married December 12th, 1788.
Mitchell, William and *Polly Bayse*, were married the 3rd day of April, 1811.
Smith, George W. and *Hannah Bayse*, were married August —, 1835.

Basye, William, was born the 20th day of September, 1759.
Logan, Jean, was born the 6th day of June, 1765.

Basye, Polly, was born the 28th day of December, 1778 or 1788.
Basye, John, was born the 29th day of October, 1790.
Basye, Anna, was born the 7th day of Jan. 1791 or 1794.
Basye, Logan, was born the 6th day of March 1797.
Basye, Hannah, was born the 26th day of Feb. 1800.
Basye, Elizabeth, was born the 1st day of March, 1803.
Basye, William, was born the 6th day of November, 1811.
Mitchell, Joseph, was born the 9th of Jan. 1812.
Mitchell, Maryan Jean, was born October 6th, 1813.
Mitchell, Eliza, was born March the 18th, 1816.
Basye, William, was born the 11th of Feb. 1834.
Smith, George Washington, was born Sept. 22nd, 1812.
Smith, John Logan Basye was born July 26th, 1843.
Smith, Georgie A., was born March 21st, 1840.
Smith, Sallie J., was born May 21st, 1836.
Basye, William, departed this life Jan. 25th, 1834.
Basye, Jane, departed this life April 5th, 1834.

Bohon Bible

(Now the property of Miss Cora Bohon of Harrodsburg, Mercer County, Kentucky.)

Bohon, Garret and *Elizabeth Basey*, were married in the year 183— October 10th.
Rupley, Geo. W. and *Martha A. Bohon*, were married December 21, 1882.
Bohon, Garrett, was born in the year of our Lord July 9, 1800.
Bohon, Elizabeth, was born in the year of our Lord March 10, 1803.
Bohon, William L., was born in the year of our Lord Aug. 9, 1834.
Bohon, Sarah Jane, was born in the year of our Lord March 26, 1836.
Bohon, Mary R., was born in the year of our Lord Sept. 19, 1838.
Bohon, Martha Ann, was born in the year of our Lord Dec. 30, 1840.
Bohon, Elizabeth, was born in the year of our Lord Dec. 6, 1842.
Bohon, John A., was born in the year of our Lord August 25th, 1845.
Edwards, Mary R., died Nov. 27th, 1901.
Rupley, George W., died Jan. 22, 1903.
Rupley, Martha Bohon, departed this life Aug. 31st, 1909.
Bohon, John A., died March 30th, 1913.

BOTTOM—CARPENTER

(This Bible is now the property of the Harrodsburg Historical Society.)

Bottom, W., was born December the 13th, 1792 (?)
Bottom, Polly, was born June 18th, 1799.
Bottom, Farris, was born April 10th, 1818.
Bottom, Mary, was born August 16th, 181— (?)
Carpenter, Nancy, was born Dec. 11th, 1861.
Carpenter, John H., was born Feb. 21st, 1864.
Carpenter, William F., was born Sept. 11th, 1838.
Carpenter, Henry W., was born May 19th, 1840. Died June 15th, 1891.
Carpenter, M——, was born April 7th, 1842.
Carpenter, Josephine, was born March 26th, 1844.
Carpenter, George Alfred, was born June 7th, 1852. Died Aug. 14th, 1858.
Carpenter, Sarah A., was born May the 16th, 1859.
Carpenter, Conrad, was born April the 12th, 1846.
Carpenter, Louisa, was born August the 14th, 1848. Died Jan. 11, 1858.
Carpenter, Lilard, was born September the 20th, 1850.
Carpenter, Mary E., was born ———. Died Jan. 18th, 1858.
Carpenter, Jacob, was born Jan. 29th, 1857.

CARLISLE

(Owned by Mr. George Chinn, Jr., of Mercer County, Kentucky, and copied by Miss Lockette Smith from Clippings from the Harrodsburg Herald dated September, 1926, and loaned by Miss Jennie Sharp of Mercer County, Kentucky.)

Carlile, Jane—daughter of *John Carlile* and *Elizabeth* his wife, was born Nov. 26th, 1746.

"*Ditto*" *Carlile, Mary*—was born May 19th, 1749.

(Note—The "Ditto" evidently means that Mary was also the daughter of John and Elizabeth Carlile.)

Carlile, Agnas—was born October 5th, 1749.
John was born May 24th, 1751.
James was born August 13, 1756.
Robert was born February 11, 1759.
Samuel was born April 2, 1762.

(Note:—"Another branch of the family takes up the record here. Apparently the Bible was heired by James for the records of the next generation begin:")

Carlile, John—son of *James Carlile*—was born January 13, 1781, was married to *Margaret McClure*, born February 17, 1789—on August 21, 1806.

Thompson, Rebecca—born January 27th, 1813—was married January 19, 1837 to *John Carlisle* of Kentucky and Virginia.

"Letha, Loaf Sugar Lump." was born December 12, 1841.

There is no mention of little Letha's marriage or death. Only that one endearing phrase in the old family Bible to show that she ever lived.

The last birth recorded is that of *John G. Carlisle.*

COMINGO

(Owned by Mrs. W. C. Carr of Mercer County, Kentucky, and copied from Clippings from the Harrodsburg Herald, dated September, 1926, loaned by Miss Jennie Sharp of Mercer County, Kentucky.)

"I, *John Comingore*, was born in the year of our Lord, 1749 on September 16. My wife, *Anne Mathis*, was born in the year 1758 on the first day of August.

DAVIS

(The H. C. Davis Bible which is now the property of the Harrodsburg Historical Society.)

Davis, James E., married to *Margaret Thompson Moore* May 31st, 1815.

Davis, James E., born 23rd of April, 1791.

Davis, Margaret T.—his wife—born the 31st of July, 1791.

Davis, Thomas S., married to *Martha Robinson* 29th of May, 1825.

Davis, Martha R., was born November the 19th, 1805.

Davis, George W., married to *Susan Cecil* the 24th of Dec. 1822.

Davis, Mary E. was born the 8th of April, 1825.

Davis, William H., was born the 19th of Feb. 1827.

Davis, Malinda A., was born Dec. the 23rd, 1828.

Davis, James, was born September 3rd, 1763.

Davis, Polly—his wife—was born January 10th, 1763.

Davis, Stephen—the first child—born March 13th, 1787.

Davis, Jessey, born (illegible) 14th, 1787.

Davis, James, born April 23rd, 1791.

(Three names illegible)

Davis, Lucy, born August 21st, 1799.

Davis, Thomas Sales, born Nov. 5th, 1801.

Davis, Harrison, born June 25th, 1804.

Davis, Archiles E., born August 14th, 1806 (?)

Vandike, Henry N.—son of *Henry* and *Fanny Vandike*, was born Dec. 11th, 1814.

McCoy, James G., was born April 13th, 1817.

McCoy, Joseph E., was born the 17th day of December, 1821.

Davis, Stephen and Elizabeth Moore were married Nov. 3rd, 1809
Davis, William, was born Sept. 7th, 1810.
Davis, Bedialjamal, was born Jan. 12th, 1814.
Davis, George B., born April 2nd, 1816.
Davis, Sally Ann, born Sept. the 8th, 1819.
Davis, Joseph H., born the 17th of October, 1821.
Davis, James G. born October 28th, 1810.
Davis, Charles W., born Feb. 15th, 1812.
Davis, John H., born Feb. 28th, 1814.
Davis, Elinder, born October 15th, 1815.
Davis, Geo. R. (no date)
Davis, Margaret, born November 1820.
Davis, Jesse F., born May 4th, 1824.
Davis, James Sr., died Dec. 6th, 1820. Aged 57 years, 1 month and 1 day.
Davis, Sally Ann, died the 16th of Oct., 1821.
Davis, Jesse Franklin died 31st of Aug. Aged 8 yrs., 3mo., and 28 days.
Davis, Mary—wife of the Rev. *James Davis*—died March 20th, 1841. Aged 78 yrs., 2 months and 10 days.

This Bible was printed in Philadelphia by M. Carey. 1816. "James Davis. This Book from his son James E. Davis. Nov. 30th 1816."

DUNN

(Dunn Family Bible now in the possession of Mr. John Dunn, McAfee, Mercer County, Kentucky.)

Dunn, Peter R. and *Mary Buchanan* married Sept. 19th, 1820. (By the Rev. Thomas Cleland.)

Dunn, Nancy, married *John W. Davis, Jr.,* February 5th, 1846. (By the Rev. John Montgomery of Harrodsburg.)

Dunn, Susan, married *Dr. John W. Powell,* May 20th, 1856. (By the Rev. John Montgomery of Harrodsburg)

Dunn, John, married *Mary C. Robeson,* Oct. 3rd, 1861. (By the Rev. James Lapsley)

Dunn, Peter R., was born the 15th day of Dec. 1794.

Buchanan, Mary, was born Jan. 26th, 1798.

(Peter R. Dunn and Mary B. Dunn became connected with the New Providence Presbyterian Church Sept. 14th, 1822.)

Dunn, Mary, the first born of *Peter R.* and *Mary B. Dunn,* was born July 3rd, 1821.

Dunn, Nancy, was born Dec. 7th, 1824 and Baptized the 7th of August, 1825.

Dunn, Elizabeth, was born the 11th of May, 1827 and Baptized the 20th of October, 1827.

Dunn, America, was born the 12th of March, 1829 and Baptized the 25th of July, 1830.

Dunn, Catherine, was born the 20th of Jan. 1832 and Baptized the 16th of July, 1832.

Dunn, Susan, was born the 15th of Feb. 1834 and was Baptized the 21st of July, 1834.

Dunn, George, was born the 25th of October, 1836 and Baptized the 20th of Aug. 1837.

Dunn, John, was born the 8th of June, 1839 and was Baptized the 4th of August, 1839.

Davis, Mary Alma—the first born of *John W.* and *Nancy Davis* was born the 5th day of April, 1847.

Davis, William Worth—was born the 22nd day of August, 1849.

Powell, Thomas Moore—first born of *John W.* and *Susan Powell* was born Dec. 6th, 1857.

Powell, William Dunn—was born June 26th, 1859.

Powell, George—was born Feb. 13th, 1862.

Powell, Anne Sinclair—was born May 9th, 1864.

Dunn, Mary—the first born of *Peter R.* and *Mary Buchanan Dunn* departed this life the 8th day of May, 1822. Aged ten months, five days.

Dunn, Elizabeth—departed this life the 15th of March, 1828. Aged ten months and four days.

Dunn, Catherine—departed this life the 16th of October, 1832. Aged eight months and twenty-six days.

Davis, Nancy Dunn—departed this life the 17th of Feb. 1850. Aged 25 years, 2 months and 10 days.

Dunn, America—departed this life the 9th of August, 1852. Aged 23 years, 4 months and 27 days.

Dunn, Mrs. Mary—wife of *P. R. Dunn*—departed this life March the 8th, 1858 at 4 O'clock, P. M. Aged Sixty years, one month and thirteen days.

Dunn, Peter R.—departed this life February 22nd, 1863 at 7 o'clock, P. M. Aged Sixty-eight years, two months and seven days.

Powell, Susan Dunn—departed this life October 7th, 1864. Aged 29 years, 7 months and 22 days.

Dunn, John—departed this life March 13th, 1869. Aged 29 years, 8 months and 5 days.

Dunn, George—departed this life May 27th, 1908. Aged 71 years, 7 months and 2 days.

Dunn, Mary Margaret Robb—wife of *George Dunn*—departed this life Sept. 27th, 1929. Aged 86 years, one month and 21 days.

ROBB—COLEMAN

(Copied from a Bible now owned by Mrs. Mattie Robb Chilton, Harrodsburg, Mercer County, Kentucky. This Bible was the property of her great grandfather, Philip Dedman and was brought from Aberdeen, Scotland, in the year seventeen hundred and fifty-eight.)

Robb, Jonas M. was born July 16th, 1831. Died Dec. 12th, 1895 at 9 o'clock, a. m.

Robb, Lucy Foster—was born ———— 1833.

Coleman, William Linfield—First husband of Lucy Foster, died Oct. 18th, 1857.

Robb, Fannie M.—First wife of Jonas Robb, died June 20th, 1855.

James, Fannie R.—daughter of William L. and Lucy Foster Coleman, died March 17th, 1899 at 9 o'clock p. m.

SHARP

(Taken from the Jacob Sharp Bible now owned by Miss Jennie Sharp of Mercer County, Kentucky.)

Sharp, Ann E.—was born July 11th, 1796.

Sharp, Abraham E.—was born Sept. 11th, 1821. Died March 6th, 1901.

Sharp, Joseph & Josiah were born Aug. 20th, 1823.

Sharp, Thomas C.—was born Dec. 28th, 1824. Died Nov. 23rd, 1908.

Sharp, William H.—was born Dec. 11th, 1826. Died Jan. 19th, 1901.

Sharp, Elizabeth R.—was born March 4th, 1829.

Sharp, Jacob S.—was born Jan. 13th, 1835.

"MUD MEETING HOUSE" NEIGHBORHOOD—BIBLE RECORDS

SCOMP—VAN NUYCE

(Taken from Bible and Court Records now owned by Mrs. Mary Rebecca Scomp Cunningham, Mercer County, Kentucky.)

Van Nest (Van Nuyce), Cornelius, Sommerset Co., New Jersey. Married *Mary Van Nuyce* (his cousin) April 10, 1781.

(They came to Mercer Co., Kentucky between 1790 and 1801. They had six children.)

Van Nuyce, Flora—daughter of *Cornelius* and *Mary Van Nuyce*. Married *Henry de Schamp (Scomp)* in 1814 in Mercer County, Kentucky.

Scomp, John Van Nuyce—son of *Flora* and *Henry de Schamp*—married Catherine Wilson in 1840.

Scomp, Mary Rebecca—daughter of *John Van Nuyce* and *Catherine Wilson Scomp*—married *J. T. Cunningham* December 11, 1883.

Van Nuyse, Mary—was born 1763 near Millstone, Somerset Co., New Jersey.

Van Nuyce, Cornelius—was born 1755 in Somerset Co., New Jersey.

Van Nuyce, Flora—daughter of *Cornelius* and *Mary Van Nuyce*—was born December 6, 1789.

Scomp (de Schamp), Henry—was born October 20th, 1785.

Scomp, John Van Nuyce—son of *Flora* and *Henry Scomp*—was born Feb. 29th, 1815.

Wilson, Cathrine Head—wife *of John Van Nuyce Scomp*—was born April 16th, 1817.

Scomp, Mary Rebecca—daughter of *John* and *Cathrine Scomp*—was born March 4th, 1855.

Van Nuyce, Cornelius, died in 1820.
Van Nuyce, Mary, died in 1845.
Scomp, Flora, died Jan. 1st, 1862.
Scomp, Henry, died June 12th, 1840.
Scomp, John, died June 22nd, 1881.
Scomp, Catherine, died Nov. 22nd, 1891.

Van Arsdale

Contributed by Miss Jennie Sharp, McAfee, Mercer Co., Ky. (Harrodsburg Herald, Aug. 13, 1926.)

Copied by Lockett Smith, 1933.

(Mayor R. S. VanArsdall of Harrodsburg, Kentucky, owns an old hand-tooled leather Dutch Bible printed 185 years ago at Dordrecht, Holland. The Bible is printed in Dutch throughout.)

Vanarsdalen, Jan—a knight in Holland born 1211.

Vanarsdalen, Symon Janson, married in Holland. (Came to the New Netherlands to examine the country about what is now New York to see if it was practical to establish in the New World a pottery for the manufacture of chinaware. Just as he was ready to return to Holland he received word that his wife and two children had died of a plague. He decided to stay in New York.)

Johnson, ———*?* second wife of *Vanarsdalen, Symon Janson.*

Vanarsdalen, Simon Johnson, married *Miss Clawson*.

Vanarsdalen, Cornelius, married *Miss Baxter.*
Vanarsdalen, Alexander, married *Dobitha Smith.*
Vanarsdalen, William Smith, married *Sarah Riker.*
Vanarsdall, Charles Suydam, married *George Ann Vannuys Terrune.*
Mayor Riker Samuel Vanarsdall married *Maud Rose.*
Vanarsdall, Ormand, married *Mabel Currens.*
Vanarsdall, R. S., their oldest child.

Cornelius VanArsdalen who married Miss Baxter came to Mercer County among the band of Dutch settlers that peopled the old Mud Meeting House community. His wife was the first person buried in the Mud Meeting House cemetery in 1800.

Part of the quaint old records in the Bible are as follows:

Marya VanArsdalen haar bock—— 22 von Augustus ent yaar 1771.

VANARSDELL NO. 2

(The Simon VanArsdell Bible now in the possession of Mrs. Louis VanArsdell of Harrodsburg, Mercer Co., Kentucky.)

Vanarsdell, Simon, was born in the year of our Lord 1818, April 14.

Vanarsdell, Harriet Ann, was born in the year of our Lord 1821, August the 17th.

Vanarsdell, Mary Catherine, was born in the Year of our Lord 1840, July the 7th.

Vanarsdell, Martha Ann, was born in the year of our Lord 1842, May the 6th.

Vanarsdell Elizabeth Jane, was born in the year of our Lord 1851, Feb. the 21st.

Vanarsdell, William Bunton, was born in the year 1857, Aug. the 5th.

Beasley, Robt. H., was born in the year of our Lord October 19th, 1846.

Beasley, Mary C. (Vanarsdell), was born in the year of our Lord 1840, July 7th.

Vanarsdell, Simon, and *Harriet Ann Bohon* were married April 13th, 1837.

Beasley, Robt. H, and *Mary C. Vanarsdell* were married June 11th, 1873.

McDonald, Robt., and *Anna Vanarsdell* were married June 4th, 1889.

Vanarsdell (?), William Bunton, died July 23, 1860.

Vanarsdell, Elizabeth, died Dec. 28th, 1863.

Beasley, Robt. H., departed this life in the year of our Lord June 20th, 1898 in the 52nd year of his life.

Vanarsdale, Harriet Ann, departed this life April 24th in the year of our Lord 1875.

Vanarsdale, Simon, departed this life May 31st, 1882.

McDonald, Anna, departed this life in the year of our Lord April 9th, 1899. In the 57th year of her life.

BACON FAMILY RECORD

Copied from OLD BIBLE formerly belonging to EDMUND BACON, of Peak's Mill, Franklin County, Kentucky; owned in 1930 by Mrs. Alexander Bacon, High St., Frankfort, Ky.

Edmund Bacon was born Oct. 11th, 1774.
Edmund Bacon Dec'd, Feb. 1819.
Mary B. Hanley was born Feb. 25th, 1779.
Edmund & Mary Bacon was marryed November 3, 1797.
John R. Bacon was born Aug. 21, 1798.
Edmund Bacon was born Feb. 29, 1800.
John Bacon Dec'd Oct. 2nd, 1801.
Samuel A. Bacon was born Jan'y 29, 1802.
Samuel Bacon Dec'd May 19th, 1802.
William A. Bacon was born May 16, 1803.
Eliza B. Bacon was born Dec. 23, 1804.
Alexander B. Bacon was born Dec. 22, 1806.
William A. Bacon Dec'd May 6th, 1808.
Richardson Bacon was born May 16th, 1808.
Mary D. Bacon was born March 20th, 1809.
Susan H. Bacon was born March 15th, 1811.
Virginia P. B. Bacon was born Jan. 9th, 1813.
Alice M. A. Bacon was born June 18th, 1815.
Sary Elizabeth Bacon was born Aug. 15th, 1817.
(In different handwriting):
Edmond R. H. Bacon was born April 12th, 1828.

(Copied June 11th, 1930, by Mrs. Jouett Taylor Cannon, Secretary Kentucky Historical Society).

FORD BIBLE RECORD—

Copied from old Bible contributed by Mrs. Mary B. Herring, Georgetown, Kentucky.

(Title-page of Old Testament missing).
Title-page of NEW TESTAMENT:

THE
NEW TESTAMENT
OF OUR
LORD AND SAVIOUR
JESUS CHRIST

Newly translated out of the
Original Greek
And with the Former
Translations
Diligently Compared and Revised.

Philadelphia
Printed by Matthew Carey
No. 122, Market Street
1813.

BIRTHS—

William Ford the first Son of Nathaniel and Hannah Ford, was born May 16th 1816.

Mary Ford the first daughter of Nathaniel Ford and Hannah Ford was born February 5th 1818.

Nathaniel Ford was born October the Twenty-ninth in the year of our Lord 1783.

Hanah (Cromwell*) Ford was born July the twelvth in the year of our Lord 1789.

William Ford was born May the Sixteenth in the year of our Lord 1816.

Mary Ford was born February the fifth in the year of our Lord 1818.

Harriot Ford was born May the Nineteenth in the year of our Lord 1819.

DEATHS—

Nathaniel Ford Departed This Life September 4th, 1833.
Harriot Ford Departed this life, November 23rd, 1843.
Mary Randolph Departed this life, March the 10th, 1877.
Hannah Ford Departed this life, January the 4th, 1881.

BIRTHS—

William H. Randolph was born December the 6th, 1844.
Harriet F. Randolph was born July 31st, 1846.
John Walker Randolph was born Oct. 19th, 1849.
Francis D. Randolph was born Oct. 4th, 1853.
Marietta Randolph was born Feb. 18th, 1859.

The Ford Bible Record above was copied from the Bible presented to the Historical Society by Mrs. Mary B. Herring, of Georgetown, Kentucky.

---

*The name Cromwell was interlined in different hand and ink.

COTTRELL BIBLE RECORDS

Copied and contributed by Mrs. Charles A. Wahking, Louisville, Ky., from old Bible owned in 1929 by Mr. Evans W. Floyd, Louisville.

(Bible printed in 1816-17, at Brattleborough, Vt.)

Births

Richard Cottrell was born Oct. 26, 1779.
Anna Clarke was born June 10, 1777.
Margaret Cottrell was born Oct. 12, 1800.
Benjamin Cottrell was born Jan. 15, 1803.
George Cottrell was born Sept. 10, 1804.
Nancy Cottrell was born Sept. 26, 1815.
Shepard Cottrell was born Jan. 27, 1817.

Marriages

Richard Cottrell and Anna Clarke were married Jan. 11, 1829.
Richard Cottrell and Deoshy Cottrell, his second wife, were married September, 1829.

Deaths

Richard Cottrell departed this life Nov. 11, 1829.
Anna Cottrell departed this life Aug. 9, 1828.
*Dicey Cottrell departed this life 1863.
Benjamin Cottrell departed this life Sept. 6, 1828.
George Cottrell departed this life April 4, 1841.
Shepard Cottrell departed this life April 11, 1838.
William S. Floyd was born Oct. 14, 1812.
William S. Floyd and Nancy Cottrell were married July, 1838.
Nancy Floyd died Jan. 9, 1885.
William S. Floyd died Sept. 6, 1888.

Births

Annie M. Floyd was born Sept. 26, 1839.
Jesse Minor Floyd was born March 14, 1841.
Mary Belle Floyd was born Nov. 20th, 1843.

*Note by Mrs. Wahking:—"Dicey and Deoshy were the same person, and she was an Elliott before her marriage to Richard Cottrell as his second wife."

John William Floyd was born Sept. 14, 1846.
Richard Taylor Floyd was born March 14, 1847.
John Levi Floyd was born Jan. 22, 1850.
Jacob B. Floyd was born Jan. 12, 1853.
George E. Floyd was born Nov. 12, 1855.
Lucy Ella Floyd was born May 14, 1867.

*MARRIAGES

Annie Floyd (daughter of William S. Floyd), married James U. Brown, April 22, 1861.

Richard Taylor Floyd married Edna Forman (b. July 5, 1841), who was the widow of James Van Dyke.

DEATHS

John William Floyd died Sept. 24, 1846.

Jesse Minor Floyd departed this life July 9, 1857. "Blessed are the dead who die in the Lord."

SMITH FAMILY RECORD

From Bible printed in 1826, and copied by Mrs. Charles A. Wahking, 1365 South First St., Louisville, Kentucky.

Henry J. Smith born April 24, 1809.

Henry J. Smith married Ellen Page Nov. 7, the year of our Lord 1834.

Ellen Page, the daughter of Levy Page and Elizabeth, his wife, was born March 10, 1814.

Levy Page Smith was born March 29, 1836.
Alonzo N. Smith was born Nov. 27, 1838.
Steven H. Smith was born June 28, 1840.
Mary L. Smith was born May 10, 1842.
Emmeline Smith was born May 30, 1845.
William Smith was born Feb. 10, 1847.
Ellen Page, wife of Henry J. Smith departed this life March 23, 1881.

---

*Note by Mrs. Wahking:—"These Floyd records were on a paper in the old Cottrell Bible."

Note by Mrs. Wahking:—"I cannot find who Anne Clark Cottrell was the daughter of."
"The Cottrell graveyard lies four miles from Normandy, Spencer County."
"William S. Flyod was the son of John Levi Floyd and his mother was a Smith before her marriage to John Levi Floyd. His full name was William Smith Floyd."
"The Floyd family lived in Spencer and Shelby counties."

OLD BIBLE RECORDS

Copied and contributed by Miss Ruth Beall
Hart Chapter, N. S. D. A. R., Winchester, Ky.

GRISWOLD-PARSONS RECORD

Records from the Bible of Lieutenant-Colonel Marshfield Parsons, of Lyme, Conn. Bought in 1803, when he was 70 years old. Now (June, 1930) in possession of Miss Anne Axton, 363 Crescent Ave., Winchester, Ky.

Matthew Griswold was married to Phebe Hyde, 21st May, 1683
Phebe their Daughter, Born, August 15th, 1684
Elizabeth, Born, Novr. 19th, 1685
Sarah, Born, March 19, 1687
Matthew, Born, Sept. 15, 1688
John, Born, December 22, 1690
George, Born, August 13, 1692
Mary, Born, April 22, 1694

Sarah
Thomas } Not Recorded in the Town Records
Deborah & Patience

Mathew Griswold, after the death of his wife, Married to Mary Lee as may appear by the following—Whereas there is a purpose of Marriage between Mr. Matthew Griswold and Mrs. Mary Lee both of Lyme, it is agreed & covenanted between them 1st That whatever Estate the said Griswold shall have with or by virtue of his marriage with the sd Lee, according to Inventory, she shall have full liberty to dispose of as she pleases by will, or in her life time to her children, & in case she should die with out a Will, it shall be equally divided between her Daughters. And the sd Griswold doth hereby Bind himself, his heirs, Executors & Assigns, to make it good to them. That is to say, so much as he shall Receive of her Estate. And in case he should outlive her, he engages to leave her in as good an Estate as he found her. 2ndly, she doth wholly refer herself to the pleasure of the sd Griswold in case he should died before her, to give her any thing, or nothing, of his own Estate, above what he had with her, any Law to the Contrary, Notwithstanding, in testimony whereof they have hereunto set their hands—And in case she should have a child, or children, by the sd Griswold, she shall make them equal Sharers in her Estate, with her Daughters that she hath already & not more. May 30th 1705.

In presence of
  Moses Noyes
  John Lee
  Thos Lee

{ John, son of Sd Matthew was Married to Hannah, Daughter of Sd Mary June 23d, 1713 }

Matthew Griswold
her
Mary X Lee
mark

Moses Noyes, was the Parson of the Parish

John Griswold was married to Hannah Lee, June 23rd, 1713
Revd Jonath Parsons was Married to Phebe Griswold Decr 14, 1731
Marshfield Parsons, 23, was married to Lois Wait, 20, Octr 9th, 1755
Marshfield Parsons, 34, was married to Abigail Marvin, 20, Novr 20th, 1766
Marshfield Parsons, 50, was Married to Abigail Waterman, 44, Jany 15th 1783
Marshfield Parsons, 61, was Married to Phebe Griffing, 58, Octr 10th 1793
John Parsons, 22, was married to Joanna Mather, 21, Feby 25 A 1779
John Parsons, 29, was married to Lois Wait, 20, Oct 1, A. D. 1786
Elijah F. Tracy, 27, was married to Abigail Parsons, 28, March 5 1817
John Parsons Tracy & Eliza Beck, married Aug. 19, 1841
Isaac Harrison Axton and Lois H. Tracy married Jan. 8, 1867

BIRTHS

The children of John & Hannah Griswold were:—
Matthew, Born March 25th 1714
Phebe, Born, April 22d 1716
Thomas, Born, Feby 15, 1719
Hannah, Born, Jany 10th 1724
Lucy, Born July 6th 1726
Sarah, Born, Decr 2d 1728
Clarina, Born, May 30th 1731 and Died April 9th 1732
Clarina, Born, Feby 9th 1733
Deborah, Born March 1st 1735
John, Born, May 15th 1739 and Died Jany 4th 1742
Lydia, Born, June 1742

The children of Revd Jonath and Phebe Parsons were—
Marshfield, Born Feby 7th 1733
Jonathan, Born, April 25th 1735
Saml H. Born, May 14th 1737
Thomas, Born, April 25th 1739
Ezra, Born, Jany 2d 1742 & Died the 13th, Aged 11 days
Phebe, Born, Octr 7th 1743 & Died April 28th 1746, Aged 2 yrs., 6 mo, 21 days
A Daughter still Born Jany 6th 1746
So far Lyme Records. The other children Viz.: Phebe, Lucia, **Lydia** & Clarina—& two sons were Born at Newbury.—as follows—viz:—
Phebe. Born, March 6th 1748
A son still Born July 16th 1750
Ezra, Born, July 20th 1751, and died, August 23d
Lucia, Born, Decr 25th 1752

Lydia, Born, April 3d 1755
Clarina, Born, June 7th 1756 and died August 13th

The children of Marshfield & Lois Parsons—were—
John, Born, March 9th 1757
William. Born, June 27th 1759
A Daughter, still Born, March 20th 1761
William. Died, August 14th 1761, Aged 2 years, one month & Seventeen days

Children of John & Joanna Parsons:—
Lois born Novr 26, A. D. 1729
Abigail born, August 23 A. D. 1732
Deborah, born August 26 A. D. 1734

Children of John & Lois Parsons:—
Joanna, Born, July 31 A. D. 1787
Abigail, born, October 12 A. D. 1788
Phebe, born April 15 A. D. 1790
William born July 30 A. D. 1791
Lucy, born July 9, A. D. 1793
Lydia, born July 14 A. D. 1795
Marshfield born March 11 A. D. 1798
A Son born & died May 10 A. D. 1800
Richard Wait born Aug 19 A. D. 1801
Thomas Griswold born Nov 11 A. D. 1803
John born December 15 A. D. 1805
George, born Jany 2 A. D. 1808
Elizabeth born July 30 A. D. 1810
John Griswold Esqr. died Sept 29th 1764—in his 74th year
Mrs. Hannah Griswold died May 11th 1773, in her 79th year
Rev. Jonath Parsons died July 19th 1776, in his 71st year
Mrs. Phebe Parsons died Decr 26th 1770 in her 55th year
Mrs. Lois Parsons died July 6th 1764, Aged 28 years, 6 months & 22 days
Mrs. Abigail Parsons died August 22d, 1782, Aged 35 years & 7 months
Mrs. Abigail Parsons died March 14th 1793, Aged 53 years & 11 months
Col. Marshfield Parsons died Jany 13th A. D. 1813, Aged 79 years & 11 months
Mrs. John Parsons died May 22 A. D. 1815, Aged 56 years & 2 months
William Parsons died May 31, A. D. 1818, Aged 21 years & 10 months
Mrs. Joanna Parsons died Jany 31, 1786, Aged 28 years, 3 months & 18 days
Abigail Parsons died Octr 29, A. D. 1784. Aged 2 years & 2 months
Joan Parsons died May 17, 1817, Aged 29 years, 10 months
Lucy Parsons died May 12, 1818, Aged 24 years & 10 months
Lois Parsons Smith died August 24, 1819, Aged 30 years & 9 months

Thomas Griswold Parsons Died Sept. 26, 1820, Aged 17

Capt. Jonathan Parsons of Newburyport, Died at sea, Decr 28th 1784 in his 30th year

Samuel Holden Parsons Esqr of Middletown, Died Novr 17th 1789 in his 53d year

Capt. Thomas Parsons of Newburyport, sailed for the West Indies Feby 10th 1772 and not heard of after But supposed to be drove into the Bay of St. Mary's in a gale, and there Murdered by the Inhabitants, in his 33d year

Marshfield Parsons Esqr Died on Wednesday Janr 13th 1813, Aged seventy-nine year & 11 months.

Children of Elijah Fitch & Abigail Parsons Tracy:—

John Parsons born Jan. 18, A. D. 1818
Lois Smith born August 10, 1819
Mary Elizabeth born Oct 29, 1820
Elizabeth Fitch born May 16, 1822
Joan Morgan born Oct 6, 1824
Elijah born Nov. 12, 1826
Elijah F. Tracy Died June 24th 1831, aged 41 years, 1 mo & 6 days
Abigail Dide Sepr 8th 1863, aged 74 years, 10 mo & 22 days
John Parsons Tracy, died Jan 1877
Elizabeth Beck Tracy died Nov. 1884
Lois Tracy Axton died March 5, 1909
Isaac H. Axton died March 13, 1900

Copied by Ruth Beall, Hart Chapter, D. A. R., Winchester, Ky.

TWYMAN-HAGGARD

Records from the Bible of John G. Twyman, who lived 7 miles East of Ruckerville, Clark Co., Ky. Bible published 1859 by the American Bible Society, N. Y. Instituted in the year MDCCCXVI. Bible now (May 1931) in possession of D. P. C. Haggard, 7 miles East of Ruckerville.

John G. Twyman was born August the 17th 1837
Gusta Ann Twyman was born Aprile the 4th 1842
Henry Linzy Twyman was born July the 4th 1863
Lony May Twyman was born September the 6th 1873 } Twins
Kelly Jay Twyman was born September the 6th 1873 }
Chester A. Haggard was born Oct. 9, 1890
Gusta B. Haggard was born Feb. 21, 1893
Clifton Haggard was Born Feb 27, 1868
Ward Haggard was born July 29, 1895
Bulah Haggard was born Aug. 20, 1896
Orna May Haggard was born Mar. 5, 1900
Rutha Belle Haggard was born Apr. 21, 1904

John G. Twyman and Gusta Ann Todd was married in the year of our Lord and our love September the 25th 1862

Clifton Haggard and Lona May Twyman was married in A. D. and love Oct. the 29, 1888

Kelly Jay Twyman died August 16th 1874
Gusta Ann Twyman died Aprile the 1st 1875
John G. Twyman died April the 21, 1877
Mary W. Twyman died March 10, 1881
Gusta B. Haggard died August 19, 1893
Ward Haggard died August the 29th 1895
Rutha Belle Haggard died Sept. the 13th, 1904

Copied by Ruth Beall, Hart Chapter, D. A. R., Winchester, Ky.

STUART

Records from the Bible of James Stuart, who lived on the Iron Works pike, five miles East of Winchester, Ky. James Stuart was a Revolutionary soldier. Bible printed in Brattleborough, Vermont, 1816. J. Holbrook's stereotyped copy. First edition. Now in possession of Halley family, 415 E. Broadway, Winchester, Ky.

James Stuart was born Dec. 23rd 1790
James Stuart was born December 23rd 1791
Susan Stuart was born December the 18th 1800
William G. Stuart was born 7th April 1837
Charles J. Stuart was born January 30th 1840
Richard G. Stuart was born February the 15th 1843
Samuel G. Stuart was born August 13, 1822
Lucy Stuart was born December 13, 1824
Mary Stuart was born March 17, 1827
Maria Stuart was born September 2nd 1829
Elizabeth F. Stuart was born July 6th 1832
Thomas Stuart was born October the 9th 1834
Sam G. Stuart was married Dec. the 18th 1845
Maria W. Stuart was married January the 9th 1850
Thomas H. Stuart was married Dec. the 14th 1854
Elizabeth F. Stuart was married May the 1st 1856
Mary Stuart was married October the 13th 1856
William G. Stuart was married October the 27th 1859, 1st 2nd time 26th Nov. 1868
Lucy Stuart Died May 21st 1826
Richard G. Stuart died March 1st 1848
Maria W. Halley Formerly Maria W. Stuart Died Sept 3rd 1854
Samuel G. Stuart died March 10 inst 1872

Susan Stuart Died March 7th 1865
Thomas H. Stuart Died October 3rd 1866
Samuel G. Stuart Died March 10th 1872
Maria L. Stuart wife of S. G. Stuart Died July 20th 1875
James Stuart Died February 4th 1876
Mary Stuart Darnaby Died Feb. 14th 1909
William G. Stuart Died Dec. 25 1909
Elizabeth F. Stuart Halley Died Mar 17 1912
Chas. J. Stuart Died Aug 14 1912
James Stuart married November 6th 1821
Susan Greene Stuart was born Dec. 18 1800 and died Mar 1865
James Stuart was born Dec 23 1790
James Stuart died Feb 4, 1876

May 13, 1931.

Copied by Ruth Beall, Hart Chapter, D. A. R., Winchester, Ky.

Barkley Grave Yard

Barkley grave yard on the Lexington pike, four and one-half miles West of Winchester, Ky.; farm now owned by Courtney Taylor.

William Barkley, born May 1, 1775; died July 5, 1833.
Nannie Barkley, Jan. 22, 1829.
Matilda McMillan, born July 21, 1816.
William McMillan, born Dec. 13, 1839; died Dec. 18, 1839.
Ella Barkley, born 1850; died Aug. 24, 1856.
Whitie Barkley, born April 1, 1853; Jan. 29, 1856.
Lizzie N. Barkley:—Sept. 3, 1855; April 11, 1859.
S. Moore Barkley:—Aug. 8, 1852; Jan. 11, 1856.
Lane, son of S and A. Barkley, born Aug. 21, 1850; died Feb. 28, 1870.

From grave yard on farm now owned by Gatewood Gay.
Sallie Linville, born Dec. 15, 1834.
Sarah Linville, born July 15, 1834.

May 13, 1931

Copied by Ruth Beall, Hart Chapter, D. A. R., Winchester, Ky.

BIBLE RECORD OF ROBERT AND FRANCES HARRIS

Copied verbatim from family Bible in my possession

Robert an Frances Harris their childrin
Elizabeth Harris wa born in year 1766 in may 17
Saley Harris was born November 26th 1767
Frances Harris in September the 14th 1769
Foster harris was born in July the 5 1771
John Harris in July the 9 1773
An Harris June th 4th 1775
Polley Harris in November th 20 1777
Henry Harris September 20 1779
......................(torn page).........Harris November 5 1781
....................Harris 1783
...................................February 28 1786
..................................1788.

* * * * * * *

On a page inserted and sewn in with blue thread is the following:

Albert G. Lancaster was born Jan. 6th 1826
Mary Ann Lancaster was born March 9th 1828
Henry B. Lancaster was born December 27th 1829
Eliza Jane Lancaster was born July 2nd 1832

(At the bottom of the page is written something about William E. Harris, but it is unreadable.)

On the reverse of this inserted page is the following:

James Harris was born Apreil th 6th 1803
Polina Harris was born August the 22nd 1805
Simeon B. Harris was bornd August the 19th 1808
Susannah Harris was borned July the 12th 1812
Mary Harris was borned March the 24th 1817
William E. Harris was borned August the 1th 1819
Henry M. Harris was borned Apriel th 25th 1822

* * * * * * *

   The William E. Harris, b. 8-1-1819, was William Elliott Harris, my grandfather born in Madison Co., Ky., came to Missouri in 1838 with his brother-in-law, Jeremiah P. Lancaster, who had married his sister, Paulina Harris ("Polina"). William Elliott Harris, and Paulina Harris Lancaster were the children of *Henry Harris, b. 9-20-1779, married Jane Manion, on Aug. 19, 1801.* (Ky. Reg. Madison Co. Marr. p. 87). Other marriages of this family are recorded in Madison Co. from 1797 on. Any and all information concerning this family is desired.

Mrs. Paul R. Davis

Bible Records

JOHNSON

Family Bible of George W. Johnson, Scott County, Kentucky, Provisional or Confederate Governor of Kentucky from November, 1861, until his death at Shiloh, April 9, 1862. Given to the Society, with the Viley Bible below, by Mrs. William H. Coffman, Louisville, August, 1959.

BIRTHS

Eliza W. Johnson was born July 15, 1834.
Willa Viley Johnson was born March 4, 1837.
One Born Sept. –, 1841.
Madison Conyers Johnson was born August 16th, 1842.
Martha Lydia Johnson was born September 7th, 1845.
Junius Ward Johnson was born September 14th, 1847.
Warren Viley Johnson was born October 5th, 1849.
Henry William Johnson was born August 6th, 1852.
Euclid Lane Johnson was born February 7th, 1856.
George W. Johnston, son of J. Stoddard Johnston and Eliza W. Johnston, was born April 24th, 1862.
Mary Hancock Johnston their daughter was born August 31st, 1866.
Emily Johnson, daughter of W. V. Johnson and Lilly Johnson, was born at Marion, Ala., August 17th, 1863.
George W. Johnson, Jr., was born in Ky. May 13, 1865.
John Madison Johnson, son of M. C. Johnson and Adele Johnson, was born July 28th, 1866.
Ann E. Payne Daughter of Geo. V. and Martha L. Payne was born February the 27th, 1872.
Wm. J. Payne, son of Geo. V. and Martha L. Payne, was born Sep. 1st, 1877.
Margaret Allen Payne, daughter of Geo. V. and Martha L. Payne, was born August 4th, 1881.
Martha Payne Coffman, daughter of Wm. H. and Anne Coffman, born Nov. 17, 1899.

Ann Eliza Viley was born April 25th, 1815.
> Her Parents—Willa Viley & Lydia Smith.
>
> Grand Parents—George Viley & Martha A. Jeans; Rhodes Smith & Eunice Thomson.
>
> Great Grand Parents—Viley & _____; Wm. Jeans & _____; Wm. Smith & Mary Rhodes; Wm. Thomson & Ann Rhodes.
>
> Great Great Grand Parents—John Rhodes & Mary Crawford; John Smith & _____; Samuel Thomson & Molly McDonald; John Rhodes b. 1697, d. 1775, & Mary Crawford, b. 1703.

DEATHS

Warren Viley Johnson died December 31st, 1852.

Geo. W. Johnson, as a soldier of the Confederate Army, was wounded in the battle of Shiloh, on the 5th day of April 1862, and died April 6, 1862.

Ann E. Johnson wife of Geo. W. Johnson died August 8th, 1875.

Madison C. Johnson, Jr., died Nov. 24th, 1879, at his home in Hinds Co., Miss.

Martha L. Payne, wife of Geo. V. Payne, died Aug. 20, 1896, at her home in Georgetown.

Junius Ward Johnson died Mch. 16, 1919, when his home at _____ _____, Miss., was destroyed by cyclone.

Dr. W. H. Coffman died Nov. 13, 1925, at Georgetown, Ky.

Willa Viley Johnson died May 4, 1913, at Colorado, Texas.

We do solemnly state, that we will never hereafter, play at cards, for money—July 4th, 1845—George W. Johnson, James L. Allen, Thomas P. Johnson, Willa V. Johnson, W. M. Johnson, E. J. Williams, H. P. Roberts, W. W. Johnson.

In evil hours I have violated this pledge. But with the grace of God it shall henceforth be sacred—W. V. Johnson, March 4th, 1857. M. C. Johnson, W. H. Sellers.

MARRIAGES

George W. Johnson to Ann Eliza Viley—August 20, 1833.

J. Stoddard Johnston to Eliza W. Johnson, June 13th, 1854.

Willa Viley Johnson to Lilly Tilford, Oct. 22nd, 1860.

Madison C. Johnson, Jr. to Adele Greavis, of Miss. November 8th, 1865.

George Viley Payne to Martha L. Johnson Dec. 22nd, 1870.
Henry V. Johnson to Rosa M. Parish Feb. 24th, 1876.
Junius Ward Johnson to Fannie Winter Willis, of Miss., May 3, 1881.
Wm. H. Coffman to Anne E. Payne—June 27, 1895.
Martha Payne Coffman to James Luther Moss, Oct. 7, 1926.

VILEY*

Family Bible owned by George Viley, Scott County, and in 1893 bequeathed by his grandson, George W. Viley, of "The Oaks," Scott County, Kentucky, to Mrs. William H. Coffman, who donated it to the Society.

MARRIAGES

George Viley and his wife Martha Ann Janes married March 6th, 1785.

Samuel Viley and his wife Polly Suggitt was married December 29th, 1816.

William Payne and Albina D. Viley was married December 8th, 1840.

John M. Viley and Susan A. Long was married July 28, 1846.

George W. Viley and Williena N. Green were married April 24th, 1877.

BIRTHS

Elizabeth Viley was born Feby. 3, 1786.
William J. Viley was born Feby. 10th, 1788.
Samuel Viley was born Jan. 9th, 1790.
Warren Viley was born Feby. 7th, 1792.
Aletha Viley was born Nov. 18th, 1793.
George Viley was born Nov. 20th, 1795.
John Viley was born Jan. 1st, 1797.
Marthan Viley was born Dec. 16th, 1799.
Meriah Viley was born June 16th, 1801.
Cyrene Viley was born Dec. 10, 1803.
Horatio Viley was born Jan. 13th, 1806.
Metilda Viley was born September 16th, 1808.
James McConnell was born January 7th, 1820.
George W. Viley, son of Samuel Viley and Polly Viley, was born July 1st, 1818.

*See also the article on the Viley family, pp. 570-579, this volume.

Albina D. Viley was born May 12th, 1821.
John Milton Viley was born September 17th, 1823.
Elizabeth Marion Viley was born June 19, 1826.
Mary E. Viley was born March 21, 1848.
James S. Viley was born January 4, 1850.
John M. Viley was born December 21, 1852.
Prislla L. Viley was born May 3, 1855.

DEATHS

George Viley, Jr. died September 16th, 1797.
Warren Viley died Nov. 12th, 1812.
George Viley, Sr. died Nov. 1st, 1814.
Elizabeth McConnell died January 21st, 1820.
Horatio Viley died Feby. 3rd, 1824.
Martha Viley died June 13th, 1832.
Elizabeth Marian Viley died July 27th, 1827.
Polly Viley, wife of Samuel Viley, died August 27th, 1839, aged 41 years, 4 months, 25 days.
Albina D. Payne, wife of William Payne, died August 13th, 1849.
George Viley, Sr., died November 1st, 1814.
Martha Viley, wife of George Viley, Sr., died June 13th, 1832.
Aleatha Bunch, wife of Rodes Bunch, died Sept. 4th, 1838.
Samuel Viley died April 7, 1859.
John M. Viley died April 28th, 1891.
George W. Viley died August 15, 1893.
John Suggitt, Sr. died December 12th, 1834, aged 85.
Mildred Suggitt died July 11th, 1834, aged 78.
Edgecomb P. Suggitt died August 11th, 1838.
(See also JOHNSON)

BLACKBURN

Family Bible of Dr. Luke Pryor Blackburn, of Woodford and Franklin counties, Kentucky, eminent authority on yellow fever, Surgeon in the Civil War under General Sterling Price, and Governor of Kentucky, 1879-1883. Deposited on loan with the Society, August, 1960, by Eugenia Blackburn, Curator of the Society's Museum.

MARRIAGES

Theresa M. Graham and Joseph C. S. Blackburn married February 16th, 1858.

E. M. Blackburn and Lavinia S. Bell were married Sept. 3rd, 1809.

George E. Blackburn and Isabella P. Burch (?) married August 4th, 1831.

Thompson B. Flournoy and Frances Ann Blackburn married Feb. 17th, 1827.

Luke P. Blackburn and Ella Bosworth were married Nov. 24th, 1835.

Thompson M. Parish and Mary P. Blackburn married Jan. 18th, 1838.

Wm. E. Blackburn and Henrietta Everett married Jan. 6th, 1846, 7 o'clock Tuesday evening.

C. H. Blackburn and Frances J. Hale married Sept. 22nd, 1847, half 7 Wednesday evening.

Jilson P. Johnson and Cassandra Flournoy married March 1st, 1849.

B. F. Blackburn and Dianna Hamilton were married 1st November, 1855, Chicago.

James Blackburn and Em Everett were married November 20th, 1855.

Judge B. S. Morris and Mary B. Parish were married November 21st, 1855.

Henry Blackburn and Mary Bryant were married Oct., 1854.

Luke P. Blackburn and Julia P. Churchill were married Nov. 17th, 1857.

E. M. Blackburn, Jr. and Charlotte Calhoun, Jan. 21st, 1858.
Grandson:

William E. Blackburn and Jennie Alford were married at the Grand Central Hotel, Cincinnati, 28 Oct. 1874.

BIRTHS

E. M. Blackburn was born born Feb. 10th, 1787.

Lavinia S. Bell was born March 23rd, 1794.

George E. Blackburn was born July 6th, 1810, 4 o'clock A. M.

John Bell Blackburn was born Nov. 29th, 1811, 2 o'clock P. M.

Frances Ann Blackburn was born May 28th, 1813, 4 o'clock A. M.

Luke P. Blackburn was born June 16th, 1816 at sunrise in the morning.

Edward Lewis Blackburn was born Dec. 18th, 1817, 8 o'clock P. M.

Mary Prudence Blackburn was born July 11th, 1819, on Sunday, one hour before sunset.

Elizabeth Jane Blackburn was born April 3rd, 1821, Tuesday, 10 o'clock A. M.

William Edwin Blackburn was born Feb. 14th, 1823, on Friday, 10 o'clock A. M.

Henry Berry Blackburn was born March 26th, 1825, Saturday evening.

Churchill Horace Blackburn was born 13th Dec. 1827, Thursday, 6 o'clock P. M.

Edward Mitchell Blackburn was born Sept. 3rd, 1829, Friday, 4 o'clock A. M.

Breckenridge Flournoy Blackburn was born Feb. 25th, 1832, 8 o'clock P. M.

James Weir Blackburn was born April 30th, 1834, Wednesday, 10 o'clock P. M.

Joel C. Stiles Blackburn was born Oct. 1st, 1838, 1 o'clock A. M., Wednesday.

Lavinia B. Flournoy was born Nov. 28th, 1829, Friday, 12 o'clock.

Cassandra Flournoy was born March 10th, 1832, 10 o'clock A. M.

Mary Parish Flournoy was born July 19th, 1844, 4 o'clock P. M.

Cary Bell Blackburn was born Saturday, 29th, April, 1857.

William E. Blackburn was born Sept. 13th, 1847, Sunday, 4 o'clock.

Lavinia Bell Blackburn was born August 27th, 1849, Sunday evening.

Samuel E. Blackburn was born March 26th, 1857, 7 o'clock A. M.

Joseph Morris Blackburn was born July 26th, 1859, 17 minutes to 1 o'clock A. M.

GREAT GRAND CHILDREN

Henrietta E. Hempstead born at the old homestead on Thursday night 11 o'clock Jan. 9th, 1868.

DEATHS

Frances Ann Blackburn departed this life Nov. 7th, 1834.

Prudence Blackburn, an old ancestor, departed this life June 14th, 1836, 6 o'clock P. M.

John Bell Blackburn departed this life Aug. 2nd, 1813.

Edward Lewis Blackburn departed this life Sept. 14th, 1818.

Lavinia B. Flournoy departed this life Dec. 25th, 1842.

George E. Blackburn departed this life Oct. 21st, 1847, on board the Empire Mississippi river with his family around him

Wm. E. Blackburn departed this life June 17th, 1849, 20 minutes after 4 o'clock P. M.

Em E. Blackburn departed this life 12th April 1857, 9 o'clock, in the 21st year of her age. The loved wife has passed away from earth to her home in the beautiful Heaven.

On Thursday the 27th of August, 1857, Little Sammy, infant son of James and Em Blackburn passed away like the sweet rose of summer.

These two were my loved treasures.

Jennie, wife of William E. Blackburn died 3 Sept., 1875, leaving a little son twelve days old to comfort the desolate heart of the Father and to the care of **Him** whose promises never fail to the Orphan.

Henrietta Hempstead died May 18th, 1887. (Clipping)

CROCKETT*

Family Bible of Anthony Crockett, 1756-1838, of Mercer and Franklin counties, Kentucky. Deposited on loan with the Society, August 11, 1960, by Mrs. Frank H. Kincheloe, Charleston, West Virginia, with the Morris Bible below.

BIRTHS

Anthony Crockett was born November 19th, 1756.

Mary Crockett was born April 11th, 1760.

Polly Crockett was born February 9th, 1781.

Sally Crockett was born January 29th, 1783.

William R. Crockett was born November 25th, 1784.

Margaret Crockett was born February 2nd, 1787.

Samuel B. Crockett was born February 18th, 1789.

Overton W. Crockett was born February 14th, 1791.

Elizabeth Crockett was born March 10th, 1793.

Martha Crockett was born June 1st, 1795.

Fountain B. Crockett was born May 6th, 1797.

Granville S. Crockett was born December 24th, 1799.

*For additional information on the Crockett family see *Genealogies of Kentucky Families* (Vol. A-M), 222-224.

Kitty Crockett was born December 19th, 1801.
Dandridge S. Crockett was born June 2nd, 1804.
Mary Vaughan was born May 25th, 1807.
Mary A. M. Acton was born March 5th, 1814.
Richard E. Crockett was born September 12th, 1827.
Sallie C. Crockett was born January 25th, 1839.
Florence Augusta Crockett was born March 4th, 1859.
Mattie Crockett was born August 13th, 1860.
Ada Lee Crockett was born September 18th, 1862.
William R. Crockett was born June 23rd, 1865.
Rosana Johnson Crockett was born March 26th, 1867.
Lelia Moss Crockett was born July 25th, 1870.
Ann Rebecca Crockett was born April 30th, 1872.
Billy Acton was born Dec. 10th, 1835.
Mary Jane Acton was born Feb. 3rd, 1838.
George Anthony Crockett was born December 16th A. D. 1826.
Susan Mary Crockett was born January 2nd, 1829.
Edmund Vaughan Crockett was born April 6th, 1831.
William Overton Crockett was born November 15th, 1834.
James Granville Crockett was born March 15th, 1836.
(F.?) A. Crockett born March 4, 1859.
Mattie Crockett born Aug. 13, 1860.
A. L. Crockett born Sept. 18, 1862.
W. R. Crockett born June 23, 1865.
R. L. Crockett born March 26, 1867.
Lelia Moss Crockett born July 25, 1870.
Nellie Lee Morris born Aug. 31, 1883.
Grace Bell Morris born May 16, 1885.
Born to Grace Newman on August 1, 1907, Cornelia Newman.
Born to Grace Newman on Sept. 28, 1909, Eleanor Newman.
Born to Grace Newman on Feb. 5, 1912, William Morris Newman.
Born to Grace Newman on May 24, 1924, Nell Katherine Newman.

MARRIAGES

Caleb W. Merchant, Nellie Lee Morris married Oct. 28, 1903.
William C. Newman, Grace Bell Morris married Oct. 10, 1906.

DEATHS

Margaret Crockett departed this life January 17th, 1788.

Mary Crockett, wife of A. Crockett, departed this life 1st Sept. 1818.

Anna Maria Crockett departed this life August 14th, 1835.

Ann Rebecca Crockett departed this life December 4, 1856.

Died Sept. 25, 1907, Cornelia Newman.

Richard E. Crockett died January 3rd, 1874.

Sallie C. Crockett departed this life June 17th, 1872.

Ann Rebecca Crockett departed this life July 15, 1872.

MORRIS

DEATHS

E. Loisce G. Morris, died 1874, aged 40 years, My Dear sister.

Sarah A. Morris, my oldest sister, died January 29th, 1876, aged 56 years, My Dear sister.

Jeptha T. Morris died on the 4th day of July, 1848, aged 23 years.

Mildred H. Morris died September 5th, 1855, aged 19 years.

Mrs. Wineaford Morris died on 14 January, 1861, aged 62 years, My Dear Mother.

Mr. James Morris died February 17th, 1864 on ? , aged 70 years and 8 months, My Dear Father.

My Brother Thos. H. Morris died Oct. 7th, 1875, aged 64 years and 6 months, My Dear Brother.

Wineaford Morris, My Mother, aged 62 years at her Death 14th Jan. 1861.

BIBLE RECORDS

Copied by Mrs. L. N. Taylor, Lexington, Kentucky

Bible Records of William Tarlton Taylor, and Elizabeth Hampton Taylor. of Pulaski County, Ky.

Bible bought 1803. The records copied in Bible by Wm. T., Junior, at request of Wm. T., Sr.

William Tarlton Taylor, b. 8/24, 1759. Died 2/6, 1811. (Rev. soldier, Loudon Co., Va.) Wife Elizabeth Hampton, b. 3/25, 1762 (dau. of Jeremiah), m. Aug. 4, 1778. Children:

1. Levi Tarlton Taylor, b. Loudon Co., Va., 4/26, 1800, m. Nancy Danning, 1/6, 1799.
2. John H. Taylor, b. Loudon Co., Va., 1/27, 1782, m. Annie Weeks, 1/8, 1807.
3. Tarlton Taylor, b. Loudon Co., Va., 12/11, 1784, m.
4. Sallie Taylor, b. Loudon Co., Va., 6/9 1787, m. Burgess French, 4/30, 1807.
5. Hampton H. Taylor, b. Loudon Co., Va., 12/6, 1789, m. Sharlott Rector, 2/3, 1814.
6. Nancy Taylor, b. Loudon Co., Va., 10/6, 1792, m. Reuben Smarr, 11/16, 1809.
7. Ignatius Taylor, b. Loudon Co., Va., 8/29, 1795, m. Mary Batson, 12/14, 1819.
8. Eliza Taylor, b. Loudon Co., Va., 2/28, 1798.
9. Jenefer H. Taylor, b. Loudon Co., Va., 3/22, 1801, m. Rebecca Boyle, 12/20, 1827. Marriage recorded in Spencer Co., Ky.
10. Joseph Taylor, b. Loudon Co., Va., 3/15, 1804.

1. Levi Tarlton Taylor and Nancy Danning (Downing?) Taylor's children:
Alfred Taylor, 10/11, 1799.
Elizabeth Taylor, 3/25, 1801.
Ellender Taylor, 12/18, 1802.
Wm. Tarlton Taylor, 8/26, 1804, m. Elizabeth Miner.
Levi Tarlton Taylor, Jun., 7/20, 1806.
Abednego Danning Taylor, 7/7, 1808.
Joseph Hampton Taylor, 5/18, 1810, m. Catherine ———.
John T. Taylor, 2/21, 1812, m.
Levi Tarlton Taylor, m. 1/15, 1839, Leah Combs.

2. John H. and Annie Weeks Taylor's children:
William T. Taylor, 7/26, 1808.
Elizabeth Taylor, 3/15, 1810.
Sarah Ann Taylor, 1/15, 1812.
Will recorded Taylorsville, Ky.
3. Tarlton Taylor. (No record.)
4. Sally Taylor and Burgess French's children:
Luiza French, 10/16, 1808, m. James A. Williams, 4/18, 1827.
Mariah French, 9/28, 1810.
Susannah French, 10/5, 1813.
Mahala French, 5/19, 1817.
Matilda Ann French, 7/9, 1819.
John W. French, 6/2, 1822.
Sarah Elender French, 9/26, 1825.
5. Hampton H. Taylor and Sharlott Rector Taylor's children:
William R. Taylor, 1/12, 1816.
Nim H. Taylor, 12/11, 1818.
Sarah C. C. Taylor, 2/6, 1820.
Cinty Susan Taylor, 8/29, 1822.
Joseph A. Taylor, 2/13, 1825.
6. Nancy Taylor and Reuben Smarr's children:
Elizabeth Smarr, 11/7, 1810.
William T. Smarr, 5/1, 1813.
John H. Smarr, 11/29, 1815.
J. Edward Smarr, 4/12, 1818.
Robert W. Smarr, 7/28, 1820.
7. Ignatius and Mary Batson Taylor's children:
John William Taylor, 9/1, 1820.
Thomas H. Taylor, 8/26, 1822.
James L. Taylor, 3/9, 1825.
Elizabeth Marion Taylor, 4/28, 1828.
Some more recrods:
Starling Warren, b. 10/17, 1775.
Vincent Warren, b. 4/9, 1779.
Nancy Warren, b. 2/11, 1780.

Leah Warren, b. 12/30, 1783.
Catherine Taylor, b. 8/24, 1799.
Catherine Taylor, wife of Joseph Hampton Taylor, died 4/3, 1870.
Joseph H. Taylor, died 5/12, 1898.
Joseph H. and Catherine ———— Taylor's children:
Leona E. Taylor, 3/2, 1833, m. 8/16, 1851. (Name not given.)
Rebecca Ann Taylor, 3/7, 1835, m. 8/17, 1854. (Name not given.)
Oliver Perry Taylor, 3/25, 1837.
Martha Frances Taylor, 12/13, 1843, m. 9/1, 1864, James D. Shearer.
Joseph H. Taylor, m. 2nd wife, 9/27, 1870, Madeline Davis. Children:
John William Taylor, 2/5, 1873. (This man has Taylor Bible.)
Joseph Jones Taylor, 3/24, 1875-12/18, 1875.
William T. Taylor, departed this life February 8th, 1811, being in his 52nd year.
Elizabeth Taylor, deceased the 23rd day of November, in the year 1857.
Elizabeth Taylor, Senior, deceased the 11th of September, 1857.
Sarah Elizabeth, daughter of James and Peggy Jane Coomer, b. 5/6, 1842.
Sidney Goddard, son of James and Peggy Jane Coomer, b. 8/25, 1843.
Ann Jones Coomer, b. 12/17, 1846.
Nellie Goddard Coomer, b. 4/11, 1849.
Mary Ann Foster, b. 8/13, 1852.
Sarah Catherine Foster, b. 12/14, 1853.
Eliza Jane Foster, b. 11/2, 1855.
Vincent Warren Taylor, b. 3/3, 1845.
Marcus Edwin Shearer, oldest child of J. D. and Mattie F. Shearer, born 7/27, 1865.
Joseph Napoleon Shearer, b. 2/19, 1868.
Sid Coomer's Mose (Col.) was born Sept. 12, 1859.
Bible published 1802. Bought by Wm. Tarlton Taylor, May, 1803. Price $8.00.

I. Robert Buchanan, and Mary Jamison Buchanan Bible.

Printed by Alexander Kincaid, MDCCLXXV.

To be used in Churches of Edinburg.
Children:
James Buchanan, born 9/20, 1777.
Jean Buchanan, born 5/4, 1780. (Called Jane.)
John Buchanan, born 5/26, 1782.
Mary A. Buchanan, born 9/21, 1784.
Margit Buchanan, born 12/11, 1788.
Edward Buchanan, born 4/1, 1791.
Robert Buchanan, born 6/3, 1794.
William Buchanan, born 8/16, 1796.
Josiah Buchanan, 8/17, 1798, m. 3/16, 1820.
Andrew Buchanan, born 9/27, 1801.
Jane Knox, born 6/1, 1804.
John Hamilton Buchanan, born 2/9, 1821.
William H. Buchanan, born 1/4, 1823.

Note.—Robert and Mary Buchanan were both born in Ireland. They were in Washington Co., Va., at the time of the Revolutionary War. Mary died in Va. Robert died at his daughter, Jane Hubbell's, Pulaski Co., Ky., in 1831 or 1832, aged 90. Jane Knox was the wife of Andrew Buchanan, and evidently the two last named were their children.

II. *Robert Adams, and Rebakah Willey Adams' Bible.

Owned by Judge Napier Adams, Somerset, Ky.

Robert Adams, born, 1751. Died, 11/17, 1816. (Buried at Ansel, Ky.)
Rebekah Willey, born 5/29, 1758. Died, 8/27, 1817. (Buried at Ansel, Ky.)
Above married 4/2, 1778.
Children:
Alexander, born 4/1, 1779, m. Mary Morrow, 12/1, 1803.
Sally, born 12/24, 1780, m. Ansell Stroud, 1/30, 1805.
John, born 3/10, 1782, m. Rhoda Atkinson, 11/6, 1807.
Matty, born 3/19, 1786, m. Robert Wallace, 6/6, 1805.
James, born 7/25, 1789, m. Betsy Kerr, 10/24, 1813.
Ginney, born 1/1, 1793, m. Elias Woods, 3/14, 1815.
George Washington, born 8/15, 1796, m. Nancy Morrow, Dec., 1816.

*(Robert Adams came to Ky. from South Carolina.)

Old Newelle Bible Records

Elizabeth Collvil, b. April 27, Anno (torn off).

Janet Black, b. Feb. 11, Anno 174 (too dim to read last figure).

Christian Black, b. Nov. 4th, 1745.

Joseph Black, b. Feb. 22, Anno (torn off).

Mathew Black, b. Jan. 21, Anno 17— (torn off).

Elizabeth Black, b. Dec. 12, 17— (torn off).

Samuel Newell, b. Nov. —— (dim) Anno (torn off).

Sarah Newell, b. Jan. —— (dim) —— (torn off).

Next Page

Samuel Newelle, Sr., b. Nov. 4, 1754.

Jean Montgomery, alias, Newelle, b. about Oct. 1764.

Esther M. Newelle, b. Sept. 25, 1783.

Samuel Newelle, Jr., b. Mch. 25, 1786. (m. Nancy Owens.)

Margit E. Newelle, b. June 3, 1788. (m. Wm. Owens.)

John M. Newelle, b. Sept. 20, 1790. (m. Margaret Beatty.)

Susannah Newelle, b. Nov. 4, 1792. (m. Andrew Evans.)

Dorcas Newelle, b. Mch. 7, 1795. (not married.)

Elizabeth Collvil Newelle, b. Aug. 24, 1797. (Not married.)

Joseph Black Newelle, b. July 28, 1800. (m. Jane Kinkead.)

William T. Newelle, b. May 8, 1803.

Jean Newelle, b. Mch. 13, 1806. (m. James Evans.)

(The above records were copied from the old family Bible of Samuel Newelle (b. Virginia 1754), the first sheriff of Pulaski County, Kentucky, and were rescued from the burning house in about 1868, by one of Samuel Newelle's sons, Joseph Black Newell.)

The Bible is now owned by Mrs. F. E. Tibbals (Theobald), of Somerset, Kentucky, granddaughter of Joseph B. Newelle.

APPENDIX B

A FEW OLD FRANKLIN FAMILIES

That Part of Franklin County, Kentucky, Between the Kentucky River and South Elkhorn Creek, and South of the Georgetown Turnpike.

Since the organization of the District of Kentucky and its division into three counties (1780), this portion of Franklin has been a part, first of Fayette, one of the original counties, afterward (1788) of Woodford, until the formation of Franklin (1794). It was well settled as early as the beginning of the nineteenth century, mainly by emigrants from Virginia, many of whom had been soldiers of the Revolution. Since its settlement, and to the present day, this has always been considered a choice and desirable part of the county.

That early highway of the pioneers, which, in some places, followed a much older buffalo trail, long known as the Leestown road, and which lay between Lexington and the old settlement of Leestown (founded by the Lees and Cyrus McCrackin, on the Kentucky river just below and now a part of the present city of Frankfort), traversed this portion of Franklin, and is still an important county road, though it no longer leads to the place which gave it the name.

Filson's map locates both the settlement and the highway and also "Col. Marshall's Office" in what is apparently this locality of Franklin, near South Elkhorn creek.

It is known that Marshall possessed large tracts of land here, which he sold at considerable profit to the immigrants. The official records of Fayette, of which this region was a part until 1788, have been destroyed, but after this date we have preserved those of Woodford and Franklin. In addition to these, the early history of this locality is recorded in that invaluable "Church Book"* of the old Forks of Elkhorn Baptist Church, preserving local history in a manner very similar to that of the Parish Registers and Vestry Books of Virginia, whose value as historic authority is so clearly recognized. A brief account of the organization of this Church, so long ministered to by William Hickman, has been given in a previous article.†

These pioneer families of this part of Franklin, who were not associated with this church are exceptional.

While the spiritual welfare of this community was so well ministered to, their intellectual needs were not neglected. An excellent school was established in close proximity to the church. Many of those who received their early training here lived to extreme old age, though often far removed from the scenes of their youth, but wherever located, they were invariably characterized throughout life, by a moral and intellectual refinement indicating not only a favorable heredity and environment, but a careful youthful training as well.

Roughly outlined, all that fertile tract between South Elkhorn and the present

---

*Placed for safety in the Southern Baptist Theological Seminary at Louisville.
†"Register" of January, 1906.

Versailles turnpike was, at the beginning of the nineteenth century, the property of comparatively few persons. One of these was John Major, Sr.,* a Revolutionary soldier and a man of considerable wealth for those days. With his large household, he had emigrated in 1785 from King and Queen county, Va., and settled here on his grant of one thousand acres, which was soon after increased by the purchase of five hundred acres additional, from the Marshall lands adjoining.

His dwelling, or manor house, as it was then generally designated, and which was in existence until destroyed by fire shortly prior to the Civil war, occupied the present site of "Weehawken," illustrating this article. John Major, Sr., was largely instrumental in organizing the Forks Church, and the first religious assembly of this congregation, which is also the first on authentic record within the present bounds of Franklin, was that meeting conducted in January, 1788, in the old Major house. On the death of John Major, Sr., in 1808, his estate was divided among his large family of children, the main and central tract, containing the manor house, becoming the home of his youngest son, Lewis Redd Major, whose wife was Elvira, daughter of General David Thomson, a veteran of the War of 1812. Many of the Major children of two generations were born here, the last being those of Lewis R. and Elvira Major, their son John, and beautiful daughters, Ann Redd and Evelyn.

Very near the manor house was the home of an older son of John Major, Sr., John Major, Jr., On the death of the latter's wife, Judith Trabue, in 1817, he emigrated to Christian county, Kentucky with his children and other relatives.

Not far from these homes were those of two other brothers, both of which are still standing. The older of these two structures, now called "Ingleside",* was built in 1793 by Thomas Major for his bride Susanna Trabue, and was occupied by them and by their son, Olive Trabue, a soldier of the War of 1812, until the latter's death in 1846. Adjoining "Ingleside" was the estate of the other brother, James Major, on which the old residence still stands, with an older gambrel-roofed building, originally intended for a cotton factory, but later, when abandoned for this purpose, utilized as a schoolhouse which was taught by Lucy Cosby and Jane Major, two young ladies of the family. A sister of these brothers, Susanna Major, first the wife of Robert Wooldridge and afterward of Ritchie Boulware, lived adjoining. Of the other children of John Major, Sr., William and Elizabeth Redd, wife of John Price, Jr., were dead by 1795. Frances, wife of Nathaniel Thomson, lived in Woodford, Martha, wife of Charles Sanford, lived in Henry county, and Mildred Taylor, the youngest, wife of Powhatan Wooldridge, lived in Christian county, to which she and her husband had gone from Franklin, and from whence they finally went to Missouri.

After the departure of John Major, Jr., to Hopkinsville, his farm was purchased by Dandridge C. Freeman, who with his wife, Martha Fox, and family, occupied it for many years. They were people of means and were prominently connected in this and other localities. In later years

---

*See Major geneology in "Register," for May, 1905.(*Genealogies of Kentucky Families* (Vol. A-M), 721-728.)

*Register of May, 1905.

748

the house has been partially destroyed, and being reconstructed, became the very handsome country house of John Hendricks, formerly Attorney-General, but is now the Gordon Academy, a private school for boys.

After the death of Olive T. Major, "Ingleside" was owned by the Giltners, Craigs, and others, until it came into the possession of its present owner a number of years ago. It is now the beautifully appointed suburban home of Chas. E. Hoge, a native Virginian, but having for many years large business interests in Kentucky, the State of his adoption, with his headquarters at Frankfort, long the home of himself and family.

Lewis R. Major removed to Missouri with his family in 1833, accompanying that of his father-in-law, General Thomson, where they settled and laid out Georgetown, named for General Thomson's Kentucky home. Another son-in-law of General Thomson, who emigrated with them, George R. Smith, founded the present city of Sedalia.

After this departure of Lewis R. Major to Missouri, "Weehawken" the old Major home, (Mr. French Hoge's residence), with about five hundred acres surrounding became the property of the Trabues, in whose possession it remained until recent years, when its present owner, S. French Hoge, a son of Charles E. Hoge, of "Ingleside, purchased it and has done much to restore and preserve the beauty of the estate.

James Major also emigrated to Missouri, where he lived to a great age, dying at the beginning of the Civil War. His farm adjoining "Ingleside," was purchased by the Jett family about 1835, which still has a large connection in this locality, now known by their name. The main farm is now the property of the estate of the late H. P. Mason.

The Trabues, who so long resided at "Weehawken," were of distinguished Huguenot ancestry. The first of the family in America was Antoine Trabue a native of Montabaun,* France, and member of the Huguenot church there, who being compelled to flee from France on the revocation of the Edict of Nantes, found refuge from religious persecution in the Huguenot colony at Lausanne, Switzerland, from whence he came to the French settlement in America, located at the old Indian Manakin-town, on James river, above Richmond, Virginia, where he died in 1724, aged fifty-seven years. After his death,

---

*In the possession of Mrs. Z. F. Smith, a direct decendant of Antoine Trabue, is a copy in French, of the church letter given to him on his departure from France, signed by the Pastor and deacons, translated as follows: "We, the undersigned, certify that Antoine Trabue, native of the city of Montauban, twenty or nineteen years of age, dark chesnut hair, having a small cicatrice under the left eye, has always professed the reform religion, just as his parents did, without his ever having committed any scandal that has come to our knowledge, other than that which the violence of the late persecutions in France have caused him to commit; which God has given him the grace to abandon, and for which he has made reparation. We recommend him to the divine Providence and to the love of our brethren.

Done at Lausanne, this 15th day of September 1689.

(Signatures.)

VERHERS, formerly minister of the church of Dittemare and of Montanban.

Balli, pastor of the church in Langueduc. and five Deacons.

749

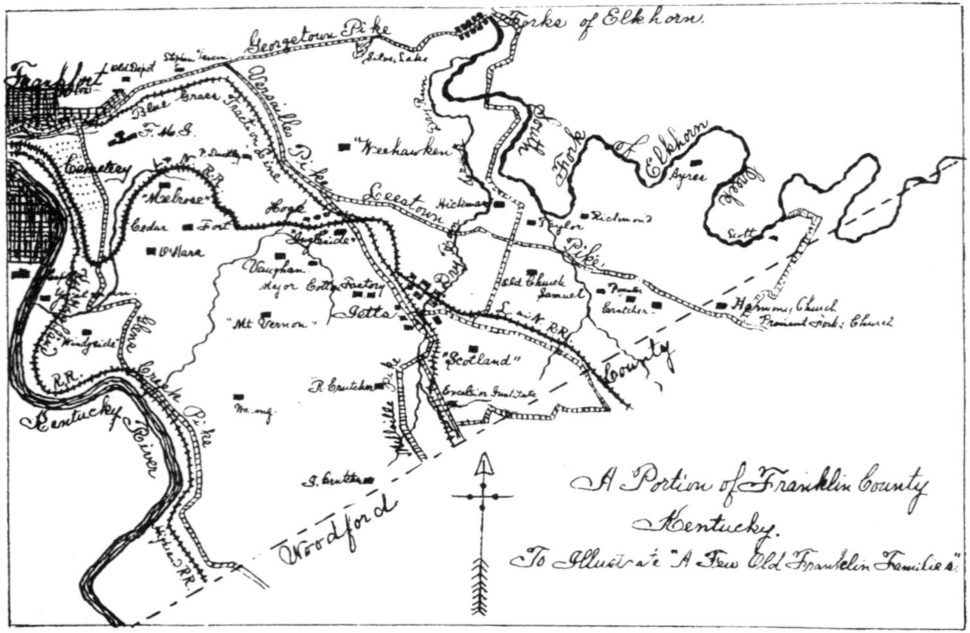

his wife, Magdalen,* married Pierre Chastain. Antoine and Magdalen Trabue had five children, Jacob, Anthony, Magdalen, wife of Pierre Guerrant; Judith, wife of Stephen Watkins, and John James, the youngest, who married Olymphia Dupuy, a grand-daughter of the famous Huguenot, Bartholomew Dupuy. These have many descendants, many of whom have long been located in Kentucky, and particularly the line of John James Trabue. His wife, Olymphia Dupuy, born Nov. 12, 1729, lived with her younger daughters, in Franklin at one time and was a member of the Forks church. She died in her ninety-third year, at the home of her son, Edward Trabue, in Woodford county, opposite Tyrone, and was buried there.

Judith, wife of John Major, Jr., and Susanna, wife of Thomas Major, were daughters of John James Trabue and Olympia Dupuy. Elizabeth Minter, wife of James Major, was their grandchild; Chastain Trabue, the former owner of "Weehawken," was also their grandchild, son of their son, Stephen Trabue. Elizabeth Trabue, the wife of Chastain Trabue, was the daughter of their son, James Trabue. Stephen F. J. Trabue, a son of Chastain and Elizabeth Trabue, and whose wife was Alice Berry, of Oldham county, was the last of his family who lived at "Weehawken."

Adjoining the plantation of John Major, Sr., was that of another wealthy planter, Nathaniel Sanders, also instrumental in establishing the Forks church and one of its first converts. It was by the persuasion and inducements offered by these two men, that William Hickman was located here on a donated farm, adjoining theirs, where the faithful minister lived and served his flock for the space of a half century. John Major, Sr., and Nathaniel Sanders were the first deacons of this church. Of the seven children of Nathaniel Sanders, his son, Lewis Sanders, was a noted lawyer, and served as Secretary of State under Governor Breathitt, afterward emigrating first to Natchez, Mississippi and then to California. His wife was Margaret Hubbell Price, a daughter of John Price, Jr., and his second wife, Susan Gano, who was a daughter of that famous Baptist minister, John Gano, whose last earthly resting place is the old deserted grave-yard of the Fork church.*

Lewis Sanders and Margaret Price,

---

*There is a difference of opinion as to the maiden name of Antoine Trabue's wife. An old Trabue family-tree gives her name Magdalen Le Fevre. Since the discovery of her will in the Henrico records it is presumed that she was a daughter of Jacob Flournoy, also a prominent Huguenot emigrant, because in this will she appoints her beloved brother, Francis Flournoy, her executor. The Flournoy family-book, carefully preserved from those times does not show such a connection. In the light of this seemingly conflicting evidence it would seem that Magdalen Trabue, was, very likely, a daughter of Jacob Flournoy's third wife, Magdalen Prodhom Verreuil, by her first marriage, being at the time of her marriage to Jacob Flournoy, the widow of Moses Verreuil, a Dutch merchant of Rouen, who emigrated to Virginia with the Huguenots, and died shortly after. His wife Magdalen Prodhom was the granddaughter of the Huguenot minister at Lousanne. These brought several of their children to America and one of these latter may have been Magdalen, wife of Antoine Trabue.

*See Register for January, 1904.

his wife, had thirteen children—seven sons, only one of whom married, and six daughters, five of whom married. These were Eliza, wife of J. B. Haggin, Susan Gano, wife of Lloyd Tevis; Edith, wife of A. C. Hunter; Laura E., wife first of George Voorhies, second of Jas. P. Amsden, and Ezza, wife of Isham Railey.

The Hickman farm on which the original log house, built in 1787, is still standing, has had many owners since the death of William Hickman in 1834* In this neighborhood, previous to 1800, were also the homes of Ritchie Boulware, whose son, Ritchie, was the second husband of Susanna Major, also that of Edmund Wooldridge and Elizabeth Watkins, his wife, whose son, Powhatan Wooldridge, married Mildred Taylor Major.

Above Hickman's, on Elkhorn, was the old Head farm, once owned by Colby Taylor, now by Jerry D. Taylor. On the opposite side of the Leestown road from this, Robert W. Scott built a house of the materials obtained from the demolition of the old Forks Meeting-House,* which stood just behind this house, since owned by the Freemans and Bedfords, but now the residence of Samuel Mason.

Further up Elkhorn, stands the old Richmond house, for many years the property of Duane Brown, whose family was earlier located near the Meeting-House.

On the opposite side of the Leestown road from this, the Hicklins lived, and near them at an early period, the Samuel family, whose original residence is still standing. Robert Todd, the father of Mary Todd, wife of Abraham Lincoln, once lived here, and authentic tradition states that President Lincoln visited here at that period. On Elkhorn, near the county line, was the Ayres stock-farm, and above that the homes of Bartlett Crutcher, and that of Thos. Scott, the last once known as the Davis farm. In the locality, partly in Woodford and partly in Franklin, many small farms have long been occupied by branches of the Crutcher family, all descendents of Henry Crutcher, Sr., a volunteer and quarter-master in some of the campaigns of George Rogers Clark.*

Henry Crutcher, Sr., brought his family to Kentucky in 1795 from Caroline county, Virginia and died here in 1807. He had three sons. The eldest, Isaac Crutcher (1767-1837) was for many years the Baptist minister at Mount Pleasant, near Steadmantown. His home place, near Jetts, now occupied in part by a descendant, Redd Crutcher, was partly in Woodford. The two younger sons of Henry Crutcher, Sr., Henry (1780-1852), and Reuben (1782-1863), were the only children of his second wife, Martha, daughter of William and Ann Beazley, of Caroline. All these were finally members of the Forks Church, though they had earlier worshiped at Mount Pleasant. It is very unusual in the Church-Book to chronicle a death, but the following is recorded—"Sister Martha Crutcher died January 10, 1843, aged ninety-five years and nine months." Though living to this ripe age, Martha Beazley Crutcher

---

*A picture of this old house with description may be found in the "Register" for May, 1904.

*English's "Conquest of the Northwest."

retained the faculties of her mind clear and vigorous to the last. In her old age she would entertain her children of the third generation with vivid descriptions of the scenes of her Virginia home during the thrilling days of the Revolution, of which she was probably the last surviving witness in this portion of the county. She was buried by the side of her husband in the old church-yard, where many other pioneers lie in the sleep of peace.

The three simple homes of the three brothers, built in the beginning of the nineteenth century, are still standing after the lapse of more than one hundred years. That of Isaac Crutcher, a tenant house since his death; that of Henry Crutcher remodeled and long the home of the Poynters; while that of Reuben Crutcher, is the home of his grand-son, Lewis Crutcher, and his wife who was Effie Britton, of Shelby county.* Nearby is the home of Mary French Crutcher, a grand-daughter of Martin and Juliet Calhoun Hardin, and widow of John Crutcher, son of the second Henry Crutcher. On another part of the original Crutcher farm nearby is the residence of N. Maffit Crutcher and wife, Ellen Giltner. He is a grand-son of the second Henry Crutcher. Between the Leestown and Versailles turnpikes, and on both sides of the Louisville and Nashville railway, is an historic estate, long celebrated for its beauty and fertility as well as for the elegant mansion, now adorning it. This is known as "Scotland," for many years the property of Robert W. Scott, who built the present beautiful dwelling. It now belongs to the widow and heirs of the late H. P. Mason, a native of Virginia, who located here about twenty years ago, being associated in business with Chas. E. Hoge, of "Ingleside." In pioneer times, "Scotland" belonged to the Ware family and afterward it became the home of that distinguished statesman, Martin D. Hardin, who died and was buried here in 1823. Elizabeth Logan, wife of Martin D. Hardin, survived him and married Porter Clay, a brother of the great Commoner, Henry Clay. This place was the early home of the Hardin children, one of whom, John J. Hardin, was an officer in the Mexican War, where he distinguished himself by heroic courage and brilliancy of action. He was mortally wounded while bravely leading the Illinois troops to victory at Buena Vista. An inscription in a place of honor on the Battle Monument at Frankfort reads:

"By order of the Legislature the name
of Col. J. J. Hardin,
of the 1st Illinois Infantry,
A Son of Kentucky,
Who fell at the Battle of Buena Vista,
Is inscribed hereon."

On the Versailles turnpike, near the county line, is located "Excelsior Institute," a private school of excellent standing, established and since conducted by the family of J. K. P. South, a minister of the Christian church. This was formerly the property of Hubbard Taylor and wife, Catherine Taylor, daughter of Reuben Taylor, of Clark county. Between the Versailles turn-

---

*The writer of this article is largely indebted to these occupants of the oldest Crutcher home for many interesting and historical facts of this region.

pike and the Kentucky river are a number of farms which have had comparatively few changes of owners in a century. Among these is that of the late Washington Crutcher, son of Richard and Pamelia Berry Crutcher, and grandson of Isaac Crutcher, the Baptist minister, whose pioneer residence is located here. Redd Crutcher, a son of Washington and Virginia Redd Crutcher, now lives on this place, in his father's dwelling, erected about thirty years ago. West of this there were two farms, belonging in former days to Thomas and Jeremiah Hall. A daughter of the former, Sarah Hall, was the second wife of Isham Hawkins, of Woodford, whose children are the only living descendants of Thomas Hall. Jeremiah Hall married Mary, daughter of Thomas Wooldridge. The only trace of the home of these is an old family graveyard in which are memorials of the Halls, Hardins, Wooldridges and others.

In the same locality, but nearer Jetts, were two other homes, well known since early days. One, called "Mount Vernon," originally belonged to the Blantons, but for many years, was the home of Levi Crutcher, whose wife Rebecca Dixon, was a niece of Archibald Dixon and grand-daughter of the pioneer Cyrus McCrackin. It is still in the possession of the children of Levi and Rebecca Crutcher. Levi Crutcher was the son of Henry and Susanna Hancock Crutcher and grandson of Henry and Martha Beazley Crutcher.

The other, a farm of considerable size in the early nineteenth century, belonged to the Vaughans. On it are now two residences, both very old. The older of these was the homestead of Edmund Vaughan and his family, now a tenant house; the other, a substantial brick, situated between this latter and "Ingleside," was built for Edmund Vaughan, son of Edmund Vaughan and his first wife, Sarah Samuel. This last is now the home of John Hanly. Edmund Vaughan and his first wife had other children besides Edmund Vaughn. By the second wife, Susanna Thomson* there were two children, Jas. Vaughn, who married Charlotte Ashmore Hawkins—these have no descendants living—and Mary Vaughn, wife of Dandridge Crockett, a son of Anthony Crockett, of Revolutionary fame, who lived near Bridgeport in Franklin county.

On the Versailles turnpike, opposite "Weehawken," there stood until recently, when it was destroyed by fire, the country residence of Peter Dudley, a distinguished officer of high rank in the War of 1812. General Dudley's town house on St. Clair street, Frankfort, was demolished several years since. The wife of General Dudley, was Maria Garrard, daughter of James Garrard, second Governor of Kentucky. They had no children.

Near the intersection of the Leestown and Versailles turnpikes, the site of an old tavern, known as Fosters, is marked by a cabin and a deserted graveyard.

---

*Susanna Thomson, the second wife of Edmund Vaughan, Sr., was a native of Louisa county, Virginia. Her father, Anthony Thomson, was a soldier of the French and Indian War, who located in Woodford county, Kentucky, 1785. He was, until his death in 1794, a deacon in the Old Forks of Elkhorn Church. His wife was Ann, daughter of Henry Bibb, of Fredericksville Parish, Louisa county, Virginia, who was a so of Benjamin Bibb, of King William county, Virginia.

At the intersection of the Versailles and Georgetown roads and opposite the Major farm, was that of the Ellis family, related to the Garrards, Fosters, Ayres and others.

At one time the largest and richest estate in Franklin was historic "Melrose." The mansion, still in existence, was on a commanding site and surrounded by woodlands and many well watered and fertile fields, formerly several square miles in extent. Near the foot of the hill on which the house stands, there was a pioneer settlement, and about a half mile away, on the crest of the hill, there was a refuge for the scattered settlers known as Cedar Fort, to which everyone in the surrounding country might resort when threatened by the Indians.

At least one attack of the savages on this little settlement resulted fatally, as authentic tradition records that, being surprised at one time, the settlers made a hasty retreat to the fort, but one of their number, a lame man, was overtaken and massacred, shortly after leaving his house.

Following these early days, this almost princely domain came into the possession of Isham Talbot, a native of Bedford county, Virginia, who emigrating in youth to Kentucky, became a celebrated lawyer and was a Senator both of the State and the nation. His wife was Margaret Garrard, a daughter of Governor Garrard. She died at "Mount Lebanon," her father's home in Bourbon, a number of years before her husband, who died at "Melrose" in 1837. After Isham Talbot's death, Ambrose Dudley, an upright and courtly gentleman, whose wife, Eliza Talbot, was the Senator's daughter, lived here with his family until about the time of the Civil War. Since that time much decreased in extent, it was used by the Dudleys as a summer home, until purchased some years ago by Kentucky to serve as an experimental farm for the Normal and Industrial Institute, a State institution for the training of its negroes. Cedar Fort, not far from "Melrose," was situated on an old highway* no part of which is now in existence, which entered Frankfort on the river bank just below the tunnel.

On the other side of Cedar Fort from "Melrose," the famous O'Hara Academy was once conducted.

The founder of this academy was Kane O'Hara, an Irish gentleman, who had received a collegiate training, which turned out to be his most valuable possession. Being compelled to flee the English persecution in Ireland, he escaped to America, bringing with him little, save his education. He settled in Kentucky, first at Danville, where his gifted son, the soldier-poet, Theodore O'Hara, was born in 1820. In the poet's infancy his parents removed from Danville to Woodford county, but soon after located in this spot, where they remained until just after the Mexican war—that conflict immortalized by the sword and pen of their distinguished son—when they removed to a farm on Elkhorn, some miles below Frankfort.

---

* It was over this road that LaFayette made his triumphal progress from Frankfort to Versailles, and not over the Georgetown-Versailles turnpike as erroneously supposed. Some time since a well known Louisville paper, containing a picture of the Stephens Tavern (where Santa Anna was once a constrained guest), stated that LaFayette lodged here when journeying toward Lexington, which was a mistake.

where the father died soon after. In all these places, Kane O'Hara conducted an academy and lived and died distinguished in his profession, but it was that spot near Cedar Fort that is best associated with his fame, which was as well, the boyhood home of the poet. This was the home of the author of the immortal "Bivouac of the Dead," during those years of life when the human organism is most sensitive to its environment. It is then, if ever, young men see visions. Inclined to meditation tinged with sadness, he spent many a thoughtful hour amid the soothing solitude of the Frankfort cemetery (near his early home), which suited just such a soul as his, for it is embowered in loveliness, crowns a height that is surpassingly picturesque, and commands a view fine enough to tempt the pencil of a master."

Within its hallowed enclosure, it is meet that the poet should finally rest, amid the beloved scenes of his youth, and within the shadow of his own "Marble minstrels' voiceless stone"
"No impious footsteps here shall tread
  The herbage of your grave ,
Nor wreck, nor change, nor winter's blight
Nor Time's remorseless doom,
  Shall dim one ray of holy light
That gilds your glorious tomb."

A house built and occupied by the Downey family stands where O'Hara's Academy once stood. Between this and the "Big Eddy" of the Kentucky river is that marshy tract locally known as Trumbos, so called from the family owning it, in part, in recent years. In former days it was largely the property of Charles Julian and John U. Waring. That of the latter was for many years the home of Richard Kidder Woodson, now of James Wakefield. Further down the river, and on the Glens Creek pike, is a considerable estate known as "Windyside," formerly the property of Thomas Page, more recently that of the Walcutt family, and now the handsome suburban home of Gilbert Mastin.

Between this and Frankfort were once a number of smaller places, situated on the old roadway, all of which, like it, have long since disappeared, save one, now a portion of "Windyside" belonging formerly to the Scearce family. On the banks of the Kentucky river and nearly opposite the new Capitol, stood until recently a house, known in the pioneer days as Yeatmans. Here at the mouth of a small creek, bearing the same name, flat-boats were constructed for the purpose of trade with the then Spanish port of New Orleans.

On the heights above is the Frankfort Cemetery, formerly a part of "Melrose," as was the adjoining beautiful site, now that of the Kentucky Feeble Minded Institute, but which was in ante bellum days the location of Dr. Lloyd's celebrated school for girls.

George Crutcher Downing.

APPENDIX C

THE FAMILIES KINKEAD, STEPHENSON, GARRETT, MARTIN, AND DUNLAP*

By LAURA KINKEAD WALTON

The following records of the Kinkead family represent no original work on my part, but merely an attempt to collect such papers as are in my possession under one head. Unfortunately, genealogical research requires both time and money, and, though I have reason to believe the dates and facts herein stated are true, there are a number of minor points that could be cleared up with ease (as all the sources are known and available) if one were only on the spot to verify them.

According to Misbet's** "Heraldry", "The Kincaids were in possession of Kincaid in 1280, as is provided by a charter extant. Kincaid, Laird of Kincaid, of Stirlingshire, for his galant services in rescuing the Castle of Edinburg from the English in the time of Edward I. was made Constable of said Castle, and his posterity enjoyed that office for a long period, carrying the Castle in their Armorial Bearings in memory thereof to this day."

A memorandum brought to this country by an early Kincaid seems most interested, however, in the fact that the first Kincaid was Roderick John Campbell, who, after his valiant service, for which he was given the name and estates of Kincaid was given in marriage the daughter of the Duke of Montrose, and who's son William Kincaid distinguished himself in battle and at home. William Kincaid was a descendant of the Earl of Huntington, who was the third son of David the first King of Scotland. He was a first cousin of Robert Bruce and of John Baliol. He was with Baliol when King Edward defeated him at Tweed in 1296, and was with William Wallace when he was defeated at Falkirk and also with him until he was betrayed in 1303. He was with Robert Bruce when he defeated Edward I. at Bannochburn in 1314, and was Knighted there by Bruce for bravery. He was with Sir John Douglas when he started, with the heart of Bruce, to the Holy Land in 1329. He was with Sir James Douglas when he was killed in battle with the Moors in Spain and returned to Scotland with the heart of Bruce in 1329. He married Julia McDowell in 1330, and died in 1350.

Ten generations later (And I have all the names and dates of these so far as they pertain to my own family) Joseph Kincaid, a staunch Presbyterian, renounced the Lairdship in his native land on account of religious convictions which forced him to leave Scotland, during the troublous revolution of 1688, and went to the north of Ireland. Robert Kincaid, his son (1686–1730) had a son Thomas, who married Margaret Lockhart and emigrated to America, and settled at Carlisle, Pennsylvania. The date of his emigration is unknown to me and though I am of the impression that he married in Ireland I have no data to prove it. However I do know that Margaret Lockhart Kincaid was also of the same religious persuasion and probably came from the same locality.

Thomas Kincaid left Carlisle and went to Augusta County Virginia in 1747,

*Excerpted from "Historic Meeting at Pisgah Church," by Laura Kinkead Walton, *The Register of the Kentucky Historical Society*, Vol. 37 (Oct. 1939), 283-321.
**For *Misbet's* read *Nisbet's*.

757

and died there in 1752. This fact is set forth in a bill in Chancery, filed for "William Kincaid, a minor, by his next friend James Lockhart".

William Kincaid, the eldest son of Thomas Kincaid and Margaret Lockhart, was born at Carlisle, Pennsylvania, January 9th, 1739, and died in Woodford County, Kentucky, May 30th, 1820. He moved to Augusta County, Virginia, with his parents and remained there until after the Revolutionary War. On November 30th, 1756 he married Eleanor Guy.

Eleanor Guy Kincaid was a woman of great courage, prepared for the rigors of pioneer life. She was of the same Scotch-Irish ancestry. Her maternal great Grandfather had fought in the siege of Londonderry and what was more important her great Grandmother had lived through it, and she had been brought up on tales of its horrors. In later years she told these stories to her grandchildren, rivaling Macaulay in the vividness of her description of the ferocity of those times. She, like her husband, had a background of strong religious belief, for which men had suffered and died, and her faith was tried to the uttermost in the savage adventure that befell her.

In a letter from her grandson, to his son (my great uncle), the story of her capture and escape from the Indians is told far better than I can tell it and I give it in his own words.

Cane Spring, April 20th, 1847

Dear Blackburn;

You request that I should give you some of your great grandmother's early history. I am at a loss where you wish me to begin, but I suppose I may go back as far as I have any dates. She was born August 17th. 1740. Was married to your grandfather November 30th 1756 Was taken captive by the Indians April 14th. 1764, from Augusta County, Virginia, twenty miles from Staunton, on the road to the Warm Springs. She had, when she was taken, three children, the eldest a daughter, seven years old, the second a son four years old, the youngest, your Aunt Hamilton, two years old.

When the Indians came to the house, your grandfather had but a short time left. He had eaten his dinner, and gone to the fields out of sight of the house, to plough. Your grandmother was sitting just inside the door spining, the children were playing at the door, when, suddenly, they screamed, as though alarmed, and before she had time to rise, an Indian jumped in at the door, there were five of them four men and a boy. They immediately went to packing up the clothing; they cut open the beds, throwing out the feathers. Several persons had brought their clothing there, believing it to be the most secure place in the neighborhood, and intending to come and build a fort there. They took all their clothing. There were two guns in the house, and a new saddle; they took all. She said it was astonishing the load that they carried. The Indians had never come as early in the season before, and their visit was utterly unlooked for at the time.

Your grandfather did not return to the house until night. You may imagine his feelings when he came and found things as they were. He immediately turned out to raise a company to pursue them, and started the next morning and followed them for two or three days, but the difficulty of keeping on the trail was too great.

They were very careful to leave as little (trail) as possible. She said she frequently broke limbs of bushes, until the Indians noticed it and made her quit. When they left the house, they went up the side of a hill, in view of the house, and stopped and sat down on a log, staying some time, and fixed her and the children for traveling. They made her pull off her shoes and put on moccasins, on her and the two oldest children. She was in three months of having an infant.

When they got all fixed, one of the Indians, who spoke good English turned to her and said it was the Great Spirit that put her in their hands. She told him she knew it; but the thought passed through her mind that that same Great Spirit was able to take her out of their hands before six months.

When they started, she had the child two years old to carry. The little boy gave out after traveling several days. Two of the Indians stopped behind with him; when they came up he was not with them, and she saw him no more. After traveling several days, going up very high and steep mountains, she fell and was not able to get up. The Indians called to her to come along, but she lay still. One of them came, broke a switch and whipped her severely. She said she never felt it. While he was whipping her, she turned her head and looked at him; he instantly drew his tomahawk. She turned her face from him and waited to receive the blow, but he did not strike. She made the exertion and got up, and went to the other Indians. They took the child from her, set her on a log, and sat on each side of it, and appeared to be holding council, whether to kill it or not. After talking together some time, they asked if the child would have black eyes. She told them it would. One of them remarked her hair was very black. They immediately decided. One of them that had the saddle fixed it on your grandmother's back, so that it gave her the use of her arms, which was a great relief to her. He set the child on top of his pack, which she said was a heavy one, and carried it to the towns.

In two days they got home. He gave the child to one of his sisters who had lost a little one, and she saw it no more until it was given up about six months after. When it was taken from her it spoke English remarkably well for one of its years, and when she next saw it, it could not speak a word of English, but spoke Indian well. Nothing very material transpired until they got to the Indian town. They went through the mountains to

Kenawah, where they had left their canoes, and went by water most of the way thereafter.

Soon after getting to the Indian's home she was adopted into the family of King Bever, and was treated as one of them. She was, for a large portion of the time she was with them, at Zanesville. When the time arrived for her to be confined, they would not let her stay in the town, but sent her to the woods, the squaws attended her and carried her food. Her Infant was born July 25th 1764.

The fall after, an army was sent against the Indians. commanded by General Boquette (I think his name is spelled). The Indians were alarmed and agreed to make peace and bring in all the persons they held as captives, when upwards of two hundred persons were given up, and among them your grandmother, her infant three months old and the one two years old, the oldest having taken sick and died during the summer.

Your grandfather was with the army when the little girl was given up. Your grandmother knew her immediately, but he could not recognize her, and was in great uneasiness, until her mother asked him if he did not recollect having bled her in the foot. He said he did, and stripped off her moccasin. There was the mark. The Great Spirit was kind to her, and delivered her out of their hands in just six months from the time she was taken captive. They returned to Augusta County, from where she was taken, and remained there until 1789, and then moved here, where they lived until her death.

I have given you an account of your grandmother's history-Perhaps all you wish to know. You know how I dislike writing. I did not think it would make such a long story, I intended to copy it when I began, but for fear you should want it, I will send it as it is; perhaps you can read and understand it. Let me hear from you shortly and tell me if it will do.

                    Your affectionate Parent.
                        JOHN KINKEAD.

The annals of Augusta County substantiate this letter and also its contents is related in brief in Boquet's Exposition against the Ohio Indians in 1764 page 78.

As you have heard William Kincaid volunteered in Colonel Boquet's expidition and was rewarded by being reunited with his wife and children. He must have had his doubts as to the safety of his former abode or else he was better off and decided to get nearer to civilization for in 1765 he bought from Samuel Hodge a tract of land on the Great Calf Pasture River where he resided until he came to Kentucky. (The old house still stands in a fine state of preservation.) And there he resided unmolested until 1789. He served as Lieutenant and Adjutant, later as Captain in the Revolution. Records show that he marched in command of a company from Staunton in March 1777 to a block house on the west fork of the Monongalia River . . . Again in 1780 he served as captain of Militia and was allowed certificates for service in land grants in January, 1780, and again February 15th, 1780.

It was about the time of the Revolution that the spelling of the name was changed from Kincaid to Kinkead. Various reasons have been given for the change but I have always thought that the deplorable weakness in that regard in his descendants may have come from him and account for it.

In 1789 there was quite a movement from Augusta County to Kentucky. The laws of the State of Virginia concerning the domination of the Episcopal Church sat heavily on the consciences of the Scotch-Presbyterians and they resented the many inconveniences they entailed, so a number of them moved together to Woodford County, Kentucky, built a church and made their lives around it, and called it Pisgah.

William Kinkead and his wife bought a lovely place known as Cane Spring and lived there the remaining of their days leaving it to their son John Kinkead when they died, he on May 30th, 1820, and Eleanor Guy Kinkead on October 9th, 1825. They both lie buried in Pisgah churchyard.

CHILDREN OF WILLIAM KINKEAD.

Margaret Kinkead	born	Sept.	25th	1757	Died in infancy.
Andrew	"	"	Feb.	25th	1760	Killed by the Indians.
Isabella	"	"	April	10th	1762	Married Andrew Hamilton.
Andrew	"	"	July	25th	1764	
Agnes	"	"	Nov.	1st	1766	Married Alexander Black.
William	"	"	June	6th	1769	Married Anne Dunlap.
Eleanor	"	"	Aug.	31st	1771	
Margaret	"	"	Sept.	10th	1772	
Susanna	"	"	Apr.	20th	1775	
Guy	"	"	Mar.	14th	1779	
Rebecca	"	"	July	25th	1782	
John	"	"	Dec.	25th	1784	Married Margaret Trotter Blackburn

MISS BRADLEY: "Pardon me if I add a bit of personal history. The little Isabella Kinkead of whom Mrs. Walton has just told you; who was stolen by the Indians; whose life was spared because of her very black hair; who was adopted by King Beaver; later brought in with the prisoners after Boquet's treaty and restored to her family; grew to young womanhood and married Andrew Hamilton; this little Isabella was the great-grandmother of my own precious Mother and the one for whom she was named. My Mother not only inherited the name

Isabella, but also the very black hair that saved the life of the first little Isabella and caused her to be adopted by King Beaver."

"Bancroft says, 'The arrival of the lost ones formed the loveliest scene ever witnessed in the wilderness. Mothers recognized their lost babies; sisters and brothers, scarcely able to recover the accent of their native tongue, learned to know that they were children of the same parents.' "

"At the meeting in June splendid biographies of Major Samuel Stevenson and his wife Jane Gay Stevenson were given by Mrs. Oscar Elmore, but she insisted that in this publication we use the following which were written by Mr. R. S. King, Head of the Mechnical Engineering Department Georgia School of Technology, Atlanta, Georgia."

MAJOR SAMUEL STEVENSON.

Samuel Stevenson was born March 11, 1744. He married Jane Gay, daughter of James Gay, on May 22, 1771. He died in Pisgah, Kentucky, the 17th of December, 1825. Their children were James, Thomas, Robert, John, William, Alexander, Samuel, Martha, Mary and Jane.

Genealogists in London, England, furnish a strong evidence that the Stevensons were descended from an officer of that name in the Army of William the Conqueror, who for services rendered at the Battle of Hastings, was rewarded with a grant of land in Scotland, South of Glasgow, the Parish and Town of which still bears the name of Stevenson, to this day. One of the family, Sir Hugh Stevenson was High Constable of Scotland.

The Coat of Arms is identical with the Coat of Arms of the Stevensons of the Counties of Derby and Lincoln, England, as given in the Herald's Visitation of 1622, viz.—Gu on a Bond ar, three leopards' faces vertical. Crest a gard, or. Family tradition has it that our Scotch-Irish ancestor was in the Siege of Londonderry. That the Family came from Ireland to America seems well established.

Samuel Stevenson was the youngest of six brothers, who all came to Kentucky, but is the only one buried in Pisgah Church yard. The spelling of the name used here is Stevenson because in most records it is spelled that way—sometimes Stinson. The spelling Stephenson is usually taken as belonging to the English Branch. The Scotch spelling was almost always with a "v". The Scotch home of the family was Lanarkshire, Scotland.

Whether Samuel was born in Virginia or not is not definitely known. It is more than likely that it was not as according to Kegley's Virginia Frontier the first group of families to move into the Valley of Virginia came there in 1744. The group that settled that year on the Calf Pasture was,—Alex. Dunlap, Robert Crocket, Henry Gay, Robert Gay, James Lockridge, John Graham, John Preston, William Warwick, John Campbell, John Wilson, John Kinkead, William Elliott, Jr., William Hamilton, William Gay and some others. In 1749 we notice the first Stevenson (Stinson) name—James, along with John and Thomas Meek, Andrew Kinkead and Andrew Hamilton.

After Braddock's defeat practically all of these people, lead by their pastor, Rev. Alexander Craighead moved to Mecklenburg County, North Carolina. However some of them remained in the pastures and later moved into Kentucky—these were the Kinkeads, Armstrongs, Elliotts, Clarks, Hamiltons, Carlyles, Hicklins, Lockridges, McIlvaines, and Meeks. They settled near Pisgah in February, 1784.

Little is known concerning the early childhood of Samuel Stevenson. That he spent practically all of it in the pasture region is almost certain. Here he was subjected to many Indian raids and to duty in the Colonial Troops. According to Family traditions his mother was killed in the massacre of Kerr's creek, which occured on July 17, 1763. The Rev. Samuel Brown, a descendent of Dr. Brown, who was pastor of the Providence, describes this raid in an issue of the Lexington, Va., Gazette. This Samuel Brown's mother was Mary Moore, daughter of James Moore of Abb's Valley in Rockbridge Co., Va. He says only one thing saved many—The Old Timber Ridge Church was filled, and the Rev. John Brown was preaching—the alarm came during the intermission between morning and afternoon worship. Not much attention was paid to the report. All had assembled for the second service when a messenger had arrived from Kerr's Creek—all was confusion and dismay, the congregation fled in every direction where they thought safety could be found. This did not save Samuel's mother as she was killed on the way home from this meeting.

During Dunmore's War Samuel Stevenson came in contact with many men from Pennsylvania, who have since become well known to American History—Kenton, Todd, Patterson, Boone, The McConnells and others. Samuel Stevenson was related to George Rogers Clark by marriage.

Kentucky Historical Register, Volume 21, page 108, says—a certificate book shows that Samuel Stevenson claimed 1,000 acres on Elkhorn "to include his cabin built in the year 1776"; page 119 says: Thomas Stevenson, by Col. Logan, claimed 1000 acres on a branch of Dick's River improved in 1776. This would seem to indicate that Samuel's brother Thomas was along. In order to prove title to land in Kentucky it was necessary to plant a crop of corn and if possible to erect a cabin the walls of which must be at least four feet high. These certificates were granted by the Virginia Land Commission 1779-80, Court sitting at Bryan's Station on Elkhorn. Jan. 4, 1780—To Samuel Stevenson 1000 acres at the State price on Shannon's Run, about one and one half miles from the mouth of said run waters of Elkhorn to include his cabin built in 1776.

According to records in the Veteran's Bureau, Washington, Samuel Stevenson enlisted July, 1778, as a private in Capt. John Williams Virginia Company under Col. George Rogers Clark and was stationed at Kaskaskia and served until May 31, 1779. His pension application states that he was in the service at various times until the close of the war, amounting to three or five years in all and that in addition to the above he served with the Virginia troops under Captains William McConnell, James or John Brown, and Col. Benjamin Logan and was in a battle on the Miami River against the Shawnee Indians.

Samuel Stevenson, his brother John, who held the rank of Sergeant and his son John, nephew of Samuel, took part in Clark's memorable military meneuver. Samuel, as noted, re-enlisted in Captain William's Company and served a year to guard Kaskaskia while Clark went on to take Cahokia.

Putting all accounts of English, Roosevelt and others together of the taking of Vincennes and Kaskaskia, we can scarcely over estimate the bravery of the attack or the significance of the capture. It was the turning of the key that unlocked the great Northwest to the American Government.

Details of Col. Clark's successes as narrated by Captain Montgomery at Williamsburg, and the presence of Capt. Rockeblave and other British prisoners created a fever of excitement. The Virginia Legislature recognized the importance of the conquest by immediate and unanimous vote of thanks to Col. Clark and his soldiers. Five years later, The State, ceding the territory to the general government, reserved one hundred and fifty thousand acres for officers and men engaged in the conquest of Illinois.

While the Stevensons were serving in Illinois, preparations were being made back on the Greenbrier for moving to Kentucky. On May 31, 1779, Samuel Stevenson was discharged from Capt. Williams Company as his time of enlistment was up and he desired to return to his Greenbrier home and to his family. His excursions through the fertile lands of Kentucky made him impatient to remove to the new country with his family and there to raise his family in the richest of Kentucky forests and pastures.

Samuel Stevenson, his brothers John, William and Thomas, who was killed at the Blue Licks, all formed a party with some of their neighbors and moved out to Kentucky in the fall of 1779. James Stevenson, a son of John, says (in the Draper MSS.), "My father moved out from the calf pasture, didn't get ready in time to come out with Uncle Sam and Aunt Jane as he had intended. When my father got to Boonsbourough, there was not a sign of a blaze, or trace, to there from Lexington and Uncle Sam set out to meet us; was so glad to hear we had come. So happened that we that we did not pass each other. Met just about half way between the two places."

Samuel Stevenson was the leader of the third party to leave the Greenbrier. That he must have been well skilled in the method of scouting and knowing all the Indian signs etc., is attested by the fact that they were not once disturbed by the Indians, altho the party ahead of him was attacked on more than one occasion. Capt. James Gay and Alexander Dunlap, Jr., were among other members of the party. This party arrived at Lexington on October 27, 1779. From the Greenbrier District and the Calfpasture the Pioneers generally traveled by the wilderness road. Longer in miles and slower in time of passage, and beset with dangers and hardships also, it was, on the whole, considered less dangerous and less troublesome than the Pennsylvania Routes.

According to the Galloway Family record the first four white women in Lexington were Jane Gay Stevenson, Mrs. Barton, Mrs. Johnson, and Mrs. William Galloway.

Fine weather in the spring encouraged a renewal of immigration, Lexington having many newcomers who built cabins outside of the stockade. But these improvements were checked in June by the fate of Ruddell's and Martin's Stations. On the second of August Samuel Stevenson, together with his brothers John and Thomas left Lexington as members of Capt. Patterson's Company to join Col. George Rogers Clark's campaign against the Shawnee Indian Villages on the Little Miami and Mad Rivers. The villages and the growing crops were destroyed. The value in this lay in the fact that the Indians, having no longer any corn to subsist on, were obliged to spend their time and powder and shot on game instead of the white settlers, and the Kentucky Pioneers had two years of comparative quiet to follow.

1782 saw the two most thrilling chapters in the History of Kentucky—the Siege of Bryan's Station and the Battle of the Blue Licks. Samuel Stevenson took part in these two battles as did also his brothers John, William and Thomas, the latter losing his life at the Battle of the Blue Licks. The Stevensons made up a part of the sixteen horsemen who reached Bryan's Station under Capt. Patterson.

These two disasters coming one upon the other, might well have discouraged forever the settlement of Kentucky. Once again the settlers decided to attack the Indians in their villages and strongholds. Clark, Logan and Patterson raised one thousand men to attack the indians. They destroyed their crops and villages. Only one man was lost. The campaign was one of intimidation. The Stevensons were again in the Campaign against the Indians.

In 1784 Samuel Stevenson moved out to Pisgah and together with the Gays, Dunlaps, McIlvaines, and others built up the Pisgah Community. The Pisgah Church and school house were the first of the community buildings to be built. The floor of the second meeting house was laid of tongue and grooved cherry. Samuel Stevenson contributed heavily to it.

Once more the Pioneers were threatened by invasion of the indians. Col. Clark and Col. Logan again commanded the troops. They took the towns of Macocheek and McKeestown. In this campaign many Indian Chiefs were engaged—Red Jacket, Tecumseh, Mclunthe, Little Turtle, Logan and Big Corn. This was really the last Indian Campaign of Samuel Stevenson altho he was called out against the Wiah Indians.

Samuel Stevenson rose to the rank of Major in the Kentucky State Militia. He spent his remaining days on the Pisgah plantation and is buried in the Pisgah Church yard. He died 1825.

JANE GAY STEVENSON

"Whither thou goest I will go, where thou lodgest I will lodge."

Our first definitely known ancestors according to records in this country were William Gay and his wife Margaret Hamilton, said to be the daughter of Alexander Hamilton. The father of this William Gay was one of the defenders of Londonderry or Derry as it is usually called. State papers frequently refer to Londonderry and the settlement of the County it is in as "The settlement of Ulster". William Gay was born after the siege took place but no doubt heard many of the details from his parents. Our Bible records do not give the christian name of our Londonderry defender.

We know that William Gay came here with his children. The English home of the Gays was near Warwickshire, England. From there they went to Ulster in the North of Ireland, then to Londonderry.

According to importation records in Orange County, Virginia, William Gay appears before the Court and proves his importation by way of Philadelphia. He does not name his wife but he does name his six sons—William, James, Robert, Samuel, Henry and John and a daughter Eleanor, who at that time must have been about a month old. The statement is made in some Histories that William Gay died in Ireland. This record proves that this is not true. Eleanor was born August 17, 1740. William Gay indicated his intention to take up land in the Valley of the Shenandoah.

Along about 1730 there were a large number of Scotch-Irish Families came to America and most of them entered by the way of the Port of Philadelphia. The path of migration was by way of Chester, Lancaster and Cumberland Counties, Pennsylvania and then down the Valley of the Shenandoah. Some of the Families traveled the entire road while others stayed in Lancaster County. However the Campbells, McElroys, McDowells, Grahams, Gays, Kinkeads, Elliotts, Stevensons and many other of the Families who helped to settle the Valley of Virginia came in about this time and by this route.

After the sojourn of the Gays in Pennsylvania they moved into the Borden Tract, which is now included in Rockbridge County, Virginia, and known as the Pastures. This territory was originally in Augusta County. James Gay, father of Jane Gay, one of the sons of William Gay, built a fort as protection for his family and the neighbors. These hardy pioneers came into the Valley and built their cabins and started to clear ground for their crops. This being hard and dangerous work as the Indians were not all favorable to the settlement of white men on lands that they claimed were their favorite hunting grounds. James Gay was married twice, his first wife, mother of Jane Gay Stevenson, being killed by the Indians the first time Kerr's Creek was taken in 1758. The last name of this second wife is not known but he mentions her in his will as Jean. James Gay came from Ireland when he was a boy and in all probability was born there. His first wife was supposed to have been Jean Warwick and is so given by some.

Quite early on a Thursday morning, Nov. 15, 1750 (O. S.), a daughter was born to James Gay and his wife. Tradition tells us that it was a bright clear day. The woods had taken on their bright autumnal hues. The crops were all in, the early settlers were preparing for the long winter, when hunting would be the chief occupation and the main source of meat supply. Time was also used to put all farming equipment into shape and to do the necessary weaving of cloth. The Gay neighbors were other members of the Gay family, the Kinkeads, Dunlaps, Elliotts, Grahams, Lockharts, McIlwains and others of the early Scotch-Irish who sought homes in the Calf Pastures. They had come in from Pennsylvania mostly from Lancaster and Cumberland Counties. James Gay had already settled on his land by 1743. Their cabins were fairly close together to give protection from Indians.

Jane was the name of the daughter born 1750 to James Gay and his wife and as her life was a very eventful one, and as she left some record of her travels and doings in the Draper Manuscripts and elsewhere we are going to let her tell the story of her life and the events and mode of living during her time.

Jane says, "Where we lived was about 35 miles from Staunton. No Lexington then. The country was newly settled. We attended Providence Meeting House. Old Mr. John Brown preached there then. The men carried their guns to meeting, as regularly as the congregation met. Communion service generally lasted three to four days."

"I was forted from the time I was 7 years old, 1757, and was never rid of the Indians until I moved to Pisgah, Ky. The first fort I was in, a little girl was taken out of it, but from July to November older than me. She was but seven years old and was seven years gone; until Brocade's (Bouquet's) campaign. We walked out and got some haws. They, some of the company pulled down the limbs, and handed us some of the haws. I wouldn't go any farther. And when I came, went into another cabin, wouldn't go into Mammy's, she would know I had been out. Presently the alarm came. They had gone about two hundred yards farther and the Indians took them."

"Carr's Creek (Kerr's Creek) was in about seven miles of us. We were on the Calf-Pasture. Mother was killed when I was about 8 years old (1758)."

"The settlement on Carr's Creek was taken twice. The first time it was taken, Aunt escaped to the woods. (Eleanor Gay Kinkead.) She had but two children then, and while she escaped that way the route of the indians was down the river."

The Rev. Samuel Brown, a descendant of Dr. Brown who was Pastor of the

Providence Meeting House (Presbyterian) describes this raid in an issue of the Lexington, Virginia, Gazette. The following is an abstract of that article.

How soon do the exciting scenes of childhood pass into oblivion. On July 17, 1763, The Massacre of Kerr's Creek occurred. Few people passing up and down this beautiful valley of Kerr's Creek realize the horrible destruction that swept the inhabitants of this place.

There was reason to believe the place had been spied upon and meditated upon some weeks before this terrible catastrophe. Two boys James Tilford and his brother were returning from school, one evening when they saw a naked man in their path hiding behind a tree trying to keep the tree between them and him. They ran home and gave the alarm—nothing much was thought until after the massacre.

The second and still worse disastrous invasion of Kerr's Creek came later. Jane Gay says—"The second time it was taken I had an Uncle and a Cousin killed. This Aunt (Eleanor Gay Kinkead) and her three children were taken prisoners and carried to the Indian towns."

By this time Jane was coming into young womanhood and she says—she often swam the calf pasture river on her back. Said she would reap all day and swim and dance and frolic or fish at night.

Jane Gay said the people were very much and frequently molested by the Indians. And on this account the men would carry guns with them and have them always ready and within reach, and while at work they would be on the lookout lest cunning scouts in ambush would shoot them down while they endeavored to earn their living by the sweat of their brows.

Jane Gay says, "Samuel Stevenson and I knew each other for years,—we were cousins you know, his mother and my mother being sisters. For some time Sammie and I planned on being married and finally set the day, this was on ... May 22, 1771. Our wedding was no different than other weddings at that time."

"We started housekeeping in Augusta County, Virginia, near my father's home. Our first child was born on April 21, 1772. He was named for my father —James Gay. Our daughter Martha, named for her grandmother, was born on February 23, 1774. This was the year of Dunmore's War. All of the able bodied men were called out for service. The Continental militia consisted of all men able to bear arms. The Stevensons and Gays served under Col. Andrew Lewis and were in the battle of Point Pleasant. They were in the west Augusta Battalion under Major John Connolly. This Battle was fought on Oct. 10, 1774, at the mouth of the Great Kanawa River. Chief Cornstalk commanded the Indians. (Theodore Roosevelt in his "Winning of the West" says this Battle was the first in which blood was shed for American Liberty and was the beginning of a war which ended at Yorktown.) Col. Lewis had 1100 men at Point Pleasant. Captains Andrew Lockridge, Samuel Wilson, John Skidmore commanded some of the companies. Capt. McClanahan's Company of Augusta County formed with Capt. Lewis a line around the Camp to guard it. For a detailed description of this Battle see Morton's History of Highland County, Virginia, Chapter 10.

"We moved to the Greenbriar in 1775," says Jane Gay, "the year after the Battle of the Point."

"Where we settled on the Greenbrier (in Pocohontas County, West Virginia)," says Jane Gay, "there were but one or two families that were not Dutch and half Dutch in that whole settlement. But never was a settlement of kinder people. They were great for dancing and singing."

"Our daughter Mary was born in December 23, 1778," says Jane Gay, "while Samuel was with George Rogers Clark's Illinois Regiment. My husband was with Capt. John Williams' Company and was stationed at Kaskaskia July 17, 1778, to May 31, 1779. His brother John also served in this campaign.

"In 1776," says Jane Gay, "my father, James Gay, Samuel Stevenson, Ben Blackburn and William Elliott, went out to Kentucky in April and got back in June I think." It seems that this same year Samuel Stevenson and John Gay and some others went up into Ohio to "spy" out the land. Sammie found time to tomahawk some land claims in Woodford County, Kentucky, and afterwards moved onto them. The trip into Ohio carried them up to Zanesville, where Dunlap afterwards located some claims and Stevenson located his land in Green County, Ohio.

"In the fall of 1779," says Jane Gay, "Sammie and I determined to move to Kentucky and make our home. Sammie had already spied out the land and had selected our future home. This became later known as the Asparagus Patch of Kentucky. My husband was selected as the leader of a group, who desired to move into 'Old Kentucky'. When we started to Kentucky we were 100 miles back from Daddy's.

"John McKinney, the School Master, came out with us. He was nearly killed at the 'Battle of the Point'. After leaving the Greenbrier settlement we never traveled a Sunday and it must have been 70 miles we traveled in Powell's Valley. This cavalcade was so well organized Indians followed it for miles hoping to find a point of attack, but finally gave up and let them through without interference. After leaving Blackmore's Station we didn't see the smoke of a chimney until we reached Boonesborough." Jane says, "We came to Lexington in October 1779. It had been settled the previous April. There were every sort of people there and that is what took us away. We had no notion of raising our children among that sort of people."

"Francis McConnell was the first man I knew when I got to Lexington. I had known the McConnells in Pennsylvania."

"We went down to McConnells Station 2nd of April, 1780. It took its name from Frances McConnell, and lay between Frances and William McConnell's places, and about one and one quarter miles from Lexington. Right where Royall's Mill now is—on the railroad. There was a graveyard there. James,

Francis and William McConnell were cousins to Alexander and John McConnell". (Draper.)

Aunt Jane says, "We raised four crops, and then moved out. That was in March 1, 1784. Crop raised 1780-81-82-83. The meeting house was built in 1785. Mr. Rankin gave us time about with Lexington. He preached at first out here in private houses." Samuel gave ten acres of land to the congregation and two acres for the meeting house and grave yard. The meeting house was called Pisgah and is said to be the first Church established in Kentucky. The Kentucky Academy was soon founded at Pisgah, General Washington and John Adams gave to it each $100; but in 1798, the Academy and Transylvania Seminary united to form the Transylvania University at Lexington. Nearly all the present members of the Church are the descendents of the original families and own the lands which their ancestors won. (Note.—For more than 125 years the doors to Pisgah Church have not been closed on a Sunday.)

One writer says concerning Pisgah Church—"It was in Wild March weather in the year 1784 that Samuel Stevenson and Jane Gay, his wife, came from the Fort in Lexington to live in their log cabin, their new home erected on the lands which they had surveyed in the new Kentucky country. It stood upon the wooded point of land just west of the present site of the Church. The house had been built by Stevenson with the help of his brothers-in-law, Alexander Dunlap and John Gay, with their friend Moses McIlvain. In the same season was built the homes of Dunlap and Agnes Gay, his wife, of John Gay and Sally Lockridge; of Moses McIlvain and Margaret Hodge. These homes were within a mile of each other and each near to a spring of water. The grant of land had originally been acquired and the claim located by Samuel Stevenson. He and Dunlap had each married sisters of John Gay. These were Scotch-Irish Virginians all from Augusta County in Virginia."

For many years Jane Gay occupied her cabin home raising a large family and taking an active part in the neighborhood affairs. Aunt Jane was for many years bed-ridden before her decease on the eighth of February, 1845, aged 95 years.

Children of Samuel Stevenson and Jane Gay.
James, b 1772, married Ann Galloway.
Martha, b 1774.
John, b 1776, Mar. Catherine Kilpatrick, Major War 1812.
Mary, b 1778, 2nd Wife of James Cox.
Samuel, b 1781, m. 1st Eliz. Clark, 2nd Harriett Webb.
Thomas, b 1783, m. Mary Steele.
Robert, m. 1st Sarah Cohagen, 2nd Eliz. Ramsey.
Jane, 1st wife of James Cox.
William, b 1791, married Peggy Scott.
Alexander, b 1791.

BIBLIOGRAPHY.

History of Orange County.
Draper Manuscripts.
Lexington Virginia Gazette.
History of Lancaster County, Pa. By Rupp.
History of Rockbridge County. By Morton.
History of Pocohontas Co., W. Va. By Martin.
The Scotch-Irish. By Hanna.
Abstracts of Augusta County. By Chalkley.
Winning of the West. By Roosevelt.
History of Highland County. By Morton.
History of Bath County. By Morton.
Pension Records, Washington, D. C.

WILLIAM GARRETT
By Louise Garrett Graddy.

A grand old elm stands sentinel in the middle of the beautiful little Pisgah graveyard. Yearly its spread grows greater as if eager to cast its welcome shade over more of our loved ones buried near. Under one outermost branch lies a cracked and moss embroidered stone slab which only young eyes may read "In memory of William Garrett departed this life 1820, age 71 years." Beside him lies his wife Elizabeth Black Garrett, and nearby one of his daughters Jane Garrett Long. Jane lived to the age of 100 years 2 months and 27 days and it is said there were 100 vehicles in her funeral procession.

William Garrett was one of Kentucky's earliest pioneers. Little is known of his early life. He was born in Pennsylvania in 1749 of Scotch-Irish Presbyterian parents. It has been handed down "By word of mouth" from generation to generation in the Garrett family that William came to Kentucky about 1775, returned soon to Virginia, fought in the Revolution and came back to Kentucky in the early 1780's to settle the 1000 acres of land secured by preemption.

The important thing often in a historical sketch of a man is to prove or disprove, by recorded sources, family tradition. Only through the inspiration of Miss Katherine Bradley could the writer, a great-great-granddaughter of William Garrett, have undertaken this task.

In the Court House at Lexington Kentucky are two very old volumes of Commissioners land Certificates. In Vol. 1 page 236, we find recorded "William Garrett this day claimed a preempt of 1000 acres of land at the State price in the District of Kentucky, on account of of marking and improving the same in the year of 1776, lying on one of the East branches of Clear Creek about three miles from the Fork of this Creek, to include his improvements satisfactory proof having been made to the Court that said Garrett has a right to a preempt of 1000 acres of land to include the above location and a certificate be issued accordingly". This hearing was at Court continued and held by the Commissioners of Kentucky District for the adjusting of land titles to unpatented lands at St. Asaphs (now Stanford, Ky.) the 21st day of April 1780. It is important to note that this original document states that William Garrett marked and improved this land as early as 1776. Over 300 acres of this original tract situated on the Nicholasville and Versailles Road in Woodford Co. six miles from Versailles are still in possession of the great-great grandchildren.

In searching for record of William Garrett's military service we found in Dunmore's Wars, Thwaites and Kellog, Page 421, a list of men who came to Kentucky with their leader James Harrod of Pennsylvania in 1774 establishing a Fort known as Ft. Harrod.

This list of names was copied by Gen. McAfee from Jas. Harrod's own Company Book owned by Margaret Fauntleroy, Harrod's step-daughter. It is therefore absolutely authentic. The list is recorded in McAfee paper 14 J 128 Wisconsin State Library, Madison, Wisconsin. Harrod and his men went back to fight in the battle of Point Pleasant returning again to Kentucky May 1775. William Garrett's name appears in H. J. Ekenrodes "List of Colonial Soldiers of Virginia" reference being made to the McAfee list.

As to William Garrett's Revolutionary service, the U. S. War Department lists him as serving during the Revolution for 2 yrs. as a private in the infantry Co. 3, Reg. 2. He is also mentioned as "soldier" in the infantry in Revolutionary War Records by Brumbaugh and in other such records. The writer wishes to trace more carefully this matter of Revolutionary service.

In Draper Mss. 11 C. 216-217 Robert Guyn states that he came to Kentucky from Augusta Co. Va. by the Wilderness Road in the fall of 1784 and that William Garrett, the Black family and Thos. Woods came out in spring of 1785. Do not these recorded dates coincide very closely with the verbal ones handed down through the family? There can be no question but that the William Garrett marking land in 1776 and the William Garrett traveling back and forth with Harrod in 1774 and 1775 are one and the same. We then find him, according to family tradition and Draper Mss. record, returning to Kentucky in 1785 after the Revolution to settle down for life on his "preempt" as he speaks of it in later land deeds.

Elizabeth Black, the wife of William, was the daughter of Joseph Black a Scotch Irish Presbyterian of Augusta County, Virginia. One of the earliest wills recorded in Woodford County is that of Joseph Black, an old man in 1796. The marriage date of William and Elizabeth Garrett has not been traced but was prior to 1779 as the eldest daughter Jane was born in that year.

Elizabeth and William Garrett had two sons, James and John Garrett, the latter a captain in the war of 1812; and six daughters, Jane, Nancy, Martha, Elizabeth, Polly and Sarah. The Garrett family were members of the Old Ebenezer Church in Woodford County. William Garrett helped to build the old stone building and his name appears early as an officer in the Old Ebenezer

Church Book. His Grandson, Robert Garrett, was the first of that name to belong to Pisgah Church but the earlier members of the family are buried there.

The first Garrett home in Kentucky was a log house. Several such houses were built on the original preemption. Jane Garrett Long lived in one of them until her death in 1879. About 1812 William Garrett built a simple but beautiful stone house. Prof. Newcomb of the University of Illinois, an authority on Colonial Architecture, pronounced this house a perfect example of very early Kentucky architecture and included pictures and measured drawings of the house in his recent valuable book. Four large frame rooms and porch were added to the stone portion by John Garrett, William's son. A magnificent Burr Oak, the most remarkable in this part of the country, with a measured circumference of 24 feet and a spread of 116 feet stands in the beautiful avenue at Oakland, the name of this fine old home. William Garrett's great-great-great grandchildren play under the oak's mighty boughs. Each Sunday the family from neighboring counties gather at Oakland, a family still interested in the same simple beautiful things as was its founder, the farm and how to tend it well, the church and how to best further its interests the family and how to keep it closely knit by love and high ideals. Thus the heritage of William Garrett, pioneer, soldier, churchman, farmer and home builder passes on from generation to generation.

RECORD OF WILLIAM MARTIN

William Martin was born in Augusta County, Virginia March 8th, 1762. The earliest record we have is that of his military service as its appears in Pension Records, Appendix D:

"He enlisted for two years in Albemarle County, Virginia February 16th, 1776 and served in the company of Capt. Mathias DeWitt, 7th Virginia Regiment commanded by Colonel Dangerfield. He was discharged at Valley Forge. He is known to have been in the battle of the Brandywine.

He removed to Kentucky in 1779 and in 1780 was drafted and served in the company of Capt. John Morrison in the regiment of Colonel Todd. Later, while in garrison duty at Lexington watching movements of Indians, Capt. William McConnell succeeded to command of his company. In 1782 he was again chosen to go on an expedition up the Ohio River under Capt. Robt. Patterson. They went as far as the Big Bone, but were forced to return overland because of lack of force to accomplish the purpose of the expedition, namely to establish a fort at Big Bone. Later William Martin went on the expedition under George Rogers Clark against the Indians in Miami Valley, and he was at the Battle of the Blue Licks. He left the service in 1784, having served continuously since 1780. This period plus the two years service in the East already mentioned make a total of six years of Revolutionary War service."

From the above we note that William Martin enlisted just prior to his 15th birthday. It would be interesting if possible, to follow this gallant youth especially through the two years of his enlistment in the regiment of Colonel Dangerfield. We are told that he was at the battle of Brandywine. We know that the troops there were in very bad condition, many were without shoes and they had little food. He was probably with Washington when he crossed the Delaware. He ended his enlistment at Valley Forge where some were discharged from lack of food and clothing.

In 1779 William Martin with two or more of his brothers came to Kentucky. That year Robert Patterson made a settlement and called it Lexington. He built a cabin (said to have been built in 1776). Many settlers came to Lexington in the year 1779 and William Martin was among them. The winter of 1779-80 was terribly hard. Food was scarce. The streams were frozen over. Wild animals came to the station for food. There was much suffering. Family tradition has it that William Martin brought his old mother over the mountains with him to Kentucky. Tradition also says that he built the first chimney ever built in Lexington either for his own cabin or it may have been for Robert Patterson's cabin previous to 1779. The cabins previous to 1779 were merely log pens without a roof or doors.

In 1781 he with his brothers Hugh and Samuel were among those who drew lots at Lexington. These lots were on the town branch, now Water Street, Lexington.

In 1785 when a colony came out from Lexington and settled in the Pisgah community, he settled on land nearer Versailles on what is now called the Big Sink Pike. The land was then settled by three plans, by pre-emption, military grants and land warrants. We do not know which plan he followed. When a grandson was asked why he did not take more land, it was said that he only took what he could use. We have not heard of any litigation over his settlement as many settlers had. It was on this settlement that he built the log cabin which stands today. There were puncheon floors and all the inside woodwork was of walnut which will last another hundred years. It was built on high ground from which the men could watch for Indians while the women washed or did other outside work.

It was April 11th 1799 that he married Letitia McClannahan of Pendleton County and from that union there were twelve children, six daughters and six sons. Settled on land which has been in cultivation 150 years and which last year produced the best corn and tobacco in the county, he raised his 12 children. (Note: one of his daughters, Jane, married James McAfee of the McAfee brothers)

In these days of the early settlement as soon as enough were gathered, they built a church or the settlement went to pieces. In this settlement Pisgah was the church and Father David Rice was instrumental in its founding. Presbyterians and warm patriots, coming from Valley of Va., "an austere, a thoughtful race, they preferred the peaceful pursuits of agriculture to the wild license of the hunters life and constituted a manly and virtuous yeomanry; of whom "Washington is reported to have said that should all his plans be crushed and but a single standard left him, he would plant that standard on the Blue Ridge, make the mountain heights his barrier and rallying round him the noblest patriots of the valley, found under better auspices a new republic in the west."

Here in the cabins and cane breaks of the wilderness they faced the hardships without fear having the same elevated, "uncompromising and indomitable spirit that formerly stood up unflinchingly for Christ's Crown and Covenant at the foot of the heath-clad Grampians. It is from the Kirk of Scotland in her days of depressions and cruel trial that the Presbyterians of Kentucky delight to deduce their origin."* They came here from the Valley of Virginia and their posterity are a tall, muscular and industrious race. They have inherited from their forefathers independence and integrity of character, exemplary morals, and a deep reverence for the institutions of religion. These people left their native country for a wilderness for conscience sake and naturally hugged religion closer the more they were persecuted and it might be reasonable to expect that among their first duties was to erect the altar where they pitched the tent and this can be truly said of all these revered and honored today.

A noble Heritage. MRS. WM. HENRY MARTIN, Midway, Ky.

(Note William Martin's Military Record was taken from Appendix D. New York, Chas. T. Dillingham 1880. Louisville, Ky. Public Library, R. 929-2. Book M. 381, given by F. M. Calkrell.)

Children of William Martin and his wife Letitia McClannahan:

Names	Died	Married
Agnes		John Stogdell
William	at 72	unmarried
Ann D.	sixty five years ago	unmarried
Martha		James Martin
Washington		Miss Offutt
Hugh		
Joseph		Talitha Martin
Jane		James McAfee
Elijah		Lou Allen Creason
John		Mary Ann Alexander

(This John was an Elder at Pisgah.)

The Martins came from the Tinkling Spring and Timber Ridge Churches in Virginia.

---
* Davidson's History of Presbyterian Church in Kentucky.

MISS BRADLEY: "In the biographies given today are included two women—because each had rendered military service. Eleanor Guy (or Gay) Kinkead had been captured and taken prisoner by the Indians and Jane Gay Stevenson, who says in the Draper manuscript 'I was forted from the time I was seven years old until I came to Pisgah.'"

"A third woman lies buried here whom we feel should be honored too. She is Agnes Gay Dunlap, a niece of the former and sister of the latter. We have been told that her husband, Col. Alexander Dunlap Jr. was one of the four founders of Pisgah, but one whose history has *not* been told today because he is not buried here. Alexander Dunlap and Agnes Gay were married in Virginia 1768 and she endured the hardships of pioneer life there; kept the home and children while her husband went on various military campaigns and later came with him to Kentucky in 1784 and remained in this community until her death on August 5, 1804, and lies buried in this Churchyard. Her husband, Alexander Dunlap, had located lands in Ohio, and three of the children of Alexander and Agnes had married and gone there to make their homes, and after the death of his wife Agnes, Alexander went to Ohio, spent the few remaining years of his life with them and died there. But there were others of their children who remained in this community and some of their descendants are in this audience today."

"Agnes Gay Dunlap was the daughter of James Gay and his first wife and from them inherited those stern qualities of character which enabled her to endure the same hardships and courageously face the same dangers as her husband and father; and we deem it a privilege to place on her grave a palm leaf denoting the same honor as we will give to other soldiers whose names we are honoring."

INDEX

---, --- 65, 75, 81, 118, 358, 411, 414, 415, 416, 417, 418, 421, 433, 462, 515, 533, 575, 578, 579, 626, 673, 682, 736
--- (Col.) 654
--- (Mr.) 84
Abraham 237
Aggy 668
Agnes 10, 710
Agnese 55, 80
Alan 317
Alexander 202, 317
Alferret 708
Amanda 236
Ann 18, 184, 186, 711
Anne 76
Annie 711
Anthony 711
Arthur 97
Asa 459, 461
Babe 703
Behethdod 395
Behethland 395
Belle 352
Blackburn 758
Booker 421, 423
Buck (" Old Uncle ") 570
Caroline 348
Catherine 17, 673, 744
Catherine E. 57
Clay 429
Cript 16
Criss 711
Daphne 266
David 16, 422, 423
Dicy 422, 424
Dorothy 179, 370
Edward 621
Eleanor 170, 372
Elizabeth 17, 22, 202, 353, 355, 451, 465, 486, 626, 662, 663, 679
Ellen 460
Ellen (Aunt) (?) 435
Ellender 362
Emily 711
Emma 469
Ephraim 459, 461
Ephriam 459, 461
Frances 354, 361, 362, 416
George 711
George Washington 708
Giles 713
Grace 422, 423
Harry 619

---, (cont.)
Henry 16
Hettie (Aunt) 695
Hetty 18, 52
Hut (Uncle) 442
Indy 266
Isabel 527
Isabella 337, 762
Jack 266, 459, 461
James 317, 708
Jane 330, 338, 416, 419, 434
Jane (Aunt) 764, 770
Jean 317, 677
Jemey 487
Jemima 459, 461
Jenny 619
Jeremiah 413
Jim 237
Jim (Uncle) 44
Jimmy 472
Joanne 236
Johanna 236, 547
John (?) 413
John 696
Jone 417
Judith 421, 429, 451, 457
Julia 674, 711
Julia A. 676
Leanna 488
Letty 459, 461
Lewis 422
Louisa 349
Lucy 237, 256
Lucy A. 351
Lue 708
Malinda 360
Mammy 767
Margaret 237, 360, 451, 457
Margery 686
Maria Jane 708
Marie 496, 508
Martha 711
Martha Ann 236, 359
Martha J. 360
Martha O. 67
Mary 73, 236, 238, 250, 259, 298, 525, 626, 662, 663
Mary A. 348
Mary Frances 696
Maude Lee 696
May 65, 227, 459, 461
Mayfield (?) 266
Mi--- 423
Mile 421, 422
Mill 423
Milley 422

---, (cont.)
Milly 423
Moll 459, 461
Mose 745
Nan 421, 422, 423
Nancy 16, 56, 73, 533
Nancy A. 354
Nann 459, 461
Nolly 421, 422
Notly 423, 424
Olive 333
Pearl 226
Phebe 668
Phill 422, 423
Posey (?) 693
Rebecca 17
Reuben 422
Reubin 423
Robert 711
Rosine 490
Ruth 16
St. Clair (?) 24
Sally 236, 237, 481
Sam (Uncle) 764
Sarah 35, 362, 465
Sarah R. 57
Sarelda 362
Sary 266
Scipio 98
Shelton 303
Sollomon 421, 422
Solomon 423
" Sudie " 307
Susane 626
Susanna 76
Tiller 422, 423
Tom 708
Tomy 302
Walter 317
Washington 237
Willem 547
William 395
Wils'e 634
Winnie 423
Winny 422
Winnie (" Old ") 424
Winny (" Old ") 421, 422
---len, John (Mr.) 423
---sings, --- 423
A., Richard 16
Abbey, Edwin A. (Mr.) 275
Abbott, Thomas 626
Accord, John 336
Acheson, Benedicta von Schilling 72
Marcus Wilson 72
Ackerman, Ralph 35
Acton, Billy 742
Mary A. M. 742

779

Acton, (cont.)
  Mary Jane 742
Ada 26, 27
Adair 116
  --- (Governor) 591
  Alexander 591
  Eliza 591
  Isabella 135-136, 136, 182
  Isabella McCalla 131
  John (General) 136, 182
Adam 216
Adams 679
  --- (Mrs.) 652
  Alexander 745
  Annie 40
  Betsy 419, 431
  David Hampton 679
  David Thomson 591
  Dolly 679
  Elizabeth 679
  Elizabeth --- 679
  Elizabeth Nancy 679
  Evelyn C. 647
  Evelyn Crady 637
  Evelyn Crady (Mrs.) 652
  Francis 679
  George Washington 745
  Ginney 745
  Hortense 130
  James 745
  Jane 679
  John 745, 770
  John, Jr. 679, 680
  John, Sr. 679
  Julia 591
  Lowry 679
  Lucinda 354
  Mary 36, 419, 679
  Mary E. 132, 222
  Mary Jane 679
  Matty 745
  Nancy 679
  Napier (Judge) 745
  Rebakah Willey 745
  Robert 591, 745
  Rosalie (Miss) 46
  Sally 745
  Sidney 679
  Traves 679
  Virginia 591
  Wm. 679
Addams 595
  A. (Mrs.) 187
  Abram 596
  Abram (Dr.) 596
  Mary Townsend 162
Addison, --- 276, 283
Adington Baron, ---
  (Lords of) 201
Adriensen, Jooste 554
Agin, William 131
Ahaz 683
Albertson, Lula F. 118
Alden, --- 263
Alderson, Anna 150
Aldgatha 26
Aleen, Jane 422
Aleshire 335
  Benedict 335, 336
  Catherine 335
  Elizabeth 336
  Jacob 336
Aleson 27
Alexander 679, 680, 681

Alexander, (cont,)
  --- 375
  --- (Mr.) 496
  A. J. 680
  Albert Lister 257
  Alice Seeley 681
  Andrew 402
  Andrew J. 375, 402, 680
  Andrew Jonathan 680
  Apoline 375
  Apolline 402, 680
  Charles 680
  Charles Williams 681
  E. J. 681
  Eliza 680
  Eliza Jane 680
  Emily 402
  Frances Agatha 680
  Geo. M. 402
  J. R. 681
  J. Regis 680, 681
  James Robert 680
  Jane 680
  John Campbell 681
  John R. 680
  John Regis 680
  Lister 257
  Lucille Laura Estelle 257
  M. F. 680
  Mariamne 680
  Marian F. 680, 681
  Marie Agatha Henriette Sophie 680
  Mary Ann 775
  Mira 680
  Myra 402
  Percy 257
  Robert 625, 680
  Robert Andrew 680
  Taliaferro 257
  Thomas Biddle 680
  William 680
Alford, --- (Dr.) 243
  Jennie 739
Alfred, Martha 236, 237, 242
  Patsy 241, 242
Allan, Algernon (Dr.) 566
  Algernon Sidney (Dr.) 565
  Elizabeth 691
Allen 228, 414
  --- (Aunt) (?) 437
  --- (Judge) 427, 435
  --- (Mr.) 414
  --- (Mrs.) 425
  Alfred W. 697
  Caroline Hobson 140
  Chas. 567
  David 420
  Dorothy Railey 140
  Eliza 657
  Elizabeth 644
  Frank S. 691
  Hannah 707
  Harriet Lowry 476
  Henry (Governor) 115
  Henry (Major) 425
  Henry T. 421
  Henry T. (Major) 426
  Henry T. (Major-

Allen, (cont.)
  General) 414
  Ira 19
  Isaac 657
  James 707
  James L. 736
  Jane 424, 426
  Jane Tandy 425
  John 87, 421, 422, 424, 425, 426, 653
  John (Col.) 685
  John (Judge) 421, 425, 427, 429
  John (Major) 425
  John (Mr.) 422
  Jos. (Dr.) 568
  Joseph 228
  Joseph (Dr.) 568
  Louisa 568
  Mary 414
  Mary Wright 659
  Philip 19, 53 (See also Philip Patton)
  Polly 466
  Richard 417, 420
  Sallie Jane 657
  Sally Jane 657
  Sally L. 19, 53
  Sara 653
  Sarah 568
  Shelby L. 140
  Shelby L., Jr. 140
  Tandy 437
  V. W. 573
  W. 629
  Will H. 95
  William Henderson 498
Allin, Tho. 237, 240
Allison, Minnie 149
Alsop, Benj. 493
  Benjamin 493
  Carrie 140
  James 493
Altsheler, Brent 236
Ambler, Mary Willis 108
Amos, Henry 699
Amott, John 424
Amsden, Jas. P. 752
  Laura E. Sanders Voorhies 752
Ancell, --- 264
  Samuel 265
Anderson, --- 118
  --- (Miss) 272, 400
  --- (Mr.) 194, 195, 196, 396, 583
  Albert G. 120
  Albert Gallatin (Dr.) 120, 122
  Alberta 119
  Ann 567
  Ann McPheeters 119
  Annie Yeatman 118
  Caroline McPheeters 118
  Cornelia Francis 118
  Cyrus 118
  David 117, 121
  David Thompson 120
  Edna Francis 118
  Edward Clifford, Jr. 222-223
  Edwin Lilbourne 118
  Elizabeth 119, 584, 588, 589
  Elizabeth Maria 120
  Fannie 120

Anderson, (cont.)
  Fannie Corrall 118
  Fannie Elizabeth 119
  Fanny 654
  Francis Elizabeth 119
  G. 514
  Henry T. (Rev.) 504
  James McPheeters 118
  Jane Randolph 119
  Jeff Randolph 197, 199
  Jefferson Randolph 204
  Jefferson Randolph (Mr.) 194, 195
  John 690
  Joseph Easton 120
  Joseph R. (General) 600
  Juliet Mitchell 118
  L. C. (Mrs.) 453
  Lelia 504, 515
  Lilbourne Morris 120, 122
  Lillian 120
  Lillian Belle 120
  Lola 301
  Lucile 118
  Lutie Garnett 120
  M. 653
  Margaret Thompson 118
  Martha 692
  Martine 120
  Mary 113, 567, 654
  Mary Alby 119, 122
  Mary Catharine 119
  Mary G. 120
  Nelson 584, 588
  Polly 18
  Rufus Easton 118, 121
  Rufus Easton, Jr. 118
  Russell Easton 118
  Russella Easton 118, 119
  Samuel 121
  Samuel Shepherd 119, 122
  Sarah Elizabeth 117
  Thomas 62, 121, 654
  Thos. (Col.) 653
  Thomas L. 121, 122
  Thos. L., Jr. 122
  Thos. L., Sr. 122
  Thomas Lilbourne 117
  Thomas Lilbourne, Jr. 118, 119
  Tuthill 118
  Walter 120, 122
  Walter A. 120
  William 202
  William Russell 118, 121, 122
  William Russell, Jr. 122
  William Russell, Jr. (Rev.) 118
Andrews, --- (Miss) 217
Andros, --- (Governor) 558
  Edward (Sir) 205
Angus, Archibald (Earl of) 27
Anstrother 365, 397
Anstruther 397
Anthony, Emmerson 479
Antle, Harriett 528
  Jacob 528

Antle, (cont.)
  Thomas 528
Apperperson, Richard (Capt.) 682
Apperson, --- (Miss) 32
  Ann 681
  Anne 682
Applegate, Elizabeth 157
Appleton, Hattie 221
  Mehitabel (Hattie) 221
Arbuckle, Matt 533
Archer, Adair Pleasants 133
  Edmund Minor 133
  Sheppard 133
  William Wharton 133
  William Wharton, Jr. 133
Ardery, Julia S. 258
  W. B. (Mrs.) 656
Ardis, --- 626
Arience, --- 554
  Anneken 550
Ariencesen, Jooste 554
Ariens, Anneken 549
Armistead, Anthony 586
  John (Col.) 212
  Patsy (Miss) 272
Armstrong 331, 332, 341, 714, 763
  --- 331
  --- (Doctor) 22
  Abel 331
  Ann 332
  Ann (Stuart) 331
  Bess Barr 698
  Elizabeth 334
  Elizabeth Taylor 142
  Jane 331
  John 331, 336
  John L. 714
  John Lapsley 714
  Mabel 696
  Mabel F. 696
  Mary 334
  Mollie Towles 696
  Nancy 334
  Polly 333, 334, 335
  Prudence 336
  Rawleigh D. 696
  Rawleigh D., Jr. 696
  Richard 331, 336
  Robert 331, 333, 334
  Rosanna 331
  Ruby D. 696
  Samuel 334
  Sarah 331
  Thomas 320, 331, 332, 333, 334, 342, 344
  William 331, 334
Arnold, Anna M. 301
  David 301
  John L. 301
  Lucy 301
  Maria (Tapp) 301
  Mary K. 301
  Randie E. 301
  W. E. 644, 652
  William A. 301
  William Clay 161
Arnoll, Jno. 422
Arnot, Hugo 225
  Lilas 225
Arran, --- (Countess of) 26

Ashburn, John 419
Ashby, --- (General) 411
  --- (Mr.) 410
  Ann 411, 498
  Elizabeth 411
  John 411
  Martha 411
  Mary (Tibbs) 451, 460
  Mary Wade 411
  Sarah 411
  Turner (Governor) 384
  William 384, 411, 460
  Wm. (Dr.) 411
Ashley, --- 406
  --- (General) 175, 406
  Thompson 406
  William H. (General) 175
Ashley Folville, --- (Knight of) 492
Ashmore, Charlotte 108, 111, 168, 175, 176, 203, 219, 385
  Samuel C. 535
  William E. 544
  William Edward 203
Ashurst, Jacob 510
Askins, Betsey 407
Asmead, I. 708
Atchison, Sarah 707
Athey, Reba 163
Atkinson, Elizabeth 516
  Rhoda 745
  Rubena 301
  Thomas 497
  Winnie 2, 3
Atwood, George F. 126
  Legrand 126
  Thomas C. 126
Austin, John B. 672
Avent, Edgar 577
  Elizabeth 577
Averill, Alice B. 103
  Christine 103
  Louise 103
  Marvin D. 103
  Mary Virginia 103
  Robert 103
  William 103
Avery, Mary Brand (Mrs.) 575
Awbrey, Dorothy 662
  Henry (Captain) 662
Axton, Anne (Miss) 727
  Isaac H. 730
  Isaac Harrison 728
  Lois Tracy 730
Ayers, Phil. E. 686
Ayres 750, 752, 755
  Ann Elizabeth 687
B., --- (Mrs.) 245
Babbage, Richard G. 77
Bacon 679, 681, 723
  --- 415
  Albert 682
  Albert Gallatin 681
  Alexander (Mrs.) 723
  Alexander B. 723
  Alice 681, 682
  Alice E. 682
  Alice M. A. 723
  Amanda 681, 682

781

Bacon, (cont.)
  Ann 681
  Anna 681, 682
  Anne 682
  Anne A. 681
  Anne Apperson 682
  Belle Talbot 33
  Benedict 681, 682
  Caroline M. 682
  Charles 682
  Charles P. 681, 682
  Edmond R. H. 723
  Edmund 681, 682, 723
  Eliza B. 723
  Elizabeth 681, 682
  Elizabeth (Mrs.) 683
  Elizabeth P. 681
  James 681, 682
  James Haggin Albert 682
  James W. 681, 682
  John 681, 682, 710, 723
  John M. 681, 682
  John Mosby 681
  John R. 723
  Langston 681, 682
  Laura 681
  Lyddall 681, 682
  Lyddall (Captain) 681, 682
  Maria 681
  Mary 723
  Mary D. 723
  R. R. 682
  Richard A. 681, 682
  Richard Apperson 681
  Richardson 723
  Romulus Riggs 682
  Sallie 32
  Sally W. 681
  Samuel 723
  Samuel A. 723
  Sarah Cordelia 681
  Sarah J. 682
  Sarah Ware (Miss) 681
  Sary Elizabeth 723
  Susan 681, 682
  Susan H. 723
  Virginia P. B. 723
  W. A. 33
  W. W. 681
  William A. 723
  Williamson 681, 682
  Williamson W. 681
Backhoven, Jennie Francis 132
Baer, Mabel Van Dyke 613
Bagby, John 591
Bailey 179
  ---- 71
  Alfred 228
  Elizabeth Belle 142
  John 21
  Landon Thomas 581
  Leola 301
  Loretta M. 124, 144
  Lucy Dupuy 161
  Sarah 180, 384, 404
Bainbridge, Eleanor 700, 701
  Eleanor James McIntosh 700
Baker, --- (Col.) 477
  E. D. (Col.) 477

Baker, (cont.)
  Isabelle Ball 228
  Jessie Gresham 228
  John Hopkins 228
  Mara Bracken (?) 3
  Mary 712
  Mary Elizabeth 36
  Rachel 77
  S. 304
  S. W. 36
  Sheridan, Jr. 36
Baldwin, --- 630
  William Edwin 68
Baliol, --- 757
  John 757
Ball, 406
  --- (Miss) 360
  Ann Figg 645
  Burgers (Col.) 388
  Charles (Lieut.) 652
  Charles (Mrs.) 645
  Esther 426
  Francis M. 132
  Francis M., Jr. 132
  James 360
  James Hilary 647
  Malinda (?) 360
  Robert (Lieut.) 652
  Susan Martha 72, 406
  Wm. (Capt.) 271
Ballantine, Frank S. (Rev.) 78
Ballard 146
  --- 35
  Addison C. 141
  Anna Belle 141
  Anna Lee 141
  Bland 711
  Camden Montague 140
  Camden Winlock 140, 141
  Caroline Varry 142
  Curtis Warren 142, 146
  Effie Winlock 141
  Elizabeth 142
  Elizabeth Armstrong 142
  Elizabeth M. 142
  Emma Louise 140
  Fielding Edward 140
  Fielding Montague 141
  Florence Effie 141
  Frances 589
  Gertrude 119
  John Allen 142
  John Norvil 142
  John Thomas 140
  Jonathon Young 141
  Joseph James 140, 141
  Joseph James, Jr. 141
  Lavinia 141
  Lavinia Harrison 141, 143
  Margaret 141
  Mary Peyton 141
  Nancy Peyton 141
  Nancy Winlock 141
  Susan Mary 141
  Victoria Reynolds 141
  William Jordan 142
Balli, --- 495, 749
Balling, Mary 110
Balmone 355
Balmore, --- (Mr.) 355
Baltimore, --- (Lord) 250, 255

Bancroft, --- 281, 762
Bane, --- (Mr.) 406
Banister, Augusta (Miss) 273
Bankhead, --- (Col.) 399
  Charles 221
  John 221
  Thomas M. R. 221
  William 221
Banks 180
  --- 568
  --- (General) 389
  Frances 404
  Frances (Mrs.) 404
  Francis 385, 404
  Francis Pannill 385
  Gerard 404
  Katherine 173, 216
  Thomas 456
Banton, --- 377
  --- (Mrs.) 377
  R. T. 377
Barbee, Frances 664
  Joseph 341
Barbour, --- (Mrs.) 97
  Fanny 411
  J. O. 143
  John (Dr.) 411
  Joseph (Judge) 96
  Joseph Railey 143
  Philip 411
  Thomas 411
  Thomas (Dr.) 384, 411
  William S. 104
Barclay, Sallie Goodloe 152, 154
Barefield 353
Barker 337, 340, 527
  --- 337
  --- (Mrs.) 340
  Elizabeth 340
  Isabella ? 340
  Isabella 337
  Shelby 303, 304
  Thomas 341
Barkley, 732
  A. 732
  Ella 732
  Lane 732
  Lizzie N. 732
  Nannie 732
  S. 732
  S. Moore 732
  Whitie 732
  William 732
Barksdale, --- (General) 611
  --- (Mr.) 611
  Nathaniel 612
  Peter 612
  Trabue 514
  William 514
  William H. 514
Barnes, Anna (Miss) 146
  Anna E. 143
  F. A. (Rev.) 106
  John 591
  Kate 649
  Mary 65
  Wood 643, 652
Barnett, Elizabeth 186
  Jane 532
  Joel 399
  Robert 658

Barr, --- 625
   James O. 511
   Juliet Maude 511
Barrows, Mary (Mrs.) 271
Barry, Mary 156
Bartholomew, St. 537
Bartlett, --- (Mrs. Dr.) 544
   Martin 499
   Theresa 477
Barton, --- (Mrs.) 765
   Beatricia 162
   David 603
Bascom, Edith Maude 163
Basey, Elizabeth 715
   John 240
Baskett, Cammilla 103
Bass, Robert A. 157
Bassett, Grace 31
Basye, Anna 715
   Edmond 451, 455, 456
   Edmond (Mrs.) 454
   Elizabeth 715
   Hannah 715
   Jane 715
   John 715
   Josias 487
   Logan 715
   Phoebe McCausland 80
   Polly 715
   Sarah Payne 57
   William 57, 62, 715
Bateman, Bonnie May 503
   Claude 503
   Dupuy 503
   Dupuy, Jr. 503
   John 503
   John W. 503
   Ralph 503
Bates, 114, 135
   --- (Miss) 178
   Edward 114
   Edward (Hon.) 178, 187, 188
   Fleming (Hon.) 114
   Frederick (Governor) 114, 178, 187, 188
   James Woodson (Gov.) 178
   James Woodson (Hon.) 115, 178, 187, 188
   John 200
   Susan Fleming 653
   Thomas Fleming 178, 187
Bathurst, Edward (Sir) 265
   Lancelot 265
   Mary 265
Batson, Mary 744
Battersby, Richard Stanley (Dr.) 122
Battersley, Richard Stanley (Dr.) 119
Batterton, --- (Mrs.) 49
   Fred (Mrs.) 49
   W. G. 31
   W. G. (Mrs.) 32
Battey, Henry Halsey (Dr.) 227
   Mary Sinclair 227
Batts, John 393
   John M. 379
   John Minor 396
Baughman, --- 22

Baumgartner, Jacob 338
Baxter, --- (Miss) 722
   --- (Mrs.) 278
   Martha Antoinette 290
   Martha (Mendenhall) 290
   Martha Mendenhall (Mrs.) 278, 293
   Wm. Edwards 294
Bayles, Mary Evaline 261
Bayless, Benjamin (Capt.) 631, 635
Bayley, Mary 84, 85
   Pearce 84
   Sarah 404
Baylor, Robert 431
Bayne, Howard R. 383
   Martha 184, 185
Baynham, Elizabeth 492
Bayse 714
   Hannah 714
   Polly 714
   William 714
Baysey, Edmond (Mrs.) 454
Beale, Byron Sunderland 172
   Carrie Marie 172
   Cornelius William 151, 172
   Earle Gordan 172
   Edna Elizabeth 172
   Ruth Burnley 151, 172
   William A. 151
   William Stuart 151, 172
Beall, Betsy Brooke 285
   Margaret 466
   Mary S. 708
   Ninian 466
   Patsy 285
   Rachel 466
   Robert M. 285
   Ruth 730, 731, 732
   Ruth (Miss) 688, 691, 706, 708, 727
Bealle, Brooke 286
   Robert 286
   Robert (Lieut.) 286
Bean, John R. 705
   John Smith 705
   Mary M. 705
   Minnie 705
Beasley, Mary C. (Vanarsdell) 722
   Robt. H. 722
Beattie 339, 340
   --- 339
   Francis 320, 339
   Jane 339
   Rosannah 339
Beatty, Eliza 591
   Margaret 746
   Martha Stuart 163
   Mary Stuart 167
   Thomas Stuart (Dr.) 167
Beauchamp, Isaac 625
Beaumont, Mary Gabriella (Randolph) 226
   Myron H. (Col.) 226
   Myron Holley 226
Beavers, Averill 501
   Herschel 501
   Lois 501
   William A. 501

Beazley, Ann 752
   Martha 752
   William 752
Beck, Eliza 728
   James B. (Hon.) 572
Beckley, --- 421, 425
Beckner, Jacob L. 695
   Lucien (Mr.) 695, 696
   Nancy 695
Bedford, 752
   Edwin 263
   Franklin 48
   H. Clay 48
   Henrietta 48
   Matt H. 48
   Samuel 48
Bedinger, John C. 36
   Mary Amanda 36
Beecher, Helen Louise 645
   Walter (Mrs.) 645
Beheler, Bettie 672
Belcher 346
   Phoebe 346
Belfied, T. H. (T. W. ?) 266
   T. W. ? 266
Belfield, T. W. 265
   Thomas Wright 265
Bell, --- 271, 331
   --- (Miss) 592
   Amarilla 223
   Ann 591
   Clement 280, 281
   Clement, Esq. 280
   Clement (Mrs.) 279
   David 700
   David (Dr.) 700
   Elizabeth 19, 575
   Elizabeth (Weir) 591
   Francis C. 575
   J. Franklin (Gen.) 568
   James 331
   Jefferson 591
   John 568, 591
   Judith (Thomson) 591
   Lavinia S. 739
   Mary Shepherd 708
   Othy 708
   R. A. 575
   Robert 591
   Samuel 591
   Sarah 85
   Sarah F. 575
   Sidney Sayre 102
   Thomas 591
   Thomson 591
Bellfield, Nancy 465
Bellmore 355
Bellomy 355
Belvoir, --- (Baron of) 660
Bennett 609
   --- 609
   --- (Judge) 608
   --- (Mr.) 640
   Ambrose Lee 609
   Caddie 609, 611, 612
   Caswell (Judge) 608, 609
   Dick 611
   Dick (Major) 609
   Elizabeth 159
   Fayette 611

Bennett, (cont.)
　John 417
　Richard (Major) 609
　Sherwood 470
Bent, --- 606
Bentheim, Otto (Count
　of) 547
Benton, Angelyn 515
　Mortimer Murray
　　(Rev.) 515
　William Terry 515
Bergen, --- 554
Berkeley, Anne 218
　Edmund (Col.) 218
　Edmund, Jr. 218
　William 217
　William (Governor
　　Sir) 415
Berkley, --- 609
　Muriel 492
　Thomas (Lord) 492
　William 454
Bernard, Anna 574
　Anne Corderay 574
　Richard 574
Berry, Alice 751
　Alice Elizabeth 511,
　　520
　Anna 532
　Bessie 140
　Edmund Taylor 511,
　　520
　Elizabeth 372
　James 533
　John 338
　Margaret 372
　Mary Norris 163, 167
　Milton 672
　Robert Mallory (Rear
　　Admiral) 511
　Washington 520
　William (Surgeon)
　　511
Berryman, Annie 103
　Barbour 104
　Bessie 103
　Buford 104
　Cary M. 103
　Church 103
　Claude 103
　Clifford 103
　Cornelia 103
　Edw. H. 104
　Emma Woodson 103
　Francis 592
　Frank P. 105
　Frank P., Jr. 105
　George Railey 104,
　　107
　Hervey 103
　James Sthreshley 102
　James T. 102, 103
　Jane 107
　Jane Railey 104
　John 101, 105, 107
　John W. 102
　Julia 104
　Kate 105
　Kate Theresa 102
　Lela 104
　Mary A. 103
　Mary Elizabeth 101
　Mary Virginia 104
　Mattie 104
　Mattie Woodson 104
　Mollie 103
　Newton 105

Berryman, (cont.)
　Price 102
　Robert 104
　Robt. H. 103
　Robert Handy 103
　Robert S. 102
　Sarah A. 33
　Sidney Robertson 105
　Stuart Robinson 103
　Sue M. 103
　Theresa Willis 102
　Theresa Woodson 104
　Walter 104
　Wilhelmina 105, 125
　Willis N. 104
Betersworth, Alen O. H.
　Jerry ? 693
　Almorium ? 693
　Argalus 693
　Argalus Jefferson 693
　Armerie 693
　Arominto Coly 693
　Pasy ? 693
　Posey --- ? 693
　William 693
Bethea, Daisey Margaret
　536
　Richard W. 536
　Robert Cochran (Dr.)
　　536
Bethel, Carlyle 68
　Gracey Hobbs Luckett
　　68
Bethoe 26
Bettersworth, Adonis 693
　Ann Flo 693
　Arthur W. 693
　W. 693
　Wiliam 693
　William 693
Betts, Albert Raymond 118
　Albert Raymond, Jr.
　　118
　Thos. Jeffries
　　(Capt.) 224
Bevan Asperen, ---
　(Earl of) 547
Beverley, Elizabeth 216,
　232
　Lucy 231
　Maria 231
　Peter 232
　Peter (Colonel) 216
　Susanna 232
Beverly, --- (Miss)
　183
　Elizabeth (Miss)
　　108
　Harry 431
Bibb, 590, 682
　--- 684
　--- (Mrs.) 684, 685
　Ann 590, 754
　Benjamin 590, 754
　Burnley 684
　Charles 590
　Charles Scott 684,
　　685
　David 590
　Edward Booker 683,
　　684
　Edward C. 683, 684
　Eliza 683
　Elizabeth 590, 684
　Eugene B. 683, 684
　Fleming 673
　G. R. (Dr.) 683

Bibb, (cont.)
　George 685
　George Burnley Breck-
　　enridge 685
　George M. 683, 684,
　　685
　George M. (Judge)
　　377
　George N. 685
　George Nehemiah 685
　Harriet Critenden 685
　Harriet Crittenden
　　685
　Helen 410, 411
　Henry 590, 754
　James 683, 684
　John 590, 683, 684
　John B. 683, 684
　John H. 410
　John M. 411
　Joseph H. T. 685
　Kate 410, 411
　Lucy 683, 684
　Lucy B. 683
　Lucy Booker 683
　M. S. 685
　Martha T. 684
　Martha Tabb 684
　Mary 683
　Mary Ann 683, 684
　Mary E. 685
　Mary E. T. 685
　Mary S. 685
　Mary Scott 684, 685
　Patsy 685
　Patsy (Miss) 684
　Pendleton 410, 411
　R. 683
　R., Jr. 683, 684
　R., Sr. 684
　Rd. 684
　Richard 679, 683, 684,
　　685
　Richd., Jr. 683, 684
　Richard, Sr. 682, 683,
　　684
　Robert Crittenden 685
　Robert Fleming 590
　Rr., Sr. 684
　Sarah P. 684
　Scott 685
　Susa. Eliza 683
　Susanna 683
　Susanna Elizabeth 683
　T. P. A. 684, 685
　T. P. Aticus 685
　T. P. Atticus 679, 684
　Thomas 590, 683, 684
　Titus Pomponius Atti-
　　cus 684
　William 683
Bibbs, Mary Maslin 516
Bickley, Matilda 527
　William (Sir) 527
Bierley, Elizabeth Ada-
　line (Miss) 315
Big Corn 765
Bigbee, Geo. 407
Biggarstaff, Elizabeth
　163
Bigger, William, Sr. 683
Biggs, Freda 536
Bigod, Hugh 660
　Roger 660
Binford, F. (Mr.) 603
Bingaman, Lucy Ann 306
Bird, Elizabeth 417

784

Bird, (cont.)
 John 417
Birke, --- (Mr.) 411
Birney, David B. (General) 375
 James G. 375
 Jas. G., Jr. (Col.) 375
 Julia 247
 Julia (Miss) 247
 Wm. M. (General) 375
Bixenstein, Myrna 676
Black, 772
 --- 320
 Alexander 761
 Benjamine Wyly 155
 Charles Railey 155
 Christian 746
 Dorcas 320, 327
 Elizabeth 746, 772
 Francis 592
 Janet 746
 Joseph 746, 772
 Katurah 327
 Mathew 746
 Mayo Walton 155
 Samuel 320, 327
 Samuel (Rev.) 320, 327
 W. W. (Dr.) 155, 165
 Wiliam 16
 William 16
 " Black Agnes of Dunbar " 214
Blackburn, 738
 --- (Miss) 248
 B. F. 739
 Ben 769
 Breckenridge Flournoy 740
 C. H. 739
 Cary Bell 740
 Churchill 594
 Churchill Horace 740
 E. M. 739
 E. M., Jr. 739
 Edward Lewis 740, 741
 Edward Mitchell 740
 Elizabeth Jane 740
 Em 741
 Em E. 741
 Eugenia 738
 Frances Ann 739, 740
 George E. 739, 741
 Granville 159
 Henry 739
 Henry Berry 740
 J. C. S. (Hon.) 572
 James 739, 741
 James Weir 740
 Jennie 741
 Joel C. Stiles 740
 John Bell 739, 740
 John S. 223
 Joseph C. S. 739
 Joseph Morris 740
 Lavinia Bell 740
 Luke P. 739
 Luke P. (Gov.) 139
 Luke Pryor (Dr.) 738
 Margaret Trotter 761
 Mary P. 739
 Mary Prudence 740
 Prudence 740

Blackburn, (cont.)
 Sammy 741
 Samuel E. 740
 William E. 739, 740, 741
 William Edwin 740
Blackerby, Lunonta Battaille 152
Blackfish 235
Blackwell, --- 45
 Eran 51
 Mary 108, 112, 167
 Mary W. 162, 167
 R. P. 625
Blair 179, 366
 --- 71
 --- (General) 375
 --- (President) 274
 Andrew 402
 Cary M. 402
 Christine 402
 Colbert Powell 70
 Elizabeth Hill 70
 Frances P. 402
 Francis P. 402, 606
 Frank P. (General) 375
 Geo. M. 402
 Gladys 126, 572
 James 402, 560
 Lucinda Montgomery 70
 Martha 70
 Mary (Miss) 400
 Molly Morgan 71
 Sarah 376, 400
 Sarah (Miss) 400
 Thomas Johnston 70
Blake, George 626
Blakemore, 146
 Annabine 143
 Edmonia 141, 143
 Edna C. 142
 Effie Carrie 141, 143
 Fielding Winlock 141, 143
 George Robert 141, 143
 George Robert, Jr. 141, 143
 Henrietta 142
 James Marcus 142
 Joseph William 142
 Robert Emmet 142
 Robert Emmet, Jr. 142, 143
 Thomas Ballard 141, 143
 Thomas S. 142
 Virginia Hill 143
 William Thomas 142
Blanchan, Cathrine 558
Blanchard, Robert 287
Bland 184
 --- (Miss) 183
 --- (Mrs.) 592
 E. U. 517
 Ewing 181
 Frances 231
 Mary 112, 184, 201, 234
 Richard 112, 184, 201, 216, 234
 Richard (Hon.) 181
 Richard, Jr. 234
 " Silver Dick " 181, 592
 Theodore (Colonel)

Bland, (cont.)
 272
 Theoderic 234
 Theoderic (Col.) 231
 Theoderick 112
 Theodoric 265
 Theodoric (Colonel) 265
Blankenship, Arminta 356
 Caroline 147
 F. C. 147
 Ferdie C. 147
 Richard 347
Blanton 754
 B. H. 682
 Elizabeth (Miss) 439
 James W. Bacon 682
 Thomas 591
 Willis 710
Bledso, Moses 422
Bledsoe 434, 439
 --- 438, 439
 Abraham 439
 Dulcena M. 434
 Hannah 453, 462
 Hiram 428
 Hiram (Col.) 428
 Isaac 439
 Jacob 439
 James 438, 439
 Jessie 435
 Jesse I. 430, 431
 Jesse J. 434
 John 439=
 Joseph 439
 Joseph (Judge) 428
 Judith (Ward) 438
 Lucy Jameson (Mrs.) 434
 Lucy Virginia 434
 Margaret 428
 Moses 421, 430, 434, 435
 Moses (Rev.) 431, 434
 Pamela Audress 434
 Sallie B. (Tandy) 431
 Sally 424, 438
 Sally B. 422
 William 439, 453, 462
Blincoe, Jeffrey (Sir)= 601
 Martha Jones 600
 Mary 600
 Sampson 600, 601
 Thomas 601
Blinshall, James 674
Blythe, --- 328
 --- (Mr.) 327
 James 328
Boblett, V. (Mrs.) 642
Bodie, John 370
Bodley, Mary Bartholomew 278
 Thomas (General) 278
Boggess, Earle Montrose 163
 Richard Oates 163
Boggs, Lewis A. 590
Bohannon, Susan 271
Bohon,715
 Cora (Miss) 714, 715
 Elizabeth 715
 Garret 715
 Garrett 715
 Harriet Ann 722

785

Bohon, (cont.)
  John A. 715
  Martha A. 715
  Martha Ann 715
  Mary R. 715
  Sarah Jane 715
  William L. 715
Boler, Wm. 625
Bolin, --- (Mr.) 428
  Catherine 185
Bolling, --- 231
  Archibald 231
  Jane 183, 230
  John 230
  John (Col.) 229
  Lucy 217
  Mary 191, 200
  Mary (Kennon) 230
  Robert 217
  William 231
Bonaparte, Jerome 639
  Napoleon 639
Bonnell, --- 578
Booker, James 146
  Lucy 683
Boon, Matilda Wilson (?) 711
  Nancy 711
  William 711
Boone 186, 274, 523, 686
  --- 279, 290, 763
  --- (Col.) 92
  Daniel 235, 236, 258, 468, 511, 523, 649, 686
  Daniel (Lieutenant) 91, 93
  Elizabeth 686
  George 286, 523
  Lucy 523
  Mary 523
  Miriam 286
  Sarah 686
  Squire 686
Bootelingh, A. 633
Boquet, --- 760, 761
  --- (Colonel) 760
Boquette, --- (General) 760
Borden, 340
  --- 320, 322, 331
  Benjamin 320
  Benjamin, Jr. 323, 331
  Benjamin, Sr. 320, 323, 331
Bostwick, --- (Mr.) 406
Boswell, William Elliott (Col.) 481
  William Elliott (Major General) 481
Bosworth, Ella 739
  Ellen 254
  Sarah E. 254
Bottom, 716
  Farris 716
  Mary 716
  Polly 716
  W. 716
Botts, John Minor 396
Boucher, William F. 615
Boude, Annie 85
  Benjamin 85
  Devall 85
  Eliza 85
  Hannah 85
  Henry 85
  Jack 85

Boude, (cont.)
  James 84, 85
  John 85
  Letitia 85
  Samuel 84, 85
  Susan 85
Boulden, Sallie 159
Boulware, Ritchie 748, 752
  Wm. (?) 625
Bountiful, --- (Lady) 246
Bouquet, --- 767
  --- (General) 321
Bourne, J. M. 412
  Sally 21
Boutwell, Mary 398
Bowen, Adaline 527
Bowles, Alfred 120
  Herbert 676
  Katharine 120
Bowman, --- 58, 626
  --- (Mr.) 359
  Elizabeth 126
  Lilburn Edward 151
  Lucy Railey 151
  Thomas 151
Bowmar, --- 241
  --- (Mr.) 139
  Catharine Hunter 160
  Charlotte Thornton 159
  Daniel M., Sr. 138, 139
  Elizabeth 160
  Fannie Adams 159
  Herman 159
  Joseph Marshall 159
Bowyer, 374, 402
  --- (Col.) 398
Boyd, Alice Webster 71
  Bessie 68
  Charles Mayo 155
  Fannie 676
  Frederick W. (Rev.) 155, 165
  Frederick William 155
  James Railey 155
  John 68, 676
  John (Rev.) 71
  Katherine Patterson 155
  Loyd Tilghman 155, 165
  Marie 68
  Mary Railey 155
  Mollie 673, 676
  Sallie Anna Shipton 71
  Walter Stuart 155
  William 674, 676
Boyde, Corinne 517
Boyle, Amanda M. 709
  Frances Eliza 710
  J. F. 585
  John F. 709
  John Francis 709
  John N. 585, 709, 710
  John Neagle 585
  M. N. 709
  Mary Eliza 709, 710
  Rebecca 744
Boynton, Grace 163
Bracken, Mary 2, 3
Braddock, --- 6, 321, 418, 763
Bradford 452, 460

Bradford, (cont.)
  --- 475
  Anna 452
  Fielding 615
  Hannah 451, 452, 453, 458, 459, 460
  James M. 475
  John 452, 458, 460
  John (Mr.) 421, 423
  Mary 458
  Mary Belle 164
  Mary (Marr) 458
  Sarah 451, 458, 459, 460
  Simon 622
Bradle, Alice 492
  Wm. 492
Bradley, --- (Miss) 761, 776
  Katherine (Miss) 771
Bradshaw, --- 45, 271, 330
  --- (Mrs.) 330
  John 330
  Mary E. 707
Brag, --- 302
Bragg, R. 568
Branch, Martha 194
  R. G. 655
Brand, Abram Owen 72
  Abram Owen, Jr. 73
Branham, Edward 499
  Eliza Stuart 355
  Elizabeth 355
  Elvira 355
  John 355
  Joseph 355
  Laura A. 355
  Martha 355
  Palina 355
  Rebecca 355
  Riley 355
  Wiley 355
  William 355
Brannan, Daniel 498
Bratton, 330, 340, 345
  --- 330
  Adam 330, 345
  Ann 330
  Robert 330
Breathitt, --- (Governor) 751
  Harvie Whitlock 400
  James 376, 400
Breck, Daniel (Judge) 325
Breckenridge, Cabell 576
  Clifton 576
  Frances 576
  John Owen 576
  Mary 576
Breckinridge 290
  --- 13, 286
  --- (Dr.) 582
  C. R. 40
  Catherine Carson 40
  Clifton Rodes 40
  John C. 571
  John C. (General) 576
  Martha 290
  Robert J. (Rev.) 582
Breight, Constance 676
Brent, Hannah 84
Bridges, --- 538

786

Bridges, (cont.)
  Eliza (Ellis) 336
  Elizabeth 336
  John 336
  John L. 297, 298
Bridwell, Margaret M. 622
Briggs, --- (Dr.) 407
  James McDonald 108
  Mollie 130
Bright, --- (Senator) 285
  Augusta 513
  George Moore 285
  Horatio 513
  Jesse D. (Senator) 285
  Judith 68
  Michael Graham 285
Brightwell, William 625
Brinegar, 679
  George 710, 711
  George B. 711
  Matilda 710, 711
  Matilda Boone 710
Brinker, Mary Coleman 499
  Morton 499
Brinkley, --- 627
Brinley, Mary Frothingham 79
Britt, Amelia Hughes (Mrs.) 35
  G. W. Hughes 36
  William H. 36
Brittenham, Lucy 629
Britton, Effie 753
  Henry 243
Broaddus, John (Major- U.S.A.) 254
  Martha 254
  William (Major) 270
Broadhurst, Cyrus N. (Rev.) 157
  Cyrus N., Jr. 157
Broadnax, William 599
Broadwell, Stuart 479
Brocade, --- 767
Brock, --- 230
  --- (Dr.) 269
  --- (Mr.) 602
  R. A. (Dr.) 267
Brockenborough, John (Dr.) 221
Brockenbrough, --- (Dr.) 376, 377, 395, 399
  Gabriella 400
  John 400
  John (Dr.) 377
  Mary 400
Brockman, Elizabeth 432
  Frances N. 432
  Samuel 432
  William E. 29
  William Evart 25
  William L. 432
Brodhead, Daniel 663
Brodnax, Austina 273
  John Slaughter 273
  Mary 273
  Robert Withers 273
Broerson, Jan 556
Brokaw, Dura 148
Brokenbrough, John (Dr.) 395
Bromfield, Madison 354
Bronaugh, Anna 697
  John 301

Bronaugh, (cont.)
  Wm. (Col.) 391
Bronston, --- (Mr.) 37
  Charles J. 37
  Charley 37
  Sallie A. 37
  Susie Hughes 37
  Thomas S. 37
Brooke, Dunbar 402
  Frances 662
  John 115
Brooks, Eliza Jane 680
  Elizabeth 680
  James A. 689
Browder, George Tingley 529
Brower, Marie Leslie 163
Browing, Robert Vincent 119
Brown 349, 476
  --- 192
  --- (Col.) 1
  --- (Dr.) 763, 767
  --- (General) 383
  --- (Miss) 410
  --- (Mr.) 166
  --- (Mrs.) 166
  Adelaide C. 686, 687
  Agnes Steele 156
  Alexander 453
  Anderson 625, 628
  Ann (Cannon) 687
  Barbara Lucretia 647
  Belle Manning 607
  Carolyn Allen 478
  Catharine Louise 156
  Catherine Cox 645
  Charles 647
  Charles C. 645
  Charles Rowland 156
  Charlie Wood 645, 652
  Charlotte Hudson 607
  Christopher 477
  Christopher C. 326
  Clementine 162
  Cora Johnson 648
  Daniel 349, 410, 477
  Daniel Calvin 476
  David 477
  David Allen 475, 476, 477
  David Allen (Mrs.) 474, 475
  Dorothy Allen 477
  Dorothy Thornton 156
  Duane 752
  Edwards 479
  Eliza 475, 477
  Eliza Jane 479
  Eliza Smith 477
  Elizabeth 349, 645, 647
  Fannie 647
  Fannie Cox 648
  Francis (Mr.) 488
  Frank J. (Mrs.) 643
  George 647
  George Adams 156
  George Washington 648
  Hannah 476
  Harriet Jane 477
  Harriet Lowry 477
  Helen Gordon 162
  Helen Margaret 156
  Isabel 476, 644
  James 476, 686, 687
  James (Capt.) 764

Brown, (cont.)
  James Isaac 648
  James U. 726
  James William 687
  Jay Taylor 478
  Joel B. 479
  John 476, 647, 648
  John (Capt.) 333, 764
  John (Mr.) 767
  John (Rev.) 320, 763
  John Howe 476
  John Mason (Col.) 387
  Joseph 33
  Laura Loretta 647
  Malachi Styron 648
  Marcia 648
  Martha Jane 648
  Mary 575, 648
  Mary Catherine 647
  Mary Elizabeth 478
  (Mary) Matilda 349
  Matilda 349
  Matthew 476
  Nathaniel 456
  Norton Jonathan 648
  R. Alexander 156
  Robert Alexander 156
  Robert G. 503
  Sadie 530
  Sallie 648
  Sallie C. 482
  Sallie Clara 477
  Samuel 622, 763
  Samuel (Rev.) 763, 767
  Sandy 156, 166
  Sarah Elizabeth 120
  Thornton Lee 156
  Washington 648
  William 192, 568
  William (Rev.) 474
  William Bartlett 476, 477
  William H. 479
  William Joseph 477
  William M. 474
  Wm. Warren 607
Browne, Nell 575
Brownfield, Erma Catherine Cabell (Mrs.) 687
Browning, 179
  Betsey 410
  Cassia 409, 410
  Charles 382, 384, 405, 408, 409, 410, 411
  Charles E. 384
  Elizabeth 405, 409, 410
  Fanny 410
  Francis 409, 410
  Genevieve Elizabeth 119
  George 410
  James 410
  John 409, 410, 411
  John (Capt.) 382
  Joseph 409, 410
  Lafayette 406
  Lee Tatlow 119
  Lloyd 410
  Loyd 409
  Lucy 409, 410
  Mary 405
  Mary Ann Pendleton 384

Browning, (cont.)
  Mary Ann Pendleton,
    (cont.) 409-410
  Milly 410
  Molly 410, 411
  Nancy 409, 410
  Polly 409, 410
  Sally 409, 410
  Sarah ? 534
  Shadrach 410
  Wm. 409, 410
  Willis 409, 410
  Wylie Morrison 119
Bruce, --- 757
  Charles 384, 404
  Lavinia 394, 408
  Mary 202, 223
  Robert 202, 214, 757
Bruehl, Robert 34
  W. A. R. 34
Bruen, John 82
  Rebecca 82
Brumbaugh, --- 772
Brumleigh, Annie 577
Brun, M. W. 125
  Mary Woodson 125
Bryan, --- (Miss) 577
  B. H. 681
  Elizabeth 682
  Elizabeth Bacon 682
  Howard 682
  Sarah 529
Bryant, --- 427
  Mary 739
  Sallie 698
  Sarah 534
Buchanan, Andrew 745
  Andrew (Major) 523
  Edward 745
  James 745
  Jane 745
  Jean 745
  John 320, 338, 745
  John (Col.) 62
  John Hamilton 745
  Josiah 745
  Margaret 62
  Margit 745
  Mary 718, 745
  Mary A. 745
  Mary Jamison 745
  Robert 745
  Samuel 326
  William 745
  William H. 745
Buck, Charles 251
  John 251
  Thomas 251
Buckner, 687
  --- 411
  --- (Miss) 411
  --- (Mr.) 676
  Aylette (Judge) 411
  Aylette Harvey
    (Judge) 384
  Bailey 384
  Baly (Mr.) 411
  Calhoun 411
  Harriet 687
  John 411
  Richard 411
  Sam (Dr.) 411
Buckridge, B. S. 130
  Carolyne 130
  Mary Elizabeth 130
Buffington 359
  Martha Ann (?) 359

Buffington, (cont.)
  P. C. 359
Buford, --- (Mr.) 700
  Abram (Col.) 357
  Le Grand 470
  Wm. 700
  William R. (Mr.) 700
Bukley, Rhoda 644
Bulbert, --- 91
Bulkley, Sarah 132, 136
Bull, --- (Miss) 392, 403
  John C. 84
  Mariah 536
Bullard, William 581
Bullitt, Irene (Smith)
    (Mrs.) 577
Bullock, Annie 575
  Desha 575
  Elizabeth 121, 575
  Elizabeth Randolph 120, 122
  Jane Railey 117, 121
  John 272
  John (Captain) 122
  John, Jr. (Capt.) 117, 121
  John Rodes 575
  Lydia 575
  Maria 100, 107
  Maria B. 575
  Maria Patterson 120, 122
  Thomas W. 575
  Waller 575
Bunch, Aleatha 738
  Rodes 738
Buntin, Mary 235
Bunton, Mary 243
Burbridge, Sarah 688
  Thomas 688
Burch, Anna 576
  Carr 577
  Clifton Rodes 576
  George 576, 577
  George V. 576
  Isabella P. (?) 739
  James 576, 577
  John 577
  Malvina 576
  Marion 576, 577
  Martha 576, 577
  Mary 576, 577
  Mary Cyrene 576
  Milton 576
  Sallie 576
  Sarah 576
  Susannah 526
  William 576, 577
Burchfield, Elizabeth 629
Burdell, --- (Mr.) 643
Burden, Benjamin 60
Burgess, 357
  --- 357
  --- (Miss) 359
  Edward 352, 357
  Edward, Sr. 357
  George 357
  George R. 357
  Geo. Raymond (Mrs.) 76
  Gordon 357
  John 357
  Mary Jane 683
  Nancy 357, 359
  Nancy Ann 357

Burgess, (cont.)
  Reuben 357
  Strother 357
  William 357
Burgin, Sallie Johnson
    (Mrs.) 688
Burk, --- 539
Burke, --- 267, 369
  John 221
Burks, Lucy Jane 151, 153
Burnam, Robert R. (Mrs.) 705
Burnett, Gilbert 168
  John Calhoun 168, 182
  John Calhoun (Mrs.) 112
  Marie 102
  Theodore L. 168
Burney, Anna Railey 106
  Harriet 105
  Margaret 105
  P. H. (Rev.) 105
  Philo 105
Burnley, --- (Mrs.) 685
  Cornelia 151, 154
  Frances Ann 684
Burns, Martha (Guyther)
    (Mrs.) 602
Burr, A. D. V. 600
Burris, Jane 418
  Sarah Ann 521
  Sarah Ann (Miss) 521
  Thomas 416, 418, 521, 522
Burrus, Ann 690
  Sarah Ann (Miss) 521
  Thomas 521
Burton, --- 243
  Mary 412
Burwell, Lewis 218
  Lucy 229
  Nathanael (Col.) 229
  Nathaniel 233
Bush, --- 673
  Archie 673
  Armine 673
  Catherine --- 673
  Charles 673
  George 673
  Isaac 673
  Jane 673
  Josiah 673
  Peter 673
  Philip 431
  Rebecca 673
  Walter 673
  William 422, 424, 673
Bustard, --- (Mr.) 339
Buster, --- (Mr.) 339
  Claudius 338
  John 3
  Mattie 2
Butcher, Hannah 488
  Thomas 488
  William 487, 488
Bute, --- (Countess of) 26
  --- (Earl of) 317, 321
  --- (Lord of) 317, 319
  John Stuart 317
Butler, --- 63
  O. E. (Col.) 377
Button, Jane H. 673
Byram, Augustus 696
  Valentine 696

788

Byrd, --- 321
   --- (Col.) 321
   William 560
Byrom, Henry 415
Byron, --- (Lord) 622
Cabell 210, 229, 420, 431, 453, 687
   --- (Mrs.) 599
   Ann 230
   Anne 112, 182
   Frank (Prof.) 687
   John 687
   Joseph (Col.) 112, 182
   Robert Henry (Dr.) 117
   Thomas J. 687
Cable, Lucy Reed 464
   Mary 475
   Philander L. 464
   William 591
Caesar 202
Caldwell 505
   Ann Eliza 513
   Ann Jane 513
   Augusta 513
   Catherine 514
   David 260
   Elizabeth 51
   Elizabeth Haskins 513, 517
   George Alfred 500, 513, 514
   George Danforth (Capt.) 513
   Isaac 513, 514
   Isaac Palmer 514
   James Guthrie 513
   James Guthrie (First Lieut.) 513
   John 260
   John P. (Corp) 513
   Julia 513
   Junius 513
   Junius (Serg.) 513
   L. 676
   Margaret 260, 514
   Margaret (Phillips) 260
   Mary 514
   Mary Phoebe 513
   Nancy 513
   Phoebe Lucretia 513
   Robin Adair 514
   William 500, 513, 514
   William B. 500
   William Beverly (M. D.) 513
Calendar, Margaretta 72
Calhoun, --- 376
   Charlotte 739
   Lennie (Adams) 591
Calkrell, F. M. 775
Call, Elizabeth 328
   Hamilton 328
Callahan, Charles 328
   Mary 328
Callaway, --- (Col.) 92
   John 2
   Richard 533
Calloway, --- 241
   Elijah 241
   Keziah 468
   Kizzie 468
   Richard (Col.) 468
Calmes, (See also De La Calmes)

Calmes, (cont.)
   Isabel 251
Caltavoturo, --- (Count de) 225
Calvert, Balls 409
   Betsy 409
   Edward 409
   George 382, 409
   Jerry 409
   John S. 409
   Kitty 409
   Lidia 409
   Lucy 409
   Nancy 409
   Ralls 409
Calvin, --- 540
Cameron, --- 578
   --- (Rev. Mr.) 277
   Archibald (Rev.) 292, 293
   Brodnax 273
   Emeline 705
   Gabrielle 273
   George 273
   Helen 273
   James 578
   Nancy 578
   Polly 578
Camm, John (Captain) 431
Campbell (See also Compbell) 278, 336, 586, 766
   --- 60
   --- (Mr.) 349
   --- (Mrs.) 569
   Alexander 2, 336
   Arthur (Dr.) 622
   Elizabeth (Henry) 582
   George (Sir) 28
   Helen 158
   Jane (Miss) 84
   John 762
   Justine Tandy (Mrs.) 435
   Lemira Ann 34
   Margaret 28
   Marion Francis 680
   Mary 46, 47, 402, 529
   Nancy 347
   Orpha 565, 566
   Rachel 33
   Roderick John 757
   Sarah 581
   Whitaker Hill 566
   William (General) 582
Camus 202
Cannon, 679, 686, 687
   --- (Mrs.) 689
   Ann 686, 687
   Betsy 686
   Burton, Jr. 686
   Catherine B. 687
   Elijah 686
   J. T. 686
   Jno. 653
   John H. 686, 687
   John W. 686, 687
   Jouett Taylor 682
   Jouett Taylor (Mrs.) 681, 684, 686, 688, 690, 710, 723
   Joseph 686, 687
   Louisa Lucretia 686, 687

Cannon, (cont.)
   Mary 686
   Mary G. 686
   William 654, 686, 687
   William Lindsey 686
Cant, David (Major) 493
Canterberry, America 358
   Eleanor 363
   Henry 364
   John 358, 364
   Ralph 364
   Reuben 358
Caperton, --- (Miss) 392, 403
   --- (Senator) 403
Capet, Hugh 201, 660
Car, --- (Mr.) 420
Carden, 687
   Anna 687
Cardwell, Mary 714
   Mary S. 581
Carey, Jane 109
   M. 700, 718
   Mathew 681
   Matthew 724
Carle, Mary 711
   Mercy 711
Carley, Grace 75
Carlile, Agnas 716
   Elizabeth 716
   James 716
   Jane 716
   John 331, 716
   Letha (Loaf Sugar Lump) 717
   Margaret (--- Wanless) 331
   Mary 331, 716
   Robert 716
   Samuel 716
Carlisle, 716
   John 716
   John G. 717
   Letha (Loaf Sugar Lump) 717
   Mary S. 132
Carlton, James S. 687
   Louisa Lucretia 687
Carlyle, 763
Carmichael, Elizabeth 27
Carnegie, --- 65
Caro, Carso S. 225
Carpenter, 716
   Conrad 716
   George Alfred 716
   Henry W. 716
   Jacob 716
   John H. 716
   Josephine 716
   Lilard 716
   Louisa 716
   M.--- 716
   Mary E. 716
   Nancy 716
   Nannie 572
   Sarah A. 716
   William F. 716
Carr, --- (Miss) 409
   Ann 280
   Barbara 420
   Dabney 229
   Edward 625
   Elizabeth Ann 261
   John 420
   W. C. (Mrs.) 717

Carrick, --- (Earl) of
  214
  John 322
Carrington, Mary 654
Carroll, Augusta
  (Smith) 479
  Charles Van Bergen
    479
  Edith Lyle 479
  Lucinda 462
  Minnie 105
Carson, --- 606
  Kit 606
  Patsy 303
Cart, John 560
Carter, 599
  --- (Colonel) 395
  --- (Counselor) 486
  --- (" King ") 230
  --- (Miss) 272
  Agnes 259
  Anne 184
  Cal 371
  Calvery 359
  Calvin 359
  Charles 217, 218
  Colbury 359
  Eliza J. 359
  Elizabeth 217
  Jewell 691, 692
  John 221
  John H. 359
  Lucile 691
  Macie 147
  Mary E. 359
  Maud 691, 692
  Minnie 132
  Octavia 359
  Robert 459, 560, 561
  S. H. 692
  Sarah 222
Carteret, Philip (Governor) 556
Carthral, John 399
  Mary 399
Cartmell 329, 331, 340
  --- 60, 330, 331, 333,
    337
  Andrew 331
  Elizabeth 331, 333
  Henry 331, 333
  John 329, 331, 345
  Samuel 331
  Thomas 341
  William 331, 341
Cartmill, Eliza 56, 73
  Jacob 73
Cartwell, --- 562, 563,
  564
Cary, --- 199
  Alice 101
  Ann 208, 221, 396
  Anne 108, 110, 176,
    181, 183, 219, 220,
    221, 225, 231
  Archibald 396
  Archibald (Col.) 181,
    183, 219, 229, 231
  Arthur 102
  Edward Humphrey 102
  Eliza 231
  Elizabeth 102, 231
  Evaline 123, 144
  George Hamet 101
  George Hamet, Jr. 102
  Graddy 102
  Hallie 102

Cary, (cont.)
  Henry 231
  Hettie 600
  James 102, 600
  Jane 183, 229, 231
  Jane Railey 102
  John B. 102
  Julia Ann 123, 144
  Logan Wickliffe 102
  Martha Woodson 102
  Mary 102, 231
  Mary (II) 231
  Mary Clifton 102
  Mary E. 123, 144
  Mathew 682
  Mattie 102
  Rhoda 102
  Sarah 231
  W. M. (Capt.) 210
  William 123, 144
  William Woodson 124,
    144
  Wilson Jefferson 220
  Wilson M. (Capt.)
    199, 209
  Wilson Miles 600
  Wilson Miles
    (Capt.) 221
Case, Bopher 35
  Leonard, Jr. 35
  Leonard, Sr. 35
  Mary 35
  Meshack 35
  Reuben 35
  Sarah 35
  William 35
Casey, --- 7
  Peter 6
Cassady, --- 63
Cassidy, Fanny 222
Castaing 507
Castleman, --- (Miss)
  421, 430, 435
  Ada Mayo 164
  Anna Cabell 431
  Caroline 681
  David 164
  Elise Kane 164
  George A. 464
  Lucie Cabell 453
  Sarah 368, 386
Castner, Marion 68
Cates, --- 518
Catesby, --- 374, 603
  --- (Miss) 374
  Mark 603
  Robert 603
Catlett, Henrietta 251
  John 170, 391, 402
Cave, 462, 463
  Ann 453, 462
  Banjamin 453
  Benjamin 453, 462,
    463, 467
  Nancy 453
  William 485
  William (Rev.) 463
Cavanaugh 463
  Philemon 463
Cavenaugh, 463
Cecil, Ellin C. 339
  Narcissa P. 411
  Susan 717
Cespedes, Maria 225
Chaffin, --- (Lieut.)
  400
Chafin, Simon 352 , 353

Chafon, A. E. 353
  " Lemon " 353
Chalfant, Josephine 109
Chalkley, --- 13, 60, 433,
  771
  Lyman 334
Chamberlain, Mabel 130
Chambers, --- 31
  Agnes 673
  Bird 46
  Elizabeth Buford 504
  Elizabeth Buford
    (Mrs.) 515
Chandler, Amanda Park
  (Mrs.) 697
  John Temple (Maj.)
    697
  John Temple, Jr. 697
  Ruth 147
Chapman, 346, 363
  --- 336
  --- (Dr.) 366, 400
  Asa 674
  Elizabeth 674, 677
  Ella 400
  Elvira 383, 411
  Emily (?) 400
  Emily Louise 225
  Frances 674
  Frances D. 674
  George 363, 346, 673,
    674
  Isaac 363
  Jemima 353
  John 400
  John Biddle 225
  Margaret 674
  Mary Gabriella 225
  Nancy 674
  Nathaniel 388
  Nathaniel (Dr.) 225
  Pearson (Dr.) 600
  Polly 674
  Rebecca Biddle 225
Chappell, Dean Jennings
  123, 144
  Elmer Louis 123, 144
  James 123, 144
  John 123, 144
  Walker 123, 144
Charlemagne 660
Charlick, Grace 132
Chastain 495, 507
  James 192
  Pierre 495, 508, 751
Chaucer, --- 365
Cheadle, John 113
Cheatham, --- (Mr.) 515
  Martha 517
Chef, Martha Cabell 687
Chenault, David 522, 523
  Tom (Mr.) 523
Chenoweth, Arthur 535
  John 535
  Nancy R. 535
Chesney, Ann 1
  Polly 1
Chesnut, Garrard 697
Chew, --- 523
  Larkin 523
  Samuel (Dr.) 256
Chichester, Arthur Mason
  (Capt.) 78
  Lydia W. 78
  Washington Bowie 78
Childers, Elizabeth 66
  Gracey 66

790

Childers, (cont.)
  Irene 66
  James Francis Wm. 66
  John 672
  Lula 66
  Mary Stacker 66
  William 66
Childress, Abram 672
  Ampsa P. 672
  Caswell J. R. 672
  Cynthia F. 672
  Henry 672
  Jane G. 672
  Joel 672
  John 672
  John A. 672
  Nancy 672
  Rachel 672
  Robert 672
  Sarah 672
  Verda 676
  Verlinda (Mrs.) 677
  William 672
Chiles, John Henry 41
  Mary Rogers 41
  Richard 41
  Sally 41
  Sarah Johnston 41
Chilton, Alvin O. 527
  Anne 527
  B. F. 527
  Dora 527
  Eve 527
  George T. 527
  Henry S. 527
  James F. 527
  Jeff 527
  John B. 527
  Mary Susan 527
  Mattie Robb (Mrs.) 720
  Millard 527
  Notley 527
  Ransdall 527
  Robert 527
  Smith (Captain) 527
  Thomas 185, 527
  Thomas (Rev.) 185
  Thomas, Jr. 185
  William P. 527
Chinn, --- 421, 435
  --- (Judge) 435
  --- (Mr.) 426, 435
  --- (Mrs.) 425, 429
  Amanda 470
  Franklin 470
  George (?) 712
  George 238
  George, Jr. (Mr.) 716
  Joseph 574
  Mary (Scott) 470
  Milley 424
  Raleigh 426
Chisholm, --- (Miss) 583
  Sarah 359
Chism, Sarah 359
Chiswell, --- 218
  Elizabeth 218
  John (Col.) 218
  Lucy 218
  Mary 218
  Susanna 218
Chrisman, Chas. 653
Christerson, M. E. 313
  T. J. 313

Christerson, (cont.)
  Willie F. 313
Christian, Katherine 40
Church, Sallie Steele 102
  Seville 101, 137
Churchill 190, 191, 198, 199, 208, 209, 210, 212
  Armistead 213
  Judith 175, 176, 181, 183, 184, 190, 191, 195, 196, 197, 198, 199, 208, 209, 210, 211, 212, 213
  Julia P. 739
  William 198, 200, 212, 213
  William (Col.) 196, 198,200, 212, 213
Cilley, --- (Congressman) 185
Claget, Dudley Malcolm 119
  Edith 119
  Eleanor 119
  I. Anderson 119
  John Robertson 119
  William H. 119
Clagett, Anderson 122
  Dudley 122
  William H. 122
Clagott, Amy 465
Clairborne, --- 609
  --- (Mr.) 488
  Billy 487
Clapham, William 414
Clapp, Russell (Rev.) 79
Clark, 192, 193, 763
  --- 764, 765
  --- (Col.) 511, 518, 764, 765
  --- (General) 58, 59, 60, 187
  --- (Miss) 495
  --- (Mrs.) 32, 34
  Absolum 192
  Allen 330
  Ann 192, 420, 569
  Asa W. 192
  Asa Winslow 192
  Bannister 192
  Christopher 656
  Christopher (Dr.) 656
  Cynthia 192
  Eliz. 770
  Eliza 192
  Elizabeth (Mrs.) 684
  Garner 192
  George Rogers 420, 752, 763, 769, 773
  George Rogers (Col.) 511, 514, 518, 763, 765
  George Rogers (General) 55, 58, 59, 61, 63, 186, 291, 563
  Godfrey 192
  Henry Conyers 575
  Israel 192
  J. A. (Mr.) 193
  James Robert 141
  James Robert, Jr. 141

Clark, (cont.)
  Jeff D. 575
  Jeff D., Jr. 575
  Jesse 192
  Jo Ballard 146
  Joe Ballard 141
  John 192, 420, 694
  John Asa 193
  John B. 192
  John Rodes 575
  John T. 575
  Jonathan 420
  Julius Graves 51
  Julius Graves, Jr. 51
  Levi 192
  Mary 192
  Mary Elizabeth 575
  Mildred Campbell 141
  Nancy 192
  Obedience 192
  Prudence 192
  R. M. (Mrs.) 32
  Reuben M. 51
  Robert 658
  Sara G. 4
  Sara G. (Mrs.) 34
  Sarah 192, 694
  Spicy 192
  Stuart Heth 141
  Virginia Rosalie 51
  William 192
  Wm. (Gov.) 387
  Wm. (Mr.) 656
Clarke, 192
  --- (Mr.) 246
  Anna 725
  Robert 613
  Susan 84
  William Newman 529
Clarkson, 669
  Anselm 515
  Ellott 34
  Hiram 664
  James 664
  Thomas 664
Claunch, F. 3
Clawson, --- (Miss) 721
Claxon, Sarah 470
Clay, 263, 346, 499
  --- 121, 476
  Charles 356
  Charles L. 364
  David 347
  Edward 499, 512
  Eleazer (Rev.) 516
  George W. 240
  Harry B. 47, 49
  Henry 88, 431, 504, 512, 753
  Henry (Mrs.) 431
  Jane 504
  Jane B. 516
  John 476
  John Carter 49
  John Frank 49
  Laura Hume (Mrs.) 49
  M. Hume 49
  Mary 346
  Mitchell 345, 346, 347, 360, 363
  Patience 346, 363
  Phoebe (Belcher) 346
  Porter 753
  Samuel, Jr. 263

791

Clay (cont.)
  Sidney Green 262
  Tabitha 347
Clayton, Joseph 218
  Nancy 393, 394, 408
  P. 403
  Philip 516
  Philip (Major) 270
  Susan 270
Cleck, J. F. 36
Cleland, Thomas (Rev.) 718
Clemans, --- (Miss) 659
Clemens, Juliet 272
Clemons, Jane 311
Clemson, Margaret 639
Cleveland, --- (President) 181
  Emma 572
  Jas. 572
  Kirtley 572
  Robert 572
  W. H. 572
  Wm. T. 572
Clifford, Robert (Sir) 214
Clift, G. Glenn 622
Cloninger, Valentine 338
Clopton, --- (Miss) 406
Clough, --- (Mrs.) 471, 483
  George 415
  James Lee Whitley 471
  P. W. (Mrs.) 484
  Pershing Wilson 471
  Sarah (French) 483, 484
  Susan Harriet 471
Cloverdale, --- 259
Cloyd 345
Cobb, Agnes (Miss) 272
  Irene 65
Cobbs 589,
  Ann (Walton) 261
  Charles (Captain) 261
  Frances 261
  J. M. 273
  Jane 583, 584, 589, 709
  Judith 584, 589, 709
  Mary Lewis 584, 589
  Robert 584, 589, 709
  Samuel 583, 584, 589
Coburn, Ann (Mrs.) 634
  Mary 632
  Wilson (Dr.) 632
Cochran, --- (Miss) 500
  Caroline Bullitt 511
  Gavin H. 511
  S. P. (Mr.) 635
Cocke, Elizabeth 603
  Martha 115, 217
  Wm. (Dr.) 603
Cockrill, Dura Louise 148
  Egbert Railey (Rev.) 148
  H. C. 148, 153
  Henry Clifton 149
  Louise Mayo 148
  Pocahontas 149
  William 619
Coffee, Elizabeth 313
  Jessie 313
  Polly 311

Coffer, Hetty Gay 17
Coffey, Hugh 329
  Sally 523
Coffman, Anne 735
  Martha Payne 735, 737
  W. H. (Dr.) 573, 736
  W. H. (Mrs.) 86
  Wm. H. 735, 737
  Wm. H. (Dr.) 570
  William H. (Mrs.) 735, 737
Cogar, George 574
  Marion 574
Cogghill, Patrick 625
Coghill, E. S. 417
Cohagen, Sarah 770
Colby, Mary 535
Cole, Elizabeth 350
Coleman, 720
  --- (Miss) 413
  Ambrose 368
  Ann 72
  John 368
  John W. 51
  Louise 51
  Lucy 383, 391, 392, 402
  Lucy Foster 720
  Mary Ann 565
  N. D. 712
  Nancy 368
  Sarah E. 499
  Strother 368
  Susan 368, 514
  Susanna Strother Watkins 368
  Susannah 385
  Thomas 169, 170, 368, 385
  Wm. 380, 466
  William L. 720
  William Linfield 720
Collier, Clarence Calvert 141
  Helen Elizabeth 141
  Kirby Smith 141
Collin, --- 597
  Lewis 63
  Richard 63
Collins, --- 93, 94, 250, 253, 279, 281, 541, 544, 596, 630
  Elizabeth 579
  Lewis 613, 669
  Lillian 579
  Minnie 152
  Richard D. 579
  Richard H. 669
  Tabitha 591
Collvil, Elizabeth 746
Colmes, Marquis 544
Colpatrick IV 27
Colston, Francis 266
  Lucy 223
  William 265
Colton, Mary 337-338
Columbus, --- 550
Colve, --- (Governor) 556
Colvin 327
  Susan 327
Colyer, Sallie Dillingham (Mrs.) 688
Combs, Benjamin 251
  Leah 744
Comingo 717

Comingore, John 717
Compbell (See also Campbell)
  Alexander 2
Conant, Carrie 407
Conger, Ralph (Dr.) 105
Connell, Darby 342
Connelly, Darby 337
Conner, Sarah 628, 675
Connolly, Darby 342
  John (Major) 768
Conrad, J. W. 8
Constant, Mary 472
Conway, Albert (Dr.) 403
  Edwin 456
  Frank 403
  Geo. (Capt.) 488
  Philip C. (Dr.) 403
  Sarah 456
Conyers, --- (Lady) 88
  Ann Holland 464
  Ann Holland (Lady) 83
Cook, --- 713
  Charles C. (Mrs.) 449
  George Tandy 449
  John (Capt.) 1
  Justine S. 449
  Margaret 712, 713
  Merriam L. 449
  Nancy 355
  Rachel 348, 356
  Sadie Estelle 162
  William 360
Cooke, Elizabeth 493
  Frances 492
  Giles 84
  John 493, 653
  Lettie ? 713
  Margaret 712
  Mordecai 419
  Mordica 492
Cooley, Frederick Earl 698
  Mildred 698
  Sarah Margaret 698
Coolidge, 228
  Algernon 221
  Ellen R. 221
  Harold Jefferson (Mr.) 221, 228
  Joseph 221, 228
  Joseph R. 221
  Joseph Randolph 228
  Sidney 221
  Sidney (Lieut.) 221
  Thomas Jefferson 221
Coolige 110, 181
  --- (Mr.) 181
Coomer, Ann Jones 745
  James 745
  Nellie Goddard 745
  Peggy Jane 745
  Sarah Elizabeth 745
  Sid 745
  Sidney Goddard 745
Coons, John 625
Cooper, Carrie 535
  Chas. J. 469
  Chas. J., Jr. 469
  Daniel 159
  Daniel (Mrs.) 166
  Dick 535
  Frank 535
  Franklin 535

Cooper, (cont.)
  John Daniel 159
  Mary Eleanor 159
  Mary Louise 47
  Rachel 578
  Sallie 37
  Sarah 711
  Sue 535
  Thornton 159
  Timothy 711
  Wickliffe (Col.) 568
Copedge, Charles 487
Copeland, Bessie N. 123, 144
  Ella W. 123, 144
  James S. 123, 144
  Jesse J. 123, 144
  John Herbert 123, 144
  Joseph F. 123, 144
  Robert W. 123, 144
  Susie S. 123, 144
Coppedge, Charles 457
  John 457
  Judith 457
  William 457
Corbin, Gawin 265
Corley, 527
  Aquilla 526
Corly, Mary Ann Maddox 526
Corncello, Jno. 422
Cornick, Anna 261
  Olivette (Phelps) 261
  Richard 261
Cornock, Anna 261
Cornstalk 768
Cornwallis, --- 19, 345, 378, 398, 524, 610
Cornwell 327
  Betsy 333
  Elijah 333
Corse, --- 402
Corwin, Ann 631
Cosby, --- (Mr.) 583
  Elizabeth Ann 512
  Fortunatus 405
  Lucy 748
  Lucy Dupuy 511
  William H. 512
Cospatrick 26
Cospatrick III 26
Costen, Ann 686
  Henry 686
Coston, Ann 686
  Rosanna 686
  Rosey Ann 686
  Sarah H. 686
Cotton, --- (Col.) 545
  Elizabeth 649
  George T. 545
  Geo. T. (Mrs.) 545
  John 480
  Susan 147
  Susannah Smith 480
Cottrell 725, 726
  Anna 725
  Anne Clark 726
  Benjamin 725
  Deoshy 725
  Dicey 725
  George 725
  Margaret 725
  Nancy 725
  Richard 725
  Shepard 725
Couch, --- (Mr.) 254

Coughton, --- (Baronet of) 492
  --- (Lord of) 492
Coulbourn, --- (Miss) 628
  J. 629
  M. 627
  Sarah 628, 629
Coulton, Joseph 320, 338
  Mary 337-338
  Robert 320
Coupland, Nancy 229
Courtney, Delia Edith 158
  Sarah ? 534
Coverdale, Miles 551
Covington 179
  --- 405
  Francis 382, 410
  Gilla 410
  John 410
  Lucy 405
  Mary 654
  Mildred 405
  Nancy 410
  Peggy 410
  Polly 410
  Robert 382, 410
  Susan 410
  Wm. 382, 410
  Wm. Strother 410
Cowan, Addie L. (Miss) 296
  Eliza 568
  Elizabeth 296, 568
  George S. 296
  John 568
  Luke 149
Cowherd 687
  Francis 687
Cowin, Sue Will--- 296
Cown, Donald Joseph 36
  Mary Shaw 36
  Max 36
  Sallie Hughes 36
  William E. 36
Cox, 647, 669, 679, 687
  Adam 536
  Archibald 687
  Azro 536
  Burr Harrison (Dr.) 157
  Chesterfield 700
  Claudius C. 536
  Curran 625
  David 648
  Edward 536
  Elizabeth B. 687
  Fannie 647
  Fannie Moriah 647
  Fannie Moriah Hull 647
  Frank 647, 648
  Fredrick 687
  Geo. H. 700
  Isaac 647, 648
  Isaac Russell 647
  Isaac Russell (Major) 647
  James 647, 648, 770
  James (Brigadier General) 647
  James (General) 647
  John 627, 664
  John P. 687
  John P., Jr. 687

Cox, (cont.)
  Jonathan 648
  Jonathan Wood 647, 648, 652
  Joseph 226
  Judith G. 687
  Julia 226, 573
  Louisa 648
  Lucie Ann 687
  Martha 664
  Mary 647
  Mary Catherine 647, 648
  Mary Jane 157
  Mary Sue 536
  Nancy 687
  Ora 157
  Palmer Sargeant 536
  Pearl (Mrs.) 535
  Polly 648
  Polly Wood 647, 648
  Sallie Hughes 648
  Samuel 664, 687
  Samuel Turner 157
  William 627
Cox-Ball, Mary Catherine 642
  Mary Catherine Wood 646
  Polly Wood 646
Coxe, 643
  --- 559
  Daniel 559
  Daniel (Colonel) 559
Cozine, Eliza A. W. 243
Crabb, Charles J. 134
  Charles Layton 134
  Elizabeth 134
Crabtree, L. B. 676
Crady, B. A. 648
  M. N. 648
  Mary Wood 652
  William Henry 648
  Wood 648, 652
Cragg, Talliferro 431
Craig, 522, 749
  --- 447, 606
  D. P. 439
  E. W. 467
  Edward 440
  Edwin S. 161, 166
  Eliza 308
  James 594
  James T. (Dr.) 440
  John S. 440
  Joseph 440
  Lewis 440
  Lucy 498
  Lutitia 440
  Mary 568
  Perlinia 440
  Sally 440
  Sarah 462
  Toliver 462
  Walton 439, 447
  William 440, 594
Craighead, Alexander (Rev.) 763
Crane, Ada Johnson 649
  J. M. (Mrs.) 389
  Joseph Minor 412
  Margaret 260
  Robert 260
Cranford, John 664
Crask, Elizabeth 415
Craven, Frederick M. 143

Cravens, Margaret 23
Crawford, 534, 572
--- 393
--- (Countess of)
  26
  Brown Craig 102
  David (Captain) 572
  Elizabeth Page 308
  George Cary 102
  Maggie J. 301
  Mary 572, 736
  Newton G. 102
  Robert Irvin 102
  Sarah Mary 132
Creason, Lou Allen 775
Creed, Maria 622
Crego, George Floyd 73
Crews, David 523
Crickton, --- (Viscountess) 26
Crinan 26
Crisp, Mary 502
Crittenden, --- (Col.) 545
  Caroline 124, 127, 175
  Frances ? 416
  Henry 416
  John Allen (Col.) 545
  John J. 121
  John J. (Hon.) 175
  Robt. H. 685
  Virginia (Mrs.) 544, 545
  Virginia Jackson
    (Mrs.) 537
Crocket, Robert 762
  William Overton 592
Crockett 741
  --- (Col.) 398
  --- (Mr.) 411
  A. 743
  A. L. 742
  Ada Lee 742
  Alex 625
  Ann Rebecca 742, 743
  Anna Maria 743
  Anthony 741, 754
  Anthony (Colonel) 592
  Dandridge 754
  Dandridge S. 742
  Dandridge Spottswood 592
  Edmund Vaughan 592, 742
  Elizabeth 741
  Emma 592
  (F.?) A. 742
  Florence 592
  Florence Augusta 742
  Fountain B. 741
  George 592
  George Anthony 742
  Granville S. 741
  James 16, 592
  James Granville 742
  Joseph, Jr. 120, 122
  Kitty 742
  Lelia Moss 742
  Margaret 741, 743
  Martha 741
  Mary 741, 743
  Mary Vaughn 754
  Mattie 742
  Overton W. 741
  Polly 741

Crockett, (cont.)
  R. L. 742
  Richard E. 742, 743
  Rosana Johnson 742
  Sallie C. 742, 743
  Sally 741
  Samuel B. 741
  Sarah (Ellison)
    (Mrs.) 592
  Susan M. 592
  Susan Mary 742
  W. R. 742
  William Overton 742
  William R. 741, 742
Croghan, --- 387
  --- (Major) 387
Crom, --- 558
  Geertje 556
  Gysbert 558
Cromwell 724
  --- 28, 588
Cropper, Bela 623
Crosthwaite, Aileen 104
  John W. 104
  Mary Virginia 104
Crouch, Richard 456
Crow, Letta 119
Crozier, --- 415
Crtucher, (See also
  Crutcher)
  Flora 503
Crumbaugh, Elizabeth 65
Crume 643
  Agnes Snyder 649
  Anise 649
  Anna 649
  Beatrice 649
  Benjamin 649
  Benjamin (Lieut.) 652
  Benjamin Wood 649, 652
  Daniel Burr 649
  Elise 649
  Elizabeth 649
  Elizabeth Ellen 649
  Elizabeth Wood 649
  Emma 649
  Jackie 649
  John 649
  John Bruce 649, 652
  John Robert 649
  John Robert (Colonel) 652
  John William 649
  Jonathan Robert 649
  Jones 649
  Joseph P. 643, 649
  Joseph Wood 649, 652
  Keith 649
  Lelia 649
  Mamie Figg 645
  Mary 649
  Mildred Emily 649
  Mundy 649
  P. Burr (Mrs.) 645
  Philip Burr 649
  Robert 649
  Thomas 649, 652
  William Ernest 649
  William Ernest (Dr.) 649
  Woodie 649
Crump, --- (Mrs.) 682
  Elizabeth Judith 116
Crutcher, (See also
  Crtucher) 750, 752, 753

Crutcher, (cont.)
  Anna 503
  Anna B. (?) 503
  Anna Lee 503
  Asa 503
  Bartlett 752
  Earle 503
  Eddie 503
  Gesse Grady 515
  Henry 503, 752, 753, 754
  Henry, Sr. 752
  Isaac 752, 753, 754
  J. 750
  J. H., Jr. 503
  Jesse Graddy 503
  Jessie 503
  John 753
  Laura B. 711
  Laura Boon 711
  Levi 754
  Lewis 753
  Maria 572
  Martha 752
  Martha Beazley 752, 754
  Mary 503
  Mary D. 711
  Mary French 753
  Mattie 503
  N. Maffit 753
  Nancy G. 710
  Pamelia Berry 754
  Pittman 503
  R. 750
  Rebecca 754
  Redd 752, 754
  Reuben 752, 753
  Richard 503, 754
  Richard L. 503
  Robert (?) 503
  Susanna Hancock 754
  T. G. 710, 711
  Thomas G. 710
  Virginia Redd 754
  Washington 754
Crutchfield 679, 687
  Amanda 688
  An E. 708
  Ann E. 688
  Delfina 688
  George N. 688
  Harriet 688
  Hester 688
  Hester C. 688
  Hulda 688
  Huldah 687
  Janet 687
  Jenette 688
  John C. 687, 688
  John R. 688
  Mary C. 688
  Mary E. 688
  Sally 688
  Sally W. 688
  Tacy F. 688
  William W. 688
Cuick 547
  Jan V (Lord of) 547
  Johanna (?) 547
Cuick and Grave, Johanna (Lady of) 547
Culpepper, --- (Lord) 602
Culton, Joseph 320
  Robert 320
Cummings, Jenet 688

Cummins, Charles (Rev.)
   339
  Eliza 390
  W. H. 629
Cunningham, Isaac (Captain) 564
  J. T. 721
  Maria 48
  Maria D. 47
  Mary 123, 144
  Mary Rebecca Scomp (Mrs.) 720
  Rebecca 564, 565, 566
Curd, F. 676
  John 95, 96
  Mary 95, 96
Curl, Mary Ann (Mrs.) 658
Currens, Mabel 722
Currier, Guy 79
Curry, Ella 576, 577
Curtis, --- 609
  Edwina 677
  John 560
Custis, 581
  --- (Widow) 184, 581
  Edmund 626
  Mary Randolph 184
Cuthbert, Isabella Parlby 222
Cutter, Wm. Richard 263
Cutts, --- (Lord) 276
Dabney 179, 180
  --- (Miss) 413
  Belle Moore (Mrs.) 511
  Cornelius 382
  E. S. 40
  Elizabeth Prewitt 40
  John 170, 367, 382, 404
  Kitty Prewitt 40
  Susan 367, 384
  Susan (Miss) 404
  Susanna 169, 170, 179, 180, 382, 388
  Susannah 372, 386, 387 387, 388, 392, 393
  Wm. Pape (Judge) 376
Dade, Frances 67
  J. B. 403
  Philip 403
  Randolph 567
  Townshend (Capt.) 403
Dale, Perlina 698
Dallas, Mae Martha 536
Dameron, Dorothy 486
  Elizabeth (Dennis) 486
  George 451, 457, 458, 486
  George (Mrs.) 456
  James P. 499
  Lawrence 486
  Margaret (Taylor) 486
Dammann, John Francis, Jr. 133
Dandridge 389
  Alexander Spotswood (Captain) 272
  Wm. 560
Dangerfield, --- (Colonel) 773, 774
Daniel, --- (?) 254

Daniel, (cont.)
  Ann Goode 605
  Anna 224
  Hezekiah Goode 605
  J. E. 106
  Jennie C. 605
  Jno. 653
  Joseph 106
  Peter Vivian (Judge) 233
  William Pride 605
  Willie Sue 106
Daniels, Thomas (Rev.) 710
  Walker 710
Danley, B. F. 585
  Ben F. 709
Danning, Nancy 744
Darling, Mattie 573
Darlington, James Lister 471
Darnaby, George 677
  Mary Stuart 732
Darnall, Elizabeth 662
Darnell 628
  --- 468
  --- (Mr.) 148
  --- (Mrs.) 484, 485
  Aaron 146, 147, 148, 625
  Aaron H. 147
  Ann Elizabeth 147
  Attalanta 147
  Catharine 147
  Charles 147
  Charles Randolph 101, 137, 147
  Dunlap C. 147
  Elizabeth Pope 146
  Ermina (Mrs.) 483
  Ermina Jett 467
  George Lewis 147
  Harvey Randolph 147
  Isham Randolph (Judge) 147, 148
  James S. 147
  John 147
  John R. 147
  John R., Jr. 147
  John Robb 147
  M. C. (Mrs.) 623
  Mahala 147
  Mathew C. 148
  Mathew Cotton (Dr.) 147
  Mayme 147
  R. R. 625
  Randolph 147
  Randolph Railey 146, 628
  Ruth Elizabeth 147
  Samuel Pepper 147
  Sarah E. 147
  Shapley 147
  Southey 147
  Southy W. 147
  Varsalina 147
  Virginia 147
  W. W. 147
Daukhearts, Sebastian 551
Davenport, --- (Miss) 406
  Glover 272
  Jesse 590
Davidge, Benjamin (Judge) 19

Davidge, (cont.)
  Susan 19
Davidson, --- 292, 775
  Bessie 147
Davies 211
  --- (Mrs.) 696
  H. L. 198
  Henry Landon 211
  Judith 211
  Judith Fleming 199
  Judith Fleming Randolph 211
  Margaret (Mrs.) 695
  Nicholas 190, 198, 199, 210, 211, 212
Daviess, Hannah 503
Davis 5, 717, 752
  --- 493, 514, 692, 708
  Amanda 84
  Archiles E. 717
  Bedialjamal 718
  Ben 498
  Benjamin 237, 625
  Catherine 632
  Charles W. 718
  Charlotte Railey 160
  David 695
  Eleanor 579
  Elinder 718
  Elizabeth 676
  Garrett (Hon.) 262
  George B. 718
  Geo. R. 718
  George W. 717
  H. C. 717
  Handy T. 628
  Hannah 490
  Hardin 439, 676
  Harriet 695
  Harrison 717
  James 717, 718
  James (Rev.) 718
  James, Sr. 718
  James E. 717, 718
  James G. 718
  James Riley 535
  Jeff 377, 707
  Jefferson 180, 601
  Jefferson (President) 367, 368
  Jesse F. 718
  Jesse Franklin 718
  Jessey 717
  John H. 718
  John W. 719
  John W., Jr. 718
  Joseph H. 718
  Laban 5, 7
  Lucy 717
  Madeline 745
  Malinda A. 717
  Margaret 718
  Margaret T. 717
  Martha 567
  Martha R. 717
  Mary 695, 718
  Mary Alma 719
  Mary E. 717
  Nancy 719
  Nancy Dunn 719
  Paul R. (Mrs.) 734
  Polly 717
  Robert 4, 5, 13, 567
  Sally Ann 718
  Sammy 9
  Samuel 532

Davis, (cont.)
  Samuel T. 674
  Samuel Turner 676
  Sarah 5
  Sarah Wade 243
  Stephen 717, 718
  Theophilus 579
  Thomas S. 717
  Thomas Sales 717
  William 718
  William H. 717
  William O. 160, 166
  William Worth 719
Davit, --- 334
  William 334
Dawes, Ephraim Pennington 301
  Ephraim Pennington, Jr. 301
  Frances Mariah 301
  James Stephenson 301
  John Andrew 301
Dawson, --- (Mr.) 585
  Phoebe 336
  William (Rev.) 232
Day, Presley 712
Dayton 201
de Albini, William 660
De Choiseul 218
de Clare, Gilbert 660
  Richard 660
de Fahnarburg, ---
  (Baron) 367
de Fahnenburg, ---
  (Baron) 393
de Hart, Abigail 116, 117
de Hume (See also Hume)
  Galfridus 27
  John (Sir) 27
  Patrick (Sir) 27
  Roger (Sir) 27
  Thomas (Sir) 27
de Joux, Benjamin 507
De La Calmes, --- (Marquis) 251, 253
  Isabel 251, 253
de la Marre, Jean Baptiste 452
de la Muse, --- (Marquis) 507
de Lacie, John 660
de Potestad, Emily Mildred 225
  John Henry 225
  Luis Emilio 225
  Manuel Henry 225
  Marie Eugenie 225
  Mary Gabriella 225
  Robert E. Lee 225
de Potestad- Fornari, Barbard Luis 225
De Priest, Martha 254
de Quincy, Saire 660
de Richeboug, Claude Philippe 507
de Roos, Robert 660
de Schamp, Flora 721
  Henry 721
de Spinets, Guy (Sir) 492
  Eleanor 492
De Telere 636
De Vere 201
Dean, John 236, 237
  Margaret 355
  William E. 354

Dean, (cont.)
  William P. 439
Dearing, James 629
Deatherage 405
--- 405
  Robert 382
  Wm. 410
Debnam, Wm. 493
Debow, Elizabeth 516
  Helen Terry 516
  Henry 516
Decatur, --- 367, 376, 400
Dedman, Philip 720
del Strother, Alen 365
  William 365, 369
del Wallington, Jean 365
Delaporte, Mariamne (Made.) 680
  Marie Agatha Henriette Sophie 680
  Pierre Victoir 680
Delaware, --- (Lord) 695
Delay, 337, 341
  Henry 337
DeLong, Bettie Payne 87
  W. F. 87
Demarest, Letitia M. 132
Dempsey, Louise 227
DeNeus, Alice 633
  Alitje 633
Denison, Daniel 260
  Elizabeth 260
  Patience (Dudley) 260
Dennett, John 417
Dennis, Elizabeth --- 486
  John 486
Dent, John 525
  Lydia 525, 526
Denton, Thomas 92
Depp, J. 677
  Martha 674, 676
  Phebe D. 692
Derritt, Diana 673
DeRoulac, J. R. 147
Dervall, --- 24
Desportes, Henriette 70
Devere, Pearl 120
Dewell, Charles 647
DeWitt, Mathias (Captain) 773
Dick, Franklin 375, 402
  Wm. A. Evans 402
Dickens, Asberry 400
  Fanny 400
  Frances M. 210
  Frank 400
  Harriet 400
Dickenson, --- (Capt.) 329
  Adam 329, 330
  John 330, 333
  John (Capt.) 333
Dickerson, --- (Miss) 411
  Mary 673
Dickey, Emma 36
Dickins, --- (Miss) 199, 210
  Albert White 226
  Asbury 225
  Ellen Arnot 226
  Emily 226
  Fanny M. (Miss) 199

Dickins, (cont.)
  Frances Margaret 225
  Frances Margaret (Miss) 199, 208
  Francis Asbury 225, 226
  Francis Asbury, Jr. 225
  Harriot Wilson 225
  Lilas Arnot 226
  Mary Randolph 225
  Medora Braxton 225
  Randolph 226
  (Thomas Mann) Randolph 226
  Virginia Fleming 226
Dickinson, --- 329
Digges, Catherine 273
  Dudley 273
  J. Singleton (Judge) 273
Dilingham, Henry H. 688
  Vachel 688
Dillard, Elizabeth 382
Dillian, Eliza J. 674
Dillingham, 688
  Amanda F. 688
  Chas. T. 775
  Elihu 688
  Elizabeth 688
  Henry B. 688
  John P. 688
  Joshua 688
  Paulina 688
  Solomon 688
  William 688
Dillman, Eugene 137=
Dillon, Agnes 223, 224
  Amanda 672
  Eliza J. 676
  Margaret J. 592
Dimmitt, John 120
  John J. 120
  Rosa 120
Dinwiddie, --- 320
  --- (Gov.) 320, 321, 388
  --- (Rev. Mr.) 272
Diuguid, Jas. 440
Divers, Rhoda 672
Dixon, Archibald 754
  Rebecca 754
Dobson, 690
  Frances 690
Dodd, Jane 692
  Mary Ann 327
Dodge, --- (Mr.) 75
Dodson, Ada 650, 672
  Adra 650, 672
  Fletcher (Mrs.) 650, 652
  George O. 530
  J. P. (Mrs.) 650, 652
Dogan, Fountain Eli 315
Doherty, John 56
  Mary 55, 56, 57, 59, 64, 80
Dohoney, William 664
Doiser, Daniel B. 664
Donahoe 610
  --- 610
  Elizabeth 610
  Thomas 610
Doniphan, --- 108
  --- (Miss) 219

796

Donley, Samuel Waddy 710
Donly, Samuel Waddy 709
Donnally, John 329
Donohoe 609, 610, 611, 612
   --- (Col.) 611
   --- (Grandfather) 610
   --- (Grandma) 610, 611-612, 612
   --- (Grandmother) 611
   --- (Grandpa) 611
   --- (Major) 610, 611
   Archie (Col.) 611
   Archie (Major) 610, 612
   Dixon 611
   Saunders (Colonel) 611
   Thomas 610, 611, 612
Doolan, --- 511
Dooley, F. 675
   Reuben 258
Dooly, Elizabeth Anne 675
   Eloise 675
   Fitzhugh 675
   Irene 675
   Martha Neal 675
Doom 650
   --- (Colonel) 645
   Ben (Colonel) 645, 650
   Cassandra Phillips 645
   Elizabeth 644-645
   Elizabeth M. 644
   Lizzie 650
   Miriam Samuels 650
   William 650
Dorden, Mary J. 156
Doremus, E. W. (Mrs.) 598
Dorsey 67
   Charles 255
   Greenberry 584
   Matilda 709
Dougherty, Kate 514
   Mary 64
   William 329
Douglas 573, 574, 609
   --- 25
   --- (Baron of) 26
   James (Sir) 757
   John (Sir) 757
   Katharine 160
   Nancy 573
   William (Colonel) 573
Douglass 230, 481, 669
   --- 204, 207, 229
   --- (Countess of) 26
   Jane 664
   Mae 160
   William 664, 665
   William (Rev.) 204
Douthatt, --- (Mr.) 379, 399
Downes, Sallie Wood 43
Downey 756
   Harriet 641
   Jane 635
   John 641
Downing 570
   Betsy 578
   Eleanor 579
   Ellen 578
   Elvina 578

Downing,(cont.)
   Frances 578
   Francis 570
   George 578
   George C. 585, 593, 594
   George Crutcher 756
   George Viley 578
   Henrietta 578
   Henrietta Viley 570
   James (Hon.) 579
   John 578
   Mary (Polly) 578
   Nancy 578
   Polly 578
   Ruth Ann 578
   William 578
Downman 573
   William 574
Dowsing, wm. 192
Doyle, Conan (Mrs.) 275
Dragoo, Amanda Jane 35
Drake, A. S. (Col.) 271
   Adaline (Mrs.) 612
   Adaline Bennett (Mrs.) 608
   Eliza 271
   Townsend (Rev.) 84
Drane, Canning (Judge) 499
   Charles 68
   Chas. Haddox 68
   Edward C. (Dr.) 499
   Joseph S. (Dr.) 499
   Lucy 68
   Mary Louise 68
   Roberta Luckett 67
   Walter Harding 67
   William 68
   William McClure 67
   William McClure (Mrs.) 64
Draper 91
   --- 235, 236, 238, 241, 242, 243, 514, 615, 626, 764, 767, 770, 771, 772, 776
   --- (Dr.) 243
   L. C. 501
   Lyman C. 242
   Lyman C. (Dr.) 241
Driggs, --- (Dr.) 85
Drummond, Bettie 627
du Bois 560
   --- 554, 563
   Catherine 554, 555
   Catrynda 558
   David 558
   Isaac 563
   Jacob 558, 559, 560
   Louis 554, 556, 558
   Rebecca 563
   Sara 554, 558, 559
   Sarah 554, 559, 560
Dudley 755
   --- (General) 754
   Ambrose 755
   Frederick R. 131
   John W. (Mr.) 618
   Margaret Adair 131
   Maria Garrard 754
   Peter 689, 754
   Thomas 260
Duffield, Richard 412
   Richard (Mrs.) 389

Duke 534
   Eskridge 273
   Helen 273
   John S. 273
   Mary 273
   R. T. W. 273
   R. T. W., Jr. (Judge) 273
Dunaway, Elizabeth 530
   John 488
   Warren 530
Dunbar 25
   --- (Baron of) 26
   --- (Countess of) 26, 214
   --- (Earl of) 25, 26, 27, 214
   Patrick, Earl of (Sir) 27
Duncan 26, 406, 534
   --- (Mr.) 542
   Abner 242
   Annie Laurie 530
   Asa 242, 243
   Benjamin Lee 651
   Catharin (Mrs.) 438
   Charles 530, 534
   Charles Talbott (Dr.) 243
   Daniel 242
   Elizabeth 530
   Elizabeth (Patsy) 243
   Garrett 62
   Green 243, 644
   James 242, 408
   John K. 530
   John Ray 243
   Joseph 530
   Lorena 530
   Madden 243
   Martha 644
   Martin 242
   Martin, Jr. 242
   Mary 236, 242, 393, 394, 530
   Mary (Miss) 408
   Mary Ray 242, 243
   Mildred 534
   Millie 534
   Nimrod 410
   Oscar 530
   Patsy 243
   Polly 242
   Sally 95
   Samuel 530
   Sarah --- 534
   Seeny 408
   Talbott 243
   Wm. B. 409
Duncan Seton, --- (Viscountess of) 26
Dundas, --- (Baron of) 26
Dunkley, Clarissa 694
Dunlap 341, 765, 767
   --- 769, 770
   Agnes 776
   Agnes Gay 776
   Alex 762
   Alexander 770, 776
   Alexander, Jr. 764
   Alexander, Jr. (Col.) 776
   Anne 761
   Eliza 700

Dunlap, (cont.)
  Elizabeth 23
Dunmore, --- 763, 768, 772
  --- (Governor) 511, 518
  --- (Lord) 15, 344, 511
Dunn 718
  America 719
  Augustine 22, 23
  Catherine 719
  Eleanor 22, 23, 72, 383
  Elizabeth 22, 719
  Ellen 516
  Eva 23
  George 719, 720
  Hannah 22
  Harry L. (Mrs.) 608
  James 22, 23, 53
  John 22, 53, 718, 719, 720
  John (Mr.) 718
  Joshua 23
  Mackay 23
  Mamie McRoberts 23
  Margaret McRoberts 23
  Martha 22
  Mary 23, 718, 719
  Mary (Mrs.) 719
  Mary B. 718
  Mary Buchanan 719
  Mary Harvey 23
  Mary Margaret Robb 720
  Nancy 718
  P. R. 719
  Peter R. 718, 719
  Richard 23
  Sally Ann 23
  Sarah 23
  Sarah Ann Patton 22
  Susan 718, 719
  Sybil 22
Dupee, G. W. 467
Dupui, James 510
  Jean Jaque 510
  Judith 510
  Olimpe 510
  Philippe 510
  Susane 510
Dupuy (duPuy) 467, 495, 499, 501, 502, 584
  --- 497
  Achsa 498
  Ann Stark 497
  Augustine 499
  B. H. (Rev.) 497, 501, 509
  B. W. (Rev.) 496
  Bartholomew 496, 497, 498, 501; 505, 508, 509, 510, 584, 751
  Bartholomew (Captain) 496, 497
  Bartholomew (Count) 467
  Bartholomew, Jr. 497
  Beverly W. 496
  Eliza (Miss) 496
  Eliza Ann 499
  Elizabeth 467, 497, 498, 510
  J. L. (Dr.) 496
  James 498, 499, 510, 584
  James (Rev.) 497

Dupuy (duPuy),(cont.)
  Joel 498
  John 498, 510
  John (Rev.) 497
  John James 497, 508, 509, 510, 584
  Joseph 498, 499
  Judith 498, 510
  Judith Coleman 499
  Martha 497, 498
  Martha Turner 498
  Mary 497
  Mary Motley 497, 499
  Mildred D. 499
  Nancy 498, 499
  Olympe 508, 511
  Olymphia 496, 497, 499, 504, 751
  Olympia 751
  Peter 497, 509
  Sarah 499, 584
  Stark (Rev.) 497
  Susanna 497, 510
  Susanna La Villain 584
  Susanne 498
Durfee, Kate 103
Durrett, R. T. (Col.) 58
Duvall, Ben T. 151
  Lot 702
  Louisa M. 702
  Lucy 702
Dwight, Edmund 221
Dyer, 4, 10, 13
  --- (Mr.) 7
  Eleanor 20
  Esther 4, 13
  Hannah 4, 10, 11, 12
  Hester 4
  James 4, 5, 8, 9, 12 13
  John 4
  Roger 4, 5, 8, 10, 11, 12, 13
  Sarah 4, 7
  William 4, 7, 12, 427, 431
Dymoke, Edward (Sir) 589
  Frances 589
Dysart, James (Capt.) 339
  Mable 697
E., --- 627
Earle, (?) 114
Eastham, Frances 382
  Francis 387
Easton, Archibald 535
  Arthur Z. 535
  DeWorth 535
  Russella 118, 121
Eastridge, Rachel 672
Eaton, James S. 120
  Martha Anderson 120
Eberhardt, Fred W. (Rev.) 471
Ecard, John 336
Eckard, John 336
Eckeurode, H. J. 563
Ecton, Martha 124, 145
Eddleman, Fannie 649
Edmiston 323
  --- 320
  --- (Mrs.) 340
  Betsy Stuart 339
  John 320

Edmiston, (cont.)
  John S. 340
  William 320. 338
  William Campbell (Gen.) 339-340
Edmonson, Margaret Montgomery 39
Edson, --- 323, 341
  George 317
Edward, John, Senr. 689
Edwards 601, 602
  --- 294, 604, 605, 607
  --- (Captain) 383, 406
  --- (Gov.) 466
  --- (Major) 603
  Benjamin 466
  Charles Eugene 147
  Esther (Steele) 294
  F. 625
  George Randolph 147
  John 286, 601
  John, Jr. 623
  John N. 603, 604
  John Swann 602
  Mamie 156
  Margaret Beall 466
  Mary 628
  Mary R. 715
  Moses 623
  Ninian (Gov.) 326, 466
  Ninian (Hon.) 602
  Ninian W. 326
  Ninian W. (Judge) 602
  Sarah 601
  Thomas, Senr. (Mr.) 488
  Thos. S. 395
  Thomas W. 147
  Virginia Pearl 147
  Wiley 147
Egmont, Fuentes y (Count) 225
Egremont, --- (Lord) 321
Ekenrode, H. J. 772
Eley, --- 576
Elfreth, Mary 655
Elgin, Mary 22
Elgira 26
Elkin, Robert (Rev.) 521
Ellen, --- (Aunt) (?) 435, 437
  (See also Allen)
Elley 679, 688
  Edward 688, 689
  Elizabeth 688
  Esther 688
  George 688, 689
  Henry 688, 689
  Nancy 688
  Polly 688
  Polly Herndon 688
  Sally 688
  Sarah 688
  Thomas 688
Ellinwood, Calvin 694
Elliott 341, 763, 766, 767
  --- 345, 472
  --- (Mr.) 472, 585
  --- (Mrs.) 425
  Ann 341

798

Elliott, (cont.)
  Archie 472
  Charles Stuart (Dr.) 164
  Doeshy 725
  Dicey 725
  Elizabeth 341
  Griffith 472
  Hallie 472
  Harry 472
  James 451, 471, 472, 478, 480, 485
  James (Rev.) 472
  James Stuart 341
  Jane 485
  Jane (Taylor) 472, 484
  Jane Taylor Plummer 472
  Jimmy ? 472
  John 341
  John James 472
  Lewis (?) 472
  Mary 332, 341, 345, 346, 472
  Mary (Constant) 472
  Milton (Mrs.) 690, 696
  Mormon 472
  Ralph 341
  Richard 337, 341, 344, 345, 346, 357
  Richard (Col.) 332
  Rita 472
  Robert 341
  Susannah 341
  Temple 472
  Tom 472
  William 341, 769
  William, Jr. 762
  William B. 472
  William R. 472
Ellis, 672, 677, 755
  --- (Mrs.) 401
  Alfred 673
  Armine 673
  Asa 673
  Betty 677
  Catherine 677
  Drusilla T. 449
  Elizabeth 677
  George 3, 115, 673, 677
  George A. M. 677
  Isaac 673
  J. C. 676
  James 330
  James C. 673, 676
  James M. M. 677
  James Tandy 435
  Jane 673
  John 454, 455, 673, 674, 677
  Josiah B. 673
  Julia A. P. 672
  Katherine 673
  Martha 673
  Mary 673, 674
  Varlinda J. 672
  William 673, 677
Ellison, Sarah Elizabeth 592
Elmore, Oscar (Mrs.) 762
Elston, Cora 530
  Lee 530
  Lena Ann 529

Elston, (cont.)
  Lewis 530
  Roy 530
  William 530
Ely, --- 358, 359
  --- (Countess of) 26
  Lewis B. 281
  William 349
Elting, Cornelius 559
  Cornelius, Jr. 560
Emack, John D. 577
Embrey, --- 618
Embry, --- (Miss) 576
  Talton 533
  William 21
Emerson, Ruben 308
Emmons, Orra 707
Emory, Anna 71
English, --- 752, 764
  James W. (Capt.) 406
  Martha A. 406
  Martha Ann 72
  William Hayden 61
Ennolds, --- 629
Enrma 26
Eppes, John Wayles 229
Erskine, --- (Mr.) 398, 402
  --- (Viscountess) 26
  Amos 535
Erwin, Dudley 578
  Elizabeth 578
  Johnson 578
  Victor 578
  Ward 578
  Wm. 407
Esmay, Irving Bliss 161
Espy, David 45
Estill, --- (Mr.) 398, 402
  Alice Garth 40
  Amanda Fry 40
  Anna Price 40
  Daniel Sheffer 41
  Elizabeth Prewitt 41
  George Castleman 40
  Howard S. 40
  Jacob S. 40
  James 656
  John 321
  Katherine Rodes 40
  Laura 48
  Laura Sheffer 41
  Martha 40
  Martha Prewitt Van Meter 39
  Martha Rodes 39
  Naomi Sheffer 41
  Omie Wierman Sheffer 40
  R. C. 40
  R. Julian 40
  Rachel Wright 656
  Robert C. 40, 41
  Robert Rodes 41
  Robert Whitridge 40
  Samuel 338
  Samuel (Col.) 330
  W. W. 40
  W. W. (Mr.) 48
  Wallace 656
  William 41, 656
  William R. (Colonel) 40

Estill, (cont.)
  William Rodes 40
  William Rodes (Colonel) 39
  William W. 40, 41
Evans 185
  Andrew 746
  Edward 625, 638
  James 746
  John (Col.) 391, 403
  John (Mrs.) 413
  John Wainwright 119
  Lucinda 355
  Richard 347
  Samuel 303
  Sarah 638
  Thomas 350
  Wainwright 119
  William 349
Eve 216
Everett 679
  --- 451, 456
  Em 739
  Henrietta 739
  Mary (Mrs.) 454, 455
  Nancy 689
  Samuel 689
  Wm. N. 689
Everhart, Catharine 156
Ewing, --- (Mrs.) 250
  George 511
  Mary 515
Eyre, John (Col.) 632
Fahnarburg (See de Fahnarburg)
Fahnenburg (See de Fahnenburg)
  --- (Baron) 403
Fahs, Lilly Herbert 574
Fairfax, --- (Lord) 366, 371, 375, 378, 381, 399, 465, 562
  George 481
Fakker, Jacomytge 562
Fall, Anne Apperson 682
  Elizabeth 682
  James Slater 682
  Philip S. 368, 681, 682
  Phillip S. (Rev.) 247
Fallon, P. D. 75
Fannin, Amy 358
  Isaac Newton 358
  Rachel 355
Fannon, Amy 358
Fargeson, Ann 395
Faris, Eliza 653
  Richard 653
Farley, --- (Miss) 438
  Henry 346
Farmer, Rob 469
  Sidney French 469
Farra 632
  Oliver H. 102
Farrar, Elizabeth 684
  Mary (Mrs.) 230
Farris 185
  William 311
Farrow, Catherine 468
  Susanna 468
Farwell, Mary 69
Faulkner, John 102
Fauntleroy, Margaret 772
Feemster 341

Feemster, (cont.)
  Thomas 345
Feltere, Erasmus 559
Fenwick, --- 553
Fergerson, --- (Rev.) 78
Ferguson 643, 650, 651, 652
  Abraham 672
  Abraham L. 33
  Ann 651, 652
  Ann McCown 649
  Anna Hughes 37
  Arthur (Mrs.) 434
  Arthur D. (Mrs.) 434
  Catherine 651
  Catherine Wood 651
  D. G. 672
  Dougal G. 672, 673
  George 672
  Henry E. 672
  James C. 34
  James W. 33
  Joseph 643, 651, 651-652
  Joseph (Reverend) 651
  Julia A. 672
  Lucy E. 33
  Maggie B. 33
  Mary 362, 672
  Matilda R. 33
  Morris 673
  Nancy 421, 426, 428
  Robert 37
  Robert H. 33
  Sallie A. 672, 674
  Sarah 651
  Thomas 673
  Thomas C. 672
  Van B. 651
  Volney W. 33
  William 651
  William H. 651
  William P. 33
  William S. 651
  Yetmon 673
Ferra, --- 632
Ferrell, --- (Mr.) 354
Ferril, William 354
Ferris, Elizabeth 113, 177
Fessenden, --- 691
Ficklin, Charles 390
Field 370
  --- 94
  John (Colonel) 270, 271
  Mary 194
  Rachel 70
  Susannah 271
Fielding, Edwin 457, 488
Fields, --- (Mr.) 602
Figg, Christopher Columbus 645
Filson 747
  Margaret 20
Fincel, --- 469
Finley, --- (Miss) 406
  Mary 185
  Robert W. 258
Finnell, --- 430
Finx, --- (Mr.) 409
Fishback, Catharine C. 126, 160
  Catharine Mary 126

Fishback, (cont.)
  Emma Woodson 126
  Ezza Railey 126
  George M. 126, 127
  George Taylor 126, 160
  George Taylor, Jr. 126, 160
  Jane Lyle 126
  Lucy 565
  Randolph Railey 126
  William Hunter 126
Fisher, (See also Von Fisher) 271, 669
  --- 22, 444
  Stephen 271
  Susannah 271
  Susannah (Miss) 270
Fiske, --- 551
  --- (Professor) 551
Fitch, John 644
Fitzhugh, 117
  Mary (Mrs.) 372, 390
  Nellie 150, 153
  William 217
Fitzwilliam, Rd. 560
Fleet, --- (Captain) 502
Fleming 116, 117, 191, 195, 200, 208, 208-209, 209, 210, 590
  --- (Miss) 201
  Charles 177, 190, 200, 212, 218
  Charles (Col.) 200
  Elizabeth 200
  Elizabeth Anne 226
  John 189, 191, 198, 200, 210, 211, 212
  John (Col.) 110, 200
  Judith 108, 110, 110-111, 169, 176, 189, 190, 191, 195, 196, 197, 198, 199, 200, 208, 209, 210, 212, 213, 218, 219
  Mary 340
  Robert 200
  Susanna 200
  Susannah 200
  Tarleton 177-178, 178, 189, 198, 200, 210, 211, 212, 218
  Tarleton, (Sir) 177
  Thomas 200, 212
  Thomas (Sir) 177, 200
  Ursula 113, 114, 129, 135, 136, 177, 178, 187, 182, 200, 653
  William 200
Fletcher 695
  Anna 696
  Catherine 696
  Mary 696
  Mollie 694
  Nancy 696
  Rachel 695, 696
  Rebecca 696
  Robert (Gen.) 695
  Rutha 696
  Thomas 695, 696
  Thomas (Col.) 695
Flournoy 495, 751
  Cassandra 739, 740

Flournoy (Cont.)
  David (Dr.) 654
  Francis 751
  Jacob 505, 751
  Laetitia 49
  Lavinia B. 740, 741
  Magdelain 505
  Mary Parish 740
  Thompson B. 739
Floyd, (See also Flyod) 726
  --- (Col.) 62
  Annie 726
  Annie M. 725
  Evans W. (Mrs.) 725
  George E. 726
  Jacob B. 726
  Jesse Minor 725, 726
  John (Governor) 62
  John Levi 726
  John William 726
  Lucy Ella 726
  Mary Belle 725
  Nancy 725
  Richard Taylor 726
  William S. 725, 726
  William Smith 726
Fluke, A. J. 130
  George 130
  Vivian 130
Flyod (See also Floyd)
  William S. 726
Fogg, --- (Mr.) 498
  Benjamin 498
  Dione 498
  Elizabeth 498
  James 467
  Joel 498
  John 498
  Joseph 498
  Lucy 498
  Mary 451, 498
  Mary M. 467
Folk, Evora 530
Fontain 495
  --- (Capt.) 405
Fontaine, Parson 405
Foote, --- 62
Ford 723, 724
  --- 470
  --- (Secretary) 420
  Bourn G. 303, 304
  Bourne G. 304
  Edward 197, 203, 219
  Frances 692
  Hanah (Cromwell) 724
  Hannah 724
  Harriot 724
  J. S. 304
  John 692, 693
  John S. 303
  John, Sr. 692
  Katherine 693
  Mary 724
  Nathaniel 724
  William 142, 724
  Worthington Chauncey 319
Fore, Lud 709
  Mary Jane 709
  Samuel 709
  Sarah Adoline 710
Foree, L. 585
Forkner, --- (Colonel) 500
Forman, Edna 726

Forman, (cont.)
  Ezekiel 634
Forsee, A. R. 439
  Eliza Ann 444
  Elizabeth 484
  Elizabeth T. 483
  Emily 439
  Granville 439
  James Nichlaus 439
  John 441
  John William 439
  Judith (Ward) Bledsoe 438
  Martha (Mrs.) 441
  Mary 439
  Peter 468, 484
  Sallie 439
  William 438, 468
  Wm. B. 443
Forsythe, Eliel 664
  James 308
Fortescue, Dorothy 492
  John (Sir) 492
Fossett, Mary 626
Foster, 754, 755
  --- 568, 629
  --- (Dr.) 636
  Annie (Miss) 636
  Catharine 160
  E. H. 101
  Eliza Brown 478
  Eliza Jane 745
  Elizabeth 69
  Ezekiel 631
  George 510
  Harrison Edward 478
  James 497
  Lucy 720
  Martha 510
  Mary 510
  Mary Ann 745
  Nat (Dr.) 636
  " Puss " 478
  Sarah A. 31
  Sarah A. Deadman 31
  Sarah Catherine 745
  Stephen 645
  Stephen Collins 287
  Susanna 510
Fountain, James 584
Fowler, Wm. T. (Mrs.) 687
Fowlkes, Emma 655
Fox, --- (Mrs.) 634
  Arthur 633, 635
  Elizabeth 634
  Elizabeth Brown 648
  Henry 83
  John Poland Moses Linton Isaac Howard 647
  Joseph (Colonel) 590
  Martha 748
  Matilda 631, 635
  Will 298, 303
  William 297, 298
Foy, Emmett 70
  Virginia 70
  Winthrop 70
Franklin, Catharine 104
  Ellen Baford 104
  Lucy 673
  Robert B. 104
  Walter D. 103
Fravir, --- (Miss) 17
Frazier, --- 283
  Alexander 202
  Elizabeth 231

Frazier, (cont.)
  Joseph 126
  Margaret 202
  Sarah E. 101, 126, 137
Freeman, 752
  Dandridge C. 748
French 471, 472, 483, 484
  --- (Dr.) 419
  --- (Miss) 413
  --- (Mr.) 379, 399
  Alice 471
  Alice Lee 471
  Amanda (Chinn) 470
  Anne 469
  Benjamin 470
  Benjamin Quinn 471
  Burgess 744
  Catherine 470
  Clara 469
  Daniel 391, 402
  Elizabeth 471
  Emma --- 469
  Florence 469
  Franklin 471
  Harriet Pryor 471
  Isaac 469
  J. Wickliffe 469
  James 468, 469
  James II 468
  Jane 470
  Jay 469
  Jennie 469
  John W. 469, 744
  John Wickliffe 470, 471
  Joseph 469, 470
  Joseph L. 469
  Keziah 468
  Laura 469
  Luiza 744
  Mahala 744
  Margaret 124, 145, 170, 367, 391, 393, 402
  Mariah 744
  Martha Wingate 469
  Mary 227
  Mary Katherine 470
  Matilda Ann 744
  P. (?) 21
  Polly 469, 485
  Polly (Taylor) 468, 469, 483, 484
  Richard 468
  Richard C. 470
  Richard Calloway (Dr.) 471
  Robert Lee 471
  Sallie 469
  Sally Taylor 744
  Sarah Ann 470
  Sarah Elender 744
  Sidney 469, 470
  Stephen 470
  Susan 469
  Susannah 744
  Wickliffe 471
  William 451, 468, 469, 471, 474, 485, 575
  William (Captain) 468
Frick, --- 65
  Caroline 150
Frog, --- (Capt.) 398

Frog, (cont.)
  --- (Miss) 398
  John 397, 399
  John (Capt.) 402
Frogg, John 373, 374, 375, 379
  John (Capt.) 379
  John, Jr. 374
Froman, --- 439
Frost, Lucinda 237, 241
  Margaret 227
Fry, --- (Miss) 394, 408
  --- (Mrs.) 398
  Amanda F. (Miss) 41
  Joshua 388
  Mary Dunbar 226
  Smith D. 226
Frye, A. S. (Mrs.) 18, 22
  Archie Spears 23
  Margaret Mc. R. D. 53
Fugate, --- 3
  Cole 3
  Jane 3
  Martha 3
  Polly 3
  William 3
  Winnie 3
Fulkerson, William 356
Fuller, Esther 185, 186, 187
Fulton, Anne 24
Fuqua, Katherine 591
  Mary 591
Furgeson, Ann 388
  Anna 382
Furr, Stephen 460
G., --- (Mrs.) 246
Gad 682
Gadby, Gabriel 300
  John 300
Gadsby, --- 89
Gaines 179, 413
  --- (Gen.) 405, 413
  --- (Mr.) 410
  B. O. 615
  B. W. (Mrs.) 271
  Benjamin W. 271
  Daniel 250
  Edmund Pendleton (General) 367, 405
  James 382, 405
  Mary 306
  Mary E. 271
  Mary Martha (Miss) 307
  R. P. 625
  Robt. 625
  Sarah 250
  Squire 574
  Squire, Jr. 574
  Thomas 382, 405
  Thomas (Mr.) 413
Gainsborough, --- (Earl of) 85
Gale, Robert D. 625
  Villore 625
Gallaway, Joseph 256
  Sophia 256
Galloway 765
  --- (Mrs.) 765
  Ann 770
  David (Mr.) 488
  William 488
Galt 478

Galt, (cont.)
　William A. (Rev.)
　　478
Gamble, --- (Miss) 411
Gano, John 751
　Stephen F. (Dr.) 88
　Susan 751
Gardiner, Julia 221
Gardner 345
　Cynthia 345
　Harriet Eliza (Bradford) 477
　Harriet May 477
　Henson 345
　Hiram Edwin 477
　Mary 704
　Patton 345
　Samuel C. 345
　Susanna 613
Garfield, --- 259
Garland 533
　--- 273, 600
　Bettie 273
　Catherine M. 272
　Elizabeth Bibb 590
　Mary Rice (Miss) 272
　Nathaniel 590
　Rice 272
Garley, Mary (Berry) (Mrs.) 573
Garlick, Braxton 225
　Mary C. Webb 225
　Medora Braxton 225
Garlington, Elizabeth (?) 486
　Marie 391
Garner, Julia 143
Garnes, --- (Mr.) 406
Garr, Mary Magdalene 271
Garrard, 679, 689, 690, 755
　--- (Governor) 755
　Ann Elinor 690
　Ann Ellinor 689
　Daniel 689, 690
　Elizabeth 690
　Elizabeth Mountjoy 689, 690
　James 689, 690, 754
　James, Jr. 689
　John 689, 690
　Maria 689, 690, 754
　Mary 689, 690
　Nancy 690
　Peggy 689, 690
　Sarah 690
　William 689, 690
Garrett 771, 772, 773
　--- 771
　Elizabeth 772
　Elizabeth Black 771, 772
　James 772
　Jane 772
　John 772, 773
　Martha 772
　Nancy 772
　Polly 772
　Robert 773
　Sarah 772
　William 771, 772, 773
Garrison, Mary 536
Garth, Alice D. 40
　Belle 134
　Jefferson 134

Garth, (cont.)
　John M. 134
　Mattie 134
　Susanna 134
Gartman, Arabella 651
Garvey, Prestons 423
Garvin, Sallie Ann 698
Gascoigne 452
　Alice 451, 452, 456, 486
　Thomas 454
Gaskins 454, 489
　--- 454
　Alice 451, 452, 456, 486
　Dorothy 489
　Thomas 454
Gate, --- (General) 515
Gates, --- 500
Gatewood, Elva 51
Gathright 192
Gaugh, --- 14
　--- (Mr.) 14
Gay 765, 766, 767, 768
　--- (Mr.) 14
　Agnes 770, 776
　Alice (Miss) 248
　Augustus 51
　Benjamin 17, 51
　Benjamin P. 18, 23
　Benjamin Patton 17, 51
　Betty 51
　E. 48
　Eleanor 766
　Elizabeth 51
　Elizabeth H. 51
　Elizabeth Hume 47
　Elva Gatewood 51
　Ester 17
　Gatewood 51, 732
　Georgia 574
　H. Burton 228
　H. Burton, Jr. 228
　Henry 23, 762, 766
　Hetty 23
　J. D. 48
　J. D. , Jr. 51
　Jacob Douglas 51
　James 14, 17, 18, 23, 762, 766, 767, 769, 776
　James (Captain) 18, 23, 764
　James D. 47, 48
　Jane 762, 766, 767, 768, 769, 770
　Jean --- 767
　John 17, 23, 766, 769, 770
　Katherine Claggett 568
　Lizzie 48
　Lizzie H. (Mrs.) 49, 50
　Louise 228
　Lucy 51
　Maria 48
　Robert 23, 762, 766
　Robert McCreary 51
　Ruth 102
　Sally Patton 17
　Samuel 23, 766
　Sarah 657
　Sarah Patton 18
　Thresa McCreary 51

Gay, (cont.)
　W. D. 51
　W. D. (Dr.) 51
　William 23, 762, 766
Gayle, --- (Widow) 226
Gedney, Eleazer 73
　Ruth 73
Geiger, --- 668
　Fred (Captain) 671
　Jacob 671
Gelre, --- (Count of) 549
　Otto, (Count of) 547
Gelre and Cuick, Willem (Duke of) 547
Gentry, Lavinia 150
George, Alice Lee 225
　Joseph 368
　St. Elmo (Rev.) 575
　William 368, 386
Gester, (See also Keister)
　Hanna 12
　Hannah 12
Gex, J. A. 447
Gibbons, --- 626
　Betty 457
　Judith 457
Gibson, --- (Miss) 411
　Andrew Crawford 578
　Ann 640
　Betsy 578
　Eleanor 578
　Elizabeth Lee 568
　Gregg (Dr.) 640
　John Crawford 578
　Nancy 578
　Nannie Pottinger 640
　Susan 640
　Susan Cotton 578
　William 12
Gilbert, Aquilla 328
　Emily 328
　Ezekiel 328
　Isaac 328
　Jane 328
　Polly 328
Gilchrist, Catharine 133
　Edward 133
Giles, --- (Miss) 406
　Charles 405
Gilham, Reginald 133
Gill, Bettie 500
　Charles W. 512
　William 517
Gillenwater 529
　--- (Dr.) 529
Gillespie, Hugh 329
　Thomas 329
Gillett, A. 627
Gilliam, --- (Mr.) 267
Gillock, Kittie 677
Gills, Moe 712
Gilmer, --- (Gov.) 366, 370
　Charles L. 399
　Elizabeth 399
　George B. 399
　George R. 379
　James Jackson 399
　John 399, 403
　Mary Merriweather 398
　Peachey R. 399

Gilmer, (cont.)
  Peachy B. 398
  Peachy M. 379
  Peachy R. 375
  Peachy Ridgeway 398
  Thomas 398, 399
  Thomas M. 379, 398
  William Benjamin
    Strother 399
  Wm. Benjamine Strother
    379
Gilmoore 305
  Anny 306
  David 306
  James 306
  Jefferson 306
  John 305
  Robt. 305
  Samuel 306
  William 306
  Winston 306
Gilmore 295
  Anderson 303
  Anderson Smith 303
  Cyrenius 303
  Elizabeth E. 302
  James 302, 303
  Jeeffrson 303
  Jefferson 302, 303
  John 303
  Mary Martha 302, 303
  Robert 301, 302, 303,
    304
Gilmour, Martha 305
Giltner, 749
  --- (General) 529
  B. 625
  Ellen 753
Gisbertson, John (of
    Meteren) 554
Gist, --- 377
  --- (Colonel) 300
  Mordecai 19
  Nathaniel (Colonel)
    296, 299, 431
  Sarah 431
Gittings, Victoria (
    (Miss) 613
Given, --- (Miss) 83
  R. F. 126, 572
Givens, Agnes 147
  Virginia 147
  William 330
  William A. 147
Glass, David 20, 568
  Hugh M. 568
  Marg. 568
  Margaret Jane 568
  Sarah Paxton Steele
    568
  Zack 18
Glassell, --- (Miss)
    403
Glenn, Dan 568
  David 642
  Frances 627
  Martha S. 340
  Nancy 642
Gleson, Peyton 568
Glidewell, Mary 350
  Nash 350
Glousester, --- (Duke
    of) 437
Glover, --- (Lane) 572
  --- (Mrs.) 572
  Annie 577
Godby, Gabriel 300

Godby, (cont.)
  John 300
Godden, Jane 658
Godfrey, 490
  Frederick 490
  Mathew 490
  Sarah 490, 491
Godwyn, (See also Good-
    win)
  Harold 50
Goebel, --- (Governor)
    146
Goetschie, Anna 82
  Maurice (Rev.) 82
Goff, Ann Prewitt 51
  Ben Douglas 51
  Ben Douglas, Jr. 51
  Benjamin 51
  Benjamin Douglas 15
  Bessie Spahr 15
  Strauder D. 51
  Thomas 16
Goggin 634
Gonoe, Daniel 363
Gooch, --- (Gov.) 560
  William 430
  William (Governor)
    562
Goode 350, 598, 599
  Benjamin 350
  Daniel C. 350
  Daniel C., Sr. 353
  Ed. 654
  Edward 653
  Elizabeth 350
  Elizabeth (?) 353
  Elizabeth J. (Haw-
    kins) 350
  G. Brown 350
  Jemima 350
  John 350, 568
  John Collier 350
  Lucinda 350
  Mary 350, 598, 599
  Mary (Glidewell)
    350
  Nancy 350
  Narcissa 353
  Reuben J. 353
  Robert (Col.) 599
  Sarah 350
  Susannah 350, 352
  William 350
  William H. 350
Goodloe, Carrie (Miss)
    697
  William (Judge) 697
Goodwin, (See also God-
    wyn) 690
  --- (Mr.) 583
  John 690
  S. S. 62
Gordon, --- (Mr.) 488
  George W. (Maj.
    Gen.) 271
  John 338, 509
  Mollie 152, 154
Gore, Andrew 94
  Douglas 646
Gossett, --- (Mrs.)
    305
  F. 304
  Fountain 303, 304,
    305
Gough, Elizabeth S.
    (Mrs.) 395
  Hattie 163

Gough, (cont.)
  Rebecca 101, 137
Gould, Francis 116, 117
  Nathan 694
Goulder, Alice 158
  Charles N. (Rev.)
    158
  Ernest Preston 158
  James William 158
  Ruth 158
Govertz, Cornelia 633
Govertz van den Wyngaert,
    Tobias 633
Gow, Emily 512
  James 512
Gracey 57, 64, 80
  Charles 65
  Elizabeth 68
  Ellen 66
  Frank 66, 68
  Frank Patton 65, 68
  George 57, 64, 68,
    80
  George Tilford 65
  Hope 66
  Iola 66
  Irene 66
  James 57, 64
  James Nelson 64
  James Nelson, Sr. 57
  John 57, 64
  Judith 68
  Julien 66
  Julius 66
  Kate 65
  Laura 66
  Louise 66
  Lucy 66
  Lucy Castner 68
  Maria Tilford 66
  Martha Nelson 57, 65
  Mary 66
  Mary Beaumont 68
  Matthew 65, 68
  Matthew Lyon 57, 65,
    68
  Mildred 65
  Minnie 66
  Rebecca 57, 64
  Robert 68
  Sarah Bright 68
  William 57, 65, 68
  William Adolph 64
  William Robert 66
Graddy, Fanny 102
  Louise Garrett 771
  Lucy 51
Graden, Thos (Mrs.)
    569
Grafton, Philip 589
Graham 766, 767
  --- 89, 476
  --- (Dr.) 89
  C. C. (Dr.) 89, 236
  Christopher 330
  Christopher C.
    (Dr.) 236
  Eliza 243
  George 278
  Hannah 285, 286
  Jane 330
  John 762
  John (Mr.) 488
  Mary 40
  Mary Elizabeth 151,
    172
  Richard (Major) 634

Graham, (cont.)
  Robert 27, 330
  Robert (Rev.) 40
  Samuel S. (Col.)
    629
  Theresa M. 739
Grandin, Samuel 82
  Sarah 82
Grant, 686
  --- 712, 713
  --- (General) 273
  --- (Mr.) 373
  Elizabeth 686
  Elizabeth Boone 686
  John 372, 373, 617
  Margery --- 686
  Rebecca 686
  William 686
Grason, --- (Colonel)
    296
Grat, Squire 712
Grattan, Eliza Frances
    399
Graves, --- (Miss)
    388
  --- (Mr.) 432, 544
  Albert G. 432
  Amelia 419, 431
  Ann R. 433
  Augustus 51
  Ben 51
  Charles T. 432
  Charles Tandy 432,
    433
  Claiborne 432
  Claibourne 419
  Clairborne G. 432
  Clairbourne 432
  Edna Elizabeth 140
  Eleanora Burnley 51
  Elizabeth H. 51
  George S. 140
  Harriet Amanda Patton
    Hughes 52
  Isaac F. 432
  Jacob, Jr. 51
  Jacob Hughes 50
  Jacob Hughes, Jr. 51
  James 51
  Jane 51
  Jane Hughes 32, 51
  Jane Rachel 25, 51
  Jane Rachel Hughes 50
  John (Col.) 388
  Joseph 50
  Julia 140
  Julia Mary 51
  Margaret 578
  Mary Goodwin 50
  Robert Benjamin 41,
    50, 51
  Ruth 140
  Sallie Elizabeth 51
  Sally (Tandy) 432
  Sarah 432
  Thomas 420
  William 431, 432
  William P. 432
Gray, (See also Grey)
    484, 485
  --- 486
  --- (Captain) 485,
    486
  --- (Miss) 498
  --- (Mr.) 411
  --- (Mrs.) 485
  Annie M. 473, 476

Gray, (cont.)
  Benjamin 473, 485
  Daniel 403
  Dave (Mrs.) 413
  Elizabeth T. 468
  Emma Duncan (Mrs.)
    243
  George 391, 402, 413
  H. P. 517
  Hattie (Miss) 273
  Jemima 451, 473, 485
  John 20
  John D. 451, 467, 484,
    485
  Louise 577
  Mary Jane 468
  Mattie 408
  " Mimy " 473
  N. E. (Mrs.) 692
  Nancy Taylor 468
  Presley 485
  Presley (Colonel)
    485
  Sally Ann 468, 484
  Victor (Mrs.) 164
  William 485
Grayson, --- 377
  --- (Colonel) 299
  William (Colonel)
    300
Greaff, Eve Anna 85
Greavis, Adele 736
Greely, Horace 528
Green 370
  --- 345, 541, 576,
    610
  --- (Col.) 111
  Ada 407
  Ann Coleman 72
  Annie 407
  Austin 407
  Benjamin Franklin 407
  Betsey 406
  Charity 603
  Charles (Rev.) 84
  Clemmie 407
  Cora 407
  Daniel S. 407
  Eleanor 465
  Eleanor Dunn 72
  Ethel 72, 407
  Francis 407
  Francis W. 407
  Francis Wyatt 72, 383,
    406
  Frank W. 407
  Gertrude 407
  Grace N. 407
  Irene W. 155
  James 407
  James Olive (Dr.)
    407
  Jennie 407
  Jennie Crumpler
    (Mrs.) 46
  John 407
  John Ball 407
  John English 72, 407
  Joseph 406, 407
  Joseph M. 407
  Joseph Strother 72
  Keeziah 407
  Lawrence 407
  Lucy 406, 567
  Lucy Strother 72
  Mabel 407
  Mable 72

Green, (cont.)
  Martha 407, 576
  Martha Ann English
    72
  Martha Nelson 73
  Martine S. (Mrs.)
    120
  Mary (Ball) 465
  Matilda S. 155, 165
  Mildred 72, 407
  Mollie 407
  Moses 403
  Moses (General)
    392, 393
  Nancy 406
  Nester C. 407
  Neville 407
  Norva 407
  Norvin 72, 407
  Norvin (Dr.) 383,
    406
  Norwin English 407
  Pinckney Frank 407
  R. G. 21
  Rennie 407
  Robert 4, 72, 383,
    406, 465
  Sallie 36
  Strother 407
  Susan Martha Ball 72
  Susan T. (Mrs.)
    397
  Susannah Thornton 407
  T. M. 427
  Thos. 567
  Thos. M. 111
  Thos. M. (Col.) 112
  Thomas Marshall 197
  Thomas Marshall
    (Col.) 111
  Thompson 407
  Thornton 407
  Tom (Mr.) 202
  Virginia 157, 166
  Warren 407
  William 72, 161, 383,
    406, 407
  William N. 85
  Williena N. 737
  Willina 575
Greenaway, John 340
Greene, 201
  Nathaniel (Gen.)
    344
Greenfield, Mary 466
Greenlaw, --- (Baron
    of) 26
Greenlee, James 320
  Mary 327
Greenwell, Sallie
    (Mrs.) 648
Greenwood, Mary F. 394,
    409
Greer, George Cabell
    414, 417
  Isaah 672
  Sarah 672
Gregory (Gregorie)
    499
  Joseph 344
  Martha Ward 599
  Mary 395
  Pauline (Miss) 501
  Richard 599
Gresham, Susan (Mrs.)
    399
Grey, (See also Gray)

Grey, (cont.)
　J. P. 577
　Katherine 577
　William 577
Gribble, A. M. 105
　A. M., Jr. 105
　Andrew W. 105
　Anna 105
　Chas. King 105
　Elizabeth 106
　Elizabeth Randolph 105
　Jennie 105
　Robert Fonda 106
　Robt. Fonda, Jr. 106
　Samuel 105
　Theodore 106
Griffin, Elizabeth 387
　George 387
　Wm. 218
Griffing, Phebe 728
Griffith 690
　--- 690
　Belle (Mrs.) 699
　Calvin 690, 691
　Charles 691
　Clemons, Jr. 691
　Elenore E. 691
　John M. 690
　Marian (Hon.) 449
　Marinday 691
　Mary 691
　Nannie 124, 145
　Samuel a. 690
　Samuel A. 691
　Spenser 690
Griffiths, Clemons 690
　Marinda 690
Grigg, John 709
Grimes, --- (Miss) 83
　Charles 32
　Lucy 112, 184
　Mary 32, 511
Grishon, Julia Ann 425
Griswold, 727
　--- 727
　Clarina 728
　Deborah 727, 728
　Elizabeth 727
　George 727
　Hannah 728
　Hannah (Mrs.) 729
　John 727, 728
　John, Esqr. 729
　Lucy 728
　Lydia 728
　Mary 727
　Mathew 727
　Matthew 727, 728
　Patience 727
　Phebe 727, 728
　Sarah 727, 728
　Thomas 727, 728
Grosenbaugh, Royal 226
Grosjean, Julia Allen 429
　Julia Ann 425
Grotius 547
Groves, --- (Miss) 184, 232
　Frederick A. (Mrs.) 429
　John (Col.) 395
　William 185
　William Jordan 185
Grubb, George 354
　Isaac 354

Grubb, (cont.)
　Julia Ann 354
　Sarah 354
Grubbs, Lucy 673
Grymes, John 560
　John Randolph 233
　Lucy 233, 234
　Mary 233
　Philip 217, 233
　Philip, Jr. 233
　Susan 233
Guelph, Judith 437
Guerrant, 573
　Daniel 508, 573
　Judith 496, 573
　Magdalen Trabue 573, 751
　Peter 496, 508, 573
　Pierre 751
Gufton, Susie Effie 118
Gum, Nell Park 697, 699, 700
　Robert (Mrs.) 697, 705, 707
　Robert Park 698
　Robert R. (Mrs.) 679, 694
　Robert Richardson 679, 698
Gummere, Francis Barton 79
　Francis Barton, Jr. 79
Gunn, R. H. 157
Gunnins, Betsy 616
Gunnoe, Daniel 363
Guthrie, --- 240
　--- (Senator) 500
　Ann Augusta 500, 513
　Elizabeth Anne 351
　Irby 351
　James 513
Guy, Eleanor 758
Guyn, Robert 772
Gwin, Drusilla 580
　Margaret 328
Gysbertsen Van Meteren, Jan 553
Haas, Jacob 606
Hackley, A. B. 696
　Mary Frances --- 696
　Richard S. 220
Haddon, John 337, 342
　William 330
Hagan, Jennie 673
Hager, --- 338
　Daniel 338
　George 338
　John 338
　John, Sr. 338
　Joseph 338
　Margaret 224
　Rachel 338, 353
Haggard, 679, 691, 730
　Bulah 730
　Chester A. 730
　Clifton 730, 731
　D. P. C. 730
　David D. 691
　Elizabeth 691
　Franky 691
　Garrett 691
　Gusta B. 730, 731
　James 691
　John T. 691
　Lewis 691
　Martin 691

Haggard, (cont.)
　Mary 691
　Matilda 691, 708
　Milly 691
　Nancy 691
　Orna May 730
　Pleasant 691
　Rutha Belle 730, 731
　Sarah 691
　Ward 730, 731
Haggin, Eliza Sanders 752
　J. B. 752
　Sarah Jane 681
Hahn, Susan 568
Halbert, Susanna 643
　Thomas, Sr. 643
Haldeman, John (Mrs.) 187
Hale 573
　--- 355
　George 574
　Peter 355
　Sarah 355
　Smith 573, 574
　Susanna Smith 573
　Susannah Smith 573
　Zachariah 355
Hales, Frances J. 739
Haley, Catharine 161
Hall, 754
　--- 515
　Allen 308
　Ann Gibson (?) 640
　Benjamin Logan 308
　Catherine B. 253
　Catherine Bainbridge 251
　Catherine Wood 643
　David Stevenson 308
　Eleanor James 640
　Elizabeth Logan 308
　Fannie 692
　H. C. 416
　Isaac 643
　Jeremiah 754
　John 308
　John (Dr.) 565, 566
　Maria Isabella 308
　Mary (Polly) 192
　Mary Prudence 306
　Moses 308, 309, 314
　Moses, Jr. 308
　Nancy 4
　Nathan H. 665
　Nicholas Snowden 640
　Olivia Winchester 325
　Polly 192
　Sallie 575
　Sarah 386, 395, 754
　Sarah Bainbridge 251, 253
　Susannah 496
　Thomas 754
　Uriel Sebree (Hon.) 87
　William A. 87
　Woodford 308
Halley, (See also Holley) 731
　--- 53
　Elizabeth F. Stuart 732
　Maria W. 731
　Sarah 613
Halloway, --- (Miss) 274
Halsell 687

Halsell, (cont.)
  Precious L. 687
Hamblin, Nancy 116
Hamel, --- 557
  Jan 556
  John 557
Hamilton 340, 341, 656, 763
  --- 245, 331, 341
  --- (Aunt) 758
  --- (Grandfather) 658
  --- (Grandmother) 658
  --- (Miss) 342
  Abner 341
  Agnes 557
  Alexander 766
  Andrew 658, 659, 761, 763
  Andrew (Governor) 557
  Archibald 329, 331, 341
  C. 298, 299
  Dianna 739
  Edgar 530
  J. C. 699
  James 330
  Jane 659
  John 329, 330, 331, 337, 338, 341, 342, 344, 658
  Margaret 659, 766
  Martha 656, 659
  Mary 329, 331, 342, 344, 659
  Mary (Stuart) 341
  Orie P. 298
  Paulina 694
  Peggy 338
  Ruth 657
  S. M. 319
  Sarah 658, 659
  William 320, 342, 344, 657, 658, 659, 762
Hamlake, --- (Baron of) 660
Hammock, John 420
Hammon, 669
  Charles Franklin 668
  Edward 668
  Frances 666, 668
  Jesse Franklin 668
  Jesse Franklin (Judge) 666
  John 666
  Martha Ann 668
  Martha Ann Paget 666
  Stratton O. 660
Hampton, 679
  --- (Miss) 270
  Alfred Howard 680
  Cynthy 680
  David 679
  David, Jr. 680
  David Reed 680
  Elizabeth 679, 680, 744
  Elvie C. 143
  Geo. Washington 680
  Jeremiah 744
  John 680
  John Andrew Jackson 680
  Mary 680

Hampton, (cont.)
  Nancy 680
  Sarah 680
  Wade B. 680
Hancock, Caroline 387
  George 386, 387
  George (Col.) 387
  Jno. Strother 387
  Julia 387
  Mary 387
  Pearl 675
  Pearle 675
Hands, Catherine Gertrude 129
Handy, Ann 629
  Betty 626, 627
  Charlotte 627
  Evelyn Crady 648
  George 501
  Henry 627
  James 627
  John 627
  Joshua 627
  Mary 501
  Nancy 627
  Peggy 627
  Sarah 627
  Sydney S. (Mrs.) 648
  William 627
Hanley, Mary B. 723
Hanly, John 754
  S. G. (Mr.) 248
Hanna, --- 771
  --- (Mr.) 92
Hannah, --- (Mr.) 92
Hannibal 420
Hansbrough, --- (Mr.) 408
  George Woodson (Col.) 394, 408
  Hamilton 394, 408, 409
  Hamilton (Mrs.) 394
  John S. (Rev.) 408
  John Strother (Rev.) 394
Harbison, Agnes 569
  David 569
  Pauline 569
  Wm. 568
Hardage, Elizabeth --- 465
  James 465
  Lydia 464, 465
  Sarah 465
Hardaway, Pattie (Miss) 400
Harden, Marie 575
Hardesty, Bert 149
  Bertie Railey (Mrs.) 153
  Egbert 149
  Frank 149
  John 149, 150
  Louis 150
  Mayo 150
  Shortridge 150
Hardin 490, 505, 753, 754
  --- (Col.) 498
  Bayless 54
  Bayless (Mr.) 482
  Bayless E. 462
  Ben 501
  Caroline 512

Hardin, (cont.)
  Charles (Judge) 501, 512
  Charles, Jr. 512
  Elizabeth Logan 753
  J. J. (Col.) 753
  Jane 512
  John 512
  John J. 753
  Joseph H. 591
  Julia (M. D.) 512
  Juliet Calhoun 753
  Mark (Col.) 308
  Martin 753
  Martin (Rev.) 512
  Martin D. 753
  P. Watt (Attorney General) 501
  Parker, Jr. 512
  Parker H. 512
  Parker Watkins 512
  Susan Mary 161, 166
Harding, J. 687
  Jasper 687
Harker, Charles M., Jr. 273
  Charles M., Sr. 273
  Charles Matson, Jr. 273
  Edith Ridgway 273
  Elizabeth Walker 273
  Mary 273
  Mary (Miss) 273
  Mary Haines 273
Harlan, Lula Overton 692
  Nancy Robinson (Chenoweth) 535
Harlin, 679, 691
  A. D. 691, 692
  Andrew Depp 691, 692
  Andrew Depp, Jr. 691
  Clay 691
  Esther Elizabeth 691
  Grover 691, 692
  I. C. 691, 692
  J. B. 692
  John B. 691
  Lola 691, 692
  Mary 691
  Mary Ann 691
  Nellie W. 691
  Phebe D. 691
  Phebe Depp 692
  Phebe E. 691
  Phebe Edna 692
  Ralph Travis 691
  Renie T. 691
  Rine 691
  Robert Clay 691
  S. C. 691, 692
  Samuel Seay 691
  Sarah L. 691
  Sarah Lela 692
  W. R. 692
  William R. 691
Harllee, William Curry 536
Harlow 679, 692
  Alexander P. 692
  Amanda J. 692
  B. F. 692
  B. F. (Mrs.) 692
  Benjamin F. 692
  Emely F. 692
  Fannie H. 692
  Fannie Hall 692
  Frances M. 692

Harlow, (cont.)
  Harriet Byron 692
  James L. 692
  Jane Eliza 692
  John H. 692
  Kathrine 692
  Martha Ann 692
  Mary F. 692
  Susan 693
  W. D. 692
  W. E. 693
  William D. 692
  William E. 692, 693
Harmon, George D. 530
Harness, Hannah 565
  Sarah 564
Harp, --- (Miss) 577
Harper 187
  --- (Mr.) 504
  Anne (Mrs.) 398
  Barbara Ann 184, 185, 186
  J. 630
  Lillian Dupuy Van Culin 518
  Ned 692
  Thomas Roberts 516
  William 186, 187, 625
Harper(s), --- 514
Harriman 75, 77
  Albert C. 130
  Albert C. Jr. 130
  Anne 75, 76
  Belle 130
  Briggs 130
  Caroline Mayo 131
  Elizabeth Belle 130
  Emmeline 75
  Ethel Borden 75
  Georgianna 130
  Grace Virginia 131
  Helen 131
  Herbert 76
  J. Borden 75
  James 75
  Jennie 130
  John Hulsey 130
  John McCutchen 131
  Joseph 75
  Joseph Halsey 130
  Leslie M. 130
  Lillie 76
  Louise 131
  Lucile 130
  Mary Margaret 130
  Oliver 75, 77
  Oliver, 1st 75
  Oliver, 2nd 75
  Regis A. 131
  Robert L. 131
  Robert S. 130
  Russell 129
  Russell, Jr. 130
  Susannah 535
  William Adams 130
  William P. (Dr.) 129, 130, 135
  William P., Jr. (Dr.) 129, 135
  William Peyton 129
Harris, --- 733
  --- (Miss) 592
  A. V. 151
  Addie Dunlap 315
  Alexander Henry 125
  An 733
  Ann 613

Harris, (cont.)
  Annie 105
  Elizabeth 733
  Emma Railey 125
  Foster 733
  Frances 733
  Henry 733, 734
  Henry M. 733
  James 733
  Jemima 583
  John 605, 733
  John Leonard (Dr.) 125
  Lola Bell 503
  Margaret Calhoun 222
  Margaret Leonard 125
  Mary 733
  N. 625
  Patsy 583
  Paulina 733
  Polina 733
  Polley 733
  Robert 733
  Saley 733
  Simeon B. 733
  Susannah 733
  W. E. 512
  William E. 733
  William Elliott 733
Harrison 21
  --- 121
  --- (General) 187, 498
  --- (Governor) 279
  --- (Miss) 83, 109
  --- (Mr.) 14
  --- (President) 586
  Albert 434
  Ann 4, 17, 18, 21, 24, 515
  Ann Elgin 24
  Ann Patton 17, 22, 24
  Anna 24
  Anna Patton 18
  Anne 217, 503
  Anne Carter 217
  Benjamin 17, 24, 182, 217, 231, 232, 233
  Benjamin (Governor) 83
  Cabell (Rev.) 112, 182
  Carter 110, 174, 183
  Carter H. 182, 230
  Carter Henry 112, 182, 230
  Daniel 14, 17, 18, 21, 22, 23, 24
  Daniel (Captain) 23
  Daniel (Mr.) 15
  Ellen Wayles (Mrs.) 209
  Elvira 233
  Hannah 17, 24, 212, 213
  Howard 228
  Isaiah 23
  Jane Cary 220
  Jane Nicholas 223
  Jefferson Randolph 223
  Jesse 23
  Jilson 434
  Lucy 217, 232
  Margaret 21, 24
  Margery 17

Harrison, (cont.)
  Micajah Volney 434
  Nannie 118
  Patton D. 17, 20, 21, 22, 24
  Patton Daniel 22
  Peyton 112
  Randolph 112, 228, 230
  Robert 112, 230
  Robert Carter 112, 182, 228
  Sarah Moore 23
  Susanna 182
  Susannah 270
  Sybil 613
  Wm. (Captain) 613
  William B. 223
  William H. (General) 503
  William Henry 182, 599
Harrod, --- 772
  James 772
  Wm. (Capt.) 58
Hart, --- 688, 706, 708, 727, 730, 731, 732
  Joel T. 262
  Nat 277
  Nat (Col.) 242
  Nathaniel 242, 582
  Nathaniel (Colonel) 431
  Nathaniel, Sr. (Col.) 582
  Susanna Preston 582
  Virginia 582
Hartson, Joseph 226
Harvey, John (Sir) 114
  Judith 535
  Onisephorus 489
Harvie 366, 367
  --- (Mrs.) 376
  Anna 401
  Blair 400
  Brockenbrough (Dr.) 400
  Charles 400
  Courtney 400
  Daniel 398
  Edwin J. 376, 400, 401
  Edwin J. (Col.) 377
  Eliza 400
  Ellen 401
  Emily 401
  Fanny 400
  Gabrella 366
  Gabriella 208, 219, 225, 376, 395, 396, 399
  Gabriella Augusta 400
  Irving 400
  Jacqueline B. 400
  Jacqueline B. (General) 376
  James 400
  Jaquelin B. (General) 367
  John 219, 400, 401
  John (Col.) 225, 366, 376, 381, 395, 399
  John (Mrs.) 401
  John (Sir) 177
  John, Jr. 376

Harvie, (cont.)
  John B. 400
  John Strother 400
  Julianna 401
  Katherine Ellen 401
  Lewis 376, 400
  Lewis E. 376, 400
  Lewis Edwin 376, 400, 401
  Llewellyn Jones 400
  Margaret 376
  Margaretta 401
  Martha 400
  Mary 223, 400, 401
  Mary Whitlock 400
  Nancy 398
  Pattie 400
  Sarah 400
  Seddon 400
  Susan 401
  Virginia 376, 401
  Wm. Old 400
  Wm. Wallace 401
Hase, (See also Hawes)
  Sarah 12
Haselrigg, (See also Hazelrigg)
  --- 588
Haskell, Frank 68
Haskins 501
  Ann 654
  Elizabeth 500, 501, 513
  Elizabeth (Hill) 508, 513, 514, 516
  Jane 500, 501, 513, 516
  Martha 501, 504, 515
  Mary 500, 501, 514
  Robert (Col.) 500, 501, 508, 513, 514, 515, 516
  Thomas 510, 654
Hassinger, Susan 105
Hatch, Cyril 76
  Grace M. 156
  Rutherford 76
Hatcher, Ben 497
  Benjamin 510
  Mary 510
  Robert 515
  Susanna 510
Hathaway, Pattie 376
Havermyer, --- 76
Haversham, --- (Baron) 588
Hawes, (See also Hase)
  --- (Mrs.) 8, 9
  Elizabeth (Gold) 259
  Hannah 4, 9
  Henry 4
  Peter (Mrs.) 7
  Sarah Dyer 4, 13, 14
Hawkins 170, 180, 366, 368, 385
  --- (Capt.) 170
  Anna Gabriella 400
  B. F. 625
  Bejamine Dabney 395
  Catharine 147
  Catharine Keith 108, 111, 139, 169
  Catherine (Miss) 139
  Catherine Keith 101, 137, 386

Hawkins, (cont.)
  Charlotte Ashmore 395, 592, 754
  Elijah 575
  Emma 527
  Frances 325
  I. 625
  Isham 754
  Isham Keith 203, 368, 386, 395
  Jacob 527
  James K. 395
  John 376, 377, 381, 395, 400, 401
  Joseph 527
  Katherine Keith 173, 174, 175, 177, 179, 395
  Lew (Miss) 441
  Lucy 368, 385, 386, 395, 404
  Lucy J. 468
  Margaret 376
  Margaretta 400
  Mary 462, 575
  Moses 368, 385, 395, 404
  Moses (Capt.) 169, 170, 179, 180, 368, 384, 385
  Moses, Jr. 386
  Sallie 527
  Sally 404
  Sarah 368
  Sarah Bailey 385, 404
  Sarah Cordelia 629
  Steven 527
  Susan 404
  Susan Strother 395
  Susannah H. (Mrs.) 271
  Susannah Strother 385, 404
  Thomas W. 689
  W. B. 575
  W. W. 468
  William 625
  William Strother 108, 111, 169, 175, 176, 179, 203, 368, 385, 395, 404
Hawthorne, Bess L. 521
Hay, Samuel 320
Hayden, --- 213, 537, 538
  --- (Mr.) 213
  Horace Edwin (Rev.) 212
  Noah G. 240
Haydon, --- 586, 590
  Charles 705
  John 301
  Sue (Mrs.) 307
Hayes, --- (Mr.) 531
Haymaker, Jesse N. 712
Hayney, Henry 347
Hays, --- (President) 390
  Charles 320
  John 320
  Samuel Quintus 691
Hayward, W. W. (Rev.) 414
Hazelrigg, (See also Haselrigg)
  Ely 696

Hazen, --- (Col.) 596
Hazzard, --- 555
Head 752
  Martha Ann 471
Headley, Katherine 41
Heale, Bettie 574
  George 574
  Priscilla Downman 574
  William 574
Hearn, Andrew 625
  Sarah 629
  Warren 629
Heckscher, Ledyard 73
Hedger, Harry 149
  J. A. 149
Hedges, Soloman 559
Hedpeth, James 699
Helm, --- 511
  Ann Elizabeth 155
  Elizabeth 165
  William Duvall (M. D.) 513
Helms, Richard 488
Helton, Jesse 362
Hemphill, Minnie 102
Hempstead, Henrietta 741
  Henrietta E. 740
Henderson, --- 274
  Alexander 429
  Andrew 151
  Elizabeth (Miss) 273
  Nathaniel (Capt.) 265
  Sarah 656
  William 151
Hendrick, --- (Miss) 600
Hendricks, --- (Miss) 599
  Francis 363
  John 749
Hendricks of Laeckervelt, --- 554
Hendricksen, Femmetjen 554
  Macyke 554, 557
  Macyken 558
  Roelof 556
Hendrygksen, Macyke 554
Hening, --- 91, 430, 433
Henning, --- 61, 93, 405
Henry, --- (?) 254
Henry, Alexander 125
  Alexander (Rev.) 105, 125, 127
  Alexander, Jr. 105, 125
  Arthur McG. 46
  Catharine Clifton 105, 125
  Elizabeth 582
  Emma Railey 125
  Emma Yeaman 105, 125
  Frank Berryman 105, 125
  Gano 46
  Hallie 46
  James 125
  John 341
  Margaret 125
  Margaret Ellen 223
  Mary 125, 626
  Patrick 63, 366, 374, 402, 567
  Patrick (Gov.) 281, 344, 582

808

Henry, (cont.)
  Randolph 125
  Robert 68
  Robert P. 18
  Susanna 366, 374
  Susanna (Miss) 402
  Thomas 46
  Urey 68
  William 125
Henson, --- 345
Henton, Mildred 591
Herndon, --- 477
  Clara 124, 144
  Jemima 673
  Rector 124, 145
  W. L. 124, 144
  Waller 35
Herring, Mary B. (Mrs.) 723, 724
Hertford, --- (Earl of) 660
Hevener, --- (Miss) 9
Hewett, Alfred M. 71
  Fay Lenora 71
Hewitt, Amy 407
  Emily Cook 71
Hewlett 591
Hewlitt, Elizabeth Kendal 412
Hickley, Sarah 243
Hicklin, 341, 752, 763
  Hannah 328
  James (Capt.) 328
  Jane 328
  Thomas 330
Hickman, 750, 752
  --- 479
  Catherine 39
  Edwin 420
  John (Dr.) 592
  Paschal (Capt.) 87
  Paschal (Colonel) 246
  William 747, 751, 752
  William (Rev.) 474
  William, Sr. (Rev.) 479
Hiden, M. W. 460
  Philip Wallace (Mrs.) 460
Hider, Adam 12
Higbee 632
  --- 632
Higdon 679
  Ann A. 693
  I. 693
  Isaac A. 693
  Ishmael 693
  James Newton 693
  Joseph 693
  Joseph A. 693
  Joseph Allen 693
  Joshua W. 693
  Margaret 693
  Margaret Anna 693
  Martha 693
  Martha Jane 693
  Ozias H. 693
  Ozirres L. 693
  Rachel R. S. 693
  Sarah T. 693
  Sarah Thompson 693
  Susan Mariah 693
  William Jasper 693
Higgins, Aaron 674
  John S. 311
  Lola 158

Hildreth, Gano 48
Hill 501, 508
  --- 669
  A. P. (General) 606
  Annie Marshall 34
  Bettie K. 306
  Eliz. 567
  Eliza 307
  Elizabeth 70, 508, 515
  Fred J. 640
  Henry 256
  James 192
  John 457, 516
  Joseph Kent 640
  Lucy Ann 306, 307
  Maggie C. 307
  Margaret 256
  Margaret C. 306
  Marshall 34
  Martha Susan 306
  Mary Ann 306
  Mary Ellen 640
  Mary Hughes 34
  Mary Prudence 307
  Permelia H. 306
  Rebecca Jane 306, 307
  Ross 227
  Samuel Henry 306, 307
  Sarah 256
  Sarah J. 409
  T. D. 306, 307
  Thomas D. 306
  William Kimmel 640
  Wm. Thomas 306
Hillyar, Sallie 140
Hilton, Benjamin 362
  Eliphaz 362
  Jesse 362
  John 362
Hind, Lee H. 36
  Lucile 36
  R. M. Samuel 36
  S. Wayne 36
Hines, Richard Percy 226
  William 592
Hinker, --- 377
Hinton, Elizabeth W. (Mrs.) 40
  Thomas, Jr. 623
Hisky, Joseph 640
Hite, --- (Dr.) 403
  Abraham 563
  Edmund 403
  Eliza 403
  Fontaine 403
  Isaac 403
  Joost 563
  Jost 562
  Mary 513
Hiter, Laura 161
Hites, A. 20
Hoard, --- (Miss) 270
Hobacker, Philip 700
  Robert 700
Hobbs 67
  Ann Manyard 584
  Deborah 584
  E. D. 670
  Elizabeth 584, 709
  Joseph 584
  Joshua 584
  Lucrecia L. 161
  Mary 584
  Rachel 584
  Sarah 584
  Susan 584

Hobbs, (cont.)
  Susan E. 67
Hobson, Samuel 510
Hockaday, Irvine 565
  Lucy 565
Hockaway, Lucy 564
Hocker, Edward Berry 163
  James E. 163, 167
  Leonidas Oates 163, 167
  Lon O. 163
Hockinsmith, --- 604
Hodge, --- (Mrs.) 657
  Abraham 536
  Andrew 657
  James 659
  John 659
  Margaret 770
  Paulina 657
  Samuel 760
Hodgen, Isaac 500
Hodgson, --- 369
Hogan, --- (Mrs.) 710
  Richard 92
  Smith D. (Mrs.) 710
Hoge 750
  Charles E. 749, 753
  French (Mr.) 749
  Moses (Rev.) 655
  S. French 749
  S. French (Mr.) 519
  Stephen French (Mr.) 520
Hogg, --- 274
Hogsett, Anna Lee 141
  William Rankin 162
  William Sloan 162, 167
Hoidale, Andrew D. (Dr.) 159
  Porter Madeira 159
Holbrook, J. 731
  John 703
Holcombe, Jno. 567
Holford, Dorothy (Lady) 82
Holiday, Nancy 348
  Polly 358
  William 348
Holladay, Nannie 224
Holland, --- 629
  --- (Lord) 83
Holley, (See also Halley) 53
  Henry 22
  Sibbee 22
Hollingsworth, --- (Mr.) 409
  Virginia 409
Hollinsead, Jeremiah 668
Holloway, Catherine 633
  Irene 104
  S. 17
  Thomas 632
Holman 573
  --- 433
  James 573
  James, Sr. 573
  Jane 573
  Sarah 573
  Tandy 433
Holmes 313
  Dudley (Mrs.) 311
  Dudley V. 312
  Eliza 313
  Eliza Emily 312

Holmes, (cont.)
  Ephriam Pennington 313
  John W. 312
  Mary Jane 462
  Rhoda (Miss) 295
  Samuel 311, 312, 313
  Samuel M. 312
Holt, Mary 407
Holton, Mary 592
Homes, --- (?) 60
Hood, Theodora 468
Hooker, William 48
Hoop, Annie 155
  Elizabeth 356
  Jane 356
Hooper, Elizabeth 116
Hopewell, John 564
Hopkins, --- 241
  H. Hanford (Dr.) 638, 641
  James (Mr.) 248
  Jane 92
  Mary 17
  Sam'l. (General) 683
  Tannah 626
Hoppin, --- (Mr.) 618
  Charles 671
  Charles A. 661
  Charles Arthur 618, 669
  Charles Arthur (Mr.) 618
Hopple, Matthew 84
Hord 713
  --- (Miss) 274
  Lysander (Judge) 545
  Margaret 572
Horigon, --- (?) 302
Horine, H. P. 240
Hornsby, John 457, 487
Horseley, Sarah P. 683
Horsley, Alice 655
  Mary 690
Horton, Tobias 454
Hotten, --- 192
Hough, Edmond 626
Houston, --- 605
  --- (General) 498
  James 263
Hovey, Edith Lou 77
Howard 117, 679, 693
  Allan Randolph 227
  Benjamin 693
  Benjamin, Jr. 693, 694
  Benjamin, Sr. 693
  Betsy 227
  Catherine Elizabeth 693
  Clarence Randolph 227
  Clark 227
  Creed 692
  Eleanor 693
  Frances Randolph 227
  Francis Key 227
  John Beale, Junr. 614
  John Lamar 227
  Jonathan 694
  Lavinia 693
  Mary 693
  Matthew 693
  May --- 227
  Montgomery 694
  Nancy 693

Howard, (cont.)
  Rebecca 693
  Thirza 116
  Thomas 693
  William (Dr.) 227
  William Key 227
  William Key, Jr. 227
  Zerelda 694, 697
Howe 687
  --- 347
  --- (Mrs.) 696
  Isabelle 490
  John William 346, 347
  Sallie W. 687
Howell, 669
  Ada 577
  Lina 165
  Lina L. 156
Howson, John 455
  John (Capt.) 457
  Leonard 454
Hubard, James L. 222
  Louisa 222
  Robert Thruston 222
Hubbell, Jane 745
Hucheson, (See also Hutcheson, Hutchison)
  Charles Gregory, Jr. 162
Hudson, --- 551, 552
  Addie 296
  Daniel 296
  Henry 454, 551
  Henry (Captain) 551
  J. 629
  Susan 692
  Tabitha 359
Hueston, --- (Messr) 278
  Elizabeth 278
  Jane 278, 290
  Jane (Mrs.) 277
  Jane (Steele) 278
  Mary 246, 278
  Nancy 278
  Robert 278
  Sarah 278
  Susan 278
  William 278
Huey, James 329
Huff, --- 626
  H. P. 101
  Susan Withers 101
Hugart, 329, 341
Huggins, Ann Laura 689
  Ann Mary 689
  Bettie R. 689
  Clement Williams 689
  Clemmy Depp 689
  Elizabeth 689
  Elizabeth Ann 689
  Ellen J. 689
  Eugenia B. 689
  Harry Munford 689
  Howard 689
  Howard Malcolm 689
  James Pendleton 689
  John T. 689
  John Thomas 689
  Lizzie 689
  Lizzie Lawrence 689
  Malcolm 689
  Nellie 689
  Rosa 689
  Samuel W. A. 689
  Sarah J. 689

Huggins, (cont.)
  Sarah Jane 689
  Wm. Ed. 689
  William Edmund 689
  Zion R. 689
Hughart, Jane 656
Hughes 34, 36
  --- 428, 429, 451, 462
  --- (Major) 98, 425, 427
  --- (Mr.) 426
  --- (Senator) 426
  Alexander Franklin 35
  Amelia 36
  Ann 33
  Anna 37, 591
  Anna Pearl 36
  Annie 34, 36
  Augustus 37, 43
  Bela 429
  Betsey 410
  Blanche 428
  C. J. , Jr. (Senator) 429
  Caroline Donaldson 35
  Catherine 33
  Catherine, Sr. 33
  Charles (Senator) 426
  Chas. J., Jr. (Senator) 427
  Clay ? 429
  Cooper 37
  Cornelius 33, 34, 35, 42
  Delilah Case 35
  E. E. 164
  E. Lee 36
  Edward Ward 164
  Elizabeth 677
  Elizabeth Hume 41
  Elizabeth Patton Hume 37
  Elliott 425, 429
  Elliott, Jr. 425
  Elliott M. 428
  Elliott McNiel 427
  Emily 36
  Gabriel 427, 428
  Gabriel Tandy 426, 428
  George 33, 35
  Harriet 42, 43
  Harriet (Aunt) 44
  Harriet (Miss) 43
  Harriet Amanda 42
  Henry Clay 427, 428
  Jack 35
  Jacob 33, 34, 36, 37, 38, 40, 41, 42, 43, 49, 50
  James 329, 410
  James Henry 34, 35
  Jane 33, 41, 427, 428
  Jane (Mrs.) 379
  Jane Rachel 50
  John 33, 34, 35, 410
  John Christian 35
  John D. 120
  John Henry 34
  John T. 36
  Joseph 35
  Joseph Case 35
  Joseph Coleman 36
  Julia (Miss) 41
  Julia Ann 37

Hughes, (cont.)
  Julia Ann Smith 37
  Julia Mary 39
  Kate 37
  Katherine 37
  Lacy 37
  Lucy 426
  Margaret 426, 427, 428
  Margaret Ward 164
  Martha 35
  Mary 33, 34
  Mary Adams 36
  Mary Case 35
  Mary Christian 35
  Mary E. 36
  Mary Frances 36
  Mary Menefee (Miss) 426
  Mary Patterson 35
  Merrett W. 36
  Michael 33
  Michael C. 36
  Milly 410
  Neil 34
  Pearl 36
  Rachel 33
  Rachel (Campbell) 35
  Rebecca 36
  Rebecca Patterson 35
  Robert 33, 407
  Robert Henry 37
  Robert Owen 34
  Robert Perry 35
  Roderick Perry 35
  S. W. 428
  Sallie Case 35
  Samuel W. 425, 426
  Sara 653
  Sarah 35, 405
  Sarah --- 35
  Sarah A. 36
  Sarah J. 673
  Susan 37, 427, 428
  Tho. 408
  Thomas 33, 36, 37, 410, 425, 427, 428, 429, 625
  Thomas (Major) 421, 422, 425, 426, 427, 428
  Thomas Elliott 164
  Willlam 37, 382, 408, 410, 426, 427, 428
Hughlett, --- 454
  James 382
  John 454
Hughs, --- (Capt.) 398
Hulett, E. M. (Hon.) 603
  James 405, 407
  Susannah 405
Hull, --- (Miss) 410, 411
  Fannie 564
  Fanny 565
  Henry 565
  Isaac (Captain) 647
  Martha Bell 348
Hume, (See also de Hume) 25, 26, 27, 28, 29
  --- 31, 35
  --- (Baron of) 26
  --- (Countess of) 26
  --- (Earl of) 25, 26, 27

Hume, (cont.)
  --- (Lord of) 27
  Abraham 25, 28
  Alexander 25, 29
  Andrew 28, 29
  Andrew (Sir) 28
  Anne Maria 48
  Benjamin T. 32
  Benjamin Talbot 32
  Betsy 17
  Carrie L. (Miss) 29
  Charles 28
  D. J. 32
  David 28
  David (Sir) 25, 27, 28
  David J. 32
  David P. 33
  Eliza Hutchcraft 32
  Elizabeth 33, 47, 48
  Elizabeth Patton 33
  Elizabeth Stevens 49
  Ester Patton 24
  Esther Patton 32, 33, 44, 47, 49
  Frances 25
  Francis 28, 29
  George 25, 27, 28, 29
  George (Sir) 27, 28, 29
  Hannah 29
  Isabel 25, 28
  Jacob 29
  James 29
  Jean 28
  John 17, 18, 24, 25, 29, 30, 31, 32, 33, 44, 47, 49
  John (Sir) 28
  John R. (Dr.) 28
  John S. 32
  Julia 17, 44, 47
  Julia Patten 45
  Laura Frances 48, 49
  Margaret 25, 28, 29
  Martha A. 33
  Mary C. 48
  Mary F. 32
  Matilda 33
  Matthew D. 47, 48, 49
  Matthew Dyer 47, 48
  Milme (Colonel) 28
  Ninian 25, 28, 29
  Orlando V. 32
  Patrick 25, 28, 29
  Patrick (Sir) 25, 28
  Robert 29, 49
  Sallie B. 33
  Sallie L. 33
  Sally 31
  Samuel C. 32
  Sarah 17, 29
  Thomas 28
  Will P. 32
  William 29
  William, Lord of (Sir) 27
  William P. 32
  William P., Sr. 33
  William Patton 32
Humphrey, Geo. 407
Humphries, Ann Catharine 135
  Ann Catherine 131
Hunloke, --- 557

Hunloke, Edward 556
Hunt, John 393, 403
  Mary Elizabeth 693
  Ruth 655
  Theodosia 367, 392, 393, 403
  Thos. 390
Hunter 389, 396
  A. C. 752
  Andrew 389
  Belle 577
  Cyrene 126
  Daniel (General) 389
  Edith Sanders 752
  Elizabeth Pendleton 389, 390, 412
  Etta 697
  Jane 272
  Joshua (Rev.) 272
  Josiah 272
  Josiah E. (Dr.) 272
  Lizzie 572
  Mary 124, 127
  Mary Elliott 390, 412
  R. M. L. 389
  Robert 272
  Robt. M. T. 376
  Selina 272
Huntington, --- (Earl of) 757
Huntly, Alexander (Earl of) 202
Hunton, Alexander 459
Hurlbut, Denison 70
  Emma, Jr. 70
Hurst, --- 451, 458
  Kemp 489
  Suckey 459, 461
Husban, Polly 53
Husband, Polly 53
Huse, --- 435
  --- (Aunt) 435
Husten, John 443
Huston, Craig 512
  Joseph M. 512
  Judelle MacGregor 512
  Polly 18, 19, 53
Hutchcraft, Eliza 32
  Thomas 32
Hutcheson, (See also Hucheson)
  Charles Gregory 162
  Elizabeth 162
Hutchins, Elizabeth 250
Hutchison, Chas. E. 409
  Emma Belle 409
  Geo. Wm. 409
  Henry Strother 409
  Thomas J. 409
Hutson, Margaret 323
Hyde, Phebe 727
Hylton, Jesse 362, 363
  Martha 362, 363
  Nathan 362, 363
  Violet (Pennington) 362
Igo, Mary 691
Inge, Hibernia (Miss) 515
Ingles, Ada Alice 101
Inloe, William H. 152
Innes, Anne 217
Inskeep, Bettie 563
  Joseph 563
  Tabitha 563
Inskip, --- 15

811

Irby, Anna Marie 536
  Richard 536
  Robinson L. 147
Isham 189, 195, 201, 216
  Anne 189
  Catharine 110
  Henry 110, 173, 189,
    201, 216
  Katherine 189, 201
  Katherine Banks 173
  Mary 108, 110, 111,
    112, 173, 174, 175,
    177, 181, 183, 189,
    201, 216
Jack, William A. 157
Jackson 137, 537, 539,
    544
  --- 5, 378
  --- (General) 185,
    387, 445, 516
  --- (President)
    136, 182
  Alice 544
  Alice (Mrs.) 544
  America 544
  Andrew (General)
    387
  Andrew (President)
    222
  David 544
  Eliza 544
  Eliza Ann 657
  Helen Page 469
  J. Craik 469
  John 544
  John G. 84
  Kezziah 664
  Maria 544, 545
  Mary Ann 683
  Mary Lafon (Mrs.)
    542
  Mary Virginia (Mrs.)
    545
  Richard (Mrs.) 545
  Richard G. 542, 544,
    545
  Richard Gilbert 544
  Sally 544, 545
  Sally (Miss) 537,
    544
  Stonewall 84, 325,
    392, 403
  Virginia 544, 545
  William 418, 544
Jacobs 679, 694
  Achsah 694
  Benj. 694
  Benjamin Franklin 694
  Caroline Hoyt 694
  Clark 694
  Edwin Arnold 694
  Emeline 694
  Emiline Amelia 694
  Enoch 694
  Ferrand 694
  Francis Clark 694
  Geo. Washington 694
  H. W. 699
  Henry Whitney 694
  Isaac Newton 694
  Jane 514
  Lucy J. 707
  Mary Berilla 694
  Nathan 694
  Nathan Jr. 694
  Nathan, Sr. 694
  Samantha 694

Jacobs, (cont.)
  Sarah 694
  Sarah Clark 694
  Sarah Eliza 697
  William Loring 694
Jacquimin, Richard 149
Jacquimine, Richard 153
Jaffray, Florence 75
Jameison, Mande 118
James 366, 639, 640, 641
  --- 639
  A. J. 303
  Achshah 638
  Alice 391
  Benjamine 391
  Chas. Redmon 575
  Daniel 638, 639, 640,
    641
  Daniel (Major) 639,
    641
  Drusilla 638
  Elizabeth 638
  Fannie R. 720
  George 391
  John 390, 391, 638,
    641
  John, Jr. 391
  Joseph 638, 640
  Joseph (Colonel)
    641
  Katherine 593
  Lucy 638, 639
  Lucy Wood 639, 641,
    642
  Margaret 638, 640
  Mary 130, 170, 372,
    388, 390, 412, 413
  Mollie 391
  Nancy 391
  Pratby (Major Sir)
    639, 640, 641
  Rebecca 638, 640
  Sidney Ann 639
  Sir Pratby (Major)
    639, 640, 641
  Susanna 638
  William 391, 488
  Zealand 639, 641
Jameson, Betty 262
  Elizabeth " Betty "
    262
  John 321
  Lucy Ann 434
Jamison, Blanche 226
Janes, Elizabeth 570
  Joseph 570
  Martha Ann 570, 737
  William 570
Jans, Anne Jan 554
  Jooste, J. M. of Me-
    teren 558
  Lysbeth 558
Jans Van Meter, Joost
    559
Jans Van Meteren, Joost
    558
Janse Van Meteren, Joost
    558
Jansen Vander Vliet,
  Dirck 73
  Hendrica 73
January, James 278
Janzoon, Maas 549
Jeanes, Martha Ann 570
Jeans, --- 736
  Martha A. 736
  Wm. 736

Jefferson 194
  --- 139, 213, 521
  --- (Miss) 400
  --- (Mr.) 221
  --- (President) 221,
    229, 376, 400
  Anna Scott 229
  Charles (M. D.) 513
  Elizabeth 229
  Field 194
  Jane 181, 182, 229
  John 194
  Lucy 181, 229
  Maria 229, 517
  Martha 110, 176, 181,
    191, 208, 221, 222,
    229, 396
  Mary 229
  Peter 109, 112, 173,
    174, 180, 181, 184,
    218, 228, 230
  Peter (Mrs.) 98
  Randolph 229
  Thomas 99, 110, 112,
    169, 180, 194, 201,
    213, 229, 267, 377,
    521
  Thomas (Capt.) 194
  Thomas (President)
    173, 208, 213, 221
Jeffries, Mamie 529
Jefse, (See also Jefsy,
  Jesse, Jessee)
  Mary Eliza 709
  Samuel Waddy 709
Jefsy, Ephriam G. 709
Jegue, Peter 556
Jenkins, --- (Miss)
    409
Jennert, Joshua 666
Jennings 89, 206
  --- (Miss) 88
  Ann 83, 84, 593
  Ariana 232
  Edmund 206, 232-233
  Edward 206
  Louise 39
  Sarah 170, 367, 404
  Jeremiah 683
Jesse (See also Jefse,
  Jefsy, Jessee)
  --- (Mr.) 625
  Ephriam 709
  M. F. 709
  Samuel Waddy 709
  Sarah Adaline 709
  Susan M. 709
  Thos. 469
  William G. 709
Jessee, Ephraim 585
  Millard 585
  Samuel Waddy 585
  William G. 585
Jett 749, 750
  Catherine (Newton)
    465
  Ermina 147
  Thomas J. 147
Jewell, William 607
Jillson, W. R. (Dr.)
    622
  Willard Rouse (Dr.)
    435
Job 473, 480
Johnson, 735, 738
  --- (?) 721

812

Johnson, (cont.)
--- 263, 468, 607, 735
--- (Miss) 84
--- (Mrs.) 35, 765
Adele 735
Aletha 711
Alice B. 711
Andrew 625
Ann E. 736
Annie 573
Betsy 86
Bettie 591
Case 544
Cave 617
Cecil 152
Charles 35
Claude 35
Eliza C. 573
Eliza W. 573, 735, 736
Elizabeth 18, 19
Emily 735
Emily M. 573
Emma Brown 711
Euclid 573
Euclid Lane 735
Fayette 41
Francis (Mrs.) 544
George W. 573, 594, 735, 736
George W. (General) 573
George W., Jr. 735
Hamilton 573
Henry V. 573, 737
Henry William 735
Isaac 623, 625
Isaac, Jr. 623
J. Stoddard (Col.) 187, 291
James 533
Jemima 85, 597
Jemima Suggett 597
Jilson P. 739
Jo. E. (General) 376
Job 700
John D. 501
John M. 522
John Madison 735
John T. (Rev.) 574
Joseph E. 377
Junius 573
Junius Ward 573, 735, 736, 737
L. F. 464
L. L. (Col.) 88
Lilly 735
Louise 35
Lucy 533
M. C. 735, 736
Madison C., Jr. 736
Madison Conyers 88, 573, 735
Margaret (?) 360
Margaret R. Robertson 700
Martha L. 573, 575, 737
Martha Lydia 735
Mary 679
Mary B. 573
Mary S. 574
Matilda 533
P. (Major) 41
Polly 533
R. M. 89

Johnson, (cont.)
Richard ? 89
Richard 533, 574
Richard (Colonel) 523
Richard M. 86
Richard M. (Colonel) 84, 187
Richard M. (Vice-President) 597
Robert 86, 573
Robert (Col.) 574-575, 578, 597
Robin 86
Sallie 533, 574, 597
Sally 578
Sally Chiles 41
Sarah 35
Thomas 630
Thomas P. 736
Virginia 600
W. M. 736
W. V. 735, 736
W. W. 736
Warren Viley 735, 736
Whittington 630
Willa V. 573, 736
Willa Viley 735, 736
William 86, 523, 573
William (Gen.) 88
Wm. B. 573
Wm. Ransom (Col.) 600
Johnston, --- 302
Adam 616, 617
Albert Sidney (General) 170, 367, 387
Albert Sydney 85
Claude (Mrs.) 34
Eliza E. 573
Eliza W. 735
George W. 573, 735
Harris 573
Henrietta 367, 387
J. Stoddard 86, 735, 736
J. Stoddard (Col.) 573
J. Stoddard, Jr. 573
Jane 131
Joseph E. (Gen.) 367, 400
Lucy 399
Mary H. 573
Mary Hancock 735
Robert 131
Rufus P. (Rev.) 513
Sarah Elizabeth 256
Wm. Preston 387
Johnstone, Andrew 27
Mariota 27
Jones, 179, 192, 265, 366, 367, 395, 602, 603
--- 603
--- (Mr.) 411, 426
--- (Mrs.) 267, 375, 399
Albert 655
Alla Gay 13
Alla Gay (Mrs.) 5, 25
Amanda Elizabeth 471

Jones, (cont.)
Ann Cary (Randolph) 221
Ann Thomas 470
Anna 376, 377
Anna Gabriella 381, 395, 401
Ap Catesby 602
B. F. (Major) 607
Bathurst 267
Bessie Cary 106
Cadwallader 370
Cadwallader (Col.) 270, 271
Catesby 459, 461
Catherine Chappel (Mrs.) 654
Cynthia 658
Edward 471
Edward A. 106, 108
Elizabeth 265, 375, 376, 377, 381, 401
Ethel 69
Florence 471
Frances Anne 270
Frances Malcolm 677
Francis Anne 271
Francis B. 377
Francis Buckner 221
Frederick 602
Gabriel 176, 366, 373, 375, 377, 378, 379, 397, 399, 401
Gabriel (Captain) 270
Gabriel (Mr.) 399
Gabriel (Mrs.) 375, 399, 413
Gabriella 376, 377, 395
George Woodson 107
H. L. (Mr.) 602
Hannah 28
Howard 471
Howard M. 677
Howard Malcolm 675
Howard Phillip 471
Israel (Major) 192
James 454, 455, 470
James F. 377
James Sidney 470
James William 470
Jane 265, 602
Jean Luckett 677
Jekyll 264, 267
John 375
John Gabriel 399
John Swann 602
Joseph F. (Mr.) 265
Koziah 192
L. H. (Mr.) 603
Lawrence 574
Lewis H. (Judge) 265
Louis 471
Margaret 376, 377, 381, 395, 399, 401
Margaret (Miss) 694
Martha 601
Martha Ann 528
Mary 265, 471
Mary Alice 470
Mary Ann Nesbit 607
Mary Crenshaw 655
Mary Octavia 607

Jones, (cont.)
  Mattie Estelle 107
  Nellie 103
  Newland 698
  Philip 602
  Randolph 221
  Richard 270
  Robert 240
  Roger 602, 603
  Roger (Capt.) 267, 602, 603
  Roger (Mr.) 267
  Russell 470
  Sally 265
  Sarah Katherine 470
  Shelton 265
  Skelton 264, 265, 267
  Strother 296, 375, 376, 377, 381, 401
  Strother (Captain) 299, 300
  Strother (Mr.) 399
  Susan Markham 107
  Taylor 516
  Thomas 265
  Thomas (Col.) 602, 603, 655
  Thos., Jr. 488
  Thomas ap Thomas 265
  Thomas Dawson 470
  Vincent R. (Mrs.) 672
  Vivian Amanda 471
  Wesley Howard 640
  William 69, 528, 601, 602
  William French 470
  William Russell 470
  William Strother 221, 377
  Wm. Strother, Jr. 377
Joost Van Meteren, Jan 553, 554
Joosten, --- 557
  Cathrin 558
  Geertye 557
  Geertze 557
  Gysbert 557
  Jan 555, 556, 557, 558
  Jane 557
  Jooste 557
  Jooste Jans 557
  Lysbeth 557, 558
Joosten Van Meteren, Jan 554, 558
Jordaen de Cahiliser, Michael 550
Jordan 116
  --- (Miss) 403
  Elizabeth 113, 115
  Samuel 200
Jorley, --- (Miss) 406
Jouett, --- 289, 293
Jourdan, Elizabeth 399
Joux, (See de Joux)
Jove 660
Joyce, Edith 77
  Thomas 594
Julian, Charles 756
Jump, Peter 314
Kamera, Eva 226
Kates, Frederick Ward 613
Kavanaugh 463
  Adelia 628
  Ann 628

Kavanaugh, (cont.)
  Ann (Mrs.) 404
  Ann (Cave) 463, 467
  Anna 169, 170, 180, 382, 385
  Benjamin Taylor 161
  Bishop H. H. (?) 161, 166
  Charles William 161
  David Ella 161
  Elizabeth 451, 453, 460, 462, 463, 479
  H. H. (Bishop) (?) 161, 166
  John Hubbard 161
  Nancy 467
  Philemon 169, 170, 385, 404, 453, 462, 463
  Sarah ? 534
Kavanuagh, Bishop H. H. (?) 254
  H. H. (Bishop) (?) 254
Kavenaugh, Elizabeth 452
  Philemon 453
  Phillip 453
Kaylor, Elizabeth Pringle 396
Kean, Jefferson Randolph (General) 224
  Lancelot Minor 224
  Louis Randolph 224
  Martha (Pattie) Cary 224
  Pattie Cary 224
  Robert Garlick Hill 224
  Robert Garlick Hill, Jr. 224
Kearney, Kate 224
Keats, --- (Mrs.) 247
Keene, John 466
Kegley, --- 762
Keim, --- (Mrs.) 199
  George de Benneville 226
  John May 226
  Theodora 199
  Theodora (Mrs.) 199, 210
Keister (See also Gester)
  Frederick 4, 10
  Hannah 10
  James 10
Keith 98, 177, 194, 195, 201, 202
  --- (Bishop) 219
  --- (Capt.) 176
  --- (Parson) 176
  Alexander 108, 202, 219
  Catharine 108, 111, 169, 385, 386
  Charlotte Ashmore 108
  Elizabeth 167, 197, 203, 219
  George 177, 202
  Ida Blanche 150
  Isham 111, 202, 219
  Isham (Capt.) 108, 111, 168, 175, 176, 178, 187, 385
  Isham (Lieut.) 368
  Isham (Mr.) 202
  James 108, 177, 202

Keith, (cont.)
  James (cont.) 219,
  James (Judge) 112, 202
  James (Parson) 201, 202
  James (Rev.) 108, 111, 139, 169, 175, 176, 177, 190, 194, 195, 197, 198, 209, 219, 385
  James Francis Edward 177, 202
  John 108, 111, 219
  Katherine 175, 176, 179, 203, 368
  Kittie 111
  Mary 203
  Mary Elizabeth 108, 109, 111, 167, 168, 176
  Mary Isham 209
  Mary Randolph 108, 111, 176, 219, 366
  Robert (Bishop) 177, 202
  Robert (Mr.) 202
  Thomas 219
  Thomas R. 112
  Thomas Randolph 108
  William (Sir) 202
Keller, --- (Mr.) 237
  --- (Mrs.) 241
  Catherine 236, 241, 242
  Frances 515
  Jane 513
  Raymond 160
  Raymond, Jr. 160
  Sam'l. 240
  Samuel (Mr.) 237
  Sam'l. D. 240
Kelley, Hannah 18, 19
  James 530
  Martha 658
  W. M. (Mrs.) 65
Kellog, --- 772
Kelly, Annie 70
  Blanche 65
  Elisha 70
  Elizabeth 335
  Geraldine 120
  J. Howard 120
  J. Howard, Jr. 120
  James 65
  Julia 70
  Lily 65
  May --- 65
  W. M. 65
  Warfield 70
  William, Jr. 65
  William C. 65
  Zarilda 65
Kelso, 329, 341
  Hugh 323
  Margaret 323
Kelvin, --- (Lord) 586
Kendrick, Nancy 271
Kennedy 396
  Ann 91
  Anthony 389
  Clifton 103
  John Pendleton 389
  Julia 223
  Willie Marcia 103
Kenner 358
  David 358

Kenner, (cont.)
  Granville 358
  Hansford 358
  Henry 358
  Lafayette 358
  Louisa 358
  Margaret 358
  Mary F. 358
Kennerly 389, 395, 396
Kennon 178
  Elizabeth 114, 178, 187
Kenny, James 20
  Matthew P. 20
  Rebecca 20
Kent, Joseph (Governor) 640
Kenton, --- 763
  Eleanor 44
  Rachel 45
  Thos. 45
Kenyon, --- (Miss) 388
  Abram 373
  Francis Elizabeth 396
  Sallie 389
Kerby, Mary 499
Kercheval, Samuel 559, 562, 563
Kerr, --- (Dr.) 565
  Betsy 745
  Elizabeth 512
  James 589
  Matthew M. 599
Ketcham, Elizabeth 596
  Elizabeth T. 132
  Hannah 596
  Stephen 596
Key, --- (Bishop) 368
  Alice 699
  Lucy Thornton 368
  Martin 420, 420-421
Keyes, Idelie (Miss) 286
  Idelle 287
  Martha Elizabeth 419, 433
Keyser 631, 633, 636
  Dirch Gerritz 634
  Dirck 631, 633
  Dirck Gerritz 633
  Elizabeth 631, 633
  Gerritz 633
  Leonard 633
  Peter 633
Kidd, Emma 699
Kilbuck 5, 6, 7, 8, 9
Kilpatrick, Catherine 770
  Jenny 314
Kimberlin, Effie 549
  Palser 656
Kimberly, Catharine 170
  Mollie 170
Kimbrough, Elizabeth 576
Kimmel, --- (Colonel) 640
  --- (General) 639, 640
  Agnes Gibson 640
  Anthony 639
  Anthony (General) 639
  Anthony Z. 640
  Anthony Z. (Colonel) 640
  Ellen 640
  Gregg 640

Kimmel, (cont.)
  Mary 640
  Mary Morgan 639
  Mary Morgan (Miss) 640
  Michael 640
  Pratby 640
  Pratby James 640
  Sidney Ann 641
  Sidney Ann (James) 640
  Thomas Morgan 640
  William W. 640
Kimmell, Elizabeth Marshall (Miss) 640
Kincaid 329, 341, 757, 761
  --- (Laird of) 757
  Alexander 745
  Eleanor Guy 758
  Elizabeth 328
  Hugh 327
  James 329
  Joseph 757
  Margaret Lockhart 757
  Robert 231, 757
  Thomas 757, 758
  William 757, 758, 760
Kincannon, Martha D. 340
Kincheloe, Frank H. (Mrs.) 741
  John 704
King, Addison 336
  Allie F. 712
  Ann Venable 569
  Anna 105
  Archibald (Dr.) 512, 520
  Asa 676
  Baxter 569
  Charles 149
  Davis 569
  Douglas Wheeler 173, 174, 175, 177, 179, 184, 186
  E. A. 149
  Eliza 569
  Eliza Jane 512
  Elizabeth Woodson 105
  Ella 676
  Ella C. 106
  Ellen 105
  Florence 683
  George 569, 676
  Gideon 711, 712
  Hattie 105, 106
  Hugh 105
  Jas. 569
  Jennie 105
  Jennie Catherine 105
  Lucy Woodson 105
  Maggie D. 105
  Mary Ann 512
  Mary E. 676
  Mary Louise 159
  Mary P. 712
  Pattie Markham 106
  Philip 569
  Prudence 336
  R. S. (Mr.) 762
  Samuel A. (Rev.) 105, 107
  Samuel Arthur 105
  Samuel Arthur, Jr. 105
  Susan M. 512
  Thomas H. 674, 676

King, (cont.)
  Walter 105
  Walter Blackburn (Dr.) 105
  Walter Blackburn, Jr. 105
  William 625
  William M. (Rev.) 105, 107
  William M., Jr. 106
  Willie 106
King Beaver 761, 762
King Bever 760
Kingsbury, Susan M. 670
Kinkaid, Alexander 290
Kinkead 757, 761, 763, 766, 767
  --- 656
  Agnes 761
  Andrew 761, 763
  Eleanor 761
  Eleanor Gay 767, 768, 776
  Eleanor Guy 761, 776
  Elizabeth 659
  Guy 761
  Hattie 46
  Isabel 659
  Isabella 761, 762
  Jane 746
  John 760, 761, 762
  John D. 105, 107
  Margaret 761
  Rebecca 761
  Susanna 761
  William 761
Kinnear, Andrew 358
  Hannah 358
Kinnerly 395
  Catherine 386, 391, 393
  James (Capt.) 386
  Mary 382, 386, 393
Kirk, Henry I. 630
Kirkham, Agnes Hugh (Campbell) 336
Kirkpatrick, Wm. 286
Kirtley, --- 713
  Elizabeth Railey 164
  Roberta Ward 164
  W. Lacey 164
Kitchener, --- (Lord) 316
Kitchner, --- (Lord) 305
Klasettler, Annie (Miss) 441
Kleiser, Anna Elizabeth 565, 566
  Jonas Marks 566
Klementynowska, Zoya 226
Knight, --- (Mrs.) 135
  John 488, 653
  John Alexander 580
  Sallie Lane 308
Knox, Cornelia 224
  Jane 745
Koen, Arthur Roy (Dr.) 536
Kreiger, --- (Captain) 555
  John C. 104
  Martin 555
  Martin (Capt.) 554
Kyle, Hester Roberta 134
  Matilda (Mrs.) 399

Kyle, (cont.)
  Robert 338
L---, Frances 423
La Calmes, De (See
  De La Calmes)
La Villain, Susanna
  (Countess) 496
Lackland, --- 579
Lacy, Benj. Watkins, Jr.
  225
Ladd 350
  Nancy Annis 351
Lafayette, --- 514, 524,
  639, 654, 755
  --- (Gen.) 345
Lafferty, 330, 340, 345,
  --- 329, 330, 333
  Agnes 330
  Alexander 330
  Clara 330
  Elizabeth 330
  James 330
  Jane 330
  Jane --- 330
  John 330
  Martha 330
  Mary Ann 329
  Mattie 330
  Nancy 330
  Polly 330
  Ralph 329, 330, 331,
    333, 343, 345
  Ralph Stuart 335
  Rebecca 330
  Robert 330
  Sarah 330
  Steele 330
  William 330
  William Stuart 330
Lafon 537, 539, 540
  --- 540
  --- (Captain) 540,
    541, 542
  --- (Mrs.) 538
  Lucy Letitia 544
  Maria 545
  Maria (Mrs.) 544
  Maria Upshaw 540, 541,
    542
  Mary 537, 538, 542,
    545
  Mary (Miss) 542
  Mary Virginia 544
  Nicholas 538, 539,
    544, 545
  Nicholas (Captain)
    540
  Nicholas (Mrs.) 539,
    540
  Thomas 540
Laidley, --- 558
Lakin, Joseph 359
  Sarah 359
  Sarah Jane 359
Laloo, John 56
Lamar, Mirabeau B. 603
Lamb, --- (Colonel)
  74
  Luda 573
Lambert, --- 588
Lancaster 679, 695
  --- (Grandfather)
    695
  --- (Grandmother)
    695, 696
  Albert G. 733
  America 695

Lancaster, (cont.)
  Annie 705
  Catherine 695
  Eliza Jane 733
  Harriet Davis 695
  Henry B. 733
  Jeremiah P. 733
  John (Major) 696
  Joseph 695, 696
  Joseph Manerva 695
  Mary 695
  Mary Ann 733
  Nancy 695
  Paulina Harris 733
  Rachel 695, 696
  Rebecca 695
  Samuel 695
  Samuel S. 695
  Thomas 695
Lander, James 20
  Mary 20
Landersdale, ---
  (Duchess of) 26
Lane 464, 465, 481,
  --- 631, 635
  --- (Aunt) 635
  --- (Mr.) 254
  Aaron 465
  Amy 465
  Andrew 466
  Ann 83, 573, 575
  Ann Carr 466
  Ann Wilson 465
  Anne 463, 464, 465,
    466
  Anny 465
  Betty 465
  Dorothy 110
  E. P. 23
  Elizabeth --- 465
  Elvira 466
  Hannah 465
  Hardage 466
  Hardage (Dr.) 466
  Harvey 466
  Heath H. 466
  Henry 466
  James 463, 464, 465,
    480
  James, Jr. 465
  James, Sr. 465
  James Beall 466
  James Hardage 465
  Jane 464, 466, 480,
    482
  John (Colonel) 464
  John (Dr.) 465
  Joseph (Col.) 465
  Julia 466
  Karenhappuch 480
  Kearn H. 466
  Kenenhuppuck 466
  Keron 466
  Kerren Happuch 466
  Kerrenhappuch 466
  Keturah 466
  Lydia 452, 465, 466,
    474, 479, 480, 481
  Lydia Hardage 463,
    465, 480
  M. L. 572
  Mary 126
  Moses 465
  Samuel 466
  Sarah 465, 466
  Sarah --- 465
  Sarah (Hardage) 465

Lane, (cont.)
  William 465, 466
  William (Captain)
    482
  William Armistead 465
  William Carr 465, 466
  William Hardage 466
Langhorn, John T. 84
Langhorne 85
  Elizabeth Brent 85
  Jennie 412
  John 85
  John Devall 85
  John Trotter 85
  Judith Fry 85
  Maurice 85
  Penelope Vertner 85
  Sarah Bell 85
  Thomas Young 85
  William (Sir) 85
  William David 85
Langley, Edward 371
Lansing, Paul 574
Lapsley, Gertrude 478
  James (Rev.) 718
Larel, A. T. 301
Lashbrooke, Peter 712
Lasosee 507
Latane, Louis 507
Latur, T. 507
Laud, Alfred D. (Judge)
  256
  Alfred Vivian 256
  Florence Laura 256
  Jennie May 256
Laughlin, Henry 34
Laverty, Ralph 330
Law, Dorothy 215
  Richard 215
Lawler, Caty 407
  John 382, 393, 407
  Michael 405, 407
  Mollie 407
  Nancy 393, 407
  Sallie 407
  Susan 407
  Susannah 405
  Susannah (Strother)
    405
Lawrence 67
  Catherine (Miss)
    229
  Elspa 535
  George 69
  Hannah 69
  Minnie 529
Laws, Emma 155
Lawson, --- 630
  --- (Gen.) 654
  Beatrice 649
Laytham, Bettie F. 530
Layton, Ambrose Young
  134
  Annie 134
  Barbara 134
  Benjamine Pleasants
    134
  David W. 134
  David W., Jr. 134
  Douglass Young 134
  Douglass Young, Jr.
    134
  Edward S. 134
  Elizabeth 134
  Francis 134
  Hugh P. 134
  Jennie 134

Layton, (cont.)
  Kelby Vance 134
  Nannie 134
  Susan L. 134
  T. K. (Dr.) 134, 137
  Thomas K., Jr. 134
  Whitney 134
Le Fayre, Judith 497
Le Fevre, Magdalen 751
Le Fon 539
Le Grande, Peter 569
le Telier 636
Leaken, Joseph 359
Leaming, --- 557
Leatherby, Thomas 455
LeBaron, --- 532
Lee 184, 295, 298, 747
  --- 5, 302, 727
  --- (General) 154, 201, 601
  --- (Major) 247
  Amanda 295
  Ann 303
  Anna 300
  Anne 300
  Annie (Miss) 609
  Anny 297
  Ata Leighton 296
  Benjamin 300
  Bethel 297
  Betsy 297
  Charles 297
  Charles B. 300
  Charles Bethal 300
  Curice 420
  David 303, 536
  Dewey 298
  Dewit-Clinton 296
  Dewitt Clinton 295, 296, 305
  Drewry 297
  Drury 300
  Edward P. 636
  Elizabeth 299, 386
  Ezekell Tom 295
  Ezekiel Thomas 296
  Faunt 295
  Ferol Sargent 536
  Fitzhugh L. 296
  Frank Brown 536
  Frankie (Miss) 295
  Frederick 295
  Hancock 373
  Hannah 727, 728
  Harry 112
  Henry 5, 112, 184, 201, 234, 609
  Henry (General) 609, 636
  Henry (Mrs.) 544
  Henry, Jr. 184
  James 296, 297, 298, 299, 300, 305
  James B. 300
  James G. 302, 303
  Jennings Bryan 536
  John 297, 300, 544, 727
  Joseph 295
  Kendall 574
  Lancelot 265
  Leland Frank 536
  Letitia Atwell 246
  Lewis 297, 299
  " Light Horse Harry " 184, 378, 389, 412,

Lee, (cont.)
  " Light Horse Harry " (cont.) 609
  Lizzie 295
  Lucy Coleman 631
  Margaret 530
  Martha 295, 302, 303
  Mary 300, 727
  Mary (Mrs.) 727
  Nancy Ellen 296
  Oural Herman 536
  Pauline 303
  Polly 297
  R. E. 377
  Rhodaett (Miss) 315
  Rhodett 295
  Richard 539
  Robert E. 112, 184, 201
  Robert E. (General) 112, 213, 234, 601, 609
  Ruby Monzella 536
  S. E. 304, 305
  Sally 297
  Silah B., Jr. 295
  Silas 295, 298
  Socrates 295, 296
  Socrates E. 296, 303, 304
  Thos. 727
  Vivian Lorraine 536
  W. R. 303, 304
  Walter M. 296
  William 295, 297, 299
  William R. 295, 296
  Willis 300
  Willis (Major) 247
  Willis Green 297, 300
Leeds, Evangeline 103
Leeman, Elizabeth 69
Legette, Mary E. 536
Lehugh, Peter 451, 460, 488
Leigh, --- (Mr.) 481
  A. Lawrence (Mr.) 481
Leinster, --- (Earl of) 83
Leitch, John 591
Leithell, Rebecca 24
LeMaster, Nathaniel Field 162
  William Pope 162
Lemon, --- (Mr.) 85
Lemond, 686
  Agness Vernor 686
  Augustus William 686
  Eliza Boone 686
  Frances Augusta 686
  J. 686
  James 686
  John James 686
  Mary Grant 686
  R. 686
  Rebecca Knox 686
  Sarah Grant 686
Leonard, Charlotte 499
Leslie, Annie 530
  Frank 201
Lester, Joseph 515
Letcher, --- (General) 601
  Robert Perkins 700
  Samuel M. (Dr.) 700

Levilain, John, Jr. 509
  John, Sr. 510
  Susanna 508, 509
Levilaine, Jean 510
Levillon, Susanne (Countess) 508
Lewellen, John White 516
Lewellyn, Joseph 254
Lewis 179, 366, 374, 378, 402, 432, 481, 493, 589
  --- (?) 254
  --- 3, 374, 402
  --- (Capt.) 769
  --- (Col.) 768
  --- (Miss) 398
  --- (Mr.) 83, 644
  --- (Mrs.) 413
  Abadiah 567
  Addison 485
  Agatha 374, 379, 398, 402
  Amelia Clay 565, 566
  Andrew 378, 398
  Andrew (Col.) 768
  Andrew (General) 374, 402
  Ann 229, 378, 379, 399
  Anna 229
  Benjamin 398
  Betty Washington 286
  Charles 109, 229, 356, 378, 398, 516
  Charles (Col.) 321, 342, 344, 378, 398
  Charles, Jr. 229
  Charles, Jr. (Captain) 181
  Charles H. (Col.) 378
  Charles Lilburne 181
  Daniel (General) 378, 379
  Edna Elizabeth 151
  Elizabeth 379, 398, 432
  Ellen Joel 286
  Fanny 399
  Fielding 286, 377
  Florence (Miss) 273
  Frances 181
  Francis 181
  Gab. 683
  Gabriel 377
  Howell (Major) 286
  Hugh 567
  Huldah 590
  James 433
  Jane 398, 399
  Jane Meriwether 584, 589
  John 324, 366, 376, 377, 378, 381, 398, 401, 492, 493, 517
  John (Col.) 378, 565
  John (Major) 589
  John (Mr.) 474
  John F. 378, 397
  Jno. K. (Rev.) 273
  Judith 220
  Kitty 575
  L. L. (Judge) 378, 379

Lewis, (cont.)
  Margaret 379, 398
  Mary 182, 398, 492, 493, 583, 584, 589, 684
  Meriwether 387
  Mildred 567
  Mildred E. 409
  Nancy 689
  Nellie (Miss) 248
  Nicholas 420
  Robert 584
  Robert (Colonel) 493, 589
  Samuel (General) 398
  Sarah 432, 653
  Sarah Ann 644
  Sarah Travers 590
  Sheffy (Dr.) 379
  Sophia 379, 399, 574
  Theo. 424
  Thomas 366, 373, 374, 375, 378, 379, 397. 398, 399, 573
  Thomas (Hon.) 565
  Thomas Willis 172
  Thornton 565, 566
  Waller 432
  Warner 218
  Wm. 653
  William (Col.) 220
  William A. 420
  Wm. B. Strother 378
  William Lynn 324
Liddell, Francis (Sir) 28
  Isabel 28
Lightfoot, --- (Major) 270
  --- (Miss) 217
  Annie 271
  Francis 217
  Wm. 170, 391, 402
Ligon, Seth 116
  Thos. (Gov.) 115
Lilburne, Jane 228
  John 228
Lile, Peter 17
Lillard, --- 239
  Ephriam 574
  Jno. 625
  John L. 239
  Margaret 629
  Martha 574
Lincoln, --- 326, 477
  --- (Mr.) 177
  --- (President) 114, 187, 752
  A. 694
  Abe (Mrs.) 156
  Abraham 42, 317, 752
  Abraham (President) 326, 602
Lindenberger 71, 81
  Anna Emory 72
  Annie 407
  Edward 71
  Eliza 71
  George 71, 72
  Harry 72
  J. Hopewell, Jr. 71
  Jacob Hopewell 71, 81
  Laura 72
  Lily 72
  Mary 72
  Sarah 72

Lindenberger, (cont.)
  W. J. 75
  William H. (Dr.) 71
  William James 71, 81
Lindsay, J. C. 447
  James 281
  Jane 279
  John C. 447
  Joseph 281
  Joseph (Col.) 92, 94
  Luvina (Grimes) 262
  Marie Louise 262
  Nimrod Long (Colonel) 262
  W. B. (Hon.) 449
Lindsey, --- 518
  Alex C. 686
  Genevieve (Miss) 690
  Mary G. 687
  William 529
  William Talbot (Mrs.) 689
Linville, Sallie 732
  Sarah 732
Lippincott, Augusta Elizabeth 79
  Deborah Scull 79
  Dorothy Muir 79
  John Haines 79
Lipscomb, --- 421
  Francis 422
Lister, --- (Judge) 256
  Albert Dunlap 256
  Albert Garland 256
  Florence 256
  Josiah Dunlap (Judge) 256
  Laura Elizabeth 256
  Ophelia Virginia 256
  Sarah Virginia 256
Litt, Polly 362
Little, --- (Miss) 109, 182
  Elizabeth (Miss) 229
  William 631
Little Turtle 765
Littlepage 679, 696
  Ann 696
  Dorathea W. 696
  Dorothea W. 696
  Frances A. 696
  Frances S. 696
  James S. 690, 696
  James S., Jr. 696
  John M. 696
  Mariah M. I. 696
  Mary 696
  Mary S. 696
  Richard 696
  Richard W. C. 696
  Robert B. 696
Littleton, Esther 626
Livandais, Marie Josephine 152
Lizenby, William 459, 461
Lloyd, --- (Dr.) 756
Lockert, Carrie 106
Lockett 66
  Brittaen 510
  Frances 655
  Henry 655
  James 497, 510

Lockett, (cont.)
  Joel 510
  John 510
  Lucius 655
  Mary 502, 503, 655
  Mary Clay 655
  Napoleon 655
  S. L. (Col.) 655
  Selina 655
  Stephen 655
  Susanna 510
  Virginia 655
  William Ballard 65
  William Ballard (Mrs.) 65
Lockhart 767
  James 758
  Margaret 757, 758
  Nancy 409
Lockridge 763
  Andrew (Captain) 768
  James 762
  Sally 770
Logan 765
Logan 295, 301, 309
  --- 304, 765
  --- (Col.) 763, 765
  --- (Miss) 84
  --- (Mr.) 408
  Ann Eliza 607
  Benjamin 308
  Benjamin (Col.) 764
  Betsy 308
  David 308, 309
  David Stephenson 301
  Edeth 314
  Elizabeth 301, 309, 314, 567, 753
  George 308
  Hugh 308
  J. M. 304
  James B. 301
  Jas. Harvey (Rev.) 568
  Jane 714
  Jean 714
  John 301, 308
  Johnson,(Dr.) 607
  Malinda 301, 308
  Malinda (Mrs.) 301
  Margaret 308
  Margaret A. 301
  Mary 301, 308
  Mary V. 607
  Mathew 309
  Polly 308
  Thomas 301, 309, 314
  W. H. 303, 304
  William C. 301
Logwood 211
Lomax, --- (Judge) 398
  --- (Miss) 379
  Elizabeth 267
  John T. (Judge) 378
  Lunsford, Esq. 267
Lomay, Linsford 388
Londes, Rosa Ann 172
Long, --- 334
  Alexander 334
  Andrew 30
  Benjamin Ritchie 31
  Esther 31
  Harrison Hume 31
  Harrison M. 31
  Hume H. 32
  James Henry 31

Long, (cont.)
  Jane Garrett 771, 773
  John 30
  John H. 664
  Lou Ritchie 32
  Lucy 623, 627
  Mary Sue 31
  Reuben 625
  Susan 575
  Susan A. 737
  T. 627
  William John 31
Longest, Ann 687
  James 687
  John Richard 687
  William Powell 687
Longmoor, --- (Mrs.) 596
  Loula B. (Mrs.) 596
  W. W. 596
  W. W. (Mr.) 596
  W. W., Sr. (Mrs.) 595
Looney, Jane 379
Loudoun, --- (Earl of) 321
Lovat, --- (Viscountess) 26
Love 542
  --- (Mrs.) 542
  Ephraim 13
Lovelace, --- (Governor) 556
Loving, Elizabeth 515
Low 75, 76, 81
  Anne --- 76
  Edward 77
  Frederick Joyce 77
  Jabez Baker 77
  James 75, 77, 81
  James, Jr. 77
  John 76
  Joseph Tompkins 77
  Joseph Tompkins 1st 77
  Joseph Tompkins 2nd (Dr.) 77
  Joseph Tompkins 3rd 77
  Laura 75, 77
  Mary Mott 77
  Nathaniel 76
  Nelson 77
  Susanna --- 76
  Thomas 76
Lowell, Mary 221
Lowery, --- 340, 357
  John 320, 340
  Robert 340, 357
  William 340, 356
Lowry, David 657
  David Wright 657
  Jordan Scott 104
  Martha S. 657
  Rebecca 657
  Robert G. 104
  Robert Mitchell 657
Lucas, Mary E. (Mrs.) 147
Lucket, Roberta 68
Luckett 66
  Alfred 67
  Edward Rankin 68
  Frances 68
  Gracey Hobbs 68
  Leven 66
  Lou Lue 67

Luckett, (cont)
  Mary E. 704
  Mary Stacker 67
  Samuel 1st 66
  Samuel 2nd 66
  Thomas Dade 66, 67, 68
  William 66
  William Gibson 285
Luggett, --- (Miss) 270
Luneford, Lewis 459
Lupton, Lancaster P. (Capt.) 606
Luther, --- 540
  Martin 633
Luthy, Carroll 479
  George 479
Lyle 571
  Annot Mary 131
  Cornelia Elizabeth 163
  Cornelius Railey 163
  Ernest Thornton 163
  J. Irvine 163
  Joel I. 157
  Joel Irvine 163
  Joel Irvine, Jr. 163
  John 131
  John T. 131
  Marion T. 157
  Matthew 11, 55
  Pauline 131
  Robert 131
Lyman, Anne 217
Lynde, Cornelius 133
  George Pleasants 133
  Isabel Adair 133
  Margaret Emily 133
  Samuel A. 133, 136, 182
Lynn, --- (Laird of Loch) 54, 62, 63, 79, 366
  Geo. (Dr.) 569
  Jean 140
  Margaret 378
  Sarah 54, 62, 63, 79
  William 54, 63, 79
Lyon, Catherine E. --- 57
  Chittenden P. 57
  Chittenden P., Jr. 57
  James Nelson 57
  Martha A. 57
  Mary Ann 57
  Matthew P. 57
  Sarah R. --- 57
Lyons, Salemna 673
  Sally 673
Lytle 278
  --- (General) 278, 636
  --- (Messr.) 278
  --- (Mr.) 277
  Anne 286, 287
  Elizabeth 287
  Jane 286, 287
  John 286, 287
  Joseph 287
  Josephine (Miss) 636
  Mary 278, 287, 290
  Mary (Mrs.) 277
  Mary Steele 292
  Nancy 278, 292

Lytle, (cont.)
  Robert Todd (General) 287
  Sarah 287
  William 287
  Wm. (Col.) 291
  William (General) 278, 286
  William Haines 287
Macaulay, --- 202, 366, 540, 758
MacBeth 26
MacDonnell, Alexander Railey 153
  Jane Randolph 153
  T. D. S. 153
Macey, Pattie Railey 101, 127, 138
  Railey Woodson 101, 127, 138
  Robert Ward 101, 126, 137
  Robert Ward (Mrs.) 128
  Robert Ward, Jr. 101, 127, 138
  Sadie 101, 127, 138
MacGregor, Chastine Elizabeth 512
  Judell 500
  Mathilde Lewis 512
  Thomas A. (Dr.) 512
Machen, Willis B. 57
MacKenny, Alexander 418
MacKenzie, --- 555
Mackey, Alonzo W. 118
Macklin 483, 484
  --- (Mrs.) 483, 484
  Bedford 483
Macon, Charlotte Nelson 224
Maconichie, --- (Dr.) 403
Maddox 526, 527
  Elijah 192
  Ella 407
  John 528
  Lucinda 394
  Lucinda Owsley 409
  Lula 529
  Notley 526
  Susanna Burch 526
  William 94
  Wilson 192
Madeira, Frederick 159
  Louise 159
  Pauline 159
Madison 179, 395
  --- (Bishop) 366, 397
  --- (Capt.) 402
  --- (General) 392
  --- (Mr.) 391, 402
  --- (Mrs.) 542
  --- (President) 87 374, 395, 586, 611
  Agatha 374, 401, 402
  Agatha Strother 401
  Dolly 542
  Elizabeth 401
  Gaul Thomas 374, 395
  George 374, 375, 401
  James 84, 374, 401
  James C. 374
  John 60, 366, 373, 374, 375, 397, 399, 401. 402, 431

Madison, (cont.)
  John (Mrs.) 413
  Letitia 392, 403
  Margaret 374, 375
  Martha M. 680
  Myra 375, 402
  Roland 402
  Rowland 374
  Sarah 568
  Susanna 401
  Susanne 374
  Thomas (General)
    366, 374, 395, 402
  Wm. 401
  Wm. (General) 403
  Wm. (Mrs.) 401
  Wm. I. 401
  Wm. Strother 374
Maffitt, Clarence Dudley 65
Magee, Thomas R. (Major) 481
Magoffin, William Roland 696
Magruder 527
Mahon, --- (Infant) 568
  Archibald 568
  Eliza 568
  Jas. 568
  Jane 568
  Judith 568
  Martha 568
  Mary 568
  Wm. 568
  Wm. (Rev.) 568
Major 500, 748, 749, 750, 755
  Ann Redd 748
  Benjamin 517
  Chastain 517
  Eliza 517
  Elizabeth Minter 751
  Elizabeth Redd 517, 592, 748
  Elvira 748
  Elvira Thomson 748
  Evelyn 748
  Frances 592
  James 512, 748, 749, 751
  Jane 748
  John 500, 517, 592, 748
  John, Jr. 748, 751
  John, Sr. 748, 751
  John James 517
  Joseph 625
  Joseph Winter 517
  Judith 751
  Judith Trabue 748
  Lewis R. 748, 749
  Lewis Redd 748
  Lucy 395
  Mildred Taylor 748, 752
  Olive T. 749
  Olive Trabue 517, 748
  Susanna 748, 751, 752
  Thomas 500, 517, 520, 748, 751
  William 748
  William T. 517
Majors, Lucinda (Mrs.) 271
  Lucy 386
  Margaret 706

Makemie, --- 286
  Francis (Bishop) 286
  Martha 286
  Martha Breckinridge 286
  Rebecca 286
Maldred 26
Mallet, Stephen 509
Malone, Julia 516
  Julia White Fields 697
Malredus 26
Manahan, John E. (Dr.) 487
Manion, Jane 734
Manley, Christine 504
Manly, Christiana Hans 516
Mannon 359
  Eliza 359
Mansfield, Virgil L. 675
March, --- (Earl of) 25
Marchmont, --- (Earl of) 28
  Alexander II, Earl of 28
Marchmount, --- (Earl of) 25, 28
Marischal, --- (Earl of) 202
  George, Earl of 202
Markee, Ann 563
Markell, Cornelia Thompson 118
  George William 118
  Harry Hamilton 118
  Harvey Hamilton, Jr. 118
  Juliet Mitchell 118
  Russell Yeatman 118
Markham, George W. (Dr.) 106, 107
  Lucy Fleming 106, 108
  Martha Woodson 106, 108
  Pattie 108
  Thomas Railey (Rev.) 106, 108
  William Fleming 106, 107, 108
Markley, Ann Randolph 147
  John 147
  Maria Louise 147
Marks, Elizabeth 399
  Hastings 229
  Merriweather 399
  Nancy 399
Marnix, 555
Marquis, Dorothy Jean 47
Marr, John 452, 460
  Mary 452, 453, 460
Marre, de la (See De La Marre)
Marsh, B. B. 658
  Richd. 488
Marshall 111, 176, 179, 366, 748
  --- 747
  --- (Chief Justice) 65, 201, 203, 367, 401, 564
  --- (Col.) 176, 747, 26
  --- (Countess of)
  --- (Miss) 401
  Acton 702

Marshall, (cont.)
  Ann Lewis 377
  Ann Maria 377
  Annie 100
  Betty 626
  Charles 366, 377
  Charles Edward 85
  Edward C. 109
  Esther 626
  H. 63
  Humphrey 121
  Humphrey (General) 111, 168
  J. M. 65
  John 111
  John (Chief Justice) 108, 176, 213, 219, 376, 377, 387, 400
  John James (Judge) 85
  Josephine 109, 126
  Judith L. (Mrs.) 83, 85
  Louis 109
  Louis (Dr.) 108
  Mary 367, 376, 400, 627, 628
  Mary Keith 111
  Robert 626
  Robert Nairne 626
  Thos. 702
  Thos. (Capt.) 111
  Thomas (Col.) 108, 111, 176, 219, 366, 377
  Thos. F. 109, 111
  William 58
Marshell, Thomas (Col.) 203
Martian, Elizabeth 574, 589
Nicholas (Capt.) 574
Nicholas (Colonel) 589
Martin 243, 533, 573, 775
  --- 59, 238, 544, 771
  Agnes 775
  Ann D. 775
  Anna Rodes 532, 533
  Annie Woodson 124, 145
  Anthony 573
  Azariah, Sr. 533
  Betty 626
  Caroline Jane 496
  Catherine Jane 573. 574
  Elijah 775
  Elizabeth 222
  Ernest 124, 145
  Esther Smith 573
  Evalina 402
  F. R. 124, 144
  Henry Newell (Professor) 600
  Hugh 774, 775
  James 496, 573, 616, 617, 775
  Jane 774, 775
  John 207, 573, 775
  Joseph 420, 775
  Judith 437
  Judith (Miss) 437

820

Martin, (cont.)
  Laura 124, 144
  Lucille Long 31
  Lucille Long (Mrs.) 31
  Margaret 573
  Martha 775
  Mary 568
  Mary Ann (Rapine) 573
  Minerva 2
  Pierre 573
  Polly 523
  Robt. 568
  Sallie 310
  Samuel 774
  Sarah Holman 573
  Sid 604
  Talitha 775
  Thomas 616, 617
  Washington 775
  Wesley 437
  William 238, 533, 773, 774, 775
  William H. 573
  Wm. Henry (Mrs.) 775
  William Holman 496, 573
  William W. (Rev.) 564
Martion, Henry 437
  Judith (Miss) 437
Marvin, Abigail 728
Mashburn, H. H. (Mrs.) 650
  H. H. (Rev.) 650
  Miriam 650
Mason, --- 236, 238, 241, 243
  Ann 662
  Charles 223
  Francis (Sir) 528
  George 390, 587
  George (Colonel) 587
  H. P. 749, 753
  James M. 376
  Jefferson Randolph 223
  John 422, 424
  John Enoch 223
  Joseph 419
  Kathryn Harrod 235
  Lucy Wiley 223
  Margaret 662, 663
  Mary 390
  Samuel 752
  Thomson 587
  Wilson Cary Nicholas 224
Massey, Lee (Rev.) 84
Masters, John G. 301
Mastin, Geo. R. (Mrs.) 197
  Gilbert 756
  Grace Murray 197
  T. L. (Dr.) 576
Maston, --- (Dr.) 577
Mather, Joanna 728
Mathews, Baldwin 574
  Claude (Gov.) 466
  Francis (Capt.) 574
  Mary 574
  Samuel (Gov.) 574

Mathis, Anne 717
Matson, Mary 33
Matthew, Thomas 259
Matthews. --- (Gov.) 399
  Emma 149
  George 329
  John 320
  Jozie Mae Turner 525
  Marcellus 672
  Otho F. 122
  Otho Floyd 119
  Preston V. 120
  Richard 329, 331
  Sampson 329
  Sarah Lee 120
  Walter (Dr.) 529
  Walter (Mrs.) 525
Mattox, Eliza 653
Maupin, Cornelia 152
Maxey, Elizabeth 254
Maxwell, --- 24
  James (Capt.) 1
  Margaret 17, 21
May, --- 275
  John 513
  Will 529
Mayer, --- (Miss) 220
Mayes, Henry 488
Mayfield, R. M. (M. D.) 1
  R. N. 3
  R. N. (Dr.) 2
Mayo 98, 116, 117, 145, 166, 167
  Addison F. (Dr.) 129, 135
  Addison F. , Jr. 129
  Adeline Livingston 228
  Anna Lillian 129
  Arthur Randolph 228
  Caroline L. 130
  Catharine Swann 116
  Catherine Randolph 129
  Cynthia F. 358
  Daniel 116
  Dixie Railey (Mrs.) 153
  Edward C. 227
  Edward Everitt 129
  Elizabeth 116, 148, 153, 167
  F. E., Jr. 130
  Francis Gertrude 129
  Francis Sweeny 116
  Frederick E. 130
  George Anna 135
  George D. 227
  George Washington 227
  Georgianna 129
  Joan 116
  John 116, 117
  John (Col.) 116, 117
  Joseph 116
  Joseph E. 150
  Jouette 116
  Julia 117
  Laura Rutherfoord 227
  Lewis 358
  Lewis Randolph 228
  Louise 228
  Marie 117
  Mary 116, 155, 164, 165, 166, 167

Mayo, (cont.)
  Nancy 116, 140, 145, 146, 167
  Peyton Randolph 130
  Railey 150
  Randolph 228
  Robert (Dr.) 117
  Thirza Howard 116
  Thomas Jefferson 129
  Thomas Mann Randolph 227
  Thurza Howard 286
  William 116, 129, 135, 145
  William (Col.) 116, 117, 135, 145, 153, 164, 167
  William (Major) 116, 117
  William, Jr. 167
  William Frederick 129
Mays, Elisha 359
  Rebecca Jane 359
McAdams, Harry Kennett (Mrs.) 243
McAdon, Mary E. 149, 153
McAfee 278, 327, 714, 772, 774
  --- (Captain) 293
  --- (General) 772
  Alabama 714
  Anne 714
  Charles 124
  Charles Elmore 123, 144, 145
  Clinton 104
  Dwight 104
  E. E. 123
  E. Elmore 144
  Elizabeth J. 714
  Henry 104
  Henry Whitney 694
  Indiana 714
  Irene 104
  James 774, 775
  James M. 714
  Jane 243
  John 238
  John J. 714
  Kate J. 694
  Lady Rachael 123, 144
  Margaret W. 714
  Mary 17
  Polly 714
  Rice 714
  Robert 714
  Robt. (Mrs.) 695
  Robt. W. 694
  Sallie E. 695
  Samuel 714
  Samuel W. 714
  Viola A. 123, 144
  William C. 714
  William Leroy 123, 144
McAlister 185
  Charles 695
McAllister, --- 432
McBrayer, Sarah 162, 166
McBride, Melva 675
  P. D. 101, 137
  William 243
McCall, James (Mr.) 488
McCann, Susie 32
McCarrig, Ana (?) 636
McCarthy, Mary F. 605

821

McCarthy, (cont.)
  S. A. 416, 417
McCartney, Andrew 339
McCarty, --- 692, 708
McCasland, James 625, 627
McCauley, James 341
McCausland, Phoebe 57, 61
McChesney, H. V. , Sr. (Mrs.) 608
McClain, Daniel 337
McClanahan, --- (Captain) 379, 769
  --- (Mr.) 410, 411
  Lucy 410
McClannahan, --- (Captain) 398
  Letitia 774, 775
McClellan, Sarah 408
McClelland, Mary 476
McClintock, Della 575
McClung, Will 11
McClure, Abram 498
  Achsah 498
  Alexander 498
  Bartlett 498
  James 324
  John Alexander 324
  Joseph 324
  Malcolm 324
  Margaret 716
  Mary 324, 498
  Robert 324
  Samuel 324, 498
  Walker 324
  William 324, 498
McConchie, --- (Dr.) 392
  Susan 383
McConitry, --- (Miss) 406
McConnell, 763, 769
  Adelia 478
  Alexander 770
  Andrew 478
  Augusta (Rogers) 478
  Belle 577
  Cyrene 577
  Eliza 572
  Elizabeth 572, 577, 738
  Emma 577
  Frances 769
  Francis 769, 770
  George 572
  Henry 577
  Henrye C. (?) 577
  Hunter 572
  James 572, 577, 769-770, 737
  James (General) 572, 577
  Jane 428
  Jane (Miss) 428
  Jane Sandidge 428
  John 770
  John M. 126
  Kate H. 572
  Margaret 572
  Martha 126, 127, 572
  Mary 576, 577
  Payne 577
  Robert 572, 577, 591
  Robin 572
  Sarah Miller 572

McConnell, (cont.)
  William 572, 769, 770
  William (Capt.) 764, 773
  Wm. Thompson 572
McCorkle, Winfield P. 712
McCormick, J. B. 124
McCoun 278, 327
McCown 644, 645
  --- (Dr.) 645
  Alexander 644
  Ann Wood 644
  Annie 645
  Burr 644
  Elizabeth Doom 645
  Emaline 645
  Harrison Wood 652
  Harrison Wood (Dr.) 644, 645
  James 644, 645
  Laura Doom 645
  Sarah Jane 645
  William 645
McCoy, --- 605
  Arthur 604
  James G. 717
  Joseph E. 717
McCrackin, Cyrus 747, 754
  Rosa 574
McCrary 345
  David Stuart 345
  John 345
  Robert 345
  Robert (Col.) 345
McCreary, Harriet 51
  James B. 37, 51
  James Bennett 37
  Kate Hughes 37
McCue, John (Rev.) 334
McCulloch, George 563
  Zadah 134
McCullock, Hannah 563
McCullough, --- 409
  Samuel D. 622
McCurdy, --- 306
McCutchen, Grace 131
  Isabella 131
  John D. 131
  John D., Jr. 131
  Louise 131
McDaniel, --- (Mr.) 89
  William 89
McDaugh, John 57
McDavid, Edward T. 131
  Emma Catherine 131
McDonald, --- 592
  Amanda Jane Park 697
  Anna 722
  Bertha 697
  Douglas De La Gal 697
  Edward Dysart 697
  Edward Henry 697
  Edward Henry (Dr.) 697
  Lilian 697
  Mary 568, 697
  Mattie 697
  Molly 736
  Norman Simpson 697
  Robt. 722
McDougal, Genevieve 160
McDough, John 80

McDowell 179, 766
  Agatha 375
  Alexander Railey 149
  Elizabeth 517
  Jane Randolph 149
  John (Capt.) 323
  Julia 757
  Lucinda 375
  Mary 130, 375
  Sallie 512
  Samuel 326, 375
  Samuel (Judge) 375
  T. D. S. 149
  Wm. (Judge) 374, 375
  Wm. M., Jr. 375
McElhany, --- (Capt.) 398
  Mary (Mrs.) 379
McElroy 766
  Hugh (Mrs.) 501
  Samuel T. 568
McFarland, Jennie 159
McFerran, James C. 574
  Viley 574
McFerren, Clara 692
McGarry, Hugh (Col.) 92
McGarth, Richard Allen 23
McGary, --- 238
  Catherine 238
  Hugh 235, 236, 238
McGaughey, Ann 45
  Arthur 45, 46
  Arthur (Colonel) 44, 45
  Arthur (Lieutenant) 44
  Arthur II 44
  Arthur Kenton 46
  Charles 44
  Eleanor 45
  Ellen Kenton 45
  Harriet 46
  Hume 46
  Jane 45
  John 46
  Lavinia 45
  Norman 46
  Rachel 45
  Robert 46
  Thomas 45
McGee, Betty 327
  Dorothy 327
  Edward 578
  George 577, 578
  Ira 578
  James 327
  Molly 327
  Robert 578
McGinniss, Thomas 395
McGinty, Ann (Kennedy) Wilson Poage Lindsay 91, 93, 94
  James 94
McGoffin, Jennie 512
McGrath, Annie M. 700
  Lula 675
McGrau, --- (Mr.) 401
McGregor, Chastain 499
  Matilda 499
  Tom A. (Dr.) 499
McGuire, John A. (Elder) 528
McHatton, Bettie 577, 578

McHatton, (cont.)
   Charles 577
   Fannie 577
   James 577
   Minor 577
   Robert 577
McHenry 490
   --- (Mrs.) 490
   Hannah 490
   Henry D. 490
   Henry D. (Mrs.) 490
   John Hardin 490
   John James 490
   Isabella Howe 490
   Lemuel Hardin 490
   Mary Taylor 490
   Morton D. 490
McIlhaney, --- (Miss) 696
McIlvain, Annie Wright 658
   John W. 658
   Moses 770
McIlvaine 763, 765
McIlwain 767
McIlwaine, Sally Walthall 223
McIntire, Mary 224
McIntosh, David G. (Col.) 600
McKamie 278, 288, 293
   Francis 290
   Francis (Rev.) 245, 288
   Jane 245, 293
   Martha 288, 290, 293
   Martha Breckinridge 288
   Robert 288
McKay, Alexander 329
   James 329, 331
   Sarah 29
McKeag, Catherine 131
   Henry 131
McKee, Logan 469
   Samuel 701
McKenney, Jennie 50
   Sallie Ferguson 51
   William 51
McKibben, --- (Mr.) 85
McKinley, John (Capt.) 4
McKinney, Gertrude 34
   Irine 530
   John 769
McKittrick, Jane Armstrong 331
   Robert 331
McLaughlin, James 338
McLuer, Emer (Miss) 441
McLunthe 765
McMahon, Mary 596
McMakin, Adams Carithers 104
McMeekin, Laura 576
McMiehan, Josie 575
McMillan, Matilda 732
   William 732
McMullen, Samuel 334
McMullin, Alvinx 72
   Beverly 72
   Clarence 72
   Florence 72
   John H. 72
   Nelson Van Buskirk 56, 61, 72

McMullin, (cont.)
   Norval Van Buskirk (?) 72
McMurtrie, --- (Dr.) 63
McMurtries, --- 63
McNeilly, Hannah 314
McPheeters, Annie 118
McRoberts, Annie 140
   Charles C. 310
   Mamie 23
   Margaret 310
   Margaret Taylor 310
   Rebecca 310
Mead 116, 117, 349
   --- (Bishop) 564
   Benjamin 348, 349
   Cynthia 348, 349, 361, 362
   Dorothy Randolph 103
   Elizabeth 349
   Elizabeth (Brown) 348, 349
   H. J. 103
   Henry 351, 356
   Lalla 103
   Malinda 351, 356
   Mary Belle 103
   Robert 349
Meade, --- (Bishop) 201, 231, 370, 375, 399
   --- (Mr.) 411
   Anna May 529
   Anne 231
   David 231
   Edmonia (Miss) 400
   Richard Kidder (Col.) 231
   Shannon 529
Meaken, --- (Mrs.) 380
Means, Hugh 334
Mechteld, --- (Duke of) 547-549
Medley, Mildred 382
   Milly (Miss) 405
Meek 763
   --- 330
   John 763
   Thomas 763
   William 330
Meikleham, David Scott (Dr.) 222
   Ellen Wayles 222
   Esther 222
   Esther Alice 222
   Thomas Mann Randolph 222
   William 222
Melehoir, --- (Miss) 400
Melrose, --- (Baron of) 26
Mendenhall, John (M. D.) 286, 293
   Martha Breckinridge (Steele) 290
Menefee, --- (Miss) 426
   Benjamin 406
   Milly 406
   Nancy 406
   Sally 406
   Wm. 406
Menifee 179
   Marie 35
   Mary 35

Menifee, (cont.)
   Wm. 383
Menzies, C. C. 573
Mercer, George 322
   Jane 1
   John Fenton 322
Merchant, Caleb W. 742
Merchison, Jessie 151
Meredith 533
Meriwether, Charlotte Nelson 224
   Frances 265
   Frances (Morton) (Mrs.) 96
   Francis 265
   Jane 584
   Lucy 265
   Mary 265
   Mary Walker 224
   Nicholas 584
   William 266
Merrill, --- (General) 375
Merritt, --- (Miss) 392, 403
   Catherine 338,
   Martha 358
   Samuel 338
Mershon, Aaron 146
   Benjamin 146
   Elemander 146
   Jane Railey 146
   Lavinia 146
   Minerva 146
   Orlander 146
   Randolph Darnell 146
   Virginia 146
Messer, William 349
Metcalfe, --- (Governor) 285
   Anna M. (Mrs.) 635
   John 192
   Keturah 285
   Sue 164
Meteren 547
   --- (Lord) 549
   --- (Lord of) 549, 550
   Jooste, Jans, J. M. of, 558
Meteren and Kerkwick, --- (Lord of) 550
Meux 690
   Ann 690
   Frances 690
   James 690
   John 690
   John G. 690
   Richard 690
Meyer, Beverly 469
Meyers, Edward J. 147
Michaux, --- 569
   Abraham 569
   Abram 569, 654
   Ann 569, 654
   Anne 569, 653, 654
   Eliz. 567
   Eliza. 569
   Jacob 567, 569, 653, 654
   Jas. 569
   Jane 569
   Jno. 569
   Judith 569
   Nannie 569
   Paul 569

Michaux, (cont.)
    Susan 569
Middleton, --- (Mr.)
    462
    Charity 66
    James 577
    John 66
    Mary 180
Milam, --- 45
    W. E. (Rev.) 124,
    145
Miles, --- (Colonel)
    34
    Annie H. (Mrs.)
    201
    Annie Hawkins 368
    Enos 623
    Florida E. 565
    Isaac 625
    Samuel 625
Miller, --- 14, 524
    --- (Mr.) 14, 15,
    406
    Alexander 11, 55
    Alexr. 11
    Barbara 668-669
    Craig 648, 652
    Ellen 151
    Hanna 703
    Hannah 580, 581
    Harvey W. 300
    Isaac Wood 652
    Jane Gaines 325
    John Thomas 645
    Joseph (Captain)
    652
    Joseph Alexander
    (Captain) 652
    Joseph Llyod
    (Lieut.) 652
    Laura 645
    Mabel (Miss) 648
    Mary 653
    Matthew 669
    Merle 648
    Rodney 648
    W. H. 524
    William 12
    William (General)
    325
    William C. 6
    Wilson B. 648
Milligan, George 44
Milliken, --- 45
Mills, 592
    --- (Miss) 592
    Ann 418, 431
    Elizabeth 615
    Emily 565
    Nathaniel, Sr. 419
    Ogden, Jr. 76
    Rebecca 666
    Robert 415
    Rogers Will 620
    Sarah 419, 432
Milton 249
    Kittie ? 247
    Mary Willis 247
    William 247
    William E. 247
    William E. Kittie ?
    247
Miner, Elizabeth 744
Minor 116
    Agatha 578
    Alice Thomas 578
    Anna Hyde 133

Minor, (Cont.)
    Caroline 133
    Catharine Pleasants
    133
    Edmund Christian 133
    Edmund Christian
    (Judge) 133, 136
    John 381
    Louise McLain 133
    Thomas 578
    Virginia Adair 133
    Vivion (Captain)
    523
Minter, Anthony 512
    Elizabeth 497, 512,
    751
    James 512
    Jane 512
    Jane Trabue 501
    Jeremiah 512
    John Trabue 512
    Joseph 499, 512
    Joseph (Rev.) 512
    Judith 512
    Martha 512
    Nancy 501, 512
    Sarah 512
    Tabitha 512
    William 512
Minton 687
    Jackson G. 687
Misbet, --- 757
Mitchell, --- 360
    Bonnie Smith 470
    Eliza 715
    Fred 625
    Hamilton 657
    James 261, 657
    Joseph 715
    John 329
    Mark 341
    Martha 657
    Maryan Jean 715
    Michael 625
    Rosanna 623
    Ruth 657
    Sallie 412
    Sarah 657
    Sarah Wright 659
    Thomas 657
    Virginia 181
    William 625, 657, 714
Mize, Will 694
Moahan, Sarah 487
Mobeley, Keziah 299
Mobely, Keziah 299
Mock, Rose 649
Molenax, Janekken 558
Momford, --- (Miss)
    401
    Wm. (Col.) 401
Moncure, --- (Mr.) 390
    R. C. L. (Judge)
    390
Monod, Frederic (Rev.)
    70
    Henri 70
Monroe, --- (Mr.) 391,
    402
    --- (President) 154
    Andrew 591
    Ben (Judge) 591
    Elizabeth 591, 602
    James 5, 591
    James (President)
    602
    John (Judge) 265

Monroe, (cont.)
    Mary 591
    Mary K. 591
    Rachael 591
    Thomas Bell (Judge)
    591
Montague, Peter 248
Monteiro, Moses T. 509
Montfort, Elizabeth 527
    Frances 529
Montgomery 278
    --- (Captain) 764
    --- (Mr.) 248
    Alexander Rennick 247
    Cynthia 591
    Edith 247
    George Berryman 104
    James 159, 248, 320
    James (Rev.) 335
    James Todd 247
    Jane Railey 104
    Jean 746
    John 247, 248
    John (Rev.) 247,
    334, 718
    Jno. B. 104
    John Gilbert 70
    Kate 247
    Letitia 247
    Lettie 248
    Lilian 247
    Lillian 248
    Lucinda 70
    Martha Neely 70
    Mary 104, 247, 248
    Mattie Woodson 104
    Oak 159
    Paul 159
    Robt. 104
    Robert Fry 104
    Thomas 247, 248
Montignani, William C.
    71
Montrose, --- (Duke
    of) 757
Moody, Mary B. 142
    Matilda 668
    Matilda Paget 666
    Robert 666
Moore, --- 412
    --- (Mr.) 390
    --- (Mrs.) 390
    --- (Parson) 247
    Anderson W. 120
    Caroline 643
    Cato (Mrs.) 389
    Clifton Albert 120
    Eleanor 282, 283
    Elizabeth 718
    Evelina Watts 711
    Fannie Belle 120
    Florence Lamar 227
    G. W. 710, 711
    George Edgar 157
    George W. 710
    Georgia Lee 120
    Georgie 573
    Gertrude 479
    Hesseltine Marshall
    226
    J. P. 390
    James 763
    Jane 327
    John 323, 329, 330,
    335
    John L. 625
    Leonard 228

Moore, (cont.)
  Margaret 327, 335
  Margaret Thompson 717
  Mary 544, 763
  Matilda B. 711
  Nancy 335
  Nannie 566
  Quinton 696
  Rebecca 493
  Robert 533
  Roscoe Edward 120
  Sallie 567
  Samuel 335
  Sarah 334, 335
  Sarah Elizabeth 120
  Sarah French 471
  Thomas 23
  Thomas B. 709
  Thomas Edward 709
  Thomas R. 566
  Walter B. 120
  William 493
  Wm. (Major) 492, 493
  William Whitley 471
Moorehouse, M. C. 254
Moorhead, --- 635
  --- (Dr.) 636
  John (Dr.) 635
  John (Sir) 636
  Robert (Dr.) 635
Moorman, --- 568
  Agnes 569
  John 568
  Margaret 471
Moran, Elizabeth Jane 262
  Nancy A. 261
Morancey, --- 164
Moray, --- (Earl of) 214
More, John 430
Morehead, Chas. (Gev.) 575
  Charles S. (Governor) 541
  Henry (Dr.) 342
  Katie 575
Morgan, --- 569, 707
  E. W. 300
  John H. (Gen.) 571
  John Hunt (General) 262
  Mary 640
  Mary Rollington 640
  Molly 71
  Samuel 360
  Sarah 686
  " Stonewall " 571
  Thomas 640
Morison, Catherine 28
Morley, --- 588
  Samson 569
Morris 490, 741, 743
  Alicia 84
  Asa 84
  B. S. (Judge) 739
  Ballard Emmanuel 142
  Charles 648
  E. Loisce G. 743
  F. O. (Rev.) 670
  Frank Sidney 142
  Garnet Elizabeth 143
  Garnett S. 143
  Gouveneur 220
  Gouverneur 221
  Grace Bell 742

Morris, (cont.)
  Hannah Ann 84
  Hugh 84
  Isaac 626
  James (Mr.) 743
  James Scearce 143
  Jeptha T. 743
  John Speed 224
  Julius 142
  Marcus Blakemore 143
  Margaret Nelson 143
  Margaret Reid 142
  Mary 84
  Mary Jane 407
  Mildred H. 743
  Nathan G. (Col.) 113
  Nellie Lee 742
  Orville 650
  Penelope 84
  Ruth 140
  Sarah 490
  Sarah A. 743
  Susan 84
  Thos. H. 743
  William 84, 490, 490-491, 530
  William, Sr. 490
  William Emmet 143
  Wineaford 743
  Wineaford (Mrs.) 743
Morrison, --- 410
  Bessie 517
  James 59
  John (Capt.) 773
  John Rowan (Dr.) 511
Morrow, Jackson 364
  Mary 745
  Nancy 745
  O. H. 673
Morton, 432
  --- 13, 769, 771
  --- (Miss) 567, 653
  --- (Mr.) 397
  --- (Mrs.) 92, 95, 189
  Caroline Bruce 78
  Charles 419, 432
  Daniel 432
  Elijah 419, 432
  Elizabeth B. 390
  Elizabeth (Hawkins) 432
  George 366, 373, 375, 419, 432
  Henry 399, 419, 432
  J. P. 671
  James Williams (Judge) 78
  Jennie C. (Mrs.) 95, 189, 279, 483
  Jennie Chinn (Mrs.) 608
  John 419, 432
  John P. 613
  Jos. 654
  Joseph 567, 653
  Judith 567
  Mary 567, 569, 654
  Mollie Tandy 419
  Nancy 419, 432
  Oren 329
  Quin 567
  Quin (Colonel) 567
  Sam'l. 567

Morton, (· cont.)
  Thomas 653, 654
  Wm. Quin 567
Mosby 116
  Alfred 105, 125
  Lydia 133, 136
  Virginia Cary 133, 136
Moseby, Arthur 151
  M. A. 151
Moses, Claudine 575
Moss, --- (Dr.) 175
  Betsy 21
  Elizabeth 175
  James Luther 737
  John 22, 417
  Mary 577
Mote, Sally (?) 440
Motley, Mary 497
  Sarah 580
Mott, Mary Ann 73
  Mary Varum 77
Mottrom, John (Colonel) 662
Mount, Alice Holmes 140
  Bessie 140
  Charlotte Amanda 140
  Ella Morris 140
  James 140, 145
  Jo Ann 140
  John James 140
  John McRoberts 140
  Joseph Railey 140, 145
  Margaret 140
  Mary Maude 140
  Robert Morris 140
  Ruth Berry 140
  Sara Railey 140
Mountjoy, Elizabeth 689
  Phyllis 690
  William 690
Muhlenberg, --- 514
Muir 69, 70, 78, 82
  Alice King 79
  Augusta Elizabeth 79
  Clara 78
  Elizabeth 644
  Isabel Brown 644
  Jasper 644
  John 82
  John (Lieutenant) 78
  John Brinley 79
  John Wallingford 79
  Mamie Figg 649
  Maria Wurts 78
  Mary 78
  Ophelia 79
  Ophelia (Miss) 54
  Peter Brown 644
  William 70, 78, 82
  William Morton 78, 79
  William S. 54
  William Sawtell 78, 79
Muldrough, William 329
  Wm. (Col.) 122
Muldrow, Elizabeth 120
Mullins, Judith E. 515
Murphrey, J. 625
Murphy, Fanny 516
  Hester Ann 534
  Martha Foster 224
Murray, --- (Earl of) 201
  Henry 331, 342

Murray, (cont.)
  Rosanna Armstrong 331
Murrell, --- (Dr.) 605
Murry, --- (Countess of) 26
Muse, de la (See de la Muse)
Musik, Charles 577
  Daisy 577
  Edwin 577
Myers, Madge 675
Nair, James M. 278
Nairne, Betty 626
  Esther 626
Nantz, --- 654
Napoleon 600
Nash, Elizabeth 530
  Frank (Gen.) 326
  Katie Lee 581
  Mary 460
  Mary Virginia 326
  Robert 488
Neal, Mary Tribble (Mrs.) 522
  Sarah 262
Neale 679, 696
  Anne Rainey 697
  Benjamin Howard 694
  Eliza Anne 697
  James 696, 697
  James, Jr. 697
  James M., Jr. 697
  Margaret Jones 694
  Wiliam L. 697
  William Lewis 694, 697
Neblett, Beatrice 530
  Mary 531
  Ollie 531
  Robert 530
  Thomas E. 530
Neel, Eurie Pearl Wilford 350
Neely, Martha 70
Neiddefer---, Louise 704
Neighbor, Elizabeth B. 499
Nelson, 57, 73, 79, 80, 81, 337
  --- (Mr.) 600
  Augustine O. 57, 73
  Benjamin F. 57, 73
  Cornelius Van Buskirk 57, 73
  David Patton 56, 73
  Eliza (Mrs.) 271
  James 56, 73
  John 73, 74, 75
  John (Capt.) 56, 73, 74, 75, 79, 80
  Jones 576, 577
  Julia 57, 74
  Marcus L. 57, 74
  Margaret 57, 74
  Mary 218
  Mary --- 73
  Mary Ann 57, 74, 80, 81
  Nancy 57, 74
  Nancy --- 56, 73
  Polycarpus 73
  Rebecca 583
  Robert 234
  Sarah 56, 73, 81
  " Scotch " Tom 218
  Thomas 73

Nelson, (cont.)
  Thomas (Governor) 233
  Tom 218
  William 583, 584, 589
  William (Col.) 218
Nentley, Emma 579
Netherbud, Mary 653
Netland, --- (Earl of) 26
Neville, Amelia 286
  James (Capt.) 93
  Joseph (General) 286
  Lydia 516
Newburn, William 231
Newcomb, --- (Professor) 773
Newell, James (Capt.) 1
  Joseph Black 746
  Margaret 1
  Samuel 1, 746
  Sarah 746
Newelle, 746
  Dorcas 746
  Elizabeth Collvil 746
  Esther M. 746
  Jean 746
  John M. 746
  Joseph B. 746
  Joseph Black 746
  Margit E. 746
  Samuel 746
  Samuel, Jr. 746
  Samuel, Sr. 746
  Susannah 746
  William T. 746
Newman, Cornelia 742, 743
  Eleanor 742
  Grace 742
  Lucy 105
  Margaret White 101
  Maude 150
  Moses 358
  Nell Katherine 742
  William C. 742
  William Morris 742
  Susan Withers 101
  W. W. 101
Newton, --- 604
  --- (Miss) 389
  Clare Montgomery 119
  Clarence H. (Rev.) 118
  Clarence Hitchcock 122
  Francis May 119
  Harriett Ann 119
  Lurlene 470
  William Russell 119
Nicholas, Elizabeth 233
  Jane Hollins 221, 222
  Robert Carter 233, 599
  Wilson Cary (Governor) 222
Nicholls, Guy Winthrop 76
  Mary Margaret (Miss) 76
  Winfield J. 76
Nichols, John 626
  S. S. 62
Nicholson, --- 456
  James 456

Nicklin, Benj. Patten (Col.) 396
  J. B., Jr. 396
  J. B. III (Lieutenant) 396
  John Bailey 396
Nicol, Ann (Miss) 246
Nisbet, Milus 512
  Milus Cooper (Dr.) 512
Nix, John 567
Noble, Alice 132
  Bertha Demarest 132
  Carl 132, 136
  Catherine Pauline 131
  Charles 132, 136
  Charles (Rev.) 132, 136
  Elizabeth 132
  Enid 132
  Fannie Ketcham 132
  Franklin Pleasants 132
  George Adams 132
  George Pleasants 132, 136
  George Pleasants (Rev.) 132
  Henry Prime 132
  Henry Prime, Jr. 132
  Henry T. (Dr.) 132
  Isabella Pleasants 131
  Jean 132
  John Adair 132
  Joseph Franklin 132, 136
  Joseph Franklin (Rev.) 131
  Katherine Pleasants 132
  Manly O. 132
  Mary 131
  Mary Elizabeth 132
  Mason 132
  Mason (Rev.) 131, 132, 136
  Mason, Jr. 132, 136
  Mason, Jr. (Rev.) 136
  Rosalind 132
  Rose 132
Noel, Anne Maria 681
Noftsinger, Peter 338
Noland, Jesse 532, 533
  Sallie 533
Norfolk, --- (Earl of) 660
Norman, Courtney 384
Normandy, --- (Duke of) 201
  Richard, Duke of 26
Norris, John 642
Northop, Nellie 147
Northumberland, --- (Earl of) 25
  Cospatrick, Earl of 26
  Uchtred, Prince of 26
Norton, 179
  Brooke Minor 513
  Caldwell 513
  Ernest 513
  J. M. Robinson 515

Norton, (cont.)
　James Stephens (1st
　　Lieut.) 513
　Minnie 513
Norvell, 599
　Martha 599
　Moses 622
　William 599
　Wm. (Hon.) 599
Noyes, Moses 727
Nuckles, Louisa 87
Nuckols, --- (Mrs.)
　　89
　Cecil 575
　George Watkins (Dr.)
　　580
　Louise 575
　Nancy 704
　Robert C. 575
　S. V. (Mrs.) 93
Nugent, Neel M. 670
Nunn, Nancy Farris 123,
　　144
Nutt, Eliza (Mrs.) 488
　John 487, 488
　John (Mr.) 488
　Joseph 488
　William 488
Nutting, Wallace 205
O'Bannon, Florence 529
　Ida B. 125
O'Bryan, Lucinda 516
O'Donahoe, Elizabeth
　　(Miss) 610
Offutt 481
　--- (Miss) 775
　--- (Mrs.) 84
　Benj. F. 578
　Eliza 481
　Elizabeth 573
　Elizabeth Ann 710
　Finch 569
　Reuben 576
　Robert 86
　Sue Ford 576
Ogden, Charity 712
Oglesby, --- (Gov.)
　　479
　John G. 479
　Joseph B. 686
　Rosanna 687
O'Hara 750, 755, 756
　--- 543
　--- (Mr.) 542
　Kane 755, 756
　Kean 542, 543, 545
　Mary Helen 542
　Reuben R. 57
　Theodore 542, 755
　Zarilda 64
Oldham, Mabel 475
Olds, Moses 528
Olie, Jans Derick 549
Olin, --- (Mr.) 75
Oliver, --- 419
　John 74, 333
　Sarah Elizabeth 481
Olliver, John 57
Olney, Margaret 492
　Robert (Sir) 492
Olson, Griffin 131
　John 131
　John Thomas Miller
　　652
　Robert 652
O'Neal, Lucy Mahin 104
　Nellie 591

Orde, John 369
　Thomas 369
Ormes, Rica 530
Ormonde, --- (Duke of)
　　283
Orr, --- (Miss) 602
Ortelius, Abraham 552
　Ortillia 552
Ortels, Abraham 552
　Ortillia 552
　William 552
Orton, Benjamin Ford
　　133
　Elen Adair 133
Osborne, Attalanta Toft
　　626
　Gabriel Glenn
　　(Capt.) 271
　Harrison 226
　Lucy 271
　Nancy Jones 271
　Phillip 271
Otis, Richard W. 670
Overton, Lula 692
Owen, Abram 498
　Abram (Col.) 498
　Ann Elizabeth 34
　Clark Lewis (Col.)
　　498
　Elizabeth 498
　Harriet 498
　James Dupuy 498
　Juliet 308
　Lucy Wooten 498
　Martha Dupuy 498
　Nancy 498
　Sanford 627
　Sarah 192, 583
　Susan 498
Owens, 1
　--- 421
　Amanda 408
　America 409
　Avy 1
　Clarence 1
　David D. 1
　J. M. (Dr.) 1
　Jack 1
　James 1
　Jane 1, 3
　John 1
　John (Col.) 1
　Levina 1
　Martin 1
　Mary Evelyn 694
　Nancy 1, 746
　Perry 1
　Rebecca 1
　Reuben 1
　Sam 694
　Samuel 1
　Sarah 1
　W. Allen 1
　William 1, 746
　Wm. K. 1
Owings, 255
　Beall (Dr.) 640
　Rachel Ruth 640
　Richard 255
Owsley 173, 184, 185,
　　186
　--- (Capt.) 301
　Ann --- 184
　Ann Bayne 185
　Annie H. 101, 137,
　　169
　Annie Harper 173, 174

Owsley, (cont.)
　Annie Harper 173, 174,
　　174, 179, 184, 185,
　　186
　Anthony 185
　Bryan Young 185
　Ellen 185
　Harry Bryan (Mr.)
　　184, 186
　Henry 184, 185
　Henry Bryan 185
　Henry Ebsworth 184,
　　185, 186
　Henry Hawkins 185
　John 184, 185, 186
　John (Rev.) 186
　John Ebsworth 185
　Johnathan (Major)
　　185
　Mary Middleton 185,
　　186
　Mike (Judge) 185
　Thomas 184, 185, 186
　Thomas (Captain)
　　184
　Thomas Taylor 185
　William 185, 186
　William (Gov.) 185
　Wm. Logan 118
　William Logan, Jr.
　　118
Oxford, --- (Bishop of)
　　665
　--- (Earl of) 201
Pace, M. R. 698
Packenham, --- (General) 185
Packingham, --- 603
Page 209, 211
　Carter (Major) 231
　Elizabeth 726
　Ellen 726
　Frank 35
　George Hughes 35
　Judith 195
　Levy 726
　Mann 199, 561
　Mann (Hon.) 213,
　　218
　Maria Judith 108,
　　110, 176, 178, 181,
　　190, 213, 218
　Mary 217, 218
　Mary Hughes 35
　Mary Judith 199, 218
　Mary Mann 223
　R. C. M. (Dr.) 209
　Thomas 756
Paget, 665, 666, 667
　--- 416
　Benjamin Bryan 666
　Bernard Charles Tolver (Major-General) 665
　Edmund 665
　Elizabeth (Lady)
　　665
　Francis 665
　Jonathan 663, 665,
　　666, 668
　Joseph 666
　Joshua 666
　Margaret 666, 668
　Margaret Wright 665,
　　666
　Margaret Wright
　　(Mrs.) 667

Paget, (cont.)
  Martha Ann 666
  Matilda 666
  Pamela 666, 668
  Reuben 665
  Richard (Sir) 665
  Theophilus 665
  William 665, 666, 668
  William (Sir) 665
Pagett, Edmund 415
  Margaret 668
Paine, Verpyle 280
Palen, Frederick Pomeroy 228
  Frederick Pomeroy, Jr. 228
Pallas 660
Palmer, Edward 18, 19
  Rebecca 20
  Thomas 488
Pankey, Jane 478
  Thomas Lorton 478
Pannill 385
  --- (Mrs.) 413
  --- (Widow) 180
  David 385, 404
  Frances 404
  Joseph 385
  Sarah 169, 170, 386
  Sarah (Mrs.) 404
  Sarah Bailey 180, 384, 395
  Sarah Bailey (Mrs.) 179, 367
  Sarah Bailey Morton 404
  Sarah (Bayly) (Mrs.) 463
  William 169, 170, 384, 385, 404, 463
  Wm. R. 404
Papworth, --- 267
Pardue, Leone 675, 677
Parish, Mary B. 739
  Rosa M. 737
  Thompson M. 739
Park 679, 697
  --- 697
  Amanda Jane 697
  Ann Bronaugh 697
  Asa 699
  Barbara 699
  Charity 688
  Charlie Whitney 697
  Edward McDonald 697
  Elihu 697
  Elihu Scott 698
  Eliza Fillmore 697
  Fannie Waugh 697
  Francis Bronaugh 697
  Geo. Clark 697
  Harry Morton 697
  Joe 697
  John, Sr. 699
  John Simpson 697
  John Wesley 697, 698
  Mariam 699
  Mark 698
  Mary E. 697
  Matilda 697, 698
  Miriam 699
  Nell Marshall 698
  Robert White 697
  Simpson 697
  Susan 699
Parke, Ann 582
  John 705

Parke, (cont.)
  Samuel Snoddy 705
Parker 499
  --- (Mr.) 84, 85
  Cecelia Jane 151
  Matilda 673
  Thos. 625
Parkes, Elizabeth Ann 705
  Margaret Jane 705
  Nancy 706
Parks, --- (Mr.) 601
  Carrie Roberta 162, 167
  D. Z. M. 700
  John Price 700
  Mary Belle 700
Parlou, Nancy (Miss) 438
Parremore, John 455
Parrett, Wm. 459, 461
Parris, Martha A. 708
  Thomas 708
Parrish, Irene 673
  John 87
  John (Mrs.) 648
  Mary Phil 574
  Rosa 573
Parrott, Ella 149
  Joseph V. 149
Parry, J. C. (Judge) 603
Parson, Maria 712
  Mary McAfee 695
  Wm. Frank 695
Parsons 727
  --- (Daughter) 728, 729
  --- (Son) 728, 729
  Abigail 728, 729
  Abigail (Mrs.) 729
  Charles F. (Judge) 196
  Chas. F. (Hon) 196, 197
  Charles Francis 227
  Clarina 728, 729
  Deborah 729
  Elizabeth 712, 729
  Ezra 728
  George 729
  Joan 729
  Joanna 729
  Joanna (Mrs.) 729
  John 728, 729
  John (Mrs.) 729
  John Randolph 227
  Jonath (Revd.) 728, 729
  Jonathan 728
  Jonathan (Capt.) 730
  Jos. 653
  Lois 729
  Lois (Mrs.) 729
  Lucia 728
  Lucy 729
  Lydia 728, 729
  Marshfield 728, 729
  Marshfield, Esqr. 730
  Marshfield (Col.) 729
  Marshfield (Lieut.-Colonel) 727

Parsons, (Cont.)
  Phebe 728, 729
  Phebe (Mrs.) 729
  Richard Wait 729
  Robert Battey 227
  Sam'l. H. 728
  Samuel Holden, Esqr. 730
  Silenus deWitt 227
  Thomas 728
  Thomas (Capt.) 730
  Thomas Griswold 729, 730
  William 729
Pary, Everdt 556
Pasteur, William (Dr.) 194, 219
Paten 54
Patis 54
Patrick, --- (Sir) 27
Patrick, Herod 695
  Joseph Manerva 695
  Spicer (Gov.) 376, 401
Patten 64
  James (Capt.) 64
  Margaret 535
Pattershall, Frances 29
  William 29
Patterson 687
  --- 763, 765
  --- (Capt.) 765
  --- (Miss) 399
  Anna 682
  Betsy 639
  Charles 682
  Elizabeth 534
  Ethel 223
  George 515
  Jane 280
  Lucinda Anne 227
  Mary 34
  Regina D. 687
  Robert 280, 281, 774
  Robt. (Capt.) 773
  Robert (Colonel) 280, 682
  Sally 503
  Susan A. 155
Pattie, Coleman (Dr.) 592
  John 625
Patton 4, 15, 52, 54, 59, 60, 62, 63, 64, 79, 345
  --- 13
  --- (Capt.) 54, 55, 56, 57, 58, 59, 60
  --- (Col.) 388
  --- (Mr.) 9, 14, 514
  --- (Mrs.) 59
  Agnes 10, 11, 55
  Agnese 10, 55, 60
  Agnese --- 55
  Agness 10, 11
  Alice 21
  Ann 17, 20 ,23
  Ann --- 18
  Banjamin W. 19
  Benjamin 17, 19
  Benjamin W. 18, 19, 19-20, 20, 21, 53
  Benjamin W. (Mrs.) 19
  Catherine --- 17
  D. S. 20

Patton, (cont.)
Daniel S. 19
David S. 18, 19, 20
Desha 106
Edward Jones 106
Eliza 16, 17, 19
Eliza W. 403
Elizabeth 19, 20, 22, 53, 54, 60, 61, 62, 80
Elizabeth --- 17, 22
Elizabeth Randolph 106
Ester 17, 18
Esther 16, 17, 18, 25, 31, 52
Esther Dyer 17, 22, 23
George Ann 20
George S. 392, 403
Hannah 21
Henry 54, 62, 63, 79
Hester 12, 19, 20
Hetty 17, 18
Hetty --- 18, 52
Hugh M. 392, 403
Isaac 392
Isaac W. 403
Isabel 10, 55
Isabell 10, 55
James 10, 11, 13, 14, 17, 18, 19, 20, 21, 22, 53, 55, 61, 63, 388
James (Captain) 54, 55, 56, 57, 58, 60, 61, 62, 63, 64, 73, 79, 80
James (Col.) 54, 60, 61, 62, 63, 80, 323, 345
James (Mrs.) 59
James F. 392, 403
James T. 20
Jesse 20
John 4, 10, 11, 13, 17, 18, 21, 22, 52, 53, 55, 60, 61, 80
John (Captain) 10, 54, 55, 56, 60, 61, 62
John, Jr. 4, 10, 13, 54
John, Sr. 13
John D. 18, 19, 20, 52, 53
John Dyer 18
John M. 21, 392, 403
John M., Jr. 392
John T. 19; 20, 53
John William 22
Louisa N. 20
Mackey 22, 53 (See also Nackey)
Maggie Lee 161
Margaret 10, 17, 19, 20, 21, 54, 55, 56, 57, 62, 63, 80
Margaret St. (Mrs.) 20
Margaret St. Clair 18, 20 ,21
Mariah 19, 20
Martha 56, 63, 73, 80
Mary 17, 56, 57, 62, 63, 64, 68, 80
Mary Ann 16, 17, 19,

Patton, (cont.)
Mary Ann (cont.) 20
Mary Doherty 57
Matthew 4, 5, 9, 10, 13, 14, 15, 16, 17, 18, 19, 20, 21, 22, 23, 24, 52, 54
Matthew, Jr. 15, 17, 18, 20, 21
Matthew, Sr. 14, 18, 19
Matthew D. 19
Matthew Thompson 22
Nackey 53 (See also Mackey)
Patsy 56, 63, 80
Peggy 18, 56, 57, 63, 80
Philip 53
Phoebe McCausland Basye 58
Polly 17, 18, 19, 22, 56, 57, 63, 64, 80
Rebecca 17, 18, 19, 20, 52
Rebecca --- 17
Richard 22
Robert 18, 19, 20
Robert G. 20
Robt. Grier 106
Robt. Grier, Jr. 106
Robert W. 403
Roger 14, 15, 16, 17, 18, 19, 20, 52
Roger Dyer 17
St. Clair 18
Sally 17, 21
Sally Ann 23
Samuel 10, 54
Sarah (?) 16
Sarah 17, 18, 20, 23
Sarah Ann 22, 53
Sarah Lynn 54, 62, 63
Sibbea H. 53
Sibbee Holley 22
Thomas 21
W. Tazewell 392, 403
William 10, 11, 14, 15, 17, 18, 20, 24, 25, 54, 55
William (Hon.) 25
Wm. M. 403
Pauley, Elizabeth 360
Paulger, Helen Verry 142
John William 142
Paumile, Sarah Bailey 382
Paxton, Katie 23
Mary 514
Payne 88, 464
--- 591, 664
--- (Dr.) 393, 404
--- (Mr.) 88, 89
Albert 157
Albina D. 738
Alice 85
Alicia 83, 84
Alicia Ann 84
Amanda 85
Ann 464
Anna 84
Ann E. 735
Anne 470
Anne E. 737
Anne (Lane) 464
Annie 158, 573

Payne, (cont.)
Asa 84, 86, 87, 90, 574
Asa, Sr. 86
Asa (Colonel) 86
Bell 84, 85
Benj. 84, 85
Benj. Clark 84
Benjamin 85
Betsey 86, 87, 464
Catharine 157
Charles Wesley 157
Clara 84
Cornelia 85
Cyrus 86, 87
Daniel McCarty 83
Della 157
Dennis 18
Devall 84
Devall, Jr. 84, 85
Dolly 84
Edward 83, 88, 158, 464, 569
Edward, Sr. 84
Edward T. 158
Edwin 85
Eliza 84, 85
Eliza R. 576
Elizabeth 48, 83, 85, 573
Elizabeth Baxter 84, 85
Elizabeth V. 575
Ella 513
Eloise 85
Emeline 87
Emmeline 86
Fannie 158
Frank 87
Franklin 86, 87
George 48, 85, 578, 653
George V. 573, 575, 753, 736
George V. (Judge) 86
George Viley 737
Hazel Oro 157
Henry 83, 85, 89, 464, 573, 575
Henry (Judge) 463, 464, 466
Henry C. 575
Henry Conyers 88, 464, 575
Henry Conyers (Col.) 575
Hugh 84, 85
Innis 85
J. Walter 48
Jack 84
James 83, 84, 85
James Sanford 157
Janette 575
Jeff 84
Jilson 83
John 83, 84, 85, 86, 87, 575
John (General) 86, 87, 89
John (Sir) 83, 464
John F. 89, 578
Julia 85
June J. 48
Katharine 149
Katherine 575, 577
Lee 158

829

Payne, (cont.)
　Letitia 84, 85
　Lewis T. 574
　Louis T. (Mr.) 89
　Lucinda 84, 85
　Lucy 157, 542
　Luella 575
　Lydia 464, 574
　M. Douglas 158
　M. Hume 48
　Maggie 157
　Margaret 84, 85
　Margaret A. 573
　Margaret Allen 735
　Maria Gay 48
　Maria (Williams)
　　(Mrs.) 576
　Martha 393, 394, 408
　Martha Ann 158
　Martha L. 735, 736
　Mary 84, 85, 158
　Mary E. 575
　Matilda 84
　Mollie 85
　Nancy 86, 464
　Nathan 158, 464
　Newton 86, 87
　Penelope 84
　Ralph Glenn 157
　Richard 86, 87
　Richard Howson 459,
　　461
　Robert 86, 87, 575,
　　576
　Robert (Sir) 83
　Romulus 575
　Ruby 157
　Sallie 85, 86, 158,
　　575
　Sally 86
　Sanford 83, 84
　Susan 85
　Theodocia 451
　Theodosia 83, 463,
　　464
　Thomas 85, 575
　Thomas H. 575
　Thomas H. (Col.) 88
　Thomas Jefferson 86,
　　87
　Thomas T. 84
　Viley 575
　William 83, 84, 85,
　　87, 88, 157, 575,
　　737, 738
　William (Sir) 83
　William, Jr. 83, 84
　William, Sr. 83, 84
　William A. 157
　William J. 86, 87,
　　573, 735
　William P. 84
　William Vernon 157
Paynes, --- (Miss) 569
Payton 179
Peace, Philip P. 514
Peak, James 87
　John 481
　Mary L. 575
Pears, Susannah 689
Pearson, Laura Louise 77
　Theodore 77
　Victoria Evans 77
Peart, Sarah G. 471
Peay, Nancy 498
Peck, --- 575
　Jacob 338

Peck, (cont.)
　Joseph 338, 339
　William 339
Pedan, Samuel 704
Pedego 679
　Amanda 698
　Elizabeth S. 698
　Ellen D. 698
　Ellen Depp 698
　George T. 698
　H. M. 698
　Henry M. 698
　Isaac Alonza 698
　James G. 698
　John M. 698
　John W. 698
　Joseph 698
　Martha J. 698
　Mary A. 698
　Perlina 698
　Sarah E. 698
　Sarah L. 698
　William 698
Peeples, --- (Mr.) 14
Peery, Narcissa Bowdry
　432, 433
Pegram, James W. 599
　James W. (Major) 600
　James West 600
　John (Gen.) 599,
　　600
　John (Major General)
　　600
　Mary 600
　Virginia 600
　Wm. R. J. (Brigadier
　　General) 600
Pemberton, Ann 592
　Richard 592
Pence, Luther 469
　Sallie French 469
　W. L. 469
Pendleton, 179, 370, 389
　--- (Miss) 384
　--- (Widow) 409
　Albert 404
　Albert G. 383, 411
　Benj. 412
　Benjamine 396
　Benjamine (Mrs.)
　　389
　Catherine Thornton
　　396
　Edmund 411
　Edmund (Judge) 395
　Edward 383, 407
　Edward (Judge) 383
　Edward (Mrs.) 394
　Elizabeth 395
　Elvira 384, 393
　French 411
　Harry (Capt.) 407,
　　409=
　Henry 383, 395, 396
　Henry (Col.) 383
　James 383, 388
　James (Col.) 395,
　　410
　James F. 411
　James French 411
　John 419
　John S. 410, 411
　John S. (Hon.) 367
　John Strother 170,
　　383
　Nancy 395
　Nathaniel 380

Pendleton, (cont.)
　Nathaniel (Capt.)
　　395
　Sallie Strother
　　(Mrs.) 394
　Sally Strother 409
　William 383, 388,
　　393, 395, 410, 411
　William C. 411
Penick, E. A. (Rev.)
　685
Peniston, Sallie 408
Penky, Rebecca (Smith)
　3
Penn, Fannie 600
　Parmelia 654
　William 57, 64, 600,
　　695
Pennick, Matilda 568
Pennington, E. L. 311
　E. Lewis 312
　Elizabeth 312
　Elizabeth Vardeman
　　312
　Eph. D. 312
　Eph. R. 312
　Ephriam 311
　Jane Clemons 312
　Kity Ann 312
　Lindsay Ephrum 312
　Polly 312
　Saley E. 312
　Tom M. 312
　Violet 363
Pepdie, Nichola 27
Peper, E. S. 713
Pepper, --- 713
　Ada 163
　E. S. 712
　Sarah E. 147
Percival, Emma 151
Perine, Sue 226
Perkins, Elizabeth 535
　Permelia 566
　Rachel 672
Pero, --- (Capt.) 495
Perreau, --- (Capt.)
　495
Perrin, --- 280, 470,
　482, 543
　Archibald 481
Perrott, Anne 116
Perry, Daisy 530
　Elisha K. 530
　Emma 35
　James 419
　Mary 308
　Matilda 629
　Micajah 206
　Robert 278
　Roderick 623
Person, Margaret F. 700
Peter, Alisonia 249
　James Todd 249
　Lettie Lee 249
　R. A. 249
　R. A. (Mr.) 248
　Robert Arthur, Jr.
　　249
　Virginia Cary 249
Peterman, Jacob 358
　Lucy 358
Peters, Eliza 591
　Martha 697
Peterson, --- (Mrs.) 9
　Ed. 675, 677
Pettus, Anna 698, 699

Petty, --- (Miss) 410,
    411
  Dorothy 697
Peyton, 679, 698
  --- 60
  Agatha Garnett 401
  Allen Y. 401
  Ann Frances 401
  Anne Guffey 698
  Benj. H. 401
  Bernardine 401
  Craven 698
  Elizabeth 401
  Francis (Capt.) 66
  Garnett 374, 401
  J. Lewis 342, 565
  James 401
  John Bowse 401
  John H. 401
  John Howe 374, 401
  Juliet 401
  Letitia 66
  Margaret 698
  Margaret Moore 698
  Mary Jane 698
  Sally T. 401
  Susan M. 401
  Valentine (Col.) 66
  Wm. Madison 401
  Wm. Preston 401
  Yelverton 698
  Yelverton, Jr. 698
Phelphs, Jarret 534
Phelps, --- 523
  Elizabeth 534
  Henrietta 515
  Jarret 534
  John 261
  Josiah 534
  Mary Williams 261
Philbert, --- (Mr.)
    673
  Armine 673
Phillips, Cassandra 645
  James 371
Pickerill, Evelyn 308
Pickett, --- 392, 403
Picrel, Richard 662
Pierce, Benj. 263
  E. 499, 501
  Franklin 500, 513
  Margaret 512
Pignatelli d'Aragon,
    Joseph (Prince)
    225
Pike, --- 543, 603
Pindell, Elizabeth Augusta 478
  Frances Adelia 478
  Harry M. 478
Piper, Helen 382, 383,
    384, 410
  Helen Frances 698
  James (Col.) 383
  Virginia Park 698
  William Steele 697
Pirtle, Alfred 671
Pitman, Asa 502, 503
  H. D. 586
Pittman, 501
  --- (Mrs.) 502
  Ann 502
  Anna 502
  Anna A. 504
  Anna Asa 515
  Anna R. 504
  Anne Belle 503

Pittman, (cont.)
  Arthur Anderson 503
  Asa 502, 503, 515
  Asa M. Walker 503
  " Asie " 502
  Cora 503
  Edward 503
  Edward F. 503
  Edward Francis 515
  George 503
  George Trabue 504,
    515
  Hattie 503
  Ida May 503
  James 503
  Jean 503
  Judith 503
  Marie 503
  Martha 503
  Martha J. 503
  Martha Jane 515
  Nancy Trabue 503
  Nannie M. 503
  Trabue 503
  W. Daviess, Jr. 503
  William Daviess 503
  William H. 512
  William Haskins 515
  Williamson H. 502,
    503
  Williamson P. 503
Pitzer, A. White (Rev.)
    600
Place, Caroline Leslie
    132
Plantagenet 665
Pleasant 98
  Benjamin F. 236
  Tarleton Woodson 115
Pleasant's, Benjamine
    Franklin 131
Pleasants, 115, 117
  --- (Gov.) 135
  --- (Miss) 583
  Adair 132, 136, 182
  Ann 109
  Ann Catherine 131,
    136
  Ann S. 113, 115
  Anna 182
  Anna (Mrs.) 113,
    115
  Archibald 113, 115
  Benjamin F. 182
  Benjamine 136
  Benjamine F. 135, 136
  Caroline Fleming 116,
    129, 135, 145, 167
  Catharine Noble 133,
    136
  Catherine Cellers 134
  Dorothy 132
  Elizabeth Randolph
    134, 136
  George B. 133
  George W. 136, 182
  George W. (Judge)
    132, 136
  George Woodson 131
  Hampden (Hon.) 178
  Isabel Adair 133
  Isabella 136
  Isabella Adair 133,
    182
  J. Hall (Dr.) 613
  James 109, 112, 113,
    115, 116, 168, 169,

Pleasants, (cont.)
  James (cont.) 178,
    181, 230
  James (Gov.) 110,
    114, 115, 168, 169,
    178, 181, 187-188,
    230
  Jane 230
  John 109, 113, 115,
    116, 135, 178, 181,
    206
  John Adair 133, 134,
    136, 182
  John Hampden 114
  John L. 113
  Johnathan 230
  Joseph 113, 115, 206
  L. McLain 133
  Louise McLain 133
  Lydia Mosby 133
  Martha 115, 167, 178,
    181, 182
  Martha Randolph 109,
    112, 113, 129, 135,
    168
  Mary Webster 133
  Mathew 109, 113, 115,
    129, 132, 134, 135,
    136, 167, 181, 182
  Mathew F. 136, 182
  Mathew Franklin 133,
    134
  Nannie Buell 132,
    136, 182
  Pauline 114, 115, 131
  Peyton Randolph 131,
    135
  Robert 220
  Roberta Kyle 134
  Rosaline Harrison 133
  Samuel 230
  Sarah 115
  Susan 230
  Susanna 113, 115, 129
  Susanna Randolph 114,
    115
  Tarleton Woodson 113
  Thomas Jefferson 134
  Ursula 113, 115
  Virginia Mosby 133,
    136
Plummer, Jane Taylor 471
  Ophelia 250, 471
  Ophelia V. 256
  Rachel (Hobbs) 471
  William 451, 471
Poage, (See also Pogue,
    Pougue) 91
  --- 94
  --- (Mrs.) 94
  --- (Sergeant) 93
  Ann 91
  Ann Kennedy Wilson
    93, 94
  Elizabeth 91, 92
  John 92
  Martha 91
  Robert 91, 93, 94
  Robert (General) 94
  William 91, 92, 93,
    94
  William Lindsay 94
Poague, William 93
Pocahantas 190, 191
Pocahontas 110, 183,
    201, 230

831

Podesta, --- (Mr.)
  366, 400
  Emily Chapman 400
Poe, Christine 471
Pogue, (See also
  Poage, Pougue) 91,
  92
  Amanda (?) 92
  Amaziah 92
  Ann 92
  Elizabeth 92
  Joseph 92
  Martha 92
  Mary 92
  Polly 92
  Robert 92
  William 92
  William Lindsay 92
Poindexter, --- (Miss)
  270
  Ann 589
  Elizabeth (Miss)
    272
  James 590
  John, Jr. 272
  Sarah 272
  William 590
Polk, 91, 630
  Benjamin 630
  James (Mr.) 85
  James K. (President) 672
  Leonidas K. 601
  Priscilla 629
  Rebecca 628
  Robert 91
  Sally 630
  Sarah 628
  W. H. 630
Pollard, --- (Miss)
  254
Pollock, Bertha L. 133
  Mary Ann 307
  Nancy 285
  Samuel D. 306
Pollok 91
  Robert 91
Polworth, --- (Baron
  of) 26
  --- (Viscountess)
    26
Pontefract, --- (Lord
  of) 660
Poole 640
  Achshah 641
  Basil 641
  Bushrod 640
  Charles Edgar 641
  Claire 641
  Cordelia 641
  Daniel 640
  Edward 641
  Emma 641
  Frederick 641
  Henry 640
  Henry Thornton 641
  Joseph James 640
  Lucy 640, 641
  Lydia 641
  Margaret 640, 641
  Margaret James 640
  Mary 641
  Matilda 640
  Narcissa 641
  Sarah 641
  Thornton 640
Poore, Mary Jane 271

Pope, 179
  --- (Widow) 222
  Anne 661
  John 387
  Nathaniel (Lieut.-
    Col.) 661, 662
Poper, James 454
Popplewill, Lutitia
  (Tandy) Craig
  441
  Richard (Mr.) 441
Porter, --- (Miss) 248
  Alice 158
  Alice C. 536
  Asa 434
  Bettie 159
  Charles 159
  Charles Randolph 159
  David I. 158, 166
  David Irvine 159
  Edward Lacey 159
  Edwin CLark 159
  Elfreda Oak 159
  Elizabeth Richardson
    (Mrs.) 254
  Jane E. 499, 501, 511,
    517, 518
  John 434, 629
  Mary 159
  Pauline 159
  Robert 511
  Sara 653
  Thornton 159
  William 630, 710
  William, Jr. 710
  Woodford 159
Porterfield, William 224
Portwood, Belle 104
  Emma 103
Posey, Albert (Dr.)
  103
  Edith 103
  Genevieve 103
  W. Horace 103
  William 658
Post, Elizabeth 69
  Thomas 69
Postlewaite, John 684
  Polly 684
Potestad, de (See de
  Potestad)
Potter, Mary 85
Pougue (See also Poage,
  Pogue)
  William 93
Povall, Jno. 653
Powell, Anne Sinclair
  719
  Elizabeth Whiting 412
  George 719
  J. 627
  John D. 686, 687
  John W. 719
  John W. (Dr.) 718
  Susan 719
  Susan Dunn 720
  Thomas Moore 719
  William Dunn 719
Powers, --- 482
  --- (Mr.) 409
  John C. 53
  Joseph 339
  Nicholas 398
Poynter, 753
Poyntz, Dorothy 186
Poythress, Annie 112
Prall, Hannah 271

Prather, Margaret 574
  Thomas 405
Pratt, Adriana 259
Prentice, Caroline 130
  George D. 490
Prescott, Elizabeth
  Tucker 224
Presley 602
Presnell, Theodore David 608
Preston 179, 366, 387
  --- 13, 401, 421
  --- (Col.) 1
  Alice 158
  Ann Sophonisba 582
  Caroline 387
  Charlotte 158
  Eleanor 158
  Elizabeth 60, 374,
    401
  Elizabeth Patton 54,
    60, 61, 62, 80
  Ellen 401
  Francis (Gen.) 582
  Henrietta 387
  Hontas 158
  James M. 158
  James Oak 158
  John 54, 60, 61, 62,
    80, 401, 762
  John L. 233
  Josephine 387
  Letitia 62
  Maria 387
  Martha Elowise 158
  Mary 387
  Mary Louise 158
  Robert Irvine 158
  Sally Y. 401
  Sarah (Campbell)
    582
  Sophronisba 182
  Sophy 112
  Susan 401
  Susanna 582
  Susanna Smith 582
  Susannah Smith 62
  Thornton Porter 158
  Walter 401
  William 60, 62, 374,
    387, 582
  Wm. (Col.) 375
  William (General)
    170, 367, 387
  Wm. (Major) 387
  Woodford Campbell
    158
Prewitt, Catherine
  Hickman 39
  David 39, 40
  Elizabeth 39
  Elizabeth Hume 39
  Elizabeth S. 40
  Jacob S. 39
  Julia Hughes 39
  Julia Katherine 40
  Margaret Montgomery
    Edmonson 39
  Martha 39, 40
  Martha C. 564, 565
  Martha Estill 40
  Martha Rodes Estill
    40
  Nelson 565
  Richard H. 39
  Richard Hickman 39,
    40

Prewitt, (cont.)
    Robert (Uncle) 43
    William C. 39
Price, --- 218
    --- (General) 604,
      605, 607
    Alice Cary 101
    Catherine Fox 412
    Daniel B. 101
    Daniel B. (Major)
      325
    Elizabeth Redd Major
      748
    James 354
    Jennie Cary 101
    John 218
    John, Jr. 748, 751
    John Upshaw (Mr.)
      542
    Justus Albert 529
    Kitty 388, 389, 396,
      412
    Louise 102
    Margaret 751
    Margaret Hubbell 751
    Mary Louise 101
    Nathaniel 569
    Richard (Capt.) 538
    Samuel 622
    Samuel (Col.) 251
    Samuel (Hon.) 374
    Sterling (General)
      159, 738
    Thomas (Captain)
      642
    Virginia 352
    W. F. 35
    Wm. 569
    Wm. H. 1
Prichard 349
    A. M. 349
    Charles 459, 461
    James 347, 349
    William 349
Prickett, John (Rev.)
    526
Prime, Emma M. 131
Prince, --- (Mr.) 407
Pritchard, --- (Mr.)
    428
    Charles 488
Procter, George M. 713
    John R. (Professor)
      712
    Lucy 713
Proctor 679, 712
    --- (Mr.) 656
    Anne Maria 713
    Geo. M. 713
    John Robert 713
Prodhom, Magdalen 751
Prodhomme 495
    Magdalene 495
Pryor 95, 96, 97
    --- (Judge) 95, 96
    --- (Mrs.) 201
    Ann Eliza 95
    C. (Miss) 438
    Fanny 409
    Fanny W. 408
    Green Lewis (Dr.)
      471
    Jack 95, 96
    Jack (Capt.) 95
    James (Judge) 95
    James R. 95
    John 95, 525

Pryor, (cont.)
    Martha Ann Head 471
    Mary Catherine 95
    Nancy 95
    Nathaniel 57, 80
    Polly 95
    Rebecca 653
    Samuel 95, 96, 97,
      430
    Samuel (Col.) 96
    Sarah Head 471
    Will S. 97
    Wm. S. 95
    William S. (Judge)
      95, 96, 499
    William Samuel
      (Judge) 96
Pugh, --- (Miss) 251
Pullen, Eliza 339
    James 339
Pulliam, --- 419
    Jerusha 419
    Joseph 419
Purcell, Benjamin Ladd
      133
    Benjamin Ladd, Jr.
      133
    John Adair 133
    Lydia Mosby 133
    Martha Webb 133
Purviance, --- 258
    David 258
Pyles, Jesse 529
    Madison (Dr.) 57
    Madison (Mrs. Dr.)
      61
Quarles, Sarah 430
Quinby, Upcher (Mr.)
    538
Quincey, Josiah 263
Quinn, B. T. 469
    B. T. (Rev.) 470
    Cynthia Nall 470
    Richard 470
    Sallie (French) 470
Quisenberry 418, 524
    --- (Rev.) 522
    A. C. 418
    Aaron 418
    Anderson Chenault
      524
    James 418, 522
    Joyce 418
    William 431
Ragan, Laura 697
Railey 98, 99, 110, 111,
    112, 113, 115, 116,
    117, 127, 135, 139,
    146, 148, 153, 165,
    166, 167, 168, 169,
    170, 172, 175, 176,
    182, 183, 189, 195,
    197, 200, 208, 369,

    --- 630
    --- (Mr.) 188, 191,
      196, 369
    Ada 164
    Agnes Morancey 164
    Alexander 156
    Amanda 145
    Amanda Malvina 140
    Ann Catharine 142
    Ann Maria 152, 154,
      155, 165
    Anna 109, , 113, 115,
      129, 135, 136, 167,

Railey, (cont.)
    Anna (cont.) 168,
      182
    Anna Barnes 143
    Annabell 150
    Annette 164
    Annie Farris 124, 144
    Annie Harper 175
    Arthur 149
    Aubrey Lee 124, 145
    Augustus Randolph 156
    B. H. 147
    Belle 163
    Bertha 123, 124, 138,
      144, 145
    Bertha Hontas 101, 137
    Bertie 149
    Bertie Hardin 161
    Beverly Randolph 150
    Bonnie B. 162
    Boone 124, 145, 167,
      182
    Bradley Stone 164
    Branch 150, 153
    Branch, Jr. 150
    Cabell Breckinridge
      151, 153
    Cabell Percival 151
    Caroline 123, 124,
      126, 144, 145
    Caroline Crittenden
      125
    Caroline Green 155
    Carrie Pleasants 151
    Carter Harrison 150,
      153
    Carter Henry 150
    Catharine 127, 150
    Catharine C. 126
    Catharine Steele 163,
      167
    Catharine Swann 156,
      165
    Cecil 142
    Chapman 155
    Charles 116, 139, 145,
      148, 149, 155, 156,
      164, 165, 166, 167,
      168
    Charles, Jr. 155, 165
    Charles A. (Dr.)
      146
    Charles Elmer 164
    Charles Gordon 152,
      154
    Charles Keith 151
    Charles Lilburn 151
    Charles Logan 163
    Charles Logan, Jr.
      164
    Charles Randolph 142,
      155, 156, 165
    Charlotte 158, 166
    Collins Daniel 152
    Cornelia 158, 163
    Cornelia Jane 152
    Daniel 150, 153
    Daniel Mayo 148, 153
    Dick 138
    Dixie 150
    Drake Carter 125
    E. Bayard 164
    Earl Pleasants 151
    Edith Hunter 126
    Edward Hood 151
    Edward T. 124, 145
    Edwin 151, 156

Railey, (cont.)
Egbert 149, 153
Egbert W. 150
Elise 164
Elizabeth 122, 123, 127, 143, 146, 149, 151, 182
Elizabeth Belle 151, 152
Elizabeth C. 117, 120
Elizabeth Jane 149, 153
Elizabeth Randolph 124
Elizabeth White 161
Elizabeth Woodson 100, 120
Ella 149
Ellen 156
Emily 157
Emma 125, 126, 127, 150, 572
Emma Catharine 152
Emma Inloe 152
Ernest H. 155
Estelle 124, 145
Eva 149
Ezza Sanders 752
F. G. (Rev.) 154
Francis 157
Francis Sweeney 164
Frank 155
Fleming G. (Rev.) 99, 152, 154, 182-183
Fleming G., Jr. 152
Gabriel Webster 162
George Alfred 143
George Woodson 100, 107, 120, 121, 122
Georgie Ellen 100, 120
Grace B. 151
Grace Churchill 150
Hampden Pleasants 149
Hampden Pleasants, Jr. 149
Hattie 164
Haydon W. 124, 145
Henry Heath 150
Henry Newell 158
Hervie Otie 155
Hilton Howell 156
Howard Williams 152
Hunter 572
Ida Dixon 125
Irvine 164
Isabella 124, 145
Isabella Watson 151
Isham 125, 127, 129, 169, 752
Isham (Dr.) 109, 114, 115, 127
Isham Keith 108, 167
Isham R. 127
Isham Randolph 109, 113, 123, 127, 128, 146
Isham Tarleton 124, 144
J. Garner 143
James 126, 139, 140, 145, 146, 150, 153, 155, 165, 572
James Alexander 156
James Faulkner 151
James Green 155

Railey, (cont.)
James Pleasants 151, 154
Jane 101, 107, 139, 146, 147, 148, 168
Jane Price 150, 153
Janette 143
Jennie 149, 155, 165
Jennie Farris 101, 137, 169, 173, 174, 175, 177, 179, 184, 186
Jerry 149
John 98, 99, 100, 107, 109, 112, 117, 121, 123, 127, 129, 135, 137, 138, 139, 143, 145, 146, 147, 148, 153, 154, 155, 158, 164, 167, 168, 171, 172, 174, 176, 230
John (Col.) 172, 173, 182
John, Jr. 100
John, Sr. 112
John A. 124, 145
John A., Jr. 124, 145
John Barclay 152
John Crittenden 125, 127
John Daniel (Col.) 151, 154
John Gipson 143
John Hubbard 157
John Martin 148, 149, 150
John Martin, Jr. 153
John Martin, Sr. 153
John Randolph 124, 145, 150, 151, 152
John Slaughter 162
John Watson 149
John Woodson 123, 127, 144
Jordan 127
Joseph 156
Joseph Jordan 143, 146
Joseph Lewis 142
Joseph R. 145
Joseph Randolph 116, 140, 145, 146, 167
Joseph W. 124, 145
Josephine 101, 126, 137, 161
Josiah Woodson 127
Judith 177
Judith Woodson 100, 107, 108, 112, 137, 138, 173, 174, 175, 177
Katherine Keith 368
Laura 101, 156
Laura L. 138
Lavinia Harrison 140
Lawrence Amsden 109, 126
Leonidas Clay 163
Lewis Clark 156, 161, 166
Lilburn Burnley 151
Lilburn Randolph 152, 154
Lilburn Rogers 151, 153, 154
Lilburn Rogers, Jr. 152

Railey, (cont.)
Linwood Walker 152
Logan 138, 163, 165, 167
Logan J. 152
Louis 124, 145
Louise Sharon 126
Loula 142
Lucy 105, 107
Lucy Belle 152
Madie Matilda 155
Margaret Ann 125
Margaret Crittenden 161, 166
Margaret Jane 156
Margaret Kavanaugh 158
Margaret Sanders 125
Mark Hardin 110, 114, 115, 161
Martha 126, 177, 572
Martha Virginia 151
Martha Woodson 100, 127, 137
Martin 116, 145, 148, 149, 153, 154, 164, 167
Martin H. Steele 161
Martin Hardin, Jr. 162
Mary 101, 107, 113, 126, 157, 572
Mary Agnes 162
Mary Ann 162, 167
Mary Cecelia 151
Mary Eliza 165
Mary Elizabeth 124, 144, 151, 155
Mary Ellen 152
Mary Hardin 161
Mary L. 156
Mary Lucy 152
Mary Slaughter 162
Mary Stuart 125
Matilda Green 157
Mattie 124, 145
Merritt Maupin 152
Morton Sanders 125
N. P. 124, 145
Nancy 127
Nancy Scott 157, 166
Oliver 149
Oliver Daniel 149
Oretta Virginia 143
Orville Browning 125
P. I. 100 , 137
P. I., Jr. 101, 126, 137, 138
P. I., Sr. 107, 108, 112, 138
P. Woodson 101, 137
Pattie 168
Peachey Lee 143
Peter I. 173, 174, 177
Pocahontas 149, 150, 153
R. H. 395
Randolph 108, 109, 111, 112, 113, 115, 124, 127, 129, 135, 139, 148, 150, 164, 167, 168, 169, 572
Randolph, Jr. 125, 175
Randolph, Sr. 176, 178, 181, 182
Randolph Burks 152

834

Railey, (cont.)
  Randolph Stroud 152
  Randolph Woodson 126
  Richard 138, 156
  Richard H. 138, 139
  Richard Henry 100,
    108, 137, 138, 139,
    169, 173, 174, 175,
    177, 179, 386
  Robert L. 124, 145
  Robert McConnell 126
  Robert Tarleton 163,
    167
  Robert Tarleton
    (Judge) 178
  Robert Woodson 124,
    145
  Rose Malvern 152
  Roy 162
  Russell 164, 165,
    167
  Ruth Ann 157
  Sadie 148, 149, 153
  Samuel 157, 158, 166
  Samuel Lindsey 157
  Samuel Wheeler 112,
    168, 169, 181, 182
  Sarah 100, 107, 137
  Sarah Catharine 142
  Sarah Elizabeth 163
  Sarah Pleasants 162
  Sina Keene 142
  Sterling Anglairs
    151
  Sterling Price 151,
    153
  Sue Nevis 126
  Susan Ann 124, 144
  Susan Emory 161
  Susanna 106, 107
  Tarleton 124, 162,
    166, 167
  Thomas 100, 107, 109,
    113, 127, 128, 129,
    156, 169, 173, 174,
    177
  Thomas, Jr. 100, 107,
    137
  Thomas Jefferson 101,
    138
  Thomas Tarleton 163
  Thomas Tarlton 167
  Thornton 158
  Vivian 152
  W. E. 189
  W. E. (Mr.) 188,
    191
  W. T. 124
  Walter 152
  Watson 158
  Wesley 152
  Wesley Harris 157
  William 109, 113, 127,
    128, 129, 137, 138,
    139, 164, 168, 169,
    174, 175, 177, 572
  William Baxter 152
  William E. 111, 129,
    138, 172, 187, 189,
    194, 195, 200, 369,
    381, 386, 463
  Wm. E. (Hon.) 196
  William E. (Mr.)
    189, 208, 209
  William Edward 101,
    137, 139, 169, 173,
    174, 175, 177, 179

Railey, (cont.)
  William Edward
    (cont.) 180, 184,
    185, 186
  Wm. Edward (Mrs.)
    187
  Wm. H. 127
  William Hunter 126
  William Hunter, Jr.
    126
  William James 142
  William Mayo 156, 165
  William Montgomery
    151
  William Randolph 100,
    137
  Willie Virginia 152
  Woodson 138
  Woodson Tarleton 145
Raine, Eliz. 567
Rainey 499
  Anna 696
Raleigh 171, 172
  John 171
  Walter (Sir) 171,
    172
Ralston, Jane 4
Ramey, Jonathan 443
Ramsey, Eliz. 770
Ranck, George W. 613
Randall (See also Rans-
  dall)
  --- 201
  Alexander B. 223
  James 528
  Luther 528
  Mary 528
  Morgan 528
  Sallie 528
  Thomas 528
Randolph 98, 111, 112,
    114, 116, 117, 139,
    166, 168, 170, 172,
    173, 179, 181, 183,
    184, 189, 191, 194,
    195, 196, 197, 201,
    204, 206, 207, 208,
    211, 212, 213, 215,
    219, 221, 225, 366,
    369
  --- 206, 207, 599
  --- (Councillor)
    216, 217
  --- (Miss) 224
  --- (Mr.) 399
  Agnes 214
  Allan 227
  Allen 400
  Ann 211, 217, 231
  Ann Cary 221, 377
  Anna 109, 112, 113,
    115, 116, 168, 169,
    178, 181
  Anne 217, 230
  Anne Cary 220, 221
  Ariana Jennings 233
  Arianna 233
  Archibald Cary 183,
    220, 229
  Arthur 228
  Avery 214
  Benjamin 217
  Benjamin Franklin 222
  Beverley 5, 216, 217,
    220, 233
  Beverly 183
  Beverly Strother 390

Randolph, (cont.)
  Brett 231
  Brett, Jr. 231
  Caroline Ramsay 224
  Cary Anne Nicholas 223
  Cary Ruffin 223
  Clara 228
  Clara Haxall 227
  Cornelia Jefferson
    221
  David Meade 220, 231
  Dorothea 113, 173,
    174, 177, 178, 180,
    230
  Dorothy 99, 107, 109,
    112, 114, 127, 129,
    135, 138, 169, 187
  Dorothy Law 215
  Edmonia 233
  Edmund 183, 217, 599
  Edmund (Captain)
    183
  Edmund Jennings 233
  Edward 206, 232
  Edward (Captain)
    216, 232
  Elizabeth 98, 99, 100,
    107, 109, 112, 117,
    121, 123, 127, 129,
    135, 137, 138, 139,
    145, 146, 147, 148,
    153, 154, 155, 164,
    167, 168, 169, 173,
    180, 182, 184, 201,
    216, 217, 218, 220,
    229, 230, 231, 232,
    233, 234
  Elizabeth McIntire
    224
  Elizabeth Wilson 227
  Ellen 221
  Ellen Wayles 221, 223,
    228
  Frances Howell 226
  Francis D. 724
  Francis Meriwether
    224
  Francis Nelson 224
  George Geiger 224
  George Washington 220
  George Wythe 222
  Harriet 220, 400
  Harriet F. 724
  Harriet Hackley 227
  Harriet Wilson 226
  Harrison 217
  Henry 110, 173, 183,,
    206, 214, 215, 216,
    230, 231
  Henry Cary 220
  Henry Patterson 227
  Isaetta Carter 222
  Isham 110, 178, 183,
    204, 206, 216, 228,
    229
  Isham (Captain) 98
  Isham (Col.) 109,
    111, 112, 114, 116,
    135, 139, 169, 173,
    174, 178, 180, 181,
    182, 183, 187
  Isham, Jr. (Capt.)
    109
  Jack 201
  James Lingon 390, 412
  James Madison 222
  Jane 109, 112, 169,

Randolph, (cont.)
　Jane (Cont.) 173, 174, 180, 194, 213, 228, 229, 231
　Jane Cary 220
　Jane DeHart 228
　Jane Hollins 224
　Jane Margaret 222
　Jane Nicholas 224
　Jane Rogers 229
　Johannes, Eques 232
　John 176, 183, 199, 206, 207, 209, 214, 220, 231, 232, 233, 399, 599, 600
　John (Dr.) 207, 208, 220, 222
　John (Sir.) 183, 214, 216, 232, 233
　John Brockenborough, Jr. 226, 227
　John Brockenburough 226
　John Hager 224
　John Walker 724
　Joseph 232
　Joseph W. 215
　Judith 108, 110, 176, 183, 184, 190, 194, 195, 198, 209, 210, 211, 212, 218, 219, 220, 231, 232
　Judith Churchill 176, 181
　Judith Fleming 190, 198, 199, 210, 211,
　Julia Minor 224
　Lewis Carter 222
　Lewis Jackson 222
　Lingon 390
　Louisa Gabriella 227
　Louise 226
　Lucy 217, 218, 233
　Lucy Bolling 217, 220
　Margaret 400
　Margaret Douglass 224
　Margaret Harvie 225
　Margaret Smith 222
　Maria Jefferson Carr 223
　Maria Judith 218
　Marietta 724
　Martha Jefferson 181
　Martha (Patsy) Jefferson 223
　Mary 109, 176, 178, 181, 183, 184, 190, 204, 209, 216, 218, 219, 220, 222, 223, 229, 230, 231, 232, 233, 400, 724
　Mary Buchanan 223, 224
　Mary Gabriella 225, 226
　Mary Isham 108, 110, 111, 139, 169, 175, 176, 177, 190, 194, 195, 197, 198, 201, 202, 212, 213, 218, 219, 228, 385
　Mary Jane 225
　Mary Louisa 227
　Mary Walker 224
　Meriwether Lewis 222, 224

Randolph, (cont.)
　Meriwether Lewis, Jr. 224
　Norman V. (Major) 215
　Patsy 223
　Paul 227
　Peter 216, 217, 220
　Peter (Judge) 215
　Peyton 217, 233, 599
　Richard 108, 110, 173, 183, 199, 206, 209, 210-211, 214, 215, 216, 220, 229, 230, 231, 232
　Richard, Jr. 230
　Richard, Sr. 183
　Richard Kidder 217
　Robert 214, 215, 217
　Robert Carter (Dr.) 183
　Robert Livingston 227
　Robert Mann 222
　Ryland 231
　Sarah 231
　Sarah Nicholas 224
　Septimia Ann 222
　Strother 412
　Susan 231, 233
　Susanna 110, 112, 182, 230
　T. J. 2nd 224
　Theoderic Bland 231
　Thomas 108, 110, 111, 169, 175, 176, 181, 183, 184, 189, 190, 191, 194, 195, 196, 197, 198, 199, 200, 201, 204, 205, 206, 207, 208, 209, 210, 211, 212, 213, 214, 216, 218, 219, 228, 229, 230, 231
　Thomas (Col.) 210, 211
　Thomas (Sir) 214
　Thomas, Jr. 109
　Thomas Beverly 220
　Thomas Esten 229
　Thomas Eston 220
　Thomas Isham 183, 229
　Thomas Isham (Captain) 182, 183
　Thomas Jefferson 221, 222
　Thomas Jefferson, (Colonel) 110, 181
　Thomas Jefferson, Jr. 224
　Thomas Jefferson, III 224
　Thomas M. 211
　Thomas Mann 108, 181, 208, 211, 219, 396, 399, 400
　Thomas Mann (Col.) 176, 178, 181, 183, 187, 376, 377, 395, 396
　Thomas Mann (Gov.) 110, 176, 181, 377, 396
　Thomas Mann, Jr, 181, 191
　Thomas Mann, 1st 110, 196, 197, 198, 199,

Randolph, (cont.)
　Thomas Mann, 1st (cont.) 200, 207, 208, 209, 211, 212, 213, 218-219, 220, 221, 225, 231
　Thomas Mann, 2nd 110, 207, 208, 220, 221, 229
　Thomas Mann 2nd (Governor) 222
　Thomas Mann, 3rd 208, 225, 227, 228
　Thomas Mann, 4th 227
　Thos. Mason (Col.) 395
　Tom Mann (Col.) 399
　Virginia 220, 221
　Virginia Minor 224
　W. C. N., Sr. (Dr.) 224
　William 108, 110, 111, 112, 173, 174, 175, 176, 178, 181, 182, 183, 189, 190, 195, 196, 198, 199, 201, 204, 205, 206, 207, 208, 209, 210, 211, 212, 213, 214, 215, 216, 217, 218, 219, 220, 221, 228, 229, 230, 231-232, 232, 233, 234
　William (Councillor) 217, 218
　William, Jr. 108, 109, 183, 216
　William, 1st 217, 231-232, 232, 233
　William, 2nd 216, 217
　William, 3rd 176
　William Fitzhugh 220
　William H. 724
　William Lewis 223, 224
　William Mann 222, 224
　William Mayer 220
　Wilson Cary Nicholas (Dr.) 224
　Wilson Cary Nicholas, Jr. (Dr.) 224
Rankin, --- (Mr.) 770
　Edmonia 68
　Mary 130
Rankins, Elizabeth 576
　Jessie 576
　Malvina 576
　Paul (Dr.) 576
　Penelope 576
　Rodes 576
　Wagner 576
　Wm. 576
Ransdall (See also Randall)
　Alice 527
　Ann 528
　B. Franklin 527
　Carrie 527
　Elizabeth 527
　Eveline 527
　Frank 527
　Fulton 527
　George 527
　Hannah 566
　Isabel 527

Ransdall, (cont.)
  Isabel --- 527
  Jasper 527
  Jennie 527, 530
  John 527, 528
  Joseph 527, 528
  Kate 527
  Lucinda 527
  Lucy 527
  Martha 527
  Martha J. 527
  Mary 527, 528
  Nancy 528
  Notley 527
  Sallie 527, 530
  Smith 527
  Susan 527
  Thomas 527
  Virginia 527
  Wm. 527 ,528
Rapine, Antoine 573
  Margaret 573
  Mary Ann 573
Ratcliff, --- 664
Ray 241
  --- 235, 236, 238,
    239, 241, 242, 243
  --- (General) 235,
    238
  --- (Miss) 568
  --- (Widow) 236
  Amelia 242
  Catherine 241
  Harry 237
  Harvey 237, 241, 243
  Harvey T. 243
  Henry 242
  James 235, 236, 237,
    238, 239, 240, 241,
    242
  James (General)
    235, 244
  James, Jr. 241, 243
  Jane 241
  Jefferson 237, 241,
    243
  Jess 242
  Jesse 236, 237, 241
  John 235, 237, 241,
    243
  John (Dr.) 241,
    242, 243
  Lucinda 241
  Martha 243
  Millie 238
  Milly 236
  Patsy 241, 243
  Polly 242
  Polly Duncan 241
  William 235, 236, 237,
    239, 241, 242
Rayleigh 172
Rayley 172
Read, --- (Judge) 713
  Ann Mayo 272
  George 493
  Mildred 493
Reade, George (Col.)
    574, 589, 608
  Mildred 574, 589
  Mildred (Windebank)
    589
  Robert 589
Reading, Coulter Steele
    568
  David Glass Venable
    568

Reading, (cont.)
  James Edward Lee 568
  John Windell 568
  Katherine 568
  Margaret Dryden 568
  William Thomas 568
  Windell Gay 568
Reager, Elizabeth 57, 80
Reames, Jane 155
Reams, Jane 165
  Mary 165
Reburn, Robert 309
Rector, Sharlott 744
Red Jacket 765
Redd, Agatha Minor 578
  Drucilla 352
  Elizabeth 578
  Elizabeth --- (Mrs.)
    710
  Mordica 578
Redford 679, 698
  --- (Mr.) 673
  A. H. 652
  B. F. 699
  Bessie 699
  Caroline Rebekher 699
  Eliza A. 699
  Emely S. 699
  Emely Susan 699
  Frances 699
  Francis 699
  Frank 699
  H. L. 699
  Hawood Leslie 699
  Henry 699
  Jam (?) Robert 699
  John Edward 699
  M. R. 699
  Margaret E. 699
  Margarette Ruth 699
  Mary 699
  Mucther (?) Frances
    699
  P. H. 698, 699
  Robert 699
  Ruth 699
  Sally A. 699
  Thomas William 699
  Tom 699
  William Durward 699
  William P. 699
Reece, Cornelia 104
Reed, Bettie 401
  Ella 146
  Fannie 146
  Gertrude Beale 227
  James 226
  John 338, 568
  Martha 428
  Mattie 146
  Ross 146
  Thomas 401
Reese, Ed. 104
Reid, A. W. 706
  Anderson Woods 705
  Andrew 326
  Elizabeth 706
  Henry A. 705
  John M. 705
  Marshall B. 134
  Marshall B., Jr. 134
  Oscar L. 134
  William S. 705
Remy, Anna 465
  Betty 465
  Jacob 465
  James 465

Remy (cont.)
  John 465
  Lydia 465
  Samuel 465
  Sanford 465
Renick, Alexander 293
  Matilda 33
  William (Major) 659
Rennick 245, 246, 278
  --- (Mr.) 247
  --- (Mrs.) 247
  Alexander 245, 246
  Alexander H. 246
  Alisonia 247
  Alisonia Bibb 247
  Atwell 247
  Catherine 247
  Catherine Martyn 247
  Eliza 247
  Henry 247, 248
  Henry Swigert 247
  John 246, 278
  John Alexander 247
  Joseph 246
  Julia 247, 248
  Louisa 247
  Louisa Workham 247
  Mary 246
  Mary Willis 247
  Thomas Todd 247
  Willis Lee 247
Reno, --- (Mr.) 85
Reuben 682
Reynolds, G. Y. 104
  John Houston 516
  Leila Tandy (Mrs.)
    428
  Susan 140
  Varnette Gregg 140
Rhoade, --- 558
Rhodes, Ann 736
  Anna 275
  Elizabeth 275
  John 736
  Mary 736
  N. O. 558
  Waller 275
Ricardson, (See also
    Richardson)
  Samuel Q. 253
Rice 349, 534
  --- 22
  --- (Judge) 349
  Charles 534
  David (Father) 774
  Elizabeth Turner 533
  Elmer 407
  James 349, 533, 534
  James M. 349
  James M. (Judge)
    358
  Martin 534
  Rebecca 347
Richard, Elizabeth 469
  Helen 469
Richardson (See also
    Ricardson) 250,
    252, 253, 679, 699
  --- 253
  --- (Col.) 254
  Alice 251
  Ann 251
  Ann Eliza 699
  Barbara A. 700
  Benjamin 254
  Beverly Randolph 148
  Caroline 254

Richardson, (cont.)
  Charles 254
  Charles Bruce 254
  Daniel (?) 254
  Daniel 250, 255, 256
  Daniel Couch 254
  David 250, 254
  David Porter 254
  Dudley 679, 699
  Eli 700
  Elijah 250
  Eliza 254
  Elizabeth 250, 251, 256, 699
  Elizabeth M. 700
  Emma 254
  Felix 254
  Felix Allen 254
  Felix R. (Hon.) 254
  G. B. 148
  George 254
  Harriet 254
  Henry (?) 254
  John 250, 251, 254, 256, 699, 700
  John, Jr. 699
  John Corly (Capt.) 253
  John Croley 251
  John Samuel 254
  Joseph 250, 251, 255, 256
  Joseph Leslie (Rev.) 516
  Judith 254
  Lewis (?) 254
  Lucretia 251
  Mara E. 700
  Margaret 251, 254, 255, 256
  Mariam Park 699
  Marquis 251
  Martha 254, 700
  Martha DePriest 254
  Mary 251
  Mary Ann 250, 699
  Mary E. 700
  Mathews 251
  Matilda 694, 699
  Mayme (Miss) 273
  Milcah 251
  Miriam 251
  Nathan 255, 256
  Nathaniel 250
  Ophelia Virginia 250, 256
  Paulina 699, 700
  Polly 254
  Rebecca 493
  Richard 250, 251, 255, 256
  Robert 254
  Robert T. 254
  Sallie 254
  Samuel 250, 251, 254
  Samuel, Jr. 254
  Samuel Calmes 251
  Samuel Calmire (Calmes) 251
  Samuel Marquis Calmes 251, 253
  Samuel Q. 253
  Samuel Q. (Col.) 252
  Sarah 250, 251, 700
  Sarah Gaines 250
  Shelton 699

Richardson, (cont.)
  Simpson P. 699
  Sophia 250, 251
  Susan Frances 700
  Thomas 250, 251, 254, 255, 256
  Victoria 251
  William 250, 251, 254, 255, 256, 493
  William, Jr. 251, 253, 255
  William, 1st 255
  William, 2nd 250
  William Hall (Dr.) 253
  Wm. M. 699
  Wm. S. 700
  Woodson P. 699, 700
Richeboug, de (See de Richeboug)
Richman, John 563
Richmond, 750, 752
  --- (Miss) 704
  --- (Duke of) 83
Ridge, John 347, 348
Ridgeley, Franklin 472
  Mary Jane 472
  Nicholas 472
  Temple 472
Ridgely, 475
  Sophia N. 475
Ridings, J. R. 23
Riestap, --- 547
Riffle, 337
Riggs, --- (Miss) 349
  Abigail 76
  Alice 681
  Sarah A. 348
  William F. 349
Right (See also Wright)
  Ann 665
  Anne 665
  Annie 665
  John 665
  Mildred 665
  Peggy 665
  Reubin 665
  Richard 665
Rightenour, Agness (Miss) 315
Rightmire, J. Baxter 118
  Marguerite Thompson 118
Rufus Anderson 118
Riherd, Frank 677
  Joe 677
  W. T. 675, 677
Riker, Sarah 722
Riley, --- 89
  Ben Carleton 143
  Catharine 151
  Charles A. (Dr.) 143
  Clarence A. 143
  Courtland 143
  Gipson Railey 143
  Kenneth 143
  Sarah 694
Ringo, Caroline 529
  George 529
  Sarah 528
  Sarah Bryan 529
Rion, Georgien 658
Risher, Laura 106
Ritchie 31
  B. P. 32
  Ben 32

Ritchie, (cont.)
  Benjamin P. 31
  Benjamin Patton 31
  Elizabeth Julia 31
  George 78
  James 31
  James Henry 31
  John Silus 31
  Lizzie 32
  Louise 31
  Mary 78
  Mary Esther 31
  Mary Louise 31
  Philip 31
  Sallie Hume 31
  Sarah Lizzie 31
  Susanna 31
  William 631
  William Hume 31
Rittenhouse, --- 631, 635
Ritter, Sallie 704
Roach, B. F. (Judge) 577
  Edward 354
Robards, Horace 655
  Horace (Col.) 655
  Wm. 655
Robb 720
  Fannie M. 720
  Jonas 720
  Jonas M. 720
  Lucy Foster 720
  Robert G. 227
Roberson, John 261
Roberts, --- (Dr.) 648
  Betsey 578
  Boanerges 684
  Boanerges (Dr.) 683
  D. D. (Dr.) 648
  E. M. 576
  Eliz. 683
  Elizabeth 393, 404
  H. P. 736
  Irene 648
  John (Major) 393, 404
  Paul 576
  Rosa 214
  Rose 215
  Russell 648
  Susanna Elizab. 684
  Susanna Elizabeth 684
  Thomas 214, 215
  W. F. 613
  William Edward 648
Robertson 669, 679, 700
  --- 8, 351
  --- (Judge) 700
  Alexander 700
  Alexander H. 700
  Alexander Hamilton 701
  Bainbridge 701
  Beverley (General) 401
  Charles H. 351
  Charlotte 700
  Charlotte Corday 700, 701
  Eleanor 700, 701
  Eleanor J. 701
  Eleanor McIntosh 700, 701
  Elizabeth 700
  George 700, 701, 702

Robertson, (cont.)
  George, Jr. 701
  George S. McKee 701
  George Samuel McKee 701
  Helen Virginia 315
  James 3rd 700
  James B. 700
  James Bainbridge 701
  James K. 700
  Jane 700
  Lindsay Vardaman 315
  Margaret 700
  Margaret Eliza 700, 701
  Margaret R. 700
  Martha 700
  Martha Jane 701
  Mary Oden 701
  Mary Oden Epes 701
  Nora 119
  Susanna 700
  Trimble Benson 315
  Wade H. 700
  Wm. David 700
Robeson, Mary C. 718
Robinson, 570
  --- 476
  --- (Miss) 270
  Ann 569
  Catharine 266
  Harriet 254
  James F. 570
  Jane Ann 706
  John 218, 266, 560
  Leonard 569
  Martha 717
  Philip P. 710
  Polly 84
  Samuel 308
Robnett, Annie Lee 658
  Alice 658
  James 658
  John 658
Rochette, Moses 569, 654
  Susannah 569, 654
Rochester, Henrietta 513
  Nathaniel (Mrs.) 375
Rockeblave, --- (Captain) 764
Rodes 534, 572, 593
  Ann 572, 593
  David 589
  John 572
  Mary 533, 572
Rodgers, Etta 130
  Frank 130
  J. F. 130
Rodman, William 116
Roe, Annie 160
Rogers 258, 259
  --- 259, 421, 423
  --- (Col.) 482
  --- (Miss) 10, 13, 54, 55, 80
  Adriana Pratt 259
  Alice 262
  Amelia Clay Lewis Van Meter 546
  Andrew 261
  Ann Walton 261
  Anna Elizabeth 263
  Anne Cornick 258
  Annie Cornick 262
  Arthur C. (Col.) 482

Rogers, (cont.)
  Benjamin 261
  Benjamin F. 262
  Charles 228, 466
  Charles Christopher 263
  Christopher 263
  Edmund 689, 691, 692, 693, 698, 704
  Elizabeth 261
  Elizabeth Ann Carr 261
  Elizabeth Denison 260
  Elizabeth Gold Hawes 260
  Frances (Cobbs) 261
  Harvey 262
  Harvey Addison 262
  Hugh Brent 263
  J. R. 263
  James R. 258, 262
  James R. (Captain) 258
  Jane 109, 112, 114, 169, 173, 174, 178, 180, 181, 182, 183, 228
  Jason (Capt.) 387
  John 259, 261
  John (Rev.) 259, 260
  John (Rev. Dr.) 260
  John II 259
  John III (Rev.) 260
  Lindsay 263
  Louise 262
  Margaret 260
  Margaret Caldwell 261
  Margaret Crane 260
  Marie Lindsay 262
  Marie Louise 262
  Martha Whittingham 260
  Mary 41, 517
  Mary --- 259
  Mary " Mollie " Katherine 263
  Mollie 263
  Nathaniel 258, 261 263
  Nathaniel (Rev.) 260
  Nathaniel Purviance 261
  Polly 87
  Rebecca 695
  Richard Reid 262
  Samuel 695
  Thomas 260, 261, 263
  Warren 262
  Warren B. 262
  Warren Brown 262
  Warren Moran 262
  William 258, 259, 260, 261, 262, 263
  William, Sr. 263
  William Skillman 263
Rollington, Mary 640
Rolstone, Jane 4
Rook, James H. 476
Roosevelt, --- 764, 771
  Theodore 768
Rose, --- 427, 458
  Hosea 458
  Leroy 458
  Lewis (Captain) 535
  Maud 722

Rose, (cont.)
  Parmenas 458
  Rebecca 535
  Sarah 458
  Susan 110, 114, 115
Roseberry, Henrietta 263
Rosecrans, --- (Gen.) 604, 605
Ross, Alexander (Rev.) 357
  C. I. 298, 299
  John 256
  Margaret 130
  Mary Cameron 412
  Nettie (Miss) 248
  Norman 30
  William C. 130
Rout, --- (Mr.) 577
Rouzee, Agnes 681
  Maria L. 681
  Philemon 681, 710
Rowan 278, 291
  --- (Judge) 278, 287
  John 286, 287, 650
  John, Esq. 668
  John (Senator) 291, 292
  Mary 286
Rowe, --- (Dr.) 226
  Nellie 226
Rowland, Allen 157, 166
  Charles Wesley 157, 166
  Harriet M. 163, 167
  Margaret 157
  Martha 157, 166
Royall, Joseph 114, 173
  Joseph (Capt.) 178, 187
  Mary 113, 114, 177, 178, 187, 653
Rucker, Eugene 575
  Katherine P. 575
  Maria P. 575
  Mary Allison 575
Ruddell, --- 59
  --- (Mr.) 581
Rudy 669
Ruffin, Cary Randolph 223
  Eliza McDonald 223
  Frank (Col.) 401
  Frank Gildart 223
  Frank Gildart, Jr. 223
  George Randolph 223
  Jefferson Randolph 223
  Julian (Mrs.) 496
  Nicholas 400
  William Roane 223
  Wilson Cary Nicholas 223
Ruggles, Jane 356
  Robert 356, 358
Rumford, --- (Count) 586
Rumsey, Jean (Miss) 613
Runersen, Hendrix 557
Runnolds, Sarah 404
  Tabitha 404
Rupard, Waller 706
Rupert, Edward 81
  Elon W. 74- 75
Rupley, George W. 715

Rupley, (cont.)
  Martha Bohon 715
Rupp, --- 771
  Anna 103
Russam, --- 629
  Mitchell 629
Russell, --- (Miss)
    182
  Arrey 351
  Elizabeth 129
  James Dudley 141
  Margaret L. 351
  Mary Clark 141
  T. R. 351
Rutherfoord, Laura 227
  Thomas 227
Rutherford, Barbara 76
  Lewis Maurice 76
  Margaret 76
Rutledge, Edward 331
  Sarah Armstrong 331
Ryland, Elizabeth 215
Sabb, Ann 324
St. Aldegonde, ---
    (Lord of) 555
St. Clair, --- (?) 24
  --- (General) 498
  Alexander 338
  Francis 129
  Mary 339
St. Vrain, --- 606
Sale, Edith Tunis 207
  Fanny E. 517
Sallee, Mary 512
Salter (See also Sutton)
  Edna 53
  Samuel 750, 752
  --- (Dr.) 471
  Ann (Nancy) 96
  Benjamin 498
  Edward 498
  Eleanor 498
  James 625
  Mary Motley 498
  Nancy 96
  Richard Gray 498
  Sarah 682, 710, 754
  Washington 498
  William 96, 498, 710
Samuels, Miriam 650
Sanders, --- (Rev.
    Mr.) 325
  Edith 752
  Eliza 752
  Ezza 125, 127, 752
  Henry Berryman 102
  Howard 102
  Jonathan 591
  Laura E. 752
  Lewis 751
  Nathaniel 751
  Robert (Rev.) 325
  Robert Stuart
    (Rev.) 325
  Samuel 443
  Susan Gano 752
Sands, --- 75
  George Winthrop 75
  Geo. Winthrop, Jr.
    76
  Samuel Stevens I 75
  Samuel Stevens II 75
  Samuel Stevens III
    75, 76
Sandusky, Mary E. 157
Sanford, Charles 748

Sanford, (cont.)
  Henry Gansevoort, Jr.
    77
  Henry Gansevoort, Sr.
    77
  Louise Mott 77
  Martha 748
Santa Anna, --- 755
Sargent 534
  Ada Opal 536
  Coral Turner 536
  Jacob 535
  Jessie Ruby 536
  John 535
  John S. 536
  John Stephen 535
  Margaret 535
  Margaret Pearl 536
  Paul Turner 536
  St. John 536
  Samuel Stephen 532,
    536
  Stephen 535
  William 535
Sarlls, James 439
Sarver, William 363
Saunder, --- 590
Saunders, Celies (Captain) 412
  Hortense 36
  Keziah (Miss) 612
  Romulus 612
Saurin, --- 569
  M. James 569
Savage, Alice 179, 372,
    377, 380
  Andrew J. 356, 362
  Andrew M. 356
  Anthony 179, 370,
    371, 380
  Isaac M. 362
Sawtell 69, 78, 79, 81,
    82
  Albert Barnes 70
  Augusta Elizabeth
    70, 71, 78, 82
  Cornelius 69
  E. N. (Rev. Dr.)
    78
  Edward Newton 70, 71
  Eli Newton (Rev.
    Dr.) 69, 71, 81,
    82
  Emily Martha 71
  Emma 71
  Ephraim (Lieut.)
    69
  Esma 71
  Frederic Henri 70
  Hezekiah (Lieut.)
    69
  James Low 71
  John 69, 79
  Julia Coster 71
  Obadiah 69
  Ophelia 70, 71
  Richard 69
  Richard Blair 71
  Royal Montgomery 71
  Sarah Ann Huntingdon
    69
  Walter 71
Sawyer, Ethel 530
  Sophia 77
Sawyers, Rachel 656
Sayle, Wm. (Dr.) 654

Sayles, Henry (Mrs.)
    704
Scantlin, Elizabeth 438
  Moses 438
  Polly 438
  Reubin 438
Scarborough, Edmund
    (Col.) 626
Scarse, Elizabeth 512
Scearce 756
  Elizabeth 104
Scearse, Annabel 160
Schamp, de (See de
    Schamp, Scomp)
Schenck, Harriet A.
    (Miss) 447
Schepmos, Derick 554
Schilling, Pauline 36
Schofield, --- (Mr.)
    84
Schroeter, George Freeman 162
  George Railey 162
  Hallie Emory 162
  Lula Agnes 162
  Mark Lewis 162
  Pattie 162
  Susie Mae 162
  William Freeman 162
Scobee, Caty 17
  Robert 17
Scomp (See also de
    Schamp) 720
  • Catherine 721
  Catherine Wilson 721
  Cathrine 721
  Flora 721
  Henry 721
  John 721
  John Van Nuyce 721
  Mary Rebecca 721
Scott 117, 679, 702
  --- 121, 476
  --- (General) 345
  --- (Gov.) 185
  Alexander C. 702
  Alonzo 702
  Ann 591
  Archibald 569
  Charles 685
  Charles (General)
    296, 684
  Charles (Major-
    General) 684
  Daniel 109, 230, 702
  Fannie E. 702
  Fredrick R. 412
  George (M. D.) 511
  Hattie (Miss) 469,
    702
  Henry Clay 702
  James 702
  James (Dr.) 590
  James M. (Dr.)
    590
  James McClure 590
  John 511
  John A. 702
  John H. 702
  John Thomson 590
  Jno. W. 684
  Laura 66
  Laura J. 702
  Leslie Thomas 702
  Levi H. 702
  Levi H. (Mr.) 702
  Lewis M. 702

840

Scott, (cont.)
  Lewis Witherspoon 702
  Louisa Duvall 702
  Louise 263
  Martha T. 683
  Martha Tabb 684
  Mary 231, 655
  Mary A. 702
  Mary Ann Lewis 590
  Mildred (Thomson) 590
  Nancy Jane 702
  Olympia 511
  Peggy 770
  Polly 684
  Robert G. (Mrs.) 374
  Robert W. 752, 753
  S. 514
  Sidney Buford 412
  Susannah 702
  Susannah Witherspoon 702
  Thos. 752
  Walter (Sir) 222
  Walter L. 702
  William Lloyd 702
  William T. 511
  Winfield (General) 117, 538
Scudder, Emma 631
Seals, Elizabeth 534
  Mary McCormick 534
Searcy 580, 679, 702
  Edmond 594
  Edmund 580, 580-581, 581, 703
  Hanna 703
  Hannah 703
  Hannah Miller 580, 594
  Harriet 581, 703
  Harriett 703
  James 696
  Maria 580, 581, 594, 703
  Mary Eleanor 581
  Mary Ellenor 703
  Mary Ellenor Smith 703
  Maude Lee --- 696
  Richard 581, 703
  Richard Edmund Plummer 703
Searles, Flavilla 574
  Mary 106
Seay, Mary 692
  Mosby (Rev.) 577
Sebastian, --- (Judge) 407
  Wm. 407
Sebree, Uriel (Maj.) 87
Seiter, Herman Raymond 159
  Herman Ridgely 159
Selby, L. 627
Selden, Joseph 114
  Sarah 412
Sellers, W. H. 736
Semple, Jacob 625
  William 623
Senour, Philip (Mr.) 444
Senteny, Fannie 119
Sessions, Charlotte Whitley 159

Sessions, (cont.)
  Susie 572
  Whitley 159
Sewell, Basil 641
  Diana 641
  James 641
  John Wood 641
Seybert, --- 7, 8
  --- (Captain) 7, 8
  Jacob 6
  Nicholas 7, 9
Seymour, Abel 563
Shackelford, Elizabeth 713
  Geo. 713
  George Scott 224
Shackleford 522
  Lucy 713
  Seth B. 713
Shaddown, Jane (Smith) (?) 3
  John 2
  Lewis 3
  Reuben 2
Shade, --- (Captain) 34
  Henry (Captain) 34
Shaffer, (See also Sheffer)
  Elizabeth Hume 39
Shands, A. R. (Dr.) 40
  A. R. , Jr. 40
Shanks, Archibald 481
  Jane 184, 185
Shannon, Samuel (Rev.) 338
Sharp 720
  Abraham E. 720
  Ann E. 720
  Elizabeth R. 720
  Harriet 688
  Jacob 720
  Jacob S. 720
  James G. 120
  Jennie (Miss) 714, 716, 717, 720, 721
  Joseph 720
  Josiah 720
  Thomas C. 720
  William H. 720
Sharpe, William R. 688
Shaw 327
  Abner 327
  Andrew 327
  Catherine 320, 327
  Darkis 327
  Dorcas 327
  Jane 327
  John 327
  Joseph W. 36
  Juliet 36
  Mary 322, 326, 327
  Middleton 210
  Robert 36
  Ruth 36
  W. E. (Dr.) 36
  W. E., Jr. 36
  William 36, 327
Shealy, George 625
Shearer, F. C. 513, 517
  Gertrude Alice 158
  J. D. 745
  James D. 745
  Joseph Napoleon 745
  Leonora 158
  Marcus Edwin 745

Shearer, (cont.)
  Mattie F. 745
  Mellville Preston 158
  William 158
Sheets, William 230
Sheffer, (See also Shaffer)
  --- 41
  Harriet 41
  Harriet Hughes 40
  J. Howard 39, 40
  Jacob Hughes 40
  John Howard 41
  Julia Hughes 40
  Julia M. 39, 40
  Laura Jane 40
  Omie 41
  Omie Wiermann 40
  Ruth Wierman 39
Sheffey, Daniel 398
Shefflett, Anderson 150
  Lilburn 150
  Mary Jane 150
Sheffy 345
  Daniel 379
Shegarie, --- (Madam) 43
Shelbourn, Anna 699
  Anne 699
  James 699
  Mary 699
  Pettus 699
  Salla 699
  Sephus 699
  Silas 698, 699
  Susanna 699
  William 699
Shelburn, James 698
  Polly 699
Shelby, --- 603, 604, 605
  --- (Gov.) 185, 582
  Alfred 582
  Isaac 702
  Susannah Hart 680, 682, 684, 688, 690, 702
Sheldon, George R. 75
  Gertrude 75
Shelton 265, 260
  Emma Lavinia 409
  Frank 409
  George 409
  James 265
  James R. 409
  John Thomas 409
  William 409
  Wm. N. 409
Shepherd, Peter 528
  Robert 403
  Thomas (Col.) 559
Sherlock, James 371
Sherman, --- 440
Sherrill, Susan 458
Shields, --- 378
  Jane 334
  John 334
Shipley, Eliza 306
Shipp, Colby 689
  Edmund 591
  Richard 623
  Sally 689
  Sarah 689
Shirley, Ann Mary 689
  Ann Mary (Huggins) 689

841

Shirley, (cont.)
　George 657
　John W. 689
Shivens, William R.
　(Col.) 516
Sholl, Bettie 694
Short, 352
　--- (Widow) 353
　Ann ? (Widow) 353
　Catherine 352
　Elisha 352
　John 1
　Milt (?) 2
　Milton 3
　Nancy 353
　Reuben 1
　Thomas 353
　Wesley 1
　Winifred 352
Shortridge, Mary (Johnson) (Mrs.) 572
Shourd, --- 560
Shourds, --- 559
Shreve 687
　John 687
　Lizzie 514
　Lizzie (Miss) 500
Shroader, Mary Ann 338
Shropshire, Clay
　(Mrs.) 5
Shuck, Andrew 192
Shumate, Celia 28
Sibert, Samuel Franklin 142
　Samuel Franklin, Jr. 142
Sibley, Ann (Mrs.) 563
Sickles, Laura (Mrs.) 429
Simms, Hugh 152
　Richard 420
Simpkins, Jean Mary 40
Simpson, --- (Gov.) 391
　Elizabeth 41
　Mary 160
　R. W. 391
Sims, Elizabeth 51
Sinclair, John 27
　Mariotta 27
Singleton 462
　--- 530
　Betty 462
　Charles 529
　Jane (Taylor) 462
　Jeconias 451, 462
　John 462
　Manoah 462
　Mary Ruth 462
　Mason 462
　Samuel 462
　Susan 462
　William 462
Sink, Lelia 676
Sitlington 329
Sizemore 350
　Anderson 350
　Elizabeth Ann 351
Skelton 265, 267, 268, 269
　--- (General) 267
　Bathurst 229, 267
　James 265, 266, 269
　Jane 266
　Jane (Mrs.) 265
　John 267

Skelton, (cont.)
　Lucy 267
　Martha (Mrs.) 267
　Martha (Wayles) 229
　Meriwether 267
　Reuben 267, 268
　Sally 265, 266
Skidmore, Edy 356
　John (Captain) 768
Skiles, N. H. (Mrs.) 243
Skillman, Christopher 263
　Henrietta (Payne) 263
　Katherine 263
Skinker, John 371, 380
Skipworth, Mary 217
　Mary (Miss) 229
　William (Sir) 217
Skirven, William 626
Slane, Carl 478
　Harry Pindell 478
Slaughter 270, 271, 272, 275, 370
　--- 62, 273, 275, 599
　--- (Col.) 270
　--- (Governor) 275
　--- (Judge) 392, 403
　--- (Miss) 270, 274, 275
　Althea 273
　Anne 271
　Augustine (Surgeon) 274
　Augustine S. 270
　Augustine Smith 271
　Austin Smith 271
　Austina 273
　B. G. (Col.) 271
　B. Rosalie (Dr.) 273
　Benjamin Gabriel 271
　Cadwallader 271
　Caroline 403
　Catherine 273
　Catherine Lightfoot 273
　Celeste Pauling 273
　Charles 270, 272, 273, 274
　Charles (Dr.) 273
　Charles Alexander 273
　Charles Rice 272, 273
　D. F. 403
　D. F. (Dr.) 392, 403
　Daniel 403
　Daniel French 392, 403
　Edith Ridgway 273
　Edmonia 272
　Eliza 403
　Elizabeth 270, 272, 273
　Elizabeth A. 272
　Frances 271
　Francis 270, 271, 274
　Francis Lightfoot (Private) 274
　Gabriel 272, 274

Slaughter, (cont.)
　Gabriel (Governor) 270, 271, 274, 275, 593
　Gabriel Stout 271
　Gabriel Webster 114, 115
　George 270
　George (Colonel) 270
　George S. 271
　Henry Clay 272
　Henry Clay, Junior 272
　Isaac Hite Williams 21
　J. 170, 391, 402
　James 270
　James (Colonel) 270
　James A. 271
　James E. (General) 392
　James E. S. (General) 403
　James P. Garland 273
　Jesse 270, 274
　John 270, 271, 274, 403, 589
　John (Col.) 270
　John (Dr.) 272
　John Field 271
　John Flavel 273, 274
　John Flavel, Jr. 273
　John H. (Col.) 109, 114, 115
　John P. 272
　John Poindexter (Dr.) 272
　John S. (Lieutenant) 274
　Lawrence 271
　Lawrence (Lieut.) 271
　Lawrence Cadwallader 270
　Lucy 21, 392, 402
　Lucy B. 684
　Margaret 392
　Martha Jones 270
　Martha Randolph 109, 114, 115, 161
　Martin 275
　Mary 273, 403
　Mary Duke (Miss) 273
　Mary E. 273
　Mary James 273
　Mary Lewis 589
　Mary Roberta 273
　Mary Smith 272
　Matilda 271
　Mildred 271
　Monroe 273
　Nancy P. 272
　Nathaniel (Private) 274
　Nicolas Cabell 272
　P. (Capt.) 403
　P. (Major) 403
　P. French (?) 21
　Pauline 272
　Phil (Capt.) 403
　Phil (Mrs.) 413
　Philip 403
　Philip (Dr.) 271
　Philip, Jr. 270

842

Slaughter, (cont.)
　Phillip 392
　Phillip (Capt.)
　　383, 391, 392, 402
　Phillip (Major)
　　392
　Reuben 271
　Richard 270
　Robert 270, 271, 273,
　　274
　Robert (Col.) 270,
　　271, 274, 275
　Robert (Lieutenant)
　　274
　Robert, Jr. 270
　Robert Burr 273
　Robert F. 271
　Robert G. 273
　Robert Harrison 272
　Robert Harrison
　　(Dr.) 272
　Robert Lewis 589
　Robert V. 271
　Rosalie 273, 274
　Rosalie (Miss) 275
　S. Garland 273
　S. Jackson 272
　St. Lawrence 270
　Sallie 392
　Sally 403
　Sam. Augustus 273
　Samuel 270
　Samuel G. (Dr.)
　　273
　Samuel Garland 274
　Samuel Maurice (Dr.)
　　273
　Sarah 272
　Simeon 271
　Simeon D. 271
　Stephen 271
　Susan 273, 392, 403
　Susan (Miss) 274
　Susan Agnes 272
　Susan Hord 114
　Susanna Hord 115
　Susie 273
　Tho. S. 683
　Thomas 270, 274, 275
　Thomas (Lieutenant)
　　274
　Thomas K. 274
　Thos. S. 684
　W. A. 272, 275
　Waddy Thomson 589
　Walter 275
　William 270, 274
　Wm. (Ensign) 274
　William (Lieut.)
　　274, 275
　William Austin 273
　Wm. B. 270
　Willis 273
Slavens, John 241
Slayback, --- 604
　--- (Gen.) 604
Sleeper, --- (Mr.) 108
　Alethea Halbert 106
　Benjamine P. 106
　Fabius M. 106, 108
　Francis D. 106
　Lockert 106
　Lucy Fleming 106
　Markham 106
　Martha Margaret 106
　Mary Woodson 106

Sleeper, (cont.)
　Pattie Markham
　　(Mrs.) 107
　Susan Margaret 106
　Thos. Markham 106
　Wm. Markham 106
　William Markham, Jr.
　　106
　William R. 106
Sleet, C. C. 36
Sloan, --- (Mr.) 624
　Alfred Baxter (Dr.)
　　162, 167
　Alfred McCready 163
　Alice Patton 163
　Annie 271
　Charles Clarence 162
　E. L. (Mrs.) 711
　Edith Bascom 163
　Edith Terrill 162
　Helen Ewing 162
　Martha Brown 162
　Mary Roberta 162
　Olive J. 163
　Robert Tarleton
　　(Dr.) 162, 167
　Roberta Lee 163
　Roberta Tarleton 162
　Rowland Boggess 163
　Sarah Lee 162
Small, John 674
Smallwood, Heabeard
　　(Captain) 300
　William Sheldon 163
Smarr, Elizabeth 744
　J. Edward 744
　John H. 744
　Nancy Taylor 744
　Reuben 744
　Robert W. 744
　William T. 744
Smart, David P. 434
　Moses Bledsoe 434
　Tabitha 626
Smith 465, 474, 480,
　　481, 572, 573, 679,
　　704, 726
　--- 299, 475, 558,
　　579, 656, 664, 726,
　　736
　--- (Capt.) 270
　--- (Dr.) 704
　--- (Infant) 703
　--- (Major) 345,
　　476
　--- (Miss) 410, 602
　--- (Mr.) 254, 409
　Abelard Temple 501
　Abigail 23
　Abraham 13
　Agatha 109
　Albert (Dr.) 603
　Alonzo N. 726
　Amelia 481
　Ann 192, 481, 569
　Ann T. 705
　Anna 576
　Anna Maria Stevenson
　　703
　Anne 466, 653, 654
　Anne Whitney 579
　Annie 481
　Augusta 479
　Augustine (Capt.)
　　270
　Austin 493
　Basil G. 704

Smith, (cont.)
　Basil Gaither 679,
　　704
　Bazilia 704
　Belle 402
　Benedict 679, 704
　Benjamin 480
　Benjamin Luckett 704
　Bernice 675
　Betsey 481
　Blanche 407
　Bradford Temple 474,
　　478, 480
　C. M. 326
　Catherine 514, 532
　Charles 466, 482
　Clater 480
　Clator 480, 481
　Clayton 480
　Cynthia Williams 706
　Daniel 297, 298, 299-
　　300, 514, 668
　Daniel D. 690
　David 576
　DeWitt W. 479
　DeWitt Wickliffe 478,
　　479
　Dobitha 722
　Donie 676
　Dorothy 577
　E. A. 706
　E. B. (Mrs.) 702,
　　708
　Edward 403,
　Edward B. 705
　Edward Jaqueline 223
　Eleanor 402
　Eliza 402, 472, 475,
　　477
　Eliza. 568
　Eliza Adelia 478
　Eliza Jane 474, 476,
　　477
　Elizabeth 214, 215,
　　349, 480, 572
　Elizabeth Jane 480
　Elizabeth Wilde 479
　Ellen Page 726
　Ellie 674
　Emmeline 726
　English O. 664
　Enoch 465
　Esther 496, 573
　" Extra Billy " 466
　F. (Mr.) 355
　Fannie 694
　Fannie Lightfoot 227
　Fleetwood 579
　Francis 265, 266, 582
　Francis (Major) 375
　Francis (Sir) 492
　Francis Whitney 579
　Fred E. 450, 475
　G. 484
　Garland 311
　George 298, 431, 466,
　　467, 480, 481, 496
　George (Rev.) 573
　George A. 466, 482
　George A. (Rev.)
　　392, 402
　George Alexander 466,
　　482
　Geo. D. 466
　George Hugh 392, 402
　George R. 749
　George W. 714

Smith, (cont.)
  George Washington 715
  George William 265
  Georgie A. 715
  Gustavus 481
  Hannah Hardage 481
  Hardage 466, 482
  Hardridge 482
  Henry 392, 402, 413
  Henry (Col.) 390
  Henry J. 726
  Hettie (Palmer) 514
  Hezekiah P. 704
  Humphrey Marshall 704
  Isaac 347, 392, 402
  Isaac A. 704
  James 466, 482, 576, 577, 629
  James W. 466
  Jane 374, 375, 401, 466, 481
  Jane Lane 482
  Jane Shaddown (?) 3
  Jay 475, 476
  Jemima 480
  Jessie Taylor 476
  Jo. Desha 579
  John 4, 502, 574, 736
  John (Captain) 551
  John (Col.) 493
  John (Major) 574
  John Ambler (Mrs.) 379
  John Logan Basye 715
  John Taylor 450, 475, 479, 480
  Joseph 3, 420, 451, 452, 465, 466, 473, 474, 475, 479, 480, 481, 485
  Joseph (Mrs.) 473
  Joseph S. 479
  Joseph Sidney 473, 475, 476, 477, 480
  Judith Guerrant 573
  Julia 577
  Julia V. 475
  Julian 704
  Junius Johnson 579
  Kate Q. 704
  Kerrenhappuch 466
  L. E. 703
  Lane 466, 481
  Laura Gibson 579
  Laurence (Col.) 270
  Leonidas 704
  Levy Page 726
  Lidia 452
  Lillian Berry 579
  Lina 468
  Llewellyn Holton 704
  Llewelyn Holten 704
  Lockett 721
  Lockette 714
  Lockette (Miss) 716
  Lois Parsons 729
  Lucinda Elizabeth 703, 704
  Lucinda Thurston 581
  Lucy E. 704
  Lydia 466, 481, 482, 572, 736
  Lyle 478
  M. Ellie 676
  Marcellus 704

Smith, (cont.)
  Margaret 169, 250, 255, 386, 466, 482
  Margaret Wilmore 706
  Maria 705
  Maria Brown 706
  Maria Louise 703
  Maria M. 704
  Marie Gibson 579
  Martha 577
  Martha S. 704
  Martin 440
  Mary 270, 492, 704
  Mary Ann 468
  Mary E. 501, 704
  Mary E. Luckett 704
  Mary Elizabeth 709
  Mary Jane 465
  Mary L. 726
  Mary Mathews 574
  Mary Rodes 572
  Mary Temple 479
  Matilda B. 705
  Meriwether 265
  Micajah 475, 481
  Micajah Wickliffe DeWitt 474, 478, 480
  Milly 481
  Milton 576
  Mittie Robb 227
  Nancy 466, 481, 704
  Nancy Jane 709
  Nancy Nuckols 704
  Nancy Snoddy 705
  Nathaniel 480, 481
  Nicholas 584, 709, 710
  Nimrod 347
  Penton (?) 3
  Pete 479
  Philip (Capt.) 574
  " Puss " 476
  Quintus M. 704
  R. H. 703, 704
  Rebecca 532
  Rebecca Penky (?) 3
  Rhodes 736
  Rice 468
  Richard Hewlitt 412
  Robt. 568
  Robert (Dr.) 581
  Robert H. 703, 704
  Robert H. (Dr.) 581, 594
  Robert Thurston Knight 703
  Rodes 572
  S. F. 676
  Sallie 577
  Sallie J. 715
  Sally 466, 474, 479, 481, 485
  Sally Taylor 450, 472, 474, 475, 484
  Sally Temple 481
  Samuel 431, 466, 481
  Samuel B. 412
  Sarah 452, 479, 480, 493, 574
  Sarah Louise 703
  Sarah Oliver 481
  Sidney Andrew 478
  Steven H. 726
  Susan 467
  Susan M. 704
  Susanna 582

Smith, (cont.)
  Susannah 62, 347, 466, 480
  Temple 452, 465, 466, 474, 475, 478, 479, 480, 481
  Temple II 481
  Temple III 481
  Thad Richardson 118
  Theodosia (Mrs.) 604
  Thomas 214, 215, 420, 498, 573
  Vickie 676
  Vincent 450, 475
  W. B. 706
  W. Basil (Mrs.) 689, 691, 692, 693, 698, 704
  W. J. (Mr.) 645
  W. J. (Mrs.) 645
  W. L. 101
  Warren K. 578
  Warren V. 577
  Weathers 466, 482
  Weathers (Gent.) 482
  Wethers 481, 482
  William 371, 466, 481, 498, 572, 577, 726, 736
  William (Captain) 15
  William Augustine 227
  William B. 705
  William Basil 704
  William Lane 479
  Wm. S. 412
  Withers 466, 480, 482
  Z. F. (Hon.) 504
  Z. F. (Mrs.) 494, 502, 503, 749
  Zachary 515
  Zachary F. 499
  Zackariah 499
Smither, --- (Miss) 409
Smithwick, --- (Mrs.) 189, 195, 196
  Martha (Mrs.) 195
  Martha C. D. 191
Smock, Lena 648
Snail, --- (Mr.) 237
Snead 192
  John Smith 684
  Lavinia Winn 192
  Martha Ann 684
  Mary Scott 684
  Patrick 192
  Samuel P. 684
Snedaker, Margaret 708
Sneed, Alice 150
  Benjamin 150
  Cary Anderson 150, 153
  Charles 150
  Edward 150
  Horace 150
  John A. 150, 153
  John A. (Mrs.) 154
  John Price 150, 153
  Louise Price 150, 153
  Lula Gordon 150, 153
  Mary Kerby 499
  Noble 150

Snoddy 679, 705
--- 705, 706
　Ann 705
　Betsy 705
　Cynthia 705
　Isabell 705
　James 705
　Jane 705, 706
　Jane Ann 705
　John 705
　John Kincade 705
　John Kincaid 705
　Joseph 705
　Joseph W. 705
　Margaret 705
　Nancy 705
　Patsy 705, 706
　Peggy 705, 706
　Samuel 705, 706
Snowdon, Mattie 516
Snyder, Agnes 649
Soane, Henry 215
　Judith 215
Soblet, J. 507
Somers, Eliza 84
Sorency, David 695
　Jacob 695
　Nancy West 695
　Samuel 695
Souplis, Margaret 633
South, Annie 511
　J. K. P. 753
　J. K. Polk, Jr.
　　(Mrs.) 680, 681
　Samuel 511
Southers, --- (Mrs.)
　440
Spahr, Asa 51
　Bessie 51
　Emma French 51
Spalding, Julia Sloan 704
Sparks, George W. 143
　Susan 159
Sparrow, Susan Mary 462
Spears, Mary Elizabeth
　262
Speed, James 666
　Jos. H. 655
Speilman, Daisy 162
Spencer, --- 523, 524,
　704
　Howard 75
　Susan 87
Sperry, America 359
Spicer, --- 557
　Laura M. 156
Spicir, William 444
Spiller, Henry 409
Spillman, Anna 409
Spilman, 97
Spinets, de (See de
　Spinets)
Spingall, Claude 160
　Mary Thornton 160
Spotswood 370
--- (Governor) 559
　Alexander, Esq. 433
Spottswood, --- (Gover-
　nor) 29, 270, 587
　Alexander (Gov.)
　　217
　Mary 217
Sprague, Chastine Mac-
　Gregor 512
　Ernest W. 512
　Ernest W., Jr. 512
　Frank 649

Sprague, (cont.)
　Frederick L. 76
　Helen Elizabeth 512
Sprake, George 578
　Isaac 578
　Susan 578
Spraker, Hazel A. 523
Sprigg, Eliza 84
　Thomas 256
Sprouse, Emma 362
Sprowl, John 656
Spurr, Burgess Hill 39
　Carola Jennings 39
　Julia 43
　Julia (Miss) 23, 32,
　　38, 42, 44
　Julia Hughes 39
　Laura Sheffer 39
　Martha Prewitt 39
　R. J. (Hon.) 186-
　　187
　R. J. Hughes 38, 39
　Richard 39, 186
　Richard A. 39
　Richard A. (Mrs.)
　　42, 44
　Richard Hughes 39
　Ruth (Mrs.) 187
　Ruth Sheffer 39
Stacker, George 66
　John 66
　Mary 66
Stacy, Matthew 20
Stagner, Barney 532
Stahl, Elizabeth Noel
　287
Stalnaker 337
--- 321
Stanard, --- (Mr.) 189
　W. G. 2, 189
Standard, --- 565
Standiford, Nannie 513
Standish, Ralph 636
Stanley, Augustus Owsley
　186
　P. B. 503
Stannard, --- (Mr.) 195
Stanton, Edward T. 104
　Henry T. 104
Staples, Charles R. 615
Stapp, Cerella 470
　Malita 566
Stark, Ann 497
　John (Major) 497
　Robert 530
Starke, Ann 584
Starling, --- (Miss)
　53
　Alfred Wallace 47
　Guy 47
　Guy, Jr. 47
　Nannie (Miss) 52
Stebbins. J. E. 263
Steck, Ella Georgia 697
Stedman, Alfred 592
Steel, --- (Miss) 517
Steele 117, 276, 281,
　285, 286, 288, 290,
　292
--- 276
--- (Miss) 330
--- (Mr.) 277, 279
　Adam 281, 285, 286,
　　293, 294
　Agnes Winfield 156,
　　165
　Amantha 285

Steele, (cont.)
　Andrew 277, 279, 280,
　　281, 282, 285, 320
　Andrew (Captain)
　　279, 280
　Andrew (Hon.) 281
　Anne 283
　Annie 280, 282
　Betsy Brooke 285
　Elizabeth Jane 148,
　　153
　Elizabeth William
　　280
　Esther 285, 286
　Jane (?) 338
　Jane 278, 280, 285,
　　286, 290, 292
　Jane (McKamie) 290,
　　294
　John 156, 165, 280,
　　283, 285, 338
　Jno. (Col.) 280
　John (General) 290
　John (Major) 282,
　　284, 285
　Jno. A. 283
　John A. (Hon.) 282,
　　284
　John Rowan 116, 286,
　　292
　Joseph 285, 286, 291
　Margaret 280
　Martha 285, 292, 293
　Martha Breckinridge
　　286, 293
　Martha McKamie 288,
　　290, 291, 292, 293,
　　294
　Martha McKamie
　　(Mrs.) 288, 289
　Mary 286, 290
　Minerva Fleming 285
　Nancy Polk 286
　Patsy Somers 285
　Priscilla 280
　Richard 276, 277, 281,
　　285, 286, 288, 290,
　　291, 292, 293, 294
　Richard, Esq. 276
　Richard (Sir) 276,
　　277, 279, 280, 283,
　　290
　Richard, Jr. 277
　Robert 281, 285
　Robert Makemie 286
　Samuel 320, 322, 338
　Samuel (Rev.) 325
　Sarah Paxton 568
　Theo. (Dr.) 282
　Theophilus (Dr.)
　　285
　Thomas 281, 282, 285
　William 280, 281, 285,
　　286
　William (Judge) 285
Steinbergen, A. 306
　Lee 307
　Mamie 307
Stephens, --- 755
　Arthur 152
　Emma 503
　Josephine 130
　Nanny 513
　Rosa 131
Stephenson 295, 298, 307,
　309, 310, 313, 314,
　315, 762

845

Stephenson, (cont.)
--- 313
--- (Mr.) 296
Alexander 310
Ann E. 313
Anna V. 310
Anna Vardiman 311
Annie Vardeman 312
Bettie 306
Bettie Hill 307
Charlie McRoberts 310
Dave Morgan 312, 313
David 308, 309, 314
E. 313
Eliza E. 313
Elizabeth Jane 312
Elizabeth (Summers) 286
Ephriam (Dr.) 310
Ephriam Thomas (Dr.) 310
George Lindsey 210
George Morgan 312
Hannah 313
Hannah B. 313
Isabelle 308
J. A. 310
J. Alexander 310
James Alexander 312
James W. 307
Jane 312
Jane Antoinette 315
Jennie Pennington 315
Joan 309
John 310
John F. 310
John Franklin 310
John Hall 267
Joseph 523
L. 313
L. O. 299, 300, 305, 309, 310
L. O. (Mr.) 295, 298, 299, 300, 301, 305, 306, 310
Lindsay 311, 313
Lindsay, Sr. 315
Lindsay Harris 315
Lindsay Orell 315
Lindsay Orell, Jr. 315
Lindsay Vardaman 295, 315
Lindsay Vardaman, Sr. 315
Lindsay Vardeman 311, 312
Lindsey, Sr. 210
Logan 306
Lola Annie 315
Malinda 308
Malindy Jane 312
Margaret 310
Margaret Lincoln 311
Marion Virginia 307
Martha 312
Martha A. 313
Martha Elizabeth 307
Mary 312
Mary E. 306
Mary Edith 312
Mary G. 310
Mills 314
Morgan Vardaman 315
Ollie May 315
P. W. 311
Patsy Ann 312
Rebecca McRoberts 311

Stephenson, (cont.)
Rebecca W. 310
Rebecca White 311
Robert 312, 314
Sallie 310
Sallie (Mrs.) 310
Sam Logan, Jr. 315
Samuel Logan (Dr.) 305, 312, 315, 316
Silas Lee 315
Stella 307
Stella A. 306
Stevie Logan 306, 307
Stevy L. 307
Stuart Hill 307
Thomas 308, 314
Thomas Logan 305
Violett Lee 315
W. P. 307
W. W. (Mr.) 91
Will Tom 310
William Alexander 315
William Gaines 307
William Lincoln 310
William Lincoln (Dr.) 311
Wm. P. 306
William Pitts 307
William T. 307, 310
William Thomas 310, 312
Willie 310
Sterling, A. 627
J. 627
Sterne, Laurence 267
Steuart 317
Stevens, Bettie 160
Douglas 160
Edwin C. 102
Eleanor 160
John B. 516
John James 160
John James, Jr. 160
John James, III 160
Mary 160
P. Stanley 152
Thornton 160
W. B. 35
Stevenson, 679, 706, 762, 763, 764, 765, 766, 768
--- 769, 770
--- (Miss) 512
Alexander 762, 770
Alice 706
Hugh (Sir) 762
Isabell 314
Isabelle 308, 309
James 762, 763, 764, 770
James Gay 768
Jane 762, 770
Jane (Aunt) ? 764, 770
Jane Gay 762, 765, 766, 767, 776
John 638, 706, 762, 764, 765, 769, 770
Joseph 523
Josiah 706
Martha 762, 768, 770
Mary 87, 762, 769, 770
Mary Jane 706
Robert 762, 770
Sam (Uncle) ? 764
Sammie 768, 769

Stevenson, (cont.)
Samuel 762, 763, 764, 765, 766, 768, 769, 770
Samuel (Major) 762
Thomas 309, 314, 762, 763, 764, 765, 770
William 4, 762, 764, 765, 770
Stevin, John 706
Stevinson, Alice 706
Augustus Vernon 706
James Mason 706
John 706, 707
John Tomson 706
Josiah 706
Leucinday 706
Margaret 706
Margaret Majors 706
Mary 706
Mary E. 706
Mary Ellen 707
Samuel 706
Thomas 706
Will 706
William 706
Williamson 706
Steward 317
Stewart 317, 318, 323, 326, 327, 328, 343, 347, 352, 354
--- 323, 328, 341
--- (Col.) 322, 374
--- (Rev.) 447
A. T. 43
Absalom 356
Adaline (Blucher) 339
Albert 356
Albert W. 356
Alexander 327, 328
Alice Minettie 356
Anderson 351
Andrew 358
Ann 341
Araminta 356
Benjamin F. 356
Betsy 336, 349
Braxton 356
Cassandra 351
Charles 351, 356
Charles Eli 356
Charles H. 355
Charles Lewis 356
Charles T. 354
Cordelia Adelaide 356
Cynthia 356
Cynthia A. 356
Cynthia Ann 356
Dabney 351
Daniel 356
Daniel C. 351, 353, 354
David 339
Dolly 327, 328
Dorothy 328
E. A. 352
Edward 328
Eli Cadwallader 356
Eliza J. 356
Eliza Jane 354
Elizabeth 149, 328, 339, 356
Elizabeth N. 356
Elmina 356
Elmira 356

846

Stewart, (cont.)
　Emily 356
　Fielding 351
　Francis Marion 356
　Frank 351
　George C. 335
　George W. 356
　Granville 356
　Harriet 356
　Harriet S. 356
　Harrison 354
　Henry 331, 356, 364
　Henry B. 364
　Hiram 352
　Hiram T. 356
　Isaac N. 354
　James 318, 327, 328,
　　331, 339, 340, 341,
　　347, 350, 356, 359
　James A. 351
　James M. 351, 356
　James Madison 356
　James N. 356
　James R. 356
　Jane 328, 355, 356
　Janet 328
　Jemima 350, 351
　Jenny 338
　John 318, 328, 351,
　　356, 364
　John (Col.) 374
　John D. 354
　Johnson 350, 356
　Joicy 356
　Joseph 339, 356
　Joseph B. 42
　Julina 354
　Landon 356
　Letitia 528
　Lewis 356
　Louisa 356
　Malinda 354, 356
　Margaret 351, 352, 354
　Marinda 356
　Martha 356
　Martha J. 356
　Marthena 354
　Mary 328, 339, 354,
　　356, 405
　Mary A. 351, 354
　Mary J. 352
　Mason 354
　Matilda 407
　Nancy 354, 356, 359,
　　405
　Nancy A. --- 354
　Nancy F. 352
　Parthena 354
　Phoebe 356
　Polly 356
　Rebecca 356
　Robert 318, 320, 328,
　　331, 339, 352, 405
　Robert T. 364
　Ruth A. 354
　Ruth Ann 356
　Samuel 339, 356
　Sarah 339, 351, 352
　Thomas 356
　Ushur 328
　Virginia 339
　W. 625
　Warren 356
　Wiley 351
　William 318, 328, 333,
　　336, 351, 352, 356
　William C. 317, 343

Stewart, (cont.)
　William G. 354
　William R. 328
　Wilson J. 351
Stievenson, John 11
Stigger, Minnie 530
Stiles, Hugh D. 649
　Woodie Crume 652
Stinson 679, 706, 762,
　　763
　James 763
　John 706, 707
　Minnie Viola 226
Stites, Eliza 514
　Jennie 130
Stith 184
　--- 198
　Elizabeth 194, 219
　John 232
　John (Capt.) 232
　Judith 194, 198, 211,
　　219
　Judith Randolph
　　(Mrs.) 211
　Mary 194, 219, 232
　William 216, 219
　William (Captain)
　　176, 184, 232
　William (Rev.) 108,
　　176, 184, 190, 194,
　　195, 211, 219, 232
Stockwell, Allen 85
Stoddard, --- 89
Stogdell, John 775
Stokes, Adele 573
Stone, --- (Capt.) 537
　--- (Miss) 673
　--- (Mrs.) 613
　Abigail 69
　Barton W. 258, 261,
　　262
　Barton W. (Rev.)
　　263
　Charles Logan 163
　Cornelia Lyle 163
　J. T. 126
　James (Deacon) 69
　Letta Brock 613
　Mary Farwell 69
　Mary H. 698
　Mary Hadley 163
　Miller 584
　Randolph F. 126
　Reba Athey 163
　William (Capt.) 537
　William G. 163
　William Haydon 163
Stonehouse, Anna 463
　Walter (Rev.) 463
Stoner, --- 523
　May Lindsay 262
　Michael 258, 522
　Robert 262
Stonestreet, Elizabeth
　　564, 565
　James 565
Storey, Ann M. 628
Storke, Behethland 170,
　　372, 382, 388, 390,
　　396 (See also
　　Stroke, Bethaland)
Storres, Graves 115
　Joshua 115
Stout, Ada P. 271
　John 271
　Louisa 686
　Olivet 271

Stovall 499
　--- (Mr.) 610
　Martha 499
Stowe, Mary 46
Stowers, William 481
Straather 397
Straathor 365
Strabo 494, 495
　Pierre 494
Stratton, Ida 407
Strawbridge, W. (Dr.)
　　629
Stringfellow, Chas. F.
　　406
　Chas. S. 383
　Horace (Rev.) 383,
　　406
　Horace J. (Rev.)
　　406
　James (Rev.) 406
Stroader, Ann 338
Strode, Willie 120
Stroke, --- (Miss) 413
　Bethaland 411 (See
　　also Storke, Beheth-
　　land)
Strother (See also del
　　Strother) 97, 98,
　　169, 170, 180, 188,
　　189, 357, 365, 366,
　　367, 369, 370, 372,
　　373, 379, 381, 384,
　　388, 393, 394, 395,
　　396, 397, 405, 408,
　　411
　--- 170
　--- (Gen.) 390
　--- (Judge) 397
　--- (Miss) 176, 370
　--- (Mr.) 388
　--- (Mrs.) 403
　--- (Sir) 369
　Abby 406
　Agatha 366, 373, 374,
　　401
　Alan, Jr. 369
　Albert Randolph 409
　Alice 373, 390, 391,
　　411
　Alice Cathrine 409
　Alonzo Bascom 408
　Ann 373, 382, 391
　　393, 394
　Anna 410, 411
　Anna Kavanaugh 385
　Anne 373, 377, 390,
　　391, 405, 407, 408,
　　409, 413
　Anne S. 405
　Anne Wolff 412
　Anthony 170, 367, 372,
　　373, 381, 382, 387,
　　388, 389, 390, 396,
　　397, 398, 404, 411,
　　412, 413
　Anthony, Jr. 388
　Anthony, Sr. 388, 390
　Archer 406
　Archer (Dr.) 394,
　　408
　Arthur 409
　Behathalind 405
　Behethdad 381, 382
　Behethland 389
　Ben Herbert 408
　Benj. 397
　Benjamin 366, 398,

847

Strother, (cont.)
  Benjamin (cont.)
    405, 412, 413
  Benjamine 169, 371,
    372, 383, 388, 389,
    390, 396
  Benjamine (Captain)
    396
  Betsey 410, 411
  Bettie 410
  Bettie Willis 411
  Betty 410, 411, 412
  C. W. (Judge) 365
  Catharine 170, 393,
    394
  Catharine Pryor 394
  Catherine 388, 391,
    393, 402, 409
  Caty 408
  Charles 406, 409
  Chas. Lewis 409
  Chas. Oscar 410, 411
  Charles R. 388
  Charles Wesley 408
  Christopher 170, 391,
    398, 402, 413
  D. H. (General) 389
  " Dabnaugh " 404
  Daniel F. 413
  Daniel French 402
  David 412
  David (General)
    373
  David H. 412
  David Hunter 367,
    412
  David Hunter (General) 170, 368, 370,
    373, 379, 388, 389
  Dorothea 398, 413
  Dorothy 169, 366, 370,
    371, 372, 391
  Dorothy --- 179
  Edwin 409
  Eleanor 169, 391, 393,
    397
  Eleanor --- 170, 372
  Eliabeth 382
  Elīnor 402
  Elizabeth 170, 373,
    374, 379, 381, 382,
    384, 387, 390, 391,
    393, 394, 395, 396,
    405, 407, 408, 411,
    412
  Elizabeth F. 413
  Elizabeth French 403
  Elizabeth Hewlitt 412
  Elvira 384, 393, 404,
    411
  Emily 389, 390, 412
  Emma 409
  Eugene T. 394
  Eugene Thomas 409
  Fanny Morton 408
  Florida 406
  Frances 170, 367, 382
  Frances Banks 367
  Francis 169, 170, 179,
    179-180, 180, 366,
    367, 372, 379, 380,
    381, 382, 384, 386,
    387, 388, 390, 391,
    392, 393, 398, 402,
    404, 405, 411, 413
  Frank Taylor 408
  French 367, 383, 391,

Strother, (cont.)
  French (cont.) 392,
    394, 402, 403, 409,
    410, 411, 413
  French (Captain)
    384, 410, 411
  French, Jr. 406
  Geeorge 413
  George 170, 381, 382,
    386, 387, 388, 389,
    390, 393, 404, 405,
    408, 409, 412
  George (Rev.) 95,
    393, 394, 397, 408,
  Geo. Duncan 409
  George F. 367, 413
  George French 367,
    391, 392, 393, 403,
    404
  Geo. Mm. 408-409
  Geo. Wm. 408
  George Woodson 394,
    408
  Gerard Banks 367
  Harriet 383, 405,
    410, 411
  Helen 384, 410, 411
  Henry 369, 394, 397,
    409, 410, 411
  Henry (Dr.) 406
  Henry (Mr.) 95,
    96, 97, 373, 380
  Hester 405
  Irvin 409
  James 169, 170, 366,
    367, 371, 372, 390,
    391, 393, 397, 398,
    402, 406, 409, 412,
    413
  James F. 404
  James French 376,
    384, 393, 403, 411
  James Lawrence 398
  James McClellan 408
  James Payne 390
  James Robert 383
  James Thomas 383
  James Wade 383, 392
  Jane 373, 374, 378,
    379, 390, 397, 398
  Jeremiah 169, 169-
    170, 366, 367, 371,
    372, 379, 380, 391,
    393, 394, 397, 398,
    402, 404, 407, 408,
    413
  Jeremiah, 1st 383
  Jeremiah, Jr. 170,
    386, 391, 393, 413
  Jeremiah, Sr. 386
  Jeremiah Pierce 408
  Jeremy 398
  John 97, 170, 367,
    381, 382, 383, 384,
    386, 387, 388, 389,
    390, 393, 394, 404,
    405, 406, 407, 408,
    409, 410, 411, 412,
    413
  John (Capt.) 381,
    382, 383, 392, 393,
    394, 404
  John (Col.) 170,
    389, 390
  John (Major) 387
  John, Jr. 382, 383,
    408

Strother, (cont.)
  John, Sr. 408
  John C. 188
  John C. (Hon.)
    394
  John Chaplin 397,
    409
  John F. (Rev.) 96
  John Fletcher 408
  John Fletcher
    (Rev.) 394
  John French 409
  John Hunt 393, 403
  John Meredith 412
  John Pryor 409
  John Pryor (Judge)
    95
  Joseph 169, 366, 371,
    372, 382, 383, 392,
    394, 398, 405, 406,
    407, 409, 413
  Kate 410, 411
  Kate Pryor 409
  Katherine P.
    (Miss) 397
  Kitty 412
  Lancelot (Sir) 395
  Lawrence 402, 413
  Lizzie 408
  Louisa 405-406
  Lucy 72, 382, 383,
    384, 403, 405, 406,
    410, 411
  Lucy C. 413
  Lula 409
  Margaret 366, 373,
    375, 377, 381, 382,
    383, 386, 387, 391,
    392, 397, 399, 401,
    403, 411, 412, 413
  Margaret (Mrs.)
    373
  Margaret Thornton
    179, 380, 381, 384,
    398
  Margaret Watts 372,
    373, 390
  Martha 408
  Mary 369, 381, 382,
    383, 388, 390, 391,
    394, 402, 405, 406,
    408, 409, 412, 413
  Mary Allen 408
  Mary Ann 406
  Mary (Duncan) 95
  Mary Elizabeth 409
  Mary Emily 409
  Mary James 388, 390
  Mary Lavinia 409
  Mary Maria 409
  Mary Stroke 412
  Mary Wade 394
  May 412
  Mildred 382, 383,
    384
  Milly 405, 407, 410,
    411
  Mollie 382, 384, 390
  Molly 409
  Nancy 383, 388, 390,
    393, 395, 405, 407,
    408, 410
  Nancy Lawler 393
  Oliver C. 409
  Oliver Peniston 408
  P. W. 413
  P. W. (Judge) 188,

848

Strother, (cont.)
P. W. (Judge) 380,
    384, 395, 412
Peggy 405, 407
Pendleton 383, 384,
    393, 406, 411
Perla 409
Phil. W. 404
Philip 408, 409
Philip W. 411
Philip W. (Judge)
    367
Phillip 388
Phillip W. (Judge)
    373, 384, 393
Pigg (?) 405
Polly 384, 408, 410,
    411
Ralph G. 188, 409
Reuben 406
Richard Henry 408
Richard Hewlitt 412
Robert 169, 366, 371,
    372, 381, 382, 388,
    398, 405, 412, 413
Robert Bruce 409
Robert Quarles 412
Sallie 384, 393, 394,
    403, 411
Sally 404, 405, 407,
    409, 410, 411
Sam Pryor 408
Samuel 388, 393
Sanford 408
Sara 404
Sarah 169, 170, 180,
    367, 368, 382, 383,
    384, 385, 386, 403,
    404, 408, 463
Sarah Ann 384, 411
Sarah B. P. 384
Sarah B. P. (Mrs.)
    404
Sarah C. 409
Sarah Catherine Kennerly 409
Sarah French 409
Sarah P. B. (Mrs.)
    404
Senaca 405, 407
Shelby French 394,
    409
Sidney 412
Solomon 393, 407
Stroke 412
Susan 404, 407, 410,
    411
Susanna 169, 170, 179,
    180, 367, 368, 382
Susannah 381, 384,
    385, 388, 393, 404,
    405
Susannah Dabney 381
Sydney 409
Theodosia 403
Thomas Nelson 412
Wade Dabney 410, 411
Wallace 409
William 169, 170, 179,
    180, 366, 367, 368,
    369, 370, 371, 372,
    373, 374, 375, 377,
    378, 379, 380, 381,
    382, 383, 384, 385,
    386, 387, 388, 390,
    391, 392, 395, 397,
    398, 399, 401, 402,

Strother, (cont.)
William (cont.)
    404, 405, 406, 409,
    411, 412, 413, 463
William, 1st 371
William, Jr. 179,
    371, 372, 379, 380,
    388, 390, 391
Wm., 2nd 411
William A. 412
Wm. D. 370
William Dabney 169,
    170, 180, 367, 384,
    385, 386, 404
Wm. Porter 412
Wm. Walker 408
Willis 410, 411
Stroud, Ansell 745
Stuart 179, 317, 319,
    328, 337, 340, 345,
    347, 350, 352, 353,
    354, 357, 363, 731
--- 319, 321, 322,
    326, 329, 340, 342,
    358, 362
--- (Miss) 398
--- (Widow) 323
A. E. 358
Absalom 333, 338,
    346, 347, 348, 350,
    352, 353, 354, 356,
    357, 358, 361, 362
Absalom B. 340
Adaline 352
Adam 354
Adia M. 348
Agnes 336
Agnes E. 336
Albert 348
Albert Gallatin 359
Albert H. 358
Albert R. 362
Alexander 323, 324,
    327
Alfred 356
Allan 359
Almrah K. 358
Alonzo David 359
Amelia Ann 348
Amelia Elizabeth 354
Amelia L. 348
America 358, 359
Amy 346, 358, 364
Anderson 351
Andrew 327, 335, 347,
    348, 355, 356, 360
Ann 329, 331, 332,
    341, 342
Ann C. 359
Ann E. 324
Ann (Lafferty) 330,
    342
Ann S. 340
Anna 346, 356, 358,
    360
Anna M. 348
Araminta 362
Archibald 319, 327
Armena 351
Belle --- 352
Benjamin F. 348, 351,
    354
Betsy 339
Bettie J. 326
Burgess 358, 359
C. I. 352

Stuart, (cont.)
Caroline 363
Caroline --- 348
Cassandra 351
Catherine 335, 346,
    360, 363
Charles 346, 347,
    348, 349, 351, 352,
    353, 354, 355, 358,
    359, 360, 361, 362,
    398
Charles A. 348
Charles B. 340
Charles C. 348
Charles F. 355
Charles J. 731, 732
Charles K. 348
Charles Lewis 363
Charlotte 360
Clay 361, 362
Clementine 353
Columbia A. 359
Columbus 362
Cora 352
Cornala 362
Curtis H. 352
Cynthia 349
Cynthia A. 349
Cynthia Ann 362
Dabney 351, 354
Dabney W. 353
Daniel C. 353
Daniel E. 359
David 339, 354, 363
David L. 339
David Todd 325
Druzilla C. 359
Edna 359
Edward 326, 362
Edwin 348
Eleanor 347, 348,
    349, 350
Eliza 335, 355, 358,
    359
Eliza Ann 325
Elizabeth 324, 331,
    332, 335, 336, 339,
    347, 348, 349, 354,
    355, 358, 359, 362,
    364
Elizabeth --- 355
Elizabeth A. 340
Elizabeth F. 731
Elizabeth (Goode ?)
    353
Ella F. 359
Ellender --- 362
Elliott 355, 356
Emily 347, 350
Emma 358, 359
Emmen 359
Emmy Lou 351
Eustatia A. 354
Fielding 351
Fletcher 359
Frances 352, 353,
    358
Frances --- 354, 361,
    362
Francis Henry 359
Francis M. 351
Francis Marion 362
Frank N. 326
G. Jefferson 353
George 336, 354
George C. 336
George E. 336, 348

849

Stuart, (cont.)
  George J. 351
  George L. 362
  George P. 354, 360, 361, 362, 363
  George S. 362
  George W. 353, 354, 355
  George Washington 349
  Gerard M. 358
  Glannis 363
  Greenville 356
  H. H. 354
  Hamilton H. 359
  Hannah 325, 326
  Hansford H. 359
  Harrison 351, 352, 353, 354, 361, 363, 364
  Harrison B. 352
  Harrison Daniel 348
  Harrison H. 363
  Harvey 347
  Henry 333, 334, 335, 346, 356, 359, 360, 361, 364
  Henry B. (?) 364
  Henry B. 352, 363
  Henry C. 363
  Henry (Cartmell ?) 363
  Henry Clay 354
  Henry F. 360
  Henry Francis 358, 359
  Henry Harrison 359, 361
  Henry R. 348
  Henry Washington 348
  Herbert 362
  Hezekiah Burgess 359
  Hiley Ann/Mary 362
  Hiley Mary (?) 362
  Hiram 347, 351, 356
  Hugh 323, 324, 327, 338, 339
  Irby W. 351
  Isaac 358
  Isaac Foster 359
  Isabella 337
  Isabella --- 337
  James 317, 319, 320, 321, 322, 323, 324, 326, 327, 328, 329, 330, 331, 332, 333, 334, 335, 337, 339, 340, 341, 342, 343, 344, 345, 346, 347, 349, 350, 351, 352, 353, 354, 356, 357, 358, 359, 361, 362, 731, 732
  James A. 359
  James A. M. 340
  James Boyd 359
  James C. 348, 364
  James E. 357, 358
  James Elliott 349, 357, 359
  James Elliott (Judge) 358
  James H. 358, 360, 362, 363
  James Hawkins 325
  James Henry 354
  James J. 354
  James M. 348, 349, 351

Stuart, (cont.)
  James Madison 351
  James T. 348
  James W. 348, 354
  Jane 324, 338, 339, 360
  Jane (Steele ?) 338
  Jannett 334
  Jemima 350, 351, 352
  Jenny 338
  Jeremiah 362
  Jeremiah F. 358
  Jesse 317, 362, 363
  John 317, 319, 320, 322, 323, 324, 326, 327, 329, 331, 332, 333, 336, 337, 338, 339, 340, 342, 344, 346, 348, 351, 355, 357, 358, 359, 360, 364
  John (Capt.) 398
  John (Col.) 326, 364
  John B. 336, 339
  John Erastus 359
  John F. 340, 353
  John H. 364
  John Hopkins 324
  John J. 351
  John M. 354, 358
  John Marshall 349
  John T. 326
  John Todd 317, 325, 326
  John Todd (Major) 326
  Johnson 347, 350, 351, 352, 353, 354
  Johnson D. 354
  Joseph 324, 327
  Joseph Sylvester 359
  Julia 354
  Julia Ann 360
  Julina 353
  Kelly 362
  Kesiah 358
  Lafayette 358, 359
  Larra B. 351
  Laverna 362
  Leander 358
  Lemuel 359
  Leroy 352
  Leslie C. 336
  Levi Todd 325
  Levicy 358, 362
  Lewis 398
  Lewis J. 353
  Louisa --- 349
  Lucinda 354, 364
  Lucy 358, 731
  Lucy A. --- 351
  Lucy E. 336
  Luther C. 348
  M. Lou 351
  Mack 351
  Malinda 360
  Malinda (Ball ?) 360
  Margaret 322, 324, 325, 326, 327, 346, 353, 362, 363
  Margaret (Johnson ?) 360
  Margaret Russell 351
  Maria 731
  Maria L. 732

Stuart, (cont.)
  Maria W. 731
  Marion 362
  Marion F. 362
  Martha 352, 354, 359, 360
  Martha A. 352
  Martha Ann 359
  Martha Ann --- 359
  Martha C. 353
  Martha E. 348
  Martha J. 359
  Martha J. --- 360
  Martin 352, 363
  Mary 322, 323, 324, 327, 329, 332, 333, 334, 337, 338, 341, 342, 346, 347, 349, 350, 353, 357, 358, 359, 362, 731
  Mary A. --- 348
  Mary Ann 359
  Mary Ann (Lafferty) 332, 344
  Mary Clay 360
  Mary E. 348
  Mary Elizabeth ? 332
  Mary Elliott 345, 357, 360
  Mary F. 359
  Mary J. 348, 354
  Mary Jane 325, 348
  Mary S. 340
  Mary Virginia 326
  Matilda 335
  Melinda 347, 351, 360
  Melissa A. 354
  Milton M. 358
  Minerva 354
  Missouri 356
  Mitchell 346, 347, 352, 353, 357, 360, 361, 362, 363
  Mollie 351
  Nancy 335, 336, 341, 349, 354, 355, 358, 360, 363, 382, 383, 394
  Nancy A. 358
  Nancy (Burgess) 358
  Nancy M. 336
  Oda T. 352
  Olive --- 333
  Ora 346, 356, 364
  Patsy 335
  Perry 363
  Phoebe 346, 360
  Polly 354, 355, 360
  Prichard 347
  Priscilla 339
  Prudence 336
  Rachel 354
  Ralph 326, 329, 330, 331, 332, 333, 334, 336, 337, 338, 341, 342, 343, 344, 345, 346, 347, 348, 350, 351, 352, 353, 355, 356, 357, 358, 359, 360, 361, 362, 363, 364
  Ralph, Jr. 355
  Ralph, (Capt.) 343
  Ralph (Col.) 358
  Rebecca 346, 349, 353, 354, 359, 361

Stuart, (cont.)
  Rebecca (cont.) 362, 363
  Reuben J. 353
  Rhoda J. 364
  Richard 346, 355, 357
  Richard G. 731
  Robert 317, 319, 320, 321, 322, 323, 324, 325, 326, 327, 329, 330, 331, 332, 333, 334, 335, 336, 337, 338, 339, 340, 341, 342, 344, 346, 352, 353, 355, 358, 359, 360, 361, 362
  Robert (Capt.) 320-321, 321
  Robert (Major) 317, 319, 326, 327, 338, 340
  Robert (Rev.) 317, 322, 324, 325
  Robert, Jr. 334
  Robert B. 359
  Robert L. 326
  Robert M. 362
  Robert Todd (Judge) 325
  Rosannah 339, 340
  Rosannah M. 340
  S. G. 732
  Sam G. 731
  Samuel 338, 339
  Samuel Campbell 336
  Samuel Davies (Rev.) 325
  Samuel G. 731, 732
  Samuel L. 339
  Sanford M. 349
  Sanford Mead 349
  Sarah 335, 346, 354, 359, 362, 363
  Sarah A. 348
  Sarah B. 359
  Sarah C. 351
  Sarah G. 354
  Sarah Jane 336, 340
  Sarah Lakin 359
  Sarelda --- 362
  Serapta 359
  Serena H. 354
  Sidney 352, 355
  Sintha 362
  Sophia 362
  Sophia Elizabeth 349
  Sue 352
  Susan 731, 732
  Susan A. 353
  Susan Greene 732
  Sylvester 359
  Tabitha 347, 359
  Theresa 359
  Thomas 731
  Thomas H. 348, 353, 354, 731, 732
  Thomas Harvey 348, 354
  Thomas Jefferson 359
  Thomas M. 351, 354
  Thomas Riley 352
  " Uncle Robert " 334
  Viola A. 359
  Virginia 351
  Virginia L. 326
  Walker 324
  Walter (Lt.) 321

Stuart, (cont.)
  Wesley 354
  Wiley 351, 353, 354
  William 317, 319, 327, 332, 333, 335, 336, 345, 346, 347, 348, 349, 351, 353, 354, 355, 357, 358, 360, 363
  William C. 363
  William G. 731, 732
  William H. 351, 353, 360
  William L. 364
  William M. 348
  William Martin 354
  William R. 354, 358, 362
  William Riley 359, 361, 362
  William T. 348
  William T. S. 340
  Wilson 352, 353, 354
  Wilson J. 351
Stubblefield, Peffie 692
Stull, Lucretia 631
Sublett, Frances 514
  Lewis 368, 500, 514
  William 514
Sublette, Anne 395
  James 514
  John 514
  Lewis 514
  Mary 395
  Philip A. 298
Suffolk, --- (Countess of) 26
Suggett, Benjamin 498
  David Castleman 498
  Jemima 86, 573, 575, 578
  Judith 498
  Lucy 498
  Polly 575
  Samuel 498
  Sophronia 498
Suggitt, Edgecomb P. 738
  John, Sr. 738
  Mildred 738
  Polly 737
Summers, --- 91
  Andrew (Capt.) 632
  Francis (Col.) 465
Sutherland, Effie (Mrs.) 648
  John 286
  Polly 285
Sutherland Fitswilliam, (Countess of) (?) 26
Sutton, (See also Salter)
  Amos 516
  Edna 22, 53
Swain, Joseph 459, 461
Swann, 117, 602
  Catharine 116, 117, 145, 153, 164, 167
  Catherine 135
  Jane 602
  John 602
  Samuel 602
  Sarah 215
  Thomas 510
  Thomas (Col.) 215
Swift, --- (Mr.) 510
Switzer, E. 339

Switzer, (cont.)
  George 339
  Nathan 339
  Priscilla 339
  Thomas 339
Swoope, Jacob 338
Symington, E. S. 229
Symms, Lee W. 124, 145
Tabb, Arthur 102
  Charles S. 102
  George Cary 102
  Mary 116, 117
  Mary Clifton 102
Talbot, 243, 580
  Benjamin 32
  Betty 478
  Charles 580
  Christina 580
  Cordelia La Fayette 61
  Cordelia Lafayette 57
  David Moil 580
  Drusilla Gwin 580
  Eliza 755
  Eliza Garard 690
  Elizabeth 236
  Ezekiel 580
  George 580
  Howard (Rev.) 478
  Isham 580, 689, 755
  John 580
  John M., M. D. 286
  John Moil 580
  John Moil (Dr.) 57
  Lucy Moil 580
  Martha A. 32
  Mary 580
  Mary Grimes 32
  Mary Lee Keister (Mrs.) 4, 10
  Mary Wiliston 580
  Matthew 580
  Nancy 408
  Providence 580
  Thomas 580
  Wiliston 580
Talbott, Elizabeth Ewen 250
  Elizabeth Ewing 255
  George 408
  Helen 408
  Isham 408
  James 408
  James W. 408
  Mary 408
  Nancy 408
  Richard 250, 255
  Sarah 408
  Seeny 408
Taliaferro, --- (Mr.) 411
  James Gorin (Judge) 257
  William (Captain) 524
Taliferro, Wm. 411
Talleyrand, --- 604
Talliaferro, John 371
  Warner 398
Tand, Knaper 439
Tandey, William 414
Tandy 414, 416, 417, 425, 426, 427, 429, 434, 435, 439
  --- 414, 415, 416, 417, 418, 421, 429, 432, 447

Tandy, (cont.)
--- (Miss) 429
--- (Castleman) 431
A. J. 428
A. W. (Rev.) 416, 419, 431
Acchillez 422
Acchillis 422
Achillas 428
Achilles 421, 429, 430
Achillis 423
Agnes 417, 418
Akillis 435
Amelia 432
Amelia (Graves) 432
Andrew Jackson 428
Ann 416, 417, 418, 419
Ann (Mills) 431, 432
Annis 428
Archillis 421, 424
Boon 438
Carroll 448, 449
Carroll S. 447, 449
Catharine 440, 441
Charles 428, 441
Charles Scott 428
Daniel 438
David 426, 437, 438
David (Dr.) 430
David Castleman (Dr.) 431
Drucilla 449
Drusilla 440
Drusilla T. 444
Edward 428, 441
Edward J. 441
Eliza Ann 439
Elizabeth 438
Emer 440
Emily 440
Ford 419, 420
Frances 416, 418, 421
Frances --- 416
Gabriel 421, 422, 423, 424, 425, 426, 427, 428, 429, 430, 431, 435
Gabriel (William) 425
George 428
Granvill 440
Granville 438
Harriet A. 448
Henry 414, 415, 416, 418, 419, 430, 431, 432, 437, 438
Henry, Jr. 415, 426, 427
Henry, Sr. 419
Henry Clay 428
Henry Jackson 419, 432, 433
J. B. 440, 442, 446, 449
J. Q. 442, 448
J--- (?) 423
Jackson 419, 432, 433
Jackson Thompson 419, 433
James 440
James B. 435
James Bledsoe 435, 436, 449
James W. 439
Jane 420, 421, 422,

Tandy, (cont.)
Jane (Cont.) 423, 424, 425, 428, 437
Jane (Miss) 427
Jane --- 416, 419, 429, 430, 434
Jennie 438
Jeptha 438
Jessie Emer 441
John 415, 416, 417, 418, 419, 420, 421, 422, 423, 424, 426, 427, 429, 430, 431, 435, 437, 438, 441, 448
John (I) 429
John J. 447, 449
John Q. A. 441
Jone 418
Jone --- 417
Judith 430, 439
Judith --- 421, 429
Junius C. 441
Justine 449
Justine A. 448
Katharine 438
Knaper (?) 439
L. B. (Mrs.) 427
Lenton 428
Lucinda 439
Lucy 421, 422, 424, 425, 428, 429
Lucy (Miss) 427, 429
Lucy Q. 421, 423
Lucy Quarles 421
Lutitia 440
Magga 441
Martha 416, 428
Martha H. 428
Marthy 438
Mary 428, 432, 438
Mary T. 441
Millie 428
Mills 419, 431, 432
Milly 421, 425, 426
Milton 438
Mollie 419
Moses 421, 422, 423, 424, 430, 437, 438, 440
Nancy 419, 438, 441
Nancy C. 441
Nappa 414
Napper 414
Narcissa Bowdry (Peery) 419
Nathaniel 419
Paschal 438
Permelia 438
R.M. 441
Ralph 419
Richard 414
Robert 426, 428, 438
Roger 415, 416, 418, 419, 427, 430, 430-431, 431, 437, 438
Roger M. 441
Russel 438
S. 446
Sallie B. 430
Sally 419, 421, 432, 434, 441
Sally Mote 440
Samuel 426, 438
Sarah 428
Sarah (Mills) 433

Tandy, (cont.)
Sarah (Quarles) 418
Sary Jane 440
Schilles 425
Scott 428, 438, 439, 441, 442, 445, 447, 448
Senit 438
Silvanus 416
Smyth 433
Sprat 438
Stephen 428
Thomas 417, 418, 428
W. H. 442, 447, 448
Walter 428
Wayland 438
William 414, 415, 416, 417, 418, 419, 420, 421, 422, 424, 425, 426, 429, 430, 434, 435, 437, 438, 440, 441, 442, 447
William (Dr.) 430
William, Jr. 430
William, Sr. 420, 427
William H. 442
William Henry 432
Willis 428, 439, 441
Willis (Capt.) 428
Tanner, Mary Jane 150
Sallie 310
Tantey, William 417
Tarleton, --- (Miss) 177, 200, 212
Banastre (Col.) 212
Judith 113, 177, 200, 653
Stephen 200, 653
Susanna 212, 218
Susannah 200
Tartar, Sam 302
Wess 302
Tarter, R. C. (Hon.) 298, 299
Tate 1, 2, 3
--- (Col.) 484
--- (Judge) 3
Asar 3
Bank G. 2
Cecil Geneva (?) 2
Edmonia 468
Geo. W. 3
H. John 2
Hannah 3
Henry 2
Homer 3
" Honest Dick " 468
Isaac 2, 3
James 2, 468
James W. 468
Jesse 2
John 2, 3
John (Col.) 2
John S. 3
Lydia 3
M. (Capt.) 2
Mara Bracken Baker (?) 3
Mary 2, 3
Mattie 3
Nancy 483, 485
Nancy Taylor Gray 468, 484
Penton Smith (?) 3
Robert 1, 2, 3
Robert M. 2, 3

Tate, (cont.)
  S. H. (Judge) 2
  Sam (?) 3
  Samuel 1, 2, 3
  Samuel (Capt.) 1
  Samuel (Major) 2
  Samuel Bracken 2
  Samuel O. 3
  Thomas L. 451, 485
  Thomas L. (Col.)
    468, 483, 484
  W. S. 3
  William O. 2
  Winnie Atkinson 3
Tatlow, Alberta Lee 119
  Fannie Anderson 119
  Lawrence 119
  Mary Louise 119
  R. Harry 119
  Richard 119
  Richard H., Jr. 119
Taylor 366, 451, 452,
    453, 458, 463, 474,
    482, 483, 489, 490,
    586, 595, 636, 745,
    750
  --- 121, 451, 456,
    457, 462, 486, 488
  --- (Capt.) 493
  --- (Dr.) 39
  --- (General) 185,
    413
  --- (Maj.) 596
  --- (Miss) 84, 85,
    377, 392, 403
  --- (Mr.) 400
  --- (President)
    586
  --- (Rev.) 484
  Aaron 451, 452, 453,
    456, 457, 458, 459,
    486, 487, 488, 489
  Abednego Danning 744
  Achsah 631, 635, 636
  Alexander 21
  Alfred 744
  Alice 455
  Alice (Gaskins) 455
  Ana 455
  Ann 456
  Annie Weeks 744
  Argail 487, 488
  Argile 459, 461
  Argle 452
  Argyle 451, 452, 453,
    456, 457, 460, 488
  Argyle (Captain)
    457
  Aron 486, 487
  Artemisia 460
  Benjamin 451, 452,
    453, 455, 457, 463,
    464, 467, 484, 485
  Benjamin P. 473
  Bennett (Col.) 223
  Betty 458
  Bradford 451, 460
  Catherine 460, 745,
    753
  Catherine --- 744,
    745
  Cave 451, 473
  Charles (Dr.) 39
  Charles M., Jr. 39
  Charlotte 223
  Cinty Susan 744
  Colby 752

Taylor, (Cont.)
  Cornelia Jefferson
    223
  Courtney 732
  Creed (Judge) 114
  Dick (General) 365,
    397
  Diedamia 490
  Dione 467
  Edith 373
  Edmund H., Sr. 682
  Edmund Randolph 223
  Edward 490
  Elias 455
  Eliza 451, 473, 744
  Elizabeth 386, 451,
    454, 455, 458, 463,
    464, 467, 473, 483,
    484, 485, 487, 490,
    626, 744, 745
  Elizabeth, Sr. 745
  Elizabeth --- 451
  Elizabeth Hampton 744
  Elizabeth Kavanaugh
    463
  Elizabeth (Kave-
    naugh) 484
  Elizabeth Marion 744
  Elizabeth Prewitt 39
  Ellen --- 460
  Ellender 744
  Emily 386
  Fanny 664
  Foushee T. 460
  George 386, 636
  Godfrey 490
  Grayson Bradford 460
  Hampton H. 744
  Hancock 171, 180,
    385, 386
  Hannah 460
  Hannah (Bradford)
    460
  Harriet 460
  Hubbard 753
  Ignatius 744
  J. Bennett 233
  J. Swigert (Mr.)
    681
  James 415, 455, 457,
    490, 586
  James (Col.) 383,
    386, 395
  James L. 744
  James W. 460
  James William 490
  Jane 363, 451, 462,
    471
  Jane Randolph 223
  Jefferson Randolph
    223
  Jenefer H. 744
  Jennie 490
  Jerry D. 752
  Jessie 490
  Joel 467
  John 450, 451, 452,
    453, 454, 455, 456,
    457, 458, 459, 460,
    461, 462, 463, 464,
    467, 473, 474, 479,
    482, 483, 484, 485,
    486, 487, 488, 596
  John (Major) 595,
    596
  John (Rev.) 452,
    453, 458, 459, 461,

Taylor, (cont.)
  John (Rev.)
    (cont.) 462, 463,
    465, 468, 469, 471,
    474, 481, 483, 484,
    486, 488
  John II 457
  John, Jr. 455, 456
  John C. R. 223
  John F. 460
  John H. 744
  John P. 473
  John T. 744
  John W. 485
  John Wickliffe 451,
    472, 473, 484, 485
  John William 744, 745
  Joseph 451, 457, 458,
    459, 461, 462, 467,
    484, 485, 486, 487,
    488, 744
  Joseph (Rev.) 483,
    484, 498
  Joseph A. 744
  Joseph H. 745
  Joseph Hampton 744,
    745
  Joseph Jones 745
  Joseph P. 386
  Judith 457
  Judith --- 451, 457
  L. N. (Mrs.) 744
  Lazarus 451, 452,
    453, 454, 456, 457,
    458, 459, 460, 461,
    467, 486, 487
  Lazerus 487
  Leanna 451, 460, 488
  Lemuel 490
  Leona E. 745
  Leroy 458, 459, 461
  Levi Tarlton 744
  Levi Tarlton, Jr. 744
  Louisa 648
  Louise 503
  Lovey 490
  Lucretia 460
  Lucy 467, 493
  Margaret 451, 457,
    458, 486
  Margaret--- 451, 457
  Margaret R. 223
  Margaret Randolph
    223
  Mariam 490
  Mariam White 490
  Martha 455, 635
  Martha Frances 745
  Martha Jane 490
  Martha (Thompson)
    586
  Mary 383, 395, 396,
    451, 456, 457, 485
  Mary Batson 744
  Mary Fogg 467
  Mary Jane 464
  Mary (Vesey) 486
  Mary (Vezey) 456,
    457
  Matilda 473
  Matty 473
  Meredith Fleet 460
  Mildred C. 21
  " Mimy " Gray 473
  Moncure Robinson 223
  Moses 455
  Nancy 451, 467, 473,

Taylor, (cont.)
　Nancy (cont.) 484,
　　485, 490, 664, 744
　" Nancy " 457
　Nancy Danning 744
　Nancy (Downing ?)
　　744
　Nannie 85
　Nim H. 744
　Oliver Perry 745
　Parmenas 458
　Philip Fall 710
　Polly 451, 468, 472,
　　474, 484
　Priscilla 596
　Rebecca Ann 745
　Reuben 753
　Reuben (Capt.) 493
　Richard 368, 386,
　　457
　Richard (Col.) 169,
　　170, 171, 180, 367,
　　384, 385, 386, 404,
　　463
　Richard (General)
　　369
　Richard (Lieut.-
　　Col.) 404
　Richard S. H. 628,
　　629
　Robert 635, 636
　Sadie Bacon Critten-
　　den (Mrs.) 681
　Sallie 744
　Sallie Jane 473
　Sally 21, 401, 451,
　　452, 462, 463, 465,
　　466, 472, 473, 474,
　　480, 481, 484, 744
　Sarah 147, 367, 386,
　　455, 479
　Sarah (Mrs.) 368
　Sarah Ann 744
　Sarah (Bradford) 458
　Sarah C. C. 744
　Sarah Frances 511, 520
　Sarah Strother 463
　Septimus 596
　Septimus (Dr.) 596
　Sharlott Rector 744
　Stevens Mason 223
　Suckey 451, 458
　Sukey 489
　Susan ? 458
　Susan Beverly 223
　Susanna 489
　Susannah 451, 457, 462
　Tarlton 744
　Theodosia (Payne)
　　463, 464, 465, 466
　Therriat 455
　Thomas 414, 417, 451,
　　453, 454, 455, 456,
　　460, 490
　Thomas H. 744
　Togerton R. 254
　Vincent Warren 745
　Virginia 512
　Wick 473
　Wilder ? 460
　Wilder 451, 458 , 462
　Wildey 458, 460, 488
　Willey 458, 460
　William 451, 452, 453,
　　454, 455, 456, 457,
　　458, 459, 460, 461,
　　473, 487, 490

Taylor, (cont.)
　Wm. Dabney 386
　William H. 473
　William R. 744
　William T. 744, 745
　Wm. T., Jr. 744
　Wm. T., Sr. 744
　William Tarlton 744,
　　475
　Winifred 185
　Zach (General) 180
　Zach (President)
　　369
　Zachary 463
　Zachary (General)
　　169, 170, 180, 385
　Zachary (General
　　President) 367
　Zachary, Jr. 386
　Zachary, Sr. 386
Taylour, John 454
Teague, Ivan 529
Teats, Caroline (Mrs.)
　　448
　John P. 442
　Magga B. (Mrs.) 442
Tecumseh 6, 187, 765
Temple, Elizabeth 480
　Lutie 155
　Margaret 5
Templeton, Maggie 161
ter Wimple, Elizabeth
　　633
Terrell, Chiles (Mrs.)
　　538
　Cordelia (Mrs.)
　　537, 537-538
　Elizabeth (Miss)
　　274
　Thos. (Mr.) 538
　Thos. F. 538
Terrill, Della 150
　Edmund (?) 432
　Elizabeth E. 681
Terrune, George Ann
　　Vannuys 722
Terry 505
　Aloah 504
　Alvah L. 501
　Alvah Lamar 515
　Alvah Lamar, Jr. 516
　Bettie 504
　Buford 504
　Elizabeth 515
　Elizabeth Buford
　　Chambers 516
　George W. 515
　Helen 516
　John Loving 516
　Mary 504
　Mary C. 515
　Maude 504
　Maude Baker 516
　Napoleon Buford 516
　William 504, 515
　William (Mrs.) 515
　William, Jr. 515
Tevis, Lloyd 752
　Matilda H. 523
　Robert 584
　Susan Gano Sanders
　　752
Tharp, Ballard Montgom-
　　ery 141
　Graham Ely 142
　Jeptha Montgomery
　　141

Tharp, (cont.)
　Rachel Mayo 142
　William Ely 142
　William Henry 129
Thatcher, Gene Shelly
　　(Mrs.) 481
Thayer, John H. 237
Theobald, F. E. (Mrs.)
　　746
Therriat, Elizabeth 451,
　　455, 456
　William 455
Thomas 669
　--- 255, 666, 674
　Alice 132
　Benjamin 466
　Caroline 398
　Cynthia 591
　Danford (Professor)
　　576
　Edward (Mrs.) 271
　Elizabeth 576, 591
　Elizabeth Poage 93
　Harriet 658
　James 658
　James M. (Captain)
　　263
　Jennie 658
　John 92, 658
　John (Captain) 181
　John Lilburne
　　(Judge) 181
　Lindsay 92
　Lucy Jane 499
　Margaret 658
　Martha Rebecca 658
　Mary Witherspoon 576
　Minnie 66
　Morris 658
　Morris, Jr. 658
　N. E. 301
　Oswald 92
　Pamela 668
　Peter 668
　Richard 251
　Robert 591
　Rodes Burch 576
　Samuel 250
　Sarah 250, 251, 591
　Sarah Burch 576
　Susan M. 649
Thomasson, Elias 499
　Joel 499, 591
　John James (Dr.)
　　499
　Joseph 499
　Mary 499
　Nelson Bartholomew
　　499
　Poindexter 499
　William Poindexter
　　499
Thomerson, A. J. 673
　Rachel 672
Thompson 586, 587, 593
　--- 25, 238, 606
　--- (Colonel) 236
　--- (Miss) 392,
　　402, 403, 413
　Amgt. 256
　Ann 377
　Anthony 590
　Anthony (Capt.)
　　623
　Benjamin 586
　Bertie Irene 536
　Blanche Kelly 65

Thompson, (cont.)
  Carolyne 130
  Cornelia 118
  Dale M. (Mrs.) 482
  Dale Moore 477
  Dorothy Brown 451, 452, 460, 483
  Ed. Porter (Captain) 593
  Elizabeth 256
  Frances 586
  George C. 237, 240, 375
  George T. 516
  Gertrude 131
  Hugh S. 593
  Jeff (Col.) 254
  John 238
  John (Rev.) 377, 587
  Joseph A. 130
  Josephine 130
  Julia 51
  Leticia 87
  Martha 586
  Mary 62, 572
  Mary E. 685
  Mary Neale (Mrs.) 693, 696, 698
  Mathew 591
  Moses D. 119
  Nancy 345
  Nancy A. 356
  Phillip R. 384
  Pres. 86
  Rebecca 716
  Rhodes 263
  Robert Coleman 65
  Roger 586
  Samuel 256
  Sid 86
  Waddy 593
  Waddy (Judge) 593
  William 62, 345, 586
  William Brown 477
  William E. 536
  Wm. F. 384, 411
Thomson 572, 583, 584, 586, 587, 588, 590, 592, 593
  --- 583
  --- (General) 749
  Anderson 589, 591
  Ann 587, 589, 591
  Ann Bibb 584, 589, 590, 591, 592, 754
  Ann Pemberton 592
  Ann Rodes 572, 593
  Ann Waddy 583, 584
  Anthony 584, 589, 590, 591, 592, 754
  Charles 86, 586
  Cynthia 591
  David 587, 588, 589, 590, 591
  David (General) 593, 748
  Eleanor 589, 590, 591
  Eliza 574
  Elizabeth 275, 591, 592, 593
  Elizabeth Anderson 584, 590
  Elvira 748
  Eunice 572, 736
  Frances 589, 748

Thomson, (cont.)
  Frances (Major) 591, 592
  Garland 589
  George 588
  George (Colonel) 588
  Hannah 587
  Henry 592
  Henry Bibb 592
  John 583, 588
  John Thomas 591
  Judith 583, 587, 590, 591, 592
  Katherine 592
  Louisa 591
  Lucy 589
  Margaret 592
  Martha 587
  Mary 584, 587, 590, 591, 592, 593
  Mary Garland 583, 584, 589
  Mary Lewis Cobbs 584
  Maurice 587, 588
  Maurice (Gentleman) 587
  Mildred 590
  Nathaniel 591, 592, 748
  Nelson 583, 584, 589
  Parthenia 591
  Paul 588
  Paulina 591
  Reuben 591
  Richard 592
  Robert 583, 587, 588, 590, 591, 592
  Robert (Major) 588
  Robert Alexander 591
  Robert Thomas 591
  Sally 583
  Samuel 593, 736
  Sarah 591, 592
  Sarah (Thomas) 591
  Stevens 586, 587
  Susanna 589, 590, 592, 754
  Waddy 584, 588, 589, 590, 591, 593
  Washington 591
  William 275, 572, 586, 588, 591, 592, 593, 736
  William (Sir) 586
  Winifred 591
Thorndike, Sarah 76
Thorne, Susan 109
Thornton 97, 602
  Alice Savage 179, 371
  Charles Randolph 161
  Charlotte 160, 166
  David 127, 161, 166
  Davy 158
  Edwin 161
  Edwin Kavanaugh 161, 166
  Eleanor 160, 166
  Elizabeth 159, 160, 166
  Fannie 376, 377, 381
  Francis 179, 370, 371, 372, 377, 380, 398, 413
  Hontas 161, 166
  James 161, 368, 385
  James Simpson 160

Thornton, (cont.)
  James T. 160
  Mabel 161
  Margaret 179, 371, 372, 379, 380, 388, 390, 391, 398, 413
  Mary 160
  Mary Anderson 157
  Mary Eleanor 158
  Minnie 160
  Prudence 96
  Robert A. 387
  Sallie 125, 127
  Sarah 536
  Stanley 161
  Susan Catharine 156, 166
  Thomas F. 156, 165
  Wilbur Hobbs 161
  Wm. 388
  Woodford Railey 161, 166
  Woodson Stanley 161
Thorp, --- 604
Thrall, John 363
Threshley, Juliet 544
  S. (Major) 538
Thrift, --- 466
Thro, Emma 130
Throckmorton 135, 492
  Elizabeth 493
  Frances 493
  Gabriel 492
  George (Sir) 492
  John 492, 493
  John (Sir) 492
  Lucy 492, 493
  Mary 492, 493
  Mordica 492, 493
  Robert 492, 493
  Robert (Col.) 493
  Robert (Right Hon.) 492
  Robert (Major) 493
  Robert (Sir) 492
  Sarah 493
  Thomas 492, 493
  Warner 493
Thurman, Lucy 515
Thurmond, Dicey 309
  Nancy 309
Thurston 580, 587, 679
  --- (Dr.) 594
  Edmund Plummer 703
  Elizabeth 580
  Ezekiel 580, 594
  Harvey 580
  John 580
  Louisiana 580
  Lucinda 580
  Lucinda E. 594, 703
  Lucinda Elizabeth 581, 703
  Maria 703, 704
  Maria L. 703
  Maria L. M. 709
  Maria Louise 581, 585
  Maria Louise Miller 594, 703
  Maria Searcy 581, 594
  Mary 580
  Mary Plummer 703
  Mary Talbot 580, 594
  Paulina 580
  Plummer 580, 594
  Robert 580, 594, 703, 704

855

Thurston, (cont.)
  Robert (Capt.) 580
  Robert (Dr.) 580,
    581, 594
  Seth 580
  Walker 594
Thwaites, --- 772
Tibbals, F. E. (Mrs.)
  746
Tibbs, Foushee 460
Tichenor, Charles 705
  Nannie P. (Mrs.)
    704
✓ Tilford, Elizabeth
  Crumbaugh 65
  James 768
  John 65
  Lilly 736
  Lily J. 573
  Maria 65, 68
Tilghman, Richard 225
Tillman, --- (Captain)
  525
Tillou, Katherine Vig-
  neau 78
Timberlake, M. 254
  Margaret 226
Tobin, Michael 488
Todd, --- 763
  --- (Colonel) 773
  --- (Judge) 542
  A. T. 249
  Alexander 248, 249
  Alexander Rennick 247
  Alexander Thomas 247
  Alice 249, 630
  Alisonia 247
  Anna Marie 326
  Anne Maria 247
  Charles (Mr.) 542
  Elizabeth P. 326
  Frances 326
  Frank (Lieutenant)
    248
  Gusta Ann 708, 731
  Hannah 325, 326
  James (Mrs.) 542
  James M. 248, 249
  James Madison 247
  James Madison, Jr.
    249
  Jane (Briggs) 325
  Letitia 247
  Letitia Lee 247
  Lettie Lee 248
  Levi 424
  Levi (General) 325
  Lillian 249
  Louis Franklin 247,
    248
  Lucy Payne 247
  M. W. 248
  Mary 326, 752
  Mary Lee 247
  Mary Willis 248
  Minnie 407
  Nettie 249
  Robert 287, 752
  Robert Smith 326
  T. J. 248
  Thomas (Judge) 542
  Thomas J. 247, 248
  Thomas Jay 247
  William Johnston 247
  William M. (Mr.)
    248
  William M., Jr. 248

Todd, (cont.)
  William Montague 247
  Willie 248
Toler 349
Toliver 356
  Hampton 356
Tolle, Sam 672
Tomlin, Stephen 456
Tompkins, Annie Eliza-
  beth 70
  Emma 70
  G. M. 422
  George Stuart 70
  Guinn 424
  Joseph 70
  Joseph Tate 69
  Julia 70
  Lucy 69
  Ophelia 69
  Samuel 69
  Sarah 69
Tomson 586
Toulmin, Lucy 689
Towels, Mary L. 696
Towles, Elizabeth Ann
  696
  Mary F. 696
  Mary Frances 696
  Mary Littlepage 696
  Price Curd 696
  Rawleigh D. 696
Townley, Lawrence 493
Trabo 495
Trabu 495
Trabue 494, 495, 499,
  501, 502, 503, 504,
  505, 506, 517, 520,
  573, 584, 749, 751
  --- 511, 514
  --- (Mr.) 520
  --- Phoebe 499
  A. E. (Mr.) 507
  Aaron 512, 516, 517
  Alice 500, 505
  Alice E. 520
  Alice Elizabeth 512
  Ann 515
  Ann Elizabeth 512
  Annie B. 517
  Anthony 495, 504,
    507, 508, 517, 751
  Anthony (Sieur)
    507
  Anthony, Jr. 496, 508
  Anthony E. (Mr.)
    507
  Anthony Edw. Dupuy
    516
  Antoine 494, 495,
    499, 505, 507, 749,
    751
  Ben (Dr.) 504
  Benjamin Franklin
    (M. D.) 515
  Benjamin McDowell
    517
  Benjamin McDowell
    (M. D.) 517
  Buford 516
  Caroline 495, 496
  Charles 517
  Charles C. 504
  Charles Clay 516
  Charles Henry Clay
    516
  Chastain 751

Trabue, (cont.)
  Chastain Haskins 511,
    517
  Clark 496
  Corinna 514
  Cynthia 516
  Cynthia Ann 516
  Daniel 500, 501, 510,
    511, 514, 518
  Daniel, Jr. 514
  E. F. 511
  Edmund 500
  Edmund F. 517
  Edmund Francis 511,
    520
  Edw. 511
  Edward 500, 501, 502,
    504, 508, 510, 515,
    516, 517, 751
  Edward Haskins 513,
    517
  Eliza 515
  Elizabeth 500, 502,
    504, 510, 511, 515,
    516, 517, 518, 751
  Elizabeth Ann 517
  Elizabeth Burns 517
  Elizabeth Dupuy 516
  Elizabeth Haskins 500
  Elizabeth Mary 516
  Ellen 515
  Emily 517
  Etta H. 517
  Fannie 504
  Frances 515, 517
  George 502, 504, 515
  George W. 504, 516
  George Washington 515
  George Washington, Jr.
    516
  Hannah J. 517
  Harriet Olympia 517
  Haskins D. 517
  Helen 504
  Helen M. 517
  Henrietta Jane 512
  Henry Joseph (M. D.)
    512
  Horace 517
  Isaac Haskins 512
  Isaac Hodgens 512
  Jacob 495, 496, 508,
    751
  James 499, 501, 511,
    514, 515, 517, 518,
    751
  James (Mr.) 500
  James Upton 500
  James Woods Walker 516
  Jane 499, 510, 512
  Jane Clay (Mrs.)
    504
  Jane E. 516
  Jane Woods Clay 516
  Jean 510
  John 495, 496, 499,
    501, 510, 512, 514,
    515
  John E. (M. D.)
    516
  John George Washington
    516
  John James 495, 496,
    497, 499, 501, 508,
    510, 511, 517, 751
  Joseph 504
  Joseph B. 515

Trabue, (cont.)
  Joseph Thomas Crutcher 516
  Judelle 512
  Judith 495, 496, 500, 508, 510, 511, 514, 517, 748, 757
  Judith Helen 512, 515
  Laura Alice 513, 517
  Leatitia 515
  Leroy P. (M. D.) 517
  Lillie 504
  Little 500
  Lucinda 500
  Lucinda Cochran 511
  Lucy Ellen 513, 517
  Macon (Mr.) 507
  Magdalen 499, 573, 751
  Magdalene 495, 496
  Magdalene Prodhomme Verrueil 495
  Magdelaine 508
  Magdelaine (Flournoy) 507-508
  Magdelene 512
  Magdelene Prodhomme 495
  Magdeline 510
  Marie --- 496, 508
  Marion Frances 512
  Marion South 511
  Martha 500, 510, 515, 516, 517, 520
  Martha Ann Sommerville 516
  Martha Haskins 502
  Martha (Patsy) 515
  Martha T. 512
  Mary 500, 502, 510, 511, 514, 515
  Matilda Jane 513, 517
  Matilda O. 516
  Mattie 504
  Mattie Y. 517
  Nancy 502, 503, 513
  Nancy H. 503
  Nancy Haskins 502, 515
  Nancy Lucretia 513, 517
  Nellie E. 516
  Olimpe 510
  Olympe 510, 517
  Olympe duPuy 508
  Olymphia Dupuy 503, 504
  Olympia 515
  Patsy 515
  Phoebe 500, 512
  Pierre 494
  Pierre (Messener) 495
  Presley 515
  Prince Edw. 516
  Rebecca 516
  Richard 500, 514
  Robert 511, 515
  Robert Berry 511, 520
  Robert P. (Col.) 515
  Robert Paxton (Col.) 514
  Robert Wood Howell 516
  S. F. J. 519

Trabue, (cont.)
  Sallie 514, 515
  Samuel 500, 510, 517
  Sarah 514
  Sarah Elizabeth 516
  Stephen 500, 501, 510, 513, 516, 751
  Stephen F. J. 751
  Stephen Fitz- James 500, 511, 517, 518, 520
  Stephen Fitz- James, Jr. 511, 520
  Stephen Fitz- James, 3rd 511
  Susan 500, 516
  Susanna 510, 517, 520, 748
  Trabue ? 500
  Virginia Taylor 511
  Willett 500
  Willett C. 511, 520
  William 499, 500, 501, 510, 513, 514, 515, 517
  William Berry 511, 520
  William Chastain 512
  William Dunn 516
  William H. 517
Tracy 74, 80
  Abigail 730
  Abigail Parsons 730
  Alfred Ripley 80
  Augustus Early 80
  Charles F. 57, 74, 81
  Charles Frederick 80
  Deborah Thomas 80
  Edward 57, 74, 80, 81
  Edward F. 57, 74, 81
  Edward Nelson 57, 80, 81
  Elijah 730
  Elijah F. 728, 730
  Elijah Fitch 730
  Eliza Ripley 80
  Elizabeth Beck 730
  Elizabeth Fitch 730
  Frederick (Capt.) 80
  Henry Nelson 80
  Joan Morgan 730
  John Nelson 57, 74, 80, 81
  John Parsons 728, 730
  Lois H. 728
  Lois Smith 730
  Mary Elizabeth 730
  William 346
  William Thomas 80
Travers 573
  Elizabeth 574
  Million 574
  Raleigh (Colonel) 574
  William 76
Travis, --- (Mr.) 68
  Mary E. 528
  Rine 692
Treanor, Lorena 530
Triangel, --- (Lord of) 550
Tribble 521, 523
  --- 522, 523
  --- (Mr.) 521, 522
  Andrew 521, 522, 523, 524

Tribble, (cont.)
  Andrew (Rev.) 521, 522, 523
  Dudley 523
  Frances Tandy 522
  George 521, 523
  John (General) 523
  Martha (Patsy) 523
  Mary 523
  Nancy 523
  Patsy 523
  Peter Burris 522, 523
  Sally B. 523
  Samuel 523
  Sarah Ann 522
  Sarah Ann Burris 522
  Silas 523
  Thomas 523
Trimbell, Jon 302
Trimble, --- (Judge) 408
Triplett, George W. 471
  Ophelia 471, 472
  Ophy 472
  Rebecca Wagner 471
  Thomas 471
Trist, H. B. (Dr.) 221
  Martha Jefferson 221
  N. P. 221
  Thomas Jefferson 221
Trousdale, Mary 311
Troutman, Ora 649
  Ray 652
  Vergil (Mrs.) 648
True, Iva 130
Trueheart, William 115
Truman, Richard 654
  Rich'd. 653
Trumbo 679, 707, 756
  A. L. 707
  Adam 707
  Adam A. 707, 708
  Adam L. 707
  Andrew 707
  Betsy 707
  Clay 707
  Deborah 707
  Doratha 707
  Elizabeth 707
  Ella Lee 707
  Frank 707
  Hannah 707
  Hannah S. 708
  Henry Whitney 707
  Isaac 707
  J. A. 707
  Jacob A. 707
  Jake 707
  Jake A. 707
  James B. 707
  James F. 707
  Jimmy 707
  John 707, 708
  John A. 707
  Lucy E. 707
  Lucy J. 707
  Maggie L. 707
  Margaret 707
  Mary E. 707
  Nancy 707
  Nannie 707
  Rachel 707
  Ruthann 707
  Sallie A. 707
  Sarah 707
  Sarah (Mrs.) 708

Trabue, (cont.)
  Sarah Eliz. 707
Tubbs, Caroline 68
Tuck, Richard 350
Tucker, 389
  --- (Mrs. Colonel)
    43
  Amanda 35
  Jane 115, 116
  Mary 653
  Robert J. 603
  Sallie 166
  Sarah 157
  Sue 306
  Thomas J. 306
  William (Captain)
    587-588
Tull, John 625
  Joshua 623
Tune, --- 443
  --- (Dr.) 443
Turberville, --- 465
  George 465
Turner 525, 527, 531,
    532, 533, 534
  --- 528, 532, 533
  --- (Mr.) 83
  Andrew 532
  Anna 149, 160, 532
  Anna Martin 535
  Annie L. 530
  Barnett 532
  Barton 527
  Bettie 529
  Caroline Ringo 531
  Carrie 529
  Catherine 532
  Charity 532
  Charles 526
  Charles Edwin 160
  Charlotte 159
  Clara 526
  Cornelius 532
  E. R. (Dr.) 531
  Eda Ruth 529
  Edward 525, 526, 532,
    532-533, 533
  Edward, Sr. 532, 533
  Edwin Thornton 160
  Eleanor 526
  Eleanor Jane 532
  Elizabeth 84, 525,
    526, 530, 533, 534
  Ella Steele 160
  Elleander 533
  Fannie 160
  Fountain 532, 533,
    534
  Frank Laytham 530
  Franklin 530
  Fulton 529
  George 529
  George A. 535
  George Campbell 529
  George R. 529, 530
  Harry McDougal 160
  Hassell 530
  Helen 530
  Henry 529
  Hontas Virginia 160
  Irine 530
  James 530, 532
  James Polk 529
  Jane 527
  Jarrett 535
  Jesse 532
  John 525, 526, 532,

Turner, (cont.)
  John, (cont.) 533
  John Coblin 529, 530
  Jonathan 532
  Joseph 526, 530
  Joseph B. 528
  Joseph Burch 527, 528,
    529, 531
  Joseph Chester 529
  Joseph Samuel 528,
    529
  Joshua 526, 527, 528,
    529
  Jozie Mae 529
  Lena 529
  Leonard 529
  Lester 160, 530
  Lester N. 160
  Louis E. 87
  Lydia 526
  Maria Anna 535, 536
  Martha 528, 529
  Martha Ann Jones 529
  Martha Jane 527
  Martin 533, 534, 535
  Martin Samuel 536
  Mary 526, 527, 529,
    533
  Mary --- 525
  Mary Ann 526, 527,
    528
  Mary E. 535
  Mary Elizabeth 529,
    530, 535
  Mary Logan 160, 166
  Mary Lula 529
  Mieba 525
  Mildred 532
  Mildred A. 535
  Minnie 529
  Nancy 533
  Nancy --- 533
  Nellie 526, 533
  Nelly 526
  Notley 527
  Oliver S. 535
  Orva 530
  Patria Ballard 529
  Patsy 526
  Patterson 532
  Phillip 532
  Polly 527, 533
  Randal 526
  Randolph 526
  Robert 657
  Robert Lee 530
  Ruth 525
  Sallie 533
  Sally 526
  Samuel 525, 526, 527,
    533, 534, 535
  Samuel, Jr. 527
  Samuel Dallas 536
  Sarah 532, 533
  Sarah Olive 529, 530
  Sarah Virginia 535
  Susan Jane 536
  Susannah 526
  Talton 532
  Theodocia 87
  Theodosia 84
  Thomas 525, 532, 533,
    534, 535
  Thomas Duncan 536
  Thomas Jefferson 529
  Thomas Samuel 527
  Ulysses 159, 166

Turner, (cont.)
  Ulysses, Jr. 160
  Vincent 533
  Virginia 530
  Wahala Clement 536
  Wanda Thelma 536
  William 526, 529,
    532
  William Jones 528,
    529
Turney, --- (Miss) 49
  Rebecca 693
Turpin, Mary 627
  Rufus Edgar 129
Tussell, Ellen 472
Twyman 679, 708, 730
  Buford 125
  David Lewis 708
  David R. 708
  Elizabeth W. 708
  Elizabeth Watts 708
  Ezza Railey 125
  Franky A. 708
  Franky Ann 708
  George Allin 708
  Gusta Ann 730, 731
  Henry Linzy 730
  John D. 687, 708
  John G. 708, 730,
    731
  John Garrett 708
  Kelly Jay 730, 731
  Lona May 731
  Lony May 730
  Lucy R. 708
  Martha A. 708
  Mary W. 731
  Matilda 708
  Pleasant H. 688, 708
  Sarah Ann 708
Tyler 179, 373
  --- 405, 460, 489,
    618, 636
  --- (President)
    383, 405, 586,
    685
  Alice Strother 374
  Anne 374
  Charles, Jr. 481
  Frances (Mrs.) 36
  Francis 373, 378
  H. 620, 621
  Henry 373, 374
  John 374
  Lee 530
  Mary 374
  Thos. G. Strother
    373
  Walter 636
  Watt the 636
Tyndale, --- 259
Uchtred 26
Upcher 537
  Abel 537, 538
  Arthur 537, 538
  John 537
  Thos. T. 538
  William 537
Upshaw 537, 539
  Cordelia 538
  Edwin 538
  Hannah 538
  Horace 538
  John 537, 538
  Lucy 538, 544
  Maria 538, 541
  Sally 538

858

Upshaw, (cont.)
　William 538
　William (Dr.) 538
Upsher 537
Upshur 537
　Thos. G. 537
Ushur, Edward 328
　Margaret 328
Usselton, John 336
　Sally 336
Utter, J. W. 575
Valentine, Sarah 490
Van Aerssen, Emerentia 550
　Jacques 550
Van Arsdale (See also Vanarsdale) 721
Van Beest 549
　Anneken 549
　Gertje 549
Van Beeste, Otto 550
Van Boxmeer, --- 550
Van Buren, Martin (President) 651
Van Buskirk 56, 69, 71, 73, 75, 81, 82
　--- 81
　Charlotte 56, 81
　Cornelius 56, 71, 73, 77, 81
　Emmeline 56, 75, 77, 81
　John 81
　Mary 56, 71, 81
　Nelson 54
　Ophelia 56, 69, 71, 81, 82
Van Buuren, --- (Count) 549
Van Cleef, Neltje 553
Van Cruick Van Meteren, Cornelia 550
Van Cuick Van Meteren 547
　Hendrix 549
　Jan 550
　Johan (Captain) 550
　Johanna 549
　John 549
　John (Captain) 549
　Josina (Lady) 550
　Willem 549
Van Culin, DuPuy 516
　Lillian Dupuy 516
　Samuel (Mr.) 504
　Samuel Ware 516
　Trabue 516
　William Townsend 516
Van De Graphe, Eliza Jane (Brooks) 680
Van der Vecken, Marie 550
Van Dyke, James 726
Van Haeften, Otto 549, 550
Van Herinjnen, Jutten 550
Van Houten, Jr. du Bois. 549
Van Inbrock, Gysbert (Dr.) 555
Van Mator, John 557
Van Meter 553, 558, 560, 565
　--- 566
　Abram 565, 566
　Amelia Ellen 566
　Ann 563, 564

Van Meter (cont.)
　Anna Rebecca 565, 566
　Annette 566
　Benjamin 565, 566
　Benjamin F. 565
　Benjamin F. (Dr.) 566
　Benjamin Franklin 566
　Catherine 563
　Charles L. 565
　Edwin 565
　Eliza Caroline 565, 566
　Elizabeth 559
　Elizabeth K. 566
　Emma 566
　Evaline B. 566
　Everitt 566
　Fannie 565
　Frank B. M. 566
　Garret 563
　Garrett 563
　Hannah 564
　Hendrick 559
　Henry 559, 563
　Hilda 563
　Isaac 559, 561, 562, 563, 564, 565, 566
　J. Brown 565
　Jacob 563, 565
　Jacob (Colonel) 564
　Jan 559
　Jan Gysbertsen 553
　Jessie 565
　John 559, 562
　John D. 566
　Jonas K. 566
　Joost Jan 559
　Joseph 566
　Kate 566
　Leta Mary 566
　Louis M. 565
　Louis Marshall 565
　Louis Marshall (Lieut.) 566
　Louis Marshall, Jr. 566
　Lucy 565
　Lysbeth 559
　Maria B. 566
　Martha Prewitt 39
　Mary 559
　Mary Belle 566
　Nannie 566
　Nelson Prewitt 565
　Rebecca 559, 563, 564
　Sallie 565
　Sallie M. 566
　Sarah 563
　Sarah Ann 565, 566
　Scott 565
　Solomon 564, 565
　Susan 564
　Susan Tabitha 565, 566
　T. W. L. 24
　Tabitha 564
　Thomas C. 565, 566
　Thomas M. 566
　Thomas Matthew 566
　Thomas Wright Lewis 566
　Walter M. 566
Van Metere 547

Van Metere, (cont.)
　Aert 549
　Jasper 549
　John Cuick 549
　Willem 549
Van Meteren 546, 547, 548, 551, 552, 553
　--- 550, 551
　Adriaan 549, 550
　Anna 549
　Anneken 549
　Arnt 550
　Balthaser 549
　Barbara 549
　Cathrin 554, 558
　Cornelia 549
　Cornelius 549, 550, 551
　Diske 550
　Emanuel 552
　Emanuuel 552
　Emmanuel 550, 551, 552, 555
　Geertje 554
　Geertje Crom 556
　Geertye 557
　Geertze 557
　Gertruida 549
　Gertyje 549
　Girty Jans 556
　Goosen 550
　Gysbert 550, 554, 557
　Hendrix 558
　Isaac 558
　Jacob 550, 551, 552
　Jan 549, 550, 554, 555, 556, 558
　Jan Joost 553, 554
　Jan Joosten 552, 554, 555, 556, 557, 558
　Jasper 549
　Joan 549
　Johan 549, 550
　Johan (Captain) 549
　Johann 549, 550
　Johanna 549
　Joost Jan 559
　Joost Jans 558
　Joost Janse 558
　Jooste 557
　Jooste Jans 554, 555, 557
　Jr. Jasper 549
　Krine Jansen 554
　Kryn Jansen 554
　Lysbeth 554, 557, 558
　Macyken 556
　Marie 549
　Marie Barbara 549
　Maximilliaen 550
　Melchoir 549, 550
　Rebekka 558
　Roelof 549
　Waalberg 550
　Willem 550
Van Meteren Van Cuick, --- 550
　Goosen 549
　Jooste ? 549
Van Meteren Van Meteren, William 549
Van Metre 546, 552, 553, 559, 560, 562
　--- 561
　Hannah 562
　Henry 562

859

Van Metre, (cont.)
  Isaac 546, 559, 560,
    562, 563
  Isaac, Jr. 560
  John 559, 560, 561,
    562
  Sarah 560, 562
Van Nest, Cornelius 720
Van Neste, Joris 557
Van Nuyce 720
  Cornelius 720, 721
  Flora 721
  Mary 720, 721
Van Nuyse, Mary 721
Van Pelt 632
  --- 632
Van Sickle, Martha 336
Van Swearengen, Thomas
  466
Van Winkle, Rip 476
Van Zant, Amelia 677
  Joe 677
Vanarsdale, (See also
    Van Arsdale)
  Harriet Ann 722
  Simon 722
Vanarsdalen, Alexander
  722
  Cornelius 722
  Jan 721
  Marya 722
  Simon Johnson 721
  Symon Janson 721
  William Smith 722
Vanarsdall (VanArsdall)
  Charles Suydam 722
  Ormand 722
  R. S. 722
  R. S. (Mayor) 721
  Riker Samuel (Mayor)
    722
Vanarsdell (VanArsdell)
  722
  Anna 722
  Elizabeth 722
  Elizabeth Jane 722
  Harriet Ann 722
  Louis (Mrs.) 722
  Martha Ann 722
  Mary C. 722
  Mary Catherine 722
  Simon 722
  William Bunton 722
Vance, --- (Mr.) 625
  Benj. (Mrs.) 544
  Maude 134
  Sallie (Miss) 84
  Samuel 333
Vandegraff, Abraham S.
  280
  Wm. (Governor) 280
Vander Vliet, Dirck
    Jansen 73
  Hendrica Jansen 73
Vanderbilt, Anne
    man Sands Ruther-
    ford 76
  William Kissam, Sr.
    76
Vandike, Fanny 717
  Henry 717
  Henry N. 717
Vardaman, Annie 315
Vardeman 313
  Ann 311
  Eliza Emily 311
  Elizabeth 311

Vardeman, (cont.)
  Jane 311
  Jeremiah 311, 313
  John Christopher 313
  John T. 311
  Martha 311
  Mary 311
  Morgan 311, 312, 313
  Patsy 311
  Polly 311, 313
  William 311, 313
Varnon, Maria W. 658
Varry, Helen M. 141
Vaughan 750, 754
  Edmund 592, 754
  Edmund, Sr. 754
  James 395, 592
  Mary 742
  Mary Ann 592
  William 514, 592
Vaughn, Jas. 754
  John 57, 80
  Mary 754
  Nancy 57
Vaux, Katherine 492
  Nicholas (Lord) 492
Venable 114, 116, 135,
  567
  Abraham 567, 568, 654
  Abraham B. (Hon.)
    114
  Abraham N. (Hon.)
    115
  Abram 419, 654
  Agnes 568, 654
  Ann 568, 569
  Betty 654
  Caroline 567
  Chas. 568
  David Glass 568
  Dorathea 568
  Eliz. Hill 567
  Eliza 568, 569, 654
  Eliza. 569
  Eliza Woodson 654
  Elizabeth Cowan 568
  Elizabeth McRoberts
    567
  Frances 569
  Geo. 567
  Hampden 567
  Hugh Lewis 568
  Jacob 567
  James 567, 568
  Jane 569
  John 567, 568, 569
  John C. 568
  John Cowan 568
  Jos. 654
  Joseph 567
  Joseph (Dr.) 594
  Joseph Glass 568
  Josiah 567
  Judith 568
  Lucy 567, 569
  Martha 567, 568, 569,
    654
  Martha Davis 654
  Mary 567, 568, 569
  Mary Eliza 568
  N. 654
  Nancy 568
  Nathaniel 567, 568,
    569, 654
  Rich'd. M. 654
  Robt. 568
  Sam'l. 567, 568

Venable, (cont.)
  Sam'l. (Col.) 654
  Samuel W. 654
  Sarah 568
  Sarah Steele 568
  Thos. 654
  William 567, 569, 654
  Wm. H. 568
  William Thompson 568
Verhers, --- 749
Vermeil, Moyse 508
Vernon, --- 534
Verreuil, Moses 751
Verreuit, Magdalen
    Prodhom 751
Verrueil, Magdalen 573
  Magdalene 495
  Moise 495
  Moses 495
Verry, Sarah Ann 142
Vertiers. --- 495
Vertner, Daniel 84
  John D. 84
Very, Mary A. 493
Vese 452, 456
Vesey 452, 456
  Ann 451
  George 452
  Mary 451, 452, 453,
    486
Vezey 452, 456
  Ann 455, 456
  George 455, 456
  Joan 455, 456
  Mary 456, 458
  Thomas 456
Vezy 452
Vickery, William 333
Viele, --- (Gen.) 412
  Emily 412
Viley 570, 735, 737
  --- 575, 736
  Albina 575
  Albina D. 737, 738
  Aletha 737
  Alethia 576
  Andrew Jackson 571,
    575
  Ann E. 573, 574
  Ann Eliza 736
  Betsy Flournoy 575
  Breckinridge 572,
    574
  Catherine 575
  Charles Morehead 575
  Cyrene 576, 577, 578,
    737
  Edward 575
  Elizabeth 572, 575,
    576, 577, 737
  Elizabeth Marian 738
  Elizabeth Marion 738
  Fannie P. 575
  George 570, 572, 575,
    576, 578, 736, 737
  George, Jr. 738
  George, Sr. 738
  George W. 574, 575,
    737, 738
  Henrietta 570, 578
  Horatio 578, 737,
    738
  James S. 738
  John 576, 577, 737
  John M. 737, 738
  John Milton 738
  Jno. Rodes 575

Viley, (cont.)
　John Rodes (Major) 574
　John T. 575
　John Warren 574
　Keen 576
　Leland 575
　Logan 576
　Lydia 575
　Lydia May 574
　Lydia Smith 571
　Maria 575, 577
　Martha 576, 738
　Martha A. 574
　Martha A. Janes 572
　Martha Ann Janes 570
　Martha J. 574
　Marthan 737
　Martinette 496, 574
　Mary 575
　Mary A. 575
　Mary Breckinridge 575
　Mary E. 738
　Matilda 578
　Meriah 737
　Metilda 737
　Milton 575
　Polly 737, 738
　Prislla L. 738
　Sallie 575
　Sallie H. 575
　Samuel 575, 576, 737, 738
　Stoddard J. 574
　Warren 496, 571, 572, 573, 574, 575, 576, 737, 738
　Willa 575, 576, 736
　Willa (Capt.) 571
　Willa J. 572
　Willa Janes 572
　Willa S. 575
　William J. 737
Vincennes, --- 563
Vinson, --- 440
　Cumfort 444
　Eli 444
　Elijah 440
　Georg 440
　George 440
　John 440
　Sally 440
　Susanna A. 444
　William 440
Virden, James 670
Voires, Emmett 527
　James 527
　Jefferson 528
　Nathaniel 528
　Willard 528
　William 527
Von Fisher, --- (Baron) 271
Von Schilling, Cecilia 72
　Ernest (Baron) 72
　Ernst John72
　Nicholas 72
Voorhies, George 752
　Laura E. Sanders 752
Vories, Eliza 527
　Martha 527
　W. L. (Dr.) 529
Waddell, Addison (Dr.) 325
　Cornelia St. Clair 325

Waddell, (cont.)
　Joseph A. 565
Waddells, --- 62
Waddleton 610
Waddy 580, 581, 582, 583, 586, 587, 588, 593, 679
　--- (Captain) 583
　Adoline 709
　Adromache 583
　Albert Samuel 709
　Amanda M. 585, 709
　Amanda Malvina 709
　Ann 583, 584, 589
　Ann J. 584
　Anthony 582, 583
　Cecil Clendenin 581
　Elizabeth 486, 581, 582, 583, 710
　Frances 582, 583
　Frances E. 585
　Frances Eliza 709
　Garland 583
　George William 581, 709
　George William Thurston 703
　Jane 582
　Jane Cobbs 584, 589
　John 486, 582, 583, 584. 589
　Joseph Owen 709
　Judith 582
　Katie Nash 581
　Lucinda Ida 703, 704, 709
　Lucy 583
　M. L. 703, 709
　Maria 703
　Maria Louise 581, 703, 709
　Maria Louise Miller 703
　Maria Louise Thurston 581
　Mary 581, 582, 583
　Mary Lewis 585, 709
　Mary P. 583
　Mildred 582, 583
　Nancy 709
　Nelson 583
　Noble 581
　Owen 583
　Patsy Harris 583
　Robert Burns 583
　Robert Samuel 581, 703
　Sally 583
　Sally Thomson 583
　Samuel 581, 582, 583, 584, 587, 589, 592, 708, 709
　Samuel (Capt.) 583
　Sarah 582, 583
　Sarah A. 585
　Sarah Adaline 709
　Susan M. 585, 709
　Susan Mildred 709
　Thomas 486
　Thomas Miller 709
　Thomson M. 581
　Thomson Miller 581, 703, 704
　Thurston 581
　W. L. 703, 709
　William 583
　William L. 703

Waddy, (cont.)
　William Landon 581
　William Lewis 581, 585, 594, 703, 709
Wade 179
　--- (Mr.) 401
　James 405
　Jonas 82
　Martha Sawtell 71
　Mary 170, 381, 382, 383, 393, 405, 407
　Mary T. 516
　Mary Willis 405
　Norman Sawtell 71
　Phebe 82
　Phoebe 78
　Ralph B. 71
Waffendall, Mary 372
Waggoner, Elizabeth Green 512
　Lucy 515
Wagner, Marie Ann 359
　Nellie 143
Wahking, --- (Mrs.) 725, 726
　Charles A. (Mrs.) 725, 726
Wainscot, Dicie 250
Wait, Lois 728
Wake, Frank 66
　Russell 66
Wakefield, James 756
　James Marcus 711
　William Daniel 711
Walcott, Anna 39
Walcutt 756
Walhn, Judith Ann 137
　Parham 137
Walke, Anthony 231
　Anthony (Rev.) 231
Walker 357, 603
　--- 390
　--- (Dr.) 321
　Alexander 320, 323
　Allen J. 123, 144
　Allen K. 123
　Allen Kendrick 144
　Charles 348, 357
　Edna M. 123, 144
　Eleanor 348, 357
　Elizabeth 164, 323, 324
　Frank Kendrick 123, 144 144
　Hallie N. 123, 144
　J. Brisben 412
　James 320, 323, 614
　James (Capt.) 323
　James (Dr.) 613
　Jane Hammer 323
　Jane Hummer 323
　Jean 323
　John 320, 323, 324, 376
　John B. 367
　John Brisban 396
　John Brislan (Gen.) 390
　Joseph 703
　Joseph Welch 581, 703
　Judith 534
　Julia E. 123, 144
　Louise Norwood (Mrs.) 686
　Margaret (Hutson) 324

Walker, (cont.)
  Margaret (Kelso) 324
  Mary 323, 324
  Mary (Culton) 324
  Mary Eleanor Searcy 581
  Mary Ellenor 703
  Minnie N. 123, 144
  Samuel 320
  Sophia Bailer 703
  Stephen 534
  Susanna 614
  William 324, 357
Wall 595
  --- (Miss) 254
  J. Sutton 595
  John 595
  John (Captain) 595, 596
  Mary Taylor 596
  William K. (Judge) 596
Wallace, --- 8, 405
  Albert 45, 46
  Albert H. 45
  Alfred Henry 47
  Alfred Henry, Jr. 47
  Alfred Honer 46
  Alfred Horner 46
  Andrew 134
  Andrew (Mrs.) 137
  Arthur McG. 46
  Bessie Beazley 47
  Henry Dade 46, 47
  Henry Dade, Jr. 47
  Howeson Hooe 47
  Howson Hoe (M. D.) 46
  John W. 46
  John Whitlock 47
  Julia Hume 46
  Julia McGaughey 46
  Kate Macrae 47
  Lucy Whitlock 46
  Margaret Campbell 47
  Maria Withrow 46
  Mary Amos 47
  Mary Wharton 47
  Nell (Miss) 47
  Nell Kenton 46
  Robert 745
  Robert McG. 46
  Sara Clarke 47
  Thos. H. 46
  Wilbur 131
  William 757
  William S. (Dr.) 326
Waller, Ann 416
  Edward 416
  Henry 85
  William 416
  Winifred 251
Wallingford, David (Lieut.) 69, 79
  Elizabeth Leeman 69
  Martha 69, 79
Wallingsford, Hiram 84
Wallington, (See del Wallington)
Wallis, Oliver 382
Walshes, --- (Professor) 443
Walter, Booker 419
Walthall, 502
Walton, --- (Mrs.) 761

Walton, Laura Kinkead 757
Ward 571, 597, 598, 602, 603, 669
  --- 604, 605, 606
  --- (Capt.) 607
  --- (Col.) 409
  --- (Major) 603, 604
  --- (Mr.) 600, 601, 605
  --- (Mrs.) 601, 602
  A. Harry (Hon.) 598
  Alice 600
  Andrew 597, 598
  Anna Davis 164
  Annie 607
  Benjamin 598-599, 599, 600
  Benjamin, Jr. 233
  Channing Moore 601, 607
  Charles Blincoe 600, 607
  Charlotte Warner 607
  Cornelia Channing 607
  Daniel French 411
  David A. 664
  Edmond 599
  Edmonia Kerr 600
  Edmund 600
  Edward 164, 604, 605
  Edward Greene 603
  Edward Greene (Captain) 607
  Edward L. 607
  Edwin (Mr.) 598
  Elizabeth 578, 597
  Estelle 600
  Evelyn Douglas 600
  Fanny 600
  Florence Landon 600
  George 597, 598
  George E. 607
  George Edward 599
  George Edward (Major) 603
  George Viley 577, 578
  Georgiana 599, 600
  Henry Tayloe 600, 607
  Hugh Campbell 605, 607
  James 577, 604, 605, 658
  James (Capt.) 598
  James Hervey 658
  James Pegram 599, 600
  James T. 603
  Jennie Daniel (Mrs.) 605
  John 411, 597, 607, 663
  John (Dr.) 598
  John Edmund 605, 607
  Joseph 598
  Josephine 603
  Judith 438
  Junius 577, 578, 597
  Logan 164
  Logan Railey 164
  Lucy E. 599
  Lucy Randolph 600
  Malvina 597
  Maria 233, 599, 600
  Martha 578, 599, 600
  Martha Jane 658

Ward, (cont.)
  Martha Norvell 600
  Martha Wright 659
  Mary 599, 603, 663, 664
  Mary F. 605
  Mary Goode 599
  Mary Margaret 658
  Mary Virginia 600
  Mathew 598
  Matilda 600
  Mildred 407
  Nancy Edmonia 599
  Naomi Ruth 658
  Nathaniel (Rev.) 260
  Paulina Jane 600
  Polly 597
  Quincy (Judge) 598
  Randolph Goode 601, 607
  Rebecca 658
  Robert J. 597, 598
  Roberta 164
  Ruth 658
  Sallie 597
  Sally 598
  Sally Johnson 578
  Samuel Goode 599, 605
  Seth 598, 599, 600
  Seth (Colonel) 598
  Seth Edmund 605, 607
  Soth 598
  Theodosia 603
  William 407, 597, 598, 605, 607
  William (Colonel) 384, 411, 578, 598
  William (General) 597, 598
  William (Mrs.) 597
  William B. 607
  Wm. H. 605
  Wm. N. (Mrs.) 602
  William Norvell 599, 600
  Wm. Norvell (Captain) 606
  Wm. Norvell (Rev.) 600
  William Russell 658
  Zebulon (Col.) 598
Warden, --- (Rev.) 411
Wardlaw, Jenny 324
  Virginia (Jenny) 324
Wardlow, John 11
Ware 710, 753
  Agnes 710
  Agnes --- 710
  Clara 710
  Clary 710
  Edmund 710
  Elizabeth 681, 682, 710
  James 710
  James (Dr.) 710
  James, Sr. 710
  John 710
  Nellie D. 125
  Nicholas 710
  Rebessa 710
  Richard 710
  Samuel 710
  Sarah 710
  Sarah Samuel 682

862

Ware, (cont.)
  William 682, 710
Warfield, William
  (Mr.) 14
Waring 252, 750
  --- 253
  Anna 221
  Charles Julian (?)
    756
  Dorcas 287
  John U. 253, 756
Warmouth, James 152
Warner 492
  --- 492
  --- (Captain) 493
  Augustine 493, 574
  Augustine (Captain)
    492, 493
  Augustine (Colonel)
    493, 589
  Elizabeth 493
  George 493
  Isabella 493, 589
  Mary 493, 574
  Mildred 493, 589
  Mildred (Reade) 589
  Nancy 707
  Robert 493
  Sarah 493
Warren, --- (Mr.) 354
  Eliza J. 352
  Leah 745
  Mary C. 460
  Nancy 744
  Starling 744
  Vincent 744
  William, Jr. 460
  William H. 354
Warring, --- 538
Warwick 337
  Jacob 342, 344
  Jean 767
  John 342, 344
  William 762
Wash, Mary P. 354
Washburn 669
  Hiram 664
Washington 372, 388, 426,
    481, 618, 660, 661,
    662, 666, 669, 671
  --- 2, 6, 34, 78, 86,
    290, 291, 319, 320,
    321, 322, 373, 378,
    397, 398, 402, 464,
    774, 775
  --- (Col.) 401
  --- (General) 233,
    383, 387, 397, 401,
    427, 542, 563, 581,
    770
  --- (Mr.) 372
  --- (President) 180,
    183
  Anne 661, 662
  Augustine 373, 388,
    395
  Augustus 372, 395
  Betty 401
  Burchard 389
  Bushrod 396, 412
  Catherine 377
  George 317, 319, 372,
    426, 464, 481, 539,
    559, 660, 661
  George (Colonel) 6,
    274, 320

Washington, (Cont.)
  George (General)
    345, 589, 660, 661,
    662
  George (Major) 542
  George (President)
    184
  John 618
  John (Captain) 660,
    661
  John (Colonel) 661,
    662, 665
  L. J. 397
  L. Q. (Col.) 391
  Lawrence 388, 415,
    427, 493, 589
  Lawrence (Capt.)
    661
  Lawrence (Reverend)
    669
  Lund 391
  Margaret (Butler)
    669
  Mary 426
  Peter G. 391, 397
  Robert 390, 391
  Townshend 618
Wason, Thomas 658
Wassemaker, --- 556,
    557
Waterhouse, Alice 35
Waterman, Abigail 728
Watkins 501, 502, 653,
    654
  Agnes 654, 655
  Ann 501
  Ben 503
  Benj. 654
  Benjamin 502, 512
  Betty Jane 655
  Caroline W. 512
  Catharine 119
  Catherine 655
  Constance 653, 654
  Eliz. 567
  Eliza 653
  Elizabeth 654, 752
  F. B. (Dr.) 655
  Fanny Anderson 654
  Frances 655
  Frances S. 655
  Francis 567, 654
  Francis N. 655
  Henrietta 655
  Henry 502, 654
  Henry (1st) 502
  Henry (2nd) 502
  Henry E. 655
  Isaac 580
  Jacob 501
  James 502
  Joel (Dr.) 655
  John 544, 654
  Jos. 655
  Joseph 501, 502, 510,
    512
  Joseph (Major) 503
  Josephine 655
  Judith 502, 503
  Judith Trabue 751
  LaFayette, Esq. 406
  Lizzie Ann 655
  Lucy 501
  Margaret C. 655
  Mary C. 655
  Nancy 139, 140, 145,
    146

Watkins, (cont.)
  Nicholas 256
  Rachel 653
  Richard 654
  Richard V. 655
  S. W. (Rev.) 655
  Selina A. 655
  Stephen 496, 508, 509,
    751
  Stephens 502
  Susan 502, 653, 655
  Thomas 654
Watling, (See also
    Watlington)
  Armistead (Colonel)
    612
  John (Captain)
    (?) 612
  Paul (Captain)
    (?) 612
  Rowland (?) 612
Watlington, (See also
    Watling) 608, 610,
    611
  --- (Grandma) 610,
    611
  Armistead (Col.)
    611
  Armistead (Coloney)
    (?) 612
  Betsy 612
  Elizabeth 612
  Frances Donohoe 608
  Frances Donohoe
    (Miss) 609
  Harry (Sir) 608
  John 610
  John (Capt.) 609-
    610, 610, 612
  Nancy Ann 608
  Paul (Captain) 612
  Rowland 612
Watson, Jane Elizabeth
    148, 153
  Lindsey 517
  Mary 150, 153
Watt, --- 59
Watts, Elizabeth 691
  Jane 395
  Margaret 170, 179,
    366, 371, 372, 373,
    374, 375, 377-378,
    378, 379, 397, 398,
    399
Waugh, Elizabeth 591
Waughop, Elizabeth 602
Wayland, Catharine 438
  John W. 13
  Sally (Miss) 438
Wayles, --- (Mr.) 267
  John 229
  John, Esq. 267
  Martha (Patty) 267
  Patty 267
Wayne, --- 401, 405, 498,
  --- (General) 345,
    374, 378, 383, 398,
Weakley, Hattie Thomp-
    son 141
Weakly, Cecil Waddy
    (Mrs.) 708
  Charles (Mrs.) 703
Weathers, Arch 649
Weaver, --- 304
  W. M. 304
  William M. 303
Webb, --- (Infant) 691

863

Webb, (cont.)
  Andrew 691
  Anne Rogers 432
  Augustine 432, 433
  E. Paul 691
  Ethel 226
  Harriett 770
  J. A. 692
  Joe Harlin 691
  Joseph 488
  Lucy (Crittenden) 433
  Phebe Edna 691, 692
  Sallie 97
  Virginia Tucker 226
  William Augustine (Captain) 226
Webster, George 230
  Isaac 109, 113, 115
  Isaac, Jr. 113
  Sarah 109, 113, 115, 127
Weeks, Annie 744
Weems, --- (Dr.) 410, 411
Weidman 632
Weiseger, Eliza Richison 680
Weisenbach, Katharine 164
Welch, Carl 39
  James 689
  John 311
  Nancy 689
Welderburn, --- (Baron of) 27, 28
  --- (Earl of) 27
  --- (Lady) 27
Wellford, Robert (Dr.) 232
Wells 534
  Mary 576
Weslin, --- (Knight of) 492
West 613, 695
  --- (Dr.) 615
  Ann 184
  Benjamin 695
  Benjamin Franklin 622
  Catherine 622
  Dorothy 619, 620, 621
  Dorothy --- 618
  Edward 613, 615, 616, 617, 619, 620, 622
  Edward, Jr. 613, 615, 618, 622
  Edward, Sr. 615, 618
  Edwd 619
  Eliza Mills 622
  Elizabeth 614, 616
  George (Col.) 84
  George William 614, 615
  George William (Mr.) 614
  Hannohretta 622
  Hugh 613, 614
  James 615, 616, 619, 620
  Jane 622
  John 613, 614, 616, 618, 619, 620, 621
  John B. 622
  Lewis 616
  Lynn (Captain) 615
  Margaret 614, 615
  Maria Creed 622

West, (cont.)
  Mary A. 698
  Nancy A. 695, 696
  Patterson Bain 622
  Peggy 616
  Polly 616
  Sally 616
  Sarah 615, 622
  Sarah Brown 622
  Susanna 614
  Sibyl 614, 615
  Sybil 614
  Thomas 215, 616, 620
  Thomas (Captain) 84
  Thomas Lewis 622
  William 614, 616, 619, 620
  William (Reverend Dr.) 613, 614, 614-615, 615
  William Edward 622
  William Wills 617
Westfall 337
  William 337
Weston, Elizabeth 626
Weyman, Mary 158
Whaley, --- 466
  Catherine 695
  James 695
Wheat, Zachariah (Judge) 514
Wheeler, Elizabeth 167, 182
  Fannie 673
  John 673
  W. H. (Mr.) 503
Wherry, Rosann 430
  Thomas 429, 430
White 533, 668, 687
  --- 712
  --- (Col.) 599
  --- (Miss) 66, 401, 410, 411
  --- (Mr.) 400
  A. S. (Senator) 226
  Albert S. 226
  Albert S., Jr. 226
  Albert Smith 226
  Arthur Cox 226
  Augustine 101
  Barbary 355
  Betsy 600
  Betty 458
  Charles Russell 226
  Claudia Amelia 677
  Claudie 675
  Claudie A. 675
  Daniel 355
  E. 712
  Eliza 599
  Elizabeth H. 687
  Ellen 101
  Frances Howell 227
  Gabriella Randolph 226
  Harriot 226
  Herbert 226
  J. 712
  Jacob (Dr.) 523
  James (Dr.) 401
  James B. 101
  Jerusha 523
  John 432
  Joseph Barton 515
  Joseph H. 401
  Lawson 101
  Lloyd 667

White, (cont.)
  Lydia 667
  Margaret 490
  Mariam 490
  Martha A. 523
  Mary 102
  Mary Gabriella 227
  Pearl --- 226
  Randolph 226
  Randolph, Jr. 226
  Rebecca Jane 697
  Sallie 394
  Samuel (Col.) 600
  Sandy 101
  Soloman 355
  Steven 626
  Thomas Phillip (Dr.) 137, 138
  Virginia 432
  William 490
  William Steele (Dr.) 137
Whiteman 337, 631, 632, 636
  Ann 632
  Benjamin 632, 633
  Benjamin (General) 632
  Catherine 632
  Clarissa 632
  Elizabeth 631, 632, 635
  Hester 632
  Jacob 632
  John 632
  Letitia 84
  Lewis 633
  Martin 632
  Mary 632
  Wendell 632
Whitesides, Sara Wood 652
  William Miller (Capt.) 652
Whitley 173, 184, 185, 187
  --- (Col.) 186, 187
  Ann 186, 187
  Elizabeth 314
  Nancy 184, 185
  Solomon 186
  Thomas 186
  William (Col.) 187
  William C. 186
  William C. (Col.) 185, 186,
Whitlock, --- (Mr.) 401
  Kate E. 46
  Kate Edgar 46
  Mary 401
Whitney, Anne Elizabeth 578
  Berilla 694
  Cynthia 673
  Eleanor 579
  Electra 694
  Frances (Dr.) 578
  Loamy 673
Whittingham, Martha 260
  Mary (Lawrence) 260
  William 260
Whittington 626
  --- 625, 626
  Ann 627
  Anna 628, 629
  Arthur 626
  Atlanta 626

Whittington, (cont.)
　Attalanta 146, 623, 628
　Betsy 626, 629
　Betty 626, 627, 628, 629
　Caroline 629
　Charlotte 629
　Edna 629
　Edward 630
　Edward Henry 629
　Eleanor 630
　Elijah 628
　Eliza 627
　Elizabeth 627, 630
　Elizabeth --- 626
　Esther 626, 627
　Fanny 629
　George 626
　Gertrude 626
　Hannah 626, 627
　Hannah Handy 628
　Henry 625, 628
　Henry Haynes 628
　Hervey 628
　Hester 630
　Humphrey M. 625, 629
　Isaac 627, 628, 629
　Isaac Stevenson 628
　James 628, 629, 630
　Jane 629
　Jeanett 627
　Jemima 628
　John 626, 627, 628
　John Drummond 630
　John Long 628
　John Nairne 627
　Joshua 623, 625, 626, 628
　Kate 629
　Katherine 627
　Leah 627
　Littleton 623, 625, 626, 627, 629
　Lucy 623, 625
　Lucy Long 625
　Maria 627
　Maria L. 103
　Mary 626, 627, 628, 629
　Mary --- 626
　Matthew 626
　Milcah 629
　Nancy 628, 629
　Peggy 630
　Priscilla 630
　Sally 627
　Sam C. 625
　Samuel Shannon 628
　Sarah 626, 630
　Sarah Drummond 627
　Smart 626
　Southey 626, 627, 630
　Southey Fossett 627
　Southy 629
　Stevenson 629
　Susane --- 626
　Tabitha 626, 630
　Thomas 625, 628, 629
　Thomas Wishart 628
　Ursula 626
　W. H. 625
　William 623, 624, 625, 626, 627, 628, 629
　William (Captain) 623, 626
　William (Colonel)

Whittington, (cont.)
　William (Col.) 623, 624, 626
　William Fitz 626
　William Wishart (Dr.) 629
　Wm. Handy (Rev.) 628
Whorwood, Margaret 492
　William 492
Wichard, Bina 704
Wickliff, John D. 513, 517
Wickliffe 472, 473
　Ann 661
　Margaret 387
　Rebecca Hunter 102
Wierman, Ellen 227
Wigginton, Alpha S. 152
　Tillie 152
Wigginton, May Wood 645, 652
Wight, --- (Dr.) 225
　H. Theodora 226
　Hattie Randolph 225
　Henry Theodore 225
　Hezekiah 228
Wigner, Marie Ann 359
Wigton, --- (Earle of) (?) 114
Wilde, Betty 451, 452, 453, 457, 458, 459, 486, 488
Wilder, Betty (?) 451, 457, 458, 459
Wildey 488
　Betty 486, 488
Wildy, Betty 486, 488
Wiley, Eli 534
　Eliza Jane 534, 535
　John 534
　Maria Ann 535
　Samuel 534
Wilford, Agnes 492
　James (Sir) 492
　Thomas 492
Wilhoit, James T. 385
Wilhoyte, Allen Sims 141
　Anna Florence 141
　Norval Joseph 141
　Samuel Sims 141
Wiliston, Mary 580
Wilkerson, Mamie 529
Wilkins, Horace 47
Wilkinson, --- 541
　--- (General) 498, 538, 541
　James (General) 541
Willer, W. H. 532
Willey, Rebekah 745
William, --- (Capt.) 764
　Claude (Mrs.) 33
　Ralph, Esq. 298
　Thomas 559
Williams 370
　--- 604, 641
　--- (Capt.) 764
　--- (General) 24, 642
　--- (Miss) 242, 243, 407
　--- (Mrs.) 89
　A. 303
　Ben. W. 125
　Benjamin ? 578
　Benjamin 658

Williams, (cont.)
　Brown 604
　Campbell 158
　Caroline 578
　Catherine 642
　" Cerro Gordo " 24
　Charles 577
　Claude (Mrs.) 48
　Claude S. 41
　Claude S. (Mrs.) 40
　Cynthia 706
　D. A. (Col.) 605
　E. J. 736
　Eleanor 403
　Elisha 335
　Eliza 403
　Elizabeth 577
　Ellenore 533
　Erastus 149
　Eva 149
　Fannie Bullitt 578
　Fielding 599
　George 577
　Irene 577, 392
　Isaac H. 402, 403
　Isaac Hite (?) 21
　Jael (Harrison) 463
　James 24
　James (Dr.) 577
　James (General) 367, 392, 393, 403
　James A. 744
　Jefferson 705, 706
　Joel P. 236
　John 24, 185, 642
　John (Capt.) 763, 769
　John Augustus 24
　John James 392, 403
　John Stuart 24, 125
　Kate 577
　Lucy 403
　Lucy Ann 383, 403, 411
　Lydia 185
　Mamie 24
　Margaret 577
　Maria 86, 577, 578
　Marjorie 125
　Martha 577
　Mary 89, 515, 534
　Merrit 577
　Merritt 86
　Minor 86, 571, 577, 578
　Mollie Elliott 24
　Nellie 692
　Neva (Miss) 242
　Ophelia 392
　Otho Holland (General) 642, 649
　P. French 392, 403
　Patton D. 24
　Phelia W. 402
　Preston H. 101
　Railey Woodson 125
　Ralph 298
　Ruth 578
　Samuel 24
　Sarah 392, 403
　Sarah Ann 463
　Shadrack 533
　T. J. C. 639
　Thomas 559
　Viley 578
　William 463
Williamson, --- (Mr.) 37

Williamson, (cont.)
  C. P. (Rev.) 37
  Eliza (Miss) 257
  Fannie L. 142
  H. M. 92
Williams, Minor 576
Willis, --- (Mr.) 84
  Fannie W. 573
  Fannie Winter 737
  Lucy 223
  N. P. 254
  Sallie 104
  Sarah 254
  Theresa 102
Willoughby, Louise 129
Wills, Elijah 708
  Euclid 349
  Franky Ann 708
  Lizzie 691
  Lucy R. 708
  Sympson 708
Willson, Fenelson R. 517
  Harriet (Miss) 399
  Jesse 347
  Letitia 517
  Olympia 517
  Slater (Rev.) 517
  Tasley ? 465
Wilmore, Charles S. 705
  Elizabeth 705
  John Williams 705
Wilson 644, 679
  --- 93, 711
  --- (Infant) 711
  --- (Miss) 346
  A. P. 143, 146
  Abner 710, 711
  Ann 91, 465, 466
  Arthur 500
  B. L. 676
  Benjamin 241
  Benjamin (Capt.) 342
  Benjamin (Mr.) 242
  Benjamin (Mrs.) 242
  Carrie 500
  Catherine 721
  Cathrine Head 721
  D. 677
  Daniel 585
  Daniel E. 709
  Edgar 52
  Eliza 285
  Elizabeth 644
  Elizabeth Allen 642
  Elizabeth Foster 69
  Elizabeth McCormick 124, 145
  Elizabeth Vaughn 225
  Eugene 500
  Fenelon 500
  Frances Eliza Waddy 709
  George 330
  George Robert 671
  Hamilton 84
  Harriot 227
  Harriott 225
  Harry A. 106
  Harry Allen 106
  Helen Vaughan 709
  Helen W. 709
  Hogen 500
  Isaac (Captain) 285
  James 347, 465
  James D. 52
  Jane 236, 241

Wilson, (cont.)
  Jasper Muir 644
  Jerry 572
  Joanna 69
  Joel H. 711
  Joel Hampton 710
  John 69, 91, 762
  Jonathan Wood 644
  Joseph 642, 643, 644
  Joseph (Dr.) 124, 145
  Joseph Glass 642, 643, 644
  Kitty 228
  Lavinia 44
  Lena (Miss) 500
  Lucinda 511
  Lydia 711
  Lydia G. 710
  Lydia Garner 710
  Mamie (Miss) 500
  Martha 91, 693
  Martha Louisy 711
  Martha Moriah 644
  Mary 84, 85, 500
  Mary E. 711
  Mary Elizabeth 711
  Matilda 711
  Matilda (Mrs.) 711
  Matilda B. 710
  Matilda Boon 711
  Mattie 710
  Mattie Lou 711
  Nancy G. 710
  Nancy Grubs 710
  Olympia 517
  Orlando 500
  Oscar 52
  Presty 644
  Priscilla 644
  Rhoda 644
  Samuel (Captain) 768
  Sarah Ann 644
  Susan M. 129
  Susanna 642
  Susanna Wood 644
  Thomas 225
  Upton 644
  William 710, 711
  William, Sr. 710
  William B. 710
  William Boon 710
  Wood 644, 649, 652
Wimple, Elizabeth ter 633
Winchell, Fannie 118
Winchester, --- 402
Winchetser, --- (Earl of) 660
Windebank, Frances Dymoke 589
  Mildred 589
  Thomas (Sir) 589
Wine, Linda Kennedy (Mrs.) 28
Wingate, --- (Miss) 470
  Isaac 469, 470, 591
  Jane (Snead) 470
  Jane (Sneed) 591
  Lavinia 591
  Martha 469
Winlock, Effie 140
Winn, John G. 39
  John G., Jr. 39
  Richard P. 39
  Sarah Elizabeth 39
Winnall, Grace 141
Winslow 192

Winsor, Justin 551
  Justine 552
Winston, --- (Miss) 254
  David 517
  Dudley 513
  George Alfred 513
  John Dudley (M. D.) 513
  Joseph 517
  Louise 35
  Mary 285, 392, 403
  Nanny Hite 513
  Sarah 177, 178, 187, 192
Winter, --- 451, 458
  Margaret 456, 457, 458
  Thomas 486
Winthrop, --- (Gov.) 711
Wintter, Deidtrich 249
  Mary W. 249
  William E. 249
Wisdom, Wm. Bell 573
Wishart, Ann 626
  Elizabeth 627
Withers 481
  --- (Miss) 480
  Augustine 101
  Augustine, Jr. 101
  Maria 101
  Mary Woodson 101
  Nancy 480
  Susan Railey 101
Witherspoon, --- (Rev. Dr.) 154
  Alice 576
  Anna 503
  Clifford 503
  Ellen 496
  Ellen Douglas 574
  Ethel 496, 574
  Fannie 702
  Ford 503
  Guy 503
  Horace Trabue 503
  John 702
  Johnson 702
  Lewis (Dr.) 574
  Lewis J. 702
  Lewis Johnson (Dr.) 574
  Lister 572, 574
  Lister (Mr.) 496
  Lister , Jr. 574
  Martha 515
  Martinette Viley 579
  Nancy 702
  Robert 574, 702
  Sallie 702
  Sarah 702
  Sarah (Johnson) 702
  Warren Viley 574
  Warren W. Viley 496
Witt, Hart 694
Wolff, Anne Bayne (Mrs.) 390
  Anne Doyne 396, 412
Wolfolk, Alice 432
  Elizabeth Lewis 432
  John 432
Womack, M. 568
  Samuel 285
  Sarah 653

Wood 631, 632, 636, 637,
 639, 640, 641, 643,
 644, 648, 651, 652
Aaron 641
Achsah 635
Adele 410, 411
Agnes 504, 655
Andrew 631, 632, 633,
 634, 635
Ann 631, 632, 643,
 644, 650
Ann Ferguson 637, 652
Barbour 411
Benjamin W. 631
Betsy 634, 635
Blanche 410, 411
Catherine 631, 635,
 642, 643, 651
Catherine Williams
 637, 643, 651
Chalmers 411
Chalmers Bourbon 410
Charles 631, 632,
 634, 635, 636
Charles, Sr. 638, 641
Charles G. (Mr.)
 651
Cora V. 655
Daniel 643, 645, 647,
 650
Daniel Benton 650
Daniel D. 651
David 631, 635
Dolly 631, 632, 634
Eddie 410, 411
Edward 410, 411
Edwin 650
Eliza W. 655
Elizabeth 631, 632,
 634, 643, 648, 649
Elizabeth Whiteman
 633
Frances 655
Francis P. 655
French 410, 411
George 631, 632, 633,
 634, 635
Glenn 650
Grayson 152
Hannah 631, 635
Henry A. (Dr.)
 655
Hester 631, 632
Hilliard (Dr.) 67
Hilliard O. 67
Hilliard O., Jr. 67
Ida (Mrs.) 158
Jack 643
James 85, 638, 641
James (Rev.) 335
Jas. D. 655
Jennie 650
John 631, 638, 641,
 643, 651
John Benton 645, 649,
 650, 651
John McLeod 650
Jonathan 637, 638,
 641, 642, 643, 645,
 648, 649, 651, 652
Jonathan Clinton
 649
Jonathan Clinton
 (Dr.) 637, 649,
 650, 651, 652
Joseph 637, 638, 641,
 642, 643, 644, 645,

Wood, (cont.)
 Joseph (cont.)
 650, 651
 Joseph (Colonel)
 641
 Joseph, Jr. 638, 641,
 642
 Joseph, Sr. 641
 Joseph Putnam 649,
 650
 Josephine 655
 Kate 650
 Lucy 638, 639, 640
 Lydia 643
 Mac 643
 Martha O. --- 67
 Mary 631, 638, 641,
 642
 Mary Catherine 643,
 647
 Mary J. 351
 Mary Lily 650
 Michael 631
 Miriam 650
 Nathaniel 643
 Otho 643, 649, 650
 Otho Williams 649
 Polly 643, 647, 648
 Robert 641
 Roger 410, 411
 S. Chesley 655
 Sallie 651
 Sarah 638, 643
 Selina 655
 Susan M. 655
 Susanna 643, 644
 Thomas 638, 641, 643
 Wade Dabney 411
 Ware Dabney 410
 William 351, 635, 641,
 643, 651
 William Kilcrease 651
 William R. 632
Woodford, Lucy Clay 39
Woodrow, Joshua 325
Woodruff 679
 Almira 712
 Ann --- 711
 Enos 712
 Ezra 712
 John 711
 John I 711
 John II 711
 John III 711
 Sophia 712
 Timothy 712
 Timothy II 712
Woods 333
 Agnes G. 516
 Andrew 91
 Andrew A. 165
 Andrew Alfred 155
 Andrew Alfred, Jr.
 156
 Benjamin 278
 C. Clarence 156
 Charles Railey 156
 Elias 745
 Elizabeth Helm 156
 Emily Eugenia 103
 Eugene D. 103
 Francis D. 103
 Harvey 242
 Henry Newton 156
 James Brison 156
 John 333
 Marvin Averill 103

Woods, (cont.)
 Robert 622
 Robt. Harvie 103
 Sarah 333
 Thos. 772
 William Railey 156
Woodson 98, 111, 113,
 114, 116, 117, 129,
 135, 139, 175, 178,
 188, 191, 193, 418,
 653
 --- (Col.) 174
 A. M. (Judge) 114,
 178, 188
 Agnes 567, 569, 653,
 654
 Albert R. 411
 Albert Robertson 410
 Benj. 653
 Benjamin 653
 Caroline 178, 187
 Charles (Col.) 114,
 178, 187
 Charles (General)
 114, 178, 188
 Chas. Oscar 410, 411
 Daniel (Gov.) 115,
 178
 Dorothea 182
 Dorothea (Randolph)
 230
 Edgar 410, 411
 Eliz. 569
 Eliza 653, 654
 Elizabeth 113, 653
 Frederick Tarleton
 (Major) 114, 178,
 187
 H. M. (Mr.) 114,
 129
 Isham 113
 Jacob 653
 Jane 113, 115
 John 113, 177, 230,
 653
 John (Col.) 99, 107,
 109, 112, 113, 114,
 127, 129, 135, 138,
 169, 173, 174, 175,
 177, 178, 187
 John (Dr.) 113,
 114, 177, 178, 187,
 191-192, 192
 Jno. 3rd 654
 John Stephen 113
 Jonathan 653
 Jos. 569, 653
 Joseph 653
 Josiah 113, 114, 177,
 178, 187, 569, 653
 Josiah (Major) 113,
 175
 Judith 109, 113, 128,
 129, 137, 138, 168,
 174, 175, 177, 178,
 187, 567, 569, 653,
 654
 Lucy 113
 Many Willis (Mrs.)
 276
 Martha 100, 107, 109,
 113, 128, 129, 173,
 174, 175, 177, 178,
 187, 653
 Mary 101, 113, 653,
 654
 Mary Tucker 653

867

Woodson, (cont.)
  Nannie 113
  Obadiah 653, 654
  Phillip 101, 107, 113
  Richard 192, 569, 653,
    654
  Richard Kiddar 247
  Richard Kidder 756
  Robert 113, 177, 192,
    653
  Robertson 410, 411
  S. 569
  Sara 653
  Sarah 113, 192
  Silas (Gov.) 114,
    178, 179, 188
  Stephen 207, 653
  Susanna 109, 113, 115,
    116, 123, 127, 128,
    129, 135, 175, 181
  Susannah 178
  Tarleton 113, 114,
    135, 136, 177, 178,
    181, 187, 200, 653
  Tarleton (General)
    114, 178, 187
  Tarlton 129
  Tucker 653
  Urey 188
  Urey (Hon.) 178
  Ursula 178
  Virginia 161
  William 418, 653
  Wm. French 410, 411
Woodville, --- (Mr.)
  410
Woodward, H. M. (Hon.)
  56, 73
Wooldridge 754
  Belle Slaughter
    (Moss) (Mrs.)
    577
  Edmund 752
  Josiah 500
  Mary 754
  Mildred Taylor Major
    748
  Powhatan 748, 752
  Powhattan 577
  Robert 748
  Thomas 754
Woolfolk, Joseph 590
Woolfork, Turner 498
Woolley, Abraham (Col.)
  387
Woolridge, --- 515
  Claiborne 515, 517
  Daniel 515
  Josiah 515
  Judith 511, 515
  Levi 515
  Livingston 515
  Martha 515
  Mary 515
  Samuel 515
  Samuel, Jr. 127
  Seth 515
  Stephen 515
Woolsiscroft, Helen 35
  John 35
  Sarah 35
Wormeley, --- (Widow)
  213
  Elizabeth (Armi-
    stead) 212
  James (Capt.) 233
  Judith 213, 218

Wormeley, (cont.)
  Ralph (Hon.) 212
  Ralph Randolph (Rear
    Admiral) 233
Wormley, --- (Miss)
  233
  --- (Widow) 199
  Elizabeth 198
  Judith 199, 200
  Ralph 198
Wornum, --- 451, 458
  Betty 457
  Elizabeth 457, 459,
    461
Worth, --- (Gen.) 401
Worthington, Betsey
  (Mrs.) 86
  Scota 631
Worthy, Caroline 285
  Caroline Dupre 282
Wrainwater, Silas 302
Wright, (See also
  Right) 656, 664,
  665, 666, 669
  --- (Infant) 657
  Adam 656
  Amanda 658
  Amanda J. 692
  Andrew H. 657, 659
  Andrew William 658
  Ann 663, 664, 665
  Anne (Washington)
    660, 662
  Annie McIlvain 658
  Clarence Jones 658
  Edwin 657
  Elizabeth 656, 663,
    664
  Elizabeth --- 662
  Elizabeth Ann 663
  Elmira 664
  Emma 565, 566
  Eunice 103
  Frances 664
  Francis (Major)
    661, 662
  Gabriella 664
  George 664
  Isaac 657, 658
  Isaac Kelley 658
  James 656, 659
  James, Sr. 658, 659
  James Gay 657
  James R. 657, 658,
    659
  James Wilson 658
  Jane 656, 657
  Jennie, Sr. 658
  John 412, 656, 657,
    658, 659, 662, 663,
    664, 665, 669
  John, Sr. 658
  John Alexander 658
  John Ward 658
  John Wason 657
  Joseph F. 663, 664
  Juda 362
  Laura 658
  Lorenzo D. 664
  M. T. 692
  Margaret 658, 663,
    665, 666, 668
  Margaret Jane 657
  Maria Belle 658
  Martha 656, 657, 658,
    659, 664
  Martha Ann 657

Wright, (cont.)
  Martha Hamilton 658,
    659
  Martha Wilsie 658
  Mary 87, 102, 657
  Mary --- 662, 663
  Mary Ann 658
  Mary Annie 657
  Mildred 664, 665
  Mildred Ann 664
  Nancy 656
  Peter 656
  Peter, Jr. 656
  Polly 664
  Rachel 656
  Rebecca 656, 657, 658,
    659, 664
  Reuben 663, 664, 665
  Richard 662, 664, 665
  Richard (Captain)
    662
  Ruth 658
  Sallie Keziah 658
  Samuel 664, 665
  Sarah 656, 657, 664
  Susanna 664
  Thomas 656, 664
  William 656, 657, 662,
    664
  William, Jr. 657, 658
  William, Sr. 657, 659
  William Lindsay 658
  William McIlvain 657
  William Volney 658
  Wurts 78, 81
  Daniel 62, 78, 82
  John 82
  John Conrad (Rev.)
    82
  Maria Wade 78, 82
Wynkoop, Annah 562
  Anne 562, 563
  Annetgie 562
  Garritt 562
Yager, Leroy 447
Yancey, --- (Miss) 378
  Layton (Col.) 399
  Stephen 576
Yancy, Fanny (Mrs.)
  379
Yates, --- (Mr.) 410
  Catherine 232
  Geo. 410
  Polly 410
  Robert (Rev.) 232
  William (Rev.) 232
Yealy, Mary Russella 36
  Russell 36
Yeaman, George F. 126
  Ida 134
  M. V. P. (Rev.) 126
Yeardley, George (Sir)
  192
Yeatman (?) 756
Yerby, Peggy 457
Yocum, Amelia 236
  Catherine 238
  Matthias 236
Yolley, Wm. 407
Yoolley, --- (Miss)
  406
Yorick, 138
York, --- (Duke of)
  287
  Minnie 118
Yorke, Dorothy 260
Yost, Elizabeth 109

Young 537, 539, 544,
    672, 679, 712
--- (Col.) 544
--- (Son) 675
A. G. 544
Amanda 675
Amanda J. 674
Amanda Jane 676
Ampsa P. 675, 677
Ampsa P., Jr. 675
Anne 677
Anne Maria 712, 713
Annie Lillian 676
Armine Catherine 674,
    676
Asa 673, 674
Asa D. 672, 675
Asa E. 674, 676
Bennett H. (Colonel)
    279
Catherine B. 675, 677
Douglas (Mrs.) 544
Douglass 134, 136
Edgar 676
Eleanor 677
Elizabeth Randolph
    (Mrs.) 137
Ellis 676
Eugene Yetmon 675
Eugent Yetmon 675
Fannie J. 676
Frances 675
Gaeorge C. 677

Young, (cont.)
George 674
George C. 672, 674,
    675
George Chapman, Jr.
    677
George D. 676
Hannah 185
Hardin 676
Horace C. 675
Horace Chapman 675
Jades 674
James 674, 676
James M. 674
James W. 676
James W. E. 675
Jane 677
Jean --- 677
John D. 422, 424
John S. 676
Johnson (Mr.) 695
Judith 712
Julia --- 674
Julia A. --- 676
Lillian Frances 677
Lola 675
Lola A. 675
Louise Hurlbut 224
Lucy 713
Margaret 713
Mary 328, 633, 635,
    636
Mary F. 674

Young, (cont.)
Mary J. 676
Mary White 675, 677
Merritt 544
Minnie 676
Mollie 674, 676
Oscar 676
Paul L. 675, 677
Richard (Col.) 544,
    633
Richard M. 544
Robert 712, 713
Sam T. 675
Saml. H. T. 713
Samuel T. 675
Sarah E. 675
Susan Frances 677
Susan Railey 137
Susanna Railey 134
Thomas 713
Verlinda Jean 677
Virginia M. 675, 677
W. T. 712
William 674
Willoughby T. 712,
    713
Yutt, --- (Dr.) 406
Ziegler, --- 306
Zimmerman, --- (Miss)
    270
Zoll, --- (Mr.) 248
Zorn, Ferda 513

ADDENDA

Gwinn, Sallie 407   Jacob, John I. 405   Jacob, John Jeremiah 405